To Mamma
from Bomar and Yvonne
Christmas 1988

The Unabridged

Crossword Puzzle

Dictionary

The Unabridged Crossword Puzzle Dictionary

A. F. SISSON

DOUBLEDAY & COMPANY, INC.
Garden City, New York

Library of Congress Card Number 62–15910

Copyright © 1963 by Doubleday & Company, Inc.

All Rights Reserved

Printed in the United States of America

This book was first published in 1963 under the title *The Unabridged Crossword Puzzle Word Finder*.

TO RUTH

How to Use This Dictionary

Main entries are set in lower case letters, as "initial." The synonyms follow in small capital letters, as "FIRST, LETTER, HEAD, INCIPIENT, START, BEGINNING, ORIGINAL," and are indented. Subentries are set in italic letters, as *"ornamental letter,"* and are indented:

initial FIRST, LETTER,
  HEAD, INCIPIENT,
  START, BEGINNING,
  ORIGINAL
ornamental letter
  PARAPH, RUNE
payment ANTE,
  DOWN, DEPOSIT

The Unabridged
Crossword Puzzle
Dictionary

A

A AY, PER, EACH, ALPHA

A-one ACE, TOPS, FIRST, BEST, FINEST

aa LAVA

aardvark ANTEATER

Aaron's *brother* MOSES
father AMRAM
mountain HOR
rod MULLE(I)N, PLANT
sister MIRIAM
son ABIHU, ELEAZER, NADAB

abaca HEMP, LINAGA, LUPIS

Abaddon ABYSS, APOLLYON, PIT, SATAN, HELL

abaft AFT, ASTERN, BACK, BEHIND, REAR-(WARD)

abalone ASSEIR, EAR, ORMER, SHELL, SEA-EAR, MOLLUSK

abandon CAST, SCRAP, DROP, JUNK, YIELD, RESIGN, REJECT, RELINQUISH, DISCARD, WAIVE, FOREGO, DESERT, MAROON, RASHNESS, LEAVE

abandoned LOST, CORRUPT, DERELICT, DISSIPATED, DEPRAVED, UNBRIDLED, FORSAKEN

abase DISGRACE, DISHONOR, MORTIFY, SHAME, DEGRADE, DEPOSE, HUMBLE, HUMILIATE, LOWER, DENIGRATE

abash AWE, HUMBLE, SHAME, EMBARRASS, MORTIFY, CONFOUND, HUMILIATE

abate END, VOID, SLOW, WANE, DECREASE, LESSEN, MODERATE, DIMINISH, SUBSIDE, ALLAY, SLAKE, REMIT, LET UP, ANNUL, EBB, REDUCE, DEDUCT, OMIT, NULLIFY, QUASH

abbe MONK, CLERIC, PRIEST

abbess AMMA

abbey ABADIA, PRIORY, CONVENT, MONASTERY, NUNNERY, CLOISTER

abbot COARB, ABBAS

abbreviate CLIP, CUT, TRUNCATE, PRUNE, ABRIDGE, CONTRACT, CONDENSE, SHORTEN, CURTAIL, DIGEST, EPITOMIZE, DOCK

A.B.C. Power ARGENTINA, BRAZIL, CHILE

Abderite STUPID, DEMOCRITUS, SIMPLETON, YOKEL

abdicate SURRENDER, VACATE, LEAVE, RETIRE, QUIT, RENOUNCE, ABANDON, RESIGN, REMIT, DEMIT, RELINQUISH, CEDE, FOREGO

abdomen PAUNCH, PLEON, BELLY, THARM
fluid in ASCITES

abdominal VENTRAL, VISCERAL, HEMAL, C(O)ELIAC
limb PLEOPOD
organs VISCERA

abduct STEAL, CAPTURE, LURE, TAKE, KIDNAP

abecedarian TYRO, NOVICE, LEARNER, BEGINNER

Abel's *brother* CAIN, SETH
parent ADAM, EVE

aberration SLIP, LAPSE, FAULT, ERROR, DEVIATION, MANIA, DELUSION, HALLUCINATION

abet ASSIST, AID, SUPPORT, ENCOURAGE, HELP, SUCCOR, SUSTAIN, BOOST, COACH, ESPOUSE, UPHOLD, BACK, EGG, INSTIGATE, FOMENT, INCITE, SUBSIDIZE

abhor SHUN, DESPISE, ABOMINATE, DISLIKE, LOATHE, DETEST, HATE, EXECRATE

abhorrence HATE, AVERSION, ODIUM, DISLIKE, LOATHING, HATRED, ABOMINATION

abide LINGER, TARRY, LIVE, STAY, LAST, ENDURE, EXIST, REMAIN, RESIDE, SUBMIT, (A)WAIT, BEAR, BIDE, REST, TOLERATE, DWELL

Abiel's *grandson* SAUL, ABNER
son KISH, NER

abies FIR, CONIFER, PINE, TREE

Abigail's *husband* NABAL, DAVID

Abijah's *father* DAVID
son ASA

ability ENERGY, FORCE, POWER, POTENCY, CAPACITY, SKILL, FACULTY, TALENT, CALIBER, CAPABILITY, EFFICIENCY, IN-

GENUITY, APTITUDE

abject LOW, MEAN, WRETCHED, MISERABLE, DEGRADED, BASE, SERVILE, PALTRY, IGNOBLE, SORDID, VILE, HELOT

abjure ESCHEW, RECALL, REVOKE, DENY, REPUDIATE, SPURN, RENOUNCE, RECANT, FORSWEAR, RESIGN, RETRACT

able EXPERT, SMART, STRONG, FIT, EFFICIENT, SKILLFUL, COMPETENT, CLEVER, CAPABLE, DEXTROUS, ADEPT

ablution BATH, CLEANSING, BATHING, BAPTISM

abnegate FOREGO, DISAVOW, REJECT, DENY, REFUSE

abnormal QUEER, ABERRANT, ECCENTRIC, IRREGULAR, UNNATURAL, ERRATIC
desire ONIOMANIA

abode HOUSE, ESTATE, INN, HUT, SEAT, HABITAT, HOME, LODGING, ADDRESS, RESIDENCE
of dead AARU, ARALU, ORCUS, SHEOL, HADES
oriental DAR

abolish END, ERASE, BLOT, EXTERMINATE, REPEAL, ABROGATE, ANNUL, CANCEL, EFFACE, QUASH, NULLIFY, ABATE, DISCONTINUE, RESCIND, REVOKE, DESTROY, KILL

aboma BOA, BOM, SNAKE

abominate LOATHE, DETEST, HATE
See "abhor"

abomination EVIL, CURSE, CRIME, AVERSION, PLAGUE, REPUGNANCE, ANTIPATHY

aboriginal SAVAGE, FIRST, NATAL, PRIMITIVE, PRIMARY, BEGINNING

aborigine SAVAGE,

NATIVE, AUTOCHTHON, INDIAN

abortive VAIN, FUTILE, IDLE

abound TEEM, SWARM, LUXURIATE

abounding RIFE, TEEMING, REPLETE

about RE, IN RE, CIRCITER, CIRCA, ANENT, SOME, CONCERNING, NEAR(LY), ALMOST, AROUND

above UP, OVERHEAD, ALOFT, OVER, OER, ATOP, HIGHER, UPON, BEFORE, PAST, BEYOND, EXCEEDING
combining form SUPER, SUPRA, HYPER

abrade FRET, GALL, GRATE, GRIND, RUB, WEAR, CHAFE, RASP, IRRITATE, ERASE, FILE

abraded RAW, SCRAPED, CHAFED, LEVEL, FLAT, ERASED, SMOOTH

Abraham's (Abram's)
birthplace UR
brother NAHOR, HARAN
father TERAH
grandfather NAHOR
nephew LOT
son ISAAC, ISHMAEL, MEDAN, SHUAH, ZIMRAN, JOKSHAN, ISHBAK, MIDIAN
wife SARAI, SARAH, KETURAH, HAGAR

abramis CARP, BREAM, FISH

abrasive EMERY, SAND, ERODENT, CORUNDUM, PUMICE, QUARTZ

abraxas AMULET, CHARM, GEM, STONE

abri SHELTER, DUGOUT, SHED, COVER

abridge LIMIT, SHRINK, CONDENSE, DIMINISH, CURTAIL, CUT, DOCK, SHORTEN, ABBREVIATE, RETRENCH

abridgement PRECIS, SKETCH, DIGEST, COMPEND, EPITOME, SYNOPSIS

abroad ASEA, ASTIR, AWAY, OFF, DISTANT

abrogate *See* "abolish"

abrupt RUDE, CURT,

SHORT, HASTY, SUDDEN, RUGGED, BLUNT, TERSE, FAST, CRAGGY, SHARP, STEEP, SHEER, VIOLENT, UNEXPECTED, BRUSK

Abruzzi, *town in* ATRI

Absalom's *captain* AMASA
father DAVID
slayer JOAB

abscess ULCER, SORE, BOIL, FESTER, MORO, LESION

abscond GO, SCRAM, HIDE, ELOPE, FLY, DEPART, DESERT, ESCAPE, QUIT, FLEE, RUN, BOLT, DECAMP

absence WANT, LACK, DEFICIENCY, VACANCY, VOID, VACUUM, WITHDRAWAL, FREE, BLANK, DRY, AWOL, FURLOUGH, LEAVE

absent AWAY, GONE, LACKING, ABSTRACTED, OFF

absolute PERFECT, POSITIVE, FULL, PURE, FREE, PLENARY, SHEER, REAL, UTTER, DEAD, TOTAL, SIMPLE, TRUE, COMPLETE, ENTIRE, WHOLE, CERTAIN, DOWNRIGHT, AUTHORITATIVE, UNALIENABLE
being ENS

absolutely YES, YEA, AMEN, WHOLLY, POSITIVELY

absolve CLEAR, RELEASE, FREE, REMIT, ACQUIT, PARDON, DISCHARGE, SHRIVE, CLEANSE, FORGIVE, FINISH, EXONERATE, LIBERATE, EXCUSE, EXEMPT

absorb FIX, RIVET, TAKE, ASSIMILATE, SOAK, DRINK, SUCK, ENGULF, PREOCCUPY, ENGROSS, IMBIBE, CONSUME, DEVOUR, OCCUPY, COMBINE, UNITE

absorbed INTENT, FIXED, RAPT, ENGROSSED

absquatulate FLEE,
ELOPE, DECAMP
abstain REJECT,
SPURN, REFUSE,
WAIVE, DISUSE, SPARE,
DENY, CEASE, FAST,
WITHHOLD, DESIST,
REFRAIN, FORBEAR
abstemious SOBER,
MODERATE, TEMPER-
ATE
absterge WIPE, PURGE,
BATHE, CLEAN
abstract IDEAL, THEO-
RETICAL, RECONDITE,
EXCERPT, PRECIS,
COMPEND, DEED,
BRIEF, SUMMARY,
EPITOME, SYNOPSIS,
TAKE, STEAL, DRAW,
PART, ABSORB, DIVERT,
SEPARATE, ABRIDGE-
(MENT), CULL
being(s) ENS,
ENTIA
abstruse REMOTE,
ACROATIC, HIDDEN,
ESOTERIC, OBSCURE,
DEEP, SUBTLE, PRO-
FOUND, RECONDITE,
MYSTIC, ACROAMATIC
absurd DROLL, SILLY,
FALSE, WILD, INANE,
STUPID, ASININE,
FOOLISH, SENSELESS,
RIDICULOUS
abundance OPULENCE,
AFFLUENCE, STORE,
WEALTH, LIBERTY,
GALORE, SUFFICIENCY,
PROFUSION, PLENTY,
BOUNTY
abundant LUSH, AM-
PLE, RIFE, PLENTIFUL,
COPIOUS, REPLETE,
TEEMING
abuse REVILE, RAIL,
VIOLATE, RUIN, FLAY,
CURSE, VILIFY,
BERATE, SCOLD, HARM,
HURT, MALIGN, IN-
JURE, MISTREAT,
MAR, SPOIL, CALUM-
NIATE, ILL-TREAT,
MISUSE, VIOLATE
abusive charges MUD,
SLANDER, LIBEL
abut BORDER, REST,
TOUCH, JOIN, ADJOIN
abutment PIER, BUT-
TRESS

abyss CHAOS, DEEP,
VORAGO, DEPTH, HELL,
PIT, GULF, CHASM,
ABYSM, GORGE,
GEHENNA, INTERVAL
Abyssinia See
"Ethiopia"
acacia LOCUST, BABUL,
ARABIC, TREE, SIRIS,
GUM
academic QUODLI-
BETIC, LEARNED,
CLASSIC, SCHOLASTIC,
ERUDITE, SCHOLARLY,
THEORETICAL, COL-
LEGIATE, RIGID,
FORMAL
academician DEAN,
PROF(ESSOR), DO-
CENT, DOCTOR
academy SCHOOL,
COLLEGE, SEMINARY,
LYCEE, ANNAPOLIS,
WEST POINT,
LYCEUM, USMA,
USNA
Acadian CAJUN
acanthopterygian
PERCH, BASS, FISH
acarus MITE, INSECT
acaudal ECAUDATE,
ANUROUS, TAILLESS,
BOBBED
accede LET, ALLOW,
COMPLY, CONCUR,
CONCEDE, CONSENT,
ACQUIESCE, YIELD,
ASSENT, AGREE
accelerate RUN,
HASTEN, STIMULATE,
SPEED, DRIVE,
EXPEDITE, HURRY,
QUICKEN, RACE,
URGE, FORWARD,
DISPATCH, THROTTLE,
REV, GUN
accent BURR, INFLEC-
TION, BROGUE, BEAT,
PULSE, THROB, ICTUS,
SOUND, RHYTHM, UN-
DERLINE, PRONOUNCE,
STRESS, EMPHASIS,
TONE, MARK, INTONA-
TION
accented syllable
ARSIS
accept AGREE, ADMIT,
BELIEVE, ADOPT,
TAKE, ALLOW, AS-
SENT, HONOR, AP-
PROVE, RECEIVE,
ESPOUSE, MARRY

as an equal NOSTRI-
FICATE
accepted standard PAR,
NORM, TYPE, PAT-
TERN, SAMPLE
access ROUTE, PORTAL,
GATE, DOOR, ADIT,
ROAD, PATH, ADMIT-
TANCE, ENTRY, FIT,
ENTREE, ENTRANCE,
WAY, AVENUE, AP-
PROACH, PASSAGE,
STREET
accessory ALLY, AIDE,
TOOL, ABETTOR,
HELPER, ASSISTANT,
ACCOMPLICE, CON-
FEDERATE, AUXILIARY,
ADDITIVE, ADJUNCT,
SCARF
accident LUCK,
CHANCE, FORTUITY,
CONTINGENCY, HAP,
CASUALTY, INJURY,
MISHAP, EVENT,
DISASTER
acclaim EXTOL, CHEER,
ROOT, ECLAT, LAUD,
PRAISE, CLAP, SHOUT,
APPLAUD
acclamation CRY,
PLAUDIT, VOTE,
SHOUT, APPLAUSE,
CHEER, APPROBATION
acclimate SEASON,
HABITUATE, ACCUS-
TOM, INURE
acclivity SLANT,
HEIGHT, ASCENT,
SLOPE, INCLINE,
RISE, HILL,
PITCH, GRADE
accolade OSCAR,
MEDAL, KISS, AWARD,
HONOR, EMBRACE
accommodate BOARD,
LODGE, HOUSE, BOW,
DEFER, FAVOR, ADAPT,
YIELD, HOLD, FIT,
SUIT, OBLIGE, HELP,
ADJUST, CONFORM,
SERVE, AID, LEND,
GIVE
accompany LEAD,
PILOT, ESCORT, AT-
TEND, SQUIRE,
CHAPERON, CONVOY,
JOIN, FOLLOW, CO-
EXIST, CONCUR
accomplice AIDE,
CHUM, ALLY, BUDDY,
CRONY, COLLEAGUE,

CONFEDERATE, PAL, ACCESSORY, ABETTOR, HELPER

accomplish ACHIEVE, CONSUMMATE, END, FINISH, FULFILL, COMPLETE, PERFORM, EXECUTE, DO, ATTAIN, EFFECT, ENACT, SUCCEED

accomplished DONE, ATTAINED, ENDED, APT, ADEPT, EXPERT, TALENTED, PROFICIENT, CONSUMMATE

accomplishment CRAFT, ART, ACHIEVEMENT, LEARNING, TALENT

accord UNITY, CONCERT, HARMONY, GIVE, GRANT, BESTOW, JIBE, UNITE, HARMONIZE, TALLY, ACCEDE, AGREE

accordance AGREEMENT, CONFORMITY, CONCORD

accordingly THUS, THEN, THEREFORE, SO, HENCE

accost SALUTE, GREET, HAIL, ADDRESS, SPEAK, MEET

account TALE, NARRATIVE, RECITAL, STORY, REPORT, RELATE, NARRATE, RECITE, COMPUTE, RATE, VALUE, WORTH, DEEM, CREDIT, TAB, BILL

accountant CPA, AUDITOR, BOOKKEEPER

accouter ARM, OUTFIT, DRESS, GIRD, ARRAY, EQUIP

accredit ENDORSE, VOUCH, SANCTION, APPOINT, DEPUTE, ALLOT, AUTHORIZE, LICENSE, COMMISSION, CERTIFY, APPROVE

accretion INCREASE, SUM, DEPOSIT, GROWTH, GAIN, COHERENCE, EXUDATE

accrue REDOUND, GAIN, WIN, EARN, ENSUE, ISSUE, ARISE, RESULT, INURE, GROW, AC-

CUMULATE, COLLECT, PILE, ADD, ACQUIRE

accumulate HEAP, PILE, STACK, ACCRUE, COLLECT, AMASS, AGGREGATE, GATHER, HOARD, ACQUIRE, STORE

accumulation FUND, HEAP, PILE, STACK, MASS, INTEREST, DIVIDEND

accurate CAREFUL, TRUE, RIGHT, NICE, TRUTHFUL, CORRECT, EXACT, PRECISE

accuse CENSURE, INCRIMINATE, SLUR, BLAME, CHARGE, INDICT

accustom ADAPT, SEASON, INURE, FAMILIARIZE, TOUGHEN, ADDICT, ENURE, ACCLIMATE, TRAIN, HABITUATE, HARDEN, DRILL

ace A-ONE, TOPS, EXPERT, ADEPT, ONE, UNIT, JOT, PIP, BASTO, POINT, MARK, AVIATOR, FLYER

ace-queen combination TENACE

acerb SOUR, HARD, HARSH, SHARP, BITTER, TART, ACRID

acetaldehyde ETHANAL, ETHYL

acetic acid VINEGAR

acetone BUTANONE, ACETOL, KETONE

acetose ACETOUS, SOUR, ACID

acetylene ETHINE, TOLANE, TOLAN

Achates FRIEND

ache PANG, THROE, TWINGE, STITCH, RACK, PAIN, THROB, HURT, SMART, LONG, PINE, DESIRE, ANGUISH

achieve GAIN, EFFECT, FINISH, EARN, ACCOMPLISH, REACH, COMPLETE, WIN, END, GET, ATTAIN, DO, REALIZE, PRODUCE

achievement ACT, ACTION, EXPLOIT, DEED, FEAT, PER-

FORMANCE, ACCOMPLISHMENT

Achilles' *father* PELEUS

horse XANTHUS

mother THETIS

slayer PARIS

achiote ANNATTO, ARNATTO, ARNATTA, TREE

achira CANNA, HANDLESS, ACHEIRIA

acid SHARP, HARSH, DRY, OLEATE, AMINO, ULMIC, BITTER, HARD, VINEGAR, SOUR, TART, ACRID

combining form ACER(O), OXY

radical ACYL, ACETYL, MALONYL, BENZOYL

acidity ACERBITY, ACOR

acknowledge ADMIT, CONFESS, ANSWER, RECEIPT, GRANT, NOD, REPLY, PUBLISH, DISCLOSE, OWN, SIGN, THANK, AVOW, RECOGNIZE, ASSENT, OBSERVE, REWARD

acme ZENITH, APOGEE, PEAK, ACE, TOP, HEYDAY, CAP, APEX, CLIMAX, SUMMIT

acolyte NOVICE, LEARNER, HELPER, BOY, SATELLITE

acomia BALDNESS

aconite BIKH, MONKSHOOD, REMEDY

acorn(s) NUT, MAST, OVEST, CAMATA

dried CAMATA

shaped BALANOID

acquaint FAMILIARIZE, APPRISE, POSSESS, KNOW, SCHOOL, TEACH, TELL, NOTIFY, INFORM

acquainted VERSANT, CONVERSANT

acquiesce BOW, YIELD, SUBMIT, CHIME, CONSENT, ASSENT, ACCEDE, AGREE, CONCUR

acquire REACH, ADD, ANNEX, GRAB, SNATCH, SEIZE, TAKE, BUY, GAIN, REAP, GET, LEARN, EARN, OBTAIN, PROCURE, COLLECT,

WIN, AMASS, DEVELOP, RECEIVE, STEAL

acquit EXCULPATE, PARDON, REMIT, RELEASE, DISCHARGE, EXCUSE, CLEAR, FREE, ABSOLVE, PAY, LIBERATE, VINDICATE, COMPORT, CONDUCT

acre, 1/4 *of* ROD, ROOD

acrid BITTER, KEEN, SURLY, CAUSTIC, SOUR, SHARP, CORROSIVE, ACID, BITING, PUNGENT, UNSAVORY

acrimonious SURLY, IRATE, SHARP, CAUSTIC, ACID, BITTER, GRUFF, ACRID, MAD, ANGRY

Acrisius' *daughter* DANAE

acroamatic ESOTERIC, ORAL, ABSTRUSE, SECRET, PROFOUND, ARCANE

acrolith STATUE, CARYATID

acropolis HILL, FORT, CITADEL

across OVER, SPAN, TRANSVERSE, ATHWART, ABROAD

prefix TRAN(S), DIA

acrostic PUZZLE, AGLA

act KARMA, DRAMA, PLAY, DEED, EXPLOIT, WORK, MOVE, SHIFT, CONDUCT, BEHAVE, COME, DO, FEAT, ACTU, ACTUS, EMOTE, PERFORM, LAW, ORDINANCE, STATUTE, BILL, APE

acting by turns ALTERN, ALTERNATE

action FRAY, FIGHT, PUSH, OPERATION, BATTLE, STEP, DEED, VENUE, JOB, ACT, PROCESS, PRAXIS, SUIT, CASE, WORK, EDICT

field of STAGE, ARENA, BOWL, STADIUM

to recover TROVER

word VERB

active ALERT, BRISK, ALIVE, ASTIR, AGILE, SPRY, BUSY, ATHLETIC

activity RALLY, STIR, ACTION, OPERATION, MOVEMENT, LIFE

actor(s) CAST, RETINUE, TROUPER, THESPIAN, BARNSTORMER, STAGER, HISTRIO(N), HAM, PLAYER, MIME, DOER, STAR, SUPER, PERFORMER, LEAD, INGENUE, AGENT

cue HINT, PROMPT

group of TROUPE, TROOP, COMPANY, CAST

lines ROLE, SIDE

part ROLE

actress INGENUE, STAR, DIVA, SOUBRETTE

actual MATERIAL, REAL, TRUE, VERITABLE, EXISTING, POSIT, GENUINE, CONCRETE, FACTUAL, SUBSTANTIAL

being ESSE

actuality BEING, FACT, EXISTENCE, REALITY

actuate IMPEL, MOVE, MOTIVATE, OPERATE, RUN, EXCITE, DRAW, URGE, STIR, SHARPEN, START, ROUSE, EGG, INSTIGATE, INDUCE, COMPEL, PERSUADE, ENLIVEN, DRIVE

acumen INSIGHT, ACUTENESS, DISCERNMENT, SAGACITY, PERSPICACITY

acute SHARP, QUICK, SHREWD, KEEN, POIGNANT, POINTED, FINE, HIGH, ASTUTE, URGENT

angle, crossing at CHIASMA

adage PROVERB, SAW, SAYING, APHORISM, MOTTO, DICT, MAXIM, AXIOM, TRUISM, BROMIDE

Adam and Eve PUTTYROOT, PLANT

adamant GRIM, STUBBORN, SOLID, STONY, HARD, UNMOVED

"Adam Bede" author ELIOT

Adam, Norse ASK, ASKR

Adam's *grandson* ENOS, ENOCH

needle YUCCA

other wife LILITH

rib EVE

son CAIN, ABEL, SETH

teacher RASIEL

adapt ADJUST, HARMONIZE, RECONCILE, CONVERT, CHANGE, TEMPER, INURE, REGULATE, CONFORM, FIT, SUIT, AGREE, EQUALIZE

add INCREASE, JOIN, ANNEX, AFFIX, AUGMENT, AGGREGATE, FIGURE, SUM, TOTAL, TOT, RECKON, CAST UP, TOTE, FOOT, SAY, GIVE

adda LIZARD, SKINK

added to AND, EKE, PLUS

adder VIPER, SNAKE

addict DEVOTEE, FAN, ENTHUSIAST, FIEND, HABITUATE, ACCUSTOM, USER, BUFF

addiction DISPOSITION, HABIT, ENSLAVEMENT, SURRENDER

Addison JOSEPH, THOMAS, ATTICUS, CLIO

addition PREFIX, CODICIL, RIDER, ELL, ENCORE, PLUS, ADDENDA, INCREASE, ENLARGEMENT, TAB, TOO, ELSE, AND, ALSO, EKE

additional MORE, OTHER, EXTRA, NEW, FRESH, ELSE

addle(d) AMAZE, AGITATE, UPSET, ASEA, MUDDLE(D), PUTRID, SPOIL, IDLE, BEWILDER(ED)

address HOME, RESIDENCE, ABODE, ACCOST, CALL, APPROACH, HAIL, SPEAK, DIRECT, GREET, COURT, WOO, PRAY, TACT, TURN, AIM, SUE, APPEAL, POINT, EASE, POISE, SKILL

adduce PRESENT, MENTION, ALLEGE, QUOTE, CITE, ASSIGN, ADVANCE, NAME, OFFER, GIVE

adeps FAT, LARD

adept ADROIT, MASTER, ARTIST, PROFICIENT,

DEXTEROUS, SKILLFUL, EXPERT, APT, ABLE, CONSUMMATE, SKILLED, VERSED

adequate FIT, MEET, PROPER, ABLE, DUE, EQUAL, SATISFACTORY, AMPLE, SUFFICIENT, ENOUGH

Adhem ABOU

adhere STICK, GLUE, LINK, JOIN, AFFIX, CLEAVE, CLING, PERSEVERE, HOLD

adherent AIDE, IST, DISCIPLE, VOTARY, ITE, ALLY, FOLLOWER

adhibit APPLY, AFFIX, ATTACH, ADMIT, USE

adipose SQUAT, FAT, OBESE, PURSY, SUET, TALLOW, LARD

adit ACCESS, ENTRANCE, DOOR, STULM, PASSAGEWAY, APPROACH

adjacent NEAR, CLOSE, NEXT, TOUCHING, NIGH, ABUTTING, CONTIGUOUS, BORDERING

adjective, *demonstrative* THIS, THAT, THESE, THOSE

adjoin ABUT, TOUCH, BORDER, MEET, CONTACT

adjourn SUSPEND, DEFER, END, POSTPONE, DISCONTINUE, STAY, PROROGUE, DEFER, DELAY, CONTINUE, PROCRASTINATE

adjudge AWARD, DEEM, RATE, TRY, JUDGE, GIVE, RULE, ALLOT, DECREE, ORDAIN

adjudicate ACT, TRY, HEAR, SETTLE, RULE, DECIDE, JUDGE

adjunct ADDITION, ANNEX, APPENDIX, PART, ACCESSORY, AID, HELP, AUXILIARY, ADDITIVE

adjure PLEAD, PRAY, BID, ASK, CHARGE, BIND, COMMAND, ENTREAT, APPEAL, REQUEST, BESEECH, CRAVE

adjust ADAPT, FIX,

SETTLE, SET, TRIM, SQUARE, (AT)TUNE, FIT, TRUE, REGULATE, RANGE, STRAIGHTEN, EQUAL, RATE, ALIGN, LINE, EQUALIZE, PREPARE

adjutage TUBE, NOZZLE, SPOUT, PIPE, OPENING

adjutant AIDE, ALLY, HELPER, OFFICER

bird STORK *See under "bird"*

adjuvant AID, HELP

ad lib IMPROVISE, OFFHAND

admeasure METE

Admetus' *wife* ALCESTIS

administer DIRECT, RUN, HUSBAND, MANAGE, GOVERN, APPLY, RULE, CONTROL, GIVE, DOSE, TREAT, DISPENSE, SUPPLY, CONDUCT, DISTRIBUTE

administration REGIME, RUN, SWAY, RULE

Admiralty island MANUS

admire LOVE, ESTEEM, IDOLIZE, VENERATE, VALUE, WORSHIP, RESPECT, PRIZE, REGARD, WONDER, MARVEL, ADORE, EXTOL, REVERE, HONOR

admired POPULAR, IDOLIZED, WORSHIPED, ADORED

admission CONCESSION, CONFESSION, DISCLOSURE, ENTRY, INGRESS, CONSENT, ACCESS, ADIT, ENTREE, FEE, CHARGE, TICKET

admit PERMIT, SUFFER, ALLOW, CONCEDE, PROFESS, RECEIVE, ADHIBIT, INDUCT, ENROLL, ACCEPT, TAKE, MATRICULATE, INITIATE, CONFESS, GRANT, ACCEDE, OWN, INCLUDE

admixture TINGE, ALLOY, BLEND, SHADE, FLAVOR, SOUPCON

admonish CHIDE, AD-

VISE, WARN, CAUTION, SCOLD, REPROVE, REBUKE, COUNSEL

admonisher MONITOR

ado FLURRY, EFFORT, TROUBLE, BUSTLE, FUSS, POTHER, STIR, WORK, HUBBUB, TO-DO

adobe BRICK, CLAY, MUD, HOUSE, MUDCAP

adolescence TEENS, NONAGE, YOUTH, MINORITY, PUBERTY

adopt ESPOUSE, TAKE, EMBRACE, BORROW, ASSUME, FOSTER, MAINTAIN, FATHER, APPROPRIATE, NATURALIZE

adore EXALT, EXTOL, PRAISE, LAUD, DOTE, LOVE, WORSHIP, ADMIRE, IDOLIZE, ESTEEM, REVERE

adorn DECORATE, ORNAMENT, GARNISH, EMBELLISH, DECK, BEAUTIFY, DRESS, GRACE, TRIM

ad patres DEAD

Adriatic, *island in* LAGOSTA, LASTOVO

resort LIDO

river to PO, PIAVE, BOSNA, ADIGE, DRIN(I), KERKA (KRKA), RENO

wind BORA

adrift ASEA, LOST, DERELICT, UNANCHORED, UNMOORED, LOOSE

adroit HANDY, SMART, HABILE, NEAT, DEFT, CLEVER, EASY, DEXTEROUS, ADEPT, EXPERT

adulterate DENATURE, DEBASE, MIX, WEAKEN, DILUTE, CORRUPT, DEFILE, TAINT

aduncuous HOOKED, BENT

advance LOAN, PROCEED, MARCH, RISE, PROGRESS, AID, HELP, GO, GAIN, PREPAY, CREEP, INCH, WORM, PUSH, PLACE, PAY, SERVE, ASSIST, SPEED, LIFT, ELEVATE, RAISE, PROPOSE, PROMOTE,

INCREASE, PROSPER,
THRIVE, PROGRESS,
SUCCEED, PASS

advanced FAR, AHEAD

advantage AVAIL,
PROFIT, EDGE, START,
STEAD, USE, ODDS,
GAIN, LEVERAGE,
FAVOR, HELP, UTILITY,
SERVICE, SUPERIORITY

adventitious FOREIGN,
CASUAL, EPISODIC, AC-
CIDENTAL, INCIDENTAL

adventure GEST(E),
QUEST, DANGER, RISK,
HAZARD, ENTERPRISE,
VENTURE, PERIL,
CHANCE, EXPERIMENT

tale GEST(E)

adversary RIVAL, FOE,
ENEMY, ANTAGONIST,
OPPONENT, COMPETI-
TOR

adversity MISERY,
MISFORTUNE,
TROUBLE, WOE, DIS-
TRESS

advertisement AD,
BILL, NOTICE,
ANNOUNCEMENT,
BLURB, COMMERCIAL

advice COUNSEL, LORE,
REDE, NEWS, IN-
FORMATION, INSTRUC-
TION, CAUTION,
TIDINGS, NOTICE

advise GUIDE, AC-
QUAINT, TELL, IN-
FORM, NOTIFY, WARN,
CONFER, REVEAL, AP-
PRISE, COUNSEL

adviser EGERIA, MONI-
TOR, NESTOR, AIDE,
COUNSELOR, IN-
STRUCTOR, TEACHER,
LAWYER, ATTORNEY,
DOCTOR, PHYSICIAN,
PREACHER

advisory URGING,
HORTATIVE, HORTA-
TORY, EXPEDIENT,
PRUDENT

advocate BACK, ABET,
PRO, PATRON, SUP-
PORT, APOLOGIST,
PLEAD, LAWYER,
FAVOR, SCHOLAR,
COUNSELOR, BAR-
RISTER, ATTORNEY,
PREACHER

adytum SHRINE,
SANCTUARY, SANCTUM

Aegean Sea, *ancient
people(s)* SAMIAN,
SAMIOTE, LELEGES,
PSARA, PSYRA

arm of SAROS

gulf SAROS

island IOS, NIOS,
SAMOS, COS, MELOS,
LEROS, SCIO, SIROS,
ANDROS, TENOS, KEOS,
NAXOS

river to VARDAR,
MARISTA, STRUMA

aeger SICK, ILL, EX-
CUSE, AEGROTAT

Aegir's *wife* RAN

aelurophile CAT LOVER

Aeneas' *father*
ANCHISES

follower ACHATES

great grandson BRUT

wife CREUSA

Aeneid, *first word of*
ARMA

Aeolian *lyricist*
SAPPHO

Aeolus' *daughter*
HALCYONE

aeonian LASTING,
ETERNAL, INFINITE

aerolite METEORITE

aerose BRASSY

aerostat BALLOON, AIR-
SHIP

aerugo RUST, PATINA,
VERDIGRIS

Aesir *See* "gods,
Norse"

Aether's *father*
EREBUS

Aetolian *prince*
TYDEUS

afar AWAY, OFF, DIS-
TANT, REMOTE, SAHO

affable URBANE, OPEN,
FRIENDLY, SOCIABLE,
GRACIOUS, FRANK,
SUAVE, CORDIAL,
COURTEOUS, LIKABLE,
CHARMING

affair OCCASION,
EVENT, PARTY, IN-
TRIGUE, PLOY,
LIAISON, MATTER,
OCCURRENCE, BUSI-
NESS, BATTLE

affect HIT, STIR,
MOVE, CONCERN,
TOUCH, INFLUENCE,
POSE, AIR, SHAM,
SWAY, DRIVE, IMPEL,
THRILL, ALTER,

CHANGE, INTEREST,
IMPRESS, FEIGN

affectation AIR, POSE,
SHAM, PRETENSION,
MANNERISM, HYPOC-
RISY, PIETISM,
FOPPERY

affection LOVE, RE-
GARD, ESTEEM, LIKING,
MALADY, AILMENT,
FEELING, FONDNESS

affectionate FOND,
TENDER, DOTING,
WARM, LOVING,
DEVOTED, AMOROUS,
FRIENDLY

affeer ASSESS, CON-
FIRM

afferent ESODIC,
ASCENDING, BEAR,
CENTRIPETAL, SEN-
SORY

affiance PLIGHT,
PLEDGE, BETROTH,
ENGAGE

affiliate JOIN, UNITE,
CONNECT, MERGE,
ADOPT, ASSOCIATE,
INCORPORATE,
BRANCH

affinity RELATION, RAP-
PORT, KINSHIP,
ATTRACTION, SYM-
PATHY

affirm ASSERT, AVER,
SWEAR, VOUCH,
STATE, DECLARE,
ALLEGE, TESTIFY

affirmation OATH,
VOW, WORD, DECLARA-
TION, DEPOSITION,
AFFIDAVIT

affirmative AYE, YEA,
YES, AY, AMEN,
POSITIVE, DECLARA-
TIVE

affix JOIN, SUBJOIN,
SEAL, STAMP, FASTEN,
ATTACH, ADD, PIN,
STAPLE, CLIP, SIGN

afflatus BREATHING,
FURY, FUROR, FRENZY,
INSPIRATION, IM-
PULSE, VISION

afflict PESTER, AIL,
HARASS, HARRY,
GRIEVE, HURT,
BURDEN, TRY, VEX,
BESET, TROUBLE,
RACK, GRILL, PAIN,
DISTRESS, TORMENT,
INFECT

affliction GRIEF, SOR-
ROW, CROSS, EVIL,
WOE, SCOURGE, AIL-
MENT, SICKNESS,
DISEASE, HURT,
CALAMITY, PAIN

affluence EASE,
WEALTH, RICHES,
OPULENCE, FORTUNE,
PLENTY, PROSPERITY,
SUFFICIENCY

afford PRODUCE, GIVE,
GRANT, LEND, MAN-
AGE, BEAR, SUPPLY,
YIELD, ENDURE

affray MELEE, BATTLE,
COMBAT, SCARE,
ALARM, BRAWL,
STRUGGLE, SCUFFLE,
RIOT, STRIFE

affright CONFUSE,
ALARM, SCARE, DAUNT,
AGRISE, COW, APPALL,
TERRIFY, INTIMIDATE

affront INSULT, SLIGHT,
NETTLE, PEEVE, SLAP,
ASSAULT, PROVOCA-
TION

affy BETROTH, ES-
POUSE, TRUST, RELY,
CONFIDE

Afghan RUG, BLANKET,
COVER(LET)

Afghanistan *ameer*
SHERE
capital KABUL
city HERAT, KABUL
coin PUL, ANANIA
language PASHTO,
PUSHTU
pony YABU, YABOO
prince AMIR, AMEER
stock SEMITIC
tribe SAFI, ULUS

aficionado FAN,
DEVOTEE, FOLLOWER,
AMATEUR

afloat BUOYED, ADRIFT,
UNFIXED, ASEA

aforesaid PRIOR,
DITTO, ANTECEDENT,
FOREGOING, PREVIOUS

afraid SCARED,
ALARMED, FEARFUL,
TIMOROUS, FRIGHT-
ENED, AFFRIGHTED

afreet JINEE, JINNI,
AFRIT(E)

afresh ANEW, AGAIN,
ANON, ENCORE,
NEWLY, REPEATED,
OVER

Africa, African, *ancient*
region PUNT
animal SURICATE,
CIVET, GENET, POTTO,
ZORIL, NANDINE,
AOUDAD, ARUI
antelope B(E)ISA,
BLAUBOK, ELAND,
GEMSBOK, KOB,
KOODOO, ORIBI, KUDU,
NAGOR, TOPI, GNU,
REITBOK, ORYX, KOBA,
ZENU See "antelope"
ass, wild QUAGGA
assembly RAAD
Atlantic port DAKAR
baboon DRILL
bass IYO
beer POMBE
bird See under "bird"
blaubok ETAAC
boss BAAS
buffalo NIARE
bustard KORI, PAAUW
camp LAAGER, BOMA,
LAGER
cane IMFE, IMPHEE
cape RAS, YUBI
(JUBY), VERT
carnivore RATEL,
SERVAL
catfish SHAL, SCHAL,
DOCMAC
cattle NIATA
charm GRIGRI, GREE-
GREE, JUJU
chief KAID
residence of TATA
city CAIRO, DAKAR,
MONROVIA, ORAN,
TUNIS
civet NANDIN(E)
coin RUPIE, PESA,
TOQUE, AKEY
colonist BOER
cony DAMAN
council RAAD
country ALGERIA,
TUNISIA, LIBYA,
EGYPT, SUDAN, KENYA,
GAMBIA, SENEGAL,
UGANDA, TOGO, CHAD,
DAHOMEY, ERITREA,
GABON, MALI,
SOMALIA, RHODESIA,
GUINEA, CONGO,
ANGOLA, GHANA,
NIGER(IA), CAME-
ROUN, MOROCCO,
LIBERIA
desert SAHARA,
LIBYAN

dialect TAAL, SAHO,
GEEZ, SWAHILI, FANTI,
AKAN, TWI
district RUANDA,
NUBIA, RAND
dunes ERG
eyeworm LOA
family BANTU, TSHI
farmyard WERF
fetish JUJU, GRIGRI,
GREEGREE
fly KIVU, TSETSE
fox ASSE, FENNEC,
CAAMA
garment TOBE, HAIK,
KAROSS
gazelle ADMI, MOHR,
ARIEL
giraffelike animal
OKAPI
gold-bearing ridge
RAND, WITWATERS-
RAND
Gold Coast city
ACCRA, AKKRA
grass FUNDI, ALFA,
ESPARTO
grassy country
VELD(T)
gulf GUINEA, SIDRA,
GABES
gully DONGA, NUL-
LAH
harp NANGA
headland RAS, KOP
helmet TOPI, TOPEE
hemp IFE, SISAL,
PANGANE
hill KOP
hornbill TOCK
horse disease SURRA
house TEMBE
hunt SAFARI
hut(s) KRAAL
instrument GORA(H),
NANGA
jackal DIEB
king SELASSIE, NEGUS
lake NYANZA, CHAD,
SHAT, NYAS(S)A,
VICTORIA, TANA,
RUDOLF, INONGO,
DEBO, TUMBA
language TAAL,
BERBER, BANTU,
SWAHILI, ASHANTI,
SOMALI, EGBA, AKKA,
AKIM, EGBE, EWE,
YAO, SUDANIC,
YORUBA
legislative assembly
RAAD

livestock FE
master BAAS
measure CURBA, DOTI,
DARAH
monkey MONO,
MONA, GUENON,
COLOBUS, GRIVET,
WAAG, GUEREZA
mountain pass NEK
mountains ATLAS
mud house TEMBE
native See "tribe" be-
low ASHANTI,
DAMARA, FULA(H),
ZULU, BOER
negro EGBA
northern coastal region
BARBARY
nurse AYAH, AJA
ostrich RHEA
palm RAPHIA,
RAFFIA
peasant KOPI
pigmy, pygmy AK-
KA(N), BATWA,
ABONGO, OBONGO
plant IXIA, UZARA
plateau KAROO
port DAKAR, ORAN,
TUNIS, LAGOS
province LAGOS
race See "tribe" be-
low SOMALI
reebok, reedbuck
NAGOR
region TIBU, RAND
religious sect ABELITE,
COPTIC
residence TATA,
TEMBE
river See under
"river"
rug KAROSS
scrub BITO
secret society MAU
servant(s) VOLK
sheep ARUI, AOUDAD
snake ELAPS, BOA
genus BITIS
soldier ASKAR(I),
SPAHI
sorcery OBEAH
sorghum IMPHEE,
IMFE
stock FE
stockade BOMA,
KRAAL
tableland KAROO
title SIDI
town IFNI, BOMA,
STAD(T), SAFI

tree OLAX, ASSAGAI,
COLA, KOLA, ARTAR,
AKEE, BAOBAB, BITO,
SHEA, ODUM, ODOOM
tribe IJO, VITI, YAO,
BONI, BANTU, ABO,
LURI, ASHANTI, AKKA,
BARI, GOLO, MADI,
RIFF, BERBER, ZULU,
KAFIR
W. Africa GA,
EWE, IBO, KRU,
AKIM, EFIK, EKOI,
NAMA, HABE, TSHI,
EGBE
valley DAAL, WADI,
WADY
village KRAAL,
STAD(T)
wild ass QUAGGA
wild sheep AOUDAD,
ARUI
wolf AARD
wood TEAK, EBONY
worker(s) VOLK
worm LOA
Afrikaans TAAL
aft ABAFT, ASTERN,
AFTER, BEHIND, BACK,
POSTERIOR
after PAST, BEYOND,
BEHIND, LATER,
ABAFT, ASTERN
prefix POST, META
aftermath UPSHOT,
RESULT, ISSUE,
EFFECT, ROWEN,
STUBBLE, EAGRASS,
ROWETT, PROFIT,
LOSS
afterpiece EPODE,
EXODE, POSTLUDE
afterthought RUE, RE-
GRET, REFLECTION,
MEMORY
afterward LATER,
THEN, THEREAFTER,
SUBSEQUENTLY
ag SILVER
Agag, *slayer of*
SAMUEL
again ANON, AFRESH,
BIS, OVER, ANEW,
EFT, MORE, ENCORE
against VERSUS, VS,
ANTI, AVERSE, CONTRA
prefix ANTI, CONTRA,
NON
Aga Kahn KARIM
son ALY
agalite TALC
agalloch wood GAROO,

ALOES(WOOD), EAGLE-
WOOD
agama LIZARD, GUANA,
IGUANA
Agamemnon's *brother*
MENELAUS
daughter IPHIGENIA,
ELECTRA
father ATREUS
son ORESTES
wife CLYTEMNESTRA
agar-agar GELOSE
agaric FUNGUS
agate MARBLE, ONYX,
QUARTZ, RUBY,
ACHATE
agave AGAUE, AMOLE,
ALOE, DATIL, MAGUEY,
MESCAL, SISAL,
PULQUE
fiber ISTLE, PITA,
SISAL
age MATURE, DEVELOP,
EPOCH, AEON, EON,
ERA, RIPEN, YEARS,
PERIOD, DAY, TIME,
OLAM, SENESCE
at same COEVAL
grow old SENESCE
moon on June 1st
EPACT
old SENESCENCE
pertaining to GERIAT-
RIC, SENILE
study of NOSTOLOGY
Agean See "Aegean"
aged FEEBLE, INFIRM,
MATURE, RIPE, OLDEN,
NESTORIAN, ANILE,
SENILE
agency OFFICE, ME-
DIUM, BUREAU,
INSTRUMENTALITY,
INFLUENCE, LEVER,
ORGAN, FORCE,
MEANS, HAND,
MEDIA
agendum LITURGY,
RITUAL, SLATE
Agenor's *daughter*
EUROPA
father ANTENOR
son CADMUS
agent MEANS, ORGAN,
MEDIUM, CHANNEL,
FACTOR, REEVE,
ATTORNEY, ACTOR,
ENVOY, SPY, SALES-
MAN, PROTECTOR,
GENE, DOER, IST,
FACIENT, BROKER,

OPERATOR, DEPUTY, PROXY

agglomerate MASS, LUMP, HEAP, PILE

aggrandize BOOST, LIFT, MAGNIFY, ADVANCE, EXALT, ELEVATE, DIGNIFY, PROMOTE

aggravate VEX, ANGER, ENLARGE, IRRITATE, PROVOKE, IRK, ANNOY, ENHANCE, NAG, TWIT, WORSEN, INCREASE, EXACERBATE, EXAGGERATE

aggregate ALL, WHOLE, AMOUNT, TOTAL, SUM, ACCRETION, GROSS, COLLECT(ION)

aggression WAR, ATTACK, OFFENSE, INVASION, RAID, ASSAULT

aggrieve WRONG, OPPRESS, PERSECUTE, INJURE, HURT, HARM, AFFLICT, TRY, HARRY, PAIN

agile DEFT, ADROIT, QUICK, BRISK, LITHE, ACTIVE, NIMBLE, LISSOME, LISH, SPRY, ADEPT, LIVELY

agitate IRK, VEX, IMPEL, DRIVE, MOVE, ROCK, SHAKE, ROUSE, FRET, STIR, SEEK, CHURN, SEETHE, ALARM, AROUSE, ACTIVATE, TEEM

agitation FLUTTER, DANCE, QUAKE, QUIVER, JERK, JAR, JOLT, RIPPLE, SHAKE, JOG, TREMOR, DITHER, DISTURBANCE, TURMOIL, ENERGY, MOTION, ALARM

aglet LACE, SPANGLE, STUD, TAG, AIGLET, STAYLACE

agnate AKIN, KINDRED, COGNATE, ALLIED

Agni KALI

agnomen EPITHET, NICKNAME, SURNAME, ALIAS, NAME

agnostic SKEPTIC, DOUBTER, UNBELIEVER

agnus LAMB, DEI, BELL, SHRUB

ago YORE, ERST, GONE, PAST, SINCE, AGONE, SYNE

agog KEEN, AVID, EAGER, EXPECTANT, IMPATIENT, EXCITED

agonize BEAR, SUFFER, TORTURE, STRAIN, RACK, TORMENT

agony DOLOR, PANGS, ACHE, TRIAL, THROE, PANIC, ANGUISH, ANXIETY, PAIN, TORTURE, SUFFERING

agouti PACA, RODENT

Agra tomb TAJ (MAHAL)

agree UNITE, TALLY, SQUARE, GIBE, JIBE, CONCUR, GRANT, MATCH, ACCORD, ASSENT, CONSENT, ACCEDE, ALLOW

agreeable GOOD, DULCET, SUAVE, AMENE, CONSONANT, LIEF, EASY, SUITABLE, PLEASING

agreeableness of letters EUTONY

agreement ENTENTE, CONTRACT, TREATY, CARTEL, ACCORD, DEAL, UNDERSTANDING, PACT, COMPACT, COMPROMISE, HARMONY, CONCERT, UNISON, FIT, NOD, MISE

agrestic RURAL, RUSTIC, BUCOLIC, UNPOLISHED

agriculture, *goddess* CERES (DEMETER)

overseer AGRONOME, AGRONOMIST

Agrippina's *son* NERO

aground, run STRAND

agua TOAD, WATER

Ahab's *wife* JEZEBEL

Ahasuerus' *minister* HAMAN

ahead BEFORE, LEADING, AFORE, ONWARD, FORWARD, ANTERIOR

Ahiam's *father* SACAR

Ahira's *son* ENAN

Ahriman's *angel* (*spirit*) DEEV, DIV

ai SLOTH

aid UPHOLD, BACK, ASSIST, TREAT, FAVOR, SUPPORT, RESCUE, RELIEF, SUCCOR, HELP, SERVE, ABET, KEY, PONY, SECOND, BEFRIEND, COACH, BOOST

Aida's *lover* RADAMES

aide ASSISTANT, ADJUTANT, HELPER

aiglet AGLET, POINT, TAG

ail FAIL, PAIN, PINE, SUFFER, AFFLICT, DECLINE, FALTER

aim INTENT, PURPOSE, GOAL, END, COURSE, BENT, DESIGN, ENDEAVOR, DIRECT(ION), ESSAY, TRY, POINT, BUTT, LEVEL, LAY, TRAIN, ASPIRE

air AERO, SKY, VENT, AERATE, ETHER, OZONE, WIND, TUNE, SONG, AURA, MIEN, ASPECT, BEARING, UTTER, CACHET, WELKIN, AER, AERI, POSE, MANNER, MELODY, VOICE, BROACH, TELL

artificial POSE

combining form ATMO, ATM, AER, AERO

component ARGON, NITROGEN, OXYGEN

craft GYRO, PLANE, HELICOPTER, ZERO, MIG, JET

foul STENCH, STINK, FETOR, FOETOR

open ALFRESCO

pertaining to AURAL, AERO, ATMO

race marker PYLON

runway TARMAC, STRIP

spirit of ARIEL, SYLPH

tight HERMETIC, HERMETICAL

upper ETHER

warm OAM

airplane GYRO, COPTER, PLANE, JET, ZERO, MIG

carrier FLATTOP

cockpit CABIN

marker PYLON

part AILERON, WING, FUSILAGE

runway TARMAC, STRIP

shelter HANGAR

throttle, to GUN, REV

airs PRECISENESS, PRETENSION, MANNERISM, AFFECTEDNESS, VANITY

airship BLIMP, PLANE, GYRO

air trip or voyage HOP, FLIGHT

airy ETHEREAL, AERIAL, JAUNTY, GAY, RARE, THIN, LIGHT, FLUFFY

aisle ALLEY, LANE, PASS, PASSAGE, WALK, WAY

ait ISLE, EYOT, HOLM, ISLET

ajaja JABIRU, SPOONBILL, BIRD

Ajax's *father* TELAMON

akin NEAR, RELATED, ALLIED, AGNATE, GERMANE, SIB, (A)LIKE, SIMILAR

Akmolinsk's *capital* OMSK

Alabama *county* BIBB, CLAY, COOSA, DALE, HALE, LEE, PIKE

river COOSA

alacrity CELERITY, HASTE, SPEED, RAPIDITY

alameda PROMENADE, WALK, MALL

alamo MISSION, SHRINE, FORT, POPLAR, TREE

alan, aland, alant DOG

alantin INULIN

alar WINGED, PTERIC, AXILLARY

alarm TOCSIN, CLOCK, SIREN, WARNING, BELL, BUZZER, FRIGHT, UPSET, DAUNT, APPALL, SCARE, ALERT, STARTLE, SOS, PANIC, FEAR, DISMAY, LARUM

alas AY, ACH, OCHONE, OCH, HEU, OIME(E), AH

Alaska, *city or town*

NOME, JUNEAU, SITKA, UMIAT

garment PARKA

island ATTU, PRIBILOF, ADAK, TANAGA, KISKA, ATKA

group FOX, RAT, NEAR, ALEUTIAN

river YUKON

Albania, *capital* TIRANA, TIRANE

city or town OPP, PUKE (PUKA)

coin LEK

dialect TOSK, GHEGHISH

king ZOG

lake SCUTARI

people GEG, GHEG, TOSK, CHAM

river See under "river"

tribe See "people" *above*

Albion ENGLAND

alchemy MAGIC, THAUMATURGY

alcidine bird AUK, PUFFIN, MUREE, GUILLEMOT

Alcinous' *daughter* NAUSICAA

alcohol ETHANOL, VINIC, ETHYL, LIQUOR, RUM, GIN

from idose IDITE, IDITOL

radical AL

alcoholic WINY, BEERY, SPIRITOUS, INTOXICATING

beverage RUM, MEAD, NEGUS, GIN, WHISKEY, BEER, ALE, LAGER, WINE

content, increased NEEDLED, LACED

solid STERIN, STEROL, CHOLESTEROL

Alcott heroine MEG, AMY, JO, BETH

alcove CUBICLE, NICHE, ORIEL, RECESS, BAY, NOOK, DORMER, GABLE

aldehyde derivative ACETAL

alder ARN, SAGEROSE, BUSH

genus ALNUS

ale STOUT, BOCK,

LAGER, FLIP, PURL, ALEGAR, MUM

house PUB

alembic CUP, RETORT, VESSEL, STILL, FURNACE

Alencon product LACE

Aleppo BEREA, BEROEA, ALEP, HALEB

alert SHARP, KEEN, ACUTE, READY, QUICK, WARY, AWARE, PERT, AWAKE, PREPARED, CAREFUL, AGILE, NIMBLE, BRISK, WATCHFUL, ACTIVE, ALIVE, ALARM, TOCSIN, SIREN

Aleut ATKA, UNALAKA

Aleutian island ATTU, ATKA, KISKA, UMNAK, ADAK

alewife WALLEYE, HERRING, POMPANO, ALLICE, FISH

Alexander, *born* PELLA

Alexandria, *patriarch* PAPA

theologian ARIUS

alfresco OPEN, OUTSIDE, AIRY, OPEN-AIR, OUTDOORS

alga NORI, DIATOM, SEAWEED, ROCKWEED, NOSTOC

genus PADINA, ALARIA, DASYA

algarroba CALDEN, CAROB, TREE

algebra term NOME, EQUATION

Algeria POMARIA, ALGERIE

cavalryman SPAHI, SPAHEE

city or town BLIDA, ORAN

commune SETIF

measure PIK, TARRI

medicinal earth TFOL

ruler DEY

seaport BONA, BONE, ORAN

weight ROTL

algesia ACHE, PAIN, ALGESIS

Algonquin *See under* "Indian"

alias NAME, ELSE, TITLE, OTHER,

EPITHET, PEN NAME, PSEUDONYM
Ali Baba's *brother* CASSIM
word SESAME
alibi APOLOGY, PRETEXT, PLEA, EXCUSE
alidade DIOPTER
alien CONVEY, DEED, REMOTE, STRANGE, ADVERSE, INVADER, FOREIGN, IMMIGRANT, FOREIGNER, UNSYMPATHETIC, INCONSISTENT, IRRELEVANT
alienate WEAN, DEMISE, ESTRANGE, CONVEY, DEED, TRANSFER, ABALIENATE
alight PERCH, ROOST, LAND, ARRIVE, DISEMBARK, SETTLE, LODGE, STOP, DESCEND
align TRAM, TRUE, LINE, RANGE, ARRAY, ADJUST
alike UNIFORM, LIKE, IDENTICAL, SAME, AKIN, SIMILAR, DUPLICATE, CONGRUENT, TWINS
combining form ISO
aliment FOOD, PAP, PABULUM, MANNA, NOURISHMENT, NUTRIMENT, RATIONS
alive AWARE, VITAL, ACTIVE, LIVING, SENSIBLE, BEING, SPRY, BRISK, ALERT, QUICK, ANIMATED, KEEN, BREATHING, ASTIR, AGILE, BUSY, ATHLETIC
alkali REH, USAR, SODA, LYE
alkaloid CAFFEIN(E), ARABINE, ARICIN(E), ESERIN(E), CODEIN(E), PHYSOSTIGMINE, MORPHINE, STRYCHNINE, COCAINE, ATROPINE
hemlock CONIN(E), CONIINE
mustard SINAPIN(E)
poison CURARE, CURARI
all ENTIRE, GROSS, PLENARY, FULL, EVERY, WHOLE, SUM,

TOTAL, TOTO, AGGREGATE, COMPLETE
combining form PAN, OMNI
religions, believer OMNIST
allan GULL
allanite CERINE, ORTHITE, SILICATE
Allatu ARALU
allay HELP, RELIEVE, ABATE, TEMPER, SOOTHE, MITIGATE, LESSEN, CALM, COOL, EASE, ASSUAGE, ALLEVIATE, QUIET, PALLIATE, QUENCH
allege SWEAR, AVER, AVOW, DEPOSE, RECITE, CITE, STATE, DECLARE, CLAIM, AFFIRM, ASSERT
alleged *force* OD, ODYL
allegiance DUTY, LOYALTY, HONOR, FEALTY, HOMAGE, FIDELITY, OBEDIENCE
allegory PARABLE, MYTH, FABLE, TALE, APOLOGUE, METAPHOR
alleviate CURE, TEMPER, LESSEN, ALLAY, EASE, CALM, SOOTHE, LIGHTEN, MITIGATE, MODERATE, MOLLIFY, DIMINISH
alleviation RELIEF, PALLIATION
alley MALL, ALLEE, WALK, PASSAGE, BLIND, LANE, AISLE, BY-WAY, WAY
alliance LEAGUE, TREATY, ACCORD, CONFEDERATION, UNION, COALITION
allied LINKED, UNITED, COGNATE, (A)KIN, KINDRED, AGNATE, SIMILAR, RELATED, ANALOGOUS
alligator LAGARTO, CAYMAN, CAIMAN, NIGER, JACARE, YACARE
pear AVOCADO, AGUACATE
allocate DOLE, DEAL, RATE, ALLOT, ASSIGN, AWARD, METE, SHARE, APPORTION

allot RATION, GRANT, ASSIGN, SHARE, GIVE, METE, CAST, DEAL, DOLE, RATE, AWARD, BESTOW, DISTRIBUTE, PRESCRIBE, AUTHORIZE
allow CONCEDE, ACKNOWLEDGE, CONFESS, AUTHORIZE, SANCTION, GRANT, DEFER, STAND, YIELD, TOLERATE, LET, ADMIT, SUFFER, LOAN, LEND, PERMIT, LEAVE
allowance DOLE, GRANT, ODDS, EDGE, TARE, TRET, RATING, SHARE, PORTION, LEAVE, SIZE, RATION, BOT(E), GIFT, SALARY, ALLOTMENT, STIPEND
for waste or weight TRET, TARE
alloy MIXTURE
black metal NIELLO
Chinese PAKTONG, PACKTONG
copper and zinc BRASS
gold and silver ASEM
iron and carbon STEEL
lead and tin TERNE
mending SOLDER
nickel and steel INVAR
pewterlike BIDRI, BIDREE, BIDRY, BIDDERY, BIDERY
tin and copper PEWTER
yellow AICH, BRASS
alloyed BASE, SPURIOUS
"All's Well That End's Well" *character* LAFEU, BERTRAM, DIANA
allude HINT, REFER, SUGGEST, IMPLY, CONNOTE, INTIMATE, ADVERT, INSINUATE
allure LURE, TRAP, DECOY, SEDUCE, WOO, ENTICE, CHARM, BAIT, TEMPT, BEGUILE, ATTRACT, MOVE
allusion INKLING, HINT, INSTANCE, INTIMATION, INNUENDO
alluvial *clay* ADOBE
deposit SILT, MUD, PLACER, WASH, DRIFT, DELTA

fan DELTA
matter GEEST
ally BACKER, HELPER, FRIEND, LEAGUE, UNION, PAL, AIDE, JOIN, CONFEDERATE, ASSISTANT, ASSOCIATE, AUXILIARY
allyene PROPYNE, ALLENE
almain GERMAN, DANCE, ARMOR, ALLEMANDE, ALMAN
almandine SPINEL, ALMANDITE, GARNET
almandite GARNET
almighty GREAT, OMNIPOTENT, POWERFUL, PUISSANT
almond AMYGDALA, NUT
liqueur RATAFIA
Malay KANARI
oil AMARIN(E)
Persian BADAM
almost NIGH, ANEAR, NEARLY, APPROXIMATELY
alms CHARITY, DOLE, GIFT, GRATUITY, BOUNTY, DONATION, BENEFACTION
box ARCA, RELIQUARY
alnus ALDER, BIRCH, TREE
Aloadae OTUS, EPHIALTES, GIANTS
aloe PITA, AGAVE, MAGUEY, PLANT
powder of PICRA
aloft HIGH, UP, ABOVE, OVERHEAD, SKYWARD
alone LORN, ONLY, DETACHED, SOLUS, APART, ONE, SOLO, SINGLE, SOLITARY, LONE, ISOLATED, UNAIDED
along ON, BESIDE, ONWARD, FORWARD
aloof FROSTY, ABACK, DISTANT, RESERVED, REMOTE, COOL, COLD, SILENT, PROUD, APART, OFF, SECLUDED
Alp PEAK, MOUNT
alpaca (L)LAMA, PACO
like GUANACO
alpha FIRST, CHIEF, DENEB
alphabet PRIMER, ORDER, ABC, LETTERS

character OGAM, OGHAM, OGUM
early RUNE
Hindu SARADA
Kashmir SARADA
old RUNE
teacher of ABECEDARIAN
Alpine *dress* DIRNDL
dwelling CHALET
herdsman SENN
primrose AURICULA
wild goat IBEX, STEINBOK
wind FOEHN, BORA
Alps, *Austrian* TYROL (TIROL)
highest peak BLANC
Italian DOLOMITES
pass CENIS, SIMPLON, COL, BRENNER
peak BERNINA
Yugoslav JULIAN, DINARIC
already NOW
alsike CLOVER
also TOO, BESIDES, LIKEWISE, AND, EKE, PLUS, DITTO, SAME
also ran LOSER
altar SHRINE, CHANCEL, ARA, CHANTRY
carpet PEDALE
cloth HAPLOMA, EPENDYTES, COSTER, FRONTAL
curtain RIDDEL, COSTER
enclosure about BEMA
offering ALTARAGE
platform PREDELLA
rail SEPTUM
screen REREDOS
shelf GRADIN, RETABLE
top MENSA
alter CHANGE, MODIFY, VARY, QUALIFY, MUTATE, ADAPT, TEMPER, SHIFT, MOVE, ADJUST, TURN
ego FRIEND, SELF
altercate BICKER, SPAT, TIFF, DISPUTE, QUARREL
alternate ELSE, OTHER, VARY, ROTATE, RECUR, SWAY, RECIPROCATE, SHIFT, OSCILLATE, SUBSTITUTE, RINGER
alternative OR, EITHER,

CHOICE, OPTION, ELECTION, PREFERENCE
althorn ALTO, SAX, SAXHORN
although EEN, EVEN, WHILE, ALBEIT, NOTWITHSTANDING
altiloquence BOMBAST, LOFTINESS, POMPOSITY
altitude HEIGHT, ELEVATION, STATURE, PEAK, APEX, LOFTINESS
barometer OROMETER, ALTIMETER
altogether ALL, WHOLLY, COMPLETELY, QUITE, ENTIRELY, COLLECTIVELY, NUDE
aluminum *compound* WAVELLITE
hydroxide (ore) BAUXITE, BAUXITITE
alveary BEEHIVE, HIVE
alveolate PITTED, HONEYCOMBED
alveus CHANNEL, BED, TROUGH, DUCT
always AY, AYE, EVER, EER, FOREVER, ETERNALLY, UNCEASINGLY, UNIFORMLY, HABITUALLY
ama CUP, VESSEL, AMULA, CANDLENUT, CHALICE
Amadis' *beloved* ORIANA
amadou PUNK, TINDER
Amalekite *king* AGAG
amalgamate FUSE, MIX, MINGLE, BLEND, MERGE, COMBINE, UNITE, MARRY
amalgamation *process* TINA
amanuensis SCRIBE, TYPIST, STENO, SECRETARY, TRANSCRIBER, RECORDER, SCRIVENER
amaryllis AGAVE, LILY, GIRL, SHEPHERDESS, SWEETHEART
amass HOARD, PILE, MASS, STACK, HEAP, GATHER, ACCUMULATE, COLLECT, STORE
amateur TYRO, TIRO, DABBLER, NOVICE,

DILETTANTE,
VOLUNTEER, BE-
GINNER, VOTARY, HAM
amative, amatory
AMOROUS, EROTIC,
ARDENT, LOVING,
PASSIONATE
amaze IMPRESS,
ASTONISH, STUN, STAG-
GER, ASTOUND, DUM-
FOUND, SURPRISE, BE-
WILDER
Amazon *cetacean* INIA
estuary PARA
forest area SILVAS
ambage PATH, CIRCUIT,
QUIBBLE, AMBIGUITY,
CIRCUMLOCUTION
ambary DA, FIBER,
CORDAGE
ambassador NUNCIO,
LEGATE, AGENT,
ENVOY, MINISTER,
DIPLOMAT, DEPUTY,
REPRESENTATIVE
amber YELLOW, RESIN,
ELECTRUM, AMBER-
GRIS
fish MEDREGAL
ambiguity PARADOX,
OBSCURITY
ambiguous CRYPTIC,
VAGUE, DARK,
OBSCURE, DOUBTFUL,
DUBIOUS, UNCERTAIN,
EQUIVOCAL
ambit LIMIT, CIRCUIT,
COMPASS, EXTENT,
SCOPE, SPHERE,
BOUNDS
ambition PURPOSE,
WISH, HOPE, DESIRE,
ASPIRATION, INTEN-
TION
ambitious BOLD,
EAGER, AVID, KEEN,
ASPIRING, EMULOUS,
SHOWY
amble *See* "saunter"
ambrosia *genus* RAG-
WEED
ambry NICHE, PRESS,
CUPBOARD, CLOSET,
PANTRY, REPOSITORY
ambulate MOVE, WALK,
GAD, HIKE
ambush SNARE, LURE,
NAB, CATCH, THREAT,
DISGUISE, TRAP,
COVER, BLIND, WAY-
LAY
ameliorate AMEND,

HELP, BETTER, RE-
FORM, EMEND, IM-
PROVE, PROMOTE
amen YEA, VERILY,
EUOUAE, ASSENT,
TRULY, ASSUREDLY,
AMON
amenable PLIANT,
OPEN, SUBJECT,
LIABLE
amend MEND, REPAIR,
ATONE, ENLARGE,
REVISE, BETTER, DOC-
TOR, IMPROVE,
CHANGE, CORRECT,
RECTIFY, REFORM
amends REDRESS,
ATONEMENT, EXPIA-
TION, RECOMPENSE,
APOLOGY, REPARATION,
COMPENSATION, RE-
WARD
amenity JOY, EASE,
MILDNESS, SUAVITY,
GENIALITY
Amen-Ra's *wife* MUT
ament CATTAIL,
CATKIN
amerce MULCT, TREAT,
FINE, SCONCE, AFFEER
America, American
YANK (includes
South America)
artist HOMER, MARIN,
BENTON, MOSES,
EAKINS, RYDER, WOOD,
STUART, FLAGG
author BAUM,
ADAMIC, ASCH, ALGER,
WYLIE, FERBER,
KANTOR, HERSEY,
MORLEY, COOPER, AL-
COTT, CABELL, HARTE,
JAMES, LEWIS, STOWE,
WARD, WOLFE, COBB,
BUCK, BEACH, BENET,
DANA, DAVIS
balsam TOLU
bandmaster SOUSA
bird *See under* "bird"
black snake RACER
cartoonist NAST,
CAPP, FISHER, BRIGGS
cavy PACA
century plant ALOE
chemist UREY,
PAULING, MARK,
FLORY, SEABORG,
RUMFORD
coin (*U.S.*) BIT,
CENT, NICKEL, DIME,
EAGLE, DOLLAR

composer COPELAND,
SOUSA, FOSTER, NEVIN,
BERLIN, KERN
deer WAPITI
desolate region PUNA
discoverer of ERIC,
CHRIS, COLUMBUS
dramatist ODETS,
BARRY, CROUSE,
MILLER, WILLIAMS,
INGE
editor BOK, WHITE,
OCHS
educator MANN, KERR,
DEWEY, JAMES, ELIOT,
BUTLER
elder SAMBUCUS
elk WAPITI
elm ULMUS
engineer EADS
explorer BYRD, PIKE,
LOGAN, LONG, BOONE,
LEWIS, CLARK
finch JUNCO
fir ABIES
flag maker ROSS,
BETSY
guinea pig (*cavy*)
PACA
herdsman LLANERO
hero, legendary
BUNYAN
humorist ADE, COBB,
NYE, ROGERS, TWAIN
illustrator FLAGG
Indian *See under*
"Indian"
inventor EDISON,
BELL, FITCH, FULTON,
HOWE, MORSE,
WRIGHT, HOE
of colored photo
IVES
journalist BROUN,
DANA, OCHS, PYLE,
WHITE
jurist HOLMES, TANEY,
JAY, MARSHALL,
STORY, CHASE, TAFT,
STONE, REED, HAND
jute MALLOW
linguistic stock ONA
lion PUMA, COUGAR
monkey TEETEE, TITI
naturalist BAIRD,
SETON, BEEBE, MUIR
novelist *See* "author"
above
painter *See* "artist"
above
patriot REVERE,
ALLEN, HALE, OTIS

philanthropist BARTON, FORD
philosopher JAMES
physician MINOT, RUSH, MAYO, REED
physicist TELLER
pianist DUCHIN, LEVANT
pioneer BOONE, CROCKETT *See* "Explorer" *above*
plains PAMPAS, PRAIRIE
plant See under "plant"
playwright See "dramatist" *above*
poet POE, STEIN, FROST, LANIER, TOWNE, NASH, MILLAY, RILEY, BENET, EMERSON, BRYANT
president (*U.S.*) ADAMS, TYLER, POLK, PIERCE, GRANT, HAYES, TAFT, ABE, IKE, CAL, TEDDY
raccoonlike animal COATI
rodent PACA, CAPYBARA, GOPHER
ruminant LLAMA, ELK, WAPITI
sculptor CALDER, BORGLUM
serpent ABOMA, BOA, RACER
socialist DEBS
spruce PICEA
staghorn SUMAC
suffrage leader CATT, ANTHONY
tiger JAGUAR
toad AGUA, BUFO, RANA
ungulate TAPIR
vine GUACO
wild cat EYRA
wind PAMPERO
yew HEMLOCK
Amerind INDIAN, UTE, ONEIDA, CREE, SAC *See under* "Indian"
memorial post XAT
amiable TENDER, KIND, WARM, LOVABLE, GENIAL, FRIENDLY, KINDLY, SWEET, ENGAGING, WINSOME, COURTEOUS, LOVING
amice EPHOD, CAPE,

HOOD, ALMUCE, COWL, TIPPET
amidin(e) STARCH
amidst AMID, MIDST, AMONG(ST), WITH
amino acid LEUCIN(E), CYSTIN(E), GLYCIN(E), VALIN(E), ALANIN(E), PROLIN(E), SERIN(E)
aminobenzene ANILINE
amiss WRONG, IMPROPER, INACCURATE, ERRONEOUS, INCORRECT
amity ACCORD, FRIENDLINESS, CONCORD, PEACE, FRIENDSHIP
ammonia compound DIAMINE, AMIDE, AMINE
ammoniac plant OSHAC
Ammonite *king* HANUN, UZZIAH
ammunition ARMS, BULLETS, SHOT, AMMO, POWDER, BOMBS, ORDNANCE, MATERIEL, SHRAPNEL, MUNITION
holder TRAY, GUN
wagon CAISSON
amoeba PROTEUS, OLM
amole AGAVE, SALT, PLANT
among BETWEEN, AMID, MIDST, IN, WITH
Amon's *wife* MUT
amor LOVE, EROS, CUPID, AMOROSO
Amorite *king* SIHON, OG
amorous LOVING, EROTIC, FERVENT, ARDENT, IMPASSIONED, TENDER
amorphous CHAOTIC, FORMLESS, VAGUE, IRREGULAR
amount SUM, TOTAL, QUANTITY, AGGREGATE, NUMBER, WHOLE, DEGREE, PRICE
amour-propre PRIDE, CONCEIT, EGOISM, VANITY, SELF-LOVE
ampere WEBER
ampersand AND, ALSO, PLUS
amphibia(n) HYLA, RANA, TOAD, FROG,

ANURA, OLM, CAUDATE, PROTEUS, NEWT, SALAMANDER, EFT
immature TADPOLE, POLLIWOG
amphibole URALITE, EDENITE, HORNBLENDE, TREMOLITE
amphitheatre CIRQUE, ARENA, CAVEA, AUDITORIUM, OVAL, STADIUM, BOWL
seat SELLA
amphora URN, VASE, JAR
ample BIG, GREAT, COPIOUS, ENOUGH, PROLIX, PLENTY, LARGE, SPACIOUS, FULL, ABUNDANT, MUCH
amplification factor MU
amplify MU, DILATE, EXPAND, PAD, SWELL, ENLARGE, EXAGGERATE
amputate SEVER, CUT, LOP, PRUNE, CURTAIL
amula AMA
amulet FETISH, CHARM, TOKEN, TALISMAN, PERIAPT
amusement DIVERSION, SPORT, PLAY, FUN, JEST, MIRTH, ENTERTAINMENT, RECREATION, PLEASURE
amusing DROLL, FUNNY, RISIBLE, LUDICROUS, COMIC, FARCICAL, DIVERTING
amygdala ALMOND, TONSIL
Amy's *sisters* MEG, BETH, JO
ana EVENTS, MEMORABILIA, SAYINGS
anaconda ABOMA, BOA, SNAKE
Anacreon's *birthplace* TEOS
anagram REBUS, GAME, TRANSPOSITION
analgesic ASPIRIN, CODEIN(E), OPIUM, ANODYNE
analogous (A)LIKE, SIMILAR, RELATED, AKIN, COGNATE, ALLIED

analogue PARALLEL, COUNTERPART, CORRELATE

analysis TEST, STUDY, CLARIFICATION, SYNOPSIS, DISSECTION, REDUCTION, INVESTIGATION, TITRATION, ASSAY

analyze TEST, PARSE, ASSAY, TITRATE, DISSECT, PART, DIVIDE, RESOLVE, INVESTIGATE

Anam, *chief city* HUE
tribe MOIS

Anamese *boat* GAYYOU
measure GON, MAU, NGU, LY, QUO, SAO, TAO, TAT, DAM, HAO, MAO, PHAN, TAC, THAT, THUOC
weight TA, BINH, DONG, FAN, HAO, LI, NEN, YEN, QUAN

Ananias' *wife* SAPPHIRA

anaqua ANAMA, TREE

anarchy CHAOS, RIOT, DISORDER, LICENSE, MISRULE, CONFUSION, REVOLT

anathematize CURSE, BAN, CENSURE, SENTENCE, MALEDICT, DENOUNCE

Anatolian *goddess* MA

anatomy STRUCTURE, BODY, SKELETON, ANALYSIS
of animals ZOOTOMY

Anaximander, *first principle* APEIRON(A)

ancestor ADAM, ELDER, PARENT, FAMILY, STOCK, SIRE, FOREFATHER, PROGENITOR, PRECURSOR
common SEPT
remote ATAVUS

ancestral AVAL, AVITAL, HEREDITARY, PATRIMONIAL, FAMILIAL
spirits MANES, LARES

ancestry RACE, PATERNITY, LINEAGE, FAMILY, PEDIGREE
relating to ATAVISTIC, ATAVIC

anchor MOOR, KEDGE, FASTEN, BIND, ATTACH, SECURE, RIVET, (AF)FIX, CONNECT
bill of PEE, PEAK
lift CAT
lifter CAPSTAN
part FLUKE, PALM, ARM
ring TORE, TOROID
small GRAPNEL
tackle CAT
timber GROUSER

anchorage DOCK, MOORAGE, ROADSTEAD, HARBOR, LOCATION, REFUGE

anchoret EREMITE, ASCETIC, ANCHORITE

anchorite MONK, STYLITE, HERMIT, RECLUSE, PILLARIST, ASCETIC

anchovy SPRAT

ancient ELD, OLD, AGED, PRIMEVAL, HOARY, ARCHAIC, PRIMAL, PRISTINE, PRIMITIVE
country GAUL, DACIA, PARTHIA, EDOM, CANAAN, GALILEE, SHEBA, ELI(A)S
festival, Thebes AGRANIA
sign RUNE
vessel CRUSE

and PLUS, ALSO, AMPERSAND, ET

and not NOR, NEITHER

Andalusia *province* JAEN

Andean *bird* CONDOR
cold region PUNA
deer PUDU
grass ICHU
tableland PARAMO, PUNA
tribe ANTI, CAMPA

andiron DOG, FIREDOG, HESSIAN

andrenid BEE

android ROBOT, AUTOMATON

Andromeda's *father* CEPHEUS

anecdotage ANA, DOTAGE, SENILITY

anecdote TALE, SKETCH, STORY, JOKE, NARRATIVE, YARN, EVENT

anele ANOINT, SHRIVE

anemic LOW, WAN, PALE, WATERY

anent ABOUT, WITH, ON, RE, CONCERNING

anesthetic GAS, ETHER, OPIATE, SEDATIVE, STOLID, OBTUSE, DULL

anfractuous WINDING, SINUOUS, TORTUOUS, SPIRAL

angel SERAPH, CHERUB, EGREGOR, BACKER, SPIRIT, GUARDIAN
apostate EBLIS
death AZRAEL
Jupiter ZADKIEL
music ISRAFIL, ISRAFEL, ISRAFEEL
"Paradise Lost" BELIAL, URIEL
resurrection ISRAFIL
ruled air and winds RUCHIEL

angelin YABA, TREE

angelus BELL
painter of MILLET

anger ROIL, VEX, IRK, NETTLE, FURY, TEMPER, PIQUE, BILE, RILE, FUME, IRE, TEEM, TIFF, RAGE, CHOLER, PROVOKE, ANNOY, INCENSE, HUFF, WRATH, SPLEEN, GALL

angered IRED, SORE, EXASPERATED

angle FISH, PEAK, CORNER, POINT, FORK, RAVELIN, ASPECT, GUISE, ARRIS, INTRIGUE, SCHEME, SLANT, BEND, ELBOW, KNEE
acute AKIMBO
forty-five degree OCTANT
having none AGONIC
of leaf and axis AXIL
of pipe TEE, ELL, ELBOW
of stem AXIL

Anglian *kingdom* DEIRA

Anglo-Saxon *armor* HAUBERK
army FYRD
assembly GEMOT(E), MOOT, MOTE
coin SCEAT, ORA, MANCUS
council HEPTARCHY

court GEMOT(E), MOTE

freeman THANE, THEGN

god WODEN, ING See under "god"

historian BEDE

infantry FYRD

king EDGAR, INE

letter EDH, ETH

lord's attendant THANE, THEGN

minstrel SCOP

money See "coin" above

nobleman THANE, THEGN

poem BEOWULF

poet SCOP

scholar BEDE

sheriff REEVE, GEREFA

slave ESNE

tax GELD

angry SORE, IRATE, HUFF(ED), MAD, CROSS, IREFUL, PROVOKED, CHAFED, WROTH, INDIGNANT

anguillad EEL

anguish ACHE, PAIN, REGRET, DOLE, GRIEF, WOE, REMORSE, THROE, AGONY, DOLOR, PANG, MISERY, TORMENT, RACK

angular SCRAWNY, BONY, GAUNT, THIN, SLIM, POINTED

measure, unit MIL

anhydrous DRY, ARID

anile DOTING, OLD, FOOLISH, SIMPLE, SENILE, OLD-WOMANISH

aniline dye BENZOL(E), MAGENTA

animal(s) FAUNA, BEAST, BRUTE, BIPED, QUADRUPED, MAMMAL, CREATURE, CARNAL, FLESHY, PHYSICAL, SENSUAL

anatomy of ZOOTOMY

and plant life BIOTA, BIOS

arboreal TARSIER, LEMUR See "arboreal" and "monkey"

body of SOMA

burrowing WOMBAT, MOLE

carrying young MARSUPIAL

cat tribe OUNCE, TIGER, LION, LEOPARD, COUGAR, PUMA

coat or pelt PELAGE, SKIN, FUR, HIDE

domestic ASS, DOG, CAT, HORSE, HOG, COW, PIG, RAM, SOW, MULE, MARE, SHOAT, STOCK, BEEF

fat SUET, LARD, LANOLIN, CETIN, TALLOW

footless APOD

giraffelike OKAPI

imaginary SNARK, GRIFFIN, CENTAUR

legs used as oars REMIPED

leopardlike OUNCE, PUMA, COUGAR

life, simple form of AMEBA, AMOEBA

long-bodied ANNELIDAN, ANNELIDIAN

molt of EXUVIAE

pelt See "coat" above

pertaining to ZOIC

pet CADE, COSSET, LAMB, CAT, DOG

sea CORAL See under "sea"

S. America COATI, AFARA, LLAMA, ALPACA, GUANACO

spotted DAPPLED, PIEBALD, PIED

starch GLYCOGEN

study of ZOOLOGY

ten-footed DECAPOD

tree TARSIER, LEMUR See "arboreal"

water OTTER, BEAVER, WHALE, SEAL, WALRUS

young WHELP, CALF, KID, BABE, FOAL, CUB, LAMB See "young"

animals with no nervous system ACRITA

animate STIR, DRIVE, MOVE, INSPIRE, QUICKEN, CHEER, LIVEN, IMPEL, FIRE, ENSOUL, ACTIVATE, VITALIZE, STIMULATE, INVIGORATE, EXCITE, INDUCE

animated ALIVE, BRISK, GAY, VITAL, QUICK, SPRIGHTLY, BLITHE, LIVELY

animosity HATE, SPITE, RANCOR, HOSTILITY, ENMITY, DISLIKE, HATRED

anion ION

opposed to CATION

anise DILL, CUMIN, ANET

ankle TARSUS, TALUS, CUIT, COOT, HOCK

bone(s) TALI, ASTRAGALI, TARSALIA, CALCIS, TALUS, ASTRAGALUS

iron BASIL, FETTER

pertaining to TALARIC, TARSAL

anlage PROTON, RUDIMENT

anna COIN, HOATZIN, HOACTZIN, STINKBIRD

¼ of PICE

annalist RECORDER, CHRONOLOGIST

Annamese See "Anamese"

Annapolis student PLEB(E), MIDSHIPMAN

annatto URUCU, DYE

Annie Oakley MOZEE, PASS, TICKET

anneal FUSE, TEMPER, SMELT, TOUGHEN

annealing chamber LEER, LEHR

annex AFFIX, ATTACH, ACQUIRE, ADD, JOIN, ELL, APPEND, UNITE, CONNECT

annihilate ABOLISH, ABATE, ERASE, END, WRECK, DESTROY, QUENCH, RAZE, RUIN, EXTERMINATE, EXTINGUISH, KILL, SLAY

anniversary FETE, FESTIVAL, CELEBRATION, MASS, ANNUAL

annotate GLOSS, EXPLAIN, NOTE, ELUCIDATE, ILLUSTRATE

annotater NOTER

announce PUBLISH, BROADCAST, REPORT, DIVULGE, REVEAL, HERALD, TELL, PROCLAIM, BRUIT,

BLAZON, ADVERTISE, INFORM, ASSERT
announcement BULLETIN, BLURB, NOTICE, NOTIFICATION, MANIFESTO
announcer HERALD
annoy VEX, TEASE, HARASS, DISTURB, MOLEST, TROUBLE, BOTHER, IRRITATE, PAIN, IRK, BAIT, BORE, DEVIL, NAG, PESTER, EGG, TRY, ROIL, UPSET, FRET, TEASE, WORRY, BADGER, CHAFE, HARRY, HECKLE, HECTOR
annoyance PEST, THORN, NUISANCE, WEED, INSECT
annual ETESIAN, YEARLY, FLOWER, PLANT, PERIODICAL, BOOK
income RENTES
annuity INCOME, TONTINE, PENSION
annul REVOKE, CASS, CANCEL, UNDO, REPEAL, RESCIND, RECALL, RETRACT, QUASH, ABROGATE, NULLIFY, DESTROY, ABOLISH, ERASE
annular ROUND, CIRCULAR, ORBICULAR, RINGED
reinforcement SPUT, HOOP
anodyne SEDATIVE, OPIATE, BALM, SALVE, NARCOTIC, PALLIATIVE, REMEDY
anoint SMEAR, ANELE, FAT, OIL, SALVE, CROWN, CREAM, GREASE, CHRISM, CONSECRATE
anomalous ODD, ABNORMAL, ATYPICAL, STRANGE, IRREGULAR, PECULIAR, ECCENTRIC, ABERRANT
anon LATER, ONCE, SOON, THENCE, AGAIN, ANEW, AFRESH, SHORTLY, FORTHWITH, AFTERWARD
anonymous INCOGNITO, NAMELESS

opposite to ONOMATOUS
another NEW, FURTHER, SECOND, ALIAS, DIFFERENT
anserine GOOSE, STUPID, DULL, STOLID
answer RESULT, REPLY, ECHO, RETORT, DEFENSE, MEET, SATISFY, FULFILL, REJOIN, RESPONSE, REBUTTAL, SOLUTION, LETTER
ant EMMET, PISMIRE, ANAY, MIRE, TERMITE, MYRMICID, ANAI, FORMICID
leaf-cutting ATTA
nest FORMICARY
queen MICROGYNE, GYNE
stinging KELEP
white ANAI, ANAY, TERMITE
worker ERGATES, NEUTER
antagonist RIVAL, FOE, ENEMY, COMPETITOR, ADVERSARY
antagonistic INIMICAL, HOSTILE, DISSONANT
Antarctic *explorer* COOK, BYRD, ROSS, SCOTT, WILKINS
mountain SIPLE
ante BLIND, STAKE, POT, BET, WAGER, PRIOR, FORMER, PREVIOUS, BEFORE
anteater ECHIDNA, PANGOLIN, MANIS, AARDVARK, TAMANDUA
antecedent PRIOR, FORMER, CAUSE, REASON, ANTERIOR, PREVIOUS, FOREGOING, FORETASTE, ANTICIPATE
antedating PREMUNDANE
antelope GAZEL(LE), TAKIN, YAKIN
African KOB, KONZE, KUDU, NAGOR, ORIBI, ORYX, WANTO, STEINBOK, BEIRA, BONGO, TOPI, KOBA, POKU, PUKU, ADDAX, OTEROP, BLESBOK, SAIGA, ASSE, BISA,

GUIB, IMPALA, DUIKER, CHIRU, ELAND, KOODOO, GEMSBOK, GNU, PALLAH, BEISA, SASSABY
ancient PYGARG, ADDAX
China DZEREN
Egyptian BUBALUS, BUBAL(E)
European CHAMOIS
genus ORYX
goatlike GORAL, SEROW, CHAMOIS
Himalayan CHIRU, GORAL
Indian NILGAI, NYLGAU, SASIN
large ORYX, GEMSBOK, BEISA
like BOVINE, BOVID
red buck PALLAH
Siberian SAIGA
Somaliland BEIRA
striped BONGO
Tibet CHIRU, GOA
antenna FEELER, AERIAL, PALP
insect, end of CLAVA
anterior PRIOR, BEFORE, FORE, PREVIOUS, VENTRAL, FRONT
anteroom LOBBY, FOYER, HALL, ENTRY, VESTIBULE
anthelion AUREOLE, HALO, NIMBUS, ANTISUN, COUNTERSUN
anthem SONG, MOTET, ANTIPHONY, HYMN, PSALM
anther STAMEN, TIP, POLLEN
anthesis BLOOM, BLOSSOM
anthocyanin ENIN, DENIN, CYANIN, OENIN
anthologize COMPILE
anthology ANA, CORPUS, GARLAND, COLLECTION, BOOK
anthozoan CORYL, POLYP
anthracite, *inferior* CULM
anthrax BOIL, CARBUNCLE, PUSTULE, CHARBON

anthropoid APE, LAR, GIBBON, GORILLA, ORANG-UTAN

antibiosis ANTITOXIN, SULFA

antic DIDO, PRANK, CAPER, DROLL, COMIC, GAMBOL, MERRY, WILD

anticipate AWAIT, EXPECT, HOPE, THWART, BALK, FORE-(SEE), ANTEDATE, PREPARE

anticlimax BATHOS, DECREASE

antidote EMETIC, REMEDY, SODA, SMILE, CHECK, CONTROL, CURE, RESTORATIVE

Antigone's *mother* JOCASTA

sister ISMENE

antimony SB, KOHL, STIBIUM, PARADOX, ANOMALY

pertaining to STIBIAL

antipathist HATER

antipathy HATE, AVERSION, RANCOR, ANIMUS, REPUG-NANCE, DISLIKE, DIS-GUST, LOATHING, HORROR

antiquity OLD, PAST, ANCIENT, AGO, YORE, ELD, PALEOLOGY, AGED, ARCHAEOLOGY

antiseptic EUPAD, IODINE, METAPHEN SALOL, ALCOHOL

acid BORIC

Antisthenes CYNIC

antithetic(al) OPPOSITE

antitoxin(s) SERUM, SERA

antler HORN

branch PRONG, BAY, BEZ, BROW, BEAM, TYNE, TINE, CROWN, ROYAL

unbranched SPIKE, DAG, DAGUE, HORN, PRICKET

antlia PUMP, CON-STELLATION

"Antony and Cleo-patra" character EROS, PHILO, AGRIPPA, GALLUS, MENAS, IRAS, TAURUS

Anu, *consort of* ANAT

anvil INCUS, STITHY, TEEST

bone INCUS, AMBOS

Anvil City NOME

anxiety DREAD, ALARM, PANIC, DOUBT, WORRY, CARE, CONCERN, FEAR, ANGUISH, UNEASINESS, DISQUIET, MISGIVING, SOLICITUDE

anxious AFRAID, UPSET, UNEASY, RESTLESS, EXPECTANT, AGOG

any AN, ONI, ALL, SOME, PART

of various stars DENEB

anything AUGHT

high flown E LA

of least value PLACK

remote FORANE

aorist TENSE, PAST, TIMELESS

aoudad ARUI, SHEEP

Apache *chief* GERON-IMO

jacket BIETLE

apart ASIDE, SOLUS, SPLIT, ALOOF, ALONE, AWAY, ENISLED, SEPARATE, DIVORCED

apartment FLAT, SUITE, DIGS, ROOM(S), CHAMBER

apathetic STOIC, STOLID, UNFEELING, IMPASSIVE, INERT, COOL, UNMOVED

apathy PHLEGM, DOL-DRUMS, UNCONCERN, TORPOR, LASSITUDE, INDIFFERENCE

ape SIMIAN, MONKEY, GORILLA, GIBBON, LANGUR, ANTHRO-POID, LAR, PRIMATE, MAHA, ORANG, SIAMANG, MOCK, IMITATE, COPY, MIMIC, PARROT, COPYCAT, TROGLO-DYTE, PORTRAY, SIMULATE

apeman ALALUS

apercu GLANCE, SKETCH, PRECIS, DIGEST, INSIGHT

aperture OPENING, PORE, VENT, ORIFICE, RIMA, BORE, HOLE, SLIT, GAP, PERFORA-TION, CLEFT, CRACK, MOUTH, WINDOW, OSTIOLE

apetalous flower TREMA, CACTUS

apex ACME, CACUMEN, NOON, TOP, ZENITH, VERTEX, PEAK, APOGEE, SUMMIT, CLIMAX, CUSP, TIP, POINT, CRISIS

belonging to APICAL, CACUMINAL

covering EPI

elbow ANCON

rounded RETUSE

aphasia ALALIA

aphid APHIS, LOUSE, PUCERON

aphorism ADAGE, AXIOM, DICTUM, MAXIM, PROVERB, SAW, MOTTO, EPIGRAM, PRECEPT, APOTHEGM

aphoristic GNOMICAL, GNOMIC

Aphrodite URANIA, VENUS

father ZEUS

mother DIONE

sweetheart ARES, HEPHAESTUS

temple site PAPHOS

apiaceous herb or plant NONDO, CELERY, PARSLEY, CARROT, ANISE

apiary HIVE, SKEP

apician EPICUREAN, GLUTTONISH

apidae *genus* BOMBUS, BEE

apiece SERIATIM, PER, EACH

aplomb ASSURANCE, POISE, SURETY, TACT, STABILITY, RESOLU-TION

apocarp ETAERIO, STRAWBERRY

apocopate ELIDE, SHORTEN

apocryphal book TOBIT, ESDRAS, BARUCH, JUDITH, MACCABEES

apogee CLIMAX, PEAK, ACME, ZENITH, APEX

apograph COPY, REP-
LICA, ECTYPE,
IMITATION

apoidea APINA, BEE,
APIS, APIDAE

Apollo CASTER,
MERCURY
and Artemis DELIANS
birthplace DELOS
festival DELIA,
APOLLONIA
giant killed by OTUS,
EPHIALTES
mother LATONA,
LETO
sage of ABARIS
seat of ABAE
site of oracle DELOS,
DELPHOS
son ION
twin ARTEMIS,
DIANA

Apollyon DEVIL,
ABADDON, SATAN,
BEELZEBUB, ARCH-
FIEND

apologue FABLE,
MYTH, STORY, PARA-
BLE, ALLEGORY

apology PLEA, ALIBI,
PARDON, AMENDS,
REGRET, EXCUSE,
EXPLANATION

apoplexy plant ESCA

apostate TURNCOAT,
DESERTER, PERVERT,
DISLOYAL, RAT,
RENEGADE, SECEDER,
HERETIC, CONVERT

apostle JOHN, ANDREW,
MATTHEW, PAUL,
JUDE, JUDAS, PETER,
JAMES, SIMON, PHILIP,
DISCIPLE, MESSENGER,
PREACHER, TEACHER,
APPRENTICE, FOL-
LOWER, BARTHOL-
OMEW, THOMAS

apostles, *teaching of*
DIDACHE

apothegm SAYING,
SAW, MAXIM, ADAGE,
PROVERB, MOTTO,
DICTUM

appal(l) HORRIFY,
SHOCK, DISGUST,
REVOLT, DAUNT, DIS-
MAY, TERRIFY

apparatus MACHINE,
GEAR, TACKLE, OUT-
FIT, TOOL, DEVICE,
GADGET, INSTRUMENT,
UTENSIL, MECHANISM,
DINGUS

apparel ATTIRE, DRESS,
ROBE, ARRAY, OUTFIT,
EQUIPMENT, RAI-
MENT, GARB

apparent DISTINCT,
CLEAR, MANIFEST,
PATENT, PLAIN,
OBVIOUS, VISIBLE,
OVERT, PROBABLE

apparition SPIRIT,
SPOOK, HA(U)NT,
WRAITH, GHOST,
DREAM, REVENANT,
SHADE, VISION,
PHANTOM, SPECTRE

appeal PLEA, EN-
TREATY, BEG, PETI-
TION, SUIT, ASK,
SEEK, SOLICIT, EN-
TREAT, PRAYER, INVO-
CATION, IMPLORE,
REQUEST

appealing CATCHY,
CLEVER, CUTE

appear EMERGE, LOOM,
ARRIVE, COME, SEEM,
ENTER, (A)RISE,
ISSUE, LOOK, DAWN

appearance AIR, GUISE,
MIEN, SIGHT, SHOW,
LOOK, ASPECT, VIEW,
DISPLAY, SEMBLANCE,
ARRIVAL

appease MODIFY,
PACIFY, MOLLIFY,
SLAKE, SOOTHE,
SATISFY, MODERATE,
CALM, PLACATE,
QUIET, ALLAY

appellation EPITHET,
NAME, TITLE, STYLE,
COGNOMEN, DESCRIP-
TION

append ADD, ADJOIN,
JOIN, AFFIX, HANG,
ANNEX, ATTACH, SUB-
JOIN, FASTEN, CLIP,
PIN

appendage TAIL, TAB,
AWN, PENDICLE,
STIPEL, CAUD, AD-
JUNCT, CODICIL,
RIDER, SUFFIX, PS

appetite TASTE, GREED,
EDACITY, URGE, YEN,
LUST, HUNGER, DE-
SIRE, RELISH, GUSTO,
CRAVING, ZEST,
OREXIS, WANT
morbid ADEPHAGIA,
PICA, BULIMIA
want of ASITIA

appetizer CANAPE,
ZEST, RELEVE,
RELISH, SAUCE

applaud ENDORSE,
EXTOL, LAUD, PRAISE,
CLAP, CHEER, HUZZA,
COMPLIMENT

applause ACCLAIM,
BRAVO, ECLAT, SALVO,
HAND, PRAISE,
PLAUDITS, CHEER
reaching after CAPTA-
TION, ESURIENCE

apple POME, ROSE,
SORB, SHEA,
CRAB, CUSTARD,
QUEENING, RUSSET,
SPY, WINESAP, PIPPIN
acid MALIC
crushed POMACE
genus MALUS
immature CODLIN(G)
juice CIDER
like fruit QUINCE,
POME
love TOMATO
Persian PEACH
seed PIP, PUTAMEN
shaped POMIFORM
tree genus MALUS
wild CRAB, DOUCIN

appliance TOOL, UTEN-
SIL, APPLICATION,
APPURTENANCE,
GADGET

applicable FIT(TING),
SUITABLE, APT, MEET,
PROPER, RELEVANT,
APPROPRIATE, USEFUL

application USE, FORM,
BLANK, STUDY,
PRACTICE, EFFORT

apply EMPLOY, USE,
UTILIZE, PUT, ASK,
PERTAIN, DEVOTE,
TOIL, LABOR, GRIND,
SOLICIT, WORK,
PERSEVERE, APPOSE,
DEDICATE

appoint NAME, SET,
ASSIGN, ORDAIN,
EQUIP, NOMINATE,
PLACE, ELECT, ARM,
OUTFIT, DECK, ARRAY,
PRESCRIBE, DESIGNATE,
DECREE

appointment DATE,
SET, TRYST, ORDER,
DIRECTION, EQUIP-

MENT, ASSIGNATION, INTERVIEW, RESERVATION

apportion DOLE, ALLOT, RATE, METE, RATION, PARCEL, GRANT, ASSIGN, ALLOCATE, ARRANGE

apportionment DIVISION, DEAL, DISTRIBUTION, ALLOWANCE, DIVIDEND

apposite APT, FIT, PAT, TIMELY, PERTINENT, GERMANE

appraise RATE, ASSESS, ASSAY, (E)VALUE, ESTIMATE, JUDGE, EVALUATE, ADJUDGE, AJUDICATE

appreciate PRIZE, ESTEEM, VALUE, CHERISH, LOVE, REALIZE, JUDGE

apprehend DETAIN, COP, TAKE, CATCH, NOTE, NAB, BELIEVE, FEAR, DREAD, PERCEIVE, SEE, KNOW, GRASP, ARREST, SEIZE

directly INTUIT, INTUE

apprehension WORRY, PANG, DREAD, FEAR, ARREST, ALARM, CAPTURE

apprentice TRAINEE, TYRO, TIRO, LEARNER

apprise TELL, REVEAL, DISCLOSE, INFORM, NOTIFY, ADVISE, WARN

approach NEAR, ADIT, COME, ROAD, STALK, ESSAY, TRY, ADVANCE, IMPEND

approbation FAVOR, PLAUDIT, ESTEEM, SANCTION, REGARD, CREDIT, REPUTE, RESPECT, PRAISE

appropriate PREEMPT, TAKE, STEAL, USURP, BORROW, GRAB, PAT, DUE, APT, PROPER, FIT, ALLOT, TIMELY, MEET, SUITABLE, HAPPY, ADD, GERMANE, CONFORMABLE

approval ECLAT, ENDORSEMENT, SANC-

TION, SUPPORT, AMEN

approve ACCEPT, LIKE, SUPPORT, RATIFY, ENDORSE, OK, CONFIRM, COMMEND, VALUE

approximate NEAR, CLOSE, APPROACH(ING), ABOUT, CIRCA

approximately NIGH, NEARLY, ALMOST, ABOUT, ROUGHLY

apricot ANSU, UME, FRUIT

cordial PERSICO(T)

disease BLIGHT

apron BIB, BISHOP, TIER, SHIELD, FLAP, BRAT, BOOT, TOUSER, TARMAC, RUNWAY

apropos HAPPY, PAT, TIMELY, FIT, MEET, OPPORTUNE, SUITABLE, APT, APPROPRIATE

apt FIT, CLEVER, SKIL(L)FUL, QUICK, PAT, DEFT, EXPERT, MEET, PROPER, LIKELY, LIABLE, SMART, CONSONANT, DOCILE, WILLING

apteryx MOA, KIWI, BIRD

aptitude FLAIR, GENIUS, LEANING, TALENT, GIFT, KNACK, BENT, TURN, FACULTY, ABILITY

aqua WATER

aquamarine BERYL, BLUE

aquarium GLOBE, POND, TANK, BOWL, POOL

aqueduct CONDUIT, CANAL, CHANNEL

of Sylvius ITER

Aquinas work SUMMA

Arab, Arabia(n) NOMAD, SARACEN, OMAN, TATAR, SEMITE, SLEB, YEMEN, SAUDI, BEDOUIN, HIMYARITE, WANDERER, HORSE

abode DAR, TENT

alphabet ALIF, BE, TE, SE, JIM, HE, KHE, DAL, ZAL, RE, ZE, SIN, SHIN, SAD, DAD, TA, ZA, AIN, GHAIN, FE, QAF, KEF,

LAM, MIM, NUN, HE, WAW, YE

ancient country SHEBA (SABA)

beverage LEBAN, LEBBAN

boat DHOW

chief AMIR, EMIR, REIS, EMEER, SHEIK, RAS

city or town ADEN, DAMAR, HAIL, JIDDA, MEDINA, MECCA, MEKKA, SANA(A), SABYA, MAREB, TAIF, WEJH SANA(A)

cloak ABA

coin CARAT, DINAR, KABIK

demon EBLIS, GENIE, JINN(EE), AFRITE, AFRIT, AFREET

desert DAHNA, NEFUD, SYRIAN, NEJD, SAHARA

devil prince EBLIS

district or region TEMA, ASIR, HEJAZ, TAIMA, NEJD (NAJD)

drink LEBAN, LEBBAN

father ABU, ABOU

flour SAMH

garment ABA, HAIK, BURNOOSE

gazelle CORA

gulf KUTCH

headkerchief cord AGAL

jasmine BELA

jinni See "demon" above

judge CADI, KADI

kingdom NEJD, NEDJED, IRAK, IRAQ

ancient MINAEAN, SABA(EAN)

land FEDDAN

letter See "alphabet" above

lyric GAZEL, GHAZAL

measure ARDEB, COVID(O), DEN, SAA, ARDAB

Medina tribe AUS

milk, sour LEBAN, LEBBAN

mirage SERAB, SARAB

monarchy YEMEN

"Nights," character in SINBAD, AMINA, AGIB, ZOBEIDE

nomad SARACEN, SLEB

oasis JOWF

peninsula SINA(I)
physician RHAZES
poet KAAB, ANTAR
porridge SAMH
protectorate ADEN
region See "district"
above
robe ABA
romance ANTAR
ruler EMIR, EMEER
See "chief" above
scholar ULEMA
script NESKI, NESKHI
scripture ALCORAN,
KORAN
seaport ADEN, MOCHA
shrub KAT
spirit See "demon"
above
state YEMEN, OMAN,
ASIR
sultanate OMAN,
MAHRA
tamborine TAAR
teacher ULEMA
tent village DOUAR
title SIDI
toga ABA
town See "city"
above
extinct MAREB
tree KAFAL
tribe ASIR, AUS, KEDAR
tribesman IBAD, SLEB
Utopia KAIF, KEF
vessel DHOW
wagon ARABA
weight KELLA, NEVAT,
CHEKI, DIRHEM,
KELLA(H), BAHAR,
ARTABA, CRAT, DANIK,
FARZIL
wind SIMOON,
SIMOOM
Arabic acid ARABIN
arable TILLABLE,
FERTILE
land LAINE
Araceae family ARUM,
TARO
member of ARAD
araceous AROID
plant CABBAGE, LILY,
TARO, ARUM
arachnid SPIDER, MITE,
SCORPION, TICK
trap WEB
arachnida ACERATA
arada LAND
Arafura Sea *island*
group ARU
Arakanese MAGHI

aralia plant FATSIA
Aramaic *city, O.T.*
ARPAD, ARPHAD
deity RIMMON
dialect SYRIAC
Aram's *children* UZ,
HUL, MASH, GETHER
Arawakan tribe GUANA
arbalest CROSSBOW
arbiter REFEREE,
JUDGE, UMPIRE,
CRITIC, ADVISER
arbitrary DESPOTIC,
THETIC, WILLFUL,
TYRANNICAL, ABSO-
LUTE, IRRESPONSIBLE,
IMPERIOUS, CAPRI-
CIOUS, SEVERE
dictum DOGMA
arbitrator MUNSIFF,
REFEREE, JUDGE,
UMPIRE, ARBITER
arbor PERGOLA,
BOWER, TRELLIS, GAR-
DEN, ORCHARD, RE-
TREAT, ABODE
arboreal DENDRAL
animal AI, UNAU,
SLOTH, DASYURE,
MARTEN, LEMUR *See*
"monkey"
arc CURVE, BOW,
ORBIT
chord of SINE
arcade ARCATURE,
PORTICO, GALLERY,
COLONNADE, STREET
Arcadian BUCOLIC,
RUSTIC, SHEPHERD,
RURAL, PASTORAL
god LADON
king LYCAON
princess AUGE
arcane HIDDEN, SECRET
arcanum SECRET, MYS-
TERY, ELIXIR, REMEDY
arch CUNNING, SLY,
CLEVER, ROUGISH,
COY, IMPISH, SAUCY,
PERT, CURVE, ARC,
VAULT, FORNIX, BEND,
OGIVE, SPAN, BOW,
SUPPORT, BRIDGE,
CHIEF, PRINCIPAL,
PRIME, GREAT
fiend DEVIL, SATAN
pointed OGIVE, OGEE
Roman ALETTE
archaic OLD, ANCIENT,
HISTORIC, OBSOLETE,
VENERABLE, ANTI-
QUATED

archangel URIEL,
MICHAEL, SATAN,
GABRIEL, RAPHAEL
archbishop ABP, MET-
ROPOLITAN, PRIMATE
Canterbury BECKET
Mayence HATTO
archbishopric SEE
arched VAULTED,
COPED, CAMBERED,
CONCAVE
archer CUPID, BOW-
MAN, CLIM, CLYM,
SAGITTARY, TELL
archery target CLOUT
archetype IDEAL, EX-
AMPLE, MODEL,
PARAGON, ORIGINAL,
PATTERN, PROTOTYPE,
SAMPLE
architect BUILDER,
ARTIST, ARTISAN,
AUTHOR
design of EPURE,
PLAN, PRINT, STRUC-
TURE, DIAGRAM
architectural *order*
IONIC, GOTHIC, GREEK,
NORMAN, ROMAN,
CORINTHIAN, MODERN,
DORIC
pier ANTA
archive ANNAL,
RECORD, LIBRARY,
MUSEUM, DOCUMENT
arctic NORTHERN,
POLAR, COOL, ICY,
COLD, CHILLY, FRIGID,
GELID, BOREAL,
GALOSH, SHOE
base ETAH
explorer BYRD, ERIC,
KANE, PEARY, ROSS
jacket ANORAK
transportation UMIAK,
SLED, OOMIAC
Arctic Ocean, *river to*
DVINA, TANA, (TENO),
MEZEN, PECHORA,
ONEGA, OB, LENA
arctoid URSINE, BEAR-
LIKE
arcuate BOWED,
ARCHED, CURVED,
HOOKED
ardent WARM, EAGER,
AVID, KEEN, FERVENT,
INTENSE, BEAMING,
FEELING, LOVING,
GLOWING, FIERY,
ENTHUSIASTIC

ardor HEAT, ZEAL, PASSION, ELAN, VERVE, ZEST, GUSTO, GLOW, FERVOR, DESIRE, FEELING, LOVE

arduous HARD, DIFFICULT, STEEP, LOFTY, TIRESOME, LABORIOUS

are, *1/100 of* CENTARE

area SPACE, TRACT, TERRITORY, EXPANSE, ZONE, REGION, BELT, SIZE, EXTENT, VOLUME, ENVIRON(S), SCOPE, SCENE, SPHERE, REALM, SURFACE, RANGE, FIELD, PURLIEU
small CLOSET, AREOLA, CELL

areca BETEL, PALM

arefy DRY, WITHER

arena OVAL, FIELD, RING, HIPPODROME, COURT, SPACE, SPHERE, RINK, STAGE, SCENE, THEATER, STADIUM, CIRCUS, COCKPIT, REGION, AREA

arenose SANDY

areola SPOT, RING, INTERSTICE, PIT

Ares MARS
parent HERA, ZEUS, ENYO
sister ERIS

argali AOUDAD, SHEEP

Argentina, *city or town* ACHA, AZUL, BAHIA, PARANA, PUAN, GOYA, SALTA
measure SINO
plain(s) PAMPA(S)
province or territory NEUQUEN, ESTERO, FORMOSA, TUCUMAN, SALTA, JUJUY, CHACO, PAMPA
tree TALA

argillaceous SLATY, CLAYEY, DOUGHY, SPONGY, CLEDGY

argo BOAT, SHIP, ARGOSY

Argolis, *vale of* NEMEA

argonaut JASON

argosy BOAT, SHIP, VESSEL, CRAFT, FLEET, GALLEON

argot CANT, FLASH, SLANG, LINGO, JARGON, PATOIS, DIALECT

argue MOOT, ORATE, WORD, PROVE, REBUT, DEBATE, DISCUSS, REASON

argument FUSS, HASSLE, DEBATE, POLEMIC, DISPUTE, EVIDENCE, CASE, PROOF, REASON, GROUND, TOPIC, THEME, DISCOURSE, CONTENTION, DISCUSSION, TEXT, WORDS

argumentative ERISTIC, FORENSIC, CONTROVERSIAL, RHETORICAL

argyles HOSE

arhat LOHAN, MONK, SAINT

arid JEJUNE, LEAN, DRY, STERILE, DESERT, BARE, BARREN, PARCHED, DULL, UNPRODUCTIVE, UNINTERESTING, BALD

Aries RAM
mother of ENYO

Arikara REE, INDIAN

aril POD

arise ACCRUE, AWAKE, BEGIN, REAR, DERIVE, RISE, MOUNT, SOAR, SURGE, TOWER, STEM, FLOW, ISSUE, LIFT, RAISE, ASCEND, EMERGE, ORIGINATE, HAPPEN, EXIST, APPEAR

arista BEARD, AWN, APPENDAGE

aristocrat LORD, PARVENU, ELITE, PATRICIAN, GRANDEE, NOBLE

Aristophanes *title* FROGS

aristophanic WITTY, COMIC, BROAD

Aristotle's *birthplace* STAGIRA, THRACE
disciple of PERIPATETIC
school LYCEUM
teacher PLATO
work ETHICA, ORGANON, NICOMACHEA

Arius, *disciple of* ARIAN

Arizona, *city or town* TEMPE, TUCSON, YUMA, PHOENIX
county GILA, PIMA, PINAL, YUMA
flower SAGUARO
river GILA

ark REFUGE, SHELTER, RETREAT, ASYLUM, BOAT, CHEST, BOX
landing place ARARAT

Arkansas county CLAY, DREW, LEE, PIKE, POLK, POKE, SCOTT, YELL

arm LIMB, MEMBER, BRANCH, BOUGH, FIRTH, FIORD, INLET, FORTIFY, WING, MIGHT, WEAPON, STRENGTH(EN), POWER, FORCE, ENERGY, OUTFIT, EQUIP, INSTRUMENT, PROVIDE
band MANIPLE, BRASSARD
bone HUMERUS, ULNA, RADIUS
pertaining to BRACHIAL
pit AXILLA, CHELIDON, ALA, OXTER
sleeve hole SCYE
walk arm in OXTER

armada FLEET, ARMY, NAVY, FLOTILLA, SQUADRON

armadillo APAR(A), PEVA, MATACO, PELUDO, TATU, PEBA, POYOU
giant, Argentina PELUDO
Brazil TATU, TATOU
S. America POYOU, PEBA, PEVA, TATOU(AY)
three-banded APAR(A), MATACO

armadillolike extinct animal GLYPTODON

armed band POSSE, HOST, ARMY, NAVY

Armenia(n), *Biblical* MINNI
capital ERIVAN, YEREVAN
Catholic UNIAT
mountain ARARAT

armhole of garment SCYE, MAIL

armistice PEACE, TRUCE, LULL, RESPITE

armor MAIL, PLATE, SHIELD, EGIS, TACE, GRAITH, CUIRASS, CULET, TASSE, CUISH, CRISSE, DEFENSE, MATERIEL, ARMS

bearer ARMIGER, SQUIRE

head SCONCE

horse BARDS, BARDES

horse's head TESTIERE

leg JAMB(E), CUISH, CUISSE, TUILE, TUILLE

parts of CREAVE, CUIRASS, LORICA, TASSE(T)

protective PANOPLY, AEGIS, SHIELD

shoulder AILETTE

skirt TACE, TASSE(T)

armored vehicle TANK

army TROOPS, SOLDIERS, HOST, FORCE, CROWD, THRONG, HORDE, MILITIA, LEGION, BATTALION, MULTITUDE

car JEEP

chaplain PADRE

depot BASE

engineer SAPPER

follower SUTLER

food CHOW

installation POST, FORT, CAMP

old English FYRD

provisioner SUTLER

army officer BRASS, GENERAL, MAJOR, LIEUTENANT, COLONEL, CAPTAIN

aroid TANIA, TARO, TANIER

aroma NIDOR, SAVOR, ODOR, SCENT, SMELL, STINK, STENCH, FETOR, FRAGRANCE, PERFUME, BOUQUET, SPICE

aromatic SPICY, PUNGENT, BALMY, PIQUANT, REDOLENT, SAVORY, ODOROUS, FRAGRANT

fruit NUTMEG

gum MYRRH

herb ANISE, CLARY, NONDO, MINT

medicinal leaves BUCHU

seed ANISE

spice CLOVE, MACE

substance BALSAM

weed TANSY

around ABOUT, NEAR, ENCIRCLING, CIRCA

combining form PERI

arouse ROUSE, WAKE(N), STIR, EXCITE, WHET, STIMULATE, SUMMON, ACTUATE, EVOKE, RALLY, KINDLE, REVIVE, PIQUE, MOVE, DRIVE, IMPEL, FIRE, THRILL, ANIMATE, INSPIRIT, RAISE, EXCITE, (EN)LIVEN

arpeggio ROULADE, SWEEP

arquebus support CROC

arraign CITE, INDITE, INDICT, ACCUSE, SUMMON, CHARGE, TRY, PROSECUTE, IMPEACH, DENOUNCE

arraignment CENSURE, CHARGE, ACCUSATION, HEARING

arrange(d) ALIGN, ETTLE, PLAT, FILE, LINE, FIX, SET, DISPOSE, STAGE, ORDER, RANGE, SORT, PLAN, DESIGN, SCHEME, ADJUST, ADAPT, CLASSIFY

in layers STRATOSE, TIERED, LAMINATED

in threes TERNATE

side by side APPOSE

arrangement COLLECTION, PLAN, FILE, INDEX, SETTLEMENT, SCHEME, DISPOSITION, ORDER

combining form TAX(I), TAXO, TAXEO

arras TAPESTRY, DRAPERY

array APPAREL, DRESS, ATTIRE, GARB, DECK, ROBE, CLOTHE, ADORN, ALIGN, POMP, ORDER, LINE, ARMY, HOST, MARSHAL, MUSTER, SERIES, ASSEMBLAGE, MULTITUDE

arrest COLLAR, DWARF, NAB, HALT, COP, RESTRAIN, STOP, SIST, SEIZE, CAPTURE, CHECK, HINDER, RETARD, SUSPEND, THWART, BALK, DELAY, DETAIN, TAKE, CATCH, JAIL, STUNT, APPREHEND, OBSTRUCT

arris PIEN(D), ANGLE, PEEN

arrival ADVENT

arrive ATTAIN, COME, FLOW, REACH, HAPPEN, APPEAR, LAND

arriviste SNOB, PARVENU

arrogance PRIDE, DISDAIN, CONCEIT, HAUTEUR, EFFRONTERY, EGOTISM, INSOLENCE, BOLDNESS

arrogant CAVALIER, BOLD, PROUD, HIGH, LORDLY, LOFTY, UPPISH, IMPUDENT

arrogate USURP, CLAIM, SEIZE, TAKE, GRAB, ASSUME

arrow SHAFT, BOLT, MISSILE, POINTER, DART, REED

end NOCK

feathered VIRE

fit to string NOCK

handle STELE

maker BOWYER, FLETCHER

poison INEE, SUMPIT, ANTIAR, CURARE, UPAS, URALI, WOORALI, WAGOGO

shaped SAGITTAL, BELOID

short SPRITE

spinning VIRE

arrowroot ARARU, ARARAO, CANNA, MARANTA, TACCA, PIA, MUSA

arrowworm SAGITTA

arroyo GULL(E)Y, CHANNEL, WATERCOURSE, HONDO

arsenic AS

mixture SPEISS

of copper ERINITE

arsis ICTUS, BEAT, RHYTHM

opposed to THESIS

arson BURNING, FIRE, CRIME

arsonist PYRO-(MANIAC)

art CRAFT, SKILL, CUNNING, SCIENCE, TECHNIC, ARS, WIT, ARTIFICE, KNACK, TRADE, CALLING, BUSINESS
style DADA
Artemis UPIS, PHOEBE, DELIA(N)
brother of APOLLO
artery STREET, ROAD, AORTA, ROUTE, WAY, COURSE, CONDUIT, PATH, VESSEL
large AORTA
neck CAROTID
pulse of ICTUS
artful POLITIC, PRACTIC(AL), WILY, CUNNING, ADROIT, SMOOTH, SUAVE, SLY, FOXY, TRICKY, CRAFTY, DECEITFUL, DESIGNING, STEALTHY
arthritis GOUT
remedy ACTH, CORTISONE
arthropoda PHYLA, CRAB, SPIDER
arthrotome SCALPEL
Arthur, King *See* "King Arthur"
artichoke BUR, CANADA, CYNARA
Chinese CHOROGI
leafstalk CHARD
article OBJECT, THING, STORY, ESSAY, THEME, REPORT, ITEM, AN, THE, CLAUSE, PLANK, PAPER, PARAGRAPH
Arabic AL
French LA, LE, LES, UN, UNE(S)
German DER, EIN, DAS
Spanish EL, LA, LAS, LOS
articulate VOCAL, FLUENT, ORAL, GLIB, UNITE, JOIN, JOINTED, DISTINCT, CLEAR, LINK, UTTER, ENUNCIATE, SPEAK
artifice TRICK, CRAFT, GUILE, FEINT, RUSE, ART, WILE, DEVICE, CUNNING, FINESSE, SKILL, CONTRIVANCE, INVENTION, DECEIT, PLAN
artificial FALSE, SHAM, ERSATZ, SPURIOUS,

UNNATURAL, FORGED, FAKE(D), AFFECTED, FICTITIOUS, SYNTHETIC
artillery ARMS, GUNS, CANNON, ORDNANCE
discharge RAFALE, SALVO
artisan CRAFTSMAN, ARTIST, WORKMAN, HAND, MECHANIC, OPERATIVE
artist MASTER, PAINTER, SCULPTOR, ADEPT, DAB, EXPERT, WIZARD, ETCHER, SKETCHER
medium TEMPERA, OILS
artistic strewing SEME
artless SIMPLE, NAIVE, NAIF, CANDID, OPEN, PLAIN, GUILELESS, FRANK, UNAFFECTED, UNDESIGNING
arts, *three liberal* TRIVIUM
arum CUCKOOPINT, AROIDES, TARO, ARAD, AROID, PLANT
water CALLA
Aryan MEDE, SLAV, CAUCASIAN
deity ORMUZD, ORMAZD
god of fire AGNI
of India HINDU
as QUA, WHILE, SIMILAR, LIKE, FOR, SINCE, THUS
far as TO
usual SOLITO
written STA, STET, SIC
asafetida LASER, FERULA, HING
Asa's *father* ABIA
ascend *See* "arise" RISE, UPGO, CLIMB, SCALE
ascendancy MASTERY, INFLUENCE, POWER, AUTHORITY, SWAY, CONTROL, SUCCESS
ascending MOUNTING, RISING, CLIMBING
ascent RISE, LEAP, UP-SWING, HILL, STEPS, STAIRS, STY, RAMP, ACCLIVITY, GRADIENT, INCLINE, SLOPE, GLORY
ascertain FIND, LEND,

DISCOVER, UNEARTH, LEARN, DETERMINE
ascetic ESSENE, HERMIT, STOIC, YOGI, MONK, RECLUSE, AUSTERE, SEVERE, STERN, FRIAR, NUN, ANCHORET, ANCHORITE, DEVOTEE
ascot SCARF, TIE, RACECOURSE, TAN
ascribe REFER, IMPUTE, CREDIT, AS-SIGN, CITE, CHARGE, ALLEGE, GUESS, AT-TRIBUTE, BLAME
ascription of praise GLORIA
aseptic STERILE, BARREN, CLEAN
Asgard, *bridge to* BIFROST
ash EMBER, CINDER, CLINKER, CORPSE, ROWAN, SORB, ASE, FRAXINUS, TREE
Africa ARTAR
fruit KEY, SAMARA
mountain ROWAN, RON
ashamed ABASHED, CONFUSED, MEAN, BAD
ashen CINEREOUS, PALE, LIVID, GREY, GRAY, WAN, WAXEN, PALLID, GHASTLY, GRIM, BLANCHED
Asherite AMAL
Asher's *daughter* SERAH, BERIAH
father JACOB
son USUI, JIMNAH
ashes, *pertaining to* CINERARY
ashkoko CONY, DAMAN
ashy *See* "ashen"
Asia, Asian, Asiatic
antelope SEROW
bird MYNA, PITTA
coin See country in-volved
country KOREA, IRAK (IRAQ), IRAN, SIAM, INDIA, CHINA, LAOS
cow ZO, ZOH, ZOBO
desert GOBI
Eskimo YUIT, INNUIT
evergreen BAGO
feline OUNCE, TIGER
gangster DACOIT
imamate YEMEN

kingdom ELAM, IRAQ
(IRAK), ANAM, KOREA,
NEPAL
lake BAIKAL,
BALKHASH
Minor, city of MYRA,
MYUS, TROY, USHAK,
ISSUS, SARDIS, HARAN,
TARSUS, PERGA
  *district, province, or
country* LYCIA,
LYDIA, CILICIA,
IONIA, IZMIR
(SMYRNA), CARIA,
PONTUS, TROAS
(TROAD)
  mountain(s) IDA,
ALAI
  old name for
ANATOLIA
  river HALYS
  southeast (old
name) CILICIA
nomad KIPCHAK,
TATAR, ARAB, MONGOL
official IMAM
open tract MAIDAN
people HUNS, SERES,
SERIC
plague CHOLERA
plain CHOL
plant RAMIE, SESAME
range ALAI
river See under
"river" MEKONG,
ILI, OB, YALU, AMUR
rodent MARMOT, PIKA
sardine LOUR
sea ARAL, AZOV
seaport SINOPE
shrub TEA, TCHE,
THEA
storm TYPHOON,
MONSOON
  snowstorm
BURA(N)
tableland PAMIR
tree See under "tree"
ASAK, NARRA,
BANYAN, ASOK(A)
tribe TAI, TURKI,
UZBEG, UZBEK
weapon ADAGA
windstorm BURA(N),
MONSOON, TYPHOON
aside AWAY, GONE,
OFF, PRIVATE,
WHISPER, APART,
ALOOF, LATERAL(LY)
asinine IDIOTIC, INEPT,
SILLY, OBTUSE, DENSE,
NUTTY, STUPID,

SIMPLE, FATUOUS,
CRASS, DULL, DOLTISH,
SENSELESS, FOOLISH
ask PRAY, SUE, PLEAD,
BEG, ENTREAT, QUIZ,
QUERY, QUESTION, IN-
TERROGATE, INQUIRE,
INVITE, PETITION,
IMPLORE, REQUEST
askew (A)WRY, AGEE,
ALOP, AMISS, ASKANT,
CROOKED, OBLIQUE,
ATWIST, DISTORTED
asleep DORMANT, ABED,
DEAD, SLUMBERING,
LATENT
asp URAEUS, VIPER,
SNAKE
aspect MIEN, LOOK,
PHASE, STAGE, SHAPE,
FACE, VISAGE, CAR-
RIAGE, AIR, GUISE,
FACET, SIDE, ANGLE,
SITUATION, BEARING,
FEATURE, COUNTE-
NANCE, VIEW, AP-
PEARANCE
  general FACIES
aspen APS, ASP, QUAK-
ING, POPLAR, TREE,
TREMBLE
asperse VILIFY, LIBEL,
REVILE, SLANDER,
SLUR, DEFILE, ABUSE,
MALIGN, CALUMNIATE,
DISPARAGE, VITU-
PERATE, LAMPOON,
BESPATTER, BESMIRCH,
BLACKEN, DEFAME,
TRADUCE
asphyxia ACROTISM,
APNOEA, APNEA, SUF-
FOCATION
aspic GELATINE,
LAVENDER, ASP,
CANNON, JELLY
aspire LONG, HOPE,
SEEK, DESIRE, AIM,
PANT, STRIVE, COVET,
THIRST, PINE, CRAVE,
WANT
ass ONAGER, QUAGGA,
DONKEY, JACKASS,
DOLT, BURRO, FOOL,
SIMPLETON, BLOCK-
HEAD
  combining form ONO
assail BESET, ATTACK,
BOMBARD, ASSAULT,
STORM, BUFFET, IN-
VADE, MALIGN, AC-
CUSE

Assam *capital* SHIL-
LONG
  dialect LHOTA, AO,
AKA
  mongoloid GARO
  shrub TEA, TCHE
  silkworm ERI, ERIA
  town LEDO
  tribesman AHOM,
AKA, GARO, AO, NAGA
assart CLEARING, GRUB
assault CHARGE, ONSET,
SIEGE, ATTACK, RAID,
STORM, SMITE, SLUG,
STRIKE, BEAT, POUND,
ASSAIL, AGGRESSION,
BOMBARD, BUFFET,
INVADE, ONSLAUGHT
assay TRY, TEST,
PROVE, ANALYSIS, AT-
TEMPT, EFFORT
assayer TRIER, EX-
PLORER, TESTER
assaying vessel CUPEL,
CUP
asse CAAMA, FOX,
HARTEBEEST
assemblage CAUCUS,
POSSE, LEVY, CONVOY,
SWARM, FLOCK, HERD,
THRONG, CROWD,
PACK, HOOKUP, COL-
LECTION, GROUP,
BODY, BUNCH,
CLUSTER, MASS,
LEVEE, ARMY
assemble MEET, MASS,
MUSTER, GATHER,
UNITE, CONGREGATE,
CONVENE, COLLECT,
CONVOKE
assembly SESSION,
BEVY, DIET, SYNOD,
PARTY, TROOP, BAND,
PRESS, COMPANY,
CONGRESS, LEGISLA-
TURE, PARLIAMENT,
GROUP, COUNCIL,
MEETING, SOCIETY
  full PLENA
  hall KIVA
  place, Greek AGORA
assent ACCEDE, AMEN,
GRANT, NOD, AGREE,
CONCUR, YIELD, AL-
LOW, ACQUIESCE, AC-
CORD
assert AVOW, DECLARE,
SAY, AFFIRM, STATE,
CITE, ALLEGE, AVER,
(DE)POSE, VOICE,

POSIT, SWEAR, MAIN-
TAIN, AVOUCH
assess VALUE, MISE,
RATE, PRICE, CHARGE,
TAX, TOLL, EXTENT,
LEVY, MEASURE, SCOT,
CESS, WORTH, RECKON,
TITHE, APPRAISE, IM-
POSE
assessment SCUTAGE,
TAX, LEVY, DUTY, IM-
POST, TOLL, TARIFF,
RATAL, TITHE, SCOT,
PRICE
assessor JUDGE, RATER,
ADJUDICATOR
asset(s) GOODS,
CAPITAL, ESTATE,
CREDIT, MEANS,
PROPERTY, EFFECTS,
MONEY, ACCOUNTS
asseverate AVER,
(A)VOW, SWEAR, DE-
CLARE, STATE
assign ALLOT, FIX,
SEAL, SET, GIVE, DEAL,
DOLE, DELEGATE,
CEDE, CHARGE,
IMPUTE, TRANSFER,
DEFINE, RATE, AP-
PORTION, CONVEY,
REFER, COMMISSION
assignation TRYST,
DATE, APPOINTMENT
assignor CEDENT
assimilate DIGEST,
MERGE, ABSORB,
BLEND, FUSE, MIX,
INCORPORATE, ADAPT,
METABOLIZE
assist ABET, AVAIL,
SPEED, HELP, AID,
SECOND, SUPPORT,
BACK, ESCORT,
BENEFIT, SQUIRE,
NURSE, BEFRIEND,
SERVE, SUCCOR,
COACH, BOOST, RE-
LIEVE, SUSTAIN, FAVOR
assistance ALMS, DOLE,
GIFT, HELP, AID,
FURTHERANCE,
PATRONAGE
assistant AID(E), ALLY,
SERVANT, COHORT,
SECOND, ABETTOR,
CLERK, AUXILIARY,
HELPER, HAND, AD-
JUTANT, NURSE,
SQUIRE, MATE, AS-
SOCIATE, PARTNER

assistants STAFF,
MATES, CREW, AS-
SOCIATES, HELPERS
assize COURT, OYER,
TRIBUNAL
associate COMBINE,
JOIN, UNITE, RELATE,
LINK, MIX, MERGE,
COLLECT, HOBNOB,
CHUM, CRONY, MATE,
ALLY, BUDDY, COL-
LEAGUE, COHORT,
HELPER, AIDE,
COMRADE, PAL,
CONSORT, FRIEND,
FELLOW, COADJUTOR,
PARTNER, HUSBAND,
WIFE, SPOUSE
association GILD,
GUILD, UNION, CLUB,
ORDER, FIRM, LODGE,
CARTEL, SOCIETY,
SODALITY, PARTNER-
SHIP, COMPANY,
ALLIANCE
football SOCCER
merchants' HANSE
Russian ARTEL
secret CABAL, LODGE
assonance PARAGRAM,
PUN, RHYME
as soon as ONCE
assort ARRANGE,
CLASSIFY, SORT,
ORDER, RANK, GROUP,
TYPE, FILE
assortment MIXTURE,
BATCH, LOT, COLLEC-
TION, SET, SUITE
assuage ALLAY, PACIFY,
CALM, MITIGATE,
MODERATE, MOLLIFY,
COMPOSE, SOOTHE,
COMFORT, RELIEVE,
EASE
assuasive SOOTHING,
EMOLLIENT, LENITIVE,
LENIENT, EASEFUL
assume DON, ADOPT,
PREMISE, INFER, TAKE,
ACCEPT, MASK, AF-
FECT, SUPPOSE,
SIMULATE, BELIEVE,
USURP, FEIGN,
CLOTHE, CLOAK, UN-
DERTAKE, PRETEND,
ARROGATE
assurance FAITH,
CREDIT, TRUST, NERVE,
SECURITY, CERTAINTY,
PROMISE, EF-

FRONTERY, BRASS,
APLOMB, COOLNESS
assure SECURE,
CERTIFY, PLEDGE,
PROMISE, INSURE,
ENHEARTEN, WAR-
RANT, GUARANTEE
assuredly CERTES,
SURE(LY), IN-
DUBITABLY, TRULY,
UNDOUBTEDLY,
VERILY
Assyria, Assyrian
ASSHUR, ASSUR, ASHUR
ancient capital CALAH,
NINEVAH (NINUS),
ANTIOCH
city ARBELA, HARA,
OPIS
*god or goddess See
under "god" or
"goddess"*
king PUL (PHUL),
SARGON
queen SEMIRAMIS
river ADHIAN, ZAB
astacidae CRAB,
LOBSTER, CRAWFISH,
CRAYFISH
asteism RAILLERY,
DERISION, IRONY
asterisk STAR, MARK
astern REAR, ABAFT,
(B)AFT, OCCIPUT,
AFTER, HIND, BACK
asteroid, *first* CERES
nearest earth EROS
asthmatic PURSY,
OBESE, PUFFY,
WHEEZY
astir AGOG, VIGILANT,
EAGER, UP, GOING,
ACTIVE, ALERT,
ROUSED, EXCITED,
MOVING, ABOUT
Astolat, *lily maid*
ELAINE
astonish SURPRISE,
AMAZE, IMPRESS,
STRIKE, TOUCH, AF-
FECT, STARTLE, CON-
FOUND, STUPEFY,
ASTOUND, OVER-
WHELM
astound AMAZE, STAG-
GER, STUN, STARTLE,
ALARM, TERRIFY,
SHOCK, SURPRISE,
EXCITE
astrakhan KARAKUL
(CARACUL), CLOTH,
APPLE

astral STARRY,
STELLAR, LAMP,
SIDEREAL, STARLIKE
fluid OD, ODYL(E)
astray LOST, WRONG,
AMISS, DEVIATE,
(A)WRY, WANDERING,
ERRING, SINNING,
FAULTY
astringent SOUR, ACID,
TART, STYPTIC, ALUM,
STERN, AUSTERE
gum KINO
astrologer JOSHI,
MERLIN,
NOSTRADAMUS
astrological belief
SIDERISM
astronaut GLENN, CAR-
PENTER, POPOVICH,
NIKOLAYEV,
TITOV, GAGARIN
chimpanzee ENOS
astronomical URANIC,
DISTANT, FAR, LARGE,
HUGE, IMMENSE,
COLOSSAL
cloud NEBULA
cycle SAROS
instrument ABA,
ARMIL, ORRERY,
SEXTANT
measure APSIS
astronomy, muse of
URANIA
astute KEEN, SHREWD,
CANNY, CLEVER,
QUICK, SHARP, WILY,
SLY, FOXY, CUNNING,
WISE, SKILLED, ACUTE
asunder (A)TWAIN,
APART, DIVIDED,
SEPARATED
as well as AND
"As You Like It"
character AMIENS,
JAQUES, OLIVER,
ADAM, CORIN, CELIA,
PHEBE
asylum RETREAT,
ALTAR, HOME, HAVEN,
REFUGE, SHELTER,
ARK, COVER, HARBOR,
SANCTUARY
at THE, AU, AL, TO, ALS,
ATTEN
all EVER, ANYWAY,
ANY, AUGHT, AVA
home HERE, IN, TEA,
PARTY, RECEPTION,
LEVEE

last ULTIMATELY,
FINALLY
same age COEVAL
Atahualpa INCA,
INDIAN
ataman HETMAN, COS-
SACK, HEADMAN,
CHIEF, JUDGE
atap NIPA, PALM
ateles paniscus COAITA,
MONKEY
atelier STUDIO
athanor FURNACE,
OVEN
Athapascan INDIAN
Athena PALLAS, ALERA,
MINERVA, ATHENE
armor EGIS
pertaining to ALEA,
PALLADIAN
temple PARTHENON
Athens, Athenian
ATTIC(A)
architect ICTINUS
assembly BOULE,
PNYX
astronomer METON
clan OBE
coin CHALCUS,
CHALKOS
founder CECROPS
general NICIAS,
PHOCION
harbor PIRAEUS
hill ACROPOLIS
judge DICAST
king CODRUS, CECROPS
lawgiver SOLON
maker DRACO
magistrate ARCHON,
DRACO
market place AGORA
room ADYTUM,
ATRIUM, CELLA
sculptor PHIDIAS
temple NIKE, ZEUS
athirst AVID, DRY,
PARCHED, KEEN,
EAGER, AGOG, ARID
athletic LUSTY,
BRAWNY, STALWART,
AGILE, POWERFUL,
STRONG, BURLY,
ROBUST, SINEWY,
STRAPPING, ACRO-
BATIC, VIGOROUS
event MEET, GAME,
AGON, RACE
field OVAL, GRID,
ARENA, STADIUM
prize MEDAL, CUP,
RIBBON

athwart TRAVERSE,
ACROSS, SIDEWISE,
OBLIQUE
Atlantides *See*
"Hesperides"
atlas MAINSTAY,
SATIN, MAPS, TITAN,
BONE, LIST, BOOK
Atlas' *daughter*
CALYPSO
mother CLYMENE
Atli's *wife* GUDRUN
atloid ATLANTAL
atmosphere AIR, AURA,
FEELING, SAVOR, TONE,
QUALITY, ETHER
gas of ARGON, ZENON,
NITROGEN, OXYGEN
atoll TARAWA, BIKINI,
ISLAND, REEF
atom CORPUSCLE, BIT,
ION, IOTA, MONAD,
DASH, PARTICLE,
SPECK, MOTE, TITTLE,
WHIM, WHIT, MITE,
JOT, TINGE, SHADE
part PROTON
atomic MOLECULAR,
MINUTE
machine BETATRON,
RHEOTRON
physicist BOHR,
MEITNER, MILLIKAN,
PAULI, COMPTON,
UREY, FERMI, RABI
atomy MOTE, PIGMY,
PYGMY, MITE
atone AMEND,
EXPIATE, REDEEM,
AGREE, HARMONIZE
atonic sound SURD,
UNHEARD
atrabiliar, atrabilious
MOROSE, GLUM,
SULLEN, MELANCHOLY
atramental INKY,
BLACK
Atreus' *brother*
THYESTES
father PELOPS
Atridae, *father of*
ATREUS
atrocious SAVAGE,
GROSS, RANK, IN-
FAMOUS, VILLAINOUS,
HEINOUS, CRUEL, BAD,
FLAGRANT, AWFUL,
EXECRABLE, ODIOUS,
VILE
atrophy STUNT,
STULTIFY, EMACIA-

TION, RUST, SHRINK-
(AGE)
atrous BLACK, EBON
attach FASTEN, PEND,
TIE, ADD, APPEND,
ARREST, SEIZE, ANNEX,
LOVE, CONNECT,
(AF)FIX, LINK, BIND,
UNITE, JOIN, COUPLE,
HITCH
attached ADNATE,
AFFIXED, FOND,
JOINED
by base SESSILE
attack SPASM, ICTUS,
FIT, STROKE, FIGHT,
STORM, BATTLE, PUSH,
ACTION, ONSET, BESET,
FORAY, ASSAIL,
ASSAULT, BLITZ, OF-
FENSE, AGGRESS,
OPPUGN, CHARGE,
RAID, THRUST,
CENSURE, STRIKE
mock FEINT
attain WIN, GAIN,
ACHIEVE, REACH, SUC-
CEED, EARN, END, GET,
PROVE, SECURE, AC-
QUIRE, EFFECT,
PROCURE, AC-
COMPLISH, OBTAIN,
ARRIVE
attainment SKILL,
WISDOM, ACCOMPLISH-
MENT, FEAT
attaint DAMN, DOOM,
TAINT, KILL, SLAY,
DEFILE, CORRUPT,
POLLUTE
attar OTTO, PERFUME,
OIL, ESSENCE
attempt BEGIN, START,
ESSAY, TRY, EFFORT,
TRIAL, SEEK, SAY,
ENDEAVOR, SHOT,
STAB, UNDERTAKE,
VENTURE, ASSAY
attend EAR, HEAR, FOL-
LOW, HEED, LISTEN,
MIND, WATCH,
HARK(EN), SERVE,
TEND, ESCORT, SQUIRE,
WAIT, NURSE, FOSTER,
HO(A), ACCOMPANY,
GUARD
attendants SUITE,
RETINUE, TRAIN,
GUARDS
attention EAR, LISTEN,
HEED, NOTICE,
NOTE, REGARD, STUDY,

CARE, OBSERVANCE,
RESPECT
getter AHEM
attentive ALERT, IN-
TENT, WARY, POLITE,
CIVIL, WATCHFUL,
MINDFUL, CIRCUM-
SPECT, CAREFUL
attenuate THIN, DE-
CREASE, RAREFY,
WEAKEN, DILUTE, SAP,
WATER, REDUCE
attest VOUCH, SEAL, AD-
JURE, AFFIRM, SWEAR,
PROVE, CERTIFY, CON-
FESS
attic GARRET, LOFT,
CLASSICAL
Attica, *alien resident of*
METIC
city ATHENS
historian XENOPHON
subdivision DEME
Attila HUN, ETZEL
attire ADIGHT, ARRAY,
GARB, GUISE, LIVERY,
REGALIA, DRESS,
CLOTHE(S), OUTFIT,
ARM, ROBE, VEST
in armor PANOPLY
attitude POSE, STAND,
POSTURE, POSITION,
ANGLE, SLANT,
BIAS, MIEN,
ASPECT, PHASE,
DISPOSITION, FEELING,
SET, BEARING, AIR
attorney LAWYER,
DEPUTY, AGENT,
PROXY, FACTOR,
SOLICITOR, COUNSEL-
(L)OR, ADVOCATE
attract (AL)LURE, BAIT,
DRAW, PULL, TAKE,
CHARM, INTEREST,
FASCINATE, ENTICE,
SEDUCE, INVITE,
ENAMOUR, IN-
FLUENCE, TEMPT,
MAGNETIZE
attraction MAGNET,
GRAVITY, AFFINITY,
CHARM, WITCHERY,
SHOW
attractive CUTE,
TAKING, LOVELY, FAIR,
PRETTY, BONNY,
WINSOME, CHARMING,
ALLURING,
PLEASING, BEAUTIFUL
attribute IMPUTE,
ASCRIBE, ASSIGN,

REFER, CHARGE,
BLAME, SYMBOL,
QUALITY, OWE, PLACE,
POWER, TYPE, MARK,
TOKEN, BADGE, SIGN,
CREDIT, FIX,
PROPERTY, CHARAC-
TERISTIC
attribution THEORY,
ETIOLOGY
attrition WEAR,
ABRASION, FRICTION,
ANGUISH, REGRET,
SORROW, GRIEF
attune KEY, TUNE,
HARMONIZE, ADAPT,
ADJUST, AGREE,
TEMPER, ACCORD,
PREPARE
au GOLD
auction BRIDGE, SALE,
DISPOSAL, VENDUE,
SELL, VEND, BARTER,
TRADE
audacious BRAZEN,
SAUCY, BOLD, BRAVE,
BRASH, RASH, DARING,
FEARLESS, INTREPID
audacity NERVE,
TEMERITY, CRUST,
COURAGE, DARING,
BRASS, GALL, METTLE,
SPIRIT, RASHNESS,
PRESUMPTION, IM-
PERTINENCE, IM-
PUDENCE, INSOLENCE
audad *See* "aoudad"
Audibertia RAMONA
audience EAR, HEAR-
ING, ASSEMBLY,
PUBLIC, FANS,
RECEPTION
audit SCAN, CHECK,
PROBE, INQUIRE,
INSPECT, EXAMINE,
ACCOUNT
auditor HEARER, AP-
POSER, CENSOR, AC-
COUNTANT, CPA,
LISTENER
auditorium HALL,
THEATRE, THEATER,
ODEUM
auditory OTIC, ORAL,
AURAL, ACOUSTIC
au fait EXPERT, SKILL-
FUL, PROPER,
PROFICIENT
auger GIMLET, BORER,
WIMBLE, TOOL
cutting edge LIP

augment SWELL, ADD, EKE, EXPAND, DILATE, INCREASE, MAGNIFY, ENLARGE

augur(y) PORTEND, BODE, OMEN, PRESAGE, DIVINE, FORESEE, SIGN, TOKEN, BADGE, AUSPEX, MARK, SOOTH-SAYER, SEER, PROPHET

august GRAND, NOBLE, EXALTED, MAJESTIC, VENERABLE, AWFUL, STATELY, IMPOSING, REGAL

August 1, *in England* LAMMAS

auk MURRE, ROTCH(E), ARRIE, PUFFIN, GUIL-LEMOT, DOVEKIE, BIRD

family ALCIDAE

genus ALLE, ALCA, URIA, GUILLEMOT

razor-billed MURRE, FALK

aula HALL, COURT, EMBLIC

Auld Hornie DEVIL

aura BUZZARD, HALO, FEEL(ING), SAVOR, TONE, AROMA, ODOR, ATMOSPHERE, EMANA-TION

aural AURICULAR, OTIC, AUDIBLE

aureate ROCOCO, ORNATE, GOLDEN, YEL-LOW

aureola GLORIA, LIGHT, HALO, NIMBUS

au revoir ADIEU, GOODBYE, ALOHA, ADIOS, TA-TA

auricle PINNA, TRUMPET, EAR

auricula plant PRIM-ROSE

auricular OTIC

auriferous GOLDEN

Auriga, *star in* CAPELLA

aurochs BISON, TUR, URUS

Aurora DAWN, EOS

tears of DEW

aurorian EOAN, ROSEATE, EASTERN, DAWNLIKE

aurum GOLD

Ausonia ITALY

auspice AEGIS, AID, SIGN, FAVOR, IN-FLUENCE, PATRONAGE, OMEN, PROTECTION, CARE, GUIDANCE

auspicious FORTUNATE, BENIGN, LUCKY, HAPPY, PROPITIOUS, FAVORABLE, OP-PORTUNE, HOPEFUL

Austen JANE

austere ASCETIC, HARSH, STERN, SEVERE, RIGOROUS, SOBER, EARNEST, GRAVE, SERIOUS, FORMAL, STIFF, RELENTLESS, HARD, RIGID, COLD, FRIGHTFUL, FRIGID

Australia, Australian AUSSIE

acacia MYALL, MULGA

arboreal animal DASYURE

bee KARBI

beef-wood BELAH

bird EM(E)U, EMEW, KOEL, COOEY, WEKA, LOWAN, LEIPOA, MALLEE

boomerang KILEY

cape YORK, HONE

city or town PERTH, MANLY

cockatoo GALAH

fern NARDOO, NARDU

fish TREVALLY, MADO

gale BUSTER

hawk KAHU

horse WALER

hut MIMI, MIAMIA

island NEPTUNE

lake EYRE, FROME, WELLS

lizard GOAN(N)A

mahogany GUNNUNG

manna LAAP, LERP, LAARP

marsupial KOALA, TAIT, KANGAROO, WOMBAT

mountain BLUE

native MYALL

cry of COOEE, COOEY

ostrich EMU

parrot LORY

peninsula EYRE

pepper KAVA

seaport SYDNEY

settler BASS, COOK

sheep shearing fold BOARD

shield MULGA

shrub HOYA, CORREA

soldier ANZAK

throwing stick WOMERAH, WOMMALE

tree KARI, TUART, KARRI, BOREE, GOAI, BELAH, PENDA, MYALL, GUNNUNG, MULGA, KOWHAI, GMELINA, MEDLAR, MARARA, WILGA

tribal group KOKO

water mole PLATYPUS, DUCKBILL

wild dog DINGO

Austria, Austrian

amphibian OLM

city or town LINZ, WELS, GRAZ, STEYR, KREMS

coin GULDEN, HELLER, DUCAT, KRONE, CROWN, FLORIN, ZEHNER, LIRA

dance DREHER

measure MUTH, FASS, SEIDEL

psychiatrist ADLER, FREUD

rifleman JAGER

river See under "river"

weight UNZE

authentic CORRECT, RIGHT, ACTUAL, EXACT, REAL, GENUINE, TRUE, ORIGINAL, VERITABLE, RELIABLE, PROPER, PURE, CERTAIN, OFFICIAL

author See "writer" PARENT, WRITER, MAKER, INVENTOR, BEGETTER, PRODUCER

authority POWER, RIGHT, TITLE, DYNASTY, REGIME, POLICE, SWAY, RULE, WEIGHT, CREDIT, PRESTIGE, EXPERT, ADEPT, ARTIST, COM-MAND

authorize(d) LEGAL, ENTITLE, ALLOW, LET, LICENSE, PERMIT, SANCTION, PATENT, COMMISSION

auto CAR, JALOPY, SEDAN, COUPE, ROADSTER, CONVERTI-BLE, RACER autobiographical sketch VITA, MEMOIR

autochthon(ous) NATIVE, ABORIGINE

autocrat CZAR, TSAR, DICTATOR, DESPOT, MONARCH, MOGUL, SOVEREIGN

autograph SIGNATURE, NAME

automaton ANDROID, GOLEM, ROBOT

autopsy NECROPSY

autumn FALL, HARVEST-TIME

flower ASTER

auxiliary SUB, ALLY, HELPER, AID(E), COADJUTOR, MATE, ANCILLARY, PARTNER, BRANCH, ASSISTANT, CONFEDERATE, SECONDARY

avail USE, SERVE, DO, HELP, SUFFICE, BENEFIT, PROFIT, AID, APPLY, UTILIZE, ADVANTAGE, SUCCEED

available FREE, OPEN, HANDY, READY, CONVENIENT, USABLE, FIT, ACCESSIBLE, ATTAINABLE, OBTAINABLE, PRESENT

avarice GREED, CUPIDITY, AVIDITY, RAPACITY

avast STOP, HOLD, CEASE, STAY

ave HAIL, FAREWELL

avellane HAZEL, FILBERT, NUT

avenaceous OATY

avenge RETALIATE, REVENGE, (RE)PAY, PUNISH, CHASTISE, VINDICATE, REQUITE

avenger NEMESIS, VINDICATOR

avenging spirit FURY, KER, ATE

avenue GATE, ARTERY, PIKE, ROAD, STREET, DRIVE, MALL, PASSAGE, ENTRY, WAY, ACCESS, ALLEY

avens GEUM, HERB

aver ASSERT, STATE, DECLARE, AVOW, AFFIRM, SWEAR, ALLEGE, PROTEST

average NORM, PAR, MEAN, MEDIAL, NOR-

MAL, MEDIOCRE, RULE, STANDARD, MEDIAN, FAIR, USUAL, SO-SO, ORDINARY

averse LOTH, LOATH, AGAINST, RELUCTANT, BALKY, UNWILLING, OPPOSED

aversion to society ANTHROPOPHOBIA

avert TURN, WARD, FEND, PREVENT, DETER, SHEER, THWART, PARRY, RETARD, SHIELD, DODGE, DEFLECT, DIVERT, BEND, TWIST, MOVE

Avesta *division* YASNA, GATHAS, YASHTS, VISPERED, VENTIDAD

translation of ZEND

avid EAGER, GREEDY, DESIROUS, LONG, KEEN, AGOG, ANXIOUS, ATHIRST, CRAVING

avifauna ORNIS, BIRDS

avocado AGUACATE, PEAR, COYO, CHININ, ALLIGATO, TREE

avocation HOBBY, VOCATION, WORK, CALLING, TRADE

avocet GODWIT, BIRD

avoid ELUDE, ESCHEW, EVITATE, HEDGE, AVERT, FLEE, FLY, VOID, SHUN, SHIRK, SLACK, DODGE, ESCAPE

avouch AVER, AFFIRM, AVOW, ASSERT, SWEAR, DECLARE

avow(al) OATH, DEPONE, SWEAR, OWN, CONFESS, ADMIT, DEPOSE, ACKNOWLEDGE, ASSERT

await BIDE, EXPECT, LOOK, HOPE, STAY, TARRY, IMPEND, PEND

awake STIR, ROUSE, WAKE, AWARE, ALIVE, ALERT, HEEDFUL, ATTENTIVE, LIVELY, VIGILANT, ACTIVE, CAREFUL

award BOUNTY, BONUS, TONY, MEDAL, OSCAR, PRIZE, ALLOT, GRANT, MEED, ACCOLADE, KISS, BESTOW, CON-

FER, GIVE, PRESENT, CONSIGN, ADJUDGE

aware HEP, CONSCIOUS, MINDFUL, RECK, ALERT, COGNIZANT, ALIVE, SURE, SENSIBLE, VIGILANT, WATCHFUL

away OUT, ASIDE, FRO, OFF, ABSENT, GONE, FAR, DISTANT, REMOTE, APART

prefix AB, AP, APO, APH

awe RESPECT, FEAR, DREAD, ESTEEM, REGARD, DAUNT, COW, VENERATION, REVERENCE, WONDER

aweather, *opposite* ALEE

awesome EERY, EERIE, APPALLING, AWFUL

aweto WERI, CATERPILLAR

awkward GAUCHE, CLUMSY, LOUTISH, INEPT, INAPT, UNGAINLY, STIFF, WOODEN, RIGID, BUNGLING, MALADROIT, PONDEROUS, UGLY

awl BROACH, PUNCH, NEEDLE

awn AVEL, ARISTA, BARB, BEARD, BRISTLE

awned ARISTATE

awning SHELTER, TENT, TILT, CANOPY, BALDACHIN, CANVAS, COVER, SHADE

awry AGEE, AMISS, AGLEY, ALOP, EVIL, OBLIQUE, ASKEW, DISTORTED, CROOKED

ax, axe ADZ, HATCHET, POLEAX, TOOL

pickax(e) GURLET

axil ALA, STEM, WING, ANGLE, RECESS

axilla ARMPIT, OXTER, AXIL

axillary ALAR

axiom RULE, MAXIM, LAW, THEOREM, SAW, MOTTO, PROVERB, TRUISM

axis SHAFT, PIVOT, LEAGUE, HUB, CEN-

TER, SPINDLE, SPOOL, DEER
of vertebrae AXON
power GERMANY, JAPAN, ITALY
axle AXIS, SPINDLE, PIVOT, SKENE, ARBOR, BAR, PIN, HUB, SPOOL
near center AXILE, HUB
aye (FOR)EVER, AY, YEA, YES, PRO, ALWAYS
aye-aye LEMUR
Azerbaidzhan *capital* BAKU
Azores *island* FAYAL, PICO, FLORES
port HORTA
volcano PICO
azote NITROGEN
Aztec *country* AZTECAN
god XIPE, EECATL, MEZTLI
hero NATA
  wife of NANA
language NAHUATL, AZTECAN
temple TEOCALLI, TEOPAN
azure BLUE, CERULEAN, BICE, CELESTE
azygous ODD, SINGLE
azym(e) BREAD
opposed to ENZYME
azymous UNLEAVENED

B

B BE, BEE, BETA
baa BLEAT
Baba ALI
babbitt LINE, FILL, FURNISH, METAL, NOVEL
babble CHATTER, PRATTLE, GOSSIP, RAVE, BLAB, TALK, SPEAK, GIBBER, GURGLE, BLAT, PRATE, PURL, GAB, CHAT, JABBER, BLATHER, PALAVER, TATTLE, TWADDLE
babel CLANG, DISCORD, JARGON, RACKET, DIN, TUMULT, CONFUSION
Babel, *site of tower* SHINAR

Babism, *creed* BAHAISM
baboon CHACMA, PAPA, MANDRILL, DRILL, APE
babul ATTALEH, ACACIA, LAC, MIMOSA, VERA, GUM, TREE
pods of GARAD
baby BABE, CHILD, TOT, INFANT, BAIRN, HUMOR, PAMPER, SPOIL
carriage PRAM, STROLLER, (GO)CART
crib, Xmas. CRECHE
food PAP, MILK
napkin BIB
outfit LAYETTE
room NURSERY
Babylonia, Babylonian SUMER(IAN), ACCAD, ELAM, SUSIANA, ELAMITE, CHALDEA, SHINAR
abode of dead ARALU
ruler of abode NERGAL
Bacchus SIRIS
chaos APSU
city, ancient AKKAD, CUNAXA
coin STATER
deity See under "god"
division ELAM, SUMER
Earth Mother ISHTAR
god or goddess See under "god" *or* "goddess"
hero ETANA
language ACCAD, AKKAD
lunar cycle SAROS
monarch, legendary ALOROS
people SUMERIAN(S), ELAMITE(S)
priestess ENTUM
river TIGRIS, EUPHRATES
tower ZIGURAT
weight MINA
bac VAT, CISTERN
baccarat term BANCO
baccate PULPY
bacchanal cry EVOE
bacchanalia ORGY
Bacchus, *cry for joy (song)* IACCHUS
bachelor CELIBATE,

MISOGYNIST, AGAMIST, KNIGHT, CRAPPIE
bacillus GERM, VIRUS
back ABET, SUPPORT, FAVOR, ASSIST, AID, HELP, SECOND, ENDORSE, NOTUM, HIND, DORSUM, TERGUM, AFTER, FRO, REAR, RETURN, REGRESS, STERN, AFT, POSTERIOR, BACKWARD, ABAFT, RETREAT, RETIRE
combining form RETRO
door POSTERN
lying on SUPINE, PASSIVE
of insect(s) NOTUM, NOTA
of neck NAPE, SCRUFF
out FUNK
pertaining to DORSAL, TERGAL, NOTAL
prefix RE, RETRO
toward RETRAL, RETRAD
zoology NOTUM, NOTA
backbite MALIGN, VILIFY, SASS, ASPERSE, ABUSE, SLANDER, DEFAME
backbone VERTEBRA, CHINE, SPINE, RIDGE, GRIT, GUTS, SAND, PLUCK, METTLE, SPIRIT, NERVE
back country BUSH, STICKS
backgammon term BLOT, GAMMON
back scratcher STRIGIL
backslide LAPSE, RECEDE
backward SLOW, TARDY, LOATH, AVERSE, RETRORSE, STUPID, DULL, DENSE, ATYPIC, SLUGGISH, REARWARD, REVERSED
backwater RETRACT, BAYOU
bacon slice RASHER
bacon work NOVUM, ORGANUM
bacteria, bacterium AEROBIA, AEROBE,

GERM, VIRUS, AEROBACTER
anti ANTISEPSIS, ASEPSIS
destroyer LYSIN, ALEXIN
bacteriologist's *wire* OESE
bad BASE, WANTON, EVIL, ILL, WICKED, LOW, VILE, POOR, AMORAL, BANEFUL, UGLY, MEAN, DEPRAVED, WRONG, CORRUPT, SPOILED, NAUGHTY
combining form MAL, CAC(O)
custom CACOETHES
luck AMBSACE
mannered person GOOP
badge EMBLEM, ENSIGN, FLAG, PIN, STAR, BUTTON, LABEL, SIGN, TOKEN, MARK, NOTE, SYMBOL, INSIGNE
sheriff's STAR
badger PATE, BAUSON, CHEVY, WOMBAT, HECKLE, FRET, HARRY, PLAGUE, TEASE, BAIT, RIDE, ANNOY, VEX, IRK, WORRY, PESTER, PERSECUTE, TAUNT
cape HYRAX, DAMAN, CONY
Dutch DAS
Europe BROCK
genus MELES
honey RATEL
like animal PHAMI, RATEL
Java TELEDU
State WISCONSIN
Badland mountain BUTTE
baffle FOIL, BALK, BLOCK, POSE, COD, THWART, FAZE, ADDLE, EVADE, DEFEAT, HINDER, PUZZLE, FRUSTRATE, CHECK, BEWILDER, PERPLEX
bag CASE, POUCH, SAC(K), ASCUS, ETUI, RETICULE, SACHET, SATCHEL, PURSE, NET, COP, STEAL, CYST, SNARE, BAIT, TRAP,

CATCH, NAB, CAPTURE, ACQUIRE
canvas MUSETTE
net FYKE
spore ASCUS
bagatelle TRIFLE, GAME, VERSE
baggage DUNNAGE, LUGGAGE, MINX, HUZZY, WENCH, TRAPS, IMPEDIMENTA, GEAR
bagnio PRISON, BATH, BROTHEL
bagpipe MUSETTE
pipe of CHANTER, DRONES
play SKIRL
sound of SKIRL
bah ROT, PAH, PSHAW
Bahama Islands *capital* NASSAU
island BIMINI, ABACO, ANDROS, ELEUTHERA
baikie GULL, STICK, STAKE
bail ANDI, BOND, LADE, DIP, PLEDGE, SECURITY, LADLE, SCOOP, SPOON, DISH, SURETY, BUCKET, HOOP, HANDLE, COURT, CONFINE
Baile's *father* BUAN
Bailey, Old PRISON, JAIL
bailiff REEVE, AGENT, FACTOR, OFFICER
bait DECOY, LURE, BRIBE, TRAP, TEMPT, SNARE, TRY, AFFLICT, BADGER, RUFFLE, PLAGUE, WORRY, HECTOR, CHEVY, RIDE, HARASS
to drop DAP, DIB
bake ROAST, DRY, HARDEN, FIRE, COOK, BROIL, PARCH, GRILL, STIFFEN
with crumbs SCALLOP
baker('s) ROASTER, OVEN
bird HORNERO
dozen THIRTEEN
itch RASH, PSORIASIS
kneading trough BRAKE
shovel PEEL
bakie VESSEL, TROUGH

baking *chamber* OVEN, OAST, KILN
dish RAMEKIN
pit IMU
Balaam's *beast* ASS
balance OFFSET, EVEN, POISE, REST, LEVEL, BALLAST, REMNANT, (AT)TUNE, ACCORD, AGREE, EQUAL, CREDIT, SCALE, EXCESS, SURPLUS, FIRM, SET, WEIGHT, COMPOSURE, SANITY, SERENITY, EQUILIBRIUM, REMAINDER, CONTROL
of sails ATRY
weight RIDER
balas SPINEL, RUBY
balata gum CHICLE
balcony BRATTICE, SOLLAR, STOOP, PORCH, GALLERY, PIAZZA, VERANDA
bald EPILATED, POLLED, BARE, MERE, PLAIN, NAKED, NUDE, SEVERE, HAIRLESS, BASE, UGLY
Bald(e)r, *slayer* LOK(I), LOKE
parent ODIN, FRIGG
wife NANNA
balderdash ROT, NONSENSE, DRIVEL, TRASH, JARGON
baldicoot MONK, COOT
baldness ALOPECIA, ACOMIA
baldric GIRDLE, BELT, ZODIAC
bale EVIL, ILL, PACK, BUNDLE, PARCEL, HARM, INJURY, RUIN
of figs SEROON, SERON
Balearic *island* MINORCA, MAJORCA
language CATALAN
baleen WHALE(BONE)
baleful MALIGN, SINISTER, NOXIOUS, DEADLY, RUINOUS, WRETCHED
baleise FLOG
balibago HAU, MAJAGUA, TREE
balk REBEL, STOP, SHY, HINDER, THWART, BAFFLE,

FOIL, REAR, FRUS-
TRATE, BEAT, LICK,
BLOCK, IMPEDE,
FALTER, WAVER
in fishing COND
Balkan *ridged area*
BILO
Balkis SHEBA
ball PELLET, ORB,
GLOBE, IVORY, SPHERE,
SHOT, BULLET, GLOB-
ULE, MARBLE, DANCE,
PARTY
game RUGBY,
CRICKET, PELOTA
low LINER
rice or meat PINDA
wood KNUR
ballad SONNET, DERRY,
LAY, SONG
ballast BALANCE, TRIM,
POISE, WEIGHT,
STABILITY
ballet DANCE, DRAMA,
MASQUE, CHOREOG-
RAPHY, PANTOMIME
jump JETE
skirt TUTU
turn FOUETTE
balloon BAG, AEROSTAT,
BLIMP, AIRSHIP,
DIRIGIBLE
basket CAR, GONDOLA,
NACELLE
ballot VOTE, ELECT,
POLL, VOICE, CHOICE,
TICKET
balm ANODYNE, BAL-
SAM, UNGUENT, SALVE,
SOLACE, EASE, COM-
FORT, OINTMENT,
RELIEF
of Gilead BALSAM
balmy MOONY,
DREAMY, SOFT, GEN-
TLE, BLAND, MILD,
WARM, SUNNY,
LENIENT, SOOTHING,
SWEET, FRAGRANT
balneation BATH
balsam STORAX, BDEL-
LIUM, TOLU, COPAIBA
Balt, Baltic YOD,
LETT, ESTH
Finn. VOD
gulf RIGA
island ALSEN, DAGO,
OESEL, FARO
seaport REVAL, RIGA,
TALLINN, REVEL
slav LETT
tribe LETT

Baltic Sea, *river to*
ODER (ODRA), PEENE,
WILSA, DVINA
Baluchistan *capital*
QUETTA
city QUETTA, KALAT
division or province
LUS
grain JOWAR
mountain pass BOLAN
race BRAHOES
river DASHI, NAL
ruler KHAN, SIRDAR
state KALAT, KHELAT
town BAGH
tribe REKI
tribesman MARI,
MURREE
Baltimore *stove*
LATROBE
team ORIOLES, COLTS
balustrade BARRIER,
BANISTER, PARAPET,
BALCONET(TE)
Balzac HONORE
bam HOAX, TRICK,
WHEEDLE
Bambi DEER
bamboo REED, CANE
shoots, pickled ACHAR
bamboozle TRICK,
DUPE, GULL, HOAX,
(BE)FOOL, DELUDE,
CHEAT, DECEIVE,
DEFRAUD
ban TABU, TABOO,
CURSE, EXCLUDE,
DAMN, BAR, BLOCK,
HINDER, EXECRATE,
FORBID, OUTLAW, EN-
JOIN, EDICT, CON-
DEMN, PROHIBIT
office BANAT
banal CORNY, PLATI-
TUDINOUS, JEJUNE,
FLAT, STALE, TRITE,
INANE, VAPID, SILLY
phrase CLICHE
banana, *Abyssinia*
ENSETE
bunch STEM, HAND
like PLANTAIN
plant MUSA, PESANG
Bana's *daughter* USHA
band STRIP, TAPE,
BELT, STRAP, GROUP,
TIE, SET, CIRCLE,
HORDE, MOB, CLUB,
ORDER, STRIPE,
CROWD, FILLET,
FASCIA, COMBO, BOND,
LINK, TAENIA, RING

brain LIGULA
fasten garment
PATTE
leader(s) CHORAGI,
MASTER, MAESTRO,
CONDUCTOR, MC
narrow STRIA, STRIAE,
TAPE
teeth RADULA
bandage TRUSS, FIL-
LET, LIGATE, SPICA,
SWATHE, CINCTURE,
TIE, SUPPORT
nose ACCIPITER
bandit PICAROON,
THIEF, ROBBER,
BRIGAND, OUTLAW,
THUG, BURGLAR, PAD,
GANGSTER, CORSAIR,
CATERAN, HOOD,
LOOTER, REAVER,
CROOK, LADRONE,
FOOTPAD, DACOIT,
PIRATE, MOBSTER,
HIGHWAYMAN, FREE-
BOOTER, MARAUDER,
CACO
bandmaster SOUSA
bandoline POMADE
bandy SWAP, TRADE,
DISCUSS
bane PEST, POISON,
VENOM, CURSE, PAIN,
NUISANCE, EVIL,
VIRUS, TOXIN(E),
SCOURGE, UPAS
baneful VILE, NOXIOUS,
BAD, EVIL
bang CUDGEL, RAP,
SLAM, SLAP, CLAP,
BEAT, IMPEL, THUMP,
POUND, SOUND
Bani's *son* UEL,
AMRAM
banish EXILE, DISMISS,
EXPEL, DEPORT, DIS-
PEL, PUNISH, EJECT,
EXPATRIATE, OSTRA-
CIZE
banjo, *Japanese*
SAMISEN
bank BRAE, DUNE,
SAND, SLOPE, MOUND,
RIPA, STRAND, COAST,
HEAP, RIDGE, BEACH,
BRINK, SHORE, SHOAL,
BAR, REEF, RELY,
COUNT, STACK, MASS,
PILE, RECKON, TRUST,
DEPEND, KNOLL,
DEPOSITORY
clerk TELLER

pertaining to river
RIPARIAN
bankrupt BREAK,
SMASH, FAIL(URE),
BROKE, DRAIN, RUIN,
QUISBY, INSOLVENT,
STRIP, BARE, SAP,
DEPLETE(D)
banner GONFALON,
BANDEROL(E), PEN-
NANT, FLAG, SYMBOL,
BADGE, ENSIGN,
COLOR, JACK, SIGNAL,
SALIENT, ORIFLAMME
banquet FEAST,
JUNKET, MEAL,
DINNER, FEED,
REGALE, DINE
banshee SHEE, FAERY,
FAIRY, FAY, GOBLIN,
SIDHE
bant DIET, FAST
banteng TSINE, OX
banter JOSH, ASTEISM,
CHAFF, JEST, TWIT,
PERSIFLAGE, BADI-
NAGE, RALLY, QUIZ,
KID, RAG, GUY, RIB,
DERIDE, WIT,
RIDICULE
Bantu DUALA, ZULU,
VIRA, YAKA, PONDO,
VILI, BASUTO, RORI,
RAVI, WARUA, RUA,
MAKUA, KAFFIR,
KAFIR, WARORI, KUA,
MAKWA
language ILA
tribe YAKA
tribesman DUALA
banxring TANA, TAPAIA,
SQUIRREL
baobab leaves LALO
baptismal FONTAL,
SPRING
font BASIN
baptize DIP, NAME,
SPRINKLE, CHRISTEN
baquet TUB, TROUGH,
SCUTTLE
bar RAIL, BETTY, FID,
ROD, DETER, SALOON,
SNAG, SHOAL, BANK,
REEF, LAW, BENCH,
COURT, BOLT, HINDER,
PREVENT, BLOCK, DAM,
CLOSE, SHUT, LOCK,
POLE, GRATING,
EXCLUDE
door RISP, STANG,
LOCK
legally ESTOP

soap frame SESS
supporting ROD
barb FLUE, JAG,
SPINE, NAG, ARROW,
HOOK, THORN, SPEAR,
BEARD, SPIKE
feather RAMUS, HARL,
HERL, PINNULA
Barbados native BIM
barbarian ALIEN,
SAVAGE, RUFFIAN,
HUN, VANDAL, GOTH,
BRUTE, PHILISTINE,
RUDE, UNCIVILIZED
N. Africa BERBER
barbarity FERITY,
BRUTALITY, CRUELTY,
FEROCITY
barbarous CRUEL,
FELL, HARSH, RUDE,
ROUGH, CRUDE,
BRUTAL, WILD,
SAVAGE, UNCIVILIZED,
FIERCE
Barbary *ape* SIMIAN,
MAGOT
States MOROCCO,
ALGIERS, TUNISIA,
TRIPOLI
barbecue BAKE, ROAST,
GRILL, BROIL
barbed UNCINATE,
BENT, HOOKED,
SPIKED
wire obstacle ABATIS
barber SHAVER,
FIGARO, TONSOR
bard POET, DRUID,
RUNER, SCOP, VATES,
MINSTREL, SCALD,
MUSICIAN
Goth RUNER
river of AVON
Wales OVATE
bare MERE, BALD,
NUDE, STRIP, NAKED,
EMPTY, SIMPLE,
DIVEST, REVEAL,
EXPOSE, SHEER, MANI-
FEST, SCANTY, STARK
barely MERELY, FAINT,
JIMP, HARDLY,
SCARCELY
bargain PALTER, PACT,
COMPACT, DEAL,
TRADE, MISE, AGREE-
MENT, CONTRACT,
TREATY, DICKER,
NEGOTIATE
barge HOY, PRA(A)M,
TENDER, FLOAT,
SCOLD, SHREW,

VIXEN, BARQUE,
PRAHAM, SCOW
barium BA
sulfate BARITE
bark BOAT *See*
"boat" BAY, YAP,
YIP, YELP, CORTEX,
RIND, HIDE, SKIN,
PEEL, SHELL, BAG,
PELT, HOWL, YELL
aromatic SINTOC
bitter NIEPA, NIOTA,
CINCHONA
cloth, mulberry TAPA
having CORTICATED
inner CORTEX, BAST,
LIBER
medicinal COTO,
QUININE (CINCHONA),
MUDAR, MADAR, CASCA
pertaining to
CORTICAL
rough exterior ROSS
strip of ROSS
tonic CANELLA
tree BAST, RIND
yercum MADAR,
MUDAR
barker PISTOL, TOUT,
SPEILER, JUMPER,
DOG
barking iron SPUD
barley, *four-rowed*
BIG, BIGG
six-rowed BERE
steeped MALT
water PTISAN, TISANE
barm YEAST, LEAVEN
barn BYRE, MEW,
STALL
barnacle, *acorn* SCUTE,
VALVE
barometer, *type of*
ANEROID
barometric line
ISOBAR
baron FREEMAN,
NOBLE, PEER
baronet SIR, BART
baronial GRAND,
SHOWY
baroque ORNATE,
ROCOCO, EXTRAVA-
GANT, IRREGULAR
barrack CASERN(E),
CAMP
barracuda SENNET,
SPET, PELON, FISH
barrage ATTACK, OB-
STRUCTION, BARRIER

barrel KNAG, KEG,
TIERCE, BUTT, TUN,
HOGSHEAD, CASK
herring CADE
maker COOPER
slat STAVE
small KEG, KILDER-
KIN
support GANTRY,
GAUNTRY, HOOP
tobacco TUN, HOGS-
HEAD
barren DULL, STUPID,
STERILE, EFFETE,
STARK, BARE, BALD,
NAKED, NUDE, ARID,
GELD, DRY, SEVERE,
UNFRUITFUL, STERN
land USAR, DESERT,
REH
barricade BARRIER,
ROADBLOCK, ABATIS,
BAR, OBSTACLE,
FENCE, DEFENSE,
PRISON
barrier WALL, FENCE,
SCREEN, DAM, BAR,
PRISON, HEDGE,
HINDRANCE
barrister ATTORNEY,
LAWYER, COUN-
SEL(L)OR,
ADVOCATE, COUNSEL
barrow MOUND,
TUMULUS, GRAVE,
BANK, DUNE, HILLOCK
Barstow, Mrs. Montagu
ORCZY
bartender MIXER
barter DEAL, TRADE,
SWAP, DICKER, PER-
MUTE, TRAFFIC, COM-
MERCE, VEND, SELL,
AUCTION, EXCHANGE,
TROKE, RECIPROCATE,
HAWK
bartizan TURRET,
LOOKOUT
basal lobes, *mosses*
ALA
base SITE, SEAT,
FLOOR, GROUND,
BASIS, FOOT, SUPPORT,
CAMP, ESTABLISH,
LOW, VILE, IMPURE,
MEAN, SORDID, SER-
VILE, SPURIOUS, IN-
FERIOR, CHEAP,
WORTHLESS, VULGAR,
FOUL, PETTY, BAD,
BOTTOM

architectural SOCLE,
PLINTH
attached by SESSILE
hit BINGLE, LOOPER,
SINGLE
marker BAG
of bird's bill CERE
of column DADO,
PATTEN, PLINTH
on balls PASS
root RADIX
baseball team NINE
baseless IDLE, GROUND-
LESS, FALSE
basement CELLAR,
BASE
bash SWAT, BAT,
MASH, WHAM, WHOP
Bashan king OG
bashful SHY, MODEST,
BLUSHING, TIMID,
COY, VERECUND,
SHRINKING, SHEEPISH,
RETIRING
Bashkiv capital UFA
basic FUNDAMENTAL
basilica LATERAN,
CANOPY, SHRINE,
TEMPLE, CHURCH
part of APSE
basin BOWL, VESSEL,
SINK, HOLLOW,
VALLEY, LAVER,
CHAFER, PAN, FONT,
STOUP, DOCK
geological TALA
ornamental CUVETTE
basis PREMISE, BASE,
SUPPORT, GROUND,
AXIOM, LAW, FOUNDA-
TION, BOTTOM, ROOT
bask REVEL, APRICATE,
SUN, LUXURIATE,
REJOICE, WARM
basket HAMPER, CRATE,
PAN(N)IER, KISH,
CORF, CABAS, SKEP,
MAUND, GABION,
CORB
fig CABA, TAPNET
fish CORF, CAUL,
CAWL
fruit POTTLE, PUN-
NET
hop-picker's BIN
kind of TUMBRIL,
CAUL, TUMBREL,
CAWL
pelota CESTA
water-tight WATTAPE
wicker BASSINET,
HANAPER, HAMPER

willow OSIER,
PRICKLE
work CABAS, CABA,
SLARTH, SLATH
basketball *player*
CAGER, GUARD, FOR-
WARD, CENTER
team FIVE
term DRIBBLE, BLOCK,
FOUL
Basque IBERIAN
cap BERET
game PELOTA
numeral SEIS, DOS
province BISCAY,
ALAVA
bass LOW, DEEP, FISH
African IYO
European BRASSE
basswood LINDEN
bast BARK, PHLOEM,
RAMIE, FIBER
basta ENOUGH, STOP
baste CUDGEL, THRASH,
SEW, LARD, COOK,
CANE, DRUB, PUNISH
bat ALIPED, SEROTINE,
NOCTULE, VAMPIRE,
RACKET, CLUB, STICK,
BRICK, SPREE
fish DIABLO
flying CHIROPTERA
fruit PECA
mining SHALE
S. America VAMPIRE
species PIPIS-
TREL(LE)
wingfooted ALIPED
Bataan *bay* SUBIC
city BALANGA,
BALAYAN
bath DIP, PLUNGE,
SHOWER, SWIM, TUB,
BALNEATION
bathe SUFFUSE, BASK,
LAVE, WASH, STEW,
ENWRAP, IMMERSE
bathing suit TRUNKS,
BIKINI, MAILLOT
Bath's *river* AVON
Bathsheba's *husband*
URIAH, DAVID
baton WAND, SCEPTRE,
SCEPTER, ROD,
TRUNCHEON, STICK
race RELAY
batrachia TOADS,
FROGS
batter FRUSH, PASTE,
RAM, SLOPE, DENT,
POUND, SMASH,
DESTROY, BEAT,

BRUISE, MAIM,
CRIPPLE
cake WAFFLE
battery ARTILLERY,
BOMBARDMENT,
PARAPET, CELL
plate GRID
battle FIGHT, COMBAT,
CONTEST, ACTION,
PUSH, BRUSH, WAR,
ONSET, COPE, AT-
TACK, KICK, ASSAIL,
PROTEST, SKIRMISH,
(AF)FRAY, COM-
PETITION
area SECTOR, ARENA,
TERRAIN
array ACIES, HERSE,
ORDER
cry AUX-ARMES
English CRESSY
formation HERSE,
DEPLOY
medieval ACRE
Texas ALAMO
trophy SCALP, RIB-
BON, MEDAL
WW-I MARNE,
VERDUN, VALMY
WW-II BULGE, BA-
TAAN *See* "World
War II"
battlefield ARMAGED-
DON, GETTYSBURG,
SHILOH
"Battle Hymn of the
Republic" author
HOWE
battlement CRENEL,
PINION, EMBRASURE,
RAMPART, MERLON
battologize ITERATE,
REPEAT
batty CRAZY, SILLY
bauble GEWGAW, TOY,
TRINKET, TRIFLE,
GIMCRACK
Bavarian *city* HOF
lake WURM
river ISAR, SAALE
weight GRAN
bawl CRY, YELL,
HOWL, HOOT,
SQUALL, BOOHOO
out See "scold"
bay INLET, BIGHT,
SINUS, VOE, GULF,
COVE, FIORD, ESTUARY,
SOUND, RECESS, NOOK,
NICHE, CREEK, COLOR,
LAUREL
color ROAN

State MASSACHU-
SETTS, MASS.
wreath LAUREL
bayard HORSE
Baylor University, *site
of* WACO
bayonet STAB
plant DATIL
Spanish YUCCA
bazaar(s) AGORA, FAIR,
EXPOSITION, SALE,
MART, EMPORIUM,
EMPORIA
be EXIST, BREATHE,
OCCUR, ARE, LIE,
LIVE, SUBSIST
beach SAND, COAST,
STRAND, PLAYA,
SHILLA, SHORE,
BANK, RIPA
cabin CABANA
beacon SIGN, FANAL,
PHAROS, FLAG, SEA-
MARK, SIGNAL, LIGHT,
WARNING
light CRESSET,
LANTERN
on a summit PIKE
Beaconsfield DISRAELI
bead(s) DROP, BUB-
BLE, FOAM, SPARKLE,
SIGHT, GLOBULE
roll LIST, ROSTER
string of ROSARY,
CHAPLET
beadle OFFICER,
MACER, CRIER, SUM-
MONER, BEDELL
beady GLOBULAR,
SMALL, ROUND,
GLISTENING
beagle HOUND, BRUTE,
SPY, DETECTIVE,
SHIP, DOG
beak NIB, BILL, NEB,
TUTEL, NOSE, LORUM,
SPERON, ROSTRUM,
SNOUT
ship's BOW, RAM,
PROW
trim with PREEN
without EROSTRATE
beaker BOCAL, CUP,
GLASS, TASS, GOBLET
beam T-BAR, I-BAR,
TEMPLET, TEMPLATE,
RAY, SILE, SHINE,
CABER, GLOW, JOIST,
TIMBER, STUD, FLASH,
GLINT, RAFTER, SUP-
PORT, LIGHT, RADIATE
beaming BRIGHT, RADI-

ANT, ROSY, LUCENT,
GAY
beamy RADIANT, JOY-
OUS, MIRTHFUL,
BRIGHT, LUCENT,
SPARKLING
bean LIMA, URD,
LENTIL, HARICOT,
PINTO, SOY(A),
TONKA, CASTER,
KIDNEY, CALABAR,
POLE, NAVY, HEAD
Asian MUNG(O),
GRAM
calabar alkaloid
ESERIN(E)
English MAZAGAN
eye(s) HILA, HILUM
kidney HARICOT
lima HABA
locust CAROB
Mexico FRIJOL(E)
plant SENNA, LOCUST
poisonous CALABAR
seed of LENTIL,
HARICOT
tree AGATI, CATALPA
bear CARRY, ENDURE,
YIELD, TOTE, WEAR,
TAKE, MOVE, SHIFT,
HOLD, CONTAIN,
BREED, ABIDE, STAND,
BROOK, BEGET, TOL-
ERATE, SUFFER,
RENDER, SUSTAIN,
TRANSPORT, CONVEY,
PRODUCE, POLAR,
BLACK, KOALA,
BROWN, GRIZZLY
Alaskan KADIAK,
KODIAK
Australian KOALA
brown URSUS
genus URSUS
Hindu BHALU
honey MELURSUS
Syrian DUBB
bearcat PANDA
beard AVEL, ANE,
AWN, ARISTA,
GOATEE, VAN DYKE,
WHISKERS, DEFY
bearded ARISTATE,
AWNY, BARBATE,
HAIRY, HIRSUTE
grain AWN, ARISTA,
WHEAT, RYE
bearing ATTITUDE,
MANNER, AIM, AIR,
PORT, MIEN, ORIENT,
COURSE, TREND,
CARRIAGE, FRONT,

DEMEANOR, PRESSURE, THRUST
plate GIB
beast *See* "animal" ASS, BURRO, LLAMA, ANIMAL, BRUTE, PARD, MONSTER, BEHEMOTH, QUADRUPED
beat ICTUS, ACCENT, RHYTHM, THROB, PULSE, PULSATE, TEMPO, DRUB, LACE, WALLOP, LARRUP, WIN, WAP, ROUT, SMITE, SLAP, CUFF, BOX, CRUSH, PUMMEL, SLUG, TRACK, COURSE, STRIKE, BATTER, CLOUT, SWAT, BRUISE, CONQUER, DEFEAT, BASTE, TAN, WHOP, FLOOR, KO
into plate MALLEATE
nautical TACK
Scot. TOWEN
beatify BLESS, HALLOW, SANCTIFY, ENCHANT, TRANSPORT, GLORIFY
beatitude BLISS, JOY, FELICITY, ECSTASY
beau BLADE, GALLANT, FLAME, SWAIN, FOP, DANDY, DUDE, BUCK, TOFF, SPARK, SWELL, NOB, COXCOMB, SWEETHEART
beaut LULU
beautiful LOVELY, BONNY, FAIR, TEMPEAN, COMELY, SUPERB, ELEGANT, GRACEFUL, PRETTY
combining form CALLI, BEL
beautify (BE)DECK, ADORN, TRIM, GARNISH, PRIMP, PREEN, PRUNE, DECORATE, GILD, EMBELLISH
beauty GLOSS, GRACE, CHARM, POLISH, STYLE, BELLE
beaver CASTOR, HAT, RODENT
cloth KERSEY
skin PLEW
State OREGON
because INASMUCH, SINCE, FOR, AS
bech-de-mar JARGON

bech-de-mer TREPANG, WORM
Bechuanaland tribe BANTU, KAFFIR
beckon SIGNAL, SUMMON, CALL, INVITE
becloud DIM, OBSCURE, HIDE, DARKEN
become BEFIT, ACCORD, TURN, CHANGE, PASS, SUIT, GRACE, BESEEM, ADORN, BEHOOVE
bed BUNK, DOSS, LAIR, LITTER, PAD, BILLET, PALLET, COT, COUCH, SACK, BASE, SUPPORT
dry stream DONGA
frame STEAD, STOCK
small BASSINET, COT, PALLET, CRIB, CRADLE
bedbug CHINCH, CIMEX
Bede ADAM
bedeck PRINK, ADORN, TRAP, TRIM, DECK, GARNISH, PREEN, PRUNE, ARRAY, BEDIZEN
bedlam NOISY, NOISE, TUMULT, HUBBUB, ASYLUM
Bedouin ARAB, NOMAD
headcord AGAL
official SHEIK, CADI
tribe HARB
bedroom CABIN, CUBICLE, FLAT, BERTH, COMPARTMENT
bee APIS, DOR, NOTION, GATHERING, PARTY
Australian KARBI
family APIDAE
genus APIS
girl named for MELISSA
glue PROPOLIS
house HIVE, SKEP, APIARY, ALVEARY, GUM
keeper APIARIST, SKEPPIST
male DRONE
nest building CARDER
plant BALM
pollen brush of SCOPA
tree LINDEN
wild DINGAR
beech FAGUS, BUCK, MYRTLE, TREE

genus FAGUS
beechnut MAST
beef, *cut of* BARON, ROUND, LOIN, FLANK, RIB, CHUCK, STEAK, BRISKET, SIRLOIN
dried BUCAN, BUCCAN
in onions MIROTON
beefy HEFTY, STRONG
Beehive State UTAH
beer LAGER, BREW, PORTER, BOCK, ALE, STOUT, GROG
ingredient HOPS, MALT
jug MUG, TOBY, STEIN
king GAMBRINUS
moistening wood with CISSING
mug SEIDEL, STEIN, POURIE, TOBY, FLAGON, SCHOONER
shop PUB, SALOON
spiced FLIP
unfermented GYLE
beef plant HOPS, BREWERY
beery MAUDLIN, MUDDLED
beeswax, *pertaining to* CEROTIC
substitute CERESIN
beet CHARD, MENGAL, SUGAR
genus BETA
sugar SUCROSE
Beethoven *composition* NINTH, SONATA, EROICA
opera FIDELIO
beetle AMARA, MELOE, CHAFER, HISPA, SCARAB, STAG, WEEVIL, CARABUS, BEAN, PROJECT
click DOR, ELATER
downy BUZZ
early stage LARVA
family ELATERIDAE
gaudy LADYBUG
grain CADELLE
grapevine THRIP
ground AMARA
horny substance of CHITIN
oil MELOE
rhinoceros UANG
sun AMARA
wing cover SHARD
wings, upper ELYTRA
wood SAWYER

befall COME, HAP,
TIDE, OCCUR, CHANCE,
BETIDE, BECHANCE,
HAPPEN
befit SUIT, BECOME,
HARMONIZE, FIT, AP-
PROPRIATE
before AHEAD, SOONER,
FRONT, CORAM,
AVANT, ERE, DAWN,
PRECESSION, GERM,
(A)FORE, ANTERIOR,
INITIAL, FROM, ANTE,
PRIOR, FORMER, SAID,
FORWARD, ALREADY
now GONE, OVER,
ENOW
prefix ANTE, PRE,
PRAE
beg IMPLORE,
BESEECH, ASK, PETI-
TION, SUE, CADGE,
CRAVE, PLEAD, PRAY,
ENTREAT, SOLICIT,
SUPPLICATE
beget PROCREATE,
CREATE, GENERATE,
BEAR, YIELD, GET,
SIRE, ENGENDER
begetter PARENT,
PATER, SIRE, FATHER,
MOTHER
beggar MENDICANT,
SUPPLIANT, PETI-
TIONER, IDLER, LAZAR,
PAUPER, STARVELING,
PARIAH
beggarly MEAN, PETTY,
ABJECT, CHEAP,
SORRY, INDIGENT,
NEEDY, POOR, PALTRY
begin (A)RISE, OPEN,
START, FOUND,
SPRING, ENTER,
INITIATE, LEAD,
ORIGINATE, COM-
MENCE
beginner DEBUTANTE,
ENTRANT, TYRO, TIRO,
PUPIL, STUDENT,
NEOPHYTE, AP-
PRENTICE, RECRUIT,
TRAINEE, POSTULATE,
CANDIDATE, BOOT,
NOVICE, NOVITIATE
beginning BIRTH, RISE,
SEED, ONSET, ALPHA,
ORIGIN, EGG, GERM,
NASCENT, DEBUT,
OPENING, INCEPTION,
INITIAL, OUTSET,
INITIATION, INCIPIENT,

EMBRYONIC,
RUDIMENTARY
begone SCAT, HISS,
OUT, AROINT, AVAUNT,
GET, WHISK, DEPARTED
begrime SOIL, DIRTY
beguile COZEN, LURE,
VAMP, BETRAY, DUPE,
GULL, (BE)FOOL,
TRICK, HOAX, WILE,
DIVERT, DELUDE,
CHEAT, AMUSE
behalf SIDE, BENISON,
INTEREST, BENEFIT,
SUPPORT, PROFIT,
STEAD
behave ACT, TREAT,
BEAR, CONDUCT,
ACQUIT, WORK,
DIRECT, FUNCTION,
DEPORT
behavior COURSE,
CONDUCT, MIEN,
ACT(ION), DEED,
BEARING, AIR, PORT,
MANNER
behemoth HUGE,
BEAST, HIPPO
behest BID, MANDATE,
ORDER, RULE, LAW,
COMMAND
behind AREAR, ASTERN,
BACK, SLOW, AFT,
AFTER, ABAFT, LATE,
TARDY, REARWARD,
POSTERIOR
behold VOILA, ECCE,
LO, SEE, VIEW,
SURVEY, OBSERVE,
ESPY, LOOK, WATCH,
DISCERN
beige TAN, ECRU, HOPI,
GREGE
being(s) ENS, ENTITY,
EXISTENCE, ESSE,
LIVING, TROLL,
ONTOLOGY, LIFE,
PERSON(S), CREA-
TURE, MORTAL,
HUMAN, REALITY
abstract ENS, ENTIA
actual ESSE
in front ANTEAL
mythological
CENTAUR
simple MONAD
spirit of ESSE, ENTIA,
ENS
Beja HAMITE
son IRI
Bela's *son* EZBON,
UZZI, IRI

belaying cleat KEVEL,
BOLLARD, BIT
beldam(e) FURY,
ALECTO, TISIPHONE,
CRONE, HAG, VIRAGO,
JEZEBEL, VIXEN,
ERINYS
beleaguerment SIEGE,
ASSAULT
Belem PARA
Belgium, Belgian
FLEMING, WALLOON
canal YSER
city LIEGE, BRUGES,
GHENT, ALOST *See*
"town" *below*
commune ATH, AATH,
ANS, TAMINES, AALST,
ALOST, NAMUR, BOOM,
MOL(L), JETTE, ZELE,
VORST, GENK
(GENCK), GEEL,
RONSE, UCCLE
(UKKEL), LIER, AALST
(ALOST)
currency BELGA
dialect WALLOON
Gaul, tribe of NERVU,
REMI
lowland POLDER
marble RANCE
measure VAT
professor AGREGE
river YSER, MEUSE,
LYS, DYLE, LEIE,
SCHELDE, SAMBRE
spring TONGRES, HUY,
SPA
town ALOST, ATH,
G(H)ENT, OSTEND(E),
MONS, YPRES, ANS,
ZELE, UCCLE, JETTE,
HUY, HAL, GILLY,
GHEEL, DOUR, BOOM
violinist YSAYE
Belial DEVIL, SATAN
belief CREDIT, FAITH,
TRUST, TROTH, FAY,
CREDO, CREED, SECT,
DOGMA, MIND, VIEW,
TENET, CREDENCE
believe DEEM, CREDIT,
TROW, TRUST, ACCEPT,
THINK, JUDGE, SUP-
POSE,
believer IST
in all religions
OMNIST
in God DEIST,
THEIST
in reality of matter
CARTESIAN

belittle DWARF, SLIGHT,
DECRY, DETRACT,
DENIGRATE,
DIMINISH, REDUCE,
LESSEN, MINIMIZE,
DISCREDIT, DE-
PRECIATE

bell CODON, CAMPANA,
KNELL, CARILLON,
GONG, TOCSIN,
ALARM, SIGNAL,
CALL, CHIME, RING,
CAMPANE
tower BELFRY,
CAMPANILE
town ADANO

belladonna MANICON,
PLANT, REMEDY
derivative
ATROPIN(E)

bellicose MILITANT,
WARLIKE, IRATE, MAD,
HOSTILE, PUGNACIOUS,
CONTENTIOUS

Bellini opera NORMA
sleepwalker AMINA

bellow ROAR, SHOUT,
BAWL, CRY, YAP,
ULULATE

belly BULGE, PAUNCH,
THARM, ABDOMEN,
PLEON

belong APPERTAIN,
INHERE, OWN, RELATE,
APPLY, BEAR

belonging to a people
ENDEMIC

belongings CHATTELS,
TRAPS, EFFECTS,
MEANS, ASSETS, GOODS,
PROPERTY, ESTATE

beloved one
INAMORATA, IDOL,
LOVE, DEAR, DARLING

below FLAT, NEATH,
SOTTO, BENEATH,
UNDER, INFERIOR
combining form
INFRA

belt GIRDLE, BAND,
STRIP, ZONE, CIRCUIT,
CINGLE, BALDRIC,
CESTUS, CEST,
CORDON, SASH,
AREA, TRACT,
REGION, RING
conveyor APRON
Jewish ZONAR
sword BALDRIC(K)

bema CHANCEL,
SANCTUARY, STEP,
PACE, PLATFORM

bemoan DEPLORE,
(BE)WAIL, LAMENT,
SOB, GRIEVE, SORROW,
MOURN

bemuse *See* "confuse"
DISTRACT, ADDLE

bench SEAT, SETTEE,
COURT, BAR, BOARD,
EXEDRA, TRIBUNAL,
PEW, SIEGE, SETTLE,
DISCARD
hook CRAMP
judge's BANC

bend STOOP, FLEX-
(URE), CROOK, IN-
FLEX, KINK, SAG,
CROUCH, NID, WARP,
BUCKLE, FORK, BOW,
CURVE, TURN, ANGLE,
BULGE, TWIST, DIVERT,
INCLINE, DEVIATE,
SUBMIT
form a COPE
in timber SNY

bending LITHE, PLIANT,
SUPPLE

Benedictine title DOM

benefactor PROMOTER,
DONOR, PATRON,
AGENT, FRIEND,
ANGEL, SAVIOR

benefice, *first fruit of*
ANNAT

beneficiary HEIR, USER,
LEGATEE

benefit HELP, AVAIL,
BEHOOF, BOOST, BOON,
BOOT, INTEREST, SAKE,
PROFIT, GAIN, GOOD,
ASSIST, AID, BETTER

benevolent KIND,
LIBERAL, AMIABLE,
LOVING, CHARITABLE

Bengal *bison* GAUR
boat BATEL
capital DACCA
city DACCA, PATNA
cotton ADATI
district NADIA
groom SAICE, SYCE
native KOL, BANIAN
quince BEL, BAEL
singer BAUL
thrush NURANG

benign KIND(LY),
GENIAL, SUAVE, BLAND,
GRACIOUS, FRIENDLY,
GENTLE

benne SESAME

bent PRONATE,
HOOKED, SWAYED,
CROOKED, TASTE,

TURN, KNACK, GIFT,
GENIUS, FLAIR,
BIAS(ED), TENDENCY,
PENCHANT, DISPOSI-
TION, LEANING, IN-
CLINATION

benthonic plant
ENALID

benthos FAUNA, LIT-
TORAL, FLORA

benumb HEBETATE,
DEADEN, STUPEFY,
BLUNT

benzene hydrocarbon
XYLENE

bequest WILL, LEGACY,
HERITAGE, TESTA-
MENT, DEVISE, GIFT

berate SCOLD,
CENSURE, UPBRAID,
RATE, CHIDE, JAW,
WIG, RAIL, REVILE,
REPROVE

Berber KABYLE,
HAMITE, MOOR, HAR-
(R)ATIN, RIFF
dialect TUAREG,
TUAREK
tribe RIFF, TIBU,
DAZA, TUAREG,
TUAREK, TIBBU

Berea ALEPPO
grit SANDSTONE

bereave DEPRIVE,
DIVEST, STRIP,
DESPOIL, ROB

bereft LOST, DESTI-
TUTE, POOR

beret BIRETTA, TAM

berg FLOE, BARROW,
ICE, MOUNTAIN

beriberi, *Jap.* KAKKE

Berkshire *race course*
ASCOT
village ASCOT

berm TERRACE, BANK,
BRIM, SHELF, PATH,
LEDGE

Bermuda *arrowroot*
ARARU, ARAROA
grass DOOB

Bernecia, *founder of*
IDA

berry CURRANT, BACCA,
HAW, DEW, BLACK,
SALAL, CRAN, FRUIT
like BACCATE

berserk MAD, MANICAL,
BRAVO, PIRATE, WAR-
RIOR, FRENZIED, EN-
RAGED

berth BUNK, BED,
BILLET, LODGING,
POST, JOB, PLACE,
POSITION, OFFICE,
for ship SLIP, DOCK
bertha CAPE, CANNON,
COLLAR
beseech SOLICIT, BEG,
CRAVE, PRAY, PLEAD,
APPEAL, ADJURE, SUE,
OBTEST, OBSECRATE,
ENTREAT, SUPPLICATE,
ASK
beseeching PRECATIVE
beset HARRY, OBSESS,
SIT, ATTACK, PESTER,
WORRY, INFEST, AS-
SAIL, SURROUND
beshrew CURSE,
EXECRATE
beside BY, NEAR,
ABREAST
combining form
PAR(A)
besides ALSO, FURTHER,
AND, THEN, TOO,
OVER, YET, ELSE,
EXCEPT
besiege STORM,
PLAGUE, PESTER,
OBSIDE, BESET, GIRD,
BELEAGUER, ATTACK,
SOLICIT
besmear, besmirch
SMOTTER, DAUB, SOIL,
BESLIME, TAINT,
COVER
besom BROOM, MOP,
SWEEP, HEATHER
bespangle STUD, STAR,
ADORN
bespeak ADDRESS,
ORDER, SHOW, HINT,
ARGUE, ATTEST,
IMPLY, ACCOST
best UTMOST, A-ONE,
CHOICE, MOST,
LARGEST, ELITE,
FINEST, SUPERIOR,
VANQUISH, OUTWIT,
BEAT
combining form
ARTIST(O)
bestow GRANT, AID,
ADD, GIVE, RENDER,
CONFER, AWARD,
DONATE, PRESENT, BE-
QUEATH, DIVIDE
bet HEDGE, STAKE,
WAGER, GAMBLE,
PLAY, POT, ANTE,
PLEDGE, LAY, RISK

fail to pay WELSH,
WELCH
in roulette BAS
betake REPAIR,
JOURNEY, RESORT
betel *leaf* BUYO, PUAN
pepper ITMO, IKMO
seed CATECHU
tree ARECA
Betelgeuse STAR
Bethlehemite BOAZ
betide BEFALL, HAP,
CHANCE, OCCUR
betimes EARLY, SOON,
ANON
betoken DENOTE,
PRESAGE, AUGUR,
SHOW, EVINCE, AT-
TEST, INDICATE,
SIGNIFY, FORESHADOW
betray BEGUILE,
PEACH, SELL, TRICK,
DELUDE, TRAP, SNARE,
GULL, MISLEAD, RE-
VEAL, BLAB, DISCLOSE,
DECEIVE, TELL
betrayer SEDUCER,
TRAITOR, JUDAS
betroth AFFY, TOKEN,
PLEDGE, AFFIANCE,
PLIGHT
better EMEND, TOP,
IMPROVE, (A)MEND,
HELP, AID, CORRECT,
RELIEVE, DEFEAT, RE-
FORM, ADVANCE, PRO-
MOTE
betting *machine* PARI-
MUTUEL
system PARLAY
between AVERAGE,
AMONG, BETWIXT,
INTERMEDIATE
law MESNE
prefix INTER, META
bevel BEZEL, EDGE,
ASLANT, SNAPE, CANT,
MITER, MITRE,
CHAMFER, OBLIQUE
out REAM
beveled edge BEARD,
WANE
beverage TEA, NEGUS,
GROG, CIDER, ALE, ADE,
BEER, COFFEE,
LIQUOR, DRINK,
POTABLE, POP, MORAT,
NECTAR, WATER,
MILK
oriental RAKEE, RAKI,
ARRACK, SAKE
Polynesian KAVA

S. America MATE
stand CELLARET
bevy COVEY, FLOCK,
HERD, DROVE, PACK,
FLIGHT, SCHOOL,
SWARM, COMPANY,
ASSEMBLY, MUL-
TITUDE
bewail GRIEVE,
LAMENT, WAIL, WEEP,
CRY, DEPLORE, SOR-
ROW, BEMOAN, RE-
GRET
beware AVOID, SHUN,
ESCHEW
bewilder PUZZLE, CON-
FUSE, PERPLEX, DAZE,
STAGGER, ADDLE,
BAFFLE, FOIL, DIS-
TRACT, MUDDLE,
ASTONISH
bewildered AMAZED,
ASEA, CONFUSED,
ADDLED, DAZED
bewilderment DAZE,
PERPLEXITY, CON-
FUSION
bewitch HEX, CHARM,
ENAMOR, ENSORCEL,
TAKE, THRILL, DE-
LIGHT, FASCINATE,
ENCHANT, EXCITE,
EXORCISE
bewray DISCLOSE, RE-
VEAL, BETRAY, TELL,
SHOW
Beyle, Marie Henri
STENDAHL
beyond BY, PAST,
YONDER, ULTRA, OVER,
ABOVE, FURTHER, BE-
SIDES, SUPERIOR
prefix ULTRA, META
bezel TEMPLATE,
FACET, RIM, BASIL,
SEAL, BEVEL, EDGE,
CROWN, FLANGE
bezoar ANTIDOTE,
COPROLITE, GOAT,
ANTELOPE
goat PASAN(G)
bhang HEMP
product of MAJOON
bharal TUR, NAHOOR,
SHEEP
Bhutan pine KAIL
bias BENT, SLOPE,
PARTIALITY, BIGOTRY,
TENDENCY, SLANT, IN-
CLINE, SWAY,
PREJUDICE, DISPOSI-
TION

bibelot CURIO,
TRINKET
Bible, Biblical
animal REEM
ascetic order ESSENE
book GENESIS,
EXODUS, JOSHUA,
RUTH, SAMUEL, KINGS,
EZRA, ESTHER, JOB,
PSALMS, ISAIAH,
DANIEL, HOSEA, JOEL,
AMOS, JONAH, MICAH,
NAHUM, HAGGAI,
MARK, LUKE, JOHN,
TITUS, PETER, JUDE
apocryphal TOBIT,
ESDRAS, BARUCH,
JUDITH, MACCABEES
character See "name"
below
charioteer JEHU
city or town AVEN,
ASHUR, AKKA(D),
ARVAD, ARAD, AIN,
BYBLOS, BOZRA,
BETHEL, CALLAH,
CANA, DAN, DEBIR,
ERIDU, ELIM, EDREI,
GADARA, GATH, GAZA,
GEBA, HAZOR,
HARAN, JERICHO,
JOPPA, KISH, MAMRE,
NINEVAH, NEZIB,
ON(O), PETRA
(SELA), PAU, RESEN,
SODOM, SIDON, SUSA,
SIN, TYRE, TARSUS,
ZOAR, ZER
coin SHEKEL, MITE,
TALENT, DARIC,
STATER, DRACHM
country SEIR, EDOM,
CANAAN, GALILEE,
MOAB, AMMON,
CHALDEA, ARAM, PUL
desert PARAN
disease PLAGUE,
LEPROSY
driver JEHU
edition RV, AV *See*
"version" *below*
garden EDEN, UZZA
garment SADIN,
CETHONETH, SIMLAH,
BEGED, CESUTH,
TSAIPH, PETHIGI
giant ANAK, EMIM,
GOLIATH
horned animal REEM
hunter NIMROD
king OMRI, BERA,
SAUL, AGAG, DAVID,

TIDAL, BIRSHA, ZOAR,
AHAB, AHAZ
kingdom MOAB,
ELAM, ISRAEL, JUDAH,
JUDEA
land See "region"
below NOD, OPHIR,
ZUPH, TOB, SHUAL,
CANAAN, ZOBA(H),
GILEAD, MORIAH
language ARAMIC
Latin version
VULGATE
line of STICH
Luther's translation
WARTBURG
measure KOR, EPHA,
CUBIT, EPHAH,
GERAH, BEKA, SHEKEL,
MANEH, TALENT
(KIKKAR), DIGIT,
PALM, SPAN, REED,
LOG, HIN, BATH, CAB,
SEAH, (H)OMER
money See "coin"
above
mountain ARARAT,
HOR, SINAI, HOREB,
NEBO, EBAL, EZEM,
EZER, EZRA, GADI,
ABARIM, HERMON,
PEOR, TABOR,
SION, MORIAH
name ANAK, ANANI,
ARAM, AROD, AROM,
EBAL, EBED, ER, EZEL,
GOG, GADDI, IRA, IRAD,
IVAH, ISHMAEL, JAEL,
MAGOG, MERAB, NER,
NOD, ON, REBA, UCAL,
VASHTI, VASHNI
ornament URIM,
THUMMIM
ox REEM
pause SELAH
place ENDOR, SHILOH,
TOBIE
plain(s) JERICHO,
MOREH, MAMRE, PIL-
LAR, TABOR
pool SILOAH, SILOAM
priest, high ELI,
AARON
prophet See
"prophet" ELIAS,
AMOS, EZRA, ELIJAH
queen SHEBA, VASHTI,
ESTHER
region GILEAD, PHUT,
CYRENE, LIBYA, UZ,
UR, MIDIAN, KEDAR,

OPHIR, DUMAH, ELAM,
DAN, ZIN
reproach RACA
river KISHON, JORDAN,
ARNON, ZAB, ABANA,
NILE
sacred object URIM,
THUMMIN
sea SALT (DEAD),
GALILEE, RED,
GENNESARET, TIBERIAS
shepherd ABEL
spy CALEB
tower BABEL, EDAR,
SILOAM
town See "city"
above
vale or valley SIDDIM,
ELAH, BACA, SHAVEH,
SALT
version RV, GEEZ, AV,
VULGATE, ITALA,
DOUAY, SYRIAC,
BOHAIRIC
weapon SLING
weed TARE
weight See "measure"
above
well SIRAH
wilderness PARAN,
THECOE, SIN
word SELAH, TOPHET
worthless RACA
Zoroastrian AVESTA
bibliotheca LIBRARY,
BIBLE
bibulous DRUNK, SOT,
TIPPLING
bicker ARGUE, DISPUTE,
PETTIFOG, SPAT, TIFF,
FIGHT, BATTLE, WAR,
WRANGLE, CAVIL
bicycle for two
TANDEM
bid ENJOIN, OVERTURE,
TENDER, OFFER,
ORDER, INVITE,
DIRECT, CHARGE, CALL,
CITE, ASK, REQUEST,
DECLARE, PROCLAIM
biddy HEN
bier CATAFALQUE,
PYRE, LITTER, COFFIN,
GRAVE
bifurcation BRANCH,
FORK, WYE, SPLIT
big VAST, LARGE,
BULKY, HUGE, GREAT,
GRAND, MASSIVE,
MONSTROUS, MIGHTY,
POWERFUL
shot VIP

bighorn ARGALI, SHEEP, AOUDAD

bight LOOP, BAY, NOOSE, GULF, BEND, COIL, INLET, COVE

bigot ZEALOT, FANATIC

bile GALL, CHOLER, VENOM

bilingual DIGLOT

bilk GYP, HOAX, TRICK, CHEAT, DECEIVE, SWINDLE

bill SCORE, DUN, CHARGE, NOTE, BEAK, LIST, TAB, TICKET, NIB, NEB, ACT, STATUTE, LAW, POSTER, STATEMENT, PLACARD, MONEY
anchor PEE
bird's NEB, NIB, BEAK
  area at base CERE
  protuberance at NEB, CERE
stroke MASSE, PICK

billet POST, POSITION, JOB, PLACE, BERTH, OFFICE, LODGE, NOTE, LETTER, EPISTLE

billfold WALLET

billiards POOL
rod CUE
shot CAROM, MASSE

billingsgate ABUSE, VULGARITY, OBLOQUY, RIBALDRY, VITUPERA-TION

billionaire NABOB

billow WAVE, SEA, SURGE, SWELL, BREAKER, ROLLER, RIPPLE, BULGE, UN-DULATE

billy CAN, CLUB, CUDGEL, COMRADE, GOAT

bin for fish KENCH, CANCH

binate DOUBLE, TWO-FOLD, PAIRED, COUPLED

bind SWATHE, TAPE, STRAP, TRUSS, GIRD, ROPE, TIE, RESTRAIN, SECURE, FASTEN, OBLIGATE, CONFINE, JOIN, LINK, UNITE, PINION, BANDAGE, CONNECT, MARRY
combining form DESMO

to secrecy TILE, TYLE
with fetters GYVE, TIE, IRON, HANDCUFF, SHACKLE

binding, *limp* YAPP
machine BALER

binge HIT, SOAK, SPREE, PARTY, BEANO

bingo LOTTO, KENO, GAME
forerunner of LOTTO

binnacle PYX, COM-PASS, NEEDLE

biography VITA, LIFE, MEMOIR, RECOUNT, HISTORY

biological BIOTIC(AL)
factor GENE
fissure RIMA

biology GENETICS

bion, *opposed to* MORPHON

bipennis AX(E), WEAPON

birch BETULA, FLOG, STICK, TREE

bird(s) AVES, ORNIS, FOWL, AVIFAUNA
adjutant STORK, ARGALA, HURGILA, MARABOU
African LORY, LOURI, TURAKOO, TURACO(U)
ajaja SPOONBILL, JABIRU
alcoid AUK, PUFFIN
Andean CONDOR
Antarctic PENGUIN
apteryx KIWI, MOA
Arctic BRANT, FULMAR, TERN
area from bill to eye LORE
Asian MINA, PITTA, MYNA
auk PUFFIN, ALCA, MURRE, ROTCH(E), ARRIE, GUILLEMOT, DOVEKIE
Australian KOEL, EMEW, EMU, LEIPOA, MALLEE, LOWAN, WEKA, COOEY
baker HORNERO
beak NEB, NIB, ROSTRUM, BILL
bill NEB, NIB, BEAK
black ANI, MERL(E), DARR, ROOK, CROW, OUSEL, OUZEL, RAVEN
blue JAY, IRENA

bobolink ORTOLAN, REED
bob-white COLIN, QUAIL
Brazilian AR(R)A, TOUCAN, CARIAMA, URUBU, SERIEMA
butcher SHRIKE
carrion VULTURE, URUBU, BUZZARD
catcher FOWLER, CLAPNET
Cent. Amer. CONDOR, GUAN
chacalaca GUAN
cockatoo ARA(RA), ARRA, MACAW
columbine DODO
coraciiformes See "non-passerine" *below*
corncrake RAIL
corvine CROW, DAW, RAVEN
courlan LIMPKIN
covey BROOD, FLOCK
crane genus GRUS
  like CHUNGA
crocodile SICSAC, TROCHILUS, PLOVER
crotophagine ANI
crowlike CORVINE, ROOK, RAVEN, DAW, CHOUGH
Cuban TOCORORO, TROGON
cuckoo ANI, KOEL, COCCYGUS
dabchick GREBE, GALLINULE
diving LOON, AUK, GREBE
dodo DIDUS
dog POINTER, SETTER
dove See "dove"
duck See "duck"
dunlin STIB, SAND-PIPER
eagle See "eagle"
E. Indian song SHAMA
egg collector OOLOGIST
Egyptian IBIS, BENU, SICSAC
emulike CAS-SOWARY
European GLEDE, REED, SEDGE, TEREK, MERL(E)
  finch SERIN
extinct AUK, DODO, MOA, ROC, MAMO
falcon See "falcon"

false wing ALULA
finch TOWHEE, MORO,
SERIN, CANARY, SPINK,
REDPOOL, BUNTING,
SISKIN
  like GROSBEAK,
  CHEWINK, TANAGER
  yellow SERIN,
  CANARY
fish hawk OSPREY
flightless DODO, EMU,
MOA, KIWI, WEKA,
OSTRICH, PENGUIN,
RATITE
  genus APTERYX,
  NOTORNIS
flock COVEY, BROOD,
BEVY, DROVE, GAGGLE,
LITTER
flycatcher PEEWEE,
REDSTART, VIREO
frigate IWA
fulmar NELLY,
MALDUCK
gallinaceous order
RASORES
gallinae See
"gallinae"
game GROUSE, QUAIL,
DUCK
garruline JAY
genus ICTERUS,
ANSER, OTIS, CRAX,
RHEA, PITTA, SULA,
STERNA, MORIS
glede KITE
goose See "goose"
goose genus ANSER,
BRANT, CHEN
guan ORTALIS,
CHACALACA, PIPILE
gull MAA, MEW *See*
"gull"
  like JAEGER, SKUA,
  TERN
Hawaiian OO, IWA,
IIWI, MOHO, ALALA,
MAMO *See* "Hawaii"
hawk CARACARA,
GOSHAWK, SHIKRA,
KITE *See* "hawk"
heron EGRET, IBIS,
BITTERN *See* "heron"
honey-eating MOHO,
IAO, MANUAO
house NEST, AVIARY
humming COLIBRI,
TROCHILUS, SYLPH,
AVA, RUBY, LUCIFER,
WARRIOR, TOPAZ,
STAR, RUFOUS, SAPPHO
hunting FALCON

iao MANUAO
ibis GUARA
Indian, MINA, MYNA,
SHAMA, SARUS,
ARGALA, LOWA, RAYA,
AMADAVAT, KOEL
insectivorous VIREO,
FLYCATCHER, PEEWEE
jackdaw KAE, DAW,
CROW, GRACKLE
  genus CORVUS
jaeger SKUA, ALLAN,
SHOOI, GULL
jaw, part of MALA
jaylike PIET, MAG-
PIE
keelbill ANI, ANO
kite ELANET, GLEDE
lamellirostral GEESE,
SWANS, DUCKS,
FLAMINGO, MER-
GANSER
lanioid SHRIKE
large KIWI, ROA, EMU,
GUAN, KITE, MOA,
OSTRICH, EAGLE,
CONDOR
larklike PIPIT
life ORNIS, AVIFAUNA
limicoline AVOCET
long-legged WADER,
AGAMI, STORK, CRANE
long-necked SWAN
loon See "loon"
lyre genus MENURA
macaw ARA, ARRA,
ARARA, ARARAUNA,
PARROT
magpie PIET, MAG,
PYAT, MADGE
manuao IAO
marine See "sea"
below
marsh SORA, STILT,
SNIPE, BITTERN
mound LEIPOA,
MEGAPOD(E)
mouse COLY, SHRIKE
mythological ROC,
HANSA, SIMURG(H)
New Zealand LOWAN,
KIWI, MOA, TUI,
WEKA, TITI, HUIA,
KOKO
  extinct MOA
  mutton OII
  parrot KEA
nighthawk PISK
Nile IBIS
non-passerine HOO-
POE, TODY, KING-

FISHER, HORNBILL,
MOTMOT
one year old AN-
NOTIN(E)
oriole LORIOT, PIROL,
BALTIMORE
oscine TANAGER,
VIREO, CROW
osprey HAWK
ostrich See "ostrich"
owl LULU, WEKAU,
BARN, BARRED,
SNOWY, UTUM, ULLET,
HAWK, SCREECH,
SURN *See* "owl"
parrot See "parrot"
parson TUI, POE,
ROOK
partridge See "par-
tridge"
passeriform IRENA
passerine SPARROW,
PITA, STARLING
peewee PHOEBE,
LARK, LAPWING
pelicanlike SOLAN
pertaining to
AVIN(E), AVIAN,
ORNITHIC
  singing OSCINE
petrel TITI
pigeon GOURA, NUN,
FANTAIL, CARRIER,
DOVE, POUTER, TUR-
BIT, JACOBIN, TUM-
BLER, PIPER, HOMER,
ISABEL, CUSHAT
plant-cutter RARA
plover See "plover"
plumed EGRET
prey HAWK, OWL,
EAGLE, KITE, KESTREL,
RAPTORES, ELANET
psittaceous PARROT
puff BARBET
puffin AUK
quail COLIN, LOWA
See "quail"
  like TINAMOU,
  TURNIX
rail CRAKE, MOHO,
SORA, WEKA, SEDGE,
COOT, COURLAN,
ORLOTAN
rain PLOVER
Raptores HAWK,
EAGLE, VULTURE,
OWL
ratite EMU, MOA,
EMEU, OSTRICH, CAS-
SOWARY
raven, Hawaii ALALA

ring dove CUSHAT
Samoan IAO, MANUAO
sandpiper REEVE,
 DUNLIN, TEREK, STIB
 See "sandpiper"
scratch for food
 RASORES
sea ERN(E), GULL,
 SCOTER, MURRE,
 GANNET, KESTREL,
 TERN, CAHOW, SKUA,
 SCAUP, PETREL,
 FULMAR, SULA,
 PUFFIN, AUK
shore AVOCET, SORA,
 STILT, WADER, WIL-
 LET, SNIPE, PLOVER,
 CURLEW, SANDPIPER
short-tailed BREVE
Sinbad's ROC
small TODY, WREN
snipe GODWIT, CUR-
 LEW, GRAY, DUCK,
 JACK, WILSON
song PIPIT, SHAMA,
 OSCINE, CANARY,
 WARBLER
 organ of SYRINX
S. America GUAN,
 TOUCAN, CONDOR,
 WARRIOR, SYLPH,
 RARA, TURCO,
 SERIEMA, ARA
spoonbill AJAJA,
 JABIRU, SCAUP, DUCK
starling STARNEL,
 MINA, MYNA, SALI
stib DUNLIN
stitch IHI
stork MARABOU,
 ADJUTANT, ARGALA
 like IBIS, HERON,
 PELARGIC
swallowlike MARTIN,
 TERN, SWIFT,
 MARTLET
swimming GREBE,
 SWAN, DUCK, GOOSE,
 GULL
talking MINA, MYNA,
 PARROT, CROW
tern DARR, PIRR, KIP,
 NODDY, STARN
three-toed STILT
thrush OUSEL, OUZEL,
 SHAMA, VEERY,
 MAVIS *See* "thrush"
titlark PIPIT
toe CLAW, TALON
 part of LOMA
toucan TOCO

towhee CHEWINK,
 FINCH
tropical MANAKIN,
 JACAMAR, TROGON,
 JACANA, TOUCAN,
 TODY
trumpeter AGAMI
turkeylike CURAS-
 SOW, LEIPOA
unfledged QUAB,
 EYAS
upupoid HOOPOE
vulture URUBU *See*
 "vulture"
wading COOT, CUR-
 LEW, HERN, UMBER,
 UMBRETTE, STILT,
 HERON, IBIS, JACANA,
 RAIL, SORA, TERN,
 STORK, CRANE,
 AVOCET, BITTERN,
 GODWIT, SNIPE
warbler PIPIT
waxwing CEDAR
weaver MUNIA, TAHA,
 BAYA, MAYA
W. Indies ANI, TODY
wing, part of ALULA
wingless KIWI
woodpecker CHAB,
 PILEATED, DOWNY,
 HAIRY, PICULET,
 WRYNECK, FLICKER
wood robin MIRO
yellow-billed CUCKOO
yellowhammer
 FINCH, FLICKER,
 SKITE, BUNTING
young FLEDGLING,
 CHICK, POULT
birl ROTATE, SPIN,
 TOSS, REVOLVE
birth GENESIS, BEGIN-
 NING, ORIGIN, CRE-
 ATION, DELIVERY,
 NATIVITY, LINEAGE
 before PRENATAL
 by NEE
 pertaining to NATAL
 rate NATALITY
birthday poem
 GENETHLIACON
birthmark MOLE,
 NEVUS
birthstone, *Jan.*
 GARNET
Feb. AMETHYST
Mar. BLOODSTONE,
 JASPER
Apr. DIAMOND, SAP-
 PHIRE
May EMERALD

June AGATE
July TURQUOISE
Aug. CARNELIAN
Sept. CHRYSOLITE
Oct. BERYL
Nov. TOPAZ
Dec. RUBY
bis AGAIN, ENCORE,
 TWICE, REPEAT
Biscay
 island YEU, RE
 language
 BASQUE *See* "Bas-
 que"
biscuit CRACKER,
 COOKIE, ROLL, BUN,
 CAKE, WAFER, PANAL,
 RATAFEE, RATAFIA,
 RUSK, SCONE, SNAP,
 PANTILE
bisect HALVE, SPLIT,
 CLEAVE, SEPARATE,
 DIVIDE
bishop, *Alexandria*
 ARIUS
 cap MITRE, MITER,
 MITRELLA
 chess ALFIN
 first year revenue of
 ANNAT
 office of DATARIA
 of Rome POPE
 ray OBISPO
 robe ALB, CHIMER(E)
 See "vestment" *be-
 low*
 seat SEE, APSE, BEMA,
 CATHEDRA
 staff CROSIER
 of office CROOK
 title PRIMATE, PREL-
 ATE, ABBA
 vestment COPE,
 GREMIAL, CHIMER(E),
 ROCHET, ALB
 weed AMMI, GOUT-
 WEED
bishopric DIOCESE,
 SEE, EPISCOPATE
 raise to MITRE
bismer MOCK, DIS-
 GRACE
bison AUROCHS, BUF-
 FALO, BOVINE,
 BONASUS
 India GAUR
bistro BAR, TAVERN,
 RESTAURANT
bisulcate CLOVEN,
 CLEFT, SPLIT
bit ACE, IOTA, JOT,
 MOTE, MITE, PIECE,

SNAFFLE, ATOM,
WHIT, MORSEL, ORT,
SNAP, SPLICE, CRUMB,
TOOL, DRILL, CURB,
PART, PORTION,
SPECK
bite STING, NIP, EAT,
CHAMP, CHAM,
MORSEL, GNAW,
CHEW, CRUNCH,
NIBBLE, SNAP
biting ACRID, CRISP,
CUTTING, RACY,
CAUSTIC, COLD,
PUNGENT, PAINFUL,
DISCOURTEOUS, CEN-
SORIOUS, MORDANT
of nails PHANERO-
MANIA
bitter ACRID, AMARA,
ACERB, SORE, IRATE,
AIGRE, PAINFUL,
ACRIMONIOUS
sentiment ACRIMONY,
HATE, BILE
bitterness ACOR, RUE,
ATTER, MARAH, ACHE,
PAIN, ENMITY, BILE,
ACRIMONY, HATE,
GALL, RANCOR
bitters LIQUOR, TONIC
bitumen ASPHALT, TAR,
PITCH, ELATERITE
shale BAT
bivalve CLAM, OYSTER,
PANDORA, MOLLUSK,
DIATOM, SCALLOP
fresh water MUSSEL,
UNIO
genus PINNA, ANOMIA
bivouac ENCAMP,
ETAPE, CAMP
bizarre OUTRE, GRO-
TESQUE, EXOTIC,
QUAINT, QUEER,
DAEDAL, CURIOUS,
ODD(ISH), FANTASTIC,
FANCIFUL, RIDICU-
LOUS, UNCONFORMA-
BLE
Bizet opera CARMEN
Bjornson hero ARNE
blab TATTLE, GOSSIP,
PRATE, BETRAY, CHAT,
REVEAL
black DHU, JET,
EBON(Y), INKY,
SABLE, NOIR, RAVEN,
NIGRINE, SOOTY,
TARRY, SHINE, POLISH,
DARK, ATROUS,
MURKY, PITCHY

alloy NIELLO
and blue spot EC-
CHYMOSIS, BRUISE,
SHINER,
art EVIL, MAGIC,
SORCERY
bird CROW, RAVEN,
ROOK, ANI *See under*
"bird"
combining form
MEL(A), MELAN(O)
diamond COAL, OIL
fish SWART, TAUTOG
gram URD, PULSE,
PEA
gum TUPELO, NYSSA
haw SLOE
blackamoor NEGRO
blackboard SLATE
blacken JAPAN, INK,
POLISH, SHINE,
BESMIRCH, SLANDER,
DEFAME, DENIGRATE
blackened SOOTED,
SOOTY
blackguard GAMIN,
KNAVE, VILIFY,
SLANDER, SCOUNDREL,
VILLAIN
blackhead COMEDO
blackheart CHERRY
blackish SWART
blackjack GAME,
CARAMEL, CLUB
blackleg CHEAT,
SWINDLER, APOSTATE
blackmail BRIBE,
EXTORT, COERCE
blackmailing EXTOR-
TION, CHANTAGE,
BRIBERY
Blackmore *heroine*
LORNA
black saltwort GLAUX
Black Sea EUXINE,
PONTUS
ancient country near
CIMMERIA, CIRCAS-
SIA, CRIMEA, THRACE
pertaining to PONTIC
port ODESSA, VARNA,
SOCHI
river to DANUBE,
PRUT, BUG, DNIESTER,
DON, KUBAN, INGUR,
RION (PHASIS),
DNIEPER (DNEPR)
blacksmith FARRIER,
STRIKER, SMITHY,
STITHY, PLOVER
shop ANVIL, SMITHY,
STITHY

blackthorn SLOE, HAW
blackwater PYROSIS
black widow SPIDER
blackwort COMFREY
bladder SAC, VESICLE,
BLISTER
combining form ASCO
kelp SEAWEED
blade CUTTER, EDGE,
SWORD, KNIFE, LEAF,
DANDY, SPORT, BIT,
TOLEDO, GRAIN, OAR,
SPIRE, BUCK, GAL-
LANT, FOP, PROPEL-
LER
blague LIE, HOAX,
HUMBUG, CLAPTRAP,
RAILLERY
blah NONSENSE, RUB-
BISH, BUNK
blain BLISTER, BULLA,
SORE
blake PALE, WAN,
COLORLESS
Blake's *symbol* ZOAS
blame GUILT, CHARGE,
REPROACH, CONDEMN,
ACCUSE, ASCRIBE,
FAULT, ONUS, CEN-
SURE, CALL, OBLOQUY,
ODIUM, SHEND
blanch ARGENT,
ETIOLATE, WHITEN,
BLEACH, PALE, FADE
bland AFFABLE, GRA-
CIOUS, MILD, SOFT,
SMOOTH, FLAT,
GENTLE, SUAVE,
URBANE, KIND(LY),
BENIGN, LENIENT,
AMIABLE, SOOTHING,
COURTEOUS
Bland, *pen name*
NESBIT
blandish COAX, AL-
LURE, CAJOLE,
CHARM, WHEEDLE
blank BARE, EMPTY,
CLEAN, FORM, UN-
FILLED, VACANT, VOID,
VACUOUS
blanket AFGHAN, BROT,
COTTA, PONCHO,
QUILT, SERAPE,
THROW, MANTA,
STROUD, SHEET,
COVER(ING), LAYER
horse MANTA
blare BLAST, PEAL,
FANFARE, BLAZON,
TRUMPET

of trumpet TANTARA,
FANFARE, TANTARARA
blasé WEARY, SATI-
ATED, SATED, SUR-
FEITED
blast ATTACK, EXPLO-
SION, GUST, DIS-
CHARGE, GALE, WIND,
FLAW, BANG, SPLIT,
BLIGHT
furnace, section of
BOSH
stone in TYMP
blasted RUINED,
BLIGHTED, SERE
blatant COARSE, NOISY,
GLIB, VULGAR, GROSS,
VOCAL, OBTRUSIVE,
LOUD, SILLY
blaubok ETAAC,
ANTELOPE
blaze FIRE, FLAME,
FLARE, MARK, SHOT,
SPOT, GLARE, GLOW,
BURN, FLASH,
GLEAM, LIGHT
star NOVA
bleach LIGHTEN,
BLANCH, ETIOLATE,
DYE, WHITEN
bleacherite ROOTER,
FAN
bleachers STANDS
bleaching vat KEIR,
KIER
bleak RAW, COLD,
DESOLATE, DREARY
bleakfish SPRAT, BLAY,
BLEY
"Bleak House" *heroine*
ADA
bleared RHEUMY,
DUSKY, INKY
bleb BULLA, BLISTER,
PUSTULE, BUBBLE,
VESICLE
bleed FLOW, SHED,
EXUDE, EXUDATE,
LEAK, ESCAPE, EXTORT
blemish BLOT,
MACULE, MAR, SCAR,
DEFECT, FLAW, IN-
JURY, SLUR, TACHE,
BRUISE, ROT, SPOT,
MOLE, STAIN, TAINT,
MARK, STIGMA, FAULT,
LACK, WANT, SULLY,
TARNISH, DEFACE-
(MENT)
blench FLINCH, PALE,
QUAIL, SHUN, EVADE,
ELUDE, RECOIL,

SHAKE, SHIRK,
SHRINK, AVOID
blend MERGE, SHADE,
CREAM, TINCTURE,
MIX, TINGE, FUSE,
GRADATE, MINGLE,
UNITE, COMBINE,
COALESCE, AMALGAM-
ATE, HARMONIZE
of colors RUN,
SCUMBLE
blended FONDU
blesbok NUNNI,
ANTELOPE
bless SAIN, FAVOR,
THANK, PRAISE, CON-
SECRATE, HALLOW,
MACARIZE, BEATIFY,
EXTOL, ADORE,
SANCTIFY, APPROVE
blessed HOLY, SACRED,
DIVINE
blessing BENISON,
BOON, GRACE, AP-
PROVAL
blight RUST, BLAST,
RUIN, SMUT, NIP,
FROST, ROT, DESTROY,
WITHER, MILDEW
blind SHADE, SHUTTER,
SEEL, STAKE, POT,
ANTE, BET, WAGER,
DECOY, IGNORANT,
SCREEN, PRETEXT
alley IMPASSE, CUL-
DE-SAC
flower girl NYDIA
impulse ATE
printing for BRAILLE
staggers GID
blindness CECITY,
ANOPSIA, ABLEPSY,
ABLEPSIA, SIGHTLESS,
IGNORANCE
blink WINK, FLASH,
TWINKLE, IGNORE,
SHUN, NICTATE,
NEGLECT
bliss FELICITY, RAP-
TURE, PLEASURE,
ESCTASY, JOY
blissful ECSTATIC,
SEELY, HAPPY,
BLESSED, HOLY
blister *See* "bleb"
blithe GAYSOME, AIRY,
GAY, MERRY, GLAD,
HAPPY, JOVIAL, JOLLY,
SPRIGHTLY
blitz ATTACK, RAID
blizzard PURGA, GALE,
STORM, BURAN, SNOW

bloat SWELL, TUMEFY,
PUFF, FERMENT,
INFLATE, DISTEND,
EXPAND
blob MASS, MARK,
SPLOTCH, BLOT,
BLEMISH, SPLASH,
BUBBLE, WEN, DROP
bloc PARTY, FACTION,
RING, CABAL
block DAM, HINDER,
INHIBIT, STYMIE,
CHECK, BAR, ARREST,
FOIL, THWART, BESET,
NOG, MASS, OBSTRUCT,
SQUARE, STREET, ROW,
BARRICADE, HEAD
architectural MUTULE
falconry PERCH
flat MUTULE, TILE
hawser BITT
house FORT
ice SERAC, CUBE
mechanical PULLEY
metal (type) QUAD,
QUOD
pedestal plinth SOCLE,
DIE
small TESSERA
wood CUBE
blockhead DUNCE,
STUPID, NINNY, DOLT,
ASS, FOOL, IDIOT,
OAF, SIMPLETON
blond(e) GOLDEN,
YELLOW, FLAXEN,
LIGHT, FAIR
blood GORE, FLUID,
SERUM, SAP, CRUOR,
KIN, RACE, MOOD,
WAR, GALLANT,
LINEAGE
bad HATE, ANGER
clotted CRUOR
color SANGUINE
combining form
HEMA, HEMO, HAEMO
emulsion CHYLE
feud VENDETTA
fluid SERUM, PLASMA
of the gods ICHOR
pertaining to HEMAL,
HEMIC, HAEMAL,
HAEMIC
plasma SERA, SERUM
poisoning PYEMIA
stagnation STASIS,
CLOT, CRUOR, GRUME
thirsty SAVAGE, WILD,
FIERCE, FERAL
vessel VAS, VEIN,

ARTERY
rupture of RHEXIS
bloodless ANEMIC
state ATONY, LAN-
GUOR, ANEMIA
blood money CRO
bloodsucker TICK,
VAMPIRE, LEECH
bloody GORY, SAN-
GUINARY, CRUEL
bloom BLOSSOM,
FLOWER, DOWN,
FUZZ, HEYDAY, DEW,
YOUTH, RIPEN,
FLOURISH, PRIME,
FURZE
bloomer TROUSER,
MISTAKE, ERROR,
LAPSE, BULL, BONER,
SLIP
bloomery HEARTH,
FORGE, FURNACE
blooming again
REMONTANT
blossom DEVELOP,
FLOWER, BUD, POSY,
BELL, BLOOM, BLOW
keels CARINAE
blot BLUR, SULLY,
SMEAR, STAIN, ERROR,
DELETE, BLEMISH,
EXPUNGE, EFFACE,
ERASE, DESTROY,
STIGMA, BRAND,
TAINT, SPOT
blotch MOTTLE,
MACULA, BLEB, BULLA,
STAIN, BLEMISH,
PATCH, BLAIN
blotter PAD, BLAD,
BOOK
blouse SMOCK,
TUNIC, WAIST,
SHIRT
blow KNOCK, DINT,
PANT, SLOG, CLOUT,
CONK, ONER, STRIKE,
HIT, SLAP, WHACK,
BUFFET, RANT, BRAG,
VAUNT, WHIFFLE,
INFLATE, ENLARGE,
WIND, GALE, BOAST,
CRIG, CALAMITY,
DISASTER
blowzed RUDDY,
FLUSHED, RED
blubber FAT, WEEP,
CRY, WAIL, WHIMPER,
WHINE, SWOLLEN,
THICK
cut FLENSED, LIPPER
to strip FLENSE

bludgeon CUDGEL,
MACE, BAT, CLUB,
WEAPON
blue TURQUOISE,
COBALT, AZURE, TEAL,
INDIGO, BICE, PERSE,
SMALT, AQUA, DE-
JECTED, SAD, DISMAL,
GLUM, LOW, MELAN-
CHOLY, GLOOMY
bird JAY, IRENA
gray SLATE, CESIOUS
green CALAMINE
jacket SAILOR, TAR,
GOB
jeans LEVIS, CHINOS
penciler EDITOR
vitriol BLUESTONE
blue and lemon
BELTON
blueback TROUT, HER-
RING, SALMON
Bluebeard's *wife*
FATIMA
bluefin WEAKFISH,
SAURY, BASS
bluegrass POA
blueprint DIAGRAM,
MAP, SKETCH, DRAFT,
TRACE, PLOT, PLAN
blues DUMPS,
MEGRIMS, MELAN-
CHOLY, DESPONDENCY
bluff BANK, CLIFF,
CRUSTY, RUDE, CURT,
HOAX, MISLEAD, BRAG,
ROUGH, PLAIN, OPEN,
FRANK, CANDID,
HEARTY, STEEP,
SHORT, UNCIVIL,
IMPOLITE
blunder SLIP, BOTCH,
BULL, BONER, BREACH,
MESS, ERR(OR),
MISDO, LAPSE, FAULT,
SOLECISM, GAFF,
BUNGLE, FAIL(URE)
blunt DULL, POINT-
LESS, ASSUAGE,
OBTUND, BRUSQUE,
OBTUSE, CURT, BALD,
FRANK, RUDE, PLAIN,
GRUFF, BLUFF, INERT,
BENUMBED
in emotivity HEBE-
TATE
blur SMEAR, BLOB,
BLOT, MACULE, SPOT,
CLOUD, DIM, OBSCURE,
DEFECT, SULLY,
STIGMA

blurb AD, RAVE, AN-
NOUNCEMENT, PUFF
blush RUBESCENCE,
GLOW, COLOR, MAN-
TLE, FLUSH, TINGE,
REDDEN
blushing ROSY,
ERUBESCENT, EMBAR-
RASSED
bluster SWAGGER,
ROAR, BOUNCE, RANT,
RODOMONTADE,
THREATEN, BULLY,
BRAVADO
boa ABOMA, SCARF,
SNAKE
Boadicea people ICENI
boar APER, BARROW,
HOG, SUS
head HURE
Hindu VARAHA
board(s) PANEL,
PLANK, DEAL, FARE,
MEALS, KEEPS, FEED,
EATS, HOUSE,
LODGE, DIET, STAGE,
CABINET, COUNCIL,
TRIBUNAL
spring OPPORTUNITY,
WAGON
boast BRAG, GAB,
VAPOR, VAUNT, CROW,
RAVE, FLAUNT, EXULT,
PREEN, BOMBAST,
BLOW, SWAGGER
boaster JINGO,
RODOMONT, BRAG-
GART, BRAVADO
boastful PARADO,
THRASONICAL
speech RODOMON-
TADE, GASCONADE,
KOMPOLOGY
boat *See* "ship"
BARK, CRAFT, TUB,
TUG, VESSEL, SKIFF,
DORY, DUGOUT,
LINER, STEAMER,
COBLE, KETCH,
CANOE, CRAFT, GIG,
ARK, CAT, TROW,
TRAWLER, PINNACE,
BIRLINN, CARVEL,
RAFT
African DHOW
Aleutian BIDAR
ancient British
CORACLE
armed galley
TRIREME, BIREME,
UNIREME
Bolivian BALSA

brace THWART
Chinese SAMPAN, BARK, JUNK
dispatch AVISO, OOLAK
Dutch YANKY, KOFF, HOOKER
duck SKAG
E. India DINGEY, DINGHY, DHONI
Egypt BARIS, SANDAL, CANGIA, FELUCCA
Eskimo OOMIAC, KAYAK, UMIAK
fast galley DROMON(D)
fishing SEALER, SMACK, SLOOP
flat-bottom BARGE, DORY, SCOW, BAC, PUNT, COBLE, BARIS, BATEAU
French CARAVELLE
front of BOW, PROW, STEM
India MASOOLA, MASULA(H), SHIBAR
Indian river ALMADIA, ALMADIE
Italian GONDOLA
Jason's ARGO
jolly YAWL
Levantine BUM, SAIC, SET(T)EE, FELUCCA
mail PACKET, AVISO
man-o-war PINNACE
Mediterranean MISTIC(O), SAIC, SET(T)EE, FELUCCA, ACCON, GAL(L)IOT
merchant ARGOSY, HOLCAD
military PONTOON
North Sea COBLE
Norwegian PRAAM, PRAHAM, PRAM
one bank of oars UNIREME
part of DECK, KEEL, SKEG, PROW, STERN, RAIL
Philippine BANCA, BANKA
racing SCULL, GIG
river FERRY
row DORY
sailing BARK, BUG-EYE, PINNACE, DONI, KETCH, YAWL, SCHOONER, BUCKEYE
Scottish SKAFFIE
shaped NAVICULAR

ship's JOLLY, GIG, YAWL
single-masted SLOOP, HOY
small SHALLOP, SCULL, SKIFF, DORY, PUNT, CANOE
square-rigged or masted BRIG, SNOW
steam TUB, LINER
steer CONN, PILOT
table GRAVY
tender HOY
three banks of oars TRIREME
three masted TERN
three oared or three rowers RANDAN
Tigris river GUFA, KUFA, GOOFAH
timber KEEL
trading BAGGALA
two banks of oars BIREME
Venetian GONDOLA, BUCENTAUR
war FRIGATE, BOYER, SUB
W. Indies MOSES, DROG(H)ER
boatman PHAON, CHARON
boat-shaped
 clock NEF
 ornament NEF
 vessel NAVICELLA
boats, *collection of* TOW, NAVY, FLEET, SQUADRON, ARMADA
boatswain, *Lascar crew* SERANG
Boaz's *son* OBED
 wife RUTH
bob DUCK, FLOAT, JERK, BOW, NOD, DAB, PENDANT, DOCK, ANGLE, SHILLING, CUT, CLIP
bobbin SPOOL, PIRN, REEL, SPINDLE
 frame CREEL
bobby OFFICER, PEELER, COP, BULL
bobcat LYNX
bobolink ORTOLAN, REED, BIRD
bobwhite COLIN, QUAIL, BIRD
bocardo *See* "bokardo"
Boccaccio classic DECAMERON

Boche HUN
bode AUGUR, PORTEND, FORETELL, PRESAGE
bodice BASQUE, WAIST, CORSET
bodkin POINARD, DAGGER, AWL, PIN, STILETTO
body LICHAM, TORSO, FORM, CORPSE, CORPUS, STIFF, CARCASS, CADAVER, TRUNK, STEM, SOMA, BOLE, BULK, MASS, SUBSTANCE, AS-SEMBLAGE
anterior part PROSOMA
cavity COELOM(E), SINUS
fluid SERUM, PLASMA, BLOOD, LYMPH, SALIVA
heavenly STAR, PLANET, COMET, MOON, ASTEROID, SUN
injury to MAYHEM, TRAUMA
joint ELBOW, KNEE, WRIST, HIP
motion, pertaining to GESTIC
of men FORCE, CORPS, MASS, ARMY, POSSE, NAVY
of vehicle BED, BOX
pertaining to SOMATIC
stimulant HORMONE, TONIC
twist FLOUNCE
zoological SOMA
Boeotian *capital* THEBES
region IONIA
Boer dialect TAAL
general BOTHA
bog FEN, MORASS, SWAMP, MARSH, MOOR, OOZE, MIRE, SINK, QUAGMIRE, SLOUGH, SYRT
manganese WAD
peat CESS, MOSS
plant ABAMA
bogey BUGABOO, BUG-BEAR, SPOOK, DEMON, GOBLIN, SPECTER
boggy FENNY, MIRY, SOFT, WET, SWAMPY

boggle ALARM, GOB-
LIN, SCARE, BALK,
JIB, SHY, HESITATE
bogus FALSE, FAKE,
PHONY, SPURIOUS,
SHAM, FICTITIOUS
bohea TEA
"Boheme" heroine
MIMI
Bohemia, Bohemian
PICARD, HUS(S),
ARTY, GYPSY
character MIMI
city PRAHA, PRAGUE
dance REDOWA,
FURIANT, POLKA
district EGER
garnet PYROPE
mountain range ERZ
religious leader
HUS(S)
boidae BOA, PYTHON,
ANACONDA, SNAKES
boil SORE, BUBBLE,
STY, ANTHRAX, RAGE,
STORM, STEW,
SEETHE, ESTUATE,
COOK, DECOCT,
EFFERVESCE, TEEM
syrup PEARL
boiler CAULDRON,
COPPER, ALEMBIC,
RETORT, KETTLE
disk SPUT
reinforcer SPUT
tube scaler SOOTER
boisterous NOISY,
STRIDENT, UNRULY,
LOUD, FURIOUS,
VIOLENT, CLAMOROUS,
EXCITABLE, STORMY
bokardo PRISON,
DOKHMA
bold BRAZEN, PERT,
DARING, BRAVE, FOR-
WARD, RASH, VALIANT,
HEROIC, NERVY,
INTREPID, FEARLESS,
PROMINENT
type DARK, TEXT
bole CRYPT, DOSE,
STEM, TRUNK, BOLUS
bolero JACKET,
WAIST, DANCE
bolide MISSILE,
METEOR
Bolivia
capital SUCRE, LA
PAZ
coin BOLIVAR
district ORURO,

POTOSI, PANDO,
TARIJA
mountain CUZCO
(CUSCO)
river BENI, ORTON
boll GROW, PERICARP,
POD, SWELL, KNOB,
BULB, CAPSULE,
ONION
bolo KNIFE, MACHETE
Bolshevik *See*
"Russia"
bolster PAD, PILLOW,
SUPPORT, AID, REPAIR
bolt FLEE, RUN, ELOPE,
ESCAPE, DREDGE,
SIFT, SIEVE, WINNOW,
SCREEN, CLOSE,
FASTEN, PIN, SHACKLE,
BAR, LOCK, LATCH,
PAWL, RIVET, TOG-
GLE, NAB, PINTLE,
GORGE, STROKE,
GULP, FLASH
bolter SIEVE, DE-
SERTER, ELOPER
bolus CLOD, LUMP,
ROCK, PILL, CUD,
MASS, WAD
bom ABOMA, BOA,
SNAKE
bomb GRENADE,
MARMITE, BLARE,
DUD
bombardment CAN-
NONADE, STRAFE,
RAFALE, SIEGE,
ATTACK
bombardon BASSOON,
OBOE, TUBA, SAX-
(HORN), POMMER
bombast FUSTIAN, GAS,
RAGE, BLUSTER,
RANT, BOAST
bombastic OROTUND,
INFLATED, GRANDIOSE,
TURGID, FLOWERY,
WORDY, TUMID,
FLUENT, VOCAL,
POMPOUS
Bombay *city* SURAT
mountain ABU
town MIRAJ, POONA
bombinate BOOM,
HUM
bombproof chamber
ABRI, CASEMATE,
DUGOUT, SHELTER
bombyx ERI, ERIA,
SILKWORM, MOTH
bonasus AUROCHS,
BISON, OX

bond CONNECTION,
ACCORD, UNION,
PLEDGE, SHACKLE,
DUTY, LINK, NEXUS,
TIE, COMPACT, RELA-
TION, VOW, SECURITY,
BOUND, BAIL, YOKE,
CEMENT, GLUE, NOTE
chemical DIENE,
VALENCE
bondage SERVITUDE,
THRALLDOM, SLAVERY,
YOKE, HELOTRY,
RESTRAINT, OBLIGA-
TION
bondland COPYHOLD
bondsman VASSAL,
CHURL, ESNE, SURETY,
PEON, SERF, SLAVE,
HELOT, STOOGE,
VILLEIN, THRALL
bone(s) OS(SA), RIB,
ULNA, TIBIA, ILIUM,
FEMUR, FIBULA,
RADIUS, HUMERUS
ankle TALUS,
ASTRAGALUS
anvil INCUS, AMBOS
breast STERNUM,
XIPHOID, GLADIOLUS
cavities ANTRA,
SINUSES
cheek MALAR,
ZYGOMA
combining form OS,
OSTEO
curvature LORDOSIS,
SCOLIOSIS, KYPHOSIS
decay CARIES
disease CARIES,
RACHITIS, RICKETS,
ARTHRITIS, OSTEITIS
ear INCUS, STAPES,
ANVIL, AMBOS
face MAXILLA, MALAR,
MANDIBLE, ZYGOMA
finger PHALANGE,
DIGIT
flank ILIUM, ILIA
forearm RADIUS,
ULNA
fragment SPICULE
heel See "tarsus"
below
inflamed OSTEITIS
leg FEMUR, TIBIA,
FIBULA, PATELLA
pelvis ILIUM, ILIA
pertaining to OSTEAL
process MASTOID,
TUBERCLE, INION
scraper XYSTER

skull VOMER, TEM-
PORAL, SPHENOID,
FRONTAL, ZYGOMA,
MAXILLA, MANDIBLE
small OSSICLE,
SESAMOID
tarsus TALUS, ASTRAG-
ALUS, CUBOID,
CALCIS
thigh FEMUR
boner *See* "blunder"
bones OSSA, DICE
boneset FEVERWORT,
THOROUGHWORT,
COMFREY, AGUEWEED,
HERB
bongo ANTELOPE,
DRUM
boniata YAM
bonito COBIA, ROBALO,
ATU, AKU, FISH
bon mot QUIP, PUN,
JEST, WITTICISM
bonnet CAP, CHAPEAU,
TOQUE, CORONET,
HOOD, COVER
resembling MITRATE
string BRIDE
bonnyclabber MILK,
CURD
bonus AWARD, PRIZE,
MEED, PREMIUM,
GIFT, SUBSIDY, CUM-
SHAW, TIP, GRATUITY
bony STIFF, LANK,
LEAN, HARD, TOUGH
boob DUNCE, FOOL,
NITWIT, ASS
booby LOSER, DULL,
STUPID, PRIZE
boojum SNARK
book WORK, FOLIO,
TEXT, TOME, BIBLE,
VOL, VOLUME, BRO-
CHURE, MSS, OPUS,
MANUAL, REGISTER,
ENTER, BLOTTER,
DIARY, LOG
back of SPINE
case FOREL, FORREL
devotional GOSPEL,
MISSAL, BIBLE
hours HORA
large FOLIO, TOME
lover BIBLIOPHILE
manuscript CODEX,
DRAFT
of feasts ORDO
of maps ATLAS
of masses or devotions
MISSAL
of nobility PEERAGE

of songs HYMNAL
ornamented cover
TOOLED
palm TARA, TALIERA
part LEAF, PAGE,
CHAPTER, SECTION
poetic CANTO
psalms PSALTER
selection PERICOPE,
EXTRACT, EXCERPT
shape and size
FORMAT
sheath FOREL
ship's LOG
title page RUBRIC
worm SCHOLAR
bookkeeping entry
DEBIT, CREDIT
boom RESOUND, ROAR,
SPAR, SPRIT, DRUM,
FLOURISH, RUMBLE,
SUPPORT
boomerang RESILE,
RICOCHET, KILEY,
RECOIL, BACKFIRE
boon GAY, JOVIAL,
BENE, FAVOR, GIFT,
GRANT, BENEFIT
boor LOUT, CARLOT,
CHURL, CAD, OAF,
CARL, CLOWN, PILL
boorish VULGAR,
GAWKY, RUDE, UN-
COUTH, STUPID,
COARSE
boost ELEVATE, KITE,
LIFT, RAISE, HOIST,
HEAVE, REAR, EXALT,
PUSH, AID, ASSIST,
ABET, HELP, BACK,
COACH, UP
boot SOCK, KICK, SHOE,
RECRUIT
bird's OCREA
Eskimo KAMIK
lace LACET, STRING
logger's PAC
stout PAC, BALMORAL,
STOGY, BROGAN
booth STALL, LOGE,
CRAME, SHOP
bootlick FAWN, TOADY,
FLATTER
booty PREY, GAIN,
LOOT, SWAG, PLUN-
DER, GRAFT, PRIZE,
SPOIL, PELF
borax TINCAL
Bordeaux wine COSNE,
BOURG, MEDOC,
CHIANTI *See* "wine"
Bordelaise SAUCE

border TIP, ABUT,
TRIM, EDGE, FLANK,
RAND, (B)RIM, VERGE,
HEM, MARGIN, SKIRT,
SIDE, LINE, FRONTIER,
MARGE, BRINK,
LIMIT, END, MARK,
ORNAMENT, PURFLE
make a raised MILL,
EMBOSS
on stamps TRESSURE
bordered LIMBATE
bore AUGER, GIMLET,
BIT, DRILL, PUNCH,
PRICK, PIERCE, TOOL,
TEWEL, DRAG, TIRE,
TEREBRATE, CALIBER,
DIAMETER, HOLE,
TIDE, EAGRE, IRK,
ANNOY
in a river EAGRE, TIDE
Boreas NORTHER, WIND
borecole KALE, KAIL
boredom ENNUI,
TEDIUM, ANNOYANCE
borings CHIPS,
FILINGS, DUST
boring tool BIT,
WIMBLE, AUGER,
GIMLET, DRILL
born NASCENT, NEE,
DELIVERED
well EUGENIC, FREE,
NOBLE
borne CARRIED, RODE
Borneo *aborigine*
IBAN, DYAK, DAYAK
ape ORANG(UTAN)
island near JAVA,
BALI, ALOR, MOA,
CELEBES, JOLO, OBI
measure GANTA(NG)
port MIRI
river KAJAN
town SERIA, MIRI
tribe DYAK, IBAN
Borodin opera IGOR
boron BORIC, ULEXITE,
BORAX
borrow TAKE, ADOPT,
COPY, STEAL
borsch base BEETS
bos BEEF, COW, NEAT,
CALF, OX, BISON
Bosc PEAR
bosh NONSENSE,
SKETCH, TRIVIA,
ROT, END, JOKE,
TWADDLE
Bosnia native CROAT,
SLAV

boss DIRECTOR, OWNER, FOREMAN, DEAN, MANAGER, MASTER, UMBO, STUD, KNOB, POLITICIAN

bot LARVA

botanical *angle* AXIL
cell SPORE, ENERGID
change CRATICULAR, PELORIA
depression VARIOLE, FOVEA
suffix ALEAE

botanist MENDEL, BROWN, THOME, RAY

botany PHYTOLOGY

botch See "bungle"

botfly larvae BOTS

both, *as a prefix*, BI, AMBI

bother WORRY, AIL, TAMPER, PUZZLE, BUSTLE, HARASS, TEASE, HARRY, NUISANCE, TROUBLE, MOLEST, PESTER, MEDDLE, PERPLEX, DISTURB

bothy, bothie COTTAGE, HUT, LODGE

bottle VIAL, COSTREL, KIT, PHIAL, FLASK, CARAFE, CRUET, JUG, CARBOY, CANTEEN, CRUSE, PIG, DECANTER, FLAGON, PRESERVE

bottom BED, NADIR, LEES, BASE, FOUNDA-TION, SOLE, FOOT, ROOT, FLOOR, DREGS, GROUND, SUPPORT
marshy SIKE

bough LIMB, BRANCH, ARM, SHOOT, TWIG, SPRIG, SPRAY

bouillabaisse STEW, CHOWDER

bouillon SOUP, CONSOMME, BROTH

boulevardier ROUE, RAKE

bounce EJECT, SPRING, FIRE, DISMISS, SACK, SPIRIT, VERVE, RESILIENCE, BOUND, LEAP, RECOIL, JUMP

bound SCUD, DART, SKIM, LEAP, LOPE, SPRING, HOP, CONFINE, (DE)MIT, BOND, BIND, END, SECURED,

TIED, TERM, VAULT, STEND, CIRCUMSCRIBE

boundary LINE, AMBIT, MERE, LIMIT, BORDER, VERGE, BOURN(E), END, FENCE, HEDGE, TERMINATION
having common CON-TERMINAL

bounder CAD, SNOB, CUB, ROUE, RAKE

bounds AMBIT, LIMIT, EDGE, RIM, OUTLINE, RESTRAINT

bounty LARGESS, BONUS, REWARD, GRANT, SUBSIDY, AWARD, MEED, PRIZE, GIFT, BOON, PREMIUM

"Bounty" captain BLIGH

bouquet AROMA, ODOR, POSY, NOSEGAY, CORSAGE, AURA, FRAGRANCE

bourne LIMIT, END, EDGE, RIM, BROOK, RILL, RIVULET, AIM, GOAL

bouse DRINK, TOPE, BOOZE, CAROUSE, HAUL, LIFT

bout CONTEST, ESSAY, ROUND, SET-TO, MATCH, TURN, CON-FLICT, TRIAL, FIGHT, JOB

boutique SHOP, BOOTH

bovine STEER, COW, CALF, BULL, OX, ZEBU, TAURINE, BOS, SLOW, SLUGGISH, PATIENT, STUPID
Asiatic YAK
hybrid CATALO

bow PROW, STEM, BEND, CURVE, SALAAM, CURTSY, CRESCENT, DEFER, YIELD, RELENT, ARCH, ARC, KNEEL, NOD, STOOP, WEAPON, CONGE
nautical BEAK, PROW, STEM
   fullest part LOOF, LUFF
   shaped ARCUATE

bowdlerize EX-PURGATE, CENSOR, PARAPHRASE

bowed ARCATE,

ARCUATE(D), STOOPED, HUMBLED

bowels COMPASSION, PITY, RUTH, COLON

bower NOOK, GROTTO, RETREAT, ANCHOR, ARBOR, KNAVE, JACK

bowfin AMIA, LAWYER, MUDFISH

bowl ARENA, STADIUM, PAN, CUP, BEAKER, VESSEL, DEPAS, SCYPHUS, CRATER, MAZER, DISH, BASIN

bowler HAT, DERBY, KEGLER

bowsprit, *lateral stay* SHROUD
part of BEE, HEEL
rests APRON, STEM

box CIST, CRATE, CHEST, CASKET, COFFIN, ETUI, COFFER, LOGE, SEAT, SPAR, SMITE, CUFF, STRIKE, HIT, PUNCH, CLOUT, SWAT, SLUG, SLAP, FIGHT, ENCLOSE, CON-TAINER, PACKAGE
alms ARCA
shaped tomb CIST

boxcars SIXES, GONDOLAS

box elder ACER, MAPLE, TREE

boxer CHINESE, LOUIS, BAER, DOG
Roman hand cover for CESTUS

boxing match See "bout"

boxwood tree SERON, DOGWOOD

boy YOUTH, BUD, BUB, SHAVER, LAD, TOT, TAD, SERVANT, WAITER, NIPPER, STRIPLING, VALET

boycott SHUN, AVOID, BLACKBALL, OSTRACIZE

Brabant, *princess or duchess of* ELSA

brace GIRD, LEG, STRUT, PAIR, COUPLE, TWO, STAY, YOKE, PROP, TRUSS, SUPPORT, CRUTCH, SHORE, STIFFEN, STRENGTHEN, REIN-FORCE, TIE, FASTEN, REFRESH, NERVE

brace and a half
THREE, TIERCE, LEASH
bracelet ARMILLA,
ORNAMENT, CIRCLE,
HANDCUFF
brachyuran
CRUSTACEAN, CRAB
bracing QUICK, TONIC,
INVIGORATING,
STIMULATING,
SALUBRIOUS
bracket CONSOLE,
CORBEL, STRUT,
GROUP, CLASS,
CATEGORY, BRACE,
LEVEL, SHELF, SUP-
PORT
bract SPATHE, GLUME,
PALEA, PALET, SPADIX
brad NAIL, PIN, SPRIG
brag CROW, PREEN,
GASCONADE, RAVE,
BOAST, SWAGGER,
STRUT, BLUFF, VAUNT
Bragi's wife ITHUNN,
IDUN
Brahma HINDU,
CREATOR
Brahman PUNDIT,
ARYAN, HINDU, PRIEST,
ZEBU
precept SUTRA, SUTTA
title AYA
braid TRIM, CUE,
LACET, RIBBON, PLAIT,
TRESS, PLAT, WEAVE,
KNIT, TAT, QUEUE,
BREDE, LACE, TRIM-
MING, ORNAMENT
knot of LACET
on coat or dress FROG
brain MIND, INTEL-
LECT, CEREBRUM,
WITS, PSYCHE
box PAN, SKULL,
CRANIUM
canal ITER
groove(s) SULCUS,
SULCI
layer OBEX, CORTEX
mater PIA, DURA, ALBA
membrane DURA,
TELA
orifice PYLA, LURA
part of PONS, CERE-
BELLUM, LOBE, STEM
pertaining to
ENCEPHALIC,
CEREBRAL
ridge(s) GYRUS, GYRI
tissue AREOLAR

track ITER
tumor GLIOMA
brake CHECK, RETARD,
CURB, FERN, THICKET,
COPSE, STOP, BLOCK,
DRAG, DELAY, HINDER,
DETER
part of SHOE, DRUM
bramble THORN, BRIER
brambly PRICKLY,
SPINY, THORNY
bran, *inferior* TREAT
branch(es) FORK,
STOLON, RAME,
VIMEN, SPRIG,
MEMBER, LIMB, BOW,
ARM, RAMUS, RAMI,
BOUGH, TWIG, SPUR,
STREAM, CREEK,
BIFURCATE, DIVERGE,
OUTLET, RAMIFY
angle formed by AXIL
combining form
CLAD(O), RAMI
like RAMOSE, RAMOUS
of nerves RAMUS
pertaining to RAMAL
branched RAMAL,
RAMOSE, RAMATE,
CLADOSE, FORKED
branches RAMAGE
three TRISKELE,
TRISKELION
branchiae GILLS
branching RAMOSE
brand KIND, SORT,
STAIN, EMBER, MARK,
BLOT, STAMP, STIGMA,
LABEL, SEAR, BURN,
TAINT, FLAW,
FLAMBEAU, TORCH,
SWORD, STIGMATIZE
brandish SHAKE,
SWING, WAVE,
FLOURISH, FLAUNT,
DISPLAY
brandling EARTH-
WORM, PARR
brandy COGNAC
and soda PEG
cordial ROSOLIO
French MARC
mastic RAKI, RAKEE
brank(s) BRIDLE,
PILLORY, PRANCE,
STRUT, CAPER
brant CHEN, QUINK,
GOOSE, SCOTER
brash BOLD, RASH,
SAUCY, FORWARD,
IMPUDENT, HASTY
brass NERVE, IM-

PUDENCE, ALLOY,
OFFICER(S), IN-
SOLENCE
man of TALOS
to imitate gold
ORMOLU
brassard, brassart
BRACER, BADGE,
ARMBAND
brassica CABBAGE,
KALE, TURNIP, RAPE,
RUTABAGA, COLE
brasslike alloy LATTEN
brassy BRAZEN, BOLD,
REEDY, CHEAP, SASSY
brat BAIRN, IMP,
MINOR, CHILD, INFANT
bravado BLUSTER,
POMP, PRIDE, SWAG-
GER, BOMBAST
brave FACE, BOLD,
HEROIC, MANLY, DARE,
DEFY, GAME, DARING,
GRITTY, INDIAN, FEAR-
LESS, DAUNTLESS, IN-
TREPID, WARRIOR,
CHALLENGE
bravo BANDIT, THUG,
GOOD, OLE, RAH, AP-
PLAUSE, DESPERADO,
INDIAN
brawl FRACAS, FRAY,
RIOT, ROW, FIGHT,
BROIL, MELEE,
SHINDY, DIN, STRIFE,
QUARREL, SCUFFLE,
REVEL, DISCORD
bray HEE-HAW, CRUSH,
GRIND, BRUISE, MIX,
POUND
brazen NERVY, PERT,
(B)RASH, CALLOUS,
INSOLENT, SASSY,
BRASSY
Brazil, Brazilian
aborigine CARIB
bird See under "bird"
cape FRIO
city or town RIO,
RECIFE, BELEM, PARA,
BAHIA, NATAL, ITU,
TUPA, LINS, JAU,
CRATO, BAGE, ASSIS,
BAIA, SANTOS
coin REIS, MILREIS,
CONTO, DOBRA
crane SERIEMA
dance MAXIXE,
SAMBA
drink ASSAI
estuary PARA
fiber IMBE

forest MATTA
heron SOCO
Indian See under
"Indian"
ipecac EVEA
island ROCAS
lagoon PATOS
measure PIPA, MOIO,
PE
money See "coin"
above
monkey SAI
nut PARA
palm See "palm"
parrot ARA, MACAW,
TIRIBA
plant JABORANDI,
YAGE, YAJE, CAROA,
IMBE
river PARA, AMAZON,
XINGU, PARANA
rubber PARA, CAUCHO
seaport NATAL, BAHIA,
CEARA, RECIFE,
SANTOS, BELAI (PARA)
state or province
ACRE, BAIA, GOIAZ,
PARANA, PARA, CEARA,
BAHIA
town See "city"
above
tree ULE, UHLE,
HEVEA, ARAROBA,
ANDA, APA, WALLABA
weight ONCA
wood EMBUIA
breach CLEFT, GAP,
RENT, FISSURE, SPLIT,
RUPTURE, CRACK,
QUARREL, VIOLATION
of etiquette GAFFE,
SOLECISM
bread BATCH, LOAF,
PONE, RUSK, FOOD,
FARE, DIET, ALIMENT,
ROLL, BUN
boiled and seasoned
CUSH
crust RIND
fried pieces CROUTONS
leavened KISRA
Passover AZYM(E),
MATZOS, MATZOTH
soaked in broth
BREWIS
spread BUTTER, OLEO
toasted SIPPET
tree seeds DIKA
unleavened AZYM(E),
MATZOS, MATZOTH
breadth SPAN, SCOPE,

EXTENT, WIDTH,
DIAMETER
break *See under* "res-
pite" FRACTURE,
SNAP, BOON, CRACK,
RUIN, OPENING, RUP-
TURE, HIATUS, TIDE,
HINT, CHANGE, REND,
DAWN, SMASH, SHAT-
TER, SEVER, SEPARATE,
TEAR
in STAVE, INITIATE,
TRAIN, BLUNDER, SLIP,
INTERRUPT
out ERUPT, RASH,
ESCAPE
breakable BRITTLE,
FRIABLE, DELICATE
breakbone fever
DENGUE
breaker SURF, COMBER,
BILLOW, WAVE, ROL-
LER
breaking down
CATACLASM,
CATABOLISM, DISRUP-
TION
breakwater JETTY,
DIKE, MOLE, QUAY,
REFUGE, PIER, OB-
STRUCTION, DAM
bream BROOM, SCUP,
FISH
Japanese TAI
sea SHAD
breast CHEST, THORAX,
BOSOM
breastbone STERNUM,
XIPHOID, GLADIOLUS
having flat RATITE
breast pin BROOCH,
PECTORAL, CLASP,
OUCH
breastplate THUMMIN,
URIM, LORICA,
POITREL, POITRAIL,
SHIELD, ARMOR
breastwork PARAPET,
FORT, FORECASTLE,
RAMPART, DICKEY
breath LIFE, WIND,
PNEUMA, PANT, PECH,
PUFF, GULP, HUFF,
RESPITE, PAUSE,
WHIFF, SIGH
of life PRANA,
PNEUMA, SPIRIT
shortness of DYSPNEA
breathe PANT, PUFF,
SNORT, ASPIRE,
SUSPIRE, UTTER,
SPEAK, RESPIRE, LIVE,

EXIST, PAUSE, WHEEZE
combining form
PNEO, PNEUMA
breathed SPIRATE
breather REST, RECESS,
BREAK, FIVE, PAUSE,
TRUCE, ARMISTICE,
REPOSE
breathing GASPING,
ALIVE, SPIRATION
organ of LUNG, GILL
orifice(s) SPIRACLE,
NARES, NOSE, PORE,
NOSTRIL, MOUTH
painful or short
DYSPNEA
smooth LENE
sound STRIDOR, RALE,
SNORE
breech BUTTOCKS,
DOUP, BORE, BLOCK,
BUTT, REAR,
POSTERIORITY,
DERRIERE
sight HAUSSE
breeches KNICKERS,
JODHPURS, LEVIS,
JEANS, TROUSERS
breeching HARNESS,
ROPE
breed REAR, RAISE,
CREATE, PRODUCE,
SIRE, BEGET, STRAIN,
CLASS, RACE, SORT,
CAUSE, BEAR, HATCH,
ENGENDER, KIND,
MULTIPLY, PROGENY
breeding TRAINING,
DEPORTMENT
place NIDUS
breeze AIR, WIND,
ZEPHYR, PIRR, AURA,
GUST, FLAW, BLAST,
GALE, RUMOR, STIR
fly WHAME
breeze on Lake Geneva
REBAT
bressumer BEAM,
GIRDER, LINTEL, SUP-
PORT
breve WRIT, MINIM,
ORDER, NOTE, MARK,
BRIEF, BIRD
breviary PORTAS(S),
COMPEND, EPITOME,
ORDO, DIGEST, AB-
STRACT
brew CONCOCT, ALE,
FOMENT, BEER, MIX,
COOK, HATCH, PLOT,
STEW, MAKE, DEVISE,
PREPARE

brewer's *grain* MALT, BARLEY, CORN, RYE
vat TUN, GYLE
yeast LOB, LEAVEN, BARM
brewery refuse DRAFF, DREGS
brewing, *amount of one* GYLE
bribe TIP, BAIT, SUBORN, BOODLE, SOP, GRAFT, TEMPT, OFFER, BUY
bric-a-brac BIBELOT, VIRTU, CURIO, KNICK-KNACKS
brick, *mix clay for* PUG
oven KILN
part of BAT
unburnt and dried ADOBE
wood NOG, DOOK, SCUTCH
bride BAR, TIE, REIN, LOOP, ROSE
of the sea VENUS
bridegroom's *gift to bride* HANDSEL
Bridewell GAOL, JAIL, PRISON, WORKHOUSE
bridge LINK, PONTOON, PONS, SPAN, CROSS, AUCTION, CONTRACT, GAME, WAY, TRAVERSE
forerunner of game WHIST
of musical instrument PONTICELLO, MAGAS
player NORTH, SOUTH, EAST, WEST
term BOOK, BID, SLAM, PASS, VOID, TRUMP, TRICK, SUIT, RAISE, BYE, SET, LEG
bridle REIN, BIT, CURB, CHECK, CON-TROL, RULE, DIRECT, STRUT, SWAGGER, SNAFFLE, RESTRAIN, GOVERN, REPRESS
brief SHORT, TERSE, COMPACT, PITHY, CURT, FLEETING, FEW, QUICK, EPITOME, LACONIC, SUMMARY, SYLLABUS, COMPENDIUM, TRANSITORY, CONCISE
briery SPINY, SHARP
brigand *See* "bandit"
bright APT, SMART,

CLEVER, QUICK, NITID, NAIF, ACUTE, KEEN, SUNNY, GAY, SHINY, VIVID, GLOSSY, ROSY, CHEERY, INTELLIGENT, WITTY, LUCID, SHINING, SHARP
to make BURN, FURBISH, CHEER, ILLUME, ANIMATE, BURNISH, POLISH, SHINE
brightness NITOR, SHEEN, SPLENDOR, LUSTER, BRILLIANCE, ECLAT, ACUMEN
brilliance ECLAT, GLIT-TER, FAME, GLORY, LUSTER
brilliant EMINENT, SIGNAL, CLEVER, RADIANT, SPARKLING, BRIGHT, SAGE, WISE, KEEN, SHINING, GOOD, GLORIOUS
brim RIM, BRINK, BLUFF, EDGE, MARGIN, BORDER, VERGE, SKIRT
brimming FULL
brine PICKLE, TEARS, BRACK, SEA, OCEAN, MAIN, SALT
shrimp ARTEMIA
bring COMMAND, FETCH, CONVEY, CARRY, TAKE, CAUSE, RISE, BEAR, GET, CON-DUCT, LEAD
forth EAN, HATCH, BEGET, BEAR
near to APPOSE
together COMPILE
up REAR, RAISE
brink EDGE, BORDER, MARGE, MARGIN, DITCH, FOSS(E), EVE, RIM, VERGE, BRIM, SHORE, SEA, END
briny SALINE, SALTY
brioche CUSHION, ROLL, PUDDING, STITCH
brisk QUICK, COOL, ALLEGRO, ALERT, SHARP, SPRY, PERKY, (A)LIVE, YARE, ACTIVE, FAST, PROMPT, KEDGE, RAPID, FLEET, SWIFT, SPRIGHTLY, NIMBLE, CHEERY
bristle SETA, STUBBLE,

BRUSH, CHAETA, RUFFLE, PALPUS, HAIR, BRIDLE, STRUT, SWAGGER, PREEN, PLUME, SPINE, PRIDE
like appendage AWN, SETA
like tip ARISTA
surgical SETA, SETON
bristled ECHINATE, HORRENT
bristly HISPID, SETOSE, ROUGH, SCRUBBY
Britain, British
ALBION *See* "England"
administrator EL-LIOT, MINTO
author See under "England"
biologist HUXLEY
cavalry YEOMANRY
channel or strait SOLENT
chief, ancient PEN-DRAGON
colony, present or former ADEN, MALTA, KENYA
composer ARNE, ELGAR
conservative TORY
financier BEIT
gun ENFIELD, STEN, BREN
king (including legend-ary) ARTEGALL, BRAN, BELI, BELINUS, LUD, BRUT, INE, ARTHUR, BRUCE, STEPHEN, OFFA, CANUTE, KNUT, HAL, HAROLD, HENRY, EGBERT(US), EDGAR, JAMES, CHARLES, GEORGE, EDRED, CNUT
legislator COM-MONER, LORD
machine gun STEN, BREN
measure AUM
naturalist SLOANE, DARWIN
orator PITT
order GARTER
parish official BEADLE
Parliamentary record HANSARD
pertaining to CYMRIC, BRYTHONIC

Prime Minister
EDEN, ATTLEE
pudding SUET
Royal Guard officer
EXON
saint ALBAN
seaport COWES
soldier ATKINS,
TOMMY
tea ELM
title DAME, EARL,
LADY, LORD, BARON
Briton, *ancient* PICT,
ICENI, ANGLE, JUTE,
SCOT, SILURE, CELT
brittle FRAGILE, FRAIL,
CRISP, SHORT, FRI-
ABLE, WEAK, FICKLE,
DELICATE, CRUMBLING
broach AWL, REAMER,
PIERCE, TAP, RIMER,
AIR, BEGIN, PUBLISH,
SHED, OPEN, LAUNCH,
VOICE, INTRODUCE,
UTTER, VENT, VEER
broad WIDE, LIBERAL,
TOLERANT, DEEP,
VAST, LARGE, AMPLE,
GENERAL
combining form LATI
broadbill RAYA,
GAPER, SCAUP,
SHOVELER, BIRD
broadcast SCATTER,
SPREAD, PUBLISH,
SEND, TRANSMIT,
SOW, SEED, TELEVISE
broaden ENNOBLE,
EXPAND, DILATE,
SPREAD, WIDEN
broadminded TOLER-
ANT, CATHOLIC,
LIBERAL, LENIENT
broadsword SCIMITAR,
KRIS, FERRARA, CUT-
LASS, SCIMITER,
CLAYMORE, BILL
brobdingnagian GIANT,
COLOSSAL, GIGANTIC
See "huge"
brocade BAUDEKIN,
KINCOB, BROCHE,
BALDACHIN, CLOTH
brocard GIBE, MAXIM,
RULE, SPEECH,
SARCASM, ELLIPSE
brocket PITA, DEER,
SPITTER, STAG,
BROCK
brogan SHOE, BOOT,
STOGY

broil GRILL(ADE),
BRAISE, FRAY, COOK,
MELEE, HEAT, ROAST,
FRACAS, SCORCH,
BAKE, ROW, BRAWL,
SCRAP
broken in back
CHINED
broker AGENT, FACTOR,
CHANGER, JOBBER,
MERCHANT, DEALER
brokerage business
AGIOTAGE
broncho buck ESTRA-
PADE
Bronte EMILY, CHAR-
LOTTE, ANNE
heroine EYRE, JANE
pseudonym BELL
bronze AES, BROWN,
ALLOY, TAN, STATUE
colored AENEOUS
film PATINA
gilded ORMOLU
Roman AES
variety LATTEN
brooch PIN, CLASP,
FIBULA, PECTORAL,
CAMEO, OUCH
brood PROGENY, FRY,
HATCH, COVEY, FLOCK,
BREED, LITTER, NEST,
FAMILY, ISSUE, OFF-
SPRING, NID(E),
COGITATE, WEEP, SIT,
MOPE, PONDER,
MULTITUDE
brook BECK, RILL,
RILLET, BEAR, ABIDE,
SUFFER, STAND, EN-
DURE, STREAM, RUN-
(NEL), CREEK
brooklet RILLET,
RUNLET
broom WHISK, BESOM,
MOP, SWAB, BRUSH,
HIRSE, BREAM
plant SPART, HIRSE,
HEATHER, CYTISUS,
GENISTA
broth SOUP, POTTAGE,
CONSOMME
brother SIB, SIBLING,
FRIAR, CADET, OBLATE,
MONK, BILLY, FRA,
FRATER, FELLOW,
PEER, PAL, BUDDY,
KIN
brought up by hand
CADE

brow CREST, RIDGE,
FOREHEAD, BRINK,
EDGE, TOP
brown DUN, TAN,
SEPIA, SENNA, SEAR,
RUSSET, SORREL,
BRONZE, TAWNY,
TOAST, COOK
and white ROAN
dark BURNET
dark reddish CUBA,
BAY, SEPIA, KHAKI,
HENNA
light TAN, TENNE,
BEIGE, FAWN, ECRU
thrasher THRUSH,
BIRD
browned RISSOLE
Brownian movement
PEDESIS
brownie NIX, NISSE,
KOBOLD, ELF, NIS,
SHEE, GOBLIN, PIXIE,
SPRITE, FAY, NIXIE
brownish tincture,
heraldry TENNE
browse GRAZE, BRUT,
CROP, NIBBLE, FEED,
PASTURE
Broz TITO
bruise ECCHYMOSIS,
BATTER, DENT, MAIM,
BRAY, INJURY, MAUL,
CONTUSE, ICTUS,
HURT, INJURE,
SHINER
bruised HUMBLE,
LIVID, HURT
bruit RUMOR, NOISE,
SOUND, TELL, REPORT,
HEARSAY, BLAZON,
RALE
brumal SLEETY,
HIEMAL, WINTRY
brume FOG, VAPOR,
MIST, HAZE, SMOG
brunette DARK, BROWN,
SWARTHY
brunt JAR, JOLT,
SHOCK, CLASH, IM-
PACT, IMPULSE,
FORCE
brush BROOM,
THICKET, SHRUB,
COPSE, FIGHT, FRAY,
ACTION, STROKE,
SKIRMISH, CLEAN
small FITCH
wire CARD
brushwood COPSE,
SCROG, BOSCAGE,

SCRUBS, THICKET, COPPICE

brushy HIRSUTE, HAIRY, SHAGGY

brusque RUDE, BLUFF, ABRUPT, BLUNT, GRUFF, CURT, SHORT, IMPOLITE, VIOLENT, DISCOURTEOUS, HASTY

brutal INSENSATE, CADDISH, CARNAL, CRUEL, COARSE, SAVAGE, FERAL, RUTHLESS, BESTIAL, RUDE

brute BEAST, RUFFIAN, SCOUNDREL, ANIMAL

Bryophyta MOSSES

Brythonic CORNISH, WELSH, CELTIC

bubal ANTELOPE

bubble GLOB, GLOBULE, SEETHE, SEED, BOIL, BLEB, BEAD, NIL, AIR, CHEAT, TRIFLE, FOAM

buccal ORAL

buccaneer CORSAIR, VIKING, PIRATE, MAROONER, RIFLER, SPOILER, FREEBOOTER, PICAROON

bucephalus HORSE, STEED, CHARGER

buck STAG, PRICKET, DUDE, SWELL, DANDY, NOB, TOFF, MALE, FOP, RESIST
African IMPALA, PALLAH
fourth year SORE
India SASIN

bucket PAIL, BOWK, SKEEL, SCOOP, TUB

Buckeye State OHIO

buckle CLASP, DISTORT, TACH(E), TIE, FASTEN, BEND, WARP, TWIST, BOW

buckler SHIELD, AEGIS, ROUNDEL

buckthorn CASCARA, RHAMN

buckwheat tree TITI

bucolic AGRESTIC, PASTORAL, RUSTIC, NAIVE, SIMPLE, RURAL, IDYL, ECLOGUE

bud SHOOT, GEMMA, BULB, CION, GERM, KNOP, BURGEON, SPROUT, GERMINATE,

BLOSSOM, GRAFT, BEGIN(NING), SPRIT
blighted BLAST

Buddha GAUTAMA, FO, SHAKYAMUNI
dialogues SUTRA
enemy of MARA
mother MAYA
tree of PIPAL

Buddhist, Buddhism
angel DEVA
cause of finite existence NIDANA
center of LASSA
Chinese FO
church TERA
column LAT
delusion MOHA
evil spirit MARA
fate KARMA
festival BON
final liberation NIRVANA
form RUPA
founder GAUTAMA
gateway TORAN(A)
god DEVA
hell NARAKA
language PALI
monastery TERA, VIHARA
monk TALAPOIN, BO, YAHAN, BONZE
monument STUPA
mother of world MAYA
nexus KARMA
novice GOYIN
ornament TEE
prayer MANI
priest LAMA, MAHATMA
relic mound STUPA
sacred city LASSA, LHASA
    language PALI
saint LOHAN, ARAHAT, ARHAT
scripture SUTRA
sect in Japan ZEN
shrine STUPA, DAGOBA, TOPE
temple VIHARA
title of respect MAHATMA
tree PIPAL
will to live TANHA

buddy CHUM, PAL, CRONY, COMRADE

budget BUNCH, BATCH, PACKET, BAG, WALLET, PLAN, PROGRAM,

PACK, PARCEL, BUNDLE, ROLL

buds, *send forth* BURGEON, DEHISCE
pickled CAPERS

buff ORANGE, TAN, YELLOW, FAN, POLISH, SHINE

buffalo CARIBOU, TIMARAU, ZAMOUSE, BISON
Celebes ANOA
European BISON
hybrid CATALO
India ARNA, ARNEE
meat BILTONG
Philippine CARABAO

buffet SLAP, STOOL, BAR, TOSS, CUFF, BASTE, BEAT, THRASH, BOX, SIDEBOARD, CREDENZA, COUNTER

buffoon CLOWN, MIMER, MIME, ACTOR, HUMORIST, ZANY, FOOL, JESTER, COMIC, STOOGE, . JAPE, DROLL, WAG, WIT, JOKER

bug INSECT, MITE, NIT, HEMIPTER, CHINCH, BEETLE, DOR, ELATER, ROACH
genus EMESA, CIMEX
June DOR

bugaboo JUMBO, MUMBO, BUGBEAR, BOGY, OGRE, SPECTER, GOBLIN, ALARM, FEAR

bugbear BOGY, BOGEY, OGRE, SPECTER, GOBLIN

buggy INFESTED, CARRIAGE, SHAY

bugle BEAD, HORN, OX, BLACK, CLARION
blare of TANTARA
call TATTOO, REVEILLE, RETREAT, TAPS
strain on MOT, BLARE
weed INDIGO, MINT

build REAR, FASHION, CONSTRUCT, FORM, MAKE, ERECT, RAISE, STATURE, FABRICATE, FRAME, FOUND, ASSEMBLE
a nest NIDIFY

builder CARPENTER, ERECTOR, MAKER, CONSTRUCTOR

of Cretan Labyrinth
DAEDALUS
building EDIFICE, PILE,
HOUSE, STRUCTURE,
FABRIC
bulb GLOBE, LAMP,
TUBER, CORM, BUD,
KNOB
edible ONION, SEGO,
POTATO, YAM
glass AMP(O)ULE
Bulbul KALA, BIRD
bulbule BULBLET,
BULBIL, BULB
Bulgar SLAV, TATAR
Bulgaria, Bulgarian
SLAV, BULGAR, TATAR
capital SOFIA
city or town RUSE,
VARNA, BYELA, VIDIN
coin LEV, LEW
measure OKA, OKE
ruler BORIS, TSAR
town See "city"
above
bulge PROJECTION,
BAG, BLOAT, SWELL,
KNOB, HUMP, JUT,
GIBBOSITY
bulging GIBBOUS,
CONVEX, FULL
bulk BODY, MAJORITY,
MASS, SIZE, VOLUME,
FORM, FIGURE, GROSS,
SHAPE, DIMENSION
bull TAURUS, ZEBU,
TORO, BULLOCK,
BLUNDER, SOLECISM,
BONER, SLIP, ERROR,
COP, BOBBY, PEELER
fighter MATADOR,
TOREADOR, PICADOR
half and half man
MINOTAUR
India ZEBU
like TAURINE
papal EDICT, LETTER
sacred APIS
young STOT
bulla SEAL, BOSS,
KNOB, STUD, BLISTER,
VESICLE
bulldoze BULLY,
BROWBEAT, COW,
SCOOP, DIG, RAM,
FORCE
bullet TRACER, SHOT,
SLUG, MISSILE, BALL
expanding DUMDUM
size CALIBER
bulletin REPORT,
MEMO, NOTICE, STATE-

MENT, ANNOUNCE-
MENT, PUBLICATION,
POSTER
bulletproof shelter
ABRI, MANT(E)LET
bullfinch ALP, OLF,
OLP, NOPE, HEDGE,
OLPH
bullion BAR, INGOT,
BILLOT, MASS
bullock STEER, STOT,
BOVINE
bully TYRANT, HECTOR,
FRIGHTEN, COW,
SCARE, FINE, GOOD,
BROWBEAT, RUFFIAN,
SHANNY
tree BALATA
bulrush TULE,
SCIRPUS, SEDGE,
CATTAIL, PAPYRUS
bulwark SCONCE, BAIL,
RAMPART, CITADEL,
BASTION, FORT,
PARAPET, BREAK-
WATER, WALL
bum TRAMP, HOBO,
IDLER
bumble BEE, BITTERN,
BULRUSH, BUNGLE,
BLUNDER, BRAMBLE,
BEADLE
bump COLLIDE, KNOCK,
STRIKE, HIT, BULGE,
SWELLING, LUMP,
PROJECTION
bumper GLASS, TOAST,
WHOPPER, CARANGID,
BOWL, GOBLET, GOOD,
FINE, BUFFER
bumpkin SWAB, BOOR,
LOUT, YOKEL, OAF,
CLOD, RUBE, GAWK,
CLOWN, CHURL, BEAM,
BOOM
bun WIG, ROLL, CAKE,
TAIL, STEM, STALK,
JAG
bunch TUFT, FAGOT,
LOT, SET, BUDGET,
WISP, PACK, CLUSTER,
CROWD, GROUP,
BUNDLE, BALE,
PARCEL, COLLECTION
bund DAM, DIKE, QUAY,
LEAGUE
bundle BINDLE, BOLT,
HANK, SHEAF, BALE,
PACK(ET), PARCEL,
BUNCH, ROLL, HURRY
bung CORK, PLUG,
MAUL, STOPPER

bungle ERR, BOTCH,
GOOF, SPOIL
bunk HOKUM, BED,
BERTH, SLEEP, ABIDE,
DWELL, LODGE, COT
bunker BIN, SANDHOLE,
CRIB, HAZARD
bunko CHEAT, SWINDLE
bunting ETAMINE,
PAPE, FLAGS, COT-
TON, FINCH, BIRD
bunyip SHAM, IM-
POSTER, HUMBUG
buoy DAN, DEADHEAD,
FLOAT, RAISE, SUP-
PORT, ELATE,
LEVITATE
buoyant ELASTIC,
CHEERFUL, LIGHT,
SPRINGY, HAPPY, GAY,
BLITHE, SPIRITED,
HOPEFUL
burbot EELPOUT, LING,
COD, LOTA, FISH
genus LOTA
burd LADY, MAIDEN,
WOMAN
burden WEIGHT, LOAD,
CHARGE, BIRN, CUM-
BER, ONUS, TAX,
CARGO, FREIGHT,
LADING, CLOG,
FARDEL, OPPRESS,
CARE, REFRAIN,
TROUBLE
bearer ATLAS, AMOS,
AMASA
burdock LAPPA, CLITE,
HURR-BUR, PLANT
bureau DESK, DRESSER,
OFFICE, CHEST, DE-
PARTMENT, AGENCY
burfish ATINGA
burgeon BUD, SHOOT,
GROW, SPROUT
burglar *See* "bandit"
burgonet MORION,
HELMET
burgoo STEW, PUD-
DING, GRUEL
Burgundy wine
PINOTS, VOLNAY *See*
"wine"
burial INTERMENT
case CASKET, COFFIN,
BOX
litter BIER
mound LOW, TUMU-
LUS, GRAVE, BAR-
ROW
one who wraps for
CERER

pile PYRE
place GRAVE, TOMB,
CEMETERY
buried IMBEDDED,
HIDDEN, SUNKEN
burin GRAVER, TOOL
burke MURDER, SLAY,
KILL, SMOTHER,
SHELVE
burl LUMP, KNOT,
PIMPLE, PUSTULE
burlesque FARCE,
COMEDY, PARODY,
MIME, TRAVESTY,
CARICATURE, IMITA-
TION, RIDICULE,
OVERDO, APE, MOCK,
COPY
burletta FARCE,
OPERA, DRAMA
burly FAT, OBESE,
STOUT, HUSKY,
FLESHY, LUSTY,
BULKY
Burma, Burmese
Buddhist MON
chief BO, BOH
city or town RAN-
GOON, AVA, AKYAB,
PEGU, MANDALAY,
PROME
coin BAT, KYAT,
MU, PE
dagger DOW, DAH
division ARAKAN,
PEGU
gate TORAN
gibbon LAR
girl MIMA
governor WUN, WOON
knife DAH, DHAO,
DOW
language WA, PEGU,
KACHIN, CHIN, LAI,
KUKI
measure BYEE, TENG,
DHA, DAIN, LAN,
PALGAT, TAIM, THA
monk BO
musical instrument
TURR
native WA, LAI,
PEGUAN, KACHIN,
MON, SHAN
peasant TAO
people CHIN, KACHIN,
WA
river IRRAWADDY,
SUTANG, SALWIN,
SALWEEN
robber DACOIT
shelter ZAYAT

spirit or demon NAT
state SHAN, WA
town See "city"
above
tree ACLE
tribe TSIN, KUKI,
CHIN, SHAN, WA,
KACHIN
tribesman LAI
weight RUAY, MOO,
TICAL, VIS(S), TICUL,
TEN, CANDY, KAIT,
MAT
burn CENSE, CHAR,
SCALD, SEAR, SERE,
RAZE, CREMATE,
SCORCH, FLAME,
OXIDIZE, FIRE, INCIN-
ERATE, BLAZE, SINGE,
GLOW, SMOLDER,
BROOK, RILL,
CONSUME
mark caused by
BRAND
midnight oil LUCU-
BRATE
surface SINGE,
SCORCH
burned USTULATE,
CHARRED
sugar CARAMEL
burning CALID, EAGER,
(A)FIRE, CAUTERY,
IRATE, MAD, ARDENT,
FERVENT, HOT, ANGRY
bush WAHOO
crime of ARSON
burnisher AGATE,
POLISHER, TOOL,
BUFFER
burnsides BEARD,
WHISKERS
burr CIRCLE, PAD,
WHETSTONE, HALO,
KNOT, RIDGE, NAP,
BRIAR, RING, CORONA,
WASHER, WHIRR,
BANYAN
burrow TUBE, HOLE,
MINE, ROOT, TUNNEL,
FURROW, EXCAVATE,
DIG
burrowing animal
MOLE, ARMADILLO,
SURICATE, GOPHER
bursar TREASURER,
CASHIER
burst REAVE, REND,
ERUPT, RUPTURE,
BREAK, SHATTER,
EXPLODE, SPLIT,
SPROUT

bursting DEHISCENCE
bury COVER, INTER,
INHUME, INURN,
CONCEAL, CACHE,
CLOAK, VEIL, HIDE,
SECRETE, ENTOMB,
INEARTH, SHROUD
bush BOSCAGE, CLUMP,
TOD, SHRUB, THICKET
burning WAHOO
of hair SHAG
bushel(s) GOBS, LOTS
¼ of PECK
40 WEY
bushing LINING, PAD-
DING, DRILL
Bushman SAN, SAAN,
ABATUA, WOODSMAN,
QUNG
bushwacker GUERILLA,
SCYTHE
bushy DUMOSE,
DUMOUS
hair SHAG
heap TOD
business TRADE,
GAME, CRAFT, GEAR,
WORK, JOB, TASK,
STINT, CHORE, ER-
RAND, AFFAIR, COM-
MERCE, OFFICE, MAT-
TER, CONCERN,
THING, INDUSTRY,
LINE, EMPLOYMENT,
VOCATION
memorandum NOTE,
AGENDUM
pertaining to
PRAGMATIC
trust FIRM, CARTEL,
TRADE
buskin SHOE, TRAGEDY,
BRODEQUIN
buss DECK, DRESS,
SMACK, KISS,
VESSEL
bustard genus OTIDAE,
OTIS *See under*
"Africa"
bustle POTHER,
TUMULT, STIR, ADO,
FRISK, TO-DO, FUSS,
RUSTLE, FLURRY,
MOTION, TOURNURE,
ENERGY, HASTE,
ACTIVITY, AGITATION
busy ENGAGED, INTENT,
HUMMING, DILIGENT,
EMPLOYED, SEDULOUS,
LIVELY
busybody QUIDNUNC,
MEDDLER

but YET, ONLY, STILL, HOWEVER, EXCEPT, SAVE, WITHOUT, MERE, HOWBEIT, NEVERTHELESS, UNLESS

butcher SLAUGHTER, KILL, BUNGLE, SPOIL, MURDER

bird SHRIKE

hook GAMBREL

butler SPENCER, SERVANT, STEWARD

butt GOAD, RAM, TUP, CASK, TARGET, PUSH, BREECH, THRUST, BUNT, HALIBUT, STUB, STUMP

one-third of TERCE, TIERCE

butter, *artificial* OLEO

coloring ANNATTO

like OLEO, CACAO, BUTYROUS

pertaining to BUTYRIC, CAPRICA

semi-fluid GHEE

substitute OLEO, SUIN(E)

tree SHEA, FULWA, PHULWARA

tub FIRKIN

butterfish GUNNEL, BLENNY

butterfly IO, VANESSA, SATYR, IDALIA, KIHO, MORPHO, URSULA

fish BLENNY

lily MARIPOSA

peacock IO

butterine OLEO

buttery PANTRY, SPENCE, LARDER

button BADGE, BOSS, BUD, KNOB, STUD, BUCKLE, HOOK, PEARL, FASTEN, CHIN

ornamental STUD

part of SHANK

buttress STAY, SUPPORT, PROP, PIER, COUNTERFORT

against a mole PILA

buy SHOP, MARKET, GET, ACQUIRE, PAY, PURCHASE, BRIBE, REDEEM

buyer VENDEE, EMPTOR, AGENT, PURCHASER, CUSTOMER

buzz HUM, RING, WHIR, WHIZ, CALL, RUMOR, HISS

buzzard AURA, BEETLE, GLEDE, CURLEW, HAWK, FOOL

American BUTEO

bald OSPREY

honey PERN

moor HARPY

buzzer BEE, BELL, SIGNAL, ALARM

by ASIDE, WITH, AGO, AT, PAST, PER, NEAR, CAUSE, BESIDE, ALONG(SIDE), ANON, ABUT, CLOSE

word of mouth ORAL, PAROL

bygone FORMER, OLDEN, ELAPSED, PAST, YORE

Byron hero LARA

bystander WITNESS

byway ROAD, STREET, LANE, ALLEY, DETOUR

byword PROVERB, PHRASE, SAYING, MOTTO, CATCHWORD, MAXIM

Byzantine *coin* BEZANT

empress IRENE

mosaic ICON

C

C CEE, HUNDRED

caama FOX, ASSE, HARTEBEEST

cab TAXI, HACK, HANSOM

cabal PARTY, PLOT, JUNTO, BLOC, RING, CLIQUE, INTRIGUE, FACTION

cabbage CHOU, WORT, COLE, SLAW, BORECOLE, KALE

kind COLZA, KOHLRABI, KALE, SAVOY, KRAUT

like RAPE

salad SLAW

tree ANGELIN (YABA)

worm LOOPER

caber BEAM, POLE, SPAR, RAFTER

cabin COACH, HUT, SHED, SHACK, BERTH, SALOON, COTTAGE, HOVEL

locomotive CAB

cabinet ROOM, COUNCIL, BOARD, CASE, ALMIRAH, BUHL, BUREAU, CHEST, MINISTRY

open shelved ETAGERE, WHATNOT

cable WIRE, ROPE, TELEGRAM, LINK

cabling RUDENTURE, MOLDINGS

cabochon STONE, GEM, ORNAMENT

caboose CAB, CAR

ship's GALLEY

cacao

extract FAT, BUTTER

seed powder BROMA

cachalot WHALE

cache CONCEAL, HIDE, SECRETE, BURY, SCREEN, TREASURE, STORE, STOREHOUSE

cachet WAFER, SEAL, STAMP

cachexic ILL, MORBID, SICK, DEATHLY

cacholong OPAL

cackle LAUGH, CHATTER, CANK, CHAT, GOSSIP, TALK, KECKLE, SNICKER, TITTER, TWADDLE

fruit EGG

cactus *See under* "plant"

fruit COCHAL

plantation NOPALRY

cad BOUNDER, HEEL, SCOUNDREL

cadaver CORPSE, SKELETON, BODY, STIFF, CARCASS

caddis fly worm CADEW

cade JUNIPER, BARREL, CASK, KEG, PET, LAMB

cadence MODULATION, TONE, LILT, SWING, METER, RHYTHM, THROB, PACE, SOUND

cadent FALLING, DESCENDING, RHYTHMICAL

cadet SON, YOUTH, JUNIOR, PLEB(E), STUDENT, MIDSHIPMAN

cadge BEG, MOOCH,
SPONGE
cadmium CD
Cadmus' *daughter*
INO, SEMELE
father AGENOR
sister EUROPA
wife HARMONIA
caduceus WAND,
SCEPTER, STAFF,
SYMBOL, INSIGNE
Caesar, *assassin*
BRUTUS, CASSIUS
colleague BIBULUS
conspirator against
CASCA
death place of NOLA
mother AURELIA
robe TOGA
sister ATIA
site of famous message
ZELA
weed fiber ARAMINA
caesura BREAK, PAUSE,
REST, INTERVAL
caffein(e) THEIN(E),
ALKALOID
cage PRISON, PEN,
BARS, BASKET, BOX,
ENCLOSURE, CONFINE,
RESTRAIN
for hauling MEW
cahoots LEAGUE,
PARTNERS, COLLUSION
Cain's *brother* ABEL,
SETH
parent ADAM, EVE
son ENOCH
cairngorm QUARTZ
caisson BOX, CHEST,
WAGON, CASE
disease BENDS
caitiff BASE, DESPI-
CABLE, VILE, WICKED,
MEAN
cajole FLATTER,
BLANDISH, BEGUILE,
PALP, CHEAT, COAX,
WHEEDLE, DECOY,
ENTICE, TEASE
cake BANNOCK, BATTY,
CONCRETE, WIG(G),
HARDEN, SCONE,
BAKE, FLOE, TORTE,
BUN, MASS, TART,
CRUST
corn PONE
round TORTE
seed WIG(G)
tea SCONE
walk MARCH, STRUT
calaba TREE, BIRMA

calabar bean ESERE
alkaloid ESERIN(E)
calaboose JAIL,
PRISON, STIR,
BASTILLE, BRIG,
JUG, GAOL
calamitous EVIL, DIRE,
WOEFUL, SAD, AVERSE,
UNLUCKY, HAPLESS
calamity WOE, BLOW,
DISTRESS, TROUBLE,
MISERY, DISASTER,
WRACK, REVERSE,
TRIAL, WRECK, RUIN,
HARDSHIP, ADVERSITY
calcar SPUR, OVEN
calcareous *deposit*
TARTAR, STALAGMITE,
SPAR, STALACTITE
skeleton CORAL
calced SHOD
calcium *carbonate*
TUFA
oxide LIME
phosphate APATITE
sulphate GYPSUM,
HEPAR
calculate COMPUTE,
ESTIMATE, COUNT,
AVERAGE, RECKON,
WEIGH, STUDY,
PONDER, FRAME,
RATE, DETERMINE
calculator ABACUS,
TABLE
calculous GRITTY,
STONY, SANDY
Calcutta *hemp* JUTE
measure KUNK, RAIK,
DHAN, JAOB
weight RAIK, PANK,
PALLY
calderite GARNET
caldron, cauldron
BOILER, KETTLE,
VAT, POT, VESSEL,
RED
Caleb's *son* HUR
calefaction HEAT,
CAUMA
calefy WARM, HEAT
calendar DIARY,
JOURNAL, DOCKET,
TABLE, REGISTER,
EPHEMERIS, ALMANAC
church ORDO
former JULIAN,
MAYAN
calenture FEVER,
SUNSTROKE
calf, *cry of* BLAT,
BLEAT, BAA

motherless MAVERICK,
DOGIE
of leg, pertaining to
SURAL
skin of KIP
caliban BEAST, SLAVE
deity of SETEBOS
witch mother
SYCORAX
caliber BORE,
DIAMETER, DEGREE,
ABILITY, CAPACITY,
TALENT, GAUGE,
BREADTH
calibrate MEASURE,
STANDARDIZE
calico, *India* SALLO(O)
printing LAPIS, TEER
calif *See* "caliph"
California ELDORADO
bay MONTEREY
city or town NAPA,
CHINO, FRESNO,
AZUSA
college or university
MILLS, UCLA, USC
county INYO, KERN,
LAKE, MONO, NAPA,
YOLO, YUBA
fish SPRAT, SUR,
RENA, REINA, CHI
fort ORD
lake SODA, BUENA,
OWENS, MONO,
TAHOE, CLEAR,
EAGLE, HONEY,
GOOSE
motto EUREKA
mountain PALOMAR
pass SONORA,
DONNER
rockfish REINA,
RENA
sea SALTON
shrub SALAL
wine area NAPA
caliginous DIM,
OBSCURE, MISTY,
FOGGY, DARK
caliologist's *study*
NESTS
caliph ALI, IMAM,
OMAR, OTHMAN
fourth ALI
calk OCCLUDE, CLOSE,
COPY, SILENCE, STOP,
NAP, TOOL
call YELL, SUMMON,
BID, CRY, PHONE,
DUB, VISIT, NAME,
CLEPE, TERM, CITE,

INVITE, MUSTER,
DIAL
forth EVOKE, SUM-
MON, ELICIT, IN-
VOKE, SIGNAL
out EVOKE, MUSTER
together CONVOKE,
MUSTER
callan(t) BOY, LAD,
FELLOW, CUSTOMER
calligrapher PENMAN,
COPYIST, ENGROSSER
calling JOB, (A)VOCA-
TION, METIER, PUR-
SUIT, TRADE, WORK,
BUSINESS, OCCUPATION
callous HARD, TOUGH,
INSENSIBLE, UNFEEL-
ING, OBTUSE, HORNY,
TORPID, INDIFFERENT
callow IMMATURE,
GREEN, UNFLEDGED
calm PLACID, STILL,
SEDATE, COOL,
SERENE, BALMY,
MILD, STOIC, LULL,
ABATE, QUIET,
PLACATE, TRANQUIL,
SMOOTH, HALCYON,
ALLAY, COMPOSED,
PEACEFUL
calmness ATARAXIA
calorie, calory THERM
calumet PIPE
calumniate BELIE,
LIBEL, SLANDER,
MALIGN, VILIFY,
REVILE, ASPERSE, AT-
TACK, DEFAME, ABUSE,
ACCUSE, SCOLD
calumniator THERSITES
calumny SLANDER,
SLUR, LAMPOON,
SCANDAL, ASPERSION,
DEFAMATION, LIBEL
calyx CUP, LEAVES
division of SEPAL
of flower PERIANTH
cam TRIPPET, LOBE,
COG, WIPER, CATCH
projection LOBE
camail HOOD, GUARD,
TIPPET, MAIL
camalig HUT, CABIN,
STOREHOUSE
camarilla CABAL,
CLIQUE, CELL, JUNTO,
RING, CHAMBER
Camarines Norte city
DAET, PARACALE
camas(s) LOBELIA

Cambodia CAMBOJA,
CAMBODGE
ancient capital
ANGKOR
native KHMER
river MEKONG, SEN
seaport KAMPOT
Cambria WALES *See*
"Wales"
zone of OLENUS
Cambridge *boat races*
LENT
honor exam. TRIPOS
student SIZAR,
OPTIME
camel DROMEDARY,
MEHARI, OONT,
DELOUL, TYLOPOD
female NAGA
hair cloth CAMLET,
ABA
keeper OBIL
thorn ALHAGI
two-humped
BACTRIAN
camelidae LLAMAS
camellia JAPONICA
cameo ANAGLYPH,
RELIEVO, RILIEVO,
CARVING, SCULPTURE,
GEM
material ONYX,
SARDONYX
camera CHAMBER,
DEPARTMENT
dark OBSCURA
light LUCIDA
part of LENS,
FINDER, SHUTTER
platform DOLLY
revolving PANORAM
shot STILL, FLASH,
SNAP
Cameroon *people*
SARA
tribe ABO
camlet PONCHO,
CLOAK, FABRIC
Camorra MAFIA
camouflage FAKE, CON-
CEAL, DISGUISE,
HIDE, SCREEN
camp SHELTER,
BIVOUAC, ETAPE,
TABOR, POST
pertaining to CASTRAL
campaign PLAN,
OPERATION, CRUSADE,
DRIVE
camphor BORNEOL,
ALANT, MENTHOL,
REMEDY

campion genus SILENE,
PLANT
campus QUAD, FIELD,
GROUNDS
camus work REBEL
can CONSERVE, PRE-
SERVE, TIN, CON-
TAINER, VESSEL,
JAIL, JUG, MAY,
COULD
Canaan city or town
HAZOR, AI
Canaanite *See*
"Hebrew"
Canada, Canadian
airport GANDER
bay HECLA (GRIPER)
canal SOO, WELLAND
cape CANSO
free grant dist.
MUSKOKA
Goose genus
BRANTA
Indian See under
"Indian"
island HARE
lake SEUL, TESLIN,
GRAS, CREE
land measure
ARPENT
lynx PISHU
park JASPER, YOHO
pea VETCH
peak, highest LOGAN
penalty, law DEDIT
peninsula GASPE
physician OSLER
policeman MOUNTIE
province ONTARIO,
ALBERTA, QUEBEC,
MANITOBA, YUKON
river NELSON, OT-
TAWA, YUKON, PEEL,
LEAF
squaw MAHALA
turpentine BALSAM
canaille RABBLE,
MOB, RIFFRAFF
canal DUCT, RACEWAY,
MEATUS, OPENING,
CONDUIT, CHANNEL,
STRAIT, WATER(WAY),
SOO, SUEZ, PANAMA,
WELLAND, KIEL, ERIE,
LYNN, ZANJE
bank BERM(E)
side opposite towpath
BERM(E)
slack water LODE
Canal Zone city
ANCON, COLON

Canary *island* PALMA
seed ALPIST
canasta play MELD
cancel EFFACE,
 DELETE, ANNUL,
 ERASE, DELE, BLOT,
 VOID, POSTMARK,
 QUASH, RESCIND,
 REVOKE, ABOLISH,
 REMOVE, REPEAL,
 ABROGATE, OBLITER-
 ATE, REPUDIATE
candent GLOWING,
 HOT
Candia CRETE
candid IMPARTIAL,
 BLUNT, FRANK, OPEN,
 HONEST, PLAIN,
 FAIR, JUST, SINCERE,
 ARTLESS, NAIVE,
 INGENUOUS, HONORA-
 BLE
candidate list SLATE,
 ROSTER
Candiot(e) CRETAN
candle DIP, WAX,
 TAPER, CIERGE,
 LIGHT
 holder SCONCE,
 LAMPAD
 melt and run down
 SWEAL
 wax TAPER, BOUGIE
candlenut tree AMA,
 BANKUL, KUKUI
candlestick SCONCE,
 LAMPAD
 branched GIRANDOLE,
 CANDELABRUM,
 CHANDELIER
 ornamental PRICKET,
 LUSTRE
 three-branched
 TRICERION
candy PRALINE,
 LOLLY, SWEET,
 FONDANT, NOUGAT,
 TAFFY, CONFECTION,
 CARAMEL, COMFIT
candytufts IBERIS,
 FLOWER
cane MALACCA, STEM,
 RATTAN, STICK,
 BAMBOO, ROD,
 STAFF, PUNISH,
 SCOURGE
 sugar SUCROSE
  disease of SEREH
cangue PILLORY
canine DOG, CUR, PUP,
 PUG, CANIS, FICE

See "dog"
 tooth LANIARY
canna ACHIRA, PLANT,
 FLOWER
cannele REP, FABRIC
cannibal ANTHROPOPH-
 AGITE, SAVAGE
cannibalism EXOPHAGY
cannikin CUP, CAN,
 BUCKET
cannon MORTAR,
 HOWITZER, CRACK,
 ARTILLERY, ORDNANCE
 ball MISSILE, PELLET,
 SHOT
 early ROBINET
 knob at breech
 CASCABEL
 old-time ASPIC,
 SAKER
 part of CHASE, RIM-
 BASE, BORE, BREECH
 projecting boss TRUN-
 NION
 reinforcing hoop
 FRETTE
 small MINION, ROB-
 INET
 stick for firing LIN-
 STOCK
cannular TUBULAR,
 HOLLOW
canoe DUGOUT, BOAT,
 SKIFF *See* "boat"
 Africa ALMADIA
 Arctic KAYAK,
 OOMIAK, UMIAK,
 KAIAK
 Cent. Amer. PITPAN
 dugout PIROGUE,
 PIRAGUA
 large BUNGO
 Malabar TONEE
 Malay PROA
 Philippine BANCA
 seagoing PAHI
 skin-covered BIDAR,
 BAIDARA
canon CRITERION, LAW,
 RULE, PRECEPT,
 STATUTE, HYMN,
 SONG, AXIOM,
 STANDARD, LAUD,
 CLERGYMAN
 enigmatical NODUS
 music NODUS
canonical hours NONE,
 SEXT, VESPERS,
 TIERCE, PRIME, LAUDS,
 COMPLINE
canonicals ROBE, ALB,
 COPE, COWL, STOLE

can opener KEY
canopy TESTER,
 AWNING, COPE,
 VAULT, SKY, CEIL,
 BALDAQUIN, COVERING,
 SHELTER, SHADE
 over altar BALDACHIN,
 BALDAQUIN
 over bed or tomb
 TESTER
canorous MELODIOUS,
 CLEAR, MUSICAL,
 SONOROUS
cant JARGON, ARGOT,
 PATOIS, LINGO,
 SLANG, DIALECT,
 HIELD, TILT, TIP,
 CAREEN, THROW,
 CAST, TOSS, LEAN,
 SLANT, BEVEL, PRE-
 TENSE, HEEL, LIST
canter RUN, PACE,
 RACK, GALLOP,
 WHINER
Canterbury *archbishop*
 LANG, BECKET
 gallop AUBIN
cant hook PEAVY,
 PEAVEY, TOOL
canticle SONG, ODE,
 BRAVURA, HYMN,
 LAUD, ANTHEM,
 CANON
canto FIT, PACE,
 PASSUS, BOOK, AIR,
 MELODY, TENOR
canvas DUCK, TUKE,
 SAIL, TARP, BURLAP,
 SCRIM, TARPAULIN,
 TEWKE, TENT,
 PICTURE, PAINTING
 covering TILT, TARP,
 TARPAULIN
 like fabric WIGAN
 waterproof TARP-
 (AULIN)
canvass SIFT,
 EXAMINE, INQUIRE,
 PEDDLE, DISCUSS,
 DEBATE, SOLICIT,
 CAMPAIGN, IN-
 VESTIGATE
canyon *mouth* ABRA
 wall DALLE
canzonet SONG,
 MADRIGAL, CENTO,
 AIR, BALLAD
caoutchouc *source*
 ULE, CAUCHO
cap BEANIE, BERET,
 TOP, ETON, TAM,
 COVER, CLOCHE,

TURBAN, FEZ, CORK,
LID, HOOD, CORNET,
MATCH, GALERUM,
GALERUS, OUTDO,
EXCEL, SUMMIT
child's BIGGIN,
MUTCH, TOQUE
close COIF, TOQUE
covering HAVELOCK
ecclesiastical
BIRETTA, BARRET,
BERET, GALERUM,
GALERUS
Jewish MITRE
military SHAKO, KEPI,
BUSBY
night BIGGIN
oriental CALPAC(K),
FEZ, TURBAN
Roman PILEUS
Scotch BALMORAL,
TAM
sheepskin CALPAC(K)
skull PILEUS, BEANIE
capable COMPETENT,
ABLE, EFFICIENT,
APT, ACCOMPLISHED,
FIT
capacious AMPLE,
MUCH, BROAD, WIDE,
SPACIOUS, ROOMY
capacity SIZE, TALENT,
SKILL, SPREAD, GIFT,
BENT, TURN, JOB,
DUTY, KNACK, POSI-
TION, WISDOM, PLACE,
OFFICE, POWER,
FACULTY, ABILITY,
VOLUME, EXTENT,
STRENGTH, ENDOW-
MENT, INTELLECT
cape TIPPET, AMICE,
FICHU, TALMA, TANG,
MANTLE, SAGUM,
CLOAK, STOLE, WRAP,
HEADLAND,
PROMONTORY, RAS,
NESS, SKAW, SCAW
angled POINT
clerical COPE,
FANON, ORALE
elk ELAND
Florida SABLE
fur PALATINE, STOLE
Japanese ESAN, MINO
of land NESS, RAS,
PROMONTORY,
HEADLAND
Massachusetts ANN,
COD
Scotland WRATH
Turkish BABA

Cape Colony plateau
KAROO
Cape Verde *island*
SAL, FOGO
capital PRAIA
native SERER, BRAVA
Capek play RUR
capel HORSE, WALL,
ROCK, QUARTZ, SCHORL
caper HOP, SKIP, LEAP,
SPRING, CURLYCUE,
ANTIC, DIDO, PRANCE,
FRISK, GAMBOL, LEAP,
PRANK, TITTUP, JUMP,
ROMP, DANCE, SHRUB,
CONDIMENT
capillary HAIRLIKE,
MINUTE, FINE,
SLENDER, FILIFORM
capital MAJOR, GOOD,
CHIEF, MAIN, BASIC,
PRIMAL, PROMINENT,
CITY, SEAT, PRINCIPAL,
LETTER, STOCK, FATAL,
EXCELLENT, MONEY,
WEALTH
letter MAJUSCULE
capote BONNET,
MANTLE, HOOD,
OVERCOAT
caprate RUTATE, SALT,
ESTER
caprice FANCY, FAD,
QUIRK, TOY, FREAK,
MOOD, NOTION, IDEA,
IMPULSE, TEMPER,
VAGARY, WHIM(SEY)
Capricorn GOAT,
BEETLE
capriole CAPER, HEAD-
DRESS, LEAP, SPRING
capripede SATYR,
GOAT
capsheaf CROWN
capstan LEVER, HOIST,
DRUM, CYLINDER
capsule PILL,
DETONATOR, THECA,
WAFER, POD, SHELL,
PERICARP, SHEATH
captain MASTER,
LEADER, CHIEF,
SKIPPER, HEAD, COM-
MANDER
boat of GIG
of David's army JOAB
caption LEGEND,
TITLE, HEADING,
LEADER, HEADLINE,
SUBTITLE
captious CRITICAL,
CAVILING, TESTY,

CARPING, INSIDIOUS,
CAPRICIOUS, IRASCIBLE
captivate ENCHANT,
CHARM, ENSLAVE,
ENAMOR, TAKE, AL-
LURE, ATTRACT, IN-
FATUATE, PLEASE
capture SNARE,
ARREST, TRAP, NET,
LAND, CATCH, TAKE,
SEIZE, COP, NAB,
BAG, PREY, PRIZE,
LURE, GRASP
capuche COWL, HOOD
caput DOOMED, HEAD,
TOP, SECTION,
CHAPTER, COUNCIL
capybara RODENT,
CAVY, HOG
car BUS, AUTO,
TROLLEY, COACH,
CAB, SEDAN
railroad CABOOSE,
DINER, SLEEPER,
PULLMAN, PARLOR
carabao BUFFALO
caracal FUR, CAT,
LYNX
caracara HAWK
carack *See* "carrack"
caracole SNAIL,
WHEEL, SPIRAL,
PRANCE, TURN
caracul *See under*
"karakul"
caradoc BALA, KNIGHT
carangoid fish SCAD,
SAUREL
carapace LORICA,
SHELL, SHIELD, CASE
carapato TICK
caravan TREK, TRIP,
FLEET, CONVOY,
SAFARI, TRAVEL,
JOURNEY
Arab CAFILA,
KAFILA
caravansary HOTEL,
IMARET, INN, KHAN,
SERAI, HOSTEL, REST-
HOUSE
caravel NINA, PINTA,
BOAT, VESSEL
carbine MUSKET,
RIFLE, ESCOPET(TE)
carbohydrate STARCH,
SUGAR, CELLULOSE
carbolic acid PHENOL
carbon LEAD, SOOT,
COKE, COAL, CRAYON,
REPLICA, COPY,
GRAPHITE

carbonate of calcium CHALK

carborundum EMERY, ABRASIVE

carboy BOTTLE, FLAGON, JUG

carbuncle BOIL, ABSCESS, GARNET, JEWEL

carcajou WOLVERINE, BADGER, LYNX, COUGAR

card ACE, TEN, DEUCE, TREY, JOKER, KING, JACK, QUEEN, WAG, COMB, DRESS, PAM, MENU, TICKET
game GIN, ECARTE, CASINO, BACCARAT, OMBER, BASSET, BEZIQUE, CRIBBAGE, LOO, BRIDGE, FARO, HOCK, HOC, MONTE, NAP, HOMBRE, PAM, CINCH, PIQUET, ROUNCE, SKAT, WHIST, VINT, CANASTA, STUSS, TAROTS, KENO, NAPOLEON, SOLITAIRE
old OMBER
player at right of dealer PONE
playing, old TAROT, TAROC, PAM
rules author HOYLE
slam VOLE
spare hand CAT, POT, WIDOW
spots on PIPS
term CAT, PIC, MELD, BID, PASS, HAND, DEAL, RENEGE, VOID, BOOK, TRUMP, SUIT, RAISE
wild JOKER

cardinal(s) VITAL, BASIC, CHIEF, MAIN, PRINCIPAL, CLOAK, BIRD, CLERIC
assembly at Rome COLLEGE
flower LOBELIA
office HAT
title EMINENCE

cards DECK, PACK

care HEED, SCRUPLE, VIGIL, TEND, ATTEND, WORRY, TROUBLE, PAINS, ATTENTION, LOVE, YEARN, RECK, ANXIETY, CONCERN, CUSTODY, ROWAN

careen TILT, HEEL, LIST, TIP, CANT, UPSET, INCLINE, SLOPE

career PURSUIT, LIFE, PROFESSION, BUSINESS, CALLING, TRADE

careful WARY, CHARY, CAUTIOUS, DISCREET, CANNY, LEERY, WATCHFUL, GUARDED, PRUDENT

careless RASH, CASUAL, REMISS, HEEDLESS, INATTENTIVE, NEGLIGENT, NEGLECT-FUL, INDIFFERENT

caress HUG, KISS, PET, FONDLE, DANDLE, EMBRACE, CODDLE, COSSET

Carew's love CELIA

cargo FREIGHT, LOAD, LADING, GOODS, MAIL, BURDEN, PROPERTY
space in ship HOLD
take on LADE, LOAD
wrecked ship FLOTSAM

Caribbean Sea bight DARIEN

caribe PIRANHA, PIRAYA, FISH

carica PAPAYA, PAW-PAW, TREE

caricature SATIRE, CARTOON, PARODY, SKIT, LIBEL, SQUIB, COPY, APE, MOCK, MIMIC, TRAVESTY, FARCE, BURLESQUE

cark HARASS, WORRY, VEX, TROUBLE

carl CHURL, RUSTIC, HEMP, BOOR

"Carmen" composer BIZET

carnage BLOODSHED, SLAUGHTER, POGROM, BUTCHERY, MASSACRE

carnation PINK

carnelian SARD, CHALCEDONY

carnivora BEAR, CAT, DOG, FELINE, GENET, HYENA, OTTER, PUMA, RATEL, SEAL, SERVAL, TIGER, LION
reptile TUATARA

carnotite URANIUM

carob ALGARROBA, TREE

carol NOEL, MADRIGAL, SONG, LAY, WARBLE, CHANT, DITTY, ALCOVE
singer WAIT

Caroline island YAP (UAP), TRUK, PALU

carom SHOT, REBOUND, GLANCE, RICOCHET

carousal ORGY, SPREE, BINGE, FEAST, BIRLE, BOUSE, REVEL, WAS-SAIL, FESTIVAL, DEBAUCH, JAMBOREE

carp CAVIL, NIBBLE, NAG, CENSOR
fish IDE, LOACH

carpel PISTIL, LEAF, CARPOPHYL(L)

carpels, mass of SOREMA

carpenter WRIGHT, JOINER, FRAMER, CABINETMAKER, ANT
bee XYLOCOPA
pattern STRICKLE, TEMPLATE
tool of SAW, HAM-MER, PLANE, LEVEL, NAIL

Carpenter opera LOUISE

carpet KALI, MAT, TAPET, HERAT, TAPIS, FABRIC, COVERING

carplike fish IDE

carpus WRIST

carrack, carack GALLEON, BOAT

carrageen MOSS, ALGA, SEAWEED

carriage VEHICLE, LANDAU, GIG, CART, WAGON, STAGE, CALASH, SURREY, TRAP, BEARING, FRONT, POSTURE, MANNER, MIEN, PORT, DEMEANOR, GAIT, SUPPORT, CON-VEYANCE
baby GOCART, PRAM, PERAMBULATOR
kind GIG, SADO, CAR(R)IOLE, STAN-HOPE, TRAP
one-horse SHAY, TRAP, FLY, SULKY, GIG
Russian KIBITKA, TROIKA, ARABA

shackle BAR
two-wheeled GIG,
ESSED(A), VOLANTE,
SHAY, SULKY, CHAISE,
TONGA, CISIUM,
DENNET
carried TOTED, BORNE
Carroll character
ALICE, HATTER,
RABBIT, DUCHESS
carrot DAUCUS, DRIAS
deadly DRIAS
genus CARUM
carry SUPPORT, BEAR,
TOTE, TAKE, BRING,
FETCH, MOVE, SHIFT,
RIDE, LEAD, URGE,
HOLD, CONVEY, TRANS-
PORT, SUSTAIN, CON-
TAIN
away TOTE, TAKE,
ELOI(G)N, STEAL,
KIDNAP
on WAGE, RAVE, RANT,
MAINTAIN, CONTINUE,
CONDUCT
cart VEHICLE, WAGON,
WAIN, DRAY, CARRY,
TOTE, TONGA,
TUMBRIL, TUMBREL
end of GATE, TIB
oriental (Asiatic)
ARABA
two-wheeled SULKY,
GIG, SHAY
carte MENU, LIST,
CHART, MAP, DIA-
GRAM, CARD
cartel PACT, TREATY,
POOL, CORNER, TRUST,
AGREEMENT, LETTER,
SHIP
Carthage CARTHAGO
citadel BYRSA, BURSA
emblem PALM
foe CATO
fort GOLETTA
founder DIDO
god MOLOCH
goddess TANIT(H)
inhabitants POENI
language of PUNIC
pertaining to PUNIC
queen DIDO
Carthusian EREMITE,
MONK
monastery CERTOSA,
PAVIA
noted HUGH
superior PRIOR
carillon PEAL, BELLS,
CHIMES

cartograph PLAT,
CHART, MAP
carton CASE, BOX,
CONTAINER
cartoonist NAST, ARNO,
CAPP
cartridge holder CLIP
carucate LAND, FIELD,
PLOWLAND, HIDE
part of BOVATE
caruncle GILL, WAT-
TLE, COMB, PRO-
TUBERANCE, GROWTH
carve FASHION, SHAPE,
CUT, SLICE,
SERVE, HEW, FORM,
DIVIDE, PART, EN-
GRAVE, CHISEL, IN-
CISE, SCULPT, SLIT,
CHOP, SLASH, SCULP-
TURE, MAKE, APPOR-
TION
carving in stone
CAMEO
casaba MELON
case SUIT, ACTION,
CRATE, EVENT, INRO,
MATTER, SURVEY,
SHEATH, INSTANCE,
COVER, CONTAINER,
SATCHEL, BAG, BOX,
EXAMPLE, TRIAL, LAW-
SUIT, ARGUMENT,
PACK, AFFAIR, CARTON
explosive PETARD,
SHELL
grammar DATIVE, OB-
JECTIVE, NOMINATIVE,
GENITIVE, ACCUSATIVE
holding a book
FOREL, FORREL
liquor bottles
CELLARET
small TYE, ETUI,
ETWEE, TROUSSE
toilet ETUI, ETWEE
casein LEGUMIN,
PROTEIN
cash COIN, DARBY,
DUST, MONEY,
SPECIE, HEMLOCK,
CURRENCY
cashew *fruit* NUT,
ANACARD
nut oil CARDOL
cashier PURSER, TEL-
LER, BURSAR, PAY-
MASTER, TREASURER,
EJECT, EXPEL, OUST,
FIRE, SACK, DROP,
DISMISS, DISCARD,
REJECT

casing LINER, COVER,
SHEATH(ING), FRAME-
WORK, TIRE
cask BARECA, KEG,
BUTT, CADE, TUB,
TUN, VAT, TIERCE,
PUNCHEON, HOGSHEAD,
BARREL
bulge of BILGE
42-gallon TIERCE
rim CHIMB, CHIME
stave of LAG
wine TIERCE
casket BOX, COFFIN,
CASE, CHEST, ACERRA,
CIST, PYX, TYE,
RELIQUARY, PIX
for Host PYX, PIX
for relics of saint
CHASSE
Caspian Sea, *old region*
near PARTHIA
river to EMBA, URAL,
KURA, VOLGA, TEREK,
ARAS, KUMA
Cassandra SEERESS
father PRIAM
cassava AIPI, JUCA,
YUCA, TAPIOCA,
STARCH, MANIOC
genus MANIHOT
casserole STEW, RAG-
OUT, VESSEL, DISH,
MOLD
cassia HERB, SHRUB,
TREE, SENNA, DRUG
bark CINNAMON
Cassiopeia's *daughter*
ANDROMEDA
cassock GOWN,
SOUTANE, CLERGY-
MAN, PRIEST
cassowary MOORUP,
MURUP, EMU, BIRD
cast JILT, MOLT,
SLOUGH, SPEW, HURL,
HEAVE, PITCH, SLING,
THROW, FIGURE,
MOULT, MOLD, SHED,
TOSS, SCRAP, JUNK,
SUM, CALCULATE,
RECKON, TINGE, TINT,
ADD, FORM, ASPECT
castanea BEECH, TREE
castaway WAIF,
DERELICT, PARIAH,
OUTCAST, BUM,
TRAMP, STRANDED,
EXILE(D)
caste CLASS, DEGREE,
SUDRA, VARNA, PARIAH,
GOLA, JATI, MEO,

CHETTY, VAISYA, ORDER, BRAHMAN, RANK, GRADE, STATUS
agricultural MEO
group of VARNA
priestly MAGI, MAGUS
top ELITE, CREAM
caster CLOAK, CRUET, VIAL, CRUSE, PHIAL, HURLER, THROWER, PITCHER, WHEEL
castigate CHASTISE, BEAT, (BE)RATE, RAIL, FINE, CLOG, LAMBASTE, CENSURE, SCORE, REPROVE, PUNISH
castigatory PENAL, PUNITIVE, CORRECTIVE
Castile, *Northern* VIEJA
province AVILA, SORIA
river DOURO, DUERO, EBRO, ESLA
Southern NUEVA
casting mold MATRIX, DIE, MATRICE
castle CHATEAU, CITADEL, ROOK, FORTRESS, RESIDENCE, STRONGHOLD, ABODE
building DREAMING
part of KEEP, DON-JON, TOWER, MOAT
castor BEAVER, CRUET, BEAN, HAT, STAR, CASTOREUM
bean poison RICIN
eater ERI(A)
plant KIKI
Castor's *brother* POLLUX
mother LEDA
slayer IDAS
Castor and Pollux GEMINI, DIOSCURI, TWINS
casual CHANCE, RANDOM, INCIDENTAL, ACCIDENTAL, CURSORY, OFFHAND, HAPHAZARD, UNCERTAIN, CON-TINGENT, PAUPER, DRIFTER
cat PUSS, CIVET, GENET, MARGAY, FELINE, GIB, MANX, LION, TIGER, TABBY, MALTESE, TOM, GRIMALKIN, MOUSER
American MARGAY, ANGORA, OCELOT, BOB

civetlike GENET
genus FELIS, FELIDAE
hater A(E)LUROPHOBE
house MOUSER
lover A(E)LEUROPHILE
Spanish name for GATO
wild BALU, PUMA, JAGUAR, EYRA, OCELOT, MANUL, CIVET, BOB, PANTHER, SERVAL
catacomb CRYPT, VAULT, TOMB
burial niche LOCULE, LOCULUS
catafalque BIER
catalan SHARPER, THIEF, SCOUNDREL
catalog(ue) LIST, INDEX, RECORD, TABLE, ROLL, ROTA, ROSTER, CANON, TARIFF, REGISTER, INVOICE, ARRANGE, FILE
catamaran BALSA, RAFT, FLOAT, VESSEL, BOAT
S. America JANGADA
cataplasm POULTICE
catapult ONAGER, BALLISTA, SLING, CROSSBOW, SCORPION
cataract CASCADE, FALLS, LINN, FLOOD, DELUGE
catarrh COLD, RHEUM
catastrophe DISASTER, CALAMITY, MIS-FORTUNE
catcall HOOT, BOO
catch HAUL, NET, TAKE, SNARE, SEIZE, GRASP, GRAB, ARREST, INCUR, HOOK, TRAP, DETECT, LAND, SNAG, COP, BAG, ENTRAP, SNATCH, NAB, CAPTURE, RECEIVE, FASTENING
catchall BAG, BASKET, CLOSET, RECEPTACLE
catchfly SILENE, CAMPION, PLANT
catchword SLOGAN, CUE
catechu yellow GAMBIER, CUTCH, DYE
catechumen PUPIL, BEGINNER, CONVERT,

NEOPHYTE, TIRO, TYRO
category CLASS, GENUS, GENRE, SPECIES, DIVISION, ORDER, RANK, FAMILY
cater PROVIDE, PANDER, PURVEY, FEED, HUMOR, FURNISH
caterpillar ERUCA, OUBIT, CANKER, TENT, TRACTOR, WOUBIT, LARVA
hair SETA
N. Zealand AWETO, WERI
caterwaul CRY, WAIL
catfish TANDAN, HAS-SAR, MUD, CUSK, WEEVER, SHEATFISH, BULLHEAD, DOCMAC, BAGRE, CHANNEL
electric RAAD
catgut THARM, STRING, CORD, VIOLIN, HERB
cathedral DOM, OFFICIAL, CHURCH
passage SLYPE
catholic LIBERAL, GENERAL, UNIVERSAL, TOLERANT, PAPAL
order MARIST, JESUIT
cation ION
opposite ANION
catkin AMENT, SPIKE, RAG
catmint NIP, NEP, HERB
catnip CATARIA, NIP, NEP(ETA), HERB
genus NEPETA
cat-o-nine-tails LASH, WHIP
cat's-paw TOOL, CULLY, DUPE, GULL
cat's tail TIMOTHY, GRASS
cattail REREE, TULE, TOTORA, DOD(D), MATREED, CLOUD, CATKIN, AMENT, MUSK
cattle COWS, BOVINES, KINE, BEEVES, STOCK
black KERRY, ANGUS
breed of ZOBO, JERSEY, GUERNSEY, HEREFORD, ANGUS, BRAHMAN

dealer DROVER, RANCHER

dwarf DEVON, NIATA

genus NEAT, BOS, TAURUS

graze for a sum AGIST

pen BARTH, BARN, CORRAL, KRAAL, REEVE, HOVEL

stealer ABACTOR, ABIGEUS, RUSTLER

Caucasian SEMITE, OSSET, TATAR, TURK, SLAV, SVAN(E), IRANIAN

carpet KUBA

family ARYAN

goat TUR

ibex ZAC

language UDI, ANDI, AVAR, SEMITIC, LAZ(E), LAZI, IRANIAN

milk liquor KEFIR, KEPHIR, KUMISS

moslem LAZ(I)

mountaineer LAK

rug BAKU, CHILA, KUBA, DERBEND, SUMAK, KAZAK

town KUBA

tribe IMER, KURD, LAZI, LAZE, SVAN, KUBACHI

caucho ULE, RUBBER, TREE

caucus PRIMARY, ELECTION, COUNCIL, MEETING

caudal appendage TAIL

caul, *infant's* HOUVE

caulk *See under* "calk"

cauma HEAT, FEVER, WARMTH

cause CREATE, CAUSA, REASON, BASIS, KEY, SUIT, ACTION, CASE, SOURCE, ORIGIN, MOTIVE, SPRING, SPUR, GOAD, AGENT, ROOT, GROUND, PURPOSE, AIM, OBJECT, LAWSUIT

science of ETIOLOGY

causeuse SOFA, TETE-A-TETE

caustic SNAPPISH, MORDANT, PYROTIC, LYE, LIME, BURNING, ERODENT, SEVERE, BITING, ALKALINE, PHENOL, ACRID, KEEN, ACUTE,

SARCASTIC, CORROSIVE, SHARP, SATIRICAL, SCATHING, BITTER, PUNGENT, PAINFUL, GRUFF, MALEVOLENT

cauterize INUST, CHAR, SINGE, BURN, SEAR, STERILIZE

caution WARN, HEED, COUNSEL, CARE, PRUDENCE, WARNING, WARINESS, VIGILANCE, ADVICE

cautious WARY, SHY, CHARY, CANNY, FABIAN, ALERT, ACTIVE, CIRCUMSPECT, CAREFUL, DISCREET

cavalcade PAGEANT, PARADE, RAID, PROCESSION, JOURNEY, SAFARI

cavalier HAUGHTY, PROUD, KNIGHT, CHEVALIER

"Cavalleria Rusticana" *character* ALFIO, LOLA

cavalryman ULAN, UHLAN, DRAGOON, HUSSAR

Algerian SPAHI, SPAHEE

cave ANTRE, CRYPT, GROT(TO), LAIR, DEN, RECESS, CELL(AR), HOLLOW, CAVITY, COLLAPSE, CAVERN

dweller TROGLODYTE

icicle STALACTITE

inhabiting SPEL(A)EAN

science of SPELEOLOGY

cavern *See* "cave"

caviar IKRA, OVA, ROE, RELISH

fish yielding STURGEON, STERLET

cavil CARP, HAFT, CENSURE, QUIBBLE

cavities, *teeth* CARIES

cavity LUMEN, ANTRE, AULA, SINUS, ANTRUM, DENT, POCKET, HOLE, PIT, CELL, CAVE, GROTTO, CAVERN, HOLLOW, VOID, VACUUM, GEODE, CAMERA

body SINUS, AULA, ANTRUM, FOSSA

heart ATRIUM, VENTRICLE

in lode VUG

in skull FOSSA, AULA

in stone GEODE

pertaining to GEODIC, SINAL

cavort CAPER, DIDO, PRANCE, PRANK, PLAY, CURVET

cavy PACA, RODENT, PIG, CAPYBARA, AGOUTI, PONY, CAYUSE

Patagonian MARA

caw QUARK, CAWK CRY, CALL, QUAWK, CROAK

cayenne CAPSICUM, CANARY, WHIST, PEPPER

cease DESIST, HALT, PETER, QUIT, END, STINT, AVAST, FINISH, CLOSE, STOP, REFRAIN, TERMINATE, INTERMIT, PAUSE, STAY, DISCONTINUE

Cecrops' *daughter* HERSE

cedar, *Australia and E. India* TOON(A)

N. America SAVIN(E), RED, WAXWING

red SAVIN(E)

cede GRANT, YIELD, SURRENDER, LEAVE, AWARD, WAIVE, RESIGN, ABANDON, CONVEY, ASSIGN, SUBMIT, GIVE

ceiling SOFFIT, COVER

division in TRAVE

mine ASTEL

celebrity VIP, LION, STAR, NAME, FAME, GLORY, HONOR, ECLAT, REPUTE, RENOWN

celerity DISPATCH, HASTE, SPEED, HURRY, RAPIDITY, VELOCITY

celery, *wild* SMALLAGE, ACHE

celestial HOLY, URANIC, DIVINE, ANGELIC, HEAVENLY

being ANGEL, CHERUB, SERAPH

elevation of mind
ANAGOGE
cell EGG, KIL(L),
GERM, CYTODE,
NEURON(E), JAIL,
CAGE, ROOM, CAVITY,
PRISON, VAULT,
LOCULUS, COMPART-
MENT, GROUP
division SPIREM(E),
AMITOSIS, LININ
Near East SERDAB
Roman NAOS, CELLA
study of CYTOLOGY
cella NAOS
cellaret TANTALUS
cells LOCULI
honeycomb ALVEOLI
cellular ALVEOLATE,
AREOLAR, FAVIFORM,
FAVOSE
celluloid XYLONITE
cellulose, *acetate*
ACETOSE
combining form
CELLO
Celt, Celtic GAEL,
WELSH, ERSE, MANX,
IRISH, CORNISH,
BRETON, GAUL,
BRITON
abbot COARB
dart or javelin COLP
*god or goddess See
under* "god" *or*
"goddess"
land holder TANIST
language BRYTHONIC,
CYMRIC, CELTIC,
MANX
pasture COLP, COLLOP
priest DRUID
cement UNITE, STICK,
PUTTY, GLUE, JOIN,
SOLDER, MORTAR,
PASTE, ASPHALT,
COHERE
hydraulic PAAR
cemetery NECROPOLIS,
GRAVEYARD, CATA-
COMB
cenobite ESSENE,
MONK, RECLUSE,
FRIAR, NUN, MONAS-
TIC, ANCHORITE
cenoby ABBEY, PRIORY,
CLOISTER, CONVENT,
MONASTERY
censer THURIBLE
Censor CATO, CRITIC,
DETRACTOR
censure FLAY, CHIDE,

CHARGE, JUDGE,
SLATE, BLAME,
IMPEACH, REBUKE,
BERATE, REPROACH,
CONDEMN, REPRIMAND
census POLL, COUNT,
ENUMERATION, LIST
cent COIN, PENNY,
HUNDRED, COPPER
Centaurs, *father of*
IXION
center SEAT, HEART,
MIDDLE, NAVE, AXIS,
SPINE, HUB, CORE,
FOCUS, NUCLEUS,
MIDST, PIVOT, CON-
CENTRATE, CONVERGE
away from DISTAL
of interest MECCA
resembling AX(I)AL
toward MESIAL,
CENTRAD
centerpiece EPERGNE
centesimal unit
GRAD(E)
centipede MYRIAPOD,
EARWIG, VERI,
CHILOPOD
central FOCAL, AXIAL,
NUCLEAR, MIDDLE,
PIVOTAL, MIDMOST
Central America(n)
See country involved
centuries, *ten* CHILIAD,
MILLENNIUM
century plant, AGAVE,
ALOE, MAGUEY, PITA
fiber PITA, PITO
ceorl CHURL, THANE,
VILLEIN
cepa ONION
cephaloid CAPITATE
cephalopod SQUID,
CUTTLE, INKFISH,
OCTOPUS
Cepheus' *daughter*
ANDROMEDA
ceral WAXY
ceramics sieve LAUN
ceramist POTTER
cerate WAX, SALVE,
LARD
ceratose HORNY
cerberus HELLDOG,
GUARDIAN, CUSTODIAN
cere WAX
cereal, *coarse* BRAN
food FARINA, RICE,
HOMINY, GRITS,
WHEAT, MAIZE, OAT-
MEAL
genus SECALE

grass OAT, RAGI,
GRAIN, RYE, RAGGEE
cerebral MENTAL
cerebrospinal axis
BRAIN, SPINE, CORD
ceremonial fuss PAN-
JANDRUM
ceremonious SOLEMN,
STATELY, PROPER,
LOFTY, FORMAL,
STIFF, PRECISE
leave-taking
CONGE(E)
ceremony POMP,
FORM, RITE, RITUAL,
PARADE, MARRIAGE,
BAPTISM
cerium CE, METAL
cero CAVALLA, SIERRA,
PINTADO, FISH
certain SURE, TRUE,
POSITIVE, PLAIN,
ACTUAL, REAL, FIXED,
CONSTANT, CLEAR,
OFFICIAL
certificate DIPLOMA,
SCRIP, STOCK,
VOUCHER, CREDENTIAL
certify VOUCH, AS-
SURE, ATTEST, DEPOSE,
AFFIRM, SWEAR,
AVOW, TESTIFY,
VERIFY, DETERMINE,
EVINCE
cerulean AZURE, BLUE,
COELIN(E)
cervine CERVID, DEER,
STAG *See under*
"deer"
cesium CS
cespitose MATTED,
TUFTED, TANGLED,
TURFLIKE, SODDED
cess RATE, TAX, LEVY,
EXCISE, LUCK, IM-
POST, DUTY, TOLL,
TITHE
cessation REST, LULL,
HALT, DESITION, END,
STOP, LETUP, PAUSE,
STAY, INTERVAL,
REMISSION, RECESS
cetacean PORPOISE,
WHALE, SUSU, INIA,
ORC(A), DOLPHIN,
NARW(H)AL(E),
GRAMPUS
genus INIA
cetyl oil compound
CETENE
Ceylon SINHALA,
SINGHALA, LANKA

aborigine VEDDA(H)
ape MAHA, LANGUR
bay PALK
governor DISAWA
grass CHENA
hill dweller TODA
language PALI,
TAMIL
measure PARA(H),
SEER
moss GULAMAN,
AGAR, JAFFNA
native VEDDA(H)
palm TALIPOT
rice PADDY, PADI
seaport GALLE
sea sands PAAR
soldier PEON
strait PALK
tree TALA
chab(o)uk WHIP
chacalaca GUAN,
BIRD
chack SNACK, BITE,
SNAP, CLACK,
WHEATEAR
chacma BABOON
chaeta SETA, BRISTLE,
SPINE
chafe GALL, FRET,
RAGE, RUB, HEAT,
VEX, FROT, ANGER,
WEAR, ABRADE, IR-
RITATE, ANNOY, NET-
TLE, FUME, INCENSE
chaff *See* "kid"
HUSK, TRASH, BRAN,
GLUMES, HULLS,
REFUSE
chaffer HIGGLE,
DICKER, HAGGLE,
BARGAIN, SIEVE
chaffy PALEATE,
ACEROSE, PALEACEOUS,
SCALY, WORTHLESS,
TRIVIAL
chain TORQUE, GYVE,
RANGE, FETTER, RE-
STRAIN, HOBBLE, ROW,
CATENA, LINK, SERIES,
STRING, BOND, FILE,
TRAIN, SET, SUITE,
MANACLE, SHACKLE,
CONCATENATION, NET-
WORK
of quotations CATENA
chair STOOL, ROCKER,
SEAT, THRONE,
SEDAN, OFFICE
back part of SPLAT
litterlike KAGO
portable SEDAN

chalcedony AGATE,
ONYX, SARD, JASPER,
CARNELIAN, QUARTZ
Chaldean
astronomical cycle
SAROS
city UR
time cycle SAROS
chalice AMA, CUP,
GRAIL, BOWL,
GOBLET
flower DAFFODIL
pall of ANIMETTA
chalk TALC, CRETA,
CREDIT, CRAYON,
TICK, SCORE, SCAR,
BLEACH
sponge ASCON
challenge DEFY, CALL,
DARE, ACCUSE,
QUESTION, CLAIM,
INVITE, EXCEPTION,
BRAVE, SUMMONS
to duel CARTEL
chamber(s) CAMERA,
CELL, KIVA, ROOM,
LOCULUS, DIGS,
FLAT, HALL, APART-
MENT, HOLLOW
judge's CAMERA
two-legislative
BICAMERA
chambray GINGHAM,
CLOTH
chameleon ANOLI,
LIZARD
chameleonic CHANGE-
ABLE, INCONSTANT,
FICKLE
champagne AY, WINE
champion ESPOUSE,
DEFEND, ACE, SQUIRE,
KNIGHT, BACK, HERO,
VICTOR, AID, HELP,
OAK, PERSEUS
championship TITLE,
ADVOCACY, LEADER-
SHIP, SUPREMACY
chance LOT, HAP,
ODDS, TIDE, HAZARD,
GAMBLE, BETIDE,
OCCUR, KISMET,
CASUAL, FATE, LUCK,
PASS, BREAK, TIME,
RANDOM, ACCIDENT,
FORTUITY, FORTUNE,
RISK, OPPORTUNITY
combining form
TYCH(O)
chancel, *part of* BEMA
screen JUBE
seats SEDILIA

change AMEND, SHIFT,
MODIFY, COINS,
MUTATE, FLUX,
VARY, TURN, EMEND,
MOVE, COMMUTE,
MONEY, ALTER-
(ATION), TRANSFER
direction TACK, TURN,
VEER
music MUTA
subject to MUTABLE,
VARIABLE, AMENA-
BLE
changeable AMENA-
BLE, PROTEAN, FICKLE,
ALTERABLE, VARIANT,
INCONSTANT, UN-
STABLE, FITFUL,
CHAMELEONIC, MUTA-
BLE, GIDDY
changeling CHILD,
DOLT, OAF, FOOL,
DUNCE, SUBSTITUTE
channel GROOVE,
DUCT, GAT, PIPE,
STREAM, RUT, WAY,
AVENUE, ROAD, VEIN,
KENNEL, GUTTER,
DIKE, ARTERY, SINUS,
STRIA, MEANS, BED,
STRAIT, SOUND,
AGENT, ORGAN, TUBE,
CANAL, DITCH, CON-
DUIT, ROUTE, TROUGH,
CHUTE, FURROW,
OPENING
bone CANICULUS
brain ITER
goose GANNET
inland GAT, CANAL
iron BAR
longitudinal RAB-
BET
marker BUOY
mill LEAT, RACE
water GURT, DRAIN,
CANAL, SLUICE,
FLUME, PIPE, RACE,
LEAT
channeled FURROWED,
CHAMFERED, CANTICLE
Channel Island SARK,
JERSEY
measure CABOT
channels MEDIA,
STRIAE
chanson LYRIC, SONG,
BALLAD, REFRAIN
chant SONG, INTONE,
INTROIT, WARBLE,
CAROL, ANTHEM,

PSALM, SING, WORSHIP
chanticleer COCK, ROOSTER
chantilly LACE
chantry ALTAR, SHRINE, CHAPEL
chaos ABYSS, CHASM, GULF, BABEL, VOID, JUMBLE, SHAMBLES, TOPHET, MESS, DISORDER, CONFUSION
primeval fluid of NU
Chaos' *daughter* NYX, NOX
son EREBUS
chaotic MUDDLED, SNAFU, CONFUSED
chap BOY, LAD, FELLOW, CHINK, CRACK, SPLIT, CHOP, ROUGHEN, CLEFT, COVE
chape CRAMPET, CASE, SHEATH, SCABBARD, LOOP
chapeau HAT, BONNET
chapel BETHEL, ORATORY, CHANTRY, SERVICE, SANCTUARY, CHOIR
in Vatican SISTINE
chaperon ESCORT, ATTEND, PROTECT-(OR), GUARD(IAN), DUENNA, HOOD, MATRON
chaplain PADRE, CLERGYMAN, NUN
chaplet ANADEM, WREATH, FILLET, GARLAND, BEAD, ROSARY, MOLDING, CORONAL, CIRCLE, TROPHY, ORNAMENT
chapped KIBY, KIBED, CRACKED, ROUGH, SPLIT
chaps CHOPS, JAWS, FLEWS, BREECHES, BOYS, LADS
chapter SECTION, LODGE, POST, BRANCH, BODY, MEETING, ASSEMBLY, CELL, CONTINGENT
pertaining to CAPITULAR, CHAPTERAL
char BURN, SEAR, SINGE, SCORCH
charabanc BUS, VEHICLE, COACH

character QUALITY, KIND, TRAIT(S), REPUTE, STRIPE, KIDNEY, TYPE, ILK, SORT, CARD, FIBER, TENOR, CLASS, NATURE, ROLE, PART, SYMBOL, SIGN, MARK, NOTE, METTLE, SPIRIT, BENT, LETTER, EMBLEM, FIGURE
anc. Irish alphabet OGAM, OGHAM
giver TONER, PACER
indicate relative pitch NEUME
of a community ETHOS
Teutonic alphabet RUNE
characteristic TRAIT, QUALITY, CAST, SYMPTOM(ATIC), FEATURE, MIEN, PECULIARITY, LINEAMENT, DISTINCTIVE, PATHOGNOMONIC
characterize MARK, REPRESENT, DELINEATE, DISTINGUISH, DESCRIBE, PORTRAY, INDICATE
charcoal CARBON, PENCIL, CARBO, DRAWING
gas from OXAN(E)
charge RATE, COST, ADJURE, FEE, ACCUSE, TOLL, LEVY, PRICE, INDICT, ONUS, DIRECT, LOAD, BID, ENJOIN, ORDER, BLAME, ASCRIBE, CREDIT, INTRUST, IMPUTE, ARRAIGN, CARE, MANDATE, CUSTODY
combat ONSET, ATTACK, ASSAULT
charger STEED, HORSE, PLATE, DISH, PLATTER, MOUNT
chariot RATH, WAIN, ESSED(E), ESSEDA, CAR, BUGGY, AUTO
See "carriage"
for statue of a god RATH
Greek QUADRIGA
religious RATH
Roman BIGA, ESSED(E), ESSEDA

three-horse TROIKA
top CALASH
two-horse BIGA
two-wheeled ESSEDA, GIG
charioteer HUR, DRIVER, PILOT
astronomy AURIGA, WAGONER
charitable KIND, GENEROUS, HUMANE, TENDER, LIBERAL, INDULGENT, BENEVOLENT, BENIGN
charity LOVE, ALMS, DOLE, BOUNTY, PITY, MERCY, LARGESS(E), GRACE, LENITY, RUTH, GIFT
charlatan CHEAT, FRAUD, EMPIRIC, QUACK, FAKE(R), IMPOSTER, PRETENDER, MOUNTEBANK
Charlemagne's *brother* CARLOMAN
father PEPIN
hero of court ROLAND
knight PALADIN, GANO, GANELON
nephew ORLANDO
Charles' Wain DIPPER, BEAR, URSA
charlock KRAUT, MUSTARD, WEED
Charlotte Corday's *victim* MARAT
charm SPELL, GRACE, AMULET, JUJU, FETISH, TALISMAN, GRIGRI, TAKE, ALLAY, CAPTIVATE, ALLURE, ENAMOR, FASCINATE, SOOTHE, CALM, ATTRACT, PLEASE, DELIGHT, GRATIFY, MAGIC, SORCERY, ENCHANT, BEWITCH
African JUJU, GRIGRI, GREEGREE, OBEAH
neck PHYLACTERY
W. Indian OBEAH
charmer MAGICIAN, SORCERER, EXORCIST, SIREN, CALMER
charnel house OSSUARY
charpoy COT, BED

Chart | 82 | Chemical

chart GRAPH, PLAN, MAP, PLAT, RECORD, PLOT, SCHEME, DESIGN, PROJECT, DIAGRAM

charter HIRE, LET, LEASE, RENT, DEED, LICENSE, GRANT, COMMISSION, PERMIT, PRIVILEGE

chase HUNT, PURSUE, FOLLOW

chasm GULF, BLANK, VOID, HIATUS, ABYSS, CLEFT, REFT, CANYON, FISSURE, ABYSM, GAP, RIFT, BREACH, INTERVAL

chasseur HUNTER

chaste VESTAL, PURE, CLEAN, SIMPLE, MODEST, INNOCENT, VIRTUOUS, UNDEFILED

chasten PUNISH, HUMBLE, ABASE, TEMPER, RESTRAIN, MODERATE, SMITE, DISCIPLINE, REFINE, SUBDUE

chastise SPANK, TRIM, SWINGE, STRAP, BLAME, SLAP, TAUNT, WHIP, BEAT, THRASH, PUNISH, CASTIGATE, FLOG, LASH, REPROVE, REBUKE, SCOLD, CENSURE

chat PRATE, CONFAB, COZE, TOVE, GAB, SPEAK, GOSSIP, CHIN, PRATTLE, CHATTER, BABBLE, CONFABULATE

chatelaine ETUI, BROOCH, TORQUE, CLASP, PIN, HOOK, MISTRESS

Chatham PITT

chattel, to recover DETINUE

chatter TALK, YAP, BABBLE, PRATE, GIBBER, GABBLE, GAB, GAS, CLACK, JABBER, TATTLE, PATTER

chatterer MAG, JAY, PIET

Chaucer's *inn* TABARD

pilgrim REEVE

title DAN

cheap ABJECT, SORDID, SORRY, MEAN, BASE, VILE, POOR, SHODDY, LOW, PALTRY, INFERIOR

cheat COZEN, FLEECE, (BE)FOOL, GYP, STING, FOB, FUB, BILK, SKIN, DUPE, GULL, GOUGE, SWINDLE, TAKE, DECEIVE, (DE)FRAUD, FAKE, SHAM, HOAX, TRICK, JOCKEY, OUTWIT, BAMBOOZLE, HOODWINK, RENEGE, CLIP, CHISEL, BURN

cheater TOPPER, BILKER, GULL, SHARPER, TRICKSTER, KNAVE

check BRAKE, ARREST, CURB, STAY, VERIFY, NIP, BIT, REIN, DETENT, NAB, TAB, SNUB, REBUFF, STUNT, BRIDLE, BLOCK, BAFFLE, IMPEDE, HINDER, OBSTRUCT, RESTRAIN

bank DRAFT

by rein SACCADE

checkered VAIR, PLAID, PIED, VARIEGATED, CHANGEABLE

checkers DRAUGHTS, GAME

moves DYKE, FIFE, CROSS, BRISTOL

checkmate BAFFLE, DEFEAT, STYMIE, GAIN, LICK, STOP, UNDO, CORNER, THWART

cheddar CHEESE

cheek(s) TEMERITY, GENA, NERVE, SAUCE, JOWL, JOLE, GALL, CHAP(S), AUDACITY, BUCCA

bone MALAR, ZYGOMA

distended BUCCATE

muscle BUCCINATOR

pertaining to MALAR, BUCCAL, GENAL

cheep CHIRP, SQUEAK, PEEP, PULE, TWEET

cheer VIVA, RAH, BRAVO, ROOT, MIRTH, SHOUT, GAIETY, SPIRIT, REPAST, DRINK, CRY, AID, ELATE, APPLAUD, CLAP, OLE, HURRAH, HUZZA, ACCLAIM, LAUD, PRAISE, JOLLITY, GLEE, COMFORT

cheerful GAY, GLADSOME, ROSY, GLEG, JOLLY, JOCUND, SUNNY, PEART, MERRY, BLITHE, LIVELY, SPRIGHTLY, JOYOUS, HAPPY, BRIGHT

cheerless SAD, GLUM, GLOOMY, DREAR(Y), DULL, DISMAL, DEJECTED, DRAB

cheese MYSOST, CHEDDAR, COTTAGE, EDAM, SWISS, CAMEMBERT, ROQUEFORT

Belgian LIMBURGER

dish FONDUE, OMELET, RAREBIT, CAKE, SOUFFLE

Dutch EDAM, COTTAGE

French BRIE, ROQUEFORT

green SAPSAGO

inferior DICK

ingredient CASEIN

Italian PARMESAN, GORGONZOLA

knife SPATULA

maggot SKIPPER

Scotch DUNLOP

soft BRIE

Swiss SAPSAGO

whole milk DUNLOP

cheesy CASEOUS, SMART, WORTHLESS, FINE

cheetah YOUSE, YOUZE

chelonian TORTOISE, TURTLE

chemical *compound* AMIN(E), AMID(E), AZIN(E), BORID(E), CERIA, INOSITE, LEUCINE, AZOLE

element See under "element"

radical TOLYL, BUTYL, ETHYL, BENZYL

salt SAL

suffix ANE, YL, AN,
ENE, OLIC
   salt suffix ITE, ATE
chemise SHIFT,
LINGERIE, SHIRT,
SMOCK
chemist ANALYST,
DRUGGIST, ALCHEMIST,
APOTHECARY
vessel RETORT
cheri(e) DEAR
cherish AID, ADORE,
PET, SAVE, PRESERVE,
FOSTER, NURSE,
NURTURE, LOVE,
PRIZE, TREASURE,
ENJOY, LIKE, PRO-
TECT, CARE, VALUE,
ESTEEM, REVERE,
DOTE, NOURISH, SUS-
TAIN, SUPPORT,
COMFORT, INDULGE,
PROTECT
cherry CAPULIN,
RUDDY, MORELLO,
MOREL, GEAN,
AMARELLE, OXHEART,
DUKE, NAPOLEON
acid CERASIN
red CERISE
sour AMARELLE
sweet LAMBERT,
OXHEART
wild MAZZARD, GEAN,
MARASCA
cherub(s)
SERAPH(IM), SPIRIT,
ANGEL
Cheshire district
MARPLE, HOOLE, HALE
chess, *defeat at* MATE
opening MOVE,
DEBUT, GAMBIT
piece MAN, BISHOP,
CASTLE, KNIGHT,
QUEEN, KING, PAWN,
ROOK
term FIDATE
chest *See* "cabinet"
THORAX, COFFER,
CASE, KIST, ARCA, ARK,
LOCKER, BOX, COFFIN,
CASKET, TREASURY,
BASKET, CONTAINER
animal's BRISKET,
THORAX
medieval BAHUT
pertaining to
THORACIC
sound RALE, RHONCUS
Chester, Eng., pertain-
ing to CESTRIAN

chesterfield SOFA, COAT
chestnut SATIVA,
CRENATA, DENTATA,
HORSE, BROWN
Chinese LING
color MAROON, ROAN
Polynesian RATA
water LING
chevron STRIPE,
MARK, RANK, MOLD-
ING
chevrotain NAPU,
DEERLET, KANCHIL
chevy *See* "chivy"
chew GRIND, CHAW,
MANDUCATE, MUNCH,
EAT, CHAM, GNAW,
CHAVEL, MEDITATE,
QUID, CUD, CHAMP,
BITE, MASTICATE,
CRUNCH
inability to AMASESIS
chewing gum ingredient
CHICLE
chewink TOWHEE,
BIRD
Chibcha ZIPA, ZAQUA,
INDIAN
chic PERT, SMART,
STYLISH, MODISH,
NATTY, DAPPER,
SPRUCE, NIFTY, POSH
Chicago district LOOP
chicanery TRICKERY,
SOPHISTRY, RUSE,
FEINT, WILE,
DUPLICITY, CHICANE,
DECEPTION, ARTIFICE,
INTRIGUE
chicken FOWL, HEN,
PULLET, FRYER,
BROILER, LAYER
young POULT, CHICK
chick-pea GRAM,
GARAVANCE, HERB
genus CICER
chickweed ALSINE,
ARENARIA
chicle GUM, LATEX
chicory SUCCORY,
ENDIVE, PLANT, ROOT
chide (BE)RATE,
BLAME, RAKE, SCOLD,
REPROVE, REBUKE,
ADMONISH, CENSURE
chief PRINCIPAL,
LEADER, THANE,
MAJOR, ELDER,
PRIME, STAPLE,
ARCH, CAPTAIN, RAIS,
VITAL, REIS, HEAD,
MAIN, MASTER,

CAPITAL, RULER,
SUPREME, FIRST,
TITAN
magistrate SYNDIC
oriental SIRDAR, KHAN
chigoe (chigger)
FLEA, INSECT
chikara ANTELOPE
chilblain KIBE, BLAIN,
PERNIO
child BAIRN, BATA,
CHIT, TAD, TIKE,
TYKE, TOT, GAMIN,
BRAT, SON, KID, ARAB,
INFANT, BABE,
BANTLING, OFFSPRING
combining form
PAED(O), PED(O)
*dedicated to monastic
life* OBLATE
mixed blood MESTEE,
MUSTEE, OCTOROON
of light and day EROS
pertaining to FILIAL
small BABE, BRAT,
PEEWEE, BABY, TOT
childish SILLY, IM-
MATURE, NAIVE,
PUERILE, FOOLISH,
ASININE, INFANTILE,
JUVENILE, YOUNG,
CREDULOUS
childlike NAIVE,
DOCILE, MEEK, DUTI-
FUL, INNOCENT
children PROGENY,
OFFSPRING
dislike of MISOP(A)-
EDIA
of heaven and earth
TITANS
patron saint of SANTA
Chile, Chilean
aborigine INCA
capital SANTIAGO
city or town TALCA,
ANGOL, LOTA
coin ESCUDO, PESO,
CONDOR
desert ATACAMA
island HOSTE
meaning of SNOW
mineral bath COLINA,
TORO
mountain MAIPU,
PULAR
province MAULE,
ARAUCO, CAUTIN,
NUBLE
river ITATA, LOA,
BIO-BIO, MAIPU

seaport LOTA, TOME, COQUIMBA
shrub LITHI
tree See under "tree"
volcano LASCAR, LLAIMA, CALBUCO
wind SURES
chill COLD, ICE, RIGOR, ALGOR, SHIVER, AGUE, MALARIA, NIP, SHAKE, FREEZE, FRAPPE, FROST, FRIGID, GELID, DISHEARTEN
chilly ALGID, BLEAK, RAW, COOL, COLD, GELID, FROSTY, FRIGID, ICY, ARCTIC
chime CYMBAL, EDGE, RIM, BELL, AGREE, SUIT, JINGLE, CHIMB, CHINE, ACCORD, HARMONY, MELODY
chimerical UTOPIAN, ROMANTIC, WILD, VAIN, FANCIFUL, FANTASTIC, IMAGINARY
chimney FLUE, PIPE, TEWEL, FISSURE, CLEFT, TUBE, GULLY, VENT, FUNNEL, OPENING, STACK
piece PAREL, MANTEL
revolving cover COWL
chin(s) MENTUM, MENTA, CHATTER, JAW
combining form GENIO
china PORCELAIN, CROCKERY, DISH(ES), DRESDEN, ORANGE, SILK, CERAMIC
China, Chinese SERES, CATAIAN, SERIC, CATHAY, SINIC, MONGOL, CERAI
aborigine MANS, MANTZU
ancient state TSAO, CATHAY
arch PAILOU, PAILOO, PAILOW
assembly HUI
blue NIKKO
boat JUNK, BARK, SAMPAN
Buddha FO
Caucasian LOLO, NOSU
chestnut LING

city or town TSINGTAO, AMOY, PEIPING, PEKING, CANTON, SUCHOW, BATANG (PAAN), SHASI, YAAN, WUHU, URGA, TAIAN, SIAN, KIAN, TAKU, IPIN (SUCHOW)
civet RASSE
cloth MOXA, PULO, SHA, SILK
coin CASH, TAEL, TAIO, YUAN, LIANG, SEN, MACE, FAN, NEU, TICAL, TSIEN
combining form SINO, SINIC(O)
department FU, HSIEN
dialect WU, CANTON
district or division MIAO, HSIEN, CHOW
divinity JOSS
dog CHOW, PEKE
duck eggs PIDAN
dynasty HAN, KIN, WEI, MING, SHANG, HSIA, SUI, SUNG, TANG, TSIN, YIN, CHIN, CHOU, MANCHU
first HSIA
exchange medium SYCEE
factory HONG
feudal state WEI
fir NIKKO
fish TREPANG
gateway See "arch" *above*
god See under "god"
grass BON
guild HUI, TONG
harbor CHEFOO *See* "seaport" *below*
idol JOSS, PAGODA
indigo ISATIS
island AMOY, QUEMOY
jade YU
kilometer LI
kingdom WU, WEI
laborer COOLIE
language SHAN, WU, CANTON
mandarin's residence YAMEN
measure MU, HO, LI, HU, SEI, SHEN(G), FEN, TO(U), TSUN, YIN, KO, CHANG, TU, TAU, PU, LIP, CHAO, CHEUK, CHO, COBRE, FAN, FU,

KING, KISH, KOH, KUNG, MAO, PING, PO, TCHING, TCHUNG, TEKE, TSAN, YAN, YU
merchant's corporation HONG
mile LI
money PU, MACE, TAEL, YUAN, TIAO, SYCEE *See* "coin" *above*
Mongol dynasty YUAN
monkey DOUC
mountain(s) SUNG, OM(E)I
musical instrument KIN, SAMISEN
negative principle YIN
noodles MEIN
numeral, hundred TAI
thousand TSAN, CH'AN
one to ten YI(H), URH (ER), S(H)AN, SZE, WOO (WU), LUH (LIU), TSI(EH), PA, KEW (CHIU), SHIH (TSU)
nurse AMAH
official KUAN, KWAN
oil tree TUNG
one thousand cash TIAO
orange color MANDARIN
ounce TAEL
pagoda TA, TAA
pertaining to SINO, SINESIAN, SERIC, SINIC, CATAIAN
philosopher MOTI, LAOTSE, LAOTZU, MOTZU
plant GINSENG, RAMIE, RICE, TEA, TCHE
poet LIPO
positive principle YANG
pound CATTY
pottery KUAN, MING, TING
president SEN, SUN
province or state FUKIEN, KANSU, HONAN, HOPEH, YUNNAN, SIKAN, HUNAN, HUPEH, KIANGSI, SHANSI

public KUNG
race SINIC, LOLO, MONGOL
religion TAOISM
river See under "river"
root, dried GALANGAL, GINSENG
ruler YAO, YAU
sauce SOY
seaport CANTON, AMOY, CHEFOO
secret society HUI, TONG
sect TAOISM
servant AMAH
shrub TEA
silk PONGEE, TASAR, TUSSAH, SHANTUNG
silkworm SINA, AILANTHUS, TUSSER, TUSSAH
silver SYCEE
skiff SAMPAN
sky TIEN
sleeping platform KANG
society HUI, HOEY, TONG
sovereign KUBLA
tax LIKIN
tea OOLONG, CHA, CONGO(U), HYSON
temple TAA, PAGODA
territorial division See "province" above
thousand TSAN, S(H)AN
town See "city" above
treaty port AMOY
tree NIKKO, GINKGO, KINKAN, KUMQUAT
tribe HU
  Tatar TOBA, HU
vegetable UDO
wax, insect PELA
weight LIANG, YIN, LI, TAEL, CATTY, PICUL, HAO, FEN, KIN, SSU, TAN, CHIN, CHU, KWAN, LUI, SHU, TCHEN
  ounce TAEL
wind instrument CHENG, SHENG
wormwood MOXA
chine FISSURE, RAVINE, SPINE, SILK, RIDGE, CREST
chink CRACK, CRANNY, RIMA RIME, BORE,

CLEFT, RENT, FISSURE, INTERSTICE, OPENING, GAP, CREVICE, RIFT, APERTURE
chinky RIFTY, RIMOSE
Chinook WIND, INDIAN, FLATHEAD
chief TYEE
conference or pow-wow WAWA
salmon QUINNAT
chinquapin CHESTNUT, OAK
chinse CLOSE, CALK, SEAM
chip NICK, SPLINTER, FLAKE, SCRAP, BIT, FRAGMENT, COUNTER
of stone GALLET, SPALL
chipmunk HACKEE, RODENT, SQUIRREL
chipper LIVELY, PERKY, SPRY, COCKY, GAY, TWITTER
chiro FISH
chirp CHEEP, PIPE, PEEP, TWITTER, RE-JOICE
chiru ANTELOPE
chisel BURIN, GOUGE, TWIBIL, TOOL, CUT, PARE, CHEAT, CARVE, SCULPTURE, FABRICATE, FORM
ancient CELT
broad DROVE
mason's POMMEL
paring SKEW
stone CELT
chit CHILD, INFANT, NOTE, IOU, VOUCHER, RICE, SPROUT, SHOOT
chiton LIMPET, MOLLUSK, ROBE, GOWN
chivalrous BRAVE, NOBLE, POLITE, CIVIL, HONORABLE, GENTEEL, GALLANT, VALIANT, KNIGHTLY
chive CLOVE, BULBET, KNIFE, CUT, STAB, ONION
chivy, chevy CHASE, NAG, RUN, FLIGHT, PURSUE, HUNT, GAME, TEASE, CRY
chlamys CLOAK, MANTLE, GARMENT
chlorine GAS, CL
family BROMIN(E),

IODIN(E)
chlorophosphate APATITE
chock CLEAT, WEDGE, BLOCK, CHUCK
chocolate CACAO, CANDY, COCOA, DRINK
powder PINOLE, COCOA
source COCOA, CACAO
stick for mixing MOLINET
tree COLA, CACAO
choice ELITE, PICK(ED), SELECT, RARE, CREAM, BEST, A-ONE, DAINTY, DELICATE, CHOSEN, EXCELLENT, POLE, VOTE, OPTION, CHARY, DESIRE, OPT, MIND, WILL, ALTERNA-TIVE
choir vestment COTTA, SURPLICE, GOWN
choke CLOG, PLUG, DAM, BURKE, HINDER, GAG, CLOSE, STIFLE, WORRY, SMOTHER, STRANGLE, THROTTLE
choler WRATH, IRE, ANGER, RAGE, BILE, FURY, SPLEEN
choleric IRATE, IRACUND, TESTY, HUFFY, CROSS, ANGRY, MAD, FIERY, IRRITABLE, WASPISH, TOUCHY
choose VOTE, ELECT, OPTATE, CULL, OPT, PREFER, SELECT, PICK, ADOPT, ESPOUSE, EM-BRACE
jointly COOPT, ELECT
chop CHIP, CUT, HEW, MINCE, HACK, LOP, AXE, JOWL, DICE, SLIT, SLASH, CARVE, SPLIT, RIVE, CLEAVE
chopping instrument AX, AXE, HATCHET, CLEAVER
chord TRIAD, TONE, STRING, HARMONY
kind MINOR, MAJOR, SEVENTH, NINTH
ninth NONE
seventh TETRAD
chore TASK, CHARE, JOB, DUTY, STINT, WORK

chortle CHUCKLE,
SNORT, LAUGH
chorus CHOIR, ACCORD,
UNISON, SONG,
SINGERS, REFRAIN
girl CHORINE, DANCER,
SINGER
Chosen KOREA
chough CROW, BIRD
chow FOOD, EATS,
GRUB, FODDER,
FORAGE, MESS, DOG
chowchow OLIO,
SLAW, PICKLES,
HODGEPODGE,
MIXTURE, CUCKOO
Christ *stopped at*
EBOLI
thorn of NABK, NUBK
Christian *feast* AGAPE
oriental UNIAT
symbol of early
ORANT, ICHTHUS
unity IRENICS
Christianity, *promoting*
of IRENICS
Christian Science
founder EDDY
Christmas NOEL,
XMAS, YULE(TIDE),
FESTIVAL
carol NOEL, NOWEL
crib CRECHE
drink NOG
food, Dutch EEL
mummer GUISER
trim TINSEL, HOLLY
chromium CR, METAL
chromosome IDANT
chronic SETTLED,
ROOTED, FIXED,
INVETERATE, CON-
STANT, CONTINUOUS
chronicle ACCOUNT,
ANNAL(S), DIARY,
HISTORY, RECORD,
STORY, RECITAL,
REGISTER, NARRATIVE
chronological error
PROLEPSIS,
ANACHRONISM
chronometry DATE,
EPOCH, ERA
chrysalis, *early* PUPA
insect AURELIA,
KELL
chrysolite PERIDOT,
OLIVINE
chub FOOL, CHEVIN,
DACE, SHINER, CHOPA,
LOUT, MACKEREL,
BASS, FISH, DOLT

chuck FOOD, GRUB,
BEEF, CHOCK, THROW,
PITCH, TOSS, CLUCK,
LOG, LUMP, HURL
chuckle CHORTLE,
CLUCK, LAUGH,
GIGGLE, TITTER, EXULT
chum CRONY, PAL,
BUDDY, FRIEND, BAIT
chunky STOUT, THICK,
SQUAT, STOCKY,
LUMPY, GAME
church FANE, TEMPLE,
CATHEDRAL, CHAPEL,
MOSQUE, KIRK,
SYNAGOGUE, BETHEL,
TABERNACLE, PAGODA,
MASJID, DENOMINA-
TION, CONGREGATION
altar end APSE
bench or seat PEW
bishopric SEE
body NAVE
calendar ORDO
chapel ORATORY
council SYNOD
court ROTA
deputy VICAR,
CURATE
dignitary PRIMATE,
BISHOP, DEAN, ABBOT,
PRELATE, POPE
dissenter SECTARY
district PARISH,
DIOCESE
division in SCHISM
doorkeeper OSTIARY
doxology DOXA,
GLORIA
episcopacy PRELACY
judicatory CLASSIS
jurisdiction PARISH,
SEE, DEANERY,
DIOCESE
land GLEBE
leader HIERARCH,
BISHOP, CARDINAL,
POPE
middle body NEF,
NAVE
officer BEADLE,
PRESBYTER, LECTOR
official SACRIST,
VERGER, SEXTON,
ELDER, PRESBYTER,
SACRISTAN *See*
"clergyman"
papal LATERAN
court SEE
part of TRANSEPT,
BEMA, ALTAR, PEW,
PULPIT

peace device
IRENICON
reader LECTOR
reading desk AMBO,
LECTERN
recess APSE
reliquary APSE
revenue BENEFICE,
TITHES
rite LAVABO, MASS,
COMMUNION,
BAPTISM, MARRIAGE
Roman BASILICA
Scotch KIRK
seaman's BETHEL
seat PEW
stipend PREBEND
tax TITHE
traffic in anything
sacred SIMONY
vault CRYPT
warden TRUSTEE,
SEXTON
wash basin LAVABO
Churchill's *daughter*
SARAH
order GARTER
churl BOOR, HIND,
KNAVE, OAF, CARL,
CEORL, VILLEIN, LOUT,
CLOWN, VASSAL,
RUSTIC, PEASANT,
MISER, NIGGARD
churlish RUSTIC,
SORDID, CURT, BLUNT,
GRUFF, SOUR, DOUR,
RUDE, SULLEN,
CRABBED, SULKY,
SURLY
cibol ONION, SHALLOT
ciborium PYX,
CANOPY, COFFER
cicada LOCUST
cicatrix SCAR, MARK
cicatrization HEALING,
ULOSIS
cicely MYRRH, PARSLEY
cicerone CONDUCTOR,
PILOT, GUIDE,
COURIER
cichlid BOLTI, SUN-
FISH
cicisbeo KNOT,
STREAMER, RIBBON,
GALLANT, CAVALIER
Cid RUY, BIVAR,
RODRIGO, CHIEF,
COMMANDER, HERO,
TITLE, EPIC, POEM
sword of COLADA
cider, *weak* PERKIN

cigar CORONA, STOGY,
CLARO, CULEBRA,
CHEROOT, STOGIE,
BELVEDERE
fish SCAD
inferior TOBY
long thin PANATELA,
STOGY, STOGIE
mild CLARO
cigarette CUBEB, FAG,
GASPER, CIGARILLO
cilium LASH, EYELASH,
HAIR, BARBICEL
cimmerian BLACK,
GLOOMY
cinch FASTEN, BELT,
GRIP, GIRD, GIRTH,
CERTAINTY
cinchona QUININE,
BARK, TREE
cincture GIRDLE,
BALDRIC, CESTUS,
COMPASS, ENCLOSURE,
FILLET, BAND
cinder(s) SLAG,
ASH(ES), CLINKER,
EMBER, SCORIA,
DROSS, LAPILLA, GRAY
cinema SCREEN,
MOVIE, FILM,
FLICK(ER)
cinerarium
MORTUARY, URN
cinnabar ORE,
VERMILION
cinnamon CANEL(L),
CASSIA, ISHPINGO,
SPICE
stone GARNET,
ESSONITE
cinquefoil CLOVER,
PLANT, HERB, DESIGN
cion GRAFT,
DESCENDANT, SHOOT,
BUD, SCION, UVULA
Cipango NIPPON,
JAPAN
cipher NAUGHT, CODE,
MONOGRAM, ZERO,
FIGURE, NIL, NOBODY,
LETTER, SYMBOL,
DEVICE, CRYPTOGRAM
cipo LIANA, VINE
circa ABOUT, AROUND
Circe TEMPTER,
SORCERESS
father HELIOS
island AEAEA
circle ROTATE, TWIRL,
WHIRL, SWIRL, TURN,
GYRE, COTERIE,

FRIENDS, CLIQUE,
CLASS, SET, CORDON,
PARTY, INFLUENCE,
GROUP, REALM,
REGION, GIRD(LE),
DISK, CAROL, ORB,
RHOMB, RIGOL, LOOP,
RING, GLOBE, FRAME,
HOOP
celestial sphere
COLURE
of light HALO,
NIMBUS, AURA
part of ARC, SECTOR,
CHORD, SECANT,
RADIUS
circuit LAP, TOUR,
DETOUR, AMBIT,
ZONE, COMPASS,
ORBIT, ROUTE, CYCLE
of judges EYRE
circuitous WINDING,
CURVED, MAZY,
DEVIOUS, SINUOUS,
INDIRECT
circular BILL, MAIL,
LETTER, PAMPHLET,
PUBLICATION, ROUND,
DISCOID, GLOBULAR,
ORBED, ANNULAR,
CYCLOID
motion GYRE, EDDY
ornament PATERA
plate DISC, DISK
circulate SPREAD,
DIFFUSE, ROTATE,
TURN, PUBLISH,
MOVE, MIX,
PROMULGATE,
PROPAGATE
circumference BOUND-
ARY, AMBIT, BORDER,
GIRTH, PERIPHERY,
PERIMETER
circumlocution
AMBAGE, VERBIAGE,
WINDING, PERIPHRASE,
REDUNDANCY
circumspect PRUDENT,
WARY, CAREFUL,
CHARY, ALERT, AT-
TENTIVE, CAUTIOUS,
DISCREET
circumstance STRAIT,
EVENT, STATE,
EPISODE, PHASE,
PLACE, PICKLE, FIX,
ITEM, ELEMENT,
SITUATION, FOOTING,
DETAIL, INCIDENT,
FACTOR, FACT, CONDI-

TION, ENVIRONMENT,
PARTICULAR
circumvent DUPE,
TRICK, EVADE,
BAFFLE, THWART,
FOIL, BALK, CHECK,
CHEAT, COZEN, HINDER
circus rider DESULTOR
cirque CIRCLE(T),
EROSION, CORRIE,
RECESS
cistern SAC, VAT,
IMPLUVIUM, CAVITY,
WELL, TANK,
RESERVOIR, CUVETTE
citadel TOWER, ALAMO,
CASTLE, STRONGHOLD,
FORT(RESS)
cite QUOTE, MENTION,
SUMMON, ADDUCE,
CALL, TELL, ARRAIGN,
MUSTER, ALLEGE,
AROUSE, EXTRACT, AC-
CUSE
citizen VOTER,
RESIDENT, NATIVE,
ELECTOR, DENIZEN,
CIT, DWELLER,
BURGHER, OPPIDAN,
INHABITANT
citron LEMON, LIME,
CEDRAT(E), YELLOW
citrus *drink* ADE
fruit CITRON, LEMON,
ORANGE, LIME,
CEDRAT(E), GRAPE-
FRUIT
citternhead DUNCE
city TOWN, METROPO-
LIS, MUNICIPALITY
cathedral LINCOLN,
YORK, PARIS, ROME,
ELY
of God(s) ASGARD,
ZION, PARADISE,
HEAVEN
of Masts LONDON
of Palm Trees
JERICHO
of Seven Hills ROME,
ROMA
of the Violet Crown
ATHENS
of Victory CAIRO
oldest DAMASCUS
pertaining to URBAN
civet RASSE, NANDINE,
CAT
like GENET
palm PAGUMA,
MUSANG
tree-climbing RASSE

civic POLITE, SECULAR, LAY, CIVIL, SUAVE, URBANE
club LIONS, ROTARY
pertaining to OPPIDAN, URBAN
civil POLITIC(AL), KIND, COURTLY, HEND(E), POLITE, BLAND, URBANE, SUAVE, COURTEOUS
war battle SHILOH
wrong TORT
civilian dress MUFTI
civilize REFINE, EDUCATE, TRAIN, POLISH, CULTIVATE, TEACH
clad ATTIRED, ROBED, CLOTHED
claim ASK, ALLEGE, LIEN, TITLE, ASSERT, RIGHT, DEMAND, EXACT, REQUIRE, CHALLENGE, HOME-STEAD
presumptiously AR-ROGATE, USURP
clairvoyant PROPHET, SEER
clam STEAMER, SOLEN, QUAHOG, RAZOR, MOLLUSK, BIVALVE
genus MYA, SOLEN
giant CHAMA
like CHAMA, COCKLE, MUSSEL
long MYA, RAZOR
razor SOLEN
round QUAHOG
shell opening GAPE
clamor TUMULT, RACKET, BUNK, DIN, BERE, WAIL, ROAR, NOISE, OUTCRY, BLARE
clamp PIN, VISE, GRIP, CLASP, NAIL, TIE, LUG, BOLT, FASTEN(ING)
clan TRIBE, RACE CLIQUE, GENS, CASTE, SIB, SEPT, FAMILY, PARTY, SET, GROUP, FRATERNITY, CLASS
emblem TOTEM, XAT
head of THANE, ELDER, CHIEF
clandestine SECRET, COVERT, SLY, FOXY, ILLICIT, FURTIVE, STEALTHY
clang PEAL, DING,

RING, JANGLE, CLANK, CLASH
clangor HUBBUB, ROAR, DIN, UPROAR, CLANG
clannish TRIBAL, UNITED, CLOSE, SECRET
clap STRIKE, BANG, APPLAUD, CHEER, EXPLOSION
clarify PURIFY, CLEAN, CLEAR, ILLUMINATE, FREE, DEPURATE, EXPLAIN
clarinet REED
mouthpiece BIRN
clash JAR, DIFFER, COLLIDE, IMPACT, SHOCK, BOLT, BRUNT, STRIFE, DISCORD, NOISE, SOUND, CRASH, DISAGREE(MENT)
clasp HUG, ENFOLD, HASP, TACH(E), EM-BRACE, HOOK, HOLD, PIN, SEIZE, CLING, GRASP, GRIP, CLUTCH, BUCKLE, CATCH, FASTEN
class CASTE, GENUS, ILK, ORDER, RANK, FAMILY, SPECIES, RACE, TRIBE, KIND, TYPE, SORT, BREED, CLAN, DESCRIPTION, DIVISION, GENERA, GRADE, VARIETY, GROUP, SEMINAR, CATEGORY
classic STANDARD, MODEL, MASTERPIECE, BOOK, COMPOSITION
classical CHASTE, PURE, ATTIC, FIRST-RATE, GREEK, ROMAN, LATIN, MASTERLY
classification GROUP-ING, CATEGORY, SORT, GENUS, ORDER, TAXONOMY, ANALYSIS, TAXIS, SYSTEM, FILE, DIVISION, ARRANGE-MENT, NOMENCLATURE
classifier TYPER, FILER
classify TICKET, LIST, DIGEST, RATE, RANK, (AS)SORT, CATA-LOG(UE), REGISTER, TYPE, FILE, LABEL, ORDER, ARRANGE,

MARSHAL, CATEGORIZE, DISTRIBUTE, DISPOSE
clatter RATTLE, NOISE, RACKET, DIN, BABBLE, PRATE, PRATTLE
clause ARTICLE, PROVISION, PROVISO, PLANK, SENTENCE, STIPULATION, CONDI-TION, PART, PASSAGE
clavis GLOSSARY, KEY
clavus CORN, BUNION, BAND, STRIPE, CALLOUS
claw NAIL, TALON, UNCUS, UNCE, UNGUIS, UNGULA, HOOK, GRASP, SCRAPE, LACERATE, SCRATCH, DIG
of crustacean CHELA
clay BOLE ARGIL, LOESS, MUD, LOAM, KAOLIN(E), EARTH, MIRE
baked ADOBE, BRICK, TILE, TASCO
bed GAULT
box SAGGER
burned piece TESTA
calcium carbonate MARL
composition LUTE
constituent ALUMINA
covered with LUTOSE
deposit LOESS
mineral NACRITE
mold DOD
molded PUG, BRICK
pack with TAMP
plug BOTT
polishing RABAT
potter's ARGIL
prepare for pottery PUG, BOTT
rich MALM, MARL
clayey LUTOSE, BOLAR, MALMY
soil BOLE, MARL, LOESS
clean PURE, DECENT, CHASTE, UNSTAINED, TRIM, SPOTLESS, UN-DEFILED, PERFECT, MOP, SWAB, DUST, SWEEP, WASH, SCOUR, ENTIRE, EMPTY
Hebrew KOSHER
ship's bottom BREAM
cleaner RAMROD, PURER, SOAP, DETERGENT
fish SCALER

cleanse ABSTERGE,
DEPURATE, DETERGE,
PURGE, RINSE, WASH,
DISINFECT, CLEAN,
PURIFY, ELUTRIATE
cleansing WASHING,
PURIFYING, PURIFICA-
TION, ACQUITTAL,
ABLUENT
clear ACQUIT,
EXONERATE, RID, FREE,
RELEASE, LIBERATE,
VINDICATE, PELLUCID,
PLAIN, DISTINCT,
SHARP, VIVID, LIGHT,
OPEN, LIMPID, BRIGHT,
PATENT, LUCENT,
CLEAN, LOUD, NET,
FAIR, PURE, CRYSTAL,
SIMPLE, TRANSPARENT,
CLOUDLESS, EVIDENT,
OBVIOUS, VISIBLE,
CERTAIN, INTEL-
LIGIBLE, MANIFEST
clearing of land SART,
ASSART
cleat BATTEN, STRIP,
KEVEL, CHOCK, BLOCK,
BOLLARD
make fast around
BELAY
cleave ADHERE, CLING,
JOIN, LINK, UNITE,
COHERE, STICK, HOLD,
DIVIDE, SPLIT, RIVE,
REND, TEAR, RIP, CUT,
HEW, CHOP, SLIT,
DISPART, SEPARATE,
SUNDER, SEVER,
BISECT
cleaver FROE, FROW,
AX(E)
cleche(e) URDE(E),
CROSS-SHAPED
cleft CLOVEN, FISSURE,
BREACH, FORKED,
CREVICE, CHINK,
CHAP, CRACK, RIMA,
REFT, GAP, RIFT,
CHASM
Clemens TWAIN,
MARK, SAM
clement MILD,
LENIENT, MERCIFUL,
TOLERANT, KIND,
BENIGN, TENDER,
GENTLE, HUMANE,
COMPASSIONATE
Cleopatra's *attendant*
IRAS
lover ANTONY
needle OBELISK

river NILE
suicide instrumentality
ASP
clepe CHRISTEN,
NAME, BID, CALL, CRY,
APPEAL, MENTION
clepsydra CLOCK, DIAL
clergy(man) CURATE,
CANON, VICAR, DEAN,
PRIEST, ABBE, RECTOR,
RABBI, CLOTH,
CLERIC(AL), CLERK,
PULPIT, PADRE,
DOMINE, PRIOR,
PASTOR, PARSON,
DIVINE
residence MANSE,
VICARAGE, PARSONAGE
cleric *See* "clergy-
man"
hat for BIRETTA
non LAIC
vestment of AMICE,
ALB, FANON, ORALE,
CLOTH
clerk SCRIBE, SALES-
MAN, LAYMAN,
REGISTRAR, TELLER,
RECORDER, AGENT
clever APT, ADROIT,
DEFT, SMART, CUTE,
BRIGHT, QUICK, ABLE,
KEEN, ALERT, HANDY,
AGILE, EXPERT,
DEXTEROUS, SLY,
ARTFUL, SLICK, OILY,
SKILLFUL, INTEL-
LIGENT
clevis CATCH, HOOK
clew GLOBE, BALL,
SKEIN, TINT, KEY,
CUE *See* "clue"
cliche TRUISM,
BROMIDE, BANALITY
click PAWL, RATCHET,
CATCH, DETENT, TICK,
AGREE
client PATRON,
PATIENT, RETAINER,
CUSTOMER, HENCH-
MAN
cliff BLUFF, CRAG,
HEIGHT, KLIP,
CLEVE, SHORE, SCAR,
PRECIPICE, PALISADE,
SCARP
channel between GAT
climax MOUNT, SCALE,
ZENITH, ACME,
APOGEE, CAP, PEAK,
APEX, SUMMIT, TOP,
ASCEND, CULMINATION

climb RISE, SPEEL,
GRIMP, SHIN, MOUNT,
ASCENT, ASCEND,
GRADE, SCALE, CLAM-
BER, CREEP, TWINE
climbing fish ANABAS
clime REALM, REGION,
ZONE, CLIMATE
clinch CLUTCH, SEIZE,
GRIP, NAIL, CLAMP,
EMBRACE, FASTEN,
RIVET, CONFIRM,
BIND, SEAL, GET,
GRASP, SECURE, COM-
PLETE, SNATCH, HUG
cling STICK, HOLD,
CLEAVE, ADHERE,
GRASP, COHERE, RELY,
TRUST, BANK, HANG,
PERSEVERE
clingfish TESTAR
clink PRISON, JAIL,
JUG, RIME, RHYME,
JINGLE, RING, TINKLE,
SLAP, INSTANT
clinquant TINSEL,
SHOWY
clip SHEAR, SNIP,
TRIM, PRUNE, DOCK,
SHORTEN, CUT, PARE,
LOP, BARB, CLASP,
FASTEN, BLOW, RAP,
WHACK, HINDER, PACE,
HOLDER, LIP
clique RING, COTERIE,
SET, CIRCLE, PARTY,
BLOC, JUNTO, CLUB,
SODALITY, CABAL,
GANG, CONCLAVE
cloaca maxima
SEWER, DRAIN
cloak DOLMAN, GREGO,
MANTO, MANTLE,
CAPE, WRAP,
CAPOT(E), ROBE,
COVER, SHIELD, DRESS,
SAGUM, PALL, DIS-
GUISE, MASK, CON-
CEAL, HIDE, SCREEN,
VEIL, BLIND
ancient Irish INAR
hooded CAPOTE,
CAMAIL, MOZZETTA
loose ABOLLA,
PALETOT, PELISSE,
PONCHO, ROBE
Spanish MANTA
cloche HAT, COVER,
JAR, BELL
clock NEF, TIME,
METER, WATCH, BELL,

GONG, DIAL, CHRO-
NOMETER, BEETLE
astronomical
SIDEREAL
ship-shaped NEF
water CLEPSYDRA
weight PEISE
clod LUMP, GROUND,
LOAM, EARTH, SOD,
TURF, CLOWN, FOOL,
DOLT
clodpate FOOL, IM-
BECILE, DOLT, BLOCK-
HEAD
clog SABOT,
CHOPIN(E), PATTEN,
SHOE, HAMPER, BALK,
FETTER, JAM, BLOCK,
CHOKE, RESTRAIN,
CHECK, CURB, HINDER,
SHACKLE, OBSTRUCT,
IMPEDE, DANCE
with mud DAGGLE,
DAUB
cloister NUNNERY,
ABBEY, FRIARY, STOA,
PRIORY, ARCADE,
AISLE, HALL,
CONVENT, MONAS-
TERY, PIAZZA
"Cloister and Hearth"
author READE
close NEAR, IMMINENT,
INTIMATE, SIMILAR,
FINAL(E), STIVY,
END, OCCLUDE, HOT,
SILENT, TIGHT,
(DE)BAR, BLOCK, DAM,
CEASE, QUIT, STOP,
SEAL, DENSE, SHUT,
FIRM, CODA, MUGGY,
STALE, DENSE, STUFFY,
STINGY, FRUGAL, TAUT,
SECRET, RETICENT,
HUG, NIGH, FINISH,
OBSTRUCT, TERMI-
NATE, ESTOP, CHOKE,
COMPACT, NIGGARD
keep HUG
mouthed person
CLAM
securely SEAL, LOCK
the eyes SEEL
closed body cavity
ATRESIA
closely ALMOST,
BARELY, NEARLY,
JUST, COMPACTLY
closet LOCKER,
ROOM, CABINET,
AMBRY, EWRY, CON-
CEAL, SECRET,

PRIVATE, WARDROBE,
CUPBOARD
closing measure, *music*
CODA
clot COAGULATE,
LUMP, MASS, STICK,
THICKEN, JELL, CON-
CRETE, GEL, CO-
AGULUM, SOLIDIFY
cloth NANKEEN,
PLISSE, CLERGY,
NAPKIN, RAG, TOWEL
See "fabric"
baptismal CHRISOM
blemish or blister in
AMPER, RIP, TEAR,
SNAG
camel's hair ABA,
CAMLET
chalice BURSE
checkered PLAID,
TARTAN
chrisom ALB, SUR-
PLICE
coarse LINSEY,
GUNNY, BURLAP,
CRASH
  hemp GUNNY
  BURLAP
  linen DOWLAS
dealer DRAPER,
MERCER
dyed BATIK
finisher BEETLER
flaw BRACK
goat's hair TIBET,
CAMLET, MOHAIR
homespun KELT
insertion of cord
SHIRR
linen BRIN, DOWLAS,
CREA
measure ELL, NAIL,
YARD
metallic LAME
modern ACETATE,
RAYON, NYLON,
DACRON
mulberry bark TAPA
muslin ADATI
selvage LISTING,
ROON
soft PANNE, VELVET
straining TAMIS,
CHEESE, TAMMY
Tibet CAMLET
triangular piece
GORE
twilled JANE, JEAN,
SERGE, DENIM, REP
used as a dressing
STUPE

velvet PANNE
weatherproof TARP,
CANVAS
woolen TARTAN,
TWEED
wrapping TILLOT,
BURLAP
clothe ENDUE, TOG,
DRAPE, GARB, GIRD,
INVEST, VESTURE,
ATTIRE, DRESS,
ARRAY, ROBE, AP-
PAREL, DECK, SWATHE
clothes, clothing TOG-
GERY, TOGS, ATTIRE,
REGALIA, RIG, DRESS,
ARRAY, APPAREL,
VESTURE, DUDS, GARB,
GEAR, FRIPPERY,
RAIMENT, GARMENTS,
VESTMENTS, HABITS,
FROCK *See under*
"garment"
moth TINEA
Clotho, *spins* THREAD
cloud(s) CUMULUS,
NIMBUS, STRATUS,
NUBIA, CIRRUS, DE-
FECT, STIGMA, SULLY,
VAPOR, MIST, HAZE,
FOG, OBFUSCATE,
BLACKEN, STAIN,
TARNISH, SHADE,
SCREEN, SWARM
broken RACK
combining form
NEPHO
gaseous NEBULA
luminous NIMBUS
masses STRATI, RACKS,
CUMULI
nebula of comet
COMA
study of NEPHOLOGY
vapory RACK
wind-driven SCUD,
RACK
cloudy DULL, LOWERY,
FILMY, DIM,
MURKY, HAZY,
NUBILOUS, OBSCURE,
OVERCAST, FOGGY,
DISMAL, GLOOMY,
BLURRED, OPAQUE
clout SLUG, BUMP,
THRASH, HIT, STRIKE,
SMITE, BOX, CUFF,
SLAP, SWAT, BEAT,
WASHER, NAIL,
BANDAGE, PATCH,
MEND, CLOD

cloven CLEFT, SPLIT, BISULCATE
hoofed FISSIPED, SATANIC
clover MELILOT, ALSIKE, TREFOIL, LUCERN(E), MEDIC, ALFALFA, RED, PROSPERITY, LUXURY, COMFORT
three-leaf TREFOIL
clown OAF, COMIC, APER, LOUT, MIME, STOOGE, ZANY, BOOR, CHURL, FOOL, JESTER, LUBBER, BUFFOON, PUNCH, PUNCHINELLO, RUSTIC
boastful SCARAMOUCH
clownish CLUMSY, RUDE, ROUGH, RAW, GREEN, LOUTISH, COARSE, AWKWARD
cloy SATE, SATIATE, PALL, GORGE, CLOG, GLUT, SURFEIT
cloyed GORGED, FULL
club WEAPON, BAT, STICK, MACE, BILLY, SOCIETY, SORORITY, ORDER, LODGE, FRATERNITY, TEAM, ASSOCIATION
Irish SHILLELAGH
Maori MERE
service LIONS, KIWANIS, ROTARY, USO
shaped CLAVATE
social COTERIE, SORORITY, CARD, FRATERNITY
woman's SORORITY, DAR
clubfoot TALIPES
clue HINT, GUIDE, INTIMATION, KEY, TIP, BALL, THREAD, TWINE, INDICATION
clump GROVE, CLUSTER, BUNCH, TUFT, MOTT, MASS, HEAP, PATCH, GROUP
clumsy STUPID, INAPT, INEPT, AWKWARD, HEAVY, UNCOUTH, MALADROIT, GAUCHE, UNFIT, BIG, JUMBO, RUDE, GREEN, CALLOW, STIFF, TENSE, RIGID, UNWIELDLY, CUMBROUS
Cluny *product* LACE

clupeid HERRING, SHAD, SARDINE, MENHADEN, TELEOST, FISH
cluster CYME, FASCICLE, CLUMP, TUFT, KNOT, BUNCH, GROUP, COLLECTION, GLOMERULE
fibers NEP
flower CYME, RACEME, PANICLE, UMBEL
growing in ACERVATE
seven stars PLEIAD
clustered ACINIFORM, GLOMERATE, TUFTED
grains GRUMOSE
clutch GRIP, SNATCH, GRAB, CLAW, TALON, COUPLING, CLENCH, GRASP, CONTROL, POWER, CLETCH, LEVER, NEST, HATCH, SEIZE, RETAIN
clypeus SHIELD, PLATE, TISSUE
Clytemnestra's *mother* LEDA
son ORESTES
cnemis SHIN, TIBIA
coach STAGE, TRAIN, TEACH, HELP, TUTOR, BUS, ARABA, CARRIAGE, CAR
hackney JITNEY, TAXI
coachman WHIP, JEHU, FLY, FISH, PILOT, DRIVER
coagulant STYPTIC, RENNET
coagulate CONGEAL, SET, CAKE, CLOT, JELL, POSSET, GEL, CURDLE, THICKEN, CLABBER, SOLIDIFY
coal BASS, EMBER, CARBON, COKE, CINDER
bad SWAD, SMUT
bin BUNKER
brown LIGNITE
carrying box DAN, HOD, SCUTTLE
deposit, lateral face BORD
derivative CRESOL, PITCH, PARAFFIN, LYSOL
dust SOOT, SMUT, COOM(B), CULM
heat-treated COKE

immature form LIGNITE
miner COLLIER
refuse CULM, COOM(B), SLAG, CINDER, CLINKER
scuttle HOD
size EGG, PEA, CHESTNUT
volcanic SCORIA
wagon CORB, CORF, TRAM
waste COOM(B), CULM, GOAF, GOB
coalesce MERGE, UNITE, FUSE, BLEND, COMBINE
coalescence FUSION, LEAGUE, UNION
coalfish SEY, PARR, BESHOW, POLLACK, SAITHE
coarse ROUGH, CRUDE, HARSH, GROSS, RIBALD, RUDE, LOW, CRASS, VULGAR, BROAD, BAWDY, RAW, GREEN, CALLOW, IMPURE, INELEGANT, RANDY, DIRTY, UNPOLISHED
coast LAND, SEASIDE, BEACH, SEABOARD, LITTORAL, SHORE, RIPA, STRAND, BANK, SLIDE, GLIDE
dweller ORARIAN
pertaining to LITTORAL, ORARIAN, RIPARIAN, COASTAL
Coast Guard *woman* SPAR
coat COVER, CRUST, PLASTER, PAINT, GLAZE, PLATE, PROTECT, SHELL, JACKET, JERKIN, ULSTER, RIND, TUNIC, TOGA, JOSEPH, TOPPER, CUTAWAY, LAYER
animal's PELAGE, SKIN, PELT, HIDE, FUR, WOOL, HAIR
camel's or goat's hair ABA
coarse CAPOT(E)
double-breasted REEFER, REDINGOTE
hair MELOTE
long REDINGOTE
long-sleeved CAFTAN

loose PALETOT, SACK, MANTLE, ROBE
mail ARMOR, HAUBERK
man's close fitting SURTOUT
monk's MELOTE
with an alloy TERNE
coating *on copper or bronze* PATINA
inside of boiler FUR
on tongue FUR
coax LURE, TEASE, ENTICE, TEMPT, URGE, CAJOLE, WHEEDLE, FLATTER, PERSUADE
cob LEADER, HORSE, CHIEF, EAR, SWAN, GULL, MEW, LUMP, MUFFIN
black-backed GULL
cobalt CO, METAL
cobaltiferous arsenopyrite DANAITE
cobble DARN, MEND, PATCH, PAVE, BOTCH, BUNGLE, COBSTONE, REPAIR
cobbler CRISPIN, SHOEMAKER, SOUTER, SUTOR, PIE, DESSERT
wax CODE, PITCH
cobia BONITO, SERGEANT, COAL, FISH
cobra VIPER, NAJA, NAIA, MAMBA, RINGHALS, SNAKE
tree MAMBA
cobweb NET, TRAP, SNARE, INTRICACY
cocaine source COCA
Cochin China *capital* SAIGON
inhabitant ANNAMESE
cochlea, spiral of SCALA
cochleate SPIRAL
cock STACK, PILE, HEAP, MASS, BANK, SHOCK, FOWL, CHANTICLEER, ROOSTER, FAUCET, VALVE, RICK, YAWL, TAP
and bull story CANARD
cockade KNOT, ROSETTE, BADGE
cockatoo GALAH, COCKY, COCKIE,

ARA(RA), ARRA, MACAW
genus KAKATOE, CACATUA
cockatrice BASILISK, SERPENT
cockboat COG
cocker DOG, SPANIEL, PAMPER, CODDLE, PET, INDULGE, FONDLE, FIGHTER, SHOE, BOOT, LEGGING
cockeyed ALOP, AWRY
cockle GITH, KILN, OAST, SHELL, MOLLUSK, DARNEL, GALL, PUCKER, WRINKLE, RIPPLE
cockpit ARENA, CABIN, WELL, RING, COURT, FIELD, RINK
cockspur THORN, ACACIA, TREE
cocktail SIDECAR, MARTINI, APPETIZER, DRINK, APERITIF
cocky SMART, PERT, SAUCY, JAUNTY, CHIPPER, PROUD, CONCEITED
coco(a) PALM, TARO, CHOCOLATE, HEAD, YAUTIA
oilless BROMA
coconut husk fiber COIR
meat of dried COPRA
cocoon CLEW, POD, SHELL
thread BAVE, SILK
coco plum ICACO
cocuswood EBONY
cod BURBOT, COR, CULTUS, SCROD, CUSK, TORSK, BANK, ROCK, POLLACK, FISH
Alaskan WACHNA
like LING, HAKE, GADUS, BIB
pertaining to GADOID
coddle BABY, HUMOR, PAMPER, FONDLE, CARESS, PET, NURSE, COOK, PARBOIL
code CANON, LAW, CODEX, RULE, CIPHER, SECRET, SIGNAL, FLAG, DIGEST, PRECEPT
inventor MORSE
message in CRYPTOGRAM, CIPHER

codger FELLOW, MISER, NIGGARD, CRANK, CHURL
codicil DIPLOMA, RIDER, SEQUEL, APPENDIX, POSTSCRIPT, PROVISION
codify DIGEST, INDEX, CLASSIFY, SYSTEMATIZE
coehorn MORTAR
coelebs BACHELOR
coerce DRIVE, FORCE, MAKE, COMPEL, CURB, CONSTRAIN, BULLY, COW, MENACE, REPRESS, CHECK, RESTRAIN
coffee JAVA, MOCHA, RIO, SANTOS, BRAZIL, SUMATRA
berry exterior PULP
cup holder ZARF
extract CAFFEINE
house CAFE, INN
pot BIGGIN
root used with CHICORY
tree CHICOT
coffer CHEST, ARK, CAISSON, TRENCH, CASKET, TRUNK, DAM
coffin BOX, CASKET, SARCOPHAGUS
cloth CLOAK, PALL
pre-historic CIST
stand BIER
cog GEAR, CAM, CATCH, TOOTH, WHEEDLE, CHEAT, TENON, WEDGE
cogent STRONG, POTENT, VALID, SOUND, FORCIBLE, TRENCHANT, POWERFUL
cogitate THINK, MULL, MUSE, PONDER, WEIGH, PLAN, REFLECT, MEDITATE, CONSIDER
cognate RELATIVE, ALLIED, (A)KIN, ALIKE, KINDRED, SIMILAR, RELATED
cognizance KEN, HEED, NOTICE, MARK, EMBLEM, BADGE, KNOWLEDGE, OBSERVATION
cognizant AWAKE, AWARE, CONVERSANT, SENSIBLE, ON TO

cognize KNOW, PER-
CEIVE, RECOGNIZE

cognomen NAME,
TITLE, SURNAME,
PATRONYM(IC), AP-
PELLATION *See*
"name"

coheir PARCENER,
COPARCENER

cohere CLING, CLEAVE,
ADHERE, GLUTINATE,
STICK, GLUE, AGREE,
COINCIDE, SUIT, FIT,
UNITE

coiffure HAIRDO, HEAD-
DRESS

coil CURL, ANSA,
QUERL, TWINE, ROLL,
CIRCLE, SPIRAL, WIND,
SPIRE, LOOP, TWIST,
RINGLET, CONVOLU-
TION, TUMULT,
TROUBLE, DIFFICULTY,
CONFUSION
into ball CLUE, CON-
VOLVE

coin(s) *See under
country involved*
ORI, MONEY, QUOIN,
SPECIE, CASH, CUR-
RENCY, FABRICATE, IN-
VENT, MINT, STRIKE,
STAMP
American, early ROSA
box for METER, PYX,
TILL
collector NUMIS-
MATIST
copper CENT, PENNY
counterfeit SLUG,
RAP
edging REEDING,
MILLING, KNURLING
European, old DUCAT,
PISTOLE
front of OBVERSE
hole SLOT
medieval BANCO
pertaining to
NUMISMATIC(AL)
reverse VERSO
roll of ROULEAU
science of NUMISMAT-
ICS
sheckel, 1/20 of
GERAH
silver BATZ, DIME
silver amalgam
TESTER, TESTON, PINA
toss a BIRL
trifling DOIT, RAP

coincide CONCUR,
AGREE, JIBE, TALLY,
FIT, HARMONIZE,
CORRESPOND

coke COCAINE, COAL,
DOPE

col NECK, PASS

colander SIEVE,
STRAINER

cold GELID, BLEAK,
FRIGID, ICY, NIPPY,
RHEUM, CATARRH,
COOL, GLACIAL,
ARCTIC, CHILLED,
POLAR, FROSTY, WIN-
TRY, DULL, RESERVED,
INDIFFERENT, INSENSI-
BLE, DISPASSIONATE
biting ALGID
blooded UNFEELING,
POIKILOTHERMAL
combining form CRYO
mist DROW
pertaining to FRI-
GORIC, ICY, GELIC,
FRIGID
spell SNAP
steel BAYONET,
SWORD

Coleridge's "sacred
river" ALPH

colewort KALE, CAB-
BAGE

collapse BREAK, FAIL,
RUIN, FALL, CAVE,
WRECK, DOWNFALL,
PROSTRATION, CON-
TRACT, FOLD

collar GORGET, FICHU,
BERTHA, ETON, RUFF,
TORQUE, RING,
CIRCLET, SHACKLE,
SEIZE, NAB, CATCH
bone CLAVICLE
clerical RABAT
convict CARCAN(ET)
frilled RUFF
jeweled CARCANET
papal ORALE, FANON
plaited RUCHE
Roman RABAT
turned down RABATO,
REBATO
twisted TORQUE

collation TEA, MEAL,
REPAST, LUNCHEON,
COMPARISON, PARAL-
LEL

colleague ALLY, AIDE,
PARTNER, DEPUTY,
ASSOCIATE, ASSISTANT

collect SAVE, HOARD,
GARNER, PILE, COM-
PILE, LEVY, TAX,
(A)MASS, BAG,
SHEAVE, HEAP,
ASSEMBLE, MUSTER,
ACQUIRE, GATHER
little by little GLEAN

collection HEAP, PILE,
SET, ANA, LEVY,
MASS, STACK, AS-
SEMBLAGE, GROUP,
AGGREGATE, CROWD
of facts ANA,
ANALECTA
literary ANA, LIBRARY
of proper names
ONOMASTICON

colleen GIRL, MAID-
(EN), BLONDE, MISS,
LASS, BELLE, DAMSEL

college LYCEE,
ACADEMY, SCHOOL,
SEMINARY, UNIVERSITY
barracks DORM
building LAB
California MILLS,
UCLA, USC
Garden City
ADELPHI
Georgia EMORY
girl COED
graduate ALUMNUS,
ALUMNA
grounds QUAD,
CAMPUS, LAWN
group FRAT, SORORITY
hall AULA, DORM
Iowa COE
Kentucky BEREA
officer DEAN, PROC-
TOR, BURSAR, BEADLE,
PRESIDENT
professor DON,
DOCENT
servant GYP
treasurer BURSAR
tree ELM

collide BUMP, CLASH,
CRASH, HURTLE,
WRECK, HIT, STRIKE

collier MINER, VES-
SEL, BOAT, FLY,
PLOVER

colloquy CHAT, PAR-
LEY, TALK, DIALOGUE,
CONVERSATION, DIS-
COURSE

collude PLOT,
SCHEME, CONSPIRE,
CONNIVE

Cologne king CASPAR, JASPER

Colombia, Colombian
city or town CALI, PASTO, BUGA, BOGOTA
coin CONDOR, PESO, REAL
Indian See under "Indian"
lake TOTA
province or state CHOCO, CAUCA, VAUPES, BOLIVAR, NARINO, HUILA, CALDAS
river META *See under* "river"
volcano PASTO
weight SACO, CARGA
colonize SETTLE, FOUND, GATHER, ESTABLISH
colonizer ANT, SETTLER, OECIST
colonnade STOA, PORTICO, PERISTYLE
colonus SERF, LITUS
colophonite GARNET, ANDRADITE
colophony ROSIN
color(s) FLAG, ENSIGN, BANNER, PENNANT, JACK, SHADE, TINT, CAST, TONE, TINGE, HUE, DYE, PAINT, DISGUISE, ASH, BAY, RED, TAN, CREAM, BLUE, FAWN, GRAY, JADE, LIME, NAVY, NILE, PINK, ROSE, AMBER, BEIGE, CORAL, EBONY, HENNA, IVORY, MAUVE, MOCHA, SEPIA, UMBER, CERISE, COBALT, MAROON, SORREL, CARMINE, MAGENTA
expert at DYER, PAINTER
without WHITE, PALE, PLAIN, ACHROMA
Colorado *city* DENVER, LAMAR, PUEBLO, GOLDEN
county MESA, BACA, YUMA, WELD, KIOWA, BENT, DELTA, OTERO, OURAY, PARK
Indian ARAPAHO(E)
park ESTES
peak PIKES, ETHEL, BALDY

colorless PALLID, ASHEN, WAN, WHITE, CLEAR, BLANCHED, DULL, PALE, PLAIN, ACHROMIC
liquid ACETAL, WATER, PYRROL(E)
oil CETANE
colossal HUGE, GIGANTIC, MONSTROUS, ENORMOUS, VAST, IMMENSE, BIG, GREAT
See "huge"
colossus GIANT, TITAN, MONSTER, PRODIGY, STATUE *See* "giant"
colt FOAL, HORSE, FILLY, GUN, PISTOL
coluber SNAKE, SERPENT
Columbia University *symbol* LION
columbine bird DODO
columbo GENTIAN, PLANT, HERB
Columbus' *birthplace* GENOA
port of embarkation PALOS
ship NINA, PINTA, SANTA MARIA
Spanish name for COLON
column PILLAR, PILASTER, SHAFT, FORMATION, LINE, FILE, ROW, CYLINDER
arrange in TABULATE
base PLINTH
Buddhist LAT
figure, female CARYATID
  male TELAMON
Greek DORIC, IONIC
kind of ANTA
outward form of ENTASIS, GALBE
pertaining to COLUMNAR
ring of annulated BAGUE
shaft FUST, SCAPE
small STELE
square engaged ANTA, PILASTER
subbase STYLOBATE
support SOCLE
coma SLEEP, TORPOR, LETHARGY, STUPOR, TUFT, BUNCH, CLUSTER

comate HAIRY, COMOSE, COMPANION
comatose DROWSY, INSENSIBLE, OUT
comb CARD, CARUNCLE, CREST, CURRY, RIDGE, CLEAN, RAKE, SCRAPE
for cotton or wool TEASE, CARD
shaped like PECTINATE
combat ACTION, JOUST, COPE, STRIFE, WAR, FIGHT, BATTLE, ATTACK, ASSAIL, STORM, FURY, BRUSH, CONFLICT, CONTEST, SKIRMISH
challenge to single CARTEL
combination UNION, CARTEL, RING, CABAL, JUNTO, PARTY, BLOC, CORNER, POOL, TRUST, MERGER, LEAGUE, FACTION, COTERIE, COALITION, KEY
combine BLOC, FACTION, RING, JUNTO, CARTEL, POOL, AMALGAMATE, MERGE, UNION, CABAL, MIX, BLEND, SPLICE, MARRY, WED, JOIN, FEDERATE, ABSORB, ADD, UNITE, COOPERATE, MINGLE
combining form *See word involved*
combining power, *chemistry* VALENCE
combustion HEAT, THERM, BURNING, CONSUMING, OXIDATION
residue of ASH, CLINKER, GAS
come ARRIVE, REACH, NEAR, APPROACH, (A)RISE, ACCRUE, EMERGE, SPRING, EMANATE, ISSUE, STEM, ADVENE, ADVANCE
before PREVENE, PRECEDE
down ALIGHT, LAND
under SUBVENE
comedian BUFFOON, WIT, CARD, WAG, JESTER, ANTIC,

CLOWN, STOOGE,
COMIC, FOOL, BUFF,
BERLE, WYNN, HOPE,
SKELTON
comedy FARCE, SLAP-
STICK, DRAMA,
TRAVESTY
muse of THALIA
"Comedy of Errors"
character SOLINUS,
ANGELO, PINCH,
ADRIANA, LUCIANA,
LUCE
comely FAIR, PRETTY,
BONNY, LOVELY, BE-
COMING, FITTING,
SUITABLE, DECOROUS,
DECENT
comestible(s) MANNA,
VICTUAL, FOOD, VIAND,
EDIBLE, EATABLE,
ESCULENT
comet HALLEY'S,
BIELA'S, OLBER'S,
SWIFT'S, HOLMES',
SAPPHO, STAR, ENCKE'S
envelope or nebula
COMA
tail STREAMER
comfit PRALINE,
CANDY, SWEET, CON-
FECT(ION), SWEET-
MEAT, CONSERVE
comfort EASE,
NEPENTHE, SOLACE,
CHEER, AID, SOOTHE,
REST, REPOSE, DE-
LIGHT, RELIEF, CON-
SOLE, GLADDEN,
PLEASURE, QUILT
means of MONEY
producing EU-
DEMONIC
comfortable EUPHORIC,
COSH, SNUG, GRATI-
FYING, CONTENTED,
PLEASING
comic *See* "comedian"
FUNNY, DROLL
afterpiece EXODE
comical RISIBLE,
DROLL, FUNNY,
FARCICAL, BURLESQUE,
LUDICROUS, DIVERTING
coming ADVENT, AR-
RIVAL, IMPENDING,
DUE
comity URBANITY,
SUAVITY, CIVILITY,
COURTESY, AMENITY
command DICTATE,
PRESCRIBE, GOVERN,

RULE, EDICT, HEAD,
BECK, (BE)HEST, BID,
MANDATE, FIAT, EN-
JOIN, ORDER, ORDI-
NANCE, CALL, DIRECT,
CHARGE, CONTROL,
FORCE, MANAGE,
EXACT, REQUIRE,
COMPEL, POWER,
SWAY
the market CORNER
to a horse GEE, HAW,
HUP, WHOA
commander CID,
CHIEF, CAPTAIN,
MASTER, HEAD,
LEADER, COMMAN-
DANT, OFFICER
of fortress CAID,
ALCAIDE
commandment PRE-
CEPT, ORDER, RULE,
LAW
ten DECALOG(UE)
comme il faut PROPER,
FITTING
commemoration
MEDAL, AWARD,
SERVICE, CELEBRA-
TION, SOLEMNIZA-
TION, PLAQUE
commence (A)RISE,
OPEN, SPRING, BEGIN,
FOUND, INITIATE,
START, ORIGINATE,
INSTITUTE
commencement GRAD-
UATION, SOURCE, OUT-
SET
commend COMMIT, AP-
PROVE, PRAISE, EXTOL,
LAUD, BESPEAK, IN-
TRUST, COMPLIMENT
commensurate EQUAL,
EVEN, ENOUGH, AD-
EQUATE, APPROPRIATE,
CORRESPONDING
comment POSTIL, AN-
NOTATE, DESCANT,
ASIDE, REMARK, NOTE,
EXPOUND, EXPLAIN,
GLOSS
commentary REMARKS,
NOTES, ACCOUNT,
MEMOIR, TREATISE,
GLOSS(ARY)
commentator CRITIC,
GLOSSATOR, EXPOSI-
TOR, ANNOTATOR
commerce TRADE,
BARTER, TRAFFIC,
BUSINESS, EXCHANGE

commingle MIX,
BLEND, MINGLE,
MERGE, FUSE, UNITE,
JOIN, COMBINE,
AMALGAMATE
comminute MILL,
CRUSH, GRIND, PUL-
VERIZE, TRITURATE
comminuted FINE,
PULVERIZED
commiseration RUTH,
PITY, EMPATHY, COM-
PASSION, SYMPATHY,
CONDOLENCE
commission CHARGE,
WARRANT, BREVET,
ERRAND, TASK, PER-
MIT, PROXY, PERPE-
TRATION, ALLOWANCE,
COMPENSATION, DE-
PUTE, DELEGATE,
ORDAIN, ESTABLISH
commissure SEAM,
JOINT, MITRE,
SUTURE, JUNCTION
commit INTRUST,
PERFORM, DO, CON-
SIGN, DELIVER, ALLOT,
ASSIGN, CONFIDE,
PERPETRATE, IM-
PRISON, RELEGATE,
ARREST
committee BODY,
GUARDIAN(S), BOARD,
EXECUTOR(S), GROUP,
COUNCIL
commodity PRODUCT,
ARTICLE, STAPLE,
WARE, GOODS
common GENERAL,
AVERAGE, VULGAR,
ORNERY, CURRENT,
POPULAR, GENERIC,
LOW, REGULAR,
COARSE, SHARED,
JOINT, MUTUAL,
ORDINARY, RIFE,
PUBLIC, UNIVERSAL,
USUAL, TRITE, BANAL,
HACKNEYED, PLAIN,
TRIFLING, BASE,
PLEB(EIAN)
combining form HOMO
fellow CARL, RUCK
fund POOL, POT,
PURSE
Commoner, Great
PITT
commonly accepted
VULGATE, POPULAR
commonplace HUM-
DRUM, BANAL, TRITE,

STALE, DAILY, USUAL, TEDIOUS, PROSY, HACKNEYED, ORDINARY, DULL, PROSAIC, UNIMPORTANT, PLAIN
phrase CLICHE, TRUISM, PLATITUDE
style BATHOS
commons FOOD, KEEP, PARK, GROUNDS, PABULUM, FARE, COMMONALITY, RATIONS, PROVISIONS, QUARTERS, HALL
commonwealth REPUBLIC, STATE, COMMUNITY, PUBLIC
commotion FLARE, RIOT, POTHER, ADO, TO-DO, STIR, FUSS, TUMULT, FERMENT, WELTER, TURMOIL, BUSTLE
commune CONFER, CONVERSE, SHARE, AREA, REALM, SOIL, IMPART, CONSULT, ADVISE, PARLEY, TREAT, TALK, SPEAK, DISCUSS, DEBATE, ARGUE, COMMUNICATE, REVEAL, DIVULGE, DISTRICT, TOWNSHIP
France USSEL *See under* "France"
Netherlands EDE, EPE *See under* "Netherlands"
communion EUCHARIST, TALK, HOST, UNITY, MASS, VIATICUM, FAITH, CHURCH, CREED, SECT, CULT, FELLOWSHIP, SACRAMENT, ANTIPHON
cake WAFER
plate PATEN
table ALTAR
Communist RED, SOVIET
community MIR, TOWN(SHIP), DISTRICT, BODY, GROUP, SOCIETY, VILLAGE, PROVINCE
Comoro island MOHELI
comose HAIRY, TUFTED, COMOUS

compact ETUI, KNIT, PRESS, DENSE, TERSE, SOLID, COMPRESSED, TRIG, TREATY, BOND, SNUG, THICK, TIGHT, CLOSE, FIRM, HARD, UNIFY, TIE, BIND, PACT, CARTEL, CONTRACT, UNITED, COVENANT, AGREEMENT, BARGAIN, CONSOLIDATE, SOLID, PITHY, BRIEF
companion FELLOW, SPOUSE, WIFE, PEER, MATE, ESCORT, CHUM, PAL, ALLY, CRONY, FRIEND, COMRADE, CONSORT, PARTNER, TWIN
constant SHADOW
equal (COM)PEER COEVAL
faithful ACHATES, DOG
companionable SOCIABLE, GRACIOUS, CORDIAL, AGREEABLE
company SQUAD, CREW, GROUP, FIRM, BAND, BEVY, TEAM, TROUPE, SET, CIRCLE, CLIQUE, CROWD, MOB, HORDE, ASSEMBLAGE, BODY, GANG, FLOCK, VISITOR, GUEST, TROOP, PARTY, ACTORS
of soldiers PHALANX, BATTERY
comparative THAN, EQUAL, RIVAL, RELATIVE
compare COLLATE, EVEN, SEMBLE, RELATE, LIKEN, CONFER, TEST, CONTRAST, VIE, ESTIMATE
comparison ANALOGY, PARABLE, SIMILE, SIMILITUDE, METAPHOR
compartment PART, BIN, CELL(ULE), SECTION, DIVISION, PIGEONHOLE, REGION
compass GAIN, ATTAIN, HORIZON, ORBIT, NEEDLE, REACH, SWEEP, GYRO, AREA, BOUND(S), ENCLOSE, EXTENT, SCOPE,

AMBIT, CIRCUIT, SIZE, FIELD, SPHERE, RANGE, ENVIRON, SURROUND, ENCIRCLE, LIMIT, BOUNDARY, DEGREE
beam TRAMMEL
card ROSE
point AIRT(H), AZIMUTH, RHUMB
sight VANE
suspender GIMBAL
type of GYRO
compassion CHARITY, GRACE, LENITY, MERCY, HEART, PITY, RUTH, SYMPATHY, RUE
compel FORCE, DRIVE, PRESS, COERCE, OBLIGE, IMPEL, MOVE, ORDER, ENJOIN, CONSTRAIN, REQUIRE, ACTUATE
compellative NAME
compendium ABSTRACT, SYLLABUS, PRECIS, BRIEF, DIGEST, EPITOME, SKETCH, APERCU, BREVIARY, ABRIDG(E)MENT, SUMMARY
compensate SQUARE, TALLY, JIBE, AGREE, (RE)PAY, SATISFY, REQUITE, CORRECT, REMUNERATE, RECOUP, REWARD, ATONE, RESTORE
compensation SOLATIUM, HIRE, PAY, REWARD, SALARY, BALM, OFFSET, COUNTERPOISE, HONORARIUM
compete EMULATE, COPE, MATCH, CONTEND, STRIVE, VIE, RIVAL, PIT, STRUGGLE
competent CAPABLE, SMART, ABLE, CAPAX, ENOUGH, APT, FIT, ADEPT, SUITABLE, MEET, ADEQUATE, SANE, QUALIFIED, ENDOWED, SUFFICIENT
competition RIVALRY, STRIFE, CONTEST, TRIAL, HEAT, MATCH, GAME, OPPOSITION
competitor RIVAL, ENEMY, FOE,

ANTAGONIST, OP-
PONENT, COMBATANT,
CANDIDATE
Compiegne's *river*
AISNE, OISE
compilation DIGEST,
ANTHOLOGY, ANA,
CODE, COLLECTION,
BOOK
compile EDIT, WRITE,
COMPOSE, COLLECT,
PREPARE, SELECT, AR-
RANGE
complain GRIPE, FUSS,
FRET, WHINE, REPINE,
MOAN, YAMMER,
CHARGE, LAMENT,
(BE)WAIL, GRUMBLE
complaisant KIND,
LENIENT, AFFABLE,
POLITE, CIVIL,
OBLIGING, COMPLIANT,
GRACIOUS, COURTEOUS,
SUAVE, SMOOTH
complete FULL,
PLENARY, SOLE, END,
STARK, ALL, ENTIRE,
MATURE, UTTER, FUL-
FILL, FINISH, DO,
CLOSE, QUITE, TOTAL,
WHOLE, PERFECT,
THOROUGH, CONSUM-
MATE, CLEAN,
REALIZE, ABSOLUTE,
ACCOMPLISH
complex INTRICATE,
INVOLVED, KNOTTY,
MAZY, MIXED, MANI-
FOLD, TANGLED,
COMPLICATED, DIF-
FICULT, HARD, SYN-
DROME, NETWORK
complexion ASPECT,
HUE, COLOR, BLEE,
TINGE, TENOR, VEIN,
TEMPER, HUMOR,
MOOD, TINT, LOOK,
STATE, APPEARANCE
complicate PERPLEX,
INTORT, TANGLE, IN-
VOLVE
complicated COMPLEX,
HARD, ABSTRUSE,
TANGLED, KNOTTY,
DISORDERED, PROLIX
complication NODE,
NODUS, SNARL, PLOT,
COMPLEXUS, CON-
FUSION, INTRICACY,
DIFFICULTY
compliment EULOGY,
LAUD, EXTOL, PRAISE,

ENCOMIUM, TRIBUTE,
CONGRATULATE,
PANEGYRIC
comply AGREE, ASSENT,
YIELD, OBEY, CON-
FORM, SUBMIT,
CONSENT
component PART, ELE-
MENT, INTEGRAL,
FACTOR, MEMBER,
PIECE, ITEM,
CONSTITUENT
comport TALLY, JIBE,
BEHAVE, DEPORT,
AGREE, SQUARE, AC-
CORD, ACT, (AC)QUIT,
BEAR, BROOK, CARRY,
HARMONIZE, DEMEAN,
CONDUCT, COMPOTIER
compose FORM,
FASHION, CONSTRUCT,
DESIGN, MAKE, WRITE,
DISPOSE, ADJUST
type SET
composed SEDATE,
COOL, QUIET, STILL,
SERENE, CALM, STAID,
UNRUFFLED, TRAN-
QUIL, PLACID, COL-
LECTED, WROTE,
WRITTEN
composer ABT, BACH,
BIZET, BRAHMS, BULL,
CHOPIN, CZERNY,
DELIBES, DVORAK,
ELGAR, GLUCK,
GOUNOD, GRIEG,
HANDEL, HAYDN,
LALO, LEHAR, LISZT,
MOZART, STRAUSS
(VON)SUPPE, VERDI,
WAGNER, WEBER
Aida VERDI
Carmen BIZET
Ernani VERDI
Merry Widow LEHAR
Oberon WEBER
composition OPUS,
THEME, ESSAY, PIECE,
ETUDE, NOME, RONDO,
SUITE, SONATA,
FANTASIA, MAKE-UP,
SYNTHESIS, AG-
GREGATE, MIXTURE,
MASS, FORMATION,
CONSTITUTION, COM-
POUND, INVENTION,
PICTURE, WRITING,
ARTICLE
choral MOTET
literary CENTO

nine instruments
NONET
pertaining to
SYNTHETIC,
SYNTHESIS
premise of LEMMA
sacred MOTET,
HYMN
compositor TYPO,
PRINTER
composure POSTURE,
POISE, MIEN,
BALANCE, QUIET,
CALMNESS, REPOSE,
EQUANIMITY
compound MIX, FAR-
RAGO, OLIO, JOIN,
UNITE, BLEND, SET-
TLEMENT, COMPOSITE,
MINGLE, COMBINE,
ENCLOSURE, HODGE-
PODGE, COMPLEX,
MEDLEY, JUMBLE
fruit PECTIN
law COMPROMISE
word, division of
TMESIS
comprehend KNOW,
GRASP, SENSE, EM-
BRACE, GET, FATHOM,
SEE, REALIZE, SEIZE,
COMPRISE, INCLUDE,
UNDERSTAND,
IMAGINE, DISCERN,
PERCEIVE, SAVVY
compress REDUCE,
DIGEST, CLING, CROWD,
FIRM, ABRIDGE, CON-
DENSE, SHRINK, DE-
FLATE, BIND, WRAP,
TIE, BANDAGE,
SQUEEZE, ABBREVIATE,
PLEDGET, STUPE, CON-
TRACT, CURTAIL
medical STUPE,
BANDAGE, PLEDGET
comprise EMBRACE,
CONTAIN, HOLD,
SEIZE, INCLUDE, IN-
VOLVE, EMBODY
compulsion FORCE,
DURESS, STRESS,
NEED, COERTION,
CONSTRAINT, IMPULSE
compulsory service
ANGARY, ANGARIA,
SLAVERY
compunction
PENITENCE, QUALM,
REMORSE, REGRET,
SORROW, SCRUPLE,
DEMUR, CONTRITION,

RELUCTANCE, MIS-
GIVING, CONSCIENCE

compute SUM, TOTAL,
CAST, ADD, FIGURE,
COUNT, RECKON,
TALLY, CALCULATE,
ESTIMATE, RATE,
ASSESS

comrade FRATER,
BUDDY, PAL, PEER,
ALLY, MATE, CHUM,
FRIEND, FELLOW,
CRONY, ASSOCIATE

con READ, ANTI, SCAN,
PERUSE, STUDY,
AGAINST, VERSUS,
MEMORIZE, DECEIVE,
CHEAT, SWINDLE,
THINK, LEARN

conation WILL,
VOLITION

conative state NISUS

concatenate CHAIN,
LINK, UNITE, CON-
NECT, JOIN

concave HOLLOW,
VOID, VAULTED, DE-
PRESSED, ARCHED,
DISHED

concavity DIP, HOL-
LOW, HOLE, DENT,
PIT, BOWL, DISH,
CRATER

conceal CLOAK, PALM,
VEIL, SCREEN, MASK,
HIDE, BURY, CACHE,
DISGUISE, SECRETE,
COVER, WITHHOLD
goods by law ELOIN,
ELOIGN

concealed LATENT,
COVERT, VEILED,
CLANDESTINE, WITH-
DRAWN, HIDDEN,
MASKED, LARVATE
combining form
ADELO

concede YIELD,
ADMIT, AGREE, ASSENT,
GRANT, CEDE, ALLOW,
WAIVE, SURRENDER,
OWN, ACKNOWLEDGE

conceit IDEA, PRIDE,
VAGARY, EGO, FANCY,
VANITY, WHIM,
CAPRICE, FOLLY,
EGOTISM

conceited PRIGGISH,
VAIN, OPINIONATED,
DOGMATIC

conceive PLAN,
FRAME, THINK, BEGIN,

IDEATE, DEVISE,
FANCY, PONDER,
MAKE, CONTRIVE,
IMAGINE, SUPPOSE,
FORMULATE, UNDER-
STAND, COMPREHEND

concentrate FOCUS,
FIX, AIM, CENTER,
GATHER, UNIFY, MASS,
HEAP, PILE, THICKEN,
ESSENCE, CONDENSE,
CONSOLIDATE, IN-
TENSIFY, ASSEMBLE,
CONVERGE

conception IDEA,
NOTION, IMAGE,
THOUGHT, FANCY, BE-
LIEF

concern BUSINESS,
FIRM, COMPANY,
CORPORATION, RELATE,
AFFECT, TOUCH, BEAR,
PERTAIN, CARE, APPLY,
MATTER, THING,
ANXIETY, AFFAIR, RE-
GARD, INTEREST,
WORRY, EVENT, GRIEF,
TROUBLE, DISTURB

concerned BOTHERED,
ANXIOUS, WORRIED,
INTENT

concerning ANENT,
ABOUT, FOR, IN RE,
ON, RE, REGARDING

concert RECITAL, AC-
CORD, AGREEMENT,
CONCORD, HARMONY,
PLAN, DEVISE
hall LYCEUM, ODEON,
ODEUM

conch COCKLE, SHELL,
MOLLUSK

conciliate APPEASE,
EASE, PLACATE, CALM,
PACIFY, ADJUST,
PROPITIATE, RECON-
CILE, SATISFY, ATONE

conciliatory PACIFIC,
WINNING, PERSUASIVE,
MOLLIFYING, FOR-
GIVING, LENITIVE,
LENIENT, MILD,
GENTLE

concise CURT, PITHY,
SUCCINCT, TERSE,
PRECISE, SHORT,
BRIEF, NEAT, CRISP,
LACONIC, POINTED

conclude REASON,
SPECULATE, GUESS,
JUDGE, GATHER,
DEDUCE, FIGURE,

INFER, RESOLVE, END,
COMPLETE, TERMI-
NATE, GRADUATE,
REST, SETTLE, CLOSE,
FINISH

conclusion CODA,
END, RESULT,
DECISION, RESOLVE,
FINDING, PERIOD,
JUDGMENT

conclusive TELLING,
COGENT, CERTAIN,
ULTIMATE, LAST,
DECISIVE, CON-
VINCING, FINAL

concoct PLAN, HATCH,
INVENT, DEVISE, COOK,
BREW, MIX, PREPARE,
FRAME, COMPOSE

concord PEACE, RAP-
PORT, ACCORD, PACT,
AMITY, HARMONY,
UNITY, CONSONANCE,
TREATY, GRAPE

concordant UNISONAL,
AGREEABLE, COR-
RESPONDENT

concrete ACTUAL,
REAL, BETON, HARD,
SOLID, TANGIBLE,
DEFINITE, FIRM,
SOLIDIFIED, COM-
POUND

concretion CLOT,
PEARL, MESS, NODULE,
CALCULUS

concur AGREE, ASSENT,
ACCORD, CHIME, HAND,
UNITE, JIBE, CONSENT,
ACQUIESCE, APPROVE,
COINCIDE

concurrent COEVAL,
UNITED, ASSOCIATED,
SYNCHRONOUS

concuss JAR, SHAKE,
SHOCK, CLASH, JOLT,
FORCE, COERCE

condemn DAMN,
BLAME, BAN, DECRY,
DOOM, JUDGE,
SENTENCE, CENSURE,
CONFISCATE, CONVICT

condense ABRIDGE,
CUT, DISTIL(L),
SHORTEN, SHRINK,
DEFLATE, REDUCE,
COMPRESS, CONCEN-
TRATE, LIQUEFY,
EPITOMIZE, HARDEN,
THICKEN, SOLIDIFY

condescend DEIGN,
STOOP, FAVOR,

OBLIGE, GRANT,
VOUCHSAFE
condign JUST, DE-
SERVED, FITTING, DUE,
FAIR, ADEQUATE, FIT,
SUITABLE, WORTHY
condiment SAUCE,
CURRY, MACE, SALT,
PEPPER, RELISH, HERB,
SPICE, SEASON, SAGE,
APPETIZER, CHUTNEY
condition IF, TERM,
STATUS, STATE, BIRTH,
RANK, PLACE, CLASS,
MODE, CAUSE, PHASE,
REPUTE, FACET,
ANGLE, CASE, PLIGHT,
PREDICAMENT, STA-
TION, PROVISO,
STIPULATION, AGREE-
MENT
condolence PITY,
SYMPATHY, RUTH,
EMPATHY
condone ABSOLVE,
REMIT, PARDON, EX-
CUSE, FORGIVE, FOR-
GET, IGNORE, ACQUIT,
OVERLOOK
condor VULTURE, COIN,
TIFFIN
conduce AID, GUIDE,
EFFECT, FURTHER,
HELP, LEAD, ADVANCE,
TEND, CONTRIBUTE,
REDOUND
conduct ACTION,
DEMEAN, RUN,
MANAGE, LEAD, WAGE,
ACT, DEED, MIEN,
BEARING, USHER,
ESCORT, GUIDE,
SQUIRE, CONVOY,
GUARD, DEMEANOR,
BEHAVIOR, SUPERVISE
conductor MAESTRO,
LEADER, DIRECTOR,
GUIDE, ESCORT,
PROPAGATOR,
CONVEYOR, GUARD,
COPPER, CICERONE
conduit SEWER, DRAIN,
MAIN, PIPE, DUCT,
CHANNEL, CANAL,
PASSAGE, TUBE, WIRE,
CABLE
cone STROBILE
retorting PINA
silver PINA
tree FIR, LARCH, PINE,
SPRUCE

coney CHERVIL, PARS-
LEY
confab(ulate) CHAT,
TALK, CONVERSATION
confection COMFIT,
CIMBAL, NOUGAT,
SWEET, PRALINE,
SWEETMEAT, CANDY,
BONBON, CARAMEL
soft molded DULCE,
FONDANT
confederate ASSOCIATE,
AID, ABETTOR, ALLY,
LEAGUE, STALL,
REB(EL), COMBINE,
UNITE, ACCOMPLICE,
ASSISTANT, PARTNER
confederation UNION,
BODY, LEAGUE, AL-
LIANCE, SOCIETY
confer DISCUSS, TALK,
PARLEY, DISCOURSE,
CONSULT, COUNSEL,
CONVERSE, AWARD,
DONATE, PRESENT,
GRANT, TREAT, ADVISE,
GIVE, BESTOW, ENDOW
conference TALK,
PALAVER, CONFAB,
SYNOD, CONGRESS,
MEETING, COUNCIL,
CONSULTATION, DIS-
CUSSION
confess TELL, ADMIT,
REVEAL, AVOW, DIS-
CLOSE, OWN, ALLOW,
DIVULGE, ACKNOWL-
EDGE, GRANT,
CONCEDE, ATTEST,
SHRIVE, MANIFEST
confession CREED,
STATEMENT, AVOWAL
confetti BONBONS,
CANDY, RIBBON, TAPE
confide (EN)TRUST,
BELIEVE, RELY, TELL,
COMMIT, DEPEND,
CONSIGN
confidence TRUST,
FAITH, SECRET,
SPIRIT, CREDIT,
BELIEF, METTLE,
CERTITUDE, COURAGE,
ASSURANCE, APLOMB,
HOPE
confidential PRIVATE,
PRIVY, INTIMATE,
ESOTERIC, SECRET,
TRUSTWORTHY
law FIDUCIARY
confine CAGE, DAM,
IMMURE, LIMIT, COOP,

STRAITEN, JAIL, RE-
STRICT, BOUND, BIND,
FETTER, BOX, HEM,
PEN, CURB, CHECK,
BOTTLE, INTERN,
IMPOUND, BOUNDARY,
BORDER, CIRCUM-
SCRIBE, IMPRISON,
INCARCERATE
confined BOUND, PENT,
ABED, JAILED, RE-
STRAINED, ILL
to the initiated
ESOTERIC
confirm ASSURE,
PROVE, RATIFY, FIX,
VERIFY, ASSENT, EN-
DORSE, AVOUCH,
SANCTION, ESTABLISH,
CORROBORATE,
STRENGTHEN
confirmed INVETERATE,
RATIFIED, FIXED, SET,
CHRONIC, FORTIFIED,
HABITUAL, INITIATED
confiscate GRAB,
CONDEMN, TAKE,
SEIZE, USURP, AP-
PROPRIATE, SEQUESTER
conflict BATTLE, BOUT,
FRAY, WAR, DISCORD,
FIGHT, CLASH, ACTION,
BRUSH, STRIFE, STRUG-
GLE, CONTEST, COL-
LISION, COMBAT, OP-
POSE, RIOT,
REBELLION, MUTINY
confound BEWILDER,
PERPLEX, AMAZE,
FAZE, RATTLE, CON-
FUSE, ADDLE, BAFFLE,
STUN, STUPEFY,
ABASH, DISCONCERT,
DISMAY, ASTONISH
confront FACE, DEFY,
BRAVE, COMPARE,
MEET, OPPOSE, CHAL-
LENGE, THREATEN,
RESIST, ENCOUNTER
confuse MIX, JUMBLE,
MINGLE, RATTLE, FUD-
DLE, ABASH, BEFUD-
DLE, DERANGE, PER-
PLEX, ADDLE, BLEND,
FLUSTER, FAZE,
AMAZE, CONFOUND,
DISTURB, NONPLUS,
BEMUSE
confused ASEA,
CHAGRINED, ADDLED,
DISORDERED, OBSCURE
type PI

confusion MUDDLE,
ADO, BABBLE, MOIL,
CHAOS, DISCORD, DIN,
WELTER, SNARL,
SNAFU, MESS, MIX-
TURE, CLUTTER,
JUMBLE, TUMULT,
AGITATION, EMBAR-
RASSMENT, DISORDER
confute REFUTE,
REBUT, DENY, EX-
POSE, SILENCE,
DISPROVE
conge BOW, CURTSY,
PASSPORT, LEAVE,
PERMISSION, DIS-
MISSAL, LICENSE,
CLEARANCE
congeal FREEZE,
HARDEN, SOLIDIFY,
STIFFEN, GEL, JELL,
ICE, SET, FIX, PECTIZE,
CURDLE, COAGULATE
capable of congealing
GELABLE
congener KIND, CLASS,
RACE, GENUS
congenital INBORN, IN-
BRED, INNATE, NATIVE
congenitally attached
ADNATE
congeries HEAP, PILE,
MASS
conglobation BALL,
SPHERE
conglomerate HEAP,
MASS, PILE, STACK,
ASSEMBLAGE
congo EEL, SNAKE,
RIVER, COUNTRY
Congo, *cool season*
CACIMBO
former capital BOMA
lake TUMBA
language SUSU,
BANGALA
plant MANIOC
river ZAIRE, ZAHIR
town BOMA, MATADI
tribe SUSU, BANGALA
congou TEA
congratulate LAUD,
GREET, SALUTE,
MACARIZE,
FELICITATE,
COMPLIMENT
congregate MEET,
HERD, ASSEMBLE,
TROOP, GATHER,
COLLECT, SWARM,
TEEM, CONVENE,
MUSTER

congregation FLOCK,
FOLD, PARISH,
CHURCH, HOST,
BRETHERN, ASSEMBLY,
SWARM, HERD
congress COUNCIL,
MEETING, ASSEMBLY,
SYNOD, CONVENTION,
CONFERENCE,
LEGISLATURE, DIET,
CONCLAVE, DAIL
conifer CEDAR, PINE,
SPRUCE, FIR, PINACLE,
LARCH, TSUGA,
THUJA
conium HEMLOCK
conjecture IMAGINE,
SURMISE, ETTLE,
VIEW, BELIEF, GUESS,
THEORY, PRESUME,
INFERENCE, SUSPECT,
SUSPICION, OPINION
conjoined parts
ADNEXA
conjugal felicity,
symbol SARDONYX
conjunction UNION,
JOINT, TIE, COMBINA-
TION, BUT, OR, IF, AS,
SINCE, NOR, AND, ET,
THAN
conjurer JUGGLER, EN-
CHANTER, SORCERER,
MAGICIAN, WIZARD,
SEER
connect BIND, GLUE,
CEMENT, BRIDGE, TIE,
LINK, (AF)FIX,
FASTEN, JOIN, UNITE,
COMBINE, COUPLE,
INTERLOCK, RELATE,
ANASTOMOSE, COM-
MUNICATE, MARRY
connected with a
purpose TELIC
connection LINK,
NEXUS, BOND, TIE,
KINSHIP, RELATIVE,
JUNCTION, AFFINITY,
RELATION
connective SYNDETIC
See "conjunction"
tissue FASCIA
connive WINK, BLINK,
OVERLOOK, PLOT,
CABAL, ABET, INCITE,
FOMENT, INTRIGUE
connubial MARITAL,
CONJUGAL,
MATRIMONIAL,
DOMESTIC

conquer PREVAIL,
SUBDUE, WIN,
TRIUMPH, BEAT, LICK,
OVERCOME, ROUT,
VANQUISH, DEFEAT,
CHECKMATE, MASTER,
DOWN, CRUSH, OVER-
THROW
conquistador CORTEZ
consanguineous AKIN,
RELATED, KINDRED
conscience THOUGHT,
CASUISTRY, COMPUNC-
TION, SENSE
conscientious FAITH-
FUL, JUST, UPRIGHT,
STRICT, RIGID,
SCRUPULOUS, EXACT,
HONORABLE, FAIR,
HONEST
conscious AWARE,
AWAKE, KEEN, ALIVE,
SENSIBLE, SENTIENT,
COGNIZANT
conscript DRAFT,
ENLIST, ENROL, RE-
CRUIT, MUSTER
consecrate ANOINT,
BLESS, HALLOW, SEAL,
DEVOTE, SAIN,
DEDICATE, DEIFY,
ORDAIN, SANCTIFY
consecrated SACRED,
OBLATE
oil CHRISM
consent ACCEDE,
AGREE, GRANT, YIELD,
CONCUR, APPROVE, AS-
SENT, COMPLY,
CONCURRENCE
consequence END,
ISSUE, WEIGHT,
SEQUEL, WORTH,
VALUE, EVENT, FRUIT,
RESULT, EFFECT, UP-
SHOT, OCCASION, IM-
PORT, REPUTE, IN-
FERENCE, CONSECU-
TION, IMPORTANCE,
INTEREST, CONCERN
consequently ERGO,
HENCE, LATER, THEN,
SO, SUBSEQUENTLY,
THEREFORE
conservative SAFE,
TORY, STABLE,
DIEHARD, REACTIONARY
conserve CAN, PRE-
SERVE, SAVE, GUARD,
SHIELD, PROTECT,
UPHOLD, JAM, JELLY
grape UVATE

consider HEED, RATE, PONDER, STUDY, EXAMINE, MUSE, DEEM, WEIGH, THINK, REASON, JUDGE, CONTEMPLATE, REGARD, DELIBERATE, REFLECT, COGITATE

considering SINCE, IF

consign DELIVER, COMMIT, ASSIGN, REMIT, SEND, SHIP, ENTRUST, MAIL, CONFIDE, SHIFT, ALLOT, RESIGN, YIELD, TRANSFER, REMAND, COMMISSION

consignee FACTOR, RECEIVER

consist LIE, RESIDE, INHERE, COMPRISE, EMBRACE, CONTAIN, HOLD, EXIST

consisting *of names* ONOMASTIC

of one word MONEPIC

consolation SOP, SOLACE, BOOBY, COMFORT, RELIEF

console COMFORT, CHEER, SOLACE, ALLAY, CALM, ENCOURAGE, SOOTHE, RELIEVE, TABLE, BRACKET, CABINET

consolidate KNIT, COMBINE, MERGE, UNITE, JOIN, POOL, BLEND, MIX, CONDENSE, SOLIDIFY, HARDEN, STRENGTHEN, ORGANIZE, COALESCE

consonant DENTAL, LENIS, SPIRANT, AGREEABLE, HARMONIOUS, CONSISTENT, FORTIS, LETTER

aspirated SONANT

hard FORTIS, FRICATIVE

pertaining to FRICATIVE, PALATAL

producing hiss SIBILANT

sound SURD

unaspirated LENE

voiceless ATONIC, LENE, SURD

consort MATE, WIFE, SPOUSE, PARTNER,

AIDE, ALLY, HUSBAND, ASSOCIATE, ACCOMPANY, MINGLE

of Siva DEVI

conspicuous SALIENT, SIGNAL, NOTABLE, MARKED, GLARING, PATENT, OPEN, VISIBLE, OBVIOUS, APPARENT, NOTICEABLE, PLAIN, CLEAR, STRIKING, FAMED, FAMOUS, PROMINENT

conspiracy INTRIGUE, CABAL, PLOT, JUNTO, RING, MACHINATION, COUP

conspire PLOT, SCHEME, PLAN, COLLUDE, UNITE, CONTRIVE, CONFEDERATE

constable BALIFF, BEADLE, COP, BULL, WARDEN, KEEPER, POLICEMAN, OFFICER

constancy, *symbol of* GARNET

constant STAUNCH, STILL, LOYAL, FAST, SET, STEADY, FIRM, EVEN, STABLE, LEAL, TRIED, FAITHFUL, SETTLED, TRUE, FIXED, ENDURING, STEADFAST, CONTINUAL, IMMOVABLE, UNIFORM, REGULAR

Constantine's *birthplace* NIS(H)

Constantinople *See* "Istanbul"

constellation ANSER, LYRA, LEO, ARA, PATTERN, ARRANGEMENT

Altar ARA

Balance LIBRA

Bear URSA

brightest star COR

Bull TAURUS

Crab CANCER

Crane GRUS

Cross CRUX

Dipper URSA

Dog CANIS

Dragon DRACO

Eagle AQUILA

Fish PISCES

Herdsman BOOTES

Hunter ORION

Lion LEO

northern AURIGA, BOOTES, CYGNUS, DRACO, LYRA, PERSEUS, SAGITTA, ANDROMEDA

Peacock PAVO

Ram ARIES

Sails VELA

southern ARA, APUS, ARGO, PAVO, VELA, INDUS, CRUX, CANIS, CETUS, HYDRA, LEPUS, LUPUS, ORION, PISCES, ALTAR

Southern Cross CRUX

Water Bearer AQUARIUS

Whale CETUS

constituent FACTOR, VOTER, PART, PIECE, DETAIL, ITEM, MEMBER, ELEMENT, COMPONENT, INGREDIENT, ELECTOR

constitute FORM, MAKE, FRAME, FOUND, APPOINT, COMPRISE, SHAPE, FORGE, COMPOSE, DEPUTE, ESTABLISH, ENACT, FIX, DETERMINE

constitution NATURE, STATE, LAW, CODE, CHARTER, PHYSIQUE, HEALTH, STRUCTURE, TEMPER, HUMOR

constitutional temperament CRASIS

constraint FORCE, BOND, COERCION, RESERVE, CAPTIVITY, COMPULSION, OBLIGATION, DURESS

constrict HAMPER, ASTRINGE, NARROW, SHRINK, CURB, BIND, LIMIT, PRESS, SQUEEZE, CRAMP, DEFLATE, TIE, COMPRESS

constrictor SPHINCTER, BOA, SNAKE

construe PARSE, RENDER, EXPLAIN, RESOLVE, ANALYZE, DISSECT, INTERPRET, TRANSLATE, INFER

consuetude CUSTOM, USAGE, HABIT, USE, WONT, PRACTICE

consuetudinary MANUAL, ORDINARY

consult ADVISE, CON-
FER, DELIBERATE,
CONSIDER, ASK
consume BURN, EAT,
SPEND, WEAR, USE,
RUST, ENGROSS, AB-
SORB, DESTROY,
WASTE, EXHAUST,
DEVOUR, DISSIPATE,
DRINK, SQUANDER
consummate SHEER,
ABSOLUTE, ARRANT,
ACHIEVE, IDEAL, END,
PERFECT, WHOLE,
ENTIRE, FULL,
FINISH(ED), COM-
PLETE, ACCOMPLISHED
consumption PHTHISIS,
TB, USE, WASTE,
DECAY, DESTRUCTION
contact TOUCH, IM-
PACT, TANGENCY,
ABUT, JOIN, SYZYGY,
ARRIVE, MEET, TAC-
TION, UNION, JUNC-
TION
contagion POISON,
MIASMA, POX, VIRUS,
INFECTION, CON-
TAMINATION, TAINT
preventative SHOT,
ANTIDOTE,
PROPHYLAXIS,
ALEXITERIC
contain HOLD, CARRY,
EMBRACE, RESTRAIN,
CHECK, HOUSE, IN-
CLUDE, COMPRISE,
EMBODY, SUBSUME,
COMPREHEND
container CAGE, CASE,
BOX, TIN, TUB, VAT,
PAIL, CUP, CAN,
CARTON, BAG, POUCH,
JAR, BOTTLE, VASE,
URN, BASKET
large glass CARBOY
contaminate DEFILE,
INFECT, SOIL, STAIN,
SULLY, TAINT,
DEBASE, SPOIL, IN-
JURE, HARM, POL-
LUTE, POISON,
TARNISH, CORRUPT,
BEFOUL
contemn SLIGHT,
FLOUT, DESPISE,
HATE, REJECT, SCORN
contemplate PONDER,
MUSE, PLAN, WEIGH,
STUDY, THINK, VIEW,

SURVEY, REFLECT,
MEDITATE
contemporaneous
COEVAL, CURRENT,
MODERN, LIVING,
EXISTING
contempt DISDAIN,
SCORN, HATE,
MOCKERY, DERISION,
DISGRACE, SHAME,
CONTUMELY, CON-
TUMACY
contemptible CHEAP,
SORRY, LOW, BASE,
VILE, DESPICABLE,
ABJECT, MEAN,
SORDID, DISHONORABLE
fellow SCRUB, SKATE,
CAD, BOUNDER, ROUE
contend COPE, WAR,
VIE, STRIVE, DEBATE,
ARGUE, WAGE, FIGHT,
RESIST, COMBAT, OP-
POSE, STRUGGLE, CON-
TEST, BATTLE, ASSERT,
CLAIM, REASON, MAIN-
TAIN
content SATISFIED,
APPEASED, GRATIFIED,
SATED, SOOTHED,
REPLETE, PLEASED,
SUFFICE, GIST,
AMOUNT, CALM, WILL-
ING
contention WAR,
STRIFE, RIVALRY,
DISPUTE, TIFF, DIS-
CORD, WRANGLE,
SQUABBLE, FEUD,
RIOT, REBELLION,
CLAIM
contest TOURNEY,
AGON, BOUT, MEET,
FIGHT, ACTION, COPE,
SUE, TRIAL, (AF)FRAY,
BRUSH, PUSH, JOUST,
CLASH, OPPOSE
DISPUTE
law SUIT, LITIGATION
contestant VIER, RIVAL
law PLAINTIFF,
DEFENDANT
continent SOBER,
DECENT, CHASTE,
PURE, TEMPERATE,
MODERATE, RE-
STRAINED, LAND,
MAINLAND, ASIA,
AFRICA
hypothetical CASCADIA
sunken or lost
ATLANTIS, LEMURIA

contingency CASE,
CHANCE, EVENT,
PROSPECT, FORTUITY,
UNCERTAINTY
contingent CASUAL,
DEPENDENT, AC-
CIDENTAL, CONDI-
TIONAL, DOUBTFUL,
UNCERTAIN
continually AY, AYE,
EVER, ETERNAL,
STEADY, PERPETUAL,
ENDLESS, CONTINUOUS
continuance ADJOURN-
MENT, POSTPONE-
MENT, DELAY
continue STAY, PER-
SIST, LAST, ABIDE,
ENDURE, KEEP,
PERDURE, REMAIN,
LINGER, EXIST,
PERSEVERE
continued SERIAL,
CHRONIC, PROTRACTED
contort WRAP, COIL,
TWIST, GNARL, TURN,
BEND, WRITHE, DE-
FORM, PERVERT
contour SHAPE, FORM,
OUTLINE, FIGURE,
PROFILE, LINEAMENT,
APPEARANCE,
SILHOUETTE
geographical ISOBASE
contract SHRIVEL,
SHRINK, NARROW,
CURTAIL, REDUCE,
LESSEN, SHORTEN,
AGREEMENT,
COVENANT, CARTEL,
PACT, MISE, TREATY,
BARGAIN, INCUR,
CATCH, LEASE,
PROMISE
addition RIDER,
CODICIL
contraction ELISION,
SHORTENING, SHRINK-
AGE, ABRIDG(E)MENT,
STRICTURE, SPASM,
CRAMP, EPITOME,
ABBREVIATION, TIS,
OER, ITS, EEN, EER
pertaining to
SYSTOLIC
contradict BELIE,
IMPUGN, REBUT,
DENY, REFUTE,
RESIST, GAINSAY, DIS-
PROVE, OPPOSE
contradiction PARADOX,
DENIAL

contraption GADGET, TOOL, DEVICE, CONTRIVANCE, MACHINE

contravene OPPOSE, VIOLATE, DENY, HINDER, THWART, INFRINGE, DISREGARD, OBSTRUCT

contravention OFFENSE, VICE, SIN, CRIME, BREACH, CONTRADICTION

contretemps SCRAPE, MISHAP, ACCIDENT, SLIP, BONER
music SYNCOPATION

contribute GIVE, SUBSCRIBE, HELP, DONATE, AID, ASSIST, FURTHER, ANTE, SUPPLY, GRANT, BESTOW, CONDUCE, CAUSE, TEND, CONCUR

contribution ARTICLE, WRITING, ESSAY, BOON, GIFT, TAX, PAY, ALMS, PRESENT, LARGESS(E), OFFERING, DONATION

contrite SORRY, SORROWFUL, HUMBLE, PENITENT, REPENTANT, RUEFUL

contrivance GEAR, SCHEME, PLAN, DEVICE, GADGET, TOOL, INVENTION, PROJECT, APPLIANCE, DESIGN, MACHINE

contrive DEVISE, MANAGE, AFFORD, PLAN, PLOT, SCHEME, DESIGN, HATCH, BREW, CONCOCT, PRODUCE

control MANAGE, REGIME, REIGN, DIRECT, LAW, POWER, RULE, SWAY, GOVERN, GUIDE, LEAD, STEER, PILOT, DRIVE, CURB, CHECK, COMMAND, DOMINATE, REGULATE, SUPERINTEND, RESTRAIN

controversial POLEMIC(AL), ERISTIC, DISPUTATIOUS

controversy SUIT, WRANGLE, SPAT, QUARREL, DEBATE, DISPUTE, DISCUSSION, ALTERCATION, CONTENTION, LITIGATION

controvert DENY, DISCUSS, MOOT, ARGUE, REBUT, REFUTE, OPPOSE, DISPUTE, CONTEST

contumely SCORN, RUDENESS, ABUSE, DISDAIN, CONTEMPT, INSULT

contuse BRUISE, INJURE, BEAT, POUND, CRUSH, SQUEEZE

conundrum ENIGMA, PUZZLE, RIDDLE

convene MEET, ASSEMBLE, GATHER, SUMMON, CALL, SIT, MUSTER, CONGREGATE, CONVERGE

convenient FIT, SUITABLE, PROPER, HANDY, HELPFUL, USEFUL

convent CLOISTER, NUNNERY, PRIORY, ABBEY

convention CONGRESS, SYNOD, CAUCUS, MEETING, CUSTOM, DECORUM, RULE, USAGE, PRACTICE, FORM, ASSEMBLY
site HALL

conventional NOMIC, FORMAL, USUAL, PROPER, RIGHT, DECENT, CUSTOMARY, REGULAR, TRADITIONAL, ACCEPTED, CORRECT, TRITE

conversation CHAT, TALK, DISCOURSE, CAUSERIE, DIALOGUE, PALAVER, COLLOQUY
of three TRIALOG(UE)

converse TALK, PARLEY, SPEAK, GOSSIP, CHAT, CONFER, DILATE, COMMUNE, CONFABULATE, REVERSE, OBVERSE, OPPOSITE

convert DECODE, FORGE, REFORM, CHANGE, MAKE, APPLY, USE, TRANSFORM, REVERSE, TRANSPOSE, ALTER, TRANSMUTE, EXCHANGE, RENEW,

PROSELYTE, NEOPHYTE, NOVICE

convex GIBBOUS, ARCHED, ROUNDED, BULGING
shaft of column ENTASIS

convey AUCTION, VEND, TRADE, BARTER, DEED, CEDE, SELL, GRANT, PASS, WILL, DEVISE, TRANSMIT, CART, BEAR, TOTE, TAKE, TRANSFER, ALIENATE, MEAN, ASSIGN, CARRY
beyond jurisdiction ELOIN, ELOIGN

conveyance SALE, DEED, GRANT, TRANSFER, DEMISE, WAFTAGE, VEHICLE, CARRIAGE, LOAD, CAR, TAXI, TRAIN, CART, TROLLEY *See* "carriage"
law DEMISE, DEED, GRANT

convict SENTENCE, DOOM, CONDEMN, LIFER, PRISONER, CAPTIVE, TERMER, CRIMINAL, FELON
collar CARCAN(ET)

conviction BELIEF, FAITH, VIEW, OPINION, SENTENCE, CREDIT, CREED, TENET, DOGMA

convinced SURE, CERTAIN, POSITIVE

convincing COGENT, POTENT, VALID, SOUND, TELLING, PERSUASIVE

convivial GAY, SOCIABLE, GENIAL, JOLLY, FESTIVE, FESTAL

covocation DIET, SYNOD, COUNCIL, GATHERING, CONVENING, CONGRESS, MEETING

convoke CALL, CONVENE, GATHER, SUMMON, CITE, BID, MEET, MUSTER, ASSEMBLE

convolution of brain GYRUS

convolvulus VINE

convoy ESCORT, WATCH, GUARD, CONDUCT, LEAD, PILOT, ATTEND, ACCOMPANY, MANAGE

convulse SHAKE, EXCITE, STIR, ROCK, AGITATE, DISTURB, LAUGH

convulsion SPASM, SHRUG, FIT, ATTACK, THROE, PAROXYSM

cony DAMAN, RABBIT, HARE, PIKA, GANAM, HUTIA, BURBOT, LAPIN

coo MURMUR, WOO

coof DOLT, LOUT, NINNY, BLOCKHEAD

cook STEAM, FRY, GRILL, SEETHE, POACH, ROAST, SHIRR, STEW, FIX, MAKE, PREPARE, BRAISE, BOIL, BROIL, SAUTE
chief CHEF, HEAD
lightly BRAISE, SAUTE
room CUDDY, GALLEY, KITCHEN

cooking, *art of* MAGIRICS, CUISINE
odor NIDOR
vessel OLLA, SPIDER, POT, PAN, ROASTER

cool COLD, FROSTY, REFRIGERATE, GELID, SERENE, PLACID, COMPOSED, CALM, NERVY, CHILLY, UNFRIENDLY, INDIFFERENT, UNRUFFLED, STAID, UNEXCITED, APATHETIC, COMPOSED, NONCHALANT, CAUTIOUS

coon MAPACH(E)

coop (EN)CASE, COTE, HUTCH, MEW, PEN, STY, JAIL

cooperate AGREE, UNITE, CONCUR, COACT, COMBINE, COLLABORATE

coordinate ARRANGE, ADAPT, SYNTONY, EQUAL, ADJUST, CLASSIFY, HARMONIZE, CONCURRENT

coot DUCK, SCOTER, DOLT, SMYTH, FOWL

cop CATCH, NAB, STEAL, TRAP, FILCH, LIFT, SNARE, BAG,

BULL, PEELER, POLICEMAN

cope VIE, WAR, RIVAL, COMPETE, STRIVE, STRUGGLE, CLOAK

copestone CROWN, COPING

coping of scarp wall CORDON

copious PROFUSE, RICH, FULL, AMPLE, PLENTY, LAVISH, LUSH, EXUBERANT, OVERFLOWING, ABUNDANT, TEEMING, REPLETE

copper CU, CUPRUM, CENT, PENNY, METAL, COP, BULL, BOBBY, PEELER, POLICEMAN, BUTTERFLY
alloy BRASS, OROIDE, RHEOTAN
combining form CHALCO, CUPRO
cup DOP
Latin for CUPRUM
sulphate VITRIOL

Copperfield, Mrs. DORA

copse BOSCAGE, BOSK, THICKET, GROVE

copy APE, MIMIC, IMITATE, ECHO, ECTYPE, EFFIGY, CARBON, DUPLICATE, REPRODUCTION, RECORD
of original REPLICA, ECTYPE, PATTERN, FACSIMILE
true EXTRACT, ESTREAT, CARBON

coquet(te) FLIRT, TRIFLE, DALLY, TOY, PHILANDER, HUMMINGBIRD

coquettish COY

coquito PALM

coraciiformes *See* "bird, non-passerine"

corah UNDYED, PLAIN

coral MADREPORE, SKELETON, RED
branch RAMICLE
cavity CALYCULUS
island KEY, ATOLL, REEF
septa PALI
snake genus ELAPS
tree DAPDAP

with porous walls PORITE

corb *See* "CORF"

corbel ANCON, TIMBER, PROJECTION

corbie CROW, RAVEN, CHOUGH, BIRD

cord LINE, STRING, ROPE, TIE, BOND, TWINE, TORSADE, RIB, TENDON, NERVE
drapery TORSADE
goat's hair AGAL

cordage fiber DA, SISAL, HEMP, PITA, ERUC, COIR, FERU, IMBE, JUTE

corded REPPED, TIED, STACKED

cordelle TOWLINE, ROPE, CORD

cordial WARM, SINCERE, GENIAL, HEARTY, REAL, ARDENT, SHRUB, LIQUEUR, VIGOROUS, FRIENDLY, COURTEOUS

cordiality ARDOR, WARMTH, REGARD, HEARTINESS, FRIENDSHIP

cordon ENSIGN, STAR, BADGE, ENCLOSURE, COPING, LINE, BRAID, LACE, STRING, CIRCLE

core HEART, NAVE, GIST, CENTER, KERNEL, PITH, NUT, HUB, FOCUS, MIDDLE, ESSENCE, SPOOL
corn COB
material of earth NIFE
of a mold MATRIX, NOWEL

corf CORB, BASKET, SKIP, DOSSER, CREEL

corinne GAZELLE

Corinth king POLYBUS

cork PLUG, STOPPER, SHIVE, FLOAT, BOBBER, OAK
tissue SUBER
wax CERIN

corking EXCELLENT, FINE, PLEASING

corkwood BALSA, BLOLLY

cormorant NORIE, SCART(H), SHAG, GLUTTON, BIRD

corn CLAVUS, MAIZE, SALT, GRAIN, SEED, GRANULATE, INTOXI-CATE
bread PONE
crib BIN
flag GLADIOLUS, IRIS
hulled HOMINY
Indian MAIZE, ZEA, SAMP
knife MACHETE
leaf BLADE
lily IXIA
meal MASA
mush ATOLE, POR-RIDGE
spike EAR, COB
corncake PONE, HOE-CAKE
corncrake RAIL, BIRD
corned SALTED
corner POOL, TRUST, CANT, COIGN(E), INGLE, ANGLE, TRAP, TREE, QUOIN, NOOK, HERNE, NICHE, BEND, ELBOW, RECESS, MO-NOPOLY, MONOPOLIZE
cornerstone COIN, COIGN(E), CURB-STONE, BASIS
cornice ASTRAGAL, DRIP, CROWN
support ANCON
Cornish *diamond* QUARTZ
town prefix TRE
cornucopia HORN
Cornwall mine BAL
corolla PETALS, PERIANTH
part of PETAL, GALEA
corollary PORISM, AD-JUNCT, TRUISM, CONSEQUENCE, RE-SULT, INFERENCE, THEOREM, DOGMA, DEDUCTION
corona AUREOLE, SCYPHUS, CROWN, GARLAND, ROSARY, CIRCLET, CIGAR, FILLET
corporal NCO
Little NAPOLEON
corporate UNITED, AGGREGATE
corporeal HYLIC, BODILY, ACTUAL, SOMATIC, REAL,

MATERIAL, PHYSICAL, TANGIBLE
corpse CADAVER, BODY, STIFF, CARCASS
fat of ADIPOCERE
corpulent FAT, OBESE, FLESHY, STOUT, PLUMP, BURLY, HUSKY, PORTLY, ROTUND, BULKY
corpus BODY, WRIT-INGS, LITERATURE
corral POUND, STOCK-ADE, STY, PEN, EN-CLOSURE, COOP
correct EDIT, (A)MEND, EMEND, FIX, ADJUST, CHECK, REPAIR, TRUE, RE-FORM, REVAMP, REVISE, RECTIFY, ARIGHT, CHASTEN, EXACT, RIGHT, PROPER, NICE, DUE, INFORM, PUNISH, OK, OKAY, PRECISE, ACCURATE
correlative MUTUAL, NOR, OR, STILL, IF, THEN, EITHER, NEITHER, RECIPROCAL
correspond WRITE, COMMUNICATE, AGREE, JIBE, SQUARE, SUIT, MATCH, FIT, EQUAL, TALLY, ACCORD, HARMONIZE
correspondence MAIL, LETTERS, HOMOLOGY, TRAFFIC, SIMILARITY
corresponding *in sound* RIMIC, RHYMIC
part ISOMERE
corridor HALL, AISLE, ARCADE, PASSAGE-(WAY), GALLERY
corrie HOLLOW, CIRQUE
corroborate CONFIRM, STRENGTHEN, ESTAB-LISH, SUSTAIN, SUP-PORT
corrode RUST, CANKER, EAT, DECAY, ETCH, GNAW, BURN, ERODE, ABRADE, CONSUME, WASTE, IMPAIR
corrosive ACID, MOR-DANT, CAUSTIC, ERODENT, DESTRUC-TIVE
corrugated CRIMPED,

RUGATE, FOLDED, WRINKLED, FUR-ROWED, RUMPLED
corrugation CREASE, WRINKLE, PUCKER, FOLD
corrupt SPOIL, DEFILE, TAINT, POISON, ROT, DEBASE, PUTREFY, CONTAMINATE, POL-LUTE, LOW, VILE, AUGEAN, BRIBE, VENAL, EVIL
corsair PIRATE, PICA-ROON, BUCCANEER, PRIVATEER, ROCKFISH, BUG
body ARMOR, COVER
corset *bone* BUSK
strip STAY, BUSK
corslet, corselet BODICE, BREASTPLATE
Corsican town BASTIA, AJACCIO
cortege RETINUE, TRAIN, SUITE, PROCES-SION
cortex BARK, RIND, PEEL, PERIDIUM
corundum SAND, EMERY, RUBY, SAP-PHIRE, ALUMINA, ABRASIVE
coruscation FLASH, GLITTER, WIT, GLEAM
corvine bird CROW, DAW, RAVEN
cosmetic HENNA, PAINT, ROGUE, MASCARA, POWDER, LIPSTICK
medicated LOTION
white lead CERUSE
cosmic VAST, ORDERLY, CATHOLIC, UNIVERSAL, HARMONIOUS
opposed to ACRONY-CAL, ACRONICAL, CHAOTIC
cosmonaut *See under* "astronaut"
cosmos REALM, EARTH, GLOBE, HARMONY, ORDER, WORLD, UNI-VERSE, FLOWER
opposed to CHAOS
Cossack TURK, RUS-SIAN, CAVALRYMAN
captain SOTNIK
chief ATAMAN, HET-MAN
elder ATAMAN

regiment POLK, PULK

squadron SOTNIA, SOTNYA

unit STANITSA

whip KNOUT

cosset FONDLE, PET, CUDDLE, CARESS, CODDLE, LAMB

cost OUTLAY, CHARGE, LOSS, PRICE, EXPENSE, PAIN, DETRIMENT

costa RIB, VEIN, MIDRIB, RIDGE

costard HEAD, APPLE, CLOWN

Costa Rican coin COLON

costrel BOTTLE, FLASK

costume GARB, ATTIRE, SUIT, DRESS, RIG, TOG, UNIFORM

cot HUT, PEN, PALLET, BED, COTTAGE, COOP, COVER, SHEATH, ABODE

Cote d'Azur RIVIERA

coterie CIRCLE, CLIQUE, SET, CAMARILLA, GALAXY, SOCIETY, JUNTO

cottage BARI, HUT, COT, CABIN, LODGE, CHALET

cotton *cloth* DORIA, SURAT, KHAKI, DENIM *See* "fabric" *below*

disease HYBOSIS

drilling DENIM

dye for SULPHIDE, COPPERAS

Egyptian PIMA

fabric JEAN, LAWN, DENIM, KHAKI, GALATEA, LENO, PERCALE, SCRIM, TERRY, WIGAN, SILESIA, SUSI, NANKIN, JACONET, NANKEEN, VICHY

filament THREAD

gauze LENO

handkerchief MALABAR

lawn BATISTE

long-staple MACO

machine GIN, MULE

seed, pod for BOLL

remover GIN

Spanish BAYAL

thread LISLE

tree SIMAL

twilled JEAN, SILESIA

variety MACO, PIMA

cottontail HARE, LEVERET, RABBIT *See* "cony"

cottonwood ALAMO, TREE

couch EXPRESS, DIVAN, SOFA, LAIR, LURK, SKULK, SLINK, SNEAK, HIDE, LIE, RECLINE, CROUCH, SQUAT, STOOP, CONCEAL, UTTER, BED, SETTEE, DAVENPORT

grass See under "grass"

pertaining to SOFANE

couchant SUPINE, PRONE, ABED, CROUCHING, SQUATTING

cougar PUMA, PANTHER, CAT

cough HACK, PERTUSSIS, TUSSIS, BEGMA

relating to TUSSIVE, BECHIC

council SYNOD, BOARD, CABAL, JUNTO, SENATE, BODY, CABINET, MINISTRY, ASSEMBLY, DIET, CONGRESS

chamber CAMARILLA

church SYNOD

national CONGRESS, DIET, DAIL

relating to CAMERAL

table cover TAPIS

counsel REDE, CHIDE, WARN, LAWYER, PROCTOR, ADVISE, ADMONISH, CAUTION, ADVOCATE

counsel(l)or MENTOR, EGERIA, LAWYER, BARRISTER, ATTORNEY

count RELY, BANK, TRUST, TOT, TOTAL, FIGURE, TALLY, SCORE, RECKON, TELL, ADD, ENUMERATE, CAST, FOOT, SANCTION, CENSUS, CALCULATE, COMPUTE, ESTIMATE, EARL, GRAF

of Mayence (*Mainz*) GAN, GANELON

of Monte Cristo DANTES

Rousillon BERTRAM

countenance FAVOR, MUG, PUSS, MIEN, ABET, FACE, VISAGE, SANCTION, ASPECT, LOOK, ENCOURAGEMENT, SUPPORT, APPROVAL, APPEARANCE

counter STAND, TABLE, SHELF, CASE, CHECK, CONTEND, COMBAT, OPPOSE

counteract CHECK, DEFEAT, OFFSET, BALANCE, OPPOSE, RESIST, THWART, HINDER, COMPENSATE

counterfeit FALSE, FORGE, QUEER, SHAM, FRAUD, FEIGN, BOGUS, COPY, FAKE, PHONY, BASE, TIN, AFFECT, SIMULATE, IMITATE

counterfoil STUB

counterirritant MOXA, SETON, STUPE, MUSTARD, PEPPER, LINIMENT

countermand ABOLISH, CANCEL, REVOKE, RESCIND, RECALL, ABROGATE, ANNUL

counterpart COPY, IMAGE, DOUBLE, TWIN, REPLICA, PARALLEL, DUPLICATE, MATCH, MATE, LIKE, COMPLEMENT

counters MEN, TOKENS, POINTS, TALLEYS, RUNS, PARRIES, COMPUTERS

countersign SIGNAL, SEAL, ENDORSE, WATCHWORD, PASSWORD, MARK, SIGNATURE

countersink REAM, CHAMFER, BEVEL

counting frame ABACUS

country TRACT, REGION, VALE, PAIS, LAND, WEALD, DISTRICT, NATION, PEOPLE, HOME, STICKS

ancient SHEBA, ELI(A)S, GAUL *See under* "ancient"

bumpkin CARL, CHURL, CLOD, YAHOO, YOKEL, SWAIN

pertaining to AGRESTIC, RURAL, RUSTIC
place VILLA, FARM, RANCH
Roman CAMPAGNA
way PATH, LANE
county DOMAIN, SHIRE, SEAT, BOROUGH, PARISH, DISTRICT
coup SCOOP, STROKE, BLOW, PLAY, STRATAGEM, ATTACK
couple BRACE, DYAD, YOKE, SPAN, TWINS, TWO, PAIR, GEMINI, UNITE, TIE, LINK, JOIN, BOND, CONNECT, TWAIN
coupled YOKED, WEDDED, GEMELED, JOINED
couples, growing in BINATE
couplet PAIR, DISTICH, BRACE, POEM
courage GRIT, HEART, METTLE, SAND, SPIRIT, SPUNK, PLUCK, NERVE, VALOR, BRAVERY, GUTS, HEROISM, DARING, AUDACITY
symbol of BLOODSTONE, MEDAL
courageous HARDY, SPARTAN, GAME, GALLANT, BRAVE, BOLD, STOUT, FIERY, FEARLESS, VALIANT, INTREPID, STA(U)NCH
courier DRAGOMAN, GUIDE, ORDERLY, MESSENGER, ATTENDANT, ESTAFET(TE), CICERONE, SCOUT
courlan bird LIMKIN
course WAY, PATH, ROTE, SERIES, PLAN, HEAT, RUN, ROUTE, PASS, LAP, TRACK, ROAD, STREET, DIRECTION, STREAM, FLOW, ARTERY, CIRCUIT, AMBIT, DRIFT, TREND, TENOR, TACK, SYSTEM, CONDUCT, SUBJECT
court JUDGE, CURIA, FORUM, FORA (pl.), TRIBUNAL, FIELD, ARENA, PARVIS,

AREA, BAR, SPARK, WOO, PATIO, BID, PALACE, SOLICIT, INVITE, CURRY, FAVOR, SUE, YARD, TRAIN, RETINUE, QUADRANGLE, HOMAGE, ATTENTION, ALLURE
action SUIT, TRIAL, CASE
assistant(s) ELISOR, JURY, CRIER, TALESMAN
bring into SIST, ARREST, SUE
call OYEZ, OYES
church CLASSIS, ROTA
circuit ITER, EYRE
city MUNICIPAL
crier BEADLE
criminal ASSIZES
cry OYEZ, OYES
English LEET, GEMOT(E)
exemption ESSOIN
hearing OYER, TRIAL, ACTION, SUIT
inner PATIO
local GEMOT(E)
Mikado's DAIRI
minutes ACTA
order WRIT, RULING, DECREE, NISI
panel JURY
royal, pertaining to AULIC
session SET, SITTING
writ SUBPOENA, SUMMONS
courteous DEBONAIR, URBANE, POLITE, CIVIL, SUAVE, GALLANT, CORDIAL, GRACIOUS, RESPECTFUL, GENTLE, GENTEEL
courtly ELEGANT, HEND(E), AULIC, POLITE, CIVIL, POLISHED
courtship ROMANCE, SUIT
courtyard PATIO, CORTILE, CURTILAGE, AREA, QUADRANGLE
cove INLET, BAY, NOOK, BIGHT, CREEK, RECESS, FELLOW
covenant AGREEMENT, PACT, CARTEL, TREATY, ACCORD,

MISE, CONTRACT, COMPACT
cover SEAL, TOP, CAP, LID, THATCH, ROOF, HAT, ARK, LINE, COAT, HIDE, LAP, COSY, SHELTER, PRESERVE, REFUGE, RETREAT, SCREEN, MASK, CLOTHE, VEIL, THICKET, QUILT, BLANKET, SHEET, CONCEAL
covered CLAD, SCREENED, HIDDEN, SHELTERED
by vines IVIED
with horny plates SCUTATE
with silky down SERICATED
covering ARMOR, APRON, TENT, AWNING, ROOF, PELAGE, TEGUMENT, TILE, CAPSULE, SHELTER, TARP, UMBRELLA, QUILT, BLANKET
covert SECRET, DEN, LAIR, LIE, PRIVY, MASKED, THICKET, SHRUBBERY, REFUGE, ASYLUM, HIDDEN, CONCEALED, SLY, LATENT
covet CRAVE, PANT, PINE, WANT, WISH, ENVY, DESIRE, YEARN, HANKER
covetous GREEDY, MISERLY, FRUGAL, AVID, EAGER, AVARICIOUS
covey BROOD, FLOCK
cow KINE, BOVINE, BROCK, VACHE, BEEF, HEIFER, DAUNT, AWE, THREATEN, BULLY, RATTLE, FAZE
barn BYRE
fish MANATEE, SIRENIA
genus BOS
hornless MOIL, MULEY
hybrid CATTABU, CATTALO
like BOVINE, COUS
sea See "fish" *above*
young STIRK, CALF, HEIFER

coward SNEAK
cowardly CRAVEN, SHY, TIMID, POLTROON, PUSILLANIMOUS
cowboy GAUCHO, HERDER, LLANERO, VAQUERO, ROPER, HERDSMAN
breeches CHAPS, JODHPURS, LEVIS
cower QUAIL, FAWN, TOADY, CRINGE, WINCE, CROUCH, STOOP
cowl HOOD, CAP, LID, BONNET
coxcomb DANDY, DUDE, FOP, BUCK, SWELL, NOB, TOFF
coy CHARY, DEMURE, ARCH, SHY, BASHFUL, MODEST, PAT, NICE, PROPER, WARY, ALOOF, DISTANT, TIMID
coypu NUTRIA, RODENT
fur NUTRIA
coze CHAT, TALK, CONVERSE
cozen BEGUILE, CHEAT, TRICK, DUPE, GULL, HOAX, DEFRAUD, SWINDLE
cozy EASY, SAFE, SECURE, HOMEY, SNUG, COVERING, QUILT, TOASTY, COMFORTABLE
retreat NOOK, DEN, NEST, INGLE, LAIR
crab FIDDLER, MAIAN, CANCER, HERMIT, CRUSTACEAN, HORSE-SHOE
claw CHELA
fiddler UCA
genus OCYPODE, UCA, MAIA
king (horseshoe) LIMULUS
mantis SQUILLA
middle portion METOPE
suborder BRACHYURA
crab apple SCROG
crack KIBE, CHINK, CREVICE, CHAP, RIFT, QUIP, FISSURE, RIME, FURROW, SNAP, POP, REND, BANG, JEST, JOKE, GAG,

BREAK, CLEFT, CRANNY, SPLIT
cracker WAFER, BISCUIT
crackle CREPITATE, CRINK, SNAP
cracksman BURGLAR, YEGG
cradle SLEE, CRECHE, CUNABULA, CADER
Christmas CRECHE
song BERCEUSE, LULLABY
craft ART, TRADE, SKILL, METIER, WORK, ABILITY, TALENT, ARTIFICE, VOCATION, ARGOSY, VESSEL, BOAT
See "boat"
craftsman ARTISAN, HAND, NAVVY, MECHANIC
crafty SLY, WILY, WISE, FOXY, ADROIT, ARCH, CUNNING, TRICKY
crag TOR, SCAR, ARETE, BRACK, CLIFF, ROCK
crake RAIL, CROW, RAVEN, ROOK, BIRD
crakow BOOT, SHOE
cram PACK, BONE, CROWD, STUFF, PRESS, LEARN, FORCE, DRIVE, JAM, GORGE, TEACH, STUDY, GLUT, FILL, GRIND, STOW
cranberry tree PEMBINA
crane JIB, DERRICK, DAVIT, GRUS, BLUE, JENNY, HERON, CORMORANT, BIRD
arm of GIB, JIB
fly TIPULA
genus GRUS
Malayan SARUS
ship's DAVIT
traveling TITAN, JENNY
craniometrical point INION, STENION, PTERION
cranium SKULL, HEAD, BRAINPAN
crank WINCH, BRACE, BRACKET, HANDLE, WIND, WIT, FANATIC, WHIM, CROCHET
cranky CROSS, TESTY, DIFFICULT, GROUCHY

crape CLERGY, CRIMP, FRIZ, CURL, BAND, MOURNING
crash SHOCK, BURST, BLAST, CLOTH, FAIL-(URE), SHATTER, SMASH, SPLINTER, SOUND
crass CRUDE, DENSE, THICK, VULGAR, DULL, DUMB, STUPID, RAW, GROSS, COARSE, RUDE, ROUGH
crate BOX, CRADLE, ENCASE, HAMPER, RECEPTACLE, CON-TAINER, VEHICLE, CAR
crater CALDERA, PIT, CONE, FOVEA, HOLE, CUP, HOLLOW
cravat TIE, ASCOT, STOCK, TECK, NECK-ERCHIEF, BANDAGE
crave LONG, BEG, HANKER, YEARN, PRAY, PINE, SEEK, SOLICIT, NEED, HUNGER, THIRST, DESIRE
craven POLTROON, AFRAID, SCARED, TIMID, DASTARD(LY), COWARD(LY)
craw CROP, MAW, INGLUVIES
crawfish, crayfish YABBY, YABBIE, CRUSTACEAN, RECEDE, WITHDRAW
crawl CRINGE, FAWN, GROVEL, LAG, DRAG, CREEP, INCH, SWIM
crayon PENCIL, CHALK, PASTEL, SKETCH, PLAN, DRAW(ING)
craze FUROR, FAD, MANIA, MODE, VOGUE, RAGE, DERANGE, MAD-DEN, IMPAIR
crazy AMOK, LOCO, REE, MAD, WILD, MANIC, POTTY, WACKY, INSANE, LUNATIC, DEMENTED, BALMY, DAFFY
creak GRIND, RASP, GRATE, SQUEAK
cream GIST, REAM, BEST, ELITE, EMULSION, SAUCE, OINTMENT, FROTH, BEAT
of tartar ARGOL

crease FOLD, SEAM,
CRIMP, PLEAT,
WRINKLE, RUCK
create MAKE, FASHION,
CAUSE, FORM, REAR,
INVENT, SHAPE,
FORGE, PLAN, DESIGN,
ORIGINATE, PRODUCE,
IMAGINE, BUILD,
WRITE, COMPOSE
creation COSMOS,
WORLD, UNIVERSE,
EFFECT, FASHION,
APPOINTMENT, MAS-
TERPIECE
creature ANIMAL,
BEAST, BEING, SLAVE,
MINION, PERSON,
MAN, INDIVIDUAL,
WRETCH, THING
creche NURSERY,
MANGER, CRIB
credence BELIEF,
CREDIT, TRUST, FAITH,
CONFIDENCE
credit IMPUTE, FAITH,
TRUST, WEIGHT, BE-
LIEF, HONOR, REPUTE,
RENOWN, ASSET,
ASCRIBE, CHARGE,
MERIT, LOAN
creed CREDO, BELIEF,
FAITH, TENET, DOGMA,
SECT, CULT, DOCTRINE,
ISM
creek ESTERO, RIO,
SPRUIT, WICK, KILL,
RUN, RIA, RILL, IN-
LET, COVE, BIGHT,
INDIAN
creel TRAP, BASKET
creep CRAWL, WORM,
INCH, GROVEL, SKULK,
STEAL, SLINK, FAWN,
CRINGE, TINGLE
creeper IVY, VINE,
WORM, SNAKE, SHOE
creeping SLOW, SER-
VILE, INCHING, TRAIL-
ING, SYCOPHANTIC
creese WEAPON, DAG-
GER, STAB, KRIS
cremation, *wife's*
SUTTEE
Cremona AMATI,
VIOLIN
crenate SCALLOPED,
SERRATED, NOTCHED
Creole MESTIZO,
PATOIS
State LOUISIANA

crepitate CRACKLE,
SNAP, RATTLE
crescent MOON, LUNAR,
LUNE, LUNULE, ROLL,
CURVE
shaped LUNATE,
LUNULAR
cresset FLAMBEAU,
TORCH, FURNACE,
BASKET, SIGNAL
crest COMB, COP,
COPPLE, RIDGE, SEAL,
TOP, TIP, CROWN,
ARETE, TUFT, PEAK,
PLUME, SUMMIT,
BEARING
sharp ARETE
crested CORONATED,
CRISTATE, PILEATED
cretaceous CHALKY
Crete CANDIA
cape KRIO(S)
capital CANEA
earth spirit CURETE
legendary king
MINOS
man of brass TALOS
monster MINOTAUR
mountain IDA
port CANDIA
cretin IDIOT
cretism LIE, FALSE-
HOOD
crevice CREVASSE,
CRACK, RIME, FIS-
SURE, SPLIT, CRANNY,
CLEFT
crew MEN, OARS,
TEAM, MOB, HANDS,
GANG, BAND, SET,
PARTY, THRONG, AS-
SEMBLAGE, MARINERS,
STAFF, FACULTY
crib STEAL, PILFER,
PURLOIN, THEFT,
PLAGIARISM, PONY,
BOX, STALL, BED, COT,
BUNKER, RACK, BIN,
MANGER, CRATCH,
HUT, HOVEL
cribbage *counter point*
NOB, PEG
cricket GAME, INSECT
genus GRYLLUS,
ACHETIDAE
position in MID-OFF,
SLIP, LEG
run BYE
team ELEVEN
term ROT, OVER,
SNICK

crime OFFENSE,
FELONY, SIN, EVIL,
FAULT, VICE, ARSON,
INIQUITY, MURDER
Crimea KRYM
city YALTA,
SEVASTOPOL, KERCH
river ALMA
sea AZOV, AZOF
tribe INKERMAN
criminal CONVICT,
FELON, CULPRIT,
INMATE, FELONIOUS,
NOCENT, BAD, DE-
PLORABLE, ILLEGAL,
CULPABLE, GUILTY
intent DOLE, DOLOSE,
MALICE
crimp CURL, FRIZ(Z),
CRINKLE, WRINKLE,
GOFFER, NOTCH,
FLUTE, PLAIT
crimson LAC, RED,
CARMINE, PINK,
BLOODY, DYE
crine HAIR, SHRINK,
SHRIVEL, MANE
crined MANED
cringe WINCE, COWER,
CRAWL, SNEAK, BOW,
YIELD, QUAIL, FAWN,
SUBMIT, TRUCKLE,
CROUCH, STOOP
cringle EYELET,
CIRCLE, DISK, ORB,
ROPE, TERRET,
GROMMET, WITHE
crinite FOSSIL, HAIRY
crinitory, crinose
HAIRY
crinkle CURL, KINK,
WRINKLE, CRIMP,
RUSTLE, WIND, BEND,
CONVOLUTION
cripple UNFIT, MAIM,
HURT, HOBBLE, HALT,
LAME, HARM, MAR,
DISABLE, IMPAIR,
INJURE, WEAKEN
crisis TRIAL, CRUX,
STRAIT, PINCH, PASS,
TURN, EMERGENCY,
CHANGE, CONJUNC-
TURE, PANIC
having no ACRITICAL
crisp FRIABLE, BRIT-
TLE, SPALT, LIVELY,
CLEAR, COLD, STIFF,
FIRM, FRESH, SHORT,
TERSE, BITING, CUT-
TING, CURLY, WAVY,
SHARP, BRIGHT,

NEW, BRISK, CRACKLING
crispin SHOEMAKER, COAT
cristate CRESTED, TUFTED
criteria METRICS, FACTS, STANDARDS, MEASURES, RULES, LAWS, NORMS, EVIDENCE
criterion CANON, MODEL, NORM, RULE, GAUGE, STANDARD, TYPE, TEST, PROOF, TRIAL, AXIOM, LAW, INDICATION
critic EXPERT, CENSOR, JUDGE, ZOILUS, BOOER, REVIEWER, CARPER, DETRACTOR
critical ZOILEAN, EXACT, CRUCIAL, SEVERE, CARPING, CAPTIOUS, DECISIVE, BORDERING, IMPORTANT, DANGEROUS, DIFFICULT, DEADLY
mark OBELISK, OBELUS
criticism REVIEW, JUDGMENT, CRITIQUE
criticize BLAME, JUDGE, FLAY, CENSURE, ROAST, SCARIFY, RIP, PAN, SLATE, ANIMADVERT, CAVIL, HIT
croaking RAUCOUS, HARSH
Croatia(n) SERB, WEND, SORB, SLAV
capital ZAGREB
city AGRAM, FIUME
territory BANAT
tribe SLAV, WEND, SORB
crochet KNIT, WEAVE, PLAIT, BRAID, TAT, HOOK
crock SOIL, SOOT, JAR, POT, SMUT, STOOL
crockery PLATES, DISHES, EARTHENWARE
Crockett DAVID, DAVY
died at ALAMO
crocodile CAYMAN, GAVIAL, MUGGER, JACARE, REPTILE

bird PLOVER, SICSAC, TROCHILUS
like GAVIAL, NAKO(O)
marsh GOA
crocus bulb CORM
croft FARM, FIELD, BOTTLE
cromlech CYCLOLITH, CIRCLE, DOLMEN
Cromwell OLIVER, NOLL
site of victory NASEBY
crone BELDAM(E), HAG, WITCH, EWE
crook BEND, CURVE, STAFF, FELON, THIEF, DEVIATION
bishop's CROSIER
crooked RENT, ASKEW, BENT, AWRY, WINDING, CURVED, DISTORTED, ZIGZAG, AKIMBO, DISHONEST, VICIOUS, CORRUPT, TRICKY, CRAFTY, DISHONORABLE, ANGULAR
crop(s) HARVEST, FRUIT, REAP, TILLAGE, GATHER, WHIP, CLIP, CRAW, MAW, STOMACH
fowl's CRAW, MAW, GEBBIE, INGLUVIES
hunting or riding WHIP, QUIRT
year's ANNONA
cross CELTIC, ROOD, MALTESE, CRUCIFIX, SWASTIKA, LATIN, GREEK, PAPAL, TRIAL, CRANKY, GO, SPAN, TESTY, TRAVERSE, CRABBY, GIBBET, MISFORTUNE, UGLY
bar AXLE
barred TRABECULATE
beam TRAVE, BAR, GRILL
fiery CRANTARA
Greek FYLFOT
piece RUNG, YOKE, SPAR, BAR, GRILL
St. Anthony's TAU
stroke SERIF
tau ANKH, CRUX
threads WOOF
word puzzle ACROSTIC, ANAGRAM
term ACROSS, DOWN
crossrow ALPHABET

crotchet FAD, VAGARY, WHIM, HOOK, FANCY, CAPRICE
crotophagine bird ANI
crouch BEND, FAWN, SQUAT, TRUCKLE, STOOP, COWER, CRINGE
crouse BOLD, BRISK, COCKY, LIVELY, CHEERFUL
crouton BIT, SIPPET, TOAST, GARNISH
crow ROOK, CAW, DAW, CORVUS, CORBIE, RAVEN, BIRD, BRAG, VAPOR, VAUNT, BOAST, SWAGGER, EXALT, CRY
Guam AGA
like CORVINE
crowd MOB, SET, HERD, POSSE, RUCK, SWARM, DROVE, HORDE, THRONG, RABBLE, FLOCK, ASSEMBLAGE, MULTITUDE, JAM, SHOAL, SERRY, PRESS, CRUSH, LEGION, ARMS, SQUEEZE, CRAM, PACK, CRAMP, INSTRUMENT
crowded THICK, COMPACT, CLOSE, SERRIED, FILLED, DENSE, PACKED
crown TOP, CREST, CAP, TROPHY, DIADEM, CORONA, TIARA, GARLAND, CORONET, LAUREL, TAJ, COIN, SOVEREIGN, ADORN, CORONATE, PATE, CHAPLET, SCEPTER, INSTALL
prince HEIR, ATHELING
crucial SEVERE, CRITICAL, ACUTE, TRYING, INTERSECTING, TRANSVERSE, DECISIVE, TELLING
cruciation TORTURE, CROSSING, TORMENT
crucible CRUSET, ETNA, POT, RETORT, DISH
cruciferous plant(s) MOSS, FERN, ALGA(E)
crucifix ROOD, CROSS
crude RUDE, CRASS, ROUGH, RAW, CALLOW, GREEN, COARSE, GROSS, VULGAR, UNCOOKED,

UNTRAINED, UNRIPE,
HARSH, UNCOUTH
cruel SAVAGE, BRUTAL,
FERAL, FELL, TYRAN-
NIC, BESTIAL, MERCI-
LESS, PAINFUL, IN-
HUMAN
cruet AMPULLA,
CASTER, VIAL, CRUSE
cruising ASEA
crumble DECAY, ROT,
SPOIL, DISINTEGRATE,
PULVERIZE, DECOM-
POSE
crumple WRINKLE,
RUFFLE, RUCK, FOLD,
CREASE, RUMPLE
crunch CHAMP, CRUMP,
MUNCH, GRIND, CHEW
cruor BLOOD, GORE
crural joint KNEE
crusader TEMPLAR,
PILGRIM
 foe SALADIN, SARACEN
 port ACRE
crush MASH, CROWD,
PRESS, DESTROY,
HUMBLE, QUELL,
GRIND, BRUISE,
BURDEN, FORCE,
SHATTER, COMPRESS,
PULVERIZE, COM-
MINUTE
crust CAKE, RIND,
SHELL, HULL, COAT-
ING, HARDEN
crustacean LOBSTER,
CRAB, PRAWN, ISOPOD,
SQUILLA, BARNACLE,
SHRIMP
 claw CHELA
 feeler ANTENNA
 fossil TRILOBITE
 genus ERYON, HIPPA,
COPEPODA, TRIOPS
 group of CARIDEA
 king crab LIMULUS
 larva ALIMA
 limb PODITE
 appendage EXITE
 small COPEPOD,
ISOPOD
crusty BLUNT, GRUFF,
CURT, BLUFF, PETTISH,
TESTY, FRETFUL,
CRABBED, SNAPPISH
crux PUZZLE, RIDDLE,
ANKH, CROSS,
DIFFICULTY
cry PISH, AVAST, HEP,
CALL, WEEP, PULE,
YELP, HUE, SOB,

HO(A), HOWL, SHOUT,
EVOE, (BE)WAIL, FAD,
MODE, RAGE, STYLE,
SIGN, GROAN, SNIVEL,
BAWL, YELL, VOGUE
 See "exclamation"
 court OYEZ, OYES
 derisive HOOT, BOO,
HISS
 disgusted UGH
 mystic, Hindu OM
 of approval OLE,
HOCH, RAH, BRAVO
 of attention HOLLA,
HEY
 of pain OUCH
 of triumph AHA
 wild EVOE
crying PULING,
CLAMANT, NOTORIOUS,
HEINOUS, URGENT,
PRESSING
cryptic OBSCURE, DARK,
VAGUE, HIDDEN,
SECRET, OCCULT,
MYSTERIOUS,
ENIGMATIC
cryptocerate bug
CORIXA
cryptogram CODE,
ACROGEN, CIPHER,
FERN
crystal LUCID, CLEAR,
GLASS, ICE, DIAMOND,
QUARTZ, HARD, TRANS-
PARENT
 gaze SCRY
 twin MACLE
crystalline PELLUCID,
CLEAR, TRANSPARENT
 acid ALANINE
 compound ATROPINE,
SERINE, OSCIN(E),
ACONITE, ALBAN,
AMARINE
 globulin VITELLIN
 hollow nodule GEODE
 mineral QUARTZ,
MICA, DIAMOND
 phenol ORCIN(E),
ORCINOL
 pine tar RETENE
 rock DIORITE,
GREISEN
 salt BORAX
 structure SPARRY,
SIDERITE
 substance UREA,
DULCIN, SCOPOLINE
crystals, dewy with
DRUSY

ctenophora NUDA,
BEROE, CESTUS,
JELLYFISH
Cu COPPER
cub CODLIN(G), FRY,
PUP, NOVICE, WHELP,
LIONET, CHILD, BRAT
Cuban bird TOCORORO,
TROGON
 castle MORRO
 fish DIABLO
 fortification TROCHA,
MORRO
 rodent PILORI, HUTIA
 tempest BAYAMO
 tobacco CAPA, VUELTA
 tree CUYA
 ward BARRIO
cube(s) DIE, DICE,
HEXAHEDRON
cubic decimeter LITRE
 measure CORD, KILO-
(METER)
 meter STERE
cubicle CELL, NOOK,
ALCOVE, NICHE, BAY,
BOOTH
cubitus ULNA, FORE-
ARM
Cuchullin's wife EMER,
EIMER
cuckoo KOEL, ANI,
BOOBOOK, BIRD, FOOL,
CLOCK
 American COCCYZUS
 India KOEL
 vulgate LARUS
cuckoopint ARUM,
PLANT
cucullate COWLED,
HOODED
cucumber PEPO,
CONGER, GHERKIN,
CUKE
 sea PEDATA
cucurbit GOURD,
ALEMBIC, MATRASS,
FLASK
cud QUID, RUMEN,
CHEW, BOLUS
cuddle SNUGGLE, HUG,
NESTLE, PET, CARESS,
FONDLE, EMBRACE
cudgel STAFF, BAT,
CANE, CLUB, STICK,
STAVE, DRUB,
FUSTIGATE, BLUDGEON,
THRASH
cue HINT, CLUE, ROD,
TAIL, TIP, SIGNAL,
WINK, NOD, INTIMA-

TION, WATCHWORD,
STICK
music PRESTO, BATON
cuerpo TORSO, BODY,
HULK, NAKED, UN-
COVERED
cuff BOX, CLOUT, SLAP,
SMITE, SLUG, SWAT,
HIT, BUFFET,
GAUNTLET, GLOVE
cuif *See* "coof"
cuirass ARMOR, MAIL,
LORIC(A), PLATE
cuisine TABLE, FOOD,
MENU
cul-de-sac IMPASSE,
POCKET, DIFFICULTY,
STRAIT
cull DUPE, GULL,
SELECT, OPT, PICK,
ELECT, PLUCK, CULLY,
ASSORT, CHOOSE
culmination ACME,
NOON, APOGEE,
ZENITH, CLIMAX,
APEX, VERTEX,
COMPLETION, END
cult SECT, FAITH,
CREED, CHURCH,
WORSHIP
cultivate REAR, GROW,
FARM, TILL, FOSTER,
TRAIN, RAISE, NURSE,
IMPROVE, REFINE,
CIVILIZE, STUDY,
PLOW, PREPARE
cultivated land ARADA,
TILTH
culture POLISH,
AGAR, ART, CIVILIZA-
TION, TILLAGE,
KNOWLEDGE, TASTE
culver DOVE, PIGEON
cumin ANISE
cummerbund SASH,
BAND
cumshaw GRATUITY,
PRESENT, TIP, BONUS
cumulate COMBINE,
HEAP, GATHER
cunabula CRADLE
cunctation DELAY
cuneiform SPHENOID,
WEDGED, WRITING
cunning ARTFUL,
CRAFT(Y), SLY, CUTE,
KEEN, DECEIT, GUILE,
RUSE, FEINT, TRICKY,
SAGACIOUS, SHREWD,
SMART, FOXY, WILY,
ASTUTE, SUBTLE,

SHARP, CHICANERY,
DAEDAL, ARTFUL
cup MUG, GLASS,
CRATER, CHALICE,
TYG, SCYPHUS,
BEAKER, GOBLET,
POTION, AMA, VESSEL
assay CUPEL, BEAKER
bearer PINCERN, SAKI
earthenware MUG
flower CALYX
Greek DEPAS,
HOLMOS, COTYLE
handle EAR, LUG
large GRAIL, JORUM
like CALICULAR,
POCULIFORM
stand ZARF
loving TYG, PRIZE,
AWARD
Olympus DEPAS
Scotch TASS
small CRUSE,
CANNIKIN, NOGGIN,
SHOT
*with two or more
handles* TYG
cupbearer SAKI,
PINCERN
of gods HEBE
cupel REFINE, TEST
Cupid DAN, AMOR,
EROS, LOVE
sweetheart of PSYCHE
cupidity AVARICE,
GREED, LUST, DESIRE,
AVIDITY, COVETOUS-
NESS
demon of MAMMON
cuplike *stand* ZARF
stone GEODE
cupola LANTERN,
DOME, FURNACE,
LOOKOUT, KILN,
TURRET
cur MUT(T), TYKE,
DOG, SNEAK, FEIST
curassow CRAX, MITU,
BIRD
curate DOMINIE,
CLERGYMAN, AGENT,
ASSISTANT
curative REMEDIAL,
MEDICINAL, HEALING,
RESTORATIVE
curb SLACK, BIT,
CHECK, REIN,
MODERATE, THWART,
BRIDLE, FOIL, BALK,
REPRESS, RESTRAIN,
SHACKLE

curd CRUD, CASEIN(E),
CLABBER, CURDLE,
CONGEAL, COAGULATE
curdle SOUR, THICKEN,
CONDENSE, CLABBER
powder to RENNET
cure CORN, REEST,
THERAPY, SALT, HEAL,
SAVE, RESTORE, DRY,
SEASON, SMOKE,
ANTIDOTE, REMEDY,
PRESERVE
with salt CORN
cure-all ELIXIR,
PANACEA,
CATHOLICON, AVENS
curio VIRTU, BIBELOT,
KEEPSAKE
curious UNUSUAL, ODD,
RARE, NOSY, SNOOPY,
QUEER, SINGULAR,
STRANGE, PRYING
curl WIND, KINK,
TRESS, FRIZ, BERGER,
RINGLET, ROLL, WAVE,
RIPPLE, SPIRAL, TWIST,
COIL, WRITHE, BEND,
CONVOLUTION
curlew GODWIT, FUTE,
WHAUP, SNIPE,
MARLIN, BUSTARD,
BIRD
Hawaiian KIOEA
curlicue PARAPH,
FLOURISH, CAPER, ESS
curling mark TEE
curly OUNDY,
CRINKLED, KINKY,
WAVY
curmudgeon CRAB,
MISER, CHURL,
NIGGARD
curn GRAIN, CORN
currant RISSEL, RIBES,
RAISIN, BERRY
currency MONEY,
COINS, CASH, BILLS,
SPECIE, CIRCULATION
current FLOW,
MOTION, GOING, IN-
STANT, RAPID, TIDE,
HABIT, STREAM,
USUAL, WAY, RIFE,
EXISTING, PRESENT,
DRIFT, TREND, TENOR,
ROUTE, ELECTRICITY,
COMMON, GENERAL,
COURSE, PASSING, LIV-
ING, CONTEM-
PORANEOUS,
COETANEOUS, COEVAL
air THERMAL

curse SWEAR, BANE, ANATHEMA, BAN, MALISON, DAMN, MALEDICT, BLASPHEME

cursed ODIOUS, EXECRABLE, BLIGHTED, VIRULENT, BAD

cursory HASTY, SPEEDY, FAST, RAPID, SHORT, BRIEF, QUICK, SWIFT, CARELESS, PASSING, TRANSIENT

curt BRUSK, BRUSQUE, BRIEF, SHORT, CONCISE, TART, RUDE, BLUNT, GRUFF, TERSE

curtail CUT, CLIP, ABATE, LESSEN, STOP, LOP, PARE, REDUCE, SLASH, ABRIDGE, SHORTEN, RETRENCH

curtain SCREEN, DRAPE, BLIND, VEIL, SHADE

curtilage AREA, COURT, YARD

curvature CURL, LORDOSIS, SCOLIOSIS, KYPHOSIS, BEND, ARC-(UATION) *See* "curve"

curve TWIST, DIVERT, VEER, ARC, BEND, CROOK, TURN, CONCAVE, CONVEX, PARABOLA, BOW, ARCH, OGEE, ESS, CIRCUIT, AMBIT

cusp of SPINODE

double point of ACNODE

outer of arch EXTRADOS

parallel to ellipse TOROID

curved BENT, ARCIFORM, ARCUATE

hooked HAMIFORM, ADUNCOUS

inward ADUNCOUS, ADUNC, HOOKED

wedge CAM

curvet CAPER, FRISK, GAMBOL, PRANK, FROLIC, SKIP, BOUND, HOP, LOPE, LEAP, TURN

half turn CARACOLE

cuscuta DODDER, PARASITE, PLANT

Cush's *father* HAM

son SEBA, NIMROD

cushat DOVE, PIGEON, BIRD

cushion HASSOCK, SEAT, BAG, PAD, PILLOW, BOLSTER

on insect's foot PLANTULA

cusk BURBOT, TUSK, TORSK, FISH

cusp APEX, CORNER, PEAK, TOOTH, POINT, ANGLE, HORN

custard FLAN, ANNONA, APPLE, DESSERT

tree See under "tree"

custody CARE, CHARGE, TRUST, CONTROL, DURANCE, GUARDIAN-SHIP, KEEPING

custom USE, USAGE HABIT, WONT, RITE, RULE, LAW, FORM, TRIBUTE, TAX, DUTY, FASHION

combining form NOMO

of peoples MORES

with force of law MOS

customer PATRON, BUYER, CLIENT, PATIENT, PURCHASER

customs MORES, LEVY, TAX, TOLL, DUTY, TARIFF, RATE, CESS

cut GASH, LOB, LOP, MOW, HEW, SEVER, SLICE, CARVE, NOTCH, SNEE, CLIP, SNIP, SAW, SLIT, TRIM, TREPAN, KERF, SHEAR, FELL, SCAR(P), INCISE, HACK, SLASH, SERRATE, BOB, SNICK, SCIND, SHORN, DOCK, ELIDE, EXCISE, DICE, SCISSION, SNUB, REDUCE, DILUTE, LESION, DIVIDE, WEAKEN, CURTAIL, SHARE, EN-GRAVING

capable of being SECTILE

horse's mane ROACH

in half SECANT, HALVE, DIMIDIATE, BISECT

short POLL, DOCK

with shears SHIRL, SNIP

wool DOD, SHEAR

cutaneous DERMAL

cuticle EPIDERMIS, SKIN, PELLICLE, INTEGUMENT

blister BLEB, BULLA

cutis DERMA, CORIUM, SKIN

anserina GOOSE PIMPLE

cutlass DUSACK, TESACK, MACHETE, SWORD

cut short ABORT, CLIP, DOCK

cutter INCISOR, SLOOP, SLEIGH, SLED, SLICER, CLIPPER, BEEF, CORKER

cutting CURT, TART, SCION, SLIP, TWIG, TRENCHANT, SHARP, KEEN, ACUTE, CRISP, MORDANT, SARCASTIC, WOUNDING, PAINFUL

off last letter APOCOPE

relating to SECTILE

cuttlebone OSSELET

cuttlefish SEPIA, SQUID, OCTOPUS

ink SEPIA

cut-up CARD, WAG, JOKER

cuvette BUCKET, POT, TRENCH, TUB, BASIN, TANK

Cybele RHEA

Cyclades island IOS, MELOS, NAXOS, PAROS, TENOS (TINOS), NIOS, ANDROS, KEOS (ZEA), SYROS (SYRA, SIRA, SIROS)

cycle PERIOD, SAROS, AGE, EON, EPOCH, CIRCLE, ROUND, WHEEL, BIKE, VEHICLE

of life (biogeog.) SERE

cyclone TORNADO, WIND, GALE, GUST, BLAST, TWISTER, STORM

cyclopean GIANT, HUGE, VAST, GIGANTIC, COLOSSAL, HERCULEAN, STRONG *See* "huge"

Cyclops GIANT, MONSTER

Cyclostomata LAMPREYS, EELS

cygnet SWAN, FOWL

cylinder BARREL, PISTON, GABION, ROLLER, PLATEN, TUBE, PRISM
printing press INKER
cylindrical TERETE
cyma GOLA, GULA, OGEE, MOLDING
cymba SPICULE
cymbal, *oriental* TAL, ZEL
Cymbeline's *daughter* IMOGEN
cymose, *inflorescence* ANTHELA
Cymric WELSH
god See under "god, Welsh"
cynic EGOTIST, SNARLER, TIMON, DOGLIKE, MIS-ANTHROPE, PESSIMIST
cynocephalus AANI, PAPIO, LEMUR
cynosure LODESTAR, POLESTAR, ATTRAC-TION
Cynthia LUNA, MOON
cyperaceous plant SEDGE
cypher *See* "cipher"
cyprinoid fish IDE, CHI, CARP *See under* "fish"
Cyprus, *Biblical name* KITTIM
capital NICOSIA
measure OKA, OKE, PIK, CASS
town PAPHOS
Cyrenaic HEDONIC
Cyrenaica measure DRA
Cyrus SUN
daughter ATOSSA
cyst BAG, POUCH, SAC, WEN
Cytherea VENUS, APHRODITE
Cyzicus, *bishop* EUNOMIUS
czar TSAR, TZAR, PETER, IVAN
Czech SLAV
capital PRAGUE (PRAHA)
city or town PILSEN, BRNO, ZLIN, TUZLA, MOST, OPAVA, AS (ASCH)
coin DUCAT, KORUNA
county UNG

leader BENES
measure LAN, SAH, MIRA
mountain TATRA
munitions plant SKODA
river See under "river"
czigany GYPSY

D

D DEE, DELTA
dab SPOT, PINCH, PAT, STRIKE, DABSTER
dabble SPLASH, TRIFLE, SPLATTER, SPRINKLE, MOISTEN, POTTER, SMATTER, MEDDLE
dabbler DILETTANTE, SCIOLIST, TRIFLER, QUACK
dabchick GALLINULE, GREBE, BIRD
Dacian AVAR
dacoit BANDIT, MURDERER *See* "bandit"
dactyl ADONIC, FINGER, TOE, PIDDOCK
dactylic hexameter EPOS
daddle TODDLE, WAD-DLE, WALK, DAWDLE
daddy longlegs SPIN-NER, TIPULID, ARACHNID, STILT, CURLEW
dado SOLIDUM, WAIN-SCOT, DIE, BASE, GROOVE
daedal CUNNING, INGENIOUS, SKILFUL, SKILLFUL, INTRICATE
Daedalus' *nephew* TALOS
son ICARUS
Dagda's *son* AENGUS
dagger DIRK, KNIFE, BAYONET, SKEAN, BODKIN, PONIARD, SNEE, STILETTO
handle HILT
Philippine ITAC
Scotch DIRK
short KATAR
stroke STAB, STOC-CADO
tapering ANLACE
Dahomey tribe FON(G), EWE

daily ADAY, DIURNAL, QUOTIDIAN, NEWS-PAPER
dainty CATE, TIDBIT, NEAT, PRETTY, FUSSY, NICE, BONNY, PETITE, LOVELY, LIT-TLE, SMALL, RARE, CHOICE, DELICATE, SAVORY
dairy LACTARIUM
dais ESTRADE, PLAT-FORM, TABLE, BENCH, CANOPY, STAGE, ROSTRUM, SUPPORT, THRONE
daisy SHASTA, GERBERA, GOWAN, MORGAN, OXEYE
dale DELL, DINGLE, VALE, DENE, VALLEY, GLEN
dam MARE, PARENT, STEM, BAR, CLOG, OBSTRUCT, RESTRAIN, WEIR, BLOCK, HINDER, IMPEDE, CLOSE
Arizona-Nevada DAVIS, HOOVER
Australia HUME
California SHASTA
Canal Zone GATUN
Egypt ASWAN
Missouri OSAGE
S. Carolina SALUDA
S. Dakota OAHE
Tennessee NORRIS
Virginia KERR
damage LOSS, SCATHE, HARM, INJURE, HURT, IMPAIR, MAR, SPOIL, RUIN, WRECK, INJURY, DETERIORATION
pertaining to NOXAL
daman HYRAX, CONY, CONEY, RABBIT
Damascus king ARETAS
damask CLOTH, LINEN, ROSE, PINK, STEEL, FABRIC
dame, *famous* RUMOR, FORTUNE
damp HUMID, MOIST, DANK, WET, GAS, DEADEN, DEPRESS
Dan, *town of* ELON
dance, dancing NAUTCH, TROT, BAL-LET, TOE, TAP, HOP, REEL, GAVOT, POLKA, HULA, WALTZ, MIN-UET, R(H)UMBA,

HORA, PAVAN(E),
ROCK, FOLK, LAVOLTA,
GALOP, TWIST, PARTY,
BALL, BAL, PROM
art of ORCHESIS,
CHOREOGRAPHY
Bohemian REDOWA
clumsily BALTER
Cuban R(H)UMBA,
CONGA
drama BALLET
English ALTHEA,
MORRIS
European KOLO,
POLKA
formal PAVAN, PROM,
FARANDOLA
French GAVOT, BAL
gay RIGADOON, GAL-
LIARD, REEL
girl CHORINE, GEISHA,
ALMA, NAUTCH,
DANSEUSE, BAYADERE,
BALLERINA, CORYPHEE
Hawaiian HULA
Hebrew HORA
Italian COURANTE,
CALATA, VOLTA
mirthful CONGA,
GALOP, CAPER
modern SHAG, TANGO,
ROCK, TWIST
muse of TERPSICHORE
negro JUBA
New Zealand HAKA
old-fashioned HORN-
PIPE, JOG, JIG,
GALOP, REEL, MINUET
partner GIGOLO
pertaining to GESTIC,
SALTANT, TERPSI-
CHOREAN
Peru CUECA
Russian KOZACHOK
school PROM
Spanish TANGO,
BOLERO
   gypsy POLO
step CHASSE, COUPE,
PAS, GLISSADE
term PLIE
Ukrainian GOPAK
weird, pertaining to
MACABRE
dancer CHORINE, ALMA,
ZORINA, BOLGER,
ASTAIRE, BALLERINA,
DANSEUSE *See*
"dance, girl"
pole POY
dandelion stalk SCAPE

dandify ADONIZE,
SPRUCE
dandle NURSE, PAT,
PET, CARESS, TOY,
DALLY, FONDLE,
TRIFLE
dandruff SCURF
dandy FOP, TOFF,
BEAN, DUDE, FINE,
GREAT, BEAU, JAKE,
NOB, BUCK, SWELL,
COXCOMB, MACARONI,
BLADE
danger PERIL, RISK,
THREAT, PASS, HAZARD,
JEOPARDY
dangerous DIRE, CRITI-
CAL, FERAL, UNSAFE,
INSECURE, OMINOUS,
PERILOUS, RISKY,
CHANCY
dangle SWING, SUS-
PEND, DROOP, LOLL,
LOP, HANG, SWAY,
WAVE, OSCILLATE,
PEND
Danish *See* "Den-
mark"
dank DAMP, HUMID,
MOIST, WET
danseuse CORYPHEE,
BALLERINA *See*
"dance"
Dante's *love* BEATRICE
Dante, *verse from*
SESTINA
Danube *fish* HUCH(O),
HUCHEN
   tributary ARGES,
DRAVA (DRAVE,
DRAU), ILLER, INN,
IPEL (IPOLY),
PRUT(H), SAVE
(SAVA), TRAUN, VAH
(VAG, WAAG), JUI
(SCHYL), NA(A)B,
RABA (RAAB)
Daphne's *father*
LADON (PENEUS)
   mother GE
Daphnis' *lover* CHLOE
dapper NIFTY, NATTY,
SMART, CHIC, POSH,
SPRUCE, TRIM,
ELEGANT
dapple FLECK, SPOT,
PIEBALD, PIED,
VARIEGATED
dare OSSE, RISK, FACE,
DEFY, BRAVE, VEN-
TURE, CHALLENGE

dariole SHELL, CUP,
PASTRY
dark MELANIC, OC-
CULT, STYGIAN, EBON,
BLACK, DIM, JOYLESS,
WAN, MURKY, MIRKY,
OBSCURE, VAGUE,
SOMBRE, SWART,
DUSKY, MYSTIC, INKY,
GLOOMY, DISMAL,
CABALISTIC, LATENT,
UNLIT
darkness MURK, SHADE,
UMBRA, GLOOM, OB-
SCURITY, IGNORANCE,
DESPONDENCY, NIGHT
   place of EREBUS
   prince of AHRIMAN,
DEVIL, SATAN
darling CHERI(E), JO,
PET, FAVORITE, LOVE,
DEAR, BELOVED
   Irish ROON, ACUSHLA
darnel COCKLE, TARE,
GRASS
dart SCUD, FLY,
HURRY, HURL, RUSH,
SPRING, CAST, THROW,
FLIT, ARROW, LANCE,
ELANCE, MISSILE,
POMPANO, FISH,
JAVELIN, LEAP,
BOUND, START
   shooter CUPID, AMOR,
EROS, BOW
Darwin's *boat* BEAGLE
das BADGER, DASSIE
dash TOUCH, TINGE,
SHADE, VEIN, STREAK,
OBELUS, SMASH, HURL,
CAST, ARDOR, ELAN,
VERVE, RACE, COURAGE
dashes OBELI
dashing GAY, SMART,
CHIC, POSH, BRAVE,
NIFTY, NATTY, PRE-
CIPITATE, SHOWY,
HEADLONG, IMPETU-
OUS, FASHIONABLE,
OSTENTATIOUS
   as of waves PLAN-
GENT
dastard CRAVEN, CAD,
POLTROON, COWARD,
MILKSOP
datary CARDINAL
date DAY, APPOINT-
MENT, TRYST, TIME,
ERA, ENGAGEMENT,
FRUIT
   on coin EXERGUE

daub PLASTER, SMEAR, TEER, SULLY, BLOB, SOIL, COVER, SMIRCH

daunt FAZE, AMATE, SCARE, CHECK, ALARM, THWART, FOIL, APPAL(L), DISMAY, COW, AWE

dauphin GUIGO, HEIR, DELPHINIUM

daut, dawt CARESS, FONDLE

David's
captain JOAB
cave ADULLAM
commander AMASA
daughter TAMAR
father JESSE
feminine of VIDA
friend ITTAI
general IRA, IGAL, ABNER, REI
minister to IRA
musician ASAPH
son AMMON, ABSALOM

davit CRANE, SPAR, HOIST

dawdle LOITER, IDLE, LAG, POTTER, POKE, DELAY, DALLY, TARRY, WAIT, STAY, TOY, QUIDDLE

dawn AURORA, DEW, SUNUP, ORIGIN, UPRISE, DAYBREAK, SUNRISE, BEGINNING, PRECURSOR
goddess of EOS
pertaining to EO, EOAN

Dax SPA

day AGE, EPOCH, ERA, DATE, TIME
book DIARY
combining form HEMER(O)
lasting one DIARY
of this HODIERNAL, HOC DIES
pertaining to DIURNAL
week FERIA

day's *journey* DIET(A)
march ETAPE
work DARG(UE), DIET(A)

daze BEMUSE, FOG, MAZE, AWE, SHOCK, CONFUSE, STUN, BEWILDER, STUPEFY, PERPLEX, ASTONISH, BLIND

dazzle BLIND, IMPRESS, DAZE, ASTONISH, SPLENDOR

dazzling GARISH, SHOWY

deacon's *stole* ORARION

dead DECEASED, EXTINCT, AMORT, DEFUNCT, INORGANIC, GONE, LIFELESS, BREATHLESS, INANIMATE, INACTIVE, INERT, LAPSED, EXPIRED, INSENSIBLE, FEY, NAPOO, OBIT, FLAT, DULL, LATE
abode of HADES, SHEOL
city of NECROPOLIS
house of OSSUARIUM, OSSUARY, MORTUARY
mass for BLACK
relating MORTUARY

deaden MUFFLE, DAMP, OPIATE, MUTE, SMOTHER, BLUNT, BENUMB

deadfall TRAP

deadly FATAL, INTERNECINE, LETHAL, TOXIC, MORTAL, MALIGN, MURDEROUS, NOXIOUS, DESTRUCTIVE, PERNICIOUS, POISONOUS

Dead Sea, *river to* JORDAN, ARNON

deaf and dumb person SURDOMUTE

deaf, *make* SURD

deafness AMUSIA, BARYECOLA, SURDITY

deal DOLE, TRADE, SALE, ARRANGE, ALLOT, GIVE, DIVIDE, ASSIGN, SHARE, METE, DISTRIBUTE

dealer MONGER, AGENT, MERCHANT, TRADER, VENDOR, DISTRIBUTOR

dean DELL, DOYEN, SENIOR, TEACHER, VALE, VALLEY
pertaining to DECANAL

dear COSTLY, EXPENSIVE, PRECIOUS, BELOVED, DARLING, LOVE(D), CHERI(E)

dearth FAMINE, WANT, PAUCITY, SCARCITY, NEED, LACK

death EVANISHMENT, MORT, DEMISE, DECEASE, EXTINCTION, END, EXIT, FINIS, QUIETUS
black PLAGUE
bringing FUNEST
mercy EUTHANASIA
notice OBIT
rattle RALE

debar ESTOP, HINDER, SHUT, BAN, BAR, PROHIBIT, EXCLUDE, RESTRAIN

debark LAND, DISEMBARK, ARRIVE

debase ABASE, CORRUPT, ALLOY, DEMEAN, TAINT, HARM, SPOIL, WEAKEN, DEGRADE, SAP, LOWER, VITIATE, DISGRACE, DENIGRATE

debased VILE

debatable MOOT

debate ARGUE, CANVASS, MOOT, REASON, TALK, PLEAD, REBUT, DISPUTE, BATTLE, ARGUMENT, ALTERCATION, CONTROVERSY
pertaining to FORENSIC, CLOTURE, QUODLIBETARY
stopping of CLOTURE

debauch BOUT, ORGY, SPLORE, INJURE, HARM, SPOIL, MAR, LURE, DEFILE, CORRUPT, DEPRAVE, SEDUCE, DISSIPATION, CAROUSAL

debauchee RAKE, ROUE, SATYR, LIBERTINE

debilitate WEAKEN, UNMAN, SAP, IMPAIR, HURT, HARM, MAR, ENERVATE, EXHAUST, ENFEEBLE

debility INFIRMITY, ATONY, LASSITUDE, FRAILTY

deblaterate GAB, BLABBER, PRATE, TATTLE

debonair SUAVE, URBANE, BUOYANT, PERKY, COCKY, CHIPPER, GAY, LITHE, GENTEEL, AFFABLE,

POLITE, GRACIOUS, CHEERY

debris TRASH, DRIBLETS, DETRITUS, ODDMENTS, RUBBISH, RUINS, REMAINS, SCREENINGS

debt IOU, LIABILITY, DUTY, CHARGE, ARREARS, SIN, FAULT, OBLIGATION, DEBIT, TRESPASS

debutante BUD, DEB

decad TEN

decade DECENNIUM

decamp FLEE, BOLT, ELOPE, FLY, ABSCOND, MOVE, VAMOOSE, ESCAPE, DEPART, SCRAM, QUIT, LEAVE, GO, EVADE, LAM

decant POUR

decanter CARAFE, CROFT, EWER, PITCHER

decapod CRAB, PRAWN, SQUID, SHRIMP, LOBSTER, CRUSTACEAN
crustacean genus HOMARUS

decay ROT, SPOIL, DEFILE, RUIN, FAIL, IMPAIR, DECLINE, DETERIORATE, PUTREFY, DECOMPOSE

decease DEMISE, FAIL, OBIT, DEATH, PASSING

deceased LATE, DEAD, DEFUNCT, LOST, GONE

deceit GUILE, COVIN, FRAUD, CRAFT, SHAM, WILE, RUSE, TRICK, FEINT, COZENAGE, DECEPTION, ARTIFICE, CHICANERY

deceitful ARTFUL, WILY, INSIDIOUS, DELUSIVE, FRAUDULENT, GNATHONIC, CUNNING

deceive MISLEAD, MASK, SILE, HOCUS, ABUSE, FLAM, GULL, ILLUDE, DUPE, BETRAY, CHEAT, COZEN, (BE)FOOL, TRICK, HOAX, DELUDE, HUMBUG

deceiver LIAR, BETRAYER, SHAM, CHEAT,

FAKER, TRICKSTER, IMPOSTER, CHARLATAN, ROGUE, SHARPER

decency GRACE, PROPRIETY, DECORUM, MODESTY

decent CHASTE, PURE, GOOD, FIT, PROPER, SEEMLY, NICE, MEET, MODEST, NOBLE, COMELY, ACCEPTABLE

deception SHAM, FRAUD, CHEAT, FAKE, RUSE, HOAX, ILLUSION, LIE, JAPE, WILE, STRATAGEM

deceptive SIRENIC HOLLOW, VAGUE, SPECIOUS, FALSE, WRONG, FALLACIOUS, ILLUSORY

decibels, *ten* BEL

decide ELECT, SETTLE, FIX, (AD)JUDGE, CONCLUDE, DETERMINE, RESOLVE, END, RULE, VOTE, RATE

decimal TEN, TENTH
circulating REPETEND

decimate SLAUGHTER, SLAY, SUBTRACT, KILL, DESTROY

decipher DECODE, UNRAVEL, SOLVE, INTERPRET

decision VERDICT, DOOM, METTLE, NERVE, RULING, VOTE, JUDGMENT, ARRET, APLOMB, DECREE, ANNOUNCEMENT, DETERMINATION, FINDING, REPORT

decisive FINAL, CRITICAL, CRUCIAL, ACUTE, CONCLUSIVE, CERTAIN, TELLING

deck ARRAY, ADORN, ENRICH, GILD, ATTIRE, DRESS, GARNISH, FLOOR, CARDS
cards PACK
lower ORLOP
post BITT
raised border COAMING
ship MAIN, LOWER, POOP, PROMENADE, ORLOP

declaim AIR, VENT, ORATE, SPOUT,

RECITE, INFORM, VOICE, UTTER, RANT, BLAZON, MOUTH, HARANGUE, DISCOURSE

declaration STATEMENT, BID, PROCLAMATION, PLEADING, AVOWAL

declare AVOW, ALLEGE, AVER, AVOUCH, UTTER, PUBLISH, SPREAD, SAY, STATE, MELD, ASSEVERATE, ASSERT, PROCLAIM, AFFIRM

decline BALK, AGE, ABATE, SINK, FAIL, DIP, EBB, SLUMP, REFUSE, REJECT, SPURN, DEMUR, DECAY, PINE, FLAG, WANE, FADE, WEAKEN, DROOP

declivity SLOPE, DESCENT, SCARP, INCLINE, SLANT, GRADE, HILL

decoction TISANE, APOZEM(A), SAPA, CREMOR, DRINK, DISH, EXTRACT, BOILING, INFUSION

decompose DECAY, ROT, SPOIL, LIQUEFY, MELT, DISINTEGRATE, ANALYZE, PUTREFY

decor DECORATION, SCENERY, MOTIF, SETTING

decorate ADORN, (BE)DECK, GARNISH, BORDER, SCRIMSHAW, ORNAMENT, TRIM
garishly BEDIZEN
with letters MINIATE
with raised patterns BROCADE

decorated NIELLED, ADORNED, BROCADED, CITED
wall part DADO

decoration NIELLO, TROPHY, MEDAL, RIBBON, CUP, TRIM, INSIGNE, ORNAMENT, EDGING, LACE
metal ware TOLE
military MEDAL, RIBBON, DSC, DSM, DSO
mineral TINSEL, PURFLE

pertaining to MEDAL-
LIC
decorous DEMURE,
NICE, DECENT,
SEEMLY, PROPER,
FORMAL, COMELY,
FIT, CALM, SEDATE,
PRIM
decorticate STRIP,
BARK, PARE, PEEL,
SKIN, FLAY, HULL,
HUSK, DEBARK
decoy LURE, TRAP,
TOLE, ENTICE, PLANT,
BAIT, SNARE, TEMPT,
DELUDE, DECEIVE,
INVEIGLE
gambling CAPPER,
RINGER
decrease DWINDLE,
EBB, WANE, ABATE,
LESSEN, REDUCE,
SHRINK, DIMINISH,
DECEIVE, SUBSIDE
decree ORDAIN, FIAT,
WRIT, ARRET, ACT,
EDICT, CANON, LAW,
NISI, JUDGMENT,
RULING, WILL, ORDER,
DICTUM, MANDATE,
APPOINT, DECISION
imperial IRADE, FIAT,
ARRET, UKASE
papal BULL
Russian UKASE
decrepit OLD, INFIRM,
FEEBLE, WEAK,
FRAIL, FRAGILE,
WORN, AGED, WASTED,
DECAYED
decry BELITTLE, DIS-
CREDIT, DISPARAGE,
TRADUCE, DETRACT
decussation CHIASMA,
INTERSECTION
dedicate DEVOTE, HAL-
LOW, CONSECRATE,
SANCTIFY, INSCRIBE
deduce GATHER,
JUDGE, INFER,
REASON, DEEM,
OPINE, THINK, DERIVE,
CONCLUDE
deduct BATE, FAIK,
TAKE, DELETE, RE-
BATE, RETRENCH, CUT,
SUBTRACT, WITHDRAW,
REMOVE
deed EXPLOIT,
GEST(E), ACT, FEAT,
RECORD, TRANSFER,
ACTION, REALITY,

FACT, FAIT, INDEN-
TURE, CONVEY,
CHARTER
deem CONSIDER,
JUDGE, OPINE,
REGARD, ACCOUNT,
RECKON, INFER,
THINK, SUPPOSE,
IMAGINE, HOLD,
GATHER
deep PROFOUND, BASS,
WISE, CUNNING, AB-
STRUSE, ASTUTE,
SEA, OCEAN
deer ELK, PITA,
BROCKET, CERVID,
MOOSE
American CARIBOU,
MOOSE, WAPITI,
ELK
antler DAG, TRES-
TINE, HORN, BEZ
Asian KAKAR, SAMBAR,
AXIS
axis CHITAL
Chile PUDU
cry BELL
fallow DAMA
family CERVIDAE
female DOE, HIND,
ROE
genus CERVUS, DAMA,
RUSA, PUDU
grass RHEXIA
India AXIS, KAKAR,
RUSA
male BUCK, STAG,
HART
muntjac KAKAR,
KAKUR
Persia MARAL
pertaining to CER-
VINE, DAMINE
pygmy, Malay
PLANDOK
red HART, OLEN,
STAG, ROE
rusine antlers AXIS
Sambar MAHA
small MUNTJAC, ROE,
PLANDOK, FAWN
S. Amer. PITA,
GUEMAL, PUDU
tail SCUT
three-year-old SORREL
Tibet SHOU
track SLOT
two-year-old
BROCK(ET)
unbranched antler
DAG

young FAWN, SPIT-
TER, PRICKET
deface SCAR, MAR,
MUTILATE, INJURE,
BLEMISH, DISTORT,
DISFIGURE, BLOTCH
defame SPLATTER,
LIBEL, VILIFY,
SLANDER, REVILE,
ASPERSE, DECRY,
DISPARAGE, MALIGN,
TRADUCE, CALUMNI-
ATE
default DEFICIT, LACK,
WANT, MORA, LOSS,
NEGLECT, DEFECT,
DEBT
defeat FOIL, CONQUER,
REVERSE, THWART,
BEAT, LICK, REDUCE,
MASTER, ROUT, CON-
FUSE, WORST, RE-
PULSE, OVERTHROW,
FRUSTRATE, FAILURE
defect BUG, FLAW,
LACK, FAULT, FAIL-
ING, FRAILTY, WANT,
NEED, BLEMISH,
CRACK, FOIBLE,
IMPERFECTION
in cloth SCOB,
SNAG
timber LAG, KNOT
defend GUARD, SHEND,
COPE, BACK, SHIELD,
RESIST, FIGHT, UP-
HOLD, SAVE, VINDI-
CATE, JUSTIFY,
ESPOUSE, OPPOSE,
SHELTER, SCREEN,
SECURE, WARD
defendant REUS,
CHAMPION
defense ALIBI, PLEA,
EXCUSE, GUARD,
PROTECTION, MAIN-
TENANCE, SHIELD,
BULWARK
in law ANSWER
making a salient angle
RAVELIN
means of ABATIS
unit NATO, SEATO,
ARMY, NAVY, MARINES,
AAF, AF
defer DELAY, STAY,
YIELD, SUBMIT,
RETARD, SLOW, AC-
CEDE, AGREE, RE-
MAND, POSTPONE,
ADJOURN, PROCRASTI-
NATE, WAIT

deference FEALTY, HOMAGE, HONOR, REGARD, RESPECT, ESTEEM, CONSIDERATION

deficiency SHORTAGE, ULLAGE, WANT, LACK, DEFAULT, DEARTH, SCARCITY

defile MOIL, TAINT, POLLUTE, PASS, SULLY, DIRTY, BEFOUL, TARNISH, RAVISH, VIOLATE, SOIL, STAIN, CORRUPT, CONTAMINATE, POISON, DEBAUCH

define ASSIGN, EXPLAIN, LIMIT, FIX, SET, INTERPRET, DEMARCATE, BOUND, SETTLE, CLARIFY, NAME

definite EXACT, PLAIN, PRECISE, SET(TLED), EXPLICIT, CERTAIN, SPECIAL, MANIFEST, APPROVED, OFFICIAL

deflate EXHAUST, EMPTY, REDUCE, HUMBLE, SHRINK, LESSEN, DRAIN, COLLAPSE

deflect TURN, DIVERT, AVERT, DEPART, VEER, CURVE, TWIST, DEVIATE, DIVERGE, SWERVE

Defoe character FRIDAY, MOLL, CRUSOE, XURY

deform CRIPPLE, DISFIGURE, INJURE, MAR, DISTORT, MAIM, WARP, MANGLE, DEFACE, SPOIL

defraud GULL, ROB, SWINDLE, GYP, CHEAT, BILK, COZEN, HOAX, DUPE, FOIL, TRICK, (BE)FOOL, HOODWINK, CHOUSE

deft ADROIT, CLEVER, EXPERT, APT, FIT, MEET, PAT, HANDY, AGILE, NIMBLE, QUICK, DEXTEROUS, SKILLFUL

defy REVOLT, BEARD, DARE, FACE, SCORN, FRONT, OPPOSE, BRAVE, CHALLENGE, SLIGHT, SPURN, FLOUT, DISOBEY, THREATEN

degrade ABASE, DEBASE, SHAME, DEMOTE, HUMBLE, DISGRACE, DISHONOR, LOWER, HUMILIATE, DEPOSE

degrading MENIAL, LOW

degree STEP, RANK, RATE, CLASS, STATION, GRADE, ORDER, PITCH, STAGE, HONOR, TERM, STANDING, MEASURE, EXTENT

kind of NTH, THIRD

dehisce GAPE, YAWN, BURST

dehydrate DRY, PARCH, BAKE, DESICCATE

deiform DIVINE, GOD-LIKE

deify EXALT, APOTHEOSIZE, IDOLIZE, ELEVATE, ENNOBLE, GLORIFY, HONOR

deign CONCEDE, STOOP, CONDESCEND, VOUCHSAFE, CONSENT

deity See "god" or "goddess"

dejected GLOOMY, MOPY, DROOPY, AMORT, BLUE, DISHEARTENED, DOWNCAST, DOLEFUL, MELANCHOLY

delate ACCUSE, DENOUNCE, REPORT

Delaware county KENT, SUSSEX

delay LINGER, RETARD, PAUSE, DETER, LATEN, DALLY, LAG, DETAIN, SLOW, HINDER, BLOCK, OBSTRUCT, IMPEDE, STAY, DEFER, LOITER, CUNCTATION, POSTPONE, PROCRASTINATE, ARREST, CHECK, STALL, CONTINUE

law MORA, CONTINUANCE

unjustifiable MORA

dele DELETE, ERASE, REMOVE, CANCEL, BLOT

delegate AGENT, ATTORNEY, LEGATE, ENVOY, COMMISSIONER, REPRESENTATIVE, DEPUTY

delete DELE, EFFACE, EXPUNGE, CANCEL, REMOVE, ERASE, BLOT, OMIT, STRIKE

deletion, last letter of word APOCOPE

restore STET

delibate SIP, TASTE, DABBLE

deliberate PREPENSE, COOL, THINK, MUSE, PLAIN, WILLFUL, WILLING, REASON, PONDER(OUS), SLOW, REFLECT, CONSIDER, COGITATE, MEDITATE, CAREFUL, CAUTIOUS

Delibes composition LAKME, SYLVIA

delicacy TACT, FINESSE, CATE, TIDBIT, KNACK, NICETY, SUBTLETY

delicate DAINTY, NICE, LACY, AIRY, WEAK, SOFT, CHOICE, MILD, LENIENT, SAVORY, FINE, FRAGILE, EXQUISITE, TENDER, SLENDER

delicious RARE, DAINTY, CHOICE, SAVORY, TASTY, SAPID, NECTAREOUS, LUSCIOUS, DELICATE, APPLE

delict OFFENSE, WRONG, VIOLATION, CRIME, TORT

delight GRATIFY, PLEASE, SATISFY, AMUSE, REGALE, DIVERT, BLISS, GLEE, JOY, MIRTH, REVEL, CHARM, RAPTURE, ENCHANT, TRANSPORT

delineate DEPICT, PAINT, LIMN, SHOW, SKETCH, MAP, OUTLINE, DRAW, DRAFT, PLOT, TRACE, RELATE, DESIGN, PLAN, FIGURE, DESCRIBE, PORTRAY

deliquesce DISSOLVE, MELT, THAW, LIQUEFY, RAMIFY

delirious MAD, RAVING, INSANE, DERANGED,

WANDERING,
FRENZIED, MANIACAL
delitescent LATENT,
HIDDEN
deliver RID, UTTER,
EMIT, DEAL, FREE,
DISCHARGE, VENT,
EXPRESS, RESCUE,
SAVE, LIBERATE, RE-
LEASE, EMANCIPATE,
REDEEM, YIELD,
CEDE, GRANT, RELIEVE
dell VALE, DALE, GLEN,
DINGLE, RAVINE,
VALLEY, DENE, GLADE
Delphi priestess
PYTHIA
delude *See* "deceive"
deluge STREAM,
FLOOD, SPATE, OVER-
FLOW, CATACLYSM,
DOWNPOUR
delusion MIRAGE,
VISION, PHANTASM,
RUSE, MOCKERY,
CHEAT, ERROR, FAKE,
DECEIT, DREAM, TRICK,
FANCY, FRAUD,
ARTIFICE, WILE,
DECEPTION
Buddhist MOHA
partner of SNARE
delve DIG, MINE, TILL,
SPADE, GRUB, DIP,
STUDY, INVESTIGATE,
PROBE
demagogue OCHLOCRAT
demand DUN, CRY,
ASK, LEVY, CLAIM,
EXACT, REQUIRE,
SOLICIT, ORDER,
DIRECT, BID, CALL,
CITE, CHALLENGE,
INQUIRE, SUMMON
demean ABASE, DE-
GRADE, DEBASE, CARRY,
BEHAVE, LOWER, CON-
DUCT, COMPORT
demeanor CARRIAGE,
MIEN, MANNER, BE-
HAVIOR, DEPORTMENT,
CONDUCT, AIR, BEAR-
ING
demented LUNY,
LOONY, MAD, CRAZED,
MANIC, IDIOTIC,
FOOLISH, DAFT,
DERANGED, MANIACAL,
CRAZY
Demeter CERES
daughter KORE

demigod HERO,
SATYR, IDOL, GODLING
demolish ELIDE,
RAZE, RUIN, UNDO,
WRECK, DESTROY,
SCRAP, WRACK, SACK,
RAVAGE, RASE, LEVEL,
OVERTHROW
demon(s) IMP, ATUA,
DEUCE, FIEND, JIN(N),
DEVA, GENIE, DEVIL,
OGRE, GOBLIN, TROLL,
DAEMON
Arabian AFREET,
JIN(N)
assembly of SABBAT
Burmese NAT
cunning DAEDAL,
OGRE, IMP
female LAMIA, MARA
Hindu ASURA
king ASMODEUS
Maori ATUA
prince of BEELZEBUB
worship of
DEMONOLATRY
demonstrate PROVE,
SHOW, EVINCE, TRY,
TEST, REVEAL, DIS-
CLOSE, EXHIBIT,
ARGUE, DEBATE,
VERIFY, ESTABLISH
demonstration TRIAL,
TEST, RIOT, SCENE,
PROOF, MANIFESTA-
TION, DISPLAY,
EXHIBITION
demonstrative
GUSHING, VEHEMENT,
THIS, THAT, THESE,
THOSE, ABSOLUTE,
PROBATIVE
demos DISTRICT,
PEOPLE, POPULACE,
DEME
demulcent BALM,
SALVE, SOOTHING,
SOFTENING,
SEDATIVE, EMOLLIENT
demur HESITATE, OB-
JECT, SCRUPLE,
WAVER, BALK, PAUSE,
STOP, DELAY, INTER-
POSE, DISSENT
demure PRIM, STAID,
COY, GRAVE, MIM,
SEDATE, NICE, PROPER,
SOLEMN, SOBER, SHY,
DECOROUS, MODEST
den CAVE, DIVE, LAIR,
HAUNT, STUDY,
CAVERN, RETREAT

wild animal's, Rome
CAVEA
denary TEN, DECIMAL
dendrophilous
ARBOREAL
denigrate DEFAME,
BELITTLE, SULLY,
VILIFY
denizen INHABITANT,
CITIZEN, CIT,
RESIDENT, DWELLER
of Hell HELLION,
SATAN
Denmark, Danish
anatomist STENO
animal AUROCHS
artist BLOCH
astronomer BRAHE
chief YARL, JARL
city or town
ELSINORE, A(A)RHUS,
ODENSE, VEJLE
coin KRONE, ORE,
HORSE, FYRK
council of state
RIGSRAAD
county SORO
dependency FAROE
(ISLANDS)
division AMT
fjord ISE
island(s) AERO,
FAROE, FALSTER, FYN
king KNUT, OLAF
legislature LANDSTING,
FOLKETING, RISDAG
measure FOD, ALEN,
POT, ALBUM, LAND-
MILL, MI(I)L, FAVN,
FLASKE, FUDER,
KANDE, LINIE, MUL,
PAEGLE, PFLUG,
PIBE, RODE, TOMME,
TONDE
parliament RISDAG
peninsula JUTLAND
physician FINSEN
physicist BOHR
prince HAMLET,
OGIER
ruler CANUTE, KLAK,
SWEYN, KNUT, AVEN,
OLAF, (C)NUT, SVEN
sand ridge SCAW,
SKAGI
seaport VEJLE
speech STOD
trading post THULE
trumpet LUR(E)
weight CENTNER,
ORT, LOD, PUND,
VOG, GRAN, KVINT,

MARK, QUINT, TONDE, UNZE, WAAG

dennet GIG, CARRIAGE

denominate STYLE, CALL, DUB, TERM, NAME, CHRISTEN, ENTITLE

denomination SECT, CULT, CLASS, CATEGORY, NAME, CHURCH

denote IMPLY, MEAN, SIGNIFY, SPECIFY, CONNOTE, INDICATE, DESIGNATE

denounce DECRY, CHARGE, ASSAIL, SCATHE, BLAME, AC-CUSE, INDICT, THREATEN, MENACE, ARRAIGN

de novo AFRESH, AGAIN, ANEW, NEWLY, OVER

dense POPULOUS, THICK, CRASS, CLOSE, MASSED, PILED, COM-PACT, HEAVY, CROWDED, TEEMING, STUPID, DULL, DUMB, OBTUSE, STOLID

density MASS, COM-PACTNESS

dent NOTCH, DINT, NICK, DINGLE, HOL-LOW, PIT, IMPRESSION

dental tool SCALER, DRILL, FORCEPS

dentate SERRATE, TOOTHED, JAGGED

dentine IVORY

denture TEETH, PLATE

denude STRIP, UNROBE, BARE, DIVEST, EXPOSE

deny NEGATE, ABJURE, REJECT, DISOWN, REBUT, RENEGE, CON-TRADICT, GAINSAY, RENOUNCE, ABNEGATE, DISCLAIM, REFUSE

deodar CEDAR, TREE

depart VEER, DEVIATE, DECAMP, RETREAT, EGRESS, VAMOOSE, EXIT, GO, FLEE, ELOPE, RETIRE, LEAVE, QUIT, SCRAM, VANISH, WITHDRAW, DIE, DE-CEASE, PERISH, RELINQUISH

departed GONE, NAPOO, OFFED, DEAD, LEFT, WENT, LATE, BYGONE

department DIVISION, DISTRICT, PROVINCE, BUREAU, STATION, REGION, SECTION

departure LEAVE, EXODUS, EXIT, RE-TIREMENT, RETREAT

depend HINGE, RELY, HANG, LEAN, REST, LOP, TRUST, COUNT, RECKON, BANK

dependency APPENDAGE, ADJUNCT, COLONY, DOMINION, PROVINCE

Hindu TALUK

dependent COL-LATERAL, CLIENT, SPONGER, MINION, SERVILE, CHILD, HANGER-ON, SUBJECT, LIABLE, OPEN, CON-TINGENT, RETAINER, VASSAL, SUBORDINATE, CONDITIONED

depict DELINEATE, LIMN, PAINT, PORTRAY, TELL, SKETCH, DRAW, DE-SCRIBE

depilate STRIP, PLUCK, SHAVE

depilatory RUSMA

deplete DRAIN, SAP, WEAKEN, LESSEN, EX-HAUST, REDUCE, EMPTY, EVACUATE

deplore (BE)WAIL, REGRET, RUE, WEEP, CRY, GRIEVE, MOURN, LAMENT

deplorable SAD, PITIABLE, CALAMITOUS, WRETCHED, BAD, EXECRABLE, TERRIBLE

depone ATTEST, DEPOSE, SWEAR, AFFIRM, TESTIFY

deport BANISH, EXILE, DEMEAN, (AC)QUIT

depose AFFIRM, OUST, AVER, TESTIFY, UN-SEAT, SWEAR, DETHRONE

deposit HOARD, STORE, SAVE, PLEDGE, PLACE, LAY, CACHE, BED, MARL, OOZE, LEES, DREGS, DUMP, PUT, SEDIMENT, SILT, PAWN

alluvial DELTA, GEEST

black tissue MELANOSIS

clay MARL

geyser SINTER

loam LOESS

river ALLUVIA, DELTA, SILT

teeth TARTAR, CALCULUS

wine cask TARTAR

depository VAULT, SAFE, BANK, DEPOT, STOREHOUSE, CACHE

depot STATION, STOP, GARE, WAREHOUSE, CACHE

depraved EVIL, VILE, DISSOLUTE, DEBASED, VICIOUS, CORRUPT, DEGENERATE, PER-VERTED, SHAMELESS, WICKED

depravity VICE, DIS-GRACE, INFAMY, LICENSE, INIQUITY

deprecate PROTEST, REGRET, DEPLORE, BEWAIL

depreciate CHEAPEN, SLUMP, FALL, BE-LITTLE, UNDERRATE, LESSEN, DECRY, DE-CLINE, WEAR, RUST

depredate PILLAGE, ROB, SPOIL, MARAUD, PREY, WASTE, PLUNDER

depress ABATE, DAMPEN, DENT, TROUBLE, AIL, LOWER, SINK, REDUCE, DIS-COURAGE, DEJECT, CHILL, SADDEN

depressed DIRE, SAD, DISMAL, LOW

depression TROUGH, COL, DENT, DIP, FOSSA, PIT, VAPORS, GLOOM, BLUES, DESPAIR, ENNUI, HOLLOW, DUMPS, CAVITY, DIMPLE

between mountains COL

deprive DIVEST, DIS-POSSESS, DENUDE,

BEREAVE, DEBAR, ROB, STRIP, DESPOIL, TAKE

depth ABYSS, EXTENT, ACUMEN, PIT, GULF, OCEAN, SEA, PROFUNDITY, SAGACITY, MIDDLE

depute SEND, ASSIGN, DELEGATE, COMMISSION, AUTHORIZE

deputies POSSE, AGENTS

deputy PROXY, ENVOY, AGENT, VICAR, FACTOR, LEGATE, REPRESENTATIVE, SUBSTITUTE

derelict ABANDONED, TRAMP, CASTAWAY, HULL, LAPSE, WRECK, FORSAKEN, LEFT, NEGLIGENT, FAITHLESS, DESERTED, OUTCAST

deride FLEER, JEER, JIBE, MOCK, SCOFF, RAG, KID, CHAFF, TAUNT, TEASE, TWIT, RIDICULE, SCOUT, LAMPOON

derive DRAW, EVOLVE, CONCLUDE, GET, EDUCE, OBTAIN, (A)RISE, ISSUE, DEDUCE, STEM, FLOW, SPRING, TRACE, INFER

dermal filament HAIR

dernier LAST, FINAL, ULTIMATE

derogate DECRY, REPEAL, ANNUL, REDUCE, LESSEN, DISPARAGE, DENIGRATE

derrick CRANE, RIG, STEEVE, HOIST, DAVIT
part of BOOM, GIN, LEG

derring-do GESTE

dervish FAKIR, AGIB, YOGI, MENDICANT, ASCETIC
headgear TAJ

descant EXPIATE, SOPRANO, COMMENT, NOTE, REMARK, ENLARGE, DILATE, TREBLE, TUNE

descendants POSTERITY, PROGENY, SEED, (S)CIONS, LITTER, ISSUE, OFFSPRING

descended ALIT, FELL, STOOPED, SANK
from same ancestor AGNATE, CONSANGUINEOUS
source ROOT, STIRPS

descent BIRTH, ORIGIN, LINE, FALL, DROP, SLIP, LURCH, HILL, DIP, DECLINE, PITCH, SLOPE, PEDIGREE, PARENTAGE, LINEAGE, SUCCESSION
line(s) of PHYLA, PHYLUM

describe DEPICT, STATE, RELATE, REPORT, SKETCH, DRAW, LIMN, TRACE, EXPLAIN, PORTRAY, PICTURE, OUTLINE

description REPORT, ACCOUNT, VERSION, SORT, CLASS, NATURE, ILK, TYPE, EXPLANATION, RECITAL, SPECIES, DISCOURSE, DEFINITION

descry SIGHT, ESPY, DETECT, SPOT, SEE, REMARK, DISCOVER, BEHOLD, RECOGNIZE, DISCERN, DETERMINE

Desdemona's husband OTHELLO

desert RENEGE, RAT, LEAVE, FORSAKE, DEPART, EMPTY, ABANDON, QUIT, DUE, MEED, MERIT, REWARD, WASTE, DESOLATE, WILD, BARREN, WILDERNESS
Africa SAHARA, LIBYAN, (EL)ERG
Asia GOBI
Gobi SHAMO
India THAR
pertaining to EREMIC, SERE
plant ALHAGI, CACTUS, AGAVE
Russia TUNDRA
watering spot OASIS

deserter RAT, APOSTATE, RENEGADE, RECREANT, TURNCOAT

deserve EARN, MERIT, WIN

desiccated ARID, DRY, SERE, PARCHED

design DESTINE, SCHEME, FORM, DIAGRAM, DRAWING, END, GOAL, IDEA, PLOT, INVENT, FIGURE, MOTIF, PURPOSE, DEVICE, PLAN, MAP, MEAN, AIM, ASPIRE, CREATE, CONTRIVE, CONTRIVANCE, DRAUGHT, DRAFT, INTENT(ION), INSIGNE, MONOGRAM

designate STIPULATE, INDICATE, DENOTE, STYLE, ASSIGN, ALLOT, MARK, ENTITLE, CALL, NAME, APPOINT, CHOOSE, SELECT, PICK, SPECIFY

desipience FOLLY, CONCEIT, TRIFLING

desirable IDEAL, RARE, ENVIABLE, CHOICE, GOOD

desire URGE, LUST, PINE, HUNGER, PANT, YEN, ASPIRE, COVET, NEED, CARE, THIRST, LONG, WISH, WANT, FANCY, CRAVE, YEARN, HANKER, ITCH, HEART, IMPULSE, AIM, ENTREAT, REQUEST, ASK, APPETENCY

desist CEASE, STOP, QUIT, FORBEAR, REFRAIN, PAUSE, DISCONTINUE

desmanthus ACUAN, HERB, SHRUB

desolate BLEAK, (FOR)-LORN, SACK, LONELY, BARREN, DESERTED, (A)LONE, CHEERLESS, DREARY, DEVASTATE(D), DEJECTED, SAD

despair SADNESS, DEJECTION, GLOOM, DESPONDENCY, HOPELESSNESS, GRIEF

despatch See "dispatch"

desperate RASH, FORLORN, WRETCHED, HOPELESS, FRANTIC

despise SCORN, DISDAIN, LOATHE, ABHOR, DETEST, HATE, SPURN, CONTEMN despoil FLEECE, REAVE, DIVEST, RUIN, INJURE, RIP, ROB, RAVAGE, SACK, PILLAGE, STRIP, DENUDE, DEPRIVE, PLUNDER, RIFLE, BEREAVE

despot AUTOCRAT, TSAR, TYRANT, DICATATOR

despumate SCUM, SKIM, FROTH, FOAM

dessert ICE, PIE, TRIFLE, COURSE, SNACK, MOUSSE, CAKE, PASTRY, PUDDING, SWEET

destination GOAL, END, MARK, WILL, WISH, FATE, LOT, DOOM, PURPOSE, DESIGN, OBJECT, AIM

destine INTEND, ORDAIN, DOOM, DEVOTE

destiny FATE, DOOM, EURE, LOT, PORTION, END, GOAL, STAR, FORTUNE
oriental KISMET

destitute BEREFT, NEEDY, (DE)VOID, BARE, BARREN, EMPTY, INDIGENT, POOR

destroy ROOT, RUIN, SACK, DECIMATE, KILL, UNDO, WRECK, ABOLISH, ERASE, DEMOLISH, RASE, RAZE, ANNIHILATE, WASTE, RAVAGE, SLAY, SPOIL, BURN

Destroyer SIVA

destroying angel, *fungus* AMANITA
Mormon DANITE

destruction RUIN, HAVOC, PERDITION, CRASH, FALL, DOOM, HOLOCAUST, TALA, DEMOLITION, MASSACRE
of species GENOCIDE

destructive ANERETIC, RUINOUS, PERNICIOUS, FATAL

desultory CASUAL, CHANCE, FITFUL, CURSORY, SLIGHT

detach UNFIX, ISOLATE, SEVER, PART, SUNDER, SEPARATE, DISJOIN, WITHDRAW

detachment PART, ITEM, PORTION, PIECE, SECTOR, SQUAD, ALOOFNESS, UNCONCERN

detail PORTION, ITEM, PIECE, SECTOR, PART, NARRATE, RECITAL, ACCOUNT, PARTICULAR, CIRCUMSTANCE

detain INTERN, KEEP, CHECK, CURB, SLOW, DELAY, HOLD, JAIL, NAB, CATCH, ARREST, RETAIN, RESTRAIN, STOP, CONFINE

detect ESPY, SEE, SCENT, SPOT, FIND, DISCOVER, DESCRY, EXPOSE, DISCERN, SMELL, HEAR

detecting device RADAR, SONAR

detective BEAGLE, SLEUTH, SPY, DICK, TEC, SPOTTER, TAILER, SHADOW

detent CLICK, TONGUE, PAWL, PIN, STUD, CATCH, FENCE, DOG

deter HINDER, PREVENT, FRIGHTEN, SCARE, RESTRAIN, DISCOURAGE, DISSUADE

detergent SOAP, CLEANER, PURGE

deteriorate WANE, WEAR, RUST, ROT, DECAY, DECLINE, EBB, CORRUPT, WORSEN, IMPAIR, VITIATE, DEGENERATE, DEPRECIATE

determine IMPEL, LEARN, DECIDE, CONTRIVE, END, SET, RULE, SETTLE, FIT, FIX, BOUND, DEFINE, RESOLVE, ADJUST, CERTIFY, LIMIT, JUDGE, ADJUDICATE, FIND

detest EXECRATE, HATE, ABHOR, LOATHE, SCORN, SPURN, REJECT, ABOMINATE, DISLIKE

dethrone DEPOSE, STRIP, REMOVE, OUST, UNSEAT

detonator CAP, EXPLODER

detour BYPASS, WIND, DIVERT, TURN, ROUTE

detract DECRY, DEROGATE, BELITTLE, ASPERSE, REDUCE, MALIGN, LIBEL, LESSEN, DISPARAGE, DEFAME, SLANDER

detriment HURT, INJURY, LOSS, DAMAGE, EVIL, HARM, COST

detritus DEBRIS, TUFF, CHAFF, RUBBISH, WASTE, GARBAGE

devastate RAZE, RUIN, WASTE, RAPE, SACK, STRIP, DESPOIL, ROB, RIFLE, PLUNDER, RAVAGE, PILLAGE, HARRY, DESTROY

devastation HAVOC, RAVAGE, RAPINE

develop EVOLVE, RIPEN, UNFOLD, GROW, AGE, MATURE, ADVANCE, EXPAND, DILATE
rapidly BOOM

development, *incomplete* APLASIA
pertaining to GENETIC

Devi, *beneficient* GAURI
consort SIVA
fierce KALI
light UMA
malignant DURGA
of parentage HAIMAVATI
riding a tiger CHANDI

deviate WARP, YAW, ERR, MISS, SHIFT, LAPSE, DEFLECT, ROVE, TURN, STRAY, DIGRESS, VEER, DEPART, SWERVE, AVERT, DIVERGE, SLEW, WANDER, TACK, VARY
suddenly MUTATE
vertically HADE

device BADGE, RUSE, TRICK, RULE, GADGET, FIGURE, TOOL, ARTIFICE, EMBLEM, INSIGNE, DESIGN, MOTIF, INVENTION, CONTRAPTION, SCHEME, PLAN, WILE, FRAUD, CONTRIVANCE

devil SATAN, DEMON, FIEND,

AZAZEL, BELIAL, WRETCH, DULE, DEUCE, DICKENS, IMP, LUCIFER, OGRE, APOLLYON, GOBLIN, BEELZEBUB, HUGON
female DEMONESS
fish MANTA, OCTOPUS, RAY, WHALE
of bottomless pit APOLLYON
tree DITA, ABROMA
devilkin IMP
devilry ART, MAGIC, ENCHANTMENT, MISCHIEF, WICKEDNESS
devious CROOKED, SLY, CRAFTY, FOXY, MAZY, SINFUL, ERRING, ERRATIC, ROUNDABOUT, WANDERING
devise FRAME, SCHEME, INVENT, MAKE, CONSTRUCT, CONTRIVE, PLAN, CONCOCT, BEQUEATH, DEMISE, LEAVE
devoid VOID, BARREN, BARE, LACKING, VACANT, EMPTY, DESTITUTE
devoir DUTY
devote GIVE, STUDY, DEDICATE, HALLOW, CONSECRATE, ADDICT, CONSIGN
devotee FAN, VOTARY, ZEALOT, IST, BIGOT, FANATIC, ENTHUSIAST, PARTISAN, BUFF
devotion ADORATION, NOVENA, ZEAL, WORSHIP, FEALTY, PIETY, FERVOR, ARDOR, LOVE, ADDICTION, DEVOUTNESS, ATTACHMENT
devotional *exercise* AVES, WORSHIP
period NOVENA, LENT
devour EAT, DESTROY, WOLF, ENGULF, SWALLOW, GORGE, GULP
devouring EDACIOUS, VORACIOUS, VORANT
devout HOLY, PIOUS, SINCERE, FERVENT, ARDENT, RELIGIOUS, SAINTLY, GODLY, SOLEMN

Dev's *land* EIRE
dew, *congealed* RIME, FROST
dewlap WATTLE, FOLD
dewy RORIC, RORAL, BEDEWED, MOIST, REFRESHING
dexterity FINESSE, SLEIGHT, MAGIC, EASE, SKILL, KNACK, ABILITY, TACT, ART
dexterous AGILE, FACILE, HANDY, ADROIT, DEFT, ADEPT, NIMBLE, APT, QUICK, CLEVER, EXPERT
dextrose SUGAR
d'Herblay ARAMIS
diabetic remedy INSULIN, ORINASE
diacope WOUND, CUT, INCISION, TMESIS
diacritic *See* "mark"
diadem TIARA, CROWN, FILLET
diagonal BIAS, OBLIQUE, HYPOTENUSE
diagram PLAN, GRAPH, MAP, SKETCH, PLOT, DRAFT, TRACE, SCHEME, CHART, GAMUT, DRAWING
illustrative ICON-(OGRAPH)
dialect PATOIS, ARGOT, IDIOM, CANT, PATTER, SLANG, SPEECH, JARGON, DRAWL
diameter CALIBER, MODULE, BREADTH, BORE, WIDTH, CHORD
diametric ADVERSE, REMOTE
diametrically opposite ANTIPODAL
diamond ICE, GEM, ADAMANT, ARENA, RING, FIELD, ADAMAS, CARBON, MINERAL, LOZENGE
blue HOPE
coarse BORT
crystal GLASSIE
cup for cutting DOP
face of FACET, BEZEL
famous MOGUL, ORLOFF, PITT, HOPE, KOHINOOR, SANCY, REGENT, JUBILEE, CULLINAN
geometrical RHOMB, LOZENGE

holder DOP, RING
inferior BORT
native CARBON
necklace RIVIERE
single SOLITAIRE
small splinterlike ROSE
wheel SKIVE
with true luster of NAIF
Diana ARTEMIS, DELIA, CYNTHIA, MOON
parent JUPITER, LATONA
sacred grove NEMUS
dianthus plumarius PINK, FLOWER, CARNATION
diaphanous SHEER, THIN, TRANSPARENT, TRANSLUCENT, PELLUCID
diaphragm, pertaining to PHRENIC
diary LOG, RECORD, JOURNAL, CHRONICLE
ship's LOG
diaskeuast EDITOR, REVISER, REDACTOR
diaspora GOLAH, GALUTH
diatonic CHORD, SCALE
opposed to CHROMATIC
run TIRADE
scale GAMUT
diatribe PHILIPPIC, TIRADE, SCREED
dib BOB, MONEY, DAP, DIP, DIBBLE, RUPEE
dice BONES, CUBE, DIE, RICE, IVORY
cheat in COG
game CRAPS
natural SEVEN, ELEVEN
six SISE, SICE, BOXCAR
dichotomy DIVISION, SPLIT, CLEFT
Dickens BOZ
character SCROOGE, MICAWBER, GAMP, URIAH (HEEP), FAGAN, OLIVER (TWIST)
dicker BARTER, TRADE, DEAL, HAGGLE
dickey COLLAR, SEAT, BIB, APRON, JACKET, MATE, DONKEY, BIRD
dictate ORDER, RULE, ENJOIN, DIRECT,

DECREE, COMMAND, REQUIRE

dictionary ONOMASTICON, LEXICON, GRADUS, CALEPIN, GLOSSARY, VOCABULARY, THESAURUS

dictum SAYING, DICTA, APOTHEGM, OPINION, STATEMENT, PRINCIPLE

didactic INSTRUCTIVE, PRECEPTIVE

dido ANTIC, CAPER, TRICK, PRANK

Dido's *father* BELUS
sister ANNA
wooer AENEAS

die CUBE, SICCA, STAMP, MOLD, LAPSE, EXPIRE, PERISH, CEASE, HAZARD, BLOCK, CHANCE
gambling DICE (pl.)
highest number on SISE, SICE, SIX
pipe DOD

diet RATION, REGIMEN, FAST, FOOD, VICTUALS, FARE, ALIMENT, ASSEMBLY, CONGRESS, COUNCIL

differ VARY, DISSENT, DIVERGE, DEVIATE, DIS-AGREE, DISPUTE, CON-TEND

difference ODDS, NUANCE, DIS-SIMILARITY, DISPARITY, MISUNDER-STANDING, DEBATE

different NEW, DIVERSE, OTHER, SUNDRY, SEPARATE, DISTINCT, UNLIKE

difficult HARD, TOUGH, ARDUOUS, PAINFUL, LABORIOUS

difficulty CAVIL, KNOT, RUB, NODUS, SCRAPE, TASK, SNAG, DILEMMA, FIX, PASS, JAM, PINCH, OBSTACLE, STRAIT, PLIGHT, BAR-RIER, CRUX, TRIAL, PICKLE, IMBROGLIO, COIL
pertaining to SPINY, CRUCIAL

diffident COY, SHY, MODEST, BASHFUL,

DOUBTFUL, RELUCTANT

diffuse PERVADE, PROLIX, WORDY, LAVISH, DISPERSE, PUBLISH, SCATTER, CIRCULATE, STREW, COPIOUS, VERBOSE

diffusion through membrane OSMOSIS

diffusive AMPLE, OSMOTIC

dig GRUB, DELVE, JAB, EXCAVATE, SHOVEL, SPADE, MINE, PROBE, EXHUME, SCOOP, PUNCH, POKE, STUDY

digest ABSORB, SHORTEN, ABSTRACT, CODE, PANDECT, SKETCH, PRECIS, APERCU, SYSTEM, EPITOME, BREVIARY, BRIEF, STUDY, PONDER, CONSIDER, METABOLIZE

digestion EUPEPSIA, PEPSIS, EUPEPSY, ABSORPTION
having good EUPEPTIC

digger, *soldier* SAPPER

digging, *fitted for* FODIENT, FOSSORIAL
tool LOY, SPADE, SLICK, SHOVEL, PICK

digit FINGER, TOE, UNIT, CIPHER, INTEGER, PHALANGE
manual THUMB, FINGER
podal TOE
shield for COT, STALL, THIMBLE

diglot BILINGUAL

dignified SEDATE, ELEVATED, AUGUST, DECOROUS, STATELY, TOGATED, MAJESTIC, COURTLY, IMPOSING

dignities DECORA

dignity REPUTE, PRIDE, DECORUM, DECENCY, VIRTUE, MERIT, ELEGANCE, GRACE, WORTH, RANK, STANDING, STATION, EMINENCE, GLORY, HONOR, STATUS, MAJESTY

digraph AE, EA, OA, OE, SH, TH

digression ECBOLE, LOOP, DETOUR, DEVIATION, EPISODE, EXCURSUS

dike DITCH, MOUND, CHANNEL, BANK, JETTY, LEVEE
military ESTACADE

diked land POLDER

dilapidate RUIN, WRECK, WRACK, ROT, DECAY, WASTE, DESTROY

dilapidation HAVOC, DISREPAIR, DOWNFALL

dilate DESCANT, EXPAND, DISCUSS, SWELL, AMPLIFY, INFLATE, DISTEND, WIDEN, STRETCH, ENLARGE

dilation EXPANSION, ECTASIS
of hollow organ ECTASIS

dilatory SLOW, RE-MISS, LATREDE, SLACK, LAX, TARDY, LINGERING, SLUG-GISH

dilemma SNARE, PICKLE, FIX, TRAP, JAM, PLIGHT, SCRAPE, QUANDARY, STRAIT, PREDICAMENT

dilettante AMATEUR, DABBLER, TYRO, NOVICE

diligence INDUSTRY, SEDULITY, ASSIDUITY, CONSTANCY, PERSE-VERANCE, PRUDENCE, VIGILANCE, CARE

diligent OPEROSE, ACTIVE, ATTENTIVE, SEDULOUS, BUSY, STUDIOUS, CAREFUL, PAINFUL

dill ANISE, ANET, HERB

dilute THIN, WATER, ATTENUATE, RAREFY, WEAKEN, QUALIFY, REDUCE, CUT

diluted THIN, WEAK, WATERY

dim CALIGINOUS, BLEAR, FAINT, FADE, DULL, DARKEN, OBSCURE, ECLIPSE, DARK, GLOOMY, DUSKY, INDISTINCT,

SHADOWY, CLOUDY,
MYSTERIOUS
diminish PLOY, EBB,
PETER, SINK, ABATE,
TAPER, REDUCE,
LESSEN, SUBSIDE,
LIGHTEN, DWINDLE,
CURTAIL, WANE
diminution DECREASE,
DECREMENT,
ABRIDG(E)MENT,
SHRINKAGE, CONTRAC-
TION
diminutive RUNTY,
PETITE, WEE, SMALL,
TINY, BANTAM, LIT-
TLE, MINUTE, PUNY,
DWARFISH
suffix ULE, ETTE, ITA
din UPROAR, BABEL,
CLASH, RACKET,
NOISE, CLAMOR,
HUBBUB
dine SUP, EAT,
FEAST
dingle DALE, DELL,
GLEN, VALE, VALLEY
dingy DIRTY, DUSTY,
OURIE, DARK, DUSKY,
GRIM, SMOKY,
BESMIRCHED, BOAT
dining room CENACLE,
SALON, REFECTORY,
SPENCE
dinner, pertaining to
PRANDIAL
dint NICK, NOTCH,
STROKE, DENT, BLOW,
FORCE, POWER
diocese CENTER,
BISHOPRIC, SEE,
EPISCOPATE, JURIS-
DICTION
Dione's *consort* ZEUS
daughter APHRODITE
Dionysus BACCHUS
mother SEMELE
diopter ALIDADE,
LEVEL
Dioscuri CASTORES,
CASTOR, POLLUX,
TWINS, ANACES
dip SOP, DAP, DOUSE,
LADE, SWIM, DUNK,
DOP, BAIL, DUCK,
SOUSE, SCOOP,
IMMERSE, PLUNGE,
LADLE, INCLINE,
SLOPE
in liquid MERSE,
IMMERSE
diphthong AE, OE, OU

diploma SHEEPSKIN,
PAPER, DOCUMENT,
CHARTER
diplomacy TACT,
FINESSE, ARTFULNESS
diplomat ENVOY,
CONSUL, ATTACHE,
NUNCIO, LEGATE,
MINISTER, AMBAS-
SADOR
diplomatic CRAFTY,
POLITIC, TACTFUL,
ARTFUL, SMOOTH,
BLAND, SUAVE,
URBANE, WILY, SHY,
POLITE
dipody SYZYGY
dipper PIET, SCOOP,
PIGGIN, DUNKER,
BAPTIST, LADLE,
GREBE
dipsacus plant TEASEL
dipsomaniac DRUNK,
SOT, SOAK, TOPER,
TOSSPOT, ALCOHOLIC
diptera FLIES, GNATS,
MOSQUITOES,
ANOPHELES
lobe of wing ALULA
dire FUNEST, BANE-
FUL, FEARFUL,
AWFUL, DREADFUL,
SHOCKING, TERRIBLE,
CALAMITOUS,
GRIEVOUS
direct BOSS, MARSHAL,
AIM, LEAD, GUIDE,
POINT, COACH, TEACH,
HEAD, CONN, STEER,
BID, MANAGE, BLUNT,
STRAIGHT, PILOT,
RULE, ORDER, IM-
MEDIATE, OPEN,
SINCERE, FRANK,
LEVEL, CONTROL,
GOVERN, COMMAND
direction BEARING,
DRIFT, TENOR, AIM,
COURSE, TENDENCY,
PRESCRIPTION, MAN-
AGEMENT, EAST,
WEST, NORTH, SOUTH
musical SOLI
without fixed ASTATIC
directly SPANG, SOON,
ANON, EXPRESSLY,
QUICKLY, PROMPTLY,
FORTHWITH, IN-
STANTLY
dirge CORONACH,
ELEGY, HYMN,
THRENODY, LINOS,

LINUS, LAMENT,
SONG, MONODY,
REQUIEM
requiem masses
TRENTAL
dirigible BLIMP, BAL-
LOON, AIRSHIP
cabin of NACELLE
dirk DAGGER, SNEE,
SWORD
Roman SICA
dirndl SKIRT, DRESS
dirty FOUL, SORDID,
VILE, FILTHY, NASTY,
SQUALID, UNCLEAN,
BEGRIMED, SOIL(ED)
disable CRIPPLE,
MAIM, GRUEL,
WEAKEN, SAP,
ENFEEBLE, HAM-
STRING, DISQUALIFY,
INCAPACITATE, INJURE
disagreeable CROSS,
NASTY, FULSOME,
UNPLEASANT, DIS-
TASTEFUL, OFFENSIVE
disagreement DISCORD,
QUARREL, SPAT,
DIFFERENCE, STRIFE,
DISPUTE, BICKER
disappear PASS,
VANISH, RESOLVE,
RECEDE, DISSOLVE
disapproval CENSURE,
CONDEMNATION
sound of BOO, HISS,
RAZZ
disavow RECANT,
ABJURE, DISCLAIM,
DISOWN, DENY,
REPUDIATE
disburse EXPEND,
SPEND, WASTE, PAY
disc MEDALLION,
DIAL, MEDAL,
RECORD, HARROW,
PLATE
plate PATEN
discard REJECT,
SLUFF, MOLT, SCRAP,
SHED, JUNK, OUST,
ABANDON, DESERT,
DISMISS, DISCHARGE
discarded SHED,
CASTOFF
place LIMBO
discern DETECT, ESPY,
READ, DESCRY, KEN,
SEE, REMARK, NOTE,
BEHOLD, PERCEIVE,
VIEW, DISTINGUISH,
DISCRIMINATE

discerning ASTUTE, ACUTE, JUDICIOUS, SHARP

discernment SAGACITY, TACT, INSIGHT, ACUMEN, REASON, SHREWDNESS, PERCEPTION

discharge PERFORM, DROP, BOUNCE, DISMISS, EJECT, EXPEL, OUST, FULFILL, EMIT, FIRE, SACK, SHOOT, SHOT, BLAST, SALVO, VOLLEY, SPEED, FREE, RELEASE, UNLOAD, UNBURDEN, PAY, LIQUIDATE, EXONERATE, ABSOLVE, DISCARD, CANCEL, ANNUL, LIBERATE

disciple APOSTLE, ADHERENT, SCHOLAR, PUPIL, STUDENT, FOLLOWER, VOTARY, IST
Biblical JAMES, JOHN, PETER, JUDAS
chief PETER

disciplinarian MARTINET, TSAR, TZAR, TYRANT

discipline CONTROL, TRAIN, GUIDE, CURB, CHASTEN, TEACH, LEAD, PUNISH, CORRECT, BRIDLE, CHECK, DRILL, CHASTISE, INSTRUCT, ORDER

disclaim DENY, DISOWN, REJECT, RENOUNCE, REPUDIATE

disclose REVEAL, TELL, SHOW, UNCOVER, EXPOSE, DIVULGE, BARE, AIR

discolored USTULATE, DIRTY, OLD, STAINED, TARNISHED, MOLDED

discomfited ROUTED, BAFFLED, FRUSTRATED, FOILED

discomfort AGONY, PAIN, ACHE, MISEASE, DISQUIET, UNEASINESS, MALAISE, TROUBLE, DISTRESS, SORROW

disconcert, FAZE, UPSET, RATTLE, ABASH, PUZZLE, BAFFLE, CONFUSE

discord WAR, CACOPHONY, VARIANCE, NOISE, STRIFE, CLASH, ENMITY, RANCOR, CONTENTION, HARSHNESS, JANGLE
goddess of ERIS

discordant *musically* SCORDATO
serenade CHARIVARI

Discordia ERIS

discount REBATE, LESSEN, IGNORE, BELITTLE, ALLOWANCE, DRAWBACK, DISREGARD, DEDUCT-(ION)

discourage DASH, DETER, OPPOSE, DISHEARTEN, DAUNT, DEPRESS, DEJECT, DISSUADE

discourse TALK, DESCANT, PRELECT, HOMILY, SPEAK, SCREED, SERMON, DISSERTATION, ARGUE, LECTURE, PARLEY, TREATISE, CONFER, CONVERSATION, COLLOQUY
art of RHETORIC

discover FIND, ESPY, LEARN, UNCOVER, DIVULGE, REVEAL, DETECT, IMPART, UNEARTH, BARE, DISCERN, ASCERTAIN, DESCRY, DISCLOSE

discredit REVILE, SHAME, ASPERSE, DOUBT, QUESTION, DISREPUTE, SCANDAL, SMEAR, OBLOQUY, IGNOMINY, DISHONOR, ODIUM, DISPARAGE, IMPEACH

discreet PRUDENT, WARY, CAUTIOUS, POLITIC, JUDICIOUS, CIRCUMSPECT, HEEDFUL, CAREFUL

discretion TACT, PRUDENCE, WILL, TASTE, FINESSE, CAUTION, SENSE, JUDGMENT, CHOICE, DIPLOMACY, RESERVE, LIBERTY

discriminate SEPARATE,

DISCERN, RECOGNIZE, DISTINGUISH, SECERN, DIFFERENTIATE

discrimination BIAS, TASTE, ACUMEN, WISDOM, SENSE, INSIGHT, PENETRATION, DISCERNMENT, PERCEPTION

discus DISK, QUOIT, PLATE
thrower DISCOBOLUS

discuss EXPLAIN, DEBATE, SIFT, AIR, ARGUE, EXPOUND, DILATE, CANVASS, REASON, DISPUTE, DELIBERATE

discussion TALK, CONFERENCE
group PANEL, FORUM, SEMINAR, CLASS

disdain SNOOT, ARROGANCE, SCORN, CONTEMPT, SPURN, DESPISE, CONTUMELY, HAUGHTINESS, HAUTEUR

disease ILLNESS, MALADY, DISORDER, DISTEMPER, COMPLAINT, AILMENT, INFIRMITY, PATHOLOGY, INDISPOSITION, MORBUS
animals NENTA, DISTEMPER, MANGE, SURRA
chickens ROUP, PIP, PEROSIS
declining stage of CATABASIS
diver's BENDS, CAISSON
fatal LYSSA, MALIGNANCY
fowl PIP, ROUP, PEROSIS
fungus ERGOT, TINEA
grape ERINOSE, COLEUR
jumping TIC, LATA(H)
plant SCALD *See* "plant"
malignant PLAGUE, CANCER
pertaining to CLINIC, LOIMIC
prevalent ENDEMIC
producing ZYMOTIC

science of classification NOSOLOGY
  of origin ETIOLOGY
spreader VECTOR, CARRIER, FLY
suffix ITIS, OSIS, OMA
tropical SPRUE, MALARIA
diseased MORBID, SICKLY, UNSOUND, UNHEALTHY
disembark DETRAIN, LAND, DEPLANE, DEBARK, ARRIVE
disencumber RELEASE, RID, FREE, DETACH, LIGHTEN, DISBURDEN, EASE, DISENGAGE
disenfranchisement, *anc. Greece* ATIMY
disengage FREE, DETACH, EXTRICATE, DISJOIN, WEAN, DISENTANGLE, DISEMBROIL, SEPARATE, PART, WITHDRAW
disentangle(ment) UNRAVEL, SLEAVE, FREE, SEVER, PART, SUNDER, UNTWIST, EXTRICATE, DISEMBROIL, DETACH, UNTIE, DIVORCE
disfigure SCAR, MAR, MANGLE, MAIM, DEFACE, DISTORT, WARP, IMPAIR, DEFORM, BLEMISH
disfranchisement, *anc. Greece* ATIMY
disgrace TAINT, ODIUM, SHEND, SLANDER, OBLOQUY, ABASE, SULLY, SHAME, SCANDAL, IGNOMINY, STIGMA, BRAND, BLOT, STAIN, DISHONOR, DISFAVOR, INFAMY
  public, Greece ATIMY
disguise CAMOUFLAGE, MASK, MUMM, CLOAK, COLOR, COVER, FEIGN, HIDE, CONCEAL, SHAM, AFFECT, VEIL, SHROUD, DISSEMBLE, MASQUERADE, FALSIFY
disgusting NASTY, OFFENSIVE, NAUSEOUS, LOATHSOME, REPULSIVE, ODIOUS, ABHORRENT, FOUL
dish RECIPE, BOAT, CHARGER, CRUSE, PLATE, PATINA, FOOD, PATERA, VESSEL, BOWL, CONCAVITY, PLATTER, SAUCER, VIAND, TROUGH
  main ENTREE
  stemmed COMPOTE
dishearten DAUNT, AMATE, DEJECT, UNMAN, DETER, DISCOURAGE, DEPRESS
disheveled UNKEMPT, DERANGED, MUSSED, TOUSLED, DISORDERED
dishonest UNTRUE, FALSE, CROOKED, FAITHLESS, KNAVISH, UNFAIR, FRAUDULENT, TREACHEROUS, PERFIDIOUS
dishonor SHAME, VIOLATE, STIGMA, BRAND, BLOT, STAIN, DISGRACE, IGNOMINY, SCANDAL, DEBAUCH, DEGRADE, DEBASE
disinfectant CRESOL, IODIN, PHENOL, CHLORINE, LYSOL
disinherit DISOWN, DEPRIVE
disintegrate ERODE, DECAY, CORRODE, SPOIL, ROT, PUTREFY, CRUMBLE, DECOMPOSE
disinter EXHUME, UNBURY, DIG, DELVE, UNEARTH, DISENTOMB
disk ATEN, SEQUIN, DIAL, HARROW, MEDAL, PATEN, PLATE
  hockey PUCK
  like DISCOID, DISCAL
  metal TAG
  solar ATEN
dislike ANTIPATHY, ODIUM, AVERSION, REPUGNANCE, DISTASTE
  combining form MIS(O)
dislocate LUXATE, SPLAY, DISPLACE, DISJOINT
dislodge TOPPLE, EXPEL, EVICT, DISPLACE, OUST, EJECT, REMOVE
disloyal FALSE, FICKLE, UNSTABLE, UNFAITHFUL, PERFIDIOUS, UNTRUE
dismal BLUE, DREAR(Y), JOYLESS, SORRY, GLOOMY, LONESOME, SOMBRE, MELANCHOLY
dismantle STRIP, RAZE, UNRIG
dismay APPAL(L), DAUNT, TERRIFY, FEAR, FAZE, RATTLE, FRIGHT, PANIC, ALARM, CONSTERNATION
dismiss AMAND, RELEGATE, REMUE, FIRE, SACK, DEMIT, CASHIER, SHELVE, OUST, EXPEL, CAST, DROP, BOUNCE, SHED, QUASH, DISCARD, DISCHARGE
dismissal CONGE(E), MANUMISSION
dismount ALIGHT, DESCEND, LAND, UNHORSE
disorder MESS, SNARL, RIOT, DISARRAY, HASH, PUDDLE, CHAOS, CONFUSION, JUMBLE, LITTER, MUDDLE, TUMULT, DERANGE, UPSET, TURBULENCE, DISEASE
disorderly CHAOTIC, MESSY, IMMETHODICAL, LAWLESS, TURBULENT, RIOTOUS, INDECENT
disown DENY, DISAVOW, DISCLAIM, REPUDIATE, RENOUNCE
disparage BELITTLE, DECRY, SLUR, MALIGN, ASPERSE, LIBEL, DEPRECIATE, TRADUCE, DEFAME, VILIFY, DENIGRATE, DETRACT
disparate UNEQUAL, DISSIMILAR, SEPARATE, DISTINCT
dispatch POST, KILL, SEND, SLAY, HASTE, SPEED, MESSAGE, NOTE, WIRE, CELER-

ITY, EXPEDITE,
DILIGENCE

dispel SCATTER,
DISPERSE, EXPEL,
EJECT, OUST, DIS-
SIPATE, BANISH

dispensation ECONOMY,
SCHEME, PLAN,
EXEMPTION, DISTRIBU-
TION, ALLOTMENT,
LICENSE

dispense PORTION,
PARCEL, RATION,
GIVE, DISTRIBUTE,
SELL, DIVIDE, DEAL,
DOLE, ALLOT, AS-
SIGN, EXEMPT, RE-
LIEVE, EXCUSE,
ABSOLVE, FOREGO

disperse PART, DIVIDE,
DISMISS, DISPEL,
SPREAD, SCATTER,
STREW, FACE,
DIFFUSE, DISSOLVE

displace REMOVE,
EJECT, DISPOSE, FIRE
See "dismiss"

display REVEAL, SHOW,
SCENE, AIR, VAUNT,
SPLURGE, FLAUNT,
UNCASE, BARE, EX-
POSE, PARADE,
EXTEND, EXPAND,
UNFOLD, OPEN,
EXHIBIT, POMP

displease OFFEND,
PIQUE, MIFF, PRO-
VOKE, IRRITATE,
ANNOY, VEX

disposed PROPEND,
PRONE, SETTLED,
FIXED, INCLINED,
TENDING, READY,
APT, SOLD,
ARRANGED

disposition BENT, BIAS,
MOOD, SPIRIT,
TEMPER, ANIMUS,
MORALE, NATURE,
PROCLIVITY, SALE,
APTITUDE
toward work ERGASIA

dispossess DIVEST,
EVICT, OUST, DEPRIVE,
STRIP, EJECT

disprove CONFUTE,
REFUTE, REBUT,
NEGATE

disputation DEBATE,
FORENSIC, ARGUMENT,
DISPUTE, CONTRO-
VERSY

practice of POLEMICS

disputatious SASSY,
ERISTIC, CAPTIOUS,
QUARRELSOME

dispute DISSENT,
BICKER, HAGGLE,
ARGUE, SPAR, DE-
BATE, DISCUSS,
AGITATE, STRIFE,
CONFLICT, ALTERCA-
TION, WRANGLE,
SPAT, BRAWL, SQUAB-
BLE, TIFF

disqualify DIVEST,
DEPRIVE, INCAPACI-
TATE, DISABLE,
DISBAR

disquisition TREATISE,
ESSAY, SPEECH,
SEARCH, INQUIRY

disregard IGNORE,
DEFY, NEGLECT,
SLIGHT, FORGET,
OMIT

disrepute ODIUM, DIS-
HONOR, SHAME,
SCANDAL, DISCREDIT

disseize OUST, EVICT,
DEPOSE

disseminate DIFFUSE,
SPREAD, SOW, SCAT-
TER, DISPERSE,
CIRCULATE, PUBLISH,
TEACH

dissent OBJECT, DIS-
AGREE, DIFFER,
DEMUR, BALK

dissenter HERETIC,
RECUSANT, SECTARY,
NONCONFORMIST

dissertation STUDY,
THESIS, DISCOURSE,
TREATISE, ESSAY,
SERMON, TRACT

dissimilar ODD, UN-
LIKE, DIFFERENT,
DIVERSE

dissipate WASTE,
DISPEL, SCATTER,
SQUANDER, LAVISH,
VANISH, DESTROY

dissolute FAST,
ABANDONED, LAX,
LEWD, CORRUPT,
LOOSE, DEBAUCHED,
WANTON, RAKISH,
SHAMELESS
person RAKE, ROUE

dissolve THAW, MELT,
VANISH, FADE,
LIQUEFY, END, CLOSE,
CRUMBLE, DISIN-

TEGRATE, REVOKE,
CANCEL, ABROGATE,
ANNUL, TERMINATE,
RELEASE, DIVORCE

dissolved substance
SOLUTE

distal angle AXIL

distance OFFING,
SPACE, MILEAGE,
STEP, REMOTENESS,
INTERVAL, RESERVE,
ALOOFNESS

distant (A)FAR,
FOREIGN, ALOOF,
COLD, REMOTE, BE-
YOND, AWAY,
HAUGHTY
combining form TELE

distend STRETCH,
DILATE, AMPLIFY,
INFLATE, SWELL,
EXPAND, BLOAT

distended PATULOUS,
BLOATED

distich COUPLET

distill DROP, TRICKLE,
EXTRACT, PURIFY,
VAPORIZE

distilling *device*
ALEMBIC, STILL
tube MATRASS

distinct DEFINITE,
SHARP, CLEAR,
SPECIAL, SINGLE,
PLAIN, SOLE, LUCID,
SEPARATE, MANIFEST,
AUDIBLE, VISIBLE,
PROMINENT

distinctive *air* CACHET
mark BADGE,
CACHET, RIBBON,
MEDAL, INSIGNIA

distinguished NOTA-
BLE, NOTED, CELE-
BRATED, PROMINENT

distort DEFORM,
TWIST, WARP, TURN,
GNARL, BEND, CON-
TORT, PERVERT,
MISINTERPRET

distortion TWIST,
TORSION, WARP,
DEFORMITY, WRYNESS,
MISREPRESENTATION,
FALSEHOOD
head to one side
LOXIA

distract DIVERT,
AMUSE, CONFUSE,
ADDLE, PUZZLE, UP-
SET, BAFFLE, BALK,
MYSTIFY, PERPLEX

distracted FRANTIC, CRAZY, MAD, INSANE, RAVING, WILD, CONFUSED, AMUSED

distraught AGITATED, CRAZED, DISTRACTED

distress TRY, PANG, PAIN, RACK, DISTRAIN, GRILL, TRIAL, TROUBLE, GRIEF, WOE, ACHE, DOLOR, AIL, AGONY, HARASS, HARROW, AFFLICTION, CALAMITY, DISASTER, MISERY, TRIBULATION, SORROW, TORMENT

distribute DEAL, DOLE, ASSIGN, METE, ALLOT, DIVIDE, RATION, PRORATE, PORTION, SHARE, CLASSIFY, ASSORT, ARRANGE

distributee HEIR

district SECTOR, SPHERE, FIELD, CANTON, DEMESNE, PALE, REALM, TRACT, REGION, WICK, AREA, PRECINCT, ZONE, BELT, CIRCUIT, PROVINCE, WARD, QUARTER, TERRITORY
Old Eng. court SOC, SOKE

distrust DOUBT, FEAR, SUSPICION, MISGIVING, SUSPECT

disturb UPSET, AGITATE, ALARM, SCARE, FAZE, RATTLE, DERANGE, SHIFT, MOVE, MEDDLE, EXCITE, MOLEST, WORRY, SHAKE, STIR, DISORDER, CONFUSE, ANNOY, VEX, RUFFLE, AROUSE

disturbance RIPPLE, RIOT, TUMULT, FIGHT, FRACAS, COMMOTION, DISORDER, TURMOIL, HUBBUB, AGITATION

disyllabic foot
TROCHEE

ditch CANAL, FOSS, MOAT, SAP, TRENCH, DIKE, ACEQUIA, RELAIS, FOSSE, CHANNEL, DRAIN, CONDUIT, ZANJE
slope SCARP

dithyramb HYMN, POETRY, ODE

dithyrambic WILD, BOISTEROUS

diurnal DAILY, QUOTIDIAN, JOURNAL, BUTTERFLY

divagate DIGRESS, STRAY, WANDER, RAMBLE

divan SETTEE, SOFA, COUCH, DAVENPORT, SALOON

diverge BRANCH, FORK, VEER, DIFFER, PART, DIVIDE, SEPARATE, VARY, DEVIATE, TURN, ALTER

diver's *disease* BENDS, CAISSON
gear FLIPPER, TANK

diversify VARY, VARIATE, DAPPLE, SPOT, CHANGE, ALTER

diversion PLAY, SPORT, AMUSEMENT, RECREATION, PASTIME, ENTERTAINMENT, DISTRACTION, DEVIATION

divert AMUSE, AVERT, PARRY, DEFLECT, DISTRACT, TURN, VEER, BEND, CURVE, TWIST, DIGRESS, CHANGE, ALTER, PLEASE, BEGUILE, DECEIVE

divest STRIP, TIRL, BARE, UNCLOTHE, DENUDE, DISPOSSESS, UNCOVER, DOFF

divide SUNDER, DIVORCE, RATION, SPLIT, DEAL, DOLE, RIVE, REND, SEPARATE, APPORTION, CLEAVE, FORK, PART, ALLOT, LOT, SEVER, SHARE, BISECT, DISMEMBER, ALIENATE
into feet SCAN
into number of parts MULTISECT
in two parts BISECT, HALVE

divided HALVED, SPLIT, ZONED, APART, CLEFT
by linear sinus BIFID
nearly to base PARTITE

dividend BONUS, SHARE, EARNING, MELON

dividing wall(s) SEPTUM, SEPTA, PARTITION

divination AUGURY, ACUMEN, INSIGHT, FORETELLING, PRESAGE, PROPHECY, OMEN, PREDICTION
by dreams ONEIROMANCY
by figures GEOMANCY
by forehead METOPOMANCY
by rods RHABDOMANCY, DOUSING
by stars or straws, burning SIDEROMANCY

divine FORESEE, PREDICT, DISCERN, FORETELL, GUESS, HOLY, CELESTIAL, SACRED, BLESSED, GODLIKE, SPIRITUAL, ANGELIC, MINISTER, PASTOR, PARSON, CLERIC
communication ORACLE
spirit NUMEN
word GRACE, LOGOS
work THEURGY

"Divine Comedy"
author DANTE

divinely inspired
ENTHEAL, ENTHEATE

diving *bell* NAUTILUS
bird GREBE, PELICAN, LOON, AUK

divinity DEITY, IDOL, THEOLOGY *See* "god" or "goddess"
Hebrew ADONAI, ELOHIM, JAH, YAH, YAHEW, JEHOVAH
individual opinion on THEOLOGOUMENON

division PART, SCHISM, SECTION, PORTION, PIECE, FRACTION, DISJUNCTION, CATEGORY, SEGMENT, DISUNION, VARIANCE, CLASS, DISCORD
primary EOGAEA
restricted MEER, MERE

divorce law TALAK

divot SOD, TURF, CLOD

divulge DISCLOSE, CONFIDE, TELL, REVEAL, TATTLE, GOSSIP, BETRAY, IMPART, BLAB, PUBLISH

dizziness VERTIGO, WHIRLING, GIDDINESS
pertaining to DINIC(AL), VESTIBULAR

Dneiper tributary BUG, DESNA, PSEL (PSIOL), SULA

do PERFORM, WORK, SOLVE, SERVE, SWINDLE, EFFECT, COMMIT, ACCOMPLISH, SETTLE, ANSWER, SUFFICE, SUIT, CHEAT, COMPLETE, SUCCEED

docent TEACHER, LECTURER

docile TRACTABLE, GENTLE, TAME, PLIANT, PLIABLE, YIELDING

dock JETTY, PIER, WHARF, BASIN, SLIP, BANG, CUT, CLIP, CURTAIL, TRUNCATE, SHORTEN, WEED
post BOLLARD, PILE
ship's BASIN, BERTH, SLIP

doctrine LOGIC, DOGMA, ISM, LORE, THEORY, CREED, TENET, CABALA, PRINCIPLE, OPINION, PRECEPT, MAXIM, RULE
secret ESOTERY
single principle HENISM, MONISM

document WRITING, RECORD, DEED, WILL, PAPER, CERTIFICATE, INSTRUMENT, LETTER
provisional SCRIPT, NOTE, MEMO, DRAFT
true copy ESTREAT, CARBON

documents ARCHIVES, ANNALS, CHRONICLES

dod FIT, SULK, HUFF, DIE

doddering FOOLISH, INANE, ANILE, INFIRM, SENILE, AGED

Dodecanese island COS, KOS, COO, RHODES, RODI, PATMO(S)

dodge AVOID, PALTER, PARRY, DUCK, EVADE, QUIBBLE, ARTIFICE

dodo genus DIDUS

doe HIND, TAG, TEG, DEER

doer FEASOR, ACTOR, OPERATOR, AGENT

doff DIVEST, STRIP, VAIL, REMOVE

dog SHADOW, FOLLOW, TRAIL, TRACK, HUNT, CATCH, FOOT, WRETCH, RASCAL, SPORT, POM, MASTIFF, CUR, DANE, WHELP, ALCO, CHOW, FEIST, POOCH, MUTT, PUG, CANINE, CANIS, BASSET, PEKE, POINTER, BULL, PUP
Arctic HUSKY, MALEMUTE, SAMOYED(E)
Australian wild DINGO
bird POINTER, SETTER
Buster Brown's TIGE
combining form CYN(O)
duck hunting TOLLER, RETRIEVER
extinct breed TALBOT
fictional ASTA, ARGUS, TOBY, TIGE
fierce KOLSUN, BANDOG, BULL, DHOLE, MASTIFF
fire ANDIRON
fish See under "fish"
genus CANIS
hero RAB
house KENNEL
hunting ALAN, TALBOT, BASSET, HOUND, GRIFFON, BLOODHOUND
India DHOLE
like JACKAL, HYENA, WOLF
Russian SAMOYED(E)
Scotland SEALYHAM
short-eared ALAN
short-legged BEAGLE
small POM, FEIST, TIKE, ALCO, PUG, PEKE, TYKE

star SIRIUS, CANICULA
swift WHIPPET, GREYHOUND
Thin Man's ASTA
tropical ALCO
T.V. CLEO, LASSIE
underworld CERBERUS
wild DHOLE, COYOTE, DINGO, JACKAL

dogbane *fruit* ABOLI
tree DITA, APOCYNUM

dog days CANICULE

doge, *office of* DOGATE

doggerel MEAN, TRIVIAL, ABSURD, RHYME, VERSE

dogie CALF, MAVERICK

dogma BELIEF, TENET, DOCTRINE, CANT, VIEW, CREED, ISM

dogmatic saying DICTUM, LEVITISM

dogs FEET

dogwood CORNUS, OSIER, CORNEL, SUMAC, TREE
genus CORNUS

doily MAT, NAPKIN, PAD

doings ADO, HUSTLE, ACTIVITY

doldrum(s) CALM, TEDIUM, BOREDOM, ENNUI, DULLNESS, DUMPS, LISTLESSNESS, DEJECTION

dole ALMS, PITTANCE, METE, ALLOT, GRIEF, SORROW, WOE, REGRET, TRIAL, MISERY, PART, SHARE, PORTION, GIFT, GRATUITY, DISTRESS

doleful DISMAL, DREE, SAD, RUEFUL, WOEFUL, MELANCHOLY, GLOOMY, DREARY, DARK

doll PUPPET, TOY, PREEN, PRIMP, GIRL, WOMAN

dollar BUCK, BEAN, PESO, BILL, COIN, MONEY
German TALER
Spanish PESO

dolly CART, TRAY, CAR, TRUCK, LOCOMOTIVE, DOLL

dolphin BOUTO, PORPOISE, DORADO, DIVE, WREATH, SUSU, INIA

dolt IDIOT, CLOD, OAF, DUNCE, ASS, LOON, SIMPLETON, FOOL, NUMSKULL
like genus INIA
domain BARONY, DEMESNE, ESTATE, EMPIRE, REALM, AREA, REGION, ZONE, DISTRICT, DOMINION, PROVINCE, TERRITORY, PROPERTY
dome CUPOLA, ROOF, THOLUS, HEAD
domestic CLOTH, SERVANT, NATIVE, MAID, TAME, LOCAL, HOME, INTERIOR
establishment MENAGE
domicile ABODE, HOME, HOUSE, RESIDENCE, DWELLING, MANSION
dominate RULE, SWAY, BULLY, MASTER, CONTROL, PREVAIL, COMMAND, INFLUENCE
domineer BOSS, BLUSTER, LORD, BULLY, TYRANNIZE, HECTOR
Dominican measure ONA
dominion CONTROL, SWAY, POWER, COLONY, RULE, GOVERNMENT, COUNTRY, REALM, OWNERSHIP, RIGHT, TITLE, SOVEREIGNTY
domino CLOAK, AMICE, MASK, IVORY, DICE, HOOD, COSTUME
spot on PIP
dominoes MUGGINS, MATADOR, GAME
domite TRACHYTE
donate BESTOW, GIVE, CONFER, GRANT, CONTRIBUTE
done OVER, COOKED, THROUGH, ENDED, EXECUTED, ACCOMPLISHED, EXHAUSTED, FINISHED
donkey ONO, ASS, BURRO, FOOL, NEDDY, SIMPLETON, SECONDARY, AUXILIARY
combining form ONO

England MOKE, NEDDY
Don Quixote's *steed* ROSINANTE
doohickey DINGUS, GADGET, THINGUMBOB
doom DESTINY, FATE, CONDEMN, DAMN, LOT, PORTION, SENTENCE, END, DESTRUCTION, JUDGMENT, DEATH
door GATE, PORTAL, INLET, ENTRANCE, PATH, OPENING, ENTRY, AVENUE, PASSAGE(WAY)
back POSTERN
handle ANSA, KNOB
knocker RISP
part of JAM, RAIL, STILE, SILL, PANEL, MULLION
Persian DAR
doorkeeper OSTIARY, TYLER, TILER, PORTER, JANITOR
doric *capital, part of* ABACUS
fillet bottom of frieze TAENIA
frieze, space bet. triglyphs METOPE
dormancy LATENCY, TORPOR, SLEEP, QUIESCENCE, ABEYANCE
dormant ASLEEP, TORPID, INERT, LATENT, IDLE, COMATOSE, LETHARGIC, INACTIVE
dormice, pertaining to MYOXINE
dormouse LEROT, GLIS, LOIR, RODENT
dorsal NEURAL, NOTAL, TERGAL, NERVE, VERTEBRA
opposed to VENTRAL
pertaining to NEURAL, NOTAL, TERGAL
Dorsetshire borough POOLE
dose POTION, BOLUS, DRUG, DRAUGHT, QUANTITY, PART
dosseret ABACUS
dossier RECORD, FILE, HISTORY
medical CHART
dossil SPIGOT, TENT, PLEDGET

dot PERIOD, POINT, DOWERY, SPECK, IOTA, SPOT, WHIT, STIPPLE, SPECKLE, VARIEGATE
dotage AGE, SENILITY, IMBECILITY
dote DRIVEL, RELISH, ENJOY, FANCY, LIKE, LOVE
dotted PIEBALD, PINTO, PIED
dotterel DUPE, MORINEL, GULL, PLOVER, BIRD
double DUAL, BINATE, DUPLEX, TWIN, SUBSTITUTE, FOLD, COUPLED, PAIRED, DUPLE, TWOFOLD, TWICE, COUNTERPART, INSINCERE, DECEITFUL, DUPLICATE
cross RAT, GYP
dagger DIESIS
faced ANCIPITAL
ripper SLED, BOB-SLED
doubloon ONZA, COIN
doubt PAUSE, HESITATE, DISBELIEF, DUBIETY, MISTRUST, WAVER, DEMUR, QUESTION, SUSPICION, MISGIVING, SKEPTICISM, DISSENT, UNCERTAINTY
dough MONEY, NOODLE, DUFF, CASH, PASTA, PULP, PASTE
fried SPUD
doughnut SINKER, BAGEL, FRIEDCAKE, CRULLER
doughty BRAVE, BOLD, INTREPID, COURAGEOUS, FEARLESS, VALIANT, HEROIC, STRONG
dour GLUM, SULLEN, SURLY, GRIM, STERN, RIGID, OBSTINATE
dove INCA, NUN, CULVER, TUMBLER, PIGEON, COLUMBA
genus COLUMBIDAE
murmur COO
ring CUSHAT
dovekie AUK, ROTCHE, GUILLEMOT
genus ALLE
dovetail TENON, FIT, SUIT, JOIN, TONGUE,

GROOVE, AGREE, IN-
TERSECT, INSERT
dowel PIN, PEG,
TENON, PINION
dower DOT, BEQUEST,
GRANT, DONATION,
EQUIP, OUTFIT, GIFT,
ENDOW
dowitcher SNIPE, FOWL
down UNDER, ALOW,
BELOW, NAP, DOWL,
FUZZ, EIDER, DUNE,
LEA, FLOOR, SAD, LOW,
GRUDGE, SICK
combining form
CAT(A), CATH
facing PRONE,
PRONATE, PROSTRATE
downfall RUIN, DIS-
GRACE, REVERSE, TRAP,
DROP, DESCENT, RAIN,
DESTRUCTION,
FAILURE, MISFORTUNE
downright BLUNT,
FLAT, STARK, ARRANT,
CANDID, PLAIN, OPEN,
FRANK, SIMPLE,
SHEER, CLEAR,
EXPLICIT, HONEST,
SINCERE, DIRECT,
ABSOLUTE
downy SOFT, FLUFFY,
FLOCCULENT, PILAR,
PUBESCENT, VILLOUS,
LANATE, LANUGINOUS
dowry *See* "dower"
doxy DOCTRINE,
OPINION, BELIEF,
PARAMOUR, MISTRESS
doyen DEAN, SENIOR
doze CATNAP, DROWSE,
NAP, SLEEP, SLUMBER
drab DUN, DULL,
MONOTONOUS
drachma, *1/20 or 1/6*
OBOL
draft PROTOCOL,
SKETCH, BREEZE, DE-
SIGN, COPY, DRAW,
DRINK, PLOT, DRAM,
LEVY, LOAD, NOTE,
MONEY, CONSCRIPT,
MUSTER, CALL, DRAW-
ING, CURRENT, DE-
MAND, CLAIM, GULLY,
GORGE, SELECTION,
CHECK, WRITE
architectural EPURE
drag SNIG, HAUL, HALE,
TUG, TOW, PULL,
DRAW, HARROW, LAG,
DAWDLE, INCH, CLOG,

OBSTACLE, SLEDGE,
IMPEDIMENT
dragoman AGENT,
INTERPRETER, GUIDE
dragon OGRE,
MONSTER, DUENNA,
PIGEON, TRACTOR,
MUSKET, LIZARD,
DRAKE, DRACO
Chinese LUNG
fly genus ODONATA
Greek BASILISK
head, Hindu RAHU
Norse myth. FAFNER,
FAFNIR
of darkness RAHAB
tail, Hindu KETU
two-legged, winged
WIVERN, WYVERN
dragon's teeth sower
CADMUS
drain DEPLETE, EMPTY,
WEAKEN, EXHAUST,
DISSIPATE, SAP, SEWER
TRENCH, DITCH,
CHANNEL, CULVERT,
TAP, CONDUIT, SLUICE,
PIPE
drake DUCK, DRAGON,
GALLEY
dram DRAFT, DRINK,
NIP, SLUG, WEIGHT
drama THEATER,
STAGE, ART, PLAY,
OPERA, SPECTACLE,
TRAGEDY, COMEDY,
FARCE, BURLETTA,
MASQUE, MASK
dance BALLET
introduction of
PROTASIS
main action EPITASIS
pertaining to
HISTRIONIC
sudden reverse in
PERIPETIA
dramatic TENSE,
SCENIC, VIVID, STAGY,
THEATRICAL,
HISTRIONIC, THESPIAN,
TRAGIC,
OSTENTATIOUS, SHOWY
dramatize ENACT,
STAGE
drapery, *on bed* PAND,
VALANCE, TESTER
drastic RADICAL,
SEVERE, STERN,
POWERFUL, VIOLENT,
VIGOROUS
draught DOSE, POTION,
PLAN, COPY, DESIGN,

DEPTH, DRINK *See*
"draft"
draughts CHECKERS,
GAME
Dravidian TAMIL,
HINDU
language TAMIL,
TULU, TODA, KOTA
draw DRAFT, ETCH,
TRACE, LIMN, SKETCH,
DELINEATE, PAINT,
WIN, ATTRACT, ELICIT,
INDUCE, TIE, TOLE,
TOW, TUG, REMOVE,
ENTICE, INHALE,
EVOKE, HAUL,
(AL)LURE, PULL,
DRAG, HALE, DRAIN,
SIPHON
away ABDUCE,
ABDUCT, DIVERT
back WITHDRAW, RE-
TREAT, WINCE, RE-
COIL, RETRACT
close STEAL, AP-
PROACH, NEAR
forth EDUCE, DERIVE,
ELICIT, TUG, PULL
out ATTENUATE, PRO-
TRACT, CONTINUE,
ELICIT
tight FRAP, PULL,
BIND
together COUL, FRAP,
ASSEMBLE
up TUCK
drawback DEFECT, DIS-
ADVANTAGE, FAULT,
FLAW, HINDRANCE
drawer TILL, TRAY,
ARTIST
dray CART, WAGON,
SLEDGE
dread AWE, FEAR,
HORROR, TERROR,
PANIC, ALARM, AP-
PREHENSION
dreadful AWFUL, DIRE,
SHOCKING, TERRIBLE,
FRIGHTFUL, HORRID,
BAD, FEARFUL
dream VISION,
FANTASY, DELUSION,
MUSE, SCHEME,
VAGARY, FANCY,
ILLUSION
day REVERIE, VISION,
FANCY
dreams, *god of* ONIROS
pertaining to
ONEIROTIC, ONEIRIC

dreamy SOOTHING,
LANGUID
dreary ALANGE,
DISMAL, DULL,
SOMBER, INSULAR,
DESOLATE,
MELANCHOLIC,
GLOOMY, DARK, DREAR,
CHEERLESS, LONELY,
TIRESOME, BANAL
dredge TRAIN, SIFT,
DRAG, RAISE
dregs SORDOR, SILT,
DRAFF, LEES, DROSS,
SCUM, REFUSE,
SLUDGE, RESIDUE,
MAGMA, SEDIMENT,
GROUNDS, REMAINDER,
SORDES, FAEX
drench DOUSE, IMBUE,
HOSE, SOAK, SOUSE,
WET, SATURATE, SOG,
SOP, RET, STEEP,
PERMEATE
drenched DEWED,
ASOP, WET, SOAKED
dress ATTIRE, DECK,
DIGHT, RIG, TOG(S),
CLOTHE, GARB, AC-
COUTER, ADORN,
GOWN, PREEN, PRE-
PARE, GARNISH,
BANDAGE, ARRAY,
ROBE, APPAREL,
RAIMENT, HABILI-
MENT, SCOLD See
under "garment"
feathers PREEN
leather TAN, CURRY,
TAW, TEW
looped part POUF
riding HABIT,
JODHPURS, BREECHES
right ALINE, ALIGN
trimming GIMP,
LACE, BRAID
dresser BUREAU,
VANITY, TABLE, CHEST
dressmaker MODISTE,
SEAMSTRESS
term GODET, GUSSET,
GORE
dribble TRICKLE, DROP,
DRIP
dried ARID, SERE,
DESICCATED
drift TENOR, INTENT,
HEAP, AIM, PILE,
TREND, FLOAT,
COURSE, BEARING,
DIRECTION, PURPOSE,
TENDENCY, MEANING

drill BORE, PIERCE,
TRAIN, DISCIPLINE,
PREPARE, TEACH,
PRACTICE, EXERCISE,
PROBE, ENTER,
GIMLET, AUGER
drink SWALLOW, SIP,
SWIG, QUAFF, TOPE,
IMBIBE, SUP, GUZZLE,
TIPPLE, NOG, TOAST,
ADE, ALE, NIPA,
TODDY, BRACER, SHOT,
GROG, DRAM, PUNCH,
BEVERAGE, POTION,
FLIP, FIZZ, SLING,
SOUR, SODA, PONY,
WATER, MILK, COFFEE,
TEA, BEER
ancient MORAT
Arabian BOZA
brandy, spiced
SANGAREE
brewed ALE, BEER,
PORTER, STOUT, BOCK,
LAGER
Christmas NOG,
WASSAIL
gruellike CAUDLE
habitually TIPPLE,
TOPE, SOT
Hindu SOMA
honey MEAD, MORAT
of the gods NECTAR
oriental SAKE
palm NIPA
plant juice SOMA,
NIPA
rum BUMBO, BOMBO
Russia VODKA
soft ADE, POP, SODA
South Seas AVA,
KAVA
Tatar KUMISS
wine, water and sugar
NEGUS
drinking *bowl*
MAZER
cup CYLIX, KYLIX,
FACER, MUG, TOBY,
TANKARD, STEIN
horn RHYTON
pledge in PROPINE,
PROSIT, TOAST
vessel MUG, JORUM,
TYG, TIG
word PROSIT
drip LEAK, SILE, SEEP,
TRICKLE, OOZE
drive LANE, ALLEY,
RIDE, STREET, ROAD,
ACTUATE, PUSH,
SHOVE, URGE, CALL,

MOTOR, INCITE,
IMPEL, PROPEL,
STEER, FORCE,
COERCE, MOVE,
THRUST, HURL, PRESS,
COMPEL, CONSTRAIN,
DIRECT, PILOT
away DISPEL
back REPEL
in TAMP, NAIL
drivel DOTE, DROOL,
WASTE, FRITTER,
SLAVER, SLOBBER,
NONSENSE, TWADDLE
driveler DROOLER,
DOTARD, IDIOT
driver JEHU, WHIP,
MOTORIST, HAMMER,
COACHMAN,
CHARIOTEER, CHAUF-
FEUR, PILOT
camel SARWAN
drizzle MIST, MIZZLE,
RAIN, SHOWER,
SPRINKLE
droll ODD, BUFFOON,
JESTER, ZANY,
RISIBLE, COMIC,
WITTY, PUNCH,
CLOWN, FOOL, WAG-
GISH
saying GIBE, TAUNT,
QUIP, JEST
dromedary MEHARI,
CAMEL
like BACTRIAN
drone HUM, IDLER,
BEE, SLUGGARD, SOUND
droop SINK, BEND,
PINE, LOP, FADE, SAG,
WILT, FLAG, NOD,
DANGLE, SLOUCH,
DECLINE
drooping ALOP
drop DRIP, MINIM,
DRIB, GUTTA, SINK,
BLOB, BEAD, FALL,
OMIT, TRICKLE, DIS-
CARD, SACK, FIRE,
BOUNCE, GLOBULE,
EARRING, BIT, SHED,
LOWER, DUMP,
LEAVE, DESCENT,
PENDANT
by drop GUTTATIM
gently FLOW, DAP
like GUTTATE
sudden HANCE, PLOP
dropsical EDEMIC,
HYDROPIC, PUFFY
dropsy EDEMA

dross SCORIA, SCUM, SCOBS, SLAG, CINDER, REFUSE, DREGS, CHAFF, TRASH, SULLAGE
of iron SINTER
drought THIRST, NEED, ARIDITY, DEARTH, DRYNESS, INSUFFICIENCY
plant GUAR, XEROPHYTE
drove CROWD, FLOCK, HERD, RODE, GAGGLE, PACK, BEVY, SWARM, SCHOOL, ASSEMBLAGE, MULTITUDE
of horses ATAJO
drowse SLEEP, DOZE, DOVER, NOD, SLUMBER, NAP
drowsiness TORPOR, LETHARGY, OSCITANCE, DULLNESS, SLUGGISHNESS
drudge HACK, PLOD, SLAVE, FAG, GRUB, TOIL, LABOR, MOIL, GRIND
drug DOPE, OPIATE, SULFA, DOSE, NARCOTIC, MEDICINE, REMEDY
drugged bliss KEF, KIEF, KEIF, KIF(F)
drugget MAT, RUG, CLOTH
Druid, *priestess of opera* NORMA
stone SARSEN
drum BEAT, HILL, RIDGE, TATTOO, TABOR, TABRET, KETTLE, REPEAT, DUB, TIMBREL, BONGO, BARREL, CYLINDER, CARP, TYMPANUM, TIMBAL
ear TYMPANUM
India NAGARA
low beat DUB, RUFF
Moorish ATABAL
oriental ANACARA, TOM-TOM
roll at sunrise DIAN
small TABOR
string SNARE
tighten FRAP
W. Indies GUMBY, BONGO
drunk FULL, SOAKED, LIT, SODDEN, POTTED,

POTTO, INEBRIATED, OILED
drunkard DIPSOMANIAC, SOT, SOUSE, TOPER, TIPPLER
drunt DRAWL, PET, GRUMBLE
drupe CHERRY, PEACH, PLUM, APRICOT, TRYMA
drupe stone NUTLET, PIT, PUTAMEN
drupetum ETAERIO, RASPBERRY
druplet ACINUS, GRAIN
dry AREFY, BLOT, SERE, SEC, ARID, BRUT, THIRSTY, SICCATE, XEROTIC, WIPE, PRESERVE, CYNICAL, UNMOISTENED, SAPLESS, PARCHED, DULL, DEHYDRATE(D), DESICCATE(D)
combining form XERO
as a narrative JEJUNE
dryad NYMPH, DRYAS
dry goods dealer DRAPER, MERCER
drying SICCATIVE
spread for TED
duad DYAD, TWO, DUALITY, PAIR, COUPLE
dual DOUBLE, TWIN, BINARY, TWOFOLD
dub CALL, NAME, POKE, THRUST, STYLE, TITLE, TERM, DESIGNATE, DRUMBEAT, BUNGLER
dubious SHADY, SEAMY, VAGUE, DOUBTFUL, UNDECIDED, UNCERTAIN, HESITANT
duck FOWL, PEKIN, SMEW, SCOTER, TEAL, WIDGEON, EIDER, GANNET, MERGANSER, SCAUP, BOW, CRINGE, EVADE, STOOP, DODGE, DIP, MERSE, CLOTH, SOUSE
Arctic EIDER
Chinese MANDARIN
Europe SHELDRAKE
flock of SORD
genus AYTHYA, ANAS, AIX, NYROCA, ANSERES, CLANGULA
hawk FALCON

large MUSCOVY, PATO
like COOT, DECOY
lure DECOY
male DRAKE
pertaining to ANATINE
pintail SMEE, WIDGEON
river TEAL
sea EIDER, SCAUP, SCOTER
sitting DECOY
small SMEW
surf SCOTER, COOT
wild GADWALL, MALLARD
duckbill PLATYPUS, MAMMAL
duckweed LEMNA
duct CANAL, PIPE, TUBE, RACE, VAS, CHANNEL, FLUE, CONDUIT, AORTA, PASSAGE(WAY)
ductile SOFT, ELASTIC, TRACTABLE, COMPLIANT, DOCILE, FLEXIBLE, FACILE, PLASTIC, MALLEABLE
ductless gland THYMUS, PINEAL, THYROID
dude FOP, JOHNNY, COXCOMB, MACARONI, DANDY
dudeen PIPE
dudgeon IRE, PIQUE, MALICE, ANGER, RESENTMENT, INDIGNATION
due PROPER, RIGHT, DEBT, DUTY, REWARD, REGULAR, OWED, FIT, SUITABLE, CHARGE, JUST, LAWFUL, PAYABLE, OWING
duel CONTEST, TILT, COMBAT, CONFLICT, FIGHT
duet DUO, PAIR, SONG
dugout ABRI, PIROGUE, CANOE, BOAT, SHELTER
duke's realm DUCHY, DUKEDOM
dulcet SOFT, SWEET, TUNEFUL, ARIOSE, HONEYED, HARMONIOUS, CHARMING, AGREEABLE, MELODIOUS
dulcimer PSALTERY, CITOLE, CANUN, SANTIR, ZITHER

dull HEBETATE,
(BE)NUMB, DENSE,
INERT, DIM, OBTUSE,
DUMB, CRASS, STOLID,
PALLING, DRAB, PROSY,
BLUNT, DRY, JEJUNE,
VAPID, OBTUND,
STOGY, LEADY, LOGY,
STUPID, DOLTISH,
DEAD, DINGY,
APATHETIC, CALLOUS,
GLOOMY, DREARY,
MATTE, UNINTEL-
LIGENT, INSENSIBLE,
COLORLESS, SIMPLE
color TERNE, DUN,
FAVEL, MATTE, KHAKI
finish MATTE, MAT
statement PLATITUDE
dullard OAF, MORON,
BOEOTIAN, DUNCE
See "dunce"
dullness PHLEGM,
APATHY
dulse SEAWEED
Dumas character
ARAMIS, PORTHOS,
ATHOS
dumb APHONIC,
SILENT, MUTE, DULL,
DENSE, CRASS, VOICE-
LESS, INARTICULATE
dummy PEL, SHAM,
DECOY, SUBSTITUTE
whist MORT
dun ASK, SOLICIT, BILL,
PRESS, URGE, IM-
PORTUNE, DINGY,
DULL
color BROWN, GREY,
GRAY, TAN, KHAKI,
ECRU
dunce COOT, DOLT,
OAF, GOON, FOOL,
MORON, SIMPLETON,
IGNORAMUS, DOPE,
HALFWIT, BOOBY,
NUMSKULL, NINNY,
LOUT, ASS
dune MOUND, BANK,
DENE, RIDGE
dunk DIP, SOP, SOUSE,
SOAK
dunlin STIB, SAND-
PIPER, BIRD
duo DUET, PAIR, TWO
dupe CHEAT, COZEN,
DELUDE, TRICK, HOAX,
SUCKER, (BE)FOOL,
GULL, BILK, FRAUD,
CULL(Y), TOOL, DE-
CEIVE, CHOUSE

duplicate BIS, DUPLEX,
COPY, DOUBLE, TWIN,
CARBON, REPLICA,
TWOFOLD, FACSIMILE,
COUNTERPART,
IMITATE, IMITATION
duplicity FRAUD, GUILE,
CUNNING, DECEIT,
CHICANERY, ARTIFICE,
DISHONESTY
durable FIRM, TOUGH,
STOUT, STABLE,
STRONG, ENDURING,
LASTING, ABIDING,
CONSTANT
durance vile JAIL,
IMPRISONMENT
duration SPACE, TERM,
LIFE, PERIOD, SPAN,
TIME, LENGTH, CON-
TINUANCE
Durham district RYTON
durra MILLET,
SORGHUM, GRAIN
dusk GLOOM, TWI-
LIGHT, NIGHTFALL,
EVENING
dusky SWART(HY),
DARK, DIM, MURKY,
TAWNY, OPAQUE,
SHADOWY, CLOUDY
dust POWDER,
COOM(B), BRISS,
PILM, STIVE, ASH,
LINT, TRASH, STOUR,
DIRT, SOOT, SMUT,
MONEY
reduce to MULL,
PULVERIZE, GRIND
Dutch See "Nether-
lands"
Dutch Guiana See
"Surinam"
Dutchman HOGEN
duty TARIFF, LEVY,
RATE, CESS, FEU, TAX,
TOLL, IMPOST, EXCISE,
JOB, TASK, OFFICE,
ONUS, DEVOIR,
CHORE, STINT,
CHARE, WORK,
OBLIGATION,
RESPONSIBILITY
Hindu DHARMA
Dvorak ANTON
dwarf SHEE, ELF,
GNOME, MANIKIN,
RUNT, PIGMY, PIXY,
NIX, MIDGET, TROLL,
CRILE, DURGAN,
STUNT, SPRITE, FAY,
PUCK, BANTAM,

SESQUIPEDAL,
LILLIPUTIAN
fish-shaped ANDVARI
Scottish DROICH, URF
dwarfishness NANISM
dwarfs, *the 7* BASHFUL,
DOC, DOPEY, GRUMPY,
HAPPY, SLEEPY,
SNEEZY
dwell RESIDE,
(A)BIDE, LIVE, LODGE,
STAY, STOP, INHABIT,
TENANT, SOJOURN,
DELAY, PAUSE
dwelling HOUSE,
RESIDENCE, DAR,
IGLOO, TEPEE,
QUARTERS, FLAT,
HOME, ABODE, HUTCH,
MANSION, DOMICILE,
CABIN, COTTAGE,
PALACE
dwindle THIN, WANE,
EBB, WASTE, ABATE,
PETER, LESSEN,
SHRINK, DIMINISH,
DECREASE, DECLINE,
DEGENERATE
dyad See "duad"
Dyak IBAN
knife PARANG
dye EOSIN(E), KINO,
COLOR, IMBUE, STAIN,
TINT, TINGE
base ANILINE
blue WOAD, ANIL,
CYANINE, WAD(E)
coal tar EOSIN(E)
component AZO,
DIAZIN(E)
cosmetic HENNA
gum KINO
indigo ANIL
lichen ARCHIL,
ORCHIL, ORCHAL,
LITMUS
morindin AL, AAL
plant ANIL, CHAY,
SUMAC, ALKANET,
MADDER, WOAD,
HENNA, ANNATTO
red AURIN, CERISE,
AAL, EOSIN, ANNATTO,
ANATO, AURINE,
ALKANNIN, AL,
MORINDIN
root pigment MADDER
soot KOHL
S. America LANA
yellow ANATO,
ANNATTO

dyeing *apparatus* AGER
　chamber OVEN
　to produce marble
　　effect BATIK
dyewood tree TUA
dynamic FORCEFUL,
　VIGOROUS, LIVE,
　ACTIVE, VITAL,
　POTENT, EFFECTIVE
dynamics FORCES,
　SCIENCE, MECHANICS
dynamite EXPLOSIVE,
　DANGEROUS
　inventor NOBEL
　variety of DUALIN
dynamo GENERATOR,
　MOTOR
　inventor FARADAY
　part LIMB, STATOR,
　YOKE, COIL, BRUSH,
　ARM, PULLEY, COM-
　MUTATOR, CONDUCTOR
dynasty RULE, REIGN,
　DOMINION, EMPIRE,
　SOVEREIGNTY, LORD-
　SHIP, KINGDOM
　Chinese See under
　"China"
dysphoria ANXIETY,
　DISQUIET, RESTLESS-
　NESS
dzeren ANTELOPE
Dzhugashvili STALIN

E

E EPSILON
ea RIVER, INLET,
　DEITY, EACH
each ALL, EVERY,
　APIECE, BOTH, EITHER
　for each PER
　of each ANA
eager AGASP, AGOG,
　WILLING, AVID, KEEN,
　ATHIRST, ARDENT,
　RESTIVE, GREEDY,
　YEARNING, ANXIOUS,
　FAIN, DESIROUS,
　YARE, IMPATIENT,
　ZEALOUS, FERVENT,
　FERVID
eagle ERN(E), BERGUT,
　GIER, FALCON, HARPY,
　COIN, LECTERN,
　STANDARD
　Biblical GIER
　brood AERIE
　constellation AQUILA
　genus AQUILA
　male TERCEL

　nest AERIE, EYRIE,
　EYRY
　relating to HARPY,
　JOVE'S
　sea ERN(E)
eaglestone ETITE
eaglewood AGALLOCH,
　ALOES
eagre BORE, FLOOD,
　FLOW
ear LUG, SPIKE, KNOB,
　HEED, ATTENTION,
　HEARING, AURICLE,
　PINNA
　anvil of INCUS, AMBOS
　attachment CORN
　auricle PINNA
　bone INCUS, STAPES,
　STIRRUP, MALLEUS,
　AMBOS
　cavity COCHLEA,
　MEATUS
　combining form
　OT(O), AURI
　depression SCAPHA
　doctor AURIST,
　OTOLOGIST
　external AURICLE,
　PINNA, HELIX, CONCHA
　grain SPIKE
　hammer MALLEUS
　inflammation OTITIS
　lobe LUG, PINNA
　near PAROTIC
　outer See "external"
　above
　pertaining to OTIC,
　AURIC, LOBAR
　　to both BINURAL,
　　BINOTIC
　science of OTOLOGY
　shell OMER, ABALONE
　specialist AURIST,
　OTOLOGIST
　stone OTOLITE,
　OTOLITH
　wax CERUMEN
earache OTALGIA,
　OTALGY
early FIRST, AHEAD,
　OLD, SOON, BETIMES,
　TIMELY, SEASONABLE,
　MATUTINAL
　poetical RATH(E),
　BETIMES
earn DESERVE, GAIN,
　WIN, MERIT, SECURE,
　GET, REACH, ACQUIRE,
　OBTAIN, PROCURE,
　MAKE
earnest GRAVE, SOBER,
　SERIOUS, INTENT,

　SEDATE, STAID,
　SINCERE, DILIGENT,
　BUSY, ARDENT,
　ZEALOUS, EAGER,
　PLEDGE, PROMISE
　combining form
　SERIO
　money ARLES,
　HANSEL, HANDSEL
earnestness UNCTION,
　STUDIOUSNESS,
　SINCERITY
earnings WAGES,
　SALARY, PROFITS,
　INCOME, PROCEEDS,
　STIPEND
earth CLAY, DIRT,
　TERRA, SOIL, GROUND,
　LAND, GLOBE, PLANET,
　WORLD, ORB, ERD,
　PEOPLE, LAND
　axis HINGE
　born TERRIGENOUS,
　MORTAL, HUMAN,
　WORLDLY, TEMPORAL
　center CENTRO-
　SPHERE, CORE, BARY-
　SPHERE
　combining form GEO,
　TERRA
　crust HORST
　deified SEB, GEB, KEB,
　DAGAN, TERRA
　deposit SOIL, MARL,
　LOAM
　lump CLOD, SOD
　metallic ORE
　occur at surface
　EPIGENE
　outer portion of
　SIAL, CRUST
　pertaining to GEAL,
　TERRENE, TER-
　RESTRIAL, CLAYEY,
　TEMPORAL, WORLDLY
　pigment OCHRE,
　UMBER
　poetic VALE
　surface EPIGENE,
　CRUST, HORST
　volcanic TRASS, LAVA,
　TUFF
earthdrake DRAGON
earthenware DELFT,
　JASPER, PORCELAIN,
　CHINA, OLLA, ECHEA,
　CROCKERY, POTTERY,
　STONEWARE
　maker POTTER
earthflax AMIANTHUS,
　ASBESTOS

earthling MORTAL, HUMAN

earthly TERRENE, MORTAL, PROFANE, SECULAR *See* "earthy"

earthnut CHUFA, POD, PEANUT, GOOBER, TUBER

earthquake TREMOR, SEISM, TEMBLOR
pertaining to SEISMIC

earthstar GEASTER, FUNGUS

earthwork AGGER, FORT, MOUND, DIKE

earthworm DEWWORM, ESS, ANGLEWORM

earthy CARNAL, FLESHY, GROSS, COARSE, MORTAL, TERRESTRIAL, SENSUAL, LOW, TEMPORAL, MUNDANE

ease ALLAY, ASSUAGE, MOLLIFY, RELIEVE, SOOTHE, REST, REPOSE, LEISURE, RELIEF, QUIET, PEACE, CONTENT, FACILITY, COMFORT, ALLEVIATE, MITIGATE, ABATE

east ASIA, LEVANT, ORIENT, SUNRISE
pertaining to EOAN, ORIENTAL

East Africa *cedar* DEODAR
discoverer GAMA
house TEMBE
tribe BARI
slave vessel DHOW
sultanate ZANZIBAR

Easter PASCH(A), PAAS, PACE
feast of PASCH
festival PAAS
first Sunday after QUASIMODO
Mohammedan EED
pertaining to PASCHAL

eastern ORIENTAL, ASIATIC, ORTIVE
people SERE, AVARS
priest IMAM
ruler EMEER, EMIR
V.I.P. AG(H)A

East India SRI, TAMIL
See "India"

easy LIGHT, SMOOTH, SIMPLE, FREE, MILD, FACILE, GLIB, PAIN-LESS, LENIENT, EF-FORTLESS

job SINECURE, SNAP, CINCH, PIPE

eat(s) FEED, SUP, DINE, INGEST, CON-SUME, DEVOUR, DOWN, FOOD, GRUB, CHOW, VIANDS, FRET, ERODE, RUST, GNAW, CANKER, CORRODE
greedily GORGE, RAVEN, BOLT, GOBBLE, GULP
immoderately GLUT, SATE
in gulps LAB

eatable ESCULENT, EDIBLE

eating DINING, CAUSTIC, CORROSIVE, EROSIVE
excessively EDACITY, VORACITY
hall MESS, CENACLE, DINER

Eban ABBA

ebb RECEDE, REFLUX, DECAY, WASTE, WANE, ABATE, RETREAT, LESSEN, REGRESS, DECLINE, RETIRE, SINK
and flow TIDE, (A)ESTUS

Eber's *son* PELEG

ebullate BOIL, BUBBLE, SEETHE, STEW

eccentric CRANK, ERRATIC, ODD, GINK, STRANGE, BIZARRE, QUEER, ATYPIC(AL), IRREGULAR, PECULIAR, UNCOMMON, AB-NORMAL, CURIOUS
piece CAM

ecclesiastic PRELATE, CLERIC, PRIEST, ABBE, PADRE, CLERGYMAN, PASTOR, MINISTER, PARSON, DIVINE, VICAR, ABBOT, PRIOR, CHURCHLY, RELIGIOUS

ecclesiastical *attendant* ACOLYTE
banner LABARUM
benefice GLEBE
cap BIRETTA, CALLOT, CALOTTE, ZUCCHETTO
council SYNOD
court CLASSIS, ROTA
garment See "vest-ment" *below*
hood AMICE

jurisdiction DEANERY, SEE, PARISH, DIOCESE
seat(s) SEDILE, SEDILIA
surplice COTTA
vestment AMICE, STOLE, ALB, VAGAS, COTTA, VAKASS, EPHOD, COPE
widow's office VIDUATE

ecdysiast STRIPTEASER

echidna ANTEATER

echimyine HUTIA, CONY

echinate SPINY, BRISTLY, PRICKLY

echo REPLY, RING, RESOUND, APE, ITERATE, REVER-BERATE, REPEAT, IMITATE, ANSWER
back RESOUND, RE-BOUND

eclat GLORY, RENOWN, PRAISE, FAME, HONOR, REPUTE, BRILLIANCY, SPLENDOR, POMP

eclipse CLOUD, HIDE, DARKEN, DIM, OBSCURE, SURPASS, STAIN, VEIL, SHROUD, SULLY, SHADE, OUT-SHINE, BEAT
region of PENUMBRA

economics PLUTOLOGY, SCIENCE, HOUSE-WIFERY

economize HUSBAND, SCRAPE, SCRIMP, SAVE, STINT, PARE, RE-TRENCH

economy THRIFT, SYSTEM, SCHEME, FRUGALITY, HUSBANDRY, PARSIMONY, PLAN, ORDER

ecru BIEGE, TAN, YELLOWISH, UN-BLEACHED, BISCUIT, DOE

ecstasy JOY, BLISS, TRANCE, RAPTURE, DELIGHT, RHAPSODY, FRENZY, MADNESS

ectad, *opposed to* ENTAD

Ecuador *capital* QUITO
city or town LOJA, NAPO, MANTO, IBARRA, TULCAN, CUENCA, AMBATO

coin SUCRE, CONDOR
province (EL) ORO,
MANABI, AZUAY,
GUAYAS, CARCHI,
CANAR, AZUAY, LOJA
seaport MANTA
ecumenical council
TRENT, LYON
eczema HERPES, TET-
TER, DERMATITIS
edacity AVARICE,
GREED, APPETITE,
VORACITY
edaphic LOCAL,
AUTOCHTHONOUS
eddish ARRISH,
EDGROW, AFTERMATH,
STUBBLE
eddy TURN, TWIRL,
ROTATE, GYRATE,
CIRCLE, SPIN, WHIRL,
BORE, SWIRL, VORTEX
edema DROPSY, IN-
TUMESCENCE, SWELL-
ING, PUFFINESS
Eden GLORY, HEAVEN,
PARADISE, GARDEN,
ANTHONY, ELYSIUM
edentata group SLOTH,
AI, ANTEATER,
AARDVARK
edentate genus MANIS,
PANGOLIN
edge SKIRT, BRINK,
BORDER, LIMIT, END,
BOUND, RIM, MARGIN,
LIP, TRIM, HONE,
BANK, VERGE,
LABRUM, BRIM, HEM,
RAND, SELVEDGE, ZEST,
ARRIS, SHARPEN,
ACRIMONY, GALL,
SELVAGE, BOUNDARY,
ODDS, SIDLE
sloping BASIL, BEZEL
edging LACE, RUCHE,
TATTING, TRIM,
BORDER, FRINGE,
TRIMMING, FRILL
edible COMESTIBLE,
ESCULENT, EATABLE,
SUCCULENT
edict ARRET, ACT,
DECREE, UKASE,
MANDATE, BULL,
IRADE, RULE, LAW,
FIAT, WRIT, COM-
MAND, ORDER,
ORDINANCE,
MANIFESTO
Pope's BULL(A)

edit ISSUE, REVISE,
REWORD, REDACT,
BLUEPENCIL, CORRECT,
AMEND, EMEND,
PUBLISH
edition ISSUE, IMPRES-
SION, VERSION
editor WRITER, RE-
VISER, REDACTOR,
DIASKEUAST
editorial ARTICLE,
LEADER
Edom *chieftain* IRAM
land of IDUMAEA,
TEMA, TEMAN
educate TRAIN, TEACH,
SCHOOL, COACH,
DISCIPLINE, INSTRUCT,
PREPARE, DRILL
educated ERUDITE,
LETTERED, TRAINED,
LITERATE, CULTURED
education STUDY,
NURTURE, DISCIPLINE,
INSTRUCTION,
PEDAGOGICS, BREED-
ING
educe INFER, EVOLVE,
ELICIT, EVOKE, DRAW,
EXTRACT, DERIVE,
DISENGAGE
eel MORAY, CONGO,
CONGER, LAUNCE,
SCOURGE, WHIP,
TUNA, LAMPREY,
ELVER
fish for SNIGGLE
genus CONGER
marine CONGER
sand LAUNCE
young ELVER
eelpout BURBOT, LING,
FISH, WEASEL
eelworm NEMA,
NEMATODE
eerie UNCANNY, WEIRD,
BIZARRE, ODD, QUEER,
SPOOKY
efface DELE, EXPUNGE,
ERASE, BLOT, CANCEL,
OBLITERATE, REMOVE,
DELETE, SPONGE,
DESTROY
effect GAIN, REACH,
END, FULFILL, COM-
PASS, SEQUEL,
ACHIEVE, TAKE, RE-
SULT, DO, MAKE,
CAUSE, UPSHOT, ISSUE,
CONSEQUENCE, FRUIT,
OUTCOME, PURPORT,

IMPORT, DRIFT, PER-
FORM, CONTRIVE
effeminate GENTLE,
MILD, WEAK, SOFT,
EPICENE, WOMANLY,
UNMANLY, TIMOROUS
effervesce FIZZ,
BUBBLE, HISS, BOIL,
FOAM, AERATE, FROTH,
FERMENT, EBULLATE
effete BARREN, IDLE,
WEAK, UNPROLIFIC,
FRUITLESS, SPENT,
EXHAUSTED, OLD,
TIRED
efficacy POTENCY,
POWER, COGENCY,
COMPETENCY, FORCE,
STRENGTH, ENERGY,
VIGOR, VIRTUE,
EFFICIENCY
efficient ABLE,
CAPABLE, EXPERT,
ADEPT, SKILLED,
EFFICACIOUS, POTENT
effigy ICON, FACSIMILE,
COPY, STATUE, IMAGE,
FIGURE, LIKENESS,
PORTRAIT, DUMMY,
MANIKIN, MODEL
effluvium AURA, REEK,
FLATUS, MIASMA,
ODOR, NIDOR, VAPOR,
EXHALATION, EMANA-
TION
effluxion EMANATION,
EFFUSION, OUTFLOW,
EFFLUENCE
effort TRIAL, STRUGGLE,
CONATUS, FORCE,
STRAIN, NISUS, PAINS,
WORK, LABOR, TOIL,
MIGHT, ESSAY, EN-
DEAVOR, ATTEMPT,
EXERTION, STRIFE,
SPURT, APPLICATION,
DRIVE
effrontery BRASS,
NERVE, CHEEK, GALL,
GUTS, IMPUDENCE,
AUDACITY, PRESUMP-
TION, BOLDNESS
effulgence LUSTER,
GLOW, SPLENDOR,
BRILLIANCE, FLARE,
RADIANCE, BRIGHT-
NESS, RUTILATION
effusive GUSHY, LAVISH,
GENEROUS, OUTPOUR-
ING, EXUBERANT,
EBULLIENT

eft EVET, LIZARD, NEWT, TRITON
genus TRITURUS
eftsoon AGAIN, ANON, AFTERWARD
egg(s) OVUM, OVA, NIT
bake SHIRR
capsule OVISAC
case SAC, SHELL
collector of bird's OOLOGIST
combining form OO, OVI
dish OMELET
drink NOG
fish BERRY, ROE, CAVIAR
of insect NIT, LARVA
part of LATEBRA, YOLK, SHELL, WHITE, ALBUMEN
shaped OVATE, OVOID, OOID(AL)
shell SHARD
small OVULE, NIT
strand uniting white and yolk CHALAZA, TREADLE
tester CANDLER
white GLAIR, ALBUMEN
egg on URGE, INCITE, GOAD, SPUR, IN-STIGATE, ENCOURAGE
Egil's *brother* VOLUND
ego JIVATMA, ATMAN, SELF, ID, ME, SELFISH-NESS
egregious FLAGRANT, GROSS, SHOCKING, VICIOUS
egress VENT, OUTLET, EXIT, DOOR, ISSUANCE, DEPARTURE
egret HERON, PLUME, BIRD, FOWL
Egypt, Egyptian NILOT, GIPSY, GYPSY, MISR, ARAB, MIZRAIM, KEM
ancient capital MEMPHIS
name MISR, KEM
ape, myth, AANI
Arabic name MISR, MIZR
astral body KA
beetle SCARAB
Biblical name MIZRAIM

bird IBIS, BENU, SICSAC
boat CANGIA, BARIS, SANDAL, FELUCCA
body, mortal KHET
spiritual See "soul" *below*
bull APIS, BACIS
cape SUDR
captain RAIS, REIS
catfish DOCMAC, BAGRE
chaos NU
Christian COPT
city or town ASWAN, ASYUT, LUXOR, SAID, ISNA, ESNA, GIZA, GIZEA, TANTA, TANTIS, ZOAN, SIWA, SAIS, MEROE
  ancient ABYDOS, KARNAK, CANOPUS, NO
cobra HAJE, ASP
coin FODDA(H), KEES, PARA, PURSE, BEDIDLIK, GIRSH (GERSH), TALLARD
commander SIRDAR
conqueror AMR(U)
cosmetic powder KOHL
cotton PIMA
cross of life ANKH
dam SADD, ASWAN
dancing girl ALMA
dead region AMENTI
deity See under "god" *or* "goddess"
desert LIBYAN, NUBIAN, SAHARA
divinity See under "god" *or* "goddess"
division MAZOR, PATHROS
dog SALUKI
dye plant HENNA, HINNA
evil spirit SET, SETH
fable monster SPHINX
falcon-headed deity HORUS
fertile land GOSHEN
fish SAIDE, BICHIR, DOCMAC, LATES
fruit FIG
gate PYLON
genie HAPI
god or goddess See under "god" *or* "goddess"
governor BEY

guard GHAFIR
harelike mammal HYRAX
hawk-headed deity HORUS
man RA
headdress of ruler URAEUS
healer ARABI
heaven AARU
hieroglyphic name KEM
immortal heart AB, HATI
intelligence CHU
island RODA, PHILAE
jar CANOPIC
jini, jinii, jinee AMSET, HAPI
judge of dead OSIRIS
Khedive's estate DAIRA
king PTOLEMY, PHAROAH, RAMESES, FAUD, FAROK, FAROUK
lake MOERIS
land GOSHEN, FEDDAN
language COPTIC
lighthouse PHAROS
lizard ADDA
lute NABLE
measure ARDAB, ARDEB, CUBIT, APT, THEB, HEN, KILAH, KELE, KHET, PIK, ABDAT, APET, BAAH, GASAB, GIRBA, HON(UN), INION, KADAM, KADDAH, KERAT, KISLOZ, MILI, NEUT, OIPHI, PIC, REBEB, RO, SA, TAMA, THEBAN
monarch RAMESES
month TOTH, HATHOR, TYBI, MECHIR, PAYNI, MESORE, APAP
mountain HOREB (SINAI)
mouse JERBOA
musical performer ALMEH, ALMA
Nile deified HAPI
oasis SIWA, KHARGA
party WAFD
peasant FELLAH
peninsula PHAROS
pharoah's hen VULTURE
physician IMHOTEP
plant CUMIN
plateau TIH

policeman GHAFIR
port SAID
pound ROTL
province NOME
queen CLEO(PATRA)
  of gods SATI
rattle SISTRUM
reed BYBLUS,
  PAPYRUS, BIBLUS
royal symbol, anc.
  ASP, URAEUS
ruler KHEDIVE *See*
  "king" *above*
season AHET, PERT,
  SHEMU
serpent, myth. APETI
singing girl ALMA
skink ADDA
snake ASP, COBRA,
  HAJE
solar disk ATEN
soul or spirit SAHU,
  KA, BA, CHU, AKH
sultan SALADIN
symbol ANKH
  of sovereignty
  URAEUS, ASP
symbolic eye UTA
temple OSIRIS, IDFU,
  KARNAK, LUXOR,
  DENDERA, ABYDOS
thorn KIKAR, BABUL
title CALIPH, CALIF
tomb MASTABA
  cell of SERDAB
town *See* "city"
  above
tribesman MADI
unit of capacity
  ARDEB
  of currency GERSH,
  PIASTRE
viceroy KHEDIVE
water bottle DORUCK
water raising device
  SAKIEH, SHADOOF,
  TABUT
weight KET, KANTAR,
  KAT, OKA, KHAR, OCHA,
  OKE, OKIE(H), UCKIA,
  HEML, OKIA, UTEN
wind KAMSIN,
  KHAMSIN
eider DOWN, WAMP,
  DUCK, QUILT
eidolon IMAGE,
  APPARITION,
  PHANTOM, EMANATION
eight VIII, ETA, CARD,
  OGDOAD
combining form
  OCTA, OCTO

day OCTAN
days of feast UTAS
fold OCTUPLE
group of OCTET(TE),
  OCTAD
series of OGDOAD,
  OCTAD, OCTET
eighteen inches CUBIT
Eire *See* "Ireland"
ejaculation, *mystic* OM
eject CAST, SHED,
  MOLT, EMIT, EXPEL,
  EVICT, OUST, DIS-
  CHARGE, VOID, EXILE,
  FIRE, SPEW, SACK,
  BANISH, DISLODGE,
  SPOUT, SPURT, DIS-
  MISS, CASHIER, DIS-
  POSSESS, BOUNCE
eke ADD, INCREASE,
  ENLARGE, SUPPLE-
  MENT
elaborate ORNATE,
  COMPLICATED, DRESSY,
  INTRICATE, LABORIOUS,
  IMPROVE, REFINE,
  DEVISE, DEVELOP, EX-
  PLAIN
Elam *capital* SUSA
  father SHEM
elan ARDOR, DASH,
  SPIRIT, ZEST, VERVE,
  EAGERNESS
eland ELK, IMPOFO
elapse DIE, GO, PASS,
  RUN, LAPSE, GLIDE
elasmobranch fish
  SAWFISH, CHIMERA,
  SHARK, RAY
elastic SPRINGY,
  PLIANT, LITHE, LIM-
  BER, RESILIENT,
  BUOYANT
elate EXCITE, EXALT,
  FLUSH, PLEASE,
  CHEER, ANIMATE, EN-
  LIVEN, DELIGHT, IN-
  FLATE
elated CHEERFUL,
  PERKED, JOYOUS,
  SPIRITED, RAD,
  EXHILARATED,
  EXULTANT
Elbe *tributary* ISER,
  EGER (OHRE), ELDE,
  HAVEL, MULDE, SAALE
elbow SQUEEZE,
  ANCON, PUSH, PUNCH,
  TURN, BEND, ANGLE,
  CROWD, JOSTLE,
  NUDGE, JOINT
  bend TOPE, DRINK

  touch with NUDGE
Elcesaites, *founder*
  ELCESAI
elder PRIOR, FIRST,
  SIRE, DEAN, OLDER,
  SENIOR, SR, ANCESTOR,
  MORMON, PRESBYTER,
  TREE
  shrub or tree
  SAMBUCUS
elderly GRAY, OLD,
  AGED
eldest AINE(E),
  EIGNE, SENIOR
eldritch EERIE,
  GHASTLY, UNCANNY,
  WEIRD, FRIGHTFUL
elect SELECT, FIX,
  CALL, ORDAIN,
  DECIDE, OPT, CHOOSE,
  NAME, ELITE, PICK,
  CULL, JUDGE
electioneer STUMP,
  CAMPAIGN
elector ELISOR, VOTER,
  CHOOSER, CONSTIT-
  UENT
Electra's *brother*
  ORESTES
electric *appliance*
  IRON, TOASTER,
  HEATER, WASHER,
  DRYER
  atmosphere AURA
  atom ELECTRON,
  ANION, CATION, ION
  circuit regulator
  BOOSTER
  coil TESLA
  constituent *See*
  "atom" *above*
  detective RADAR,
  SONAR
  ion ANION, CATION
  measure *See* "unit"
  below
  particle ION, ANION,
  CATION
  terminal ELECTRODE,
  POLE
  unit VOLT, HENRY,
  AMPERE, FARAD, REL,
  OHM, ES, MEGADYNE,
  WATT, COULOMB
  capacity FARAD
  force ELOD, OD
  pressure BARAD,
  DYNE
  reluctance OERSTED,
  REL
electrode CATHODE,
  ANODE, TERMINAL

electromagnetic disk
OERSTED
electronic tube
VACUUM, KLYSTRON,
TRIODE
electrum AMBER,
ALLOY
eleemosynary
CHARITABLE,
ALMONER, DEPENDENT
elegance GRACE,
LUXURY, BEAUTY,
TASTE, DIGNITY,
REFINEMENT, LUXE,
GENTILITY, POLISH
elegant NOBLE, GRAND,
RARE, CHOICE, DAINTY,
POSH, RICH, COURTLY,
POLITE, CLASSICAL
elegiac FUNEREAL,
POEM, PLAINTIVE
elegy LAMENT, DIRGE,
REQUIEM, POEM,
MONODY, THRENODY
element PART, GERM,
ORIGIN, COMPONENT,
ITEM, DETAIL, FACTOR,
METAL, CONSTITUENT,
INGREDIENT
chemical URANIUM,
HALOGEN, SILICON,
SODIUM, SILVER,
RADIUM, NICKEL,
ERBIUM, IODINE,
HELIUM, CESIUM,
COPPER, COBALT,
XENON, CARBON,
RADON, BORON,
ARGON, ZINC, TIN,
NEON, LEAD, IRON,
GOLD
earth group ERBIUM
even valence ARTIAD
inert gas NEON,
XENON
non-metallic
BROMINE, IODINE,
BORON, SILICON
non-volatile BARIUM
of air ARGON,
NITROGEN, OXYGEN
similar ISOTOPE
white INDIUM, SILVER
elemental spirit GENIE
elementary INCHOATE,
BASIC, SIMPLE,
PRIMARY, PRIMAL,
PRIMORDIAL,
RUDIMENTARY
elemi ANIME, ELEMIN,
OLEORESIN, RESIN

elephant PACHYDERM,
MASTODON
apple tree FERONIA
boy SABU
carrying bird ROC
cry BARR
ear TARO, FERN
extinct MASTODON
goad ANKUS
keeper MAHOUT
pen KRAAL
pertaining to
PACHYDERMIC
seat on HOWDAH
stick for goading
ANKUS
trappings for JHOOL
tusk IVORY,
SCRIVELLO
young CALF
elephantine HUGE,
TITANIC, LARGE,
ENORMOUS, CLUMSY,
GIGANTIC, COLOSSAL,
IMMENSE *See*
"huge"
elevate EXALT, PRO-
MOTE, TOWER, SOAR,
HEAVE, BOOST, LIFT,
RAISE, HOIST, DIGNIFY,
ADVANCE
elevated *ground*
RIDEAU, MESA,
MOUND, RIDGE, HILL,
TERRACE
summer house
BELVEDERE
elevation RIDGE, HILL,
RISE, HEIGHT, MOUNT,
STATURE, ALTITUDE,
PROMOTION, DIGNITY,
PLAN
of mind ANAGOGE
elevator CRANE, WING,
CAGE, LIFT, CAR
elf NIX, FAY, GNOME,
IMP, OAF, OUPHE,
SPRITE, PUCK, PIXIE,
GOBLIN, FAIRY,
DWARF, SHEE, NIXIE
king ERLKING
elfkin FAIRY, FAY
elfish sprite DRAC
elicit EDUCE, EXTRACT,
STRETCH, EVOKE,
DRAW, DRAG, PULL,
WRING, EXTORT,
PUMP, DISCOVER
eligible APT, MEET,
COMPETENT, FIT,
SUITABLE, QUALIFIED,

WORTHY, DESIRABLE,
AVAILABLE
eliminate DELE, ERASE,
RID, DETACH, DROP,
OMIT, EXPEL, EX-
CLUDE, EJECT, OUST,
EVICT, SIFT, REMOVE,
ERADICATE
Elijah ELIAS, TISHBITE,
PROPHET
elision SYNCOPE,
HAPLOLOGY, APOCOPA-
TION
Eli's *son* HOPHNI,
PHINEAS
elite CREAM, GENTRY,
SOCIETY, BEST,
CHOICE, FLOWER,
TYPE
elixir ARCANUM,
PANACEA,
CATHOLICON, CURE-
ALL
Elizabeth I ORIANA
elk MOOSE, LOSH,
SAMBAR, WAPITI,
DEER, GOOSE, SWAN,
LEATHER
bark BAY, MAGNOLIA
Elkanah's *son* SAMUEL
wife HANNAH
ell WING, ANNEX,
EXTENSION, MEASURE
ellipse CURVE, OVAL,
OVATE, OBLONG
elliptical OVAL, OVATE
elm ULME, TREE,
SHRUB
borer LAMIID
fruit SAMARA
genus ULMUS, CELTIS,
TREMA, PLANERA
Elmo's *fire* CORPOSANT,
LIGHT
elongated PROLATE,
STRETCHED,
LENGTHY, EX-
TENDED, PROTRACTED
elope ABSCOND, FLEE,
ESCAPE
eloquent CICERONIAN,
ORATORICAL, GLIB,
FLUENT, VOLUBLE,
POWERFUL, IMPAS-
SIONED
else OTHER, BESIDE(S),
INSTEAD, DIFFERENT,
ADDITIONAL
elude SHUN, AVOID,
EVADE, FOIL, DODGE,
BAFFLE, ESCAPE, OUT-

WIT, FLEE, FLY, FRUSTRATE

elusive EQUIVOCAL, EVASIVE, EELY, SLICK, ELUSORY, IMPALPABLE, DECEPTIVE

elvan *See* "elf"

elver CONGER, EEL

Elysium EDEN, PARADISE, BLISS

elytrin CHITIN

elytrum of beetle SHARD

em, *half* EN

emaciated TABETIC

emaciation MACIES, WASTE, TABES, LEANNESS, LANKNESS, TABEFACTION, ATROPHY

emanate EMIT, ISSUE, SPRING, DERIVE, (A)RISE, FLOW, STEM, PROCEED, EMERGE, RADIATE

emanation AURA, VAPOR, NIDOR, ISSUANCE, EFFLUX, ISSUE, EFFLUVIUM, OUTCOME, PERFUME, ODOR

emancipate DELIVER, FREE, MANUMIT, RELEASE, UNSHACKLE, LIBERATE, AFFRANCHISE

emancipator LINCOLN, FREER, DELIVERER, MOSES

embalm PERFUME, CERE, PRESERVE, ENSHRINE

embankment BUND, DIKE, LEVEE, DUNE, MOUND, BARROW

embark BOARD, SAIL, BEGIN, ENGAGE, ENLIST, DEPART, START

embarrass ABASH, RATTLE, FAZE, DISTURB, FLUSTER, SHAME, HARASS, DISTRESS, CONFUSE, MORTIFY, DISCOMFORT, DISCONCERT, HINDER

embattled CRENELED

embellish DRESS, ADORN, ENRICH, GILD, GARNISH, ROUGE, (BE)DECK, ARRAY,

DECORATE, BEAUTIFY, ENHANCE, EMBLAZON

ember COAL, ASH, CINDER, IZLE, ISEL, CLINKER, SPARK

embezzle PURLOIN, STEAL, FILCH, LIFT, ROB, LOOT, RIFLE, MISAPPROPRIATE, DEFALCATE

embitter ACERBATE, ENVENOM, SOUR, POISON, EXACERBATE, AGGRAVATE

emblem BADGE, DEVICE, MOTIF, DESIGN, MARK, INSIGNIA, INSIGNE, FLAG, TOKEN, SIGN, SYMBOL, FIGURE, STAR, EAGLE, TOTEM
of authority MACE, FASCES, STAR, BAR, EAGLE, STRIPE(S)
of clan TOTEM
of U.S. EAGLE

emblic AULA, TREE

embodiment AVATAR, MATTER, EPITOME, INCORPORATION, INCARNATION, IMAGE
of Ptah APIS

embody UNITE, INCARNATE, ORGANIZE, PERSONIFY, INCORPORATE, INCLUDE, EMBRACE, COMPRISE

embolism OBSTRUCTION, STOPPAGE, INTERCALATION, OCCLUSION

embrace ACCOLADE, CARESS, HUG, ENARM, CLASP, EMBODY, CONTAIN, INCLUDE, GRASP, CHOOSE, SEIZE, ACCEPT, TAKE, CLUTCH, FOLD, CHERISH, RECEIVE, WELCOME, COMPREHEND, LOVE, COMPRISE, ENCOMPASS, ENCIRCLE

embrocation ARNICA, LINIMENT, FOMENTATION, STUPE, POULTICE

embroider DECORATE, ADORN, WORK, EMBELLISH, SEW, ORNAMENT, EXAGGERATE
frame for TABORET, TABOURET, RING, HOOP

embroidery BREDE

embrown TAN, DARKEN

emend CORRECT, RECTIFY, EDIT, WRITE, IMPROVE, AMEND, CRITICISE

emerald BERYL, GREEN, JEWEL, GEM

Emerald Isle EIRE, ERIN, IRELAND

emerge APPEAR, ISSUE, LOOM, STEM, SPRING, FLOW, (A)RISE, EMANATE

emergency CRISIS, PINCH, PASS, STRAIT, NECESSITY, EXIGENCY, URGENCY, DIFFICULTY

emery CORUNDUM, FILE, ABRASIVE

emetic IPECAC, MUSTARD

emigration EXODUS, REMOVAL

eminence TOR, HILL, RIDEAU, PROMINENCE, ELEVATION, HEIGHT, DIGNITY, RANK, CELEBRITY, VIP, DISTINCTION, RENOWN, REPUTE, NOTE, FAME, CARDINAL, TITLE

eminent NOTABLE, HIGH, LOFTY, FAMOUS, FAMED, ELEVATED, CONSPICUOUS, ILLUSTRIOUS, EXALTED, OUTSTANDING, PROMINENT

emir, *jurisdiction of* EMIRATE

emissary AGENT, SCOUT, SPY, ENVOY, LEGATE, MESSENGER

emit REEK, EMANATE, SHED, EXUDE, UTTER, ERUCT, EXHALE, EJECT, DISCHARGE, SPURT, SQUIRT, GUSH, OUTPOUR, ISSUE

emmer SPELT, WHEAT

emmet ANT, PISMIRE

emollient BALM, SALVE, OINTMENT, MALACTIC, SOFTENING, SOOTHING, NARD, LOTION

emolument STIPEND, FEE, GAIN, WAGE, PAY, HIRE, LUCRE, INCOME, COMPENSATION, REMUNERATION,

PROFIT, PERQUISITE,
HONORARIUM

Emory University site
ATLANTA

emotion ONDE, LOVE,
IRE, PATHOS, ELAN,
FEELING, TREMOR,
PASSION, EXCITEMENT,
AGITATION, SENTI-
MENT

emotionless STAID,
TORPID, APATHETIC,
UNFEELING

empathy PITY, RUTH,
UNDERSTANDING,
SYMPATHY

emperor TSAR, CZAR,
RULER, KING,
SOVEREIGN, MONARCH,
ATAHUALPA, MIKADO
Holy Roman OTTO
(OTHO)

emphasize ACCENT,
MARK, STRESS, AC-
CENTUATE, UNDERLINE

empiric FAKER, QUACK,
CHARLATAN, IMPOSTER

employ APPLY, PICK,
SELECT, USE, HIRE,
ENGAGE, OCCUPY,
UTILIZE, ENGROSS

employer BOSS, USER

employment *See*
"work"

empress TSARINA,
CZARINA, QUEEN

emptiness INANITION,
VOID, VACUUM

empty BARREN, VAIN,
BARE, BLANK, IDLE,
INANE, VOID, VACUOUS,
CLEAN, DRAIN, UN-
LOAD, UNOCCUPIED,
VACANT, HOLLOW,
DEVOID, DESTITUTE,
DEPLETED,
EVACUATE(D),
HUNGRY
combining form
KEN(O)

empyreal AERIAL,
CELESTIAL, ETHEREAL,
AIRY

empyrean ETHER, SKY,
HEAVEN, FIRMAMENT

emulate STRIVE, COM-
PETE, RIVAL, VIE,
COPY, APE, MATCH,
EQUAL

emyd TURTLE,
TERRAPIN

enable EMPOWER, IN-
VEST, ENDOW, PERMIT,
ALLOW, LET,
CAPACITATE

enact PASS, ORDAIN,
DECREE, ENJOIN,
PLAY, STAGE, DO

enactment CANON,
DECREE, EDICT,
ORDINANCE, LAW,
STATUTE, BILL

enamelware LIMOGES

encampment BIVOUAC,
TENT, CAMP, LOCA-
TION, ABODE

enchain ENCIRCLE,
FETTER, PIN, FASTEN,
BIND, SHACKLE,
MANACLE, RESTRAIN,
ENSLAVE, HOLD,
RIVET

enchant DELIGHT,
CHARM, PLEASE, BE-
WITCH, ENSORCEL,
ALLURE, ATTRACT,
CAPTIVATE, FASCINATE,
ENAMOR, TRANSPORT,
ENRAPTURE

enchantment CHARM,
MAGIC, SPELL, IN-
CANTATION, CONJURA-
TION, SORCERY,
NECROMANCY,
WITCHERY

enchantress CIRCE,
SIREN, WITCH,
CHARMER, SORCERESS

encircle FRAME,
HEM, ENVIRON, GIRD,
SPAN, RING, ENFOLD,
ZONE, BELT, SUR-
ROUND, CLASP, EN-
CLOSE, EMBRACE, EN-
COMPASS

enclose FENCE, HEDGE,
ENCLAVE, CORRAL,
CASE, CAGE, MEW,
ENCIRCLE, CIRCUM-
SCRIBE, ENVELOP,
WRAP

enclosed area SEPT,
PEN, CORRAL,
PATIO, FIELD, YARD

enclosure STOCKADE,
YARD, JAIL, PEN, STY,
CORRAL, CAGE, MEW,
COOP, PATIO

encomium TRIBUTE,
PANEGYRIC, EULOGY,
PRAISE, LAUDATION,
EULOGIUM

encompass GIRD,

COVER, EMBRACE, EN-
CIRCLE, INVEST, BESET

encore AGAIN, BIS,
OVER, ANEW, AFRESH,
RECALL, REPETITION,
REAPPEARANCE

anti BOO, CATCALL,
HISS

encounter MEET,
STRUGGLE, FIGHT,
SKIRMISH, BATTLE,
CLASH, FRAY, BRUSH,
ATTACK, COMBAT,
COLLIDE, DISPUTE,
ACTION, CONTEST

encourage FOSTER,
EGG, ABET, RALLY,
BOOST, HEARTEN,
CHEER, URGE, HELP,
INSPIRE, EMBOLDEN,
ANIMATE, STIMULATE,
INCITE, SUPPORT,
FURTHER, AID, COM-
FORT

Encratism, *early
leader of* TATIAN

encroach USURP, IN-
VADE, VIOLATE,
TRESPASS, ENTER,
INFRINGE

encumber LOAD, SAD-
DLE, CLOG, CHECK,
BURDEN, OPPRESS,
IMPEDE, OBSTRUCT,
HAMPER, COMPLICATE,
HINDER

encyclic PANDECT,
TREATISE, LETTER,
CIRCULAR, COM-
PREHENSIVE

encyclopedic learning,
person of
POLYHISTOR

end AIM, CEASE,
CLOSE, OMEGA, TOE,
LIMIT, TAIL, CODA,
TIP, GOAL, FINIS,
FINISH, FINALE, STOP,
HALT, PERIOD,
EXPIRE, DIE, THIRTY,
FATE, LOT, DOOM,
OBJECT, INTENT,
EXTREMITY, EXPIRA-
TION, CONCLUSION,
DENOUEMENT, DE-
STRUCTION, ANNIHILA-
TION, DISSOLUTION,
RESULT, CON-
SEQUENCE, FRAGMENT,
REMNANT, STUB,
PURPOSE, DESIGN,
TERMINATE, CON-

CLUDE, ARMAGEDDON, BOUNDARY
musical FINE, CODA
result PRODUCT
tending to TELIC
endeavor SEEK, AIM, STRIVE, ESSAY, TRY, VIE, EFFORT, ETTLE, ATTEMPT, STRUGGLE
ending CONCLUSION, DESINENT, END, CODA, DEATH
having same CO(N)TERMINOUS
endless ETERNAL, LASTING, UNDYING, INTERMINABLE, UN-LIMITED, INFINITE, EVERLASTING, PERPETUAL, INCESSANT, CONSTANT, IMMORTAL
endorse SIGN, APPROVE, CERTIFY, VOUCH, SUP-PORT, BACK, SUPER-SCRIBE, GUARANTEE, SANCTION, WARRANT, RATIFY
endow BESTOW, CLOTHE, INVEST, ENRICH, FURNISH, GRANT, AWARD, ENDUE
endowment GRANT, GIFT, TALENT, DOWER, BEQUEST, BOON, BOUNTY, PRESENT, LARGESS(E)
endue DIGEST, DOWER, (IN)VEST, SUPPLY, ENDOW, ENRICH, CLOTHE
endure TOLERATE, PERSIST, REMAIN, WEAR, SUFFER, STAND, BEAR, LAST, LIVE, BROOK, DREE, EXIST, ABIDE, UNDERGO, SUSTAIN, SUPPORT, EXPERIENCE, WITH-STAND, CONTINUE
enduring STURDY, LASTING, DURABLE
enemy FOE, RIVAL, ADVERSARY, OP-PONENT, ANTAGONIST
energize BRACE, FORTIFY, STIR, AROUSE, ANIMATE
energy MIGHT, ARM, VIM, PEP, STHENIA, BENT, ZIP, WORK, POWER, VIGOR, FORCE,

POTENCY, STRENGTH, METTLE, IMPETUS
pertaining to ACTINIC
potential ERGAL
unit of ERG, ERGON
enervate DRAIN, EX-HAUST, SAP, DISABLE, TIRE, UNMAN, WEAKEN, ENFEEBLE, DEVITALIZE, DEBILITATE
enfilade BARRAGE, RAKE
enforce COMPEL, URGE, GOAD, LASH, OBLIGE, FORCE, EXECUTE, CONSTRAIN
enfranchise FREE, RELEASE, DELIVER, EMANCIPATE, MANUMIT, LIBERATE
engage BIND, PLIGHT, PROMISE, HIRE, ENTER, PLEDGE, ENLIST, EMPLOY, USE, FIGHT, CONTRACT, ENGROSS, COMMIT, OBLIGATE, AFFIANCE, BETROTH, ATTRACT, ALLURE
engender BEGET, BREED, GENERATE, GET, SIRE, PROPAGATE, PROCREATE, BEAR
engine MOTOR, MOGUL, GIN, MACHINE, DIESEL, TURBINE, INVENTION, LOCOMOTIVE
war ONAGER, CATA-PULT, RAM, GUN, MORTAR, CANNON, MANGONEL, BOAR *See under* "military"
England, English ALBION, ANGLICAN, SILURES *See* "British"
actor OLIVIER, EVANS, DONAT, TERRY, GWENN, MAUDE, GUINNESS
actress GWYN
ancient name ALBION
Antarctic explorer SCOTT
archbishop LAUD, BECKET, LANG
architect ADAM, WREN, SCOTT
author SHAW, ROLLE, LANDOR, HENTY, MOORE, MORE, ARLEN, BACON, DEFOE, ELIOT, READE, WAUGH,

AUSTEN, HUXLEY, BELLOC, BRONTE, STERNE, WELLS, WREN, DICKENS (BOZ)
aviators RAF
bailiff REEVE
basket CAUL
canal laborer NAVVY
castle site ARUNDEL, WINDSOR
cathedral city ELY
circuit court EYRE
city YORK, ELY, LEEDS, LONDON
clergyman INGE, NEALE, WESLEY
coin GEORGE, GUINEA, GROAT, FLORIN, PENCE, ANGEL, CAROLUS, SHILLING, FARTHING
college ETON, BALIOL, HARROW
comedian TOOLE, CHAPLIN, GINGOLD
composer ELGAR, ARNE
conspirator FAWKES
county SHIRE, ESSEX, KENT, YORK, BERKS, DERBY, DEVON, HANTS, WILTS, DORSET, SURREY, SUSSEX
court EYRE, SAKE, SOC, GEMOT(E), LEET
diarist PEPYS
domain MANOR
dramatist PEELE, TOBIN, PINERO, READE, WILDE, SHAW, COWARD
early conqueror HORSA, HENGIST
editor MEE
elm CAMPESTRIS
emblem ROSE
essayist LANG, LAMB (ELIA), STEELE, AD-DISON, RALEIGH
etcher HADEN
explorer RALEIGH, CABOT, HUDSON
festival ALE
financier GRESHAM
forest ARDEN, SHER-WOOD
fortified town BERG
franchise SOC
freeman CHORL, CHURL, THANE, THEGN
free tenant DRENG
gift to bride DOS, DOT, DOWER

headland NAZE
health resort BATH
hills WOLDS, CLEE
historian BEDE,
GIBBON, CARTE, WELLS
hog ESSEX
honor exam. TRIPOS
horse dealer COPER
humorist LEAR
hymnist NEALE,
WESLEY
king CHARLES, GEORGE
See under "British"
kingdom, early DEIRA
landed proprietor
SQUIRE
lapwing TEWIT
law book FLETA
limestone OOLITE
measure PIN, CRAN
coal CORF
military academy
RMA
mine wagon ROLLEY
minister PEEL, PITT,
WALPOLE, DISRAELI
monk BEDE
musician ARNE
navigator DRAKE *See*
"explorer" *above*
noble EARL, LORD,
SIR, DUKE, PRINCE
northern tribe PICT
novelist See "author"
above
order GARTER
painter OPIE, ROM-
NEY, HOGARTH, CON-
STABLE
pamphleteer DEFOE,
SWIFT, PAINE
party TORY, WHIG,
LABO(U)R
patron saint GEORGE
philanthropist ANGELL
philosopher HUME,
BACON
playwright See
"dramatist" *above*
poet GRAY, KEATS,
ELIOT, BLAKE,
CAREW, BYRON,
POPE, SHELLEY,
BARRETT, BROWNING
early CAEDMON
laureate CIBBER
political philosopher
BURKE
pot herb CLARY
pottery, potter SPODE
prelate INGE
printer CAXTON

queen MAB, MARY,
ANNE, ELIZABETH,
VICTORIA
race course EPSOM,
ASCOT
ready money PREST
region WEALD
river See under
"river"
royal house YORK,
TUDOR, WINDSOR,
BLOIS, STUART,
HANOVER
ruler OFFA *See*
"king" *above*
scholar ALCUIN
school ETON, HAR-
ROW
schoolmaster ARAM
scientist DARWIN
serf THRALL
settlement group GA
settlers, early JUTES
sheep LONK
slave ESNE
slice of bread CANCH
socialist FABIAN
spa BATH
spy ANDRE
stone monument
CROMLECH
surgeon HADEN,
PAGET, HUNTER,
LISTER, POTT
tax EXCISE, GELD,
PREST
textile FLAX, HEMP,
JUTE
thicket SPINNEY
town ETON, ELY,
RYDE
treaty TROYES,
CARTA
tribe PICT
village BOURG
weight STONE, TOD,
MAST
West Point RMA
writer See "author"
above
English Channel, *river*
to EXE, ORNE,
RANCE, SEINE, SOMME
Englishman BRITON,
SASSENACH
engrave CHISEL, CUT,
INFIX, CARVE, RIST,
INSCRIBE, IMPRINT,
ETCH, MARK, INCISE
by dots STIPPLE
engraving PRINT,
DESIGN, PICTURE,

CARVING, ETCHING,
XYLOGRAPH
act of CELATURE,
XYLOGRAPHY
coin, ancient CAROLUS
stone INTAGLIO,
CAMEO
tool BURIN
wood XYLOGRAPH
engross COPY, WRITE,
ABSORB, FILL, EN-
GAGE, USE, APPLY,
OCCUPY
engrossed BUSY,
EMPLOYED, RAPT,
ABSORBED, INTENT,
MONOPOLIZED,
OCCUPIED
enhance EXALT, ADORN,
INCREASE, WAX, LIFT,
ELEVATE, RAISE, AUG-
MENT, EXTOL,
EXAGGERATE, AG-
GRAVATE, IMPROVE
enigma REBUS, SECRET,
RIDDLE, MYSTERY,
PUZZLE, CONUNDRUM,
QUESTION
enigmatic MYSTIC,
CRYPTIC, DARK, VAGUE,
OBSCURE, OCCULT,
RECONDITE,
PERPLEXING,
EQUIVOCAL
enisled ALONE, APART,
ISOLATED
enjoin FORBID, DECREE,
DIRECT, ORDER, BID,
WARN, BAR, PRO-
SCRIBE, PROHIBIT,
RESTRAIN, BAN, RE-
QUIRE, COMMAND
enjoy POSSESS, OWN,
RELISH, LIKE, LOVE,
HOLD, FANCY
enjoyment GUSTO,
SATISFACTION,
GRATIFICATION, DE-
LIGHT, FELICITY, HAP-
PINESS, ZEST, RELISH,
PLEASURE
enkerchief DRAPE
enlarge REAM, BORE,
EXPAND, INCREASE,
WIDEN, DILATE,
SWELL, EXALT, AUG-
MENT, EXTEND,
MAGNIFY, AMPLIFY,
AGGRANDIZE,
EXPATIATE, STRETCH
enlarging gradually
EVASE

enlighten TEACH, INFORM, EDIFY, TRAIN, SCHOOL, ILLUME, ADVISE, TELL, ILLUMINATE, INSTRUCT, CIVILIZE, EDUCATE

enlightened person ILLUMINATO

enlisted man GI

enliven ANIMATE, REFRESH, QUICKEN, FIRE, CHEER, ELATE, DIVERT, AMUSE, INSPIRE, WAKE, ROUSE, INVIGORATE, DELIGHT, EXHILARATE

enmesh ENSNARE, KNOT, SNARL, TRAP, ENTANGLE

enmity HATRED, RANCOR, ANIMUS, HATE, AVERSION, MALICE, ANIMOSITY, HOSTILITY, MALEVOLENCE, ANTAGONISM, ANTIPATHY

ennead NINEFOLD

ennui FATIGUE, LANGUOR, VAPORS, BOREDOM, TEDIUM

enormous VAST, LARGE, HUGE, TITANIC, COLOSSAL, ABNORMAL, MONSTROUS, IMMENSE, PRODIGIOUS, GIGANTIC

Enos' *father* SETH
grandmother EVE
uncle ABEL

enough AMPLE, ENOW, BUS, BASTA, PLENTY, ADEQUATE, SUFFICIENT

enrage MADDEN, ANGER, INCENSE, IRE, IRK, ROIL, INFURIATE, INFLAME

enraged IRATE, ANGERED, MAD, MANIC, IRED

enrich ADORN, INCREASE, LARD, ENDOW, IMPROVE

enroll ENLIST, SERVE, RECORD, IMPANEL, ENTER, REGISTER, ENGROSS, COIL, LIST

ens BEING, ENTITY, ESSENCE

ensiform XIPHOID, BONE

ensign OFFICER, FLAG, PENNANT, COLORS, BANNER, JACK, STANDARD, PENNON, BADGE, GONFALON
of Othello IAGO
of sovereignty REGALIA
Papal GONFALON

ensilage SILAGE, FODDER, FEED

ensnare SNIGGLE, BENET, NOOSE, TRICK, SEDUCE, NAB, COP, NET, TRAP, TEMPT, LURE, DECOY, INVEIGLE, CATCH

ensorcel BEWITCH, ENCHANT, CHARM

ensue FOLLOW, SUCCEED, HAPPEN, RESULT, DERIVE, ISSUE, STEM, ARISE

entad, *opposed to* ECTAD

entangle TWIST, SNARL, MAT, RAFFLE, EMBROIL, RAVEL, ENSNARE, ENTRAP, CATCH, INTERTWINE, KNOT, ENMESH, BEWILDER, CONFUSE

entanglement IMBROGLIO, SNARE, TRAP, NET, MESH, WEB, INTRICACY, WAR, COMPLICATION, INVOLVEMENT, QUARREL

entente PACT, ACCORD, UNDERSTANDING, AGREEMENT, TREATY, ALLIANCE

enter ADMIT, RECORD, BORE, PIERCE, TRESPASS, INVADE, BEGIN, ENROLL, JOIN, BOARD, FILE, LIST, START, INSERT, PENETRATE, REGISTER, INSCRIBE, EMBARK

enterprise EXPLOIT, ESSAY, SCHEME, PROJECT, QUEST, FEAT, UNDERTAKING, (AD)-VENTURE, ENDEAVOR, INITIATIVE

entertain DIVERT, REGALE, AMUSE, TREAT, FEED, BEGUILE, RECEIVE, WELCOME, SHELTER, LODGE, HOUSE, BOARD, FETE, HARBOR, PLEASE

entertainment SHOW, FETE, FEAST, FIESTA, PLAY, SPORT, GAME, BANQUET, FESTIVAL, REPAST, RECREATION, PASTIME, FARE
of strangers XENODOCHY

enthusiasm RAPTURE, FURY, FUROR, FIRE, FRENZY, ZEAL, FERVOR, ZEST, SPIRIT, ARDOR, VERVE, MANIA, ELAN, WARMTH, EAGERNESS, EXCITEMENT

enthusiast BUG, FAN, BIGOT, ZEALOT, DEVOTEE, FANATIC, BUFF

enthusiastic AFIRE, ZEALOUS, ARDENT, ACTIVE

enthymeme ARGUMENT, SYLLOGISM

entice SEDUCE, ALLURE, TEMPT, LURE, DECOY, TOLE, COAX, (EN)-SNARE, TRAP, ATTRACT, BAIT, INVEIGLE, CAJOLE, PERSUADE

enticement LURE, BAIT, TICE, ATTRACTION, DECOY, TEMPTATION

entire TOTAL, GROSS, ALL, WHOLE, INTACT, COMPLETE, FULL, PERFECT, UNDIVIDED, PLENARY, THOROUGH

entitle NAME, DUB, CALL, DESIGNATE, CHRISTEN, STYLE, ENABLE, MERIT

entity SOUL, BEING, ENS, EXISTENCE, THING, UNIT, ONE, ESSENCE

entourage TRAIN, FOLLOWING, RETINUE

entrance DEBUT, PORTAL, ADIT, INLET, ACCESS, WAY, DOOR, OS, POSTERN, GATE, INGRESS, MOUTH, ROAD, PASS, APPROACH, AVENUE, ENTRY, PASSAGE, STILE, INITIATION, COMMENCEMENT, INTRODUCTION, ENRAPTURE, DELIGHT

entranced RAPT, CHARMED, EN-

CHANTED, TRANS-
PORTED
entreat ADJURE,
BESEECH, HALSE,
SOLICIT, IMPLORE,
ASK, PLEAD, COAX,
BEG, CRAVE, SUE,
PRAY, SUPPLICATE
entree ADMISSION, AC-
CESS, DISH, INGRESS,
ENTRY, ENTREMET
entrepot WAREHOUSE,
DEPOT, STOREHOUSE
entresol MEZZANINE
entrust RELY, BANK,
COUNT, TRUST, CON-
FIDE, COMMIT
entry MINUTE, ITEM,
POST, CREDIT, DEBIT,
RECORD, NOTE *See*
"entrance"
entwine ENLACE,
WEAVE, TWIST,
WREATHE, ENCIRCLE,
EMBRACE, JOIN
enumerate COUNT,
NUMBER, NAME, TELL,
ADD, SUM, TOTAL,
FIGURE, RECITE,
RECKON, COMPUTE,
RECAPITULATE
enumeration TALE,
CENSUS, LIST,
CATALOG(UE)
enunciate STATE,
DECLARE, UTTER,
TELL, SPEAK, PRO-
CLAIM, EXPRESS,
ENOUNCE, PRO-
NOUNCE, ARTICULATE,
INFORM, VOICE
envelop ENFOLD,
SHROUD, WRAP, FOLD,
HIDE, COVER
envelope BURR, CASE,
SHROUD, WRAPPER,
CAPSULE, VESTURE,
COVERING
environ HEM, OUT-
SKIRT, PURLIEU, SUR-
ROUND, ENCOMPASS,
GIRD, ENCLOSE
environment SUR-
ROUNDINGS, IN-
FLUENCE, ATMOS-
PHERE, MILIEU
combining form ECO
environs TERRAIN,
AREA, VICINITY, SCENE,
LOCALE, SETTING,
STAGE
envoy LEGATE,

NUNCIO, MINISTER,
PLENIPOTENTIARY,
AMBASSADOR
envy RANKLE, COVET,
SPITE, GRUDGE, LONG,
HANKER, YEARN, PINE,
WISH, DESIRE, JEAL-
OUSY, MALICE
enzyme ASE, DIASTASE,
PEPSIN, MALTASE,
PTYALIN, OLEASE,
AMYLASE
leather making TAN-
NASE
opposed to AZYME
eon OLAM, ERA, AGE,
CYCLE
eonic ERAL
ephah, *tenth of* OMER
epic POEM, EPOS, SAGA,
HOMERIC, HEROIC,
NARRATIVE, STORY
poem EPOPEE, ENEID,
AENEID
epicarp HUSK, RIND,
PEEL
Epictetus STOIC
epicure SYBARITE,
FRIAND, GOURMET,
GLUTTON, GOURMAND,
CONNOISSEUR
epicurean APICIAN,
LUXURIOUS, APIKOROS,
HEDONIST
epidemic PEST,
PLAGUE, PANDEMIC,
GENERAL, PREVAILING,
PREVALENT, WIDE-
SPREAD, ATTACK
epidermis BARK,
CUTICLE, SKIN, PEEL
epigram ADAGE, QUIP,
MOT, SAYING, MOTTO,
SAW, POEM
couplet DISTICH
epilepsy FITS, CON-
VULSIONS
type of PETIT
Epimetheus' *wife*
PANDORA
epimyth MORAL
Epirus *native*
EPIROT(E), GREEK
town DODONA
episode EVENT,
INCIDENT, STORY,
ACTION, DIGRESSION,
ATTACK
epistle LETTER, MIS-
SIVE, BILLET, NOTE,
REPORT, COMMUNICA-

TION, LESSON, RE-
SCRIPT
epithet CURSE, (BY)-
NAME, AGNOMEN,
TITLE, APPELLATION,
DESIGNATION
epitome BRIEF, DIGEST,
ABSTRACT, ABRIDG(E)-
MENT, COMPENDIUM,
BREVIARY, SYNOPSIS,
CONDENSATION
epoch EON, AGE, ERA,
TIME, PERIOD
epochal ERAL
epode POEM,
EPISTROPHE, AFTER-
SONG
epoptic MYSTIC
equable EEN, EVEN,
STEADY, UNIFORM,
REGULAR, CALM,
SERENE, TRANQUIL
equal PAR, (A)LIKE,
PEER, SAME, CO-
ORDINATE, COMPEER,
MATCH, MEET, IDENTI-
CAL, EVEN, UNIFORM,
TANTAMOUNT,
EQUIVALENT, QUITS,
TIED
angled figure ISOGON
combining form ISO,
PARI
quantity IDENTIC, ANA
sides ISOSCELES
to three short syllables
TRISEME
equality IDENTITY,
JUSTICE, PAR, UNI-
FORMITY
equanimity POISE,
CONTROL, PHLEGM,
BALANCE, CALM,
COMPOSURE, SERENITY
equatorial TORRID,
TROPICAL
equestrian RIDER,
HORSEMAN, JOCKEY,
CHEVALIER
equilateral parallelo-
gram RHOMB
equilibrium POISE,
BALANCE, CONTROL,
SANITY, COMPOSURE,
SERENITY
want of ASTASIA
equine HORSE
water sprite KELPY,
KELPIE
equip ENDOW, OUTFIT,
DRESS, RIG, GIRD, PRO-
VIDE, ARM, FURNISH,

ACCOUTRE, ACCOUTER, SUPPLY

equipment TACKLE, ARMS, OUTFIT, GEAR, APPARATUS

equipoise BALANCE, POISE, EQUILIBRIUM

equiponderant BALANCED

equitable IMPARTIAL, HONEST, FAIR, JUST, EQUAL, UPRIGHT, UNBIASED, REASONABLE, WISE

Roman law BONITARIAN

equivalence PAR, EQUALITY, PARITY

equivalent EQUAL, (A)LIKE, SAME, IDENTIC(AL), COMMENSURATE, CONGRUENT

equivocal CRYPTIC, AMPHIBOLIC, ENIGMATIC, VAGUE, AMBIGUOUS, PROBLEMATIC, DOUBTFUL, DUBIOUS, OBSCURE, MYSTERIOUS

equivocate LIE, HEDGE, FIB, EVADE, ESCAPE, TERGIVERSATE, FENCE, PALTER, QUIBBLE, SHUFFLE, DODGE, MISLEAD

equivoque *See* "pun"

era AGE, CYCLE, EPOCH, DATE, EON, TIME, PERIOD

eradicate ERASE, UPROOT, EPILATE, ANNUL, LEVEL, KILL, ROOT, ABOLISH, RAZE, REMOVE, RASE, EXTIRPATE, DESTROY, ANNIHILATE, EXTERMINATE, REMOVE, BLOT

eral EPOCHAL

erase DELE, DELETE, CANCEL, BLOT, NEGATE, ABOLISH, EFFACE, OBLITERATE, EXPUNGE, DESTROY, KILL

ere PRIOR, RATHER, BEFORE

Erebus DARKNESS, HADES

father CHAOS

offspring AETHER, DAY

sister NIGHT, NOX

erect REAR, STANDING, UPRIGHT, VERTICAL, BUILD, RAISE, CREATE, CONSTRUCT

Eretrian ELIAN

erewhile FORMERLY, ONCE, AGO, HERETOFORE

ergo HENCE, THEREFORE, BECAUSE

ergon ERG, WORK

Eric RED

erica HEATH

Erin *See* "Ireland"

Eritrea *measure* CUBI

seaport ASSAB

ermine STOAT, WEASEL, FUR

Eros CUPID, AMOR, LOVE

beloved—PSYCHE

erotic ARDENT, CARNAL, AMATIVE, AMOROUS, AMATORY

err SLIP, TRIP, SIN, FALL, WANDER, STRAY, MISTAKE, BLUNDER, DEVIATE, MISJUDGE, LAPSE

erratic VAGRANT, NOMADIC, WHACKY, ODD, QUEER, STRANGE, QUAINT, FICKLE, ECCENTRIC, IRREGULAR, ABERRANT, CAPRICIOUS, CHANGEABLE

error(s) ERRATA, LAPSE, SIN, SLIP, BULL, BONER, MISCUE, ERR, SOLECISM, GAFFE, MISDEED

printing TYPO, ERRATUM

Erse CELT, GAEL(IC)

erudition WISDOM, LORE, SCIENCE, LETTERS, KNOWLEDGE, LEARNING

erythrina *genus* DADAP

Esau's *brother* JACOB

father ISAAC

later name EDOM

escapade VAGARY, PRANK, FROLIC, INDISCRETION, DIDO

escape DECAMP, ELOPE, EVADE, FLEE, LAM, FLY. ELUDE, SHUN, AVOID, BLOW, BOLT, ABSCOND, ESCHEW, LEAK, LEAKAGE, SEEP, OOZE

escargot SNAIL

escarpment SLOPE, FORTIFICATION

eschew ABSTAIN, AVOID, SHUN, EVADE, FORBEAR, FEAR

escolar PALU, FISH

escort ACCOMPANY, PROTECT, CONVOY, STEER, PILOT, LEAD, (AT)TEND, USHER, GUARD, SQUIRE, CONDUCT, SHIELD, CAVALIER, GALLANT, BEAU

escrow BOND, DEED

esculent COMESTIBLE, EDIBLE, EATABLE

escutcheon ARMS, CREST, SHIELD, ARMORIAL

band FESS

voided ORLE

Esdras APOCRYPHA

eskar(s), esker(s) OSAR, OS, RIDGE

Eskimo ALASKAN, ALEUT, INNUIT, YUIT, ITA

Asian YUIT, INNUIT

boat UMIA(C)K, OOMIAC, OOMIAK, KAYAK, KAIAK, BIDAR, BAIDAR

boot KAMIK, MUKLUK

curlew FUTE

dog HUSKY, MALEMUTE

garment PARKA, TEMIAK

house IGLU, IGLOO, TUPEK, TUPIK

knife ULU

memorial post XAT

settlement ETAH

Siberian YUIT

esodic AFFERENT

esophagus GULA, GULLET

esoteric OCCULT, MYSTIC, ARCANE, SECRET, ABSTRUSE, RECONDITE, PRIVATE

doctrine CABALA

knowledge GNOSIS

espalier TRELLIS

esparto grass ALFA

espionage SPYING, OBSERVATION

esplanade LEVEL, WALK, GLACIS, ROAD

espouse ADOPT, TAKE, PLIGHT, BETROTH, MARRY, WED, EMBRACE *See* "abet"

esprit MORALE, SPIRIT, INTELLIGENCE, WIT, CLEVERNESS, VIVACITY

espy SPY, SEE, NOTE, NOTICE, VIEW, BEHOLD, DISCERN, OBSERVE, DESCRY, DISCOVER, FIND

ess CURVE, SIGMA, SIGMOID, WORM

essay THESIS, THEME, ARTICLE, PAPER, COMPOSITION, TREATISE, TRY, CHRIA, STRIVE, EFFORT, WORK, ENDEAVOR
short THEME, THESIS, TRACT

essayist LAMB, ELIA, PAYNE, EMERSON, HOLMES, ADDISON, STEELE

essence ATTAR, GIST, ENS, MARROW, PITH, BEING, ENTITY, REALITY, NATURE, EXTRACT, SENSE, CORE, KERNEL, FIBER, FIBRE, SCENT, ODOR, PERFUME

essential NEEDED, VITAL, INTRINSIC, BASIC, BASAL, CHIEF, MAIN, PRIMARY, NECESSARY, INDISPENSABLE, IMPORTANT, REQUISITE, INHERENT

establish BASE, PROVE, FOUND, FIX, PLANT, SETTLE, SECURE, SET, ROOT, ENACT, ORDAIN, CREATE, BUILD, DECREE, INSTITUTE, ORIGINATE, ERECT, VERIFY

establishment, *domestic* MENAGE, HOUSEHOLD

estate ASSETS, MANOR, STATE, RANK, AL-(L)OD, AL(L)ODIUM, DEGREE, LAND, HOLDINGS, STATUS, POSITION, PROPERTY, EFFECTS, FORTUNE, SITUATION
manager STEWARD, GUARDIAN, COMMIT-

TEE, ADMINISTRATOR, EXECUTOR

esteem REGARD, REVERE, ADMIRE, HONOR, ADORE, PRIDE, VALUE, PRIZE, LOVE, RESPECT, REPUTE, CHERISH, APPRECIATE, VENERATE, WORSHIP

ester SILICATE, STEARIN, ETHER, OLEATE

Est(h)onia, Esthonian, Estonian ESTH
capital TALLIN(N), REVEL
city or town MARVA, TARTU, MUHU (MOON)
island OESEL, SAREMA, MUHU (MOON)
measure SULD, LIIN
weight NAEL, PUUD

estimate RECKON, FIGURE, METE, RANK, AIM, AUDIT, RATE, (AD)JUDICATE, (AD)-JUDGE, MEASURE, GAGE, VALUE, ASSAY, GUESS, BUDGET

estivate SUMMER

estrange ALIENATE, WEAN, PART, DIVIDE SUNDER, SEVER, WITHDRAW, DIVERT, DISUNITE

estray WAIF, DOGIE

estuary PLATA, FIRTH, FRITH, FIORD, INLET, CREEK
Amazon PARA

estuate BOIL

esurient GREEDY, HUNGRY, VORACIOUS

et al ELSEWHERE, OTHERS

etch BITE, CUT, CORRODE, ENGRAVE, DRAW, DELINEATE, FURROW

ete SUMMER

eternal LASTING, ENDLESS, EVER, PERPETUAL, UNCEASING, CONTINUAL

eternity AGE, AEON, EON, TIME, OLAM, INFINITY

etesian PERIODICAL, ANNUAL, SEASONABLE

etheostomoid DARTER, FISH

ether AIR, SKY, SPACE,

ESTER, OZONE, AMYL, HEAVEN
crystalline APIOL(E)

ethereal AERIAL, AIRY, AERY, THIN, RARE, DELICATE, LIGHT, TENUOUS, FRAGILE, FAIRY, EMPYREAL, CELESTIAL, HEAVENLY

ethical VIRTUOUS, MORAL, RIGHT, NOBLE, DECENT, CORRECT

ethics MORALS, PRINCIPLES

Ethiopia, Ethiopian ABYSSINIA(N), KAF(F)A, SEBA, CUSH, GEEZ
ancient capital MEROE
ape or baboon GELADA
battleground ADOWA
cattle SANGA
cereal TEFF
city or town NAPATA, ADOWA, ADUWA, ASMARA, GOBA, GONDAR, ASSAB, AXUM
coin BESA, GIRSH, TALARI, HARF, KHARAF
dialect TIGRE, GEEZ
See "language" *below*
district HARAR, LASTA, AMHARA, DEMBEA, BANA
division SHOA, TIGRE, MEROE
emperor NEGUS, MEMNON, SELASSIE
fly ZIMB
governor RAS
grain TEFF
hamite AFAR
ibex WALIE
king See "emperor" *above*
lake TZANA, TSANA, TANA, ZEWAY, DEMBEL
language SAHO, AMHARIC, AGOW, GEEZ, GALLA
measure TAT, CUBA, KUBA, ARDEB, BERRI
oxen GALLA, SANGA, SANGU
plant (herb) TEFF
primate ABUNA
prince RAS
province HARAGE, SIDAMO, JIMA, ILUBABOR, WALAGA,

WALLO, TEGRE,
BAGEMDER, GOJAM,
SHAWA, ARUSI, GAMO-
GOFA
queen CANDACE
river See under
"river"
territory AMHARA
title ABUNA, RAS,
NEGUS
town See "city" *above*
tree KOSO, CUSSO
tribe AFAR, AGOWS
tribesman SHOA
weight OKET, KASM,
NATR, ALADA, PEK, ROT
wolf KABERU
ethos, *opposed to*
PATHOS
ethyl *derivative*
ALCOHOL, ETHER
hydride ETHANE
hydroxide ALCOHOL
oxide ETHER
symbol ET
etiolate PALE, BLANCH,
WHITEN, BLEACH
etiquette MANNERS,
CUSTOM, MIEN,
DECORUM, PROPRIETY
Etonian holiday VAC
Etruscan *city* VEII
god TINIA
goddess MENFRA, UNI
Juno UNI
king PORSENA (LARS)
land ETRURIA
title LAR(S)
ettle AIM, INTEREST,
SUPPOSE, INTEND, TRY
etui CASE, TROUSSE,
BOX
etymon RADICAL,
RADIX, ROOT
Etzel ATILLA, ATLI
eucalypt YATE, BLOOD-
WOOD
eucalyptus
gum KINO
leaf deposit CERF
secretion LAAP, LERP,
LARP
tree YATE
eucharist *box* PIX, PYX
plate PATEN
vessel AMA, AMULA
wafer HOST
wine KRAMA
euchite VAGRANT,
MENDICANT,
ADELPHIAN

Euclid, *origin* MEGARA
eulogistic LAUDATORY,
ENCOMIASTIC,
PANEGYRICAL, COM-
MENDATORY
eulogize PRAISE,
GLORIFY, EXALT,
MAGNIFY, APPLAUD,
EXTOL, LAUD, BOOST
eulogy ENCOMIUM,
PANEGYRIC, ELOGE,
TRIBUTE, PRAISE
euouae TROPE
euphonium TUBA
euphony MELODY,
METER, HARMONY
euphorbia SPURGE,
PLANT
euphoria EASE, COM-
FORT, WELL-BEING
Euphrates tributary
TIGRIS
Eurasian *range*
URAL(S)
region TATARY
eureka AHA, TRIUMPH
red PUCE
Euripides *hero* ION
heroine MEDEA,
HELENA
play HELENA, MEDEA,
ION, ELECTRA,
ALCESTIS
euripus FLOW, STRAIT,
CHANNEL, CANAL,
FLUX, REFLUX, FRITH
Europe and Asia
EURASIA, SCYTHIA
Europe, European
LAPP, DANE, SLOVENE,
FINN, LETT, CELT,
BALT, SLAV
ancient CELT
ancient country
SWABIA, RUTHENIA,
DACIA
bird See under
"bird"
blackbird MERLE
bunting ORTOLAN
burbot genus LOTA
central region BANAT
coal basin SAAR
country, ancient
DACIA
dormouse LOIR
fish BARBEL, BOCE,
RUDD, LOTA *See*
under "fish"
ground squirrel
SISEL, SUSLIK,
SOUSLIK

health resort BADEN,
EMS, SPA
kite GLED(E)
linden TEIL
plant AZAROLE,
ALYSSUM, ORPINE
polecat FERRET
porgy PARGO
river See under
"river"
shad ALOSE, ALLIS,
ALLICE
shrew ERD
shrub FURZE
tree SORB
Eurydice's *husband*
ORPHEUS
Eurytus' *daughter*
IOLE
eutectic FUSIBLE
evacuate EMPTY,
CLEAR, EJECT, EXPEL,
PURGE, EMIT, VACATE,
ABANDON, VOID, QUIT,
FORSAKE, DESERT,
LEAVE
evade BILK, SHIRK,
SHUNT, FOIL, ESCAPE,
THWART, DODGE,
PARRY, ELOPE, ELUDE,
SHUN, AVOID, BAFFLE,
QUIBBLE, PALTER,
FLEE
evaluate APPRAISE,
ESTIMATE, RATE, AS-
SESS, VALUE, ASSAY,
JUDGE, TAX
evanesce FADE, VANISH,
DISAPPEAR
evangelist APOSTLE,
DISCIPLE, PATRIARCH,
WRITER, REVIVALIST,
MISSIONARY, LUKE,
MARK, JOHN, MAT-
THEW
Evans, Mary Ann
ELIOT
evaporate DISTIL,
EXHALE, VANISH,
VOLATILIZE, VAPORIZE
eve DAMPEN, WET,
EVENING, PM, IVA,
RIB, FEMALE, HERB
even FLAT, TRUE,
FLUSH, SQUARE, SAME,
EQUABLE, FAIR, PLANE,
TIED, LEVEL, THO,
THOUGH, SMOOTH, TIE,
UNIFORM, STEADY,
EQUAL, CALM, JUST,
IMPARTIAL, REGULAR,

PURE, PLAIN, DIRECT, BALANCE(D), EXACT

evening EVE, DUSK, PM, EVENTIDE, TWILIGHT, SUNSET
German ABEND
Hebrew EREB
party SOIREE
pertaining to VESPER, CREPUSCULAR
prayer VESPER
song SERENA
star HESPER, MERCURY, VENUS, HESPERUS, MOON

event EXPLOIT, FEAT, CHANCE, DEED, CASUS, INCIDENT, EFFECT, UPSHOT, OCCURRENCE, HAPPENING, ADVENTURE, RESULT, OUTCOME

eventide *See* "evening"

eventually LASTLY, YET, FINALLY, ULTIMATELY

eventuate RESULT, CLOSE, END, OCCUR, HAPPEN

ever ALWAYS, AYE, EER, EVERMORE, PERPETUALLY, ETERNALLY, FOREVER

Everest, *mountain near* LHOTSE
site of NEPAL

evergreen YEW, FIR, LAUREL, SPRUCE, CAROB, TOYON, PINE, CEDAR, HOLLY *See* "tree"
cedarlike DEODAR
genus OLAX, ABIES, CATHA
shrub TOYON

everlasting ETERNE, ETERNAL, AGELESS, IMMORTAL, UNENDING, CONSTANT, INCESSANT, INTERMINABLE, UNDYING, PERPETUAL, ENDLESS
plant ORPINE

everted TURNED, ECTOPIC

every ALL, EACH, ANY, ENTIRE, COMPLETE

everything ALL, TOTAL, SUM

evict CASHIER, EJECT, OUST, REMOVE, FIRE,

SACK, EXPEL, DISPOSSESS

evidence DATA, PROOF, TRACE, PROBATE, EVINCE, DEPONE, SHOW, REVEAL, ATTEST, SPEAK, TESTIMONY, ATTESTATION, VOUCHER, INDICATION

evident OPEN, PATENT, PLAIN, BROAD, CLEAR, MANIFEST, OBVIOUS, APPARENT, VISIBLE, DISTINCT, CONSPICUOUS, PALPABLE

evil(s) WRONG, VICE, SIN, HARM, HURT, BAD, ILL, BASE, LOW, VILE, NEFARIOUS, MALIGN, CORRUPT, VICIOUS, MALUM, MALA
doer SINNER, CHEAT, MISCREANT, FELON, CRIMINAL, MALEFACTOR, CULPRIT, VILLAIN, CROOK
prefix MAL
spirit BUGAN, GHOST, DEMON, DEVIL
Hebrew myth. ASMODEUS
Iroquois OKI, OTKON
of blame MOMUS
Persian DAEVA

evince EXHIBIT, SHOW, PROVE, ATTEST, DISPLAY, DISCLOSE

evoke ELICIT, EDUCE, CALL, SUMMON, PROVOKE, AROUSE, EXCITE, ENLIVEN

evolute UNROLL, UNFOLD, GROW

evolution GROWTH, DEVELOPMENT, EXPANSION, CHANGE, UNFOLDING
doctrine BIOGENY, COSMISM

evolve DEDUCE, UNFOLD, GROW, DERIVE, DISENGAGE, EMIT, EDUCE, EXHIBIT

ewe KEB, THEAVE, SHEEP
old CRONE

ewer URN, PITCHER, JUG

exacerbate IRK, INCREASE, EMBITTER, TEASE, WORSEN, IR-

RITATE, EXCITE, PROVOKE, ENRAGE, EXASPERATE, INFURIATE, AGGRAVATE

exact CORRECT, RIGHT, NICE, PRECISE, ACCURATE, EXTORT, TAKE, WREST, WRING, FORCE, IMPOSE, REQUIRE, CLAIM, DEMAND, DUE, STRICT, STERN, LITERAL, LEVY, JUST, MINUTE, ASK, TRUE, SEVERE

exaggerate STRETCH, ENLARGE, OVERSTATE

exaggerated OUTRE, EXCEPTIONAL, EXTRAVAGANT, MAGNIFIED

exalt ELEVATE, EXTOL, RAISE, HONOR, ELATE, ENNOBLE, PRAISE, GLORIFY

exalted ELATED, HIGH, NOBLE, LORDLY, PROUD, SUBLIME, MAGNIFICENT

examination TEST, QUIZ, INVESTIGATION, INTERROGATION, AUDIT, INSPECTION, PROBE, ORAL, INQUIRY, SEARCH, EXPLORATION, SURVEY, TRIAL, INQUISITION, RESEARCH

examine PRY, SCAN, SPY, AUDIT, TRY, PORE, TEST, SIFT, PERUSE, EXPLORE, PROBE, APPOSE, INSPECT, OBSERVE, CANVASS, STUDY, INTERROGATE, INQUIRE, QUESTION

example INSTANCE, PARADIGM, PATTERN, STANDARD, MODEL, IDEAL, SPECIMEN, COPY, SAMPLE, CASE, PRECEDENT, WARNING, ILLUSTRATION, PROBLEM

exasperate ANGER, VEX, GALL, IRE, INCENSE, PEEVE, ROIL, ENRAGE, ANNOY, NETTLE, PROVOKE, IRK, IRRITATE, CHAFE, EXACERBATE, INFLAME

excavate DIG, SCOOP, DELVE, SPADE, GRUB, BURROW, SHOVEL

excavation HOLE,
SHAFT, MINE, PIT,
HOLLOW, TRENCH,
CAVITY
for ore STOPE, MINE
exceed TOP, PASS,
SURPASS, EXCEL,
OUTDO, OUTSTRIP,
ECLIPSE, CAP, BEAT,
WIN
exceedingly VERY,
VASTLY, EXTREMELY,
SUPERLATIVELY
excel TOP, STAR,
PRECEL, TRANSCEND,
EXCEED, SURPASS,
WIN, OUTDO, OUTVIE
See "exceed"
excelled WON
excellence VIRTUE,
MERIT, PROBITY,
SUPERIORITY,
EMINENCE, WORTH,
VALUE
excellent BRAVO,
A-ONE, TOPS, WORTHY,
CHOICE, PRIME,
ADMIRABLE, FINE,
SELECT, GOOD,
EXQUISITE
except UNLESS, OB-
JECT, BESIDES, BUT,
BAR, SAVE, EXCLUDE,
OMIT, QUALIFY
exception DEMUR,
DOUBT, OMISSION, OB-
JECTION, COMPLAINT,
EXEMPTION, AFFRONT,
DEVIATION, OFFENSE
excerpt VERSE, EX-
TRACT, CHOICE, SCRAP,
QUOTATION, CITATION,
SELECT(ION)
excess SURPLUS, OVER-
PLUS, LUXUS, GLUT,
SATE, SUPERFLUITY,
REDUNDANCE,
PLETHORA, INTEMPER-
ANCE, DISSIPATION,
REMAINDER
excessive EXTREME,
UNDUE, OVER, EXTRA,
SURPLUS, SPARE,
SUPERABUNDANT,
EXUBERANT, INORDI-
NATE, IMMODERATE,
UNREASONABLE,
EXORBITANT
exchange BANDY,
BOURSE, TRADE, SELL,
BARTER, AUCTION,
BANK, STORE,

MARKET, PIT, SUB-
STITUTE, SHUFFLE,
SWAP
premium AGIO
exchequer TREASURY,
FISC, BANK, PURSE,
FINANCES
excise TOLL, TAX,
IMPOST, LEVY, RATE,
CESS, TITHE, DUTY,
REVENUE, CUT, RE-
MOVE, ERASE,
EXPUNGE, EXTIRPATE
excite BESTIR, AGITATE,
ELATE, ROUSE, WHET,
ROIL, RALLY, WAKEN,
FIRE, STIR, MOVE,
STIMULATE, KINDLE,
INFLAME, ANIMATE
excited (A)ROUSED,
AGOG, BREEZY, AVID,
FRENZIED, ASTIR,
ANIMATED, MOVED
excitement FUROR(E),
FURY, FERMENT,
THRILL, FRENZY,
STIR, AGITATION,
STIMULUS, BUSTLE,
TENSION, SENSATION,
PASSION
exclaim CRY, SHOUT,
CLAMOR, VOCIFERATE,
CALL
exclamation AH(A),
AHEM, ALAS, HOY,
HEM, GRR, BAH,
EGAD, FIE, HIP, OHO,
OW, PAH, POO, PHEW,
TUT, HAH, HEY, EVOE,
YAH, WOW, BAW, HUH,
TCH, UGH, WEE, YOW,
EH, HA, OH, MY
See "cry"
of disgust RATS, UGH
of exhilaration EVOE
of pain OW, OUCH
of sorrow ALAS,
ALACKADAY
of surprise GEE, AHA,
OH, WOW, GOSH, OHO
toast SKOL, PROSIT
exclude EJECT, OMIT,
(DIS)BAR, DEPORT,
LIMIT, BLOCK,
BANISH, EXILE, BLACK-
BALL, OSTRACIZE,
PRECLUDE, PROHIBIT
exclusive SOLE, ONLY,
SELECT, LIMITED,
ALONE, POSH, NAR-
ROW, SNOBBISH, CLAN-

NISH, SPECIAL, PRI-
VATE
excogitate CONTRIVE,
DEVISE, INTENT,
THINK
excoriate GALL, FLAY,
CHAFE, CURSE, SKIN,
PEEL, REVILE, SCAR,
SCORE, GOUGE,
ABRADE
excrescence LUMP,
KNOB, (OUT)GROWTH,
FUNGUS, WART
excursion JAUNT,
TOUR, TRIP, SALLY,
CIRCUIT, TREK,
CRUISE, VOYAGE,
RIDE, DRIVE, JOUR-
NEY, EXPEDITION,
WALK, HIKE
excuse ACQUIT,
ALIBI, CONDONE,
PRETEXT, PARDON,
REMIT, FORGIVE,
ABSOLVE, FREE,
JUSTIFY, EXPLAIN,
EXEMPT, OVERLOOK,
APOLOGY, PLEA,
REASON, OUT
for non-appearance
PLEA, ESSOIN
for sickness AEGER
execrable BAD, POOR,
WRETCHED, AWFUL,
CURSED, BASE, LOW,
VILE, ODIOUS,
ABOMINABLE, OF-
FENSIVE, REPULSIVE,
REVOLTING
execrate REVILE,
DETEST, ABOMINATE,
HATE, CURSE, DAMN,
IMPRECATE, ABHOR
execute (EN)FORCE,
GOVERN, RULE,
FINISH, EFFECT,
PERFORM, FULFILL,
CLOSE, MAKE, DO,
SIGN, HANG, SPEED,
ACT, SEAL, ACCOM-
PLISH, CONSUMMATE,
ACHIEVE
executive BRASS, BOSS,
JUDGE, MAGISTRATE,
PRESIDENT, DIRECTOR
exegete ADVISER,
CRITIC, INTERPRETER
exemplar MODEL,
PATTERN, IDEAL,
STANDARD, COPY,
SPECIMEN, EXAMPLE,
ARCHETYPE

exempt IMMUNE, FREE, APART, REMOVED, RELIEVE, EXCUSE, EXONERATE

exemption RELEASE, ESSOIN, IMMUNITY, PRIVILEGE, FREEDOM, DISPENSATION

exequies WAKE, RITES, CEREMONIES, OBSEQUIES

exercise PLY, WIELD, ACTION, NISUS, PRAXIS, URE, USE, DRILL, PRACTICE, DO, EFFECT, DISCIPLINE, LESSON, TASK, STUDY, EXERT, SCHOOL

exertion EFFORT, STRAIN, TUG, PULL, BOUT, SPURT, TROUBLE, PAINS, ENDEAVOR, TOIL, WORK, GRIND, EXERCISE, STRUGGLE

exfoliate SCALE, DESQUAMATE

exhalation STEAM, AURA, FUME, BREATH, VAPOR, SMOKE, ODOR, EFFLUVIUM, EMANATION

exhale BREATHE, EXPEL, EMIT, EXPIRE, EMANATE

exhaust SMOKE, JADE, EMIT, FAG, TIRE, SAP, DRAIN, DEPLETE, EMPTY, USE, WEAKEN, SPEND, SQUANDER, WASTE, CONSUME

exhausted TIRED, PETERED, DONE, SPENT, BEAT, WEAK, WEARY, EMPTY

exhibit STAGE, SHOW, AIR, EVENT, EVINCE, REVEAL, STATE, EXPOSE, PARADE, FLAUNT, FAIR, DISPLAY, MANIFEST, WEAR

exhibiting OSTENSIVE, SHOWING

exhilarate BUOY, ELATE, TITILLATE, CHEER, ANIMATE, BOOST, ENLIVEN, INSPIRE, STIMULATE, GLADDEN, FIRE

exhilaration JOY,

GAIETY, GLEE, HILARITY

exhort PREACH, URGE, INCITE, PERSUADE, WARN, ENCOURAGE, ADVISE, CAUTION

exhume DISINTER, DELVE, DIG, UNEARTH, GRUB, SPADE, DISENTOMB

exigency PINCH, STRAIT, CRISIS, ESSENTIAL, NEED, PRESSURE, URGENCY, NECESSITY, WANT, REQUIREMENT, EMERGENCY, DIFFICULTY

exiguous SMALL, MEAGER, SCANT, SPARE, SPARSE, TINY, SLENDER, FINE, ATTENUATED, DIMINUTIVE

exile BANISH, DEPORT, EXPATRIATE, EXPEL, EJECT, OSTRACIZE

exist LIVE, AM, ARE, BE, SUBSIST, BREATHE, REMAIN, ENDURE, ABIDE

existence ENS, LIFE, ESSE, BEING, STATE, STATUS, ENTITY, ANIMATION, DURATION

beginning NASCENT, BIRTH

having no NULL, VOID, DEAD, DEFUNCT

existent BEING, LIVING, EXTANT

exit DEATH, EGRESS, OUTLET, DOOR, VENT, ELOPE, ESCAPE, GOING, DEPARTURE, WITHDRAWAL, END, DEMISE

exocoetoid fish IHI

exodus HEGIRA, FLIGHT, GOING, EMIGRATION

exonerate ACQUIT, CLEAR, RELEASE, ABSOLVE, EXCUSE, REMIT, PARDON, EXCULPATE, VINDICATE, EXEMPT, FORGIVE

exorbitant DEAR, EXTREME, GREEDY, STEEP, EXTRAVAGANT,

INORDINATE, EXCESSIVE, UNREASONABLE

exorcism EXPULSION, SPELL, CHARM, INCANTATION

exordium PROEM, OVERTURE, PRELUDE, INTRODUCTION, OPENING, PREAMBLE, PREFACE, PROLOGUE, FOREWORD

exoteric PUBLIC, OPEN, EXTERNAL, OUTSIDER

exotic ALIEN, FOREIGN, PEREGRINE, OUTRE, EXTRANEOUS, STRANGE

expand SPLAY, DILATE, FLAN, GROW, WIDEN, INFLATE, STRETCH, SWELL, ADD, SPREAD, OPEN, UNFOLD, DISTEND, EXTEND, ENLARGE, INCREASE

expanse AREA, SEA, OCEAN, REACH, SPREAD, STRETCH, RANGE, SCOPE, SWEEP, ORBIT, FIELD, SPHERE, TRACT

expatiate RANT, DESCANT, ENLARGE, DILATE, SPEAK, TELL, AMPLIFY

expatriate EXILE, BANISH, DEPORT, EXPEL, PROSCRIBE, OSTRACIZE

expect (A)WAIT, DEEM, HOPE, LOOK, WISH, ANTICIPATE, RELY

expecting AGOG, ATIP, ASTIR, AWAKE

expedient STOPGAP, FIT, RESORT, SHIFT, DEVICE, MEANS, PROPER, SUITABLE, POLITIC, DESIRABLE, CONTRIVANCE, USEFUL

expedite HURRY, HASTEN, EASE, HIE, SPEED, RUSH, ACCELERATE, QUICKEN

expedition CRUSADE, DRIVE, SAFARI, CRUISE, ENTERPRISE, UNDERTAKING, CAMPAIGN, QUEST, CARAVAN, TOUR, TRIP,

JAUNT, SPEED, HASTE, HURRY, CELERITY

expel EXILE, EJECT, EXTRUDE, EVICT, BANISH, OUST, FIRE, SACK, CAST, DISLODGE, EGEST, DISOWN, RELEGATE, EXPATRIATE, DISCHARGE, DISBAR

expensive DEAR, COSTLY, RARE, LAVISH, EXTRAVAGANT, HIGH

experience UNDERGO, SEE, MEET, SUFFER, BRAVE, ENJOY, FEEL, REALIZE, KNOW, DO, KNOWLEDGE, SKILL, FACILITY, SUFFERING

experienced OLD, VETERAN, SKILLED, EXPERT, ACCOMPLISHED, VERSED, ABLE, PRO, ACE, FINISHED, SKILLFUL, WISE

experiment PROOF, TEST, TRIAL, EXAMINATION, ASSAY, ORDEAL, ENDEAVOR

expert ACE, ADROIT, ADEPT, MASTER, CRACK, APT, WHIZ, SHARK, DEFT, ARTIST, DEXTEROUS, SKILLFUL, SKILLED, CLEVER, SPECIALIST, CONNOISSEUR

expiate ATONE, PURGE, SHRIVE, APPEASE, PROPITIATE

expiation TRIAL, CROSS, ATONEMENT, SATISFACTION, REPARATION

expire EMIT, EXHALE, DIE, ELAPSE, PERISH, END, TERMINATE, CONCLUDE

explain SOLVE, SPEED, CLEAR, RESOLVE, INTERPRET, ELUCIDATE, ILLUSTRATE, EXPOUND, DEMONSTRATE, ANSWER

explanation ALIBI, EXCUSE, EXPOSITION, SOLUTION, DESCRIPTION, KEY, ANSWER

marginal notes SCHOLIA, ANNOTATIONS

of a passage EXEGESIS

expletive OATH, CURSE, THERE, VOILA, DANG, EGAD, DEAR

explicit EXPRESS, PLAIN, POSITIVE, CLEAR, OPEN, DEFINITE, LUCID, PRECISE, EXACT, FIXED, CATEGORICAL

explode FULMINATE, FIRE, POP, DETONATE, BURST, DISCHARGE

exploding *meteor* BOLIDE

star NOVA

exploit ACTION, FEAT, ACT, WORK, GEST(E), FARE, DEED, HEROISM, QUEST, ACHIEVEMENT, CLIP

explore SEEK, SEARCH, RANGE, SCOUT, TEST, EXAMINE, SCRUTINIZE, FATHOM, PLUMB, PROBE, INVESTIGATE

explorer ERIC, RAE, BYRD, GAMA, OSA, ROSS, DRAKE, HUDSON, COLUMBUS

explosion (OUT)-BURST, POP, BLAST, DETONATION, FULMINATION, CLAP, SOUND

explosive BOMB, AMATOL, CERIA, AMMO, MINE, TONITE, DYNAMITE, TNT, CORDITE, DANGEROUS

isometric mineral THORITE

picric acid LYDDITE

exponent ITE, INDEX, NOTE, SYMBOL, SYMPTOM, EXAMPLE, ILLUSTRATION, INDICATION

expose UNMASK, SHOW, PARADE, VOICE, REVEAL, RISK, AIR, BARE, UNCOVER, DISCLOSE, UNEARTH, ENDANGER, JEOPARDIZE, DENOUNCE, DENUDE

expound STATE, EXPRESS, EXPLAIN, DISSECT, ANALYZE, ELUCIDATE

express VOICE, UTTER, VENT, AIR, PLAIN, EXACT, PRECISE, SPECIFIC, DEFINITE, LUCID, CLEAR, DISTINCT, SAY, DO, SHIP, WRITE, SPEAK, DECLARE, ASSERT, STATE, ENUNCIATE, INDICATE, SIGNIFY, EXPLICIT, POSITIVE, DETERMINATE, ACCURATE, TRAIN

expression IDIOM, LOCUTION, ASPECT, PHRASE, UTTERANCE, DECLARATION, STATEMENT, WORD, SAYING, TERM

expunge EFFACE, ERASE, DELE(TE), CANCEL, OBLITERATE, DESTROY

expurgate CLEANSE, CENSOR, PURGE, BATHE, PURIFY

exquisite EXACT, DELICATE, RARE, CHOICE, DAINTY, REFINED, EXCELLENT, PRECIOUS, PERFECT

exscind EXCISE, EXTIRPATE, CUT

exsiccate DRY, PARCH, DESICCATE

extend SPREAD, EKE, JUT, PROTRACT, EXPAND, RENEW, BEETLE, SPAN, STRETCH, PROLONG, WIDEN, ENLARGE, AUGMENT, DISTEND

extended LONG

extension ARM, ELL, RANGE

extent SIZE, AREA, SWEEP, RANGE, SCOPE, REACH, DEGREE

exterior, external OUTER, CORTICAL, EXTRINSIC, FOREIGN, ALIEN, ECTAL, FALET, OUTWARD

covering HIDE, HUSK, PELT, PEEL, RIND, SKIN, CLOTHING

extinct bird AUK, DODO, MOA, ROC, MAMO

extinguish DOUSE, ABATE, ABOLISH,

ERASE, REPRESS,
SMOTHER, KILL,
BLOT, QUENCH,
QUELL, STIFLE,
CHOKE, OBSCURE,
ECLIPSE, NULLIFY,
DESTROY
extirpate ERASE, DELE,
ROOT, ERADICATE,
RAZE, RASE, KILL,
REMOVE, UPROOT,
ANNIHILATE,
DESTROY
extol PRAISE, LAUD,
EXALT, MAGNIFY,
GLORIFY, CELEBRATE,
EULOGIZE, APPLAUD,
COMMEND
extort WRING,
COMPEL, EXTRACT,
SQUEEZE, ELICIT,
DRAW, EXACT,
FORCE, WREST,
WRENCH
extra ULTRA, SPARE,
BONUS, MORE, OVER,
(SUR)PLUS, ADDI-
TIONAL, ACCESSORY,
SUPERNUMERARY,
ADDED
extract ESSENCE,
EXCERPT, QUOTATION,
JUICE, FLAVORING,
CITE, ELICIT, ESTREAT,
EVULSE, PULL,
EXTORT, REMOVE,
DERIVE, DISTIL,
WITHDRAW
from a book
PERICOPE
information PUMP,
BRAINWASH
extraction LINEAGE,
ORIGIN, BIRTH,
PARENTAGE, LINE,
DESCENT, GENEALOGY,
ELICITATION
extraneous ALIEN,
EXOTIC, OUTER,
FOREIGN, EXTRINSIC,
SUPERFLUOUS
extraordinary BIG,
HUGE, GREAT, RARE,
NOTABLE, REMARKA-
BLE, UNUSUAL,
SINGULAR, PRODI-
GIOUS, MONSTROUS,
ABNORMAL, EXCEP-
TIONAL
extravagant PROFUSE,
LAVISH, WILD, UN-
REAL, FLIGHTY,

ABSURD, E LA,
EXCESSIVE, FOOLISH,
PRODIGAL, WASTEFUL
extreme RADICAL,
LAST, FINAL, DIRE, IN-
ORDINATE, ULTRA,
END, EXORBITANT,
UTMOST, GREATEST,
HIGHEST, ULTIMATE,
DRASTIC, OUTRAGEOUS,
CONCLUSIVE, INTENSE
extremely VERY
extremity BOUND,
LIMIT, TERM, FOOT,
HAND, LEG, ARM,
LIMB, POLE, TIP,
END, EDGE, BORDER,
VERGE, TERMINATION
extricate RELEASE,
FREE, LIBERATE,
RELIEVE, RESCUE,
DELIVER, DISENGAGE,
LOOSEN
exudate, exudation
TAR, PITCH, SUDOR,
SWEAT, RESIN, GUM,
EMANATION, AURA,
EXCRETION, SAP
exude LEAK, EMIT,
FLOW, OOZE, SWEAT,
DISCHARGE, REEK,
SECRETE
exult CROW, ELATE,
LEAP, VAUNT, GLOAT,
PRIDE, REJOICE,
JUBILATE, BOAST
exultant OVANT,
ELATED, JOYOUS,
AGOG, GLAD, JUBI-
LANT, TRIUMPHANT,
EUPHORIC, HAPPY
eye OPTIC, ORB,
PEEPER, SIGHT,
OBSERVE, SEE, OGLE,
UTA, GLIM, WATCH,
STARE, VIEW, IN-
SPECT
black SHINER,
MOUSE
black pigment of
MELANIN
cavity ORBIT
colored portion IRIS
cosmetic KOHL,
KUHL
dropper PIPETTE
film NEBULA
inflammation IRITIS,
CONJUNCTIVITIS,
RETINITIS, UVEITIS
membrane(s) RET-
INA, CONJUNCTIVA

opening in PUPIL
part UVEA, CORNEA,
IRIS, PUPIL, SCLERA
pertaining to OPTIC
protector VISOR,
BLINKER, PATCH,
BLINDER, GOGGLES
shield PATCH
symbolic UTA
worm LOA
eyeball GLOBE, ORB
covering CORNEA
eyebrow SUPERCILIUM,
BREE
dye MASCARA
eyelash(es) CILIUM,
CILIA
dye MASCARA
loss of MADAROSIS
eyelid *darkener* KOHL
drop PTOSIS
pertaining to
PALPEBRAL
eyesore BLEMISH,
DEFECT
eyewash EXCUSE, AP-
PLESAUCE, FLATTERY
eyot AIT, ISLE(T)
eyre JOURNEY,
CIRCUIT, COURT
eyrie NEST
Ezekiel's *father* BUZI
(JEREMIAH)
Ezrahite HEMAN,
ETHAN, DARDA

F

F EF, EFF
fabaceous plant ERS
Fabian policy INERTIA,
DELAY, PROCRASTINA-
TION
fable MYTH, LEGEND,
LIE, APOLOG(UE),
FICTION, PARABLE,
STORY, TALE, AL-
LEGORY, FORGERY
teller of PARABOLIST,
FABULIST, FABLER
writer of AESOP,
ANDERSEN, GRIMM
fabled *animal* UNI-
CORN, CENTAUR,
BASILISK
being OGRE, DWARF,
GIANT, TROLL,
MERMAID
bird ROC
fish, upholding world
MAH
serpent BASILISK

fabric STRUCTURE, TISSUE, CLOTH, REP, FELT, LACE, WEB, RAS, DUCK, LAWN, TAPE, TAPA, TEXTURE, DACRON, CREPE, MOIRE, RAYON, NYLON, CANVAS, JEAN, MATERIAL *See* "cloth"
coarse CRASH, MAT, CAD(D)IS, BURLAP
corded REP, REPP
cotton JEAN, LAWN, DENIM, MANTA *See under* "cotton"
crinkled CREPE, CRAPE
curtain LENO, SCRIM
dealer MERCER, DRAPER
design with wax coating BATIK
figured MOREEN
heavy BROCADE, DENIM, CANVAS
hempen BURLAP
knitted TRICOT
lace ALENCON, MECHLIN, VAL
linen SCRIM
metallic LAME
plaid TARTAN
printed PERCALE, CHALLIS, CALICO
satin PEKIN
shiny SATEEN
short-napped RAS
silk See "silk"
and gold ACCA, SAMITE
Spanish TIRAZ
striped DORIA, SUSI, GALATEA
towel HUCK, TERRY
velvetlike PANNE, PLUSH, VELURE
watered silk MOIRE
woolen SERGE, MERINO, TAMISE, BEIGE, ALPACA, PRUNELLA, RATINE, RATTEEN, TARTAN, TWEED
worsted ETAMINE
fabricate BUILD, CONCOCT, MAKE, SHAPE, COIN, MINT, SCHEME, FALSIFY, FORM, FORGE, CREATE, FRAME, CONSTRUCT, MANUFAC-

TURE, FASHION, FEIGN
fabrication ROMANCE, LIE, WEB, DECEIT, GUILE, FABLE, ART, CRAFT, OPUS, FIGMENT, INVENTION, FICTION
fabricator INVENTOR, MAKER, LIAR, FORGER, FABULIST, PARABOLIST
fabulist AESOP, GRIMM, ANDERSEN, FABLER, PARABOLIST
fabulous FICTITIOUS, LEGENDARY, MYTHICAL, UNREAL, FABRICATED, APOCRYPHAL
facade FRONT, FACE, REAR
face PUSS, MAP, MUG, PAN, FIZ(Z), PHIZ, PHYSIOGNOMY, MOUE, SNOOT, VISAGE, SIDE, ANGLE, PHASE, FACET, FACADE, ASPECT, OBVERSE, COUNTENANCE, GRIMACE, MEET, ANSWER, BOLDNESS, AUDACITY, IMPUDENCE, FRONT, DEFY, DARE, DIAL
covering VEIL, MASK, YASHMAK
downward PRONE, PRONATE, PROSTRATE
guard BEAVER, MASK
with masonry REVET
facet BEZEL, CULET, FACE, SIDE, ASPECT, PHASE, ANGLE, SURFACE, FILLET
star PANE
facetious COMICAL, DROLL, WITTY, JOCULAR, MERRY, JOCOSE, HUMOROUS, WAGGISH
facile EASY, PLIABLE, READY, SMOOTH, LIGHT, DEFT, ADROIT, GLIB, PLIANT, FLEXIBLE, FLUENT
facilitate AID, FURTHER, QUICKEN, HELP, EASE, ASSIST
facility ART, MEANS, EASE, TACT, POISE, EASINESS, DEXTERITY,

KNACK, ABILITY, SKILL, ESTABLISHMENT
facsimile COPY, MATCH, REPLICA, TWIN, DUPLICATE, REPRODUCTION
fact DATUM, DEED, FAIT, FEAT, EVENT, TRUTH, REALITY, ACTUALITY, CIRCUMSTANCE, CERTAINTY
faction BLOC, CABAL, JUNTO, SIDE, CLAN, SECT, PARTY, RING, CIRCLE, CLIQUE, COMBINE, TUMULT, DISCORD
factious TURBULENT, DEMAGOGIC, WARRING, SEDITIOUS, REFRACTORY, REBELLIOUS, RECALCITRANT
factitious ARTIFICIAL, SHAM, UNNATURAL
factor PART, AGENT, BROKER, GENE, REEVE, SUBSTITUTE, CONSTITUENT, ELEMENT, CIRCUMSTANCE, INFLUENCE
factory MILL, SHOP, PLANT, WORKSHOP
factotum SERVANT, AGENT, HANDYMAN
factual TRUE, REAL, EXACT, LITERAL, GENUINE, ACTUAL, CORRECT
faculty STAFF, TALENT, COGNITION, POWER, SENSE, KNACK, FUNCTION, GIFT, BENT, TURN, FLAIR, CAPABILITY, CAPACITY, ENDOWMENT, SKILL, DEXTERITY, INGENUITY, APTITUDE, CREW, FORCE
fad CRAZE, RAGE, HOBBY, VOGUE, ISM, STYLE, MODE, CRY, WHIM, FANCY
fade DIM, DIE, PETER, WILT, WANT, PALE, DULL, WITHER, DROOP, VANISH, DISAPPEAR, EVANESCE, DECLINE, BLANCH, LANGUISH, PASS
faded DIM, DULL, FAINT, PASSE

fadge AGREE, FIT, SUIT, HARMONIZE

"Faerie Queene" *character* UNA, ATE, TALUS, DUESSA, GUYON

Fafnir's *brother* REGIN *slayer* SIGURD

fag HACK, SLAVE, MENIAL, TIRE, DRUDGE, EXHAUST, JADE, WORRY, WEARY, DROOP, SINK, FLAG, TOIL

fail LOSE, DESERT, DISAPPOINT, NEGLECT, FLOP, ERR, FLUNK, COLLAPSE, MISS, FIZZLE

failing BLOT, FOIBLE, FAULT, FRAILTY, DEFECT, LAPSE, ERROR

failure FLOP, DUD, BANKRUPTCY, OMISSION, NEGLECT, BOTCH, COLLAPSE, BREAKDOWN, NEGLIGENCE, INSOLVENCY, BUST

faineant OTIOSE, LAZY, INERT, IDLE, INACTIVE

faint FAIL, FADE, DIM, SWELT, SWOON, SYNCOPE, LANGUISH, TIMID, LISTLESS, FEEBLE, INDISTINCT, SOFT, WEAK

fair EVEN, SOSO, JUST, IMPARTIAL, UNBIASED, EQUABLE, EQUAL, LIKELY, BLOND(E), KERMIS, LIGHT, SUNNY, FINE, COMELY, SHOW, EXHIBIT, BAZAAR *pertaining to* NUNDINAL

fairness BEAUTY, CANDOR, HONESTY

fairy SPRITE, FAY, PERI, PIXIE, PUCK, NIX(IE), SHEE, KELPIE *See* "elf" *air* SYLPH *ghost* SPRITE *king* OBERON *queen* MAB, TITANIA, UNA *Serb* VILA

shoemaker LEPRECHAUN

spirit of death BANSHEE

tricky PUCK

faith TRUST, BELIEF, CREED, TROTH, CREDIT, DOGMA, TENET, CULT, CREDENCE, SINCERITY, CONFIDENCE, RELIANCE, DOCTRINE, FIDELITY *pertaining to* PISTIC

faithful LOYAL, SURE, TRUSTY, FAST, LEAL, LIEGE, STAUNCH, TRUE, DEVOTED, LOVING, TRIED, FIRM, OBEDIENT, RELIABLE, STEADFAST, SINCERE *friend* ACHATES *Old* GEYSER

fake CHEAT, TRICK, SHAM, FRAUD, DECEIT, COUNTERFEIT, IMITATION, SPURIOUS *combining form* PSEUD(O)

fakir YOGI, MONK, MENDICANT, DERVISH, MOSLEM, ASCETIC

falcon BIRD, SORAGE, KESTREL, SAKER, SACER, PEREGRINE, BESRA, MERLIN, LANNER, HAWK, TERCEL, LUGGAR, JUGGER *Arctic* GYR *Asia* LAGGAR, LUGGAR, LANNER(ET) *bait* LURE *blind* SEEL *East Indian* BESRA *English* HOBBY *European* SAKER(ET), KESTREL, MERLIN *genus* FALCO, RAPTORES *headed god* MENT(U) *India* LAGGAR, LUGGAR, SHAHIN, SHAHEEN *male* TERCEL *nestling* EYAS *prairie* LANNER *rapacious* RAPTOR *ribbon or strap for* JESS *unfledged bird* EYAS

fall(s) SPILL, DROP, PLOP, RUIN, SIN, FAIL, PLUNGE, SINK, (RE)LAPSE, SETTLE, TOPPLE, TUMBLE, DESCENT, CASCADE, CATARACT, NIAGARA, DEGRADATION, SAG, AUTUMN *preceder* PRIDE

fallacy IDOLUM, SOPHISM, ERROR, MISTAKE, ILLUSION, ABERRATION, DELUSION, MISCONCEPTION

fallal GEEGAW, FINERY, RUFF, AFFECTATION

falling CADENT, DECREASING *sickness* EPILEPSY

false UNRELIABLE, WRONG, DISLOYAL, CROOKED, SHAM, COUNTERFEIT, DECEITFUL, FEIGNED, UNTRUE, TRUTHLESS, DISHONEST, PERFIDIOUS, TREACHEROUS, FORGED, SPURIOUS, BOGUS, ERRONEOUS *combining form* PSEUD(O) *form(s) of thinking* IDOLA, IDOLUM *wing* ALULA

falsehood LIE, CANARD, TALE, FRAUD, PERJURY, FLAM, FIB, STORY, FABLE, UNTRUTH, TREACHERY, FABRICATION, MENDACITY

falsify FORGE, BELIE, GARBLE, DISTORT, MISREPRESENT, FAKE, MISSTATE, VIOLATE, DECEIVE

Falstaff's *follower* NYM *lieutenant and crony* PISTOL

falter TOTTER, TREMBLE, QUAIL, WAVER, RECOIL, FLINCH, HESITATE, STAMMER, QUAVER, STUTTER, DODDER, PAUSE

fame KUDOS, HONOR, GLORY, REPUTE, CRY, NOTE, PRICE, RENOWN, ECLAT, EMINENCE, LUSTER famed NOTED, EMINENT, NOTORIOUS, CELEBRATED, RENOWNED, ILLUSTRIOUS, NOTABLE, GREAT, HEROIC

familiar VERSANT, CLOSE, THICK, EASY, COSY, SNUG, FREE, ORDINARY, USUAL, CONVERSANT, INTIMATE, CUSTOMARY, HABITUAL, COMMON, FREQUENT
saying SAW, TAG, ADAGE, MOT, MAXIM, PROVERB

family LINE, GENS, ILK, STIRPS, GROUP, CLAN, TRIBE, SEPT, RACE, HOUSEHOLD, MENAGE, BROOD, LINEAGE, STOCK, BREED, DYNASTY
famous Italian ESTE

famous *See* "famed"

fan ROOTER, DEVOTEE, VOTARY, ADDICT, FIEND, ENTHUSIAST, BUFF, COOL, FOMENT, WINNOW, FLABELLUM, CIRCULATOR
oriental swinging OGI, PUNKA(H)
palm genus INODES
stick of BRIN, BLADE

fanatic BIGOT, LUNATIC, PHRENETIC, ZEALOT, MANIAC, RABID, VISIONARY, FRENZIED, WILD

fanatical RABID, MANIC, MAD, WILD

fanciful POETIC, BIZARRE, ABSURD, UNREAL, IMAGINATIVE, WHIMSICAL, CAPRICIOUS, CHIMERICAL, FANTASTIC

fancy DREAM, FAD, IDEA, WHIM, MEGRIM, LIKE, VISION, LOVE, ENJOY, NOTION, RELISH, CONCEPT, IDEAL, FONDNESS, CAPRICE, VAGARY, FANTASY, WHIMSEY, REVERIE, EXCELLENT, FINE

fandango DANCE, BALL, TUNE, MANAKIN

fane TEMPLE, BASILICA, SHRINE, SANCTUARY, CHURCH

fanfare SHOW, TANTARA, DISPLAY, FLOURISH

fanfaron BULLY, HECTOR, BOASTER, BRAGGART, SWAGGERER

fang CLAW, TALON, TINE, TUSK, TOOTH, NAIL

fangle CUT, FASHION, STYLE, VOGUE, GEWGAW, CONTRIVANCE

fanion BANNER, FLAG

fanning device PUNKA(H)

fanon ORALE, VANE, MANIPLE, CAPE

fantastic BIZARRE, EXTREME, ABSURD, STRANGE, ODD, QUEER, CHIMERICAL, QUAINT, OUTRE
style BAROQUE, ROCOCO

fantasy FANCY, IDEA, VAGARY, VISION, DREAM, WHIM, FREAK, HALLUCINATION, DESIRE, IMAGINATION, DAYDREAM, PHANTASM

fantoccini PUPPETS, SHOWS

fantod FUSS, PET, SULK, FIDGET

far DISTANT, AFAR, REMOTE, ADVANCED, PROGRESSED
combining form TELE

farce COMEDY, SHAM, BURLESQUE, CARICATURE, TRAVESTY, PARODY, MOCKERY, STUFFING, FORCEMEAT

farceur JOKER, WAG, CLOWN, COMEDIAN

farcical ATELLAN, RIBALD, COMIC, DROLL, FUNNY, RISIBLE, LUDICROUS, RIDICULOUS, ABSURD

fare FOOD, DIET, RATE, GO, PAY, JOURNEY, TRAVEL, PROSPER, CHARGE, VICTUALS, PROVISIONS, TABLE, BOARD, ENTERTAINMENT

farewell ADIOS, AVE, CONGE, VALE, ADIEU, LEAVE, DEPARTURE, VALEDICTION

farinaceous MEALY, STARCHY
drink PTISAN
food SAGO, SALEP, CEREAL

farm RANCH, COTLAND, CROFT, MAINS, GRANGE, PLOW, WORK, TILL, CULTIVATE
building BARN, SILO
fee MANOR
grazing RANCH
implement HEADER, RAKE, PLOW, TILLER, SEEDER, TRACTOR, DISK, DISC, HARROW
tenant COTTER, CROPPER

farmer PLANTER, SOWER, GRANGER, RYOT, HUSBANDMAN, AGRICULTURIST, TILLER, COTTER, CROPPER, TENANT
S. Africa BOER

farmhouse ONSTEAD, MANOR, VILLA, HACIENDA

farming HUSBANDRY

farmyard BARTON

faro, form of MONTE, STUSS

Faroe island BORDO, OSTERO, SANDO, STROMO, VAAGO
duck EIDER, PUFFIN
fish CHAR(R)
judge FOUD
whirlwind OE

farrow PIG, LITTER

fascia BAND, FILLET, SASH

fascicle CLUSTER, BUNDLE, GROUP, GLOMERULE

fascinate CHARM, BEWITCH, ENAMOR, ENTRANCE, ALLURE, ENCHANT, CAPTIVATE

fashion DEVISE, DESIGN, PLAN, FORM, FORGE, STYLE, MOLD, CREATE, MAKE, FIT, SUIT, ADJUST, MODEL, BUILD, PATTERN, SHAPE, CRY, FAD, TREND, USAGE, RAGE,

CRAZE, MODE, VOGUE, TIMBER, TON, FIGURE
fashionable MODISH, CHIC, NEW, SMART, NATTY, NIFTY, SPRUCE, POSH, DAPPER
fast WILD, APACE, SWIFT, FLEET, QUICK, HASTY, RECKLESS, RAPID, SECURE, TIE, LOCK, DIET
day EMBER
period LENT
fasten MOOR, ANCHOR, JOIN, LINK, BIND, TIE, LOCK, SEAL, TACK, NAIL, PIN, (AF)FIX, CHAIN, ROPE, TRAP, RIVET, HANG, SECURE, ATTACH, CATCH, BOLT, LACE, STRAP, TETHER, CONNECT, BELAY, CLING, CEMENT, GLUE
combining form DESMO
fastener PIN, PEG, CLAMP, HALTER, SNIB, HASP, NAIL, SNAP, CLASP, CLEVIS, COTTER, STAPLE, CLEAT, BOLT, CATCH
fastidious NICE, CRITICAL, DAINTY, FUSSY, EXACT, CLEAN, SQUEAMISH, PARTICULAR, DELICATE, PRECISE, PRISSY
fastigate CONICAL, POINTED
fastness CELERITY, CITADEL, FORT, FIXITY, CASTLE, STRONGHOLD
fat LARD, OIL(Y), ESTER, LIPA, SUET, GREASE, WAX, OBESE, STOUT, FLESHY, ADIPOSE, PLUMP, RICH, PORTLY, PUDGY, PURSY, CORPULENT, PYKNIC, LUCRATIVE
butter CAPRIN, OLEO
combining form STEAT(O), LIP(O), PIO
constituent STEARIN, CHOLESTEROL
goose AXUNGE
of animal TALLOW, LANOLIN, SUET, ADEPS, LARD
part of GLOBULE, OLEIN(E), ELAIN(E)
swine LARD

vegetable OLEO, OIL
wool TALLOW, LANOLIN
fat-yielding tree SHEA
fatal DIRE, LETHAL, MORTAL, DEADLY, BANEFUL, PERNICIOUS, TOXIC, POISONOUS
Fata Morgana MIRAGE
fate CHANCE, DOOM, DESTINY, KISMET, NONA, ISSUE, LOT, UPSHOT, END, RESULT, DIE, FORTUNE, OUTCOME, RUIN, DISASTER, FATALITY, STARS
Buddhist KARMA
cuts thread of life ATROPOS (MORTA)
measures threads of life LACHESIS
oriental KISMET
fated DOOMED, DESTINED, APPOINTED, PREORDAINED
Fates ATROPOS, CLOTHO, MOIRA, DECUMA, MORTA, NONA, PARCA, LACHESIS
Three MOIRA(I), PARCAE (Roman)
father PATRIARCH, PRIEST, ABBA, AMA, PADRE, FOUNDER, PARENT, DAD, PERE, SIRE, PAPA, PA(W), POP, PATER, ANCESTOR, PROGENITOR, CREATOR, BEGET, CREATE, AUTHOR
of English learning BEDE
of mankind IAPETUS, ADAM
of the gods AMEN, AMON
relating to AGNATE, PATERNAL
fatherly PATERNAL, PARENTAL
Fathers of the Oratory *founder* NERI
fathom DELVE, PROBE, TEST, TRY, PLUMMET, PLUMB, SOUND, UNDERSTAND, DIVINE, MEASURE
fatigue TIRE, BORE, FAG, JADE, TUCKER, DRAIN, DEPLETE, SAP, WEAKEN, LASSITUDE,

WEARINESS, EXHAUSTION
Fatima, *descendant of* SAYID, SEID
sister ANNE
step-brother ALI
fatten BATTEN, PINGUEFY, ENRICH, EXPAND
fatty ADIPOSE, OILY, UNCTUOUS, GREASY, OLEAGINOUS
acid ADIPIC, VALERIC, LANOCERIC
secretion SEBUM, OIL
tumor LIPOMA
fatuous IDIOTIC, INANE, VACANT, SILLY, ASININE, SIMPLE, FOOLISH, STUPID, WITLESS
faucet COCK, TAP, SPIGOT, VALVE, OUTLET, HORSE, PEG, ROBINET
faujasite ZEOLITE
fault CRIME, FAILING, BLAME, GUILT, CULPA, FOIBLE, LAPSE, FLAW, SIN, DEFECT, NEGLIGENCE, ERROR, SLIP, VICE, WRONG, BLEMISH, IMPERFECTION, INFIRMITY, WEAKNESS, PECCADILLO, FRAILTY
find CARP, CENSURE, CAVIL
in mining HADE
faultfinder MOMUS, CAVILER, CARPER, CENSURER, REPINER, COMPLAINER
faultless INNOCENT, CORRECT, PERFECT, IMPECCABLE, GUILTLESS, IMMACULATE
faulty BAD, IMPERFECT, WRONG, ERRONEOUS, AMISS, DEFECTIVE, BLAMEWORTHY
faun SATYR, DEITY
of Praxiteles MARBLE
fauna ANIMALS
Faunus' *grandfather* SATURN
son ACIS
"Faust" *author* GOETHE, GOUNOD
faux pas GAFFE, ERROR, MISTAKE, MISSTEP, SLIP, LAPSE,

BULL, BONER, BLUNDER

favor BOON, GRACE, TOKEN, BADGE, LARGESS, GIFT, PLEDGE, KINDNESS, BENEFIT, LETTER, RESEMBLE, FOR, PRO, BIAS, REGARD, OBLIGE, HELP, AID, ASSIST, PATRONIZE, ENCOURAGE, FACILITATE, EASE, SUPPORT, INDULGE, ACCOMMODATE

favorite IDOL, HERO, DEAR, DARLING, BELOVED, PET, MINION

favoritism NEPOTISM, PARTIALITY, BIAS, PREDILECTION

fawn BUCK, DOE, DEER, COWER, GROVEL, CRINGE, TOADY, BOW, COURT, WOO, CROUCH, FLATTER

fay ELF, SPRITE *See* "fairy"

faze DAUNT, DISTURB, RATTLE, ABASH, DENT, DISCONCERT, WORRY

fe IRON

feal FAITHFUL, OBEDIENT, LOYAL

fealty HOMAGE, DUTY, RESPECT, FIDELITY, CONSTANCY, LOYALTY, ALLEGIANCE

fear PANIC, AWE, PHOBIA, UG, DREAD, ANXIETY, WORRY, DOUBT, FRIGHT, ALARM, TERROR, MISDOUBT, FUNK, APPREHENSION

of being buried alive TAPHEPHOBIA

of darkness NYCTOPHOBIA

of drafts AEROPHOBIA

of fire PYROPHOBIA

of number 13 TRIAKAIDEKAPHOBIA

of open spaces AGORAPHOBIA

of pain ALGOPHOBIA

of poisons TOXIPHOBIA

fearful AWED, CRAVEN, DIRE, GRISLY, GRIM, AFRAID, TIMID, ANXIOUS, AP-

PREHENSIVE, SCARED, TIMOROUS, TERRIBLE, DREADFUL, NERVOUS, TREPID

fearless BOLD, BRAVE, DARING, GALLANT, IMPAVID, DAUNTLESS, COURAGEOUS, INTREPID, VALIANT

feast REGALE, JUNKET, PICNIC, FETE, REVEL, GRATIFY, REPAST, SPREAD, FIESTA, DINNER, BANQUET, TREAT, ENTERTAIN

funeral WAKE, ARVAL

of Lanterns BON

of Lots PURIM

of Weeks PENTECOST

feat STUNT, DEED, EXPLOIT, GEST(E), ACT, VICTORY, QUEST, DEFT, ADROIT, SPRY, TRICK

feather(s) PENNA, PINNA, PLUME, QUILL, DOWN, TUFT

barb HERL, PINNULA

base of bird's wing ALULA

bed TYE

down PLUMULE

filament DOWL

grass STIPA

having FLEDGE, FLEDGY

quill AIGRET(TE), COVERT, REMEX

scarf BOA

repair IMP

shaft SCAPE

slot SPLINE

yellow HULU

feathered PENNATE(D), FLEDGED, PLUMED, PLUMOSE

feathering ENDYSIS

featherless CALLOW

featly FITLY, NEATLY, CLEVERLY, NIMBLY, NEAT, GRACEFUL, HEROIC

feature STORY, FILM, ASPECT, TRAIT, FAVOR, FORM, SHAPE, MIEN, LINEAMENT, ITEM, MARK, CHARACTER-(ISTIC)

principal MOTIF, PLOT

feaze, feeze UNRAVEL, UNTWIST

feckless WEAK, INEFFECTIVE, SPIRITLESS

feculent ROILY, TURBID, MUDDY, FILTHY, FECAL, FOUL

federation LEAGUE, UNION, PARTY, BAND, FUSION, BODY, ALLIANCE, COALITION, CONFEDERACY

fee CHARGE, PRICE, COST, EMOLUMENT, PAY, FIEF, HONORARIUM, BRIBE, TIP, RETAINER, WAGE, TAX, DUES, COMPENSATION, GRATUITY, REMUNERATION, TOLL, REWARD, RECOMPENSE

feeble DOTTY, INFIRM, PUNY, FRAIL, POOR, DIM, WEAK, SICK, ANEMIC, LANGUID, FAINT, INDISTINCT

feed SUBSIST, NURSE, FOSTER, EAT, DINE, GRAZE, NURTURE, SUPPLY, NOURISH, SUSTAIN, SUPPORT, STRENGTHEN, FODDER

animal HAY, MASH, GRAIN, GRASS, FODDER, OATS, CHOPS

charge for cattle AGIST

feeding, forced GAVAGE

feel PALP, AIL, SENSE, SUFFER, GROPE, SAVOR, TONE, TOUCH, HANDLE, QUALITY

feeler ANTENNA, TENTACLE, PALPUS, INQUIRY

feeling PITY, ARDOR, LOVE, EMOTION, PASSION, SENSATION, SENTIMENT, ATTITUDE, OPINION, RESPONSIVENESS, ATMOSPHERE, PERCEPTION

capable of SENTIENT

loss of ANESTHESIA, ANALGESIA

show EMOTE

feet DOGS, PAWS

having PEDATE

number of FOOTAGE

pertaining to PEDARY, PODAL, PEDAL

six FATHOM

two metric DIPODY

verse of two DIPODY

without APOD, APODAL

feign SHAM, ACT,
GARBLE, PRETEND,
SIMULATE, INVENT,
FABRICATE, FORGE
sickness MALINGER
feint PRETENSE, BLIND,
FETCH, WILE, TRICK,
RUSE, ARTIFICE,
EXPEDIENT, STRATA-
GEM
in fencing APPEL
feist DOG
feldspar ALBITE,
ODINITE, LABRADORITE,
ANORTHITE
yield KAOLIN
felicitate BLESS,
MACARIZE, CON-
GRATULATE
felicitous APT, PAT,
NEAT, HAPPY, AP-
PROPRIATE, OP-
PORTUNE
felicity BLISS, HAP-
PINESS, JOY, ECSTASY,
GRACE, SUCCESS
felid CAT, LION, TIGER,
LEOPARD, PUMA,
COUGAR, OUNCE
feline CAT, CATTY,
SLY, TREACHEROUS,
STEALTHY *See*
"felid"
felis *leo* LION
pardus LEOPARD
fell BRUTAL, CRUEL,
FIERCE, GRIM, IN-
HUMAN, RELENTLESS,
SAVAGE, CUT, HEW,
PELT, HIDE, SKIN,
RIND, PEEL, DROPPED
fellow EQUAL, MATE,
LAD, MAN, BOY,
BLOKE, EGG, BOZO,
YOUNKER, BLADE,
CHAP, DICK, GALLANT,
DON, COMPANION,
COMRADE, PEER
brutish YAHOO
worthless BUM, CAD,
SPALPEEN, SCOUNDREL
fellowship SODALITY,
UNION, COMPANY, AL-
LIANCE, BROTHER-
HOOD, INTIMACY,
PARTNERSHIP, FRIEND-
LINESS, CORPORATION
felly CRAFTILY,
FIERCELY, RIM
felon WHITLOW,
CRIMINAL, OUTCAST,
CULPRIT, MALE-

FACTOR, CONVICT,
OUTLAW
felony CRIME
felt, like PANNOSE
feltwort MULLEIN,
PLANT, HERB
female DAME, GORGON,
SISTER, WOMAN, GIRL,
LADY, FEM(M)E *See*
"woman"
animal DAM *See*
animal involved
combining form
GYNE, GYN(O)
figurine ORANT
fish RAUN
fox VIXEN
red deer HIND
ruff REEVE, REE
warrior AMAZON
feminine name *See un-
der* "name"
suffix ETTE
femme fatale SIREN,
LORELEI
femur THIGH(BONE)
fen MORASS, BOG,
SUMP, SWAMP,
MARSH, MOOR,
QUAGMIRE
water SUD(S)
fence PALISADE,
SCRIME, HEDGE, WALL,
BARRIER, RAIL, EN-
CLOSURE, STOCKADE,
TILT, FAGIN, SHUFFLE,
EVADE, EQUIVOCATE,
PARR
crossing STILE
fish WEIR, NET
interwoven RADDLE
movable GLANCE,
HURDLE
picket PALE, PALING
steps over STILE
sunken AHA, HAHA
fencing *breastplate*
PLASTRON
cry SASA, HAI, HAY
dummy PEL
foot tap APPEL
hit PUNTO
maneuver APPEL
parrying position
SECONDE
position of hands
PRONATION, SUPINA-
TION
posture CARTE,
SEPTIME, SECONDE,
GUARD, OCTAVE,
TIERCE, SIXTE,

QUINTE, QUARTE,
PRIME
redoubling of attack
REPRISE
stroke BUTT, APPEL
sword FOIL, EPEE,
RAPIER
part of FOIBLE,
FORTE
term TOUCHE,
QUARTE, RIPOSTE,
PALING
thrust LUNGE,
RIPOST(E), REPRISE,
PUNTO, REMISE
fend AVERT, PARRY,
WARD, SHIFT
fenestra FORAMEN,
WINDOW, OPENING,
APERTURE, FONTANEL
fennel ANIS, AZORIAN,
PLANT
genus NIGELLA
feral DEADLY, WILD,
FERINE, FIERCE, UN-
TAMED, FEROCIOUS,
SAVAGE, RAPACIOUS
fer-de-lance SNAKE
Ferdinand II BOMBA
fere EQUAL, MATE,
PEER, PAL, ABLE,
STRONG
feretory CHAPEL,
SHRINE
feria, ferie HOLIDAY
ferment SEETHE,
YEAST, LEAVEN, TUR-
MOIL, DISORDER,
BARM, FRET, BREW,
CHANGE, BOIL, EXCITE,
AGITATE, AGITATION,
TUMULT, FEVER
active principal
ENZYME
agent to induce MUST
revive STUM
fermentative ZYMOTIC
fermented milk dessert
LACTO
fern NARDOO, BRAKE,
BRACKEN, TARA, WEKI,
OSMUND, PLANT
climbing NITO
cluster SORUS
edible TARA, ROI
genus TODEA, POLY-
PODY, PTERIS,
OSMUNDA
leaf FROND
like plant ACROGEN
male OSMUND
patches SORI

Polynesian TARA
root stock ROI
royal OSMUND
ferocious CRUEL,
 FELL, FERAL, TRUCU-
 LENT, FIERCE, SAVAGE,
 GRIM, UNTAMED,
 WILD, RAVENOUS,
 BARBAROUS, BRUTAL,
 VIOLENT, RUTHLESS,
 VANDALIC
ferret, *female* GILL
 male HOB
ferric oxide powder
 ROUGE
ferrotype TINTYPE
ferry BAC, PONT,
 TRAJECT, WHERRY,
 CARRIER, TRANSPORT,
 BOAT
fertile PROLIFIC, RICH,
 FECUND, FRUITFUL,
 PRODUCTIVE,
 LUXURIANT
fertilizer COMPOST,
 GUANO, MARL, SUPER-
 PHOSPHATE, MANURE
ferule FENNEL, ROD,
 RULER, PUNISHMENT
fervent AVID, ARDENT,
 DEVOUT, PIOUS,
 WARM, TENDER,
 SINCERE, HOT, GLOW-
 ING, FIERY, EAGER,
 VEHEMENT, PAS-
 SIONATE
fervid FIERY, HOT,
 EXCITED, ARDENT,
 AVID, AGOG, INTENSE
fervor PASSION, ARDOR,
 ZEAL, LOVE, HEAT,
 WARMTH, INTENSITY,
 ANIMATION
fester ABSCESS,
 RANKLE, ROT, COR-
 RUPT, ULCER(ATE),
 PUTREFY, SUPPURATE,
 LESION
festival FEIS, BEE, ALE,
 FEAST, FETE, PICNIC,
 FAIR, FIESTA, KERMIS,
 GALA, CARNIVAL,
 JUBILEE, HOLIDAY,
 REVELRY, BANQUET,
 CELEBRATION
ancient Greek DELIA
Creek Indian BUSK
of Apollo DELIA
festive season YULE
festivity JOY, REVELRY,
 GAIETY, CONVIVIALITY,

JOLLITY, MERRY-
 MAKING, CELEBRATION
festoon GARLAND,
 SWAG, LEI, WREATH,
 BUCRANIUM
fetch CARRY, RETRIEVE,
 BRING, TAKE, GET,
 BEAR, WRAITH, ELICIT,
 DERIVE, ACHIEVE,
 MAKE, ARRIVE, ATTAIN,
 DEDUCE, INTEREST, AT-
 TRACT, STRIKE, SWEEP,
 TRICK, ARTIFICE, TACK,
 DOUBLE
fete, *rustic* ALE
feted WINED, DINED,
 HONORED, ENTER-
 TAINED
fetich *See* "fetish"
fetid RANK, NOISOME,
 OLID, FUSTY, FOUL,
 NASTY, RANCID,
 PUTRID, STINKING,
 OFFENSIVE, MEPHITIC,
 MALODOROUS
fetish CHARM, JUJU,
 MASCOT, AVATAR, OBI,
 MOJO, ANITO,
 AMULET, PERIAPT,
 TALISMAN, OBEAH
fetter SHACKLE, CHAIN,
 HOBBLE, BOND, GYVE,
 CLOG, BLOCK, BAR,
 DAM, CURB, HAMPER,
 CHECK, BIND, TIE,
 TRAMMEL, RESTRAIN,
 BASIL
feud QUARREL, FIEF,
 VENDETTA, FIGHT,
 STRIFE, SPAT, BROIL,
 CONTENTION, (AF)-
 FRAY, CONTEST, DIS-
 SENSION
Old English law
 ESTATE, LAND
feudal *benefice*
 FEU(D)
domain FIEF
land, right of FEUD,
 FEOD, FIEF
lord LIEGE
opposed to AL(L)-
 ODIAL
service AVERA
 pertaining to BANAL
tenant VASSAL,
 SOCAGER, LEUD,
 SOCMAN
 payment by TAC,
 TAK
tenure SOCAGE
tribute HERIOT

fever FRENZY, ARDOR,
 HEAT, CAUMA,
 WARMTH, TERTIAN,
 PYREXIA, FLUSH, FER-
 MENT, FIRE, DESIRE,
 EXCITEMENT
affected with PYRETIC
chills and AGUE
intermittent QUARTAN,
 MALARIA
kind of OCTAN,
 MALARIA, MARSH, HAY,
 MILK, TRENCH,
 MALTA, TICK, ROSE,
 YELLOW, SPOTTED,
 UNDULANT, TEXAS
spot(s) PETECHIA(E)
tropical DENGUE, YEL-
 LOW, MALARIA
without APYRETIC,
 AFEBRILE
feverish HECTIC,
 FEBRILE, EXCITED,
 JUMPY, RESTIVE,
 FRANTIC, IMPASSIONED
few SCANT, SCARCE,
 RARE, LESS
combining form
 OLIG(O), PAUCI
fey DYING, DEAD,
 ELFIN, VISIONARY,
 OTHERWORLDLY
fez CAP, TURBAN,
 TARBOOSH
fiat SANCTION, EDICT,
 ACT, ORDER, LAW,
 DECREE, WRIT,
 ORDINANCE, COM-
 MAND, DECISION
fiber THREAD, STRAND,
 SHRED, CORDAGE,
 JUTE, HEMP, RAFFIA,
 STAPLE, DA, COIR,
 FERU, AMBARY, IMBE,
 RHEA, ABACA, SISAL,
 FILAMENT, CHINGMA,
 ERUC, SINEW,
 STRENGTH
bark OLONA, TERAP
century plant PITA
cordage See
 "cordage"
E. India plant RAMIE
hat DATIL
istle PITA, PITO
kind FILASSE, SISAL,
 JUTE
knot NEP
palm ERUC, AGAVE,
 RAFFIA, COQUITA,
 COQUITO

pineapple ISTLE, PITA, PITO
plant PITA, RAMIE, IXTLE, ISTLE, RAMEE, FLAX, SIDA, SISAL,
E. India SANA, RAMIE, DA, AMBARY
Tampico ISTLE
wood BAST
wool PILE, KEMP, STAPLE, NEP
fibril HAIR, FILAMENT
fibula BROOCH, CLASP, BONE, BUCKLE, PIN
fickle VOLATILE, ERRATIC, UNSTABLE, FITFUL, FLIGHTY, WAVERING, INCONSTANT, FAITHLESS, UNSTEADY, VARIABLE, CAPRICIOUS, VACILLATING, MUTABLE
fico SNAP, FIG, TRIFLE
fictile MOLDED, PLASTIC
fiction TALE, MYTH, STORY, FABLE, YARN, NOVEL, INVENTION, FANCY, FANTASY, ROMANCE, IMAGINATION, FABRICATION
fictitious FALSE, INVENTED, COUNTERFEIT, FEIGNED, ASSUMED, UNREAL, MYTHICAL, SPURIOUS, ARTIFICIAL
fictive IMAGINARY
fiddle VIOLIN, SCRAPE, TRIFLE, DAWDLE, IDLE, CHEAT, SWINDLE, POTTER
medieval GIGUE
fiddler crab UCA
fidelity HOLD, TROTH, FEALTY, PIETY, FAITHFULNESS, LOYALTY, DEVOTION, CONSTANCY, ALLEGIANCE, EXACTNESS, ACCURACY, LEALTY
symbol of TOPAZ
fidget TOSS, FANTOD, FUSS, TWITCH, FRET, CHAFE, WORRY
fidgety UNEASY, HECTIC, RESTIVE, IMPATIENT, NERVOUS
field AREA, ACRE, GLEBE, LEA, GRID, ARENA, SPHERE, DOMAIN, LIMITS,

BOUNDS, TRADE, BUSINESS, CLEARING, MEADOW, EXPANSE, RANGE, SCOPE, LOT
Biblical AGER, ANER
extensive SAVANNA(H), PLAIN
goddess FAUNA
inclosed AGER, CROFT, COURT
pertaining to CAMPESTRAL, AGRARIAN
stubble ROWEN
fiend IMP, DEVIL, SATAN, DEMON, ADDICT, MONSTER, SADIST
fiendish CRUEL, AVERNAL, SINISTER, MALIGN, HELLISH, DIABOLICAL, DEMONIAC, INFERNAL, MALICIOUS, ATROCIOUS
fierce VIOLENT, SAVAGE, CRUEL, FELL, WILD, RAGING, FEROCIOUS, FURIOUS, BARBAROUS, UNCURBED
fiery FERVENT, ARDENT, HOT, ANGRY, IGNEOUS, INTENSE, SPIRITED, FERVID, GLOWING, FLAMING
fiesta HOLIDAY, FETE, FEAST, FAIR *See* "festival"
fife FLUTE
fig(s) FICO
ball of SEROON
basket CABA(S), SEROON
genus FICUS
Italian FICO
kind of dried CARICA
like CARICOUS
marigold SAMH
Smyrna ELEME, ELEMI
fight BATTLE, MELEE, BARNEY, WAR, CONTEST, COPE, CONFLICT, ROW, STRIFE, SET TO, SCRAP, DUEL, BOUT, CLEM, (AF)FRAY, BRAWL, COMBAT, SCUFFLE, BOX, SPAR, SKIRMISH, STRUGGLE, WRESTLE, QUARREL, RIOT, TILT, ENCOUNTER, BROIL
figure SHAPE, OUTLINE, CONFORMATION,

IMAGE, SILHOUETTE, MARK, SYMBOL, DIGIT, NUMBER, NUMERAL, FORM, DOLL, TYPE, SOLID, BODY, STATUE, DEVICE, MOTIF, LIKENESS, EFFIGY, DESIGN, PATTERN, DIAGRAM, EMBLEM, COMPUTE, CAST, ADD, SUM, TOTAL, FOOT, COUNT, CALCULATE
archeology CARYATID, TELAMON
earth GEOID
equal-angled ISAGON, ISOGON
five-angled PENTAGON
four-angled TETRAGON, RHOMBUS, SQUARE, RECTANGLE
oval ELLIPSE
round CIRCLE, SPHERE, GLOBE
ten-sided DECAGON
three-angled TRIANGLE
figured FACONNE, ADORNED, COMPUTED
figure of speech TROPE, SIMILE, METAPHOR, PUN
figurine TANAGRA, STATUETTE
movie OSCAR
Fiji *island* VITI, VITA, LAU
capital SUVA
group LAU
nephew VASU
filament THREAD, FIBER, FIBRIL, STRAND, VEIN, HAIR, LINE, DOWL, HARL, TENDRIL
cotton THREAD
feather DOWL(E)
flax HARL(E)
filbert HAZEL, NUT
filch SNATCH, SWIPE, GRAB, TAKE, LOOT, LIFT, PINCH, COP, PILFER, STEAL, PURLOIN, CRIB, ROB
file RASP, ROW, ENTER, CARLET, STORE, CABINET, LINE, ROLL, LIST, RECORD, PIGEONHOLE, SMOOTH, POLISH, SHARPEN, GRIND, QUANNET
comb-maker's CARLET
flat QUANNET

half-round GRAIL(LE)
rough RASP
filet LACE, NET
filibeg KILT, SKIRT
filigree LACE, DESIGN,
OPENWORK, DECORA-
TIVE, FANCIFUL, UN-
SUBSTANTIAL
Filipino *See "Philip-
pine"*
fill PLUG, CHOKE,
PACK, CRAM, PAD,
STUFF, EXECUTE,
SUPPLY, LOAD,
SATISFY, SATE, SUF-
FUSE, PERMEATE,
PERVADE, SATIATE,
BLOCK, CALK, GORGE,
GLUT, OCCUPY
fillet ORLE, ORLO,
STRIP, BAND, RIBBON,
SNOOD, REGLET,
STRIPE
bottom of frieze
REGULA, TAEINA
for hair SNOOD, BAND
jeweled DIADEM,
TIARA
narrow LISTEL,
REGLET
fillip SNAP, EXCITE,
STIMULUS, TONIC
filly FOAL, MARE,
COLT, HORSE, GIRL
film HAZE, BLUR,
SCUM, COATING, PIC-
TURE, NEGATIVE,
X-RAY, PELLICLE,
SKIN, MEMBRANE,
NEBULA, CLOUD,
PATINA, LAYER
coated with PATINATE
green PATINA
old PATINA
thin PELLICLE, BRAT
filter PERCOLATE,
COLATURE, OOZE,
SEEP, CLEAN,
COLANDER,
STRAIN(ER), REFINE
filth SQUALOR, MUCK,
DIRT, NASTINESS, COR-
RUPTION, OBSCENITY
fimbriate HEM,
FRINGE, HAIRY
fin-footed animal
PINNIPED
fin, *spinous* ACANTHA,
DORSAL
under VENTRAL
final DERNIER, DECI-
SIVE, END, TELIC,

EXAM, LAST, LATEST,
ULTIMATE, TERMINAL,
CONCLUSIVE, DEFI-
NITE, DEFINITIVE,
COMPLETE(D)
finale CODA, END, COM-
PLETION, FINIS, CON-
CLUSION
finances PURSE, AC-
COUNTS, FUNDS,
REVENUES, RESOURCES,
INCOME
finch SPINK, SERIN,
SISKIN, REDPOLL,
CANARY, BUNTING,
BIRD
Africa FINK, MORO
America CHEWINK,
JUNCO, TOWHEE,
LINNET, BURION
canarylike SERIN
copper CHAFFINCH
Europe SERIN, TARIN
genus FRINGILLIDAE
like GROSBEAK,
TANAGER, CHEWINK
yellow SERIN, TARIN,
CANARY
find LEARN, LOCATE,
ESPY, DETECT, DESCRY,
DECIDE, CHANCE, DIS-
COVER, ATTAIN,
PROCURE, CATCH, PRO-
VIDE, SUPPLY
fault BEEF, CARP,
COMPLAIN, GRUMBLE,
CAVIL
law DETERMINE,
ASCERTAIN, DECLARE,
DECIDE, HOLD
fine TINY, SMALL,
PURE, NICE, PENALTY,
LEGER, SCOT, AMERCE,
SCONCE, GOOD,
DELICATE, FORFEIT,
EXACT, SLENDER, THIN,
DAINTY, KEEN, TAX,
SHARP, TENUOUS,
EXQUISITE, ELEGANT,
PUNISH(MENT)
for killing WERGILD,
CRO
for misdemeanor
MULCT
India ABWAB
law CRO
record of ESTREAT
finery FRIPPERY, TOGS,
GEWGAWS, TRIM-
MINGS, TRAPPINGS,
DECORATION, JEWELRY

Fingal's *cave island*
STAFFA
kingdom MORVEN
finger POINTER, FEEL,
DACTYL, INDEX, DIGIT,
TOUCH, MEDDLE,
HANDLE, PILFER,
PURLOIN
cap COT, THIMBLE
combining form
DIGITI
fore INDEX
guard COT, THIMBLE,
STALL
inflammation of
FELON, WHITLOW
little PINKY, MINIMUS
middle MEDIUS
nail half moon
LUNULE, LUNULA
pertaining to DIGITAL
ring ANNULAR
shield *See "guard"
above*
fingerling PARR,
THIMBLE, FISH
fingerprint WHORL,
LOOP, ARCH
finial EPI, APEX, TOP
finical PRUDISH,
SPRUCE, FUSSY, NICE,
FASTIDIOUS, DAINTY,
CRITICAL, SQUEAMISH,
DAPPER, FOPPISH,
METICULOUS, MINCING
finis END, CONCLUSION,
DEATH
finish END, WIN, CLOSE,
COMPLETE, ACCOM-
PLISH, EFFECT, CON-
SUMMATE, EXECUTE,
PERFECT, TERMINATE,
CONCLUDE, WIND-UP,
POLISH, SHINE,
VENEER, TAPE
finished OVER, DONE,
CLOSED, COMPLETED,
ENDED, PERFECT,
REFINED, SMOOTH,
SUAVE, EXPERIENCED,
PROFICIENT, SKILLED,
ABLE
finishing line TAPE
fink SPY, SCAB, FINCH,
BIRD, INFORMER,
SQUEALER
Finland, Finnish, Finn
VOD, VOT, VOTE,
SUOMI
bath SAUNA
coin MARKKA, PENNI
dialect KAREL

fortress
　SUOMENLINNA
god JUMALA
harp KANTELE
island ALAND
lake ENARE, INARI
legislature
　EDUSKUNTA
measure KANNOR,
　TUNNA
pertaining to SUOMIC,
　SUOMISH
seaport ABO, TURKU,
　VAASA, OULU, PORI,
　RAUMA
tribe VEPS, VOTE,
　CHUD, VOTH
fin(n)ikin PIGEON
fir *genus* ABIES
fire BLAZE, IGNIS,
　FLAME, LIGHT, BURN,
　CHAR, CONFLAGRA-
　TION, HEAT, SCORCH,
　SHOOT, SACK, DISMISS,
　EJECT, OUST, DROP,
　DISCHARGE, EXPEL,
　KINDLE, INSPIRE,
　ANIMATE, IGNITE,
　AROUSE, EXCITE, STIR,
　ARDOR, FEVER
artillery BARRAGE
basket CRESSET,
　GRATE
bullet TRACER
combining form
　PYR(O), IGNI
damp METHANE, GAS
drill CHARK
god or goddess See
　under "god" *or*
　"goddess"
having power over
　IGNIPOTENT
miss SNAP, DUD
sacrificial AGNI
worshipper
　PYROLATER
firearm GUN, GAT,
　PISTOL, WEAPON,
　ARM, MUSKET, RIFLE,
　REVOLVER, COLT
firebrand TORCH,
　AGITATOR
firecracker PETARD
firedog ANDIRON, SUP-
　PORT
fireman STOKER, VAMP
fireplace INGLE, GRATE,
　HEARTH
　back of REREDOS
　ledge HOB, SHELF,
　MANTEL

firewood bundle
　FAGOT, LENA
fireworks GIRANDOLE,
　RIP-RAP, GERB(E),
　FIZGIGS
firm BUSINESS,
　PARTNERSHIP, CON-
　CERN, COMPANY,
　CORPORATION, TIGHT,
　STAUNCH, STEADY,
　CLOSE, COMPACT,
　DENSE, THICK, STRONG,
　COMPRESSED, HARD,
　FIXED, FAST, ROOTED,
　ESTABLISHED, RIGID,
　MOOR, SECURE, SET,
　SETTLED, STABLE,
　RESOLUTE, ROBUST,
　DETERMINED
firmament HEAVENS,
　VAULT, SKY, SPHERE,
　WELKIN
firn ICE, SNOW, NEVE
firs ABIES
first PRIMUS, NEW,
　AHEAD, STAR, DEBUT,
　PRIME, INITIAL,
　MAIDEN, LEADING,
　BEST, CHIEF, FRONT,
　EARLIEST, PRIMARY,
　PRIMORDIAL, ORIGINAL,
　PRINCIPAL, HIGHEST,
　FOREMOST, CAPITAL,
　PRIMITIVE, ABORIGINAL
class A-ONE, TOPS,
　ACE
day of Roman month
　CALENDS
globe circler MAGEL-
　LAN
installment EARNEST,
　HANDSEL
letter of Arabic
　alphabet ALIF
rate OK, OKAY, SUPER,
　ACE, A-ONE
year's revenue ANNAT
firth ESTUARY, FRITH,
　KYLE, ARM, FIORD
fish ANGLE, TROLL,
　CAST, SEEK, ID(E),
　EEL, CARP, DACE,
　HAKE, JOCU, LING,
　MADO, OPAH, ORFE,
　PEGA, PETO, PIKE,
　POGY, RUDD, SESI,
　SHAD, SOLE, SPET,
　TUNA, PARGO, ROACH,
　MULLET, DARTER,
　SPRAT, DEVIL, TAUTOG,
　SMELT, LULU, CISCO,
　PERCH

amber MEDREGAL
ascend rivers
　ANADROM, SALMON,
　SHAD
bait WORMS, CHUM,
　FLY
barracuda SPET,
　SENNET, PELON
basket CORF, CAUL,
　CAWL
bass, African IYO
　European BRASSE
bat DIABLO
bin for salting KENCH,
　CANCH
bivalve SCALLOP,
　OYSTER, CLAM,
　DIATOM, MOLLUSK,
　PANDORA
black SWART, TAUTOG
bleak BLAY, BLEY,
　SPRAT
bonito SKIPJACK,
　AKU, ATU
bright colored OPAH
broken-bellied THOKE
burbot LOTA, COD,
　EELPOUT, LING
butter GUNNEL,
　BLENNY
butterfly BLENNY
California RENA,
　REINA, CHI, SPRAT, SUR
carangoid SCAD,
　SAUREL
caribe PIRAYA,
　PIRANHA
carp IDE, LOACH
cat DOCMAC, RAAD,
　MUD, CHANNEL *See*
　"catfish"
catch of SHACK,
　STRING
chopped CHUM
cigar SCAD
climbing ANABAS
clinging REMORA
cobia SERGEANT,
　COAL, BONITO
cod TORSK, SCROD,
　CUSK, BANK, BURBOT,
　COR, CULTUS, ROCK,
　POLLACK
like LING, HAKE,
　GADUS, BIB
colored OPAH, WRASSE
cow MANATEE,
　SIRENIA
crab, fiddler UCA
　See "crab"
Cuban DIABLO
cutlass SAVOLA

cuttle SEPIA, SQUID, OCTOPUS
cyprinoid BARBEL, BREAM, CHI, DACE, IDE, TENCH, ORF(E), CARP, CHUB, BLEAK, BLAY, BLEY, SPOT, RUD(D), LULU
devil MANTA, RAY, OCTOPUS, WHALE
dog SHARK, BOWFIN, BURBOT, WRASSE
snapper JOCU
dolphin DORADO, SUSU, COWFISH, INIA, PORPOISE
E. India ARCHER, DORAB, GOURAMI
eel MORAY, CONGER, LAMPREY *See* "eel"
eggs ROE, CAVIAR
Egypt SAIDE, BICHIR, DOCMAC, LATES
elasmobranch SAWFISH, CHIMERA, SHARK, RAY
escolar PALU
Europe BOCE, TIRU, TENCH, BREAM, SPRAT, BARBEL, BRASSE, ALOSE, LYRIE, LAVARET, MARENA, BOGUE, MAIGRE, MAIGER, RUDD
exocoetoid IHI
fabled, upholding world MAH
female RAUN
fence WEIR, NET
flat DAB, TURBOT, SKATE, RAY, FLUKE, PLAICE, SOLE, FLOUNDER
flounder FLUKE *See* "flounder"
flying SAURY, GURNARD
fresh water ANABAS, CRAPPIE, TROUT, LOACH, DARTER, REDEYE, BREAM, CARP, PERCH
game MARLIN, SALMON, BASS, CERO, SWORD, TARPON, TROUT
ganoid GAR, STURGEON, BOWFIN
genus MOLA, PERCA, ELOPS, AMIA, LOTA, APOGON
gig SPEAR

globe DIODON
grampus ORC(A), WHALE, KILLER
grouper MERO, GUASA, HIND
grunt RONCO, CROAKER
guachoncho PELON
half-beak IHI
Hawaiian ULUA, AWA, ALAIHI, LANIA
hawk OSPREY
herring *See* "herring"
hook GAFF, SPROAT, FLY, GIG, BARB
imperfect THOKE
India DORAB, CHENAS
Japan TAI, FUGU, PORGIE, AYU, MASU, KOI, FUNA
jelly MEDUSA, NETTLE, QUARL, ACALEPH
umbrella of PILEUS
jew MERO, GROUPER
king BARB, OPAH, CERO, SIERRA, PINTADO
lancet SURGEON
land-traveling ANABAS
largest fresh water ARAPAIMA
leather LIJA
line SNELL, CORD
with series of hooks TROT
little MINNOW, SARDINE, SMELT
mackerel *See* "mackerel"
mammal MANATEE, WHALE *See* "cetacean"
Mediterranean SARGO(N)
medregal AMBER
milk AWA, SAVOLA
mollusk *See* "mollusk"
mutton SAMA, MOJARRA, PARGO
nest-building ACARA, STICKLEBACK
net SAGENE, SEINE, TRAWL, SPILLER, FYKE
bagging of BUNT
support METER
New Zealand IHI, HIKU
Nile BICHIR, SAIDE, DOCMAC
oil ESCOLAR

oyster TOAD
parrot LANIA, LORO, SCAR(ID), SCARUS
pen for CRAWL
perch *See* "perch"
European BARSE
pertaining to PISCATORY, FINNY
pike ESOX, DORE, LUCE, GED(D)
adult LUCE
like GAR, ROBALO
pimelepteroid BREAM
porcupine DIODON
porgy SCUP, TAI, PARGO, BREAM
pork SISI
porpoise DOLPHIN, INIA, PELLOCK
ray MANTA, SEPHEN, SKATE, DORN, OBISPO
redmouth GRUNT
remora PEGA, PEGADOR
rock RASHER, RENA, REINA
salmon *See* "salmon"
salmonoid *See* "salmonoid"
sardine PILCHARD, BANG, ANCHOVY
sauce ALEC, ANCHOVY, SOY, TARTAR, GARUM
saurel SCAD, POMPANO
scale GANOID
scombroid TUNA, BONITO, MACKEREL
scorpion LAPON
sea LING, MERO, OPAH, TUNA, HAKE, COD, POLLACK
sergeant COBIA, COAL
serranoid LATES
shad *See* "shad"
shark *See* "shark"
sheat SOM
shell *See* "shell"
shiner ROACH, MINNOW, CHUB, MENHADEN
sign of PISCES
silver TARPON
skipjack BONITO, SAURY, SKIPPER, SAUREL, ALEWIFE, BLUEFISH
slender GAR, SAURY
small ID(E), SMELT, SARDINE, MINNOW

smelt SPARLING
  like CAPLIN,
  CAPELIN
soap JABON
S. America ARAPIMA,
  ACARA, CARIBE,
  PIRAYA, PIRANHA,
  PACO, PACU
Spanish RONCO
sparoid PORGY, SAR,
  TAI, SARGO(N),
  SALEMA
spear GIG, TREN,
  GAFF
spiny-finned GOBY,
  PERCH
squirrel MARIAN,
  SERRANO
sturgeon See
  "sturgeon"
sucking REMORA
sun ROACH, OPAH,
  MOLA
surgeon TANG,
  BARBER
synancioid LAFF
synodontoid TIRU
tarpon ELOPS,
  SABALO
  related to CHIRO
teleost APODA, EEL
thunder RAAD, ROACH
toad SAPO, SARPO
trap WEIR, NET,
  FYKE, SAGENE,
  SEINE, TRAWL,
  SPILLER
tree-climbing ANABAS
tropical BARRACUDA,
  SALEMA, PACO, PACU,
  ROBALO
trout MALMA, SEWEN,
  LONGE, TOGUE, RAIN-
  BOW, SPECKLED,
  BROOK
unicorn UNIE
upholding universe
  MAH
voracious CARIBE,
  SHARK, PIRAYA,
  PIRANHA
wahoo PETO
W. Indies CERO,
  SESI, PEGA, PEGADOR,
  RONCO, MARIAN,
  PETO, PINTADO
whale BELUGA *See*
  "whale"
whales, order of
  CETE
whisker BARBEL

white POLLAN,
  ANTIGA, CISCO
whiting-pout BIB
young MINNOW,
  ALEVIN, FRY, PARR,
  SPROD, SMELT
fisher WEJACK,
  PEKAN, BIRD
fisherman EELER,
  SQUAM, SEINER,
  ANGLER, PISCATOR
  hat of SQUAM
fishhook ANGLE,
  BARB, SPROAT,
  FLY, HACKLE
  attach to snell
  GANGE
  feathered FLY,
  HACKLE, SEDGE
  leader SNELL
fishing *basket* SLARTH,
  SLATH, CREEL
  gear REEL, ROD,
  LINE, HOOK, FLY,
  TACKLE, NETS
  pertaining to
  HALIEUTIC
  smack DOGGER
fishlike ICHTHYIC
  skin ICHTHYOSIS
fishpond PISCINA
fissle HISS, WHISTLE,
  RUSTLE, FIDGET
fissure(s) RIME, RIFT,
  RENT, CLEFT, SULCUS,
  SULCI, CHINK, RIMA,
  LEAK, SPLIT, SLIT,
  SEAM, CREVICE,
  CRACK, CRANNY,
  BREAK, BREACH, GAP,
  INTERSTICE, OPEN-
  ING, CHASM, FRAC-
  TURE
fist NEIF, NIEVE
fisticuffs BOUT,
  COMBAT, BLOWS,
  BOXING
fistula CAVITY, SINUS,
  REED, PIPE, TUBE
fit SPASM, PAROXYSM,
  STROKE, TANTRUM,
  PET, SPELL, ATTACK,
  SEIZURE, APPOSITE,
  RIGHT, DECENT,
  GEE, MEET, PAT,
  HAPPY, READY,
  QUALIFIED, TRAINED,
  APPROPRIATE, ADE-
  QUATE, CONVENIENT,
  LICENSED, COMPE-
  TENT, DUE, SUIT,
  APT, DULY, ABLE,

ELIGIBLE, EQUIP,
ADAPT, CLOTHE,
PROPER, FAY,
GEAR, CAPABLE,
HUMOR, WHIM,
FANCY, OUTBREAK
fitchew POLECAT
fitful VARIABLE,
  IRREGULAR, SPAS-
  MODIC, INTERMIT-
  TENT, IMPULSIVE,
  CAPRICIOUS
fitting *See* "fit"
Fiume RIJEKA
five, *books of Moses*
  PENTATEUCH
  combining form
  PENTA, PENT
  dollar bill VEE
  fold QUINTUPLE
  group of PENTAD
  in cards PEDRO
  year period LUSTRUM,
  PENTAD
five-finger OXLIP,
  CINQUEFOIL, PLANT,
  FISH
fix PLIGHT, DILEMMA,
  SCRAPE, PICKLE,
  PREDICAMENT,
  (A)MEND, REPAIR,
  SETTLE, TIE,
  FASTEN, ATTACH,
  ADJUST, FREEZE,
  PLACE, SET, DEFINE,
  BIND, LOCK, STAY,
  DETERMINE, LIMIT,
  APPOINT, RIVET,
  SOLIDIFY, CONGEAL,
  EMBED
fixed STABLE, STILL,
  STATIC, SETTLED,
  FIRM, SET, INTENT,
  REPAIRED
  routine RUT
  time ERA, DATE,
  APPOINTMENT
flaccid SOFT, LIMP,
  WEAK, LIMBER,
  FLABBY, LAX,
  YIELDING
flag GONFALON, BUNT-
  ING, BANDEROL(E),
  PENNANT, BANNER,
  SIGNAL, ENSIGN,
  COLORS, JACK, PEN-
  NON, STREAMER,
  STANDARD, FANE,
  SIGN, DROOP,
  LANGUISH, FAINT,
  DECLINE, SINK, LAG,
  PALL, IRIS

corner CANTON
flower IRIS, CALAMUS
merchant vessel
  BURGEE
military FANION,
  GUIDON, COLORS
national ENSIGN
navy BURGEE
pirate ROGER
signal CORNET
sweet CALAMUS
yacht BURGEE
flagellant(s) WHIP,
  SCOURGE, TAIL
religious ALBI
flagellate CASTIGATE,
  FLOG, LASH,
  THRASH, BEAT,
  CUDGEL
flageolet PIPE,
  LARIGOT, FLUTE,
  BEAN
Hindu BASAREE
flagitious BAD,
  WICKED, ATROCIOUS,
  HEINOUS, VILLAINOUS,
  INFAMOUS, SCANDAL-
  OUS, NEFARIOUS,
  CORRUPT, SHAMEFUL,
  DISGRACEFUL
flagon JUG, EWER,
  DEMIJOHN, CANTEEN,
  CARAFE, FLASK
flagrant ARDENT,
  SCARLET, EVIL, RANK,
  GROSS, EGREGIOUS,
  HEINOUS, RAGING,
  GLOWING, BURNING,
  NOTORIOUS, MON-
  STROUS, OUTRAGE-
  OUS, WANTON, GLAR-
  ING, ODIOUS
flagstone SHALE, SLAP,
  WALK(WAY)
flail SWINGLE,
  THRASH, BEAT,
  STRIKE, SWIPLE,
  FLOG
flair TALENT, BRAINS,
  WITS, SCENT, APTI-
  TUDE, DISCRIMINA-
  TION, DISCERNMENT,
  TASTE, LIKING,
  BENT
flake FLOCK, CHIP,
  LAMINA, SLATE,
  SCALE, LAYER, STRIP,
  SCUTE
flaky SCALY,
  SQUAMOUS
flambeau CRESSET,
  TORCH

flamboyant ORNATE,
  GAUDY, FLORID,
  ROCOCO, GORGEOUS,
  RESPLENDENT
flame ZEAL, BEAM,
  LEYE, FIRE, GLAZE,
  FLARE, GLOW, ARDOR,
  FERVOR, IGNITE,
  LIGHT, WARMTH,
  ENTHUSIASM, BURN
Flaminia ROAD, WAY
Flanders *city* GHENT,
  LILLE
flaneur IDLER,
  STROLLER, LOITERER,
  TRIFLER
flank SIDE, WING,
  BORDER, TOUCH,
  THIGH, LOIN
flannel LANA,
  DOMETT, CLOTH
flap FLY, TAG, LAP-
  (PET), BANGLE, TAB,
  FLOP, SWAY, WAVE,
  FOLD, FLUTTER,
  VIBRATE
furnished with
  LOBED
membranous LOMA
of sails SLAT
flare GLITTER, FLASH,
  FLECK, BLAZE,
  FLICKER, GLARE,
  FUSEE, FLAME,
  GLOW, DART, SHOOT,
  RISE, SPRING,
  DAZZLE, WIDEN,
  SPLAY, WAVER
flaring BELLING,
  EVASE, SHOWY
flash GLEAM, FLARE,
  SHINE, LIGHT,
  GLINT, GLITTER,
  SPARK, SHOOT,
  BLAZE, GLARE,
  GLISTEN, SHIMMER,
  SPARKLE, INSTANT,
  TWINKLING, GLANCE
flashing FLANGE,
  GAUDY
flashy SHOWY,
  OSTENTATIOUS, LOUD,
  FLAUNTING, GAWDY,
  GLITTERY, TINSEL
flask CANTEEN, BETTY,
  CRUSE, CARAFE,
  OLPE, EWER,
  FLAGON
glass MATRASS
leather GIRBA,
  OLPE, MATARA
shaped LAGENIFORM

flat INSIPID, JEJUNE,
  BANAL, STALE, VAPID,
  LIFELESS, MONOTO-
  NOUS, UNINTEREST-
  ING, DULL, EVEN,
  FLUSH, PLANE,
  PRONE, LEVEL,
  HORIZONTAL, SMOOTH,
  LOW, SIMPLE, BROKE,
  ROOMS, SUITE, DIGS
combining form
  PLANI
fish See under
  "fish"
flattened PLANATE,
  OBLATE, APPLANATE,
  EVENED, PLANED,
  LEVELED
flatter PALP, ADULATE,
  PRAISE, OIL,
  PLEASE, CAJOLE,
  FAWN, WHEEDLE,
  COMPLIMENT, COAX,
  BLARNEY, BLANDISH,
  SWAGE, BEGUILE,
  INGRATIATE
flattering GNATHONIC,
  CEREMONIAL
flattery BLARNEY,
  SOAP, OIL, PRAISE,
  SNOW, PALAVER,
  TAFFY, BALONEY,
  SYCOPHANCY, SERVIL-
  ITY, OBSEQUIOUSNESS,
  BLANDISHMENT,
  PANEGYRICS
flaunt PARADE,
  TRAIPSE, BOSH,
  BOAST, STOUT,
  EXPOSE, EXHIBIT,
  BRANDISH, FLOURISH,
  VAUNT, WAVE,
  FLUTTER, BRAG
flavor SEASON, TANG,
  SAUCE, AROMA,
  GUST(O), SAPOR,
  SAVOR, TASTE, TACK,
  ZEST, RELISH, SMACK,
  ODOR, FRAGRANCE,
  PIQUANCY, TINCTURE
flaw FAULT, MAR,
  CRACK, HOLE,
  BLEMISH, RENT,
  DEFECT, BLAST, GUST,
  GALE, BREAK, SPOT,
  FLECK, BREACH, GAP,
  IMPERFECTION, TEAR,
  RIP
flax LINT, LINUM,
  FLOWER, ANNUAL
bundle HEAD
capsule BOLL

cloth LINEN
comb CARD, HATCHEL, HACKLE
disease RUST
dust POUCE
fiber TOW
filament HARL
genus LINUM
insect DODDER, CANKER
place for processing RETTERY
refuse PAB, HARDS, HURDS, POB, TOW
seed LINSEED
soak RET
tow of CODILLA
woody portion BOON
flay SKIN, PEEL, PARE, EXCORIATE, SCARIFY, ABRADE, CHAFE, TORTURE, GRILL, RACK, CENSURE
flea CHIGOE, CYCLOPS, PULICID, INSECT, PEST
genus PULEX
water CYCLOPS
fleche BROACH, SPIRE, PARAPET
flee ELUDE, EVADE, ESCAPE, SHUN, RUN, AVOID, ELOPE, FLY, BOLT, DECAMP, ABSCOND, SKEDADDLE, VANISH, BLOW, DESERT
fleece PILE, SKIN, HAIR, CLOTH, NAP, ROB, STRIP, MULCT, SHEAR, CLIP, PLUNDER, DESPOIL, CHEAT, RIFLE, BLEED, WOOL
inferior part of ABB
fleer GIBE, MOCK, SNEER, SCOFF, JEER, FLAUNT, DE-RIDE, SMIRK, SCORN,
fleet ARGOSY, ARMADA, NAVY, FLOTILLA, SQUADRON, ESCA-DRILLE, NIMBLE, TRANSITORY, FAST, AGILE, BRIEF, SWIFT, RAPID, SPEEDY
Flemish painter RUBENS
flesh MEAT, PULP, MAN(KIND), KIN, FAMILY, STOCK, RACE

eating CARNIVOROUS, SARCOPHAGIC
like CARNOSE
pertaining to SARCOUS
fleshly CARNAL, SENSUAL, LUSTFUL, LECHEROUS
fleshy ADIPOSE, FAT, OBESE, PLUMP, STOUT, BURLY, CARNOSE
fleur-de-lis LYS, LUCE, LUCY, IRIS
fleuret EPEE, SWORD, FLOWER
flex BEND, GENU, BOW, GENUFLECT
flexible LIMBER, LISSOME, SUPPLE, LITHE, ELASTIC, PLIANT, SPRINGY, PLIABLE, FLEXIBLE, WILLOWY, DUCTILE, DOCILE
flexion of a limb ANACLASIS
flexure GENU, CROOK, FOLD, BEND, TURN, CURVE, CURVATURE
flick FLIRT, FLIP, JERK, WHIP, DAUB, STREAK
flicker BIRD, BLAZE, BLINK, FLIT, HOVER, WAVER, FLAME, GLEAM, FLUTTER, FLUCTUATE, FLARE, FAIL, FLUNK
flickering LAMBENT, FLUTTERING
flight EXODUS, HEGIRA, ESCAPE, BEVY, GAG-GLE, COVEY, WING, FLOCK, HERD, DROVE, PACK, ROUT, MIGRA-TION, MOUNTING, SOARING, TRIP, HOP
range(s) RADIUS, RADII
flightless bird DODO, MOA, PENGUIN, OSTRICH, WEKA, EMU, RATITE, KIWI
genus APTERYX, NOTORNIS
flighty BARMY, FICKLE, MAD, GIDDY, VOLATILE, MERCURIAL, FRIVOLOUS
flimflam HOCUS, TRICK, DECEPTION, HUMBUG, HOAX

flimsy SLEAZY, FRAG-ILE, FEEBLE, WEAK, THIN, SLIGHT, SLIMSY, TRIVIAL, SHALLOW, TRASHY, CHEAP, SUPERFICIAL
flinch QUAIL, BLENCH, WINCE, WONDE, FEAR, SWERVE, RECOIL, FALTER, SHRINK, WITHDRAW
fling CAST, THROW, HURL, SLING, TOSS, PITCH, HEAVE, CHUCK, FLOUNCE, SHY
flint CHERT, QUARTZ, STONE
impure CHERT
flinty HARD, CRUEL, OBDURATE
flippant FRESH, GLIB, CHATTY, PERT, SASSY, SAUCY, FLUENT, VOLUBLE, FORWARD, BOLD, FRIVOLOUS, TRIFLING, BRASSY
flirt FIKE, JILL, COQUET(TE), TOY, OGLE, DALLY, TRIFLE, TOSS, FLING, SHY, HURL, CHUCK, PHILANDER
flirtatious ARCH, COY, COQUETTISH
flit FLICKER, HOVER, FLY, DART, SKIM, SCUD, FLUTTER, GAD
flittermouse BAT
float BUOY, LURE, DRIFT, QUILL, RAFT, SWIM, WATCH, CORK, SELL, WAFT, SKIM, RIDE, GLIDE, SAIL, SOAR
floating ADRIFT, AWASH, NATANT
grass FOXTAIL
plant(s) FROGBIT, LOTUS, SUDD
wreckage FLOTSAM
flock COVEY, POD, SKEIN, BROOD, BEVY, DROVE, SET, LOT, SCHOOL, SWARM, PACK, HIRSEL, HERD, RAFT, GAGGLE, CROWD, PRESS, HORDE, MOB, HATCH, LITTER, COMPANY, MULTI-TUDE, GROUP,

TROUPE, TEAM, CON-
GREGATION, CONGRE-
GATE, GATHER
pertaining to GREGAL
floe BERG
flog LARRUP, WALE,
CAT, TAN, WELT,
YANK, CANE, WHIP,
LASH, BEAT, THRASH,
DRUB
flogging TOCO, TOKO
flood CATARACT,
CATACLYSM, SEA,
SPATE, FLOW,
STREAM, TIDE, EXCESS,
SURPLUS, DELUGE,
INUNDATION, FRESHET,
EAGRE, OVERFLOW
gate CLOW, GOOL,
SLUICE
lights KLIEG
tidal EAGRE
floor PLAYA, PAVE,
DECK, BASE, DEFEAT,
KO, STORY, BEAT,
PLATFORM, BOTTOM
covering MAT, RUG,
CARPET, TAPIS
raised border
COAMING
flooring BATTEN, TILE,
SLAB, PAVEMENT,
PARQUET, LINOLEUM
flop LEMON, FALL,
FAIL(URE), TUMBLE,
DUD, DROP, SLUMP
flora and fauna
BIOTA
floral leaves PERIANTH
Florence *gallery*
UFFIZI, PITTI
river ARNO
Florentine family
MEDICI
floret bracht PALEA,
PALET
florid ORNATE, RED,
RUDDY, RUBICUND,
ROCOCO, SHOWY,
FLOWERY; RHETORI-
CAL, FLUSHED,
MELISMATIC
style ROCOCO
Florida *city* OCALA,
MIAMI, TAMPA,
NAPLES
county BAY, CLAY,
DADE, GULF, LAKE,
LEE, LEON, LEVY,
PASCO, POLK
fish TETARD, TARPON
tree GOMART

floss SLEAVE, SILK,
THREAD, STREAM
flounder PLAICE,
TURBOT, SOLE, FLAT-
FISH, BREAM, SUN-
FISH, FLUKE, WELTER,
WALLOW, GROVEL,
STRIVE, TOIL, LABOR,
STRUGGLE, ROLL
flour *and butter* ROUX
sifter BOLTER,
SIEVE
sprinkle with DREDGE
unsorted ATA, ATTA
flourish PARAPH,
BRANDISH, GAIN,
WAVE, FLAUNT,
THRIVE, ROULADE,
PARADE, GROW,
SWING, THRASH,
WIELD, PLY, PROSPER,
SUCCEED, BOAST,
BRAG, VAUNT, FAN-
FARE, DISPLAY,
OSTENTATION
flout JIBE, JEER,
SCOFF, FLEER, SNEER,
GIBE, SCORN, SPURN,
MOCK, DERIDE, IN-
SULT, TAUNT
flow RUN, ISSUE, OOZE,
SPOUT, STEM,
STREAM, FLOOD, TIDE,
FLUX, SPRING, RISE,
DERIVE, POUR, EMA-
NATE, PROCEED, GLIDE,
WAVE, GUSH, TEEM,
CURRENT
out SPILL, EXUDE,
ISSUE, OOZE
tide EBB, NEAP, FLUX
flower BLOOM, POSY,
ELITE, ELECT, BEST,
BLOSSOM, BUD, UN-
FOLD, DEVELOP
algae genus NOSTOC
apetalus TREMA,
CACTUS
border FLOROON
buckwheat TITI
bud KNOT
burry TEASEL
butterfly lily
MARIPOSA
California State
POPPY
cardinal LOBELIA
center EYE
cluster RACEME, UM-
BEL, PANICULATE,
PANICLE, CYME
leaf BRACT

combining form
ANTH(O)
Connecticut State
LAUREL
dogrose fruit HIP
dry AZALEA, CACTUS
Egypt, sacred LOTUS
England LUPINE
envelope PERIANTH
erica HEATH
extract ATTAR, OTTO,
PERFUME
fall ASTER, COSMOS
felwort GENTIAN
forgetfulness LOTUS
fragrant JASMINE
full bloom ANTHESIS
genus ROSA,
ADONIS, VIOLA
head BLOOM *See*
"cluster" *above*
heath AZALEA, ERICA
honeysuckle SAMBUC-
CUS
   swamp AZALEA
Idaho State SYRINGA
Illinois State VIOLET
Indiana State ZINNIA
indigo ANIL
iris ORRIS, FLAG, LIS
leaf SEPAL, BRACT,
PETAL
sets of four QUAD-
RIFOLIATE
sets of three TRIL-
LIUM
lily ARUM, LOTUS,
SEGO, ALOE *See*
"lily"
   butterfly MARIPOSA,
SEGO
   corn IXIA
   palm TI, TOI
meadow BLUETS
medicinal RUE, ALOE
New England
BLUETS, RUE
New Hampshire
State LILAC
New Jersey State
VIOLET
New Mexico State
YUCCA
New York State
ROSE
nightshade BEL-
LADONNA, HENBANE,
POKEWEED
Oklahoma State MIS-
TLETOE
part of ANTHER,
BRACT, PISTIL,

SEPAL, STAMEN,
CARPEL, PETAL,
COROLLA, SPUR
Pennsylvania State
LAUREL
pink SILENE
pistil, part of CARPEL
plat BED
ragwort JACOBY
Rhode Island State
SALVIA, VIOLET
rose, Persian GUL
of Sharon CROCUS,
ALTHEA, SAFFRON
seed OVULE
shaped ornament
FLEURON
sheath SPATHE
silene PINK
spike AMENT,
SPADIX
spring CROCUS,
HYACINTH
stalk PEDUNCLE,
PETIOLE, SCAPE,
STEM
stand for EPERGNE
starwort ASTER
summit of stamen
ANTHER
Swiss EDELWEISS
Syrian RETEM,
JUNIPER
syringa LILAC
Tennessee State IRIS
turban TULIP
unfading AMARANTH
Utah State SEGO
LILY
water lily LOTUS
wind ANEMONE
Wisconsin State
VIOLET
wood sorrel OCA,
OXALIS
flower holder VASE,
LAPEL, POT
flowering *grasses genus*
STIPA
tree CATALPA, TULIP,
MIMOSA
flowerless plant
ACROGEN, FERN,
LICHEN, MOSS
flowerlike ANTHOID
flowing AFFLUX,
CURSIVE, EMANANT,
FLUX, RUNNING,
SMOOTH, FLUENT,
ABUNDANT
fluctuate WAVER, VARY,
SHIFT, SWING, SWAY,

OSCILLATE, UNDULATE,
CHANGE, VIBRATE,
VACILLATE
fluctuating, *music* RU-
BATO
fluent GLIB, GLIDING,
FACILE, EASY,
SMOOTH, READY, APT,
VOLUBLE, TALKATIVE,
FLUID, LIQUID,
COPIOUS, FLOWING
fluff NAP, LINT, PUFF,
FLOSS, ERR, MISS,
DOWN
fluid FLUX, STEAM,
VAPOR, SAP, JUICE,
LIQUID, FLOWING,
GASEOUS, FLUENT,
FLOATING
blood SERUM,
PLASMA
milk PLASMA
mythological blood
ICHOR
fluidity unit RHE
fluke BLADE, WORM,
BARB, FLOUNDER,
LUCK, ADVANTAGE
flume SLUICE, CON-
DUIT, CHUTE, CHAN-
NEL, GORGE, RAVINE
flunk FAIL, FLINCH,
MISS, SLIP, SHIRK,
RETREAT
flunk(e)y SNOB,
TOADY, FOOTMAN,
LACKEY
fluosilicate of alumi-
num TOPAZ
flurry AGITATION,
HURRY, GUST,
BUSTLE, SQUALL,
BLAST, FUSS, ADO,
STIR, POTHER, FRET,
HASTE, SPEED, CON-
FUSION, EXCITEMENT,
COMMOTION, DISTURB-
ANCE, FLUSTER
flush BLUSH, REDDEN,
GLOW, ROSINESS,
EVEN, LEVEL, FLAT,
PLANE, SMOOTH,
START, ROUSE,
THRILL, RINSE, IN-
CREASE, GROWTH,
ABUNDANT, LAVISH,
PRODIGAL, PROSPER-
OUS
flushed AGLOW,
FLORID, RED, RUBY,
SCARLET, VIGOROUS,
PROSPEROUS

fluster POTHER, MOVE,
EXCITE, UPSET,
FLURRY, RATTLE,
FAZE, ADDLE,
AGITATE, PERTURB,
DISTURB, RUFFLE,
CONFUSE, DISCONCERT,
CONFOUND
flute PIPE, FIFE,
GROOVE, CRIMP,
FLAGEOLET, PICCOLO,
WINEGLASS, SHUTTLE
ancient TIBIA
bagpipe CHANTER
Hindu PUNGI, BIN
player FL(A)UTIST,
AULETE
stop VENTAGE
transverse FIFE
flutter AGITATE, FLIT,
WAVE, FLICKER,
FLAP, BUSTLE, SHAKE,
THROB, QUIVER,
PALPITATE, HOVER,
FLIRT, TREMBLE,
BEAT, FLUCTUATE,
VACILLATE
flux FLOW, PURGE,
CURRENT, TIDE,
STREAM, FLOOD
fly INSECT, PEST,
DIPTERON, AVIATE,
SOAR, WHIR, WING,
FLOAT, DART, FLIT,
SKIM, SCUD, SHOOT,
RISE, HOVER, MOUNT,
FLUTTER, FLAP, SAIL,
GLIDE, FLEE, ELOPE,
ESCAPE, DECAMP,
ABSCOND, PASS,
ELAPSE, LAP, FLAP,
CARRIAGE, CAB
Africa ZIMB,
ZEBUB, TSETSE
artificial HARL,
SEDGE, CLARET,
CAHILL, HERL
as clouds SCUD
block PULLEY
catcher PEEWEE,
PHOEBE, KINGBIRD,
TODY
constellation MUSCA
genus MUSCA
small GNAT, MIDGE
wing(s) of ELYTRA,
ELYTRUM, ELYTRON
flyaway GIDDY, REST-
LESS, FLIGHTY, UN-
RESTRAINED
flybane *genus* SILENE
flyblow LARVA

flycatcher *bird* PEE-WEE, REDSTART, PHOEBE, TODY, KINGBIRD

flying VOLANT, BRIEF, FAST, SWIFT

fish SAURY, GURNARD

foam FUME, BUBBLE, SCUM, BARM, FROTH, SPUME, LATHER, SUDS, BOIL, RAGE, YEAST, FERMENT, SPRAY, HEAD, CREAM

fob CHEAT, SHAM, TRICK, POCKET, CHAIN, ORNAMENT

focus HEART, CENTER, NUCLEUS, CORE, HUB, HEARTH, CONCENTRATE, CONVERGE, MIDDLE

fodder STOVER, ENSILAGE, FORAGE, FOOD, FEED, STRAW, PROVENDER, OATS, CORN

storage place SILO, BARN

straw STOVER

to store ENSILE

trough for MANGER

fodgel FAT, PLUMP, STOUT, SQUAT

foe ENEMY, RIVAL, ADVERSARY, OPPONENT, ANTAGONIST

fog BEDIM, CLOUD, HAZE, MIST, VAPOR, AEROSOL, SMOG, BRUME, ROKE, STUPOR, MURK, SMOKE

horn SIREN

foggy NUBILOUS, CLOUDY, DIM, CONFUSED, MUDDLED, BEWILDERED, OBSCURE, VAGUE

fog(e)y DODO, FOGRAM, HUNKER, MOSSBACK, FOGRUM, CONSERVATIVE

foil BALK, EPEE, STOOGE, CHEAT, THWART, BAFFLE, OUTWIT, FAZE, SWORD, DEFEAT, FRUSTRATE, CIRCUMVENT, CHECKMATE, METAL, LEAF

foist FOB, PALM, INTERPOLATE, IMPOSE, THRUST

fold BEND, CREASE, FLAP, PEN, HUG, CRIMP, PLEAT, LAP, PLY, RUGA, WRAP, CLASP, DRAPE, PLICATURE, REEF, COT, COTE, FLOCK, CONGREGATION, ENVELOP, EMBRACE

of skin PLICA

folded PLICATE, CLOSED, SHUT

foliage, *mass of* SPRAY, BOUQUET, LEAFAGE

foliated LOBED, LAMELLAR, SPATHIC, LAMELLATE, FOLIACEOUS

folio PAGE, BOOK, NUMBER, LEAF, FOLDER

folk KIN, RACE, PEOPLE, KINDRED, NATION

folklore LEGENDS, CUSTOMS, BELIEFS, SAYINGS, HISTORY, TRADITIONS, SUPERSTITIONS

folkway(s) MOS, MORES, CUSTOM(S), PATTERN(S)

follicle CAVITY, SAC, TUBE, FRUIT, DEPRESSION, GLAND, COCOON

follow ATTEND, OBEY, HEED, OBSERVE, CONFORM, PRACTICE, ENSUE, NEXT, IMITATE, APE, RESULT, SUCCEED, ACCOMPANY, COPY, CHASE, TRAIL, TAIL, DOG, TRACE, PURSUE, HOUND

follower IST, ITE, FAN, BUFF, ADDICT, APER, MIMIC, COPIER, VOTARY, RETAINER, ATTENDANT, ACOLYTE, ADHERENT, DISCIPLE, PUPIL, ASSOCIATE, HENCHMAN

following TRADE, RETINUE, NEXT, SECT, AFTER, SINCE, PUBLIC, SEQUENT, SUCCESSIVE, VOCATION, PROFESSION

folly IDIOCY, DESIPIENCE, LUNACY, MADNESS, FOOLISHNESS, IMBECILITY, LEVITY, IMPRUDENCE, NONSENSE, INDISCRETION

foment INCITE, FIRE, PROVOKE, BREW, ABET, SPUT, STUPE, EXCITE, INSTIGATE, STIMULATE, PROMOTE

fomentation STUPE, EXCITATION, INSTIGATION

fond DEVOTED, LOVING, FOOLISH, SILLY, ARDENT, PARENTAL, DOTING, EMPTY, VAIN, TENDER

fondle CARESS, COSSET, INGLE, PET, CUDDLE, CODDLE, BLANDISH, INDULGE

fondness LOVE, DESIRE, LIKING, RELISH, AFFECTION, PARTIALITY, PREDILECTION

font LAVER, STOUP, SPRING, SOURCE, FOUNTAIN, BASIN

holy water STOUP

fontanel OPENING, VACUITY

food CUISINE, TABLE, MENU, MEAL, PLATE, FEAST, SNACK, ALIMENT, DIET, GRUB, CHOW, FARE, NUTRIMENT, DISH, MESS, VIANDS, PABULUM, EATS, MANNA, MEAT, FEED, FODDER, FORAGE, PAP, BREAD, SUSTENANCE, NOURISHMENT, PROVISIONS, VICTUALS, RATION, BOARD, POI

animal FORAGE, GRAIN, FODDER, FEED, GRASS, PROVENDER

choice CATES, PASTRY

combining form TROPH(O)

excessive desire for BULIMIA

lacking desire ASITIA

Latin for CIBUS

miracle MANNA

of gods AMBROSIA, AMRITA, MANNA
pertaining to CIBARIAN
perverted desire for PICA
provide(r) CATER(ER)
room for SPENCE
semi-digested CHYME
soft PAP
fool OAF, CLOWN, GOOSE, DOPE, DUPE, NINNY, MORON, JESTER, ANTIC, COMIC, STOOGE, DROLL, SAP, DOTARD, IDIOT, ASS, JERK, SIMP(LETON), DOLT, BUFFOON, BUTT, RACA, TRIFLE, DALLY, ZANY, CHEAT, TRICK, DECEIVE, GULL, COZEN
foolhardy RASH, BOLD, DARING, RECKLESS, BRASH, ICARIAN, VENTUROUS, INCAUTIOUS, DESPERATE
foolish HARISH, INEPT, MAD, INANE, SIMPLE, DAFT, SILLY, DESIPIENT, ZANY, PUERILE, ASININE, IDIOTIC, SENSELESS, WITLESS, UNWISE, NONSENSICAL, ABSURD, RIDICULOUS, IMPRUDENT
fool's *bauble* MAROTTE
gold PYRITES
stitch TRICOT
foot PAD, PAW, PES, PEDIS, DOG, HOOF, SOLE, BASE, BOTTOM, FIGURE, CAST, ADD, SUM, TOTAL, PAY, SETTLE, DISCHARGE, MEASURE, PEDESTAL
and mouth disease MURRAIN
bone of ASTRAGALUS, CUBOID, CALCIS, SCAPHOID
combining form PED(I), PEDO, POD(O)
deformity TALIPES, PLANUS
having PEDATE
lever PEDAL
like part PES

not having APOD
oar-shaped REMIPED
pertaining to PODAL, PEDAL
  sole PLANTAR
poetic IAMB, ANAPAEST, DACTYL
print, animal's PUG, TRACK, MARK, SPORE, SLOT
three-syllable ANAPAEST, DACTYL
two-syllable SPONDEE, IAMBUS, TROCHEE
football *field* GRID
pass LATERAL, FORWARD
player END, BACK, GUARD, TACKLE, CENTER
Rugby FIVES
team, American ELEVEN, RAMS, COLTS, EAGLES, BROWNS, LIONS, IRISH
term PUNT, DOWN, PASS, GOAL
types RUGBY, ASSOCIATION
footed, *large* MEGAPOD
footing BASE, BASIS, TERM, PURCHASE, FOOTHOLD, GROUNDWORK, STANDING, STATUS, CONDITION, TOTAL, FOUNDATION, SUPPORT
footless APODAL, UNSUBSTANTIAL, CLUMSY, STUPID
foot-loose FREE, NOMADIC, UNTRAMMELED
footpad WHYO, THUG, BANDIT, HOOD, ROBBER, HIGHWAYMAN, GANGSTER *See* "bandit"
footprint mold MOULAGE
footrace, *double course* DIAULOS
footstalk STRIG, PEDICEL, PETIOLE, PEDUNCLE
footstool HASSOCK, OTTOMAN
fop DUDE, NOB, ADON, BUCK, PUPPY, DANDY, TOFF, SWELL, COX-

COMB, MACARONI, POPINJAY
for BECAUSE, PRO, SINCE, AS, INSTEAD, TOWARD, CONCERNING, DESPITE, FAVORING
aye ALWAYS, EVER
example VIDE, E.G.
fear that LEST
instance E.G., AS
this case alone AD HOC
this reason HENCE, ERGO
forage FOOD, FODDER, GRUB, EATS, CHOW, HAY, PROVENDER, PLUNDER, RAVAGE, SEARCH, RAID
plant ALFALFA, CLOVER
foramen PORE, OPENING, ORIFICE, APERTURE, PERFORATION
foray INCURSION, RAID, PILLAGE, INROAD, INVASION, SALLY
forbear SPARE, STOP, FOREGO, RESTRAIN, ABSTAIN, ESCHEW, ENDURE, TOLERATE, PAUSE, WAIT, CEASE, AVOID, SHUN
forbearance MERCY, PATIENCE, GRACE, CLEMENCY, MILDNESS, ABSTINENCE, AVOIDANCE, PITY
forbearing TOLERANT, GENTLE, MILD, PATIENT, LENIENT
forbid EXCLUDE, DEBAR, ENJOIN, BAN, TABU, TABOO, INHIBIT, VETO, PROHIBIT, INTERDICT, PRECLUDE, PROSCRIBE, DISALLOW
forbidden city LHASA, LASSA
forbidding REPELLENT, UGLY, STERN, PLAIN, GRIM, ODIOUS, OFFENSIVE
force STAFF, EMPLOYEES, CREW, ENERGY, STRENGTH, VIGOR, VIM, EMPHASIS, POTENCY, COGENCY, VIOLENCE, COMPUL-

SION, COERCION,
DRIVE, ORDER,
EXACT, STRESS,
DURESS, EFFORT,
BRAWN, STRAIN,
MIGHT, DINT, COM-
PEL, VIS, IMPEL,
POWER, ARMY, NAVY,
POSSE, TROOP,
BRUNT, FACULTY
alleged OD,
ODYL(E), ELOD
brief and sudden
BRUNT
by AMAIN
down DETRUDE,
TRAMPLE, TAMP,
PACK
hypothetical See
"alleged" *above*
organized ARMY,
NAVY, POSSE,
POLICE
out EXPEL, EVICT,
OUST
unit of STAFF, DYNE
with AMAIN
forced feeding GAVAGE
forcemeat FARCE
forcibly AMAIN,
POTENTLY, COGENTLY,
MIGHTILY, VIOLENTLY,
PERFORCE
ford WADE, CROSS,
STREAM, CURRENT
Fordham's team RAMS
fore PRIOR, FRONT,
VAN, FORMER,
EARLIER, FIRST,
ANTERIOR, PREVIOUS
forearm ANTE-
BRACHIUM
bone ULNA, RADIUS
pertaining to ULNAR
foreboding MENACING,
AUGURY, OMEN,
PORTENT, PREDICTION,
PRESAGE, PREMONI-
TION, CROAKING
forecast PREDICT,
AUGUR, FORETELL,
ANTICIPATE, PLAN,
PROPHECY, CONTRIVE,
SCHEME
forecaster SEER,
PROPHET, SOOTH-
SAYER, PROGNOSTI-
CATOR
forefather SIRE, AN-
CESTOR, PROGENITOR
forefoot PAW

foregoing FORMER,
PAST, PRIOR, PRE-
FIX, PRECEDING,
PREVIOUS, ANTECED-
ENT
forehead BROW,
SINCIPUT, METOPION,
FRONS
pertaining to
METOPIC, SINCIPITAL
foreign ECDEMIC,
PEREGRINE, ALIEN,
OUTSIDE, OUTER,
ABROAD, EPIGENE,
FORANE, STRANGE,
EXOTIC, EXTRANEOUS,
EXTRINSIC, ADVENTI-
TIOUS
quarter ENCLAVE
foreigner ALIEN,
GRINGO, EMIGRE,
OUTSIDER, PEREGRINE
foremost MAIN,
CAPITAL, VAN, FRONT,
FIRST, CHIEF, BEST,
LEADING
forerun SCOUT,
ANTECEDE, HERALD,
USHER, INTRODUCE,
PRELUDE
foreshadow ADUM-
BRATE, PRESAGE, SUG-
GEST, INDICATE, PRE-
FIGURE, FOREBODE,
PROGNOSTICATE
foreshank SHIN
forest WOOD, GROVE,
WOODLAND, TIMBER,
SILVA, SYLVA
fire locater ALIDADE
glade CAMAS(S),
CLEARING
keeper RANGER
open space in CLEAR-
ING, GLADE,
CAMAS(S)
pertaining to
NEMORAL, SYLVAN
road TRAIL, RIDE
seasonally flooded
GAPO
Siberian TAIGA
small GROVE,
THICKET
treeless WOLD
trees SILVA, SYLVA
foretell PREDICT,
PROPHESY, AUGUR,
BODE, FORESHOW,
BETOKEN, PRESAGE,
PRESIGNIFY,
PROGNOSTICATE

foretelling FATIDIC,
PROPHETIC
foretoken OMEN,
AUGUR(Y), PORTENT,
SIGN, SYMPTOM
forever AYE, ALWAYS,
EVER, ETERNALLY,
CONTINUALLY, CON-
STANTLY, EVERLAST-
INGLY, PERPETUALLY,
CEASELESSLY,
ETERNITY
forewarning OMEN,
PORTENT, CAUTION,
ADVICE
forfeit PENALTY, FINE,
LOSE, SURRENDER,
MULCT
to God DEODAND
forfeiture FINE, DEBIT,
LOSS, AMERCEMENT,
CONFISCATION,
PENALTY
forge FASHION, FORM,
SMITHY, MAKE, MINT,
IMITATE, SHAPE,
FURNACE, FRAME,
FABRICATE, INVENT,
COIN, FALSIFY,
FEIGN
tongs TEW
waste SPRUE, DROSS
forget OMIT, SLIGHT,
NEGLECT, IGNORE,
OVERLOOK, DISREGARD
forgetfulness LETHE,
OBLIVION, NEGLI-
GENCE, CARELESSNESS
fruit of LOTUS
tree of LOTUS
water of LETHE
forgive PARDON,
REMIT, EXCUSE,
ABSOLVE, ACQUIT,
FORGET
for(e)go QUIT, DENY,
NEGLECT, RESIGN,
WAIVE, ABDICATE,
LEAVE, FORSAKE,
RENOUNCE
fork BISECT, DIVERGE,
(BI)FURCATE,
DIVARICATE, GRAIP,
PRONG, TINE,
BRANCH, CROTCH,
WYE
forlorn DESOLATE,
LONELY, LORN,
(A)LONE, VAIN, HOPE-
LESS, ABANDONED,
WRETCHED, ABJECT,

SOLITARY, DIS-
CONSOLATE
form CAST, CONTOUR,
MOLD, FIGURE, PLOT,
SHAPE, MAKE, FRAME,
BUILD, OUTLINE,
SCHEME, BLANK,
PLAN, DEVISE, RITE,
RITUAL, USAGE,
FASHION, INVENT,
CREATE, PATTERN,
CONFORMATION,
FORMAT, CUT, MODE,
COMPOSE, WRITE,
CONSTITUTE, MODEL,
CONCEIVE
philosophy EIDOS
formal PRIM, REGULAR,
CONVENTIONAL, STIFF,
DRESS
formation, *battle*
HERSE, COLUMN,
LINE
former EX, PRIOR,
EARLIER, PREVIOUS,
ANTERIOR, ANTECED-
ENT, QUONDAM, ONE-
TIME, WHILOM
formerly ERST, NEE,
ONCE, THEN, AGO,
HERETOFORE, AFORE-
TIME
formicid ANT
formless CHAOTIC,
FLUID, LIQUID,
ROUGH, RAW, CRUDE,
ANIDIAN, ARUPA,
SHAPELESS,
AMORPHOUS
Formosa TAIWAN
town SHOKA
formula CREED, LAW,
RULE, LURRY,
RITUAL, RECIPE,
FORM, MODEL,
PRESCRIPTION
formulate FRAME,
DEVISE, MAKE, PLAN,
COMPOSE, WRITE
forsake DESERT,
ABANDON, QUIT, RE-
SIGN, LEAVE, RE-
NOUNCE, FORSWEAR,
FOREGO, RELINQUISH
forsaken LORN,
DESERTED, REJECTED,
ABANDONED *See*
"forlorn"
fort ABATIS, DUN,
BULWARK, CITADEL,
STOCKADE, GARRISON,

FORTRESS, STRONG-
HOLD, CASTLE, POST
enclosed LIS(S)
sloping bank of
GLACIS
forth OUT, FORWARD,
ONWARD, ABROAD,
AHEAD
forthwith NOW,
DIRECTLY, IM-
MEDIATELY, IN-
STANTLY, PROMPTLY
fortification REDOUBT,
REDAN, ESCARP,
BASTION, RAVELIN,
RAMPART, TOWER
See "fort"
slope TALUS
work REDAN
fortify GIRD, EMBAT-
TLE, ARM, MAN,
BRACE, STRENGTHEN
fortress ALCAZAR,
CITADEL, KEEP, CAMP,
BASTILLE, DONJON
outwork of
TENAIL(LE)
fortuitous CHANCE,
HAP, CASUAL, RANDOM,
ACCIDENTAL, IN-
CIDENTAL, ADVENTI-
TIOUS, UNDESIGNED
fortunate DEXTER,
FAUST, BLEST, LUCKY,
HAPPY, PROSPEROUS,
FAVORED, SUCCESSFUL
fortune HAP, ESTATE,
LOT, STAR, LUCK,
CHANCE, HAZARD,
FATE, PORTION, DOOM,
BREAK, ACCIDENT,
FORTUITY, WEALTH,
RICHES, OPULENCE,
PROSPERITY, DESTINY
teller SIBYL, ORACLE,
SEER, PALMIST,
PROPHETESS
forty *days* LENT
forty-five *degree angle*
OCTANT
inches ELL
forty-two *gallon cask*
TIERCE
forty winks NAP
forward PERT, ACTIVE,
VAIN, EAGER, ON,
SEND, SHIP, FRESH,
FLIP, CONFIDENT,
BRAZEN, FRONT,
AHEAD, (A)FORE, BE-
FORE, ONWARD,
FORTH, FURTHER, PRO-

MOTE, HELP, AID, AS-
SIST, SPEED, BOLD,
ADVANCING, PROGRES-
SIVE, READY, PROMPT,
SUPPORT, TRANSMIT
foss(e) DITCH, MOAT,
TRENCH, CANAL, GRAFF
fossil RELIC, STONE,
BALANITE, PETRIFICA-
TION, FOGY, AMBER
egg OVULITE
footprint ICHNITE
mollusk DOLITE
resin AMBER,
RETINITE
shell DOLITE,
BALANITE
toothlike CONODONT
worm track NEREITE
foster REAR, BREED,
NURSE, AID, CHERISH,
SUPPORT, LODGE,
HOUSE, HARBOR,
FAVOR, OBLIGE,
NOURISH, FEED,
MOTHER, COSSET
child DALT, NURRY,
NORRY, STEPSON
foul SOILED, DIRTY,
FILTHY, NASTY,
SQUALID, FETID, GROSS,
VULGAR, COARSE, VILE,
OBSCENE, IMPURE,
POLLUTED, SULLIED,
RANK, PUTRID, ODIOUS,
NOISOME
foulard TIE, HANDKER-
CHIEF, NECKERCHIEF
found START, BEGIN,
BASE, ESTABLISH,
BUILD, CONSTRUCT,
ERECT, RAISE, SET,
FIX, ORIGINATE, IN-
STITUTE, SETTLE
treasure TROVE
foundation BEDROCK,
BED, BASE, BASIS,
GROUND, FOOTING,
BOTTOM, ESTABLISH-
MENT, SETTLEMENT,
SUPPORT
founder ORIGINATOR,
AUTHOR, FAIL, MIS-
CARRY, STUMBLE,
WELTER, SWAMP,
ASTONISH, DISMAY,
SINK, CRASH
fountain WELL, AQUA,
FONT, HEAD, SPRING,
FONS, JET, SPRAY,
SOURCE, RESERVOIR,
UPWELLING

god of FONS
nymph NAIAD, EGERIA
of youth site BIMINI
four IV
bagger HOMER, SCORE, TALLY
combining form TETRA
footed TETRAPOD, QUADRUPED
group of TETRAD
Horsemen, Biblical CONQUEST, WAR, FAMINE, DEATH
inches HAND
in-hand NECKTIE
fourgon TUMBRIL, VAN, WAGON, CAR
fourpence GROAT, FLAG, JOEY
foursome TETRAD, QUARTET, BRIDGE
fourteen pounds STONE
fourth *caliph* ALI
estate PRESS
row DEE
foveated PITTED
fowl BIRD, CAPON, POULT, COCK, HEN, TURKEY, POULTRY
gizzard GIBLET
fox CUB, TOD, VIXEN
Africa CAAMA, ASSE, FENNEC
Asia ADIVE, CORSAC
female VIXEN
flying KALONG
genus VULPES
hunter's coat PINK
killer VULPICIDE
male STAG
paw PAD
Russian CORSAK, KARAGAN
foxtail GRASS, BRUSH
foxy SLY, WILY, VULPINE, CRAFTY, CUNNING, ARTFUL
fracas *See* "brawl"
fraction PART, PARCEL, SHARE, PIECE, SECTOR, DETAIL, PORTION, BIT, SCRAP
fracture SPLIT, BREAK, CRACK, REND, RUPTURE, FISSURE
fragile FRAIL, WEAK, CRISP, FROUGH, BRITTLE, DELICATE, FRANGIBLE, FRIABLE

fragment PIECE, PART, SECTION, PORTION, DETAIL, REMNANT, SNIP, ORT, SCRAP, SHARD, BIT, WISP, CHIP, FRACTION, SWATCH
fragrance SPICE, ODOR, AROMA, INCENSE, ATTAR, SCENT, SMELL, PERFUME, REDOLENCE, BOUQUET
fragrant BALMY, OLENT, REDOLENT, AROMATIC, SPICY, SWEET
ointment VALERIAN, NARD
wood MIMOSA, ALOE, CEDAR
frail SLIM, WEAK, FLIMSY, SEELY, FEEBLE, INFIRM, SLIGHT, SLENDER, PUNY, FRAGILE, FRANGIBLE, DELICATE, BRITTLE
frailty ADAM, FAULT, DEFECT, FAILING, FOIBLE, VICE, FLAW, BLEMISH, IMPERFECTION
framb(o)esia YAWS, PIAN
frame BIN, CARCASS, CHASSIS, RACK, PATTERN, SKELETON, STRUCTURE, SHAPE, FORM, PLOT, BUILD, CADRE, MAKE, CONSTRUCT, COMPOSE, INVENT, DEVISE, CONTRIVE, FORGE, HUMOR, MOOD, FASHION, BORDER
bar of soap SESS
cloth stretching TENTER
counting ABACUS
fish line CADER, CADAR
glass making DROSSER
of mind MOOD, BENT, HUMOR
ship's table FIDDLE
skin drying HERSE
supporting TRESTLE, HORSE
torch CRESSET
framework TRUSS, SKELETON, CRADLE, CADRE, SHELL,

STRUCTURE, SUPPORT
See "frame"
France, French
airplane AVION, SPAD
among ENTRE
and ET
annuity RENTE
art group FAUVES
article LA, LE, LES, UN(E), UNES
artist See "painter" *below*
assembly SENAT
aunt TANTE
author RENAN, DUMAS, HUGO, RACINE, CAMUS, SARTRE, GIDE, LOTI, ZOLA, STAEL, VOLTAIRE, VILLON, DAUDET, BENDA, PROUST, SAND
axe HACHE
baby BEBE, ENFANT, POUPEE
bay BISCAY
beach PLAGE, RIVE, RIVAGE
bean FEVE, HARICOT
beast BETE
beauty BEAUTE, NINON
bed LIT, COUCHE
beef BOEUF
beware GARDE
bicycle VELO
bitter AMER(TUME)
black NOIR
blessed SACRE, BENI
blue BLEU
bonds RENTES
bread PAIN
brown BIS, BRUN
bulk(y) GROS
coffee CAFE
cake GATEAU
Cardinal MAZARIN, RICHELIEU
chalk TALC
champagne AY
chanteuse PIAF
cheese BRIE
chemist PASTEUR, HOLBACH
city AGEN, CASTRES, ARLES, LILLE, CAEN, RIOM, TARARE, AMIENS, AIX, PAV, CANNES, NIMES, PARIS, SENS, ALBI, ALES, TOUL, BONY
See "town" *below*
cleric ABBE

cloth DRAP, TOILE
cloud NUE(E), NUAGE
coach FIACRE
coin LIARD, OBOLE,
SCUTE, ECU, SOU, SOL,
FRANC, LOUIS D'OR,
HENRI, LILY, LIVRE,
MAIL, TESTON, RIAL
cooking style SAUTE
commune NERAC,
CENON, ANCRE,
TERARE, USSEL, PAU,
PESSAC, DOLE, REZE,
RODEZ, STAINS, CROIX,
LAVAL, LAON, SANVIC,
ALBI, VICHY
company CIE
composer BIZET,
LALO, INDY, FAURE,
HALEVY, RAVEL
concrete BETON
conqueror CLOVIS
couturier DIOR
cowardly LACHE
critic TAINE
crude CRU
dance BAL,
GAVOT(TE)
daughter FILLE
dear CHER(E)
decree ARRET
deed FAIT
department See
"province" and
"region" *below*
head of PREFET,
PERFECT
devil DIABLE
dialect PATOIS
diplomat GENET
district BRIE
down BAS
dramatist DUMAS
dream REVE(R),
SONGE(R)
dry SEC
duke DUC
dungeon CACHOT
dynasty CAPET,
VALOIS
egg OEUF
empress EUGENIE
enamelware LIMOGES
equal(ity) EGAL(ITE)
eye OEIL
exclamation HEIN
explorer CARTIER
extravagant OUTRE,
PRODIGUE
fabric LAME, RAS,
ETOFFE, TISSU
father PERE

finally ENFIN
five CINQ
fortification PARADOS
friend AMI(E)
game JEU
gift CADEAU
God DIEU
good BON
goodbye ADIEU
gorilla fighters
MAQUIS
gravy JUS
gray GRIS
grimace MOUE
head TETE
help AIDE(R)
here ICI
historian THIERS,
RENAN, GUIZOT,
SEGUR
home LOGIS, CHEZ
SOI
honeysuckle SULLA
house MAISON
illustrator DORE
impressionist MONET
income RENTE
inn HOTEL, AUBERGE
island(s) ILE,
CORSICA, OCEANIA,
OLERON, COMORO,
LOOS, YEU, IF
knife COUTEAU
lace ALENCON, CLUNY
lampoon SATIRE
laugh RIS, RIRE
leather CUIR
leave CONGE
lively VIF, GAI, VIVANT
luxury LUXE
lyric form RONDEL
maid BONNE
marshal FOCH, SAXE,
NEY, MURAT, PETAIN
material DRAP
means RESSORT
measure KILO,
ARPEN(T), MINOT,
ARE, TOISE, ELL, AUNE,
POT, VELT(E),
CENTIARE, HECTARE,
DECARE, KILAIRE,
LIGNE, MICRON,
POUCE, TOISE
merry GAI
military leader FOCH
milk LAIT
misdemeanor DELIT
month MOIS, MAI,
MARS, JUIN
morning MATIN
motion GESTE

mountain(s) JURA,
VOSGES, DORE
peak CENIS, BLANC
museum MUSEE
nail CLOU
nobleman COMTE,
DUC
noon MIDI
not MON, NE PAS
nothing RIEN
novelist See "author"
above
painter MONET,
MANET, DAUBIGNY,
DEGAS, COROT,
LEMOYNE, MILLET,
RENOIR, DOYEN,
CHAGALL, DERAIN,
BRAQUE, UTRILLO,
MATISSE, DORE
pancake CREPE
pastry BABA
patron saint DENIS
paving brick DALLE
permission CONGE
philosopher ABELARD
physicist CURIE,
AMPERE
plane AVION, SPAD
pocket POCHE
poem VERS
poet MAROT, BAIF,
VILLON
political club JACOBIN
porcelain VENDEE,
SEVRES
port CAEN, BREST,
HAVRE, SETE
pretty JOLI
pronoun MOI, TU,
ELLE(S), IL(S), NOUS,
VOUS, NOTRE, VOTRE
province AIN, AISNE,
ALLIER, ARDECHE,
ARDENNES, ARIEGE,
AUBE, AUDE, AVEYRON,
CALVADOS, CANTAL,
CHARENTE, CHER,
CORREZE, CORSE,
COTE-D'OR, CREUSE,
DORDOGNE, DOUBS,
DROME, EURE, GARD,
GERS, GIRONDE,
HERAULT, INDRE,
ISERE, JURA, YONNE,
LANDES, LOIRE,
LORIET, LOT, LOZERE,
MANCHE, MARNE,
MAYENNE, MEUSE,
MORDIHAN, MOSELLE,
NIEVRE, NORD, OISE,
ORNE, BAS-RHIN,

HAUT-RHIN, RHONE, SARTHE, SAVOIE, SEINE, SOMME, TARN, VAR, VAUCLUSE, VENDEE, VIENNE, VOSGES
priest ABBE
psychologist BINET
pupil ELEVE
railway station GARE
recruit RECRUE
refugee EMIGRE
region LORRAINE, POITOU, ANJOU, GASCOGNE (GASCONY), PICARDIE (PICARDY), NORMANDIE (NORMANDY), BRETAGNE (BRITTANY), ALSACE, BEARN, NAVARRE, BOURGOGNE (BURGUNDY)
republic ANDORRA
resort CANNES, ANTIBES, NICE, PAU
revolutionist MARAT, DANTON
ridge VIMY
river See under "river"
roast ROTI
royal family VALOIS, CAPET
ruler, early PIPPIN, PEPIN
saint, patron DENIS
savant AMYOT
saying DIT
scholar ELEVE, ECOLIER(E)
school ECOLE, LYCEE
  child ELEVE
sculptor BARYE, RODIN, ETEX, BARTHOLDI
sea MER
she ELLE
shelter ABRI, COUVERT
shield EGIDE, BOUCLIER
shooting gallery TIR
silk SOIE
silk center LYONS, ARLES
singer PIAF, SABLON, PONS, CALVE
sister SOEUR
soldier POILU, ZOUAVE, SOLDAT
son FILS
soul AME

south MIDI, SUD
southeastern SAVOY
spirit AME, ELAN, ESPRIT
stable ECURIE
star ETOILE
station GARE
stoneware GRES
storm ORAGE
street RUE
style TON
summer ETE
surgeon PARE
sweetbreads RIS
target TARGE
then ALORS, DONC
thy TES
town ST LO, AGEN, CRECY, NESLE, NERAC, RIOM, SETE, HAM, ORLY, RENNES, NIMES, NIORT, SENS, ANCRE, SENLIS, VAUX, VALMY, LUZ, LENS, PAU, DAX, AY
  See "city" above
trade license PATENTE
true VRAI
Tuesday MARDI
underground troops MAQUIS
verse RONDEL, VERS
vineyard CRU, VIGNE
wall MUR
water EAU
weight GROS, GRAMME, KILO, LIVRE, ONCE, MARC
where OU
wine See under "wine"
wood BOIS
woodland FORET
world MONDE
writer See "author" above
yellow JAUNE
franchise RIGHT, CHARTER, SUFFRAGE, VOTE, BALLOT, PRIVILEGE, IMMUNITY, ASYLUM
Old English SOC, SOKE, VOTE
Franciscan MINORITE
mission ALAMO
francolin TITAR, PARTRIDGE, BIRD
frank SINCERE, FREE, OPEN, CANDID, PLAIN, SIMPLE, NAIVE, IN-

GENUOUS, ARTLESS, DIRECT, GUILELESS, GENUINE, EXEMPT, SIGN, MARK, MAIL
frankincense OLIBANUM, THUS, INCENSE, GUM, RESIN
Frankish *king* CLOVIS
  law SALIC
  peasant(s) LITUS, LITI
  pertaining to SALIC
  vassal LEUD
frantic WILD, MAD, INSANE, AVID, CRAZED, EXCITED, PHRENETIC, FURIOUS, RAVING, DISTRACTED, FRENZIED, RABID
fraud CHEAT, SHAM, GUILE, FAKE, BUNCO, DECEIT, COVIN, IMPOSTURE, DECEPTION, DUPLICITY, ARTIFICE, HOAX
fraught LADEN, CHARGED, FULL, FILLED, BURDENED, FREIGHTED
fraxinus ASH, TREE
fray RUCTION, TIFFLE, HASSLE, RUB, MELEE, WEAR, RAVEL See "fight"
freak CAPRICE, FLAM, VAGARY, NOTION, IDEA, WHIM, FANCY, PRANK, HUMOR, QUIRK, ANTIC, CAPER, MONSTROSITY
freckle SPOT, TACHE, LENTIGO
Frederick the Great ALTE FRITZ
free ABSOLVE, DELIVER, RELIEVE, CLEAR, LAX, FRANK, UNTIE, GRATIS, RID, LOOSE(N), MANUMIT, LIBERATE, RELEASE, INDEPENDENT, UNRESTRAINED, BONDLESS, EMANCIPATE, RANSOM, AUTONOMOUS, EXEMPT, IMMUNE, GENEROUS, LIBERAL, PRODIGAL
  from discount NET
ticket PASS
freebooter CATERAN, PIRATE, CORSAIR See "bandit"
freeholder YEOMAN

freeman CEORL, THANE, THEGN

freemason TEMPLAR

freeze ICE, CHILL, CONGEAL, SOLIDIFY, BENUMB, GLACIATE, STABILIZE, KILL

freight CARGO, LOAD, BURDEN, TRAFFIC, LOADING, LADING

car GONDOLA, SIX

fremd FOREIGN, STRANGE, ALIEN

French *See* "France"

Frenchman PICARD, GAUL, PARISIAN

frenzied ENRAGED, AMOK *See* "frantic"

frenzy RAGE, MANIA, FURY, MADNESS, INSANITY, LUNACY, DERANGEMENT, DELIRIUM, ABERRATION

frequent HAUNT, GO, OFT, OFTEN, USUAL, RESORT, TURN, ITERATE, FAMILIAR, HABITUAL

fresh NEW, NOVEL, COOL, KEEN, RAW, GREEN, RECENT, BLOOMING, REVIVED, UNWILTED, HEALTHY, HARDY, VIVID, LIVELY, UNTRAINED, FLIP, SASSY, BRASSY

freshet SPATE, TORRENT, FLOOD, STREAM, CURRENT, INUNDATION

freshman TIRO, TYRO, NOVICE, PLEBE, STUDENT

fret WORRY, FUME, ABRADE, CHAFE, GALL, IRK, NETTLE, NAG, ORP, VEX, RUB, ANNOY, HARASS, PLAGUE

Freudian term EGO, ID

Frey's *wife* GERTH

friable MEALY, CRUMBLING, FRAGILE, BRITTLE, CRISP, SHORT, FRAIL

friar LISTER, MONK, FRA, MINOR, BROTHER, ABBOT

bird PIMLICO

black DOMINICAN

gray FRANCISCAN

mendicant SERVITE

Robin Hood's TUCK

white CARMELITE

fricative SPIRANT, RUSTLING, CONSONANT, HISS

friction RUB, CONFLICT, GRATING, ATTRITION, ABRASION, DISSENSION, DISAGREEMENT, WRANGLING, CLASHING

friend PATRON, ALLY, QUAKER, CRONY, CHUM, PAL, AMI(E), CONFIDANTE, INTIMATE, COMPANION, ASSOCIATE, CONFRERE, ADVOCATE, BUDDY

faithful ACHATES, DOG

false JUDAS, TRAITOR

friendly AMICABLE, KIND, AFFABLE, WARM, CLOSE, AMIABLE, BENEVOLENT, CORDIAL, FRATERNAL, NEIGHBORLY, FAVORABLE, PROPITIOUS

relations AMITY

understanding ENTENTE

Friendly island TONGA

friendship AMITY, ACCORD, COMITY, AFFINITY, ESTEEM, REGARD, FAVOR, LOVE, AFFECTION, FONDNESS, INTIMACY, FELLOWSHIP

frigate bird IWA

Frigg(a)'s *husband* ODIN

maid FULLA

fright DISMAY, HORROR, SCARE, STARTLE, FUNK, OGRE, PANIC, ALARM, AWE, FEAR, TERROR, GAST, DREAD, CONSTERNATION

frigid COLD, ICY, FORMAL, GELID, CHILLY, FROSTY, ARCTIC, COOL, LIFELESS, STIFF

frill RUCHE, JABOT, FURBELOW, RUFFLE, EDGING

fringe EDGE, BORDER, BOUNDARY, RIM, LOMA, THRUM, TASSEL, EDGING, SKIRT, ZIZITH, TRIM,

PERISTOME, FIMBRIATION

frisk SKIP, PLAY, SEARCH, CAPER, DANCE, FROLIC, SPORT, LEAP, HOP, JUMP, ROMP, GAMBOL, PRANCE

fritted EATEN, ERODED, WASTED, LESSENED

fritter DALLY, DAWDLE, BANGLE, CAKE, FRAGMENT, SHRED, DISPERSE, SCATTER, WASTE

frivolity LEVITY, FOLLY, PLAY, SPORT, FUN, JEST, TRIFLING, FLUMMERY

fro BACK, FROM, HITHER, AWAY, BACKWARD

frock ROBE, GARMENT, SOUTANE, GOWN, JAM, COAT, KIRTLE, TUNIC, MANTLE

frog POLLIWOG, ANURAN, AMPHIBIAN, TOAD, BRAID, HOARSENESS

combining form BATRACHO(S), RANI

genus ANURA, RANA, HYLA

like RANINE

pertaining to BATRACHIAN

tree genus HYLA

frolic MARLOCK, FUN, LARK, ROMP, PRANK, SPORT, DIDO, ANTIC, JEST, PLAY, CAPER, FRISK, PLOY, SPREE, PICNIC, GAMBOL, ESCAPADE, GAIETY, MIRTH

from AB, FRO, DE, SINCE

front FACADE, OBVERSE, VAN, FORE, FACE, ANTERO, MIEN, MANNER, PORT, FOREHEAD, EFFRONTERY, IMPUDENCE, BRASS, DIAL

extend the DEPLOY

in ANTEAL, FORNE, AHEAD

frontier BORDER, BOUNDARY, BACKWOODS

post FORT

frontlet TIARA, BAND, FACADE, VALANCE, FOREHEAD, FRONT-STALL

frost RIME, HOAR, ICE, FRIGIDITY, UN-SOCIABILITY

covered ICED, RIMED, HOARY

frostfish TOMCOD, SMELT, SCABBARD, WHITEFISH

frosty RIMY, ICY, COOL *See* "frigid"

froth SUDS, FOAM, SPUME, YEAST, SCUM, LATHER, LEVITY, TRIVIALITY, NONSENSE, BOSH

frothy SPUMY, TRIVIAL, EMPTY, VAIN, FRIVOLOUS, UN-SUBSTANTIAL, LIGHT

froufrou RUSTLE, STIR, LACE, HUMMINGBIRD

frow DAME, WIFE, SLATTERN, WOMAN, KNIFE, FROE

frown LOWER, LOUR, SCOWL, MOUE, GLOWER, REBUKE, DISAPPROVE

frowning GLUM, DOUR, SURLY

frozen ICED, CHILLY, GLACE, GELID, FRAPPE, CONGEALED, UN-SYMPATHETIC, FIXED

dessert ICE, MOUSSE, SHERBET

vapor FROST, RIME

frugal ECONOMICAL, CHARY, SPARE, SPARING, TIGHT, THRIFTY, SAVING, PROVIDENT, CAREFUL, UNWASTEFUL, TEMPERATE

fruit OUTCOME, EF-FECT, YIELD, RE-SULT(S), CROP, OFF-SPRING, PRODUCE, PROFIT, ORANGE, APPLE, PEAR, BERRY, NUT

aggregate ETAERIO, STRAWBERRY, RASP-BERRY, MAGNOLIA

American tree genus SAPOTA

beverage ADE, WINE

blemish BLET, SPOT

combining form CARPO

cordial RATAFIA

decay BLET, ROT

dish COMPOTE

dried PASA, PRUNE, CURRANT, RAISIN

drupaceous PEACH, CHERRY, PLUM

dry REGMA, LEGUME, NUT, ACHENE

envelope BUR(R), RIND

flesh PULP, PAP

fleshy BERRY, MELON, APPLE, ORANGE, PEAR, POME, GRAPE, TOMATO, PLUM, CHERRY

goddess POMONA

gourd family PEPO

  fruit PUMPKIN, MELON, SQUASH, CUCUMBER

hard-shelled NUT, GOURD

hybrid POMATO

jar MASON

  ring LUTE, RUBBER, GASKET

lemonlike CITRON, LIME

maple SAMARA

outer covering RIND, BUR(R)

peddler COSTER

pertaining to POMONIC, POMONAL

preserve JELLY, JAM, CONSERVE

pulp PAP

pulpy DRUPE, UVA

refuse MARC

rose HIP

science of CARPOLOGY

seller COSTER

skin EPICARP, RIND, PEEL

squeezer REAMER

tapiocalike SALEP

tomatolike POMATO

tree genus OLEA

tropical INCA, MANGO, CITRUS, ORANGE, BANANA, LIME, LEMON

yellow PAWPAW, PAPAW, PAPAYA

fruiterer COSTER

fruitful GRAVID, PROLIFIC, FERTILE, PRODUCTIVE, FECUND, RICH, ABUNDANT

fruitless IDLE, EMPTY, HOLLOW, STERILE, FUTILE, VAIN, BARREN, INEFFECTUAL, USE-LESS, UNPRODUCTIVE

frustrate THWART, DASH, FOIL, CROSS, BAFFLE, BALK, OUT-WIT, DEFEAT, DIS-CONCERT, BLOCK, CIRCUMVENT, CHECK, DISAPPOINT, ANIENTIZE

frustration DEFEAT, BALKING

frying pan SKILLET, SPIDER

fuddle MUDDLE, BOOZE, TOPE

Fuegian ONA

fuel PEAT, WOOD, COKE, COAL, GAS, OIL, COMBUSTIBLES, FOOD

supply with STOKE, FEED

fugitive EXILE, RUN-AWAY, DESERTER, REFUGEE, FLEETING, SHORT, VOLATILE, TRANSITORY, UNCER-TAIN, UNSTABLE, TEMPORAL, MOMENTARY

fugue DIATONIC, TONAL, THEME, DORIAN

answer COMES

special passage STRETTA

theme DUX

fulcrum PROP, SHORE, STAY, THOLE, SUP-PORT, BAIT

oar THOLE, LOCK

fulfill REALIZE, ATTAIN, ACHIEVE, REACH, SATISFY, MEET, EF-FECT, ANSWER, AC-COMPLISH, EXECUTE, COMPLETE, OBSERVE, OBEY, PERFORM, CON-SUMMATE

fulfillment FRUITION, CONSUMMATION

fulgent BRIGHT, RADIANT, SHINING, DAZZLING

fuliginous SOOTY, DARK, DUSKY, SMOKY, OPAQUE, DIM

full REPLETE, SATED,
COMPLETE, COMPACT,
PERFECT, MATURE,
GLUTTED, CLOYED,
GORGED, STUFFED,
BRIMMING, ENTIRE,
ROTUND, PLENARY,
OROTUND
house SRO
of cracks RIMOSE
sized ADULT, RIPE,
GROWN, MATURE
size draft or plan
EPURE
suffix ITOUS, OUS, OSE
fuller's *earth* BOLE
herb TEASEL, TEAZEL
fullness SATIETY,
SURFEIT, PLENUM,
REPLETION, PLETHORA,
PLUMPNESS, PERFEC-
TION, ABUNDANCE
fulmar MALDUCK,
NELLY, BIRD
fulsome OFFENSIVE,
COARSE, GROSS, FOUL,
SATIATING, NAU-
SEATING, SICKENING
fumble FLUB, MUFF,
ERR(OR), BUNGLE,
STUMBLE, BOTCH,
STAMMER, MIS-
MANAGE, PAW
fume STEAM, VAPOR,
RAGE, GAS, FRET,
REEK, ANGER, SMOKE,
SMELL, EXHALATION,
RAVE, BLUSTER, STORM
fuming MAD, ANGRY,
IRATE, RAGING, REEKY,
AREEK
fun SPORT, JOKE,
PLAY, JEST, FROLIC,
JOY, GLEE, MIRTH,
MERRIMENT, PRANKS,
DIVERSION, JOLLITY,
GAIETY
function OFFICE,
PARTY, FACULTY,
CAPACITY, OCCUPA-
TION, POWER, JOB,
TASK, RITE, USE,
DUTY, ROLE, ACT, END,
GOAL, OBJECT, PUR-
POSE, AFFAIR
fund(s) MONEY, CASH,
DEPOSIT, STORE, AS-
SETS, SECURITIES,
RESOURCES
fundamental BASILAR,
BASAL, BASIC,
ELEMENTAL,

ORIGINAL, PRIME,
PRIMAL, PRIMARY,
ESSENTIAL, VITAL,
CHIEF, CAPITAL,
ELEMENTARY,
RADICAL, ABC
trigonometry SINE,
COSINE
funeral RITES,
EXEQUIES, OBSEQUIES,
INTERMENT, BURIAL,
SOLEMNITIES
attendant MUTE
bell MORTBELL
oration ELOGE,
ELOGY, ENCOMIUM
pile PYRE
song DIRGE, ELEGY,
REQUIEM, THRENODY,
NENIA
funereal EXEQUIAL,
SAD, BLACK, DARK,
WOEFUL,
LUGUBRIOUS, SOMBER,
GLOOMY
funest DIRE, FATAL,
DOLEFUL
fungi *See* "fungus"
fungoid tissue TRAMA
fungous SPONGY
fungus, fungi MILDEW,
MOLD, AGARIC,
BOLETUS, YEAST, RUST,
MUSHROOM, TOAD-
STOOL, PUFFBALL,
SMUT, GEASTER,
EARTHSTAR, ERGOT
black ERGOT
cells or sacs ASCI
disease TINEA,
MYCOSIS, FRAMBOESIA
dots TELIA
edible CEPE, MOREL,
TRUFFLE, BLEWITS,
MUSHROOM
genus ERYSIBE,
AMANITA, TUBER,
BOLETUS
growing on rye ERGOT
mushroom MOREL
parasitic ERGOT,
AWETO, TINEA
plant UREDO
rye ERGOT
funicle LIGATURE,
FIBER, STALK, CORD,
FILAMENT
funk FEAR, FRIGHT,
TERROR, PANIC, SHIRK,
FLINCH, SHRINK,
COWARD

funny KILLING, DROLL,
COMIC, JOCOSE,
RISIBLE, WITTY,
COMICAL, QUEER,
LUDICROUS, FARCICAL,
LAUGHABLE,
FACETIOUS, ODD,
STRANGE, CURIOUS
fur PELAGE, COAT,
SKIN, HAIR, PELT,
FITCH, VAIR, NUTRIA,
MARTEN, SABLE,
ERMINE, MINK
bearing animal
MARTEN, GENET,
MINK, SEAL, OTTER
cape STOLE
collection PELTS,
PELTRY
garment PELISSE,
CAPE, STOLE, COAT
regal ERMINE
furbelow FRILL,
FINERY, RUFFLE,
FLOUNCE, ORNAMENT
furbish BUFF, POLISH,
SHINE, CLEAN,
BURNISH, RENEW,
SCRUB, SCOUR
Furies DIRAE,
EUMENIDES
avenging ERINYES
gracious EUMENIDES
the three ALECTO,
MEGAERA, TISIPHONE
furl BUNDLE, ROLL,
CURL, FOLD, STOW,
WRAP
fur-lined tippet AMICE
furlongs, *eight* MILE
furnace SMELTER,
KILN, ETNA, FORGE,
STOVE, HEATER,
VOLCANO
flue TEWEL, PIPE,
CHIMNEY
nozzle TUYERE
part of BOSH, GRATE
tuyere of TEWEL
furnish SUPPLY, YIELD,
CATER, LEND, ENDOW,
EQUIP, OUTFIT, ARM,
CLOTHE, APPOINT,
ENDUE, FEED, PRO-
VIDE, FIT, GIVE, BE-
STOW, GRANT, AFFORD
furnishings MODE,
DECOR, FIXTURES,
FITTINGS, TACKLE,
TOOLS, GEAR, MOVA-
BLES, EQUIPMENT,
APPLIANCES

furniture GOODS, STOCK, GRAITH, EQUIPMENT
parts of SHOOK
furor FLURRY, MANIA, RAGE, TUMULT, FURY, FRENZY, CRAZE, VOGUE, EXCITEMENT
furrow(s) RUT, TRENCH, SEAM, GROOVE, WRINKLE, CHANNEL, SULCUS, TRACK, CHAMFER, FLUTING, PLOW
having GUTTERED, GROOVED, FLUTED
in a plank RABBET
minute STRIA
notch SCORE
furrowing mark FEER, SCRATCH
fur seal URSAL
further AID, ABET, FORWARD, ADVANCE, PROMOTE, BACK, HASTEN, HELP, QUICKEN, STRENGTHEN, ENCOURAGE, MORE, FARTHER, ADDITIONAL, MOREOVER, BESIDES
furtherance HELP, RELIEF, SUCCOR, AID, PROMOTION, ADVANCEMENT
furtive WARY, SECRET, CRAFTY, WILY, ARCH, COVERT, SLY, STEALTHY, SURREPTITIOUS, SKULKING, SNEAKY
fury RAGE, IRE, ANGER, WRATH, FRENZY, VIOLENCE, VEHEMENCE, ERINYS
furze ULEX, GORSE, WHIN, WHUN, PLANT
genus ULEX
fuse MELT, SOLDER, ANNEAL, SMELT, MERGE, COALESCE, WELD, UNITE, WED, JOIN, COMBINE, BLEND, MIX, UNIFY, LIQUEFY, AMALGAMATE
partially FRIT
fusee MATCH, FLARE
fusion ALLIANCE, UNION, LEAGUE, COALITION, COMMIXTURE

fuss ADO, FIKE, FUME, TO-DO, FRET, NIGGLE, NAG, AGITATION, STIR, BUSTLE, FLURRY, PREEN, HASTE, HURRY, FIDGET, WORRY, COMMOTION, DISTURBANCE, POTHER, FLUSTER, DISPUTE, QUARREL
fussy PRISSY, FINICAL, FRETFUL, EXACT, OVERNICE
fustian BOMBASTIC, POMPOUS, TUMID, WORTHLESS, INFLATED
fustigate WHIP, BEAT, CUDGEL, STRIKE
fusty STUFFY, MUSTY, RANCID, RANK, FOUL, PUTRID, FETID, MO(U)LDY, MALODOROUS, STALE
futile IDLE, VAIN, USELESS, TRIVIAL, FRIVOLOUS, TRIFLING, FRUITLESS, INEFFECTUAL, WORTHLESS
future STILL, YET, COMING, PROSPECTIVE, LATER, FIANCE(E), HEREAFTER
fuzz LINT, FUR, DOWN, FIBERS
fylfot EMBLEM, CROSS, SWASTIKA

G

G GEE
gab *See* "chatter"
gabel(le) EXCISE, TAX, IMPOST, DUTY
gabion BASKET, CYLINDER, CAGE
gable PINION, AILERON, WALL, DORMER
gaby FOOL, DUNCE, SIMPLETON
gad ROVE, GOAD, GALLIVANT, RANGE, PROWL, STRAY, ROAM, RAMBLE, SPIKE, BAR, INGOT, WANDER, TRAIPSE
Gad's *father* JACOB
son ERI, OZNI
tribe of ERITES
gadfly OESTRID, BUSYBODY, BOTFLY, BREEZEFLY, TABANID, PEST

gadget TOOL, DEVICE, THINGUM(A)BOB, THING, CONTRIVANCE, DOODAD
Gadhelic GAELIC, IRISH, MANX, ERSE, CELT(IC) *See* "Gaelic"
gadus FISH, COD
gadwall DUCK, FOWL
Gael, Gaelic CELT(IC), ERSE, SCOT(CH), MANX, IRISH, GADHELIC
hero OSSIAN
John IAN
poem DUAN
spirit BANSHEE
warrior DAGDA
gaff SPAR, SPEAR, HOOK, SPUR, GAMBLE, ORDEAL, RAILLERY, HOAX, TRICK, FLEECE
gag CHOKE, RETCH, HOAX, JOKE, JEST, CRACK, QUIP, ANECDOTE, MUZZLE, SILENCE, THROTTLE, OBSTRUCT, MUFFLE
gain REALIZE, WIN, EARN, ATTAIN, APPROACH, REAP, EFFECT, REACH, SECURE, GET, LUCRE, PROFIT, NET, INCREMENT, ACCRETION, ACQUISITION, ADVANTAGE, BENEFIT, WINNING, INCREASE
gainsay DENY, IMPUGN, OPPOSE, REFUTE, RESIST, CONTRADICT, CONTROVERT, DISPUTE, FORBID
gait SHAMBLE, AMBLE, LOPE, STEP, WALK, PACE, STRIDE, TROT, RACK
of horse CANTER, GALLOP, PACE, TROT, LOPE, RACK, VOLT
gaiter PUTTEE, SPAT, STRAD, SHOE, BOOT, LEGGING
gala FESTAL, FESTIVAL, FIESTA, POMP, GAY, FETE, MERRY
Galam SHEA
gale WIND, STORM, BLOW, GUST, BLAST, BREEZE, TEMPEST, OUTBURST

Galician river STYR, SAN

Galilee, *town in* CANA, NAZARETH, TIBERIAS

galipot BARRAS, RESIN, SAP

gall BILE, SPITE, CHAFE, VEX, FRET, ABRADE, BITTERNESS, RANCOR, ACERBITY, MALICE, IMPUDENCE, EFFRONTERY, IRRITATE, ANNOY

gallant HERO, SPARK, BRAVE, DARING, POLITE, CIVIL, HEROIC, BEAU, SUITOR, WOOER, BOLD, COURAGEOUS, VALIANT, INTREPID, CHIVALROUS

gallantry VALOR

galled RAW, SORE, MAD, PEEVED

galleon CARRACK, ARGOSY, BOAT

cargo ORO

gallery SALON, MUSEUM, LOFT, PORCH, PIAZZA, ARCADE, BALCONY, VERANDA, PROMENADE, CORRIDOR

open LOGGIA

galley BIREME, DROMOND, TRIREME, BOAT, PROOF, TRAY, KITCHEN, FOIST *See* "boat"

Gallic chariot ESSED(E)

gallimaufry OLIO, HASH, RAGOUT, MEDLEY, HODGEPODGE, SALMAGUNDI, MIXTURE

gallinae GROUSE, QUAILS, TURKEYS, RASORES, PEAFOWLS, PHEASANTS, CURASSOWS

order RASORES

gallinule HEN, RAIL, COOT, FOWL

galloon LACE, TRIMMING

gallop RUN, PACE, HURRY, RUSH, SPEED, SCAMPER

galloping dominoes DICE

gally FLURRY, SCARE, IMPUDENT, BOLD, BITTER

galore LOTS, GOBS, ABUNDANCE, PLENTY

Galway *island* ARAN

gam HERD, SCHOOL, VISIT, TOOTH, MOUTH, LEG

gamble RISK, WAGER, CHANCE, HAZARD, BET

gambler GAMER, DICER, SHARK

accomplice of SHILL

gambling *cube(s)* DICE, DIE

pertaining to ALEATORY

place CASINO, RENO

stake MISE, ANTE, POT, BET, LAYOUT

gamboge tree family CALABA

gambol CURVET, PLAY, LEAP, CAPER, ROMP, FROLIC, SPORT, FRISK, HOP, SKIP, PRANK

game FUN, SPORT, CONTEST, MATCH, PLAY, FROLIC, AMUSEMENT, DIVERSION, PASTIME, SCHEME, STRATEGY, PLOY, PLAN, PAM, LOTTO, GOLF, POLO, BINGO, QUARRY, COURAGEOUS, BRAVE, RESOLUTE, VALIANT, DISABLED, LAME, GAMBLE

Basque PELOTA

bird QUAIL, GROUSE, DUCK

board HALMA

card See under "card"

confidence BUNCO, BUNKO

dice LUDO, DOMINOES, CRAPS

fish See under "fish"

gambling FARO, KENO, PICO, DICE, CARDS, POKER, BINGO

Greek AGON

like ninepins SKITTLES

marbles TAW

oriental HEI, FANTAN

parlor LOTTO, CARDS, DOMINOES, CHECKERS

piece MAN, DOMINO

point SCORE, TALLY, RUN, GOAL

Scottish SHINTY

shot CAROM, CANNON

Spanish OMBER

to follow STALK, DOG, HUNT

using fingers MORA

gamin ARAB, TAD, HOODLUM, URCHIN

gammon HAM, BACON, BOSH, DECEIVE, HOAX, HUMBUG, DUPE, GULL, COZEN, DELUDE, BEGUILE, MISLEAD

gamut RANGE, SCALE, SOL-FA, REACH, SWEEP, KEN, ORBIT, COMPASS, SERIES

gander GANNET, WANDER, STROLL, LOOK, GLANCE, GOOSE, STEG, SIMPLETON, FOWL

Gandhi MAHATMA

gang MOB, CREW, SET, BAND, NUMBER, COMPANY, HORDE, POSSE

Ganges *efflorescence* REH

vessel PUTELI, PUTELEE

gangling LANKY, SPINDLING, LEAN, AWKWARD

gangrene MORTIFY, ROT, NECROSIS, SPHACELUS

gangster THUG, WHYO, YEGG, RUFFIAN, APACHE *See* "bandit"

gangway AISLE, PLANK, PASSAGE(WAY)

gannet GOOSE, FOWL, BOOBY

family SULA

ganoid fish GAR, STURGEON, BOWFIN

gap CHASM, HIATUS, LACUNA, SPLIT, SPACE, BREACH, CLEFT, CREVICE, CHINK, OPENING, CRANNY, RAVINE, CRACK, INTERSTICE, BREAK, INTERVAL, RENT

gape DEHISCE, OPE, YAWN, STARE, GAZE, GLOAT, PEER, GLARE, GAP, RENT

gapes RICTUS

gapeseed STARER

gaping OPEN, CRACKED, CHAPPY, RINGENT

of plant capsule
DEHISCENCE
garb ATTIRE,
   CLOTHE(S), DRESS,
   CUSTOM, STYLE,
   HABIT, APPAREL,
   GARMENTS, VESTURE,
   RAIMENT, COSTUME,
   FROCK *See under*
   "garment"
garble DISTORT,
   MUTILATE, FALSIFY,
   COLOR, MIX, MESS,
   MISQUOTE, PERVERT,
   MISREPRESENT
garden PATCH, EDEN,
   TRACT, CULTIVATE
of golden apples
HESPERIDES
Gardner ERLE, AVA
gare DEPOT, STATION,
   WOOL, PIER, WHARF
garfish SNOOK
Gargantua's *son*
PANTAGRUEL
wife BADEBEC
gargantuan HUGE,
   GIANT, TITANIC, VAST
   See "huge"
garish FLASHY, CHEAP,
   GAUDY, SHOWY,
   BRIGHT, TAWDRY
garland ROSARY,
   ANADEM, FESTOON,
   LEI, WREATH,
   CHAPLET, ANTHOLOGY,
   FILLET, TROPHY
garlic, *root* RAMSON,
   BULB
segment CLOVE
wild MOLY
garment WRAP, CLOAK,
   COTTE, DRESS, COAT,
   GOWN, VESTMENT
   See "garb"
ancient TOGA,
   CHLAMYS, EPHOD,
   SYNTHESIS, PAENULA,
   TRABEA
Arab ABA
bishop's COPE,
   GREMIAL, ROCHET,
   CHIMER
clergy CASSOCK *See*
   "priest" *below*
fitted REEFER
Greek CHLAMYS,
   CHITON, PEPLOS
Irish, ancient INAR
knight's TABARD,
   MAIL

loose CLOAK, MANTLE,
   ROBE, CAMISE,
   SIMAR, CYMAR
Malay KABAYA,
   SARONG, CABAYA
outer CAPOTE, HAORI,
   SMOCK, ROBE,
   JACKET, PALETOT,
   PARKA
priest's ALB, COPE,
   AMICE, EPHOD, STOLE,
   CASSOCK
rain PONCHO,
   SLICKER, OILSKIN
Roman See under
   "Roman"
scarflike TIPPET *See*
   "scarf"
S. African KAROSS
tuniclike TABARD
under SHIFT, SLIP,
   BRA
women's MANTUA,
   BODICE, SIMAR,
   DRESS, SHIFT, SLIP,
   BRA
garnet PYROPE, RED,
   (H)ESSONITE,
   (H)APLOME, ALMAN-
   DITE, ANDRADITE
berry CURRANT
black MELANITE
garnish LARD, TRIM,
   (BE)DECK, ADORN,
   ORNAMENT, PARSLEY,
   CRESS
garret LOFT, ATTIC
garrot DUCK, FOWL,
   GOLDENEYE, TOURNI-
   QUET
garruline bird JAY
garvie SPRAT, FISH
gas NEON, RADON,
   ARGON, BUTANE,
   DAMP, VAPOR, FUME,
   REEK, ETHER, FUEL,
   PETROL, GOSSIP
charcoal OXAN(E)
charge with AERATE
charger AERATOR
colorless KETONE,
   ETHANE, OXAN(E)
combining form AER,
   AERO
inert ARGON,
   XENON
marsh METHANE
nitrogen and carbon
   CYANOGEN
non-flammable HE-
   LIUM

gasconade VAUNT,
   BOAST, BRAG,
   CROW, BLUSTER,
   BRAVADO
gaseous TENUOUS,
   THIN, LIGHT,
   AERIFORM
element RADON,
   NEON
hydrocarbon ETHANE
gash CUT, SLASH,
   INCISE, SLIT, SCORE,
   WOUND
gasoline PETROL,
   FUEL, GAS
gasp PANT, PUFF,
   BLOW, EXCLAIM,
   CHOKE
gastropod MOLLUSK,
   SNAIL, SLUG, WHELK,
   ORMER, ABALONE,
   LIMPET, NERITOID
genus HARPA,
   NERITA, OLIVA
marine MUREX,
   APLYSIA, TETHYS
gate ENTRY, SPRUE,
   BAB, DAR, SLUICE,
   DOOR(WAY), PORTAL,
   START, BARRIER,
   OPENING, INTAKE,
   ARCH
Persian BAB, DAR
rear POSTERN
to Buddhist shrine
   TORAN(A)
gateway DAR, TORAN,
   TORII, DOOR, GATE
Gath, *king of* ACHISH
gather REAP, ACQUIRE,
   CULL, GLEAN,
   (A)MASS, GARNER,
   MUSTER, COLLECT,
   SHEAVE, HERD, AS-
   SEMBLE, RALLY,
   CONVENE, MOBILIZE,
   CONGREGATE, AC-
   CUMULATE, HUDDLE,
   PLUCK, PICK, MEET,
   FULL, SHIRR, FOLD,
   PLAIT, PUCKER, INFER,
   DEDUCE, JUDGE, CON-
   CLUDE, DERIVE,
   COMPILE
and compare COL-
   LATE
gathered MET,
   SHIRRED
gathering PARTY, SUM,
   MOB, HORDE, PRESS,
   THRONG, CROWD,
   MEETING, ASSEMBLY,

COMPANY, CONGREGA-
TION, ABSCESS
social BEE, PARTY,
TEA
gauche AWKWARD,
CLUMSY, INEPT,
TWISTED, SKEW
Gaucho *knife* BOLO
weapon MACHETE
gaud ADORN, FINERY,
ORNAMENT, TRINKET,
BAUBLE
gaudy CHEAP, SHOWY,
GARISH, FLASHY,
VULGAR, COARSE,
GROSS, TAWDRY,
TINSEL
gauge SIZE, NORM,
RULE, MODEL,
TYPE, STANDARD,
MEASURE, ESTIMATE,
RATE, VALUE
pointer ARM, HAND
rain UDOMETER
Gaul, *anc. people*
REMI, CELT
nation AEDUI
gaulding EGRET,
HERON, BIRD
gaum DAUB, HEED,
UNDERSTAND, CON-
SIDER
gaunt BONY, LEAN,
SLIM, SCRAWNY,
LANK, SPARE, THIN,
HAGGARD, GRIM,
BARREN
gauntlet GLOVE,
CUFF, CHALLENGE
gauze MARLI,
BAREGE, CREPE,
LENO, HAZE, LISSE,
TULLE, CLOTH
gavial CROCODILE
Gawain's *father* LOT
gawk STARE, GAPE,
FOOL, CUCKOO,
BOOBY, LOUT, BUMP-
KIN, SIMPLETON,
BOOR
gay HAPPY, AIRY,
LIVELY, MERRY,
BLITHE, JOLLY,
RIANT, GENIAL,
JOVIAL, FESTIVE,
JAUNTY, VIVACIOUS,
SPRIGHTLY, SPORTIVE,
CHEERFUL
gaze GAPE, PORE,
REGARD, CON, LOOK,
SEE, OGLE, STARE,

SCAN, PEER, GLOAT,
WATCH, GAWK
gazebo PAVILION,
SUMMERHOUSE
gazelle CORINNE,
KUDU, MOHR,
DIBATAG, DAMA *See*
"antelope"
Africa MOHR, ADMI,
CORA, ORYX, SPRING-
BOK, KUDU
Arabia ARIEL
Asia AHU
Clark's DIBATAG
four-horned CHIKARA
Persia CORA
Senegambian KORIN
Sudan DAMA
Tibet GOA
gear COG, CAM, BAG-
GAGE, TOOLS,
CLOTHING, TACKLE,
OUTFIT, GARB, AP-
PAREL, HARNESS,
ARMOR, APPLIANCES,
ACCESSORIES, TRAP-
PINGS, RIGGING
first LOW
Geb's *consort* NU,
NUT
offspring ISIS,
OSIRIS
gecko LIZARD,
TARENTE
gee-gee HORSE
geese *See* "goose"
flock of wild RAFT,
GAGGLE
genus ANSER, CHEN,
BRANT
gel HARDEN, SET,
PECTIZE, SOLIDIFY,
JELLY
gelatin JELLY, AGAR,
COLLIN, COLLOID
plate (printing) BAT
gelid ICY, COLD,
FROZEN, FRIGID,
CHILLY, FROSTY
gem STONE, ROCK,
ICE, JEWEL, PRIZE,
OPAL, SARD, RUBY,
PEARL, ONYX, JADE,
DIAMOND, LIGURE,
AGATE, BERYL,
PEARL, TOPAZ,
TREASURE, MUFFIN
carnelianlike SARD
carved CAMEO
Egyptian SCARAB
face BEZEL, CULET,
FACET, COLLECT

friendship TOPAZ
good luck MOON-
STONE
health AGATE
imitation GLASS,
PASTE, STRASS
immortality EMERALD
inlaying for CRUSTA
law RUBY
love AMETHYST
modern ZIRCON,
JACINTH
peace DIAMOND
purity PEARL
relief CAMEO
rose spinel BALAS
semi-precious SARD
single SOLITAIRE
State IDAHO
truth SAPPHIRE
weight CARAT
youth BERYL
gemel TWIN
gemel(l)ed PAIRED,
COUPLED
gemmation BUDDING
gemsbok CHAMOIS,
ORYX, GOAT
gendarme TROOPER,
OFFICER, COP,
SOLDIER, CAVALRY-
MAN, POLICEMAN
gender BEGET, BREED,
SEX, NEUTER, MALE,
FEMALE, INSTRUMENT
common to both
EPICENE
genealogy DESCENT,
PATERNITY, TREE,
PEDIGREE, LINEAGE,
HISTORY, LINE
genera CLASSES, CATE-
GORIES, PHYLA,
DIVISIONS
general VAGUE, COM-
MON, RIFE, WIDE,
GENERIC, REGULAR,
HABITUAL, APPROXI-
MATE, UNIVERSAL,
ABSTRACT, BROAD,
CATHOLIC, USUAL,
WHOLE, TOTAL,
ORDINARY, RANK,
OFFICER
aspect FACIES
effect ENSEMBLE
generate BREED,
BEGET, SIRE, BEAR,
PRODUCE, YIELD,
PROCREATE, ENGEN-
DER, SPAWN, MAKE

generation AGE, CREATION, PRODUCTION, FORMATION, LIFETIME
spontaneous ABIOGENESIS
genesis NASCENCY, ORIGIN, BIRTH, BEGINNING, ORIGINATION
genial WARM, AFFABLE, SOCIABLE, KIND, CORDIAL, JOLLY, HEARTY, CHEERFUL, JOVIAL, PLEASANT, EXPANSIVE
geniculate BENT
genipap *tree dye* LANA
genius TALENT, GIFT, BENT, KNACK, TURN, FLAIR, APTITUDE, ENDOWMENT, BRAINS, INGENUITY, MASTER, SPIRIT
Genoese *family* DORIA
genos FAMILY, CLAN, GENS
genouillere KNEEPIECE, KNEELET
genre CATEGORY, SPECIES, KIND, TYPE, GENUS, SORT, STYLE
Gentiles, pertaining to ETHNIC
gentle TAME, BLAND, MILD, CALM, SOFT, BALMY, PLACID, SERENE, MODERATE, KIND, TENDER, MEEK, HUMANE, CLEMENT, DOCILE, TRACTABLE, PACIFIC, CHIVALROUS, TRANQUIL
music direction AMABILE
slope GLACIS
gentleman SIR, KNIGHT, YEOMAN, ARISTOCRAT, AMATEUR, SQUIRE
genu FLEXURE, BEND
genuflect CURTSY, BEND, KNEEL
genuine TRUE, REAL, VALID, SINCERE, PURE, SHEER, ACTUAL, HONEST, UNCORRUPT, UNALLOYED, AUTHENTIC, VERITABLE, FRANK, CERTI-

FIED, OFFICIAL, INCORRUPT
not See "spurious"
genus CLASS, ORDER, SORT, TYPE
antelope ORYX
auk ALCA, URIA, GUILLEMOT, ALLE
bear URSUS
bee APIS
beech FAGUS
bird See under "bird"
bivalve ANOMIA, PINNA
burbot LOTA
bustard OTIS, OTIDAE
cat FELIS, FELIDAE
catnip NEPETA
cetacean INIA
climbing shrub TECOMA, IVA
crane GRUS
dog CANIS
dogwood CORNUS
duck AIX, ANAS, HARELDA, CLANGULA, AYTHYA, NYROCA, ANSERES
eel CONGER
elm ULMUS, CELTIS, TREMA, PLANERA
fish LOTA, AMIA, APOGON, MOLA, PERCA, ELOPS
fox VULPES
frog RANA, ANURA
fungi AMANITA, BOLETUS, ERYSIBE, TUBER
gastropod NERITA, OLIVA, HARPA
goat CAPRA
goose CHEN, ANSER, BRANT
grass AVENA, POA, STIPA
gull LARUS, LARI- (DAE), XEMA
hare LEPUS
herb See under "herb"
hog SUS
horse EQUUS
insect CICADA, ACARUS, NEPA, EMESA *See under* "insect"
lichen USNEA, EVERNIA

lily ALOE, BESSERA, HOSTA, SCILLA
lizard UTA, AGAMA
loon GAVIA
louse APHIS
magpie PICA
maize ZEA
mint NEPETA
mole TALPA
mollusk NERITA, OLIVA, OSTREA, MUREX, CHITON
monkey CEBUS
spider ATELES
nettle URTICA
nuthatch SITTA
olive OLEA
oyster OSTREA
palm NIPA, ARECA, OENOCARPUS *See under* "palm"
peacock PAVO
perch PERCA
pigeon GOURA, COLUMBA
pine ABIES
plant See under "plant"
rat SPALAX, MUS
raven CORVUS, CORVIDAE
robin TURDUS
ruminant BOS, CAPRA
sand snake ERYX
sheep OVIS
shrub See under "shrub"
spider AGALENA, ARANEA
spider monkey ATELES
squirrel SCIURUS
swan OLOR
swine SUS
tailless amphibian RANA
tarpon ELOPS
tern STERNA, ANOUS
thrush TURDUS
tick IXODES, ARGAS, IXODIDAE, CIMEX
tortoise EMYS
tree See under "tree"
turtle EMYS, CHELONE
whale INIA
wolf CANIS
wren NANNUS

geode VOOG, VUG(G), VUGH, DRUSE, NODULE, CAVITY
geographer, *Greek* STRABO
geological *age* PLIOCENE, CENOZOIC
division EON, ERA, LIAS, TRIAS, TRIASSIC
epoch ECCA, LIAS, CHAZY, MIOCENE, EOCENE, PLIOCENE, ERIAN, MUAV, GLACIAL, HOLOCENE, SILURIAN
S. Africa ECCA
formation TERRANE, JURASSIC, TRIASSIC
group BALA, CARADOC
oldest period ARCHEAN, JURASSIC, LIAS
period See "epoch" *above*
stage RISS
subdivision TROPHIC, GAULT
vein angle HADE
geologist HUXLEY
geometric *pole* PERPOLE
geometrical *body* LUNE, PRISM, CUBE, SPHERE
figure ELLIPSE, SOLID, SQUARE
line(s) LOCI, LOCUS
point relating to curve ACNODE
premise POSTULATE
proportion PORISM
term SINE, TANGENT
theory CONICS
geometry *coordinate* ABSCISSA(S)
proponent of EUCLID, PASCAL
rule THEOREM
solid CONE, CUBE, SPHERE
term VERSOR
geophagous PICAL
geoponic RURAL, RUSTIC, BUCOLIC
geomyoid, *one of* GOPHER
Georgia *city* SPARTA,

ATHENS, ATLANTA, AUGUSTA
county RABUN, TROUP, HART, BACON, EARLY, BIBB, BURKE, BUTTS, CLAY, COBB, COOK, DADE, CRISP, HALL, LEE, LONG, PIKE, POLK, TIFT, WARE
Georgian SVAN(E)
georgic RURAL, POEM
Geraint's *wife* ENID
geranial CITRAL, ALDEHYDE
Gerar *king* ABIMELECH
gerefa REEVE, BAILIFF, SHERIFF, OFFICER
germ BUG, VIRUS, BUD, SEED, SPORE, MICROBE, EMBRYO, OVUM, EGG, OVULE, SPROUT, BACTERIUM, ORIGIN, SOURCE
fermenting ZYME
freedom from ASEPSIS
seed CHIT
German, Germany BOCHE, JERRY, ALMAIN, HUN, TEUTON
about ETWA
admiral SPEE
air LUFT
airplane STUKA
already SCHON
angry BOSE
animal TIER
approximately ETWA
archbishop of Cologne ANNO
armament works SKODA
article DAS, DER, DIE, EIN
artist DURER
astronomer KEPLER
author MANN, EBERS, FICHTE, GOETHE, GRIMM, HEGEL, HEINE, KANT, SCHILLER
away WEG
bacteriologist KOCH
bad BOSE
bank UFER
beautiful SCHON
because WEIL
bed BETT

bench BANK
blue BLAU
boat BOOT
bomber STUKA
bread BROT
breeze LUFTIG
bright HELL
but ABER
cake TORTE, KUCHEL
canal KIEL
cathedral city ESSEN, COLOGNE
chap KERL
cheese KASE
chemist BUNSEN
chicken HUHN
child KIND
city or town BONN, GOTHA, HALLE, STADT, ULM, WESEL, ESSEN, GERA, WORMS, WERDAU, UNNA, AALEN, CELLE, BORNA, PIRNA, PENIG, PEINE, GERA, DUREN, RIESA, HEIDE, HOF, KEHL, MORS (MOERS), TRIER (TREVES), SPEYER, SOEST, STADE, AHLEN, KIEL, JENA, BURG, PORZ
clean REIN
clever KLUG
clock UHR
coal region SAAR, RUHR, AACHEN, KREFELD
coat ROCK
coin MARK, THALER, KRONE, ALBUS, BATZ, CAROLIN, HELLER, PFENNIG
cold KALT
commune MARL
complete GANZ
composer ABT, BACH, HASSE, WEBER, WAGNER
corner ECKE
courage MUT
cow KUH
dam EDER
day TAG
dead TOT
dear LIEB
deep TIEF
distant WEIT
district GAU
doctor ARZT
dog HUND
door TUR

drinking salutation PROSIT
dumpling KNODEL
earl GRAF
early FRUH
earth ERDE
east OST(EN)
eight ACHT
eleven ELF
empty LEER
entire GANZ
evening ABEND
exclamation ACH, HOCH
eye AUGE
far WEIT
fat DICK
fellow KERL
field FELD
firm FEST
five FUNF
foot FUSS
forest WALD
four VIER
fruit OBST
full VOLL
glad FROH
glass city JENA
god WODAN (ODIN), DONAR, WODEN
good GUT
gray GRAU
green GRUN
guest GAST
hair HAAR
half HALB
hall SAAL, AULA, DIELE
happy FROH
hat HUT
head KOPF
heart HERZ
high HOCH
hill BERG
historian NEANDER, DAHN, MOSER
holiday FEIERTAG
home HEIM, HAUS
honor EHRE
host WIRT
hot HEISS
ice EIS
inventor DIESEL
island INSEL, FOHR
joke SPASS
knight RITTER
lady DAME
lake SEE, CHIEM, WURM
landlord WIRT
late SPAT
lazy FAUL

leaf BLATT
league BUND
left LINK
leg BEIN
legislature REICHSRAT, REICHSTAG
letter BRIEF
lyric poems LIEDER
manufacturing city GERA, FRANKFURT
mathematician LIEBNITZ
measles MASERN
measure AAM, KETTE, EIMER
metaphysician KANT
mind SINN
mister HERR
moon MOND
more MEHR
mountain(s) BERG, HARZ
mouth MUND
narrow ENG
nation VOLK
naturalist HUGEL
naval base EMDEN, KIEL
near NAHE
neat NETT
neck HALS
never NIE
new NEU
nice NETT
nine NEUN
no NEIN
nobleman GRAF, RITTER, ADLIG, EDELMANN
noise LARM
nose NASE
number ZAHL
ocean MEER
old ALT
only NUR
or ODER
outer garment ROCK
part TEIL
path WEG
people VOLK, JUTE
philologist GRIMM
philosopher HEGEL, KANT
physician ERB
physicist OHM, WEBER
picture BILD
poor ARM
president, first EBERT
prison STALAG
pronoun ICH, DU, SIE, UNS

proud STOLZ
psychologist BENEKE
red ROT
rifleman JAGER
river See under "river"
road WEG
roof DACH
round RUND
ruler, early OTTO
scholar ELZE
school hall AULA
sculptor BEGAS
sea MEER
seaport EMDEN, KIEL
seat BANK
sense SINN
sentence SATZ
shoe SCHUH
shore UFER
short KURZ
sir HERR
six SECHS
skirt FRAUEN, ROCK
small KLEIN
solid FEST
son SOHN
song LIED
soon BALD
star STERN
steel STAHL
steel center ESSEN
steeple TURM
still NOCH
stone STEIN
stout DICK
strong STARK
sun SONNE
superior OBER
sweet SUSS
table TISCH
ten ZEHN
there DORT
thick DICK
thin DUNN
thing DING
three DREI
throat HALS
time MAL, ZEIT
tired MUDE
title GRAF, HERR
today HEUTE
tooth ZAHN
tower TURM
town See "city" above
train ZUG
tree BAUM
trousers HOSE
true WAHR
two ZWEI

valley TAL
very SEHR
village DORF
wall WAND
watch UHR
watering place EMS,
  BADEN
way WEG
weight LOTH, TONNE
wet NASS
where WO
white WEISS
who(ever) WER
whole GANZ
wicked BOSE
wine WEIN, HOCK
wise KLUG
woman FRAU
wood(s) WALD(ER)
world WELT
worth WERT
year JAHR
yellow GELB
yet NOCH
you SIE, DU
young JUNG
zero NULL
germane APT, AKIN,
  RELEVANT, FITTING,
  ALLIED, APROPOS,
  RELATED, COGNATE,
  PERTINENT, SUITA-
  BLE
germinate BUD,
  SPROUT, SPRIT
Geronimo APACHE,
  INDIAN
Gershwin IRA,
  GEORGE
Gertrude Atherton
  LIN
gesso CHALK,
  GYPSUM, PLASTER
gest(e) DEED,
  EXPLOIT, TALE,
  ADVENTURE, ACTION,
  ROMANCE
gesture MOTION,
  WAVE, NOD, ACTION,
  SIGNAL
get SECURE, TAKE,
  WIN, EARN, OBTAIN,
  GAIN, ACQUIRE,
  CATCH, GRAB,
  SEIZE, BEGET, SIRE,
  BREED, PROCURE,
  REALIZE, GENERATE
  around CAJOLE, OUT-
  WIT, CIRCUMVENT,
  PERSUADE, TRAVEL
  away SCAT, SHOO,

LAM, ELOPE,
  ESCAPE, FLY, FLEE
Gettysburg commander
  MEADE, LEE
geum AVENS, HERB,
  PLANT
gewgaw BAUBLE,
  TRIFLE, BIBELOT
geyser, mouth of
  CRATER
geyserite OPAL
Ghana capital ACCRA
ghastly CADAVEROUS,
  PALE, LURID, ASHEN,
  GRISLY, GRIM, PAL-
  LID, WAN, GHOSTLY,
  GRUESOME, HIDEOUS,
  FEARFUL, SHOCKING,
  DISMAL, FRIGHTFUL
Ghent's river LYS,
  SCHELDE
ghost HAUNT,
  EIDOLON, KER, LARVA,
  SHADOW, TRACE,
  DAEMON, SPOOK,
  WRAITH, SHADE,
  SPIRIT, SPECTER,
  IMAGE, PHANTOM, AP-
  PARITION, REVENANT,
  JUBA
  combining form SCIO
  fish CHIRO
ghosts LEMURES
ghoul VAMPIRE, OGRE,
  FIEND, DEMON,
  BLACKMAILER
giant(s) JUMBO,
  ANAK, ETEN, OGRE,
  YMIR, THURSE,
  HUGE, VAST,
  TITAN(IC), COLOSSUS,
  HERCULES, MONSTER,
  CYCLOPS, CYCLO-
  PEAN, TALL,
  GARGANTUA(N),
  PANTAGRUEL, OTUS,
  EPHIALTES, LOKI,
  GOLIATH, BALOR,
  HRYM, GYGES,
  BANA, HYMER,
  HYMIR See "titan"
  and "huge"
  evil LOKI, JOTUN(N),
  GOLIATH
  Formorian BALOR
  frost HRYM
  god, Norse HYMIR,
  HYMER
  Greek myth. COTTUS,
  CYCLOPS, GYGES
  Hindu BANA

hundred-handed COT-
  TUS, GYGES,
  BRIARCUS
hundred eyes ARGUS
inhospitable sea
  HYMIR, HYMER
land of UTGARTHAR
Moab EMIM,
  ZUZIM
Norse myth.
  JOTUN(N), UTGAR-
  THA-LOKI, HYMIR,
  HYMER
Old Testament ANAK,
  GOLIATH
one-eyed CYCLOPS,
  ARGES, POLYPHEMUS
Philistine GOLIATH
primeval YMER,
  YMIR
race of ANAK
sea demon WADE
shepherd ARGES,
  CYCLOPS
storm WADE
strong TITAN
thousand-armed BANA
giantess, Celtic myth.
  DOMNU
  Norse GROA, NOTT,
  NORN
  Scand. SKULD, URTH,
  WYRD
  slain by Athena
  PALLAS
gib GUT, SALMON,
  CAT, FASTEN,
  PRISON, PROJECTION
gibber PRATE, CHAT,
  GAB, TALK
gibbet GALLOWS, JIB
gibbon APE, LAR,
  SIAMANG, WOU-WOU,
  HOOLOCK
gibbous CONVEX,
  BULGING, HUMPED,
  ROUNDED, SWELLING,
  CURVED, PROTU-
  BERANT
gibe HECKLE, SNEER,
  QUIP, JEER, SCOFF,
  FLOUT, FLEER,
  DERIDE, MOCK,
  TWIT, TAUNT,
  RIDICULE
Gibraltar, legendary
  founder of GEBIR
  point opposite CEUTA
gibus HAT
giddy DIZZY, FOOLISH,
  VERTIGINOUS, FICKLE,
  INCONSTANT, CHANGE-

ABLE, WILD, FRIVO-
LOUS, FLIGHTY
gift TALENT, FACULTY,
KNACK, BENT, TURN,
GENIUS, FLEER, ALMS,
ENAM, GRANT, FAVOR,
TIP, LAGNIAPPE,
LEGACY, DOLE, DOW,
LARGESSE, BOON,
DONATION, PRESENT,
BENEFACTION, GRATU-
ITY, BONUS, HANDSEL,
HONORARIUM, PRIZE
conciliatory SOP
gig NAP, SPEAR,
CARRIAGE, CHAISE,
ROWBOAT
gigantic TITAN(IC),
COLOSSAL, HUGE,
VAST, GIANT, ENOR-
MOUS, IMMENSE,
PRODIGIOUS, TALL,
LARGE *See* "huge"
giggle SNIGGER,
CHUCKLE, TITTER,
LAUGH, SNICKER
gila monster LIZARD
Gilbert island
TARAWA, MAKIN
gild ADORN, AUREATE,
ENRICH, BRIGHTEN,
EMBELLISH *See*
"guild"
Gileadite *judge* JAIR
gill(s) WATTLE, JAW,
BRANCHIA, COLLAR,
LUNG, BROOK,
STREAM, MEASURE
four PINT
gilt GOLD, GILDING,
MONEY, SOW, PIG
gimcrack BAUBLE,
SCHEME, TOY,
TRINKET, TRIFLE,
THINGUM(A)BOB,
GEWGAW, KNICK-
KNACK
gimmer CLASP,
HINGE, EWE
gimp JAG, NOTCH,
FISHLINE, TRIMMING,
SPIRIT, VIM
gin SNARE, TRAP,
GAME, LIQUOR,
SCHNAPPES, RUMMY
type of SLOE
ginger PEP, VIGOR,
FIRE, SPIRIT, ECLAT,
SPUNK, VIM, PLUCK,
PLANT, SPICE
genus ZINGIBER
pine CEDAR

wild ASARUM
gingerbread CAKE,
WEALTH, MONEY,
TRIM, TRIMMING
tree DOOM, DUM
gingerly CAUTIOUSLY,
CAREFULLY, TIMIDLY,
DAINTILY
ginseng ARALIA,
PANAX, PLANT,
HERB
gipsy *See* "gypsy"
giraffe CAMELOPARD
like animal OKAPI
girasol(e) OPAL, HELI-
OTROPE, ARTICHOKE,
SUNFLOWER
gird BIND, BELT,
STRAP, ENCIRCLE,
EQUIP, SURROUND,
ENCOMPASS, ENCLOSE,
BRACE, SUPPORT,
GIRDLE, STRENGTHEN
girder TRUSS, TIMBER,
BEAM, T-BAR
girdle RING, OBI, BELT,
CINCTURE, SASH,
CINGLE, BAND,
CESTUS, ENCIRCLE,
ENVIRON
pertaining to ZONAL
Roman CESTUS
saddle CINCH
sash CUMMERBUND
girl CHIT, MISS, LASS,
SIS, MINX, BELLE,
MAID, DAMSEL,
MAIDEN, SERVANT,
COLLEEN
Anglo-Irish COLLEEN
cover MODEL
graceful NYMPH,
SYLPH
lively FILLY, GIGLET
slender SYLPH
girth GIRDLE, STRAP,
BELT, BEND, HOOP,
CIRCUMFERENCE,
CINCH
gist ESSENCE, CORE,
CRUX, NUB, PITH,
KERNEL, POINT,
HEART, MARROW,
MEANING
give WAIVE, CEDE,
YIELD, IMPART,
DONATE, AWARD,
GRANT, ALLOT, DEAL,
DOLE, GIE, ENDOW,
WILL, BEQUEATH,
BESTOW, RENDER,
ACCORD, PRESENT,

CONFER, FURNISH,
SUPPLY, CONTRIBUTE,
PROFFER, PAY,
DELIVER, DEVISE
back REMISE, REMIT,
RETURN, RESTORE
forth EMIT, EXHALE,
BLAZE, PROCLAIM
law REMISE, DEVISE,
BEQUEATH
up CEDE, RESIGN,
RELINQUISH, SUR-
RENDER, FORSAKE,
ABANDON, DEVOTE
gizz WIG
glabrous BALD,
SMOOTH, SLICK
glacial ICY, ARCTIC,
GELID, FRIGID, COLD,
FROSTY, COOL,
FROZEN, CONGEALED
chasm CREVASSE
deposit MORAINE,
PLACER
hill PAHA
ice block SERAC
pinnacle SERAC
ridge(s) ESKAR,
KAME, OS(AR),
ESKER, AS(AR)
snow FIRN, NEVE
waste deposit DRIFT
glaciarium RINK
glacier(s), *erosion*
CIRQUE, CORRIE
facing STOSS
shafts MOULINS
glad HAPPY, ELATED,
FAIN, MERRY, JOY-
OUS, JOLLY, BLITHE,
PLEASED, DELIGHTED,
GRATIFIED, CON-
TENTED
tidings EVANGEL,
GOSPEL
gladden ELATE,
PLEASE, TICKLE,
GRATIFY, COMFORT,
EXHILARATE, DELIGHT,
SOLACE, CHEER, BLESS
glade LAUND, GAP,
CLEARING, FLASH,
PASSAGE
combining form
NEMO
gladiator FENCER,
ATHLETE, BOXER,
SWORDSMAN, FIGHTER,
COMBATANT
competitions LUDI
trainer LANISTA
Gladsheim ASGARD

glamour CHARM, IL-
LUSION, WITCHERY,
ENCHANTMENT,
FASCINATION, AT-
TRACTION, CAPTIVA-
TION

glance STROKE,
GLEAM, GLINT,
FLASH, GLIMPSE,
GLITTER, FLIT, DART,
HINT, ALLUDE
at SKIM, SCAN,
GLIMPSE

gland ORGAN,
THYROID, PANCREAS,
PINEAL, ADRENAL
edible NOIX, LIVER,
RIS
salivary PAROTID
secretion HORMONE,
INSULIN, ADRENALIN,
SALIVA

glare SCOWL, FROWN,
STARE, SHINE, SHEEN,
GLOSS, GAZE, GLOW,
FLAME, BLAZE, FLARE,
DAZZLE, GLOWER

glary SLICK, SMOOTH,
FROSTY, DAZZLING,
SLIPPERY

glass PANE, GOBLET,
TUMBLER, LENS,
MIRROR, CRYSTAL,
TELESCOPE, MONOCLE,
TALLBOY
artificial gems
STRASS, PASTE
blue SMALT
bubble in SEED,
BOIL, REAM
French for VERRE
handling rod PUNTY
ingredient SILICA,
SAND, POTASH
jar BOCAL, MASON
make into sheets
PLATTEN
maker GLAZIER
material for SAND,
SILICA, POTASH,
FRIT
molten PARISON
mosaic TESSERA
partly fused FRIT
piece of PANE
pour in water to break
DRAGADE
refuse CALX, CUL-
LET
scum GALL
showcase VITRINE

small VIAL, PONY,
SHOT
vial AMPUL(E),
AMPOULE
volcanic OBSIDIAN
worker GLAZIER

glassmaker's *oven*
TISAR

glasswort KALI, SALT-
WORT, JUME,
PLANT

glassy CRYSTAL,
SANIDINIC, VITRIC,
HYALINE, VITREOUS,
TRANSPARENT,
BRILLIANT
sea HYALINE

Glaucus' *father*
SISYPHUS
wife IONE

glaze ICE, COAT,
SHINE, ENAMEL,
VENEER, GLARE,
GLOSS, SHEEN,
LUSTER, INCRUST,
COVER, OVERLAY,
POLISH, COATING,
VARNISH

glazier's *diamond*
EMERIL, EMERY

glazing machine CAL-
ENDER

gleam GLINT,
CORUSCATE, RAY,
GLOW, FLASH,
SPARK(LE), GLANCE,
BEAM, GLIMMER,
LUSTER, GLITTER,

glean REAP, PICK,
GATHER, COLLECT,
CULL, HARVEST

glebe SOD, CLOD,
LUMP, SOIL, TURF,
LAND, EARTH, FIELD,
BENEFICE

glede bird KITE

glee JOY, MIRTH,
JOLLITY, DELIGHT,
MERRIMENT, GAIETY,
LIVELINESS, HILARITY

glen DALE, DINGLE,
VALE, VALLEY, DELL

gliadin GLUTIN,
PROTEIN, PROLAMIN

glib PAT, OILY, READY,
BLAND, FLUENT,
VOLUBLE, VOCAL,
FACILE, SMOOTH,
EASY, TALKATIVE,
FLIPPANT

glide SKIM, SLIP, SKI,
SKATE, SKID, SKIP,

SLIDE, SOAR, SCUD,
SAIL, COAST, FLY,
FLOAT, LAPSE,
GLISSADE

gliding over LABILE,
ELIDING

glimmer SHEEN, LEAM,
GLINT, FLASH,
SPARK(LE), SHINE,
GLEAM, GLITTER,
FLICKER, TWINKLE,
RAY, BEAM, GLIMPSE,
GLANCE, SHIMMER

glimmering INKLING,
LIGHT

glioma TUMOR

glitter FLASH, GLOW,
CORUSCATE, SPARK-
(LE), GLINT, GLISTEN,
GLISTER, GLEAM,
SCINTILLATE

gloat BOAST, GAPE,
REVEL, GAZE, STARE,
EXULT, REJOICE

globe EARTH, MOON,
ORB, SPHERE, BALL,
WORLD
fish DIODON
like ORBED,
GLOBULAR

globule BEAD, TEAR,
BLOB, MINUM, DROP,
BALL, PILL, SPHERULE

glockenspiel LYRA,
CARILLON, XYLOPHONE

gloom MURK, SAD-
NESS, DEJECTION,
DESPONDENCY, CLOUD,
SHADOW, DARKNESS,
OBSCURITY, SHADE,
BLUES, DUMPS,
VAPORS

gloomy DIM,
DREAR(Y), DARK,
DOUR, WAN, SAD,
DOLESOME, DOLOROUS,
ADUSK, MURKY,
OBSCURE, DUSKY,
DISMAL, CHEERLESS,
DOWNCAST, CREST-
FALLEN, MOROSE,
GLUM, TENEBROUS

glorify ADORE, BLESS,
WORSHIP, EXALT,
REVERE, UPLIFT,
ENLARGE, PRAISE,
EXTOL, MAGNIFY,
HONOR

glorious ECSTATIC,
ELATED, SUBLIME,
SUPERB, ILLUSTRIOUS,
RENOWNED, CELE-

BRATED, FAMOUS,
EMINENT, SPLENDID,
NOBLE, LOFTY, RE-
SPLENDENT, BRIL-
LIANT

glory KUDOS, AUREOLA,
FAME, RENOWN,
HALO, HONOR, ECLAT,
PRAISE, ADMIRATION,
BLISS

cloud of NIMBUS

gloss PALLIATE,
EXCUSE, BLINK, WINK,
EXTENUATE, EXPLAIN,
INTERPRET, LUSTER,
SHEEN, SHINE,
POLISH, GLAZE,
GLARE, NOTE, RE-
MARK, ANNOTATE,
CLOAK, MASK,
VENEER, VARNISH,
COMMENTARY, TRANS-
LATION, ENAMEL

glossy SLICK, SATINY,
BRIGHT, SLEEK,
NITID, GLACE,
SMOOTH, SHINY,
LUSTROUS, SPECIOUS

glove GAUNTLET,
MITT(EN), HAND-
WEAR

fabric KID, LISLE,
SUEDE, COTTON,
SILK, NYLON

leather MOCHA,
NAPA

shape TRANK

glow FLUSH, SHEEN,
LIGHT, SHINE, BLAZE,
GLARE, FLAME, FLARE,
BURN, RADIATE,
BLUSH, ARDOR,
WARMTH, FERVOR,
ENTHUSIASM

glowing CANDENT,
ARDENT, LAMBENT,
ASHINE, FLUSHED,
WARM, RADIANT,
FERVENT, EXCITED

glucose DEXTROSE,
SUGAR, HONEY,
SIRUP

glucoside root GEIN

glue STICK, CEMENT,
PASTE, FASTEN,
(AF)FIX

glum LOW, SULLEN,
DOUR, SURLY, SOUR,
BLUE, SULKY, MOODY,
MOROSE, DEPRESSED,
DEJECTED

glume CHAFF, HUSK,
BRACT

glut SURFEIT, SATE,
PAUNCH, PALL, GORE,
CLOY, SATIATE,
STUFF, OVERFEED

glutin GELATIN,
GLIADIN

glutinous SIZY, VISCID,
GLUEY, GUMMY,
ROPY, VISCOUS,
STICKY, ADHESIVE,
TENACIOUS

glutton GOURMAND,
CORMORANT, HELLUO,
EPICURE, GORMAND-
IZER, PIG

gluttony GREED,
VORACITY, EDACITY

glycolaldehyde DIOSE,
SUGAR

G-man FED

gnarl NUR, KNUR(R),
GROWL, KNOT, WARP,
TWIST, SNAG, SNARL,
GRUMBLE

gnash GRATE, BITE,
GRIND

gnat MIDGE, FLEA,
FLY, INSECT, PEST

gnaw CHEW, BITE,
CORRODE, NIBBLE,
CHAMP, CRUNCH,
CONSUME, ERODE,
WASTE

gnede MISERLY,
SCANTY, SPARING

gnome GREMLIN,
IMP, DWARF, GOBLIN,
NIS, BOGEY, MAXIM,
APHORISM, SAW *See*
"fairy"

German KOBOLD

N. American OWL

gnomic DIDACTIC,
APHORISTIC

gnomon of a sundial
PIN, STYLE

gnostic *representation*
ABRASAX, ABRAXAS

second century
SETHITE

gnu ANTELOPE,
KOKOON

go LEAVE, GAE, GANG,
SALLY, WORK, QUIT,
RUN, SCRAM, FARE,
EXIT, PASS, DIE,
RETIRE, BETAKE,
PROCEED, ADVANCE,
REPAIR, HIE, WALK,
WEND, JOURNEY,

TRAVEL, DEPART,
DISAPPEAR, ELAPSE,
DIMINISH, WANE,
WITHDRAW, EXTEND

about, nautical TACK,
WEAR

astray ABERRATE, ERR,
DIVERGE

away SCAT, SCRAM,
LEAVE, DEPART, FLEE

back REGRESS,
REVERT, RETURN

forth FARE, MOSEY,
TRAVEL

goa GAZELLE

goad PROD, EGG, GAD,
PRICK, SPUR, ANNOY,
BADGER, INCITE,
INSTIGATE, URGE,
IMPEL, STIMULATE,
ROUSE, WHIP

goal TALLY, POINT,
SCORE, MARK,
BOURN(E), IDEAL,
END, AIM, DESIGN,
FATE, OBJECT, CAGE,
HOME, POST, META,
DISTINCTION, PURPOSE

distant THULE, REACH,
DESTINATION

goat KID, CAD, CAPRINE,
NANNY, BILLY, VICTIM

Alpine IBEX,
BOUQUETIN

Angora CHAMAL

antelope SEROW,
CHAMOIS, GORAL

astronomy CAPRICORN

bezoar PASAN(G)

Caucasian TUR, ZAC

genus CAPRA

Himalayan GORAL,
JEMLAH, TAHR

jaal BEDEN, IBEX

like HIRCINE,
CAPRINE, LEWD

male BUCK, BILLY

Old World IBEX

pertaining to CAPRIC,
CAPRINE, HIRCINE

Rocky Mountain
MAZAME

wild TUR, KRAS, TAHR,
MARKHOR, IBEX

goatish CAPRINE,
HIRCINE, COARSE,
LECHEROUS, LEWD,
LASCIVIOUS, LUSTFUL,
SALACIOUS

goat's hair *cloth*
CAMLET, TIBET,
MOHAIR

cord AGAL
gob CHOKE, GOAF,
    MOUTH, TAR, SAILOR,
    BLOB, MASS, LUMP,
    MOUTHFUL
Gobi Desert SHAMO
lake HARA
goblet GLASS, HANAP,
    TASS, CUP, TALLBOY,
    TUMBLER
constellation CRATER
Eucharistic CHALICE
goblin ELF, TROLL,
    GNOME, BHUT, PUCK,
    POOK *See* "fairy"
German KOBOLD
Scand. NIS(SE)
goby MAPO, FISH
God DEITY, CREATOR,
    JEHOVAH, DIVINITY,
    IDOL
god(s) DEI, DI(I)
car to carry image of
    RATH
false IDOL, BAAL,
    BAALIM
home of OLYMPUS,
    ASGARD, MERU,
    EMPYREAN
god(s) *classification of*
    (*See also under*
    "god(s)," *further*
    classification of," *be-*
    low)
Anglo-Saxon, chief
    WODEN
    fate WYRD
    fertility, peace,
        prosperity ING
    thunder THOR
    war TIU
Aramic RIMMON
Arcadian LADON
Assyrian SIN, ASSUR,
    ASUR, EL, NEBO, IRA,
    ZU, NUSKU, NERGAL,
    NINIB, NABO,
    SHAMASH, ASHUR
    sky ANAT
    sun HADAD
    war ASUR, ASSUR
Aztec XIPE, EECATL,
    MEZTLI
Babylonian ANSHAR,
    SIN, EAR, LARES,
    ENLIL, OANNES, EA,
    ZU, ANU, BEL, HEA,
    IRA, IRRA, UTU, ADAD,
    ADDU, ENKI, ANZU,
    NABU, NEBO, UTUG,
    ETANA, SIRIS, BABBAR,

SHAMASH, ABU, DAGAN,
    ALALU
    chief BEL, ASUR,
        MARDUK
    earth DAGAN
    evil ZU
    healer EA
    heavens ANU
    medicine
        NINGISHZIDA
    moon SIN, NANNAR
    scribes NABU
    sky ANU
    storms ADAD, ZU
    supreme ANU, BEL,
        EAR, EA
    thunder LARES
    war IRA, IRRA
    wind ADAD
    wisdom NABU,
        NEBO
Buddhist DEVA
Carthage MOLOCH
Celtic HAFGAN, LLEU,
    LLEW, ARAWN, BELI,
    ESUS, TARANIS,
    BELINUS, GWYN, LUGH
    chief HAFGAN,
        LLEU, LLEW
    underworld GWYN
Chinese JOSS, GHOS,
    SHEN, TAO
    chief JOSS
Cymric *See* "Welsh"
Egypt MNEVIS, NUT,
    APET, AMON, MIN,
    NU, RA, SU, BES, GEB,
    KEB, SHU, TEM, TUM,
    AMEN, AMUN, SEB,
    ATMU, HAPI, KHEM,
    MENT, PTAH, SET(H),
    HORUS, TOTH, OSIRIS,
    SERAPIS, CHNEMU,
    HOR, ANUBIS,
    HERSHEF, SOBK, SEBEK
    (SEBAK)
    crocodile-headed
        SOBK
    earth GEB
    evil SET, SETH
    falcon-headed
        HORUS
    hawk-headed HOR
    heavens NUT
    incarnate MNEVIS
    jackal-headed
        APUAT
    moon KHENSU,
        TOTH
    noontime RA
    pleasure BES
    principal MIN

science TOTH
solar disk ATEN
sun AMEN, AMON,
    ATMU, HORUS,
    KHEHERA, RA, RHE,
    SHU, OSIRIS, TEM,
    TUM, CHEPERA
sunset TEM
Etruscan TINIA
Finnish JUMALA
Gaelic LER, MIDER,
    DAGDA
German ODIN,
    WODEN, DONAR
Greek DES, PAN, ZAN,
    ARES, EROS, ZEUS,
    COMUS, EURUS,
    HADES, PLUTO,
    APOLLO, AUSTER,
    CRONUS, BOREAS,
    HERMES, NEREUS,
    ONIROS, HYMEN,
    CHAOS
    Aegean Sea NEREUS
    avenging ALASTOR,
        ANTEROS
    beauty APOLLO,
        HELIOS
    chief ZEUS, PTAH,
        HADES
    dream ONIROS
    flocks PAN
    Hades PLUTO,
        HERMES
    heavens URANUS,
        ZEUS
    hurricane OTUS
    joy COMUS
    law ZEUS
    love EROS, POTHOS
    marriage HYMEN
    rain ZEUS
    rivers SELINUS
    sea AEGEUS,
        NEREUS
    sky ARGUS
    sun APOLLO,
        MENTU, PHOEBUS,
        HELIOS, HYPERION,
        MENT
    sunset ZEUS,
        ENDYMION
    underworld
        PYTHON
    vegetation DIONYSUS
    war ARES,
        ENYALIUS
    wind AEOLUS,
        EURUS
    wine BACCHUS
    youth APOLLO

Hebrew BAAL, JAH,
ADONAI, ELOHIM,
YAHWEH
  sun BAAL
Hindu AGNI, AKAL,
CIVA, DEVA, VARUNA,
DEWA, KAMA, S(H)IVA,
BHAGA, KA, VISHNU,
MANU, KRISHNA,
RAMA, VAYU
  dead YAMA
  destruction SIVA
  fire AGNI
  lightning AGNI
  love KAMA
  nature DEVA
  sea VARUNA
  sky DYAUS
  sun ADITYAS, AGNI,
  VARUNA
  triad SIVA
  unknown KA
  waters VARUNA
  wisdom GANESA
Icelandic DONAR,
THOR, LOKI, HEIM-
DALL, WODEN, ODIN,
FORSETI, BALDER,
AESIR, TYR, TIU
Irish DAGDA, LER,
DANU, DANA
  chief DAGDA
  death and fertility
  DANU, DANA
  love ANGUS
  sea LER
Italian CONSUS,
FEBRUUS, JANUS,
PICUS, TIBERINUS
Japanese AMIDA,
AMITA, EBISU, SHA,
HOTEI
  happiness EBISU,
  HOTEI
Latin, sun JANUS, SOL
Norse ASGARD, AS(A),
FORSETI, YMIR,
LOK(I), ER, TIU, TIW,
TYR, VAN, ZIO, ZIU,
FREY, HLER, HOTH,
LOKE, ODIN, THOR,
TY(RR), ULL(R),
VALE, VALI, VANS,
AESIR, BALD(E)R,
BRAGE, BRAGI, DONAR,
VANIR, BALDUR, VOR,
WODEN
  battle ODIN
  *betrothal and mar-
  riage* VOR
  blind HOTH
  chase ULL(R)

chief FENIR, ODIN,
VALI, VANIR, YMIR
clouds YMIR
commerce VANIR
discord LOKI, ERIS
dwarf TROLL
evil LOKI
fate NORN, URTH
fruitfulness FREY
heathen AESIR
justice FORSETI
king of WODEN
light BALD(E)R,
BALDUR
mischief LOKI
peace FORSETI,
FREY
poetry BRAGE, ODIN
sea AEGER, AEGIR,
NJORD, YMIR
sky TIU, ZIO
sun BALDER, FREY,
ING
thunder THOR
war ODIN, ER,
THOR, TYR
watchfulness HEIM-
DALL
Persian MITHRAS,
YIMA
  sun MITHRAS
Philistine DAGON
Phrygian MEN, ATTIS,
ATYS
Polynesian ORO,
MAUI, PELE, TANE,
ATUA, TIKI
Roman DIS, AMOR,
FAUN, JOVE, PICUS,
MARS, MORS, CUPID,
EURUS, ORCUS,
APOLLO, AUSTER,
BOREAS, FAUNUS,
VULCAN, NEPTUNE,
LAR, PAN, PALES
  chief JOVE,
  JUPITER
  dead ORCUS
  death MORS
  fire VULCAN
  flocks PAN, PALES
  Hades DIS, ORCUS,
  PLUTO
  herds PAN, PALES
  household LAR,
  LARES, PENATES
  joy COMUS
  love AMOR, CUPID
  night SOMNUS
  patron MERCURY
  sea NEPTUNE
  sky JUPITER

sleep MORPHEUS,
SOMNUS
thieves MERCURY
tutelary LAR, LARES,
NUMEN
underworld DIS,
HADES, ORCUS,
PLUTO, COG
war MARS,
QUIRINUS
wine BACCHUS
woods SYLVANUS
Sanskrit See "Vedic"
and "Hindu"
Scandinavian See
"Norse"
Semitic, household
EL
Syrian, fortune GAD
  sun HADAD
Tahitian TAAROA
Teutonic See "Norse"
Theban AMENN,
AMENT, AMON
Vedic INDRA, ADITI,
ADITYA
  dawn or sun
  ASVINS, DYAUS,
  ADITI, ADITYA
Welsh DYLAN,
GWYN, PWYLL, LLEU,
GWYDION
  dead PWYLL
  sun LLEU
*god(s), further classifi-
cation of*
Aegean Sea NEREUS
agriculture FAUNUS,
NEBO, NINGIRSU,
OSIRIS, THOR
battle ODIN
beauty APOLLO,
HELIOS
betrothal and marriage
VOR
chase ULL
clouds YMIR
commerce VANIR
crocodile-headed
SOBK
darkness SET, SIN,
LAIUS, ACRISIUS
day HOR, HORUS,
JANUS
dead ANUBIS, ORCUS,
OSIRIS, MORS,
THANTOS, PWYLL,
YAMA
death MORS, DANU,
DANA
destruction SIVA
discord LOKI, ERIS

dreams MORPHEUS,
SERAPIS, ONEIROS
earth DAGAN, GEB,
KEB, SEB
elephant-headed
GANESHA
evil LOKI, GIRRU,
NERGAL, SET, VARUNA,
ZU
faith SET, SANCTUS
falcon-headed HORUS
fertility DAGAN, FREY,
ING, OSIRIS, DANU,
DANA
fire AGNI, DYAUS,
LOGE, VULCAN, GIRRU,
NUSKU
fish DAGAN, PRIAPUS
flocks PAN, PALES
force MENT, PTAH,
SHU
fortune GAD
fruitfulness FREY
goatlike AEGIPAN
Hades PLUTO,
HERMES, DIS, ORCUS
harvest CRONUS
hawk-headed HOR,
HORUS
healer EA
health BELI,
BELENUS, OSIRIS, EA
heavens ANU,
URANUS, NUT, ZEUS
herds PAN, PALES
household LAR, LARES,
EL, PENATES, STERAPH
human sacrifice
MOLOCH
hurricane OTUS,
ALOADAE
incarnate MNEVIS
jackal-headed APUAT
joy COMUS
justice FORSETI,
RAMMAN
law ZEUS
light LUG, MITRA,
OSIRIS, SHU, BALDER
lightning AGNI,
JUPITER
love AENGUS, AMOR,
BHAGA, CUPID, EROS,
KAME, POTHOS
marriage HYMEN
medicine NINGISHZIDA
messenger of HERMES
metal work VULCAN
mischief LOKI
mockery MOMUS
moon SIN, NANNAR,
KHENSU, THOTH

mother of RHEA,
FRIGGA, CYBELE
mountain(s), of
ATLAS, OLYMPUS
music APOLLO
nature DEVA
night SOMNUS
patron MERCURY
peace BALDER, EIR,
FORSETTE, FREY
poetry BRAGE, BRAGI,
ODIN
queen of HERA
rain AGNE, ESUS,
FREY, INDRA, ING,
JUPITER, ZEUS
rivers SELINUS
science TOTH
scribes NABU
seas AEGER, ATLAS,
DYLAN, NJORD,
NJORTH, LER, NEP-
TUNE, NEREUS,
VARUNA, AEGEUS,
PONTUS, YMIR
sky ANU, COEL,
DYAUS, JUPITER, TYR,
YMIR, ARGUS, ZEUS,
ANAT, TIU, ZIO
sleep MORPHEUS,
SOMNUS
solar disk ATEN
storms ADAD, ZU
sun AGNI, AMEN,
BALDER, KHEPERA,
AMON, PHOEBUS,
APOLLO, BAAL, BELI,
UTU(G), MENTU,
FREY, HELIOS, HORUS,
TEM, ING, CHEPERA,
MITHRAS, NERGAL, RA,
SHAMASH, SOL, HADAD
sunset TEM,
ENDYMION
thunder DONAR,
JUPITER, TARANIS,
THOR, ZEUS, LARES
trade VANIR
triad SIVA
tutelary LAR, LARES,
NUMEN
underworld PYTHON,
DIS, GWYN, OSIRIS
unknown KA
vegetation ATTIS,
BACCHUS, ESUS,
DIONYSUS
victory ODIN, ZEUS
war COEL, ER, MARS,
MENT, ARES, NERGAL,
THOR, TIU, TYR, KOEL,
WODEN, ODIN,

ENYALIUS, QUIRINUS,
IR(R)A, AS(S)UR
watchfulness HEIMDAL
waters EA(R),
FONTUS, HEA, NEP-
TUNE, VARUNA
wealth PLUTUS
wind(s) ADAD,
AEOLUS, BOREAS,
EURUS, KAARE,
NJORD, VAYU
wine BACCHUS
wisdom EA(R),
GANES(H)A, NEBO,
ODIN, SABU, SIN, TAT,
THOTH, NABU
woodlands PAN,
SATYR, SILENIUS,
FAUN, SILVANUS
woods SILVANUS
youth APOLLO
goddess(es) DEA *See
also under* "god-
dess(es), classification
of," *below*
Anatolian MA
Assyrian ALLATU,
FURY, IS(H)TAR,
NANA, SARPANITU
Babylonian AI, AYA,
ERUA, NANA,
IS(H)TAR, GULA,
NINA, ARURU
    deep NANA, NINA
    earth ARURU,
    IS(H)TAR
    healing BAU, GULA
    oceans NINA
    waters ERUA
Bakongo NZAMBI
Carthage TANIT(H)
Egypt MUT, ANTA,
APET, BAST, BUTO,
ISIS, MAAT, ATHOR,
AMEN, HATHOR, NUT,
SESHAT, IRIS, SATI,
MIN, AMENTI, PAKHT,
SEKHET
    cat-headed BAST,
    PAKHT, SEKHET
    cow-headed ISIS
    heavens NUT
    hippo-headed APET
    joy HATHOR
    justice MAAT
    learning SESHAT
    life ISIS
    lower world
    AMENTI
    panopolis MIN
    rainbow IRIS
    sky NUT

truth MAAT
womanhood SATI
Etruscan MENFRA,
UNI
Greek ATE, EOS,
ALEA, DICE, DIKE,
ENYO, ERIS, GAEA,
GAIA, HERA, HORA,
KORE, NIKE, UPIS,
IRENE, METIS, ATHENA,
CLOTHO, CYBELE,
EIRENE, HECATE,
MOERAE, PALLAS,
SELENA, SELENE,
ARTEMIS, ATROPOS,
DEMETER, LACHESIS,
APHRODITE, TYCHE,
NEMESIS
  agriculture
  ARTEMIS, DEMETER
  air AURA, HERA,
  AETHER
  arts MUSE, ATHENA
  beauty APHRODITE
  chance TYCHE
  chase ARTEMIS
  chastisement
  NEMESIS
  clouds NIOBE,
  IOLE, JOCASTA,
  JACASTE
  cross-roads HECATE
  dawn EOS, ARIADNE
  destiny MOERA
  destruction ARA
  discord ERIS
  earth GAEA, GE
  fate MOERA
  fire HESTIA
  flowers CHLORIS
  ghosts HECATE
  goblins ARTEMIS
  halcyon days
  ALCYONE
  happiness EBISU,
  HOTEI
  health DAMIA,
  HYGEA
  hearth HESTIA,
  VESTA
  heavens HECATE,
  HERA
  love APHRODITE
  marriage DEMETER,
  GAEA, GE, HERA
  memory
  MNEMOSYNE
  mischief ATE, ERIS
  mist NEPHELE,
  PHRIXOS, PHRIXUS
  moon ARTEMIS,

ASTARTE, DIANA,
SELENE, SELENA, IO
night ARTEMIS,
LEDA, LETO, NYX,
HECATE
peace IRENE
plains MAIA,
MAJESTA
retribution ARA
seas DORIS, INO
sky HERA
twilight PHAEDRA,
HELEN
vegetation COTYS
vengeance ARA,
NEMESIS
victory NIKE
war ENYO
weaving ERGANE
wisdom PALLAS,
MINERVA
youth HEBE
Hawaiian, fire PELE
Hindu USHAS, UMA,
VAC, DEVI, KALI,
S(H)RI, SHREE, VACH,
LAKSHMI
  beauty S(H)RI,
  SHREE, LAKSHMI
  dawn USHAS
  destruction KALI
  luck LAKSHMI,
  SHRI, SRI
  speech VAC
  wealth SRI, SHRI
Italian CERES, DIANA,
MINERVA, OPS,
POMONA, SALUS,
VENUS
Norse DIS, HEL, RAN,
SIF, URD, ERDA, FREA,
FRIA, GERD, NORN,
RIND, SAGA, URTH,
FREYA, NANNA,
WYRD, FREYJA
  beauty FREYA,
  FREYJA, FREIA
  betrothal VOR
  death HEL, HELA,
  RAN
  destiny NORN, URD,
  URTH, MOIRA
  doom URTH, WYRD
  earth SIF
  flowers NANNA
  giant NORN, URTH
  healing EIR
  history SAGA
  love same as beauty
  marriage FRIGG(A)
  peace EIR, NERTHUS
  seas RAN(A)

sky FRIGG(A)
  wedlock SIF
Peru, fertility MAMA
Roman ARA, NOX,
NYX, OPA, DIAN(A),
IRIS, JUNO, MAIA,
NONA, SPES, CERES,
EPONA, FAUNA, FLORA,
MORTA, PARCA, TERRA,
VENUS, VESTA,
DECUMA, PARCAE,
VACUNA, TRIVIA,
AURORA
  agriculture OPS
  beauty VENUS
  birth PARCA,
  LUCINA
  corpse LIBITINA
  cross-roads TRIVIA,
  HECATE
  dawn AURORA
  death PROSERPINE
  earth LUA, TELLUS
  fertility FAUNA
  fields LARES,
  TELLUS
  fire VESTA
  flowers FLORA
  fountains FERONIA
  harvest OPS
  health SALUS
  horses EPONA
  hunting DIANA,
  VACUNA
  love VENUS
  maternity APET
  moon LUNA,
  PHOEBUS
  night NOX, NYX
  peace PAX, MINERVA
  plenty OPS
  retribution CERES
  seas SALACIA
  state VESTA
  vegetation CERES,
  FLORA
  virtue FIDES
  war VACUNA,
  MINERVA
  womanhood JUNO
Sanskrit DEVI, UMA
Teutonic See "Norse"
Theban MUT
goddess(es), *classifica-*
tion of
abundance SRI
actors MINERVA
agriculture BAU,
CERES, ISIS, OPS,
ARTEMIS, DEMETER
air AURA, HERA,
AETHER

arts MUSE, ATHENA
avenging FURY, NEMESIS
beauty FREYA, VENUS, APHRODITE, SRI, SHRI, SHREE, LAKSHMI
betrothal VOR
birth PARCA, LUCINA
cat-headed BAST, PACHT
chance TYCHE
chase ARTEMIS, DIANA, DIANE
chastisement NEMESIS, FURY
civic ALEA
clouds NIOBE, IOLE, JOCASTA
corn CERES
corpse LIBITINA
cow-headed ISIS
criminal recklessness ATE
crops OPS, ANNONA
cross-roads HECATE, TRIVIA
dawn EOS, AURORA, MATUTA, ARIADNE, ALCEMENE
death DANU, HEL, HELA, PROSERPINE
deep NANA, NINA
destiny MOERA, NORN, URTH, URD
destruction ARA, KALI(KA)
discord ERIS
doom URTH, WYRD
earth SIF, ARURU, ISHTAR, GAEA, GE, TARI, CERES, GALA, LUA, OPS, TELLUS, ERDA, HERTA, SEB
faith CLOTHO, FIDES
fate MOERA, MORTA, NONA, NORN
fertility FAUNA, MAMA, ANNONA
fields LARES, TELLUS
fire HESTIA, PELE, VESTA
flowers CHLORIS, FLORA, NANNA
fortune TYCHE
fountains FERONIA
fruit trees POMONA
ghosts HECATE
goblins ARTEMIS
halcyon days ALCYONE
harvest OPS, CARPO

healing BAU, GULA, EIR
health DAMIA, HYGEA, SALUS
hearth HESTIA, VESTA
heavens NUT, HECATE, HERA
hippo-headed APET
history SAGA
hope SPES
horses EPONA
hunting DIANA, VACUNA
infatuation ATE
joy HATHOR
justice ASTRAEA, DICE, MAAT
learning SESHAT
life ISIS
light LUCINA
love ASTARTE, ATHOR, FREYE, ISHTAR, APHRODITE, VENUS
luck LAKSHMI, SHRI
marriage GAEA, GE, HERA, DEMETER, FRIGG(A)
memory MNEMOSYNE
Memphis DOR
mischief ERIS, ATE
mist NEPHELE
moon BENDID, DIANA, ISIS, LUNA, HECATE, LUCINA, PHOEBE, PHOEBUS, SELENE, SELENA, ARTEMIS, ASTARTE, TANIT(H)
nature ARTEMIS, CYBELE
night LETO, NOX, NYX, HECATE, LEDA, ARTEMIS
oceans NINA *See* "seas" *below*
order DICE, DIKE, IRENE
ovens FORNAX
peace EIR, IRENE, PAX, MINERVA
persuasion SUADA
plains MAIA, MAJESTA
plenty OPS
rainbow IRIS
retribution ARA, CERES, NEMESIS
seas DORIS, INO, RAN(A), SALACIA
seasons HORAE
sky NUT, HERA, FRIGG(A)
speech VAC
state VESTA

storms HARPY
sun AI
trees POMONA
truth MAAT
twilight PHAEDRA, HELEN
underworld ALLUTU, FERONIA, FURY, GAEA, HECATE, HEL, LARUNA
vegetation COTYS, CERES, FLORA
vengeance ARA, NEMESIS
victory NIKE
virtue FIDES
war ANAHITA, ANATU(M), ATHENA, BELONA, ENYO, ISHTAR, VACUNA, MINERVA
waters ERUA
wealth SRI
weaving ERGANE
wedlock SIF
welfare SALUS
wisdom MINERVA
womanhood SATI, MUT, JUNO
youth HEBE
godfather SPONSOR
godly PIOUS, DIVINE, DEVOUT, RIGHTEOUS
godwit PRINE, BIRD
Goethe *hero* FAUST
home WEIMAR
goggle STARE, SQUINT, EYESHADE
goggler SCAD, FISH
allied to AKULE
Hawaii AKULE
going EXIT, ULTRA, BEHAVIOR, WAY, CURRENT, MOVING, WORKING, RUNNING, DEPARTURE, OBTAINABLE
back on APOSTASY
in INEUNT
out EXEUNT, EXIT, EXODUS
gola SIMA, OGEE, MOLDING
gold ARUM, GILT, GILDING, AU, ORO, WEALTH, MONEY, RICHES
braid ORRIS
cast INGOT
colored metal GILT, ORMOLU
combining form AURO
deposit PLACER

field OPHIR
  Africa RAND
fineness of CARAT
fool's PYRITE
imitation ORMOLU
lace ORRIS
like AUREATE
magic hoard of
  RHEINGOLD
mosaic ORMOLU
pertaining to AURIC
seeker ARGONAUT,
  MINER, PROSPECTOR
Spanish ORO
symbol AU
thin sheet FOIL,
  LATTEN
vein LODE
vessel CUPEL
washing pan BATEA
gold-brick SHIRK(ER)
  See "avoid"
"Gold Bug" *author*
  POE
Gold Coast *colony*
  TOGO
language TSHI, TWI,
  FANTI, AKAN
negro stock GA
seaport KETA, ADA
tribe AKAN, AKIM
golden YELLOW,
  AUREATE, AURIC,
  SHINING, BRIGHT,
  PRECIOUS, FLOURISH-
  ING
age SATURNIAN
bough MISTLETOE
fleece, land of
  COLCHIS
  seeker of JASON
  ship ARGO
goldenrod *genus*
  SOLIDAGO
goldlike alloy ASEM,
  ORMOLU, OROIDE
goldsmith's *crucible*
  CRUSET
golem DUNCE, BOOBY,
  ROBOT, AUTOMATON
golf *attendant* CADDY
call or cry FORE
club BRASSIE, DRIVER,
  CLEEK, IRON, MASHIE,
  PUTTER, SPOON, MID-
  IRON, NIBLICK
  head end of TOE
  socket HOSEL
course LINKS
cup RYDER, WALKER
hole CUP
poor shot SLICE

score PAR, BIRDIE,
  EAGLE
stroke LOFT, PUTT
teacher PRO
term TRAP, DIVOT,
  BAFF, CHIP, PAR,
  PUTT, SLICE, FORE,
  TEE
tournament OPEN
golfer JONES, SNEAD
poor DUBBER
Goliath's *town* GATH
gombeen USURY
Gomer's *husband*
  HOSEA
gomuti EJOO, ARENG,
  IROK, PALM
gone DEPARTED, LEFT,
  LOST, PAST, AGO, OUT,
  BROKEN, RUINED
Goneril's *sister* REGAN,
  CORDELIA
gonfalon BANNER,
  FLAG, ENSIGN,
  STANDARD
goober PEANUT
good PALATABLE,
  FLAVORABLE,
  GUSTATORY, EDIBLE,
  RIPE, MORAL, BON,
  RIGHT, PIOUS,
  WORTHY, DECOROUS,
  KIND, HONEST,
  VIRTUOUS, UPRIGHT,
  SINCERE, GRACIOUS,
  PROPER, ESTIMABLE,
  GENUINE, FAIR, VALID,
  SOUND, CHOICE,
  BENEFICIAL, FAVORA-
  BLE, EXCELLENT,
  VALUABLE, ABLE,
  SUITABLE, SATIS-
  FACTORY, VALID,
  RESPONSIBLE,
  SOLVENT, SUFFICIENT
arrangement EU-
  TAXIE, EUTAXY
fellow BRICK,
  TRUMP, PRINCE
-for-nothing MEAN,
  SHOTTEN, KET, BAD
King Henry BLITE
luck cap, newborn
  CAUL
news EVANGEL,
  GOSPEL
working order
  KILTER
goodbye ADIEU, TA-TA,
  ALOHA, ADIOS,
  FAREWELL, AVE, VALE,
  VALEDICTION

goods STOCK, WARES,
  FEE, WRACK, CLOTH,
  FREIGHT, MERCHAN-
  DISE, EFFECTS, CHAT-
  TELS, COMMODITIES,
  BONA
admission of taking
  AVOWRY
cast overboard JET-
  SAM, FLOTSAM
law BONA
movable CHATTELS
package BALE, BOX,
  CARTON
  covered by hides
  SEROON
stolen PELF, SPOIL,
  BOOTY, LOOT,
  GRAFT
sunk at sea LAGAN
goon ROUGH, THUG
  See "bandit"
goose GRAYLAG,
  BARNACLE, BRANT,
  GANNET, SOLAN,
  DUPE, NINNY,
  SIMPLETON, IRON,
  FOWL
barnacle ANATIFER,
  ANATIFA
Canada OUTARDE
cry CACKLE, HONK
fat AXUNGE
fen GRAYLAG
flock GAGGLE, RAFT
gannet SULA
genus ANSER,
  CHEN, BRANT
Godwin's GANZA
grease AXUNGE
Hawaii NENE
male GANDER
pygmy GOSLET
relating to ANSERINE
sea PHALAROPE,
  SOLAN
snow CHEN, WAVEY,
  BRANT
solan GANNET
wild BARNACLE,
  BRANT, ELK
young GOSLING
gooseberry THAPE,
  FABES, CHAPERON,
  OBSTACLE
goosefoot BLITE,
  SHRUB, PLANT
gopher RODENT,
  SNAKE
Mexican TUCAN
State MINNESOTA

gore PIERCE, STAB, CRUOR, BLOOD, GUSSET, HORN
of cloth GUSSET
gorge SATE, BOLT, GLUT, CLOY, PALL, STUFF, SATIATE, THROAT, GULLET, CANYON, FLUME, GULLY, CHASM, RAVINE, STRID, DEFILE, NOTCH, PASS, SURFEIT
Hindu NULLAH
Gorgon MEDUSA, STHENO, EURYALE
watchers for GRAEAE, DEINO, ENYO, PEPHREDO
gormandize SATE, GLUT, GORGE, STUFF, OVEREAT
gorse WHIN, FURZE, JUNIPER, SHRUB
gory BLOODY, RED, SANGUINE
gosling GOOSE, AMENT, CATKIN
gospel(s) TRUTH, EVANGEL, NEWS, TIDINGS, DOCTRINE, PRINCIPLE, CREED
harmony of the four DIATESSARON
gossamer DIAPHANOUS, GAUZY, THIN, FLIMSY, LIGHT, COBWEB
gossip CAT, CHAT, CLAVER, RUMOR, DIRT, ON-DIT, NORATE, QUIDNUNC, TATTLE, TALK, CHIN, BABBLE, CHATTER, PRATE, BUSYBODY, TALEBEARER
India GUP
tattling PIET
gossoon LAD, YOUTH, BOY
Gothic *arch* RIB
bard RUNER
goulash RAGOUT *See* "hash"
Gounod opera FAUST
gourd MELON, CALABASH, PEPO, CUCURBIT, FLASK, PUMPKIN, SQUASH
fruit PEPO, LOOFA, LUFFA
rattle MARACA

sponge LOOFA, LUFFA
gourmand GLUTTON, EPICURE, WOLF
gourmet TASTER, EPICURE, GLUTTON
gout ARTHRITIS, PODAGRA, GONAGRA
govern REIN, REIGN, BRIDLE, LEAD, RUN, REGULATE, RULE, EXECUTE, DIRECT, CURB, CONDUCT, MANAGE, CONTROL, COMMAND, RESTRAIN
government REGIMEN, SWAY, POLICY, RULE, STATE, REGIME, KINGDOM, EMPIRE, POWER, MONARCHY, AUTONOMY, GUIDANCE, DOMINION, ADMINISTRATION, COMMONWEALTH, SOVEREIGNTY, DEMOCRACY
by ten DECARCHY
by women GYNARCHY, GYNECOCRACY
control REGIE, REGIMEN
form of POLITY
lands, India AMANI
without ACRACY, ANARCHY
governor DYNAST, REGENT, VICEROY, EXECUTIVE, COMPTROLLER, DIRECTOR, MASTER, PILOT, MAGISTRATE, CONTROLLER, REGULATOR, SATRAP
Burma WOON, WUN
governors, 1 of 10 DECARCH
gowan DAISY, FLOWER
gown FROCK, SOUTANE, SULTANE, DRESS, ROBE, GARB, GARMENT
Greece CHITON
Middle Ages CYCLAS
negligee MATINEE, KIMONO
Goya *subject* ALBA, DUCHESS
grab SNATCH, TAKE, GRASP, CLUTCH, SEIZE, NAB, COP, STEAL, KIDNAP

grabble GROPE, FEEL, DIG, GROVEL, SPRAWL, GRAB
grace FAVOR, ADORN, ESTE, CHARM, TACT, ENHANCE, HONOR, MERCY, LENITY, DIGNITY, KINDNESS, PIETY, RELIGION, PRAYER, PARDON, REPRIEVE, ELEGANCE, BEAUTY
graceful EASY, GAINLY, ELEGANT, COMELY, BEAUTIFUL, NATURAL, CHARMING, APPROPRIATE, FITTING, SEEMLY, SYLPHIC
Graces, *mother of* AEGLE
one of THALIA, AGLAIA, EUPHROSYNE
gracile SLENDER, SLIM, SLIGHT, THIN, SYLPHIC
gracious BENIGN, URBANE, KIND, AFFABLE, BENEVOLENT, FAVORABLE, FRIENDLY, MERCIFUL, CONDESCENDING, TENDER, GENTLE, CIVIL, POLITE, GENEROUS, COURTEOUS
grackle MINA, MYNA, DAW, BLACKBIRD
gradation NUANCE, STEP, SCALE, SERIES, PROGRESS, ADVANCE
grade LEVEL, RANK, MARK, RATE, STEP, RATING, DEGREE, STAGE, GRADIENT, HILL, SLOPE, SLANT, INCLINE, CLASS(IFY)
gradient ASCENT, SLOPE, INCLINE, RAMP, HILL, SLANT
graduate ALUMNUS, PASS, FINISH, MEASURE, ALUMNA, LAUREATE
Graeae, *watchers for Gorgons* DEINO, PEPHREDO, ENYO
graft BUD, CION, SCION, JOINT, SHOOT, SLIP, SPROUT, BRIBE, TOLL, LABOR
taker BRIBEE

grafted heraldry ENTE
grail SANGREAL,
  SANGRAAL, BOWL,
  CHALICE, CUP, AMA,
  PLATTER
  knight of PERCIVALE,
  GALAHAD, BORS
grain SEED, MITE,
  BIT, SPECK, ATOM,
  IOTA, WHIT, SAND,
  CEREAL, KERNEL,
  OVULE, PARTICLE,
  SCRAP, JOT, TITTLE,
  WEIGHT, RYE, CORN,
  OAT, MAIZE, WHEAT,
  BARLEY, TEMPER,
  INCLINATION, FIBER
  beard AWN, ARISTA
  black URD
  broken spike CHOB
  disease SMUT, ERGOT
  exchange PIT
  gather in REAP,
  GLEAN, HARVEST
  German SPELT
  ground MEAL, FLOUR
  husk GLUME, BRAN
  measure GRIST, MOY,
  PECK, BUSHEL
  of stone or wood
  BATE
  1/20th of weight
  MITE
  pit SILO
  refuse PUG, CHAFF
  Russian EMMER,
  DURUM
  sacrificial ADOR
  shelter HUTCH, SILO,
  BARN
  shock of COP
  to be ground GRIST
gram molecular
  weight MOLE
gramercy THANKS
grammar, *logic and*
  (or) rhetoric TRIVIA,
  TRIVIUM
grammatical *arrange-*
  ment SYNTAX
  case DATIVE
  construction SYNESIS
  term PARSE, GENDER
grampus ORC(A),
  WHALE, KILLER
granary SILO, CRIB,
  BIN, ELEVATOR, STORE-
  HOUSE, GRANGE,
  GUNJ, GOLA, GUNGE
grand LARGE, STATELY,
  HOMERIC, AUGUST,
  EPIC, NOBLE,

OPULENT, LORDLY,
  MAJESTIC, DIGNIFIED,
  EMINENT, ILLUSTRI-
  OUS, MAGNIFICENT,
  SPLENDID, GLORIOUS,
  PIANO
grandchild OE, OY,
  OYE
  great IEROE
grandeur GLORY,
  MAJESTY, BEAUTY,
  VASTNESS, GREATNESS,
  POMP, SPLENDOR
grandeval AGED,
  ANCIENT, OLD
grandfather AIEL,
  PATRIARCH, ATAVUS,
  AVUS, ANCESTOR
  pertaining to AVITAL,
  AVAL
grandfather's grand-
  father TRESAIEL
grandiose NOBLE,
  MAJESTIC, HOMERIC,
  STATELY, EPIC,
  IMPOSING, BOMBAS-
  TIC, TURGID
grandmother BEL-
  DAM(E), AVIA,
  GRANDAM(E),
  ANCESTOR
grandparent, pertaining
  to AVAL
grange GRANARY,
  FARM, HEARTH,
  SOCIETY, LODGE,
  ASSOCIATION
granite, *constituent of*
  MICA, QUARTZ,
  ORTHOCLASE,
  FELDSPAR
  porphyry ELVAN
grant ADMIT, CON-
  SENT, ACCORD, SUB-
  SIDY, AWARD, CEDE,
  CONFER, LOAN, PER-
  MIT, ENAM, BESTOW,
  GIFT, YIELD, AGREE,
  GIVE, ALLOT, PRESENT,
  ALLOW, CONCEDE,
  CONVEY, TRANSFER,
  LARGESS(E)
  of rights CHARTER,
  DEED, FRANCHISE,
  CONTRACT, LEASE
granular snow field
  FIRN, NEVE
grape(s) CONCORD,
  CATAWBA, MUSCAT,
  MALAGA, NIAGARA,
  DELAWARE, FRUIT,
  BERRY, RAISIN

  brandy MARC
  bunch of BOB
  conserve UVATE,
  JELLY
  cultivation VITICUL-
  TURE, VINICULTURE
  deposit TARTAR
    relating to RACEMIC
  derivative of blue
  (O)ENIN
  disease COLEUR,
  ERINOSE
  drink DIBS, SAPA,
  WINE
  genus VITIS,
  MUSCADINIA
  juice DIBS, MUST,
  STUM
  like berry UVA
  refuse MARC,
  BAGASSE
  seed(s) ACINUS,
  ACINI
  sugar DEXTROSE,
  FRUCTOSE
  sun-dried PASA,
  RAISIN
  syrup SAPA
  vine disease ERINOSE
  white MALAGA,
  NIAGARA, MUSCAT
  wild vine LIANA
grapefruit POMELO,
  PUMELO, SHAD-
  DOCK
graph CHART, LOCUS,
  MAP, DESIGN,
  SCHEME, SKETCH,
  DIAGRAM, PLAN
graphic CLEAR,
  VIVID, LUCID, TELL-
  ING, DESCRIPTIVE,
  STRIKING
graphite LEAD,
  PLUMBAGO, KISH
grapple SEIZE,
  WRESTLE, ATTACK,
  FASTEN, KNIT, BIND,
  CLUTCH, LOCK, HOOK,
  TONG, STRUGGLE,
  GRAPNEL, GROPE,
  OPPOSE
grappling iron
  GRAPNEL
grasp HENT, EREPT,
  COMPREHEND, UNDER-
  STAND, EMBRACE,
  CLASP, GRIP, HOLD,
  SEIZE, GRAB,
  CLUTCH, CLINCH
grasping CLOSE,
  MISERLY, AVID,

GREEDY, AVARICIOUS, RAPACIOUS, COVETOUS
adapted for PREHENSILE, PREHENSIVE
grass SPART, DARNEL, LAWN, TURF, SOD, HERBAGE, ZEA
American GAMA, RYE, SESAME, POA
Asia COIX
Austrian MARRAM
bamboolike REED
beard AWN
Bengal MILLET
Bermuda DOOB
blade of TRANEEN, LEAF, SPIKE
blue POA
bull SLOUGH
bunch STIPA
carpet SMUT, LOUISIANA
cattail TIMOTHY
cereal WHEAT, RICE, MILLET, OAT, RYE, BARLEY
coarse SEDGE, REED, BROME
corn KAFFIR
couch DEVIL'S, QUITCH, REDTOP, FOXTAIL
creeping beard FESCUE
darnel TARE, RYE
devil's COUCH
ditch ENALID
dog's tail TRANEEN, BENT
dried HAY, FODDER
E. India USAR
edibles of GRAIN, SEEDS
esparto ALFA
family POACEAE
feather STIPA
flyaway BENT
fodder CORN, TIMOTHY, ALFALFA
forage MILLET, REDTOP, CLOVER, ALFALFA
fringed brome CHESS
genus COIX, STIPA, POA, ARUNDO, AVENA
hay ALFALFA, REDTOP, CLOVER, MILLET, TIMOTHY, FESCUE
hunger FOXTAIL
husk GLUME

India cereal RAGGEE
Job's-tears CROIX
Johnson SORGHUM
jointed stem CULM
Kentucky blue POA
kind BARLEY, BROME, EEL, TAPE, NARD
leaf BLADE, TRANEEN, SPIKE
Louisiana VETIVER, BENA
marsh REED, SEDGE, CANE
mat NARD
meadow POA, CLOVER, TIMOTHY, ALFALFA, FESCUE
mesquite GRAMA
millet PANIC, BENGAL
moor HEATH
oat AVENA
pasture See "meadow" *above*
Philippine COGON
poison rye DARNEL
quaking BRIZA, RATTLESNAKE
genus BRIZA
quitch COUCH
reedy, Medit. DISS
rope-making MUNG, MUNJ
rug MAT
salt SPART, ALKALI
scale GLUME, PALEA
sedge BROOM
Spanish ESPARTO
  broom SPART
stem REED, CULM
stiff or wiry BENT, REED
swamp SEDGE, REED
thatch ALANG, COGON
velvet HOLCUS
wiry BENT, POA
grasshopper GRIG, LOCUST, KATYDID
grassland LEA, SAVANNA, SWARD, VELD(T), PASTURE, MEADOW, PRAIRIE
grassy *country or plain* See "grassland"
grate JAR, RASP, GRID, CHARK, SCRAPE, RUB, ABRADE,

GRIND, BASKET, FIREBED, HEARTH
gratify EASE, ARRIDE, CONTENT, HUMOR, REGALE, TICKLE, DELIGHT, PLEASE, GLADDEN, SATISFY, INDULGE, PAMPER, OBLIGE
gratinate COOK, BROWN, CRISP
grating LATTICE, GRILL(E), PARTITION, GRID, HARSH, HOARSE, HACK, RASPY, IRRITATING, DISPLEASING
gratuitous FREE, GRATIS, WANTON, WILLING, VOLUNTARY, SPONTANEOUS
gratuity PILON, TIP, FEE, DOLE, GIFT, LAGNIAPPE, VAIL, LARGESS, BOON, FAVOR, PRESENT, DONATION, BOUNTY, CHARITY, BRIBE
gravamen CHARGE, GRIEVANCE, COMPLAINT
grave SUANT, TOMB, SEPULCHER, OSSUARY, SOBER, FOSSE, SAD, SERIOUS, QUIET, SLOW, STERN, SEDATE, EARNEST, STAID, MOMENTOUS, WEIGHTY, SOMBER, UNACCENTED, CARVE, ENGRAVE
cloth CEREMENT, SHROUD
mound BARROW, TUMULUS
gravel BEACH, SAND, ROCK, GRIT, GEEST, PUZZLE, CALCULUS
alluvial GEEST
graver CHISEL, BURIN, STYLE(T), SCULPTOR
gravestone MARKER, STELE, MONUMENT
graving tool See "graver"
gravitate DROP, FALL, SINK, TEND, INCLINE, SETTLE
gravy vessel BOAT
gray OLD, HOARY, ACIER, ASHEN, DUN, AGED, GRIZZLED,

LEADEN, DRAB, CLOUDY
combining form POLIO
matter BRAINS, OBEX, CORTEX, INTELLECT
grayling HERRING, UMBER, GOOSE, FISH
graze BROWSE, FEED, AGIST, PASTURE, NICK, RUB, SHAVE, TOUCH, BRUSH, NOURISH
cattle PASTURE, AGIST
grease LARD, AXUNGE, SUET, FAT, MORT, OIL, WAX, LUBRICATE, BRIBE
greasewood CHICO, CHAMISO, SHRUB
greasy YOLKY, OILY, PORKY, FATTY, UNCTUOUS, OLEAGINOUS, SLIPPERY, SMOOTH
great VIP, NOBLE, STAR, SUBLIME, IMPORTANT, EMINENT, NOTED, FAMOUS, AUGUST, BIG, HUGE, TITANIC, HERCULEAN, LARGE, VAST, EXTREME, NOTORIOUS, GRAND, SUPER, BULKY, IMMENSE, ENORMOUS *See* "huge"
Barrier Island OTEA
Commoner PITT
"Expectations" hero PIP
Lake ERIE, HURON, MICHIGAN, ONTARIO, SUPERIOR
number LAC, LAKH, LEGION, GALAXY, HEAP, HOST
Spirit, Indian MANITO
greater MORE, LARGER, MAJOR
grebe DABCHICK, FOWL
greed AVARICE, DESIRE, GLUTTONY, EAGERNESS, CUPIDITY
greediness EDACITY, CUPIDITY, VORACITY, AVIDITY, SELFISHNESS
greedy ESURIENT, OMNIVOROUS, AVID, STINGY, CLOSE, RAVENOUS, GRASPING, RAPACIOUS, AVARICIOUS, INSATIABLE

Greece, Greek CRETE, ARGIVE, HELLENE, (H)ELLAS, ACHAIA, ATTICA, DORIS
abbess AMMA
admiral NAVARCH
alphabet See "letter" *below*
ancient ATTICA, HELLAS, DORIS
  city CRISA, PELLA, PYDNA, ELIS, CHALCIS, ERETRIA, EUOBEA
  country ELIS
  region PHOCIS
assembly AGORA, PNYX
aurora EOS
avenging spirit ERINYS, KER, ATE
base, architecture ATTIC
bay or inlet SUDA
bondman PENEST
cape MALEA, PAPAS, ARAXOS, ARAXUS
castanet CROTALUM
Catholic UNIAT(E)
charioteer, myth. PHAETON
church ORTHODOX
  father or leader of ORIGEN, ARIUS, PAPAS
  reserved section BEMA
citadel ACROPOLIS
city or town SPARTA, LARISSA, TEGEA, ARTA, CALCIS, ARGOS, VOLOS, CHIOS
  ancient See under "ancient" *above*
  mythological SYBARIS, NEMEA
clan OBE
coin DIOBOL(ON), OBOL(US), DRACHMA, LEPTA, LEPTON, DUCAT, STATER, NOMAS, MINA, PHENIX

colony ELEA, IONIA
column DORIC, IONIC
commander NAVARCH
commonality DEMOS
community DEME
contest AGON
counsellor NESTOR
courtesan THAIS, ASPASIA
cup or bowl DEPAS, HOLMOS, COTYLE
cupid EROS
dance HORMOS, STROPHE
deity See under "god" *or* "goddess"
dialect (A)EOLIC, DORIC, IONIC
division IPIROS (EPIRUS), THRAKI (THRACE), THESSALIA (THESSALY), KRITI (CRETE)
doctor GALEN
drama MIME
dramatist THESPIS, EUPOLIS
drinking cup HOLMOS, COTYLE
earth GEOS
enchantress CIRCE, MEDEA
entertainer(s) HETAERA, HETAIRA, HETAERIA
eparchy DORIS
epic ILIAD, ODYSSEY
evil spirit MOMUS
fable writer AESOP
faction See "underground" *below*
female worshipper ORANT
festival DELIA, AGON, HALOA
foot-race course STADIA, DIAULOS
Furies ERINYES, ALECTO, MEGAERA, TISIPHONE
galley UNIREME, BIREME, TRIREME
garment CHITON, PEPLOS, CHLAMYS
geographer STRABO
gift(s) XENIUM, XENIA

god or goddess See under "god" or "goddess"
governor EPARCH, NOMARCH
gravestone STELE
gulf ENOS, ARGOLIS, SALONIKA, CORINTH, ARTA, LACONIA, PATRAS
gymnasium XYST
headband TAENIA
hero AJAX, NESTOR, THESEUS, MELEAGER, IDAS
historian XENOPHON, POLYBIUS
house, apartment in, men ANDRON
  women THALAMUS
huntress ATALANTA
immigrant METIC
island CHIOS, CRETE, ELIS, PELION, KOS, HYDR(E)A, NAXOS, IONIA, MILO, NIO, SAMOS, SCIO, PSARA, PSYRA, POROS See "Cyclades"
jar See "vessel" below
lawmaker MINOS, SOLON
leather flask OLPE
legislature SENATE, BOULE (VOULI)
letter ALPHA, BETA, GAMMA, DELTA, EPSILON, ZETA, ETA, THETA, IOTA, KAPPA, LAMBDA, MU, NU, XI, OMICRON, PI, RHO, SIGMA, TAU, UPSILON, PHI, CHI, PSI, OMEGA
  discontinued DIGAMMA
life BIOS
love PHILOS
  feast AGAPE
magistrate ARCHON, EPHOR
  chief NOMARCH
market place AGORA
marriage GAMOS
  song HYMEN
Mars ARES
marsh district LERNA
mathematician EUCLID
measure PIK(I), ACAENA, BEMA,

POUS, STADIUM, STADION, CADOS, CHEME, CHOUS, CONCHE, COTYLE, DIAULOS, DICHAS, DIOTE, DORON, HECTEIS, HEKTOS, HEMINA, KONCHE, LICHAS, MILION, PECHYS, PYGME, PYGON, STREMMA, XESTES, XYLON
mountain OLYMPUS, ATHOS, HELICON, OSSA, PARNASSUS, IDA, OITE, OETA, PELION, PILION, PARUS, VISTI
musical term NETE
musician ARION
nome, nomei ARKADHIA (ARCADIA), ARGOLIS, ARTA, ATTIKI (ATTICA), AKHAIA (ACHAEA), VOIOTIA (BOEOTIA), DRAMA, EVROS, EVVOIA (EUBOEA), ILIA (ELIS), IMATHIA, IRAKLION, IONNANIA, KAZALA, KASTORIA, KERKIRA (CORFU), KILKIS, LAKONIA (LACONIA), LARIS(S)A, LASITHI, LESVOS (LESBOS), LEVKAS (LEUKAS), MAGNISIA, MESSINIA (MESSENIA), XANTHI, PELLA, PIERIA, PREVEZA, RETHIMNI, RODHOPI (RHODOPHE), SAMOS, SERRAI, TRIKALA, FTHIOTIS (PHTHIOTIS), FLORINA, FOKIS (PHOCIS), KHANIA, KHIOS (CHIOS), KOZANI
note, music NETE
overseer EPHOR
painter GRECO
parliament BOULE
patriarch ARIUS
peninsula MOREA, ALTE (AKTI)
people DEMOS
philosopher PLATO, THALES, ZENO, GALEN, NESTOR, PYRRHO, SOCRATES
physician GALEN
pilaster ANTA

pillar STELE
pitcher OLPE
platform LOGEUM, BEMA
poet ARION, HOMER, ION, PINDAR, EUPOLIS
poetess ERINNA, SAPPHO
populace DEMOS
port See "seaport" below
portico STOA, XYST
prefect EPARCH
priest PAPA
promontory ACTIUM
province See "division" and "nome" above
public disgrace ATIMY
region DORIS
resistance group EAM, ELAS
river LERNA, PENEUS
sacred place ABATON
sage THALES, SOLON, SOCRATES
sculptor PHIDIAS, MYRON
seaport ENOS, VOLOS, PYLOS (PILOS), PATRAS
senate BOULE
serf PENEST
shrine ABATON
slab STELE
slave BAUBE, PENEST
soldier, ancient HOPLITE
song PAEON, MELOS, OICOS, ODE
soothsayer CALCHAS
sorceress CIRCE
soul or spirit PNEUMA, KER
star ASTRON
statesman ARISTIDES, PERICLES, THEMISTOCLES
storm wind LELAPS, LAELAPS
subdivision PHYLE
symbol ORANT
  music NETE, NEUME
temple, part of CELLA, NAOS
theater ODEON
time CHRONOS
tongue ROMAIC

town ELIS, SERES,
ARTA *See "city"*
above
township DEME
tribal division
PHRATRY
tunic CHITON
underground EAM,
ELAS
urn, vase PELIKE,
DEINOS, DINOS
vessel CADUS,
AMPHORA
village OBE
voting place PNYX
war cry, ancient
ALALA
warrior ACAMAS
weight OKA, OKE,
OBOL(E), MINA,
DIOBOL, DRACHMA,
DRACHME, KOKKUS,
STATER, TALENT,
TONOS
wind LELAPS,
LAELAPS
wine pitcher OLPE
wooden statue
XOANON
word LOGOS
writer LUCIAN,
AELIAN, AESOP
green VERD, FRESH,
UNRIPE, VERDANT,
RESEDA, IMMATURE,
NEW, UNSKILLED,
CALLOW, RAW,
CRUDE, YOUNG,
LEAFY, NILE, OLIVE,
JADE, EMERALD,
KELLY, VERDURE,
LAWN, GRASS
arrow YARROW
chalcedony JASPER
combining form
PRASEO
eyed JEALOUS
grayish RESEDA
kind of KELLY,
CYAN, VIRID, MOSS
light GO
Mountain State
VERMONT
sand MARL
tea HYSON
greenbacks MONEY,
NOTES, BILLS,
TENS, FIVES,
DOLLARS
greenery VERDURE,
SHRUBBERY
greengage PLUM

greenheart BEBEERU,
TREE, WOOD
greening APPLE,
SWAMP
Greenland *base* ETAH
discoverer ERIC,
RED
geological division
KOME
greenroom FOYER,
GOSSIP
greet SALUTE, HALSE,
ACCOST, HAIL, AD-
DRESS, MEET,
WELCOME, COM-
PLIMENT
greeting SALUTE,
ACCOIL, ADDRESS,
WELCOME, RECEP-
TION, SALUTATION,
KISS, AVE, HELLO,
HI, HOW
grego CLOAK,
JACKET
Gregorian doxology
EUOUAE
grenade SHELL, MIS-
SILE, BOMB
bag GIBERNE
gridiron GRILL, GRID,
FIELD, ARENA, RING,
COURT, FRAME
grief DOLOR, TRIAL,
WOE, PAIN, DOLE,
ANGUISH, REGRET,
TROUBLE, MISHAP,
SORROW, AFFLICTION,
DISTRESS, TRIBULA-
TION, MISERY, HEART-
ACHE, SADNESS,
DISASTER, FAILURE
grievance GRIPE,
WRONG, INJURY,
TORT, HARDSHIP,
BURDEN, COMPLAINT,
OPPRESSION
grieve LAMENT,
MOURN, CRY, SOR-
ROW, COMPLAIN, SUF-
FER, WEEP, RUE,
(BE)WAIL, AGONIZE,
PAIN, WOUND,
DEPLORE
grievous HEINOUS,
BAD, SEVERE,
INTENSE, DISTRESS-
ING, PAINFUL, SAD,
LAMENTABLE, DEPLOR-
ABLE, BURDENSOME,
ATROCIOUS, INJURIOUS
griffe MULATTO, SPUR

griffin MONSTER,
VULTURE
grifter's *henchman*
SHILL
grig CRICKET, EEL,
MONEY, GRASSHOP-
PER, LOCUST,
HEATHER, DWARF
grill GRATE, GRID,
GRATING, BROIL,
COOK, RACK, TOR-
MENT, AFFLICT,
TRY, QUIZ
grilse SALMON,
FISH
grim STERN, FIERCE,
CRUEL, FELL, OBDU-
RATE, GHASTLY,
GRISLY, SAVAGE,
FEROCIOUS, RUTH-
LESS, RELENTLESS,
FRIGHTFUL, DIRE,
FORBIDDING
grimace MOUE,
SCOWL, MOP, SHAM,
SMIRK, GRIN, AF-
FECTATION, PRE-
TENSE, SNOOT,
DISTORTION
grimalkin CAT, MOLL,
TOM, HAG, WOMAN
grime SOOT, DIRT,
SMUT, SULLY
grimy DIRTY, FOULED,
SULLIED, FILTHY,
UNCLEAN, SOILED
grind MASTICATE,
CHEW, CRUSH,
PULVERIZE, COM-
MINUTE, BRAY,
MULL, GRIT, RUB,
WHET, FILE, RASP,
GRATE, POWDER,
WORK, TOIL, LABOR,
CRANK
grinder MILL, MOLAR,
WHEEL, CHOPPER,
TOOTH, BIRD
grinding *stone*
METATE, MANO
substance EMERY,
ABRASIVE
grip BAG, CASE,
SATCHEL, HOLD,
SEIZE, GRASP,
CLUTCH, CONTROL,
DOMINATION, DITCH,
HANDLE, POWER,
DOMINION
gripper CLEAT, CLAW,
GRABBER, HOLDER,
HANDLE

gripping device VISE, TONGS, PLIERS, HAND, DOG

grit SAND, PLUCK, NERVE, GUTS, GALL, SPIRIT, GRAVEL, STAMINA, METTLE, BRAN

grivet WAAG, TOTA, MONKEY

groan MOAN, WHINE, SIGH, WAIL, LAMENT, COMPLAIN

grog RUM, RUMBO, LIQUOR, DRINK

grommet EYELET, RING, LOOP

groom PAGE, (H)OSTLER, DRESS, TEND, BRUSH, CURRY, TIDY, MANSERVANT, EQUERRY, PREPARE

groove FLUTE, RUT, SCORE, HABIT, SULCUS, FURROW, CHANNEL, MORTISE, SCRATCH, RABBET, ROUTINE
cut in barrel RIFLE, CROZE
in masonry RAGGLE
minute STRIA
pilaster STRIA

grope HUNT, FEEL, SEARCH, EXPLORE, PROBE, FUMBLE

grosbeak FINCH, CARDINAL, SPARROW, BIRD

gross ENTIRE, AGGREGATE, SUM, ABSOLUTE, GREAT, TOTAL, ALL, RANK, GLARING, STUPID, BULKY, FAT, CRUDE, CRASS, VULGAR, LARGE, BIG, BURLY, DULL, THICK, RUDE, UNREFINED, FLAGRANT, SHAMEFUL, CULPABLE

grotesque BIZARRE, BAROQUE, CLOWNISH, FREAK, ODD, UNIQUE, WILD, EERIE, UNCANNY, COMIC, DROLL, UNCOUTH, INCONGRUOUS, FANTASTIC, ABSURD, DISTORTED

grotto CAVE, CAVERN, GROT

grouch CRAB, GRUMBLE, GRUDGE, SULK

ground BASE, BASIS, REASON, FOUNDATION, SOIL, CLOD, CLAY, EARTH, TURF, SOD, LOAM, SWARD, AREA, REGION, PROPERTY, ESTATE, PULVERIZED, GRITTED, POWDERED, SCOPE
parcel of SOLUM, LOT, PLOT, ACRE
rising HURST, KNOLL

ground hog MARMOT, WOODCHUCK
day CANDLEMAS

groundless IDLE, FALSE, BASELESS, UNFOUNDED, UNTRUE

groundnut PEANUT, GOOBER, GOBBE, CHUFA

grounds BASIS, PROOF, REASON, FOUNDATION, MOTIVE, LEES, RESIDUE, DREGS, SEDIMENT, SETTLINGS, CAMPUS, LAWNS, SWARDS

group BAND, SQUAD, BEVY, DROVE, TEAM, HERD, KNOT, CLIQUE, BLOC, GANG, TRIBE, POSSE, CLUSTER, ARRANGE, CLASS(IFY), ASSEMBLE, ASSEMBLAGE, CONGREGATION, CONGREGATE, MASS, COLLECT(ION), MEET
of species PHYLUM, GENUS
together FILE, CLUSTER, BAND, ASSEMBLE, MEET

grouped AGMINATE

grouper MERO, GUASA, HIND, FISH

grouse PTARMIGAN, PARTRIDGE, BIRD, COMPLAIN, GRUMBLE, GROUCH
gathering of LEK
genus BONASA
Pallas' sand ATTAGEN
red genus LAGOPUS

grove TOPE, THICKET, COPSE, WOOD, STAND
mango TOPE

pertaining to NEMORAL
sacred to Diana NEMUS

grovel CRAWL, CRINGE, FAWN, CREEP, COWER, WALLOW, WELTER

grow BECOME, ACCRUE, RAISE, CULTIVATE, PRODUCE, BREED, WAX, MATURE, THRIVE, ROOT, RIPEN, INCREASE, ENLARGE, DEVELOP, EXPAND, WIDEN, SWELL, ENHANCE, AUGMENT, COME
old SENESCE, AGE, RIPEN

growing *in couples* BINATE
in fields CAMPESTRAL, AGRESTIAL
in swamps ULIGINOSE
in waste places RUDERAL
out ENATE
together ACCRETE

growl HOWL, GIRN, GNAR, SNARL, YAR(R), MUTTER, RUMBLE, COMPLAIN

growler FLOE, CAN, PITCHER, BASS, CAB, DOG

grown MATURE, RIPE, NUBILE, SEEDED
together ACCRETE

growth ACCRETION, SHOOT, TUMOR, WEN, HAIR, CORN, CLAVUS, WART, POLYP, STUBBLE, DEVELOPMENT, VEGETATION, INCREASE, FELON, ENLARGEMENT, EXPANSION
process of NASCENCY, DEVELOPMENT
retarding PARATONIC

grub SLAVE, BOB, MOIL, LARVA, MAGGOT, MATHE, DIG, DELVE, FOOD, EATS, CHOW, ROOT, DRUDGE, CATERPILLAR, PLODDER
clear of trees ASSART
tool MATTOCK

grubble FEEL, GROPE

grudge STINT, HATRED, ENVY, SPITE, DOLE, COVET, PIQUE, RANCOR, MALICE, ANGER

grue ICE, SNOW

gruel ATOLE, MUSH, PORRIDGE

gruesome GRISLY, MACABRE, GLOOMY, HORRID, SINISTER, GRIM, LURID, UGLY, HIDEOUS, GHASTLY

gruff SHORT, BLUNT, CURT, BLUFF, DOUR, SOUR, ANGRY, AUSTERE, ROUGH, BRUSQUE, CHURLISH, RUDE, HARSH, GRUMPY, DISCOUR-TEOUS

grumble MURMUR, COMPLAIN, MUTTER, REPINE, MAUNDER, FRET, CROAK, GROWL, SNARL

grumous THICK, CLOTTED, GRAINY

grunt fish RONCO, CROAKER

Grus constellation CRANE

guachoncho fish PELON

Guam *capital* AGANA
idol ANITO
port APRA
tree IPIL

guan *genus* ORTALIS, PIPILE, CHACALACA, BIRD, FOWL

Guana ARAWAKAN, INDIAN, MAJAGUA, TREE
Australian LIZARD, IGUANA

guarantee PLEDGE, SURETY, BOND, BAIL, TOKEN, GAGE, ENSURE, WARRANT, SECURITY, ASSURANCE

guarantor SURETY, SPONSOR, PATRON, BACKER, ANGEL, VOUCHER, UNDER-WRITER

guarapucu WAHOO, PETO, SHRUB, BUSH

guard ESCORT, WATCH-(MAN), POLICE, PATROL, PICKET, SENTRY, SENTINEL, KEEPER, WARDEN, FENDER, BANTAY, SHIELD, BAFFLE, COVER, PAD, HOOD, CLOAK, SHELTER, BULWARK, DEFEND, TEND, MIND, CONVOY, PROTECT, ATTEND, KEEP, CURB, BRIDLE, RESTRAIN
child's SITTER, TEACHER, TUTOR
freemason's TILER, TYLER

guardhouse BRIG, JAIL *See* "jail"

guardian TRUSTEE, COMMITTEE, WARDEN, PATRON, ANGEL, TUTOR, GUIDE, SENTRY, KEEPER, CUSTODIAN, PROTEC-TOR *See* "guard"
church relics MYSTA-GOGUE
subject of WARD
watchful ARGUS, CERBERUS

Guatemala *fruit* ANAY, BANANA
money QUETZAL(ES)

gudgeon DUPE, GULL, BAIT, FISH

Gudrun's *brother* GUNNAR
husband ATLI

guenon MONA, MONKEY, GRIVET

guerdon CROWN, PRIZE, REWARD, HONOR, RECOMPENSE, REQUITAL

guess THEORY, SUR-MISE, FANCY, ESTIMATE, JUDGE, OPINION, INFER, SPECULATE, THINK, REASON, BELIEVE, HYPOTHESIS, DIVINE, SUPPOSE, CONJEC-TURE, MISTRUST, IMAGINE, SUSPECT

guest FRIEND, CALLER, VISITOR, LODGER

Guiana, *Dutch See* "Surinam"

Guiana *tree* MORA, ICICA, GENIP

guide PILOT, STEER, TEACH, DIRECT, INSTRUCT, GOVERN, LEAD(ER), COURIER, CLEW, KEY, BOOK, MAP, MOTTO, RULE, CHART, ESCORT, CONVOY, MANAGE, CONTROL, CICERONE, LANDMARK
book BAEDEKER

guiding POLAR, DIRIGENT
star LODESTAR, NORTH, CYNOSURE

guidon FLAG, BAN-NER, STREAMER, MARKER

Guido's scale, *note in* UT, E LA, E LA MI
highest note E LA
low note UT

guild UNION, CLUB, GROUP, FRATERNITY, ASSOCIATION, SOCIETY *See* "gild"
hall statue, London MAGOG, GOG
merchant's HANSE

guile FRAUD, DECEIT, CUNNING, CRAFT, TRICK, SUBTLETY, ARTIFICE, DUPLICITY, WILES

guileless ARTLESS, SINCERE, NAIVE, FRANK, CANDID, INGENUOUS

guillemot AUK, MURRE, AWK, QUET, BIRD

guillotine, *wagon for* TUMBREL

guilt ERROR, SIN, BLAME, FAULT, CRIME, OFFENSE, CULPA-BILITY, WICKEDNESS, INIQUITY

guilty NOCENT, CULPA-BLE, LIABLE, WICKED, WRONG, CRIMINAL

Guinea, *bight in Gulf of* BENIN
corn DURRA, MILLET
tree AKEE
weight AKEY, PISO, UZAN, SERON

guinea fowl KEET, PINTADO
young of KEET

guinea pig *genus* CAVIA
male BOAR
S. America CAVY

guise CLOAK, GARB, COSTUME, FASHION,

MANNER, PRETENSE, DISGUISE, MIEN, WAY, ASPECT, HABIT, DRESS, APPEARANCE, FORM, SHAPE

guitar TIPLE
half step in pitch
DITAL
India SITAR, VINA
oriental SITAR
small UKE

guitarlike instrument
BANDORE, SAMISEN, ROTA, PANDORA, UKE

gula CYMA, OGEE, MOLDING, GULLET, THROAT

gulch ARROYO, GULLY, RAVINE, HOLLOW, GORGE, CLEFT

gulf PIT, GAP, RIFT, ABYSS, ABYSM, BAY, BIGHT, CHASM, WHIRL-POOL, EDDY, BASIN, INTERVAL, ADALIA, ADEN, ALASKA, BOTHNIA, CADIZ, GENOA, GUINEA, KUTCH, LIONS, MAN-NAR, MEXICO, PANAMA, PARIA, PERSIAN, RIGA, TONKIN, TUNIS
Arctic OB
Indian Ocean ADEN
Red Sea AQABA, SUEZ
weed SARGASSO

gull LARID, PIRR, SKUA, MEW, MAA, TEASER, ERN(E), XEMA, KITTWAKE, BIRD, FOWL, GUDGEON, CULLY, DUPE, CHEAT, TRICK, HOAX, BEGUILE, (BE)FOOL
Arctic XEMA
European MEW
genus LARI, LARUS, XEMA, LARIDAE
Jaeger ALLAN, SKUA, TEASER
laughing PEWIT
like JAEGER, SKUA, TERN
pertaining to LARINE
sea MEW, SKUA, ERN(E), COB(B)

gullet GULLY, MAW, THROAT, ESOPHAGUS

gullible SIMPLE,

CREDULOUS, UN-SUSPICIOUS, TRUSTFUL
"Gulliver" *author*
SWIFT
human brute YAHOO
island, flying LAPUTA

gully ARROYO, WADI, COULOIR, GORGE, DITCH, DONGA, GULCH, RAVINE, HOLLOW

gulp SWIG, SWALLOW, BOLT

gum CONIMA, AMRAD, RESIN, CHICLE, WAX, SMEAR, PATCH, LATEX, XYLAN, GINGIVA, ULA
arabic ACACIA, ACACIN
tree KIKAR
astringent KINO
boil PARULIS, ABSCESS
catechulike KINO, CHICLE
India AMRA
plant ULE, HULE
resin ELEMI, MYRRH, GALBANUM, LABDANUM
rubber source CAOUTCHOUC
tree BALATA, TUART, TOOART, BABUL, BUMBO, XYLAN
  black NYSSA, TUPELO
vanilla odor STORAX
white CAMPHOR
wood XYLAN

gumbo OKRA, OCRA, SOUP, PATOIS, GRASS, SOIL, MUD

gumboil PARULIS, ABSCESS

gums UVA, GINGIVAE
pain in ULALGIA
pertaining to GINGIVAL, ULETIC

gun ROD, MORTAR, RIFLE, STEN, ARM, ARMOR, WEAPON, CARBINE, CANNON, HUNT, ACCELERATE, REV
Africa ROER
anti-tank BAZOOKA
caliber BORE
catch SEAR
chamber GOMER
cock NAB, HAMMER
handle STOCK
leather case HOLSTER
lifesaving LYLE
lock part CATCH, SEAR

pointer device
DOTTER, SIGHT, BEAD
sight BEAD
stock corner TOE

gunfire SALVO, FUSILLADE

gunny sack TAT, TOE, BAG, BURLAP, SACKING

gunwale pin THOLE

gurnard CUR, ROCHET, TRIGLA, DRAGONET, FISH
genus TRIGLA

gush JET, POUR, RAIN, SPURT, STOUR, FLOW, EMIT, ISSUE, BURST, SPEW, SENTI-MENTALIZE

gusset GORE, INSERT, BRACKET

gust BLOW, BREEZE, BLAST, TASTE, GALE, PUFF, WIND, FLAW, SQUALL, BURST, RELISH

gustable GUSTATORY, TASTABLE

gusto RELISH, ZEST, TASTE, PALATE, LIKING, APPRECIATION, ENJOYMENT

gutta DROP, MINUM, SPOT, CAMPANA, TREENAIL
percha BALATA

gutter(s) CULLIS, DITCH, SPOUT, GROOVE, CHANNEL, MUD, MIRE, CONDUIT, TRENCH, GULLY
snipe ARAB, GAMIN, RAGPICKER

guttural HUSKY, VELAR, THROATY, GRUFF, HOARSE

guy BAFFLE, FOOL, EFFIGY, RIB, SHORE, ROPE, ROD, STAY, VANG, KID, RAG, JOSH, JOLLY, CHAIN, GUIDE, FELLOW, LAD, CHAP

guzzle DRINK, TUN, SOT, SWIG, CAROUSE, TIPPLE, TOPE, SWILL

gym feat KIP(P)

gymnast ATHLETE

gyp *See* "cheat"

gypsy NOMAD, ROM, CZIGANY, ZINCALO, ZIGEUNER, ROMANY, CALO, WANDERER

Czech BOHEMIAN
devil BENG
fortune BAHI
gentleman ROM, RYE
great BARO
girl CHAI, CHI
Hindu BAZIGAR
horse GRY, GRI
husband ROM
language ROMANY,
CHIB
man CHAL
married woman ROMI
non GAJO
paper LIL
sea tribe SELUNG
Spanish ZINCALO,
GITANO
steal CHOR
Syrian tribe APTAL
thief CHOR
tongue CHIB
village GAV
gyrate ROTATE, SPIN,
TWIRL, TURN, CIRCLE,
EDDY, SWIRL, RE-
VOLVE, WHIRL
gyre CIRCLE, RING,
VORTEX, EDDY
gyves IRONS, FETTERS,
SHACKLES

H

H AITCH
shaped ZYGAL
sound ASPIRATE
habeas corpus WRIT
habile APT, DEX-
T(E)ROUS, FIT, ABLE,
SKILLFUL, ADROIT,
CLEVER
habiliments GARB,
DRESS, GARMENTS,
APPAREL, COSTUME,
UNIFORM
habit RUT, WONT, WAY,
CUSTOM, USE, USAGE,
MODE, PATH, PRAC-
TICE, FORM, DRESS,
DISPOSITION,
COSTUME, DEMEANOR,
STATE, CONSTITUTION
riding JOSEPH,
JODHPURS, LEVIS,
CHAPS
habitat ABODE, RANGE,
STATION, LOCALITY,
HAUNT, REGION,
PURLIEU
habitation OCCUPANCY,
HOUSE, HOME,

DWELLING, RESIDENCE,
DOMICILE
habitual CHRONIC,
USUAL, WONTED,
CUSTOMARY, AC-
CUSTOMED, ROUTINE,
ORDINARY, FAMILIAR,
INVETERATE, COM-
MON, REGULAR
habituate DRILL,
SEASON, TRAIN,
SCHOOL, HARDEN, AC-
CUSTOM, ADDICT,
INURE, HAUNT, USE,
FAMILIARIZE, FRE-
QUENT, ACCLIMATIZE
hachure MARK, SHADE,
LINE
hacienda FARM, CROFT,
GRANGE, PLANTATION,
RANCH, HOUSE, ESTATE
hack CAB, TAXI,
VEHICLE, HEW, SLASH,
CUT, CHOP, DEVIL,
DRUDGE, VENAL,
WRITER, MANGLE,
COUGH, HACKLE,
HAGGLE, HORSE,
MERCENARY,
HIRELING, HACKNEY,
KICK, NOTCH, NICK
hackle COMB,
HATCHEL, HAGGLE,
CHOP, HACK, BRISTLES
hackney FIACRE,
COACH, COMMON,
HIRED, HORSE, DRUDGE,
CAB, TAXI
hackneyed OLD, WORN,
BANAL, TRITE, STALE,
USED, COMMONPLACE,
PRACTICED
Hades ABADDON,
ARALU, ORCUS, ABYSS,
SHEOL, UNDERWORLD,
HELL, TARTARUS
inhabitant of HEL-
LION
*place between earth
and* EREBUS
relating to SHEOLIC,
INFERNAL, HELLISH
river in ACHERON,
LETHE, STYX
haft HANDLE, BAIL,
HILT, FIX, STOCK
hag SHREW, CRONE,
WITCH, HARRIDAN,
VIXEN, BELDAM,
JEZEBEL, FURY,
VIRAGO

haggard THIN, WORN,
DRAWN, GAUNT,
ANXIOUS, SCRAWNY,
WAN, PALLID, LEAN,
SPARE, WILD, UN-
TAMED, UNRULY
Haggard novel SHE
haggle CAVIL, PALTER,
HACK, MANGLE,
BARGAIN, CHAFFER,
HIGGLE, STICKLE,
WRANGLE
hail GREET, CALL,
SIGNAL, SALUTE,
ADDRESS, ACCOST,
WELCOME, AHOY,
AVE, STORM
soft GRAUPEL
hair THATCH, TRESS,
MOP, LOCK(S), PILE,
NAP, CURL, FUR,
DOWN, FILAMENT,
CRINUS
absence of ACOMIA,
BALDNESS
arrange COIF
braid CUE, QUEUE,
PLAIT
brush of SHAG
coarse rigid SETA,
CHAETA, BRISTLE
coat of MELOTE, FUR,
PELT, HIDE
combining form
PIL(O)
cue of TAIL, BRAID,
QUEUE, PLAIT, PIGTAIL
curl RINGLET
curly CIRRI
dresser FRISEUR,
COIFFEUR, COIFFEUSE
dressing POMADE
dye HENNA
falling out of
PSILOSIS
false PERUKE, FRONT,
RAT, WIG, TOUPEE
feeler PALP, PALPUS
fillet for SNOOD, NET
fix PERM, WAVE, SET
fringe BANGS
having CRINATED,
HIRSUTE, PILOSE,
VILLOUS, BARBATE,
NAPPY, BEARDED
head CHEVELURE
head of CRINE, MOP
knot of BUN,
CHIGNON
like a tuft of COMOID,
FUZZY, SHAGGY

lock of TRESS, CURL, RINGLET
matted SHAG
molting ECDYSIS
of neck MANE
net SNOOD
pad RAT
part in LIST
pertaining to CRINAL, PILAR
plant(s) VILLUS, VILLI, PILUS, PILI
remove EPILATE, DEPILATE, TRIM, BOB, CUT
rigid SETA
roll ROACH
shirt CILICE
soft VILLUS, DOWN
standing ROACH
style TETE
unguent POMADE
wave MARCEL, PERM
wisp of TAIT, TATE, TUFT
woolly SHAG
haircloth CILICE
haircut BOB, TRIM
hairdo BANGS, BRAID, POODLE, PERM, RINSE, COIFFURE
hairiness VILLOSITY
See "hairy"
hairless GLABROUS, PELON, BALD
hairlike *process(es)* CILIUM, CILIA
hairy PILOSE, COMATE, HIRSUTE, COMOSE, CRINATE, PILAR, CILIATE, SHAGGY, VILLOUS, CRINITORY
Haiti *bandit* CACO
coin GOURDE
evil spirit BAKA, BOKO
liberator TOUSSAINT
measure AUNE
sweet potato BATATA
hakim JUDGE, RULER, DOCTOR
halberd FRAME, GLAIVE, AX(E), PIKE, STAFF, WEAPON
halcyon CALM, TRANQUIL, KINGFISHER, BIRD, PLACID, BALMY, PEACEFUL
Halcyone's *father* AEOLUS
husband CEYX
hale HEARTY, WELL, ROBUST, HEALTHY,

STRONG, HARDY, VIGOROUS, TUG, DRAG, SOUND, LUSTY, HAUL
Nathan SPY
half HEMI, DEMI, SEMI, MOIETY, PART, SEMESTER, RECESS, REST, PARTIAL, IMPERFECT
beak IHI, FISH
boot BUSKIN, PAC
breed MULE, METIS, MESTEE, MESTIZO, GRIFFE
combining form See "prefix" *below*
em EN
man and horse CENTAUR
mask LOUP
moon LUNE, ARC, CRESCENT
nelson HOLD
note MINIM
pint CUP, SMALL, MIDGET
prefix HEMI, DEMI, SEMI
score TEN
turn CARACOL(E)
witted IMBECILIC, SILLY
year's stipend ANN(AT)
Halicarnassian DIONYSIUS, HERODOTUS
halicore DUGONG
Halifax, *Marquis of* SAVILE
halite SALT, SAL
halitus AURA, BREATH, VAPOR, FOG, EXHALATION
hall ATRIUM, AULA, FOYER, ODEON, LOBBY, SALA, ENTRY, LYCEUM, DORM, CORRIDOR, AUDITORIUM, BUILDING, ROOM, PASSAGE(WAY)
athlete's GYM, XYSTUS
Odin's VALHALLA
hallow SANCTIFY, VENERATE, BLESS, DEDICATE, DEVOTE, CONSECRATE, REVERE, HONOR
hallowed BLEST, HOLY, SACRED
hallucination FANCY, ERROR, MIRAGE,

FANTASY, CHIMERA, DELUSION, FALLACY, ILLUSION, PHANTOM, ABERRATION, PHANTASM
halo AURA, BROUGH, NIMB(US), GLORY, LIGHT, AUREOLE, CIRCLE, RING
halogen BROMINE, CHLORINE, FLUORINE, IODINE, CYANOGEN
halt CEASE, LAME, MAIMED, CRIPPLED, ARREST, STOP, END, HESITATE, REST, STAND
halter HANG, NOOSE, SECURE, TIE, ROPE, STRAP, RESTRAIN, HAMPER
Ham's *father* NOAH
son PHUT, CUSH
Hamath *king* TOI, TOU
Hambletonian gait TROT
hamfatter ACTOR
Hamilton's *birthplace* NEVIS
Hamite SOMAL(I), BERBER, CHAMITE, AFAR, SAHO, COPT
Hamitic *language* AGAO, AGAU
negro MASAI
race SOMAL(I)
religion MOSLEM, COPTIC
tribe AFAR, BEJA, BENI, GALLA, BOGO, HIMA
hamlet ALDEA, VILLAGE, DORP, THORP, BURG, DUMP, TOWN, GROUPER, MIR
"Hamlet" *character* CLAUDIUS, HORATIO, OSRIC, POLONIUS, OPHELIA
scene of ELSINORE, DENMARK
Hammarskjold DAG
hammer MALLEATE, STRIKE, BEAT, DRUM, DRIVE, MALLET, POUND, KEVEL, RAM, MAUL, TRIP, MARTEL, FORGE, BEETLE
end or head PEEN, POLL
half-round FULLER

large SLEDGE, KEVEL, MAUL
lead MADGE
paver's REEL
tile OLIVER
toastmaster's GAVEL
type of CLAW, TRIP
hamper FETTER, TRAM-MEL, HOBBLE, CLOG, SHACKLE, HINDER, BLOCK, BAR, FOIL, PED, BASKET, CRATE, SEROON, HALT, IMPEDE, MAUND, MANACLE, HANAPER
Hampshire *borough* ROMSEY
district FLEET
hamstring HOUGH, LAME, MAIM, HOCK, CRIPPLE, TENDON, DISABLE
hamus HOOK
hanaper BASKET, HAMPER
hand FIST, MANUS, PAW, WORKER, HELPER, LABORER, EMPLOYEE, MAN, DEAL, LEAD, GIVE, SIDE, DIRECTION, PART, SKILL, ABILITY, TALENT, MANAGE-MENT, AGENCY, POINTER, INDICATOR, APPLAUSE, PENMAN-SHIP
bag ETUI, RETICULE, SATCHEL, PURSE, VALISE, GRIP
ball FIVES
bill DODGER, NOTICE, AD
book MANUAL, CODEX, GUIDE
combining form CHIRO, MANU
cuff BRACELET, MANACLE, DARBY
on left SINISTER
on right DEXTER
palm of VOLA, LOOF, THENAR
pertaining to CHIRAL, MANUAL
spread of one SPAN
used in writing Arabic NESKHI
handful BUNCH, GRIP, WISP, GOWPEN, MANIPLE, PUGIL(LUS)

handicap BURDEN, LISP, EQUALIZE, BET, ODDS, HINDER, RETARD, ENCUMBRANCE, DIS-ADVANTAGE, RACE
handicapper RATER
handjar KNIFE, DAGGER, KHANJAR
handkerchief BANDANNA, MALABAR, NECKCLOTH
handle ANSA, HAFT, HILT, CRANK, BAIL, KNOB, STOCK, HELVE, HANK, FEEL, SWING, EAR, PAW, THUMB, WIELD, LUG, MAUL, SELL, TREAT, PLY, DIRECT, AIM, EXAMINE, DEAL, TRADE, TITLE, MANAGE, USE, MANIPULATE
cup EAR
having ANSATE
pail BAIL
printing press ROUNCE
scythe SNATH, SNEAD
handled FELT, ANSATE, PALMED, DEALT, MANIPULATED, MANAGED
hand mill QUERN, GRINDER
hand-picked figs ELEME
hands MEN, CREW, POINTERS
off TABOO, COM-MAND, INTERDICTION
without AMANOUS
handsel EARNEST, GIFT, TEST, USE, TOKEN, FAVOR, MONEY
handsome FINE, BONNY, FAIR, LOVELY, GENEROUS, AMPLE, LARGE, PLEASING, ELEGANT, COMELY, STATELY, LIBERAL, GRACIOUS
hand's spread SPAN
handstone MANO
handwriting SCRIPT, HAND, CHIROGRAPHY, PENMANSHIP
on the wall MENE, TEKEL, UPHARSIN
handy NEAR(BY), APT, EXPERT, ADROIT, DEFT, DEXTEROUS, READY, HEP, ABLE,

SKILLFUL, CON-VENIENT, CLOSE, VERSATILE, AROUND, USEFUL
hang PEND, DANGLE, IMPEND, SWING, STICK, CLING, SUSPEND, DROOP, DEPEND, RELY, HOVER, INCLINE, DECLINE, EXECUTE, DRAPE, SWAG
down DANGLE, SUSPEND
fire PEND, HESITATE
loosely DANGLE, BANGLE, LOP, FLAP
hangdog MEAN, SNEAK-ING, BASE, ASHAMED
hanger on TOADY, PARASITE, SYCOPHANT
hanging SESSILE, DANGLING, DROOPING, DOSSER, CURTAIN, ARRAS, DRAPERY, PENDENT
hangnail AGNAIL
hank SKEIN, COIL, LOOP
hanker COVET, CRAVE, LONG, YEARN, PANT, WISH, PINE, THIRST, DESIRE
Hannibal's *father* HAMILCAR, BARCA
last battle ZAMA
Hanseatic League HANSE
hap CHANCE, FORTUNE, LUCK, LOT
haphazard RANDOM, CHANCE, AIMLESS, ACCIDENTAL
happen CHANCE, HAP, OCCUR, BETIDE, BE-FALL
happiness GLEE, FELICITY, BLISS, JOY, PLEASURE, DELIGHT, PROSPERITY
happy BLEST, COSH, FAUST, GLAD, GAY, JOYOUS, JOYFUL, FREE, MERRY, CHEER-FUL, BLITHE, LUCKY, APT, FITTING, PROPER, CONTENTED, FORTUNATE, OP-PORTUNE, PERTINENT
harageous BOLD, ROUGH

Haran's *brother*
ABRAHAM
father TERAH
son LOT
harangue TIRADE,
SPEECH, DIATRIBE,
TALK, ORATE, RANT,
SCREED, DECLAIM
haras STUD, HORSE,
FARM
harass VEX, PERSE-
CUTE, HARRY, PESTER,
BADGER, RIDE, BAIT,
BESET, HAZE, ANNOY,
WORRY, TEASE,
FATIGUE, TIRE, WEARY,
FAG, JADE, EXHAUST,
CHAFE, PLAGUE, DIS-
TRESS, TROUBLE,
MOLEST, HECKLE,
TANTALIZE, DISTURB,
TORMENT, IRRITATE,
NAG, BOTHER, HECTOR
Haratin BERBERS
harbinger HERALD,
SIGN, PRECURSOR,
INFORMER, FORE-
RUNNER
of spring ROBIN
harbor HAVEN,
SHELTER, LODGE,
HOUSE, ASYLUM,
REFUGE, SANCTUARY,
RETREAT, ABODE,
COTHON, KEEP,
SHIELD, BOARD, HIDE,
SECRETE, FOSTER,
CHERISH
master HAVENER
hard STEELY, STONY,
STERN, SOLID, FIRM,
DENSE, CLOSE, CAL-
LOUS, STRONG,
ARDUOUS, ONEROUS,
KNOTTY, NEAR, COM-
PACT, FLINTY, STUB-
BORN, ADAMANTINE,
DIFFICULT, IM-
PENETRABLE, STINGY,
UNYIELDING, IN-
FLEXIBLE, RIGOROUS,
STRINGENT, IN-
TRICATE, PERPLEXING
roll BAGEL
shell LORICA
harden GEL, INURE,
ENURE, CAKE, SEAR,
OSSIFY, SET, SEASON,
ACCLIMATE, ADAPT,
ADJUST, INDURATE,
TOUGHEN, TEMPER,
HABITUATE, AC-

CUSTOM, STRENGTHEN,
FORTIFY, BRACE,
STIFFEN, DISCIPLINE,
TRAIN, DRILL
hardship TRIAL, RIGOR,
PERIL, WANT,
DRUDGERY, TOIL,
PRIVATION, INJURY,
FATIGUE, AFFLICTION,
SEVERITY
hardy ROBUST, RIGID,
STRONG, DURABLE,
SET, HALE, LUSTY,
SPARTAN, TOUGH,
BOLD, INTREPID,
RESOLUTE, BRAVE,
STOUT, DARING,
STURDY, RUGGED,
HEALTHY
Hardy *heroine* TESS
hare PIKA, CONEY,
SCUT, RODENT, RABBIT,
BUNNY
combining form
LAG(O)
female DOE
genus LEPUS
like animal AGOUTI
male BUCK
S. Amer. TAPETI
tail SCUT
track FILE, SLOT
young LEVERET
harem ZENANA,
SERAGLIO
female slave
ODALISQUE, ODALISK
inmates ODA
relating to ZENANA
room in ODA
haricot STEW, RAGOUT
hark LIST, HEAR,
LISTEN, ATTEND
harlequin CLOWN-
(ISH), BUFFOON,
JESTER, DROLL,
PUNCH, ZANY,
SCARAMOUCH,
FANTASTIC
harm EVIL, DERE, MAR,
SCATHE, INJURE, MIS-
TREAT, ABUSE, IM-
PAIR, SPOIL, HURT,
DAMAGE, DETRIMENT,
MISCHIEF, WRONG,
WICKEDNESS, MIS-
FORTUNE
harmful ILL, MALEFI-
CENT, NOCENT, BANE-
FUL, NOXIOUS,
NOISOME, INJURIOUS,
PERNICIOUS,

DELETERIOUS,
SINISTER, DESTRUCT-
FUL
influence UPAS,
NOXA
harmless DOVISH, IN-
NOCUOUS, INNOCENT,
INOFFENSIVE, SAFE,
IMPOTENT
harmonious MUSICAL,
SYMMETRICAL,
CONGRUOUS, SPHERAL,
CONSONANT, CON-
CORDANT, MELODIOUS,
TUNEFUL, DULCET,
EUPHONIOUS, MEL-
LIFLUOUS, FRIENDLY,
CORDIAL
harmonize ATTUNE,
ACCORD, AGREE,
TALLY, SQUARE,
MATCH, ADJUST,
UNITE, RECONCILE,
BLEND, CHIME, CON-
FORM, CORRESPOND,
SYMPATHIZE
harmony CONCORD,
AMITY, TONE, KEY,
CHIME, CHORD, UNION,
CONSONANCE, ACCORD,
UNISON, ACCORDANCE,
ORDER, PEACE,
FRIENDSHIP, UNDER-
STANDING, MUSIC
harness GEAR, ARMOR,
GRAITH, EQUIP, PRE-
PARE, TAME, TACKLE,
ARRAY, HITCH
part of HAME,
TERRET, TUG, TRACE,
REIN, BRIDLE, SADDLE,
GIRTH, COLLAR
harp KOTO, LYRE,
NANGA, TRUMP,
ITERATE, REPEAT
ancient TRIGON(ON)
guitar key DITAL
ivory PLECTRUM
string CHORD
harpoon IRON, SPEAR,
GIG, JAVELIN, STRIKE,
CATCH, KILL
harpsichord CLAVECIN,
SPINET, FLUGEL
harpy AELLO, EAGLE,
PLUNDERER, OCYPETE,
CELAENO, PODARGE,
BIRD
harquebus *fork* CROC
harquebusier CARABIN,
SOLDIER
Harratin BERBERS

harridan HAG, CRONE,
JEZEBEL, VIRAGO,
STRUMPET, VIXEN

harrier HOUND, RUN-
NER, HAWK

harrow DRAG, DISK,
TILL, TEAR, CHIP,
BREAK, LACERATE,
TORMENT, DISTRESS,
VEX

harsh STERN, SHARP,
ROUGH, SEVERE, SOUR,
HARD, AUSTERE,
COARSE, GROSS, RIGID,
GRIM, ACERB, DURE,
CRUEL, RASPY, ACID,
ASTRINGENT, CAUSTIC,
GRATING, DISCORDANT,
STRIDENT, RAUCOUS,
UNKIND, RUDE, UN-
CIVIL, BLUFF, BLUNT,
GRUFF, CRUDE,
RELENTLESS

harshness RAUCITY,
RIGOR, SEVERITY,
STRIDOR, ASPERITY,
CHURLISHNESS

hart DEER, STAG

hartebeest ASSE,
CAAMA, TORA,
ANTELOPE
like BLESBOK,
SASSABY

hartshorn AMMONIA,
PLANTAIN

haruspex DIVINER,
SOOTHSAYER,
PROGNOSTICATOR

Harvard *book prize*
DETUR
ex-president ELIOT

harvest CROP, FRUIT,
YIELD, ISSUE, GROWTH,
RETURN, RESULT, OUT-
COME, PRODUCE,
GLEAN, REAP, GARNER,
GATHER, GAIN, REWARD
festival OPALIA
goddess OPS
India RABI
tick ACARID

hash GOULASH, RAG-
OUT, HARICOT,
GALLIMAUFRY,
OLLAPODRIDA,
SLUMGULLION,
POTPOURRI, RAMEKIN,
SALMAGUNDI,
RECHAUFFE, OLIO,
MEDLEY, MIXTURE,
MINCE, CHOP

hashish BHANG, CAN-
NABIS, PLANT,
NARCOTIC, HEMP

hassle FRAY, BRAWL,
MELEE, STRUGGLE,
MUDDLE

hassock FOOTSTOOL,
CUSHION, TUSSOCK,
TUFT

haste RUSH, DASH,
HURRY, SPEED,
CELERITY, DISPATCH,
ALACRITY, VELOCITY,
RAPIDITY, FLURRY,
PRECIPITANCY, SWIFT-
NESS

hasten HOTFOOT, FLY,
SCUD, HIE, HURRY,
SPEED, EXPEDITE,
ACCELERATE,
QUICKEN, SCAMPER,
SCURRY, PROMOTE

hastened HIED, RAN,
SPED, FLED

hastily APACE, IM-
PATIENTLY, SPEEDY

hasty CURSORY, RASH,
SUDDEN, QUICK, RAPID,
FLEET, FAST, SWIFT,
IMPATIENT, BRISK,
ABRUPT, SHORT,
SPEEDY, SLIGHT, HUR-
RIED, RECKLESS,
PRECIPITATE, SUPER-
FICIAL
pudding SEPON,
MUSH, SUPAWN

hat DICER, CAP,
CAUBEEN, LID, TOQUE,
BERET, FELT, TAM,
CHAPEAU, TOPPER,
BOWLER, BONNET,
BEANIE, PETASOS,
HELMET, TURBAN,
PANAMA, FEDORA,
DERBY, STRAW
ecclesiastic BIRETTA
fur used in
CON(E)Y, COONSKIN,
BEAVER, MINK,
ERMINE
hunter's TERAI
military See
"soldier's" *below*
oilskin SQUAM,
SOU'WESTER
opera GIBUS, TILE
palmleaf SALACOT
pith TOPEE, TOPI
plant, E. India SOLA
Roman PETASUS,
PETASOS, GALEA
silk TILE

soft FEDORA
soldier's SHAKO, TIN,
TRENCH, HELMET
straw BOATER,
PANAMA, BAKU
three-cornered
TRICORN

hatch DOOR, SKYLIGHT,
OPENING, LID, BAR-
RIER, WICKET, FLOOD-
GATE, GATE, INVENT,
DEVISE, CONTRIVE,
PLOT, CONCOCT, PLAN,
SCHEME, BREED,
PRODUCE, FABRICATE,
ENGRAVE

hatchet AX, AXE,
TOMAHAWK
archeological HACHE
stone MOGO, HACHE,
TOMAHAWK

hate DETEST, LOATHE,
ABHOR, DESPISE,
SCORN, DISDAIN,
RANCOR, ENMITY,
ABOMINATE,
EXECRATE, DISLIKE,
AVERSION
combining form
MIS(O)

hateful MALIGN(ANT),
AVERSE, ODIOUS,
EXECRABLE,
MALEVOLENT,
MALICIOUS, SPITEFUL,
ABOMINABLE, ABHOR-
RENT, HORRID, DIS-
GUSTING, NAUSEOUS,
REPUGNANT

hatred ODIUM, HATE,
ENMITY, RANCOR,
MALICE, ANIMOSITY,
HOSTILITY,
ANTIPATHY, AVERSION
Buddhist DOSA

hauberk ARMOR, MAIL,
COAT

haughty PROUD,
LORDLY, ALOOF, VAIN,
ARROGANT, DISDAIN-
FUL, SUPERCILIOUS,
ASSUMING, CONTEMP-
TUOUS, SCORNFUL,
INSOLENT

haul BOUSE, DRAW,
LUG, TREK, DRAG,
PULL, TUG, TOW,
SHIFT, MOVE, BOOTY,
SWAG

haulm STEM(S),
CULM, STALKS

haunch HANCE, HIP, HUCK, QUARTER

haunt NEST, DEN, LAIR, RESORT, ABODE, PURLIEU, ENVIRONS, SHADE, SPIRIT, GHOST, OBSESS, LIE, INFEST, BESET, SPOOK, FREQUENT, INHABIT, PERSECUTE

hautboy OBOE

hauteur ARROGANCE, PRIDE, HAUGHTINESS, LOFTINESS, DISDAIN, CONTEMPT

have OWN, HOLD, KEEP, ENJOY, POSSESS, OBTAIN, GET, ACQUIRE, RETAIN, CHERISH, DECEIVE, SWINDLE, TRICK

haven REFUGE, SHELTER, ASYLUM, HITHE, PORT, HARBOR, HOME, REST, COVE, BAY, INLET

havier DEER

havoc RUIN, WASTE, RAVAGE, DESTRUCTION, DEVASTATION, DESOLATION

haw SLOE, HEDGE, FENCE, BERRY, BUSH, HUM, HESITATE

Hawaii(an) POLYNESIAN
angry HUHU
apple MAILE
basket IE
bird OO, OMAO, IIWI, KOAE, MAMO, IOA, HUIA, IWA, APAPANI, IO, ALALA
bush OLONA
breech cloth MALO
canoe WAAPA
  stick or paddle IAKU
city HILO, HONOLULU
cliff PALI
cloak MAMO
cloth KAPA, TAPA, OLONO
common or profane NOA
cord AEA
crater KILAUEA
dance HULA
discoverer COOK
drink KAVA
extinct bird MAMO
farewell ALOHA

feast LUAU
fiber WAUKE
fiber basket IE
firm HUI
fish AWA, LANIA, ULUA, ALAIHI
fish poison HOLA, AUHUHU
flower decoration LEI
food POI, TARO, KALO
former president DOLE
fruit POHA
game HEI
god KANE
goddess of fire PELE
goose NENE
gooseberry POHA
harbor PEARL
hawk IO
herb HOLA, PIA, AUHUHU, APE
honey eater bird OO
island KAUAI, LANAI, OAHU, MAUI, MOLOKAI, KURE (OCEAN)
lava AA
loin cloth MALO
mountain(s) MAUNA, KEA, MAUNA LOA, WAIANAE
  range KOOLAU
mulberry bark TAPA, KAPA
musical instrument UKULELE, UKE
neckpiece LEI
octopus HEE
partnership HUI
pepper AVA
personification of light AO
pine IE
pit, baking IMU
plant TARO, KALO, OLONA
porch LANAI
precipice PALI
president, former DOLE
puffin AO
raven ALALA
royalty ALII
salutation ALOHA
seaweed LIMU
shrub POHA, AKALA, OLONA
silky fiber PULU
song MELE
starch root TARO, PIA
temple HEIAU
tern NOIO

thrush OMAO
tree KOA, OHIA, MAJAGUA, HAU, KOU
veranda LANAI
vine, basket work I-E
windstorm KONA
wreath LEI

hawk CARACARA, PEREGRINE, SHIKRA, KITE, FALCON, HARRIER, GOSHAWK, BUZZARD, BIRD, VEND, SELL, PEDDLE See "falcon"
Australia KAHU
blind SEEL
cage MEW
Europe PUTTOCK, FALCON, KESTREL
fish OSPREY
fly ASILID
Hawaii IO
headed god HORUS
leash JESS, LUNE
like OSPREY, SURN, IO
male TERCEL
moth SPHINGID, SPHINX
nest AERIE
nestling EYAS
parrot HIA
small KITE
young BRANCHER, EYAS

hawker PEDDLER, CADGER, COSTER, CHAPMAN, FALCONER, HUCKSTER, PACKMAN

Hawkeye State IOWA

hawkshaw DETECTIVE, DICK, TEC, SLEUTH

hawser ROPE
post BOLLARD, CAPSTAN

hawthorne MAYFLOWER, AZAROLE, SHRUB, TREE
fruit HAW

Hawthorne NAT

hay FEED, FORAGE, GRASS, FODDER, CLOVER, TIMOTHY, ALFALFA
bundle TRUSS, BALE
cock RICK, PIKE, COIL, COB, STACK
kind TIMOTHY, CLOVER, ALFALFA
mow LOFT
second growth ROWEN
spreader TEDDER

stack COCK, RICK, PILE, COIL, COB

hayfork PIKEL, PICKLE

hayseed RUBE, YOKEL, RUSTIC

hazard CHANCE, DARE, RISK, BET, DANGER, WAGER, PERIL, STAKE, VENTURE, JEOPARDY, ACCIDENT, CASUALTY, CONTINGENCY

hazardous PERILOUS, CHANCY, RISKY, DANGEROUS, UNSAFE, PRECARIOUS, UNCERTAIN

haze FILM, FOG, MIST, SMOG, VAPOR, BRUME, CLOUD, DIMNESS, MIASMA, PALL, SMOKE, DRIZZLE, HARASS, PUNISH, INITIATE
at sea GLIN

hazelnut FILBERT

Hazor *king* JABIN

head CAPITA, BEAN, NOODLE, POLL, CAPUT, TETE, NUT, NOB, TOP, SUMMIT, CAPTAIN, MASTER, FRONT, VAN, CHIEF, LEAD, MIND, TITLE, FROTH, PRINCIPAL, DIRECTOR, LEADER, CONTROL, SOURCE, FOUNTAIN, SPRING, BEGINNING, BLOCK, PATE, NOGGIN, CRANIUM
back of OCCIPUT, POLL, CROWN
band FRONTLET, FILLET, INFULA
covering HAIR, CAP, HAT, TAM, BERET, HOOD, CAUL, NUBIA, TOQUE, SNOOD
crown PATE, VERTEX
on Aegis of Athena MEDUSA
penny TAX
relating to CAPITAL, CEPHALIC, CRANIAL
shave TONSURE
side of LORE, LORUM
to foot CAPAPIE
toward CEPHALAD

headache MIGRAINE, MEGRIM, CEPHALGIA, ANNOYANCE, TROUBLE, POPPY
one side MIGRAINE, MEGRIM, HEMIALGIA, HEMICRANIA

headdress ALMUCE, PINNER, CAPELINE, WIG, TIARA, MITER, COIFFURE, CORONET
military SHAKO, BUSBY
sacerdotal BIRETTA, MITER
tropical TOPI, TOPEE
with veil HENNIN

headhunter, *Malay or Philippine* ITALONE

heading TITLE, LEAD, TROPE

headland CAPE, NESS, RAS, PROMONTORY, CLIFF, BLUFF, ESCARPMENT *See under* "cape"

headless STUPID, ACEPHALOUS, BEHEADED, UNDIRECTED, RASH, SENSELESS
animal ACEPHAL

headline BANNER, DISPLAY, LEADER, TITLE

headliner STAR

headquarters SEAT, CAPITOL, OFFICE, CENTER

head-shaped CAPITATED, CAPITATE

headstrong RASH, UNRULY, FORWARD, WILLFUL, PERVERSE, OBSTINATE, STUBBORN, DOGGED, VIOLENT, WAYWARD, INTRACTABLE

heady WILLFUL, RASH, IMPETUOUS, RECKLESS, INTOXICATING

heal CURE, MEND, PACIFY, REMEDY, RESTORE, RECONCILE, AMEND, REPAIR, FIX, SOOTHE

healing CURATIVE, SANATIVE, RESTORATIVE, ASSUASIVE, COMFORTING
goddess EIR
science of IATROLOGY

healthy WELL, FIT, PERT, HALE, HEARTY, SOUND, STRONG, VIGOROUS, WHOLESOME, LUSTY, RO-

BUST, SALUBRIOUS, SALUTARY
combining form SANI

heap STACK, COB, PILE, LOAD(S), RAFT, GOBS, HOARD, GATHER, SHOCK, (A)MASS, BANK, ACCUMULATE, QUANTITY, COLLECTION
pertaining to ACERVAL

hear HARK(EN), LIST(EN), ATTEND, REGARD, HEED, LEARN, AUDIT, PERMIT
ye OYEZ, OYES

hearing OYER, TRIAL, PROBE, AUDIENCE, EARSHOT, EXAMINATION, CONFERENCE, AIRING
defective SURDITY
pertaining to AURAL, OTIC

hearsay REPORT, RUMOR, TALK, GOSSIP, BRUIT, FAME, ON-DIT

heart CARDIA, COR(E), CENTER, KERNEL, PITH, GIST, INTERIOR, FOCUS, ESSENCE, TICKER, AFFECTION, COURAGE, SPIRIT, FORTITUDE, LOVE, EMOTION, BOSOM, BREAST, SOUL, MIDDLE, DISPOSITION, MOOD, FEELING
ailment ANGINA, CORONARY, MURMUR
bundle HIS
chamber VENTRICLE, ATRIUM, AURICLE
contraction SYSTOLE
dilation DIASTOLE
Egyptian AB, HATI
medicine for URAL, DIGITALIS
pertaining to CARDIAC
rest phase DIASTOLE
shaped CORDATE
sound MURMUR
valve MITRAL, AORTIC

heartburn PYROSIS, CARDIALGIA

hearten CHEER, COMFORT, ENCOURAGE, ANIMATE, EMBOLDEN, INSPIRIT, STIMULATE hearth HOME, GRATE, FIRESIDE, BRAZIER

heartless CRUEL, PITILESS, COLD, UNFEELING, MERCILESS, HARD, HARSH, BRUTAL, DESPONDENT, DESPAIRING, HOPELESS

heartsease PANSY, FLOWER

hearty HALE, LUSTY, ROBUST, SINCERE, VIGOROUS, DEEP, WARM, SOUND, EARNEST, CORDIAL, STRONG, SUBSTANTIAL, UNFEIGNED, FRIENDLY, PROFOUND

heat SPARK, CALOR(IC), ARDOR, FIRE, ZEAL, FLUSH, FEVER, FERMENT, WARMTH, AGITATION, CAUMA, EXASPERATION, EXCITEMENT, TEMPERATURE, ANGER, ACTIVITY, PRESSURE, EFFORT, BOUT, LAP
combining form THERM, CALORI
gentle TEPOR, CALOR, WARMTH
great CAUMA
pertaining to CALORIC, THERMAL
unit of THERM, CALORIE
white CANDENCY

heater ETNA, TISAR, STOVE, OVEN, FURNACE, RADIATOR, FIREPLACE

heath ERICA, MOOR, BENT, GRIG, PLAIN
berry BILBERRY
bird GROUSE
genus ERICA

heathen GENTILE, PAGAN, PAYNIM, ETHNIC, INFIDEL, IDOLATER
non-Jewish ETHNIC
non-Mohammedan INFIDEL

heather ERICA, LING, BESOM, PLANT, FABRIC

heathery area MOOR

heating vessel RETORT, ETNA, POT, PAN

heave SEND, THROW, FLING, HURL, LIFT,

HOIST, RAISE, TOSS, SWELL, BOOST, REAR, RISE, CAST, ELEVATE, PANT, KECK, RETCH

heaven UTOPIA, EDEN, SKIES, ZION, SKY, ETHER, ELYSIUM, FIRMAMENT, WELKIN, BLISS, EMPYREAN, ECSTASY, NIRVANA, VALHALLA, PARADISE
combining form URAN(O)
Scand. VALHALLA

heavenly ANGELIC, SUPERNAL, URANIAN, CELESTIAL, ETHEREAL, EMPYREAN, EMPYREAL, ELYSIAN, DIVINE, SERAPHIC, BLESSED, SACRED
being ANGEL, SERAPH, CHERUB
body STAR, SUN, PLANET, MOON, COMET, ASTEROID
path ORBIT

heavens, pertaining to URANIC, EMPYREAN, CELESTIAL

heavy MASSY, LEADEN, GLOOMY, HARD, SAD, DULL, LARGE, SLOW, INERT, HEFTY, SOLID, FIRM, WEIGHTY, PONDEROUS, MASSIVE, ONEROUS, BURDENSOME, AFFLICTIVE, GRIEVOUS, SERIOUS, GRAVE, DEEP, PROFOUND, SLUGGISH, DENSE
combining form BARY

hebdomad WEEK, SEVEN

Heber's *wife* JAEL

Hebraic ancedotal history ELOHIST

Hebrew JEW, ZION, AB, SEMITE, ISRAELITE, AMMONITE, MOABITE, EDOMITE
See "Bible"
acrostic AGLA
alien resident GER
alphabet ALEPH (ALEF), BETH, VETH, GIMEL, DALETH, HEH, VAV (WAW), ZAYIN, KHETH, TETH, JOD (YOD(H)), CAPH

(KAPH, KHAPH), LEMED(H), MEM, NUN, SAMEKH, AIN (AYIN), PEH, FEH, TSADI, KOPH, RESH, SIN, SHIN, TAV (TAW, THAV)
ancestor EBER
ascetic ESSENE
automaton GOLEM
avenger GOEL
benediction MIZPAH
bless BENSH
bride KALLAH
brotherhood ESSENE
canonical book TALMUD
Christian minister GALLAH
coin GERAH, MITE
day YOM
dialect LADINO
divorce bill GET(T)
doctrine ANIMISM, KARAISM, MISHNA(H)
drum TOPH
eternity OLAM
evening EREB
excommunication HEREM, CHEREM
father ABBA
feast of passover SEDER
   of tabernacle SUCCOTH
festival PURIM, SEDER, SUCCOTH, MOED
food inspector SHOMER
gentile GOY(IM), GOI
God, name for ADONAI, ELOHIM, YAHVEH, JEHOVA(H), ELOAH, YAVEH
Hades SHEOL
head (of) ROSH
healer ASA
herdsman AMOS
high priest AARON ELI, EZRA
holiday SUKKOTH, PURIM, PESACH
instrument TIMBREL, ASOR
Jehovah See "God" above
law TALMUD
   of Moses TORA(H)
learned man HAKAM, HAKIM

letter See "alphabet" *above*
lyre ASOR
marriage contract KETUBA
meadow ABEL
measure OMER, EPA(H), CAB, HIN, KOR, LOG, SEAH, EPHAH, BATH, CAPH, CHOROS, CHOMER, DIGIT, HOMER, KANEH, REED, LETECH, ZARETH
month TISRI (ETHANIM), HESHVAN (BUL), AB, KISLEU (CHISLEU), TEBET(H), S(H)EBAT, ADAR, VEADAR, NISAN (ABIB), IYAR (ZIF), SIVAN, TAM(M)UZ, ELUL
next of kin GOEL
non GOY(IM), GOI
offering CORBAN
order ESSENE
Passover month ABIB (NISAN)
feast SEDER
patriarch NASI, ABRAHAM, DAVID, JACOB (ISRAEL), SHEM, ISAAC
priest LEVITE, AARON, EZRA, ELI
garment of EPHOD
girdle ABNET
prophet DANIEL, AMOS, MALACHI, HOSEA, SYRUS, ISAIAH, JEREMIAH, EZEKIEL, JOEL, OBADIAH, JONAH, MICAH, NAHUM, HAGGAI, MOSES
prophetess DEBORAH
proselyte GER
psalms of praise HALLEL
quarter GHETTO
reclaimer or redeemer of property GOEL
robot GOLEM
scarf ABNET, TEL-LITH
scholar SABORA
scribe EZRA
seer BALAAM, ISAAC, MOSES
son BEN

song of praise HAL-LEL, PSALM
stringed instrument ASOR
sun god BAAL
teacher RAB(BI)
title RAB(BI)
tribe DAN, LEVITES
universe OLAM
weight GERAH, BEKAH, MANEH, SHEKEL, TALENT
word SELAH
Hebrides island IONA, UIST, LEWIS, HARRIS, BARRA, RUM, MULL, STAFFA, SKYE, JURA, SCARBA
hector TEASE, BULLY, INTIMIDATE, THREATEN, TORMENT, BROWBEAT, WORRY, HARASS
Hector's *father* PRIAM
wife ANDROMACHE
Hecuba's *husband* PRIAM
heddle(s) CORD, WIRE, GUIDE, HAR-NESS, CAAM
hedge HAW, FENCE, ROW, WEIR, BAR-RIER, LIMIT, OB-STRUCT, ENCIRCLE, ENCLOSE, SURROUND, EVADE, DODGE, TEMPORIZE
gap in MEUSE, MUSE
hedgehog ECHINUS, ERICIUS, MAMMAL, FRUIT, PLANT, POD
like animal TENREC, PORCUPINE
Hedin SVEN, EX-PLORER
heed NOTE, LISTEN, MIND, CARE, OBEY, RECK, NOTICE, AT-TEND, OBSERVE, RE-GARD, MARK, CON-SIDER, EAR
heedful VIGILANT, AT-TENTIVE, WATCHFUL, CAUTIOUS, WARY, CIRCUMSPECT
heedless RASH, WILD, MAD, REMISS, LAX, SLACK, CARELESS, IN-ATTENTIVE, NEGLI-GENT, INCONSIDERATE,

RECKLESS, PRECIPI-TATE, NEGLECTFUL
heel CALX, SPUR, KNOB, REMNANT, CRUST, CAREEN, LIST, TILT, CANT, IN-CLINE, BOUNDER, CAD, OBEY
bone CALCANEUS, CALCIS
heeling ALIST, TIPPED
heft LIFT, HANDLE, WEIGH(T), HEAVE, HAFT, BULK
hefty BEEFY
hegel work LOGIC
hegira EXODUS, FLIGHT, DEPARTURE
heifer COW, CALF, STIRK
height APEX, PITCH, SUMMIT, STATURE, TOP, RANK, HILL, ALTITUDE, ELEVA-TION, EMINENCE, ACME, ZENITH, CLIMAX, PINNACLE, LOFTINESS
of action in drama CATASTASIS
heir (IN)HERITOR, LEGATEE, SON, SCION, PARCENER, HERES, HAERES
additional stipend to ANN
Hejaz, *holy city* MECCA, MEDINA
held, *music* TENUTO
Helen of Troy, *husband* MENELAUS
lover PARIS
mother LEDA
suitor AJAX
helical SPIRAL, WIND-ING, COCHLEATE, SOLAR
helicid SNAIL
Heliopolis, *Biblical name* ON
Helios SOL, APOLLO
sister ARTEMIS
helix COIL, SPIRAL, CURVE, SNAIL
hell TARTARUS, TOPHET, HADES, SHEOL, GEHENNA, PIT, ABYSS, PERDI-TION, NARAKA, ORCUS, ABADDON, AVERNUS, INFERNO, UNDER-WORLD

Hellas GREECE

Hellen, *son* DORUS

Hellene GREEK

Hellespont, *anc. city on* ABYDOS

helm RUDDER, WHEEL, TILLER, LEAD, CONTROL, RULE, REINS, TIMON

helmet ARMET, GALEA, MORION, SALLET, CASQUE, BASINET, HEADPIECE, BURGONET, HAT, CABASSET, TOPI, TOPEE, MASK

adjustable flap VENTAIL

bird TURACOU, TOURACO

flower ACONITE, ORCHID

French HEAUME

light SALLET

lower part BEAVER

medieval HEAUME

nose guard NASAL

opening VUE

perforation OCULATUS

pith (sun) TOPI, TOPEE

Roman GALEA

shaped GALEATE

sun TOPI, TOPEE

type of BASINET, CASQUE

upper piece VISOR, VIZOR

helminth WORM

helmsman PILOT, TILLER, LEADER, STEERSMAN, QUARTERMASTER

Heloise's *husband* ABELARD

helot ESNE, SERF, SLAVE, THRALL, VASSAL, BONDSMAN, SPARTAN

help ABET, AID, CURE, SUCCOR, FIX, BACK, ASSIST, PROFIT, BENEFIT, ADVANCE, BETTER, IMPROVE, DOCTOR, SERVE, SUPPORT, SECOND, SUSTAIN, RELIEVE, ALLEVIATE, REMEDY, STAFF, SERVANTS, FACULTY, CREW

signal SOS

helper AIDE, ALLY, ANSAR, TEAMMATE, MATE, WIFE, ASSISTANT, HUSBAND, PARTNER, WORKER, AUXILIARY, HAND, SERVANT, SPOUSE

helpless LIMP, SPINELESS, FEEBLE, DEPENDENT, INCAPABLE, WEAK, POWERLESS, IMPOTENT, DISABLED, INFIRM, INCOMPETENT, INEFFICIENT

Hel's *watchdog* GARM

helve HANDLE, SHAFT, HAFT

hem FENCE, EDGE, SEW, FOLD, LIMIT, ENCLOSE, BORDER, MARGIN, HAW, HESITATE, SURROUND, CONFINE, ENVIRON, ENCIRCLE, RESTRAIN

hemlock TSUGA, HERB, TREE, CONIUM

fruit CONIUM

genus TSUGA

ground (American) YEW

poison CONIUM

hemorrhage FLOW, DISCHARGE, BLEEDING

hemp PLANT, FIBER, CORDILLA, PITA, TOW, ROPE, RINE, ROGUE

African PANGANE, IFE, SISAL

Ambary NALITA

derivative of CANNABIS, GANJA

dried leaves KEF, KIEF, BHANG

fabric BURLAP

fiber ABACA, SISAL, JUTE

India KEF, B(H)ANG, KIEF, DAGGA

loose OAKUM

Manila ABACA

narcotic CHARAS, HASHISH, CANNABIS, B(H)ANG

Philippine ABACA

plant BENG, SUNN, JUTE, ABACA, RAMIE

resin CHARAS

Russian RINE

shrub PUA, POOA

smoking KEF

hen FOWL, FEMALE

Chaucer's PARTLET

clam PISMO, SURF

harrier HAWK

mud RAIL, GALLINULE, COOT

roost PERCH

henbit *genus* LAMIUM

hence SO, AWAY, ERGO, THEN, THEREFORE, CONSEQUENTLY, BEGONE, FUTURE

henchman GROOM, PAGE, SQUIRE, DISCIPLE, ASSISTANT, WORKER, RETAINER, FOLLOWER, SUPPORTER, SERVANT, ATTENDANT, HELPER

Hengist's *brother* HORSA

henna ALCANNA, DYE, RINSE, SHRUB

henotic IRENIC, HARMONIZING

henpeck NAG, DOMINEER, CONTROL

Henry HAL

Henry II's *wife* ELEANOR

"Henry VI," *character in* CADE, HUME, VAUX, BONA

Henry VIII's *wife* ANNE, JANE, CATHERINE

widow PARR

hent GRASP, SEIZE

Hera's *husband* ZEUS

mother RHEA

rival LETO

son ARES

herald USHER, MESSENGER, CRIER, PAGE, HARBINGER, PRECURSOR, FORERUNNER, PROCLAIM, FORETELL, ANNOUNCE, BLAZON, INTRODUCE

coat of TABARD

heraldic, heraldry

animal's head CABOCHED

annulet VIRE

back to back ADDORSED

ball or plate ROUNDEL

barnacle CIRRIPED, BREY

bastardy mark BATON, BEND(LET), SINISTER
beakless and footless bird MARTLET
bearing TRESSURE, ORLE
  two curved lines GORE
beast partly visible ISSUANT
blind SEEL
black SABLE
blood-red MURREY
blue AZURE
boar GRISE
broken ROMPU
chaplet ORLE
checkered VAIR, CHECKY
cherub SERAPH
circle ANNULET, BEZANT
cleche URDE, CROSS
cross SALTIRE, RAGULY
  like CLECHE, PATONCE
curved NOWY, NEBULE
design RUSTRE
divided by bars BARRY
  into four parts PALY
  into squares COMPONY
  into three parts TIERCE
drops, seme of GUTTE
duck CANNET
either of two barrulets GEMEL
escalloped SCULES
escutcheon band FESS
facing each other AFFRONTE
fillet ORLE
flying in air FLOTANT
foreleg of beast GAMB
fur PEAN, POTENT, VAIR
gold in OR
grafted ENTE
grain sheaf GERB(E), GARB
green VERT
hairy COMATE

head of dart or arrow PHEON
headless ETETE
horizontal band BAR, FESS, FILL
leaves POINTE
left side SINISTER
lozenge shaped FUSIL, MASCLE, RUSTRE
  voided MASCLE
metal end of sheath BOTEROL
notched RAGULY
orange TENNE
ordinary BEND, SALTIRE, PALE, PALY
ornament of headpiece CREST
overlapping plates TEGULATE
partly swallowed ENGOULED
pointed URDE
purple PURPURE
red circle GUZE
  tincture GULES
scattered SEME
sheaf of grain GARB, GERB(E)
shield, border in ORLE, BORDURE
  boss UMBO
  broad vertical stripe PALE
  concealed half of SINISTER
  division of ENTE
  horizontal band across FESS
  rectangular division CANTON
  series of small VAIR
  two circular segments at sides FLANCH
  vertical position of PALY
sitting, as a lion SEJANT, ASSIS
sky blue AZURE
snake BISSE
springing up JESSANT
squirrel skin VAIR
standing position STATANT
strewing SEME
swimming NAIANT
symbol of tribe of Judah LION

term ENTE, URDE, PATTE, SEME
three part division TIERCE
tincture TENNE, VERT, AZURE, GUZE, GULES, SABLE, ARGENT, PURPURE
triangular form GYRON
turned to show back AVERSANT
turning head to spectator GARDANT, GAZE, AFFRONTE
vertical division PALE
voided escutcheon ORLE
wavy NEBULE, ONDE, UNDE
wickerwork trap WEEL
winged AILE, VOL
wings VOL
wreath ORLE, TORSE
Y-like figure PALL
Herat CARPET
herb(s) PLANT, ANNUAL, FOLIAGE, SAGE, MINT, THYME, SEDGE, YARROW, WORT, OREGANO
aromatic ANET, ANISE, HEMP, MINT, DILL, CHERVIL
arum family CALLA
Asia CICER, HEMP
bitter ALOE, RUE, TANSY
blue dye WOAD
dill ANET
dish SALAD
edible PARSNIP
Europe YARROW, WOAD, SPICKNEL, TARRAGON
eve IVA
fabulous MOLY
fragrant BALM
genus GAURA, GEUM, ACUAN, ALETRIS, ARUM, LINARIA, TACCA, URENA, CARUM, MEUM, ERVUM, CASSIA, IVA, INULA, HEDEOMA, SESSELI
ginger ALPINIA
goosefoot BLITE
grace RUE

kind of WORT,
BLITE
medicinal ALOE,
SENNA, BONESET,
TANSY
mint family BALM,
BASIL, HYSSOP
nightshade HENBANE
parsley family
CICELY, FENNEL,
ERYNGO
perennial BALM, DIGI-
TALIS, PIA, SEGO,
GEUM, MINT
pigweed QUINOA
poisonous CONIUM,
HENBANE
pot WORT, KALE
starch PIA
stinging NETTLE
sweet aromatic
CICELY
tonic BONESET
tropical SIDA
western YAMP
herbage TURF, PAS-
TURE, GRASS,
LEAVES, STEMS,
VEGETATION, FOLIAGE
Hercules' *captive* IOLE
mother ALCEME
scene of 12 labors
NEMEA
wife HEBE
herd DROVE, MOB,
RABBLE, FLOCK,
TROOP, PACK, BEVY,
GAGGLE, SCHOOL,
COVEY, SWARM,
FLIGHT, SHOAL,
CROWD, MULTITUDE,
ASSEMBLAGE, PEO-
PLE, PUBLIC, DRIVE,
TEND, GATHER, COR-
RAL
common RUCK
pertaining to GREGAL
herdsman SENN,
VACHER, VAQUERO,
HERDER
astronomy (*constel-
lation*) BOOTES
here and there ABOUT,
PASSIM, SCATTERED,
THINLY, IRREGULARLY
hereditary LINEAL,
INBORN, INNATE,
INBRED, ANCESTRAL,
PATRIMONIAL, IN-
HERITED
factor GENE

heredity ATAVISM,
INHERITANCE
heresy, pertaining to
ARIAN
heretic ARIAN,
AGNOSTIC, SKEPTIC,
DISSENTER, NON-
CONFORMIST,
SCHISMATIC
heretofore ERENOW,
HITHERTO, ONCE,
QUONDAM, FORMER,
ERSTWHILE, PREVIOUS
heritable land ODAL
heritage ESTATE,
LEGACY, LOT, SHARE,
PORTION, INHERIT-
ANCE, PATRIMONY
Hermes MERCURY,
HERALD, MES-
SENGER
father ZEUS
footgear TALARIA
mother MAIA
son PAN
hermit RECLUSE,
EREMITE, ANCHORITE,
ASCETIC, MONK,
FRIAR, NUN, CRAB,
COOKY, HUMMING-
BIRD
relating to ASCETIC
hero IDOL, STAR,
DEMIGOD, WARRIOR,
LION, PROTAGONIST,
KNIGHT, VIP
Babylonian myth.
ETANA
Euripides' play ION
first crusade TANCRED
legendary AMADIS,
PALADIN
Persian legend
RUSTAM
romantic legend
TRISTRAM
Russian epic poem
IGOR
Herodias' *daughter*
SALOME
husband HEROD
heroic BOLD, BRAVE,
EPIC(AL), VIKING,
GREAT, HUGE,
LARGE, RESOLUTE,
NOBLE, INTREPID,
COURAGEOUS, VAL-
IANT, GALLANT, FEAR-
LESS, DARING, DAUNT-
LESS, EXTREME,
ILLUSTRIOUS

events, series of
EPOS
poem EPIC, EPOS,
EPOPEE
heroin SNOW, NAR-
COTIC, DIAMORPHINE
heroine HEIDI,
DEMIGODDESS
heron AIGRETTE,
EGRET, HERLE, BIT-
TERN, CRANE, IBIS,
WADER, BIRD
flock SEDGE
green POKE
night QUA, QUAWK,
SOCO
plume AIGRETTE
small BITTERN
heroner HAWK
Hero's *lover* LEANDER
herpes SHINGLES,
ECZEMA
herring RAUN, SPRAT,
ALEWIFE, ALLICE,
SARDINE, BLEAK,
FISH
barrel for CADE
family PILCHARD
female RAUN
genus ALOSA,
CLUPEA
like CISCO, LILE,
POLLAN
measure CRAN
sauce ALEC
tub CADE
young MATIE, BRIT,
COB, SILE, SPRAT,
SARDINE
Hertha ERDA,
NERTHUS
hesitant TIMID,
AVERSE, LOATH,
AFRAID, SHY,
DUBIOUS, INDECISIVE
hesitate ER, UM,
DEMUR, HAW, HEM,
PAUSE, SHRINK,
WAVER, FALTER,
BALK, SHY, DELAY,
DOUBT, SCRUPLE,
STICKLE, BOGGLE,
VACILLATE, STAM-
MER
Hesperides ATLANTIDE,
AEGLE, HESTIA,
HESPERA
Hesperus' *father*
ASTRAEUS
mother EOS
hessonite GARNET

Hestia's *father*
 CRONOS
mother RHEA
hetaera PHRYNE,
 LAIS
heterogeneous MOT-
 LEY, MIXED, DI-
 VERSE, ASSORTED,
 DISPARATE, UNLIKE,
 DISSIMILAR, MISCEL-
 LANEOUS, INDISCRIMI-
 NATE, VARIED, IN-
 CONGRUOUS, FOREIGN
hetman ATAMAN,
 CHIEF, LEADER
hew FELL, CHOP,
 HACK, CHIP, CLEAVE,
 RIVE, SPLIT, FORM,
 DRESS, FASHION, CUT
hex (BE)WITCH,
 JINX, HAG, SPELL
hexad SEXTET
hexadecane CETENE
hexastich STANZA,
 STROPHE, SESTET
heyday VIGOR, BLOOM,
 ARDOR, SPIRITS,
 JOY, HEIGHT, PRIME,
 ZENITH, ACME,
 FLUSH
Hg MERCURY
hiatus COL, GAP,
 LACUNA, BREAK,
 PAUSE, FISSURE,
 BREACH, OPENING,
 RIFT, INTERVAL,
 CHASM, SPACE,
 RECESS
hibernate WINTER,
 SLEEP, RETIRE
Hibernia ERIN,
 IRELAND, EIRE
hickory SHELLBARK,
 PECAN, SHAGBARK,
 TREE, WOOD, NUT
genus CARYA
wattle ACACIA
hide BURY, SCREEN,
 CACHE, CLOAK, MASK,
 ENSCONCE, SECRETE,
 CONCEAL, COVER,
 SUPPRESS, SHELTER,
 VEIL, KIP, PELT,
 SKIN, COAT
away DEN, CAVE,
 LAIR, RETREAT
remove hair from
 MOON
undressed KIP, PELT
hideous REVOLTING,
 APPALLING, UGLY,

DISCORDANT, DREAD-
 FUL
hiding place CAVE,
 LAIR, RETREAT, DEN,
 CACHE, REFUGE
hie URGE, SCUD, GO,
 SPEED, HASTEN,
 HURRY, INCITE
hieroglyphics, *key to*
 ROSETTA
higgle CHAFER,
 STICKLE, HAGGLE,
 DISPUTE, DELAY,
 PEDDLE, HAWK,
 BARGAIN
high ALOFT, GAMY,
 LOFTY, TALL, SHRILL,
 SUPREME, ALT,
 RAISED, ELEVATED,
 FIRST, PRINCIPAL,
 EXALTED, (PRE)EMI-
 NENT, NOBLE, DRUNK,
 STEEP, TOWERING,
 SOARING, PROMINENT,
 DISTINGUISHED, SUPE-
 RIOR, GREAT, EX-
 PENSIVE, DEAR,
 PROUD, ARROGANT,
 HAUGHTY
combining form
 ACRO, ALTI
flown E LA
hat TILE, TOPPER
hill TOR
home EYRIE, AERIE
mountain ALP
note E LA
priest AARON, ELI
strung TAUT, TENSE,
 NERVOUS, STRAINED,
 SPIRITED
highest BEST, SUPREME
combining form ACRO
*number of a die or
 dice* SISE
point ACME, TOP
Highlander GAEL,
 TARTAN, BAIRN,
 SCOT, MOUNTAINEER
garb KILT, TARTAN
pouch of SPORRAN
highway ROAD, ITER,
 PIKE, DRIVE, STREET,
 AVENUE, THOROUGH-
 FARE, COURSE,
 ROUTE, RTE
Northwest ALCAN
hilarity GLEE, GAIETY,
 MIRTH, JOY, JOL-
 LITY, JOVIALITY, MER-
 RIMENT

hill COP(PLE), RISE,
 LOMA, LOMITA, HEAP,
 GRADE, KNOLL,
 ELEVATION, MOUNT,
 HILLOCK, ASCENT,
 HEIGHT
Africa KOP
broad-topped MESA,
 LOMA
fortified RATH
glacial PAHA, KAME
isolated BUTTE
rocky SCAR, TOR
round MORRO
sand DUNE, DENE
short KAME
slope ACCLIVITY,
 BRAE
small DOWN, DUNE
top of TOR, SUMMIT,
 PEAK
hillock TUMP, KNOLL,
 MOUND, HUMMOCK,
 MONTICLE, MORRO,
 RISE
French TERTRE
hills, *chain of* OS,
 RIDGE, RANGE
hillside BRAE, SLOPE,
 ACCLIVITY
hilt HAFT, HANDLE
hilum of an organ
 PORTA, EYE,
 NUCLEUS
Himalayan *animal*
 KAIL, OUNCE, IBEX,
 PANDA, SERON,
 GORAL
antelope SERON,
 GORAL
bird COUGH
cedar DEODAR
goat TAIR, KRAS,
 TAHR
kingdom NEPAL
monkshood ATIS
peak AKU, EVEREST,
 LHOTSE
pheasant MONAL,
 MONAUL
plantigrade mammal
 PANDA
sheep NAHOOR
tableland TIBET
territory SIKKIM
tree DEODAR, SAL,
 TOON
Himavat's *daughter*
 DIVA
Himyarite ARAB
hind ROE, DEER,
 PEASANT, REAR,

AFTER, BACK, POSTERIOR, GROUPER

hinder BACK, REAR, CRAMP, RETARD, BALK, CURB, FETTER, CLOG, CHECK, THWART, STAY, STOP, DETER, IMPEDE, EMBAR, BLOCK, BAR, DAM, HAMPER, OBSTRUCT, DELAY, ENCUMBER, EMBARRASS, HOBBLE, MANACLE, ARREST, HANDCUFF

hindrance RUB, CLOG, OBSTACLE, INTERRUPTION, RESTRAINT, ROADBLOCK, IMPEDIMENT

Hindu BABU, KOLI, TAMIL, SIKH, KOLARIAN *See also* "India"

acrobat NAT

age of world (cycle) YUGA

alkali plains USAR

ancestor of man MANU

Aryan race SWAT

ascetic YATI, YOGI

atheist NASTIKA

author of human wisdom MANU

bandit DECOIT

barren land USAR

bird MINA, KALA, BULBUL

blacksmith LOHAR

call to prayer AZAN

carriage GHARRY, GHARRI

caste KORI, SUDRA, TELI, MALI, DASI, KOLI, BANIAN, GOLA
  gardener MALI
  low KOLI, MALI
  member of JAT, TELI, DASI
  merchant BANIAN

cavalry troop RISALA

ceremonial gift KHILAT, KILLUT

charitable gift ENAM

city, holy BENARES, LASSA, LHASA

class See "caste" *above*

coin PICE

congregation SAMAJ, SOMAJ

convent MATH

cottage BARI

court officer AMALA(H)

cymbals TAL

deity See "god" *or* "goddess"

eighth avatar of Vishnu KRISHNA

demon DAITYA, RAHU, ASURA, BHUT

dependency TALUK

disciple SIKH

discount BATTA

drinking pot LOTA(H)

dye AL, AAL, ALTA

eighth avatar of Vishnu KRISHNA

ejaculation or mantra OM

essence RASA, AMRITA

estate TALUK

elephant-headed god GANES(H)A

evil spirit ASURA, MARA, KALI, BHUT

exchange rate BATTA

fabled mountain MERU

fair MELA

female slave DASI

festival DASHARA, DEWALI, HOLI, MELA

fire god AGNI

first mortal YAMA

fluid RASA

foot dye or coloring ALTA

garment SARI

gentleman BABOO, BABU

ghost BHUT

giant BANA

god or goddess See under "god" *or* "goddess"

godling DEVATA, DEWATA

goldsmith SONAR

grant of land INAM, SASAN

groom SYCE

guitar SITAR

hero RAMA, NALA

holy
  books SASTRA, VEDA
  hut BARI
  man SADH

idol PAGODA, SWAMI

ignorance, philosophy of TAMAS

incarnation AVATAR

jackal KOLA

kneeling man ASANA

lady DEVI

land grant INAM, SASAN

language, anc. SANSKRIT

law book MANU

leader SIRDAR, NEHRU GANDHI

lease POTTAH

life principle JIVA, PRANA, ATMAN

literature, sacred VEDA, S(H)RUTI
  pertaining to VEDIC

loin cloth DHOTI

lord SWAMI

magic MAYA, JADU, JADOO

mantra OM

margosa NEEM

master SAHIB, MIAN, SWAMI

meal ATA

measure HATH, KOS(S)

mendicant NAGA

merchant BANIAN, TELI

monastery MATH

money ANNA

month BAISAKH, JETH, ASARH, SAWAN, SARAWAN, BHADON, ASIN, KUAR, KATIK, KARTIK, AGHAN, PUS, MAGH, PHA(L)GUN, CHAIT

mountaineer BHIL

musical instrument SAROD, SITAR, VINA

mother goddess MATRIS

mountain, fabled MERU
  pass GHA(U)T

nobleman RAJAH

Olympus MERU

patriarch PITRI

peasant RYOT

philosophy YOGI

pillar LAT

poet TAGORE

poison from aconite BIKH

pottery UDA

prayer rug ASANI, ASAN(A)

prince MAHARAJ(A), RAJA(H), RANA

princess MAHARANI, RANEE, RANI
principle of existence PRANA, TATTVA
private apartment MAHAL
pundit SWAMI
queen RANEE, RANI
race JAT
rain serpent NAGA
reign RAJ
religion JAINISM, SIVAISM
religious adherent JAIN
  ascetic MUNI
  book RIG(VEDA), SASTRA, SHASTRA, SHASTER
  cymbals TAL
  devotee MUNI
  fair MELA
  festival PUJA
  formula MANTRA
  sect, unorthodox JAIN(A)
  teacher GURU, PIR
rice BORO
rite ACHAR
rule RAJ
sacred literature VEDA
sage RISHI, GAUTAMA, MAHATMA, KATHA
salvation MOKSHA
school, Sanskrit TOL
scripture TANTRA, SASTRA
  pertaining to TANTRIC
sect SEIK, SIKH, SADH, JAIN(A)
serpent NAGA
silversmith SONAR
social system CASTE
soldier SEPOY
soul ATMAN
sovereignty RAJ
spirit ASURA, MARA, JIVA, ATMAN, PRANA
spiritual darkness TAMAS
stele LAT
storeroom GOLA
summer residence MAHAL
swan, myth. HANSA
teacher GURU
temple DEUL, VIMANA
  tower SIKHRA, SIKAR, SIKRA
thought OM

title BABU, MIR, SIDI, NAIK, SRI
  for European gentleman SAHIB
  of respect SRI, SWAMI, SREE
trader BANIAN, BANYA
tribe JAT
twenty CORGE
universe LOKA
unknown god KA
veranda PYAL
village ABADI
viol RUANA
weaver TANTI
weight SER, MAUND
widow SATI, SUTTEE
  cremation of SUTTEE
world LOKA
worship PUJA
worshiper of Siva SAIVA
Hinduism BRAH- MANISM
  essence ATMAN
Hindustan Dravidian TODA
Hindustani URDU, HINDI
hinge JOINT, PIVOT, CENTER, AXIS, BASIS, DEPEND, ROTATE, HANG, SWING
joint PIVOT, KNEE, ELBOW
hinny HYBRID, MULE, WHINNY, NEIGH
hint ALLUDE, WINK, GLANCE, CUE, IN- TIMATE, SUGGEST, CLUE, REFER, TIP, POINTER, IMPLY, INSINUATE, INKLING
hip COXA, HUCK, HUCKLE, HAUNCH
bone(s) ILIA, ILIUM
pertaining to SCIATIC, COXAL
Hippocrates, *drug of* MECON (OPIUM)
hippopotamus, *Biblical* BEHEMOTH
hircine GOATISH, LEWD
hire RENT, LEASE, CHARTER, FEE, GET, EMPLOY, ENGAGE, LET, WAGES, PAY, STIPEND, SALARY, BRIBE, REMUNERATION
hireling ESNE, HACK,

MENIAL, SLAVE, MERCENARY, VENAL
hirsute HAIRY, SHAGGY, BRISTLY
hispid STRIGOSE, STRIGOUS, BRISTLY, ROUGH, SPINY
hiss FIZZ, SIZZLE, SPIT, SHISH
hissing FIZZ, SIBILANT, TST
historian ANNALIST, CHRONICLER, POLYBIUS, XENOPHON, SALLUST, LIVY, PLUTARCH, BEDE, GIBBON, CARTE, WELLS
history DRAMA, PAST, MEMOIRS, RECORD(S), ANNALS, STORY, AC- COUNT, CHRONICLE, TALE, NARRATIVE, TREATISE
muse of CLIO
of individual development ONTOGENY
hit SMASH, BOP, SLOG, BUFFET, FIND, BUNT, SINGLE, FLICK, STRIKE, LAM, AGREE, KNOCK, SWAT, SMITE, SLUG, BOX, CUFF, FAVORITE, COLLISION, IMPACT, THRASH, WHACK
or miss RANDOM
sign of SRO
hitch TIE, KNOT, PAUSE, FASTEN, YOKE, SNAG, MARRY, ATTACH, CONNECT, UNITE, CATCH, OBSTRUCTION, OBSTACLE, IM- PEDIMENT, JERK
hitherto YET, UNTIL
Hittite's *ancestor* HETH
capital PTERIR
hive STORE, SWARM, APIARY, COLLECT, GATHER, MULTITUDE
hives, *nettled* UREDO, URTICARIA
hoard MASS, GARNER, SUPPLY, HIDE, GATHER, PILE, HEAP, STACK, STORE, SAVE, HIVE, ACCUMULATE, DEPOSIT, STOCK, TREASURE, HUSBAND, AMASS
hoarder MISER, NIGGARD

hoarse HARSH, THICK,
HUSKY, RAUCOUS,
ROUGH, GRATING,
GUTTURAL

hoary WHITE, AGED,
GRAY, OLD,
CANESCENT, ANCIENT,
MUSTY, MOLDY,
MOULDY, VENERABLE

hoatzin ANNA, BIRD

hoax BAM, BILK,
CANARD, COD, SELL,
GAG, JOKE, FOOL,
TRICK, CHEAT, GULL,
COZEN, HUMBUG,
DECEPTION, FRAUD,
RUSE, ARTIFICE

hobbled HALT, LAME,
FETTERED, PASTERNED,
WABBLED, SHACKLED

hobby WHIM, FAD,
DOLLY, AVOCATION,
NAG, FALCON,
GARRAN, PURSUIT

hobgoblin ELF, BOGY,
IMP, PUG, PUCK,
BOGIE, SCRAT, SPRITE,
BUGBEAR, BOGEYMAN,
DEMON

hobo TRAMP, VAGRANT,
BUM, BEGGAR

hock HAM, HOX, PAWN,
WINE, HAMSTRING,
ANKLE

hockey *ball* PUCK
  cup STANLEY
  goal CAGE
  stick CAMAN
  team, ice SIX

hocus DRUG, DECEIVE,
FRAUD, CHEAT

hodgepodge STEW,
HASH, MESS, CENTO,
MEDLEY, OLIO,
MELANGE, POTPOURRI,
SALMAGUNDI,
OLLAPODRIDA

hog PIG, SWINE, BOAR,
SOW, PORKER, BEAST,
GLUTTON, SUID
  food MASH, ACORNS,
  SWILL, SLOPS
  genus SUS
  ground MARMOT,
  WOODCHUCK
  like PECCARY
  side of FLITCH,
  BACON
  weed AMBROSIA
  wild BOAR, BENE
  young SHOAT, PIG

hogfish CAPITAN,
WRASSE

hoggerel SHEEP,
HOGGET

hogget BOAR, SHEEP,
COLT, YEARLING

hognut OUABE, EARTH-
NUT, PIGNUT

hogshead TUN, CASK,
BARREL, MEASURE

hogtie HAMPER, CLOG,
FETTER *See* "hinder"

hoist JACK, HEAVE,
LIFT, REAR, RAISE,
BOOST, TACKLE,
ELEVATOR
  as anchor TRIP
  as sails HOISE

hoisting device GIN,
PARBUCKLE, DAVIT,
CAPSTAN, DERRICK,
CRANE, ELEVATOR,
LIFT, JACK

hoity-toity FLIGHTY,
SNOOTY, THOUGHT-
LESS, GIDDY,
ARROGANT, IR-
RESPONSIBLE

hokum BUNK,
NONSENSE

hold HAVE, OWN, OC-
CUPY, GRIP, CONTROL,
GRASP, CLUTCH, CLASP,
POSSESS, RESTRAIN,
CONFINE, IMPRISON,
RETAIN, DETAIN, KEEP,
SAVE, CONTAIN, STAY,
REMAIN, HOUSE,
LODGE, DIRECT,
MANAGE, CHECK, PIN,
FASTEN, HINDER,
THINK, CONSIDER,
GUARD, HATCH, AR-
REST
  back DAM, INHIBIT,
  INTERN, ABSORB,
  HINDER, DETAIN
  for nails NOG
  nautical AVAST
  off AVERT, REFRAIN
  out LAST, ENDURE,
  CONTINUE, OFFER,
  PROPOSE

holder OWNER,
TENANT, PAYEE, CON-
TAINER

holding INTEREST,
TENURE, SEAT, LAND,
TENEMENT, OPINION,
BELIEF, TENET

hole PIT, SLOT, DEN,
CAVE, VOID, CAVITY,
HOLLOW, ORIFICE,
PORE, CUP, SCORE,
EYE, DILEMMA, BORE,
BREACH, CHASM, GAP,
DENT, PERFORATION,
APERTURE, OPENING,
GULF, CONCAVITY
  breathing SPIRACLE
  for molten metal
  SPRUE
  for ship's cable
  HAWSE
  in garment for sleeve
  SCYE
  in mold GEAT

holed up LAIRED, ABED,
RETIRED

holia SALMON, FISH

holiday FERIA, FERIE,
FIESTA, VACATION,
FESTIVAL,
CELEBRATION, FETE,
PLAYTIME
  spot LAKE, RESORT,
  CAMP, SHORE, BEACH

holla CEASE, STOP,
HELLO

Holland *See* "Nether-
lands"

hollow CAVERNOUS,
FALSE, EMPTY, VOID,
CAPSULAR, SCOOP,
PIT, WEAK, VAIN,
VACANT, DENT, HOLE,
IDLE, CAVITY, POCKET,
GULF, CHASM, ABYSS,
CONCAVE, DEPRESSED,
INSINCERE, BASIN,
BOWL, CONCAVITY,
DIMPLE, VACUOUS,
VALLEY, SUNKEN
  combining form
  COELO
  in tile KEY
  narrow DINGLE

holly ILEX, HULL,
HOLM, YAPON, ASSI,
YAUPON, INKBERRY,
TREE
  European ACEBU
  genus ILEX
  India tea YAPON,
  YAUPON, ASSI
  N. Zealand OLEARIA
  sea ERYNGIUM
  shrub YAPON,
  YAUPON, ASSI
  Southern ASSI
  yaupon CASSENA

hollyhock ALTHAEA,
FLOWER

Hollywood prize OSCAR

holm AIT, EYOT, ISLET, ILEX, HOLLY, OAK
thrush MISSEL

holt COPSE, WOODS, HILL, MOUND, PLANTATION

holy SACRED, CHASTE, VESTAL, DEVOUT, PIOUS, DIVINE, CONSECRATED, HALLOWED, SANCTIFIED, BLESSED, SAINTLY, GODLY, PURE
Grail SANGREAL, SANGRAAL
   achiever of GALAHAD, PERCIVALE, BORS
oil CHRISM
one SAINT
Roman emperor OTTO (OTHO)
water vessel CRUET, STOUP, FONT

homage FEALTY, HONOR, ALLEGIANCE, OBEISANCE, DEFERENCE, WORSHIP, LOYALTY, FIDELITY, DEVOTION, REVERENCE

homaloidal EVEN, FLAT

Homburg HAT, FELT

home NEST, HABITAT, ABODE, GOAL, HEARTH, HOUSE, DOMICILE, HUT, FATHERLAND, SHELTER, INGLESIDE, FIRESIDE, RESIDENCE, DWELLING, SEAT, QUARTERS, ASYLUM
base PLATE
of gods OLYMPUS, ASGARD, MERU
of Golden Fleece COLCHIS
team HOST

homely PLAIN, SIMPLE, FAMILIAR, DOMESTIC, HOMELIKE, INELEGANT, UNCOMELY, UNADORNED

Homer's *birthplace* SMYRNA
epic ILIAD, ODYSSEY
reputed parody BATRACHOMYOMACHY

Homeric EPIC, HEROIC

homesickness NOSTALGIA

homespun RUSSET, PLAIN, DOMESTIC *See* "homely"

"Home Sweet Home" *composer* PAYNE

homily SERMON, ADDRESS, TALK, SPEECH, ORATION, DISCOURSE, EXHORTATION

hominy GRITS, SAMP, CORN, CEREAL
coarse SAMP, CORN
fine GRITS
mixture POSOLE

homo, *as a combining form* COMMON, SAME, JOINT, LIKE

homo sapiens MAN, BIPED

hondo, hondu ARROYO

Hondo island city KURE

hone STROP, SHARPEN, WHET, GRUMBLE, PINE, OILSTONE, WHETSTONE

honest SINCERE, TRUE, REAL, GOOD, UPRIGHT, JUST, OPEN, FRANK, FAIR, CANDID, HONORABLE, REPUTABLE, CREDITABLE, ESTIMABLE, GUILELESS, STRAIGHTFORWARD

honesty plant MOONWORT

honey MEL, SIRUP, SYRUP, SWEETNESS, SWEETHEART, DARLING, DEAR
and mulberry juice MORAT
badger RATEL
bear KINKAJOU
beige DORADO
buzzard KITE, PERN, HAWK
drink MEAD
eater IAO, MOHO, MANUAO, BIRD
fermented drink MEAD
source BEE, NECTAR
tube NECTARY
weasel RATEL

honeyberry tree GENIP

honeycombed ALVEOLATE, FAVOSE, RIDDLED

honeydew MELON

honeyed SUGARY, MELLIFLUOUS, SIRUPY, SWEET, DULCET
drink MEAD

honeysuckle, *swamp* AZALEA

Hong Kong bay MIRS

Honolulu, *cliff in* PALI
suburb EWA

honor GLORY, DIGNITY, FAME, ECLAT, REPUTE, HOMAGE, GRANDEUR, NOBILITY, MAJESTY, DEFERENCE, RECOGNITION, NOTICE, EMINENCE, TRUTH, FULLNESS, PROBITY, VIRTUE, DIGNIFY, ESTEEM, VENERATION, RESPECT, REPUTATION, INTEGRITY, CREDIT, ENOBLE, EXALT, PROW, RENOWN, REVERE, CITE, CROWN, PRAISE, TITLE, EULOGIZE, ACCEPT, DISTINCTION, WORSHIP, REVERENCE, GLORIFY, ADMIRATION, ADORATION, PRESTIGE, FEALTY, TRUST, FAITH, REGARD
hungering for ESURIENT

honorable ETHICAL, ILLUSTRIOUS, NOBLE, WORTHY, RESPECTABLE, UPRIGHT

honors DIGNITIES, RITES, TITLES, PRIVILEGES, DISTINCTIONS, CIVILITIES

hood HAT, CAP, COWL, COVER, CAPUCHE, SHIELD, BONNET, COIF, CLOAK, PROTECTION, BLIND, BANDIT, GANGSTER
clergyman's AMICE, VESTMENT
cloak with DOMINO, BURNOOSE, CAPOTE, PARKA
monk's AMICE, COWL, CAPUCHE, ACONITE, BEARBANE, ATIS, PLANT
part of CAMAIL

hooded CUCULLATE, COVERED

garment PARKA,
COWL, CAPUCHE
hoodoo JINX, SPELL,
HEX, SORCERY, JONAH,
BEWITCH
hoodwink DUPE,
COZEN, CHEAT, WILE,
BLINDFOLD, CIRCUM-
VENT *See* "hoax"
hoof UNGULA, FOOT,
WALK, TRAMP, DANCE
shaped UNGULATE
hoofprint PIST(E),
SPOOR, TRACK
hook GAFF, BARB,
SICKLE, REAPER,
CURVE, CROOK,
ANCHOR, HAMUS,
HAMULUS, TRAP,
SNARE, DECOY,
STEAL, SNATCH, BLOW,
FASTEN, CATCH, BEND,
CLIP, CLASP
dagger mounting for
CHAPE
engine GAB
fireplace HANGLE,
POKER
fish KIRBY, GAFF,
SPROAT, FLY, GIG,
BARB, SPOON
large GAFF, HANGLE,
CLEEK
like FALCATE,
UNCINAL
money LARI(N)
pot CLEEK, KILP, BAIL,
CROOK
shaped HAMIFORM
hooka(h) NARGILE,
NARGHILE, PIPE
hooked HAMATE,
FALCATE(D),
UNCINATE, ADUNCOUS,
BENT, CURVED
as a fish CLEEKED,
GAFFED, CAUGHT
as of elbow
ANCONEAL
prong PEW, PUGH
hook-shaped iron CROC
hooky, play TRUANT
hoop BAIL, ENCIRCLE,
EMBRACE, RING, BELT,
CIRCLET, BAND,
CRINOLINE
hooper SWAN, BIRD,
COOPER, RATING
hoosegow JAIL,
PRISON, CLINK, JUG,
COOLER *See* "jail"

Hoosier State
INDIANA
hoot BOO, WHOO, CRY,
HONK, JEER, HISS
as an owl ULULATE
hop CAPER, FRISK,
GAMBOL, DANCE,
LEAP, SKIP, CURVET,
BOUND, SPRING, JUMP,
LIMP, HOBBLE, HALT,
GO, FLIGHT, TRIP,
VINE, PLANT
bush AKEAKE,
LUPULUS
disease FEN
extract HUMULENE
kiln OST, OAST
obtained from
LUPULINIC
plant LUPULUS
stem BINE
tree PTELEA
hope SPES, ASPIRE,
OPTIMISM, FAITH,
EXPECT, AWAIT, AIM,
YEARN, PANT, THIRST,
RELY, LONG, TRUST,
COUNT, BANK,
ANTICIPATE, CON-
FIDENCE, DESIRE
goddess of SPES
symbol of OPAL
hoped for SPERATE
hopeful SANGUINE,
CONFIDENT,
OPTIMISTIC
hopeless SARDONIC,
FORLORN, LOST,
DESPERATE, SAD,
GLOOMY, GLUM,
ABJECT, DESPONDENT,
GONER, DESPAIRING,
FUTILE, VAIN, DOWN-
CAST, CRUSHED
Hophni's *father* ELI
brother PHINEAS
hopscotch stone
PEEVER
Horae EIRENE,
EUNOMIA, DIKE
Horatian poetry ODE
horde MOB, GANG,
TRIBE, PACK *See*
"crowd"
hordolum STY
horizon LIMIT,
PURVIEW, COMPASS,
REACH, RANGE, SCOPE,
SWEEP, RADIUS,
BOUND, EXPANSE
appear above RISE
arc of AZIMUTH

horizontal LEVEL,
FLAT, PLANE, PRONE,
ABED, FLUSH,
PARALLEL
horizontally ATHWART,
ACROSS
horn BUGLE, TRUMPET,
CORNU, TINE, ANTLER,
BEAKER, CUSP,
CORNUCOPIA, SPUR,
SPIKE, PRONG, CASQUE,
GORE, HOOK
crooked BUCCINA
deer PRONG, TINE,
ANTLER
drinking RHYTON
flourish on FANFARE,
TANTARA
Jewish SHOPHAR
mouthpiece BOCAL
of a crescent or moon
CUSP
of insect ANTENNA,
PALP, FEELER
on beak of bird
EPITHEMA
on deer's antler
CROCHE, TINE
pierce with GORE
Roman BUCCINA
saddle POMMEL
shaped object CORNU,
CERATOID
sounded for kill
MORT
stag's ANTLER
unbranched DAG
without MULLEY
hornbill HOMRAI,
TOCK, BIRD
horned animal GNU,
DEER, MOOSE, GOAT,
BULL
fabled UNICORN
hornet CRABRO, WASP,
INSECT
hornless POLLED,
ACEROUS, POLEY,
MULLEY, DODDIE
cow MULLEY, DODDIE
hornpipe DANCE, IN-
STRUMENT, TUNE
sailor's MATELOTE,
DANCE
horny *scale* NAIL,
SCUTE, SCUTUM,
LORICA
tissue KERATIN
horrible DIRE, GRIM,
HORRID, SHOCKING,
HIDEOUS, AWFUL,
UGLY, FRIGHTFUL,

TERRIBLE, ALARMING, FORMIDABLE, DREADFUL, FEARFUL, DISGUSTING, OFFENSIVE, UNPLEASANT

hors d'oeuvre CANAPE, APERITIF, APPETIZER, OLIVES, ANCHOVIES

Horsa's *brother* HENGIST

horse(s) COB, BIDET, ARAB, BLOCK, BEAST, PACER, STEED, EQUINE, NAG, COLT, PALFREY, PONY, FILLY, PLUG, ROAN, CHARGER, COURSER, STALLION, GELDING, MARE, SHELTIE, MOUNT, DOBBIN, STAND, FRAME, SUPPORT, TRESTLE

Achilles' XANTHUS
ankle of HOCK
Australia WARRAGAL, WARRIGAL, WALER
Barbary ARAB
blanket MANTA
breed MORGAN, ARAB, SHIRE, BARB, SUFFOLK
brown SORREL
buyer KNACKER, TRADER, COPER
check back SACCADE
chestnut ROAN
color PIED, PINTO, ROAN, BAY, SORREL
combining form HIPPO
command to GEE, HAW, HUP, WHOA, GIDDAP
cry NEIGH, NIE, WHINNY
dark ZAIN
dealer COPER, TRADER, KNACKER
decrepit SKATE, PLUG
disease SPAVIN, SURRA(H), LAMPAS, LAMPERS, HEAVES, DISTEMPER
draft breed SHIRE
driver COACHMAN, SUMPTER, JOCKEY
drove ATAJO
easy-paced PAD
eyelid inflammation HAW
family ASS, ZEBRA
female FILLY, MARE
fennel SESELI, PLANT

foot part PASTERN, FROG
forehead CHANFRIN
fresh relay REMUDA
genus EQUUS
giant, Norse GOLDFAX
goddess EPONA
guide rope REIN, LONGE
half and half man CENTAUR
half wild MUSTANG
harnessed pair TEAM, SPAN
hoof FOOT, UNGULA
last in team THILL(ER)
leap of CURVET
leg FETLOCK, INSTEP
mackerel SCAD, AKULE, TUNNY, SAUREL, BONITO, FISH
male GELDING, STALLION
man, with horse's body CENTAUR
of sun, Norse myth. ARVAK, ALSVITH
old SKATE, PLUG, ROSINANTE, JADE, GARRAN
pack SUMPTER, BIDET
pair of TEAM, SPAN
piebald PINTO
position of in race PLACE, SHOW, WIN, RAIL
prehistoric EOHIPPUS
race board TOTE
race, inferior PLATER
racing TURF
rearing of PESADE
reddish brown BAY, ROAN
relay REMUDA
resembling EQUOID, EQUINE
rider JOCKEY
round-up RODEO
set of three RANDEM
shaft THILL(ER)
shoe, calk on CALTROP
small BRONCO, NAG, TIT, SHETLAND, BIDET, PONY, JENNET, COLT
Spanish JENNET
spirited BARB, ARAB, STEED, COURSER
stable of STRING
stocky COB

swift ARAB, PACOLET, RACER
talking XANTHUS, ARION
track slope CALADE
training place LONGE
type of TROTTER, DRAFT
wheel POLER
white flecked ROAN
white streak on face SHIM, BLAZE, REACH
wild TARPAN
work AVER, GELDING
worthless JADE, CROCK, SHACK, PLUG, NAG
young COLT, FOAL, FILLY

horsehide pellet BASEBALL

horseman RIDER, JOCKEY, EQUESTRIAN, CAVALRYMAN, DRAGOON, CENTAUR

horsemanship, *art of* MANEGE

Horse Mesa Dam, *river of* SALT

horse-radish tree oil BEN

horseshoe *gripper* CALK
stall TRAVE

horsewhip CHABOUK, QUIRT, FLOG, PUNISH

hortative ADVISORY

Horus RA
father OSIRIS

hospice IMARET, INN, HOTEL, ASYLUM

hospitality to strangers XENODOCHY

host HORDE, ARMY, LEGION, MULTITUDE, SERVER, WAFER, SACRIFICE, ENTERTAINER, LANDLORD, INNKEEPER, CROWD
receptacle PYX, PATEN, CIBORIUM

hostel(ry) INN, MANSION, TAVERN, HOTEL, MOTEL, LODGE, SHELTER

hostility FEUD, ANIMUS, ENMITY, RANCOR, HATRED, ANIMOSITY, ANTAGONISM, WARFARE

hostler GROOM, OSTLER

hot STEAMY, TORRID, BURNING, CANDENT, FLAMING, SWELTERING, FIERY, FIERCE, ARDENT, ANGRY, FERVENT, EAGER, PASSIONATE, LUSTFUL, IMPETUOUS, EXCITABLE, EXCELLENT, GOOD
iron CAUTER
spring SPA, GEYSER
tempered IRACUND, CHOLERIC, TOUCHY
wine beverage NEGUS
hotel TAVERN, FONDA, HOSTEL, INN, HOSPICE, IMARET
keeper BONIFACE, HOST, PADRONE
hotspur PERCY, HOTHEAD, MADCAP
Hottentot NAMA, BALAO
aborigne NAMAQUA
cloak or rug KAROSS
encampment KRAAL
language NAMA
musical instrument GORA, GORAH
tribe NAMA
hough *See* "hock"
hound DOG, CERBERUS, BEAGLE, WOLF, BAIT, HARRY, HECTOR, DRIVE, BEDOG, RIDE, BADGER, WORRY, ANNOY, PERSECUTE
small BASSET, BEAGLE
wolf ALAN
hour(s) TIME, HORA(E)
book HORA(E)
canonical ORTHROS
See under "canonical hours"
hourly FREQUENT(LY), HORAL, CONSTANTLY, PERIODICAL
house HUT, COTE, CASINO, GRANGE, SHELTER, DWELLING, BUILDING, LODGE, INN, TAVERN, HOTEL, CASA, COVER, MAISON, MANSION, ABODE, HOME, DOMICILE, RESIDENCE, HABITATION, CHURCH, TEMPLE, SYNAGOGUE, THEATER, AUDIENCE,

FIRM, FAMILY, LINEAGE, CONTAIN, HOLD, BOARD, HARBOR, CABIN, VILLA
African TEMBE
combining form ECO
oriental SERAI
pertaining to DOMAL
ranch HACIENDA, GRANGE
rural VILLA, RANCH, FARM, GRANGE
Russian log IZBA
small CASITA, CABIN
stately PALACE, MANSION
summer GAZEBO, VILLA, COTTAGE, CABIN, SHACK
tree NEST
housefly MUSCA, FANNIA, INSECT, PEST
household MENAGE, FAMILY, HOUSE
deities LARES, PENATES
fairy PUCK
tutelaries LARES, PENATES
housel EUCHARIST
housewarming INFARE, RECEPTION, PARTY, TEA
housing PAD, COVER(ING), SHELTER, NICHE, FRAME, BOX, COWL, PROTECTION, TRAPPINGS, SUPPORT
Houston college RICE
hovel HUT, SHACK, STACK, CABIN, DEN, DUGOUT, HUTCH, SHED, SHELTER, COTTAGE, SHANTY, LEANTO
hover LURK, FLIT, POISE, HANG, SUSPEND, WAIT, LINGER, FLUTTER, WAVER, FLY
Howe ELIAS
however YET, BUT, STILL, NEVERTHELESS, NOTWITHSTANDING, EXCEPT
howitzer CANNON, GUN, SKODA
howl CRY, WAIL, BELLOW, SHRIEK, YOWL, BAWL, LAMENT, YELL, COMPLAIN, ULULATE
howler monkey ARABA
hoyden TOMBOY,

ROMP, RUDE, UNCOUTH, ROISTERING
Hreidmar's *son* REGIN(N)
hub NAVE, PITH, CORE, FOCUS, KERNEL, CENTER, MIDDLE, HEART
City BOSTON
hubble-bubble PIPE, CHATTER, CONFUSION
huckle HAUNCH, HIP
huddle CROWD, GROUP, BUNCH, LUMP, HURRY, COLLECT, JUMBLE, DISORDER, CONFUSION, MUDDLE, CONFERENCE
hue COLOR, TINT, ALARM, SHADE, TONE, TINGE, CLAMOR, CRY, COMPLEXION, SHOUTING, OUTCRY
huge TITANIC, VAST, GIANT, GIGANTIC, GREAT, IMMENSE, LARGE, BULKY, ENORM(OUS), COLOSSAL, GARGANTUAN, CYCLOPEAN, ELEPHANTINE, MONSTROUS, BROBDINGNAGIAN
hugger-mugger SLY, SECRET, CLANDESTINE, CONFUSION, MUDDLE, JUMBLE
Huguenot *leader* ADRETS
huisache POPINAC, SHRUB
hulk BODY, SHIP, HULL, VESSEL
hull POD, SHELL, STRIP, OPEN, HUSK, CALYX, BODY, HULK, RIND, PEEL, SHUCK, COVERING, CASING, FRAME, SHIP
hullabaloo *See* "clamor"
hum WHIZZ, DRONE, CROON, TUNE, BUZZ, SING, BOMBINATE, MURMUR
human HOMO, ADAMITE, MORTAL, BEING, PERSON, BIPED, MAN, WOMAN, CHILD, BOY, GIRL, HUMANE, KIND, TENDER, MERCIFUL

flesh, figuratively
CLAY
frailty ADAM
humane KIND, TENDER,
MERCIFUL, CON-
SIDERATE, POLITE,
GENTLE, LENIENT,
MILD, SYMPATHETIC,
CHARITABLE,
CLEMENT,
BENEVOLENT
humble ABASE, DEBASE,
CHAGRIN, HUMILIATE,
SHAME, DEGRADE,
MORTIFY, DEMEAN,
DEMIT, POOR, MEEK,
LOW(LY), MODEST,
UNASSUMING, SMALL,
OBSCURE, PENITENT
humbug PAH, BOSH,
CHEAT, FLAM See
"hoax"
humdinger ONER,
CORKER
humdrum DULL,
TEDIOUS, LISTLESS,
COMMONPLACE,
PROSY, MONOTONOUS,
IRKSOME, WEARY,
ROUTINE
humid DAMP, MOIST,
DANK, WET, VAPOROUS
humiliate SHAME,
ABASH, SQUELCH See
"humble"
humility MODESTY,
LOWLINESS, SUB-
MISSIVENESS, MEEK-
NESS
humming BUSY,
SPEEDY, MURMURING,
CHIUSCO, SPIRITED,
EXTRAORDINARY,
SEETHING, TEEMING,
STRONG, ACTIVE,
AGITATED, BRISK
humming-bird AVA,
STAR, RUBY, SYLPH,
RUFOUS, SAPPHO,
LUCIFER, TOPAZ,
WARRIOR, TROCHILUS,
COLIBRI
hummock KNOLL,
HILLOCK, RISE, RIDGE
humor CAPRICE,
QUIRK, MOOD, WHIM,
FUN, JEST, FREAK,
FANCY, INCLINATION,
DISPOSITION, WIT,
TEMPERAMENT,
FLUID(S), BABY,
GRATIFY, DELIGHT,

PLEASE, CATER, FAVOR,
TICKLE, SOOTHE, IN-
DULGE
ill TIFF, SPLEEN, IRE,
CROSSNESS, SULLEN-
NESS
humorist ADE, NYE,
JOKER, CARD
humorous person
CARD, WAG, CLOWN,
JOKER
Hun VANDAL, MAGYAR,
BULGAR
leader ATTILA
Hunan *river* YUAN
hundred CENTUM,
CENTURY, VILLAGE,
TOWNSHIP See "one
hundred"
ares HECTARE
centiares ARE
combining form
HECTO, CENTI
fold CENTUPLE
forty-four GROSS
links CHAIN
square meters AR(E)
thousand LAC
rupees LAK(H)
weight CENTNER,
CENTAL
hundredth of right
angle GRAD
Hungarian MAGYAR
city or town VAC,
PAPA, PECS, BEKES,
BAJA, GYOR (RAAB),
MAKO
coin See "money"
below
composer LEHAR
county ARVA
dynasty ARPAD
legislature FELSOHAZ
measure AKO
money PENGO, FILLER
mountain(s) ALPS,
MATRA
people MAGYAR
river See under
"river"
town See "city"
above
wine TOKAY
hunger DESIRE, AP-
PETITE, GREED, YEARN,
PINE, THIRST, LONG,
CRAVE, COVET,
FAMISH, STARVE,
HANKER, ACORIA
hungry AVID, EAGER,
CRAVING, VORACIOUS,

RAVENOUS, EDACIOUS,
STARVED, FAMISHED
hunky EVEN, RIGHT,
WELL, SQUARE,
LABORER
Huns, *conqueror of*
AVARS
king of ATTILA,
ETZEL
hunt SEARCH, PURSUE,
TRAIL, DIG, CHASE,
DRIVE, SEEK, SCOUR,
SCOUT, STALK, TRAP,
HOUND, HARRY,
PERSECUTE, FOLLOW,
SHOOT, POACH,
FERRET, PROBE
hunter NIMROD,
ACTAEON, ORION,
HUNTSMAN, HOUND,
HORSE, CUCKOO,
CHASSEUR, DOG
assistant to JAEGER,
JAGER, GILLIE, GILLY
hunting *bird* FALCON
cry YOI, TOHO,
YOICKS, TALLYHO
dog BASSET, BEAGLE,
SETTER, POINTER,
HOUND
expedition SAFARI,
CHASE, SHIKAR, HUNT
fond of or pertaining
to VENATIC
goddess of DIANA,
ARTEMIS
weasel FERRET
huntress ATALANTA,
DIANA, ARTEMIS
huntsman JAGER,
JAEGER
hurdy-gurdy ROTA,
LIRA, ORGAN, CRANK
hurl CAST, TOSS, PELT,
FLING, THROW, SLING,
PITCH
hurly-burly TUMULT,
UPROAR, CONFUSION,
TURMOIL, BUSTLE,
DISTURBANCE
hurrah VIVA, OLE, RAH,
HUZZA, ROOT, CHEER,
SHOUT
hurried, *music*
AGITATO
hurry PRESS, CHASE,
RUSH, CELERITY,
SESSA, TEAR, SPEED,
ADO, HIE, HASTE(N),
RACE, DASH, QUICKEN,
DRIVE, EXPEDITE,
SCURRY, DISPATCH

hurt ACHE, PAIN, DERE,
HARM, MAR, LESION,
SORE, DAMAGE,
WRONG, OPPRESS,
PANG, INJURE, CRUSH,
IMPAIR, WOUND,
GRIEVE, AFFLICT, OF-
FEND, BRUISE,
DETRIMENT
hurtful NOCENT,
NOISOME, HARMFUL,
BANEFUL, INJURIOUS,
PERNICIOUS,
DELETERIOUS,
BALEFUL, MALIGN,
DESTRUCTIVE
hurtle COLLIDE, CLASH,
FLING, DASH, STRIKE,
JOSTLE
husband MATE,
SPOUSE, MAN, PERE,
MANAGE, STORE,
CULTIVATE,
ECONOMIZE
brother of LEVIR, IN-
LAW
husbandman GRANGER,
FARMER, TILLER,
CULTIVATOR
husbandry GEOPONICS,
TILLAGE, FARMING,
THRIFT, FRUGALITY
hush ALLAY, APPEASE,
STILL, CALM, SHUSH,
SUPPRESS, SH, HSH,
REPRESS, SILENCE,
QUIET, ASSUAGE,
CONSOLE, SOOTHE,
LULL
husk RIND, BRAN,
LEAM, SHUCK, SCALE,
SKIN, SHELL, HULL,
COVERING, ENVELOPE,
BARK, GLUME, CHAFF
husky STRONG, STURDY,
ROBUST, STOUT,
BRAWNY, BURLY,
ROUGH, DRY, HOARSE,
RAUCOUS, HARSH,
GUTTURAL, ESKIMO,
DOG
hussy BAG, WENCH,
MINX, BAGGAGE, JADE,
SLUT, QUEAN
hut SHANTY, COT,
COTE, SHACK, SHED,
HOVEL, CABIN, SHEL-
TER, LEANTO
fisherman's SKEO,
SHELTER
Southwest JACAL
hutch PEN, COOP,

WARREN, HUT, CHEST,
BOX, COFFER, BIN
hyacinth STONE,
FLOWER, COLOR, BIRD
gem ZIRCON
wild CAMASS
hybrid CROSS,
MONGREL, MIX-
(TURE), MULE,
CATALO
animal HINNY, MULE,
CATALO
citrus TANGELO
equine MULE,
ZEBRULA
hydra SERPENT,
CALAMITY, EVIL,
MONSTER
Hydra Island port
MOREA, HYDRA
hydrargyrum
MERCURY
hydrate, *ethyl*
ALCOHOL
hydrazide AMIDE
hydrazoate AZID(E)
hydrocarbon PYRENE,
INDAN(E), METHANE,
BENZENE, PINENE,
XYLENE
colorless CUMOL,
CUMENE
ethyl CETENE
gaseous METHANE,
ACETYLENE
inflammable BUTANE,
BENZENE
isotope PROTIUM
liquid NONANE,
TOLUOL, TOLUENE
petroleum OCTANE
radical AMYL
solid CHRYSENE
solvent XYLENE
unsaturated
OLEFIN(E)
volatile TETROL(E),
BENZENE
white crystalline
DITOLYL, RETENE,
TOLAN(E)
hydrogen atoms, *hav-
ing two* DIBASIC
hydromel MEAD
hydrophobia LYSSA,
LYTTA, RABIES
hydrous *silicate*
STEATITE, TALC,
SOAPSTONE
sodium carbonate
TRONA
wool fat LANOLIN

hyenalike animal
AARDWOLF
hygienic CLEAN,
HEALTHY, SALUTARY,
SANITARY, HEALTHFUL
hymenopteron BEE,
WASP, ANT, SAWFLY
hymn ODE, SONG,
ANTHEM, CANTICLE,
CANON, LYRIC, PSALM,
PAEN, LAUD
book PSALTER,
HYMNAL
non-metrical
CANTICLE
sacred ANTHEM,
TRISAGION, ODE
short TRISAGION,
CANTICLE
sung in unison
CHORAL(E)
hyperbole EXAG-
GERATION
hyperbolic function
COSH
Hyperion's *son* HELIOS
hyphen DASH, MARK
without SOLID
hypnotic SOPORIFIC,
MESMERIC,
SOMNIFEROUS
condition TRANCE,
COMA, CATAPLEXY,
LETHARGY, HYPNOSIS
hypnotism *founder*
MESMER
hypnotize CHARM,
ENTRANCE
hypocrisy DECEIT,
CANT, PRETENSE,
DUPLICITY, GUILE,
SIMULATION
hypocrite TARTUFE,
PRETENDER
hypothecate PLEDGE,
PAWN, MORTGAGE
hypothesis IF, SUR-
MISE, GUESS,
THEOREM, SUPPOSI-
TION, ASSUMPTION,
POSTULATE, PROPOSI-
TION, THEORY
hypothetical force
BIOD, IDANT, OD,
ELOD
pertaining to ODIC
Hypsipyle's *father*
THOAS
hyrax CONY, DAMAN,
DAS, KLIPDAS, DASSIE,
RABBIT, RODENT
like BADGER

hyson TEA
hyssop MINT, HERB
hysteria NERVES,
    DELIRIUM, FRENZY,
    MANIA, ANXIETY
hysterical WILD,
    FITFUL, SPASMODIC,
    CONVULSIVE

I

I EGO, SELF, IOTA
*excessive use of
    letter* IOTACISM
Iago's *wife* EMILIA
iambic trimeter ANA-
    PAEST
iao MANUAO, BIRD
Iapetus' *son* PROME-
    THEUS
    wife GAEA, GE
Iasi *coin* LEU, LEY
Iberia SPAIN
Iberian SPANISH *See*
    "Spain"
    measure VARA
ibex SAKEEN, GOAT,
    BOUQUETIN, TUR,
    TEK
ibid SAME, LIZARD
    large, Philippine
    MONITOR
ibis GUARA, BIRD
ibn-Roshd AVERROES
ibn-Sina AVICENNA
Ibsen *character* ASE,
    NORA, HEDDA, GYNT
    native land NORWAY
Icarian DARING,
    FOOLHARDY, RASH
ice FROST, RIME,
    FLOE, GEM, CRYSTAL,
    SHERBET, DIAMONDS
    floe PACK, BERG, PAN
    HUMMOCK
    glacial SERAC
    mass of FLOE,
    GLACIER, BERG,
    CALF
    pinnacle SERAC
    *ridge or pile in
    slushy* SISH
    thin GRUE
iceberg BERG
    small GROWLER
iced FROSTED, GLACE,
    FROZEN, CHILLED
Iceland *bay* FAXA
    city or town VIK
    coin AURAR, EYRIR,
    KRONA
    epic EDDA

god See under
    "god"
    language NORSE
    legislature ALTHING
    literature EDDA,
    SAGA
    measure ALIN, FET,
    LINA
    monetary unit KRONA
    musician or poet
    SKALD, SCALD
    volcano HEKLA,
    ASKJA
icon IMAGE, STATUE,
    PICTURE, FIGURE,
    PORTRAIT
iconoscope FINDER
icterus JAUNDICE
ictus STROKE, BLOW,
    CONTUSION, BRUISE,
    PULSATION, ATTACK
icy COLD, GLACIAL,
    GELID *See* "frigid"
id IDEM, GENE, SAME,
    FISH, EGO
Idaho *capital* BOISE
    county ADA, BOISE,
    BUTTE, GEM, KATAH,
    LEMHI, LEWIS
    nickname GEM
    STATE
    river SNAKE
idant CHROMOSOME
ide ORF(E), FISH
idea WRINKLE, CON-
    CEPT, NOTION, BE-
    LIEF, PATTERN, VIEW,
    OPINION, IMAGE,
    THEORY, MODEL,
    SCHEME, INTENTION,
    AIM, DESIGN, FANCY,
    THOUGHT, PROJECT,
    CONCEPTION, CON-
    CEIT, PLAN, IMPRES-
    SION, THEME, PHRASE,
    INKLING
    combining form IDEO
ideal FAULTLESS, UN-
    REAL, UTOPIAN,
    COMPLETE, MODEL,
    IDOL, HERO, PATTERN,
    PERFECT(ION),
    IMAGINARY, VISION-
    ARY, IMPRACTICAL,
    CONSUMMATE, INTEL-
    LECTUAL, MENTAL
    remote THULE
    republic, imaginary
    OCEANA
    state UTOPIA, EDEN,
    OCEANA
ideate CONCEIVE,

THINK, FANCY, WISH,
    PREFIGURE, IMAGINE
idem SAME, ID
identical (A)LIKE,
    SAME, EQUAL,
    EQUIVALENT, TANTA-
    MOUNT, TWIN
ideology ISM, SPECU-
    LATION, THEORIZING,
    SENSATIONALISM
Ides, *9th day before*
    NONES
idiocy AMENTIA,
    ANOESIA, FATUITY,
    FOLLY, STUPIDITY,
    IMBECILITY, IRRA-
    TIONALITY, FOOLISH-
    NESS, INSANITY
idiom DICTION,
    PHRASE, DIALECT,
    SPEECH, TONGUE,
    CANT, PATOIS,
    STYLE, CONSTRUC-
    TION, EXPRESSION,
    ARGOT
idiot MORON, CRETIN,
    OAF, FOOL, SIMPLE-
    TON, IMBECILE,
    DUNCE, BOOBY
idle OFF, VAIN, SORN,
    DRONE, LOAF,
    OTIOSE, OTIANT,
    TIFFLE, LAZY, MOON,
    INERT, LAZE, GAM-
    MER, EMPTY, HOL-
    LOW, PETTY, UN-
    EMPLOYED, INACTIVE,
    INDOLENT, SLOTHFUL,
    VACANT, UNUSED,
    USELESS, FRUITLESS,
    FUTILE, WORTHLESS,
    TRIFLING, WASTE,
    SQUANDER, LOITER
idleness IGNAVIA,
    OTIOSITY, SLOTH,
    VANITY, FOLLY,
    TRIVIALITY
idler DRONE, LOUNGER,
    DAWDLER, SLUG-
    GARD, LAGGARD,
    TRIFLER
idol GOD, DEITY,
    IMAGE, EFFIGY,
    SYMBOL, TERAPH,
    FAVORITE, PET,
    FETISH, BELOVED,
    STAR, ADONIS, FAL-
    LACY
    Antillean ZEMI
    matinee STAR
    philosophy EIDOLON
    social LION

idolater BAALITE, PAGAN, HEATHEN, ADORER, ADMIRER

idolize ADORE, WORSHIP, ADMIRE, DEIFY, CANONIZE, LOVE

idyl(l) POEM, PASTORAL, COMPOSITION, ECLOGUE, BUCOLIC

i.e. ID EST, SAME

if PROVIDED, (AL)-THOUGH, WHETHER
ever AND, ONCE
not ELSE, NISI, UNLESS

igneous rock DACITE, BOSS, GRANITE, QUARTZ, FLINT, BASALT, PERIDOT, CHRYSOLITE

ignited LIT, AFIRE, LIVE, KINDLED, INFLAMED

ignoble SORDID, VILE, HUMBLE, LOW, BASE, MEAN, ABJECT, PETTY, PLEBEIAN, DISHONORABLE, UNWORTHY, INFAMOUS, SHAMEFUL

ignominious INFAMOUS, SHAMEFUL, SCANDALOUS, CONTEMPTIBLE, DESPICABLE, DEGRADING

ignominy DISGRACE, INFAMY, DISHONOR

ignoramus DOLT, DUNCE, NITWIT, SCIOLIST, DUFFER, NUMSKULL

ignorance ILLITERACY, BLINDNESS, NESCIENCE
Hindu philosophy TAMAS

ignorant NESCIENT, UNAWARE, RUDE, CALLOW, GREEN, SIMPLE, UNINFORMED, UNLEARNED, ILLITERATE, UNLETTERED, UNTUTORED

ignore SLIGHT, ELIDE, CUT, OMIT, SNUB, OVERLOOK, FORGET, EVADE, REJECT, NEGLECT, DISREGARD

igorots, *division of town* ATI

iguana GOANNA, LIZARD

ikon *See* "icon"

ileus COLIC

ilex HOLLY, OAK, TREE

Iliad, *herald in* STENTOR
hero ACHILLES, AJAX

Ilium TROY, FLANK, BONE

ilk KIND, SORT, TYPE, STRIPE, NATURE, FAMILY, BREED, CLASS

ill AILING, SICK, INDISPOSED, ABED, UNWELL, POORLY, EVIL, BAD, IMPROPER, UNFORTUNATE, UNFAVORABLE, WICKED, WRONG, FAULTY, HARMFUL, UNLUCKY, ADVERSE, HARSH, CRUEL
combining form MAL
humor(ed) SPLEEN, IRE, PEEVED, SURLY
smelling FETID, NOISOME, MALODOROUS
temper(ed) TESTY, SPLEEN, ANIMUS, CROSS, SURLY
will RANCOR, GRUDGE, MALICE, ENMITY, MALEVOLENCE, VENOM, SPITE

illative INFERENTIAL, DEDUCIBLE, THEN, THEREFORE

illegal CROOKED, CONTRABAND, ILLICIT, CRIMINAL, UNLAWFUL, UNLICENSED, PROHIBITED, UNAUTHORIZED
toll MALTOLT

Illinois *county* BOND, CASS, CLAY, COOK, FORD, KANE, KNOX, LAKE, LEE, OGLE, PIKE, POLK, WILL
river SPOON
town ZION

illiterate INERUDITE, NESCIENT, IGNORANT, UNTAUGHT, UNEDUCATED

illuminate DECORATE, EMBLAZE, LIGHT, (EN)LIGHTEN, EXPLAIN, ILLUME, INSTRUCT, ELUCIDATE, BRIGHTEN

illumination *in eclipse* PENUMBRA
unit LUX

illusion CHIMERA, MIRAGE, FANCY, DELUSION, APPARITION, DECEPTION, FALLACY, FANTASY, MOCKERY, ERROR

illustrate DESIGN, ELUCIDATE, ADORN, PICTURE, DELINEATE, SHOW, EXPLAIN, EXEMPLIFY, BEAUTIFY, TYPIFY

illustration INSTANCE, EXAMPLE, SAMPLE, SIMILE, PHOTO, CASE, SPECIMEN, PRINT, FIGURE, EXPLANATION, PICTURE, DRAWING, ENGRAVING, DIAGRAM

illustrious CELEBRATED, SPLENDID, EXALTED, FAMED, RENOWNED, SIGNAL, EMINENT, FAMOUS, STAR, GLORIOUS, NOTED, DISTINGUISHED

image IKON, ICON, PICTURE, IDOL, EIDOLON, IDEA, PIETA, NOTION, FANCY, EFFIGY, LIKENESS, PHOTO, STATUE, COPY, REPLICA, FORM, SHAPE, FIGURE, REPRESENTATION, SIMILITUDE, CAST, COUNTERPART, IMAGO, TERAPH
mental EIDOLON, RECEPT, IDEA
pertaining to ICONIC
religious IKON, ICON, IDOL, PIETA, ORANT

imagination DREAM, FANCY, IDEA, CONCEPT, FANTASY, IMAGE, ILLUSION

imaginative POETICAL, DREAMY, UNREAL, FANTASTIC, INVENTIVE, VISIONARY

imagine CONCEIVE, IDEATE, WEEN,

FANCY, OPINE,
DREAM, INVENT,
CREATE, THINK, GUESS,
SURMISE, BELIEVE,
SUPPOSE, PICTURE,
DEEM, ASSUME

imam ALIM, TEACHER,
MUFTI, PRIEST,
CALIPH, ALI

imbecile MORON,
GOON, CRETIN,
IDIOTIC, CHILDISH,
WITLESS, FATUOUS,
FOOL, DOTARD

imbecility FATUITY,
ANOESIA, AMENTIA,
IDIOCY, WEAKNESS,
STUPIDITY

imbibe DRINK, AB-
SORB, SOAK, STEEP,
IMBUE, ASSIMILATE,
INHALE

imbosom SHELTER,
CHERISH, EMBRACE

imbricate OVERLAP

imbroglio CABAL,
INTRIGUE, PLOT,
STRIFE, TANGLE, COM-
PLICATION, EMBROIL-
MENT

imbrue MACERATE,
SOAK, STEEP, WET,
DRENCH, MOISTEN,
STAIN, DEFILE

imbue DYE, INGRAIN,
TINGE, COLOR,
SATURATE, INFUSE,
INSPIRE, FIRE, STAIN,
TINT, TINCTURE,
PERVADE, PERMEATE

imidogen compound
AMIDE

imitate ECHO, MIMIC,
FEIGN, APE, MIME,
COPY, MOCK, SIMU-
LATE, PATTERN,
MODEL, ADOPT,
COUNTERFEIT, DU-
PLICATE, FOLLOW,
PERSONATE, REPEAT,
REPRODUCE, EMU-
LATE, FORGE

imitation MIMESIS,
PARODY, APISM,
FAKE, DUPLICATE,
COPY, FORGERY,
TRAVESTY, BURLESQUE,
MIMICRY, SHAM,
BOGUS, MODEL
gems PASTE, GLASS,
STRASS
pearl OLIVET

imitative, *color or
form* APATETIC

immanent INHERENT,
INDWELLING, SUB-
JECTIVE, LIVING

immature YOUNG,
CRUDE, CALLOW,
RAW, GREEN, UN-
RIPE, TRIVIAL,
CHILDISH, UNFORMED,
INCOMPLETE
zoology NEANIC

immaturity YOUTH,
NONAGE, INFANCY,
UNRIPENESS

immediately NEXT,
FIRST, INSTANT,
DIRECT, NEAR(EST),
CLOSE(ST), PROXI-
MATE, PROMPT,
PRESENT, PRESTO

immemorial OLD,
ANCIENT, PRIMEVAL,
HOARY

immense HUGE, FINE,
VAST, COLOSSAL,
INFINITE, TITANIC,
GIANT, LARGE, WIDE,
BIG, GREAT, FAT,
STUPENDOUS, BOUND-
LESS, MEASURELESS,
PRODIGIOUS, GIGANTIC,
TREMENDOUS, MON-
STROUS, ENORM(OUS)
See "huge"

immerse DUCK,
DOUSE, ENGROSS,
DIP, SOUSE, SINK,
DUNK, SUBMERGE,
PLUNGE, INFUSE,
BATHE, INVOLVE,
ENGAGE, BAPTIZE

immobile FIXED, SET,
FIRM, STABLE,
MOTIONLESS, STA-
TIONARY, STEADFAST,
INFLEXIBLE, RIGID,
STOLID, IMPASSIVE

immolation SACRIFICE

immoral EVIL,
WRONG, BAD, LEWD,
WANTON, VILE, COR-
RUPT, DEPRAVED,
LOOSE, SINFUL, DIS-
SOLUTE, UNPRIN-
CIPLED, PROFLIGATE,
UNCHASTE, LICEN-
TIOUS, OBSCENE

immortal UNDYING,
AMBROSIAL, PERPET-
UAL, ENDLESS,
ETERNAL, ENDURING,

DIVINE, CELEBRATED,
UNFADING, CONSTANT

immortality FAME,
ATHANASIA
Hindu AMRITA

immovable FIXED,
FIRM, STIFF, STEAD-
FAST, OBSTINATE,
CHANGELESS *See*
"immobile"

immune EXEMPT,
PROTECTED, SAFE,
FREE

immunity EXEMPTION,
LICENSE, FREEDOM,
EXONERATION,
FRANCHISE

immunizer SERUM,
VACCINE

immure CONFINE,
WALL, ENTOMB,
JAIL, INTERN, LIMIT,
CLOISTER, IMPRISON,
INCARCERATE, SE-
CLUDE, ISOLATE

immutable ETERNAL,
STABLE, FIRM, FIXED,
PERMANENT, UN-
CHANGEABLE, IN-
VARIABLE, CONSTANT

imp FAIRY, FAY,
SPRITE, BRAT, ELF,
PIXIE, DEMON,
HOBGOBLIN *See*
"fairy"

impact SHOCK, FORCE,
CRAM, BRUNT, SLAM,
STROKE, CONTACT,
CLASH, JAR, JOLT,
COLLISION, IMPRES-
SION, IMPULSE,
WEDGE

impair MAR, RUIN,
VITIATE, CRIPPLE,
WARP, DAMAGE,
HARM, HURT, LAME,
WEAKEN, DEFORM,
INJURE, DEFACE,
BLEMISH, ENFEEBLE,
ENERVATE

impale GORE, PIERCE,
SPIT, SPEAR, TRANS-
FIX, TORTURE, EN-
CLOSE, SURROUND

impalpable INTANGI-
BLE, RARE, TENUOUS,
SLIGHT, UNREAL,
DELICATE, AT-
TENUATED

impart SHARE, GIVE,
REVEAL, TELL, COM-
MUNICATE, DIVIDE,

INFORM, BESTOW,
GRANT, CONFER,
CONVEY
impartial EVEN,
EQUITABLE, FAIR,
JUST, CANDID, UN-
BIASED, DISPASSION-
ATE, HONORABLE,
DISINTERESTED
imparting motion
KINETIC
impasse STALEMATE,
DEADLOCK, HITCH,
BLOCK, CUL-DE-SAC
impassioned EXCITED,
ARDENT, FIERY,
FERVENT, HOT,
FERVID, INTENSE,
VEHEMENT, ZEALOUS,
ANIMATED
impassive STOLID,
CALM, PLACID,
SERENE, APATHETIC,
COOL, STOIC, CAL-
LOUS, STEELY,
PHLEGMATIC, HARD,
INDIFFERENT
impatient EAGER,
RESTIVE, FRETFUL,
ITCHING, CHOLERIC,
RESTLESS, HASTY,
PRECIPITATE, NERV-
OUS, IMPETUOUS,
INTOLERANT
impavid BOLD,
INTREPID, FEARLESS
impeach ACCUSE,
ARRAIGN, INDICT,
BLAME, CENSURE,
CHALLENGE, DIS-
CREDIT, ASPERSE,
CRIMINATE, CHARGE
impede BLOCK, CLOG,
RETARD, HAMPER,
HINDER, BAR, FETTER,
DAM, OBSTRUCT,
CHECK, THWART
legally ESTOP, BAR,
DEBAR
impediment BLOCK,
BARRIER, HITCH,
BAR, SNAG, OB-
STACLE, HINDRANCE,
DIFFICULTY, ENCUM-
BRANCE, DISABILITY,
STUTTER, LISP,
STAMMER
impedimenta LUG-
GAGE, BAGGAGE,
EQUIPMENT, GEAR
impel INCITE, DRIVE,
URGE, PUSH, MOVE,

ACTUATE, FORCE,
GOAD, INDUCE, IN-
STIGATE, CONSTRAIN,
COMPEL, STIMULATE,
PROPEL
impelling force(s)
MOMENTUM,
MOMENTA, IMPETUS
impend HANG, LOOM,
THREATEN, MENACE,
APPROACH
impending NEAR,
NIGH, CLOSE,
LIKELY, IMMINENT,
IMPENDENT, THREAT-
ENING
imperfect FALLIBLE,
FRAIL, ERRATIC, BAD,
WANTING, INCOM-
PLETE, UNRIPE, UN-
DEVELOPED, DEFEC-
TIVE, FAULTY,
LACKING
fish THOKE
goods FENT
prefix MAL
imperial KINGLY,
REGAL, ROYAL,
MAJESTIC, AUGUST,
SOVEREIGN, STATELY,
NOBLE, GRAND,
EXALTED, SUPREME,
COIN
officer PALATINE
structure EMPIRE
imperil ENDANGER,
RISK, JEOPARDIZE
imperious OVERRUL-
ING, COMPULSIVE,
OVERBEARING,
URGENT, ARROGANT,
PROUD, MASTERFUL,
DICTATORIAL, DOMI-
NEERING
impersonal COOL, IM-
PARTIAL, FAIR, JUST,
GENERAL, DISIN-
TERESTED
impersonate POSE,
PERSONIFY, MIMIC,
COPY, FEIGN, APE,
ACT, EXEMPLIFY,
EMBODY
impertinent IRRELE-
VANT, INAPPROPRIATE,
RUDE, INSOLENT,
SASSY, SAUCY, SUPER-
FLUOUS, IMPUDENT,
IMPISH
imperturbable COOL,
CALM, SERENE, SMUG,
UNMOVED, IMPASSIVE,

PHLEGMATIC, PLACID,
TRANQUIL
impetuous RASH,
VIOLENT, FURIOUS,
IMPULSIVE, VEHE-
MENT, SWIFT, HEAD-
LONG, QUICK, HASTY,
FIERY, HEEDLESS,
ARDENT, EAGER, SUD-
DEN, RUSHING, FERVID,
PRECIPITATE
person HOTSPUR
imphee SORGHUM,
PLANT
impiety SIN, IRREV-
ERENCE, PROFANITY,
UNGODLINESS
impious GODLESS,
PROFANE, UNGODLY,
IRREVERENT, IRRELI-
GIOUS
impish ELVISH, MALIG-
NANT, CUTE, PLAY-
FUL, SAUCY, PERT,
TRICKY, SLY, MIS-
CHIEVOUS
implant IMBUE,
(EN)ROOT, (IN)FIX,
PLANT, ENGRAFT,
IMPRESS, INFUSE,
INSTILL, INSET,
TEACH
implement KIT, TOOL,
GEAR, TACKLE, EN-
GINE, DEVICE, ARM,
INSTRUMENT, MA-
TERIAL, UTENSIL,
BROOM, BRUSH,
MOP, APPLIANCE,
EQUIP, FULFILL, AC-
COMPLISH, EFFECT,
ENFORCE, PERFORM
early flint EOLITH,
PALEOLITH, ARROW
farm See under
"farm"
pounding PESTLE,
MAUL, HAMMER
*used in hand print-
ing* BRAYER,
ROLLER
warfare, old CROC
implicate IMPLY,
INFER, INVOLVE,
CONNECT, LINK,
RELATE, JOIN, EN-
TWINE, INTERWEAVE,
ENTANGLE
implication OVERTONE,
HINT, INFERENCE
implore BEG, PLEAD,
ASK, PRAY, ENTREAT,

BESEECH, ADJURE, PETITION, SOLICIT, SUPPLICATE

imply ALLUDE, SUPPOSE, HINT, CONNOTE, INDICATE, INTIMATE, INDUCE, INFER, INVOLVE, SUGGEST, PREDICATE, MEAN, DENOTE, INFOLD

impolite RUDE INELEGANT, UNCIVIL, CURT, BLUFF, BLUNT, CRUDE, DISCOURTEOUS, DISRESPECTFUL, UNGRACIOUS, INSOLENT, SASSY, SAUCY, IMPERTINENT

imporous CLOSE, SOLID, DENSE

import DRIFT, VALUE, INTENT, TREND, TOUR, MEAN, DENOTE, SIGNIFY, SENSE, MEANING, WEIGHT, WORTH, BETOKEN, INDICATE, INTRODUCE *tax* DUTY

importance URGENCY, STRESS, WEIGHT, MOMENT, VALUE, CONSEQUENCE, PRESTIGE, CONCERN, SIGNIFICANCE

impose INFLICT, SUFFER, ENTAIL, LAY, TAX, LEVY, FORCE, IMPUTE, SUBJECT, BURDEN, ENJOIN, OBTRUDE, FOIST *upon* FOB, DUPE, PALM, FOIST, PRESUME, INFRINGE

imposing POMPOUS, STATELY, SHOWY, GRAND, REGAL, TALL, AUGUST, NOBLE, MAJESTIC, IMPERIAL, GRANDIOSE, IMPRESSIVE

impost TASK, TOLL, TRIBUTE, REVENUE, DUTY *See* "tax" *India* ABWAB

imposter FRAUD, QUACK, HYPOCRITE, SHAM, FAKE(R), CHEAT, DECEIVER, PRETENDER, RINGER, SWINDLER, PHARISEE,

CHARLATAN, MOUNTEBANK

imprecation CURSE, OATH, MALISON, MALEDICTION, EXECRATION, ANATHEMA

impregnate TINCT, FECUNDATE, PERVADE, IMBUE, ENTER, PIERCE, SOAK, STEEP, INFUSE, MIX, PERMEATE, TINGE, FERTILIZE

impresa DEVICE, EMBLEM, MOTTO

impress AWE, PRINT, INFLUENCE, DENT, STRIKE, LEVY, SEIZE, IMPLANT, STAMP, TOUCH, SWAY, MOVE, MARK, AFFECT, INCULCATE, SEAL

impression IDEA, MARK, STAMP, SEAL, PRINT, TRACE, BELIEF, EFFECT, INKLING, IMPRINT, NOTION, THOUGHT, IMAGE, FANCY, RECOLLECTION, OPINION, DENT, HOLLOW, INDENTATION

impressionable SOFT, EASY, EMOTIONABLE, EMOTIONAL, SUSCEPTIBLE, SENSITIVE, PLASTIC, RESPONSIVE

imprison CAGE, IMMURE, JAIL, LIMIT, CURB, INCARCERATE, CONFINE, RESTRAIN, PUNISH

imprisonment DURANCE, PUNISHMENT, RESTRAINT

improper AMISS, EVIL, WRONG, UNAPT, INDECENT, UNFIT, BAD, POOR, VULGAR, UNSUITABLE, INCORRECT, IMMODEST, INAPPROPRIATE, INDELICATE, UNBECOMING, INDECOROUS, UNSEEMLY

improve AMEND, BETTER, HELP, BENEFIT, REVISE, EMEND, REFORM, AMELIORATE, RECTIFY, CORRECT,

CULTIVATE, PROMOTE, ADVANCE, TRAIN, TEACH

improvise PONG, VAMP, AD-LIB, CONTRIVE, DEVISE, EXTEMPORIZE, COMPOSE, INVENT *music* VAMP

imprudent INDISCREET, UNWISE, PRODIGAL, RASH

impudence LIP, CHEEK, GALL, NERVE, INSOLENCE, PRESUMPTION, BOLDNESS, AUDACITY, EFFRONTERY, IMPERTINENCE, BRASS

impudent (MALA)-PERT, BOLD, BRAZEN, SHAMELESS, BRASSY, CHEEKY, SAUCY, SASSY, BRASH, RUDE, INSULTING, FLIPPANT, FORWARD, FRESH, *See* "impertinent"

impugn ASPERSE, BLAME, DENY, ATTACK, ASSAIL, GAINSAY, CONTRADICT, CHALLENGE, OPPOSE, QUESTION

impulse FORCE, PUSH, THRUST, SPUR, URGE, MOTIVE, IMPETUS, MOMENTUM, DRIVE, INCITEMENT, PROPENSION, INSTIGATION, INCLINATION

impulsive EMOTIONAL, HASTY, RASH, PASSIONATE, HEEDLESS, QUICK, IMPETUOUS, SPONTANEOUS

impunity EXEMPTION, FREEDOM, SAFETY, IMMUNITY, LICENSE

impure DIRTY, UNWHOLESOME, LEWD, OBSCENE, UNCLEAN, DEFILED, UNHOLY, FOUL, MIXED, ADULTERATED

impute ARET, ASCRIBE, CHARGE, CREDIT, ACCUSE, ATTRIBUTE, IMPOSE, ARRAIGN in INTO, AT, ENCLOSED, JAILED, WITHIN, HOME

the manner of A LA

respect to ANENT, IN RE

same place IBID(EM)

spite of MAUGER, YET, NOTWITHSTANDING

what way QUOMODO, HOW

Inachus' *daughter* IO

inaction INERTIA, TORPOR, STILLNESS, IDLENESS, INERTNESS

inactive INERT, RETIRED, IDLE, SUPINE, LATENT, DORMANT, OTIOSE, QUIET, DULL, PASSIVE, PEACEFUL, STILL, UNEMPLOYED, INDOLENT

inadequate LACKING, INSUFFICIENT, SHORT

inane EMPTY, STUPID, PUERILE, FATUOUS, SILLY, TRIVIAL, VOID, JEJUNE, VAPID, VACANT, FLAT, VAIN, IDLE, FRIVOLOUS, FOOLISH, POINTLESS, MEANINGLESS

inappropriate UNAPT, INAPT, ALIEN, AMISS, UNFIT, UNSUITED, UNBECOMING, INEPT, INEXPEDIENT

inapt INEPT, UNFIT, UNSUITABLE, GAUCHE, CLUMSY, SLOW, UNAPT, STUPID, AWKWARD, UNSKILLFUL

inarticulate DUMB, APHONIC, MUTE, INDISTINCT, UNINTELLIGIBLE, UNEXPRESSED, SILENT

inasmuch SINCE, FOR, AS, BECAUSE

inaugurate START, AUSPICATE, INSTALL, BEGIN, FOUND, INVEST, INDUCT, INTRODUCE, COMMENCE, INSTITUTE, INITIATE, CELEBRATE

inauspicious BAD, ADVERSE, MALIGN, HOSTILE, SINISTER, UNPROPITIOUS, UNLUCKY, OMINOUS, UNFAVORABLE

inborn INNATE, INBRED, INHERENT, NATIVE, NATURAL, INSTINCTIVE, CONGENITAL, INGRAINED

desire CONATUS

incantation SPELL, HEX, MAGIC, SORCERY, CHARM, ENCHANTMENT, WITCHERY

incarnation EMBODIMENT, AVATAR, PERSONIFICATION, IMPERSONATION

of Vishnu RAMA

incendiary FIREBUG, BOMB, FIREBRAND, AGITATOR, SEDITIOUS, INFLAMMATORY

incense MYRRH, SCENT, ODOR, SMOKE, FRAGRANCE, PERFUME, INFLAME, INCITE, NETTLE, ROIL, ENRAGE, ANGER, MADDEN, EXCITE, EXASPERATE, PROVOKE

bowl ACERRA, THURIBLE, CENSER

burn THURIFY

tree genus ICICA, BOSWELLIA

incensed ANGRY, IRATE, FIRED, STUNG, MAD, WRATHFUL, ENRAGED

incentive GOAD, MOTIVE, STIMULUS, SPUR, IMPULSE, PROVOCATION, ENCOURAGEMENT, OFFER

inch(es) CREEP, EDGE, WORM, MEASURE

part of LINE, MILL

nine SPAN, HAND

inchoate BEGINNING, INCIPIENT, PARTLY, RUDIMENTARY, INCOMPLETE, IMPERFECT, UNFINISHED

incident EPISODE, EVENT, PRONE, LIABLE, SUBJECT,

CASE, ACCIDENT, CONTINGENCY, OCCURRENCE, CIRCUMSTANCE

incidental CASUAL, MINOR, EPISODIC, SECONDARY, ACCIDENTAL, CHANCE, OCCASIONAL, EXTRANEOUS, FORTUITOUS, SUBORDINATE

incidentally APROPOS, OBITER

incipient INCHOATE, INITIAL, GERMINAL, BEGINNING

incision CUT, GASH, SLIT, PENETRATION, WOUND, SCAR, CICATRICE

incite EGG (ON), AGITATE, SPUR, ABET, URGE, (A)ROUSE, FOMENT, ANIMATE, ACTUATE, INSTIGATE, PROD, PROVOKE, GOAD

inclination MOOD, GRADE, BIAS, TASTE, SLANT, SLOPE, DISPOSITION, LIKING, PREFERENCE, PREDILECTION, BEND, BENT, PROPENSITY, PROCLIVITY, TENDENCY, NOD, BOW

incline TEND, LEAN, VERGE, RAMP, SLOPE, TILT, CANT, BIAS, SLANT, TREND, NOD, BEND, TURN, DEVIATE

inclined BENT, PRONE, APT, PROPENSE, DISPOSED, PARTIAL

to eat ESURIENT

inclose EMBAR, ENCLAVE, PEN, SURROUND, ENCIRCLE, INCLUDE, COOP, CORRAL, INCASE, WRAP, ENVELOP, SHUT IN, CONTAIN

inclosed field AGER

inclosure CORRAL, SEPT, CASE, ENCLAVE, PATIO, FIELD, PRISON

include COVER, ADMIT, EMBRACE, CONSIST, HOLD, CONTAIN, INVOLVE, COMPRISE, COMPREHEND

incognito FEIGNED, VEILED, ALIAS, DISGUISED

income FEES, USANCE, SALARY, WAGES, PROFITS, REVENUE, RENT(E)S, GAINS, RECEIPTS, ANNUITY, PENSION, WEALTH, RETURN, EMOLUMENT, DIVIDENDS, HONORARIUM

relating to TONTINE

incommode MOLEST, VEX, TROUBLE, BOTHER, HINDER, ANNOY, IMPEDE, BLOCK, DISTURB, INCONVENIENCE, PLAGUE

incomplete PART, IMPERFECT, CRUDE, INCHOATE, DEFECTIVE, DEFICIENT, PARTIAL, UNFINISHED, LACKING, IMMATURE, UNDONE

incondite CRUDE, UNREFINED, UNPOLISHED

incorporate MERGE, UNITE, BLEND, JOIN, FUSE, EMBODY, COMBINE, EMBRACE, CONSOLIDATE, MIX

incorrect BASE, WRONG, FALSE, INEXACT, FAULTY, INACCURATE, ERRONEOUS, SOLECISTIC, IMPROPER, UNGRAMMATICAL, UNSOUND, UNTRUE

naming of objects PARANOMIA

incrassate THICKEN, SWOLLEN, INSPISSATE, CONDENSE(D)

increase AUGMENT, EKE, UP, PROFIT, GAIN, RISE, RAISE, MULTIPLY, ACCRUE, RETURN, GROW, PRODUCE, SWELL, ENLARGE, DILATE, WAX, MOUNT, INTENSIFY, GREATEN, ENHANCE, ADVANCE, EXPAND, EXTEND, HEIGHTEN, AMPLIFY, INCREMENT

incredulity DOUBT, DUBIETY, SKEPTICISM, DISTRUST, UNBELIEF

incriminate FRAME, INVOLVE, ACCUSE, IMPEACH, CHARGE, INCULPATE, BLAME

incubate HATCH, SIT, SCHEME, PLAN, PLOT, BROOD, DEVELOP, GESTATE

incubus DEMON, SPIRIT, NIGHTMARE, LOAD, ENCUMBRANCE, CLOG, IMPEDIMENT, BURDEN, HINDRANCE

incumbrance CLAIM, LIEN, BURDEN, MORTGAGE, DEBT *See* "incubus"

incur RUN, RISK, CONTRACT, OBTAIN, ACQUIRE, GAIN

incursion ATTACK, FORAY, RAID, INFLUX, INROAD, IRRUPTION, INVASION

incus ANVIL, AMBOS, OSSICLE, BONE

indecent OFFENSIVE, INDELICATE, UNFIT, LEWD, IMPURE, GROSS, OBSCENE, IMMODEST, UNCLEAN, NASTY, UNSEEMLY, IMPROPER

indecisive TEETERY, IRRESOLUTE, DOUBTFUL, INDEFINITE, INCONCLUSIVE, WAVERING, SEESAWING, UNSETTLED, VACILLATING, HESITANT

indeclinable noun APTOTE

indeed ARU, VERILY, TRULY, REALLY, VERITABLY, ACTUALLY, CERTAINLY

indefatigable SEDULOUS, ACTIVE, BUSY, DILIGENT, UNTIRING, ASSIDUOUS, UNFLAGGING, PERSISTENT, UNWEARYING, TIRELESS

indefinite AMBIGUOUS, VAGUE, UNCERTAIN, INDETERMINATE, UNDEFINED, BLURRED, SMUDGED, INDISTINCT, CONFUSED, OBSCURE, EQUIVOCAL

sided figure NGON

indehiscent *fruit* SAMARA, PEPO, KEY, MELON

legume LOMENT

indent HOLLOW, DENT, DINT, NOTCH, JAG, PINK, TOOTH, SPACE, PARAGRAPH

indentation DINGE, CRENELET, JAB, NICK, NOTCH, DENT, DINT, CRENA, DEPRESSION, RECESS, HOLLOW, SPACE

of a blade CHOIL

indented EROSE, SERRATED, NOTCHED, CRENATE

indeterminate EQUIVOCAL, INDEFINITE, UNFIXED, UNCERTAIN, IRRESOLUTE, VAGUE, INDISTINCT, UNDECIDED

botany RACEMOSE

principle APEIRON

index FINGER, POINTER, FILE, CONTENTS, TABLE, HAND, DIRECTOR, GNOMON, LIST, TOKEN, NEEDLE, INDICATOR, PREFACE, PROLOGUE, EXPONENT

mark FIST

on a card PIP, TABLE

on a sundial GNOMON

India (includes East India) IND, URDU, HINDUSTAN, TAMIL

abuse GALI, GALEE

acrobat NAT

air conditioner TATTY

alcoholic drink ARRACK

animal DHOLE, ZEBU

antelope SASIN, NILGAI, NILGHAI, CHIRU

army officer TANADAR, THANADAR, JEMADAR

assembly hall KIVA

astrologer JOSHI

attendant AYAH, AMAH

bail ANDI

banker SHROFF

bean URD

bear BALOO, BALU

bearer SIRDAR

bed of a stream NULLAH

bill of exchange HUNDI

bird AMADAVAT, RAYA, SHAMA, BAYA, SARUS, ARGALA, LOWA
  song SHAMA, KOEL, MINA, MYNA
bison GAUR, GAYAL, TSINE
black wood BITI
boat DUNGA, DONGA
bodice CHOLI
bond ANDI
British rule RAJ
buffalo ARNA, ARNEE
bulbul KALA
butter GHI, GHEE
calico SALOO, SALLOO
canoe TANEE
cape DIVI
capital DELHI
  summer SIMLA
carpet AGRA
carriage RATH, GHARRY, EKKA
cashmere ULWAN
caste LOHANA, RAJPUT, TAI, MADI, MEO, VARNA, AHIR, BHIL
  low MAL, CAD(D)I, AHIR
cavalryman SOWAR
cedar DEODAR
chamber, ceremonial KIVA
chamois SARAU
charm OBI, OBEAH
chief SIRDAR, MIR, RANA, RAJA(H)
church SAMAJ
cigarette BIRI
city or town AGRA, BARODA, BENARES, SURAT, DELHI, ADONI, ARRAH, ARCOT, AVA, AKOLA, UNAO, MHOW, MAU, MAHE, DHAR, HANSI, BALLY, PATNA, SIMLA, NASIK, GAYA, GAUR, AJMER, PURI
civet cat ZIBET(H)
cloak CHOGA
cloth TAT, SURAT, SALU, SAL(L)OO, ULWAN
  strip PATA
coconut NARGIL
coin LAC, ANNA, PICE, PIE, FANAM, MOHAR, RUPEE, LAKH, TAR, CRORE, MOHUR, ABIDE, ADHA, AHMED, KANO,

AKHTER, DAM, FALOO, GUNDA
cotton cloth SAL(L)OO, SALU
cow NILGAI
crane SARUS, SARAS
cremation, wife's SUTTEE
crocodile GAVIAL
custom DASTUR
cymbals TAL
dacoit BANDIT
dancer NAUTCH
deer AXIS, CERVUS, CHITAL, GERAU, KAKAR, SAMBUR, SAMBAR, ATLAS, CHITRA
desert THAR
dialect PRAKRIT, PUSHTU, PASHTO, TAMIL, URDU
dill SOYA
disease AGROM
district SIMLA, MALABAR, DAYA, GYA
dog, wild DHOLE
drama NATAKA
drink SOMA, ARRACK, NIPA
drinking pot LOTAH
drought SOKA
drug BHANG
due HAK
dust storm PEESASH
dye AL, AAL
elephant HATHI
elk SAMBAR
English founder CLIVE
epic RAMAYANA
estate TALUK
European in SAHIB
fabric ROMAL, SALU, SAL(L)OO *See* "cloth" *above*
fair MELA, DEWALI
falcon SHAHIN, SHAHEEN, BES(A)RA, DHOTI
fan PUNKAH
farmer RYOT
festival DEWALI, MELA
fiber AMBARY, JUTE, OADAL, KUMBI
fig tree PIPAL, BOTREE
fish DORAB, CHENAS
flute BIN, PUNGI
footprint PUG
footstool MORA

former province or state See "state" *below*
fruit B(H)EL, LANSA
garment SARI, BANIAN, DHOTI
gateway TORAN(A)
gazelle CHIKARA, S(H)RI
goat, wild TAHR, MARKHOR
gorge TANGI
government estates AMANI
granary GOLA, GUNGE, GUNJ
grant ENAM
grass GLAGA, MANO, RAGI, KASA, DOORBA, KUSHA
groom SYCE, SAIS, SAICE
handkerchief MALABAR
harem SARAI, ZENANA
harvest RABI
hawk SHIKRA
head man of village PATEL
helmet TOPI
hemp DAGGA, KEF, B(H)ANG, KIEF
herb SOLA, PIA, SESAME
hill dweller DOGRA
hills GARO
hog-deer ATLAS
holy man SADHU, FAKIR
horse disease SURRA
hunting expedition SHIKAR
hut TOLDO
instrument See "musical instrument" *below*
invader SACAE
jackal KOLA
king RAJ(AH), ASA
  mythological NALA
  of serpents S(H)ESHA
laborer PALLI
lace GOTA
lady BIBI, BEGUM
land between two rivers DOAB
land grant SASAN
landing place GHAT
language SANSKRIT
leader NEHRU, GANDHI

levee DURBAR
licorice, poison ABRIN
liquor or wine SHRAB
macaque RHESUS
madder AL, AAL
mahogany TOON
mail DA(W)K
mammal TARSIER
market PASAR
master SAHIB, MIAN
matting TATTA
meal AT(T)A
measure ADOULIE,
 KUNK, RAIK, KOS(S),
 JAOB, JOW, GEZ,
 GAZ, DHA(N), KIT,
 DEPA, DEPOH,
 PARA(H), PARRAH
medicinal nut
 MALABAR
medicine man
 SHAMAN
merchant SETH,
 SOUDAGUR
midwife DHAI
minstrel BHAT
money See "coin"
 above
mountain pass
 GHA(U)T
mountain(s) ABIL,
 VINDHYA, GHAT,
 TRISUL, ABU
mulberry (A)AL, ACH
musket ball GOLI
musical instrument
 BINA, VINA, SAROH,
 SAROD, SARON, RUANA
muslin GURRAH,
 DOREA
narcotic BHANG
 hemp HASHISH,
 BHANG
nilgiri BADAGA
nurse AMAH, AYAH,
 DHAI
nut BEN
officer AMIN, AMEEN,
 JEMADAR
one hundred lakhs
 CRORE
ox GAUR
pageant TAMASHA
palanquin PALKEE
palm NIPA
panda WAH
partridge KYAH
peasant RYOT
people of N.W. JATS
pepper BETEL
philosopher YOGI
pigeon TRERON

pillar LAT
plum AMRA
police station THANA
powder ABIR
priest SHAMAN
 garment DHOTI
prince RANA
princess RANI, RANEE,
 BEGUM
property DHAN
province See "state"
 below
queen BEGUM, RANI,
 RANEE
race JAT, TAMIL,
 SWAT, VARNA
reception DURBAR
region DOAB
religious community
 PARSEE, PARSI
 festival MELA
 sect SAMAJ
rice BORO
rich soil REGUR
rifle pit SANGAR
river See under
 "river"
road PRAYA
robber DACOIT
root ATIS, ATEES
rope dancer NAT
ruler NAWAB, NABOB,
 RANA, RANI, RANEE,
 AKBAR
 military NIZAM
ruminant ZEBU
sacred city BENARES
 word OM
sailor LASCAR
savant PUNDIT, BHAT
score CORGE
sect SAMAJ, JAIN(A)
servant HAMAL,
 AMAH, MATY
shed PANDAL
sheep OORIAL, URIAL,
 SHA(PU), BARWAL
shrub ODAL, MADAR,
 MUDAR, ARUSA
silk CABECA, CORAH
sixteen annas RUPEE
skipper SERANG
snake KRAIT, BONGAR,
 KATUKA
soil, rich REGUR
soldier PEON, SEPOY
sorghum CUSH
spinning wheel
 CHARK(H)A
state ORISSA, BIHAR,
 ASSAM, DELHI,
 GUJARAT, KERALA,

 MADRAS, MANIPUR,
 MYSORE, PUNJAB,
 SIKKIM, TRIPURA
 former CUTCH
 (KUTCH), SWAT,
 OUDH, BASTAR,
 BERAR, JOHOR(A),
 BUNDI, AGRA, DHAR,
 REWA, TEHRI, TONK,
 PATAN
state lands AMANI
stool MORA
storehouse GOLA
sugar GUR, RAAB
surety ANDI
tax district TAHSIL
tax-free land ENAM
teacher GURU
title NAWAB, SAHIB,
 RAJA(H), HUZOOR,
 AYA, RANI, RANEE,
 MIAN
 of respect MIAN,
 SRI, SHREE
tower MINAR
tracker PUGGI
tree See under "tree"
tribe BHIL, KADU
turban PUGREE,
 PUGGREE
umbrella CHATTA
vegetable, any green
 SABZI
vehicle TONGA, RATH,
 GHARRY, EKKA
veranda PYAL
vessel PATAMAR,
 LOTA(H)
viceroy NABOB,
 NAWAB
village ABADI
vine GILO, ODAL,
 SOMA
viol RUANA
violin SAROD, SAROH
warrior SINGH
watchman MINA
wayside stop PARADO
weight CHITTAK,
 MASHA, MAUND, PICE,
 WANG, PAWA, PANK,
 HOEN, RAT(T)I, SER,
 SEER, TANK, TOLA,
 BHAR(A), VIS(S),
 PALA, MANGELIN,
 CATTY, RAIK, TALI,
 TAEL
whaler HOH,
 QUILEUTE
window screen TATTY
wine SHRAB

wood KOKRA, ENG,
SAL, TOON
xylophone SARON
Indian(s)
and white GRIFFE,
MESTIZO, LADINO
*blanket used in trade
with* STROUD
friend of Colonists
NETOP
great spirit MANITOU
house TEPEE,
WIGWAM, HOGAN
memorial post
TOTEM, XAT
money WAMPUM,
PEAG, IOQUA,
SE(A)WAN, BEADS,
SHELLS
ornament RUNTEE
pipe CALUMET
pony CAYUSE
tribal symbol TOTEM
war prize SCALP
water lily WOKAS,
WOCAS
wigwam TEPEE
Indian(s), *classification
of*
Aht confederacy
NOOTKA
Alabama CREEK
Alaska SITKA, ALEUT,
TLINGIT
Algonquin ARAPAHO,
CREE, MOHICAN,
NIANTIC, SAC, SAUK,
WEA, FOX, MIAMI,
SHAWNEE, MICMAC,
ABNAKI, OJIBWAY,
ALGIC, OTTAWA,
BLACKFOOT,
CHEYENNE
Amazon XINGU, TUPI,
TAPAJO
American AMERIND
See state or S.A.
country involved
Antilles CARIB
Arawak ARAUA
Arizona APACHE,
HOPI, HANO, PIMA,
YUMA, MOKI,
MOQUI, TEWA,
NAMBE, NAVAHO,
PAPAGO
Arkansas WICHITA
Athapaska TAKU,
WAHANE, NAHANI,
HUPA, LIPAN, NAVAHO
Bolivia MOXO, URO,

URU, ITE(N), MOJO,
URAN, LECA
Brazil CARIB,
GUARANI, ACROA,
INCA, TUPI, GE, YAO,
DIAU, MAKU(A),
MURA, PURI, PURU,
ARAUA, CARIRA,
CARAJA, MANAO,
BORORO, GUANA,
ZAPARO, SIUSI,
TAPUYA, BOTOCUDO
See "Tupian" *below*
Caddoan REE,
ARIKARI, ADAI, CADDO,
PAWNEE
California HUPA,
KOSO, MONO, NOZI,
POMO, YANA, MAIDU,
YANAN, SALINA,
WINTUN, YUKI(AN),
YUMAN, YUROK,
YUNAN, SERI
Canada CREE, DENE,
HAIDA, AHT, TAKU,
MOKA, TINNE, SIOUX,
NOOTKA, NAHANE,
NAHANI, ONEIDA,
ABNAKI, MICMAC,
SLAVE
Caribbean TAO, TRIO,
CARIB
Central America
ULVA, MAYA *See*
country involved
Chaco TOBA
Chibchan RAMA
Chile AUCA
Chimaquan HOH
Chitchan TUNEBO
Colombia DUIT,
MUSO, MUZO, CHOCO,
TAMA, COLIMA, TAPA,
MOCOA, PAEZE
Colorado
ARAPAHO(E)
Costa Rica VOTO,
BRIBRI, GUATUSO
Cowichanan
NANAIMO
Creek ALABAMA
Cuba CARIB
Dakota SIOUX,
TETON, MANDAN,
SANTEE, REE,
ARIKAREE, ARIKARA
Delaware LENAPE
Ecuador CANELO,
ARDAN, MAINA
Eskimo AMERIND,
ALEUT *See* "Alaska"
above

Florida CALUSA,
SEMINOLE
Fuegian ONA
Georgia CREEK,
UCHEAN
Great Lakes area
ERIE, HURON, CAYUGA
Guatemala ITZA,
MAM, CHOL, IXIL(I),
MAYA, ULVA, VOTO,
KICHE, QUICHE,
PIPIL, KERCHI, CHORTI,
LENCA, CHUBE, XINCA
Honduras MAYA,
CARIB, MORENO,
LENCA, CHORTI, PAYA
Indiana WEA, MIAMI
Iowa FOX, SAC, SAUK
Iroquoian ERIE,
HURON, CAYUGA,
MINGO, MOHAWK,
ONEIDA, SENECA
Jalisco CORA
Kansas PANI,
PAWNEE, KAW, KANSA
Karesan ACOMA, SIA
Lesser Antilles INERI
Louisiana CADDO
Manitoba CREE
Mayan MAM, QUICHE
Mestizo GRIFFE,
LADINO
Mexico CORA, AZTEC,
YAKUI, SERI, MAYA,
CHOL, OTOMI, OPATA,
TOLTEC, JOVA,
EUDEVE, MAYO, PAME,
HUICHOI, MIXE,
APACHE, TOBOSO,
MECO, JONAZ, SERIA,
TRIKE, ZOQUE, PINTO,
HUAVE, PUEBLO
Miami WEA
Mississippi TIOU,
BILOXI, NATCHEZ
River MANDAN,
TONIKAN
Montana HOHE,
CROW, BANNOCK
Muskohegan CREEK,
YAMASI, SEMINOLE
Nebraska KIOWA,
PONCA, OMAHA, OTO
New Mexico ZUNI,
TANO, ACOMA, SIA,
PECOS, TAOS, PIRO,
NAVAHO, APACHE,
KERES, ZUNIAN,
LAGUNA, TONOAN,
PUEBLO, ISLETA,
TIGUA

New York IROQUOIS,
SENECA, ONEIDA,
MOHAWK
Nicaragua MIXE,
ULVA, DIRIAN,
MANGUE, RAMA,
LENCA, CUKRA, MICO,
TOACA, ULVA, SMOO,
SAMBO
Oklahoma CADDO,
OTO(E), KAW,
ARAPAHO(E), LOUP,
CREEK, KANSA, KIOWA,
OSAGE, PONCA,
PAWNEE
Oregon COOS, KUSAN,
MODOC, CHINOOK,
YUNCA, YANAN
Panama CUNA, CUEVA,
DARIEN
Pawnee LOUP
Peru ANDE, CANA,
INCA, CHANGOS, PANO,
PIRO, INKA, YNKA,
CAMPA, BORO,
QUICHE, YUNCA,
LAMA, CHANCA, PEBA,
YAGUA
Piman CORA, MAYO,
PIMA, YAQUI, OPATA,
JOVA, EUDEVE
Plains CREE
Pueblo HOPI, MOKI,
TANA, TAOS, ZUNI,
PIRO
Quapaw OZARK,
ARKANSAS
Quechan, Quichuan
INCA, CHOLO,
AYMARA, NASCAN,
YUNCA
Salishan ATNAH,
TULALIP, TWANA
Seminole chief
OSCEOLA
Shoshonean UTE,
HOPI, MOKI, MOQUI,
P(A)IUTE, MONO,
BANNOCK, PIMA
Siouan KAW, OTO(E),
CROW, IOWA, KANSA,
MANDAN, OMAHA,
OSAGE, DAKOTA,
PONCA, TETON, BILOXI,
CATAWBA
Sonorian SERI
S. America YAO,
ANTEO, CARIB, URO,
ITE, ONA, OTA, TUPI,
GE(S), LULE, MOXO,
PIRO, TOBA, TAPUYA,
INERI, ARAWAK,

AYMARA *See* country
involved
S. Carolina YAMASI
S. Dakota BRULE
Southwest HOPI,
PIMA, YUMA, ZUNI
See state involved
Taconan CAVINA
Tanoan ISLETA *See*
"Pueblo" *above*
Tapuyan GE
Texas LIPAN, ADAI
Tierra del Fuego
ONA, FUEGIAN
Tupian ANTA, TUPI,
XINGO, TAPAJO
Uchean YUCHI
Uintah UTE
Uruguay YARO
Utah UTE, PAIUTE
Venezuela TIMOTE
Vera Cruz TOTONAC
Virginia POWHATAN,
TUTELO
Wakashan AHT
Washington HOH,
LUMMI, MAKAH, AHT,
CALLAM
Western REE, HOPI,
OTO, UTE *See* state
involved
Wisconsin ONEIDA
Wyoming KIOWA,
CROW
Yucatan MAYA
Indian Ocean *island(s)*
MAURITIUS, CEYLON,
MALDIVE, MINICOY
Indiana *county* CASS,
CLAY, JAY, KNOX,
LAKE, OHIO, OWEN,
PIKE, RUSH, VIGO,
WELLS
Indic *language* PALI
indicate SIGNIFY, BE-
TOKEN, POINT, TELL,
SHOW, DENOTE,
EVINCE, ATTEST, HINT,
REGISTER, MANIFEST,
EXHIBIT, DESIGNATE,
SPECIFY, INTIMATE
indication AUGURY,
MARK, SYMPTOM,
SIGN, INDEX, TOKEN,
NOTE, MANIFESTA-
TION, HINT, SUGGES-
TION, EVIDENCE,
PROOF
indicator ARROW, DIAL,
POINTER, VANE,
HAND, GAUGE,
REGISTER

indices TABLES, FILES,
POINTERS
indict ARRAIGN, AC-
CUSE, SUMMON,
CHARGE, BLAME, IM-
PEACH
indifference APATHY,
IMPARTIALITY,
NEUTRALITY, UN-
CONCERN, COLDNESS,
NEGLIGENCE, INAT-
TENTION, INERTIA,
STOICISM
indifferent COOL,
BLASE, APATHETIC,
NEUTRAL, AVERAGE,
MEDIUM, FAIR, UN-
BIASED, UNCON-
CERNED, DETACHED,
DISINTERESTED, LUKE-
WARM, NONCHALANT,
INSOUCIANT, STOICAL,
LISTLESS, INCURIOUS
indigence NEED,
WANT, PENURY,
STRAITS, POVERTY,
DESTITUTION, PRIVA-
TION, PAUPERISM,
TENUITY
indigenous ENDEMIC,
INNATE, NATIVE,
EDAPHIC, ABORIGINAL,
INBORN, INHERENT
indigent POOR, LACK-
ING, DESTITUTE,
WANTING, NEEDY,
VOID, PENNILESS,
INSOLVENT, IM-
PECUNIOUS
indignant INCENSED,
MAD, HOT, IRATE,
ANGRY, (A)ROUSED,
RESENTFUL, PROVOKED
indignation CONTEMPT,
DISDAIN, WRATH, IRE,
ANGER, RAGE, FURY,
RESENTMENT, DIS-
PLEASURE, CHOLER,
EXASPERATION,
DUDGEON, SCORN
indignity AFFRONT, IN-
SULT, INJURY, WRONG,
OFFENSE, OUTRAGE,
INCIVILITY, SLIGHT,
ABUSE, OBLOQUY
indigo BLUE, ANIL, DYE
bale of SEROON
bunting FINCH, BIRD
derivative INDOL(E)
essential principle
INDIGOTIN
source ANIL, WOAD

wild genus BAPTISIA

indirect OBLIQUE,
CIRCUITOUS, MIS-
LEADING, DISHONEST,
DEVIOUS, ROUND-
ABOUT, DEVIATING

indispensable VITAL,
ESSENTIAL, NEEDFUL,
REQUISITE, NECESSARY

indisposed SICK, ABED,
UNWILLING, DISIN-
CLINED

indisputable
APODICTIC, CERTAIN,
POSITIVE, SURE,
EVIDENT, INCONTESTA-
BLE, UNQUESTIONA-
BLE, UNDENIABLE,
INDUBITABLE, IR-
REFRAGABLE, OBVIOUS

indistinct FOGGY,
VAGUE, DIM, HAZY,
OBSCURE, FAINT, UN-
DEFINED, INDEFINITE,
NEBULOUS, BLURRED,
SMUDGED, AMBIGUOUS

indite PEN, WRITE,
COMPOSE, DICTATE,
INSCRIBE

individual ONE,
SINGLE, SEPARATE,
SOLE, SOUL, EACH,
(A)PIECE, DISTINC-
TIVE, UNIQUE,
PECULIAR, PER-
SON(AL), UNCONVEN-
TIONAL, BEING,
SPECIAL, ENTITY
combining form IDIO
of compound animal
ZOON
physiological BION

Indio-Aryan JAT,
RAJPUT, KHATRI

Indo-China ANNAM,
LAOS, VIETNAM,
THAILAND, CAMBODIA,
SIAM
aborigine KHA, HO,
YAO
agricultural caste
MEO
bull ZEBU
city or town HANOI,
SAIGON, VINH, PAKSE
coin SAPEK, PIASTER
country LAOS,
VIETNAM, THAILAND,
CAMBODIA
native MRU, TAI, LAO
rock TRIASSIC

tongue AO, AKA, TAI,
WA, ANU, LAI, SAC,
SHAN, MRU, BODO,
GARO
wood TEAK

indoctrinate COACH,
EDIFY, INSTRUCT,
TEACH, INITIATE,
IMBUE

Indo-European CROAT,
LETT, CZECH, SLAV,
SERB
language INDIC,
IRANIAN, ITALIC,
CELTIC, GERMANIC,
BALTIC, SLAVIC

indolence INERTIA,
SLOTH, LETHARGY,
LAZINESS, IDLE-
NESS, SLUGGISH-
NESS

Indonesian ATA,
NESIOT, DYAK,
BATTAK, LAMPONG,
IGOROT
island BALI, SUMATRA,
JAVA, BORNEO, CERAM,
CELEBES, TIMOR, OBI,
NIAS, WETAR, WE(H),
ARU, SAWU, PAG(A)I,
TIDORE, ROT(T)I
lake TOBA

Indo-Persian measure
GUZ, GAZ

indorse SECOND, SIGN,
ATTEST, VISA, AP-
PROVE, ABET, BACK,
SUPERSCRIBE, COUN-
TERSIGN, SANCTION,
SUPPORT, RATIFY,
CONFIRM

indubitable MANIFEST,
EVIDENT, SURE, UN-
QUESTIONABLE, IN-
DISPUTABLE, UN-
DENIABLE, CERTAIN

induce CAUSE, URGE,
IMPEL, INCITE, ABET,
ACTUATE, MOVE,
DRIVE, INFLUENCE,
PROMPT, LEAD,
ENTICE, ALLURE,
INSTIGATE, PERSUADE,
SPUR, MOTIVATE

inductance unit HENRY

indulge SPOIL, FAVOR,
PAMPER, YIELD, BABY,
HUMOR, CODDLE, COS-
SET, GRATIFY, PET

indulgence MERCY,
LENITY, GRACE,
FAVOR, PRIVILEGE,

LIBERALITY, KIND-
NESS, TENDERNESS,
COMPASSION, REMIS-
SION

indurate CALLOUS,
INURE, STRENGTHEN,
HARDEN(ED),
OBDURATE, STUBBORN,
UNFEELING

Indus *tribesman* GOR

industrial magnate
SHOGUN, TYCOON,
FINANCIER

industrious ACTIVE,
BUSY, ASSIDUOUS,
LIVE(LY), DILIGENT,
LABORIOUS, SEDULOUS,
ZEALOUS, PAINS-
TAKING, PERSEVERING

industry LABOR, WORK,
TRADE, BUSINESS,
TRAFFIC, SKILL,
EFFORT, TASK,
PURSUIT, ACTIVITY,
VIGOR, TOIL

inebriate DRUNKARD,
SOT, TOPER, TIPSY,
TIGHT, STUPEFIED,
SQUIFFY, IN-
TOXICATED, EXCITE,
EXHILARATE

inebriated *See* "drunk"

ineffectual FUTILE,
VAIN, IDLE, EMPTY,
HOLLOW, INEF-
FICACIOUS, UNAVAIL-
ING, WEAK, IN-
ADEQUATE, USELESS,
FRUITLESS

ineluctable IRRESISTI-
BLE, INEVITABLE,
DOOMED, FATED, IN-
ESCAPABLE

inept SILLY, UNFIT,
CLUMSY, GAUCHE,
UNAPT, UNSUITABLE,
AWKWARD, STUPID,
SENSELESS, POINTLESS,
ABSURD, FOOLISH, UN-
BECOMING

inert INANIMATE,
STILL, DULL, LATENT,
TORPID, IDLE, DEAD,
STOLID, AMORT, IN-
ACTIVE, LAZY, LIFE-
LESS, PASSIVE,
COMATOSE, INDOLENT,
LETHARGIC, SUPINE,
APATHETIC, SLOW

inevitable SURE, DUE,
NEMESIS, CERTAIN,
DESTINED, NECESSARY,

UNAVOIDABLE, DOOMED, FATED

inexperienced RAW, GREEN, UNPRACTICED, UNTRAINED, CALLOW, UNSKILLED

infamy OPPROBRIUM, SHAME, ODIUM, SCANDAL, DISHONOR, IGNOMINY, DISGRACE, DISCREDIT, DISREPUTE, OBLOQUY, ABASEMENT, VILLAINY, NOTORIETY

infant BABE, BABY, CHILD, NURSLING, PAPOOSE, CHIT, BRAT, BAIRN, TOT, MINOR

infatuate CHARM, ENAMOR, BESOT, BEFOOL, CAPTIVATE

infatuation FOLLY, MADNESS, FOOLISHNESS, LOVE

infected IMPURE, TAINTED, CORRUPT, POLLUTED, CONTAMINATED, DEFILED, POISONED

infection, *free from* ASEPSIS

infer DEDUCE, PRESUME, DERIVE, JUDGE, IMPLY, GUESS, GATHER, THINK, REASON, CONCLUDE, CONSIDER, SURMISE, ASSUME, DRAW

inference DEDUCTION, COROLLARY, ILLATION, SURMISE, IMPLICATION, CONCLUSION

inferior LOWER, POOR, LESS, MINOR, PETTY, SUBORDINATE, SECONDARY, INDIFFERENT, PALTRY, SHABBY, HUMBLE, MEDIOCRE, NETHER
as a judge PUISNE

infernal EVIL, SATANIC, TARTAREAN, MALIGNANT, HELLISH, CURSED, VICIOUS, DEMONIACAL, BAD, DIABOLIC, DEVILISH, STYGIAN, FIENDISH, MALICIOUS, DAMNABLE, WICKED, HATEFUL

inferno ABYSS, HADES, PIT, FIRE, HELL,
AVERNUS *See* "Hades"
Biblical GEHENNA
Buddhist NARAKA
Hebrew SHEOL
river STYX

infested HAUNTED, OVERRUN, BESET, PLAGUED, VEXED, TORMENTED, HARASSED

infidel ATHEIST, SARACEN, HEATHEN, PAGAN, UNBELIEVER, KAFFIR, AGNOSTIC, HERETIC

infinity OLAM, BOUNDLESSNESS, ETERNITY

infirm ANILE, SENILE, DECREPIT, GREY, FEEBLE, WEAK, UNSTABLE, FRAIL, IRRESOLUTE, AILING, SICK, DEBILITATED, VACILLATING, FALTERING, INSECURE, UNSOUND, PRECARIOUS

inflame FAN, RANKLE, ANGER, RILE, FIRE, LIGHT, IGNITE, EXCITE, STIMULATE, ENKINDLE, HEAT, INTENSIFY, INCITE, (A)ROUSE, ANIMATE, INSPIRIT, IRRITATE, PROVOKE, KINDLE

inflammable FLAMMABLE, ACCENDIBLE, PICEOUS, ARDENT, COMBUSTIBLE, EXCITABLE, IRASCIBLE
gas ETHANE
liquid METHANE, GAS
substance TINDER, PUNK, AMADOU

inflammation *suffix* ITIS

inflated DISTENDED, TURGID, BOMBASTIC, SWOLLEN, DILATED, TUMID, SHOWY, BLOATED, OVERBLOWN, POMPOUS, SORE

inflection TONE, TENOR, ACCENT, ANGLE, CURVATURE, BEND, CURVE, TURN, FLEXURE, CROOK, MODULATION

inflexible SOLID, HARD, STOUT, STRONG, ADAMANT, FIRM, GRIM,
IRON, RIGID, STIFF, TENSE, STARK, WOODEN, RIGOROUS, UNBENDING, STUBBORN, DOGGED, OBSTINATE, UNYIELDING, RESOLUTE, INEXORABLE, IMPLACABLE, STERN

inflict IMPOSE, WREAK, DEAL, TROUBLE, FOIST

inflorescent, *axial circle* WHORL
cluster CYME, RECEME, SPADIX

influence PULL, IMPEL, IMPORT, AFFECT, SWAY, WIN, WEIGHT, CREDIT, POWER, CONTROL, STIR, (A)ROUSE, BIAS, MOVE, TOUCH, AUTHORITY, MASTERY, PREDOMINANCE, PRESTIGE, INDUCE, PERSUADE

influenza GRIP(PE), FLU

influx ILLAPSE, TIDE, INFLOW, INPOURING

inform APPRISE, TELL, NOTIFY, TRAIN, TEACH, WARN, RAT, ACQUAINT, ADVISE, INSTRUCT, ENLIGHTEN

informal CASUAL, FREE, EASY, UNCONVENTIONAL, UNCEREMONIOUS, SIMPLE, NATURAL, FAMILIAR, IRREGULAR, COLLOQUIAL

information DOPE, NEWS, LORE, KNOWLEDGE, NOTICE, ADVICE, INSTRUCTION, TIP, DATA, FACTS, INTELLIGENCE, LEARNING, ERUDITION, WISDOM

informative INSTRUCTIVE, DIDACTIC, EDUCATIONAL, ENLIGHTENING

informer NARK, STOOL, DELATOR, RAT

infrequent RARE, SCARCE, SPORADIC, UNIQUE, STRANGE, UNCOMMON, UNUSUAL, SELDOM, OCCASIONAL, SPARSE infringement of copyright PIRACY, PLAGIARISM

infundibulum, contracted orifice LURA

infuse FIRE, ANIMATE, STEEP, SOAK, INSTILL, IMBUE, PERVADE, INGRAIN, MACERATE, MIX, INCULCATE, IMPLANT, SHED, INTRODUCE, INSINUATE, INSPIRE, FILL, DRENCH

infusion TEA, DECOCTION, EXTRACT, INPOURING, INSTILLATION, TINCTURE, ADMIXTURE, AFFUSION
malt WORT

ingenious CLEVER, DAEDAL, FINE, ADROIT, CUNNING, EXPERT, DEFT, HANDY, INVENTIVE, GIFTED, ARTFUL, RESOURCEFUL, SKILLFUL

ingenuous OPEN, FRANK, NAIVE, NATURAL, SIMPLE, ARTLESS, CANDID, SINCERE, HONEST, GUILELESS, STRAIGHTFORWARD, CHILDLIKE

ingest EAT, SWALLOW, CONSUME

ingle NOOK, FIRE, FLAME, BLAZE, FIREPLACE, HEARTH

ingluvies CROP, CRAW

ingot SYCEE, GAD, PIG, BAR, MOLD, CAST

ingredient PART, FACTOR, ITEM, DETAIL, COMPONENT, ELEMENT, CONSTITUENT

ingress ENTRY, ACCESS, PORTAL, ENTRANCE, ENTREE

inhabitant CIT(IZEN), DENIZEN, DWELLER, INMATE, RESIDENT, OCCUPANT
of marshes LIMNOPHILE

inhabiting the ground TERRICOLOUS

inhale RESPIRE, BREATHE, SNIFF, SMELL, INSPIRE

inharmonious OUTS, UNMUSICAL, DISCORDANT, CONFLICT-ING, INHARMONIC, JARRING

inhere CLEAVE, LODGE, STICK, ABIDE, RESIDE, BELONG

inherent NATIVE, INBORN, INTRINSIC, INNATE, INBRED, ESSENTIAL, NATURAL, BASIC, INFIXED, ABIDING, INALIENABLE, INGRAINED, INDWELLING

inheritance GIFT, ENTAIL, ESTATE, HERITAGE, LEGACY, BENEFACTION, BEQUEST, HEREDITY, PATRIMONY

inheritor HEIR, LEGATEE, PARCENER

inhibit FORBID, RESTRAIN, PROHIBIT, CHECK, BAN, ENJOIN, PREVENT, CURB, ARREST, HINDER, REPRESS, OBSTRUCT, BAR, STOP, INTERDICT, SUPPRESS, WITHOLD

inhuman BESTIAL, CRUEL, BRUTAL, FIERCE, GRIM, MALIGN, FELL, BARBAROUS, SAVAGE, RUTHLESS, MERCILESS, UNFEELING, DIABOLICAL, DEVILISH, FEROCIOUS

inimical ADVERSE, HOSTILE, HURTFUL, UNFRIENDLY, UNFAVORABLE, ANTAGONISTIC, CONTRARY

iniquity CRIME, EVIL, SIN, VICE, WRONG, INJUSTICE, ABOMINATION, WICKEDNESS, MISDEED

initial FIRST, LETTER, HEAD, INCIPIENT, START, BEGINNING, ORIGINAL
ornamental letter PARAPH, RUNE
payment ANTE, DOWN, DEPOSIT

initiate BEGIN, FOUND, START, INTRODUCE, INDOCTRINATE, TEACH, INSTRUCT,

ADMIT, INSTATE, INDUCT, INAUGURATE

inject INSERT, IMMIT, OFFER, INTROMIT, INTERRUPT, PROPOSE

injection SHOT, CLYSTER, ENEMA, INTRUSION, HINT, CONGESTION

injunction ORDER, BAN, MANDATE, PRECEPT, COMMAND, ADMONITION, PROHIBITION, TABU, TABOO

injure GRIEVE, MAR, TEEN, LAME, HURT, DAMAGE, HARM, WOUND, MAIM, SPOIL, CRIPPLE, DISFIGURE, WRONG, MALTREAT, ABUSE, INSULT, AFFRONT, IMPAIR, SULLY
by scorching SCATHE, BURN, CHAR, SINGE

injurious NOXIOUS, HARMFUL, DEADLY, DAMAGING, BANEFUL, INIQUITOUS, UNJUST, DETRIMENTAL, DELETERIOUS, MISCHIEVOUS, SLANDEROUS, ABUSIVE, PERNICIOUS

injury DAMAGE, LESION, LOSS, HARM, WOUND, TRAUMA, MISCHIEF, BLEMISH, HURT, EVIL, ILL, PREJUDICE, DETRIMENT, OFFENSE, INJUSTICE
causing MALEFIC
civil TORT
sense of UMBRAGE

ink *bag* SAC
berry HOLLY, GALLBERRY, POKEWEED
fish CUTTLE, SQUID
spreader, printing BRAYER, ROLLER

inker PAD, BRAYER, ROLLER
in lithography DABBER, TOMPION

inkle TAPE, YARN, BRAID, THREAD

inkling HINT, CUE, CLUE, INTIMATION, NOTION, WHISPER, SUGGESTION, SUSPICION

inky BLACK, STAINED, MURKY, DARK,

COLORED, MARKED,
ATRAMENTOUS
fluid MALENA
inlaid work MOSAIC,
BUHL
inlay, *metallic* TARSIA,
NIELLO
inlet PORE, ARM,
FIORD, RIA, COVE, BAY,
CREEK, ENTRANCE,
VOE, STRAIT, BIGHT
coast line STRAIT,
BIGHT
Orkney Island VOE
southern BAYOU
inn ABODE, TAVERN,
FONDA, HOTEL,
MOTEL, POSADA,
HOSTEL(RY), LODGE
Italian LOCANDA
keeper BONIFACE,
PUBLICAN, HOST,
PADRONE
Near East SERAI,
IMARET, CARAVANSARY
Spanish FONDA,
POSESA
innate NATIVE,
NATURAL, INBORN, IN-
BRED, INHERENT,
CONGENITAL,
INDIGENOUS, INSTINC-
TIVE, INGRAINED, CON-
STITUTIONAL,
HEREDITARY
inner OBSCURE, MID-
DLE, INTERNAL, IN-
TERIOR, INWARD,
INSIDE, INDISTINCT
combining form ENTO
Innisfail EIRE, ERIN,
IRELAND
innocence, *symbol of*
DIAMOND
innocent CHASTE,
PURE, UPRIGHT,
CLEAN, SPOTLESS,
HOLY, SINLESS, NAIVE,
BLAMELESS, UN-
TAINTED, UNSULLIED,
GUILTLESS, SIMPLE,
ARTLESS, INNOCUOUS
one LAMB, BABE,
INFANT, CHILD
innovation CHANGE,
NOVELTY, INTRODUC-
TION
innuendo SLUR, HINT,
ALLUSION, INSINUA-
TION, SUGGESTION, IN-
TIMATION, IMPLICA-
TION

inordinate DISORDERED,
FABULOUS, UNDUE,
LARGE, EXCESSIVE, IM-
MODERATE, EX-
TRAVAGANT
inquest ASSIZE, SEARCH,
PROBE, INQUIRY, QUIZ,
INQUISITION, IN-
VESTIGATION, JURY
inquiry QUEST, SEARCH,
QUERY, PROBE, TRIAL,
EXAMINATION, IN-
VESTIGATION, IN-
TERROGATION
insane MORBID, BATTY,
FRANTIC, MAD, CRAZY,
WILD, DERANGED,
PSYCHOTIC, CRACKED,
INCOMPETENT, UN-
SOUND, LUNATIC,
MANIACAL, FOOLISH,
EXTRAVAGANT
house for ASYLUM,
BEDLAM, MADHOUSE
to make DEMENT,
DERANGE
insanity FOLIE,
AMENTIA, MANIA,
VESANIA, LUNACY,
PSYCHOSIS, DERANGE-
MENT, DEMENTIA,
MADNESS, ABERRATION
inscribe RECORD, EN-
ROL(L), SIGN, ENTER,
ENGRAVE, MARK,
WRITE, ADDRESS,
DEDICATE, IMPRESS
inscription, *end of book*
COLOPHON
explanatory TITULUS
inscrutable
ABSTRUSE,
MYSTERIOUS, PRO-
FOUND, DEEP, DARK,
VAGUE, INEXPLORABLE,
UNFATHOMABLE, IN-
COMPREHENSIBLE
insect(s) BUG, NIT,
APHID, LERP, IMAGO,
ANT, SPIDER, ACARID,
ERI(A), BEE, BORER,
DOR, FLY, FLEA,
GNAT, MANTIS,
BEETLE, ROACH,
CICADA, DIPTERAN,
SCORPION, KATYDID,
MOTH
adult IMAGO
antenna FEELER,
PALP
end of CLAVA
back surface NOTUM

body segment ACRON,
THORAX
chirping CRICKET
dipterous MOSQUITO
eyes OCELLI, STEM-
MAS
feeler PALP, ANTENNA
female GYNE,
QUEEN
foremost part
ACRON
four-winged
BEETLE
genus CICADA,
NEPA, TERMES,
EMESA, CICALA,
MANTIS, THRIPIDAE,
ACARUS
hard covering
CHITIN
homopterous CICADA,
LOCUST, APHID
immature LARVA
larva GRUB, MAG-
GOT
lepidopterous MOTH,
BUTTERFLY
like ENTOMOID
mature IMAGO
middle division
THORAX
migratory LOCUST
molting of ECDYSIS
order of DIPTERA,
ACARINA, APTERA,
COLEOPTERA
parasitic TURCATA,
TICK, LOUSE,
CHIGOE, PEDICULUS,
CHIGGER, FLEA
pertaining to
ENTOMIC
plant APHID, THRIPS,
BEETLE, BORER
praying MANTIS
resin LAC
six-legged CHIGGER,
CHIGOE
slender grotesque
MANTIS
small APHID, CHIGOE,
CHIGGER, MITE,
FLEA
social ANT, BEE
sound CHIRP, KATY-
DID
stage in life INSTAR,
PUPA, COCOON,
IMAGO
sting ICTUS

winged WASP, GNAT, IMAGO, DIPTERAN, HORNET, FLY
wingless APTERAN, SPIDER, CENTIPEDE
wing margin TERMEN
with tail forceps EARWIG
insectivorous bird VIREO, PEEWEE, FLYCATCHER, REDSTART
insecure RICKETY, UNRELIABLE, DUBIOUS, ASEA, INFIRM, SHAKY, UNCERTAIN, RISKY, UNSAFE, HAZARDOUS, PRECARIOUS, DANGEROUS
inseminate IMPLANT, SOW, IMPREGNATE, FERTILIZE, INSTILL
insensibility ANALGESIA, COMA, APATHY, ANESTHESIA, TORPOR, LETHARGY, INSENTIENCE, INDIFFERENCE, UNFEELINGNESS, UNCONSCIOUSNESS, CARUS
insert INSET, INLAY, INFIX, STUFF, INSTILL, PANEL, GORE, IMMIT, INGRAFT, INJECT, INTRODUCE, IMPLANT, INTERPOLATE, INTERCALATE
insertion *of sound in word* EPENTHESIS
cord in cloth SHIRR
inset PANEL, GORE, GODET *See* "insert"
inside out EVERTED
insidious SLY, FOXY, ARTFUL, SUBTLE, CRAFTY, SNAKY, TRICKY, WILY, CUNNING, DECEITFUL, DESIGNING, GUILEFUL, ARCH, TREACHEROUS
insight ACUMEN, DISCERNMENT, PERCEPTION, PERSPICUITY, INTUITION, UNDERSTANDING
insignia STARS, BADGES, MARKS, BARS, REGALIA, BUTTONS, EMBLEMS, RIBBONS, DECORATIONS
insignificant PETIT, PETTY, PUNY, MINOR, MEAN, TRIVIAL,

PALTRY, TRIFLING, UNIMPORTANT, SMALL, INFERIOR, CONTEMPTIBLE, MEANINGLESS, UNIMPOSING
insincere FALSE, PHONY, DECEITFUL, HYPOCRITICAL, FAITHLESS, UNTRUE, DISHONEST, DECEPTIVE
insinuate HINT, INTIMATE, SUGGEST, IMPLY, ALLUDE, PENETRATE, INGRATIATE, INFUSE, INSTILL
insipid DRY, FLAT, STALE, VAPID, WEAK, PALL, JEJUNE, BANAL, TAME, TASTELESS, LIFELESS, DEAD, MONOTONOUS, PROSY, UNINTERESTING, DULL, HEAVY, POINTLESS
insist DEMAND, URGE, PRESS, MAINTAIN, PERSIST
insolence LIP, CONTEMPTUOUSNESS, ARROGANCE, IMPUDENCE
insouciant UNCONCERNED, INDIFFERENT, CALM, CAREFREE, UNBOTHERED
inspect CHECK, PRY, SCAN, VIEW, AUDIT, PROBE, EXAMINE, SCRUTINIZE, INVESTIGATE, SUPERINTEND, OVERSEE
inspiration AFFLATUS, SPUR, STIMULUS, FURY, VISION, INHALATION, INFLUENCE, ENTHUSIASM, INSIGHT, GENIUS
inspire IMBUE, ANIMATE, INHALE, FIRE, EXCITE, QUICKEN, BREATHE, INFUSE, ENLIVEN, INSPIRIT, STIMULATE
inspiring AWESOME, GRAND
inspissate THICKEN, EVAPORATE, CONDENSE
install SEAT, INDUCT, ORDAIN, INVEST, INSTATE, INITIATE,

OPEN, INAUGURATE, FIX, ESTABLISH
instance EXAMPLE, ILLUSTRATION, MOTIVE, CASE, REQUEST, SAMPLE, PROOF, GROUND, ITEM, DETAIL, IMPULSE, INSTIGATION, SUGGESTION, OCCASION
instant CURRENT, JIFFY, TIME, POP, TRICE, MOMENT, FLASH, PRESSING, URGENT, SECOND, IMMEDIATE
instead ELSE, PLACE, STEAD, LIEU, RATHER
instigate FOMENT, URGE, EGG, ABET, INCITE, IMPEL, GOAD, SPUR, SUBORN, STIMULATE, PLAN, PLOT, SCHEME, PROMPT, TEMPT, MOVE, PROVOKE, ACTUATE
instruct INFORM, COACH, EDUCATE, TEACH, BRIEF, EDIFY, SCHOOL, TRAIN, IMPART, GUIDE, DRILL, BID, ORDER, CHARGE, ENLIGHTEN, INDOCTRINATE, DISCIPLINE, ENJOIN, COMMAND
instruction TUITION, EDUCATION, GUIDANCE, KNOWLEDGE, INFORMATION, DIRECTION, ORDERS
art of PAIDEUTICS, DIDACTICS, PEDAGOGY
pertaining to PROPAEDEUTIC
instructive DIDACTIC, INFORMATIVE
instructor TUTOR, COACH, PROF(ESSOR), TEACHER, PRECEPTOR, MASTER, DOCTOR, DOCENT, LECTURER, LECTOR
instrument AGENT, TOOL, MEANS, AGENCY, ORGAN, VEHICLE, CONTRACT, DEED, WILL, BOND, LEASE, CHANNEL, PAPER, DOCUMENT, IMPLEMENT, UTENSIL, DEVICE,

APPLIANCE, CONTRIVANCE, MACHINE, GADGET, MEDIUM, INDENTURE
altitude ABA, ALTAZIMUTH, ALTIMETER
astronomical, ancient ARMIL
board PANEL, DASH
boring AUGER, DRILL, GIMLET
combining form LABE
copying HECTOGRAPH
expanding DILATOR, REAMER
for studying motion STROBOSCOPE
knowledge ORGANON
math. SECTOR
measuring eggs OOMETER
  electric current RHEO(METER)
  time CHRONOMETER, CLOCK, WATCH
medieval ROCTA
musical PIANO, VIOLIN *See* "musical instrument"
nautical PELORUS, SEXTANT
surveying TRANSIT, THEODOLITE
instrumental introduction INTRADA, PRELUDE, OVERTURE
opus SONATA
performance DUO, SOLO
instrumentality MEDIA, MEDIUM, MEANS, AGENCY, ORGAN, VEHICLE, AID
insubordination MUTINY, ANARCHY, DISOBEDIENCE, REVOLT, INSURRECTION, SEDITION, RIOTOUSNESS
insubstantial AIRY, FLIMSY, FRAIL, UNREAL, IMAGINARY, WEAK
insufficient LAME, SCANT, SPARSE, DEFICIENT, INADEQUATE, LACKING
insular NARROW-(MINDED), NESIOTE,

ISLED, ISOLATED, ALOOF, PREJUDICED, CONTRACTED, PETTY, LIMITED, RESTRICTED, REMOTE, ILLIBERAL
insulate COVER, SEGREGATE, SHIELD, ISOLATE, SEPARATE, DETACH, DISCONNECT
material to KERITE, CORK, RUBBER, MICA
insult FIG, FLOUT, RUFFLE, SLUR, KNOCK, ABUSE, AFFRONT, OFFEND, ABASE, INDIGNITY, INJURE, ATTACK, ASSAULT, OUTRAGE, INSOLENCE, SAUCE, CHEEK
in medicine ATTACK
insurance, *applicant for* RISK
insure SECURE, ASSURE, SHIELD, GUARD, PROTECT, GUARANTEE, UNDERWRITE, INDEMNIFY
insurgent MUTINEER, REVOLTER, REBEL, REVOLUTIONARY, INSUBORDINATE, SEDITIOUS
intact WHOLE, ENTIRE, PERFECT, ALL, FULL, UNINJURED, UNIMPAIRED, INTEGRAL, COMPLETE, SOUND, UNBROKEN, UNDAMAGED
intaglio GEM, STONE, MATRIX, MOLD, RELIEF, ENGRAVING, DIE, DESIGN, FIGURE
intangible VAGUE, INCORPOREAL, IMPALPABLE, INSUBSTANTIAL
integral ALL, SUM, WHOLE, COMPOSITE, COMPLETE, ENTIRE, TOTALITY
integrity HONOR, ENTIRETY, VIRTUE, FIDELITY, SOUNDNESS, PURENESS, RECTITUDE, PROBITY, HONESTY, SINCERITY
integument SHELL, ARIL, TESTA, HUSK, COAT, RIND, DERM, SKIN, COVERING

intellect MAHAT, MIND, BRAINS, NOUS, INWIT, MENTALITY, UNDERSTANDING, REASON, SENSE, INTELLIGENCE, COGNITION, NOESIS
intellectual MENTAL, SOPHIC, THOUGHTFUL
intelligence WIT, NEWS, TIDINGS, INFORMATION, ACUMEN, MIND, CAPACITY, ADDRESS, SKILL, KNOWLEDGE, SAGACITY, UNDERSTANDING, NOTICE, ADVICE
only NOESIS
test deviser BINET
intelligent APT, BRIGHT, ASTUTE, SMART, DISCERNING, KEEN, ACUTE, SENSIBLE, SHREWD, BRAINY, CLEVER, SAGACIOUS, ALERT
intend MEAN, DESIGN, PLAN, AIM, PURPOSE, CONTEMPLATE, STRETCH, EXTEND, RESOLVE, DESTINE
intensity DEPTH, VEHEMENCE, STRENGTH, DENSITY, SEVERITY, VIOLENCE, VIGOR, FORCE, ENERGY, HEAT, ARDOR
intent VOLITION, WILL, GOAL, OBJECT, DRIFT, PURPOSE, RAPT, DESIGN, WISH, END, EAGER, EARNEST, ENGROSSED, RESOLVED, ATTENTIVE, SEDULOUS, DETERMINED, AIM, PURPOSE, MEANING
intention PLAN, AIM, END, MOTIVE, MINT, DESIGN, GOAL *See* "intent"
inter BURY, ENTOMB, INHUME, INURN
intercalary BISSEXTILE, INSERTED, INTRODUCED, INTERPOLATED
month VEADAR
intercalate INSERT, INSINUATE, INTERPOLATE, INTERPOSE
intercept STOP, CATCH, NAB, ARREST, PRE-

VENT, OBSTRUCT, IN-
TERRUPT, HINDER,
SEIZE, BLOCK

intercessor MEDIATOR,
BISHOP

intercolumniation
SYSTYLE, EUSTYLE,
DIASTYLE

interdiction BAN,
VETO, RESTRAINT,
PROHIBITION, TABOO,
DECREE

interest AMUSE, AT-
TRACT, HOLD, EN-
GROSS, BEHALF,
SHARE, RIGHT,
USURY, TITLE, AB-
SORB, CLAIM, AF-
FECT, WEAL, SAVOR,
CONCERN, GOOD,
BENEFIT, ADVANTAGE,
PORTION, PART,
STAKE, REGARD, AT-
TENTION, PREMIUM,
DISCOUNT, PROFIT,
ENTERTAIN, ENGAGE
law RIGHT, TITLE

interfere CLASH,
MOLEST, CONFLICT,
TAMPER, MEDDLE,
INTRUDE, INTERPOSE,
COLLIDE, INTERVENE

interferometer
ETALION

interim DIASTEM, IN-
TERVAL, MEANTIME,
TEMPORARY, MEAN-
WHILE, PROVISIONAL

interior INSIDE,
INTERNAL, DOMESTIC,
INNER, INLAND

interjection EXCLAMA-
TION, EJACULATION,
CRIMINY, EH, EGAD,
OH, DEAR, ALAS,
WHEW, PSHAW, LO

interlace WEAVE,
LOCK, LINK, TWIST,
VINE, ALTERNATE,
MAT, KNIT, TWINE,
COMPLICATE, PLAIT,
DIVERSIFY, DISPERSE,
MIX, UNITE

interlude STASIMON,
PAUSE, GAP, SPACE,
REST, BREAK, RECESS,
FARCE, PLAY,
COMEDY, DRAMA,
ENTR'ACTE
short VERSICLE,
VERSET

intermediate BE-

TWEEN, MESNE, IN-
TERPOSED, INTERVEN-
ING, INTERJACENT,
MEDIAN, MIDDLE

intermission STRETCH,
BREAK, RECESS,
INTERVAL, PAUSE,
ENTR'ACTE, SUSPEN-
SION, LULL, STOP,
INTERRUPTION, REST,
RESPITE, CESSATION

intermitter RESTER

internal INNER, IN-
SIDE, INTERIOR,
INLAND, DOMESTIC,
INWARD, SPIRITUAL,
SUBJECTIVE

international *business
combine* CARTEL
language IDO, RO,
VOLAPIIK, ESPERANTO,
ARULO
organization UN,
NATO, SEATO,
UNESCO, WHO
signal SOS

interpolate FARSE,
CORRUPT, FOIST,
INSERT, INTERPOSE,
ADD, INTERCALATE,
INTRODUCE, ALTER

interpose MEDIATE,
MEDDLE, INTERFERE,
INTERVENE, INTER-
CEDE, HELP, INTRUDE,
INSERT, INTERJECT,
SANDWICH, ARBITRATE

interpret OPEN, SCAN,
READ, RENDER,
EXPLAIN, CONSTRUE,
EXPOUND, UNFOLD,
UNRAVEL, TRANSLATE,
DECIPHER, DEFINE,
SOLVE, DECODE,
ELUCIDATE, ILLUS-
TRATE

interpretation EXE-
GESIS, EXPLANATION,
TRANSLATION, EXPOSI-
TION, VERSION,
SIGNIFICATION, MEAN-
ING, SOLUTION

interpreter DRAGOMAN,
EXEGETE, LATINER,
EXPOSITOR
Near East DRAGOMAN
of Koran ULEMA

interpretive HERME-
NEUTIC, EXPLANA-
TORY, CONSTRUCTIVE

interrogation PROBE,
INQUIRY, QUIZ,

QUEST(ION), QUERY,
TEST, EXAMINATION,
INTERPELLATION,
INQUEST
mark EROTEME,
EROTEMA

interrogative WHAT,
WHO, WHERE, WHEN,
WHY, WHICH, INTER-
ROGATORY, QUESTION-
ING

interrogator PUMPER,
PROBER, INQUIRER,
INQUISITOR, QUES-
TIONER

interrupt ARREST,
CHECK, STOP, BREAK,
OBSTRUCT

intersect CROSS,
MEET, DECUSSATE,
BREAK, DIVIDE, CUT

**intersection, relating
to** NODAL, SECANT

interstice PORE,
CRACK, CREVICE,
AREOLA, ORIFICE,
RIMA, CLEFT,
CHINK, INTERVAL,
GAP, SPACE
pertaining to
AREOLAR

interval GAP, IN-
TERIM, DISTANCE,
REST, LAPSE, PITCH,
BREAK, HOLE, RECESS,
STRETCH, SPACE, IN-
TERLUDE

intervening MESNE,
PENDING, INTER-
MEDIATE, INTER-
FERING

intervolve ROLL,
WIND, COIL, WREATH,
TWIST, VINE

interweave PLASH,
PLAT, RADDLE, TWINE,
MAT, SPLICE, INTER-
TWINE, BLEND, INTER-
LACE, WEAVE, MIX,
MINGLE, PLAIT

interwoven NETTED,
RETIARY
rods, as a hurdle
WATTLE

intestine COLON,
ILEUM, GUT,
DOMESTIC, INTERNAL
combining form ILEO
division ILEUM
part of small ILEUM
pertaining to ENTERIC

intimate SECRET, CRONY, NEAR, INMOST, ESSENTIAL, ANNOUNCE, DEAR, SIB, IMPLY, REFER, HINT, ALLUDE, CLOSE, FAMILIAR, FRIENDLY, HOMELIKE, CHUMMY, SUGGEST, INSINUATE, CONFIDENTIAL, PERSONAL, INFORMAL

intimation CUE, HINT, INKLING, INNUENDO, ALLUSION, NOTIFICATION, ANNOUNCEMENT

intimidate DAUNT, ABASH, COW, BULLY, FRIGHTEN, SCARE, OVERAWE, HOUND, RIDE, BAIT, COERCE, ALARM, TERRORIZE, BROWBEAT

into AMONG, UNTIL, INSIDE, UNTO

intolerance BIGOTRY, DOGMATISM, BIAS, NARROWNESS, IMPATIENCE, PREJUDICE

intonation SONANCE, SONG, CHANT, TONE, CADENCE, MODULATION, RECITATION

intone CHANT, CROON, UTTER, SING, RECITE

intort CURL, TWIST, WIND, WREATHE, TWINE, COMPLICATE

in toto WHOLE, ALL, COMPLETE

intoxicant SOMA, GIN, WHISKEY, GROG, RUM, WINE

intoxicate EXCITE, ELATE, POISON, INEBRIATE, FUDDLE, MUDDLE

intoxicated SOSH, HEADY, LIT, DRUNK, TIGHT, TIPSY, OILED, STEWED, BOOZY, MAUDLIN, SOTTED

intoxicating HEADY

intracellular HISTONAL

intractable UNRULY, SULLEN, BALKY, ORNERY, STUBBORN, OBSTINATE, PERVERSE, CONTRARY, DOGGED, HEADSTRONG, UNMANAGEABLE, MULISH, CANTANKEROUS

intransigent UNCOMPROMISING, IRRECONCILABLE, RADICAL

intrepidity NERVE, VALOR, BRASS, COURAGE, PROWESS, GUTS, BOLDNESS, FEARLESSNESS, BRAVERY, GALLANTRY, HEROISM, DARING

intricate COMPLEX, OBSCURE, DAEDAL, DEDAL, GORDIAN, MAZY, ENTANGLED, COMPLICATED, INVOLVED

intrigue AMOUR, BRIGUE, CABAL, PLAN, PLOT, PERPLEX, PUZZLE, BEGUILE, ALLURE, CONSPIRACY, STRATEGY, RUSE, WILE, LIAISON

intrinsic INNATE, TRUE, REAL, INHERENT, INBORN, INBRED, NATIVE, NATURAL, INGRAINED, GENUINE, ESSENTIAL

introduce IMMIT, INFUSE, USHER, BROACH, INSERT, MEET, PREFACE, LEAD, INSTILL, ADMIT, CONDUCT, INJECT, IMPORT, INDUCT, PRESENT, INITIATE, INAUGURATE, INSTITUTE

introduction PROEM, EXPLANATION, PREFACE, FOREWORD, PREAMBLE, PROLOGUE

of new word NEOLOGY

to treatise ISAGOGE

introductory cry OYEZ, OYES, HEAR

intromit ADMIT, INTRODUCE, INSERT

intrude INVADE, ENCROACH, OBTRUDE, IMPOSE, INTERLOPE, INFRINGE, TRESPASS, INTERFERE

intrust BEKEN, DELEGATE, CONFIDE, COMMIT, COMMEND

intuit KNOW, SENSE, APPREHEND

intuitive SEEING, NOETIC, PERCEIVING, INSTINCTIVE, NATURAL, KNOWING

inulase ENZYME

inulin ALANTIN

inundate FLOOD, DELUGE, OVERFLOW, DRENCH, DROWN, SUBMERGE, OVERWHELM, GLUT

inure BENEFIT, HARDEN, TOUGHEN, STEEL, SEASON, ADAPT, TRAIN, SCHOOL, HABITUATE, ACCUSTOM, FAMILIARIZE, DISCIPLINE, RESULT

inurn BURY, ENTOMB, INTER, INHUME

invade RAID, TRESPASS, INTRUDE, ENTER, ENCROACH, ATTACK, PROBE, VIOLATE, INFRINGE

invalid ILL, NULL, VOID, SICK, WEAK, UNSOUND, DISABLED, BASELESS, FEEBLE, VAIN, INFIRM, FRAIL, CRIPPLE

invalidate WEAKEN, DESTROY, QUASH, VITIATE, VOID, NULLIFY, NEGATE, ANNUL, CANCEL, ABROGATE, REPEAL, OVERTHROW, VETO

invasion BREACH, RAID, FORAY, ATTACK, TRESPASS, ASSAULT, INCURSION, VIOLATION, ENCROACHMENT, INTRUSION

military FORAY, INROAD, RAID

invective CURSE, ABUSE, VITUPERATION, RAILING, CONTUMELY, REPROACH, CENSURE, DIATRIBE

inveigh RAIL, CENSURE, ASSAIL, CHIDE, DENOUNCE, BLAME, CONDEMN, REPROACH, VITUPERATE

inveigle LURE, COAX, SNARE, WIN, SEDUCE, TEMPT, WHEEDLE, DECOY, ENTICE See "coax"

invent COIN, DEVISE, FEIGN, CREATE,

FORM, SHAPE,
FASHION, PLAN,
PLOT, SCHEME, CON-
TRIVE, ORIGINATE,
CONCEIVE, CONCOCT,
DESIGN, FORGE,
FABRICATE, PRODUCE,
MAKE
invention FICTION,
FIGMENT, CREATION,
COINAGE, CONTRIV-
ANCE, DEVICE,
INGENUITY
inventor, *diving bell*
EADS
dynamite NOBEL
safety lamp DAVY
steamboat FULTON
steam engine WATT
telephone BELL
inventor's *right* PAT-
ENT
inventory STOCK,
STORE, CATALOG(UE),
LIST, RECORD, AC-
COUNT, ROLL,
REGISTER, SCHEDULE
inversely ovate OBO-
VATE
invertebrate INSECT,
MOLLUSK, SPINE-
LESS, WORM
invertebrates, *group of*
APTERA
invest ENDOW,
ORDAIN, TRUST, SIFT,
WASH, PROVE, EN-
DUE, SPEND, CLOTHE,
DRESS, ARRAY
investigate TRACE,
PROBE, EXAMINE,
INDAGATE, SEEK, IN-
QUIRE, ASCERTAIN
investigation ZETETIC,
PROBE, INQUEST,
INQUIRY, AUDIT,
EXAMINATION, STUDY,
SCRUTINY, INQUISI-
TION, EXPLORATION,
INDAGATION, RE-
SEARCH, TEST
investment COVERING,
CLOTHING, BOND,
STOCK, GARMENT,
CAPITAL, SIEGE,
LAYER, DRESS, ROBE,
HABILIMENTS
inveterate OBSTINATE,
HABITUAL, CHRONIC,
CONFIRMED, AD-
DICTED, SETTLED,
INGRAINED, HARDENED

invigorate ENCOURAGE,
STRENGTHEN, RENEW,
(EN)LIVEN, BRACE,
FORTIFY, ANIMATE,
REFRESH, STIMULATE,
ENERGIZE, VIVIFY
invigorating TONIC,
CRISP, ZESTFUL
invincible IMPREGNA-
BLE, INDOMITABLE,
UNCONQUERABLE
invite ATTRACT, BID,
ASK, BEG, SUE, TRY,
ORDER, COURT, WOO,
SOLICIT, CALL,
ENTICE, SUMMON, RE-
QUEST, CHALLENGE,
(AL)LURE, TEMPT
invocation of evil
MALISON, MALEDIC-
TION
invoke BEG, PRAY,
IMPLORE, CONJURE,
SUPPLICATE, EN-
TREAT, BESEECH,
PLEAD, ADJURE,
SUMMON
involucre WHORL,
ROSETTE, COVERING,
ENVELOPE
involute ROLLED,
CURLED, INTRICATE,
INVOLVED, SPIRALED
involve ENTAIL, LAP,
WRAP, ENSNARE, TRAP,
EMBRACE, INFOLD,
ENVELOP, IMPLICATE,
ENTWINE, COIL, IN-
CLUDE, REQUIRE,
COMPRISE, CONTAIN
involved DETAILED,
KNOTTY, HARD, COM-
PLEX, CONFUSED,
INTRICATE, COM-
PLICATED
inward ENTAD, INNER,
INSIDE, INTERNAL,
INTO, TOWARD
inwrap ABSORB,
ENVELOP, ROLL, IN-
FOLD, INVOLVE,
COVER, ENGROSS
ion, *negative* ANION
positive CATION,
KATION
Ionian *city or town*
TEOS, MYUS
gulf PATRAS
island ZANTE,
LET(T)I, KAI
(KEI), LAUT, PAXOS
ios NIOS

iota ACE, JOT, WHIT,
ATOM, TITTLE, BIT,
MITE, PARTICLE
Iowa *college* COE
college town AMES
county CASS, CLAY,
IDA, LEE, LINN,
LYON, PAGE, POLK,
SAC, TAMA
society AMANA
ipecac *genus* EVEA,
CEPHAELIS, PLANT
iracund CHOLERIC,
IRASCIBLE
Irak *See* "Iraq"
Iran, Iranian PERSIA,
IRANI, LUR, KURD
ancient capital SUSA
kingdom ELAM
people ELAMITES,
TATS
angel MAH
bird BULBUL
book, scriptures
KORAN
capital TEHERAN
carpet HAMADAN,
KALI
chief MIR
city or town JASK,
YEZD, SUSA, KHOI,
QUM (KUM), BABUL,
ISPAHAN, MOSUL,
HILLA
civil officer KHAN
coin BISTI, DARIC,
TOMAN, DINAR,
ASHRAFI, DANIM,
RIAL, KRAN, STATER,
PUL, ABASSI, LARI(N),
FLOUCH, RUPEE,
SHAHI, SIGLOS
dyestuff INDIGO
*dynasty, founder of
present* AGHA
evil spirit AHRIMAN
fairy PERI, FAY,
ELF
fire worshiper PARSI,
PARSEE
fish, myth. MAH
gate DAR
gazelle CORA
god YIMA, MITHRAS
gold coin TOMAN
governor SATRAP
grass MILLET
hero YIMA,
RUSTAM
hook money LARI(N)

king FEISAL
   ancient CYRUS,
   XERXES
language ZEND,
   AVESTA(N),
   ARYAN
lord KHAN
measure PARSANG,
   GUZ, MOU, ZAR,
   ZER, ARASNI, ARTABA,
   CHARAC, GEZ, GIREH,
   JERIB, YAVA
moon MAHI
mystic SUFI
oil center ABADAN
plant POPPY
poet OMAR, JAMI,
   SADI
prince MIRZA
province YEZD
race LUR, KURD,
   FARSI, TAJIK,
   SUSIAN
river TAB
   (ZUHREH), ZAB,
   KARUN
rug SENNA
ruler MIR, ATABEK,
   ATABEG, SHAH,
   SULTAN, FEISAL
   of realm of dead
   YIMA
sacred cord KUSTI
screen PURDAH
seaport BASRA
sect BABI, SUNNI,
   SUNNEE
sir AZAM
sixteen miscals SIR
song bird BULBUL
spirit of light ORMAZD
sun god MITHRAS
tiara CIDARIS
tile KAS(H)I
title BABA, MIR,
   MIRZA, SHAH, AZAM,
   KHAN
town See "city"
   above
   dwellers SART
trading center
   ISPAHAN
tribe NOMAD
twenty dinars BISTI
viceroy, anc. SATRAP
water vessel AFTABA
water wheel NORIA
weight MISKAL,
   MISCAL, SIR, MAUND,
   ABBASS(I), DANAR,
   DANG, GANDUM,
   PINAR, RIK, UNA

writings AVESTA
Iraq *city or town*
   HILLA, BAG(H)DAD,
   MOSUL, ANA,
   HIT(IS)
   ancient KISH
irascibility CHOLER,
   IRE, IRRITABILITY
irascible BRASH,
   TESTY, CRANKY,
   CROSS, EDGY, SURLY,
   PEEVISH, CHOLERIC,
   IRRITABLE, TOUCHY,
   WASPISH, SNAPPISH,
   HASTY, SPLENETIC,
   PEPPERY, HOT
irate ANGRY, HOT,
   WROTH, CROSS, MAD,
   NETTLED, ANGERED,
   PROVOKED, PIQUED,
   INCENSED, WRATH-
   FUL
Ireland, Irish IRENA,
   EIRE, ERIN, ERSE,
   HIBERNIA, CELT, IN-
   NISFAIL, SCOTIA
   accent BLAS, BROGUE
   alphabet, ancient
   OGUM, OG(H)AM
   ancient BLAS,
   BROGUE
   ancient capital TARA
   bay CLEW, GALWAY
   borrowed stock DAER
   cape CLEAR
   capital DUBLIN
    ancient TARA
    Northern BELFAST
   castle TARA
   chamber of deputies
   DAIL
   chisel CELT
   city or town DUBLIN,
   CORK, ATHLONE,
   ENNIS, TRALEE,
   MALLOW, TARA,
   COBH, SLIGO,
   KILKENNY
   clan SEPT, SIOL
   clansman AIRE
   cloak, ancient INAR
   coin RAP, TURNEY
   county CORK, MAYO,
   KERRY, CLARE,
   MEATH, CAVAN,
   SLIGO
   dagger SKENE,
   SKEAN, SKEANDHU
   Dane in OSTMAN
   dialect OGHAM
   district BIRR

doctor OLLAM,
   OLLAMH
dramatist SYNGE,
   YEATS, SHAW
ecclesiastic, early
   (H)ERENACH,
   PATRICK
endearment term
   ALANNAH
exclamation AR-
   RA(H), ADAD,
   AHEY, BOOH
family CINEL
foot soldier KERN
fortification LIS
freebooter RAP-
   PAREE
freeman AIRE
frock, ancient LENN,
   INAR
garment LENN, INAR
general SHEA
girl COLLEEN
goblin LEPRECHAUN
god DAGDA, LER,
   DANU, DANA *See*
   under "god"
   mother ANA, ANU
groggery SHEBEEN
indeed ARU
independence move-
   ment SINN FEIN
island ACHILL,
   BEAR, CLEAR, ARAN
king ENNA, AED
   home of TARA
laborer, class AIRE
lake LOUGH, MASK,
   REE, CONN, NEAGH,
   ERNE, CORRIB, DERG
land holding system
   RUNDALE
legislature DAIL,
   EIREANN
letter, ancient
   OG(H)AM
limestone CALP
love GRA
luck CESS
militia FENIAN
monk's cell KIL
moss SLOKE, CAR-
   RAGEEN
mountain WICKLOW,
   SPERRIN, DONEGAL,
   COMERAGH
musical festival FEIS
musical instrument
   LYRE, TIMPANI(O),
   CROWD
novelist ASHE, READE,
   SHAW

parliament DAIL
patriot EMMET,
  PEARSE
peasant KERN(E)
personified IRENA
playwright See
  "dramatist" *above*
poet RUSSELL (AE),
  COLUM, YEATS,
  FILI, PEARSE,
  TIGHE
poetical name IN-
  NISFAIL
president HYDE
princess ISEULT
protestant SASSENAGH
refugee SAER
river SHANNON,
  ERNE, CAVAN,
  BOYNE, FOYLE, SUIR
rock TRIASSIC
saint PATRICK
sea god LER
seaport TRALEE,
  DUBLIN
society FEINN
soldier KERN
song RANN
spirit BANSHEE
steward (H)ERENACH
surgeon COLLES
sweetheart GRA
town TARA, CORK,
  COBH, KILKENNY,
  SLIGO
tribe SIOL
verse RANN
violinlike instrument
  CROWD
whiskey POTEEN
white BAWN
Irena ERIN
iris ORRIS, FLAG, LIS,
  IRID, PLANT, FLOWER
iris, *layer of* UVEA
irk CHAFE, BORE,
  NETTLE, VEX, AN-
  NOY, BOTHER, FRET,
  UPSET, WEARY,
  TROUBLE, DISGUST
iron ELEMENT, METAL,
  MANGLE, PRESS,
  SMOOTH, ROBUST,
  STRONG, CLEEK,
  SHACKLE, HARD, EN-
  DURING
  combining form
  FERR(O), SIDER(O)
  for closing staves
  HORSE
  golf CLEEK
  lamp CRESSET

meteoric SIDERITE
molder's tool LIFTER
ore HEMATITE,
  OCHER, SIDERITE,
  LIMONITE, TURGITE
  sand ISERINE
pertaining to FER-
  RIC, FERROUS
process MITIS
sheet TERNE,
  PLATE
sulphur compound
  PYRITE
symbol FE
weed genus VERNONIA
irons GYVES, SHACKLES
ironwood ACLE,
  COLIMA, HORNBEAM,
  MESQUITE
irony LAMPOON,
  SATIRE, WIT,
  HUMOR, SARCASM,
  CENSURE, MOCKERY,
  RIDICULE,
  PASQUINADE
Iroquois *demon*
  OTKON
irrational ABSURD,
  INSANE, BATTY,
  STRANGE, ODD,
  QUEER, BRUTISH, UN-
  REASONABLE, SILLY,
  FOOLISH, UNWISE,
  DEMENTED, CRAZY,
  IDIOTIC, ABERRANT,
  PREPOSTEROUS,
  PSYCHOTIC
irregular EROSE,
  SPOTTY, ATYPIC,
  ABERRANT, UNEVEN,
  CROOKED, STRANGE,
  ODD, QUEER, AB-
  NORMAL, RAGGED,
  ERRATIC, DEVIOUS,
  UNUSUAL, DIVERSE,
  ANOMALOUS, DIS-
  ORDERLY
  standard ABERRATION
irregularity JOG,
  IMPERFECTION,
  DEVIATION, AB-
  NORMITY, UNCER-
  TAINTY, ASYMMETRY
irregularly toothed
  EROSE
irreligion DOUBT,
  IMPIETY, ATHEISM,
  UNGODLINESS
irrepressible, *as
  laughter* HOMERIC
irrevocable FINAL,
  STABLE, UNALTERA-

BLE, IMMUTABLE,
FIRM
irritable IRACUND,
  FIERY, SPLEENY,
  SPLENETIC, EDGY,
  IRASCIBLE, TESTY,
  CRABBY, CHOLERIC,
  HUFFY, CROSS,
  CRANKY, FRETFUL,
  TOUCHY, PEEVISH,
  PETTISH, PETULANT,
  IMPATIENT
irritant POISON,
  PTOMAINE, VENOM,
  STING
  susceptible to AL-
  LERGIC
irritate RILE, CHAFE,
  EXACERBATE, IRK,
  GET, FRET, NETTLE,
  PEEVE, ANGER, ROIL,
  RANKLE, EXCITE,
  TEASE, INCENSE, IRE,
  VEX, GALL, NEEDLE,
  PROVOKE, EXASPER-
  ATE, ENRAGE, ANNOY,
  AGGRAVATE, WORRY,
  EMBITTER, MADDEN,
  INFLAME
irritated CROSS, MAD,
  IRKED, SORE, RAW
irruption INVASION,
  INROAD, BREAK, IN-
  CURSION, FORAY,
  RAID, BURSTING
is EXISTS
Isaac's *son* JACOB,
  ESAU
Iseult's *husband*
  MARK
  love TRISTRAM
Ishmael's *mother*
  HAGAR
  son KEDAR
Isinai IGORROTE
isinglass MICA,
  KANTEN, AGAR-
  AGAR
Isis, *brother and
  husband* OSIRIS
  mother NUT
  shrine ISEUM,
  ISEIUM
  son SEPT
Islam See "Moham-
  medan"
island(s) EYOT, AIT,
  OE, CAY, KEY, ISLE
  Aegean COS, LEROS,
  SCIO, NIOS, IOS,
  SAMOS, MELOS,

ANDROS, TENOS, KEOS, NAXOS
Alaska ATTU, PRIBILOF, ALEUTIAN *See under* "Alaska"
Antilles See "W. Indies" *below*
Asia Minor IONIA
Canary (LA) PALMA
Caribbean See "W. Indies" *below*
Carolines YAP (UAP), TRUK, PALU
Channel SARK, JERSEY
China AMOY, QUEMOY
combining form NESO
coral ATOLL
Cuba PINES (DE PINOS)
Cycladean MELOS, NIO, NAXOS *See* "Cyclades"
Danish AERO, FAROE, FALSTER, FYN, FANO, ROMO (RUM), SAMSO
E. Indies BORNEO, NAIS
enchanted BALI
English Channel SARK, JERSEY
Friendly TONGA
Great Barrier OTEA
Greece COS, DELOS, SAMOS, CRETE, IONIA, RHODES *See under* "Greece"
Hawaiian See under "Hawaii"
Indian Ocean MAURITIUS, CEYLON, MALDIVE, MINICOY
Indonesia CELEBES, ARU, JAVA, BALI
Irish Sea MAN, HOLY
Italy ELBA, CAPRI, SICILY
Japan KURIL *See under* "Japan"
Jutland coast FRISIAN
legendary UTOPIA, AVALON
low KEY
Malay TIMOR *See under* "Malay"
Mediterranean CAPRI,

CRETE, MALTA, SICILY, GOZO
Micronesia BIKINI, PALAU, ELLICE, GILBERT, WAKE, GUAM, SAIPAN
Molucca CERAM, BANDA
New Hebrides TANA, TANNA
Nile River RODA, PHILAE
Pacific TAHITI, SAMOA, ELLICE, WAKE, GUAM, MUNGA, ARU, BALI *See under* "Pacific"
Philippine LUZON, PANAY *See under* "Philippine"
river AIT, EYOT, HOLM
Samoa UPOLU, MANUA, TUTUILA
small AIT, CAY, KAY, KEY, CALF
Society TAHITI
South Sea ATOLL
Sunda RAOUL, SUMATRA, JAVA, BALI, LAMBOK, TIMOR
W. Indies TOBAGO, SABA, NEVIS, ARUBA, GRENADA, JAMAICA
Isle of Man, *division of* TREEN
pertaining to MANX
Isle of Wight *borough* RYDE
islet AIT, HOLM, CAY, KEY, KAY
ism BELIEF, DOGMA, TENET, SYSTEM, DOCTRINE, PRACTICE, CULT
follower of IST
isolated ENISLED, QUARANTINED, DETACHED, SOLITARY, (A)LONE, SEQUESTERED, SEGREGATED
isomeric hydrocarbon OCTANE, TERPENE
isometric CUBIC, REGULAR, SAME, PARALLEL
isonomic SAME, EQUAL
isonomy EQUALITY
isopiestic line ISOBAR

Israel ZION, SION, JACOB *See* "Bible"
ancient city BETHEL, SAMARIA, TIRZAH
camp ETHAM
city or town RAMLE
desert NEGEV, NEGEB
king SAUL, OMRI, NADAB, ELAH, DAVID, AHAB, ZIMRI, JEHU, HOSEA
last HOSEA
plain SHARON
port JAFFA, ACRE, HAIFA
region NEGEB
scribe EZRA
issue EMANATE, EMIT, END, TERM, UPSHOT, EVENT, FLOW, SPRING, STEM, (A)RISE, EMERGE, RESULT, SPOUT, EDITION, COPY, EGRESS, EXIT, OUTLET, VENT, OUTCOME, PROGENY, OFFSPRING, PROCEED, DELIVER, DISTRIBUTE, PUBLISH
issuing EMANANT, ISSUANT, FLOWING
Istanbul *caravansary* SERAI, IMARET
foreign quarter PERA
Greek quarter FANAR
inn IMARET
isthmus NECK, LAND, STRAIT
Malay and Siam KRA
isurus SHARK
Isvara SIVA
Italy, Italian SABINE, ROMAN, PICENE, OSCAN, AUSONIA(N), VOLSCI
actress DUSE
administrative region See "region" *below*
ancient SABINE, ROMAN, PICENE, OSCAN, AUSONIA, VOLUSCI, ETRUSCAN, SAMNITE
  country TUSCANY, ETRURIA
art center SIENA
author DANTE
bandit BRIGANTE
bowl TAZZA
canal CANALE, CANALI

Celtic tribe SENONES
cheese GRANA,
  PARMESAN
chest CASSONE
city MILAN, ROME,
  ROMA, ASTI, NOVI,
  TRENT, UDINE, PISA,
  SPEZIA, ATRI, PARMA,
  NOLA, VENICE, TURIN,
  URBINO, GENOA,
  PADUA, NARO *See*
  "town" *below*
coin LIRA, SCUDO,
  SOLDO, RUSPONE,
  TESTON(E),
  MARENGO, DOPPIA,
  DENI
*colony (including
  former)* ERITREA,
  LIBIA
commune MEDA,
  AVERSA
composer GUIDO,
  ROSSINI, VERDI
condiment TAMARA
coastal region
  LIGURIA
culture, 14th Cent.
  TRECENTO
dance COURANTE,
  CALATA, VOLTA
*department or divi-
  sion See* "province"
  and "region" *below*
dear CARO
dessert SPUMONI
dome CIMA
dynasty, former
  SAVOY
explorer ABRUZZI
faction BIANCHI,
  NERI
family ASTI, ESTE,
  COLONNA, CENCI,
  DONATI
fascist leader, local
  RAS
festival RIDOTTO
flower FIORE
food PASTA, GNOCCHI,
  RAVIOLI, LASAGNA,
  LASAGNE, PIZZA
*god or goddess See
  under* "god" *or*
  "goddess"
*Greek colony in,
  ancient* ELEA,
  CUMAE
guessing game MORA
gulf TARANTO,
  VENICE, GENOA,
  SALERNO

hand MANO
harp ARPA
headland SCILLA
health resort CAPRI
historian CANTU
house CASA
inlay TARSIA
innkeeper OSTE
island SARDINIA,
  SICILY, ISCHIA,
  LIPARI, CAPRI,
  LIDO, LINOSA
lady DONNA, SIGNORA
lake AVERNO, COMO,
  BOLSENA, GARDA,
  NEMI, ALBANO
language TUSCAN,
  OSCAN
magistrate PODESTA
  chief SYNDIC
marble CIPOLIN(O)
measure CANNA,
  BRACCIO, STERO,
  STAIO, PALMA
millet MOHA, BUDA
money See "coin"
  above
mountain(s) CENIS,
  VISO, ALPS
  (DOLOMITES)
musician See "com-
  poser" *above*
name ESTE, ASTI,
  COLONNA, CENCI,
  DONATI
naval base TARANTO
noble woman MAR-
  CHESA, CONTESSA
nothing NULLA
opera house SCALA
painter LIPPI, RENI,
  CRESPI, GIOTTO,
  VINCI, LUINI,
  SARTO, SPADA,
  CANALE, ROSSI
peak CIMA
physicist ROSSI,
  VOLTA, GALILEO
plateau SILA
playing card, old
  TAROT
political party
  BIANCHI, NERI
port See "seaport"
  below
pottery FAENZA
prima donna DIVA
province ASTI,
  CUNEO, NOVARA,
  TORINO, VERCELLI,
  GENOVA (GENOA),
  SAVONA, LA-SPEZIA,

IMPERIA, BERGAMO,
BRESCIA, COMO,
CREMONA, MANTOVA,
PAVIA, SONDRIO,
VARESE, BOLZANO,
TRENTO, BELLUNO,
PADOVA, ROVIGO,
TREVISO, VENEZIA
(VENICE), VERONA,
VICENZA, UDINE,
GORIZIA, BOLOGNA,
FERRARA, FORLI,
MODENA, PARMA,
PIACENZA, RAVENNA,
AREZZO, FIRENZE
(FLORENCE),
GROSSETO, LIVORNO
(LEGHORN), LUCCA,
PISA, PISTOIA, SIENA,
ANCONA, MACERATA,
PERUGIA, TERNI,
LATINA, RIETI, ROMA,
VITERBO, CHIETI,
L'AQUILA, PESCARA,
TERAMO, AVELLINO,
CASERTA, NAPOLI
(NAPLES), SALERNO,
BARI, BRINDISI,
FOGGIA, LECCE,
TARANTO, MATERA,
POTENZA, COSENZA,
CATANIA, ENNA,
MESSINA, PALERMO,
RAGUSA, SIRACUSA
(SYRACUSE), TRAPANI,
CAGLIARI, NUORO,
SASSARI, MILANO
race, ancient
  SENONES, ETRUSCAN
region PUGLIE,
  CALABRIA, SICILIA
  (SICILY), SARDEGNA
  (SARDINIA), MARCHE,
  UMBRIA, LAZIO,
  CAMPANIA, PIEMONTE
  (PIEDMONT), LIGURIA,
  VENETO, TOSCANA
resort LIDO, COMO,
  CAPRI
river See under
  "river"
satirist ARETINO
sculptor LEONI,
  DUPRE
seaport FIUME, POLA,
  TRANI, BARI, GENOA,
  ANZIO, AVOLA, PESARO,
  SAVONA, GAETA,
  NAPLES, SALERNO
  of Rome OSTIA
secret society MAFIA,
  COMORRA

sheep MERINO
ship POLACCA, NAVE
singer PINZA, CARUSO, GIGLI
street STRADA, VIA
title SER, CONTE(SSA), MARCHESA
"toe" of CALABRIA
tour GIRO
town BRA, ATRI, MEDA, ESTE, ITRI, ASTI, POLA, ATESSA, ALBA, TIVOLI, VELIA (ELEA), VEII, STRESSA *See "city" above*
university city PISA, BOLOGNA
verse RANN
violin maker AMATI
volcano ETNA, VESUVIUS, STROMBOLI
weight LIBRA, ONCIA, DENARO
wind, hot SIROC(CO)
wine measure ORNA, ORNE
writer See "author" above
itch HANKERING, DESIRE, TINGLE, REEF, PINE, YEARN, ECZEMA, SCABIES, PSORA, PRURITUS
barber's SYCOSIS
item PIECE, ASSET, AGENDUM, ENTRY, DETAIL, PART, PARAGRAPH, ARTICLE, THING, OBJECT, ELEMENT, FACTOR, PARTICULAR, SCRAP, BIT, UNIT
itemize LIST, DETAIL
iterate REPEAT, RETELL, REUTTER
itinerary ROUTE, COURSE, JOURNEY, CIRCUIT, TRIP, GUIDEBOOK
itineration EYRE, JOURNEY, CIRCUIT, TOUR
"Ivanhoe" author SCOTT
character CEDRIC, ROWENA, ULRICA, BEOWULF
clown WAMBA
ivories TEETH, DICE, KEYS (piano)
ivorine WHITE, SMOOTH

ivory, bone black ABAISER
carving, art of TOREUTICS
dust and cement EBURINE
Latin for EBUR
like DENTINE, EBURNEAN
nut TAGUA, ANTA
source TUSK
synthetic IVORIDE
ivy VINE, LAUREL
crowned with HEDERATED
ground HOVE, ALE-HOOF
pertaining to HEDERIC
poison genus RHUS
ixtle ISTLE, PITA, FIBER
Izmir SMYRNA

J

J JAY
jaal goat BEDEN, IBEX
jab PINCH, THRUST, DIG, POKE, PUNCH, STAB
jabber BABBLE, PRATE, GABBLE, CHAT *See "chatter"*
jabberwocky RIGMAROLE, NONSENSE
jabiru IBIS, STORK
jack FLAG, ENSIGN, PUMP, HOIST, JUG, TANKARD, CLOWN, RAISE, KNAVE, CARD, OPENER, TOY, MULE, MAN, FELLOW, BOOR, CARNATION, PITCHER, SAILOR, LABORER, RABBIT, PIKE, COIN, SAWHORSE, BLENDE, BOWER, TREE
in cards BOWER, KNAVE
of clubs PAM
jackal KOLA
jackanapes BEAU, FOP, DANDY, COXCOMB, APE, MONKEY
jackass DONKEY, DOLT, FOOL, BLOCKHEAD, DUNCE, NITWIT
combining form ONO
jackdaw GRACKLE, CROW, DAW, KAE, BIRD
genus CORVUS

jacket BLOUSE, ETON, REEFER, BOLERO, JERKIN, VEST, COAT, DOUBLET, WRAPPER, JUMPER, TUNIC, COVER(ING), BIETLE, SKIN, RIND, PEEL, CASING, HULL, ACTON
Arctic hooded ANORAK, PARKA
armor ACTON
Eskimo TEMIAK, PARKA
hooded ANORAK, PARKA
Levant GREGO
like CAMISOLE
short JERKIN, SPENCER, ETON
sleeveless VEST, BOLERO
steel plated ACTON
with short flaps COATEE
woman's JUPE, JUPON, SPENCER
jack-in-the-pulpit HERB, FIGWORT, WAKE-ROBIN, PLANT, FLOWER
genus ARUM
Jacob('s) ISRAEL
brother EDOM, ESAU
daughter DINAH
father-in-law LABAN
ladder PHLOX, FLOWER
son REUBEN, JUDAH, ASHER, DAN, GAD, LEVI, SIMEON, JOSEPH, BENJAMIN, ISSACHAR, ZEBULUN, NAPHTALI
wife LEAH, RACHEL, BILHAH
jade GREEN, TREMOLITE, NEPHRITE, MINERAL, HUZZY, WENCH, HACK, QUEAN, NAG, PLUG, HORSE, FATIGUE, FAG, PALL, CLOY, WEARY, EXHAUST, YU
jaded WEARY, BLASE, DULLED, TIRED, WEARIED, WORN
jaeger ALLAN, SHOOI, SKUA, GULL, BIRD
gull SKUA, ALLAN
jag BARB, LOAD, NOTCH, DAG, PENDANT, TOOTH, DENTICULATION,

PROTUBERANCE, PINK,
DOVETAIL, SPREE
Jagannath, *place of
worship* PURI
jagged EROSE, SER-
RATE(D), ROUGH,
NOTCHED, POINTED,
RAGGED, SHARP, DRUNK
jaguar OUNCE, TIGER,
PANTHER, CAT, CAR
jaguarundi EYRA, CAT
jai alai PELOTA, GAME
racquet CESTA
jail GAOL, COOLER,
JUG, LIMBO, STIR,
BASTILE, PRISON, PEN,
BARS, CLINK, CAGE,
INTERN, IMPRISON,
INCARCERATE,
PENITENTIARY, BRIDE-
WELL, LOCKUP, COOP,
BRIG
fever TYPHUS
jam CROWD, BLOCK,
BRUISE, PRESS, CRUSH,
PRESSURE, SQUEEZE,
FIX, PLIGHT, PICKLE,
SCRAPE, MESS,
THRONG, TAMP, PACK,
JELLY, PRESERVE,
CONSERVE
Jamaica *bitter drug*
QUASSIA
Jamshid YIMA
realm of PERIS
jangling AJAR, CLASH-
ING, HARSH, DISCORD,
BABBLE, WRANGLING,
BICKERING, QUARREL-
LING, ALTERCATION
janitor SUPER,
PORTER, SEXTON,
DOORKEEPER, CON-
CIERGE, CARETAKER,
CUSTODIAN
Janizarian *chief* DEY
Japan, *Japanese* NIP-
PON, CIPANGO, NIHON,
ZIPANGU, LACQUER,
ENAMEL, VARNISH
aborigine AINO, AINU
admiral ITO
administrative div.
FU
American NISEI
ancient capital NARA
apricot UME
army reserve HOJU
badge of nobility
MON
baron HAN
battle cry BANZAI

bay ISE, OSAKA,
AMORT, TOKYO, TOSO,
MIKU
boxes, set INRO
Buddhism ZEN
cape MINO, OMA,
MELA, IRO, DAIO, SADA,
NOMO, SE, SU, JIZO,
SUZU, OKI, SAWA, YA,
TOI
capital TOKIO, TOKYO
carp KOI
case INRO
cedar SUGI
cherry FUJI
church TERA
city or town NARA,
KOBE, OTARU, YEDO,
TOKYO, CHIBA, ARAO,
ITAMI, HOFU, GIFU,
FUSE, OGAKI, AKITA,
UEDA, SAKAI, SAGA,
SUITA, OTSU, MITO,
KURE, UENO, TSU,
OITA, MUYA, KOFU,
LIDA, HAGI
largest TOKYO
class, lowest HEIMIN
clogs GETA
clover HAGI
coin RIN, SEN,
ITZEBU, OBAN(G),
NISHU, MON, RIO,
SHU, BU, KOBAN,
NIBU, YEN
commoner HEIMIN
composition HAIKAI
confection AME
conveyance KAGO
crest MON
dancing girl GEISHA
deer SIKA
department FU
division FU
door, sliding FUSUMA
drama NOGAKU, NOH
elder statesman
GENRO
emperor MIKADO,
TENNO
family crest MON
fan OGI
*feast or festival of
lanterns* BON
fish AYU, MASU, TAI,
KOI, FUGU, FUNA,
PORGIE
game GO, KEN
garment OBI, HAORI,
KIMONO
gateway TORAN, TORII
gentry SHIZOKU

glue, rice AME
god See under "god"
gold coin OBAN(G)
fish FUNA
harp KOTO
herb UDO
immigrant ISSEI, NISEI
instrument SAMISEN,
BIWA, KOTO
island HONDO,
KYUSHU, SADO, IZU,
KURIL, KIUSHU,
HONSHU
largest HONSHU
Jodo deity AMITA,
AMIDA
lake BIWA
language AINU
legislature DIET
light-skinned AINU
lute BIWA
measure CHO, RI(N),
SHO(O), TAN, SE,
KOKU, KEN, HIRO,
GO(GO), MO, KO, BU
(BOO), DJO, INC, ISSE,
ISSHO, ITTAN, JO,
SHAKU, TO, TSUBO,
SUN
mile RI
military governor
SHOGUN
monastery TERA
money See "coin"
above
1/10 of sen MO
mountain FUJI
musical instrument
SAMISEN, BIWA, KOTO
naval base KURE
news service DOMEI
nobility KUGE,
SAMURAI, DAIMIO
title KAMI
opened by PERRY
ornament, costume
NETSUKE, INRO
outcast ETA, RONIN
overcoat, straw MINO
palanquin KAGO,
NORIMON
peninsula IZU
persimmon KAKI
pill box INRO
pine MATSU
plane ZERO
plant AUCUBA, TEA
plum KELSEY
porgy TAI
pottery AWATA
prefecture KEN
premier KISHI

quince JAPONICA
race, indigenous AINU, AINO
radish DAIKON
rain coat MINO
receptacle INRO
religion, early SHINTO
rice drink SAKE
 glucose or paste AME
robe KIMONO
salad plant UDO
salmon MASU
sash OBI
sauce UDO
school of painting KANO
seaport KOBE, SAKATA, TSU, UBE, OITA, MOJI
seaweed NORI
ship MARO, MARU
shoes GETA
shrub GOUMI, JAPONICA, FUJI
sock TABI
song UTA
storm TYPHOON, MONSOON
style of painting KANO
suicide SEPPUKU, HARI-KARI, HARA-KIRI
sword CATAN, CATTAN
title KAMI
town MURA, MACHI, TOI See "city" above
untouchable ETA
vegetable GOBO, UDO
verse TANKA, HOKKU
vine KUDZU
volcano FUJI, ASO(SAN)
wasp genus TIPHIA
weight KIN, FUN, MO, RIN, SHI, MOMME, RJOO
wind MONSOON, TYPHOON
wisteria FUJI
wooden shoes GETA
writing system KANA
zither KOTO
jape JEST, JOKE, QUIP, CRACK, GAG, JEER, TRICK, FOOL, DERIDE, MOCK
Japheth's *father* NOAH
son TUBAL
japonica QUINCE, CAMELLIA, BUSH, SHRUB

jar JUG, JOLT, SHOCK, RATTLE, OLLA, EWER, CLASH, GRATE, VIBRATE, CLATTER, QUAKE, SHAKE, CONTAINER
coarse earthen TERRINE, CROCK
fruit MASON
Greek PELIKE, AMPHORA
 long-necked water GOGLET, GURGLET
ring LUTE, RUBBER
Spanish OLLA
two-handled AMPHORA
very large CADUS, DOLIUM, SITULA
wide-mouthed EWER
jardiniere POT, VASE, URN, STAND, BOWL, SOUP
jargon ARGOT, CANT, RANE, ZIRCON, SPEECH, DRIVEL, SLANG, LINGO, PATOIS, GIBBERISH, ABRACADABRA, RIGMAROLE, DIALECT, CHINOOK
jarl EARL, CHIEFTAIN, HEADMAN
jasmine BELA, JESSAMY, JESSAMINE, PAPAW, SHRUB, FLOWER
Jason's *father* AESON
love MEDEA
rival CREUSA
ship ARGO
uncle PELIAS
wife MEDEA
jasper MORLOP, QUARTZ, BLOODSTONE, RUBY
jaundice ICTERUS, JEALOUSY, PREJUDICE, BIAS, ENVY
jaunt SALLY, TREK, TRIP, TOUR, CRUISE, JOURNEY, SHAKE, JOLT, JOUNCE, EXCURSION, RAMBLE, HIKE
jaunty AIRY, PERKY, EASY, CARELESS, GAY, SWAGGERING, UNCONCERNED, NONCHALANT, FINE, COCKY, SHOWY, STYLISH, CHIC, SMART, FINICAL, SPRIGHTLY

Java, Javanese SUDANESE, MADURESE, COFFEE
badger RATEL, TELEDU
capital JAKARTA
carriage SADO(O)
civet RASSE
commune DESSA
language KAVI, KAWI
measure PAAL, KAN, RAND
mountain PRAHU (PRAHOE)
pepper CUBEB
port TEGAL
tree UPAS
village DESSA
volcano SEMERU, SLAMET
weight TALI, POND, AMAT, SOEKEL
javelin LANCE, DART, ASSAGAI, PILE, SPEAR, SHAFT, POLE
game JERRID, JEREED
jaw(s) VISE, MAW, MANDIBLE, MAXILLA, CHAP, FAUCES, SCOLD, (BE)RATE, VITUPERATE, TALK, CHAT
combining form GNATH(O)
lower MANDIBLE, CHIN
 pertaining to MENTAL
muscle MASSETER
point at angle of GONION
upper MAXILLA
jawless AGNATHIC, AGNATHOUS
Jayhawk State KANSAS
jaylike bird PIET, MAGPIE
jazz RAG, DANCE, MUSIC, RUBATO
jeer TAUNT, DERIDE, GIBE, JAPE, JIBE, HOOT See "gibe"
Jefferson's *home* MONTICELLO
Jehiel's *son* NER
Jehovah JAH, YAHVEH, YHVA, YHWA, GOD
jejune MEAGER, ARID, BANAL, DRY, STALE, VAPID, EMPTY, FLAT, BARREN, STERILE,

BARE, INSIPID, UNIN-
TERESTING
jelly JAM, CONSERVE,
PRESERVE, COLLOID,
ASPIC, GELATIN
animal GELATIN(E)
base PECTIN
fish See under "fish"
grape SAPA
like material GEL
meat ASPIC
vegetable PECTIN
Jena glass objective
UNAR
jennet ASS, DONKEY,
HORSE
jeopardy HAZARD,
PERIL, RISK, DANGER,
VENTURE
jeremiad TALE, COM-
PLAINT, TIRADE,
LAMENT(ATION)
jerk SNAP, TWITCH,
TWIST, NIDGE, TIC,
PULL, FLIP, YANK,
HITCH, TWEAK, JOLT,
SHAKE, DOLT, DULLARD
jerked beef BILTONG,
CHARQUI
Jerusalem, *anc. name*
SALEM, JEBUS, ARIEL
corn KAFIR
hill in ZION (SION)
poetic name ARIEL
Jespersen's *language*
IDO
jess RIBBON, STRAP,
LEASH
Jesse's *father* OBED
son DAVID
jessur DABOIA, SNAKE,
VIPER
jest FUN, JOKE, JIBE,
FOOL, MOT, QUIP,
WIT, WITTICISM,
LAUGH, TRIFLE,
CLOWN, MIME, GAG,
SPORT, PLAY, JOLLY,
QUIZ, BANTER,
RIDICULE, JEER,
TAUNT, MERRIMENT
jester, *roving student*
GOLIARD
Jesuit *founder* LOYOLA
saint REGIS
Jesus IHS, MESSIAH,
ANOINTED
Jesus of Nazareth, King
of the Jews INRI
jet SPURT, GUSH,
SPRAY, STREAM,
SPOUT, SHOOT, RUSH,

NOZZLE, LADLE, COAL,
PLANE, EBONY,
BLACK
jetty MOLE, PIER,
WHARF, WALL, BREAK-
WATER
Jew(s) *See* "Hebrew"
jewel GEM, STONE,
ORNAMENT, BRIL-
LIANT, LOUPE, DIA-
MOND, BIJOU,
TREASURE, JOY,
DARLING
setting BEZEL, OUCH,
DOP, PAVE
jeweler's *cup* DOP(P)
glass LOUPE
weight CARAT
jewelry BEADS,
TRINKETS, GEMS,
BIJOUTERIE, BANGLES
alloy OROIDE
facet QUOIN,
LOZENGE, BEZEL
mock or false
LOGIES, PASTE, GLASS,
STRASS
jewels, *adorn with*
BEGEM
set of PARURE
jewfish MERO,
GROUPER
Jewish *See* "Hebrew"
Jews, *dispersion of*
DIASPORA
Jew's-harp TRUMP,
TRILLIUM
Jezebel GORGON, FURY,
VIRAGO
husband AHAB
victim NABOTH
jib CHORE, BALK,
BOOM, CRANE, DER-
RICK, SHIFT, ARM, GIB,
JIBBER, STANDSTILL,
SAIL
boom SPAR
jibe AGREE,
HARMONIZE, FIT,
TALLY, SHIFT, TACK
jiffy INSTANT, SECOND,
TRICE, FLASH,
MOMENT, TWINKLING
jiggle TEETER, SHAKE,
JERK, ROCK, SWAY,
JOG
jimmy BAR, BETTY,
CROWBAR
Jimson weed DATURA,
STINKWEED
jingle RING, CLINK,

TINKLE, RHYME,
SONG, VERSE, JANGLE
jinnee EBLIS
jinni GENIE, DEMON,
SPIRIT
jitter TWITCH, FIDGET,
JERK, JUMP
jittery NERVOUS, REST-
LESS, HECTIC, UNEASY,
JUMPY, EDGY
jivatma ATMAN, EGO,
SOUL, SELF, SPIRIT
jive LINGO, JARGON,
JAZZ, DANCE, TEASE,
KID
Joan of Arc PUCELLE
Joan's *spouse* DARBY
job TASK, WORK,
CHORE, SHIFT, STINT,
CHAR, OFFICE, DUTY,
TRADE, CRAFT, POST,
POSITION, BERTH, BUY,
SELL, AFFAIR,
BUSINESS, EMPLOY-
MENT, SITUATION,
ENTERPRISE
soft SNAP, SINECURE
Job's *comforter*
BILDAD, ELIHU, BOIL
home town UZ
tears COIX, ADLAY,
ADLAI, PLANT, GRASS
jockey RIDER, TRICK,
CHEAT, MANEUVER,
SWINDLER, PAD,
CUSHION, VAGABOND,
SHARPER, KNAVE,
ROGUE, BLACKLEG
kind of DISK
jocose MERRY, DROLL,
DRY, LEPID, WITTY,
JOLLY, FACETIOUS,
HUMOROUS, WAGGISH,
FUNNY, JESTING,
COMIC(AL), SPORTIVE,
FROLICSOME,
HILARIOUS, JOVIAL
jocular FESTIVE,
CONVIVIAL, GAY,
VIVACIOUS, BLITHE-
SOME, DEBONAIR *See*
"jocose"
jog REMIND, TROT,
PUSH, STIR, MOVE,
JOSTLE, NUDGE,
NOTIFY, WARN, JOLT,
TURN
John, *in Gaelic* IAN
Irish SEAN, EOIN,
SEAGHAN
Russian IVAN

johnnycake PONE, HOECAKE

join WED, MARRY, LOCK, ADD, COALESCE, MEET, PIN, ABUT, BIND, ASSOCIATE, KNIT, RELATE, CONNECT, ENLIST, ENTER, ENROLL, UNITE, LINK, YOKE, PAIR, TIE, ANNEX, ATTACH, APPEND, COUPLE, COMBINE, CONJOIN, DOVETAIL, MITER, CEMENT, GLUE, SPLICE, CONSOLIDATE, MERGE, INCORPORATE

joint LINK, HINGE, SEAM, SUTURE, PUB, UNION, JUNCTION, ARTICULATION, INTERNODE, HANGOUT, RESORT, DIVE, DEN, UNITED, COMBINED, UNDIVIDED, JUNCTURE, HIP, KNEE, ELBOW, ANKLE, WRIST
articulated HINGE
grass CULM, STEM
lubricator SYNOVIA
make tight STEM
part TENON, MORTISE
plant stem PHYTOMER, PHYTON
put out of LUXATE, DISLOCATE, DISPLACE
right angle ELL, KNEE, TEE
sac BURSA

joke HOAX, PUN, GAG, QUIP, SALLY, JOSH, PRANK, JAPE, ANECDOTE

joker CARD, WAG, WIT, CLOWN, FOOL, DOR, JESTER, HUMORIST, BUFFOON

Joktan's *father* EBER
son OPHIR

jolly GUY, RAG, KID, BUXOM, CHEERFUL, CROUSE, JOCOSE, MERRY, JOYOUS, JOYFUL, GAY, JOVIAL, MIRTHFUL, JOCUND, WAGGISH, LIVELY, BLITHE, SPORTIVE, PLUMP, CHUBBY, LUSTY
boat YAWL

Joloano SULU, MORO

jolt SHAKE, JAR, BOUNCE, JUT, SHOCK, CLASH, BUMP, JOGGLE, JOUNCE, JERK, BLOW

jonah JINX, CRAB

Jonathan's *father* SAUL

Jordan, *ancient city* PETRA
mountain HOR, PISGAH (NEBO)
part of MOAB
valley GHOR

josh TWIT, BANTER, KID, CHAFF, RALLY, RAG, GUY, RIB, JOLLY, TEASE

Joshua's *burial place* GAASH
father NUN
tree YUCCA, REDBUD

Josip Broz TITO

joss CROWD, MASTER, IDOL, DIVINITY, IMAGE

jostle JOG, BUMP, PUSH, ELBOW, JOLT, RUSH, SHOCK, COLLIDE, SHAKE, JOGGLE, SHOVE, SHOULDER, HUSTLE, CROWD

jot ITEM, ACE, BIT, IOTA, MINIM, ATOM, MITE, POINT, TITTLE, WHIT, NOTE, GRAIN, PARTICLE, SCRAP, SCINTILLA

jotting MEMO, ENTRY, NOTE

joule, *part of* ERG

journal REGISTER, DIARY, RECORD, ORGAN, PAPER, LOG, MAGAZINE, GAZETTE, PERIODICAL

journey HADJ, HEGIRA, TREK, FARE, RUN, TOUR, PASSAGE, RIDE, TRIP, JAUNT, TRAVEL, HIKE, FLIGHT, VOYAGE, HOP, WENT, RAMBLE, ROAM, ROVE, EXCURSION, EXPEDITION, PEREGRINATION, PILGRIMAGE
course ITINERARY
division of LEG, LAP
in circuit EYRE
pertaining to VIATIC, PERIPATETIC
up ANABASIS

joust(s) TILT, COMBAT, BOUT, SPAR, TOURNAMENT

Jove JUPITER

jovial GAY, BLITHE, MERRY *See* "jocose"

jowl CHAP, CHEEK, CHOPS *See* "jaw"

joy MIRTH, BLISS, ECSTASY, GLEE, DELIGHT, GLADNESS, EXULTATION, PLEASURE, RAPTURE, TRANSPORT, BEATITUDE, HAPPINESS, FELICITY, HILARITY

joyous MERRY, ELATED, HAPPY, GLAD, BLITHE, BUOYANT, DELIGHTED, JOCUND, GAY, CHEERFUL

Judah, *anc. city* AMAN, EDER, HAZOR, ZIPH, TELEM, SHEMA, AZEM, AIN
first born ER
king AMON, AHAZ, ASA, JOSIAH, JOASH, DAVID
son ONAN

Judaism, *convert to* GER

Judas TRAITOR, BETRAYER

Judea *king* HEROD

judge(s) JUSTICE, JUDEX, EDILE, UMPIRE, REFEREE, CADI, ARBITER, ARBITRATOR, MAGISTRATE, COURT, BENCH(ER), MODERATOR, CRITIC, ADJUDICATOR, KEEPER, DEEM, OPINE, ESTIMATE, RATE, RULE, DECIDE, SETTLE, INFER, GATHER, DETERMINE, DECREE, PRONOUNCE, TRY, DOOM, CONDEMN, CONCLUDE, ADJUDICATE
bench BANC
chamber CAMERA
circuit EYRE
entry after verdict POSTEA
junior or subordinate PUISNE
of dead OSIRIS
of Hades MINOS

rigorous
RHADAMANTHUS
robe TOGA
seat BENCH, BANC
judgment ARRET,
  DOOM, OPINION,
  TASTE, SENSE,
  PRUDENCE, VIEW,
  BELIEF, WISDOM,
  ORDER, WRIT, AWARD,
  SENTENCE, DECISION,
  CONCLUSION, DIS-
  CERNMENT, UNDER-
  STANDING, DISCRETION,
  CIRCUMSPECTION, IN-
  TELLIGENCE,
  SAGACITY, CRITICISM,
  CENSURE
lack of ACRISY
judicial *assembly*
  COURT
journey EYRE
judicious WISE, CARE-
  FUL, POLITIC,
  PRUDENT, SAGE, JUST,
  FAIR, SANE, SENSIBLE,
  SHREWD, DISCREET,
  DISCRIMINATING,
  CRITICAL, CAUTIOUS,
  REASONABLE,
  SAGACIOUS, SOBER,
  SOUND, COOL
jug BUIRE, CRUSE,
  EWER, FLAGON, OLPE,
  TOBY, PITCHER,
  VESSEL, CONTAINER,
  JAIL, GAOL, PRISON,
  LOCKUP
shaped like man TOBY
Juggernaut VISHNU
juice LIQUID, SAP,
  RESIN, MILK,
  GAS(OLINE),
  ELECTRICITY
jujitsu JUDO
Juliana's *house*
  ORANGE
Juliet's *betrothed*
  PARIS
father CAPULET
lover ROMEO
"Julius Caesar,"
  character in CICERO,
  BRUTUS, CASCA, CINNA,
  PORTIA
jumble MEDLEY, MIX,
  PI, PIE, MESS, RAFT,
  BLEND, HASH, CHAOS,
  SNARL, BOTCH, CON-
  FUSE, CONFUSION, DIS-
  ORDER, HODGEPODGE,

GALLIMAUFRY, OLIO,
  MIXTURE, MUDDLE
jump JERK, HOP, LEAP,
  ADVANCE, ADVANTAGE,
  BOUNCE, EVADE, FLEE,
  START, SKIP, VAULT,
  BOUND, CAPER,
  SPRING, TWITCH
in Greek game
  HALMA
jumper BLOUSE, COAT,
  JACKET, SLED, DRILL
jumping SALTANT,
  TEEMING, HOT
rodent JERBOA
sickness LATA(H),
  PALMUS
stick POGO
junco FINCH, SNOW-
  BIRD
juncture SEAM, JOINT,
  CRISIS, PASS, STRAIT,
  STATUS, STATE,
  PLIGHT, PINCH, JUNC-
  TION, UNION, COM-
  BINATION, CONNEC-
  TION, LINKING,
  COUPLING, SUTURE
June bug DOR
junior CADET, PUISNE,
  YOUNGER, FILS, BUD,
  SUBORDINATE
juniper GORSE, CADE,
  CEDAR, SAVIN(E),
  EVERGREEN
junk TRASH, WASTE,
  SLOUGH, REFUSE,
  CHUNK, LUMP, DIS-
  CARD, SCRAP, BOAT
junker GERMAN,
  NOBLE, CONSERVATIVE
junket BANQUET,
  FEAST, DISH, PUDDING,
  DELICACY, TRIP,
  PICNIC, OUTING,
  EXCURSION, ENTER-
  TAIN
Juno HERA
consort JUPITER
messenger IRIS
junta, junto COUNCIL,
  MEETING, CLIQUE,
  FACTION, CABAL,
  RING, BLOC, PARTY,
  COTERIE, TRIBUNAL,
  COMBINATION,
  LEAGUE, CON-
  FEDERACY, SET, GANG
Jupiter ZEUS, PLANET,
  JOVE
Jupiter's *consort*
  JUNO, HERA

daughter MINERVA
satellite IO
son ARCAS
jural JURISTIC, LEGAL
Jurassic division LIAS
jurema ACACIA, TREE
jurisdiction SOKE, SEE,
  SOC, VENUE, POWER,
  SWAY, FUNCTION,
  FIELD, DUTY, RANGE,
  SCOPE, SPHERE, CON-
  TROL, LIMITS, BOUNDS,
  JUDICATURE,
  AUTHORITY, COMPASS,
  REACH, RIGHT,
  CIRCUIT, PROVINCE
ecclesiastical SEE,
  PARISH, DEANERY,
  DIOCESE
of an emir EMIRATE
jurisprudence LAW
jury PANEL, PEERS,
  VENIREMEN, JUDICES,
  DICASTS, COMMITTEE
lists PANEL
juryman, *ancient of*
  Athens DICAST
jus LAW(S),
  PRINCIPLE, RIGHT,
  POWER, JUSTICE,
  JUICE, GRAVY
just ABOUT, EVEN, AL-
  MOST, ONLY, FAIR,
  (UP)RIGHT, MORAL,
  NOBLE, ETHICAL, DUE,
  PROPER, IMPARTIAL,
  LEGITIMATE, TRUE,
  ACCURATE, EXACT,
  CORRECT, HONEST,
  SQUARE, EQUITABLE,
  RIGHTFUL, LAWFUL,
  CONSCIENTIOUS,
  HONORABLE, UN-
  CORRUPT, UNBIASED,
  PRECISELY, NEARLY,
  BARELY, SIMPLY,
  QUITE, DESERVED,
  MERITED, MERCIFUL
justice JUDGE, DOOM,
  EQUITY, RIGHT, DUE,
  DESSERTS, FAIRNESS,
  MAGISTRATE, REASON,
  VALIDITY, REWARD,
  PENALTY
goddess MAAT
of peace SQUIRE
justification DEFENSE,
  VINDICATION, WAR-
  RANT, REASON, EX-
  CUSE, ALIBI
justify EXCUSE, CLEAR,
  WARRANT, DEFEND,

VINDICATE, BACK, PROVE, SUPPORT, UPHOLD, ADJUST, APPROVE, MAINTAIN, EXCULPATE, EXONERATE, ABSOLVE, ACQUIT, EXPLAIN

justle *See* "jostle"

jut PROJECT, PROTRUDE

jute BURLAP, GUNNY, TAT, PLANT, SACKING

Jutlander DANE, GERMAN

jutting rock TOR, CRAG

jutty JETTY, PIER, MOLE, PROJECTION

juvenile MINOR, PUISNE, YOUTH(FUL), YOUNG, ACTOR, CHILDISH, PUERILE, IMMATURE, GREEN, UNDEVELOPED

Juventas HEBE

juxtaposition CONTIGUITY, CONTACT, PROXIMITY, ADJACENCY, NEARNESS

K

K KAY, KAPPA

Kaddish DOXOLOGY, HYMN, PRAYER

Kaf(f)ir BANTU, ZULU
body of warriors IMPI
language XOSA
tribe XOSA, ZULU

kafir corn SORGHUM, GRAIN

kago PALANQUIN, LITTER

kaka PARROT
genus NESTOR

kale COLLARD, BORECOLE, COLE-(WORT), CABBAGE, CASH, MONEY
sea COLE

kali CARPET, SALT-WORT, PLANT

kalinite ALUM

Kalmu(c)k ELEUT, MONGOL

Kanae MULLET, FISH

kanari ALMOND

Kandh *language* KUI

kangaroo MARSUPIAL, BOOMER, WALLABY, PADDYMELON, BILBI, BILBY
female DOE, GIN

male BOOMER
rat POTOROO
young JOEY

Kansas *county* ELK, GOVE, GRAY, LANE, LINN, LYON, NESS, RENO, RICE, RUSH, TREGO
State Flower SUNFLOWER
town IOLA, PAOLA

kapok FIBER, OIL, TREE, CEIBA

kaput DOOMED, RUINED, FINISHED, DESTROYED, DEFEATED

karakul LAMB, SHEEP, FUR, ASTRAKHAN

Karelian lake SEG

karma DESTINY, FATE, RITE, DUTY

Kartvelian SVAN(E)

Kashmir *alphabet* SARADA
town LEH

kat shrub KAFTA

katchung PEANUT, OIL

Kate, *Shakespeare's* SHREW

kava AVA, PEPPER, DRINK

kayak CANOE, KAIAK

kea PARROT

Keb *See* "Geb"

keck RETCH, BELCH, HEAVE

ked TICK

kedge ANCHOR

keel CARINA, CAPSIZE, CAREEN, TIMBER, MOLDING, UPSET, SHIP, BARGE, LIGHTER, OCHER, FOWL
part of SKEG
right angles to ABEAM
shaped CARINATE
wedge TEMPLET
without RATITE

keelbill ANI, ANO, BIRD

keen ASTUTE, BITTER, GARE, SNELL, TART, SHARP, PENETRATING, EAGER, AVID, AGOG, WAIL, WEEP, CRY, NIFTY, ACUTE, CUTTING, CLEVER, FINE, KNOWING, ARDENT, ZEALOUS, EARNEST, VIVID, INTENSE, FERVENT, VEHEMENT, PIERCING, POIGNANT, PUNGENT, CAUSTIC,

BITING, SHREWD, DISCERNING, ACRIMONIOUS, SENSITIVE

keenness EDGE, ACIDITY, PUNGENCY, ARDOR, ZEST, RIGOR, ASPERITY

keep SAVE, RETAIN, HOLD, POSSESS, MANAGE, CONDUCT, LIVING, BOARD, MAINTAIN, DETAIN, CONFINE, HIDE, RESTRAIN, REMAIN, PRESERVE, CONTINUE, WITHHOLD, GUARD, PROTECT, SUSTAIN, SUPPORT, TEND, HUSBAND, HARBOR, FEED, SHELTER, CONCEAL
in view REGARD
on course CAPE, HEAD
out BAR, EXCEPT, EXCLUDE

keeper, *door lock* RISP, STANG, NAB
Masonic door TILER
of golden apple ITHUN(N)
of marches MARGRAVE
of park RANGER

keepsake RELIC, TOKEN, SOUVENIR, MEMENTO, GIFTBOOK, CURIO, VIRTU, BIBELOT

keest SUBSTANCE, SAP, MARROW

keeve KIER, TUB, VAT, CISTERN

Kefauver ESTES

keg BARREL, CASK, CADE, FIRKIN, TUN
open a UNHEAD

kelp WRACK, WARE, SEAWEED, VAREC

kelter KILTER, ORDER, CONDITION, MONEY, RUBBISH

ken SCOPE, (PUR)-VIEW, RANGE, REACH, FIELD, SPHERE, SIGHT, VISION, LORE, PRESCIENCE, COGNIZANCE, INSIGHT, UNDERSTANDING, PERCEPTION, RECOGNITION

Kent *borough* ERITH
district PENGE

Kentish *freeman* LAET

Kentucky *college* BEREA
county BATH, BELL, BOYD, CLAY, HART, KNOX, LEE, LYON, OWEN, PIKE, TODD
Kenya *reserve* MASAI
kerchief MADRAS, CURCH, BANDAN(N)A, HANDKERCHIEF
Keresan Indian SIA, ACOMA
kernel(s) NUB, GIST, SEED, NUT, GRAIN, NUCLEUS, CORE, HEART, PIT(H), ESSENCE
having NUCLEATED
kestrel HAWK, FALCON, BIRD
ketch SAIC, BOAT, SHIP
kethib K'RI, KERE
ketone CARONE, ACETONE
kettle POT, CA(U)LDRON, PAIL, CONTAINER, POTHOLE
kettledrum NAKER, TIMBAL, ATABAL, TABOR, TIMPANO
cavalry ANACRA, TIMBAL
Moorish ATABAL
key COTTER, ISLET, ISLE, CLAVIS, CLUE, PITCH, TUNE, TONE, CLEW, PONY, MANUAL, CODE, WEDGE, CAY, OPENER, GUIDE, CRIB, EXPLANATION, ANSWER, COMBINATION, CLAMP, LEVER, BOLT, SPANNER, PIN, ISLAND, REEF
false GLUT
instrument MANUAL, CLAVIS
obstruction to other than right WARD
part BIT
pertaining to TONAL
telegraph TAPPER
keyed up AGOG, EAGER, TENSE, TUNED, TAUT
key fruit SAMARA
keynote TONIC, PRINCIPLE
sign, Greek music ISON
keystone SAGITTA, SUPPORT, WEDGE, PRINCIPLE, VOUSSOIR

State PENNSYLVANIA
founder PENN
khan INN, RESTHOUSE, CARAVANSARY, TITLE
Khedive's *estate* DAIRA
kiang ONAGER, ASS
kibe CHILBLAIN, CHAP, CRACK, SORE, ULCER, LESION
kibitzer SPECTATOR, WITNESS, MEDDLER, PUNSTER, JOKER, LAPWING, PLOVER, BIRD
kick BOOT, FUNK, PUNT, RECOIL, THRILL, GRIPE, KEVEL, OBJECT, PROTEST, RESIST, SIXPENCE, OPPOSE, REBOUND, IMPEL, DRIVE, DISMISS, REJECT, COMPLAIN(T)
kickshaw BAUBLE, TOY, TRIFLE, FOOD, DELICACY, TIDBIT, GADGET, GEWGAW
kid BANTER, JOSH, RAG, GUY, RIB, TAUNT, TEASE, TWIT, BOX, PEN, TUB, RALLY, HOAX, JOLLY, HUMBUG, GOAT, LAD, TOT, CHILD
undressed SUEDE
kidnap ABDUCT, SEIZE, TAKE, STEAL, SNATCH
kidney KIND, CLASS, SORT, TYPE, NATURE, STRIPE, ILK, TEMPERAMENT, DISPOSITION, ORGAN
Latin REN
pertaining to RENAL
stone NEPHRITE, JADE, NEPHROLITH
Kilauea *goddess* PELE
Kilimanjaro peak KIBO
kill SLAY, EXECUTE, DESTROY, MURDER, GARROTE, SLAUGHTER, MASSACRE, ASSASSINATE, DISPATCH, STRANGLE, SUFFOCATE, BURKE, BLAST, BAG, FINISH, SUPPRESS, CANCEL, DEADEN, EXTINGUISH, RUIN, END, DEFEAT, VETO, STREAM, CREEK
by stoning LAPIDATE

killing CARNAGE, FATAL, SUCCESS, CLEANUP, AMUSING, ATTRACTIVE, HOMICIDE, MURDER, SLAUGHTER
of brother or sister FRATRICIDE
of father PARRICIDE
of mother MATRICIDE
of self SUICIDE
of wolf LUPICIDE
kiln OST, OAST, OVEN, TILER, FURNACE, STOVE
kiloliter STERE
kilt FILIBEG, PHILIBEG, PHILABEG, PLEAT
pouch for SPORRAN
kilter KELTER, ORDER, CONDITION
kimono sash OBI
kin GERMANE, COGNATE, RELATED, ALLIED, FOLKS, KIND, RACE, RELATIONSHIP, CONSANGUINITY, SIBLINGS, CONNECTIONS, KINDRED, RELATIVES, FAMILY
kind BENIGN, TENDER, BENEVOLENT, HUMANE, GRACIOUS, FRIENDLY, GENEROUS, GENIAL, AMIABLE, LENIENT, INDULGENT, COMPASSIONATE, CLASS, STRAIN, SORT, ILK, GENUS, TRIBE, SEELY, GENRE, SPECIES, DESCRIPTION, NATURE, RACE, FAMILY, BREED, TYPE, GROUP, DIVISION, VARIETY, MILD, GENTLE, LOVING, AFFECTIONATE
kindle STIR, BURN, FIRE, (A)ROUSE, IGNITE, INCITE, LIGHT, INFLAME, EXCITE, WHET, FOMENT, PROVOKE, ANIMATE, START
kindly BENIGN, KIND, (CON)GENIAL, SYMPATHETIC, CONSIDERATE, HUMANE, AGREEABLE, FAVORABLE, BENEFICENT, GRACIOUS, PLEASANT
kindness LENITY, MERCY, AFFECTION,

LOVE, FAVOR, TENDERNESS, COMPASSION, CLEMENCY, GOODNESS, PHILANTHROPY, CHARITY, GRACE, BENEFACTION

kindred COGNATE, ALLIED, AKIN, KITH, TIE, SIB, RELATIONSHIP, CONSANGUINITY, AFFINITY, FAMILY, RELATIVES, CLAN, RACE

kine CATTLE, COWS, BEASTS

king SOVEREIGN, ROI, REGULUS, RULER, REX, SUPREME, MASTER, CHIEF, EMPEROR, MONARCH, CHECKER, PIN, PEG
See country involved
fish See under "fish"

King Arthur('s), *abode of* AVALON
capital CAMELOT
court site CAMELOT
fairy sister MORGAN LE FAY
father UTHER
foster brother KAY
knight GALAHAD, PALADIN, GARETH, MODRED, GAWAIN, LANCELOT, TRISTRAM, PERCIVALE, KAY
lady ENID, ELAINE
lance RON
last battle CAMLAN
magician MERLIN
nephew GAWAIN, MODRED, GARETH
palace site CAMELOT
queen GUINEVERE
resting place AVALON
shield PRIDWIN
sword EXCALIBUR
town ASTOLAT

King Canute's *consort* EMMA

kingdom REALM, EMPIRE, ESTATE, SPHERE, PEOPLE, STATE, TERRITORY, MONARCHY, SOVEREIGNTY, DOMINION, SUPREMACY, DOMAIN
ancient MOAB, ELAM
animal FAUNA
of Nimrod BABEL
vegetable FLORA

King Ferdinand BOMBA
"King Henry IV"
character HENRY (HAL), BLUNT, PERCY, SCROOP, POINS

King Lear's *daughter* GONERIL, REGAN, CORDELIA
dog TRAY

kinglet LIONET, WREN, BIRD

kingly ROYAL, NOBLE, LEONINE, AUGUST, REGAL, MAJESTIC, PRINCELY, IMPERIAL

King of Bath NASH
of Beggars CAREW
of Dwarfs ALBERICH
of Fairies OBERON
of Fomorians BALOR
of Golden Touch MIDAS
of Judah See under "Judah"
of Judea HEROD
of Serpents SHESHA
of waters AMAZON

king's *bodyguard* THANE
evil SCROFULA
letter BRIEF
topper ACE

kink KNOT, TWIST, SNARL, CURL, LOOP, BEND, ENTANGLEMENT, CRAMP, SPASM, CRICK, QUIRK, WHIM, CROCHET, ECCENTRICITY
in thread BURL

kinkajou POTTO

kinship See "kin" and "kindred"
father's side AGNAT(E)
Mohammedan law NASAB

kinsman RELATIVE, SIB, CONNECTION, RELATION

Kipling's
hero KIM
novel KIM
shere khan TIGER

kirtle SKIRT, COAT, TUNIC, PETTICOAT

Kish's *father* NER
son SAUL

kismet DESTINY, FATE, PORTION, LOT, DOOM

kiss BUSS, SMACK,

OSCULATE, CARESS, TOUCH, SALUTE, PECK
of peace PAX
sculptor of Kiss RODIN

kissing, *science of* PHILEMATOLOGY

kit OUTFIT, PACK, SET, COLLECTION, LOT, BOX, BAG, CONTAINER, KITTEN, VIOLIN

kitchen GALLEY, COOKROOM, CUISINE
garden OLITORY
tool or utensil CORER, RICER, GRATER, SPATULA, STRAINER, BEATER, OPENER

kite ELANET, GLEDE, HAWK, BIRD, RAISE, ELEVATE, TOY, SHARPER, ROGUE, RASCAL, FLY, SOAR, GALLIVANT
Europe GLEDE
genus ELANUS

kittiwake WAEG, GULL, BIRD

kitty CAT, ANTE, POOL, POT, BOWL, RECEPTABLE

kiwi ROA, MOA, APTERYX, BIRD
genus APTERYX

kleptomaniac THIEF, FILCHER, PILFERER

knack TRICK, HANG, MOCK, SKILL, ART, FEAT, EASE, TURN, GIFT, GENIUS, TALENT, DEXTERITY, ADROITNESS, ABILITY, APTITUDE, READINESS, FACILITY, CONTRIVANCE, TOY, TRINKET

knapsack BAG, KIT, POUCH, CASE, PACK

knarl GNARL, KNAG, KNURL, NODE, KNOT, KNOB, SNAG

knave ROGUE, LOREL, RASCAL, LOSEL, SCAMP, SERVANT, JACK, VILLAIN, SCOUNDREL, CHEAT, SWINDLER, SHARPER, TRICKSTER, MISCREANT
in cribbage NOB
of clubs PAM

knead PETRIE, ELT, MOLD, FASHION,

MASSAGE, MANIPU-
LATE, SQUEEZE,
PRESS, RUB
knee GENU, JOINT
bend GENUFLECT
bone PATELLA, CAP,
ROTULA
combining form
GENU
flexure GENU
kneecap PATELLA,
ROTULA, SESAMOID,
KNEEPAN
like ROTULAR
kneeling desk PRIE-
DIEU
knickknack GIMCRACK,
TRIFLE, TOY,
TRINKET, KICKSHAW,
PLAYTHING, GEWGAW,
BAUBLE
knife MACHET(T)E
DAGGER, DIRK,
BARLOW, SWORD,
BAYONET, LANCE,
BLADE, STAB, CUT,
WOUND
Burmese DAH
dealer CUTLER
Dyak PARANG
Hindu KUKRI
Irish SKEAN, SKENE
large BOLO, SNEE
Malay CREESE, KRIS
Maori PATU
Moro BARONG
one-bladed BARLOW
Philippine BOLO,
MACHET(T)E
plaster and paint
SPATULA
Spanish MACHET(T)E
surgical SCALPEL,
FLEAM, LANCET,
CATLIN
knight('s) DUB, SIR,
GALLANT, BARONET,
EQUITE, EQUES,
TEMPLAR, BORS,
RITTER, GARETH,
HIPPEUS, GALAHAD,
CAVALIER, CHEVALIER,
HORSEMAN, AT-
TENDANT, CHAMPION,
TITLE, LOVER
attendant PAGE,
SQUIRE
champion PALADIN
cloak TABARD
ensign or flag
PENNON
errant PALADIN

fight JOUST
next in order
ARMIGER
of the road TRAMP
order of GARTER,
BATH
Round Table GAWAIN,
GALAHAD, PALADIN,
TRISTRAM, LANCELOT,
PERCIVALE, KAY,
GARETH, MODRED
wife of DAME
knighthood CHIVALRY
confer DUB
knit COUPLE, JOIN,
WEAVE, BRAID, PLAIT,
LINK, UNITE, CON-
NECT, INTERLACE,
INTERLOCK, CONJOIN,
CONSOLIDATE, CON-
TRACT
knitting UNION, HANDI-
WORK, FASTENING,
NETWORK
machine guide SLEY
stitch in PURL
knob LUMP, HILL,
KNURL, BOSS,
NODE, UMBO,
TUBERCLE, PRO-
TUBERANCE, BUNCH,
STUD, HANDLE,
BUMP, HUMP, SWELL-
ING, KNOP, HEAD,
NURL, KNOLL
like NODAL
ornamental BOSS,
STUD, KNOP
pointed FINIAL
wood KNUR, BURL
knobby NODOSE, HARD,
LUMPY, HILLY,
KNOTTY
knobkerrie KIRI, CLUB,
WEAPON
knobstick RAT, SCAB,
STICK, CANE, CLUB,
BLACKLEG
knock RAP, STRIKE,
HIT, TAP, COLLIDE,
BLOW, POUND, SLAP,
CUFF, BUFFET, BOX,
BEAT, BUMP, CLASH,
DISCREDIT, CRITICIZE,
DECRY, BLAME
knee VALGUS
out KO, KAYO, BASH,
BEAUT, DILLY
knockabout SLOOP,
YACHT, ACTOR, HANDY-
MAN

knoll RISE, MOUND,
KNAP, HILLOCK, HUM-
MOCK, ELEVATION,
HILL, KNOB
knot(s) SNAG, JOINT,
NODE, TIE, TUFT,
HITCH, KNURL, GNARL,
NODUS, NODULE,
TANGLE, ENTANGLE-
MENT, COMPLICATION,
CONNECTION,
BOND, PERPLEXITY,
PROBLEM, DIF-
FICULTY, KNAG,
GROUP, SANDPIPER
fibrous NOIL, NEP
free from ENODE,
ENODATE, UNRAVEL
hair or silk NOIL
in wood KNAG
pertaining to NODAL
running NOOSE
thread BURL
tree GNARL, BURL,
KNUR
knotty INTRICATE, IN-
VOLVED, COMPLEX,
RUGGED, TANGLED
know REGARD, REVEAL,
KEN, WIST, WOT,
PERCEIVE,
(RE)COGNIZE, DIS-
CERN, ASCERTAIN, SEE,
COMPREHEND, UNDER-
STAND, DISTINGUISH,
APPREHEND
knowing HEP, SCIENT,
EPISTEMONIC, ALERT,
BRIGHT, SMART,
AWARE, COGNIZANT,
CLEVER, ACUTE,
SHREWD, SHARP,
CONVERSANT, INTEL-
LIGENT, EXPERIENCED,
INFORMED, ARTFUL,
CUNNING, STYLISH
knowledge KEN, LORE,
OLOGY, SCIENTIA,
LEARNING, ERUDITION,
CUNNING, SKILL,
SCIENCE, WISDOM,
COGNITION, INFORMA-
TION
highest, Plato NOESIS
object of SCIBILE
pertaining to GNOSTIC
without ATECHNIC,
IGNORANCE,
NESCIENCE
known COUTH,
EMINENT, NOTORIOUS,

FAMOUS, FAMED,
NOTED, FAMILIAR
knuckle SUBMIT,
YIELD, STRIKE, JOINT
bone DIB
kobold GNOME, NISSE,
HOBGOBLIN, BROWNIE,
NIS, SPIRIT
koel CUCKOO, BIRD
kohinoor DIAMOND
koklas(s) PUKRAS,
PHEASANT, FOWL,
BIRD
kokoon GNU
Kol *dialect* HO,
MUNDARI
kola JACKAL, NUT
Koran ALCORAN
chapter SURA
division of SURA
pertaining to
ALCORANIC
scholars, body of
ULEMA
section SURA
teacher ALFAQUI(N)
Korea CHOSEN
capital SEOUL
city or town PUSAN,
KAESONG, (R)IRI,
ANJU, UIJU, WONJU,
SUWON (SUIGEN)
monetary unit HWAN
port YOSU, GENSAN,
PUSAN
president, former
RHEE
reservoir PUJON
(FUSEN)
river YALU (AMNOK),
KUN (KIN)
seaport INCHON *See*
"port" *above*
soldier ROK
weight KON
Korzeniowski CONRAD
kosher CLEAN, PURE,
FIT, PROPER
meat maker PORGER
opposed to TREF(A)
kraal PEN, CORRAL,
ENCLOSURE, VILLAGE,
HUT, COMMUNITY
krimmer (LAMB)SKIN,
FUR
Kronos' *wife* RHEA
kthibh K'RI, KERE
kudu ANTELOPE
kulak PEASANT,
FARMER
Kulanapan POMO,
INDIAN

kumiss DRINK
like KEPHIR, KEFIR
Kuomintang *council*
YUAN
Kuril(e) *island*
ITURUP, CHISHIMA
kurtosis ARC, CURVA-
TURE
Kwantung *seaport*
DAIREN
kyphosis CURVATURE,
HUMPBACK
Kyushu *volcano* ASO

L

L ELL, FIFTY
Laban's *daughter*
LEAH, RACHEL
label TAG, MARK,
TICKET, BAND, FILLET,
FLAP, TASSEL, LAPPET,
INFULA, SLIP, STAMP,
STICKER, CARD,
CLASSIFY, CALL,
NAME, DESCRIBE
labellum LIP, PETAL
"La Bohème" *heroine*
MIMI
labor WORK, TASK,
TRAVAIL, TOIL, MOIL,
EFFORT, GRIND,
TROUBLE, STRESS,
DRUDGE, SERVICE,
EXERTION, PAINS,
INDUSTRY, STRIVE,
SUFFER, CHORE
for breath GASP, PANT
union CIO, AFL
laborer HAND, FELLAH,
PEON, TOTY, COOLIE,
WORKMAN, OPERA-
TIVE, CRAFTSMAN,
MECHANIC
canal NAVVY
Labrador tea LEDUM
labyrinth MAZE, PER-
PLEXITY, INTRICACY
lace EDGING, CORD,
BRAID, MIX, SNARE,
TRIM, VINE, FASTEN,
FORTIFY, STRING,
NET, BEAT, LASH,
ADORN, INTERTWINE,
COMPRESS, SPIKE
barred GRILLE
frilled RUCHE
front JABOT
gold or silver ORRIS
heavy TATTING,
GUIPURE

kind FILET, VAL,
ALENCON, ROSEPOINT
loop in PICOT
make TAT
Mechlin MALINES
metal tag AGLET,
AIGLET
opening EYELET
ornamental edge
PICOT
queen ANNE'S
square hole FILET
tip of AGLET, AIGLET
lacerate RIP, CUT,
REND, TEAR, MANGLE,
SEVER, CLAW, HAR-
ROW, WOUND, HURT,
AFFLICT, LANCINATE,
LANIATE
lachrymose TEARFUL,
SAD
lack ABSENCE, RE-
QUIRE, WANT, NEED,
DEFECT, MISS, FAIL,
DEFICIENCY, DEARTH,
PAUCITY, SCARCITY
of tone ATONY
lackey FOOTMAN,
FLUNKY, TOADY,
SERVANT, VALET,
FOLLOWER
lacking DEVOID, SHY,
NEEDED, SHORT
Laconian
capital SPARTA
subdivision (group)
OBE
laconic CONCISE,
TERSE, BRIEF, PITHY,
CURT, SHORT, SUC-
CINCT, COMPACT,
POINTED, EPIGRAM-
MATIC, SENTENTIOUS
lacquer ENAMEL,
VARNISH, JAPAN,
DUCO, LAC
lacuna GAP, SPACE,
BREAK, HIATUS
lad YOUTH, BOY,
CHAP, STRIPLING,
MATE, FELLOW,
LOVER, YOUNGSTER,
YOUNKER
ladder SCALE, RUN,
STEE, STY, STEPS
ascend by ESCALADE,
CLIMB
like SCALAR
part RUNG
lading CARGO,
FREIGHT, LOAD,
BURDEN, BAILING

ladle SPOON, SCOOP,
BAIL, DIP, DIPPER,
BOX, FLATBOARD
spout of typecasting
GEAT
ladrone ROGUE, THIEF,
HIGHWAYMAN *See*
"robber"
Ladrone island GUAM,
MARIANAS, SAIPAN
lady DAME, DONNA,
FEMALE, WOMAN,
BURD, WIFE,
MISTRESS, BARONESS,
COUNTESS, MATRON,
SPOUSE, TITLE,
MADAM, FRAU
of the Lake ELLEN,
VIVIAN, NIMUE
ladybird BEETLE, BUG
genus VEDALIA
ladyfish WRASSE
ladylove DELIA,
SWEETHEART,
MISTRESS
lag LINGER, DELAY,
IDLE, LOITER, DALLY,
SLACKEN, TARRY,
STAY, SAUNTER,
DRAG, STAVE
lagan, *relating to*
JETSAM, FLOTSAM
La Gioconda MONA
LISA
character in opera
LAURA, ENZO
lagniappe HANDSEL,
TRIFLE, GIFT,
MEMENTO, GRATUITY,
BONUS, TIP
lagomorph HARE,
PACA, RABBIT,
CON(E)Y, PIKA
laic CIVIL, SECULAR,
TEMPORAL, LAY
lair CAVE, DEN,
CAVERN, TRAP,
HOLE, BURROW,
COUCH, BED
laity LAYMEN,
PEOPLE
Laius' *son* OEDIPUS
lake LOCH, POND,
TARN, LAGOON,
MERE
Africa NYAS(S)A,
CHAD, TSANA,
RUDOLF, VICTORIA,
TANA, NGAMI
Asia VAN, URMIA,
BAIKAL

Australia EYRE,
FROME
California TAHOE,
SODA, MONO,
GOOSE *See under*
"California"
Ethiopia T(S)ANA,
DEMBEA, TZANA
Europe, largest
LADOGA
Finland ENARE,
SAIMA(A)
Garda day breeze
ORA
Geneva LEMAN
day breeze on
REBAT
George HORICON
Gobi Desert HARA
Great HURON,
ERIE, ONTARIO,
MICHIGAN,
SUPERIOR
Hades AVERNUS,
AVERNO
Hoover Dam MEAD
Iran URMIA
Italy COMO, GARDA,
BOLSENA, NEMI,
ALBANO
Mexico CHAPALA
mountain TARN
New York PLACID,
GEORGE, ONEIDA,
OTSEGO *See under*
"New York"
outlet of BAYOU
Panama GATUN
pertaining to LUCUS-
TRAL, LACUSTRINE
Russia BAIKAL,
BALKASH, ARAL,
LADOGA, ONEGA,
ILMEN, VOZHE,
LACHA, VIGO, SEG,
TOPO, KOLA, BYELO
shallow LAGOON
State MICHIGAN
Sudan CHAD, TSAD
Switzerland ZUG,
MORAT, THUN,
BIENNE, LUCERNE,
LEMAN (GENEVA)
third largest ARAL
Turkestan HARA
U.S. ERIE, HURON,
MEAD, TAHOE *See*
"Great" *above*
Wales BALA
lama, *chief* DALAI
lamb EANLING, YEAN,
EAN, CHILD,

YEANLING, FUR,
BROADTAIL,
ASTRAKHAN
breast of CARRE
bring forth (Y)EAN
female EWE
holy AGNUS
leg of cooked GIGOT
male RAM
pet CADE, COSSET
symbol AGNUS
Lamb, *pen name* ELIA
lambent GLOWING,
BRIGHT, LUCENT,
RADIANT, FLICKER-
ING, WAVERING
lame WEAK,
CRIPPLE(D), HALT-
(ING), MAIM,
HURT, HOBBLING,
LIMPING, UNSATIS-
FACTORY, INSUF-
FICIENT, FEEBLE,
POOR, DISABLED,
INEFFECTUAL
Lamech's *wife* ADAH
lamellirostral *bird*
GOOSE, DUCK,
SWAN, MERGANSER,
FLAMINGO
lament HONE, MOAN,
WEEP, MOURN, KEEN,
(RE)PINE, ELEGIZE,
RUE, CRY, (BE)-
WAIL, GRIEVE,
SORROW, COMPLAIN,
DEPLORE, BEMOAN,
REGRET, DIRGE,
ELEGY, EPICEDIUM
lamentation SIGH,
CRY, WAIL, PLAINT,
ULULATION, MOAN,
PLANGOR, JEREMIAD
lamina SCALE,
SHEET, LAYER,
PLATE, FLAKE,
BLADE
gray matter in brain
OBEX
laminated SPATHIC,
TABULAR, SCALED,
LAMELLAR, FLAKY,
FOLIATED, FISSILE
rock SHALE
lamp CRUSIE, ETNA,
LUCIGEN, TORCH,
LIGHT, LANTERN,
SUN, MOON, STAR,
EYE, LOOK
boy with ALADDIN
condensing ring CRIC
miner's DAVY

safety GEORDIE
waving in worship
  ARATI
lamplighter SPILL,
  TORCH, MATCH
lampoon SKIT, IAMBIC,
  LIBEL, SATIRE,
  ABUSE, SATIRIZE,
  PASQUINADE, RIDI-
  CULE, CARICATURE
  brief SKIT, SQUIB
lamprey EEL
lance JAVELIN, SPEAR,
  DART, BLADE,
  WEAPON, CUT,
  OPEN, PIERCE
  head MORNE
  rest FAUCRE
  sergeant CORPORAL
Lancelot's *love* GUINE-
  VERE
  loved by ELAINE
lancer U(H)LAN,
  HUSSAR, TROOPER,
  CAVALRYMAN,
  SOLDIER
lancet, *fish* SURGEON
  point of NEB
lancewood CIGUA
lancinate STAB,
  LACERATE, TEAR,
  PIERCE, REND
land FIELD, ASSART,
  ACRE, HEATH,
  EARTH, WEALD,
  SOIL, SOD, TURF,
  TERRAIN, GROUND,
  TRACT, COUNTRY,
  DISTRICT, CONTINENT,
  REGION, ESTATE, TER-
  RITORY, FARM,
  NATION, PEOPLE,
  REALM, DOMAIN,
  PROPERTY, MEADOW,
  PASTURE, WOLD,
  (A)LIGHT, PERCH,
  ROOST, CATCH, GAIN,
  WIN, DEBARK, AR-
  RIVE, REACH, DIS-
  EMBARK, CAPTURE,
  SECURE
  area TRACT
  barren GALL,
  WASTE, DESERT
  border of RAND
  by low stream HOLM
  church GLEBE
  cultivated ARADA,
  TILTH, TILLAGE
  east of Eden NOD
  ecclesiastical GLEBE
  farthest north THULE

feudal BENEFICE
  held in fee simple
  ALOD, ODAL, UDAL
  in law SOLUM
  meadow LEA
  measure ARE, ACRE,
  ROD, PERCH
  of Cakes SCOTLAND
  of Midnight Sun
  NORWAY
  of Nod SLEEP
  of Promise PALES-
  TINE, CANAAN
  of Rising Sun JAPAN
  of the Rose ENG-
  LAND
  of the Shamrock
  EIRE, ERIN, IRELAND
  of the Thistle SCOT-
  LAND
  pertaining to
  GEOPONIC, AGRO,
  REAL
  piled up CAIRN
  plowed ARADA,
  ARADO
  point of SPIT, CAPE,
  NESS, RAS
  prepare for seed
  TILL, PLOW
  return for service
  FEOFF
  reverting to state
  ESCHEAT
  Scottish ERD
  tillable ARABLE
  tract between rivers
  DOAB
  -traveling fish ANA-
  BAS
  treeless SAVANNA(H),
  PAMPAS, PRAIRIE,
  STEPPE, TUNDRA,
  WOLD
  triangular piece
  GORE, DELTA
  waste HEATH, MOOR
  without forests
  STEPPE *See* "tree-
  less" *above*
landing place PIER,
  (AIR)PORT, LEVEE,
  QUAY, WHARF, AIR-
  STRIP, AIRDROME,
  TARMAC, DOCK
landlord HOST,
  OWNER, BONIFACE,
  PROPRIETOR, INN-
  KEEPER, LESSOR
landmark BOUNDARY,
  COPA, SENAL, BENCH,
  STONE, GUIDE

Landolphia fruit
  ABOLI
landscape PAYSAGE,
  SCENE, VIEW,
  DEPICTION, PICTURE,
  PAINTING, SCENERY
landslide AVALANCHE,
  EBOULEMENT,
  VICTORY
Landtag DIET, LEGIS-
  LATURE, ASSEMBLY,
  COUNCIL
lane PATH, ROUTE,
  TRACK, ALLEY, ROAD,
  STREET, DRIVE,
  PASSAGE(WAY)
Langobard *king* AL-
  BOIN
language ARGOT, LIP,
  TONGUE, LINGO,
  PATOIS, DIALECT,
  SPEECH, IDIOM,
  DICTION, PEOPLE,
  VERNACULAR, NATION,
  UTTERANCE, PAR-
  LANCE, SLANG,
  EXPRESSION, STYLE
  Aramaic SYRIAC
  artificial ESPERANTO,
  IDO, OD, RO, SIGN
  Assamese AO
  Bantu SWAHILI
  Buddhist PALI
  Caucasian ANDI,
  UDI, AVAR
  dead LATIN
  Dravidian TAMIL
  E. Europe UGRIC
  form IDIOM
  Indo-European
  CELTIC, ITALIC,
  GERMANIC, HEL-
  LENIC, IRANIAN
  Moslem URDU, PALI,
  HINDUSTANI
  oriental THAI
  Semite AMORITE,
  ARAMIC, HEBREW,
  GHEEZ, AMHARIC,
  TIGRE
  thieves' ARGOT
  universal See "arti-
  ficial" *above*
languages, *person
  knowing all* POLY-
  GLOT
languet PROCESS,
  REED, TONGUE
languish DROOP,
  WASTE, PINE, FLAG,
  WANE, FAIL, FADE,

FAINT, WITHER, DE-
CLINE, SINK, SICKEN
languor LASSITUDE,
ENNUI, TORPOR,
BLUES, DUMPS,
INDOLENCE, LAXITY,
KEF, KIEF, KEEF,
FEEBLENESS, DEBIL-
ITY, LISTLESSNESS,
DULLNESS, DREAMI-
NESS, SLUGGISHNESS,
STAGNATION, WEAK-
NESS, LETHARGY
langur MONKEY,
ENTELLUS
lanioid bird SHRIKE
lanner FALCON,
BIRD
lantern(s) LIGHT See
"lamp"
feast of BON
lanuginose DOWNY
lanyard THONG,
WAPP, CORD, ROPE
Laodamia's *father*
ACASTUS
husband PROTESI-
LAUS
Laos *tribesman* KHA,
MEO
Lao Tse *concept* TAO
lapel REVERS, FACING,
FOLD, FLAP, REVERE,
LAPPET
lapidate STONE, PELT
lapin RABBIT, HARE,
CON(E)Y, FUR
lapis lazuli LAZURITE,
SAPPHIRE, STONE
Lapithae *king* IXION
Lapland *city or town*
KOLA
sled PULK(A)
lappet LOBE, WAT-
TLE, LAPEL, FLAP,
FOLD, STREAMER,
MOTH, LAP
on dress PAN
lapse ERROR, MIS-
STEP, SLIP, PASS,
BULL, BONER, SIN,
CRIME, FAULT, DE-
CLINE, RECEDE,
DEVIATE, SHORTCOM-
ING, INDISCRETION,
APOSTASY
lapwing PLOVER,
HOOPOE, PEWIT,
TEWIT, BIRD
larboard PORT,
LEFT

opposed to STAR-
BOARD, RIGHT
larch TAMARACK, TREE
genus LARIX
lard AXUNGE, SUET,
TALLOW, GREASE,
FAT, ENARM, EN-
RICH, GARNISH,
BEDECK, STREW,
LINE
larder BUTTERY,
PANTRY, SPENCE,
STOREROOM, PRO-
VISIONS
large BIG, GREAT,
HUGE, VAST, WIDE,
SPACIOUS, AMPLE,
BULKY, IMMENSE,
COLOSSAL, COMPRE-
HENSIVE, EXTENSIVE,
BROAD, CAPACIOUS,
COPIOUS, LIBERAL,
FAT, OBESE
combining form
MACR(O), MEG(A),
MEGAL(O)
largest fresh water fish
ARAPAIMA
land mass EURASIA
lariat NOOSE, LASSO,
REATA, RIATA,
ROPE
eye of HONDA
lark PIPIT, BIRD,
ADVENTURE, PRANK,
TRICK, FROLIC,
SPREE
genus ALAUDA
larva GRUB, REDIA,
MAGGOT, WORM,
SLUG, CATERPILLAR
beetle GRUB
final stage CHRYSALIS
fly BOT(T)
footless MAGGOT
horse fly BOT
infecting eye LOA
wingless CREEPER,
MAGGOT
larvate MASKED, CON-
CEALED, HIDDEN,
OBSCURE
Lascar SERANG,
SAILOR, BOATMAN
lash QUIRT, WHIP,
SWITCH, THONG,
SMITE, TIE, FLOG,
RATE, SCOLD,
SCOURGE, DASH,
STROKE, STRIPE,
CASTIGATE, CHASTISE,

BEAT, FLAGELLATE,
BIND, FASTEN, SECURE
lasso *See* "lariat"
last ABIDE, SURVIVE,
REMAIN, ENDURE,
HOLD, WEAR, UT-
MOST, ULTIMATE,
EXTREME, LATEST,
NEWEST, LOWEST,
OMEGA, END, TERMI-
NAL, FINAL(LY),
FINALE, CODA, HIND-
MOST, CLOSING,
EXTEND, REACH,
PATTERN, BLOCK
but one PENULT
but two ANTE-
PENULT
Last *of the Goths*
RODERICK
of the Mohicans
UNCAS
of Puritans ADAMS
of Romans AETIUS
of Stuarts ANNE
prize BOOBY, CON-
SOLATION, SOP
Supper, picture of
CENA
room of CENACLE
syllable of word
ULTIMA
lasting STABLE, DUR-
ABLE, STRONG, EN-
DURING, PERMANENT,
ABIDING, FIXED,
PERENNIAL, STEAD-
FAST, CONSTANT
latch SNECK, BELAY,
HOOK, LOCK, CATCH,
BOLT, FASTENER, GET,
RECEIVE
latchet *on a shoe*
TAP
late RECENT(LY),
TARDY, NEW, DEAD,
SLOW, OVERDUE, BE-
HIND(HAND)
at school TARDY
combining form NEO
latent CONCEALED,
HIDDEN, SECRET,
DORMANT, QUIESCENT,
UNREVEALED, POTEN-
TIAL, VEILED,
ABEYANT
later ANON, AFTER,
SUBSEQUENTLY
lateral SIDE, PASS,
FLANK
latex JUICE, SECRE-
TION, RUBBER

lath SLAT, STRIP
lathe TURRET,
CAPSTAN, CHUCK
holder MONITOR
watchmaker's MAN-
DREL
lather SUDS, SOAP,
FOAM, FROTH, SCUM,
SPUME, YEAST,
SWEAT
Latin ROMANTIC,
ROMAN, SPANIARD,
ITALIAN, CUBAN
alas VAE
another ALIO,
ALIUS
born NATUS
both AMBI
brother FRATER
bug CIMEX
but yet SED
copper CUPRUM
custom RITUS
day DIEM, DIES
deny (to say no)
NEGO
depart VADE
divination SORS
dog CANIS
door JANUA
earth TERRA
equal PAR
eternity AEVO,
AEVUM
evil MALA, MALUM
field or piece of land
AGER
force or power VIS
from DE
gentle LENIS
go VADO, IRE
he IPSE
himself IPSE
hope SPES
hymn STABAT
MATER
lamb AGNUS
land in cultivation
AGER
law LEX, JUS
learned DOCTUS
man HOMO
mind MENS
mine MEUM
mountain MONS
needle ACUS
nobody NEMO
observe NOTA
old VETUS
order ORDO
other(s) ALTER,
ALIUS, ALIA

our NOSTER
prison CARCER
same IDEM
ship NAVIS
side LATUS
sister SOROR
skin CUTIS
stone LAPIS
there IBI
this HOC
thus SIC, ITA
toad BUFO
total SUMMA,
OMNIS
unless NISI
water AQUA
where UBI
wool LANA
latitude RANGE,
EXTENT, SCOPE,
ROOM, SPACE, WIDTH,
BREADTH, COMPASS,
FREEDOM, REGION,
LOCALITY
latria WORSHIP,
SERVICE
latter LATE(R),
PAST, LAST,
MODERN, LATEST,
RECENT
lattice GRILL(E),
TRELLIS, CANCELLI,
GRATING, FRAME-
WORK, ESPALIER
Latvian LETT
capital RIGA
coin LAT, LATU
laud SING, EXTOL,
PRAISE, HYMN,
SONG, PSALM,
CELEBRATE, COM-
MEND, EXALT,
GLORIFY, MAGNIFY
laudation PRAISE,
COMMENDATION,
PANEGYRIC
laugh(s) HAW-HAW,
HA-HA, CHORTLE,
CHUCKLE, SNORT,
ROAR, FLEER, GUF-
FAW, SCOFF, JEER,
DERIDE, GIGGLE, TIT-
TER, SNICKER, SNIG-
GER, CACHINNATE
one who never AGE-
LAST, SOURPUSS
pertaining to
GELASTIC
laughable COMIC,
DROLL, RISIBLE,
LUDICROUS, FUNNY
laughing MERRY,

RIANT, MIRTHFUL,
GLEEFUL, GAY
laughter, *combining
form* GELO
provoking GELOGENIC
launch START, BE-
GIN, FLOAT, BOAT,
HURL, DESCANT,
LANCE, THROW,
CAST, DART,
LEAP, PLUNGE
laurel(s) BAY,
DAPHNE, IVY,
OLEANDER, SHRUB,
TREE, FAME, HONOR,
DISTINCTION
bay MAGNOLIA
crowned with LAURE-
ATE
Mexican MADRONA
wreath EIRESIONE
lava AA, DACITE,
BASALT, SLAG,
ASHES, ASH, TAXITE
cinder SCORIA
field PEDREGAL
fragment LAPILLUS
rough AA
round lump BOMB
sheet of COULEE
lavaliere PENDANT,
ORNAMENT,
JEWELRY
lave BATHE, WASH,
ABSTERGE, LADE,
DIP, POUR, DETERGE,
CLEAN
lavender PLANT,
FLOWER, COLOR,
PERFUME
European ASPIC
lavish FREE, PRODIGAL,
WILD, WASTEFUL,
PROFUSE, UNSTINTED,
THRIFTLESS, EXTRAVA-
GANT, ABUNDANT,
BOUNTIFUL, EXUBER-
ANT, BESTOW,
SQUANDER, GIVE,
DOTE, LUSH
law ORDINANCE, BILL,
CANON, LEX, JUS,
CODE, STATUTE,
DROIT, RULE, AXIOM,
ACT, REGULATION,
ENACTMENT, DECREE,
EDICT, ORDER, COM-
MAND, JURISPRU-
DENCE, LITIGATION
body of CODE
breaker FELON,
CRIMINAL, SINNER

decree NISI, EDICT
divine, *Roman* FAS
fictitious name in
DOE, ROE
fourth offenders'
BAUMES
German SALIC
Greek NOMOS
Latin JUS, LEX
like for like TALION
Moses TORA(H),
PENTATEUCH
one opposing ANTI-
LEGALIST, OUTLAW,
ANARCHIST
pertaining to FO-
RENSIC, LEGAL
points RES
suit LIS, ACTION,
CASE
term NISI, RES,
TROVER, DETINUE
volume CODEX
within the ENNOMIC,
LEGAL, LAWFUL,
LICIT, LEGITIMATE
lawful LEGITIMATE,
LEGAL, LICIT, DUE,
RIGHT, JUST, CON-
STITUTIONAL, VALID,
PERMITTED
lawlessness ANARCHY,
LICENSE, RIOT,
MUTINY, VICE,
ILLEGALITY, UNRULI-
NESS
lawmaker LEGISLA-
TOR, SOLON, SENATOR,
DELEGATE, REPRE-
SENTATIVE
lawn TERRACE, GREEN,
SOD, TURF, CLOTH,
CAMBRIC, COTTON,
SIEVE
Lawrence, T. E. SHAW
lawsuit ACTION,
LITIGATION, CASE,
SUIT, LIS, CON-
TROVERSY, PROSECU-
TION
lawyer SOLICITOR,
ADVOCATE, LEGIS,
JURIST, BARRISTER,
ATTORNEY, COUN-
SEL(OR)
patron saint IVES
woman PORTIA
lax LOOSE, LIMP,
SLACK, WEAK, RE-
LAXED, OPEN, REMISS,
CARELESS, SOFT,
FLABBY, NEGLIGENT,

DISSOLUTE, LICEN-
TIOUS
lay TUNE, DITTY, SONG,
LYRIC, BALLAD,
MELODY, POEM,
PAVE, PUT, PLACE,
HEAP, REST, STORE,
PLANT, BURY, INTER,
IMPUTE, BET, DE-
POSIT, IMPOSE,
ASCRIBE, SPREAD,
COAT, COVER, AIM,
SECULAR
layer COAT, LAMINA,
TIER, SLAB, FILM,
PLY, STRATUM,
PROVINE, PATINA,
BED, THICKNESS, HEN
of coal SEAM
of stones DESS
wood VENEER
layman LAIC, AMA-
TEUR
lazar LEPER, OUT-
CAST
lazy OTIOSE, SLOW,
INERT, IDLE, SUPINE,
SLOTHFUL, TORPID,
SLACK, LAX, SLUG-
GISH, INDOLENT,
INACTIVE
fellow BUM,
DRONE, IDLER, LUSK,
SLUGGARD
lea MEADOW, MEAD
lead METAL,
PLUMBUM, GRAPHITE,
CERUSSITE, ANGLESITE,
HEAD, OPEN, START,
BEGIN, DIRECT,
PILOT, CONTROL,
STEER, SET, FIX,
COUNSEL, INDUCE, AL-
LURE, DRAG, CON-
DUCT, ESCORT,
PRECEDE, FRONT,
SURPASS, EXCEL,
OUTSTRIP, ENTICE,
PERSUADE, SOLDER
astray MANG,
ENTICE, SEDUCE
black GRAPHITE,
PLUMBAGO
colored LIVID
*glass for gem mak-
ing* STRASS
mock BLENDE,
SPHALERITE
monoxide LITHARGE
ore GALENA
pellet SHOT, BUL-
LET, BB

pencil GRAPHITE
sounding PLUM-
MET
symbol PB
white CERUSE
leader ETHNARCH,
CHIEF, GUIDE, HEAD,
SCOUT, DUX, MASTER,
CAPTAIN, DUCE,
BARON, TITAN, VICE-
ROY, GOVERNOR,
PRESIDENT, KING,
OFFICER, CHIEFTAIN,
DIRECTOR, CONDUC-
TOR, VICTOR, COM-
MANDER, RULER,
TENDON, SINEW,
EDITORIAL, ARTICLE
Argonauts' JASON
Biblical MOSES
chorus CANTOR,
CORYPHAEUS
of thieves ALI
leading CHIEF,
MAIN, VAN, AHEAD,
FIRST, PRINCIPAL,
CAPITAL, FOREMOST
leaf FROND, BLADE,
PAGE, SHEET,
LAMINA
appendage STIPEL,
STIPULE
bud GEMMA
calyx SEPAL
division LOBE
fern FROND
first in plant COTY-
LEDON
flower SEPAL, PETAL,
BRACT
grass BLADE
interstice AREOLA
modified BRACT
of book FOLIO,
SHEET, PAGE
one side of PAGE
palm OLLA, FROND
part of RIB, VEIN,
STIPEL
pore(s) of STOMATA,
STOMA
secretion on LERP
shape or type PAL-
MATE, DENTATE,
CRENATE, SERRATE,
AEROSE, OVATE,
ACUTE, OBTUSE
small gland on
LENTICEL
stalk, pertaining to
PETIOLAR

vein (MID)RIB, NERVURE, COSTA
leafless APHYLLOUS
plant CACTUS
leaflet PINNA, FOLDER, DODGER, BILL, CIRCULAR, TRACT, HANDBILL, PAMPHLET, BROCHURE
leaflike appendage BRACT, STIPULE
league COMBINE, UNION, HANSE, BAND, BUND, FUSION, BLOC, ALLIANCE, ASSOCIATION, COALITION, CONFEDERATION, CONFEDERACY, AGREEMENT, COVENANT, JOIN, ALLY, LENGTH
merchants' HANSE
pertaining to FEDERAL
leak SEEP, OOZE, SPILL, ESCAPE, DRIBBLE, FISSURE, CHINK, CRACK, CREVICE, HOLE
leal LOYAL, TRUE, STANCH, FAITHFUL, TRUSTWORTHY
lean THIN, GAUNT, POOR, LANK(Y), SPARE, SLIM, SKINNY, EMACIATED, MEAGER, SCANTY, UNPRODUCTIVE, SCRAWNY, TEND, TILT, SLANT, DEVIATE, BEND, BEAR, CANT, HEEL, SLOPE, INCLINE, TIP, CAREEN, DEPEND, CONFIDE, TRUST
person RIBE
Leander's *love* HERO
leaning BENT, FLAIR, BIAS, TURN, FACULTY, GIFT, TENDING, INCLINATION, PROPENSITY, TENDENCY
lean-to ROOF, SHACK, SHED, SHELTER
leap VAULT, CURVET, SPANG, CAPRIOLE, SPRING, BOUND, JUMP, CAPER, DANCE, GAMBOL, HOP, FRISK, SKIP,

DIVE, LUNGE, SALTO, STEND
year BISSEXTILE
leaping SALTANT
learned ERUDITE, LETTERED, EDUCATED, VERSED, EXPERT, EXPERIENCED, INFORMED, SCHOLARLY
man SCHOLAR, PUNDIT, ERUDIT(E), SAGE, SAVANT
learning ART, LORE, KEN, WISDOM, CULTURE, WIT, SCIENCE, KNOWLEDGE, SKILL, EDUCATION, ERUDITION, SCHOLARSHIP, PEDANTRY, INFORMATION
Lear's *daughter* REGAN, GONERIL, CORDELIA
lease HIRE, RENT, DEMISE, LET, CHARTER, CONTRACT
leash THONG, STRAP, ROPE, LINE, CORD, JESS, STRING, BIND, HOLD, TIE, SECURE, TIERCE, THREE, CURB, RESTRAIN
leather, *alum dressed* ALUTA
bottle MATARA, OLPE
convert into TAW, TAN
drinking mug JACK
fine VELLUM, KID
fish LIJA
flask OLPE, MATARA, GIRBA
flexible ROAN, SUEDE, KID
glove CAPESKIN, NAPA, SUEDE, KID
inspector SEALER
kind of ELK, DEER, CANEPIN, KIP, KID, SUEDE
napped SUEDE
pouch SPORRAN, KIT
Russian YUFT
sheepskin SKIVER, ROAN
shoe SUEDE, CALF
soft SUEDE, NAPA, ALUTA, CHAMOIS

strap or thong RAND, WELT
leave GO, QUIT, RESIGN, RETIRE, DESERT, FLEE, FLY, SCRAM, WITHDRAW(AL), DEPART(URE), FAREWELL, CONGE, VACATE, ABANDON, FORSAKE, RELINQUISH, RENOUNCE, BEQUEATH, DEMISE, FURLOUGH, EXIT, VACATION, LIBERTY, PERMISSION, ALLOW(ANCE), SUFFER(ANCE), YIELD, CEDE, WAIVE, PERMIT, LET, STRAND
absence from college EXEAT
taking CONGE, VAMOOSE, ADIEU
leaven BARM, YEAST, ZYME, FERMENT, TAINT, TEMPER, INFUSE, IMBUE, PERMEATE, ALLOY, IMPREGNATE
leaves, *having* PETALED, FOLIATE
pertaining to FOLIAR
leavings REFUSE, WASTE, DREGS, REST, ORTS, RESIDUE, RELICS, ASH, DUST, CULLS, REMAINS, REMNANTS, FRAGMENTS, SCRAPS, PIECES, LEFTOVERS, HASH
Lebanon *capital* BEIRUT
city or town SAIDA (SIDON), SUR (TYRE), ZAHLE, HERMEL
lectern DESK, AMBO, PULPIT
lector READER, ANAGNOST
lecture SERMON, SPEECH, DISCOURSE, TALK, ADDRESS, ADMONITION, REBUKE, REPROOF, PRELECTION, JOBE, RATE, SCOLD
lecturer TEACHER, DOCENT

Leda's *lover* SWAN
son POLLUX,
CASTOR
ledge LODE, REEF,
RIDGE, BERM,
SHELF, CAY, SILL,
FRAME, VEIN,
CLEAT, PROJECTION,
APRON
ledger entry ITEM,
DEBIT, CREDIT
lee COVER, SHELTER,
PROTECTION
opposed to STOSS,
WINDWARD
leech PARASITE,
WORM, GILL,
SPONGE, TOADY,
ANNELID
leek *genus* ALLIUM,
PLANT
leer SCOFF, SNEER,
EYE, OGLE, STARE,
LOOK
lees DROSS, DRAFF,
DREGS, SEDIMENT,
SETTLINGS, REFUSE,
GROUNDS, REMAINS
Leeward island
BARBUDA, NEVIS,
ANTIGUA, DOMINICA,
ANGUILLA, MONTSER-
RAT
left QUIT, WENT,
HAW, DEPARTED,
PORT, LARBOARD,
SINISTRAL, RADICAL,
LIBERAL
aground NEAPED,
BENEAPED, STRANDED
*by mother, raised by
hand* CADE
combining form LEVO
hand SINISTER
page of book
VERSO
pitcher SOUTH-
PAW
toward APORT, HAW
leftover ORT, END,
UNDONE, HASH
leg LIMB, CRUS,
SUPPORT, PROP,
EXTREMITY, GAM(B),
COURSE, TACK, RUN,
LAP, CIRCUIT, WALK
armor GREAVE,
JAMB
bone FIBULA,
TIBIA, FEMUR
fore SHANK, SHIN,
HOCK

heraldry GAMB
joint KNEE
knee to ankle CRUS,
SHANK
pertaining to CRURAL
legal LAWFUL,
VALID, LICIT, LEGITI-
MATE, AUTHORIZED,
SANCTIONED, PER-
MITTED, OFFICIAL,
LEAL
abstract PRECIS,
BRIEF
claim LIEN, RIGHT
contestant LITIGANT,
PLAINTIFF, DE-
FENDANT
defense ALIBI
delay MORA
hearing OYER, TRIAL,
INQUEST
matter RES
negligence LACHES
order WRIT, NISI
paper DEED, WILL,
WRIT, SUMMONS,
LEASE, CONTRACT
plea ALIBI, ABATER
process CAVEAT,
DETINET, DETINUE
profession BAR, LAW
prosecution SUIT,
ACTION, CASE
right DROIT
site VENUE
tender DOLLAR,
MONEY, CASH,
SPECIE, COIN
warning CAVEAT
wrong TORT,
MALUM
legally competent
CAPAX, SANE
legate ENVOY, DEPUTY,
DELEGATE, AMBAS-
SADOR, NUNCIO,
CONSUL
legend EDDA, FABLE,
MYTH, TALE, SAGA,
CAPTION, INSCRIP-
TION, TITLE, NAR-
RATIVE, FICTION,
MOTTO, ANECDOTE,
STORY, LECTIONARY,
PASSIONAL
legendary slave woman
BAUBO, IAMBE
water sprite UNDINE
leger FINE, LIGHT,
TRIVIAL
legging SPAT,

GAMBADO, STRAD,
PUTTEE, GAITER
wearing feathered
OCREATE
leghorn HEN, HAT
legible CLEAR, PLAIN,
READABLE, DECIPHERA-
BLE, RECOGNIZABLE
legislator SOLON,
SENATOR, DELEGATE,
LAWMAKER, REPRE-
SENTATIVE
legislature DIET,
SENATE, DAIL, AS-
SEMBLY, BOULE, CON-
GRESS, PARLIAMENT,
REICHSTAG *See* coun-
try involved
having two branches
BICAMERAL
one house UNI-
CAMERAL
legitimate LAWFUL,
LICIT, LEGAL, VALID,
SOUND, GENUINE,
WARRANTED, REASON-
ABLE *See* "legal"
leg-of-mutton *or* lamb
GIGOT
legume PEA, BEAN,
CLOVER, ALFALFA,
SOYBEAN, POD,
MEDIC, LENTIL
Lehar FRANZ
leiocome DEXTRIN
leipoa LOWAN, MAL-
LEE, MEGAPODE,
BIRD
leister SPEAR, GIG
leisure OTIUM, REST,
EASE, TOOM, RE-
POSE, FREEDOM,
TIME, CONVENIENCE,
UNEMPLOYMENT
leisurely GRADUAL,
SLOW, DELIBERATE,
FREE, EASY
leitmotif, leitmotiv
MOTIVE, THEME,
TOPIC, TEXT
lemniscus FILLET,
RIBBON, BAND
lemon CITRUS, FRUIT,
TREE
grass RUSA, ROOSA
like fruit LIME
seed PIP, PUTA-
MEN
lemur AYE-AYE,
LORI(S), MAKI,
GALAGO, KINKAJOU,
POTTO, TARSIER

Asia LORI(S)
flying COLUGO
Madagascar INDRI
  genus INDRIS
ring-tailed MACACO
lemuroid POTTO
Lenaeus BACCHUS,
  WINE
lend LET, LEASE,
  LOAN, GRANT,
  FURNISH, SUPPORT,
  ACCOMMODATE, GIVE,
  IMPART, AFFORD
length EXTENT,
  DURATION
combining form
  LONGI
of forearm CUBIT
times width AREA
unit of DHA, MICRON,
  PARSEC, INCH, FOOT,
  ROD, METER, MILE
lengthen EXTEND,
  PROTRACT
lengthy PROLIX,
  VERBOSE, PRO-
  TRACTED, PROLONGED,
  LONG, TIRESOME,
  TALL
lenient EASY, SOFT,
  GENTLE, MILD,
  INDULGENT, BALMY,
  CLEMENT, MERCI-
  FUL, ASSUASIVE,
  SOOTHING, TOLERANT,
  BLAND
Leningrad *river* NEVA
lenis GENTLE, SOFT,
  SMOOTH, BLAND
opposed to FORTIS
lenitive MILD,
  LAXATIVE, PALLIATIVE,
  GENTLE, BALMY,
  SOOTHING, SOFTENING,
  ASSUASIVE, EMOL-
  LIENT, ANODYNE
lens GLASS
measurement LIGNE
simple TORIC
telephotic ADON
Lent QUADRAGESIMA
season CARENE
  (CAREME)
lenticular PHACOID
lentigo FRECKLE
lentil ERVUM *See*
  "legume"
l'envoi, l'envoy POST-
  SCRIPT, STANZA,
  VERSE
leopard OCELOT, PARD,
  JAGUAR, PANTHER, CAT

hunting CHEETAH
like PARDINE
snow OUNCE
lepadidae *family*
  BARNACLE
leper LAZAR, OUTCAST
lepidopter MOTH,
  BUTTERFLY
lepidosiren EEL
leporine animal HARE
leprechaun ELF,
  GOBLIN, PIGMY,
  SPRITE, FAIRY
leprosy LEPRA,
  HANSEN'S (DISEASE)
Lepus family HARE,
  RABBIT, CON(E)Y,
  LEPORID, PIKA
lesion CUT, GASH,
  HURT, INJURY, SORE,
  DAMAGE
less MINOR, MINUS,
  INFERIOR, LESSER,
  SMALLER, SECONDARY,
  FEWER
lessen WANE, ABATE,
  PALLIATE, SHRINK,
  FADE, DIMINISH,
  DEGRADE, REDUCE,
  SHORTEN, THIN,
  MINIFY, ALLEVIATE,
  DECREASE, ABRIDGE,
  CONTRACT, LOWER,
  DISPARAGE, IMPAIR,
  WEAKEN, BELITTLE,
  DEPRECIATE,
  MINIMIZE
lesson CLASS, TASK,
  EXAMPLE, EXERCISE,
  INSTRUCTION, LEC-
  TURE, REPRIMAND,
  REBUFF, PRECEPT,
  REBUKE, CENSURE,
  SCOLDING, WARNING,
  STUDY
let ALLOW, PERMIT,
  LEASE, RENT, HIRE,
  CHARTER, LEAVE,
  SUFFER
go UNHAND, RELEASE,
  NEGLECT, UNTIE,
  FREE, DISMISS, SPARE
it be done FIAT
it be given DETUR
it stand STET, STA
up ABATE, STOP,
  CEASE, LESSEN
lethal FATAL, DEADLY,
  MORTAL, POISONOUS,
  TOXIC
lethargic INERT,
  TORPID, COMATOSE,

DROWSY, DULL,
  SLEEPY, SLUGGISH
lethargy STUPOR,
  TORPOR, INERTIA,
  APATHY, COMA,
  DROWSINESS,
  LANGUOR, LASSITUDE,
  INDIFFERENCE
Lethe OBLIVION,
  DEATH, FORGETFUL-
  NESS, RIVER
Leto LATONA
letter NOTE, LINE,
  MEMO, EPISTLE, MIS-
  SIVE, COMMUNICA-
  TION, DOCUMENT,
  REPLY, CHARACTER,
  TYPE, SYMBOL, ELL,
  ESS, TEE
according to LITERAL
authoritative WRIT,
  BREVE
challenge CARTEL
cross stroke of SERIF
cut off last APOCOPE
early Teutonic RUNE
fine line of SERIF
for letter LITERATIM,
  LITERALLY
Germanic RUNE
initial PARAPH, RUNE
last OMEGA, ZED, ZEE
ornamental PARAPH
Pope's BULL
letters, *illuminate with*
  MINIATE
man of LITERATUS,
  SCHOLAR, SAVANT
on old manuscripts
  UNCIALS
lettuce COS, MINION,
  ROMAINE, PLANT,
  MONEY
genus LACTUCA
sea LAVER, ALGA
  genus ULVA
leucite LENAD,
  MINERAL
Levantine *garment*
  CAFTAN
ketch (boat) XEBEC,
  SAIC, SET(T)EE
valley WADI, WADY
vessel JERM
levee DIKE, DURBAR,
  QUAY, EMBANK-
  (MENT), WHARF,
  PIER, BANK, RECEP-
  TION, GATHERING
level FLAT(TEN),
  EVEN, GRADE, PLANE,
  RAZE, RASE, DESTROY,

SMOOTH, FLUSH, POINT, TRAIN, AIM, LAY, HORIZONTAL, JUST, STEADY, IMPARTIAL, TOOL
combining form PLANI
sandy ridge LANDE
to sight along BONE
leveling slip SHIM
lever CRANK, TAPPET, PEAV(E)Y, BAR, PRY, PRIZE
crossbow GARROT
lumbering SAMSON, PEAV(E)Y, CANT HOOK
leveret HARE, CONY, CONEY, RABBIT
leviathan WHALE, TITAN, SERPENT, CROCODILE, DRAGON, SHIP
levin FLASH
levitate FLOAT, RISE
Levite *composer* ASAPH
levy DUTY, ASSESS, IMPOST, IMPOSE, COLLECT, ESTREAT, TAX, FINE, CESS, RATE, SEIZE, TRIBUTE, MUSTER
lex LAW, JUS, JURISPRUDENCE
Leyte *town* DULAG
liability DEBT, DUTY, ARREAR, DEBIT, OBLIGATION, RESPONSIBILITY
halting of CESSER
liable APT, BOUND, LIKELY, SUBJECT, EXPOSED, RESPONSIBLE, OBLIGED, OPEN, ANSWERABLE, ACCOUNTABLE, OBLIGATED
liana CIPO, VINE
liang TAEL
liar CHEAT, FIBBER, ANANIAS, WERNARD, DECEIVER, FALSIFIER, HYPOCRITE, FAKER, FRAUD, KNAVE
lias system JURASSIC
libel DEGRADE, LAMPOON, SLANDER, ABUSE, SKIT, SQUIB, MALIGN, VILLIFY, DEFAME, SMEAR

liber BOOK, FREE, OPEN, ACCESSIBLE
liberal LEFT, FREE, ECLECTIC, FRANK, OPEN, PROGRESSIVE, ADVANCED, AMPLE, LAVISH, PROFUSE, LENIENT, TOLERANT, CATHOLIC, ABUNDANT, GENEROUS, UNRESTRICTED, BOUNTEOUS, OPENHANDED, BOUNTIFUL, BROADMINDED, MUNIFICENT
liberate UNTIE, FREE, REDEEM, RANSOM, ABSOLVE, DELIVER, RESCUE, DETACH, RELEASE, LOOSE, EMANCIPATE, MANUMIT
Liberian *coast* KRU
native VAI, VEI
town SINO
tribe KRA, BASSA, GI, GIBBI
liberty FREEDOM, POWER, PRIVILEGE, FURLOUGH, LEAVE, LICENSE
library AGENCY, BIBLIOTHECA, MUSEUM, GALLERY, DEN, BOOKS
libretto BOOK, TEXT, WORDS, COMPOSITION
Libyan *gulf* SIDRA
measure PIK, DRA
oasis SEBHA
port DERNA, (K)HOMS
town DERNA
lice *See* "louse"
license CONSENT, PATENT, RIGHT, APPROBATE, ABANDON, LAXITY, LIBERTY, GRANT, LET, ALLOW, PRIVILEGE, PERMISSION, LEAVE, AUTHORITY, AUTHORIZATION, FREEDOM, CERTIFICATE
for absence EXEAT
lichen(s) MOSS, PARELLA, USNEA, FUNGUS, FUNGI
apothecium TRICA
deriv. of LITMUS, ARCHIL
genus EVERNIA, USNEA
licit LAWFUL, LEGAL,

DUE, JUST *See* "legal"
lick LAP, BEAT, DEFEAT, SUBDUE, WIN, ROUT, THRASH, FLOG, BAFFLE, PUZZLE, STRIKE, BLOW, CUT, SLAP, MOISTEN
licorice ANISE
derivative ABRIN
seed (India) GOONCH
lid CAP, ROOF, TOP, COVER, HAT, CURB, CHECK
lie FIB, MENDACITY, STORY, FALSEHOOD, UNTRUTH, PREVARICATION, EQUIVOCATE, FABRICATE, DECEIT, DECEIVE, PALTER, PREVARICATE, ABIDE, REST, SLEEP, LODGE, EXIST, SUBSIST, RECLINE
in wait LURK
on back SUPINATE, REST
on face PRONATE, FELL, PROSTRATE
Liechtenstein *capital* VADUZ
commune VADUZ
monetary unit RAPPE
lieu PLACE, STEAD, ROOM
life SPARK, VITA, ANIMATION, HOURS, VIE, DAYS, VITALITY, VIGOR, SPIRIT, EXISTENCE, BIOS, COURSE, CAREER, VIVACITY, ENERGY, ZEST, BIOGRAPHY
animal BIOTA, FAUNA
past middle AUTUMNAL
prefix BIO
principle ATMAN, PRANA
prolonger ELIXIR
relating to VITAL, BIOTIC
story MEMOIR, BIOGRAPHY, VITA
without AZOIC *See* "lifeless"
combining form ABIO
lifeless AZOIC, DEAD, INERT, AMORT, FLAT, PASSIVE, DULL, LISTLESS, STIFF, RIGID,

WOODEN, DEFUNCT,
INANIMATE, EXTINCT,
TORPID, SLUGGISH,
TAME
lifetime AGE(S), DAYS,
WORLD, EXISTENCE
lift HOVE, HEAVE, REAR,
AID, HELP, RAISE,
HOIST, BOOST, SOAR,
SURGE, EXALT, FILCH,
STEAL, SWIPE, COP,
HEFT, ELEVATE,
ELEVATOR, JACK
ligament BOND, DESMO,
BAND, UNION, TIE,
BANDAGE, TISSUE
combining form
DESMO
ligature TAENIA, TIE,
SUTURE, BOND,
THREAD, BAND(AGE),
LIGAMENT
light AIRY, FLUFFY,
FINE, EASY, SIMPLE,
FACILE, GAY, CARE-
FREE, MATCH, LAMP,
LEGER, LANTERN,
FLASH, MOON, SUN,
KINDLE, FIRE, LUMEN,
IGNITE, KLEIG, ARC,
ILLUME, CRESSET,
DAYBREAK, SUNRISE,
DAWN, BRIGHTNESS,
SPARKLE, STAR, TAPER,
CANDLE, TORCH,
CLEAR, BRIGHT,
SLEAZY, LAND, PERCH,
ROOST, KNOWLEDGE
act of making
LEVITATION
around sun AUREOLE
beacon FANAL
celestial LUMINARY,
MOON, SUN, STAR
circle AUREOLE,
HALO, NIMB(US)
cloud NIMBUS
combining form
PHOT(O)
faint GLIM(MER)
handed DEFT
headed FAINT, DIZZY,
GIDDY, VOLATILE,
INDISCREET
image SPECTRE
ring of CORONA
science of OPTICS
spirit of, Persia
ORMAZD, ORMUZD
type KLEIG, ARC
unit PYR, LUX,

LUMEN, HEFNER,
CARCEL, PHOT
without APHOTIC,
BLIND, DARK
lighter SCOW, BARGE,
BOAT, MATCH
paper SPILL
Light-Horse Harry
LEE
lighthouse PHARE,
FANAL, PHAROS,
BEACON, TOWER
lightning LEVIN, FLASH
rod ARRESTER
ligneous WOODY,
XYLOID
like ENJOY, FANCY,
LOVE, RELISH, DOTE,
PREFER, ESTEEM,
CHOOSE, ELECT,
RESPECT, SAME, RE-
SEMBLE, SIMILAR, AS,
COPY, EQUAL, AKIN
allied COGNATE
suffix INE, OID
likely COMELY,
SEEMLY, LIABLE, APT,
POSSIBLE, PROMISING,
PRONE, PROBABLE,
CREDIBLE, SUITABLE
likeness PORTRAIT,
PICTURE, EFFIGY,
IMAGE, GUISE, ICON,
SIMILARITY, (RE)-
SEMBLANCE, SIMILI-
TUDE, COPY, FACSIM-
ILE, COUNTERPART,
REPRESENTATION,
ANALOGY
likewise ALSO, DITTO,
TOO, BESIDES, MORE-
OVER, FURTHERMORE
Lilith's *successor* EVE
liliaceous *plant* LEEK,
ONION, SEGO, IRIS,
TULIP, YUCCA, SOTOL
lilliputian MIDGET,
DWARF, DIMINUTIVE,
SMALL, TINY
lily FLOWER, WOKAS,
WOCAS, ALOE, IXIA,
LIS, FLAG, IRIS,
ARUM, LOTUS, TIGER,
CALLA, SEGO
African corn IXIA
butterfly MARIPOSA,
SEGO
corn IXIA
family ALOE, BESSERA,
CAMAS, SQUILL,
LILIACEAE

genus HOSTA, SCILLA,
ALOE, BESSERA
leaf PAD
palm TI, TOI
pond KELP
shaped like CRINOID
water LOTUS,
CASTALIA, NELUMBO,
WOKAS, WOCAS,
NYMPHAEA
lily maid of Astolat
ELAINE
lily-of-the-valley *root-
stock* PIP
limacea SLUGS, SNAILS
limax, *genus of* SLUGS
limb ARM, LEG,
BRANCH, BOUGH,
MANUS, WING, FIN,
MEMBER, EXTREMITY,
SCAMP, IMP, SHOOT
absence of AMELIA
adapted for swimming
NECTOPOD
to fetter GYVE, CLIP,
MANACLE, HANDCUFF,
SHACKLE, HOBBLE,
TIE
without ACOLOUS
limbate BORDERED
limber LITHE, PLIANT,
AGILE, LIMP, SUPPLE,
FLACCID, PLIABLE,
FLEXIBLE, CARRIAGE
limbo HELL, JAIL,
PRISON, LIMBUS
lime CALCIUM, CITRUS,
LINDEN, TEIL, TREE,
FRUIT, ALKALI
pertaining to
CALCAREOUS, SLAKED,
OOLITIC
slake HYDRATE
tree LINDEN, TEIL,
BASS
turn into CALCIFY
wild fruit COLIMA
limen THRESHOLD
limestone LIAS, MALM,
DOLOMITE, OOLITE,
SILICA, CAEN, POROS,
BALA
crystalline MARBLE
Irish CALP
limicoline *bird* AVOCET
limit REGULATE, FIX,
END, CONFINE, AS-
SIGN, RESTRAIN, RE-
STRICT, PRESCRIBE,
BOURN, BRIM, BRINK,
LINE, POINT, EDGE,
RANGE, MARGIN,

AMBIT, BORDER,
FRONTIER, BOUND-
(ARY), TERMINUS,
CIRCUMSCRIBE,
QUALIFY, DEFINE,
HINDER
combining form ORI
limited FEW, FINITE,
LOCAL, TRAIN, SMALL,
SCANT, RESTRICTED,
TOPICAL, RESTRAINED,
CONDITIONED, NAR-
ROW, CIRCUMSCRIBED
to certain area
TOPOPOLITAN, TOPO-
GRAPHICAL, REGIONAL,
PROVINCIAL
limn DEPICT, DRAW,
PAINT, DESCRIBE,
DELINEATE, PORTRAY,
ILLUMINATE, DECO-
RATE
limp FLABBY, FLACCID,
HALT, SOFT, FLIMSY,
LOOSE, SLACK, RE-
LAXED, HITCH, HOB-
BLE, WILTED,
FLEXIBLE
limpid CRYSTAL,
CLEAR, (PEL)LUCID,
PURE, SHEER, TRANS-
PARENT, TRANSLUCENT
linden LIME, LIN, TEIL,
LINN, TREE
Europe TEIL
line(s) MARK, ROUTE,
CORD, TAPE, WIRE,
CABLE, ROW, FILE,
RANGE, TRAIN,
DIVISION, LIMIT,
BORDER, BOUNDARY,
STRING, RAILROAD,
EQUATOR, ROPE,
STROKE, STREAK,
EDGE, COURSE, KIN-
SHIP, DESCENT, CON-
TOUR, LINEAMENT,
METIER, WORK, TRADE,
OCCUPATION, IN-
TEREST, STUFF, WAD
as ball of thread
CLEW
combining form
STICH(O)
cutting SECANT
fish SNELL, CORD
hair LEGER, SERIF,
CERIPH
joining barometric
ISOBAR
junction of SEAM,
RAPHE, UNION,

SYNCHONDROSIS,
SUTURE
math. VECTOR
not forming angle
AGONE
not meeting curve
ASYMPTOTE
of color STREAK,
STRIPE
*of no magnetic decli-
nation* AGONE,
AGONIC
of soldiers CORDON,
RANK, FILE
pertaining to LINEAR
similar temperature
ISOTHERE
the inside CEIL, FUR
thin STRIA
waiting CUE, QUEUE
with bricks REVET
with stone PAVE,
STEAN, STEEN
lineage BLOOD, LINE,
RACE, STOCK, SIB,
STRAIN, KIN(DRED),
BIRTH, DESCENT,
PROGENY, FAMILY,
SUCCESSION,
ANCESTRY, PEDIGREE,
KINSHIP
linen NAPERY, GULIX,
BARRAS, CRASH,
DOWLAS, LINGERIE,
NAPKINS, CLOTHS,
CLOTHES, SCRIM,
FABRIC, SHEETS,
THREAD
closet EWERY
coarse LOCKRAM,
BARRAS, DOWLAS
fabric SCRIM
fiber FLAX
fine CAMBRIC,
DAMASK, LAWN
household NAPERY
in charge of NAPERER
room EWERY
sail DUCK, CANVAS
Spanish CREA
table NAPERY, NAP-
KINS
tape INKLE
vestment ALB, AMICE
weaver, Biblical HURI
liner SHIP, VESSEL,
SHIM, BALL, HIT,
CASING, FACING
ling BURBOT, HAKE,
EELPOUT, FISH,
HEATHER

linger DELAY, DWELL,
HOVER, LAG, DALLY,
DRAG, CREEP, TARRY,
WAIT, REMAIN, ABIDE,
LOITER, PROCRAS-
TINATE, DAWDLE,
HESITATE, SAUNTER,
STAY
lingo CANT, JARGON,
PATOIS, ARGOT, PAT-
TER, DIALECT, SLANG,
LANGUAGE, SPEECH
linguist POLYGLOT,
CLASSICIST,
PANTOGLOT,
PHILOLOGIST
liniment ARNICA,
LOTION, EMBROCATION
link TIE, BOND, NEXUS,
CONNECT, JOIN,
UNITE, YOKE, INTER-
LOCK, MARRY, RING,
LOOP, CHAIN, SECTION,
DIVISION
in series CATENATE,
GIMMAL, CHAIN
lint DOWN, FLAX,
FLUFF, HEMP, NAP,
RAVELINGS, FIBERS,
TILMA
lion(s) LEO, CAT,
HERO, STAR, FELIS,
CELEBRITY
Bantu SIMBA
group of PRIDE
mountain PUMA,
COUGAR
myth. GRIFFIN
young LIONET,
WHELP
lip EDGE, FOLD,
FLANGE, LABIUM,
MARGIN, BORDER,
SPOUT, IMPUDENCE,
INSOLENCE, SASS,
SPEECH, WORDS
casting ladle GEAT
combining form
CHIL(O), LABIO
groove in upper
AMABILE, FILTRUM
having broad ALATE
ornament PELELE,
LABRET
pertaining to LABIAL
under or lower JIB
lipid(e) CERIDE,
STERIDE, ESTER
lipoma TUMOR
liquefied by heat
FUSILE

liquefy RUN, FUSE, MELT, THAW, SOFTEN, DISSOLVE

liqueur MARC, RATAFIA, CURACAO, GENEPI, CREME, NOYAU, COGNAC, KUMMEL, ANISETTE, BENEDICTINE, CORDIAL
cask TUN

liquid FLUID, WATER(Y), FLOWING, LIMPID, CLEAR, DULCET, MELLIFLUOUS, MUSICAL, SMOOTH
combining form ELAIO
element BROMIN(E)
fatty oil OLEIN
measure PINT, QUART, GALLON, BARREL, CUP
thick DOPE, TAR
weak BLASH
without ANEROID, DRY

liquidate PAY, SETTLE, AMORTIZE, ADJUST, DISCHARGE, SELL, CLEAR

liquor RUM, RYE, ELIXIR, JUICE, STOCK, BROTH, GIN, GROG, VODKA, BEER, WINE, SCOTCH, BRANDY, ALE
add flavor to TUN
bottle case or cabinet for CELLARET
cane RUM, TAF(F)IA
fruit RATAFIA, WINE, APPLEJACK, BRANDY
malt PORTER, STOUT, ALE, BEER, BOCK, LAGER
must ARROPE
oriental ARRACK, SAKE
rice SAKE
small glass of PONY, SHOT

liripipe SCARF, TIPPET, HOOD

lisp *See under* "stammer"

lissom(e) LITHE, SLENDER, LIMBER, SUPPLE, SVELTE, AGILE, FLEXIBLE, NIMBLE

list HEEL, CANT, TILT, CAREEN, SLANT, SLOPE, TIP, ROLL, NAME, TABLE, ROTA, ROSTER, CATALOG(UE), DIRECTORY, AGENDA, CANON, REGISTER(Y), INVENTORY, SLATE, HARK, ATTEND, PLOW
as a council ROTA
law DOCKET, CALENDAR
of candidates LEET, SLATE
of officers or men ROSTER
of persons PANEL, DIRECTORY
writing SCRIP

listen EAVESDROP, HARK(EN), OBEY, HEED, (AT)TEND, LIST, BUG, HEAR, EAR

listening AUDIENT
post ECOUTE

listing EDGE, SELVAGE, STRIPS, ENLISTMENT, SAPWOOD

listlessness ACEDIA, ENNUI, APATHY, INDIFFERENCE, MELANCHOLIA, TORPOR, LANGUOR

Liszt FRANZ
composition TASSO

lit DYESTUFF, DYE, STAIN, BURNING, INTOXICATED

litany ECTENE, ORISON, ROGATION, EKTENE, PRAYER, SERVICE, MASS, SUPPLICATION

literal REAL, EXACT, TRUE, ACCURATE, UNVARNISHED, UNEMBELLISHED, PRECISE, PROSAIC

literary LETTERED, VERSED, LEARNED, BOOKISH, LITERATE, ERUDITE, SCHOLARLY
collection ANA
criticism IRONY, EPICRISIS, SATIRE
effort LUCUBRATION, OPUS, WORK, ARTICLE, THEME, POEM
extracts ANALECTA, ANALECTS
hack GRUB
master STYLIST
scraps ANA
style PROSE, VERSE

affectation in PURISM

literate LETTERED, INSTRUCTED, EDUCATED

lithe *See* "lissome"

lithograph CHROMO, PRINT, REPRODUCTION

Lithuania(n) BALT, LETT
capital VILNYUS
city KAUNAS, KOVNO
coin LIT(AS)
lowlander ZHMUD, SAMOGITIAN
seaport MEMEL

litter BIER, COFFIN, STRETCHER, SEDAN, PALANQUIN, COUCH, BED, MESS, STREW, SCATTER, MULCH, JUMBLE, UNTIDINESS, DISORDER, RUBBISH, BROOD

little SMALL, PUNY, TINY, WEE, SCANTY, MINUTE, MEAGER, THIN, SLIGHT, PETTY, WEAK, BRIEF, FEEBLE, MEAN, CONTEMPTIBLE, PALTRY, TRIVIAL, DIMINUTIVE, SHORT, INSIGNIFICANT, INCONSIDERATE, SELFISH, ILLIBERAL, UNIMPORTANT
combining form MICR(O)
Henry HAL

littoral REGION, SHORE, COAST, BEACH, BANK, RIPA

lituate FORKED

litura BLUR, BLOT

liturgical *basin or towel* LAVABO

liturgy RITE, FORM, RITUAL

litus SERF

live ABIDE, DWELL, SUBSIST, RESIDE, LODGE, STAY, REMAIN, CONTINUE, LAST, SURVIVE, BREATHE, EXIST, ACTIVE, LUSTY, ANIMATED, GLOWING, BURNING, VITAL, ENERGETIC, VIGOROUS, LIVELY, ALERT
oak ENCINA

liveliness PEP, GLEE, ACTIVITY, VIVACITY, LILT, RAPIDITY, BRISK-

NESS, ANIMATION,
SPIRIT, EFFERVES-
CENCE
lively PERKY,
SPRY, AGILE, GAY,
CHEERFUL, GRIG,
BRISK, SPIRITED, YARE,
ACTIVE, NIMBLE,
QUICK, SPORTIVE,
VIGOROUS, VIVID,
VIVACIOUS, ENERGETIC,
EXCITING, ANIMATED,
SPRIGHTLY, BLITHE,
JOLLY, FROLICSOME,
SPARKLING, AIRY,
PIQUANT, BUOYANT,
LIGHTHEARTED, KEEN,
BRILLIANT, INTENSE
air LILT
music VIVO, ANIMATO,
ANIMOSO
liven CHEER, ROUSE,
ANIMATE
liver HEPAR, ORGAN
disease CIRRHOSIS,
HEPATITIS, JAUNDICE
pertaining to HEPATIC
secretion BILE
livid ASHEN, PALE,
PALLID, WAN, DIS-
COLORED
living EXTANT, VITAL,
QUICK, ALIVE, EXIST-
ING, FLOWING *See*
"live"
again REDIVIVUS
capable of VIABLE
dead ZOMBI, GHOST,
PHANTOM
in deep sea BATHYBIC
in seclusion
EREMITISM
Livistona *palm* FAN
Livonian LIV, LETT,
ESTH
lixiviate LEACH,
ALKALINE, LIXIVIAL
lixivium LYE, ALKALI,
BUCK
liza MULLET
lizard(s) GILA, NEWT,
EFT, SKINK, GECKO,
GUANA, SAUVEGARDE,
IGUANA, ANOLI,
CHAMELEON, MONI-
TOR, URAN
agamoid DAB(B),
HARDIM
beaded GILA
climbing IGUANA
combining form
SAUR(O)

Egypt ADDA, SKINK
fabulous winged
DRAGON, BASILISK
genus UTA, AGAMA
island of giant
KOMODO
Mexico BASILISK
monitor URAN,
VARAN(US), ANOLI
Old World AGAMA,
SEPS
Philippine IBID
sand ADDA, SKINK
serpent SEPS
spiny DAB(B)
star red HARDIM,
AGAMA
tropical AGAMA
veranoid WARAN,
GRISCUS
wall TARENTE, GECKO
llama ALPACA
wild GUANACO,
VICUNA
llano PLAIN, PRAIRIE,
LOWLAND
lo ECCE, SEE, BEHOLD,
OBSERVE, LOOK
loach COBITIS, FISH
family CARP
load FREIGHT, DOPE,
CARK, ONUS, CHARGE,
LADE, JAG, CARGO,
ONERATE, BURDEN,
ENCUMBER, CLOG,
FILL, WEIGHT, PACK,
PRESSURE, INCUBUS,
OPPRESS
loaf DRONE, LOLL,
IDLE, LOUNGE, BREAD,
MASS
loam SOIL, DIRT,
EARTH
calcareous (yellow)
LOESS
constituent of CHALK,
CLAY, SOIL, LIME,
SAND
India REGUR
loath AVERSE, ADVERSE,
RELUCTANT, UN-
WILLING, INDISPOSED,
DISINCLINED
loathe ABHOR, DETEST,
HATE, SCORN,
ABOMINATE
loathsome CLOYING,
FOUL, VILE, ODIOUS,
DETESTABLE, DIS-
GUSTING, NAUSEOUS,
REPULSIVE, OF-

FENSIVE, REVOLTING,
ABHORRENT
lob PITCH, TOSS,
STRIKE, DROOP, HANG,
THROW
lobby CORRIDOR, HALL,
VESTIBULE, FOYER,
ENTRY, SOLICIT,
INFLUENCE, PERSUADE
loblolly PINE, TREE
lobster *claw* CHELA,
NIPPER
eggs CORAL, ROE
female HEN
last somite of TELSON
part of THORAX, CLAW
related to BARNACLE,
CRAB, SHRIMP, CRAY-
FISH, LANGOUSTE
trap POT, CORF, CREEL
local EDAPHIC,
LIMITED, NARROW,
RURAL, TRAIN,
RESTRICTED,
CONFINED,
PROVINCIAL,
REGIONAL, SECTIONAL,
CHAPTER
court GEMOT
locale VENUE, SITE,
LOCUS, PLACE, SPOT,
LOCALITY
locality AREA, PLACE,
DISTRICT, NEIGHBOR-
HOOD, SITE, SITUS,
SPOT, ZONE, BELT,
TRACT, SECTOR,
REGION, ENVIRONS,
PURLIEU, POSITION,
SITUATION
confined to particular
ENDEMIC
locate FIND, PLACE,
SITE, SETTLE,
ESTABLISH, SET, DIS-
COVER
location SPOT, SITE,
BASE, POSITION,
PLACE, STATION,
LOCALITY, SITUATION
loch LAKE, POND, BAY,
MERE, INLET, CREEK
lock HASP, COTTER,
BOLT, BUTTON,
RINGLET, CURL,
TUFT, TRESS, FASTEN,
DETENT, BIND, SE-
CURE, JOIN, UNITE,
HIDE, GRAPPLE, HUG,
EMBRACE, CLASP,
JAM

detached, of wool
FRIB
locker, *archery equip-
ment* ASCHAM
lockjaw TETANUS,
TRISMUS
locksman WARDEN,
TURNKEY
locomotive *cowcatcher*
PILOT
heavy MOGUL
locomotor ataxia
TABES
Locrine's *daughter*
SABRINA
father BRUT
locus AREA, AXODE,
RANK, SITE, PLACE,
LOCALITY, DRUG,
POINT
locust WETA,
SAWYER, CICAD(A),
GRASSHOPPER,
CRICKET, KOWHAI,
CAROB, INSECT,
TREE
tree ACACIA, CAROB,
COURBARIL, KOWHAI
lode VEIN, LEDGE,
DEPOSIT
cavity VUG
lodge ROOM, HARBOR,
ROOST, SHELTER,
HOUSE, HUT, COT-
TAGE, CABIN, DORM,
BARRACKS, BILLET,
DEN, LAIR, CAVERN,
QUARTER, SOJOURN,
ACCOMMODATE, STOW,
ENCAMP, ABIDE,
DWELL, RESIDE,
BOARD, ENTERTAIN,
SETTLE, SOCIETY
*uninitiated in free-
masonry* COWAN
lofty HIGH, ANDEAN,
TOWERING, EMINENT,
TALL, ALPINE,
NOBLE, EXALTED,
ELEVATED, GRAND,
SUBLIME, STATELY,
PROUD, DISTANT,
HAUGHTY, ARROGANT,
DIGNIFIED, IMPOSING,
MAJESTIC
nest AERIE, EYRY,
EYRIE
log *contest* ROLEO
measure SCALAGE
revolve floating BIRL
roller DECKER,
BIRLER

split PUNCHEON
tool to roll CANT
HOOK, PEAV(E)Y
to skid TODE
logarithm *base* TEN
inventor NAPIER
unit BEL
logger's *boot* PAC
sled TODE,
TRAVOIS
logic, *affirmative*
PONENT
Aristotelian FORMAL,
ORGANON
Baconian INDUCTIVE
omission of step in
SALTUS
logical SANE, VALID,
COGENT, LUCID,
SOUND, CLEAR, CON-
SISTENT, DIALECTICAL,
COHERENT, PROBABLE,
LIKELY, REASONABLE
logion MAXIM, SAY-
ING, DOCTRINE,
TRUTH
lohan ARHAT, MONK
Lohengrin's *bride*
ELSA
loincloth MALO,
IZAR, PAREU,
DHOTI
Loire, *city on* OR-
LEANS, TOURS
tributary INDRE,
CHER
loiter POKE, LAG,
LINGER, IDLE, DALLY,
DAWDLE, DELAY,
WAIT, TARRY, SAUN-
TER, DILLYDALLY
Loki's *mother* NAAL
son NARE
Lolo NOSU
Lombardy *king* AL-
BOIN
lomboy PLUM
London airport
HEATHROW
art gallery TATE
club KITKAT
district SOHO
foreign quarter SOHO
hawker COASTER,
MUN
street FLEET
suburb KEW, EALING
subway TUBE
Lone Star State TEXAS
lonely DESOLATE,
DREARY, LONE, SOLI-
TARY, (FOR)LORN,

SECLUDED, INFRE-
QUENTED, ISOLATED,
FORSAKEN, DESERTED,
DEPRESSED
combining form
EREM(O)
long PROLIX, WORDY,
EXTENDED, LENGTHY,
PROTRACTED, PRO-
LONGED, TEDIOUS,
SLOW, WORRY, GRAVE,
ACHE, HONE, YEARN,
PINE, YEN, ASPIRE,
HANKER, DESIRE,
THIRST, WISH, WANT,
COVET, PANT
ago YORE
discourse DESCANT
life LONGEVITY
limbed RANGY, LEGGY
lived VIVA, VIVE
since YORE
story RIGMAROLE
suffering MEEK,
PATIENT, FORBEAR-
ING
Tom GUN, TREE,
TITMOUSE, BIRD
loo PAM, GAME
look SEEK, SEARCH,
EYE, VIEW, SCAN, SEE,
WATCH, GAZE, GLANCE,
OGLE, EXAMINE, IN-
SPECT, OBSERVE, BODE,
KEN, PORE, PRY,
SEEM, APPEAR(ANCE),
ASPECT, EXPECT,
HOPE, AWAIT, MIEN,
BEARING, MANNER,
POSE, FACE, AIR, EX-
PRESSION
obliquely SKEW,
SQUINT
pryingly PEER, PEEK,
PEEP, KEEK
steadily GAZE, SCAN,
STARE
lookout CROW'S-NEST,
CONNER, TURRET,
SCOUT, CUPOLA, VIEW,
PROSPECT, TOWER,
SENTINEL, GUARD,
SPY
loom APPEAR, SEEM,
EMERGE, WEAVE,
MODERATE, GENTLE,
LOON
harness or heddles
LEAF, CAAM
loon DIVER, GREBE,
GUILLEMOT, AUK,

BIRD, LOUT, DOLT, SIMPLETON
genus GAVIA
loop TAB, ANSA, RING, CIRCLE, NOOSE, KNOT, AMBIT, BIGHT, FOLD, BEND, LINK, CROOK, STITCH, TURN, EYE, CURVE
fabric TERRY
lace PICOT
lariat HONDA, HONDO(O)
rope BIGHT
running NOOSE
loophole MUSE, MEUSE, PLEA, OPENING, SLIT, ALIBI, EXCUSE, APERTURE, PRETEXT, OUTLET
loose BAGGY, SLACK, LIMP, FLABBY, FREE, OPEN, UNCONFINED, UNTIE, ABSOLVE, UNBIND, UNFASTEN, UNDO, UNLOCK, LIBERATE, RELEASE, (RE)LAX, SLACKEN, DETACH, DISENGAGE, CARELESS, VAGUE, REMISS, NEGLIGENT, IMMORAL, LICENTIOUS, WANTON, DISSOLUTE, LEWD, EASY
ends DAGS, SLACK, LAX, FREE
jointed LANKY
loosen EASE, RELAX, UNDO, UNTIE, OPEN, RELEASE, SLACKEN, DETACH, FREE, LIBERATE
loot BOOTY, PLUNDER, SPOIL(S), SWAG, PRIZE, PILLAGE, RANSACK, SACK, ROB, RIFLE, STEAL
lop SNIP, CUT, HANG, DROOP, OBTRUNCATE, DOCK, CROP, PRUNE, CURTAIL, DETACH
loquacious VOLUBLE, GLIB, VOCAL, GARRULOUS, TALKATIVE, BABBLING, CHATTERING
loquat BIWA, POME, FRUIT, TREE
lord LIEGE, PEER, EARL, BARON, VISCOUNT, MARQUIS,

NOBLE(MAN), RULER, GOVERNOR, DOMINEER
of a sanjak BEY
oriental KHAN
privileged PALATINE
wife of LADY
lordly DESPOTIC, UPPISH, PROUD, HAUGHTY, NOBLE, LOFTY, GRAND, DIGNIFIED, MAJESTIC, IMPERIOUS, ARROGANT, OVERBEARING
Lord's Prayer PATER NOSTER
lore WISDOM, ERUDITION, SCIENCE, LEARNING, KNOWLEDGE, TRADITION
lorelei SIREN, CHARMER
lorica CUIRASS, CORSELET, SHELL, COVERING
loris LEMUR, SLOTH
lose MISS, FORFEIT, SPILL, MISLAY, WASTE, SQUANDER, FAIL, ESTRANGE, DISAPPEAR, MISPLACE
interest TIRE, FAG, FLAG
loss DEFEAT, FORFEITURE, LEAK, MISFORTUNE, INJURY, TROUBLE, DAMAGE, WASTE, FAILURE, PRIVATION, DEATH, DEPRIVATION, DESTRUCTION, CASUALTY
lost MISSED, WASTED, GONE, LORN, ASEA, PERPLEXED, RUINED, DAMNED, OVERWHELMED, MISSING, ABANDONED, REPROBATE, IRRECLAIMABLE, SUBVERTED, DISSIPATED, CORRUPT
color FADED, PALED, BLANCHED, ETIOLATED
lot SCAD, SHARE, DOOM, FATE, BATCH, SUM, CHANCE, FORTUNE, CHOICE, PLOT, MUCH, DESTINY, LUCK, HAP, LAND, PORTION, HAZARD, PARCEL, PART, BUNDLE
lots LOADS, REAMS, GOBS, SCADS

divination by SORCERY, SORTILEGE
Lot's *father* HARAN
sister MILCAH
lottery CHANCE, PRIZE, RAFFLE, BINGO, LOTTO
choice in GIG
prize TERN, PURSE
lotto KENO, BINGO, GAME
lotus LOTE, NELUMBO, TREFOIL, MELILOT, PLANT, FLOWER
tree JUJUBE, SADR
water CHINQUAPIN
Louis XVI *nickname* VETO
Louis Viaud, *pen name* LOTI
Louise de la Ramee, *pen name* OUIDA
Louisiana(n) PELICAN, CREOLE
account book BILAN
bayou TECHE
county PARISH
parish ACADIA, ALLEN, CADDO, GRANT, SABINE, TENSAS, WINN
lounge LOLL, LOAF, IDLE, LAZE, RECLINE, DAWDLE, SETTEE, DIVAN, SOFA, ROOM
louse *genus* APHIS
immature NIT
plant APHID
lout BEND, BOW, GAWK, HIT, LOBBY, LURK, BOOR, CHURL, CLOWN, BUMPKIN, LUBBER, CLODHOPPER
love DOTE, AMOUR, (EN)AMOR, WOO, FANCY, PIETY, ARDOR, ZEAL, ENJOY, ADORE, LIKE, ADMIRE, AFFECTION, PASSION, DEVOTION, ATTACHMENT, FONDNESS, FLAME, CHARITY, REGARD, DEAR, DARLING, SWEETHEART *See* "lover"
affair AMOUR
Anglo-Irish GRA
apple TOMATO
combining form PHIL(O)

god, goddess See under "god" or "goddess"
knot AMORET
of fine arts VIRTU
of offspring PHILO-PROGENEITY
parental PHILOPRO-GENITIVENESS
potion PHILTER
tennis game ZERO
lovebird PARROT
lover BEAU, MINION, ROMEO, ADMIRER, FLAME, SWEETHEART, PARAMOUR, INAMO-RATO, BELOVED, SWAIN, LEMAN
"Love's Labor Lost"
character BIRON, DUMAIN, BOYET, DULL, COSTARD, MARIA
loving AMOROUS, AMATORY, AMATIVE, FOND, EROTIC, ARDENT, DOTING, LEAL, TRUE, BROTHERLY, AFFEC-TIONATE, KIND
combining form PHIL(O)
cup TIG, TYG, PRIZE
low BASE, SNEAKY, MEAN, ORRA, BAS, VILE, VULGAR, COARSE, DEBASED, GROSS, CHEAP, SOFT, SICK, COMMON, HUM-BLE, ABJECT, MENIAL, FEEBLE, WEAK, DE-PRESSED, BLUE, SAD, MOO, INFERIOR
lowan LEIPOA, MALLEE, BIRD
lower DIM, DIP, DEMIT, RESIGN, DEBASE, NETHER, DEMOTE, REDUCE, ABASE, SINK, DE-GRADE, DISGRACE, HUMILIATE, DECREASE, LESSEN, FROWN, GLOWER, DIMINISH, WEAKEN
deck ORLOP
topsail VAIL
lowest NETHERMOST
class animal life AM(O)EBA
point NADIR

low-lived MEAN, BASE, COMMON *See* "base"
lox SALMON, FISH
loy SPADE, SLICK
loyal LEAL, STA(U)NCH, TRUE, LIEGE, FAITHFUL, DEVOTED, DEPENDA-BLE, CONSTANT, OBEDIENT
loyalty TROTH, FIDELITY, FEALTY, HOMAGE, PIETY, AL-LEGIANCE, DEVOTION, CONSTANCY
Loyalty island UVEA (UEA), LIFU
lozenge PASTIL(LE), TROCHE, RHOMB, DIAMOND
lubber BOOR, CHURL, GAWK, LOUT, CLOWN
Lubeck LUBS, COIN, LUBISH
lubricate OIL, GREASE, ANOINT, SOAP, WAX
Lucca, *saint* ANSELM
lucern(e) MEDIC, FODDER, ALFALFA
lucid BRIGHT, PLAIN, CLEAR, VIVID, LIMPID, SHINING, RADIANT, LUMINOUS, RESPLENDENT, LU-CENT, PELLUCID, SANE, TRANSPARENT, DISTINCT, RATIONAL
lucidity SANITY, CLARITY, PERSPICUITY
lucifer SATAN, EVIL, MATCH, VENUS, PHOSPHOROUS
Lucius Domitius Ahenobarbus NERO
luck FORTUNE, HAP, CHANCE, LOT, SUC-CESS, BREAK, FATE, DESTINY, PROSPERITY, HAZARD, ACCIDENT
charm SWASTIKA
Irish CESS
lucky CANNY, HAPPY, BENIGN, MEET, BLESSED, FORTUNATE, AUSPICIOUS, FAVORA-BLE, PROPITIOUS
stroke FLUKE, STRIKE
lucrative FAT, PAYING, PROFITABLE, REMU-

NERATIVE, GAINFUL, PRODUCTIVE
lucre GAIN, GREED, PROFIT, MONEY, PELF, EMOLUMENT, RICHES, WEALTH
ludicrous JESTING, RISIBLE, COMIC, DROLL, SILLY, FUNNY, QUEER, LAUGHABLE, RIDICU-LOUS, FARCICAL, AB-SURD, BURLESQUE
Ludolphian number PI
lug EAR, LOOP, HANDLE, CARRY, TOTE, TUG, PULL, HAUL, HALE, DRAG, WORM, LOUT, BLOCK-HEAD
lugubrious MOURN-FUL, DISMAL, DOLE-FUL, SAD
lukewarm TEPID, INDIFFERENT, COOL, UNCONCERNED
lull *See under* "res-pite" SUBSIDE, CEASE, STILL, ABATE, HUSH, ALLAY, MITIGATE, CALM, SOOTHE, COMPOSE, ASSUAGE, INTERVAL, CESSA-TION, TRANQUILIZE
lumber TIMBER, LOGS, SCAFFOLDING, PLOD, ENCUMBER, TRUDGE, TRASH, RUBBISH, RUMBLE
State MAINE
lumberman SAWYER, CUTTER, LOGGER
hook PEAV(E)Y, CANT HOOK
shoe PAC, LARRIGAN
sled TRAVOIS, TODE, WYNN
luminary STAR, SUN, VIP, MOON, INTEL-LECTUAL
lummox BOOR, LOUT, YAHOO, BUNGLER
lump CLOT, MASS, NODULE, WAD, NUB, HUNK, CLOD, CHUNK, PROTUBERANCE, SWELLING, LOB, BARGE, TUMOR
clay CLOD, CLAG
on tree BURL

lumpish DULL, STOLID, INERT, GROSS, STUPID, HEAVY, BULKY, INACTIVE, SLUGGISH

lunacy MADNESS, MANIA, FOLLY, INSANITY, DERANGEMENT, CRAZINESS, FOOLISHNESS

lunar *crater* LINNE
sea or basin MARE
mountain(s) JURA, ATLAI, HAEMUS, APENNINE

luncheon SNACK, TIFFIN, TEA
dish SALAD, ASPIC

lung(s) LIGHTS, GILL, PULMO
combining form PULMO
sound RALE, BRUIT

lurch SWAY, ROLL, PITCH, SWING, SHIFT, JOLT, CAREEN, STAGGER, DISAPPOINT, DECEIVE

lure COAX, BAIT, DECOY, TEMPT, ATTRACT, SNARE, ENTICE, TRAP, INVITE, INVEIGLE, SEDUCE

lurer SIREN, TEMPTER, ENTICER

lurid RED, DARK, GRISLY, GRIM, GHASTLY, PALE, WAN, SALLOW, ASHEN, VIVID, TERRIBLE, GLOOMY, DISMAL, SHOCKING, STARTLING, SENSATIONAL

lurk SKULK, SNEAK, PROWL, SLINK, HIDE, STEAL

lurking LATENT

lush DRUNK, JUICY, SUCCULENT, RICH, LAVISH, LUXURIANT, LUXURIOUS, PROFUSE

luster, lustre GLOSS, NAIF, GLASS, SHEEN, FAME, DISTINCTION, GLAZE, GLORY, GLARE, POLISH, BRILLIANCY, GLITTER, BRIGHTNESS, BEAUTY, SPLENDOR, IRIDESCENCE, CHANDELIER
bronzelike SCHILLER

of uncut gems NAIF

lusterless DIM, DULL, MAT

lustrous BRIGHT, NITID, RESPLENDENT, SILVERY, BRILLIANT, SILKY, NAIF, SHINING, LUMINOUS, GLOSSY, RADIANT
Pearl ORIENT

lusty HEARTY, ROBUST, STOUT, STRONG, STURDY, SOUND, ATHLETIC, HALE, VIGOROUS, HEALTHFUL

lute CEMENT, CLAY, TAR, ASOR, PANDORE, THEORBO, GUITAR, UKULELE, RING

lutianoid *fish* SESI

luxuriant RANK, FERTILE, UBERTY, RICH, LUSH, ORNATE, PROFUSE, LAVISH, FLORID, EXUBERANT, PLENTIFUL, PLENTEOUS, OPULENT, PROLIFIC, TEEMING

luxuriate BASK, GLORY, REVEL, FLOURISH, DELIGHT, INDULGE

luxury EASE, JOY, DELIGHT, VOLUPTUOUSNESS, SENSUALITY, EXTRAVAGANCE, RICHNESS, GRATIFICATION
lover of SYBARITE, VOLUPTUARY

Luzon *See* "Philippine"

lyam LEASH

lyard GRAY

lycantrope WEREWOLF

lycee ECOLE, ACADEMY, SCHOOL

Lydia, *anc. capital* SARDIS
king CROESUS, GYGES

lydian EFFEMINATE, GENTLE, SOFT, VOLUPTUOUS, SENSUAL

lye BUCK, ALKALI, LIXIVIUM

lying RECUMBENT, FALSE, ABED, MENDACIOUS, DECUMBENT,

EQUIVOCATING, RECLINING
on back SUPINE

lymph CASEIN, SERUM, PLASMA

Lynette's *knight* GARETH

lynx CARACAL, PISHU, CAT
eyed OXYOPIA

lyre TRIGON, HARP, REBEC, SHELL
bird genus MENURA
like instrument CITHARA, SACKBUT, ZITHER

lyric MELIC, POEM, TUNEFUL, MELODIOUS, MUSICAL, OPERATIC
muse ERATO
ode LAY, SONG, EPODE
of 13 lines RONDEAU
poem MELIC
poet ODIST

M

M EM, MU, EMMA, THOUSAND

mabolo PLUM, CAMAGON

macabre GHASTLY, GRIM, LURID, GRUESOME, HORRIBLE

macaco LEMUR, MONKEY

Macao *coin* AVO

macaque KRA, RHESUS, MONKEY, BRUH

macaroni NOODLE, PASTE, FOOD, DUCK, DANDY, DUDE, SWELL, FOOL, BUFFOON, FOP

macaw ARARAUNA, ARA, ARARA, ARRA, PARROT, BIRD

"Macbeth" *character* BANQUO, MACDUFF, LENNOX, ROSS, ANGUS, HECATE

mace GAVEL, STAFF, STICK, MALLET, CLUB, ROD, SPICE, WEAPON, SCEPTRE
bearer BEADLE, MACER
nutmeg (ARIL)LODE
royal SCEPTRE

Macedonia, *anc. capital*
PELLA
city or town
BER(O)EA, EDESSA,
DRAMA, PYDNA
king ABGAR
macerate RET, SOAK,
STEEP, SOFTEN, OP-
PRESS, VEX, TOR-
MENT, MORTIFY
machete BOLO, KNIFE,
FISH
Machiavellian CRAFTY,
DECEITFUL, TREACH-
EROUS, CUNNING,
GUILEFUL, WILY
work PRINCE
machinate PLOT,
CABAL, SCHEME,
DESIGN, TRICK, PLAN,
CONTRIVE, DEVISE
machination CABAL,
INTRIGUE, CON-
SPIRACY, ARTIFICE,
PLOT, SCHEME
machine AUTOMATON,
SYSTEM, PARTY,
BLOC, CAR, VEHICLE,
MOTOR, DEVICE,
CABAL, MILL, GADGET,
ENGINE, TOOL,
ORGANIZATION
finishing EDGER
glazing CALENDER
grain cleaner AWNER
gun GATLING,
MAXIM, STEN
maturing cloth AGER
*ore dressing or
separating* VANNER
part CAM, TAPPET,
ROTOR, PISTON,
WHEEL
political PARTY, BLOC
rubber EXTRUDER
softening clay MAL-
AXATOR
macilent LEAN, THIN,
EMACIATED,
MARASMIC
mackerel *chub* TINKER
genus SCOMBER
horse SAUREL,
TUNNY, JUREL,
BLUEFISH
large CERO, PETO,
PINTADO, WAHOO
like SCAD, BONITO
net SPILLER
small SPIKE,
BLINKER, TINKER

Spanish SIERRA
young SPIKE
mackle, macula
BLOTCH, STAIN, SPOT,
BLOT, BLEMISH,
BLUR
mad INSANE, CRAZY,
WILD, RABID, ANGRY,
IRATE, WRATHFUL,
ENRAGED, FURIOUS,
FOOLISH, DOTING,
INFATUATED, UNWISE,
EAGER, GAY, HILARI-
OUS, DISTRACTED,
DEMENTED, DE-
RANGED, LUNATIC,
RAVING, MANIACAL,
FRENZIED, FRANTIC,
EXCITED, RASH,
SENSELESS
Madagascar *animal*
FOUSSA, TENREC,
LEMUR, INDRI,
TENDRAC
fiber palm RAFFIA
native HOVA
tribe HOVA,
MALAGASY
madam(e) SENORA,
MUM, MA'AM, MIS-
TRESS, WOMAN, LADY,
WIFE, DAME,
DON(N)A, FRAU,
FROW
Butterfly CHO-CHO-
(SAN)
Gynt ASE
madcap HOTSPUR,
RASH, ADVENTUROUS,
WILD, RECKLESS, IM-
PULSIVE
madden INCENSE,
EXCITE, CRAZE, VEX,
PROVOKE, INFURIATE,
ENRAGE
madder (and dye)
AAL, ALIZARIN,
PLANT
genus RUBIA
root pigment MULL
tree BANGCAL,
CHINCONA
Madeira Island *capital*
FUNCHAL
wind LESTE
wine TINTA *See
under* "wine"
madhouse BEDLAM,
CHAOS, ASYLUM
madness IRE, FRENZY,
RAGE, MANIA, ANGER,
RABIES, EXCITEMENT,

FOLLY, INSANITY,
ABERRATION, DEMEN-
TIA, LUNACY, FURY,
RAPTURE, ENTHUSI-
ASM, DERANGEMENT,
DELIRIUM, EXTRAVA-
GANCE, AGITATION,
ECSTASY, DISTURB-
ANCE
madrepore CORAL,
FOSSIL
Madrid *promenade*
PRADO
madrigal GLEE, POEM,
ODE, VERSES, SONG,
LYRIC
Madrileno SENOR
maelstrom EDDY, CUR-
RENT, SWIRL, WHIRL-
POOL, TURMOIL
magazine TABLOID,
PUBLICATION, PERI-
ODICAL, JOURNAL,
BOOK, ARSENAL,
ARMORY, DEPOT,
WAREHOUSE,
REPOSITORY, STORE-
HOUSE, CHAMBER
maggot GRUB, LARVA,
CAPRICE, WHIM
Magi BALTHASAR,
GASPAR, MELCHIOR,
SAGES
magic ART, RUNE,
SHOW, SPELL, DIVINA-
TION, WITCHCRAFT,
WIZARDRY, THAU-
MATURGY, THEURGY,
SORCERY, NECRO-
MANCY, ENCHANT-
MENT, VOODOO
act of CONJURATION
cube NASIK
ejaculation OM,
SESAME
goddess of CIRCE
image SIGIL
lantern MEGASCOPE
pertaining to GOETIC
symbol PENTACLE,
CARACT
wand CADUCEUS
white THEURGY
word SESAME,
PRESTO, ABRACADABRA
magical CHARMING,
GOETIC, OCCULT,
BEWITCHING
magician THAUMA-
TURGE, SORCERER,
WITCH, WIZARD,
MAGI, MERLIN,

M
N

MANDRAKE, ENCHANTER, CONJURER, NECROMANCER
word *See under* "magic"
magistrate EDILE, CONSUL, PRAETOR, PRETOR, JUDGE, JUSTICE, ARCHON, EPHOR, ALCALDE, BAILIE, MAYOR, GOVERNOR, PREFECT, SYNDIC, PUISNE, CHIEF, DOGE *See* "judge"
Athens ARCHON
chief DOGE, JUDGE, JUSTICE
magna GREAT, GRAND
magnanimous GENEROUS, LIBERAL, NOBLE, EXALTED, HONORABLE, LOFTY, UNSELFISH
magnate MOGUL, TYCOON, BARON, LORD, GRANDEE, BIGWIG, TITAN, SHOGUN
magnesium *metasilicate* TALC
symbol MG
magnet LODESTONE, POLE, CHARMER
electro SOLENOID
type BAR, HORSESHOE
magnetic flux unit GAUSS
magnific PALATIAL, GRAND, POMPOUS, IMPOSING, EULOGISTIC, SUBLIME, ILLUSTRIOUS, VAST, DIGNIFIED, LOQUENT, HONORIFIC
magnify ENLARGE, LAUD, GLORIFY, INCREASE, EXAGGERATE, AGGRAVATE, EXPAND, SWELL, DILATE, EXTOL, PRAISE, OVERSTATE, AMPLIFY
magnitude SIZE, IMPORTANCE, EXTENT, GREATNESS, BIGNESS
magnolia, *Chinese* YULAN
magnum opus WORK, ACHIEVEMENT

Magog *ruler* GOG
magpie MADGE, PIET, PYAT, CHATTERER, SCOLD, BIRD
genus PICA
maguey CANTALA, ALOE, AGAVE, PLANT
drink PULQUE
Magyar HUNGARIAN
mahatma AR(A)HAT, GANDHI, SAGE
mah-jong(g) piece TILE
mahogany RATTEEN, TOON, TREE, WOOD
pine TOTARA
streak in ROE
Mahomet *See* "Mohammed"
Mahua butter PHULWA, FULWA
maid LASS, BONNIE, MISS, GIRL, DAMSEL, CHILD, SERVANT, LASSIE
lady's ABIGAIL
of Orleans JOAN, PUCELLE
maiden DAMSEL, FIRST, INITIAL, FRESH, NEW, MAID, MISS, GAL, BURD, VIRGIN, UNTRIED, UNUSED
name NEE
turned into heifer IO
into spider ARACHNE
mail POST, DAK, DAWK, LETTERS, PAPERS, CONSIGN, PROTECT, ARMOR
boat PACKET, AVISO
coat of ARMOR, HAUBERK, BYRNIE
maim MAYHEM, INJURE, HURT, CRIPPLE, MAR, SPOIL, MUTILATE, DISABLE, MANGLE
main PRIME, CHIEF, PRINCIPAL, LEADING, FOREMOST, DUCT, PIPE, CONDUIT, VITAL, POWER, STRENGTH, FORCE, BODY, SEA, OCEAN, POTENT, MIGHTY, SHEER, UTTER
point PITH, GIST, JET, NUB, KERNEL

Maine *bay* CASCO
city SACO, BANGOR, AUGUSTA, ORONO
college COLBY, BATES
county KNOX, WALDO, YORK
island ORRS
motto DIRIGO
symbol PINE
university town ORONO
maintain KEEP, HAVE, AID, ASSERT, DEFEND, ALLEGE, AVER, AVOW, SUSTAIN, AFFIRM, CONTINUE, PRESERVE, SUPPORT, (UP)HOLD, BEAR
maintainable TENABLE, DEFENSIBLE
maintenance AID, ALIMONY, (UP)-KEEP, SUPPORT, BEHAVIOR, BEARING, VINDICATION, SUSTENANCE, LIVELIHOOD, SUBSISTENCE, PROVISIONS, DEFENSE
maize ZEA, CORN
bread PIKI
genus ZEA
S. Africa MEALIES
majagua GUANA, HUAMAGA, MAHOE, BARU, TREE
majesty DIGNITY, SOVEREIGNTY, GRANDEUR, NOBILITY, POWER, STATELINESS
major GREATER, OFFICER *See* "chief"
-domo SENESCHAL, STEWARD, MC
music DUR, DITONE
majorano LANTANA, PLANT
Majorca *city* PALMA
island IVIZA, IBIZA
majority MOST, EXCESS, GREATER, AGE, SENIORITY, SUPERIORITY, PLURALITY, MASS, BULK, PREPONDERANCE
make CREATE, FORM, SHAPE, STYLE, FORGE, PLAN, COMPOSE, GENERATE, INDUCE, FASHION, FRAME, MO(U)LD, CONTRIVE, PRODUCE,

EXECUTE, CONSTRUCT,
BUILD, FABRI-
CATE, FORMULATE,
DEVISE, GET, CAUSE,
EFFECT, SUSTAIN,
ACCOMPLISH, FORCE,
STYLE, BRAND, GAIN,
COME, ARRIVE,
CONSTITUTE
over REVAMP,
REPAIR, REDO,
RENOVATE, REFASH-
ION, ALIENATE
make-believe MAGIC,
SHAM, PRETENSE,
FEINT, PRETEND,
FEIGN(ED), PRE-
TEXT, FICTION
makeshift STOPGAP,
RESORT, EXPEDIENT,
SUBSTITUTE
Malabar *canoe* TONEE
measure ADY
people (tribe) NAIR
malacca CANE
Malacca *measure*
ASTA
weight KIP
malachite BICE,
MINERAL
maladroit CLUMSY,
GAUCHE, INEPT,
BUNGLING, AWK-
WARD, UNHANDY,
GAFFE, UNSKILLFUL
malady DISEASE, DIS-
ORDER, AILMENT,
COMPLAINT, SICKNESS,
INDISPOSITION, ILL-
NESS
malapert BOLD,
SAUCY, SASSY,
IMPUDENT, RUDE,
FORWARD, FLIPPANT,
IMPERTINENT, IN-
SOLENT
malapropos INAP-
PROPRIATE, UNSEA-
SONABLE, INOP-
PORTUNE
malaria MIASMA,
CHILL, AGUE, FEVER
remedy QUININE,
ATABRINE
Malay(an) POLYNE-
SIAN, MALACCA
boat (lugger) TOUP
canoe PROA, PRAH
chief DATO, DATU,
DATTO
city or town IPOH
cloth BATIK

coin TARO
condition LATA
crane SARAS, SARUS
customary law ADAT
dagger CRIS, KRIS,
CREESE
dress SARONG
gibbon LAR
island BALI, JAVA,
BORNEO, PENANG,
TIMOR, SUMATRA
isthmus KRA
jacket BAJU
knife KRIS, BARONG
See "dagger" above
law ADAT
measure PAU
mental aberration
LATA
mountain TAHAN
negrito ATA
ox, wild BANTENG
palm ARENG, TARA
race TAGAL,
VISAYAN, TAGALOG
region PENANG
seacoast town MA-
LACCA
seafaring tribe
BAJAU
state JOHORE,
KEDAH, PERAK
title TUAN
tree DUKU, DURIAN,
TERAP, UPAS,
LANSEH, OHIA
tribe ARIPAS, ATA
ungulate TAPIR
malcontent FENIAN,
REB(EL), INSURGENT,
AGITATOR, UNEASY,
RESTLESS, DISSATIS-
FIED, REBELLIOUS,
DISCONTENTED
Maldive Island capital
MALE
male MAN, SIR,
HAND, STAMINAL,
MANLY, BOY, HE,
VIRILE, MASCULINE,
STRONG, VIGOROUS
bird TOM
figure supporting
column TELEMON
gelded GALT,
GELDING, STEER,
BARROW, EUNUCH
plant MAS
malediction ANATHE-
MA, CURSE, MALISON,
BAN, THREAT, IM-
PRECATION, SLANDER,

DENUNCIATION,
EXECRATION
malefactor CRIMINAL,
FELON, CULPRIT,
CONVICT, OUTLAW,
EVILDOER
malevolence, malev-
olent MALIGN,
BALEFUL, SINISTER,
HOSTILE, HOSTILITY,
ENVIOUS, EVIL,
HATING, ILL,
MALICE, MALICIOUS,
GRUDGE, SPITE, BAD,
HARMFUL, RANCOROUS
malice HATRED,
REVENGE, GRUDGE,
SPLEEN, ENMITY,
EVIL, ENVY,
RANCOR, SPITE,
MALEVOLENCE,
VENOM, PIQUE, BIT-
TERNESS, ANIMOSITY
malign LIBEL,
SLANDER, DEFAME,
VILIFY, ASPERSE,
REVILE, EVIL, BALE-
FUL, HARMFUL,
MALIGNANT, CA-
LUMNIATE
malignant ILL, EVIL,
HEINOUS, BAD, CAN-
CEROUS, VICIOUS,
MALEFIC, INIMICAL,
MALICIOUS, VIRULENT,
PERNICIOUS, DANGER-
OUS, HARMFUL
spirit KER
malignity RANCOR,
GRUDGE, VENOM,
VIOLENCE, SPITE,
SPLEEN, FATALITY,
DEADLINESS,
VIRULENCE
maline NET
malison CURSE, TOR-
MENT, MALEDICTION,
EXECRATION
malkin CAT, HARE,
SCARECROW, SLAT-
TERN, DRAB, MOP,
SPONGE
mallard genus ANAS,
DUCK
malleable SOFT,
PLIANT, PLIABLE,
YIELDING, AMENABLE,
ADAPTABLE, DUCTILE
mallet CLUB, MACE,
MAUL, GAVEL, HAM-
MER
hatter's BEATER

leaden MADGE
presiding officer's GAVEL
wooden BEETLE, MAUL
mallow SIDA, ALTEA, HOCK, MAW, PLANT
family OKRA, COTTON, HOLLYHOCK
malmsey MADEIRA, WINE, MALVASIA, GRAPE
malodorous OLID, FETID, NOISOME, PUTRID, MUSTY, RANK, FUSTY, OBNOXIOUS, STINKING
malt *drink* BEER, ALE, PORTER, LAGER, BOCK, STOUT
froth BARM, SUDS
infusion WORT
mixture MALTATE, ZYTHUM
pertaining to ALY
vinegar ALEGAR, WORT
Malta *island* GOZO, MELITA
wind GREGALE, LEVANTER
maltese CROSS, CAT, DOG, LACE
maltreat ABUSE, BEAT, MISUSE, MISTREAT
malus *family* APPLE, CRABAPPLE
malvaceous plant ALTHAEA, ESCOBA, MALLOW, OKRA, COTTON
malvasia GRAPE
mameluke SLAVE, SERVANT
mammal PRIMATE, APE, MAN, WHALE, LORIS, BEAR, CAT, DOG, BAT, DEER, TENREC, HARE *See* "animal"
aquatic DUGONG, MANATEE, DOLPHIN, WHALE, SEAL, PORPOISE, WALRUS
order CETACEA
Australia MARTEN, KANGAROO, ECHIDNA, KOALA, TAIT
badgerlike RATEL
catlike SERVAL, OCELOT, JAGUAR,

TIGER, CHEETAH, PANTHER, LION
cetacean DOLPHIN, WHALE, PORPOISE
civetlike GENET
domestic COW, HORSE, CAT, DOG
flying BAT
giraffelike OKAPI
gnawing MOUSE, RAT, VOLE, RODENT
Himalayan PANDA
India ZEBU, DHOLE, TIGER
insectivorous BAT
lower order MARSUPIAL
marine See "aquatic" *above*
marsupial TAPOA, KOALA, TAIT, OPOSSUM, KANGAROO, PHALANGER
nocturnal LEMUR, RATEL
Palestine DAMAN
raccoonlike COATI
sea See "aquatic" *above*
smallest SHREW
S. America TAYRA, AI, COATI, TAPIR
swine PECCARY, HOG, PIG
Tibetan OUNCE
water See "aquatic" *above*
mammock SCRAP, FRAGMENT, CHUNK, HILL
man BEING, HOMO, MALE, PERSON, BIPED, BOZO, GUY, BIRD, PLAYER, JACK, HUMAN, MASTER, HUSBAND, LOVER, SERVANT, VASSAL, VALET, INDIVIDUAL, SOMEBODY, PERSONAGE, EMPLOYEE, MATE, SOLDIER, SAILOR, RUN, BRACE, STRENGTHEN, FORTIFY, REINFORCE, HUMANITY, RACE
brazen (brass) TALOS, TALUS
combining form ANDR(O), ANTHROP(O)

elderly SIRE, SENIOR, GAFFER, GEEZER, NESTOR, DOTARD
-like object ANDROID, AUTOMATON, ROBOT
newly married BENEDICT
of all work FACTOTUM
of Blood and Iron BISMARCK
of letters LITERATUS, SAVANT, SCHOLAR, LITTERATEUR
of Ross KYRLE
with 100 eyes ARGUS
Man, Isle of, *capital* DOUGLAS
"Man Without a Country" NOLAN
author HALE
manage TEND, WIELD, OPERATE, RUN, RULE, WORK, HANDLE, USE, CONDUCT, CONTROL, CONTRIVE, DIRECT, AFFORD, GUIDE, LEAD, STEER, HANDLE, SUPERINTEND, GOVERN, ORDER, MANIPULATE, ADMINISTER, MANEGE
manageable DOCILE, YARE, TRACTABLE, TAMABLE, CONTROLLABLE, COMPLIANT, PLIANT
management CONDUCT, CARE, DISPOSAL, ECONOMY, OFFICE, CONTROL, ADMINISTRATION, GOVERNMENT, CHARGE
manager DIRECTOR, BOSS, GERENT, OPERATOR, OVERSEER, SCHEMER, MASTER, ECONOMIST
business GERENT, AGENT, MASTER, BOSS
manakin BIRD *See* "manikin"
manas EGO, MIND, SENSORIUM
Manchu tribe DAUR, DAURI
Manchurian town PENKI, AIGUN
manciple STEWARD, SLAVE, BONDMAN, PURVEYOR

mandarin's *residence*
YAMEN
mandate LAW,
EDICT, ORDER,
BEHEST, DICTATE,
COLONY, COMMAND,
COMMISSION,
AUTHORITY, PRE-
SCRIPT, WRIT,
PRECEPT, CHARGE,
INJUNCTION, DECREE,
BIDDING
Pope's RESCRIPT
mandible BEAK, JAW,
CHOP, BONE
mandrel ARBOR,
LATHE, BOBBIN,
SPINDLE, AXLE
miner's PICK
mandrill BABOON, APE
manducate CHEW,
MASTICATE, EAT
mane JUBA, ROACH,
BRUSH, SHAG, STUB-
BLE, HAIR
manege gait TROT,
LOPE, VOLT
maneuver ARTIFICE,
RUSE, TRICK, TACTIC,
SHIFT, PLOT, SCHEME,
MANAGE, DEVICE,
RESORT, STRATAGEM,
BATTLE, MOVEMENT
manganese symbol MN
mange ITCH, SCAB,
SCURVY
cause ACARID, MITE
manger BIN, BOX, CRIB,
BUNKER, RACK,
TROUGH, CRECHE
mangle CALENDER,
MAR, BREAK, CRUSH,
BRUISE, PRESS, IRON,
BATTER, MAIM, RUIN,
BOTCH, CRIPPLE,
INJURE, SMOOTH,
FLATTEN, DISFIGURE,
MUTILATE, SPOIL,
HACK, LACERATE,
GARBLE
mango BAUNO, PEP-
PER, DRUPE, FRUIT,
TREE, PLANT
bird, India ORIOLE
fruit DRUPE
grove TOPE
mangrove GORAN
mania CRAZE, FRENZY,
LUNACY, MADNESS,
DELIRIUM, PASSION,
INSANITY, OBSESSION,
HYSTERIA

maniacal MAD,
DEMONIAC, CRAZED,
RAVING, INSANE,
DEMENTED, DE-
RANGED, FRANTIC,
HYSTERICAL, VIOLENT,
PSYCHOTIC
manicure TRIM, CLIP,
CUT, PARE, POLISH
manifest OPEN, SHOW,
EVINCE, OVERT,
PATENT, PUBLIC, DIS-
CLOSE, VISIBLE, BARE,
REVEAL, CLEAR, PLAIN,
EXHIBIT, APPARENT,
OBVIOUS, EVIDENT,
UNMISTAKABLE, IN-
DUBITABLE, PALPABLE,
DISPLAY, INVOICE,
LIST, WAYBILL
manifestation, *Hindu
religion* AVATAR
manifesto EDICT, RE-
SCRIPT, ORDER, WRIT,
OSTENT, DECLARATION,
STATEMENT
manikin PHANTOM,
DWARF, MODEL,
MIDGET, RUNT,
DOLL, PYGMY,
MANNEQUIN
Manila *airfield* CLARK
Bay boat BILALO
hemp ABACA
hero DEWEY
river PASIG
manioc CASSAVA,
TAPIOCA
maniple FANON,
ORALE, BAND, SUB-
DIVISION
manipulate WIELD,
SWING, PLY, OPERATE,
JUGGLE, HANDLE, RIG,
USE, MANAGE, CON-
TROL
manito(u) SPIRIT,
HUACA
mankind HUMANITY,
ADAM, FOLK, RACE
See "man"
manliness ARETE,
DIGNITY, HEROISM,
NOBLENESS, IN-
TREPIDITY, VIRILITY
manna LAAP, LERP,
FOOD, SNOW, JUICE
mannequin *See*
"manikin"
manner(s) ASPECT,
LOOK, MIEN, AIR,
SORT, STYLE, KIND,

WAY, TACT, POISE,
FORM, CUSTOM,
METHOD, FASHION,
MODE, MORES, USE,
WONT, HABIT, FRONT,
DEMEANOR, BEARING,
ADDRESS, BEHAVIOR,
DEPORTMENT, AP-
PEARANCE
manor DEMESNE,
HALL, MANSION,
ESTATE
mansion HOUSE,
ABODE, DWELLING,
RESIDENCE, PALACE
mantel LINTEL, LEDGE,
BEAM, SLAB, SHELF
mantle CAPE, COAT,
HOOD, CAP, FROCK,
ROBE, PALLIUM,
BLANKET, SHELTER,
SCREEN, COVER(ING),
ENVELOPE, CONCEAL,
FORM, SPREAD, PALL,
DISGUISE, FILAMENT
mantra OM, HYMN,
DHARANI, SPELL,
CHARM
Manu, *laws of* SUTRA
manual GUIDE, TEXT,
BOOK, REFERENCE,
DIAL, ENCHIRIDION,
KEYBOARD
art CRAFT, TRADE
training SLOYD, SLOID
manuao IAO, BIRD
manumit DELIVER,
FREE, LIBERATE,
RELEASE
manuscript(s) MS,
MSS, FOLIO, CODEX,
ARTICLE, DRAFT,
DOCUMENT, WRITING,
TEXT, COMPOSITION
unpublished
INEDITUS, INEDITA
manxman CELT
many DIVERS, SEVERAL,
GOBS, LOT(S), SCADS,
SUNDRY, NUMEROUS,
VARIOUS, MANIFOLD,
MULTIPLIED
combining form
MULTI, POLY
Maori *Adam* TIKI
canoe WAKA
chaos KORE
clan ATI, HAPU
club MERE, PATU
creator MAUI
dance HAKA
fish MOKI

Map 288 Marmot

food KAI
forever AKE
hero MAUI
parrot TUI
rootstock ROI
storage pit RUA
tattoo MOKO
tree RATA
village KAIK, KAINGA
wages UTU
war club MERE, PATU
map CHART, PLATE,
 SKETCH, PLAN, DRAW-
 ING, PLAT, GRAPH,
 DESIGN, FACE, DIA-
 GRAM
book of maps ATLAS
maple *cup* MAZER
seed SAMARA, KEY,
 WING
sugar spout SPILE
tree genus ACER,
 ACERACEAE
mar BLEMISH, DEFACE,
 SCAR, HURT, HARM,
 WARP, DAMAGE, DIS-
 FIGURE, SCRATCH,
 INJURE, SPOIL, RUIN,
 IMPAIR
marabou ARGALA,
 STORK, ADJUTANT,
 BIRD
marasca CHERRY
marasmus WASTING,
 EMACIATION
maraud PLUNDER, ROB,
 PILLAGE, INVADE, RAID,
 RAVAGE, FORAY
marauder, Scot.
 CATERAN
marble(s) AGATE,
 BASALT, DOLOMITE,
 MARMOR, MIB, MIG,
 TAW, HARD, MARL,
 LIMESTONE, COLD,
 INFLEXIBLE, UN-
 FEELING
Belgium RANCE
game MIB, MIG
Italy CARRARA
Roman CIPOLIN
variety DOLOMITE,
 CIPOLIN, PARIAN,
 CARRARA, SIENA
march TRAMP, PACE,
 FILE, TREAD, PARADE,
 HIKE, ADVANCE,
 PROGRESS, BORDER,
 WALK, STEP, GO
date IDES, NONES
king SOUSA

sisters AMY, MEG,
 BETH, JO
Mardi Gras *king* REX
Margaret of Anjou's
 father RENE
margarine OLEO
marge SHORE, BORDER,
 EDGE
margin FRINGE, BRIM,
 EDGE, RIM, SIDE,
 BRINK, END, TERM,
 LIMIT, CONFINE, LIP,
 VERGE, RANGE, SCOPE,
 BORDER, PROFIT
irregularly notched
 EROSE
marginal *note*
 SCHOLIUM, ANNOTA-
 TION, APOSTIL(LE)
reading, Hebrew
 K'RI, KERE
margosa NEEM, NIM,
 TREE
Mariana island ROTA
marigold ASTER,
 CAPER, COWSLIP,
 ORANGE, FLOWER
fig SAMH
genus TAGETES
marinal SALINE,
 NAUTICAL
marine NAVAL,
 OCEANIC, NERITIC,
 AQUATIC, SEADOG,
 PELAGIC, NAUTICAL,
 MARITIME, SEASCAPE
animal DUGONG,
 MANATEE, DOLPHIN,
 WHALE, SEAL,
 PORPOISE, WALRUS
bird See "bird, sea"
calcareous skeleton
 CORAL
plant ENALID, KELP
 See "seaweed"
mariner JACK(Y),
 SALT, TAR, GOG,
 SAILOR, SEAMAN
marionette man SARG
marjoram MINT,
 ORIGAN, PLANT, HERB
mark DOT, LABEL,
 SCRATCH, SIGN, NOTE,
 TRACK, PRINT, BADGE,
 BLOT, SCAR, DENT,
 STROKE, TRACE, SPOT,
 BLEMISH, STAIN,
 STIGMA, STAMP, DIE,
 IMPRESS(ION),
 VESTIGE, EVIDENCE,
 PROOF, SYMBOL,
 BRAND, INDICATE,

 DESIGNATE, ENGRAVE,
 HEED, NOTICE, EX-
 PRESS, OBSERVE, IN-
 DICATION, NOTATE,
 TRAIT, END, AIM,
 GOAL, DISTINGUISH,
 CHARACTERIZE, COIN,
 SYMPTOM, MAR,
 TALLY, SCORE, TARGET,
 TOKEN
critical OBELUS, DASH
curling TEE
diacritic BREVE,
 TILDE, UMLAUT
distinctive CACHET,
 SIGN, STAMP, INSIGNE
grammatical ASPER
identification EAR-
 MARK, SCAR, TATTOO
index FIST
of disgrace STIGMA
omission CARET, DELE
over vowel MACRON
printer's DIESIS,
 OBELISK, LINE, RULE,
 STET, BREVE, TILDE,
 DAGGER, FIST, DELE,
 OBELUS, SERIF, CARET,
 ELLIPSE, DIAERESIS
reference DAGGER,
 OBELISK
surveyor's BENCH
with scars ENSEAM
Mark Twain CLEMENS,
 SAM
marker(s) STELE,
 STELA, STONE, POST,
 SIGN, SCORER, MONI-
 TOR, COUNTER, BOOK-
 MARK, TABLET
air race PYLON
market MART, FORUM,
 RIALTO, STORE, SHOP,
 FAIR, EMPORIUM,
 BAZAAR, SALE, BUY,
 SELL, EXCHANGE,
 TRADE
place AGORA,
 EMPORIUM, PLAZA
type of FLEA
marksman SHOT,
 SNIPER
marl MALM, EARTH
marlinespike JAEGER,
 FID, SKUA
marmalade JAM
tree MAMEY, CHICO,
 SAPOTE, ACHRAS
marmoset MICO,
 TAMARIN, MONKEY
marmot BOBAC,
 BOBACK, HYRAX,

RODENT, WOODCHUCK, WHISTLER

Himalayan PIA

maroon ABANDON, ISOLATE, ENISLE, SLAVE

Marpessa's *abductor* IDAS

Marquand's *detective* MOTO

marque LICENSE, LETTER, REPRISAL

marquee SHELTER, TENT, CANOPY, AWNING

marquetry *material* BUHL, NACRE, IVORY, WOOD, SHELLS

marriage NUPTIALS, WEDLOCK, WEDDING, VOW, UNION, MATRIMONY, ESPOUSAL

absence of AGAMY

broker SCHATCHEN

combining form GAMO

hater of MISOGAMIST

non-recognition of AGAMY

outside the tribe EXOGAMY

second DEUTEROGAMY, DIGAMY

settlement DOT, DOWRY

marriageable NUBILE

marrow SUBSTANCE, KEEST, SAP, SUET, PITH, ESSENCE, MEDULLA, VITALITY

bones KNEES

marry WED, ELOPE, WELD, TIE, HITCH, WIVE, UNITE, MATCH, TEAM, JOIN, ESPOUSE, MATE, YOKE

Mars ARES

belt or band on LIBYA

discoverer HALL

pertaining to AREAN, MARTIAN

priests of SALII

satellite DEIMOS

spot on OASIS

"Marseillaise" *author* ROUGET (L'ISLE)

Marseilles *soap* CASTILE

marsh LIMAN, SWALE, SLUE, LERNA, QUAG,

BOG, FEN, MIRE, MORASS, SWAMP, QUAGMIRE, SLOUGH

bird SORA, STILT, SNIPE, BITTERN

combining form HELO

gas METHANE, FIREDAMP

grass SEDGE

harrier HARPY

hen RAIL

living in LIMNOPHILE

plant BULRUSH, IVA, TULE, CATTAIL

marshal GUIDE, DIRECT, MANAGE, RANGE, USHER, ALINE, ARRAY, ORDER, COLLECT, GATHER, ASSEMBLE, ARRANGE, LEAD, DISPOSE, ALIGN, OFFICIAL, COMMANDER, OFFICER

of France PETAIN, NEY, JOFFRE, FOCH

Marshall *island* MILI, NAMUR, EBON, RATIK, RALIK

marsh mallow ALTEA, PLANT

marshy BOGGY, FENNY, WET, PALUDAL, PALUDINE, SWAMPY, SQUASHY, SOFT

land, Italy PONTINE, MAREMMA

place SWALE, SLEW, SLUE, SLOUGH *See* "marsh"

marsupial *See under* "mammal"

marten SOBOL, FISHER, SABLE

Martinique *volcano* PELEE

martyr VICTIM, SAINT, SUFFERER, TORTURE, PERSECUTE, AFFLICT, TORMENT, AGONIZE

marvel PRODIGY, WONDER, MIRACLE, AMAZEMENT, ASTONISHMENT, ADMIRATION, SURPRISE

Maryland *county* CECIL, KENT, TALBOT, HOWARD

masculine MALE, MAS, VIRILE, MANLY, STRONG, ROBUST, POWERFUL

masjid MOSQUE

mask VISOR, DOMINO, SHIELD, SCREEN, IMAGE, COVER(ING), MASQUERADE, MASQUE, BLIND, CLOAK, VEIL, PROTECT, HIDE, CONCEAL, DISGUISE, PRETEND, SHROUD, DANCE, PRETEXT, SUBTERFUGE, EVASION

crest on tragic ONKOS

Greek ONKOS

half DOMINO

masked LARVATE, HIDDEN, DISGUISED, CONCEALED, OBSCURE

comedy SCAPINO

man UMP, UMPIRE, REFEREE

masker MUMMER, DOMINO, MASQUERADER

masonic *doorkeeper* TILER, TYLER

mason's *axe* GURLET

mixing rod RAB

mortar board HAWK

masquerade DISGUISE, COVER, HIDE, CONCEAL, DANCE, BALL, REVEL, MUM(M)

mass LITURGY, SERVICE, SACRAMENT, RITE, BODY, GOB, LUMP, UNIT, WAD, BULK, BOLUS, SIZE, MAGNITUDE, SUM, TOTAL, WHOLE, MAJORITY, HEAP, PILE, GATHER, MERGE, BLEND, FUSE, UNIFY, MATTER, CAKE, CLOT, ASSEMBLAGE, QUANTITY, AMOUNT, CONGERIES, HORDE, COLLECT(ION), NODE, TUMOR

book MISSAL

directory ORDO

meeting RALLY

musical number KYRIE, GLORIA, CREDO, SANCTUS, AGNUS DEI, DONA NOBIS

pertaining to MOLAR, MISSAL

vestment AMICE

Massachusetts *city or town* LYNN, WARE, SALEM

county BRISTOL, DUKES, ESSEX, SUFFOLK
State flower ARBUTUS
massacre KILL, CARNAGE, SLAUGHTER, HAVOC, POGROM, DECIMATE, BUTCHER(Y), SLAY, MURDER
massage KNEAD, RUB, STROKE
Massenet opera MANON, THAIS, CID
mast STAFF, POLE, ACORNS, NUTS, SPAR, SPRIT, PANNAGE
master SAHIB, CHIEF, TUTOR, HEAD, EXPERT, LEADER, GOVERN(OR), OWNER, BOY, BOSS, LORD, RAB(B)I, MAN, MIAN, EMPLOYER, SUPERINTENDENT, OVERSEER, COMMANDER, CAPTAIN, TEACHER, INSTRUCTOR, PROPRIETOR, SIRE, PRINCIPAL, DIRECTOR, ARTIST, SUBDUE, CONQUER, DEFEAT, RULE, MANAGE, LEARN, CONTROL, OVERCOME, SUBJUGATE, VANQUISH
of ceremonies MC, EMCEE
of Syracuse DION
pertaining to HERILE
stroke COUP
mastery DOMINION, COMMAND, RULE, SKILL, VICTORY, SWAY, SUPREMACY, CONQUEST, LEADERSHIP, DEXTERITY, ABILITY, PROFICIENCY, CLEVERNESS, ASCENDENCY
mastic GUM, RESIN, TREE, LIQUOR
masticate CHEW, CRUSH, GRIND, MANDUCATE, CUT, KNEAD
mastodon GIANT, MAMMUT, MAMMOTH
mat PAD, RUG, BOLSTER, DOILY, MATRIX, WEBBING, BORDER, CLOTH, INTERWEAVE, SNARL,

TWIST, WEAVE, KNOT, ENTANGLE
Mata Hari SPY
mataco APAR, INDIAN, ARMADILLO
matador's *adversary* TORO, BULL
garment CAPE
staff MULETA
sword ESTOQUE
match CAP, TALLY, COPY, MATE, BOUT, ACCORD, MARRY, HARMONIZE, FIT, PEER, PAIR, LUCIFER, VESTA, FUSE(E), LOCOFOCO, EQUAL, COMPARE, AGREE, SQUARE, MARRIAGE, COMPANION, TRIAL, COMPETITION, CONTEST, UNION, RIVAL, SUIT, CORRESPOND, COUNTERPART
matched PAIRED, ENGAGED, TEAMED
matchless ALONE, PEERLESS, UNPAIRED, UNRIVALED, INIMITABLE, CONSUMMATE, INCOMPARABLE
matchlock GUN, MUSKET, GUNLOCK
mate CHUM, WIFE, HUSBAND, SPOUSE, FERE, COMRADE, ALLY, AIDE, MARINER, PARTNER, OFFICER, COMPANION, TWIN, ASSOCIATE, CONSORT, COMPEER, EQUAL, ASSISTANT, PAIR, COUPLE, MARRY, MATCH
material STUFF, SWATCH, VENAL, REAL, PERTINENT, RELEVANT, ESSENTIAL, IMPORTANT, VITAL, WEIGHTY, TANGIBLE, NECESSARY, MOMENTOUS, TEMPORAL, SENSUAL, SENSUOUS, FACTS, DATA, CLOTH, METAL, PHYSICAL, CORPOREAL, BODILY
materia medica ACOLOGY
maternal MOTHERLY
relationship ENATION

matgrass MARRAM, NARD, PLANT
mathe GRUB, MAGGOT, MOTH
mathematical *arbitrary number* RADIX
constant PARAMETER
diagram GRAPH
function (CO)SINE
instrument NABLA, VERNIER
irrational number SURD
line VECTOR
quantity OPERAND
ratio (CO)SINE
surface NAPPE
symbol DIGIT, NUMBER, FIGURE, OPERAND, PLUS, MINUS, EQUAL
matinee LEVEE, SOIREE, PARTY, SHOW, RECEPTION, ENTERTAINMENT, NEGLIGEE
idol LION, STAR
matras, *crossbow* BOLT
matrass BOTTLE, FLASK, CARAFE, VESSEL, CUCURBIT, TUBE
matriculate ENROL(L), ENTER, ADMIT, REGISTER
matrix BED, MOLD, MAT, CAST, FORM, SHAPE, PATTERN, GANGUE, FOUNDATION, WOMB
matter TROUBLE, AIL, BODY, COPY, PITH, PUS, GEAR, MATERIAL, SUBSTANCE, ELEMENTS, ATOMS, CAUSE, TOPIC, THEME, AFFAIR, GROUND, THING, SUBJECT, STUFF, CONTENT, SENSE, DIFFICULTY, AMOUNT, QUANTITY, PORTION, CONCERN, EVENT, IMPORTANCE, SUBSEQUENCE, IMPORT, SIGNIFICANCE
of fact LITERAL
pertaining to HYLIC
philosophy HYLE
matthiola STOCK, SHRUB, FLOWER
mattock AXE, PICKAXE, HOE, ADZ, TWIBIL
mattress case TICK

mature PERFECT,
DEVELOP, ADULT,
HARDEN, INURE,
SEASON, GROW(N),
AGE(D), RIPE(N),
MELLOW, COMPLETE,
DUE, PAYABLE
mau TSETSE
maud SHAWL, RUG,
PLAID
maudlin BEERY,
TIPSY, SOPPY, MUSHY,
SLUSHY, EMOTIONAL,
SENTIMENTAL, SILLY,
FUDDLED
Maugham *heroine*
SADIE
play RAIN
maul BEETLE, MALLET,
CLUB, GAVEL, HAM-
MER, MOTH, BRUISE,
POUND, DAMAGE,
BEAT, INJURE, ABUSE,
DEFORM
mason's GAVEL
Mau Mau land KENYA
maund BASKET,
HAMPER, WEIGHT
Maupassant *character*
FIFI
Mauritius, *extinct bird*
DODO
mauve VIOLET, MAL-
LOW, LILAC, DYE,
PURPLE
maverick CALF, DOGIE,
STRAY, YEARLING
maw CRAW, CROP,
STOMACH, GULLET,
THROAT
mawkish SICKLY,
STALE, VAPID,
SENTIMENTAL *See*
"maudlin"
maxilla JAW, BONE
maxim MOTTO,
GNOME, RULE, SAW,
AXIOM, ADAGE, SAYING,
TRUTH, PRINCIPLE,
PROVERB, APHORISM,
APOTHEGM, TRUISM,
DICTUM, BY-WORD,
SLOGAN
maxims LOGIA
maximum MOST, UT-
MOST, ALL, GREATEST,
LIMIT, HIGHEST
may CAN, MIGHT
apple MANDRAKE,
PLANT
first BELTANE

fly DUN, EPHEMERID
tree HAWTHORN
Mayan MAM, MAYA,
INDIAN
year HAAB
*year-end days of
calendar* UAYEB
Mayence, *Count of*
GAN, GANELON
mazed LOST, TANGLED,
SNARLED, STUPEFIED,
BEWILDERED, PER-
PLEXED
meadow VEGA, BAAN,
LEA, MEAD, FIELD,
GRASSLAND
flower BLUETS
mouse VOLE,
ARVICOLE
meager ARID, BARE,
SCANT(Y), SLIM,
LEAN, POOR, SLIGHT,
WANTING, SPARE,
INADEQUATE,
DEFICIENT, LENTEN,
GAUNT, SPARSE, THIN,
EMACIATED, LANK,
SKINNY, BARREN,
DESTITUTE, STERILE,
JEJUNE
meal MESS, REPAST,
TIFFIN, FEED, FOOD,
EATS, COLLATION,
DINNER, FEAST,
LUNCH, SNACK, MUSH,
FARINA, GROUT,
PINOLE, FLOUR, GRAIN
evening DINNER, TEA
light BEVER, LUNCH,
SNACK, TEA, TIFFIN
mealy FARINACEOUS,
PALE, FRIABLE,
FLOURY
mean(s) MEDIAL,
MEDIUM, AVERAGE,
MIDDLING, IN-
TERMEDIATE, RULE,
NORM, PAR, DENOTE,
SENSE, IMPLY,
SIGNIFICANCE, POWER,
SIGNIFY, INTEND, CON-
TEMPLATE, PURPOSE,
DESIGN, INDICATE,
CONVEY, IMPORT,
SNIDE, POOR, IN-
FERIOR, HUMBLE,
MALICIOUS, VICIOUS,
IGNOBLE, VULGAR,
LOW, VILE, STINGY,
CONTEMPTIBLE, DE-
GRADED, MISERLY,
PENURIOUS, ABJECT,

BASE, SMALL, SORRY,
CHEAP, MEASLY,
AGENT, CHANNEL,
VEHICLE, MODE,
MONEY, WAY, BAD,
LITTLE, PALTRY
meander WANDER,
WIND, TURN, TWIST
meaning PURPORT,
INTENT, SENSE, IM-
PORT, SIGNIFICATION,
DRIFT, SIGNIFICANCE,
ACCEPTATION, PUR-
POSE, DESIGN
language
SEMANTIC(S)
without NULL
meaningless refrain
DERRY
meantime INTERVAL,
INTERIM
measles RUBELLA,
MORBILLI, RUBEOLA
measly MEAN, CON-
TEMPTIBLE *See*
"mean"
measure LITER, HAIR,
ROTL, METER, GAUGE,
DOSE, TIME, STEP,
DIMENSION(S),
CAPACITY, LIMIT,
METE, LAW, RULE(R),
COMPUTE, STANDARD,
SIZE, EXTENT,
VOLUME, WEIGHT,
UNIT
area AR(E), ACRE,
ROD, DECARE,
CENTIARE, PERCH
Biblical See under
"Bible"
capacity CASK, CRAN,
ORNA, PECK, PINT,
BUSHEL
cloth length ELL,
YARD
distance COSS, KOS,
MILE, KILO(METER)
dry PINT, QUART,
PECK, STERE, BUSHEL,
LITER, CUP, SPOON
electric OHM, MHO
See "electric, unit"
energy JOULE,
ERG(ON)
half em EN
herring CRAN
land RI, ACRE, AR(E),
CHAIN, ROD, ROOD
length (linear) TOISE,
CUBIT, MICRON, PACE,
ROD, INCH, FOOT, ELL,

HAND, MILE, YARD,
PERCH, FURLONG,
KILO(METER),
CENTIMETER, GUZ
¾ inch DIGIT
2¼ inch NAIL
two metrical feet
DIPODY
160 square perches
ACRE
liquid TIERCE, PINT,
QUART, CUP, DRAM,
MINIM, DROP, GILL,
TUN, FIFTH, SPOON,
GALLON, BARREL
Bible DRAM, HIN,
LOG
medicinal GUTTA,
MINIM, GRAM, GRAIN,
OUNCE
metric AR(E),
MICRON, LITER, STERE,
METER
cube STERE
music CODA, BAR
nautical KNOT
oriental RI, LI
printing AGATE, PICA,
EM, EN
sound DECIBEL
study of earth
GEODESY
time MINUTE,
SECOND, HOUR, DAY,
MONTH, YEAR
volume YARD, STERE,
CORD, LITER, QUART,
PINT, PECK, GALLON,
BUSHEL
weight GRAM, BALE,
POUND, TON, OUNCE
wine in cask BUTT
wire MIL
yarn LEA
"Measure for Measure"
character ANGELO,
LUCIO, ELBOW, FROTH,
JULIET
measurement METAGE,
COMPUTATION,
DIMENSION, SIZE,
AMOUNT, BULK,
VOLUME, DISTANCE
measuring instrument
ALIDAD(E), STADIA,
RULE(R), TAPE,
SCALE(S)
rod CALIPER
meat PITH, GIST, CORE,
MORSEL, FOOD, VEAL,
CHOP, LOIN, STEAK,
FLESH, ALIMENT,

NUTRIMENT, SUS-
TENANCE, VICTUALS,
PORK, BEEF, MUTTON,
LAMB
cut of BRISKET, LOIN,
CHOP, FIL(L)ET,
STEAK, RIB
dried and cured PEM-
MICAN, HAM, BILTONG,
BACON
eater CARNIVORE
eating of raw
OMOPHAGIA
fat SPECK, SUET
jelly ASPIC
pie RISSOLE, PASTY
preserve CORN,
SMOKE, DRY, SALT,
PICKLE, FREEZE
roasted on stick
CABOB, KABOB
meatless MAIGRE,
LENTEN
meatus CANAL, PAS-
SAGE, OPENING
Mecca *governor*
SHERIF, SHEREEF
pilgrimage to HADJ
pilgrims' dress IHRAM
shrine KAABA
mechanic ARTISAN,
WORKER, HAND,
ARTIFICER, CRAFTS-
MAN, OPERATIVE
mechanical IN-
VOLUNTARY, AUTO-
MATIC
man ROBOT, GOLEM,
AUTOMATON
mechanics, *branch of*
STATICS, DYNAMICS
mechanism WORKS,
SYSTEM, TECHNICS,
MEANS, RIGGING,
TACKLE, GEAR,
MACHINE, APPARATUS
medal COIN, BADGE,
PLAQUE, AWARD,
PRIZE, REWARD
medallion TABLET,
COIN, CAMEO, MEDAL,
PLAQUE, PANEL, POR-
TRAIT, DECORATION
meddle PRY, TAMPER,
OBTRUDE, FUSS,
MOLEST, INTRUDE,
MIX, INTERPOSE, IN-
TERFERE
meddlesome CURIOUS,
INTRUSIVE, OFFICIOUS,
PRAGMATICAL, INTER-
FERING

Medea's *father* AEETES
lover JASON
medial MIDDLE, MEAN,
AVERAGE, IN-
TERMEDIATE
median MESNE,
AVERAGE, MEAN, MID-
DLE
level NORM, PAR
line RAPHE
plane MESON
Median *king* REBA
mediant, *music* THIRD
mediate OPINE, HALVE,
JUDGE, HELP, INTER-
POSE, CONCILIATE,
INTERVENE, SETTLE,
HARMONIZE, INTER-
CEDE, ARBITRATE,
PURPOSE, INTEND,
PLAN
mediator ARBITER,
AGENT, JUDGE,
REFEREE, UMPIRE, IN-
TERCESSOR, ADVOCATE
medical CURATIVE,
IATRIC, THERAPEUTIC,
HEALING, MEDICINAL
file or record CHART,
CASE, HISTORY
group AMA
gum KINO, ARABIC
officer CORONER
medicate DOSE, TREAT,
DRUG, HEAL, CURE
medicated *fluid* TONIC,
LOTION, TINCTURE,
LINIMENT, EMBROCA-
TION, ELIXIR
medicinal *capsule*
CACHET
herb See under
"herb"
plant ALOE, RUE,
AGAR, HERB *See
under* "plant"
remedy ANTIDOTE,
SHOT, ELIXIR, TONIC
root JALAP, ARTAR
tablet TROCHE, PILL,
PILULE, PILULA,
PELLET
medicine, *of equal
parts* ANA
pertaining to IATRIC
science of PHYSICS,
IATRICS
universal PANACEA
mediety HALF, MOIETY,
TEMPERANCE,
MODERATION

medieval *galley* AESC,
BIREME, TRIREME,
UNIREME, GALIOT
helmet ARMET
hooked weapon
ONCIN
mediocre ORDINARY,
COMMONPLACE, SOSO,
FAIR, POOR, INDIF-
FERENT, MIDDLING,
AVERAGE, MEAN, LALA
meditate MUSE, PORE,
PONDER, STUDY,
WEIGH, REASON,
COGITATE, RUMINATE,
CONSIDER, PLAN,
CONTRIVE, THINK,
CONCOCT, CON-
TEMPLATE, REFLECT
meditation RUMINA-
TION, THOUGHT, RE-
FLECTION, DISCOURSE
Mediterranean *boat*
ACCON *See "ship"*
below
fruit AZAROLE
galley GALIOT
grass DISS
gulf TUNIS
herb genus AMMI
island GOZO, CRETE,
MALTA, SICILY, CAPRI,
ELBA
resort NICE, COMO
river to NILE, RHONE,
EBRO, JUCAR, VAR(O),
AUDE
Sea, pertaining to
LEVANT
ship SETEE, XEBEC,
ZEBEC(K), POLACCA
storm BORASCO,
BORASCA
tree OLEA, CAROB
volcanic island
LIPARI
wind SIROC(CO),
LEVANTER, SOLANO,
MISTRAL, ETESIAN,
GREGALE
medium MEAN(S),
AVERAGE, FAIR, PAR,
SOSO, VEHICLE,
AGENT, PSYCHIC,
ORACLE, MIDDLE,
MIDDLING, ORDINARY,
MEDIOCRE, AGENCY,
INSTRUMENT(ALITY),
CHANNEL, ORGAN
line of valve RAPHE
medlar MESPIL,
LARK, TREE, FRUIT

medley FARRAGO,
MELANGE, JUMBLE,
VARIETY, OLIO,
POTPOURRI,
SALMAGUNDI,
MIX(TURE), SONG,
AIR, PASTICCIO,
PASTICHE, GAL-
LIMAUFRY, HODGE-
PODGE
race RELAY
medregal *fish* AMBER
medrick GULL, TERN,
BIRD
medulla MARROW,
PITH, SPINE, CORD,
TISSUE
oblongata stripe OBEX
Medusa GORGON
sister STHENO,
EURYALE
slain by PERSEUS
meerschaum PIPE,
SEPIOLITE, SEAFOAM
meet GREET, ENCOUN-
TER, APPROACH, CON-
FRONT, FACE, EQUAL,
FIT, MATCH, SEEMLY,
SIT, CONVENE,
CONGREGATE, AS-
SEMBLE, MUSTER,
RALLY, COMBAT,
BATTLE, INTERSECT,
TRANSECT, CROSS,
RIGHT, GOOD, SUITA-
BLE, ADAPTED, AP-
PROPRIATE, EQUAL,
MATCH, SEEMLY,
PROPER, FULFILL,
CONFORM, SATISFY,
PAY
meeting DUEL, RALLY,
SYNOD, CAUCUS,
TRYST, JUNCTURE,
SESSION, SEAM, UNION,
ASSEMBLY, EN-
COUNTER, INTERVIEW,
GATHERING, COMPANY,
CONVENTION, CON-
FERENCE, CONFLUX,
JOINT, ASSEMBLAGE
megalithic *chamber*
DOLMEN
megapod MALEO,
LEIPOA, BIRD
mound-building
LEIPOA
megrim HEADACHE,
DULLNESS, CAPRICE,
WHIM, MIGRAINE,
BLUES, HYPO-

CHONDRIA, VERTIGO,
FAD, FANCY
Mehetabel CAT
melancholy ATRABILE,
SAD, ENNUI, MISERY,
SERIOUS, SOMBRE,
BLUE(S), DREAR,
DUMPS, DREAMY,
VAPORS, GLOOMY,
DEJECTED, DIS-
PIRIT(ED), DISMAL,
DOLEFUL, DEPRESSION,
HYPOCHONDRIA, SOR-
ROWFUL, UNHAPPY,
DISCONSOLATE,
DESPONDENT,
LUGUBRIOUS, DOWN-
CAST, DESPONDENCY,
HYSTERIA
Melanesian *native*
FIJI, PAPUAN
super being ADARO
melanous DARK,
BRUNETTE, MELANIC
melee RIOT, FIGHT,
SET-TO, TOURNEY,
ROW, BRAWL, SCRAP,
BROIL, AFFRAY,
SCUFFLE, SKIRMISH,
COMBAT
Melicocca *tree* GENIP
melilot CLOVER
Melissa *plant* MINT
Melkarth BAAL,
MOLOCH
mell(i), *combining*
form HONEY
mellifluous MELLOW,
DULCET, SMOOTH,
HONEYED, SWEET
mellow SOFT, MALM,
RICH, RIPE(N), OLD,
ADULT, MATURE,
TENDER, WARM,
AGE(D), SMOOTH,
SWEET, MELLIFLUOUS,
DULCET, AMIABLE,
GENIAL, JOVIAL, IN-
TOXICATED
melodic ARIOSE,
MELODIOUS
melodious ARIOSE,
DULCET, MUSICAL,
AGREEABLE, HAPPY,
TUNEFUL, HARMO-
NIOUS, ORPHIC, SWEET
melodramatic SHOWY,
GAUDY, EMOTIONAL,
GRAND, SENSATIONAL,
THEATRICAL
melody THEME, ARIA,
STRAIN, TUNE, AIR,

RHYTHM, CHIME,
SONG, DITTY,
HARMONY, UNISON,
MUSIC, MELISMA
Anglo-Indian RAGA
in sequence MELOS,
ROSALIA, ROUND
pertaining to PLAGAL
meloid BEETLE
melon CASABA, FRUIT,
PEPO, PROFITS,
WINNINGS, BONUS
pear PEPINO
tree PAPAYA
melos SONG, MELODY
melt THAW, RUN, FUSE,
RENDER, SQUANDER,
WASTE, LIQUEFY,
MOLLIFY, SOFTEN,
DISSOLVE, DISSIPATE,
SUBDUE, SWEAL
ore SMELT, CONVERT
Melville *character*
MOBY, AHAB
novel OMOO, TYPEE
member UNIT, ORGAN,
PART, PORTION,
BRANCH, PIECE,
SECTOR, PARCEL,
LIMB, ARM, LEG,
CONSTITUENT, COM-
PONENT, CLAUSE,
SECTION, DISTRICT, AS-
SOCIATE
membrane FILM,
VELLUM, SHEET,
WEB, TELA, PIA, SKIN,
FOLD, LAYER
covering brain
MENINGES, MATER,
PIA, DURA
diffusion through
OSMOSIS
fold of PLICA
weblike TELA
membranous fringe or
flap LOMA
memento RELIC,
KEEPSAKE, SOUVENIR,
CURIO, BIBELOT,
TOKEN, MEMORIAL
memo NOTE *See*
"memorandum"
memorabilia ANA,
ANTHOLOGY
memorable SIGNAL,
MARKED, DIS-
TINGUISHED
memorandum CHIT,
NOTE, IOU, MINUTE,
LETTER, REPORT,

BRIEF, RECORD, RE-
MINDER
memoria RELIQUARY,
SHRINE, CHAPEL,
CHURCH, MEMORY
memorial RECORD,
TABLET, SHRINE,
TROPHY, ARCHIVE,
MEMOIR, NOTE,
ABSTRACT, MONUMENT
memory MIND, RECOL-
LECTION, REMEM-
BRANCE, REMINIS-
CENCE
loss of AMNESIA,
LETHE, FORGETFUL-
NESS
partial loss APHASIA
pertaining to
MNEMONIC
Memphis *god* RA,
PTAH
men SONS, CREW,
MATES, HANDS,
BLOKES, SIRS,
SOLDIERS, TROOPS,
FORCES
mend HEAL, REPAIR,
COBBLE, PATCH,
DARN, HELP, RECTIFY,
FIX, RENEW, RESTORE,
CORRECT, REFORM,
IMPROVE, READJUST,
RETOUCH, AMEND,
EMEND, AMEL-
IORATE, CURE,
DOCTOR, BETTER,
TUNE
mendacity LIE, FIB,
FALSEHOOD,
DUPLICITY, DECEIT,
DECEPTION, UNTRUTH
mender TINKER, COB-
BLER, REPAIRMAN
mendicant FAKIR,
FRIAR, BEGGAR
menhaden PORGY,
MOSSBUNKER, BONY-
FISH, POGY, POGIE
meniscus LENS, DISC,
CRESCENT, CARTILAGE
Mennonite AMISH
meno LESS
Menotti GIAN-CARLO
mental INTELLECTUAL,
PHRENIC
defective MORON,
IMBECILE, IDIOT
disorder PARANOIA,
MANIA, DEMENTIA,
MORIA
faculty WITS, MIND

feeling EMOTION
state DOLDRUM,
MORALE, EUPHORIA
mentality WITS, MIND,
SENSE, SANITY, INTEL-
LIGENCE
menthaceous *plant*
CATNIP, CATMINT,
MINT
mention NAME, CITE,
REFER, MIND, ALLUDE,
DISCUSS, NOTICE,
SPECIFY
mentum CHIN
menu FARE, DIET, LIST,
CARTE
mephitic POISONOUS,
DEADLY, FOUL,
NOXIOUS
mercenary HIRELING,
HESSIAN, VENAL,
HACK, GREEDY, SORDID,
MEAN, ABJECT,
AVARICIOUS,
MYRMIDON
merchandise TRADE,
WARES, STORE, STOCK,
SELL, GOODS,
ARTICLES, COM-
MODITIES *See*
"trade"
pertaining to
EMPOREUTIC
merchant TRADER,
VINTNER, VENDOR,
DEALER, SELLER,
COSTER, DRAPER,
TRAFFICKER
guild HANSE
vessel See under
"boat"
"Merchant of Venice"
ANTONIO
character NERISSA,
PORTIA, SHYLOCK,
LORENZO, TUBAL,
JESSICA
merciless GRIM, CRUEL,
HARD, FELL, FIERCE,
FERAL, SAVAGE, RE-
LENTLESS, PITILESS,
UNFEELING, IN-
EXORABLE,
BARBAROUS, UN-
SPARING, REMORSE-
LESS, IMPLACABLE
mercurial FICKLE,
CHANGEABLE,
ELEGANT, CLEVER,
SHREWD, THIEVISH

mercurous *chloride* CALOMEL
soot STUPP
Mercury HERMES,
 PLANET, QUICKSILVER
son ELEUSIS
staff CADUCEUS
symbol HG
winged hat PETASUS,
 PETASOS
 shoes TALARIA
mercy PITY, GRACE,
 RUTH, LENITY, BLITHE,
 FAVOR, FORBEARANCE,
 BENEVOLENCE,
 CLEMENCY, QUARTER,
 LENIENCE, COM-
 PASSION, BLESSING,
 PARDON, FORGIVENESS,
 INDULGENCE, CHARITY,
 LENIENCY
show SPARE, PARDON,
 FORGIVE
mere SIMPLE, SUCH,
 SMALL, FEW, BARE,
 ONLY, SHEER, BOUND-
 ARY, LANDMARK, LAKE,
 POND, POOL, MARSH,
 FEN
taste SIP, DRAFT, NIP
merely ONLY, SINGLE,
 BARELY, PURELY,
 SOLELY, ABSOLUTELY,
 UTTERLY, SIMPLY
merganser DUCK,
 HARLE, HERALD,
 GARBILL, SMEW, DIVER
merge BLEND, MARRY,
 UNITE, FUSE, MINGLE,
 MIX, WED, JOIN, IM-
 MERSE, SINK, COM-
 BINE
merger FUSION, UNION,
 ABSORPTION, TRUST,
 AMALGAMATION,
 COMBINATION, MAR-
 RIAGE
meridian APEX,
 ZENITH, NOON, PEAK,
 ACME, MIDDAY, SUM-
 MIT, CULMINATION,
 CLIMAX
merino SHEEP, WOOL,
 FABRIC
merit DUE, EARN,
 MEED, WORTH, DE-
 SERVE, DESERT,
 VIRTUE, VALUE, RE-
 WARD, EXCELLENCE,
 HONOR, MARK, BADGE
meros THIGH

merriment FUN, GLEE,
 GAIETY, MIRTH,
 JOLLITY, HILARITY,
 JOCULARITY, LAUGH-
 TER, SPORTIVENESS,
 JOVIALITY
merry BLITHE, JOCOSE,
 JOYFUL, GAY,
 JOLLY, LIVELY,
 HAPPY, GLAD,
 SPRIGHTLY, JOVIAL,
 CHEERFUL, MIRTHFUL,
 JOYOUS, GLEEFUL,
 HILARIOUS, SPORTIVE
merry-andrew JOKER,
 ANTIC, JESTER,
 ACROBAT, MIME,
 CLOWN, BUFFOON,
 ZANY, SCARAMOUCH,
 HARLEQUIN,
 MOUNTEBANK
"Merry Widow" com-
 poser LEHAR
"Merry Wives of
 Windsor" *character*
 FENTON, FORD, PAGE,
 CAIUS, PISTOL, NYM,
 ROBIN, RUGBY
mescal CACTUS, YUCCA,
 MAGUEY, PLANT,
 SHRUB
mesh TISSUE, WEB,
 NET, GEAR, INTER-
 LOCK, ENGAGE, TRAP,
 SNARE, ENTANGLE,
 SCREEN
mesmeric *force* OD
Mesopotamia IRAQ,
 IRAK
 ancient city or town
 UR, NIPPUR, BABYLON
 boat GUFA
 city BASRA
 wind SHAMAL
mesquite ALGAROBA,
 PACAY, SHRUB, BUSH
 bean flour PINOLE
 genus PROSOPIS
mess BOTCH, LITTER,
 BEFOUL, CONFUSE,
 FEED, MEAL, DIS-
 ORDER, UNTIDINESS,
 BUNGLE, HODGEPODGE,
 MUDDLE, JUMBLE,
 PUTTER, MEDDLE
message BODE, NOTE,
 WORD, EVANGEL, RE-
 PORT, EPISTLE, LET-
 TER, CARD, WIRE,
 TELEGRAM, CABLE,
 COMMUNICATION,
 MEMO, TIDINGS, CALL

messenger COURIER,
 APOSTLE, NUNCIO,
 PAGE, ENVOY, HERALD,
 MERCURY, EMISSARY,
 PROPHET, MINISTER,
 CARRIER, FORERUNNER
 mounted
 ESTAFET(TE), REVERE
Messina *headland*
 SCYLLA, SCILLA
mestizo METIS
met SAT *See* "meet"
metal *alloy* BRASS,
 BRONZE, STEEL,
 NIELLO
 bar INGOT, I BEAM
 on door RISP
 casting PIG
 clippings SCISSEL
 coarse MATTE
 coat with PLATE,
 TERNE
 crude ORE
 decorating art NIELLO
 disk MEDAL, BADGE,
 TAG
 dross SLAG
 film PATINA
 fissure LODE
 heavy LEAD
 impure ALLOY,
 MATTE, REGULUS
 ingot GAD, PIG, BAR
 leaf FOIL
 lightest LITHIUM
 lump of PIG, ORE
 plate FOIL, LAME,
 SHIM
 pot POTIN
 refuse SCORIA, SLAG,
 DROSS
 shaper SWAGE
 suit MAIL, ARMOR
 vein LODE
 wedge SHIM
 white CALCIUM,
 SILVER
 worker WELDER,
 SMITH, VULCAN
metallic *alloy* SOLDER
 rock ORE
 containing ORY
metalware REVERE
metalwork *god* VUL-
 CAN
metamere SOMATOME,
 SOMITE, SEGMENT
metamorphosis PUPA,
 CHANGE, MUTATION,
 TRANSFORMATION,
 TRANSMUTATION

metaphor SIMILE, TROPE, ANALOGY, TRALATITION, COMPARISON
  extended IMAGE
  faulty or mixed use of CATACHRESIS
metaphysical *being* ENS
meteor LEONID, BIELID, ANDROMID, FIREBALL, BOLIDE
  exploding BOLIDE, BOLIS
meteorite *shower* ANDROMED, ANDROMEDE
meter LILT, RHYTHM, GAUGE, MEASURE, VERSE, CADENCE, PULSE, BEAT, EUPHONY, RHYME, TIME
  cubic STERE
  millionth of MICRON
  100 square AR(E)
method MODE, MEAN(S), SYSTEM, STYLE, FASHION, WAY, PROCESS, MODE, ORDER, ARRANGEMENT, MANNER, PROCEDURE, COURSE, SCHEME, RULE, REGULARITY
methodical EXACT, PRECISE, REGULAR, ORDERLY, SYSTEMATIC, FORMAL
methyl-phenol CRESOL, ANISOL
  ether ANISOL(E)
metier WORK, TRADE, CALLING, CRAFT, ART, LINE, PROFESSION, OCCUPATION, GAME, BUSINESS
metric *measure See under* "measure"
  system, combining form DECI, KILO
metrical *beat* ICTUS, PULSE
  foot ANAPEST, IAMB, IAMBUS, ARSIS
    of 4 syllables CHORIAMB, IONIC
    of 2 syllables TROCHEE
  stress of voice ICTUS, BEAT
  unit MORA

metropolitan (ARCH)- BISHOP, URBAN, PRINCIPAL, PRIMATE
Metz's *river* MOSELLE
Meuse River MAAS
mew STABLE, CAGE, DEN, CONFINE, HAY(MOW), GULL, MOLT, CRY, COB, BIRD
mewl WHIMPER, CRY
Mexico, Mexican
  agave DATIL
  American GRINGO
  basket grass OTATE
  beverage PULQUE, MESCAL
  bird TINAMOU
  blanket SERAPE
  brigand LADRONE, VILLA
  cactus MESCAL
  cat EYRA
  city or town UXMAL, TULA, TEPIC, TAXCO, JALAPA, TOLUCA, JUAREZ
  coin CENTAVO, PESO, ONZA, TLACO
  dish TAMALE, TORTILLA
  dollar PESO
  dove INCA
  drink MESCAL, PULQUE
  drug JALAP
  early dweller AZTEC, MAYA
  fiber plant DATIL, ISTLE, PITA, SISAL, IXTLE
  gopher TUZA, TUCAN
  gruel ATOLE
  hut JACAL
  Indian See under "Indian"
  lake CHAPALA
  landmark SENAL
  masonry ADOBE
  mat PETATE
  measure LABOR, CAREGA
  mixed blood MESTIZO
  noble TZIN
  octaroon ALBINO
  painter RIVERA
  peasant PEON
  persimmon CHAPOTE
  pine OCOTE, OKOTE
  plant AGAVE, SOTOL,

  CHIA, DATIL, SALVIA, SABADILLA
  soap AMOLE
  plantation HACIENDA
  porridge ATOLE
  proprietor RANCHERO
  race TOLTEC
  resort ACAPULCO
  river TONTO, FUERTE, SALADO, CONCHOS, YAQUI
  sauce TOBASCO
  scarf SERAPE, TAPALO
  seaport ACAPULCO, TAMPICO
  shawl SERAPE, TAPALO
  state TABASCO, YUCATAN, COLIMA, SONORA, JALISCO, DURANGO
  sugar PANOCHA
  thong ROMAL
  throwing stick ATLATL
  town AMECA, TECATE, ORTIZ *See* "city" *above*
  tree See under "tree"
  volcano COLIMA, JORULLO, POPOCATEPETL
  weight ONZA
mezereon DAPHNE, CAMELLIA, SHRUB
mezzanine ENTRESOL, STORY, BALCONY
Miami's *county* DADE
miasma MALARIA, TOXIN, CONTAGION
mica SILICATE, DIORITE, ISINGLASS, BIOTITE
mice *genus* MUS, VOLE
michael ORANGE
micher TRUANT, SNEAK, THIEF
Michigan *county* ALGER, BAY, CASS, CLARE, DELTA, IONIA, IOSCO, IRON, KENT, LAKE, LUCE, WAYNE
  river CASS
mickle GREAT, LARGE, MUCH, MANY
microbe GERM, AGENT, VIRUS,

BACTERIUM,
ORGANISM
microcosm WORLD,
VILLAGE, COM-
MUNITY, INSTITUTION,
UNIVERSE, MAN
Micronesian island
See under "island"
microorganism VIRUS,
GERM, BACTERIUM,
PROTOZOAN
microspores POLLEN
middle CENTER,
MESIAL, MESNE,
MEDIAL, HEART, HUB,
FOCUS, CORE, MIDST,
BETWEEN, MEDIAN,
CENTRAL, INTERMEDI-
ATE, WAIST
combining form
MEDI, MES(O)
toward MESIAD
middling AVERAGE,
SO-SO, FAIR, POOR,
PASSABLE, MEDIOCRE,
MODERATELY, TOLER-
ABLY
middlings MEAT,
FEED
mid-European
SLOVENE, SLAV
midge FLY, GNAT,
DWARF, FISH
Midianite king REBA,
EVI, ZUR, HUR
mid-lent Sunday
LAETARE
midmorning NINE
midshipman REEFER,
CADET, PLEBE
"Midsummer-Night's
Dream" character
THESEUS, EGEUS,
QUINCE, SNUG,
SNOUT, HERMIA,
OBERON, PUCK,
THISBE
mien OSTENT, GUISE,
LOOK, AIR, CAR-
RIAGE, APPEARANCE,
POISE, PORT, FRONT,
MANNER, DEMEANOR,
BEARING, ASPECT,
DEPORTMENT, BE-
HAVIOR
might POWER, FORCE,
ENERGY, ARM,
VIGOR, ABILITY,
STRENGTH, PUIS-
SANCE, MAIN,
POTENCY, INTENSITY,
EFFICACY

mighty POTENT, VERY,
POWERFUL, STRONG,
ATHLETIC, ROBUST,
VIGOROUS, STURDY,
PUISSANT, VALIANT,
BOLD, ABLE, ENOR-
MOUS, VAST, GREAT,
IMPORTANT, IN-
FLUENTIAL, WONDER-
FUL, MOMENTOUS,
REMARKABLE, EXTEN-
SIVE
mignonette LACE,
GREEN, FLOWER
genus RESEDA
plant WELD, WOALD,
WOULD
migraine CEPHALGIA,
HEADACHE, HEMI-
CRANIA, MEGRIM
migration EXODUS,
TREK
migratory ROVING,
STROLLING,
VAGRANT, WANDERING
bird GOOSE, DUCK,
ROBIN
farm hand OKIE
Mikado, court of
DAIRI
mike LOAF, LOITER,
TRANSMITTER
Milan opera house
(LA)SCALA
mild BLAND, MEEK,
GENTLE, SERENE,
PLACID, MODERATE,
TENDER, KIND,
CLEMENT, SOFT,
TAME, LENIENT,
EASY, BALMY, CALM,
MERCIFUL, COMPAS-
SIONATE, INDULGENT,
PACIFIC, SUAVE,
PLEASANT, TRANQUIL,
SOOTHING, MOL-
LIFYING, ASSUASIVE
offense DELIT,
DELICT
mildew ROT, BLIGHT,
MO(U)LD, MUST,
FUNGUS
mildness LENITY
Miled's son IR
mile, nautical KNOT
milestone STELE,
MARKER, MIL(L)IA-
RIUM
milfoil YARROW,
PLANT, HERB
milieu MEDIUM,

ENVIRONS, BET, SET-
TINGS, SURROUNDINGS
military MARTIAL,
WARLIKE, SOLDIERLY,
TROOPS, ARMY,
MILITIA, SOLDIERY
cap BUSBY, KEPI,
SHAKO
cloak SAGUM
close ranks SERRY
craft JEEP, LST,
FRIGATE, TANK
decoration See un-
der "decoration"
device CROC
division UNIT,
CORPS, ARMY, SQUAD,
TROOP, REGIMENT
engine ONAGER,
ROBINET, BOAR,
MANGONEL, CATA-
PULT, RAM, CAN-
NON, TEREBRA,
TREPAN, SCORPION
force CORPS, ARMY,
LEGION
formation ECHELON,
LINE, FILE
machine JEEP, TANK
See "engine" above
maneuver TACTIC
messenger COURIER,
ORDERLY,
ESTAFET(TE)
mine gallery ECOUTE
punishment STRAP-
PADO
salute SALVO
school ACADEMY,
POINT, RMA, VMI,
CITADEL
storehouse ETAPE,
ARSENAL, ARMORY,
DEPOT
militate FIGHT,
CONTEND
milk LAC, LATEX,
JUICE, SAP,
SECRETION, DRAIN,
EXHAUST, BLEED,
EXPLOIT, EXTRACT,
ELICIT
coagulator RENNET
curd CASEIN, TYRE,
TAYIR
curdled CLABBER,
YOG(H)URT
fermented K(O)UMISS
fish AWA, SABALO
part of SERUM,
CASEIN, WHEY
pertaining to LACTIC

sour CURD, WHEY,
  WHIG
whey SERUM
milk pail ESHIN
milkweed *fluid* LATEX
  tuft COMA
Milky Way GALAXY
mill PLANT, SHOP,
  QUERN, FACTORY,
  GRIND(ER), MACHINE,
  PRESS, ROLLER,
  KNURL, CRUSH,
  PULVERIZE, COM-
  MINUTE
  for pulverizing ore
  ARRASTRE, CRUSHER
millepore CORAL
miller MOTH
millet, *broom corn*
  HIRSE
  cereal ARZUN
  India DURR(A),
  KODA
  Italy MOHA, BUDA
  pearl BAJRA,
  BAJREE, BAJRI
  seed, like MILIARY
millimeter, *1/1000 part*
  MICRON
million millions TRIL-
  LION
  combining form
  TREG(A)
millionth part of ohm
  MICROHM
mime APE(R),
  ACTOR, IMITATE,
  COPY, MIMIC,
  JESTER, CLOWN,
  BUFFOON, PLAY
  masque COMUS
mimic APE(R),
  MIME, COPY,
  MIMETIC, FEIGN,
  SHAM, COUNTERFEIT,
  MOCK
mimicry APISM, PAR-
  ROTRY, ECHO,
  MIMESIS, APERY,
  IMITATION, CAMOU-
  FLAGE
mimosa ACACIA,
  SIRIS, GAMA, TREE
minaret STEEPLE,
  SPIRE, TURRET,
  TOWER
mince CHOP, CUT,
  HASH, SLASH, DICE,
  MINIMIZE, WALK,
  RESTRAIN, PIE
minced *meat* RISSOLE
  oath EGAD, BEGAD,

DRAT, HECK, ODS,
  LUD, GAD, GED, GEE
mind OBEY, HEED,
  NOTICE, (AT)TEND,
  RECK, REASON,
  WATCH, OPINION,
  NOTE, CARE, REGARD,
  WISH, INTENT, OB-
  SERVE, OBJECT,
  MOOD, SOUL, NOUS,
  BRAIN(S), WITS,
  REASON, SENSE,
  SPIRIT, INTELLECT,
  INTELLIGENCE,
  FACULTY, FACULTIES,
  INCLINATION, WILL,
  MEMORY
  peace of ATARAXIA
Mindanao *language*
  ATA
  native ATA
  town DAPA
  volcano APO
mine MY, BONANZA,
  PIT, VEIN, LODE,
  COLLIERY, SHAFT,
  EXCAVATION, DEPOSIT,
  SOURCE, BOMB,
  EXPLOSIVE, SAP,
  DIG, EXCAVATE
  basket CORF
  ceiling ASTEL
  coal ROB
  Cornwall BAL
  deposit VEIN,
  LODE
  deviate from vertical
  HADE
  entrance ADIT,
  PORTAL
  excavation STOPE
  horizontal passage
  STULM
  partition SOLLAR,
  SOLLER
  passage ADIT,
  STULM
  product ORE, COAL,
  IRON
  prop STULL, SPRAG,
  NOG
  roof support NOG
  rubbish SLAG, AT-
  TLE, GOAF, GOB
  shack over shaft COE
  shaft SOLLAR,
  SOLLER
    drain for SUMP
    step STEMPEL,
    STEMPLE
  sifter LUB

stepwise excavation
  STOPE
tub CORF
unsystematically
  GOPHER
vehicle TRAM
vein LODE
wall or ceiling ASTEL
worker CAGER
mineral TALC, ROCK,
  ORE, URANITE,
  COAL, CALCITE,
  QUARTZ, SPAR,
  SPALT
  adamantine DIA-
  MOND
  amorphous PINITE
  black URANITE,
  GRAPHITE, HEMATITE,
  COAL
  carbonate of calcium
  CALCITE, CHALK
  crystalline FELSPAR,
  QUARTZ, TOPAZ,
  GARNET, CALCITE,
  DOLOMITE, PYRITES,
  GALENA
  deposit LODE, VEIN,
  SINTER, PLACER
  glassy QUARTZ,
  MICA
  gray or white TRONA
  green URALITE
  hard SPINEL, RUBY,
  DIAMOND
  lustrous SPAR
  matter, mix MAGMA
  organic COAL,
  ASPHALT, TAR
  pitch ASPHALT, TAR
  plaster of paris
  GYPSUM
  pulp TALC
  resinous AMBER,
  OPAL
  salt ALUM
  *scale for determining
  hardness* MOHS
  silicate MICA
  soft TALC, GYPSUM,
  SALT
  spring SPA
  tar MALTHA, PITCH,
  ASPHALT
  vitreous QUARTZ
  water SELTERS,
  SELZER, VICHY,
  PULLNA
  whitish BARITE,
  TRONA(URAO),
  SPALT, SILVER, TALC

yellow(*ish*) PYRITE, EPIDOTE, SULFUR (SULPHUR)
miner's *box or basket* CORF, DAN
chisel GAD
lamp DAVY
mandrel PICK
pickaxe BEDE, FLANG
surveying instrument DIAL
tool GAD
truck DAN
Minerva ATHENA, AZALEA
shield of EGIS
mingle (AD)MIX, COALESCE, MELL, BLEND, WEAVE, MERGE, FUSE, UNITE, COMMIX, COMBINE, CONSOLIDATE, AMALGAMATE, INTEGRATE, COMPOUND
miniate RUBRICATE, ILLUMINATE
miniature SMALL, DIMINUTIVE
minim JOT, TITTLE, WHIT, DROP, GUTTA
minimal LEAST
minimum JOT, LEAST, TITTLE
minion FAVORITE, IDOL, CREATURE, PARASITE, DEPENDENT, HANGER-ON
minister TEND, NURSE, FURNISH, SERVE, OFFICIATE, AID, HELP, CURATE, DOMINIE, ENVOY, LEGATE, NUNCIO, OFFICER, PASTOR, CLERGYMAN, PREMIER, AMBASSADOR, PLENIPOTENTIARY
Minnesota *county* CASS, CLAY, COOK, LAKE, LYON, PINE, POLK, POPE, RICE, ROCK, SCOTT, TODD
minor SMALLER, INFERIOR, MINORITE, FRIAR, INFANT, YOUTH, BOY, LESS(ER)
music MOLLE
minority FEW, TEENS, NONAGE, PUPILAGE

Minos' *daughter* ARIADNE
mother EUROPA
minstrel BARD, HARPIST, POET, RIMER, PIERROT, SCALD, SCOP, SKALD, ENTERTAINER, GLEEMAN, JONGLEUR
Norse SKALD, SCALD
13th century wandering GOLIARD
mint HYSSOP, SAGE, HERB, SOURCE, STOREHOUSE, COIN, MAKE, STAMP, INVENT, FORGE, FABRICATE, PRODUCE
charge BRASSAGE
genus NEPETA
mountain BASIL
Spanish YERBA
minus LESS, LOSS, LOST, LACKING, WANTING, WITHOUT, DEFICIENT, NEGATIVE
quantity NONE
minuscule PETTY, CIPHER, SMALL, WEE, TINY, MICROSCOPIC
minute(s) ACTA, ITEM, NOTE, ENTRY, DETAIL, RECORD, MEMO, TRIFLING, WEE, SHORT, INSTANT, FLASH, INSIGNIFICANT, FINE, TINY, SMALL, LITTLE, CAREFUL, MOMENT
animal ANIMALCULE, GERM
organism SPORE, MONAD, GERM, BACTERIUM, VIRUS
orifice STOMA, PORE
minx GIRL, JADE, COLLEEN, DOLL, FILLY, MISS, HUSSY, QUEAN
mioga GINGER
miracle MARVEL, PRODIGY, WONDER
first CANA
worker THAUMATURGE, WIZARD, MAGICIAN
mirage SERAB, ILLUSION, VISION, DREAM, PHENOMENON

Miranda's *father* PROSPERO
mire GLAR, ADDLE, MOIL, OOZE, MUD, MUCK, SLIME, BOG, SWAMP, FEN, MARSH, SLUSH, ENTANGLE, INVOLVE
mirror CATOPTER, IMAGE, CRYSTAL, GLASS, SPECULUM, REFLECT(OR), IDEAL, MODEL, PATTERN, EXEMPLAR
pertaining to CATOPTRIC
mirth FUN, GLEE, JOLLITY, CHEER, JOY, GAIETY, PLEASURE, MERRIMENT, HILARITY, SPORT, FESTIVITY, GLADNESS
god of COMUS
miry OOZY, SLIMY, BOGGY, LUTOSE, MUDDY, FILTHY, SWAMPY, DIRTY
misanthrope HATER, TIMON, CYNIC, MISER
miscellany VARIA, MIXTURE, OLIO
mischief EVIL, DAMAGE, PRANK, HARM, WRACK, ILL, TROUBLE, MISFORTUNE, DEVILTRY
goddess ATE, ERIS
god of LOKI, LOKE
mischievous *child* LIMB, IMP, BRAT, SCAMP, DEVIL, HELLION
misdemeanor CHAMPERTY, OFFENSE, SIN, CRIME, FAULT, TORT, TRANSGRESSION, MISDEED
misdirect PERVERT, LIE
miser HOARD, NABAL, NIGGARD, SKINFLINT, HOARDER, CHURL, CURMUDGEON
miserable MEAN, PITIABLE, FORLORN, BAD, POOR, UNPLEASANT, DISTRESSED, VALUELESS, UNHAPPY, SICK, WRETCHED, AF-

FLICTED, CONTEMPT-
IBLE, DISCONSOLATE,
ABJECT, WORTHLESS
miserly CLOSE,
SORDID, NEAR,
TIGHT, GREEDY,
MEAN, COVETOUS,
AVARICIOUS, NIG-
GARDLY, STINGY,
PARSIMONIOUS, PE-
NURIOUS, GRIPPING
misery GRIEF,
PANDORA, AGONY,
DOLOR, TRIAL, UN-
HAPPINESS, ANGUISH,
WOE, DISTRESS, AF-
FLICTION, PAIN,
ACHE, SQUALOR,
TRIBULATION, DESOLA-
TION, HEARTACHE,
SUFFERING, TORMENT,
PENURY, PRIVATION
misfortune ADVERSITY,
HARM, ILL, TRIAL,
CROSS, MISHAP, BLOW,
DISASTER, CALAMITY,
HARDSHIP, TROUBLE,
SCOURGE, MISCHANCE,
CATASTROPHE, AC-
CIDENT
misgiving DOUBT,
QUALM, FEAR,
ALARM, DREAD,
FRIGHT, ANXIETY,
DISTRUST, SUSPICION,
HESITATION, AP-
PREHENSION, PREMO-
NITION
mishmash OLIO, HASH,
JUMBLE, HODGE-
PODGE, MEDLEY
Mishna(h) *festivals*
MOED
section ABOT(H)
mislay LOSE, MIS-
PLACE
mislead DELUDE,
LURE, DUPE, GULL,
DECEIVE
mismanage BOTCH,
ERR, BUNGLE,
BLUNK, MISRULE,
FUMBLE
misplay ERR,
RENIG, RENEGE,
MUFF, BOBBLE,
FUMBLE
misprision SCORN,
CONTEMPT
mispronounciation
CACOLOGY
misrepresent COLOR,

GARBLE, BELIE,
FALSIFY, MISLEAD
miss OVERLOOK,
LACK, FAIL, OMIT,
SKIP, AVOID, ESCAPE,
LOSE, MUFF, FOREGO,
WANT, REQUIRE,
OVERSIGHT, MIS-
CARRY, GIRL, LASS,
MAIDEN, DAMSEL,
SPINSTER
missal BOOK
missel THRUSH,
MISTLETOE
missile DART, ROCK,
LANCE, ARROW,
BULLET, BOLA,
PROJECTILE, SPEAR,
BOMB, THOR, NIKE,
GRENADE, ATLAS,
TITAN, POLARIS,
ZEUS
missing ABSENT, LOST,
WANTING, GONE,
AWOL
Mississippi *county*
CLAY, HINDS, LEE,
PIKE, TATE, YAZOO
River Indian SAC
missive NOTE, LINE,
LETTER, MEMO,
MESSAGE, COM-
MUNICATION
Missouri *county*
ADAIR, CASS, CLAY,
COLE, DADE, DENT,
HOLT, IRON, KNOX,
LINN, PIKE, POLK,
RALLS, RAY,
OZARK
misspelling CACOG-
RAPHY
misspent LOST,
WASTED, SQUANDERED
mist BRUME, DIM,
NEBULA, VAPOR,
STEAM, CLOUD,
SEREIN, HAZE, FOG,
SMOG, OBSCURITY,
DRIZZLE, BEWILDER-
MENT
mistake(s) ERR(OR),
SLIP, FAULT, BONER,
BLUNDER, BARNEY,
BULL, BOBBLE, CON-
FUSE, LAPSE, OVER-
SIGHT, MISCUE
in date ANACHRONISM
in syntax SOLECISM
in writing ERRATA,
ERRATUM
mister SIR, DON,

SENOR, MESSIEUR,
TITLE
mistreat ABUSE
misty NEBULAR,
VAGUE, HAZY, CON-
FUSED, INDISTINCT,
SHADOWY, BLURRY
Mitchell, Helen Porter
MELBA
mite ATOM, MOTE,
SPECK, ACARID, LOUSE,
TICK, INSECT, COIN,
PENNY, SOU, BIT,
WHIT, JOT, TIT-
TLE, IOTA, PARTICLE,
MONAD, MOLECULE,
WEIGHT
genus ACARUS
miter FILLET, GUSSET,
CAP, COWL, HAT,
TIARA, JUNCTION,
CIDARIS, HEADBAND,
BELT, GIRDLE, HEAD-
DRESS
mithridate ANTIDOTE
mitigate EASE,
ALLAY, PACIFY,
QUALIFY, DIMINISH,
ALLEVIATE, ASSUAGE,
TEMPER, ABATE,
SALVE, LESSEN,
SOFTEN, MODERATE,
PALLIATE, MOLLIFY,
SOOTHE, QUELL,
RELIEVE
mix STIR, CONSORT,
JUMBLE, KNEAD, MED-
DLE, ASSOCIATE,
BEAT, BLEND, MERGE,
FUSE, JOIN, COALESCE,
CONFOUND, UNITE,
(COM)MINGLE, CROSS,
INTERLARD, COMBINE,
ALLOY, AMALGAMATE,
COMPOUND, MUDDLE,
INTEGRATE, FIGHT
with water SLAKE,
WEAKEN, DILUTE
mixed blood, *person
of* OCTAROON,
GRIFFE, MESTEE,
MESTIZO, MUSTEE,
MULATTO, METIS
mixed type PI
mixture AMALGAM,
HASH, SALAD,
MELANGE, OLIO,
BLEND, COMPOUND,
MEDLEY, JUMBLE,
FARRAGO, SALMA-
GUNDI, GALLIMAU-

FRY, VARIETY,
MISCELLANY
mix-up SNAFU,
TANGLE, AFFRAY,
MELEE, FIGHT,
CONFUSION
Mizar, *star near*
ALCOR
mizzle MIST, DRIZZLE,
SPIT, DISAPPEAR,
DECAMP
moa RATITE,
DINORNITHID, BIRD
genus DINORNIS
Moab, *anc. people*
EMIM(S)
king MESHA,
EGLON
mountain NEBO
Moabite RUTH
moan GROAN, (BE)-
WAIL, LAMENT, CRY,
SOB, SIGH, DEPLORE,
COMPLAIN
moat FOSSE, GRAFF,
CANAL, DITCH,
TRENCH
mob THRONG, RING,
RABBLE, HERD,
DROVE, GANG, PRESS,
CROWD, HORDE,
ARMY, HOST, PEO-
PLE, MULTITUDE,
POPULACE, MASSES,
FLOCK, CLIQUE, SET,
GROUP
Moby Dick WHALE
author MELVILLE
pursuer AHAB
moccasin PAC, SLIP-
PER, SHOE, SNAKE
mocha COFFEE,
LEATHER
stone MOSS AGATE
mock JIBE, GIBE,
TAUNT, JAPE, DE-
RIDE, APE, FLOUT,
MIMIC, SCOFF,
FLEER, SNEER,
JEER, COPY,
IMITATE, RIDICULE,
COUNTERFEIT, FALSE,
PRETEND, SPURIOUS,
FEIGNED, SHAM,
DISAPPOINT, IMITA-
TION
blow FEINT
jewelry LOGIE,
PASTE, GLASS, STRASS
orange SYRINGA,
SHRUB

mockery FARCE,
SHAM, TRAVESTY,
IRONY, DELUSION,
RUSE, SCORN,
RIDICULE, CON-
TEMPT, DERISION,
FUTILITY
evil spirit MOMUS
mockingbird *genus*
MIMUS
mode DECOR, FAD,
VOGUE, STYLE,
FLAIR, CRY, RAGE,
CRAZE, TREND,
DRIFT, TENOR, WAY,
FORM, MANNER,
FASHION, CUSTOM,
METHOD
model TYPE, POSE,
IDEAL, PARAGON, SIT-
TER, GAUGE, NORM,
STANDARD, SHAPE,
MANIKIN, COPY,
DRAWING, DESIGN,
MOLD, EXAMPLE,
PARADIGM, PATTERN,
ARCHETYPE, PROTO-
TYPE, ORIGINAL,
MANNEQUIN
moderate REMIT,
(A)BATE, FRUGAL,
SOFT, MODEST,
LIMIT, MEDIUM, FAIR,
ABSTINENT, MILD,
GENTLE, BLAND,
RESTRAIN, SLOW,
TEMPER(ATE),
SPARING, ABSTEMI-
OUS, JUDICIOUS,
SOBER, COOL, REA-
SONABLE, MEDIOCRE,
DIRECT, REGULATE,
PRESIDE, CONTROL,
MODIFY, CALM
modern LATE, NEW,
NEOTERIC, RECENT,
NOVEL, FRESH,
PRESENT, NEO
prefix NEO
school of art DADA
modernist NEO
modest CIVIL, COY,
SHY, DEMURE,
DECENT, BASHFUL,
RETIRING, VIRTUOUS,
REASONABLE, MORAL,
MEEK, LOWLY,
HUMBLE, CHASTE,
PURE, RESERVED, DIF-
FIDENT, UNOBTRUSIVE,
UNASSUMING, UN-

PRETENTIOUS, BE-
COMING, PROPER
modified leaf BRACT
modify ALTER, TEM-
PER, MASTER,
AMEND, REVISE,
CHANGE, VARY,
QUALIFY, LIMIT,
RESTRICT, SHAPE,
MODERATE, SOFTEN,
LOWER, DIVERSIFY,
REDUCE, INCREASE
modulate INFLECT,
ADAPT, ATTUNE,
VARY, CHANGE,
HARMONIZE, ADJUST,
REGULATE, TEMPER,
SOFTEN, INTONE
modus MANNER,
MEANS, WAY
moguey RAFT,
MOKI(HI)
mogul LORD, MAGNATE,
NABOB, MONGOLIAN,
AUTOCRAT, PERSONAGE
Mohammed(an)
ISLAM, MAHOMET,
MUSSULMAN,
SARACEN, MOSLEM,
MUHAMMAD,
MAH(O)UN(D)
ablution before prayer
WUDU
adopted son ALI
angel of death
AZRAEL
antenuptial settlement,
wife MAHR
ark of covenant
TABUT
ascetic SUFI, FAKIR
Bible KORAN,
ALCORAN
bier or coffin TABUT
birthplace MECCA
blacksmith LOHAR
blood relationship
NASAB
body of interpreters
ULEMA
book KORAN,
ALCORAN
burial place MEDINA
calif, caliph OMAR,
ALI
cap TAJ
capturer of Jerusalem
OMAR
caravansary IMARET
chief SAYID, DATTO,
AGA, AGHA
convert, early ANSAR

creed SUNNA
crusade JIHAD, JAHAD
daughter FATIMA
diadem or crown TAJ
deity ALLAH
demon(s) JINNEE, JANN, AFRIT, GENIE, EBLIS, SHAITAN, SHEITAN
dervish(es) SADITE, SADI
devil EBLIS *See* "demon" *above*
dignitary SHERIF, SHEREEF
divorce TALAK
doctors of law ULEMA
dress IZAR
drinking cup LOTAH
Easter EED
evil spirit See "demon" *above*
fast RAMADAN
festival BAIRAM, EED
flight from Mecca HEGIRA
garment IZAR
guide, spiritual PIR
headgear FEZ, TARBUSH
headman DATTO
heirarchy ULEMA
holy city MECCA
hospice IMARET
infidel KAFIR
interpreter(s) ULEMA, MUFTI
judge CADI, KADI
kinship NASAB
law ADAT, SUNNA
lawyer MUFTI
leader AGA *See* "chief" *above*
loin cloth IZAR
lord SAYID
magistrate CADI, KADI
marriage settlement MAHR
minister VIZIR, VIZIER
month RAMADAN, SAFAR, SHABAN, SHAWWAL, RAJAB, MUHARRAM
mystic SUFI
noble AMIR, AMEER, EMIR, SAYID
non KAFIR
nymph HOURI
official HAJIB, VISIR
orthodox(y) HANIF, SUNNITE

pantheist SUFI
pilgrimage to Mecca HADJ
potentate CALIPH, CALIF, IMAM, IMAUM
prayer SALAT, NAMAZ
call to AZAN, ADAN
rug ASAN(A)
priest IMAM, IMAUM
prince EMIR, AMEER, SEID, SHERIF, SHEREEF, SAYID
relationship NASAB
religion ISLAM
rug, prayer ASAN(A)
ruler AKBAR, SULTAN, HAKIM, SHERIF, SHEREEF, NAWAB
sage ULEMA
saint PIR, SANTON
salutation SALA(A)M
scholar ULEMA
sect WAHABI
seminary ULEMA, MADRASA
shirt KAMIS
shrine KAABA
son-in-law ALI
spirit PIR, GENIE *See* "demon" *above*
state OMAN
stringed instrument REBAB
student SOFTA
successor CALIPH
supporters, early ANSAR
teacher ALIM, MOLLAH, PIR, AGA
temple MOSQUE
title IMAM, AMIR, EMIR, CALIF, CALIPH, AGA, NAWAB, SAYID, PIR, HAKI, HADJ, SIDI, SEID, SHERIF
tomb PIR
tomb city MEDINA
unbeliever KAFIR
uncle of ABBAS, ABU, TALIB
veil YASHMAK, IZ(Z)AR
viceroy NABOB, NAWAB
war, religious JAHAD, JIHAD
wife AISHA
woman's outer wrap IZAR
Mohicans, *last of* UNCAS

moiety HALF, PART, SHARE, PORTION
moil TAINT, TOIL, DRUDGE, MEDDLE, SOIL, DAUB, SPOT, DEFILE, BESPATTER, STAIN, DRUDGERY, LABOR, CONFUSION, VEXATION, WET, WALLOW, TURMOIL
moist DANK, HUMID, WET, DAMP, TEARFUL, MUGGY, SWAMPY, MARSHY
moisten ANOINT, BEDEW, DAMPEN, WET, SOAK
moisture DEW, RAIN, DAMPNESS, HUMIDITY, LIQUID, WETNESS
exposed to RET
moki(hi) RAFT, MOGUEY
molar GRINDING, CHOPPER, CRUSHING, TOOTH
molasses TREACLE, SYRUP, SIRUP, SORGHUM
molave PURIRI, TEAK, TREE, WOOD
genus VITEX
mold CAST, PLASM, FORM, MODEL, SHAPE, MATRIX, PATTERN, DIE, SOIL, FUNGUS, HUMUS, STAIN, FRAME, BODY, NATURE, KIND, MIX, KNEAD, AME
core of NOWEL
pouring hole in GIT, SPRUE, GATE
Moldavia ROMANIA
town BALTA, JASSY, IASI
molded *building material* PISE
in wax CEROPLAST
molder's *tool* FLANGE
molding LOZENGE, ROSE, CAVETTO, CHAIN, ASTRAGAL, STRIP, CABLE, SCROLL, OGEE, OVOLO, CYMA, CONGE, TORUS, REGLET, REEDING, SPLAY, FILLET, SCOTIA
concave GULA, COVING, SCOTIA, OXEYE, CAVETTO
convex TORUS, REEDING, OVOLO
curved OGEE, NEBULE

disk ornamented
BEZANTEE
egg-shaped OVOLO
flat FILLET
hollow SCOTIA
narrow REGLET,
LISTEL, FILLET
ogee CYMA, GOLA,
GULA
projection COVING
rounded TORUS,
OVOLO, BILLET
wavelike CYMA, OGEE,
NEBULE
moldy FUSTY, MUSTY,
OLD, EARTHY, DE-
CAYING, STALE
mole JETTY, PIER,
QUAY, TAPE, TAUPE,
TALPA, NEVUS,
STARNOSE, IMPERFEC-
TION, FAULT, SPOT
genus TALPA
like animal DESMAN
molecule MITE,
MONAD, PARTICLE,
ATOM, ION
component ATOM,
ION
molest ANNOY, ABUSE,
MEDDLE, INTERFERE
mollify (A)BATE,
SOFTEN, CONCILIATE,
LESSEN, MITIGATE,
ALLAY, SOOTHE, AP-
PEASE, PACIFY, TEM-
PER, RELAX, COMPOSE,
CALM, QUIET, RELIEVE,
MODERATE
mollusk, mollusca
CLAM, OYSTER, SNAIL,
CHITON, MUSSEL,
CONCH, OCTOPUS,
MUREX, SCALLOP,
SQUID, SLUG, BIVALVE,
WHELK, LIMPET, CUT-
TLEFISH
bivalve OYSTER,
CLAM, CONCH,
VENERID, MUSSEL,
CHAMA
genus LEDA,
ASTARTE, ANOMIA
double shelled
LIMPET
edible ASI, MUSSEL,
OYSTER, CLAM, SNAIL
eight-armed OCTOPUS
fresh-water CHITON,
MUSSEL
gastropod ABALONE,
SLUG, SNAIL

genus MUREX, OLIVA,
CHITON, NERITA
highest class
ARGONAUT
largest CHAMA
N. Zealand PIPI
rasp organ RADULA
sea ABALONE
shell COWRY, COWRIE
teeth RADULA
ten-armed SQUID
wrinkled shell
COCKLE
young SPAT
molt SHED, MEW,
MUTE, SLOUGH, CAST,
EXUVIATE, ECDYSIS
molten rock LAVA,
MAGMA
Molucca *island* BANDA,
MALUKU, CERAM
moment SEC, FLASH,
JIFFY, TRICE, POINT,
VALUE, IMPORT,
WEIGHT, TWINKLING,
INSTANT, SECOND,
IMPORTANCE,
CONSEQUENCE,
SIGNIFICANCE, CON-
SIDERATION, GRAVITY,
ELEMENT
monad ATOM, UNIT,
ENTITY, PARTICLE,
UNIVALENT, MOLE-
CULE, ANIMALCULE,
PROTOZOAN
monarch RULER, KING,
DYNAST, QUEEN,
EMPEROR, KAISER,
SHAH, SULTAN, CZAR,
TZAR, TSAR, AUTOCRAT,
DESPOT, SOVEREIGN,
POTENTATE, DICTATOR,
CHIEF, BUTTERFLY
greedy MIDAS
race DYNASTY
monarda TEA, MINT,
BERGAMOT, PLANT
monastery FRIARY,
ABBEY, HOSPICE,
CLOISTER, CONVENT,
PRIORY, NUNNERY,
LAMASERY
haircut TONSURE
head of ABBOT
room CELL
monastic ASCETIC,
SOLITARY, OBLATE,
MONK(ISH), RECLUSE,
CONVENTUAL,
CENOBITIC
monetary PECUNIARY,

FISCAL, BURSAL,
FINANCIAL
money GELT, FUNDS,
CASH, GRIG, SPECIE,
DUST, KALE, JACK,
DOUGH, MINA, TALENT,
WAD, CABBAGE, LET-
TUCE, WAMPUM,
GOLD, SILVER,
WEALTH, CAPITAL,
PEAG(E), COIN, PAPER,
CURRENCY, TENDER,
CUSH, MAZUMA,
LUCRE, NOTES, BILLS,
PROPERTY, POSSES-
SIONS, WEALTH *See*
"coin"
box ARCA, TILL,
DRAWER, SAFE
certificate SCRIP,
CHECK, BOND
changer CAMBIST,
SARAF, SHROFF
changing AGIO
coin MINT
coined SPECIE
earnest ARLES
found TROVE, TREAS-
URE
gift ALMS
hole for SLOT
hole in SLOT
hook-shaped LARIN,
LARI, LARREE
Indian See under
"Indian"
in Doomsday book
ORA
manual CAMBIST
1/60 talent MINA
premium AGIO
roll of WAD, ROULEAU
shell UHLLO, SEWAN,
COWRY, COWRIE,
SEAWAN, PEAG(E)
soft PAPER
sorter SHROFF,
TELLER, SARAF
standard BANCO,
SPECIE, GOLD
Yap stone FEI
monger TRADER,
VENDER, MERCER,
DEALER, TRAFFICKER,
MERCHANT
Mongol HU, TA(R)TAR,
ASIAN, BURIAT,
SHARRA, KHALKHA,
ELEUT, KALMUCK
dynasty YUAN
Siberian TATAR
tribe SHAN

Mongolia, *capital*
  URGA
coin TUGRIK
desert ORDOS, GOBI
former capital of
  Outer URGA
river PEI
conjurer SHAMAN
tent YURT
weight LAN
Mongoloid LAPP, RAIS,
  TURK, DURBAN, LAI,
  SHAN
mongoose, *crab-eating*
  URVA
mongrel MUTT, CUR,
  HYBRID, MIXED, CROSS
monition SUMMONS,
  WARNING, ADVICE,
  COUNSEL, NOTICE,
  INTIMIDATION, AD-
  MONITION, INSTRUC-
  TION, INDICATION, IN-
  FORMATION, HINT,
  CAUTION
monitor MENTOR,
  WARN, ADVISER, RE-
  MINDER, INSTRUCTOR,
  PR(A)EPOSITOR,
  COUNSELOR, OVER-
  SEER
lizard URAN,
  VARAN(US), ANOLI
monk FRA, FRIAR,
  ABBE, PADRE,
  CENOBITE, HERMIT,
  ANCHORITE, RECLUSE,
  EREMITE, ABBOT,
  PRIOR
ascetic FAKIR, DERVISH
Buddhist BO, ARHAT
community CENOBITE
early English BEDE,
  BEDA, BAEDA
Franciscan CAPUCHIN
Greek church
  CALOYER
head ABBOT
hermit ANCHORET,
  ANCHORITE, RECLUSE,
  EREMITE
hood for COWL
Moslem DERVISH
Tibet LAMA
title FRA
monkey PRIMATE,
  MONA, NISNAS, VITOE,
  TOTA, SIMIAN, APE,
  SIME, MIMIC, MEDDLE,
  TAMPER, TRIFLE, FOOL
Africa PATAS, MONA,
  WAAG, GRIVET,

GUENON, COLOBUS,
  NISNAS
arboreal GRIVET, TITI,
  TEETEE
Asia LANGUR,
  MACAQUE
bearded ENTELLUS
bonnet TOQUE
Brazil SAI
bread BAOBAB
Capuchin SAPAJOU,
  SAI, SAJOU
cebine SAI
Ceylon MAHA, TOQUE,
  WANDEROO
China DOUC
Diana ROLOWAY
genus CEBUS, ATELES
grivet TOTA, WAAG
guenon MONA,
  NISNAS, VERVET
house APERY
howler ARABA, MONO,
  STENTOR, ALOUATTE
long-tailed LANGUR,
  KAHA, PATAS
Malabar WANDEROO
mammal like POTTO,
  TARSIER
Phil. Islands MACHIN
proboscis KAHA, NOSE
  APE
sacred, India RHESUS
sapajou SAI
S. Africa VERVET,
  TAMARIN
S. America SAJOU,
  SAKI, SAGUIN, ARABA,
  TITI, TEETEE, SAPAJOU
spider genus ATELES
squirrel SAIMIRI,
  MARMOSET
tufted or bonnet ZATI,
  TOQUE
W. Africa MONA,
  PATAS
monkish MONASTIC
monkshood ATIS,
  ATEES, BEARBANE,
  ACONITE, WOLFSBANE,
  PLANT
mono, *combining form*
  ALONE, ONE, SINGLE
monogram CIPHER,
  CHARACTER, INITIALS,
  DESIGN
monolith MENHIR,
  PILLAR, OBELISK,
  STATUE, MONUMENT,
  COLUMN, SHAFT,
  STONE

monomachy DUEL,
  COMBAT
monomaniac CRANK,
  PARANOIC
monopolize CONTROL,
  OWN, HOLD, POSSESS,
  CORNER, ENGROSS
monopoly TRUST,
  CARTEL, POOL,
  CORNER, PATENT,
  COPYRIGHT,
  SYNDICATE
monosaccharide OSE,
  HEXOSE, MONOSE
monotonous DULL,
  TEDIOUS, TIRESOME,
  SAMELY, DRAB, HUM-
  DRUM, CHANGELESS,
  UNVARIED, UNIFORM,
  WEARISOME
monster OGRE, DEMON,
  BRUTE, ARGUS, GIANT,
  HARPY, GORGON,
  FIEND, CERBERUS,
  SPHINX, GHOUL,
  CHIMERA, GRIFFIN,
  MONSTROSITY, HUGE,
  MONSTROUS, ENOR-
  MOUS *See* "giant"
combining form
  TERAT(O)
fabled MINOTAUR,
  SPHINX, OGRE,
  CENTAUR, ECHIDNA,
  HARPY, GORGON,
  ARGUS
fabulous BUCENTAUR,
  HARPY, KRAKEN
female GORGON,
  HARPY
fire-breathing
  CHIMERA, DRAGON
giant OGRE
half man and bull
  MINOTAUR
half man and horse
  CENTAUR
half man and ox
  BUCENTAUR
half woman and
  serpent ECHIDNA
hundred eyes ARGUS
hundred hands GYGES
lion's head CHIMERA
medical TERAS
serpent ELLOPS,
  DRAGON
slain by Hercules
  HYDRA
monsterlike TERATOID
monstrous HUGE,
  ENORM(OUS), VAST,

COLOSSAL, HEINOUS, SHOCKING, HATEFUL, FLAGRANT, ABSURD, ABNORMAL, PRODIGIOUS, GIGANTIC, TITANIC, TREMENDOUS, OVERWHELMING, HIDEOUS, HORRIBLE *See* "huge"

Montana *city* BUTTE, KIPP, HELENA
county BLAINE, CARTER, HILL, LAKE, PARK, TETON, TOOLE
river TETON, POWDER
"Monte Cristo" *author* DUMAS
hero DANTES
month, *excess calendar over lunar* EPACT
combining form MENO
fasting RAMADAN
first day Roman CALENDS
French revolutionary NIVOSE
last ULTIMO, ULT
present INSTANT, INST
monticle HILL, KNOLL, KNOB, CONE, HILLOCK
monument MEMORIAL, DOLMEN, TOMB, RECORD, PYRAMID, ARCH, PILLAR, STATUE, SHAFT, OBELISK, MARKER, TABLET, PLAQUE, SLAB, (GRAVE)STONE, TESTIMONIAL, CENOTAPH, WORK, PRODUCTION, BUILDING
mood HUMOR, TONE, VEIN, WHIM, TEMPER, SPIRIT, SOUL, DISPOSITION, STYLE, MANNER
moon CYNTHIA, PHOEBE, LUNA, DIANA, MONTH, SATELLITE, PLANET, CRESCENT, STARE, ROAM, WANDER, IDLE, GAZE
age beginning of year EPACT
on June 1st EPACT
angel MAH(I)
apogee or perigee APSIS
area on MARE
crater LINNE

god or goddess See under "god" or "goddess"
imaginary inhabitant SELENITE
mountain(s) JURA, ATLAI, HAEMUS, APENNINE
personified SELENE, SELENA
pertaining to LUNAR, SELENIC
point CUSP, HORN
point farthest from earth APOGEE
nearest earth PERIGEE
position of OCTANT
sea or basin MARE
valley on RILL(E), CLEFT
moonstone ALBITE, FELDSPAR, ORTHOCLASE
moor DOCK, FASTEN, ANCHOR, HEATH, PLAIN, FEN, MARSH, WASTE, RIVET, SECURE, (AF)FIX, TIE, BIND, ROOT, SARACEN, BERBER, ARAB
buzzard HARPY, HARRIER
fowl or hen GROUSE
Moorish *palace* ALCAZAR, ALHAMBRA
sailboat SAPIT
tabor ATABAL
moose ELK
genus ALCES
mop WIPE, TUFT, SPONGE, SWAB, CLEANSE, POLISH, POUT, GRIMACE, HAIR
for cannon MERKIN, SWAB
mope BROOD, SULK, POUT, FRET
moppet CHILD, TOT, GIRL, DOLL, DOG
mora DEFAULT, DELAY, POSTPONEMENT, GAME
tree FUSTIC
moral ETHIC(AL), JUST, GOOD, VIRTUOUS, EPIMYTH, LESSON, ALLEGORY, PURE, CHASTE, PIOUS, TRUE, NOBLE, UPRIGHT, FAITHFUL, HONEST, RIGHT-(EOUS), HONORABLE,

MENTAL, INTELLECTUAL
fable APOLOGUE
lapse SIN, VENALITY
law DECALOG(UE)
poem, short DIT
principle SOUL
morals ETHICS, PRINCIPLES, STANDARDS, MAXIM, HABITS
description of ETHOGRAPHY
overseer CENSOR
morass QUAG, BOG, FEN, MARSH, TANGLE *See* "swamp"
Moravia, *former capital* BRUNN, BRNO
river ZLIN
moray EEL, CONGEREE, HAMLET
morbid DISEASED, GLOOMY, DARK, SICK, UNWHOLESOME, UNHEALTHY, GRISLY, HORRIBLE
mordant ACRID, EROSIVE, BITING, KEEN, SHARP, CUTTING, CAUSTIC, ACID, SARCASTIC, SATIRICAL, CORROSIVE, SCATHING
more BIS, TOO, ENCORE, BOOT, AGAIN, ANEW, EXTRA, PLUS, ADDITIONAL, OTHER, BESIDES, ELSE, FURTHER, GREATER
combining form PLE(I)O, PLIO
morello CHERRY
moreover BESIDES, ALSO, TOO, AND, ELSE, BEYOND, FURTHER, LIKEWISE
morepork BIRD, NIGHTJAR, BOOBOOK, RURU
More's *land* UTOPIA
work UTOPIA
moribund SICK, DYING
moringa *seed* BEN
morion HELMET, QUARTZ
Mormon DANITE, SMITH, YOUNG, LAMAN
founder SMITH
officer ELDER
morning EOS, AURORA, MATIN, DAWN, DAY-

BREAK, AM, SUNRISE, MORN, FORENOON
concert AUBADE
prayer or song MATIN(S), AUBADE
reception LEVEE
refresher DEW
star VENUS, MARS, JUPITER, SATURN, MERCURY, LUCIFER, PHOSPHOR
Moro LANAO, SULU
chief DAT(T)O
high priest SARIP
prince CACHIL
tribe SULU
Moroccan RIFF, MOOR, BERBER
city or town FEZ, TETUAN, IFNI See "seaport" below
coin RIAL, OKIA, OUNCE, FLOOS, FLUE, DIRHEM
general KAID
hat FEZ
infantryman ASKAR
land GISH
measure SAHH, FANEGA, MUHD, TANGIN, TEMAN, UEBA, CADEE, COVADO
region ER RIF
ruler SHERIF, SHEREFF, SULTAN
seaport AGADIR, CEUTA, RABAT, TANGIER, SALE (SALI, SLA), SAF(F)I, IFNI
tribesman KABYLE
morocco, imitation ROAN
moron IDIOT, OLIVE, HALFWIT
morose DOUR, GLUM, GRUM, SOUR, TESTY, CROSS, GRUFF, CRABBY, SURLY, SULKY, SULLEN, CHURLISH, PERVERSE, CRUSTY, MOODY, GLOOMY, SPLEENY
morphon, opposed to BION
morro HILLOCK, CASTLE, HILL, FORT
Morro Castle site HAVANA (HABANA)
Morse code ALPHABET, CIPHER, DOTS, DASHES

dash DAH
morsel SOP, SCRAP, BIT(E), ORT, SNACK, MOUTHFUL, TIDBIT, FRAGMENT
morsure BITING, BITE
mort DEAD, DEATH, DUMMY, FATAL, WHIST, SALMON
mortal HUMAN, DEADLY, DIRE, FATAL, LETHAL, EARTHLY, TERRENE, DESTRUCTIVE, GRIEVOUS, SEVERE, MAN, BEING, EARTHLING, INDIVIDUAL
mortar BOWL, HOBIT, CAP, CEMENT, PLASTER, GUN, CANNON, VESSEL
beater RAB
board CAP, HAWK
mixer RAB
pounding instrument PESTLE, BRAYER
tray HOD
"Mort d'Arthur"
author MALORY
mortification CHAGRIN, SHAME, GANGRENE, DEATH, PENANCE, HUMILIATION, VEXATION, NECROSIS
mortify PUNISH, ABASE, DENY, HUMILIATE, VEX, SUBDUE, DEADEN, HUMBLE, ABASH, EMBARRASS
mortise TENON, NOTCH, SLOT, HOLE, CAVITY, SLIP, FASTEN
and tenon JOINT
machine SLOTTER
mortuary CHARNEL, CINERARIUM, OSSARIUM, CEMETERY, GRAVEYARD, NECROPOLIS, MORGUE
car HEARSE
roll OBIT
mosaic, apply INCRUST, INLAY
gold ORMOLU
law TORA(H), PENTATEUCH
work TESSERA
Moscow, citadel in KREMLIN
3rd International COMINTERN

Moses, elder brother AARON
father AMRAM
father-in-law JETHRO
mountain SINAI
sister MIRIAM
spy for CALEB
successor JOSHUA
wife ZIPPORAH
writings of PENTATEUCH
Moslem See "Mohammedan"
mosque, central part JAMI
student SOFTA
tower MINARET
mosquito INSECT, PEST, IMAGO, ANOPHELE
genera CULEX, AEDES
larvae WIGGLERS
order DIPTERA
moss FUNGUS, PEAT, BOG, LICHEN, USNEA, SEAWEED, MONEY
Mossi language MO, MOLE
Most Holy Lord SS.D.
most noble HIRAM
mot PUN See "pun"
moth INSECT, IO, TINEAN, MUGA, LEPIDOPTER, MILLER, SPHINX, EGGER, REGAL, TUSSAH, YUCCA
genus of clearwing SESIA
genus of clothes TINEINA
silkworm ERIA, MUGA
mother AMMA, DAM, ABBESS, PARENT, NURTURE, NATIVE, VERNACULAR, MATER, MAMMA, ORIGIN, SOURCE, ANCESTRESS, FOSTER
goddess DEVI
government by METROCRACY, MATRIARCHY
of day and light NYX
of gods CYBELE, FRIGGA, RHEA, BRIGANTIA
of the Gracchi CORNELIA
of Presidents VIRGINIA
related on side of ENATIC
Tagalog INA

motion RATE, CLIP,
(A)ESTUS, SPEED,
GAIT, GESTURE, RE-
QUEST, MOVE, STIR,
PACE, IMPETUS, STEP,
PROPOSAL, ACTION,
MOVEMENT, DRIFT,
FLUX, PORT, COURSE,
TENDENCY, AGITATION,
SUGGESTION, SIGNAL
pertaining to KINETIC
producing MOTILE
motionless STILL,
INERT, FIXED,
STATIONARY,
QUIESCENT, IMMOBILE
motive REASON, PRE-
TEXT, CAUSE, SPRING,
SPUR, GOAD, AIM,
END, GROUND, DESIGN,
IDEA, FORCE, INDUCE-
MENT, INCENTIVE,
STIMULUS, IN-
FLUENCE, CONSIDERA-
TION, THEME, MOTIF,
IMPULSE
motmot HUHU, BIRD
mottled PIED, PINTO,
MARBLED, VARIEGATED,
SPOTTED, BLOTCHED,
MOTLEY, SPECKLED,
DAPPLED
motto MAXIM, ADAGE,
MOT, REASON, SAW,
GNOME, APOTHEGM,
THOUGHT, SLOGAN,
PROVERB, SAYING
mouflon SHEEP
mould, moulding *See*
"mold" *or* "molding"
moult *See* "molt"
mound TUMP, DUNE,
HILL, TEE,
TUMULUS, STEP,
RAMPART, HEAP, BANK,
BARROW, HILLOCK,
HUMMOCK, KNOLL,
BULWARK, MONTICLE,
MORRO
bird LEIPOA,
MEGAPOD(E)
mount PEAK, HILL,
ALP, HORSE, SEAT,
ASCEND, RISE, CLIMB,
SET, PLACE, FIX,
FASTEN, ARRANGE,
PACE, SCALE, SOAR
by ladders ESCALADE
Mount of Olives
OLIVET
Mount Rainier
TACOMA

mountain(s) MOUNT,
PEAK, ALP, MESA,
HEIGHTS, ELEVATION,
MASS, HEAP, QUANTITY
*See under country in-
volved*
Alps BLANC
ash ROWAN, TREE
Asia ALTAI, NANGA
Minor IDA
Biblical HOREB, SINAI,
ARARAT *See under*
"Bible"
California SHASTA,
LASSEN
chain SIERRA,
ROCKIES, TETONS,
ANDES
climbing peg PITON
combining form ORE,
OREO
crest ARETE, TOR,
PEAK
Crete IDA
fabulous See
"legendary" *below*
formation OROGENY
gap PASS, GATE, DE-
FILE *See* "pass"
below
high ALP
highest EVEREST
hollow in side of
CORRIE
India GHA(U)T
Kirgiz ALAI
lake TARN
legendary QAF, KAF,
MERU
low BUTTE, MESA
Moab NEBO
*Moses saw Canaan
from* NEBO
muses, seat of
HELICON
Nepal EVEREST,
LHOTSE
pass DEFILE, COL,
GHAT, GAP, CENIS,
CUT, DONNER
pasture ALP,
S(A)ETER
peak ALP, CIMA, CONE
peg PITON
pool TARN
range SIERRA, TETONS,
ROCKIES, ANDES
ridge SIERRA
science of OROLOGY
sickness VETA, PUNA
S. America ANDES
States MONTANA,

IDAHO, COLORADO,
UTAH, NEVADA,
ARIZONA
study of OROGRAPHY
sunset reflection
ALPENGLOW
trail marker KARN,
CAIRN
Turkey ARARAT
Turkistan ALAI
under Pelion OSSA
Wyoming MORAN
mountaineer AARON
mountebank EMPIRIC,
QUACK, FRAUD, FAKER,
CHARLATAN, PRE-
TENDER, TRICKSTER,
IMPOSTER
mourn RUE, SIGH,
(BE)WAIL, LAMENT,
SORROW, GRIEVE, CRY,
WEEP, (BE)MOAN,
DEPLORE
mournful THRENODIC,
SAD, SORROWFUL,
DOLEFUL, PITIFUL,
DISTRESSING,
MELANCHOLY,
LUGUBRIOUS,
LAMENTABLE, WOEFUL
mourning dress ALMA,
SABLES, WEEDS, CREPE
mouse VOLE, MUS,
MUR, RODENT,
WEIGHT, SWELLING,
BRUISE
bird COLY, SHRIKE
field or meadow
VOLE, METAD
genus MUS
India METAD
Old World JERBOA
shrew ERD
mouselike MURINE,
SHY, RETIRING
moutan PEONY, PLANT,
FLOWER
mouth(s) ORA, MUN,
OS, ENTRANCE, OPEN-
ING, RICTUS, ORIFICE,
INLET, BOC(C)A,
STOMA, CAVITY,
MUMBLE, VOICE,
UTTER, SPEAK,
GRIMACE, MOW, DE-
CLAIM, VERBAL
away from ABORAL,
ABORAD
disease of NOMA,
STOMATITIS, CANKER
furnace BOCCA

part(s) of UVULA,
PHARYNX, LIPS, LABIA
pertaining to
STOMATIC, STOMATAL,
ORAL
river FIRTH, DELTA
toward ORAD
wide RICTUS
with open AGAPE
move ROUSE, ACTUATE,
DRIVE, IMPEL, EXCITE,
SHIFT, CARRY, ACT,
STIR, BUDGE, DIS-
LODGE, PROPEL, IN-
DUCE, CAUSE,
ANIMATE, STIMULATE,
PROVOKE, KINDLE,
SPUR, GOAD, IN-
FLUENCE, PERSUADE,
IMPRESS, AGITATE,
PROCEED, PROPOSE,
PLAY, AROUSE,
MOTION, PROCEEDING,
CHANGE
along MOSEY
back EBB, RECEDE
boat KEDGE, PROPEL
furtively SNEAK,
SLINK, SKULK
in circles PURL,
EDDY, SPIN,
SWIRL, GYRATE
rapidly FLIT, DART,
RUN, SPEED
sidewise SLUE, SIDLE
slowly INCH, EDGE,
WORM
smoothly GLIDE,
SLIDE, SKATE
swiftly SCUD, FLY,
SKIM
movement DRIVE,
ACTION, STIR,
ACTIVITY, THEME,
MANEUVER,
MOMENTUM, (LOCO)-
MOTION, CHANGE,
CRUSADE, RHYTHM,
TEMPO
biological TAXIS
capable of MOTILE,
MOBILE
movie CINEMA, FILM,
SCREEN, FLICK(ER)
award OSCAR
combining form CINE
script SCENARIO
moving NOMADIC,
MOTILE, MOBILE,
ALIVE, PATHETIC,
ROUSING, TOUCHING,
PITIFUL, IMPRESSIVE,

INFLUENCING, PER-
SUADING, AFFECTING,
EXCITING, POIGNANT
part ROTOR, CAM,
WHEEL, COG
mow CUT, PUCKER,
POUT, GRIMACE, LOFT,
MEW, SHORTEN, DESS,
HAYSTACK, HAYRICK
mowed strip SWATHE,
SWATH
Mozambique *native*
YAO
Mozart *opera* FIGARO
Mrs. Montagu Barstow
ORCZY
much LOT, MANY,
VERY, NEARLY, LARGE,
GREAT, CONSIDERABLE,
ABUNDANT, PLEN-
TEOUS, HEAPS, GOBS,
LOTS, SCADS,
QUANTITY, ALMOST
combining form
MULTI, POLY
"Much Ado About
Nothing" character
CLAUDIO, LEONATO,
ANTONIO, HERO,
URSULA
mucilage ARABIN, GUM,
PASTE, GLUE,
ADHESIVE, CEMENT
mud MUCK, OOZE,
SLUDGE, MIRE, DREGS,
SILT, SLIME, DIRT,
LIBEL, SLANDER,
SULLAGE
bath ILLUTATION
deposit SILT
eel SIREN
living in LIMICOLOUS
rake CLAUT
volcano SALSE
mudar fiber YERCUM
muddle (BE)FOG,
ADDLE, ROIL,
UPSET, FAZE,
PUZZLE, (BE)CLOUD,
CONFUSE, FUDDLE,
STUPEFY, INTOXICATE,
CONFOUND, MESS,
SOSS, JUMBLE, SNAFU
muddy ROILY, SLAKY,
MOIST, MURKY, DIRTY,
MIRY, TURBID, SOILED,
SLIMY, BESMEARED,
OBSCURE, INDISTINCT,
MUDDLED, CONFUSED
muermo ULMO, TREE
Muezzin *call to prayer*
AZAN, ADAN

muffin GEM, CAKE,
ROLL, BREAD, BISCUIT,
SCONE, BRIOCHE
muffle MUTE, DEADEN,
STIFLE, DULL, WRAP,
COVER, ENVELOP,
SHROUD, BLINDFOLD,
SILENCE
mug STEIN, NOG,
NOGGIN, POT, TOBY,
CUP, FACE, PUSS,
VISAGE, DUPE, FOOL,
PHOTOGRAPH
mugger CROCODILE,
GOA
mulatto METIS
mulberry *bark* TAPA
beverage MORAT
cloth or paper TAPA
India AL, AAL, ACH
tree genus MORUS
mulch STRAW, COVER,
MANURE, SAWDUST,
LITTER
mulct AMERCE, FINE,
PUNISH, SENTENCE,
STEAL, FORFEIT(URE)
mule SLIPPER, SHOE,
HINNY, HYBRID,
MONGREL, JENNY,
TRACTOR
drove ATAJO
mull CLOTH, MUSLIN,
STEATIN, SWEETEN,
SPICE, GRIND,
CRUMBLE, PONDER,
THINK, BUSTLE,
COGITATE, ERR
mullet LIZA, SUCKER,
BOBO, FISH
Egypt BOURI
Heraldic STAR
Mexico LISITA, BOBO
multitude MASS,
GALAXY, HOST, MOB,
ARMY, LEGION, RUCK,
HORDE, THRONG,
MYRIAD, CROWD,
SHOAL, RABBLE, AS-
SEMBLY, PEOPLE,
SWARM, COLLECTION,
HERD, PACK, POPULACE
mumbo jumbo FETISH,
IDOL, DEMON, BUGA-
BOO, INCANTATION,
MUMMERY
mummer ACTOR,
GUISER, MIME,
MASKER, BUFFOON
mummy CADAVER,

RELIC, CORPSE,
CARCASS
spirit KA
mundane TERRENE,
SECULAR, TEMPORAL,
WORLDLY, CARNAL,
EARTHLY, TER-
RESTRIAL
municipal POLITICAL,
CIVIC, CIVIL
muniment RECORD,
ARCHIVE, DEED, DE-
FENSE, SUPPORT
Munro, H. H. SAKI
muntjac DEER, RATWA
muralist GIOTTO,
CIMABUE, (da)VINCI,
SARGENT, RIVERA,
OROZCO, BENTON
murder BURKE,
HOMICIDE, SLAY, KILL,
EXECUTE, SPOIL, MAR,
RUIN, DESTROY,
MASSACRE, ASSASSINA-
TION See "kill"
of king REGICIDE
of prophet VATICIDE
murderous FELL,
GORY, DEADLY,
BRUTAL, DESTRUCTIVE,
CRUEL, SAVAGE,
BLOODTHIRSTY,
SANGUINARY
murid PUPIL, DISCIPLE
murk DUSK, DARK,
GLOOM, DARKEN,
OBSCURE, CLOUDED,
OVERCAST, LOWERING
murmur GRUMBLE,
PROTEST, PURR,
REPINE, HUM, COO,
FRET, WHISPER, UN-
DERTONE, COMPLAINT,
WHIMPER, MUTTER,
MUMBLE
murrain FEVER,
PLAGUE, ANTHRAX,
PESTILENCE
mus *genus* RAT,
MOUSE, RODENT
Muscat *native* OMANI
muscle BRAWN,
THEW(S), BICEPS,
STRENGTH, MYON,
SINEW, TERES
contracting AGONIST
elevating LEVATOR
round TERES
straight RECTUS
muscovite MICA
muscular BRAWNY,
MIGHTY, STALWART,

STOUT, VIGOROUS,
ATHLETIC, THEWY,
BURLY, HUSKY, HALE,
SOUND, SINEWY,
STRONG, HERCULEAN
spasm TONUS
muse DREAM, PONDER,
MULL, THINK, REASON,
WEIGH, STUDY,
MEDITATE, REFLECT,
RUMINATE, COGITATE,
CONSIDER
amatory poetry
ERATO
astronomy URANIA
comedy and bucolic
poetry THALIA
dancing TERPSICHORE
epic poetry or
eloquence CALLIOPE
history CLIO
lyric poetry EUTERPE
music EUTERPE
sacred song
POLYMNIA
tragedy MELPOMENE
Muses, *the* NINE,
ERATO, URANIA,
THALIA, TERPSICHORE,
CALLIOPE, CLIO,
EUTERPE, POLYMNIA,
MELPOMENE
birthplace of PIERA
home of HELICON
sacred place of
PIERIA, AONIA
mush PORRIDGE,
ATOLE, PAP, SAGAMITE,
MEAL, PUDDING,
SUPAWN, MARCH,
WALK, TRAVEL,
JOURNEY, FLATTERY,
SENTIMENTALITY
mushroom FUNGUS,
AGARIC, MISY, MOREL,
TRUFFLE, PARVENU,
UPSTART, UMBRELLA,
HAT, BOOM, BOLETUS,
CHAMPIGNON, CEPE
cap PILEUS
disease FLOCK
parts GILLS
superior MOREL
umbrella-shaped part
PILEUS
mushy THICK, SOFT,
YIELDING, GOOEY,
SENTIMENTAL
music AIR, TUNE,
STRAIN, RHYTHM,
TIMBRE, MELODY,
HARMONY, ART,

MOTET, SYMPHONY,
MINSTRELSY See
"musical"
aftersong EPODE
all together TUTTI
Anglo-Indian melody
RAGA
beat MOTO, PULSE,
ICTUS, RHYTHM,
TEMPO
below SOTTO
bright ANIME
brisk ALLEGRO
canto PASSUS
character NOTE,
SLUR, TIE, STAVE, BAR,
BRACE, TRILL, KEY,
CLEFT, SHARP, FLAT,
REST
clear, brilliant
CHIARA, CHIARO
dying away
PERD(ENDOSI)
end of CODA, FINE,
FINALE, STRETTA
fast ALLEGRO,
VIVACE, PRESTO
flat MOLLE, BEMOL
flourish ROULADE
for 9 NONET
3 TRIO
2 DUET
god of APOLLO
grace note SANGLOT
half major tone SEMI-
TONE
hall(s) ODEON, GAFF,
CARNEGIE, (LA)SCALA,
ODEUM, ODEA
harsh APRE
high ALT
in the style of AL,
ALLA, ALLE, ALLI,
ALLO
lead PRESA
leap SALTO
less MENO
lines STAFF
little POCO
lively VIVO,
ANIMATO, ALLEGRO,
(CON)BRIO, VIVIDO,
VIVACE
loud FORTE
major DUR
scale GAMUT
third DITONE
mark SLUR See
"character" *above*
measured beat MOTO,
PULSE See "beat"
above

melodic phrase LEITMOTIV, LEITMOTIF
melodious ARIOSO
metrical composition POEM
more PIU
morning AUBADE
muse of EUTERPE
nine piece NONET
ninth NONA
non-concerted SOLO
note, Guido See "Guido"
pause CE(A)SURA
quick (CON)MOTO *See* "lively" *above*
quick passage STRETTA, STRETTO
repeat sign SEGNO
rudimentary SCALES
run ROLLE
sacred CHORAL
saint of CECILIA
set of verses DERRY
short song ODE, AIR
sign NEUME, SEGNO *See* "character" *above*
simple song AIR, TUNE, LAY, DITTY
slowly ADAGIO, LENTO, LARGO, TARDO
smoothly LEGATO, PIACEVOLE
soft PIANO
so much TANTO
sweetly, softly DOLCE
symbol See "character" *above*
syncopated JAZZ
tempo PULSE, BEAT *See* "beat" *above*
third TIERCE
three TER, TRIAD
time See "beat" *above*
too much TROPPO
twice BIS
musical MELODIOUS, HARMONIOUS, OROTUND, TONAL, LYRIC(AL), TUNEFUL, DULCET
ballad DERRY
chord TRIAD
comedy REVUE
composition OPERA, FUGUE, MOTET, ETUDE, NOME, OPUS, NUMBER, SONG, SONNET, CAROL
direction STA, SOLI

for silence TACET, CEASE
drama OPERA, BALLET
ending CODA
instrument DRUM, FIFE, HARP, ASOR, HORN, LUTE, LYRE, OBOE, PIPE, TUBA, VIOL, CELLO, SPINET, OCARINA, HELICON, PIANO, ORGAN, BUGLE, UKE, ROCTA, SITAR, SAX, VIOLIN, GUITAR, CLAVIHARP, HARMONICA, ACCORDION, MANDOLIN, TAMBOURINE
  Africa NANGA
  ancient CROWD, BANDORE, DULCIMER, PANDURA, NABLA
  bass wind SERPENT
  brass CORNET, HORN, TROMBONE, TUBA
  China SANG, SHENG, CHENG
  flutelike FLAGEOLET
  guitarlike LUTE, ROTE, UKE
  India SAROD, BINA, VINA, SITAR
  keyboard CLAVIER, MANUAL
  keyed SPINET, PIANO, ORGAN, CLAVIHARP, ACCORDION
  lutelike BANDORE, THEORBO
  lyrelike KISSAR, ASOR
  old REBEC, CELESTA, GITTERN, CITTERN
  percussion DRUM, BELLS, GONG, CYMBALS
  pipe OAT, REED
  saxhorn family ALTHORN
  six-string GUITAR, BANJO
  small drum TABOR(ET), TABRET, ATABAL
  Spain CASTANET
  stringed SITAR, NABLA, REBAB, REBEC, ZITHER, CITTERN, LUTE,

  LYRE, ROCTA, VIOLIN, VIOLA, BANJO, GUITAR, UKE
  ancient BANDORE
  ten-string ASOR
  terra-cotta OCARINA
  trumpetlike BUGLE, CLARION, TUBA
  wind FLUTE, OBOE, CLARINET, FIFE, PICCOLO, HORN, CORNET, BUGLE, TUBA
interlude VERSET
interval TRITONE, OCTAVE
medley RONDO, CENTO, OLIO, PASTICCIO, POTPOURRI
nocturne SERENADE, BARCAROLE
note, sharpening ECBOLE
passage brilliantly done CODA, BRAVURA
performance REVUE, CONCERT, MUSICALE
pipe OAT, REED
rattle SISTRUM, MARACA, CASTANET
scale, degree of GRADO
show REVUE
sound TONE, NOTE
study ETUDE
suite PARTITA
symbol CLEF, NOTE, REST, SHARP, FLAT *See* "character" *under* "music"
theme TEMA
third TIERCE
work ORATORIO, OPUS, OPERA, SONATA *See* "composition" *above*
Musketeer ARAMIS, ATHOS, PORTHOS
muskmelon ATIMON, CASABA, CANTALOUPE
muslin COTTON, CLOTH, MADRAS, NAINSOOK, MULL, SHELA, ADATI
  bag TILLOT
  E. Indies BAN
  India GURRAH, MADRAS, ADATI
  striped DORIA, DOREA
muss DISHEVEL, LITTER, CHAOS, RUMPLE, MESS, MUDDLE, DISORDER, CONFUSION,

DISARRANGE,
SQUABBLE, ROW, COM-
MOTION
mussel UNIO, NERITA,
BIVALVE, MOLLUSK,
NAIAD
genus MYTILUS, UNIO
large HORSE
part of BYSSUS
river UNIO, NAIAD
Mussulman MOSLEM,
SARACEN *See*
"Mohammedan"
must SAPA, JUICE,
MILDEW, STUM, WINE,
MOLD, OUGHT, NEED,
SHOULD, OBLIGED,
NECESSARY, REQUIRED,
ESSENTIAL, FUSTINESS
mustard SENVY, CHAR-
LOCK, SINAPSIS,
PLANT, CONDIMENT,
SEASONING
black genus NIGRA
gas YPERITE
genus BRASSICA
pertaining to SINAPIC
plaster SINAPISM
white genus ALBA
wild CHARLOCK
muster GATHER, LEVY,
MARSHAL, ENLIST,
ORDER, ARRAY, AS-
SEMBLE, EXHIBIT,
SHOW, COLLECT,
CONGREGATE,
COMPRISE, SUMMON,
DISPLAY
out DISBAND, DIS-
CHARGE, RELEASE
mustiness FUST, MOLD
musty RANCID, FUSTY,
MOLDY, BAD, FETID,
RANK, FOUL, STALE,
HACKNEYED, TRITE,
SOUR, SPOILED, DULL,
SPIRITLESS, FOGYISH,
LISTLESS, HOARY,
APATHETIC
Mut's *associate*
CHUNSU
husband AMEN
son KHONSU
mutable FICKLE,
ERRATIC, FITFUL, UN-
STABLE, CHANGEABLE,
VACILLATING, ALTERA-
BLE, VARIABLE, IN-
CONSTANT, UNSET-
TLED, UNSTEADY
mutate ALTER, VARY,

CHANGE, MODIFY,
MUTANT
mutation CHANGE,
UMLAUT, FREAK,
SPORT, ALBINO
mute DEADEN,
MUFFLE, SILENT,
LENE, MUM, SURD,
DUMB, SPEECHLESS,
UNPRONOUNCED
mutilate GARBLE, GELD,
MAIM, MAR, DEFORM,
DELETE, INJURE,
CRIPPLE, HURT, DE-
FACE, CUT, SCAR, DIS-
FIGURE, EXPUNGE,
MANGLE, DISMEMBER,
HAMSTRING, HACK
mutilation, *crime of*
MAYHEM
mutiny PUTSCH, RE-
VOLT, COUP, TREASON,
SEDITION, REBELLION,
INSUBORDINATION, IN-
SURRECTION
mutter GROWL,
MUMBLE, GRUMBLE,
MURMUR, COMPLAIN
mutton *fish* SAMA,
MOJARRA, PARGO
loin of RACK
mutual JOINT, COM-
MON, RECIPROCAL,
SHARED, RESPECTIVE
aid society GUILD,
UNION
muzhik PEASANT,
RUSSIAN
muzzle GAG, NOSE,
SNOUT, COPE,
CENSURE, SILENCE,
CLEVIS, RESPIRATOR,
MAUL, THRASH
muzzy DAZED, CON-
FUSED, MUDDLED,
STUPID, TIPSY,
BLURRED, FUZZY,
BEFUDDLED
myopic PURBLIND,
NEARSIGHTED, SHORT-
SIGHTED
myrmicid ANT
myrrh RESIN, GUM,
SHRUB
myrtle VINE, SHRUB,
LAUREL, PERIWINKLE,
CONDIMENT
N. Zealand
RAMARAMA
mysteries ARCANA
mysterious DARK,
CRYPTIC, MYSTIC(AL),

SECRET, ARCANE, OC-
CULT, ABSTRUSE, HID-
DEN, BAFFLING, IN-
COMPREHENSIBLE,
PUZZLING, CABALISTIC,
UNKNOWN,
ENIGMATICAL, IN-
SCRUTABLE, RECON-
DITE, OBSCURE,
ESOTERIC, INEXPLICA-
BLE, UNFATHOMABLE,
WEIRD, SUPERNATURAL
mystery RUNE,
ESOTERY, CRAFT,
ARCANUM, ENIGMA,
RITE, RIDDLE, PUZZLE,
STORY, SECRET, PLAY,
NOVEL, CONUNDRUM,
DOCTRINE
mystic EPOPTIC,
ORPHIC, RUNIC, OC-
CULT, ASCETIC,
MAGICAL *See*
"mysterious"
art CABALA
cry EVOE
ejaculation OM
initiate EPOPT
Moslem SUFI
pagan GNOSTIC
secret sect CABAL
word ABRAXAS, OM,
SESAME, ABRACADABRA,
PRESTO
writing CODE, CIPHER,
RUNE
mystical OCCULT,
SECRET, DARK,
SPIRITUAL, SYMBOLIC
significance
ANAGOGUE
word See under
"mystic"
mystify BEFOG,
OBFUSCATE, BE-
WILDER, PERPLEX,
FAZE, RATTLE, UPSET,
PUZZLE, BAFFLE,
HOAX
myth LEGEND, FIG-
MENT, SAGA, FABLE,
STORY, PARABLE, AL-
LEGORY, FICTION,
TRADITION, INVENTION
mythical *flying being*
GARUDA
island ATLANTIS,
UTOPIA
mythological *being*
CENTAUR *See*
"monster"

bird ROC, HANSA,
SIMURG(H)
giant See "giant"
hero AJAX
man-eater LAMIA
monster GRIFFIN
serpent APEPI

N

N EN, NU
Na SODIUM
nab *See* "catch"
Nabal's *wife* ABIGAIL
nabob DIVES, PLUTO-
CRAT, MIDAS, VICEROY,
GOVERNOR, DEPUTY,
CROESSUS
deputy NAWAB
Nabokov *novel*
LOLITA, PNIN
nacelle CHASSIS,
BASKET, SHELTER,
BOAT, COCKPIT
nacre (MOTHER-OF)
PEARL, SHELLFISH
nacreous PEARLY
nacrite KAOLIN(E)
nadir, *opposed to*
ZENITH
naevus MOLE *See*
"nevus"
nag HORSE, PONY,
GARRAN, PLUG, TOR-
MENT, BADGER, TEASE,
TWIT, PLAGUE,
HECTOR, IRRITATE,
HARASS, HENPECK
nahoor BHARAL, SHA,
SHEEP
Nahor's *wife* MILCAH
naiad NYMPH,
HYDRIAD, MUSSEL
nail TACK, SPAD,
BRAD, STUD, PIN,
SPIKE, BOSS, UNGUIS,
CLAW, TALON, HOOF,
SCALE, PLATE, DRIVE,
CLENCH, CLINCH,
FASTEN, CATCH, TRAP,
SEIZE, ARREST, SECURE
drive at slant TOE
French CLOU
headless SPRIG
ingrowing ACRONYX
marking on LUNULE
mining marker SPAD
shoemaker's
SPARABLE, BRAD
size PENNY
wooden PEG, FID

naive FRANK, ARTLESS,
OPEN, CANDID, IN-
GENUOUS, UNAF-
FECTED, NATURAL,
SIMPLE, UN-
SOPHISTICATED
naked BARE, NUDE,
BARREN, BALD, UN-
COVERED, UNCLAD,
UNDRESSED, STRIPPED,
EXPOSED, UNPRO-
TECTED, EXACT,
LITERAL, MERE,
SIMPLE, PLAIN, MANI-
FEST, CLEAR, OBVIOUS
namaycush TOGUE,
TROUT, FISH
namby-pamby INSIPID,
SILLY, VAPID, INANE,
SENTIMENTAL, CODDLE
name EPITHET,
AGNOMEN, ONYM,
MONIKER, (COG)-
NOMEN, NOUN, AP-
PELLATION, DESIGNA-
TION, SOBRIQUET,
REPUTATION, HYPOC-
ORISM, ALIAS,
PSEUDONYM,
PATRONYM, EPONYM,
CACONYM, TITLE, AP-
POINT, NOMINATE,
DESIGNATE, SET, FIX,
DUB, TERM, FAME,
CLEPE, CALL, ENTITLE,
ENUMERATE, STYLE,
ANNOUNCE, DENOMI-
NATE, IDENTIFY, MEN-
TION, CITE, REPUTA-
TION, REPUTE,
SPECIFY, INDICATE,
CHRISTEN
assumed ALIAS,
PSEUDONYM, PEN
bad CACONYM
consisting of names
ONOMASTIC
derived from father
PATRONYM
from mother
MATRONYM
family COGNOMEN,
AGNOMEN
female, meaning
a gate BAB(S)
amiable MABEL
beautiful BELL(A),
BELLE
beauty ADA(H)
beloved AMY, VIDA
bird AVA, AVIS
bitter MARY, MARA,

MOYA, MARI(E),
MOLL(Y), POLL(Y)
bright BERTA,
BERTIE, CLARA,
CLARE
chaste or pure
CATHERINE, TRINA,
KIT, KAY, KAREN
clinging IVY, IVE,
IVIA
compassionate
RUTH
daughter JAMA
destiny CARMA
eagle ARVA
fair SELMA *See*
"white" *below*
fairy, elf, etc.
FAY(E), FAE,
NAIDA, NIXIE, ELLA,
NISSA, FALA
felicity NAOMI
flower CALLA,
DAISY, ROSE, LANI
gate BAB(S)
gift DORA, DORE
goal META, NYSSA
God is gracious
JANE
good BONNIE,
BON(A)
grace ANN(A),
NINA, NANA, NITA,
NANCY
grandmother EM,
EMMA, EMILY
happy IDA
heaven(ly) JUNO,
CELIA, CELESTA,
SILE, CELESTE
high or holy ELA,
ALTA, (H)ELGA,
OLGA, HOLLY
high degree
(H)ERMA, IRMA,
IRME
honey MELISSA,
MILLIE, LISSA
hope NADA, NADINE
"I am" ESTA
inestimable TONY,
TONI, TONA
jewel CAMEO,
PEARL, OPAL, RUBY
joy AINE
lady LOLO
life VITA, ZOE, EVE,
EVA, EVELYN, EVIE
light LUCY, LULU,
LUCIA, HELEN(E),
HELENA, LORA,
NORA, ELLEN

little ETTA, ERICA
lovable MILA
maiden CORA
merit MOIRA
mistress MARTHA,
  MARTA, MATTIE,
  ZITA
ninth NONA
noble ELSE, ELSA,
  ELZA, ILSA, ETHEL
of the air AURA,
  ORA, ZORA, AUNE
one MONA
ornament ADA(H)
palm tree TAMAR
peace IRENE,
  ERIN(A), FREDA,
  IRINA, OLGA, OLIVE,
  NOLA
pearl MARGARET,
  MARGO, MAG, RITA,
  GRETA, GOGO,
  GRETTA, PEG
poem EDDA
poppy RHEA
power DYNA
prayer BEDA
prosperous ZADA
princess SARA(H),
  SARI, SAL, ZARA,
  ZADA
pure See "chaste"
  above
rainbow IRIS
regal ERICA
rejuvenation EDNA
rich ALDA, EDITH,
  OTHA, EDE
royal RANI
she HERA
shining rock SELA
snow NEVA
soul ALMA, ENID
sound ECHO
star or the starry
  ASTA, (H)ESTHER,
  STELLA
sweet HEDY
tenth DIXIE
the one UNA
true VERA
truth ALICE
white or fair GWEN,
  GWIN(NE), WENDY,
  NAN(NIE)
wonderful MIRA,
  MYRA
youth HEBE
feminine of Aloysius
  LOUISE
David VIDA
Herman ARMINA

John JEAN, JANE,
  JOAN, JANET, JAN,
  IVA
Joseph JO, JOSIE,
  JOSEPHA, FIFI,
  JOSEPHINE
Lief LOVE
Luther or Lothair
  CLOTHILDA
Oliver OLGA, OLIVE,
  NOLA
Otto ALDA, OTHA
Solomon SALOME
Vincent VICKY,
  VICKI
William WILLIE,
  WILLA, VELMA,
  VILMA, MINA, MIMI,
  MINNIE, BILLIE
first PRAENOMEN,
  FORENAME
from a city EPONYM
maiden NEE
male, meaning
  accuser WRAY
  all wise ALVIS
  amiable ELMO
  appointed, the SETH
  beloved DAVID
  bitter, the OMAR
  blessed BENEDICT,
    BEN(NY), BENNIE,
    DIXON
  blind HOMER
  borne by God
    AMOS
  bright ALBERT,
    BERT, XAVIER
  bright in fame
    ROBERT, BERT, BOB
  cautious, the CATO
  cheerful, the TATE
  chief KEN(T)
  child MOSES, MOSS,
    MOSE, MO
  comely and fair
    ALAN, ALLAN, ALLEN
  courageous or
    champion NEAL,
    NEIL
  dim-sighted CECIL
  divine reward AXEL
  dove JONAS, JONAH
  eagle AJAX, ARNO
  earth worker
    GEORGE, JORGE
  famous warrior
    LEWIS, LOUIS,
    ALOIS, LEW, LUIS,
    LUDI
  father of Ner (light)
    ABNER

  fighter BORIS
  flaxen-haired LINUS
  free FRANK,
    FRANCIS
  God's grace
    JESS(E)
  happy, prosperous
    FELIX
  he shall add
    JOSEPH, JOEY, JOE
  healer or physician
    ASA, JASON
  help EZRA
  high ELI *See*
    "noble" *below*
  high mountain
    AARON
  industrious EMIL
  judge DAN
  king CYRUS, ERIC,
    LEROY, ROY, REX
  kingly, royal BASIL
  laughter ISAAC
  lion LEO
  lord or lordly
    CYRIL, FREY, ADON,
    LARS
  Lord is God JOEL
  Lord is my good
    TOBIAS
  love LIEF
  lover of horses
    PHILIP, PHIL
  man ENOS
  noble or high
    ARTHUR, EARL(E),
    AZA, ELI
  noble fame ELMER
  noble friend ALVIN
  of the forest SILAS,
    SYLVESTER
  peace FRITZ
  prosperous FELIX
  protector of property
    EDGAR
  red-haired RUFUS
  rich OTTO
  rock or stone
    PETER, LIAS
  royal See "king"
    and "kingly" *above*
  safe TITUS
  skillful DREW
  son BENJAMIN,
    BENNIE, BEN
  supplanter JAMES,
    JACOB, JAKE, JIM
  tent dweller JUBAL
  wanderer ERROL
  warrior MARK,
    MARCO, MARTIN,

LEWIS, LOUIS, ALOIS, LUIS, LUDI, LEW
watchful IRA
white or fair-haired BOYD
wind, the KEITH
wise ALVIS
of a thing NOUN
of two terms DIONYM
pet or diminutive SOBRIQUET, POPPET, NICKNAME, HYPOCORISM
plate or tablet FACIA, PLAQUE
written backward ANANYM
named APPOINTED, NOMINATED, CITED, DUBBED, YCLEPT, ELECTED, CHOSEN, DESIGNATED
namely VIZ, SCILICET, SCIL, VIDELICET, PARTICULARLY
namesake HOMONYM
nanny NURSE, GOAT
Naomi MARA
daughter-in-law RUTH
land settled in MOAB
naos TEMPLE, CELLA, SEKOS, ADYTUM, SHRINE
nap PILE, RAS, DOWN, FUZZ, SNOOZE, DOZE, SLEEP, SIESTA, WINK, SLUMBER, DROWSE
long SHAG
raising machine GIG
to raise TEASE(L)
nape NIDDICK, SCRUFF, NUCHA, NECK, TURNIP
of sheep's neck SCRAG
napery LINEN, NAPKINS, DOILIES
Naphtalite ENAN, AHIRA
napkin TOWEL, CLOTH, DOILY, DIAPER, SERVIETTE
Naples NAPOLI
king MURAT
secret society CAMORRA
Napoleon's *battle* ACRE, ULM, JENA, WATERLOO
brother-in-law MURAT
island CORSICA, ELBA, HELENA

Napoleon III LOUIS
mother HORTENSE
nappy DOWNY, SHAGGY, WOOLLY
Naraka HELL
narcissus PLANT, FLOWER, EGOIST
loved by ECHO
narcosis SLEEP, TORPOR, COMA, STUPOR, STUPEFACTION, INSENSIBILITY, UNCONSCIOUSNESS
narcotic DRUG, ANODYNE, OPIATE, DOPE, HYPNOTIC, SOPORIFIC, BHANG, HEMP, CODEINE, OPIUM, HEROIN, MORPHINE, MARIJUANA, REEFER, ETHER
plant POPPY, MANDRAKE, HEMP
nardoo CLOVER, NARDU, PLANT
nares NOSTRILS, NOSE
narghile HOOKA(H), PIPE
narial RHINAL, NASAL, NARINE
nark SPY, INFORMER, SPOILSPORT, OBSERVE, NOTE, TEASE, ANNOY, IRRITATE
narrate RECITE, RELATE, TELL, BRUIT, RECOUNT, DESCRIBE, DETAIL, DEPICT
narrative CONTE, FABLE, TALE, REPORT, STORY, HISTORY, ACCOUNT, CHRONICLE, RECITAL
poem EPIC, EPOS
narrow CLOSE, LIMIT(ED), LINEAL, LEAN, SCANT, MEAGER, STRICT, RIGID, SMALL, LITTLE, BIGOTED, RESTRICT(ED), CONTRACT(ED), CIRCUMSCRIBE(D), CONFINED, INCAPACIOUS, DECREASE, PREJUDICED, STRAIT
combining form STEN(O)
inlet RIA
-mindedness BIGOTRY, BIAS

narrows SOUND, STRAIT
narthex PORCH, VESTIBULE, FOYER, LOBBY, ENTRY, HALL, PORTICO, STOA
nasal RHINAL, NARINE, NARIAL
nascency GENESIS, BEGINNING, BIRTH, ORIGIN
Nash, Richard BEAU
nasty MEAN, FOUL, DIRTY, FILTHY, OBSCENE, RIBALD, INDECENT, NAUSEOUS, DISGUSTING, UNCLEAN, POLLUTED, DEFILED, SQUALID, LOATHSOME, OFFENSIVE, REPULSIVE, ODIOUS, HARMFUL, DANGEROUS, MALICIOUS
natal GLUTEAL, INBORN, INNATE, NATIVE
Nata's *wife* NANA
natatorium POOL, TANK
Nathan Hale SPY
nation RACE, STATE, TRIBE, REALM, COUNTRY, PEOPLE
symbol CREST, FLAG
native INDIGENOUS, ENDEMIC, ABORIGINAL, (IN)BORN, INHERITED, INNATE, PRIMEVAL, NATAL, INNER, NATURAL, ORIGINAL, NORMAL, SIMPLE, UNAFFECTED, PRISTINE, INDIGINE, ABORIGINE, ITE, SON, TAO, DENIZEN, AUTOCHTHON, INHABITANT, CITIZEN
plant INDIGINE
natterjack TOAD
natty CHIC, NEAT, JAUNTY, TRIM, SPRUCE, NIFTY, DAPPER, SMART, POSH, TIDY, TRIG, FOPPISH
natural RAW, WILD, UNFEIGNED, UNCULTIVATED, PRIMITIVE, REALISTIC, LIFELIKE, REAL, INNATE, INBORN, NORMAL, NAIVE, UNAFFECTED, EASY, SPONTANEOUS *See* "native"
condition NORM

group RACE,
ETHNICISM
location SITUS
principle GUNA
naturalist MUIR,
ANIMIST, BIOLOGIST,
DARWIN
naturalize ADAPT,
ACCLIMATE,
HABITUATE, AC-
CUSTOM, DOMES-
TICATE, FAMILIARIZE
naturalness EASE
nature BENT, SORT,
TYPE, ESSENCE,
MOOD, KIND, STRIPE,
KIDNEY, ILK, FORM,
FIGURE, SHAPE,
SPECIES, QUALITY,
DISPOSITION, TEM-
PERAMENT, TENOR,
CHARACTER(ISTIC),
UNIVERSE
pertaining to COSMO
spirit NAT
worship PHYSIOLATRY
nausea PALL, QUALM,
DIZZINESS,
QUEAZINESS, SEA-
SICKNESS, DISGUST,
LOATHING
nauseous FULSOME,
OFFENSIVE, LOATH-
SOME, DISGUSTING,
SICKENING, RE-
VOLTING, REPULSIVE
nautical MARINE,
NAVAL, MARITIME
before AFORE
below ALOW
brace ABOX
cease AVAST
chain TYE
cry AHOY
fasten BATTEN
grommet BECKET
hook BECKET
instrument PELORUS,
SEXTANT, COMPASS
line EARING,
MARLINE, MARLING
mile KNOT
ring GROMMET,
BECKET
rope guide WAPP
side timber BIBB
stop AVAST
term ATRY, ABEAM,
ABAFT, AVAST, AHOY,
ALOW, AFORE
tighten FRAP

tilting ALIST
water's surface RYME
nautilus ARGONAUTA,
MOLLUSK
commander NEMO
Navaho *hut* HOGAN
naval MARINE *See*
"nautical"
depot BASE, SCAPA
FLOW
force FLEET, ARMADA,
SQUADRON, NAVY
jail BRIG
nave HUB, CENTER
navigate AVIATE, KEEL,
SAIL, TRAVERSE,
STEER, CONDUCT,
VOYAGE, JOURNEY,
TRAVEL, GUIDE,
DIRECT, CRUISE,
COURSE
navvy HAND, WORKER,
LABORER, NAVIGATOR
navy FLEET
near CLOSE, AT,
WITHIN, SHORT, DEAR,
NIGH, ABOUT, ALMOST,
APPROACH, TOUCH,
MATCH, NEXT, BY,
NEIGHBORING,
ADJACENT, NARROW,
STINGY, PARSIMO-
NIOUS, INTIMATE, AP-
PROXIMATE, AKIN
combining form
PAR(A)
sighted MYOPIC,
PURBLIND
nearby NEXT, ANENT,
GIN, NIGH, THERE-
ABOUTS, HANDY, CLOSE
Near East LEVANT
native ARAB, TURK
neat NATTY, NICE,
TRIG, TIDY, CLEAN,
ORDERLY, PRIM,
TRIM, TOSH, SPRUCE,
PRECISE, EXACT,
SHAPELY, CLEVER,
SMART, DAINTY,
ADROIT, CLEAR, NET,
CATTLE, COWS, BULLS,
OXEN, BOVINE
neb BILL, BEAK, NOSE,
SNOUT, TIP, PENPOINT
Nebraska *city* OMAHA
county BOYD, BURT,
CASS, CLAY, GAGE,
HALL, HOLT, KNOX,
LOUP, OTOE, POLK,
ROCK, YORK

nebulous HAZY, VAGUE,
INDEFINITE, OBSCURE,
UNCERTAIN, CLOUDY,
MISTY, NEBULAR, IN-
DISTINCT, UNCLEAR
envelope COMA,
CHEVELURE
necessary REQUIRED,
VITAL, REQUISITE,
NEEDED, ESSENTIAL,
COMPULSORY, IN-
EVITABLE, UNAVOIDA-
BLE, INDISPENSABLE,
COMPELLED,
MANDATORY
necessitate COMPEL,
FORCE, OBLIGE, EN-
TAIL, CONSTRAIN,
IMPEL, REQUIRE
necessity MUST,
MISTER, NEED, WANT,
POVERTY, FATE,
URGENCY, COM-
PULSION, CONSTRAINT,
REQUISITE, DESTINY,
REQUIREMENT, ES-
SENTIAL
of life ALIMENT,
FOOD, BREAD, WATER
neck SWIRE, CERVIX,
SCRUFF, NAPE,
COLLUM, CHANNEL,
ISTHMUS, WOO
armor GORGET
artery CAROTID
back of NAPE, NUCHA,
SCRUFF
frill JABOT, RUCHE,
RUFF
hair MANE
horse WITHERS
line VEE
of coat or vest
GEORGE
part of GULA, THROAT
pertaining to WAT-
TLED, NUCHAL
piece STOLE, BOA,
FICHU, AMICE, CRAVAT,
ASCOT, TIE, COLLAR,
BELCHER, BAN-
DAN(N)A, BIB, RUFF,
NECKERCHIEF
plumage HACKLE,
MANE
thin SCRAG
neckerchief *See* "neck-
piece" *above*
necklace BEADS,
BALDRIC, RIVIERE,
TORQUE, CHOKER,

COLLAR, HIAQUA,
CHAIN, PEARLS
necktie ASCOT, TIE,
SCARF, BANDAN(N)A
necromancer DIVINER,
EXORCIST, MAGICIAN,
SORCERER, CONJURER,
ENCHANTER, WIZARD,
SOOTHSAYER
necromancy GOETY,
MAGIC, SORCERY,
CONJURATION
necropsy AUTOPSY
nectar HONEY, DRINK,
WINE, AMRITA,
MANNA, AMBROSIA,
ELIXIR
of gods AMBROSIA
nectareous DELICIOUS,
SWEET, SAVORY
need LACK, REQUIRE,
CRAVE, WANT, WISH,
STRAIT, DESTITUTION,
NECESSITY, REQUISITE,
POVERTY, DEFECT,
PENURY, EXIGENCY,
URGENCY, EXTREMITY,
INDIGENCE, PRIVATION,
COMPULSION
needle BODKIN, ACUS,
OBELISK, EYELETEER,
INDICATOR, POINTER,
SEW, RIDE, HOUND,
HECKLE, VEX, IR-
RITATE, EMBROIDER
bug genus RANATRA
case ETUI, ETWEE
combining form ACU
finisher EYER
gun DREYSE
medical HYPO
pointed ACERATE,
ACEROSE
sea GAR(FISH)
shaped ACICULAR,
SPICULAR, ACIFORM
needlefish GAR,
TELEOST, PIPEFISH,
EARL
needlework SAMPLER,
SEAM, SEWING,
EMBROIDERY,
EDGING, PICOT
needy POOR, NECES-
SITOUS, INDIGENT,
DESTITUTE
negate NULLIFY, DENY,
REFUTE, ANNUL, DIS-
AVOW
negation NO, NULLITY,
VETO, NYET, OBLIT-

ERATION, ANNIHILA-
TION, DISCLAIMER
negative NAY, NAE,
NOPE, NOT, NOR,
DENIAL, FILM, X-RAY,
NEGATE, NEUTRAL,
NULLIFY, CONTRADICT
ion ANION
pole CATHODE
prefix NON, IM, UN
neglect SHIRK, OMIT,
SLIGHT, FORGET, DE-
FAULT, NEGLIGENCE,
FAILURE, IGNORE, DIS-
REGARD, OVERLOOK,
DESPISE, INATTENTION
neglectful REMISS,
CARELESS, SLACK, LAX,
NEGLIGENT, HEEDLESS,
INATTENTIVE
negligence LACHES,
DISREGARD, INDIF-
FERENCE
negligent LAX, REMISS,
SLACK, NEGLECTFUL,
INDIFFERENT, CARE-
LESS
negotiate DICKER,
DEAL, TREAT, CONFER,
CONSULT, ADVISE,
PARLEY, ARRANGE,
BARGAIN, SELL,
MANAGE, CONDUCT,
DIRECT, TRANSACT,
SETTLE, CONCLUDE,
TRANSFER, ASSIGN
negotiation DEAL, PAR-
LEY, TREATY
negrito ATA, ITA
Africa AKKA, BATWA
Malay ATA
New Guinea KARON
Philippine ATA, AETA
negro LURI, ETHIO-
PIAN, HUBSHI, HOT-
TENTOT, BUSHMAN
Africa DAHOMAN, VEI,
VAI
Beni(n) EBOE, IBO
dance JUBA
dialect GULLAH
Egypt NUBIAN
ghost JUBA
Gold Coast GA, TSHI,
AKIM, FANTI
Liberia GREBO, KROO,
KRUMAN
Niger IBO, NUPE,
EBOE
secret society EGBO,
MAU

Sudan HAUSA, EGBA,
YORUBA
tribe EWE, EVE
white and MESTEE,
MUSTEE
negroid, *Mediterranean*
HAMITE
Africa AKKA, BANTU,
KAFFIR, PONDO,
TEMBU
Kordofan NUBA,
NUBIAN
pigmy AKKA, BATWA
neighborhood PUR-
LIEU, VICINITY,
VENUE, AREA, DIS-
TRICT, LOCALITY, EN-
VIRONS, PROXIMITY,
COMMUNITY, SECTION,
REGION
neighboring ACCOLENT,
ADJACENT, BORDERING,
CONTIGUOUS, VICINAL,
NEARBY
neither right nor wrong
ADIAPHOROUS
Neleus's *son* NESTOR
nelumbo LOTUS, LILY
nemesis AVENGER,
AGENT, RETRIBUTION,
PENALTY, FATE
nemoral SYLVAN
neophyte CONVERT,
TYRO, NOVICE, BE-
GINNER, CATECHUMEN
See "novice"
neoplasm TUMOR,
GROWTH
neoteric LATE, MOD-
ERN, NEW, NOVEL,
FRESH, RECENT
Nepal *capital* KAT-
MANDU (KATH-
MANDU)
coin MOHAR, ANNA
district or area TERAI
mongoloid RAIS
mountain EVEREST,
LHOTSE
native KHA
peak API
people RAIS
ruler RANA
tribesman AOUL
warrior GURKHA
nephelite LENAD, MIN-
ERAL
nephew NEPOTE
nephrite JADE, TREMO-
LITE

Neptune, *Celtic* LER
  discoverer of planet
    GALLE
  scepter or sign TRI-
    DENT
  son TRITON
Nereid *chief* THETIS
Nereus' *wife* DORIS
nerfling ID, IDE, FISH
Nero TYRANT, FIDDLER
  successor GALBA
nerol ALCOHOL
nerve GRIT, VIGOR,
  STEEL, CRUST, COUR-
  AGE, CHEEK, GALL,
  SAND, GUTS, SINEW,
  TENON, ENERGY,
  STRENGTH, PLUCK,
  COOLNESS, ENDUR-
  ANCE, IMPUDENCE,
  AUDACITY, BRAZEN-
  NESS, VAGUS, SCIATIC
  cell NEURON
    extension AXON(E)
  center BRAIN, CORTEX,
    PLEXUS
  combining form
    NEUR(O)
  cranial VAGUS, OPTIC
  element NEURONE
  motor EFFERENT
  network(s) RETE,
    RETIA, PLEXUS
  sensory AFFERENT
nervous JITTERY,
  TENSE, TIMID, EDGY,
  RESTIVE, TIMOROUS,
  FEARFUL, SENSITIVE,
  TOUCHY, EXCITABLE,
  HIGHSTRUNG, APPRE-
  HENSIVE, RESTLESS,
  UNEASY, IRRITABLE
  malady TIC, APHASIA,
    NEURITIS
ness CAPE, HEADLAND,
  RAS, PROMENTORY
nest NID(E), LAIR, DEN,
  NIDUS, HAUNT, BED,
  ABODE, RETREAT, RE-
  SORT, COLONY, AERIE,
  BROOD, SWARM
  build AERIE, NIDIFY,
    NIDIFICATE
  builder BIRD, MOUSE,
    ANT, WASP, HORNET,
    BEE
  building fish ACARA,
    STICKLEBACK
  eagle's AERY, AERIE
  insect's NIDUS
  of boxes INRO
  squirrel's DRAY, DREY

nestle LIE, SNUGGLE,
  CUDDLE, SHELTER,
  CHERISH, SETTLE
nestling BIRD, BABY,
  EYAS, FLEDGLING,
  POULT
Nestor SAGE, SOLON,
  COUNSELOR
net FABRIC, GIN, TOIL,
  TRAP, WEIR, SNARE,
  ENTANGLE, CATCH,
  SNOOD, CAPTURE,
  CLEAR, SEINE, MESH,
  FYKE, PROFIT, GAIN,
  WEB
  bag RETICULE
  fish *See under* "fish"
  like RETIARY
  of fine threads RETI-
    CLE
  work RETE, PLEXUS,
    RETICULUM *See*
    "network"
nether DOWN, INFER-
  NAL, LOWER, UNDER,
  BELOW
Netherlands (including
  "Dutch") HOLLAND,
  FRIESLAND
  aborigine CELT
  anatomist RAU
  badger DAS
  boat *See* "ship"
    below
  botanist (DE)VRIES
  capital AMSTERDAM
  city UTRECHT, (THE)
    HAGUE, LEYDEN *See*
    "town" *below*
  coin RIDER, GUILDER,
    STIVER, DOIT,
    DAALDER, FLORIN,
    GULDEN, RYDER,
    SUSKIN, CROWN
  colonist BOER
  commune EDE, EPE,
    BREDA, OSS, DELFT,
    ZWOLLE, BAARN, AS-
    SEN, ZUILEN, ZEIST,
    WEERT, VUGHT,
    VOORST, SOEST,
    SNEEK
  cupboard KAS
  dialect TAAL
  island CELEBES,
    ARUBA, TEXEL
  measure KAN, AAM,
    AUM, STOOP
  merchant's league
    HANSE
  painter LELY, LIS,

  HALS, EYCK, DOU,
  HOET, BOSCH
  poet DECKER
  political party GEU-
    ZEN
  possession BORNEO,
    SURINAM
  province DRENTE
  river MAAS, WAAL,
    EMS, LEK, SCHELDT
  scholar ERASMUS
  seat of government
    (THE) HAGUE
  ship KOFF, GALLIOT
  town EDAM, BREDA,
    EDE, SLUIS (SLUYS),
    TIEL, SNEEK, OSS
  uncle EME
  village EDE
  weight ONS, LOOD,
    POND, WICHTJE,
    ONZE, KORREL
  woman FROW
netted RETIARY, INTER-
  WOVEN
netting MESH, SCREEN
nettle PLANT, PIQUE,
  IRK, VEX, STING, IRRI-
  TATE, URTICA, OFFEND,
  TROUBLE, RUFFLE
  See "annoy"
  genus URTICA
  rash HIVES, URTICARIA
network(s) MESH,
  PLEXUS, PLEXA, WEB,
  RETICULUM, RETE,
  RETIA, SYSTEM,
  SCHEME, COMPLEX,
  NBC, ABC, CBS
  arterial VAS
  nerve PLEXUS, RETE
neume SEQUENCE
neural NERVAL, DOR-
  SAL
neurite AXONE
neuroglia GLIA
neutral INDEFINITE,
  NONCOMBATANT, IM-
  PARTIAL, INDIFFER-
  ENT, UNBIASED
  color BEIGE
  equilibrium, having
    ASTATIC, BALANCED
Nevada *city or town*
  RENO, ELKO, ELY
  county ELKO, LYON,
    NYE, STOREY,
    WASHOE
neve ICE, SNOW, FIRN
never NOT, NARY
nevertheless YET,

HOWEVER, STILL, BUT, NOTWITHSTANDING

nevus MOLE, FRECKLE

new LATE, FRESH, NOVEL, NEOTERIC, YOUNG, RECENT, BEGINNING, ANOTHER, YOUTHFUL, MODERN, ORIGINAL, UNACCUSTOMED, UNUSED, RENOVATED

combining form NEO

New Caledonia *bird* KAGU

New Deal agency NRA, CCC, NYA, TVA

New Englander YANK

newfangled NOVEL

Newfoundland *cape* RACE

log house TILT

New Guinea PAPUA

city or town SORON, WAU, LAE, WEWAK

export COPRA

gulf HUON, PAPUA

harbor LAE

island JOBIE, ARU, PAPUA

native PAPUAN

people KARON

port LAE, BUNA

river FLY, SEPIK, DIGUL

tribesman KARON

wild hog BENE

New Hampshire *county* COOS

mountain FLUME

State flower LILAC

New Hebrides *island* EPI (API), TANA (TANNA), EFATE

port VILA

New Jersey *county* BERGEN, ESSEX, HUDSON, MERCER, MORRIS, OCEAN, PASSAIC, SALEM, SUSSEX, UNION

river TOMS

New Mexico *art colony* TAOS

county OTERO, TAOS, EDDY, LEA, LUNA, MORA

Indian See under "Indian"

region, old name CIBOLA

resort TAOS

river GILA

State flower YUCCA

town RATON

turpentine tree TARATA(H)

village TAOS

New Testament *book* MARK, LUKE, JOHN, ACTS, TIMOTHY, TITUS, PETER, JUDE, MATTHEW

last word of AMEN

New York *city* GOTHAM, OLEAN

county ERIE, ONEIDA, ULSTER, LEWIS, ESSEX, GREENE, TIOGA, YATES

lake See under "lake"

mountain SLIDE, BEAR

subway IRT, BMT, IND

university or college ALFRED, CORNELL, VASSAR, ELMIRA, HOBART, COLGATE

New Zealand(er) MAORI, KIWI, ANTIPODES

bell bird MAKO

bird HUIA, KOKO, WEKA, KIWI See under "bird"

extinct MOA

caterpillar WERI, AWETO

cattail RAUPO

compensation UTU

corn KANGA

evergreen TAWA, TARATA(H), TOATOA

fern PTERIS

root ROI

fish HIKU, IHI

fort PA, PAH

harbor OTAGO

island OTEA, NIUE

lake TAUPO

locust WETA

morepork RURU, PEHO

native MAORI

owl RURU

palm NIKAU

parrot KAKA, KEA

pigeon KUKU

pine RIMU

plant KARO

raft MOKI

rail bird WEKA, KOKO

shark MAKO

shrub KARO, RAMARAMA, GOAI, TUTU, KOWHAI

stockade PA(H)

tree See under "tree"

tribe ATI, HAPU

vine AKA

wages UTU

war club MERE

weapon PATU

wingless bird WEKA, APTERYX

wood robin MIRO

news EVANGEL, TIDINGS, WORD, ADVICE, NOTICE, REPORT, INTELLIGENCE, DOPE, INFORMATION

beat SCOOP

item LOCAL

paragraph ITEM

service ANETA, TASS, DOMEI, AP, REUTERS, INS

stand KIOSK

newt EFT, TRITON, SALAMANDER, AXOLOTL, EVET

next LATER, BESIDE, AFTER, NEIST, NEAR-(EST), THEN, IMMEDIATE, SHORTEST, ADJACENT, FOLLOWING, CLOSEST, WISE, INTIMATE

in order, combining form EKA

nexus LINK, TIE, BOND, CHAIN, CONNECTION

ngaio KIO, TREE

nib BILL, BEAK, POINT, PRONG, KINK

nibble PECK, BROWSE, GNAW, NAB, BITE, CHAMP, NIP, PILFER

Nicaragua *city or town* MANAGUA, LEON

nice PLEASANT, AGREEABLE, SUBTILE, DELICATE, ACUTE, EXACT, DISCERNING, FINE, NEAT, FASTIDIOUS, QUEASY, DAINTY, APT, FUSSY, REFINED, MODEST, RESERVED, PROPER, DEMURE, FIT, PRECISE, MINUTE, ACCURATE, PLEASING, KIND, THOUGHTFUL, CONSIDERATE, GOOD, EXCELLENT, EXQUISITE, DELIGHTFUL, PRUDISH, FINICAL, CRITICAL, DISCRIMINATING niche BAY, CUBICLE, ALCOVE, NOOK, APSE, RECESS, COVERT, RETREAT

nick DINT, DENT, SCORE, MAR, NOTCH, CHIP, GOUGE, JAG, CUT

nickel JITNEY, JIT, COIN
alloy INVAR, MONEL, KONEL
symbol NI

nickname MONIKER, ALIAS, AGNAME, HYPOCORISM, SOBRIQUET, MONICA, AGNOMEN, COGNOMEN

nictitate WINK, BLINK, TWINK, NICTATE, TWINKLE

nide NEST, BROOD, LITTER

nidor AROMA, SAVOR, SCENT, ODOR, SMELL

nidus NEST, REPOSITORY, CORE, SOURCE, ORIGIN

nieve FIST, HAND, NEIF

nifty FINE, EXCELLENT, SMART, CLEVER, ATTRACTIVE, STYLISH, ENJOYABLE

Niger, *mouth of* NUN

Nigeria *capital* LAGOS
city or town EDE, BENIN, BIDA, KANO, IWO, OYO, YOLA, JOS
native IJO, IBO, EBOE, ARO, BENI
region BENIN
river NIGER, BENUE
seaport LAGOS
state NUPE
town See "city" *above*
tribe IBO, IJO, BENI(N), EBOE, EKOI

niggard MISER, CLOSE, TIGHT, PIKER, AVARICIOUS, STINGY, COVETOUS

nigh (A)NEAR, AT, CLOSE, ADJACENT, CONTIGUOUS, NEIGHBORING, ADJOINING, ALMOST, NEARLY

night EVE, DARKNESS, DEATH, OBSCURITY, PM
combining form NYCT(I)(O)
goddess See under "goddess"

wandering at NOCTIVAGANT

nighthawk PISK

nightingale PHILOMEL, BULBUL, BIRD, FLORENCE
Swedish LIND, JENNY

nightmare ALP, INCUBUS, DREAM, VISION, FANCY, ILLUSION, MESS, FIEND

nightshade BELLADONNA, HENBANE, POKEWEED, PLANT, HERB

night watchman SERENO, GUARD, SENTRY

nihil, nil NOTHING

Nile RIVER *See also* "Egypt"
bird IBIS
boat CANGIA, BARIS
dam ASWAN
catfish BAGRE, DOCMAC
city or town on CAIRO, ARGO, ABRI, IDFU, ISNA, QUS, QINA, ASYUT
falls RIPON
fish BICHIR, BAGRE, DOCMAC, SAIDE
floating vegetation SUDD
island RODA, PHILAE
native NILOT
negro JUR, SUK, LUO
region NUBIA
relating to NILOTIC
ship's captain RAIS, REIS
source of TSANA
tribe SUK, BARI, MADI
valley depression KORE

nimble DEFT, SPRY, AGILE, GLEG, LISH, BRISK, PROMPT, ALERT, LIVE(LY), SPRIGHTLY, SUPPLE, SWIFT, QUICK, DEXTEROUS, RESPONSIVE, SENSITIVE

nimbus AURA, AUREOLA, GLORIA, HALO, VAPOR, CLOUD

nimiety EXCESS, REDUNDANCY, SUPERABUNDANCE

nimrod HUNTER, RULER

nincompoop DOLT, WITLING, ASS, SIMPLETON, FOOL, NINNY, BLOCKHEAD

nine ENNEAD, TEAM, IX
angled figure NONAGON
combining form ENNEA
day's devotion NOVENA
group of NONET, ENNEAD
headed monster HYDRA
inches SPAN

ninepins KEELS, SKITTLES, KAYLES

Nineveh *founder* NINUS

ninny BLOCKHEAD, DOLT, LOUT, IDIOT, FOOL, SIMPLETON, DUNCE, GOOSE

ninth ENNEATIC
day before ides NONES
recurring every NONAN

niobe FUNKIA, HOSTA, PLANT, HERB

Niobe's *brother* PELOPS
father TANTALUS
husband AMPHION
sister-in-law AEDON

nip BLAST, CHILL, FROST, CHIP, BITE, PINCH, CHECK, WITHER, CUT, GIBE, TAUT, VEX, PECK, COMPRESS, SQUEEZE, SNATCH, STEAL, SARCASM, DRINK, SIP, DRAM, DRAUGHT, TANG, BLIGHT, SWALLOW

nipa ATAP, ATTAP, PALM, DRINK

nipper CHELA, CLAW, HAND, BITER, BOY, INCISOR, LAD, COSTERMONGER, CUNNER, CRAB

nippers PLIERS, PINCERS, TONGS, FORCEPS

nis NIX, BROWNIE, KOBOLD, NISSE

nisi UNLESS

nisus EFFORT, IMPULSE, ENDEAVOR, POWER, STRIVING

Nisus' daughter SCYLLA

niter SALTPETER

nitid GAY, SPRUCE, SHINING, BRIGHT, GLOSSY, LUSTROUS

niton RADON

nitrogen GAS
combining form AZO
compound AZIN(E)
old name AZOTE

nitroglycerin(e) GLONOIN, TRINITRIN, TNT

nitwit BOOB, DUNCE, FOOL *See* "ninny"

niveous SNOWY, WHITE

nix NO, NOTHING, NOBODY, SPIRIT *See* "fairy"

no BAAL, NAE, NYET, NONE, NAY, NOT, NIX, DENIAL, NOTHING
one NEMO, NONE, NIX, NOBODY

Noah's *father* LAMECH
grandson ARAM
pertaining to NOETIC, NOACHIAN
son JAPHETH, SEM, SHEM, HAM

nob HEAD, HANDLE, BLOW, KNAVE *See* "fop"

Nobel prize winner RABI, FERMI, HESS, ROOT, BUCK, ROSS, KOCH, HULL, BOHR, WIEN, KREBS, ADLER, PAULING, ENDERS, BORN, LAMB, KUSCH, YANG, LEE, TAMM, FRANK, SEGRE, CURIE, GOLGI, BRAGG, STARK, HABER, ASTON, PREGL, KROGH, DIRAC, BOSCH, UREY, DEBYE, KUHN, DALE, STERN, PAULI, HAHN, DIELS, DAM, DOISY, CORI, HENCH

nobility RANK, GENTRY, ELITE, PEERAGE, DIGNITY, GRACE, STATUS, STATION, GRANDEUR, SUPERIORITY, ELEVATION, EMINENCE, ARISTOCRACY

noble SUPERB, EPIC, GRAND, STATELY, MORAL, JUST, IMPERIAL, AUGUST, EXCELLENT, MAGNIFICENT, IMPOSING, WORTHY, LOFTY, BROAD, SPLENDID, FINE, PURE, HIGH, ILLUSTRIOUS, FAME, HIGHBORN, RENOWNED, GENEROUS, LIBERAL, ARISTOCRATIC, FAMOUS, EMINENT

nobleman DUKE, COUNT, EARL, BARON, THANE, LORD, PEER, ARISTOCRAT, GRANDEE, MARQUIS
lowest BARON

nobleness of birth EUGENY

nobody JACKSTRAW, NONENTITY, NEMO
Latin NEMO
Spanish NADIE

nocent HURTFUL, GUILTY

noctuid MOTH, WORM

nocturnal *carnivore* RATEL
mammal BAT, LEMUR

nocturne LULLABY, SERENADE, PAINTING

nod DOZE, SIGN, BOW, WINK, BECK, SALUTATION, SLIP, ERR, SALUTE

node KNOT, KNOB, NODUS, TUMOR, SWELLING, PROTUBERANCE, JOINT, POINT, PLOT, ENTANGLEMENT, COMPLICATION, DIFFICULTY *See* "nodule"
of a poem PLOT
of a stem JOINT

nodule KNOT, MASS, LUMP, BUMP, NODE, GRANULE, TUBERCLE
stone GEODE

Noel CHRISTMAS, XMAS, CAROL

noggin GILL, MUG, PATE, DRINK, HEAD, NOODLE, CUP

noise SOUND, CLAMOR, BLARE, CLANG, RACKET, DIN, BABEL, (UP)ROAR, ALARM, BRUIT, AIR, ROUT, STRIDOR, REPORT, SCANDAL, GOSSIP, CLATTER, OUTCRY, ADO, TUMULT, HUBBUB, PANDEMONIUM, RUMOR, CONFUSION

noisily LARUM

noisome FETID, NOXIOUS, FOUL, RANK, RANCID, NASTY, DESTRUCTIVE, HARMFUL, UNWHOLESOME, DISGUSTING, OFFENSIVE, PERNICIOUS

noisy STREPITANT, CREAKY, LOUD, BLATANT, TURBULENT, CLAMOROUS, RIOTOUS, BOISTEROUS, VOCIFEROUS, TUMULTUOUS, UPROARIOUS

nomad GYPSY, ARAB, SARACEN, ROVER, WANDERER, SEMITE

nomenclature TERM, NAME, ONYMY, DESIGNATION, REGISTER, TERMINOLOGY

nominal PAR, TITULAR, TRIVIAL, OSTENSIBLE, SUBSTANTIVAL, NUNCUPATIVE, NEGLIGIBLE
recognizance DOE

nominate NAME, SELECT, PROPOSE, ELECT, DESIGNATE, APPOINT

nonage MINORITY, PUPILAGE, INFANCY, IMMATURITY

nonce OCCASION, PURPOSE, PRESENT

nonchalant INSOUCIANT, COOL, ALOOF, INDIFFERENT, UNCONCERNED, CASUAL, CARELESS

nonconformist REBEL, HERETIC, SECTARY, DISSENTER, RECUSANT, BEATNIK, BOHEMIAN

nonconformity RECUSANCE, NEGLECT, REFUSAL, DISSENTION, DISAGREEMENT

nonentity NULLITY, NOBODY, CIPHER, NOTHINGNESS, INSIGNIFICANCE, NONEXISTENCE

nonessential ADVENTITIOUS, UNNEEDED, INCIDENTAL, EXTRANEOUS, UNNECESSARY

in religion
ADIAPHORUS

nonesuch MODEL,
PARAGON, PATTERN,
UNRIVALED, UN-
EQUALED, MATCHLESS,
NONPAREIL

nonmetallic mineral
SPAR

nonpareil TYPE,
SUPREME, PARAGON,
UNRIVALED, PEERLESS,
NONESUCH

non-passerine bird
HOOPOE, TODY, KING-
FISHER, HORNBILL,
MOTMOT

nonplus MYSTIFY,
PUZZLE, STUMP,
PERPLEX(ITY), FAZE,
RATTLE, BAFFLE,
QUANDARY, POSER,
DISCONCERT, CONFUSE,
FLOOR

nonsense TRASH, ROT,
TOSH, BLAH, PISH,
HOOEY, POOH,
FOLDEROL, BLATHER,
AMPHIGORY, TRIFLES,
BALDERDASH, AB-
SURDITY, TRIPE,
FOLLY, TRUMPERY,
TWADDLE, DRIVEL,
CLAPTRAP, FLUM-
MERY, SILLINESS,
FRIVOLITY, TRIVIA

creature GOOP, SNARK,
SMOO

noodle(s) FARFEL,
HEAD, BLOCKHEAD,
SIMPLETON, PASTA

cases RAVIOLI

nook HERNE, CANT,
COVE, RECESS,
CORNER, RETREAT,
NICHE, BAY, ALCOVE

noon MIDDAY,
MERIDIAN, CULMINA-
TION, APEX

no one NEMO, NOBODY

noose LOOP, LASSO,
HITCH, ENSNARE,
SNARE, CATCH

norm MODEL, RULE,
AVERAGE, MEDIAN,
PAR, TYPE, STANDARD,
PATTERN, NORMA

norma PATTERN,
SQUARE, GAUGE,
TEMPLET, MOLD,
TEMPLATE

normal NATURAL,
JUST, MEAN, PAR,
USUAL, STANDARD,
SCHOOL, REGULAR,
TYPICAL, ORDINARY,
PERPENDICULAR,
ANALOGICAL, CUSTOM-
ARY, AVERAGE

Normandy *bagpipe*
LOURE

capital ROUEN

cheese ANGELOT

department CALVADOS,
EURE, MANCHE, ORNE

early conqueror
ROLLO

Norn SKULD, URTH,
WYRD

Norse DANE, SCANDI-
NAVIAN, NORWEGIAN,
OGIER

Adam BURE, BURI,
ASK(R)

bard SAGAMAN, SCALD,
SKALD

chieftain YARL, JARL,
ROLLO

collection of songs
EDDA

deity ODIN, RAN,
THOR, VALI, WODEN,
WODAN *See under*
"god"

chief group AESIR

dialect NORN

epic EDDA

explorer ERIC, LEIF

first man See "Adam"
above

giant FAFNIR, JOTUN,
MIMIR, LOKI, YMER,
YMIR, JOTUNN

giantess GROA, NATT,
NORN, NOTT

*god or goddess See
under* "god" *or*
"goddess"

guardian of Asgard
HEIMDALL(R)

hero EGIL(L)

king, myth. ATLI

letter RUNE

literature EDDA

lore RUNE

navigator ERIC

nobleman JARL

night NATT, NOTT

plateau FJELD

poem RUNE

poet SCALD, SKALD

poetry RUNE, RUNIC

queen of underworld
HEL(A)

saint OLAF

serpent, myth.
MIDGARD

tale SAGA

tsar ROS

viking ROLLO

warrior, myth.
BERSERKER

watchdog, myth.
GARM(R)

wolf, myth. FENRIR

north ARCTIC, POLAR

Africa See "Africa"

America See
"America"

Carolina cape FEAR,
HATTERAS

county ASHE, CLAY,
DARE, HOKE, HYDE,
LEE, NASH, PIT,
POLK, WAKE

river TAR, NEUSE,
PEE DEE

sound CORE

university DUKE

Dakota city MINOT,
FARGO

county CASS, DUNN,
EDDY

pole discoverer PEARY

Sea port EMDEN,
BERGEN, BREMEN,
HULL

river to ELBE,
WESER, EMS, RHINE,
ALLER, DEE, TEES,
MEUSE (MAAS),
EIDER, TYNE

star LODESTAR,
POLARIS, POLESTAR,
CYNOSURE

wind BOREAS

northern BOREAL,
HYPERBOREAN,
SEPTENTRIONAL,
ARCTIC

bear RUSSIA, POLAR

constellation URSA,
ANDROMEDA, CYNO-
SURE

northernmost inhabited
land THULE

Norway NORGE

bird RYPE,
PTARMIGAN

capital OSLO

city or town OSLO,
BERGEN, SKIEN

coin KRONE, ORE

composer GRIEG

division or county
AMT
early ruler HAAKON
governor AMTMAN
inlet FIORD, FJORD
island SOROY, HITRA
king OLAF
legislature STORTING,
LAGTING, ODELSTING
measure FOT, POT
patron saint OLAF
river TANA (TENO),
RANA, KLAR
seaport NARVIK, BODO,
TROMSO, MO, MOSS
town See "city"
above
weight LOD, PUND
writer IBSEN
northwest highway
ALCAN
nose NOSTRILS, NARES,
NOZZLE, NASUS, CONK,
NEB, BEAK, PROW,
SNOUT, PROBOSCIS,
MUZZLE, MUFFLE,
SCENT, SNIFF, SMELL,
DETECT
ailment CORYZA,
COLD, OZENA, CATARRH
bee's LORE
cartilage SEPTUM
flat PUG, SNUB
having flat SIMOUS
having large NASUTE
openings NARES
pertaining to NASAL,
RHINAL, NARIAL
partition SEPTUM,
VOMER
snub PUG
nosebleed EPISTAXIS
nosegay POSY,
BOUQUET, CORSAGE,
ODOR, PERFUME,
SCENT
noselite LENAD,
MINERAL
nostalgia LONGING,
HOMESICKNESS,
MELANCHOLIA
nostology GERIATRICS
Nostradamus
PROPHET, SEER,
ASTROLOGER
nostrils NARES *See*
"nose"
Nosu LOLO
not NONE, NARY,
NOUGHT, NEGATION
in style PASSE, OUT
long ago LATELY

prefix IR, IL, IM, NON,
UN, IN
so great FEWER,
SMALLER, LESSER
wanted SUPERFLUOUS,
DE TROP
notch DENT, INDENT-
(URE), CRENA, JAB,
NICK, GROOVE, CUT,
NOCK, SCORE, GAP,
DEFILE, DINT, HOL-
LOW, INDENTATION,
DEGREE, STEP, PEG
notched EROSE, SER-
RATE(D), CRENATE(D)
irregularly EROSE
note SEE, VIEW, ESPY,
ATTEND, HEED, OB-
SERVE, (RE)MARK,
SIGN, TOKEN, CHIT,
CHECK, IOU, LOAN,
TONE, TUNE, SONG,
STRAIN, MELODY,
MINUTE, RECORD, DIS-
PATCH, REPORT, AN-
NOTATION, OBSERVA-
TION, FAME, RENOWN,
IMPORTANCE, REPUTA-
TION, DISTINCTION,
EMINENCE, MEMO,
MEMORANDUM, LINE,
BILLET, LETTER
double whole BREVE
eighth MORA, UNCA
endorsement or
guarantee of AVAL
explanatory
SCHOLIUM
half MINIM
high E LA
marginal ADVERSARIA,
ANNOTATION,
SCHOLIUM
musical BREVE,
PUNCTUS, HALF,
WHOLE, QUARTER,
EIGHTH, SEMIBREVE
sharpening of
ECBOLE
sounded at kill MORT
tail of FILUM
whole SEMIBREVE
notebook DIARY,
ADVERSARIA, JOURNAL,
LOG, RECORD
noted GREAT, FAMOUS,
FAMED, EMINENT,
CELEBRATED, NOTORI-
OUS, DISTINGUISHED,
REMARKABLE, RE-
NOWNED, ILLUSTRIOUS

notes, Guido's scale
See "Guido"
succession of STRAIN,
GAMUT, TIRALEE
nothing TRIFLE,
NAUGHT, NOT, NIHIL,
NIL, NIX, BLANK,
ZERO, NULL, NONEN-
TITY, BAGATELLE,
CIPHER, NOUGHT, NO-
BODY
more than MERE
notice AD, POSTER, IN-
FORMATION, WARNING,
ANNOUNCEMENT, AT-
TENTION, COGNIZANCE,
INTELLIGENCE, AD-
VICE, NEWS, ORDER,
REMARK, BULLETIN,
SEE, (E)SPY, ALLUDE,
DISCERN, OBSERVE,
REGARD, HEED,
KNOWLEDGE, MEN-
TION, PERCEIVE
notify APPRISE, IN-
FORM, TELL, DECLARE,
PUBLISH, ANNOUNCE,
ACQUAINT
notion OMEN, IDEA,
VIEW, BEE, OPINION,
WHIM, BELIEF,
THOUGHT, THEORY,
CONCEPT(ION),
GADGET, SENTIMENT,
APPREHENSION, IN-
CLINATION, FANCY,
KNICKKNACK
notoriety ECLAT, FAME,
RENOWN, HONOR,
GLORY, REPUTE,
PUBLICITY, NOTORI-
OUSNESS
notwithstanding EVEN,
YET, DESPITE, THO, AL-
THOUGH, HOWBEIT,
NEVERTHELESS, HOW-
EVER
nougat CONFECTION,
CANDY, NUTSHELL
noumenal ONTAL, REAL
noun THING, NAME
common gender form
EPICENE
form CASE, GENDER
indeclinable APTOTE
suffix ERY, ET, IER,
ION, FER, ISE, IST, ANA
two cases DIPOTE
verbal GERUND
nourish AID, FEED,
FOSTER, NURSE, SUP-
PORT, MAINTAIN,

CHERISH, STIMULATE, EDUCATE, NURTURE, PROVIDE, TRAIN, SUCCOR

nourishing ALIBLE, ALMS, NUTRITIOUS, RICH, NUTRITIVE, HEALTHFUL, WHOLESOME, STRENGTHENING, INVIGORATING

nourishment FOOD, ALIMENT, MANNA, PABULUM, KEEP, DIET, NUTRITION, NUTRIMENT, SUSTENANCE

nous MIND, INTELLECT, REASON, UNDERSTANDING

nouveau riche PARVENU, UPSTART

nova STAR

Nova Scotia ACADIA, ACADIE
bay FUNDY
cape CANSO, SABLE, BRETON, GEORGE
port TRURO

novel EPIC, STORY, ROMANCE, NARRATIVE, TALE, FICTION, BOOK, PROSE, FRESH, RARE, NEW, STRANGE, UNUSUAL, MODERN, RECENT, UNCOMMON, NEOTERIC

novelty FAD, INNOVATION, CHANGE, NEWNESS, FRESHNESS

novice TYRO, TIRO, YOUNKER, NOVITIATE, BEGINNER, STARTER, AMATEUR, HAM, NEOPHYTE, STUDENT, PROBATIONER, INITIATE, APPRENTICE, LEARNER, PUPIL, ABECEDARIAN *See* "beginner"

now TODAY, HERE, YET, PRESENT, FORTHWITH, SINCE, IMMEDIATELY, CURRENT, EXISTING, EXTANT, INSTANT, NONCE

Nox NYX
brother EREBUS
father CHAOS

noxious EVIL, BANEFUL, NOISOME, NOCENT, PERNICIOUS, HURTFUL, PUTRID, FETID, INJURIOUS,

CORRUPTING, PESTILENT, INSALUBRIOUS, UNWHOLESOME, DESTRUCTIVE, HATEFUL, OFFENSIVE, HARMFUL, DEADLY

nozzle VENT, SPOUT, OUTLET, NOSE, SNOUT, BEAK, GROVEL

nuance SHADE, VARIATION, GRADATION

nub JAB, KNOB, NOB, SNAG, CORE, HEART, GIST, HUB, EAR, PITH, POINT, KNOT, PROTUBERANCE, LUMP, KEY, KNUB

nubia CLOUD, WRAP, SCARF

Nubian NUBA, BARABRA
musical instrument SISTRUM

nubilous CLOUDY, FOGGY, MISTY, VAGUE, OBSCURE, INDISTINCT, INDEFINITE

nucha NAPE, NECK

nuclear *element* PROTON
machine BETATRON

nucleus SEED, CORE, CADRE, HUB, FOCUS, HEART, CENTER, GERM, KERNEL, ROOT, CELL, MIDDLE, MIDST

nude BARE, EXPOSED, UNDRESSED, NAKED *See* "naked"

nudge GOAD, PROD, PUSH, KNUB, POKE, NOG, JOG

nudibranch SNAIL, CONCH, MOLLUSK

nugae JESTS, TRIFLES

nugatory TRIVIAL, FUTILE, VAIN, IDLE, TRIFLING, EMPTY, HOLLOW, WORTHLESS, INVALID, INEFFECTUAL, INOPERATIVE, INEFFECTIVE, USELESS, INSIGNIFICANT

nugget LUMP, MASS, SLUG, GOLD

nuisance BORE, PAIN, PEST, BANE, ABOMINATION, ANNOYANCE, PLAGUE, EVIL, STING, VEXATION, INCONVENIENCE

remover ABATOR

null INVALID, VOID, USELESS, NUGATORY, INSIGNIFICANT, NONEXISTENT

nullah RAVINE, GORGE, WATERCOURSE, GULLY

nullify CANCEL, VOID, VETO, ABROGATE, NEGATE, UNDO, ANNUL, OFFSET, INVALIDATE, REPEAL, ABOLISH, REVOKE, COUNTERACT, NEUTRALIZE

numb DAZED, DULL, RIGESCENT, HEBETATE, STUPID, DEADEN(ED), INSENSIBLE, TORPID, CLUMSY, HELPLESS

number LOTS, AMOUNT, SUM, TOTAL, WHOLE, DIGIT, MANY, QUANTITY, FIGURE, SURD, COUNT, (E)NUMERATE, RECKON, CALCULATE, COMPUTE, NUMERAL, MULTITUDE, AGGREGATE, ISSUE, COPY
describable by SCALAR
extra ENCORE
indefinite LAC, STEEN
irrational SURD
pure SCALAR
under ten DIGIT
whole INTEGER
least whole UNIT

numbered, *Biblical* MENE

numerical prefix TRI, UNI

numerous MANY, MULTIPLE, SEVERAL, SUNDRY, DIVERS, LARGE, COPIOUS, GREAT, BIG, PLENTIFUL, ABUNDANT, THRONGED, CROWDED, LEGION, LOTS, MYRIAD, PROFUSE, GALORE, TEEMING

numinous AWE

numskull DOLT, LACKWIT, LOGGERHEAD, DUNCE, BLOCKHEAD

nun SISTER, RECLUSE, PRIESTESS, VOTARESS, CLOISTRESS
bird MONASE, TITMOUSE

dress HABIT, WIMPLE
head ABBESS,
  MOTHER, AMMA
hood FAILLE
nuncio MESSENGER,
  LEGATE, AMBASSADOR,
  ENVOY, REPRESENTA-
  TIVE *See* "ambas-
  sador"
nuncupative ORAL,
  SPOKEN, DESIGNATIVE
nunnery CLOISTER,
  CONVENT
nunni BLESBOK,
  ANTELOPE
nunting SCANT,
  CLUMSY, UNGAINLY
nuptial(s) HYMENAL,
  BRIDAL, MARITAL,
  MATRIMONIAL,
  WEDDING, MARRIAGE,
  ESPOUSAL
nuque NAPE, NECK
nurse AMAH, AYAH,
  NANNY, SISTER, SIT-
  TER, BONNE, REAR,
  TEND, CARE, FOSTER,
  CHERISH, FEED, PRO-
  MOTE, FURTHER,
  NOURISH, NURTURE,
  ENCOURAGE, SUCKLE
nursery, *day or public*
  CRECHE
nurture CHERISH,
  TEND, CARE *See*
  "nurse"
nut(s) CORE, PITH,
  SEED, FRUIT, ACORN,
  BEN, BETEL, KOLA,
  PECAN, ALMOND,
  MAST, KERNEL,
  PROBLEM, HEAD,
  FOOL, DOLT, EC-
  CENTRIC
pertaining to NUCAL
tanning BOMAH
nutation NOD, NOD-
  DING, OSCILLATION
nut bearing NUCIFER-
  OUS
nuthatch *genus* SITTA,
  BIRD
nutmeg CALABASH,
  SPICE, TREE
husk MACE
nutria COPYU, FUR
nutriment FOOD, ALI-
  MENT, DIET,
  PABULUM, SUPPORT,
  KEEP, NOURISHMENT,
  NUTRITION, SUS-

TENANCE, SUBSIST-
  ENCE, VIANDS, PROV-
  ENDER
nutritive ALIBLE,
  NOURISHING, RICH,
  NUTRITIOUS,
  STRENGTHENING,
  WHOLESOME
Nut's *children* RA, ISIS,
  OSIRIS
consort GEB, KEB
nutty FLAVORFUL,
  ZESTFUL, PIQUANT,
  RACY, LOVING, SPICY,
  AMOROUS, ENTHUSIAS-
  TIC, GAGA, ZANY,
  CRAZY, CRACKBRAINED,
  QUEER, ECCENTRIC,
  FOOLISH, DEMENTED
nuzzle BURROW, ROOT,
  FONDLE, NESTLE, DIG,
  SNUFF, CARESS, PET
nymph(s) DRYAD,
  LARVA, PUPA, HOURI,
  OREAD, SYLPH, MAIA,
  CIRCE, NAIAD, NEREID,
  MUSE, ECHO, DAMSEL,
  MAIDEN, HAMADRYAD,
  OCEANID, BUTTERFLY,
  NIXIE, KELPIE,
  UNDINE, SPRITE, PIXY
beloved by Pan
  SYRINX
changed into laurel
  tree DAPHNE
fountain NAIAD,
  EGERIA
Hesperid AEGLE
in love with Narcissus
  ECHO
laurel DAPHNE
Moslem HOURI
mountain OREAD
queen MAB
sea NEREID, SCYLLA,
  SIREN, OCEANID, UN-
  DINE
tree DRYAD,
  HAMADRYAD
water NAIS, UNDINE,
  NAIAD
wood DRYAD
nyssa *genus* TUPELO,
  TREE
nystagmus TIC, WINK
Nyx NOX
daughter ERIS, DAY,
  LIGHT
father CHAOS
personified NIGHT

O

O OMICRON, CIPHER,
  ZERO, CIRCLE, OVAL,
  OH
Scotch OCH
oaf IDIOT, BOOR, DOLT,
  FOOL, SIMPLETON,
  BLOCKHEAD, DUNCE,
  CHANGELING
oak TREE, HOLM,
  CLUB, BRAVE, STRONG
bark CRUT
California ENCINA,
  ROBLE
fruit ACORN, MAST,
  CAMATA, BELLOTE
genus QUERCUS
holm ILEX
immature fruit
  CAMATA
Jerusalem AMBROSE
nut See "fruit" *above*
nut or fruit of ACORN
turkey CERRIS
types BARREN, WHITE,
  BUR, LIVE, BLACK,
  PIN, HOLLY, POST,
  SCRUB, CHESTNUT,
  SWAMP, RED, WILLOW,
  WATER, HOLM
white ROBLE
oar POLE, BLADE,
  SPOON, PADDLE,
  SCULL, PLY, ROW(ER)
blade PEEL, WASH
flat part PALM, PEEL
fulcrum THOLE, OAR-
  LOCK, ROWLOCK
part LOOM, PALM
shaped REMIFORM
oasis WADI, SPRING,
  SPA, MERV, BAR
Asia MERV
oast KILN, OVEN
oat(s) GRAIN, FOOD,
  FEED, PIPE, POEM,
  SONG
genus AVENA
head PANICLE
paid in lieu of rent
  AVENAGE
oath VOW, BOND,
  CURSE, AITH, WORD,
  PROMISE, ATTESTA-
  TION, BAN, PLEDGE,
  BLASPHEMY, IM-
  PRECATION, MALEDIC-
  TION, AFFIRMATION,
  EXECRATION
minced See under
  "minced"

obdurate FIRM, HARD, MULISH, STONY, CALLOUS, IMPASSIVE, PERVERSE, REFRACTORY, HARSH, SEVERE, RUGGED, ROUGH, OBSTINATE, STUBBORN, DOGGED, INFLEXIBLE, INTRACTABLE, SULLEN, INERT, BALKY, UNYIELDING

obeah VOODOO, CHARM, FETISH

obedience RESIGNATION, SUBMISSION, ALLEGIANCE, COMPLIANCE, SUBSERVIENCE, FEALTY, SUBJECTION

obedient AMENABLE, DOCILE, TAME, SUBMISSIVE, COMPLIANT, TRACTABLE, DEFERENTIAL, DUTIFUL, RESPECTFUL, YIELDING, OBSEQUIOUS, FAITHFUL, DEVOTED, PLIANT

Obed's son JESS(E)

obeisance BOW, HOMAGE, FEALTY, CONGEE, SALAAM, CURTSY, DEFERENCE, SALUTATION

obelisk GUGLIA, PYLON, NEEDLE, SHAFT, DAGGER, MONUMENT, COLUMN, PILLAR, OBELUS, MARK

Oberon FAIRY, KING, OPERA, POEM
wife TITANIA

obese PUDGY, FAT, FLESHY, LIPAROUS, CORPULENT, TURGID, PUFFY, PURSY, STOUT, PLUMP, ADIPOSE, PORTLY, PYKNIC

obey HEED, MIND, HEAR, EAR, YIELD, SUBMIT, DEFER, COMPLY, OBSERVE, FOLLOW

obfuscate MUDDLE, CONFUSE, DARKEN, PERPLEX, STUPEFY, CLOUD, OBSCURE, BEWILDER, DIM

obi SASH, GIRDLE, FETISH, CHARM

obit DECEASE, DEATH, REST, RELEASE, OBSEQUIES, SERVICE, MASS, NOTICE, OBITUARY, NECROLOGY

object PURPOSE, IDEA, MOTIVE, GOAL, END, AIM, DESIGN, MATTER, REALITY, PARTICULAR, PHENOMENON, SIGHT, ARTICLE, SPECTACLE, POINT, CARE, MIND, INTENTION, DISAPPROVE, DEMUR, BALK, KICK, PROTEST, REMONSTRATE, CARP, OPPOSE
of art CURIO

objection BAR, EXCEPTION, PROTEST, REMONSTRANCE, SCRUPLE, QUIBBLE, QUARREL, CAVIL

objective SAKE, AIM, GOAL, END, FAIR, UNBIASED, DETACHED, IMPERSONAL, REAL, ACTUAL, REALITY, INTENTION

objet d'art CURIO, FIGURINE, VASE, BIBELOT

objurgate CHIDE, REPROVE, JAW, CURSE, DAMN, BAN, REBUKE, REPREHEND, BERATE

obligation CONTRACT, OATH, VOW, IOU, TIE, DEBT, BOND, DUTY, MUST, ONUS, BURDEN, LOAD, RESPONSIBILITY, COMPULSION, AGREEMENT, PROMISE, CHECK, NOTE, NECESSITY

obliged FAVORED, BOUND, PLEASED, PLEDGED, OBLIGATED, GRATEFUL, CONSTRAINED

oblique BEVEL, CROOKED, DEVIOUS, AWRY, ASKEW, (A)SLANT, EVASIVE, INDIRECT, INCLINED, TILTED, SIDELONG, OBSCURE, UNDERHAND, SINISTER

obliterate SPONGE, EXPUNGE, ERASE, RAZE, RASE, DESTROY, DELE, EFFACE, CANCEL, BLOT, ABOLISH, ANNUL, EXTIRPATE, ANNIHILATE

oblivion AMNESTY, SILENCE, LETHE, NIRVANA, LIMBO, FORGETFULNESS, PARDON

obloquy CENSURE, BLAME, ABUSE, CALUMNY, CONTEMPT, DISGRACE

obnoxious HATEFUL, RANCID, ODIOUS, VILE, REPUGNANT, DETESTABLE, BLAMEWORTHY, FAULTY, OFFENSIVE, REPULSIVE, OBJECTIONABLE

oboe HAUTBOY, REED, MUSETTE, SHAWM, SZOPELKA

obscuration ECLIPSE

obscure HARD, OCCULT, DEEP, VAGUE, CRYPTIC, AMBIGUOUS, NAMELESS, DIM, MURKY, FOG, BEDIM, DARK(EN), ECLIPSE, CLOUD(ED), HUMBLE, LOWLY, DELUDE, OVERSILE, DUSK(Y), GLOOMY, RAYLESS, DOUBTFUL, INDISTINCT, INDEFINITE, MYSTIC, ENIGMATIC(AL), HIDE, DISGUISE, CONCEAL, COVER, SHADOW(Y), UNKNOWN

obscurity CLOUD, FOG, GLOOM, DARKNESS, OBSCURATION, INCONSPICUOUSNESS, SECLUSION, PRIVACY

obsecrate BESEECH, ENTREAT, PRAY, SUPPLICATE

obsequies FUNERAL, WAKE, RITES, SERVICE, OBIT, MASS

obsequious SERVILE, SLICK, DUTIFUL, SLAVISH, MENIAL, SYCOPHANTIC, CRINGING, FAWNING, FLATTERING, SUBSERVIENT, TOADYING

observation NOTICE, ESPIAL, IDEA, REMARK, REGARD, ASSERTION, OPINION, VIEW, NOTE, ATTEN-

TION, REFLECTION,
COMMENT

observatory TOWER,
LOOKOUT, LICK,
PALOMAR

observe HEED, FOL-
LOW, ADHERE, ABIDE,
CELEBRATE, OBEY,
REGARD, PERCEIVE,
MARK, BEHOLD,
NOTICE, EYE, SEE,
SOLEMNIZE, COM-
MENT, REMARK, SAY,
EXPRESS, MENTION,
UTTER, DETECT,
WATCH, KEEP, LO,
NOTE, NOTA

obsess HARASS, BESET,
HAUNT, PREOCCUPY

obsession MANIA,
CRAZE

obsidian LAVA, IZTLE,
IZTLI

obsolete RARE, BYGONE,
PASSE, ANCIENT, OLD,
ARCHAIC, DISUSED,
DEAD, PAST,
ANTIQUATED, DIS-
CARDED

obstacle BAR, DAM,
HINDRANCE, DRAW-
BACK, SNAG, OBSTRUC-
TION, IMPEDIMENT,
DIFFICULTY, BARRIER,
ROADBLOCK

obstinate DOGGED,
RESOLUTE, UNRULY,
FIXED, STUBBORN,
STIFF, FIRM, DOUR,
SET, MULISH, SULKY,
TENACIOUS,
PERTINACIOUS, IN-
TRACTABLE, UNYIELD-
ING, INFLEXIBLE,
PERVERSE, HEAD-
STRONG, REFRACTORY,
OBDURATE, WILLFUL,
RENITENT

obstruct STAY, HINDER,
IMPEDE, INHIBIT, AR-
REST, CHECK, CLOSE,
CHOKE, OCCLUDE,
BLOCK, PLUG, DAM,
BAR, CLOG, STOP,
BARRICADE, RETARD,
HAMPER, OPPOSE

obtain REACH, ARRIVE,
SECURE, ACQUIRE,
GAIN, EARN, GET, WIN,
PROCURE, ACHIEVE,
EXIST

with difficulty EKE,
INCH

obtrude IMPOSE,
THRUST, INTRUDE, IN-
TERFERE, MEDDLE,
EJECT

obtruncate LOP, HEW,
RETRENCH, SHORTEN,
BEHEAD, DECAPITATE

obtund BLUNT, DULL,
QUELL, DEADEN

obtuse DULL, STUPID,
BLUNT, INSENSITIVE

obverse FRONT, FACE,
COUNTERPART

obvious CLEAR, PLAIN,
EXPOSED, MANIFEST,
VISIBLE, OPEN, GROSS,
PATENT, EVIDENT,
SUBJECT, LIABLE,
PALPABLE, DISTINCT,
APPARENT

not SUBTLE, HIDDEN,
OCCULT, ARCANE,
SECRET, PROFOUND,
RECONDITE

obvolution FOLD,
TWIST

oca OXALIS, SORREL,
PLANT

O'Casey SEAN

occasion CAUSE,
REASON, JUNCTURE,
TIDE, NEED, CHANCE,
BREAK, OPPORTUNITY,
TIME, EVENT, NONCE,
OCCURRENCE, CONDI-
TION, HAPPENING,
INCIDENT, FUNCTION,
CEREMONY

occasional OLD,
SPORADIC, SCARCE,
INCIDENTAL, AC-
CIDENTAL, CASUAL,
IRREGULAR, IN-
FREQUENT

occident WEST,
HESPERIA

occidental WESTERN,
HESPERIAN, PONENT

occult CRYPTIC, HID-
DEN, MYSTIC, ARCANE,
SECRET, UNREVEALED,
UNKNOWN, RECON-
DITE, SUPERNATURAL,
ABSTRUSE, MYSTERI-
OUS, LATENT,
ESOTERIC, CONCEALED

occultation ECLIPSE,
CONCEALMENT

occultism CABALA,
MAGIC, MYSTERY

occupant TENANT,
RENTER, RESIDENT,
HOLDER, INHABITANT,
DWELLER, INMATE,
INCUMBENT

occupation TENURE,
BUSINESS, LINE,
CRAFT, WORK, JOB,
CALLING, NOTE,
PURSUIT, TRADE,
GAME, CONTROL, PRO-
FESSION, EMPLOY-
MENT, VOCATION,
POSSESSION, USE,
SPHERE, CAREER,
BERTH

occupied TOOK, CAP-
TURED, BUSY, ACTIVE,
INTENT, KEPT, HELD,
RAPT

occupy AMUSE,
ENGAGE, POSSESS,
HOLD, KEEP, HAVE,
INTEREST, INHABIT,
EMPLOY, USE, TAKE,
ENGROSS, PERVADE,
FILL

occur (A)RISE,
CHANCE, BETIDE,
HAP(PEN), ENSUE,
BEFALL, COME,
EVENTUATE, APPEAR,
EXIST

occurrence EVENT,
EPISODE, JUNCTURE,
HAPPENING, INCIDENT,
APPEARANCE, ITEM,
CIRCUMSTANCE

occurring *at eight day
intervals* OCTAN

at nightfall
ACRONICAL,
ACRONYCAL

at regular intervals
HORAL

at twilight
CREPUSCULAR

every fourth year
PENTETERIC

every seven days
HEBDOMADAL

hourly HORAL

ocean SEA, BRINE,
DEEP, MAIN, POND,
DRINK, EXPANSE

on the ASEA

route LANE

Oceania POLYNESIA,
MELANESIA,
MICRONESIA

sacred object ZOGO

oceanic MARINE, PELAGIC, NAUTICAL, NAVAL

Oceanus' *wife* TETHYS

ocellus EYE(LET), STEMMA

ocelot LEOPARD, CAT

ocher PIGMENT, ORE

India or Spain ALMAGRA

red TIVER

yellow SIL

octave EIGHT

of a feast UTAS

Octavia's *brother* AUGUSTUS

husband ANTONY

octopus HEE, POULP(E), SQUID, CUTTLE, MOLLUSK

secretion INK

octoroon MESTEE, MUSTEE, METIS, MESTIZO

ocular OPTIC, ORBITAL, VISUAL, OPHTHALMIC

odd UNIQUE, COMICAL, DROLL, PECULIAR, STRANGE, SINGULAR, ECCENTRIC, QUEER, QUAINT, CURIOUS, UNUSUAL, ERRATIC, EXTRA(ORDINARY), LEFT, LONE, UN-MATCHED, UNPAIRED, SINGLE, AZYGOUS

job man JOEY

oddity SINGULARITY, IDIOSYNCRASY, PECULIARITY, QUEER-NESS, ECCENTRICITY

odds EDGE, HANDICAP, ADVANTAGE, CHANCE, VARIANCE, DIF-FERENCE, DISCORD, DISPARITY, IN-EQUALITY, PROBA-BILITY

and ends BROTT, ORTS, SECONDS, REFUSE, FRAGMENTS, REMNANTS, SCRAPS

ode MONODY, POEM, SONG, LYRIC, PINDARIC

odeon HALL, THEATER, ODEUM, GALLERY

odic, *electric force* ELOD, OD

Odin WODEN, WODAN

brother VE, VILI

daughter-in-law NANNA

father BOR

son BALDER, TYR, VALI

wife RIND(R), FRIA, FRIGG

odious UGLY, HATEFUL, REPUGNANT, DIS-GUSTING, OFFENSIVE

odium HATRED, AVERSION, DISLIKE, ABHORRENCE, DETESTATION, ANTIP-ATHY, REPULSIVE-NESS, OPPROBRIUM, DISGRACE

odor AROMA, FUME, FRAGRANCE, SMELL, FETOR, SCENT, NIDOR, PERFUME, RED-OLENCE, EFFLUVIUM

of cooking FUMET, NIDOR

odorous REDOLENT, AROMATIC, BALMY, OLENT, FRAGRANT, PERFUMED, ODORIFER-OUS

odylic ODIC, OD, ODYL(E)

Odysseus ULYSSES

See "Ulysses"

dog ARGOS

father LAERTES

friend MENTOR

king of ITHACA

"Odyssey" *author* HOMER

Oedipus'

daughter ANTIGONE

father LAIUS

mother JOCASTA

sister CREON

son ETEOCLES

oestrid fly larva BOT

oeuvre WORK, OPUS

of FROM, OFF, BY, WITH, ABOUT, DE

each ANA, PER

this day HODIERNAL

off (A)FAR, ABNORMAL, WRONG, AGEE, ASIDE, AWAY, REMOTE, DISTANT, OPPOSITE, FROM, REMOVED, INACCURATE

offend AFFRONT, ANNOY, INSULT, OUT-RAGE, PIQUE, CHAFE, VEX, VIOLATE, HARM, HURT, TRANSGRESS, DISPLEASE, RASP, MIFF, MORTIFY, IR-RITATE, PROVOKE, GRATE, NETTLE, GALL, ANGER

offense FELONY, CRIME, FAULT, GRIEF, PIQUE, HUFF, INSULT, VICE, ATTACK, AS-SAULT, TORT, BREACH, MALUM, SIN, EVIL, WRONG, ONSET, AG-GRESSION, DIS-PLEASURE, AFFRONT, MISDEED, TRANSGRES-SION, MISDEMEANOR, UMBRAGE, RESENT-MENT, INDIGNITY, OUTRAGE

against law DELICT, CRIME, FELONY

civil TORT

offensive REPUGNANT, UNSAVORY, FOUL, FETID, AGGRESSIVE, OBNOXIOUS, ABUSIVE, DISGUSTING, REVOLT-ING

offer PRESENT, HAND, BID, TENDER, PROFFER, PROPOSE, EXHIBIT, SHOW, PROPOUND, VOLUNTEER, ATTEMPT, UNDERTAKE, AFFORD, SUPPLY, PROPOSAL, OVERTURE, THREATEN

up OBLATE

offering GIFT, BID, DONATION, CONTRIBU-TION, SACRIFICE, OBLATION, PRESENT

as a vow CORBAN

resistance to force RENITENT, RE-CALCITRANT

offhand CASUAL(LY), EXTEMPORE, IM-PROMPTU, HASTY, ABRUPT, UNPRE-MEDITATED, UN-STUDIED, CURT, EX-TEMPORARY, AD LIB, INFORMAL, BRUSQUE, READILY, CARELESS, SOON

office POST, FUNCTION, STATION, JOB, DUTY, TASK, WORK, STINT, METIER, SERVICE, TRUST, CHARGE, POSI-TION, CAPACITY, ROOM, BUREAU, AP-POINTMENT, SITUA-TION

priest's MATIN

relinquish DEMIT,
RESIGN, RETIRE, QUIT
officer ADJUTANT,
SHERIFF, COP, AGENT,
MINISTER, FUNC-
TIONARY, CONSTABLE,
BAILIFF
assistant to AIDE,
DEPUTY
Brit. royal guard
EXON
non-commissioned
CHIEF, CORPORAL,
SERGEANT
of king's stables
AVENER
official VIP, BASHAW,
FORMAL, APPROVED,
AUTHORITATIVE,
SANCTIONED, TRUE,
CERTAIN, CERE-
MONIOUS
approval VISE, VISA
decree UKASE, WRIT
sent by king MISSUS
weights SEALER
officious MEDDLING,
INTRUSIVE, MEDDLE-
SOME
offshoot SHOOT, SPRIG,
BRANCH, LIMB, ROD,
ISSUE, SON, SCION,
MEMBER, DESCEND-
ANT, ADJUNCT
ogee *See* "molding"
Ogier NORSEMAN,
DANE, PRINCE, HERO
ogle GLANCE, LOOK,
EYE, LEER, MARLOCK
ogre HUGON, DEMON,
MONSTER, BUGBEAR,
GIANT, BRUTE
Ohio *city or town*
LOGAN, ATHENS,
XENIA, AKRON, KENT,
BEREA
county ROSS,
UNION, LOGAN, NOBLE,
ATHENS, BROWN,
ADAMS, PIKE, ERIE,
KNOX, LAKE, WOOD
oil GREASE, OLEUM,
FAT, LUBE, LARD,
WAX, CREAM,
PETROLEUM, PAINT-
ING, LUBRICATE,
SMEAR, SMOOTH,
BRIBE, FLATTER
bottle CRUET
combining form OLEO
dry well DUSTER
fish ESCOLAR
flask OLPE

flax seed LINSEED
fragrant ATTAR,
CEDAR
lamp LUCIGEN,
LANTERN
made from butter
GHEE
ointment OLEAMEN
orange blossom
NEROLI
pertaining to OLEIC
rub with ANOINT,
GREASE
skin SEBUM
tree TUNG, EBOE,
MAHWA, POON
well gone wrong
GASSER
oillet EYELET
oilseed SESAME, TIL
oilstone HONE, WHET-
STONE
oily FAT, SMOOTH,
SLIPPERY, GLIB,
OLEOSE, GREASY,
BLAND, UNCTUOUS,
OLEAGINOUS, OLEOUS,
SERVILE, FATTY,
SEBACEOUS
substitute in fats
OLEIN
ointment BALM, NARD,
SALVE, BALSAM,
CEROMA, POMADE,
UNGUENT, GREASE,
REMEDY
application EMBROCA-
TION
Biblical SPIKENARD
Oisin's *father* FIONN
O.K. ROGER, RIGHT
Okinawa *capital* NAHA
town SHURI
Oklahoma *city or town*
ADA, ENID, ALVA
county GARVIN,
BRYAN, MAJOR, CADDO,
ELLIS, KIOWA, OSAGE,
ADAIR, KAY, LOVE
Indian See under
"Indian"
mountains OZARK
river RED
State nickname
SOONER
okra BENDY, GUMBO,
BENDEE, PLANT
old MATURE, GRAY,
SENESCENT, ANILE,
AGED, ELD(ERLY),
SENILE, OGYGIAN,
DATED, STALE,

ANCIENT, ANTIQUE,
ARCHAIC, ANTIQUATED,
OBSOLETE, WEAK,
FEEBLE, SHABBY,
WORN, FORMER,
EXPERIENCED,
QUONDAM, MEDIEVAL
age, pertaining to
GERONTAL, GERONTIC
study of
GERIATRICS,
NOSTOLOGY
fashioned QUAINT,
ANTIQUATED, FOGRAM,
FUSTY, PASSE
refrain FA LA
Sod ERIN
Testament See
"Bible"
land of riches
OPHIR
last word of CURSE
object URIM
people PHUD, PHUT
writer ELOHIST
time YORE, ELD,
QUONDAM, LATE,
FORMER
womanish ANILE
olden ANCIENT, BY-
GONE, FORMER,
MEDIEVAL
older SENIOR, STALER,
ELDER
oleaginous OILY,
FAWNING, SANC-
TIMONIOUS,
UNCTUOUS *See*
"oily"
oleander *genus*
NERIUM, SHRUB
oleoresin BALSAM,
ANIME, ELEMI, TOLU
olive DRUPE, TREE,
FRUIT
fly genus DACUS
genus OLEA
inferior MORON
stuffed PIMOLA
wild OLEASTER
olive oil, *combining
form* ELAIO
olla-podrida MEDLEY,
OLIO, HODGEPODGE,
OLLA, POTPOURRI
Olympian ZEUS
(JUPITER), POSEIDON
(NEPTUNE), HADES
(PLUTO), HESTIA
(VESTA), HERA
(JUNO), ARES
(MARS), ATHENA

(MINERVA), APOLLO,
APHRODITE (VENUS),
HERMES (MERCURY),
ARTEMIS (DIANA),
HEPHAESTUS
(VULCAN)
Olympic *cup bearer*
GANYMEDE
game site ELIS
inhabitant See
"Olympian"
Olympus, *region by*
PIERIA
Hindu MERU
Oman *capital* MUSCAT,
MASQAT
coin GAJ
Omar Khayyam's *country* IRAN (PERSIA)
omber card BASTO
omega LAST, END
omen AUGUR(Y),
MARK, SIGN, PRESAGE,
FORBODE, AUSPICE,
TOKEN, PORTENT,
PROGNOSTIC, FORE-
SHADOW
omers, *ten* EPHA(H)
omicron LITTLE,
SHORT, TINY
ceti STAR, MIRA
ominous SINISTER,
MENACING,
THREATENING, FATE-
FUL
omission CUT,
NEGLECT, FAILURE,
ERROR, OVERSIGHT,
ELISION, PRETERITION,
EXCLUSION, DEFAULT,
PRETERMISSION,
GUILT
mark of CARET
of vowel ELISION
pretended
PARALEPSIS
omit NEGLECT, SLIGHT,
DROP, OVERLOOK,
PASS, IGNORE, LET,
DELE(TE), SPARE,
SKIP, PRETERMIT,
DISREGARD
in pronounciation
ELIDE
omneity ALLNESS,
WHOLE
omni ALL, EVERY-
WHERE, OMNISCIENT
Omri's *successor* AHAB
on AT, IN, UPON, ATOP,
FORWARD, ONWARD,
ATTACHED, AHEAD, BY

onager ASS
once ERST,
FORMER(LY),
QUONDAM
oncorhynchus genus
SALMON
on-dit RUMOR, REPORT,
GOSSIP
ondoyant WAVY, UNDY
one SINGLE, SOLE,
UNO, ACE, AN, UNIT,
ONLY, INDIVIDUAL,
UNDIVIDED, UNITED,
SAME, IDENTICAL,
COMMON, UNITY, PER-
SON
after the other
SERIATIM
behind the other
TANDEM
combining form
MON(O), UNI, HENO
footed UNIPED
hundred and forty four
GROSS
hundred thousand
LAC
rupees LAKH
instructed in secret
system EPOPT
million millions
TRILLION
combining form
TREG(A)
prefix See "combining
form" *above*
Scot. AE, YIN
sided ASKEW,
UNILATERAL,
PREJUDICED, PARTIAL,
UNJUST
spot ACE, BUCK,
DOLLAR
tenth of a rin MO
thousand MIL
thousand square
meters DECARE
twelfth of an inch
LINE
one and one-half, *com-
bining form* SESQUI
one hundred percent
PURE, ALL, TOTAL
O'Neill *heroine* ANNA
one's self, *belief in*
SOLIPSISM
onion BOLL, CEPA,
CIBOL, SCALLION,
BULB, SHALLOT, PLANT
bulb SET
genus ALLIUM
like CHIVE, LEEK

small ESCHALOT,
SCALLION, SHALLOT
Welsh CIBOL
only SOLITARY, SINGLE,
SIMPLY, SOLE(LY),
BUT, (A)LONE,
MERELY, SAVE,
SINGLY, EXCLUSIVELY,
EXTREMELY, BEST,
FINEST, BARELY
onomasticon DIC-
TIONARY, LIST, GLOS-
SARY, VOCABULARY
onomatopoeic IMI-
TATIVE, ECHOIC
onslaught ATTACK,
BRUNT, ONSET,
ASSAULT, AFFRAY,
CHARGE, STORM,
ONRUSH
on this side CIS
onus BURDEN, LOAD,
DUTY, INCUBUS,
WEIGHT, TASK, OBLIGA-
TION, CHARGE,
RESPONSIBILITY
onward ON, AHEAD,
ADVANCING, PROGRESS-
ING, FORTH, FORWARD,
ALONG
in time AKE,
ETERNALLY
onyx CHALCEDONY,
QUARTZ
oopak TEA
oorial SHA, URIAL,
SHEEP
ooze EXUDE, SLIME,
LEAK, SEEP, SIPE,
MUD, SOAK, DRIP,
PERCOLATE, FILTER,
ESCAPE, MIRE,
MARSH, BOG
opah CRAVO, FISH
opal HYALITE, RESIN,
GEM
fire GIRASOL
precious NOBLE
opaque DIM, DARK,
OBSCURE, DULL,
CLOUDED, STUPID,
OBTUSE, MUDDY,
VAGUE, ABSTRUSE,
THICK, UNINTELLIGI-
BLE
open PUBLIC, AJAR,
UNCOVER(ED),
CANDID, MANIFEST,
VACANT, ACCESSIBLE,
AVAILABLE, EX-
POSE(D), UN-
FASTEN(ED), LIABLE,

OVERT, PATENT,
AGAPE, UNSEAL(ED),
PLAIN, FRANK, UN-
CLOSE(D), UNRE-
SERVED, INGENUOUS,
UNOBSTRUCTED, UN-
PROTECTED, EVIDENT,
EXTENDED, SINCERE,
UNFEIGNED, UNCLASP,
GENEROUS, LIBERAL,
RESPONSIVE, AP-
PARENT, OBVIOUS,
HONEST, ARTLESS,
VISIBLE, CLEAR, FREE,
UNDECIDED, UN-
FOLD(ED), EXPANDED,
UNLOCK, BROACH, UN-
TIE, BEGIN, RUPTURE,
CRACK, BURST, EX-
PAND, SPREAD, UNDO,
CUT, WIDEN, ENLARGE,
START, COMMENCE,
INITIATE, SHOW, EX-
HIBIT, REVEAL,
LIBERALIZE
air, in ALFRESCO
country WEALD,
VELDT, WOLD
court AREA, PATIO,
OYER
gape DEHISCENCE
passage in woods
GLADE, PATH, TRAIL
plain VEGA
shelved cabinet
ETAGERE, WHATNOT
opener(s) KEY
in poker JACKS, PAIR
opening PASSAGE,
HOLE, SPACE, BAY,
HIATUS, SINUS, SLOT,
GAP, RIFT, RIMA,
GATE, DOOR, TEAR,
EYELET, OS,
FENESTRA, FORAMEN,
VENT, STOMA, SLIT,
WINDOW, BREACH,
MEATUS, CANAL,
APERTURE, ORIFICE,
PERFORATION, CLEFT,
GULF, FISSURE, RENT,
FLAW, LOOP(HOLE),
INTERSTICE, CAVITY,
PORE, CAVE, BEGIN-
NING, FIRST, COM-
MENCING, COMMENCE-
MENT, INTRODUCTION,
INTRODUCTORY, IN-
ITIATION, INITIATORY,
DAWN, OPPORTUNITY,
CHANCE, VACANCY
in chess GAMBIT

in mold INGATE
mouth-like STOMA
of ear BURR, CANAL,
MEATUS
slitlike RIMA
small PORE
openings, *zoological*
STOMATA
opera AIDA, THAIS,
CARMEN, FAUST,
TOSCA
aria SOLO
Bellini NORMA
Bizet CARMEN
Bungert CIRCE
Carpentier LOUISE
comic actor BUFFO
Delibes LAKME
Flotow MARTHA
glass BINOCLE,
LORGNETTE
Gounod FAUST
hat GIBUS, TOPPER
Leoncavallo ZAZA
Mascagni IRIS
Massenet MANON,
SAPPHO, THAIS
Mussorgsky BORIS,
GUDUNOV
Paderewski MANRU
Parker MONA
Puccini BOHEME,
TOSCA
scene SCENA
singer PONS, MELBA,
CARUSO, GIGLI, CAL-
LAS, DIVA
Strauss SALOME, BAT
Verdi AIDA, OTELLO,
ERNANI
Wagner RIENZI, PAR-
SIFAL
Weber OBERON
operate MANAGE, CON-
DUCT, PILOT, STEER,
DRIVE, WORK, RUN,
ACT, MAN, FUNCTION,
EFFECT, MANIPULATE
operator MANAGER,
DRIVER, PILOT,
BROKER, MAKER,
DEALER, AGENT,
ACTOR, PERFORMER,
DOER, MANIPULATOR,
SPECULATOR, TRADER,
SURGEON, DENTIST
operculum COVER,
PLATE, FLAP, LID,
OPERCLE
ophidian SNAKE, REP-
TILE, SERPENT, CON-
GER, EEL

opiate DRUG, DOPE,
HEMP, ANODYNE,
OPIUM, NARCOTIC,
SEDATIVE, TRANQUIL-
IZER, SOPORIFIC
opine DEEM, THINK,
JUDGE, SUPPOSE, BE-
LIEVE
opinion CONCLUSION,
DECISION, ESTIMATE,
CONVICTION, JUDG-
MENT, IDEA, MIND,
ESTEEM, DOCTRINE,
TENET, BELIEF, VIEW,
NOTION, CONCEP-
T(ION), IMPRESSION,
SENTIMENT, ESTIMA-
TION, PERSUASION
expressed CREDO
opium *alkaloid* CODE-
INE, MORPHINE, NAR-
COTINE, PAPAVERINE
seed MAW
source POPPY
opossum, *S. Amer.*
QUICA, SARIGUE
water YAPOK
oppidan URBAN, CIVIC,
TOWNSMAN
oppilate BLOCK, OB-
STRUCT, CLOG
opponent ANTAGONIST,
RIVAL, FOE, ENEMY,
ANTI, ADVERSARY,
COMPETITOR, ASSAIL-
ANT
opportune HAPPY, FIT-
TING, READY, APT,
TIMELY, APROPOS,
PAT, SEASONABLE,
CONVENIENT, EXPEDI-
ENT, SUITABLE,
FAVORABLE, PROPI-
TIOUS, AUSPICIOUS,
FORTUNATE, LUCKY,
APPROPRIATE
opportunity OCCASION,
OPENING, SEASON,
CHANCE, BREAK, TIDE,
TIME, ROOM, JUNC-
TURE
oppose MEET, DEFY,
FORCE, RESIST, IM-
PUGN, CONTEND, FACE,
CROSS, REPEL, COPE,
FIGHT, BATTLE, WAR,
WITHSTAND, COUN-
TERACT, CONTRAVENE,
THWART, OBSTRUCT,
COMBAT, CONFRONT,
OPPUGN, GAINSAY, AN-
TAGONIZE, CLASH

opposed MET, FACED, FRONTED, COPED, PITTED, OPPOSITE, ADVERSE, HOSTILE, INIMICAL

opposite CONTRA(RY), ANTI, HOSTILE, POLAR, ANTAGONISTIC, ANTITHETIC(AL), REVERSE, OTHER, CONVERSE, INCOMPATIBLE, REPUGNANT, CONTRADICTORY, ADVERSE, COUNTER, OPPOSING, ANTIPODAL

opposition HATE, DISCORD, ANTIPATHY, FRONTING, FACING, RESISTANCE, OBSTACLE, HOSTILITY, ANTAGONISM, CONTRAST

oppress CRUSH, RACK, LOAD, ABUSE, WRONG, AFFLICT, BURDEN, EXTINGUISH, SUPPRESS, OVERPOWER, TRAMPLE, SUBDUE, DEPRESS

oppressive HOT, SULTRY, TORRID, TYRANNICAL

opprobrium SHAME, ABUSE, REPROACH, CONTEMPT, DISDAIN, INFAMY, ODIUM, DISGRACE, IGNOMINY, DISREPUTE

oppugn OPPOSE, DISPUTE, ASSAIL, ATTACK, COMBAT, RESIST, THWART, CRITICIZE, CONTROVERT

Ops' *consort* SATURN
early associate CONSUS
festival OPALIA

opt CHOOSE, WISH, (S)ELECT, PICK, CULL, DECIDE

optic EYE, VISUAL, OCULAR

optical *apparatus* LENS, GLASS
illusion MIRAGE
instrument ALIDADE

optimistic JOYOUS, GLAD, ROSEATE, ROSY, HOPEFUL, SANGUINE, EXPECTANT

option CHOICE, DISCRETION, FUTURE, PREFERENCE, (S)ELECTION, PRIVILEGE, ALTERNATIVE

opulent RICH, LAVISH, SHOWY, LUSH, BARONIAL, PLUSH(Y), WEALTHY, AFFLUENT, FLUSH, MONEYED, LUXURIANT, PROFUSE, ABUNDANT

opus ETUDE, STUDY, WORK, COMPOSITION, LABOR

oquassa TROUT, FISH

oracle AUGUR, SEER, SIBYL, MENTOR, SAGE, PROPHET, REVELATION, SOOTHSAYER
Apollo's DELPHIC
pertaining to PYTHONIC

oracular VATIC, PROPHETIC, PYTHONIC, PORTENTOUS, SAGE, WISE, AMBIGUOUS, MYSTERIOUS

oral VOCAL, VERBAL, ALOUD, PAROL(E), SPOKEN, MOUTHED, SAID, VOICED
declaration, describing NUNCUPATIVE

orange *bowl site* MIAMI
Chinese MANDARIN
flower oil NEROLI
genus CITRUS
kind of OSAGE, SEVILLE, NAVEL, BLOOD
peel ZEST, RIND
seed PIP
seedless NAVEL
tincture TENNE

orangewood *tree* OSAGE

oration, *funeral* ELOGE, ENCOMIUM, EULOGY

orator SPEAKER, ADVOCATE, RHETOR, PERORATOR, SPELLBINDER

oratorical RHETORICAL, ELOQUENT

oratorio, *coda in* STRETTO

oratory CHAPEL, BETHEL, CHANTRY, ELOQUENCE, ELOCUTION, RHETORIC

Oratory, Fathers of, *founder* NERI

orbed LUNAR, ROUND, GLOBATE, SPHERICAL

orbit EYE, TRACK, PATH, ELLIPSE, RANGE, RADIUS, KEN, SWEEP, SCOPE, CIRCUIT, AMBIT, REGION, ORB, BALL

orbital point APSIS, APOGEE, NADIR

orc GRAMPUS, WHALE, DRAGON, OGRE, DOLPHIN

orchestra *circle* PIT, PARTERRE

orchid, *African genus* DISA
appendage CAUDICLE
edible root SALEP
genus DISA, LISTERA
leaves for tea FAHAM
male PURPLE, CULLION
part of ANTHER
plant drug SALEP
pods, derivative of VANILLA
powder SALEP
tea FAHAM
tuber SALEP

ordain APPOINT, ESTABLISH, CONSECRATE, PRESCRIBE, ORDER, INVEST, FROCK, CALL, SEND, ARRANGE, PREPARE, ENACT, WILL, DECREE, DESTINE, INSTITUTE, PREDESTINE, COMMAND, COMMISSION

ordained LEGAL, DUE, PRESCRIPT

ordeal TEST, TRIAL, GAFF, CRUCIBLE, EXPERIENCE

order SOCIETY, GENRE, SEQUENCE, REGULATION, REQUISITION, ARRANGEMENT, PEACE, CLASSIFICATION, WRIT, SYSTEM, MANDATE, CLASS, WILL, BROTHERHOOD, INJUNCTION, RANK, FRATERNITY, METHOD, TRANQUIL(L)ITY, RULE, PRECEPT, DIRECT(ION), EDICT, REGULATE, ARRANGE, ENJOY, CHARGE, CLUB, LODGE, KIND, SORT, (A)LINE, ORDAIN,

DICTATE, TYPE, ARRAY, BID, COMMAND, DIRECT, DISPOSE

orderliness SYSTEM

orderly PROPERLY, TRIM, PEACEABLE, PEACEFUL, AIDE, SERVANT, MESSENGER, TRIG, TIDY, NEAT, REGULAR, METHODICAL, SYSTEMATIC

ordinal NUMBER, BOOK

ordinance RITE, CEREMONY, EDICT, CANON, PRECEPT, LAW, ASSIZE, RULE, ORDER, STATUTE, DECREE, DECRETAL, ENACTMENT, PRESCRIPT

ordinary CUSTOMARY, REGULAR, LOW, BANAL, USUAL, PLAIN, NORMAL, VULGATE, AVERAGE, COMMON, BOOK, TAVERN, NOMIC, PROSY, INEXPERT, JUDGE, LALA, HABITUAL, UGLY, SIMPLE
court of PROBATE

ordnance ARMS, GUNS, CANNON, AMMUNITION, MORTAR, ARMOR, MATERIEL
of 17th Cent. RABINET

ordo DIRECTORY, BOOKLET, PUBLICATION, CALENDAR, ORDER

ore IRON, TIN, MINERAL, METAL, ROCK, COIN, HEMATITE
box FLOSH
deposit LODE, MINE
earthy-looking PACO
excavation STOPE
fusing plant SMELTER
horizontal layer STOPE
impure SPEISS
iron pigment OCHER, OCHRE
loading platform PLAT
method of cleansing VANNING
receptacle MORTAR
trough for washing STRAKE
vein LODE, SCRIN
worthless MATTE, SLAG, DROSS

oread NYMPH, PERI
See "fairy"

Oregon *capital* SALEM
county GRANT, COOS, POLK, LAKE, LINN, LANE, UNION, WASCO
inlet or bay COOS
mountain HOOD
range CASCADE
university site EUGENE

orellin, *coloring principle* BIXIN

Oreortyx *genus* QUAIL

Orestes' *sister* ELECTRA
wife HERMIONE

orf(e) IDE, FISH

organ MEDIUM, MEANS, AGENT, AGENCY, JOURNAL, MAGAZINE, NEWSPAPER, VOICE, MEMBER, EYE, EAR, HEART, LIVER, INSTRUMENT
flutter device TREMOLO
interlude or prelude VERSET
original SYRINX
pipe FLUTE, REED
stop BASSOON, DOLCE, CELESTA, OBOE, VIOLA, DOLCIAN, MELODIA, ORAGE, TIERCE, DOLCAN

organic INHERENT, VITAL, CONSTITUTIONAL, ORGANIZED, FUNDAMENTAL, STRUCTURAL
body ZOOID
compound AMINE, KETOL
radical ETHYL
remains, without AZOIC

organism MONAS, SYSTEM, BODY, AMOEBA, ANIMAL, PLANT, MONAD, PERSON, INDIVIDUAL, BEING
of certain plants SPORE
potential IDORGAN
swimming on sea NEKTON

organization OUTFIT, STRUCTURE, UNIT, SETUP, CADRE, ARMY, FRAME, SKELETON, FIRM, BUSINESS, COMPANY, ARRANGEMENT,

SYSTEMATIZATION, ASSOCIATION, SOCIETY

organize DESIGN, FASHION, FOUND, BEGIN, START, ARRANGE, FORM, PLAY, SYSTEMIZE, DISPOSE, CONSTRUCT, ADJUST, COORDINATE, ESTABLISH, PRODUCE, INSTITUTE

organized *body* CORPS, ARMY, NAVY, POSSE

orgy RITE, BINGE, REVEL, CAROUSAL, BOUT, DEBAUCH

oribi ANTELOPE

oriel BAY, WINDOW, DORMER, RECESS

Orient ASIA, EAST, LEVANT

oriental LEVANTINE, EASTERN, BRIGHT, ORTIVE, ASIAN, PRECIOUS
beverage ARRACK
booth SOOK
bow SALAAM
caravansary IMARET, KHAN
carpet KALI
cart ARABA
Christian UNIAT
coin PARA, SEN *See* country involved
destiny KISMET
dish PILAU, PILAW
dulcimer SANTIR
dwelling DAR
fish TAI
gate DAR
guitar SITAR
hospice IMARET
inn SERAI
kettledrum ANACARA
laborer COOLIE
man servant HAMAL
market SOOK
measure DRA, PARA(H) *See* country involved
mendicant priest FAKIR
motel SERAI
nurse AMA(H), IYA, AYAH
palanquin DOOLEY, DOOLIE
patent BERAT
people, ancient SERES
pine MATSU
plane tree CHINAR
porgy TAI
potentate AGA

prince KHAN
ruler SHAH, SULTAN, AMIR, AMEER, EMIR, EMEER
salute SALAAM
servant AMAH
ship DHOW
skipper RAIS, REIS
tamarisk ATLE(E)
tambourine DAIRA
taxi RICKSHA(W)
title SRI, SAHIB
vessel SAIC, DHOW
weight ABBAS, MISKAL, ROTL, SHI(H)
orifice PORE, OSTIOLE, HOLE, MOUTH, OPENING, CAVITY, VENT, OS, OUTLET, APERTURE, PERFORATION
brain LURA
origin START, GERM, BEGINNING, ANCESTRY, STOCK, PROVENANCE, PARENTAGE, NATURE, SEED, BUD, FONT, SOURCE, NEE, BIRTH, ROOT, RISE, SPRING, FOUNTAIN, COMMENCEMENT, CAUSE, FOUNDATION, OCCASION, DERIVATION, INCEPTION, PROVENIENCE, GENESIS, OUTSET, DAWN
original PRIME(VAL), NEW, FRESH, UNIQUE, PRISTINE, INITIAL, FIRST, NOVEL, GENETIC, NATIVE, PRIMITIVE, ABORIGINAL, PRIMORDIAL, PRIMARY, INDEPENDENT, CREATIVE, INVENTIVE, FONTAL
design TYPE, MODEL, PATTERN, ARCHETYPE, EXEMPLAR
originally FIRST, INHERENTLY, PRIMARILY, INITIALLY
originate INSTITUTE, PRODUCE, PROPAGATE, DERIVE, INVENT, CREATE, EMANATE, CAUSE, START, BEGIN, (A)RISE, COIN, STEM, SPRING, INITIATE, CONCEIVE, EMBARK

oriole LORIOT, PIROL, BIRD
genus ORIOLUS
orison PRAYER
Orkney *bay* VOE
fishing bank HAAF
freehold ODAL, UDAL
hut SKEO
island, HOY, POMONA, SANDAY
largest island POMONA
tower BROCH
ormolu GOLD, GILT, ALLOY, VARNISH
ornament (BE)DECK, GARNISH, ADORN(MENT), DECORATE, EMBELLISH, BEAUTIFY, BEDIZEN, EMBLAZON, SPANGLE, SEQUIN, BROOCH, RING, BRACELET, SEME, DECOR, OUCH, FRET, SCROLL, GUTTA, AMULET, SPANG
circular ROSETTE
raised BOSS, STUD
ornate ELEGANT, FLORID, SHOWY, FANCY, GAY, ROCOCO, FLOWERY, ORNAMENTED, ELABORATE, EMBELLISHED, PRETENTIOUS, OSTENTATIOUS, ADORNED
ornery STUBBORN, MEAN, LOW, BASE, UNMANAGEABLE, CRABBED, ORDINARY, INSIGNIFICANT
orogeny UPHEAVAL
Orozco *specialty* MURAL
Orpheus' *birthplace* PIERIA
parent APOLLO, CALLIOPE
ort SCRAP, END, LEFTOVER, MORSEL, BIT, CRUMB, REMNANT, TRIFLE
orthorhombic *mineral* IOLITE
ortolan BUNTING, BOBOLINK, SORA, BIRD
os BONE, MOUTH, OPENING, ESKER
Osaka bay port KOBE
oscillate VIBRATE, FLUCTUATE, WAVE, ROCK, SWAY, WAG,

SWING, WAVER, VARY, CHANGE
oscine bird VIREO, CROW, TANAGER
oscitate GAPE, YAWN
osculate KISS, BUSS, TOUCH
osier WILLOW, WAND, SALLOW, TWIG, ROD
band WITHE, WICKER
Osiris' *brother* SET(H)
parent GEB, NUT
son ANUBIS, HORUS
wife ISIS
osprey HAWK, OSSIFRAGE, BIRD
osseous BONY, SPINY, LITHIC
ossicle BONE, MALLEUS, INCUS, STAPES, AMBOS
ossuary TOMB, GRAVE, URN
ostentation PAGEANT, BOAST, DISPLAY, FLOURISH, SHOW, SHOWINESS, EXHIBITION, PARADE, SPECTACLE, ARRAY, CEREMONY, FLAIR, ECLAT, POMP, DASH, POMPOSITY, VAUNTING, PRETENTIOUSNESS, GLITTER
osteoma TUMOR
ostiole STOMA, ORIFICE, OS, APERTURE, PORE
ostracize DEPORT, EXILE, EXPEL, BAN(ISH), BAR, EXCLUDE, CENSURE, PUNISH
ostracoderm, *order* ANASPIDA
ostrich NANDU, RHEA
feather BOA, PLUME
genus RHEA, STRUTHIO
like bird EMU, EMEU, RATITE, RHEA
Otaheite *See* "Tahiti"
otary SEAL
Othello MOOR
character in play CASSIO, IAGO, EMILIA, BIANCA
lieutenant IAGO
wife DESDEMONA
other ELSE, ALTER(NATE), DIFFERENT, ADDITIONAL, MORE,

SECOND, LEFT, FUR-
THER, FORMER
combining form
ALLO, HETER(O)
otherness ALTERITY,
DIVERSITY
others RESIDUE, REST
and ET AL(II)
otherwise OR, ELSE,
ALIAS, DIFFER-
ENT(LY)
in music OSSIA
otic AURAL, AUDITORY,
AURICULAR
otidium EAR, OTOCYST
otiose UNEMPLOYED,
HOLLOW, VAIN,
EMPTY, INACTIVE,
IDLE, SUPERFLUOUS,
INDOLENT, FUTILE,
STERILE, USELESS,
INEFFECTUAL
otologist AURIST
otter *genus* LUTRA
sea KALAN
ottoman STOOL, FOOT-
STOOL, SEAT, COUCH
See "Turkey"
ouch BROOCH, CLASP,
FIBULA, BEZEL, EX-
CLAMATION, OW
ought NAUGHT, CI-
PHER, MOTE, SHOULD,
MUST, BEFIT, OBLIGA-
TION, DUTY, BEHOOVE,
ANYTHING
ounce, ⅛ *of* DRAM
oust EXPEL, EJECT,
EVICT, DEPOSE, FIRE,
SACK, CASHIER, DIS-
SEIZE, REMOVE, DIS-
LODGE, DISPOSSESS,
DISMISS, DEPRIVE,
DISCARD
out FROM, AWAY, EX,
ODD, END, FORTH,
ABROAD, EXTIN-
GUISHED, REVEALED,
PUBLIC, DISCLOSED,
BEGONE, SCRAM, SCAT
of date PASSE
prefix EC, ECTO
out-and-out ARRANT,
SHEER, UTTER, ER-
RANT, COM-
PLETE(LY), WHOLLY,
ABSOLUTE
outbreak REVOLT,
VIOLENCE, BREAK,
RASH, RIOT, ERUPTION,
EXPLOSION, ROW, CON-
FLICT, INSURRECTION

outburst FLARE, GALE,
STORM, SPATE, OUT-
BREAK, OUTCROP,
BLOWER, VIOLENCE,
REVOLT
outcast EXILE, LEPER,
PARIAH, ISHMAEL, RE-
JECT(ED), DEGRADED,
REPROBATE, EXPATRI-
ATE, CASTAWAY
Japan ROWIN, ETA
outcome EFFECT, RE-
SULT, AFTERMATH,
FATE, LOT, ISSUE,
EVENT, END, DENOUE-
MENT, UPSHOT, CON-
SEQUENCE
outcry CLAMOR, BEL-
LOW, SHOUT, NOISE,
YELL, BRUIT, SCREAM,
SCREECH, VOCIFERA-
TION, TUMULT, COM-
PLAINT, PROTEST, OB-
JECTION, ROAR
outdo (SUR)PASS, EX-
CEED, EXCEL, BEST,
TOP, CAP, WIN, BEAT,
OUTSTRIP, DEFEAT,
CONQUER, OVERCOME
outer FOREIGN, ALIEN,
EXTERNAL, EXTERIOR,
ECTAL, UTTER, OUT-
WARD, OUTSIDE
opposed to ENTAL
outfit OFFICE, BUSI-
NESS, GARB, GEAR,
GETUP, UNIT, SUIT,
KIT, EQUIP(MENT),
TACKLE, TROOP,
CLOTHES, PARAPHER-
NALIA, ENDOWMENTS,
REQUIREMENTS,
GROUP, ORGANIZA-
TION, RIG, FURNISH-
INGS
outlandish OUTRE,
ODD, BIZARRE,
STRANGE, FOREIGN,
EXOTIC, ALIEN, QUEER,
FANTASTIC, BARBA-
ROUS, UNCOUTH,
FREAKISH, IRREGULAR,
RIDICULOUS, PECUL-
IAR, REMOTE
outlaw TABU, PRO-
SCRIBE, TABOO, BAR,
BAN *See* "bandit"
oriental RONIN, DA-
COIT
outlet ISSUE, EGRESS,
DOOR, SPOUT, TAP,
FAUCET, PASSAGE, ES-

CAPE, SOCKET, PORT,
EXIT, VENT, LOOP-
HOLE, STREAM, MAR-
KET, OPENING, GATE
outline ADUMBRATE,
SKETCH, PLAN, MAP,
PROFILE, ABRIDG(E)-
MENT, DRAW, DRAFT,
TRACE, PLOT, CON-
TOUR, DELINEATION,
SUMMARY, COMPEN-
DIUM, FEATURES, SIL-
HOUETTE
outlook FRONTAGE,
SCOPE, PURVIEW,
VISTA, WATCH, PROS-
PECT, TOWER, LOOK-
OUT, PROBABILITY,
VIEW(POINT), EX-
PECTATION
outlying *district*
PURLIEU, ENVIRON,
SUBURB, NEIGHBOR-
HOOD
outmoded DATED,
PASSE, OLD, USED, OB-
SOLETE
output HARVEST, CROP,
TURNOUT, YIELD, PRO-
DUCTION, PRODUCE
outrageous HEINOUS,
FLAGRANT, SHOCKING,
MONSTROUS, ATRO-
CIOUS
outre STRANGE, BI-
ZARRE, EXTRAVAGANT
outrigger PROA, BOAT
out-rival ECLIPSE, EX-
CEL, OUT-VIE, DEFEAT,
WIN, SURPASS
outside OUTER, ALIEN,
FOREIGN, EXTERIOR,
EXTERNAL
combining form ECTO
outspoken LOUD,
FRANK, BLUNT, FREE,
CANDID, BOLD, UN-
RESERVED, PLAIN,
ARTLESS
outstanding SALIENT,
SIGNAL, UNPAID, STAR,
A-ONE, UNSETTLED,
OWING, DUE, UNCOL-
LECTED, DISTIN-
GUISHED, PROJECTING,
CONSPICUOUS, PROMI-
NENT, REMAINING,
UNFULFILLED
outstrip (SUR)PASS,
OUTRUN, LEAD, OUTDO,
BEST, EXCEL, TOP,
CAP, WIN

outward ECTAD, EX-
TRINSIC, OUTER, EX-
TERNAL, EXTERIOR,
OUTSIDE, VISIBLE, AP-
PARENT, SUPERFICIAL,
FORMAL
turn EVERT

outwit EUCHRE, BALK,
BEST, FOIL, DEFEAT,
CHEAT, DECEIVE,
BAFFLE, DUPE, CIR-
CUMVENT, SWINDLE,
DEFRAUD, VICTIMIZE,
COZEN, GULL, FRUS-
TRATE, OVERREACH

outwork OUTDO, BEST,
RAVELIN, TENAIL(LE),
DEFENSE, LUNETTE

ouzel PIET, THRUSH,
OUSEL, BIRD

oval ELLIPTIC(AL),
OVATE, OVOID, OBLONG

ovate *inversely* OBO-
VATE

oven KILN, OAST,
STOVE
annealing glass LEER,
LEHR
mop SCOVEL
Polynesian UMU

over SUPERIOR, SET-
TLED, EXCESS, SUR-
PLUS, UNDUE, ENCORE,
ATHWART, MORE,
THROUGH, ALSO,
ACROSS, TOO, ANEW,
BEYOND, AGAIN, PAST,
BY, ABOVE, ENDED,
DONE, ATOP, COVER-
ING, PREEMINENT,
FINISHED, GONE, EX-
CESSIVE, DEAD,
STOPPED
and above ATOUR,
ATOP, BEST
prefix SUPER, SUPRA,
SUR, HYPER

overact EMOTE, OUTDO

overawe COW, DAUNT,
SUBDUE, ABASH,
BROWBEAT, INTIMI-
DATE, FRIGHTEN,
SWAY

overbearing CAVALIER,
ARROGANT, PROUD,
LORDLY, DICTATORIAL,
IMPERIOUS, OPPRES-
SIVE, DOMINEERING,
SUPERCILIOUS,
HAUGHTY, OVER-
POWERING, AGGRES-
SIVE

overcoat ULSTER, CA-
POTE, BENNY, TOP-
COAT
close fitting SURTOUT
loose RAGLAN, PALE-
TOT
sleeveless INVERNESS

overcome LICK, DE-
FEAT, CATCH, EX-
CEED, BEST, SUPPRESS,
SURMOUNT, UPSET,
ROUT, AWE, DOMI-
NATE, RULE, SUBDUE,
CONQUER, VANQUISH,
SUBJUGATE, OVER-
WHELM, CRUSH, DIS-
COMFIT, PREVAIL,
PROSTRATE, DOMI-
NEER

overdue ARREAR, LATE,
TARDY, UNPAID, UN-
SETTLED, BELATED

overflow OUTLET,
VENT, EXCESS, DEL-
UGE, SPATE, TEEM,
EBULLIENCE, SWARM,
ABOUND, REST, FLOOD,
INUNDATE, OVERRUN,
SUPERABUNDANCE,
PROFUSION, SURPLUS,
REDUNDANCE

overhanging BEETLE,
EAVE, PROJECTING,
IMPENDING, SUS-
PENDED, PROJECTION,
JUTTING, THREATEN-
ING

overhead ALOFT,
ABOVE, UPKEEP, COST,
MAINTENANCE

overjoyed ELATED,
JUBILANT, TRANS-
PORTED, ENRAP-
TURED, DELIGHTED

overlay LAP, CEIL,
COVER, SMOTHER, OP-
PRESS, HIDE, OBSCURE,
SUPERIMPOSE

overloaded SATED,
PLETHORIC, SUR-
CHARGED, BURDENED

overlook MANAGE,
SUPERINTEND, SLIGHT,
FORGET, OMIT, MISS,
SKIP, SPARE, IGNORE,
INSPECT, SUPERVISE,
DISREGARD, NEGLECT,
EXCUSE, FORGIVE,
PARDON, SURVEY

overpower AWE, MAS-
TER, BEAT, SUBDUE,
WIN, CONQUER, OVER-
WHELM, VANQUISH,
CRUSH, SUBJUGATE

overreach STRAIN,
CHEAT, COZEN, DUPE,
DECEIVE, OUTWIT, CIR-
CUMVENT, DEFRAUD,
EXAGGERATE, EXTEND,
PASS

override VETO, NUL-
LIFY, HARASS, DEFEAT,
ABROGATE, OPPRESS,
SUPPRESS

overrun INFEST,
SWARM, TEEM, RAV-
AGE, DEVASTATE, DE-
SPOIL, SPREAD

over-scrupulous PRUD-
ISH, STRICT

oversee DIRECT, MAN-
AGE, SURVEY, INSPECT,
WATCH, SUPERVISE,
SUPERINTEND, OVER-
LOOK

overseer MASTER, SU-
PERVISOR, BOSS, SU-
PERINTENDENT, IN-
SPECTOR, FOREMAN

overshadow DARKEN,
DIM, ECLIPSE, SHEL-
TER, DOMINATE, OB-
SCURE, CLOUD

overshoe BOOT,
ARCTIC, RUBBER,
GALOSH

oversight LAPSE,
CHARGE, ERROR, SLIP,
GAFFE, INSPECTION,
DIRECTION, CONTROL,
MISTAKE, OMISSION,
BLUNDER, FAULT,
INATTENTION, FAILURE

overspread PALL, FOG,
COVER, SCATTER,
STREW

overt OPEN, PATENT,
PUBLIC, EVIDENT,
MANIFEST, APPARENT,
OBSERVABLE, OBVIOUS,
UNCONCEALED

overtake CATCH,
REACH, REJOIN, PASS,
ATTAIN, SEIZE, IN-
VOLVE

overthrow ROUT,
CONQUER, VANQUISH,
DEFEAT, LEVEL, TOP-
PLE, UPSET, WORST,
UNHORSE, SUBVERT,
DERANGE, DEMOLISH,
RUIN, DISLODGE, DE-
STROY

overtop DWARF, EXCEL, TRANSCEND, SURPASS, EXCEED, ECLIPSE

overture MUSIC, PROEM, TENDER, PRELUDE, BID, OFFER, PROPOSAL, PROPOSITION, OPENING, REQUEST

overturn SUBVERT, CAPSIZE *See* "overthrow"

overwhelm DELUDE, FLOOD, CRUSH, BEAT, BURY, DROWN, QUELL, SWAMP, SUBMERGE, OVERPOWER, SUBDUE, DEFEAT, CONQUER, VANQUISH, DESTROY

Ovid work MEDEA, AMORES, FASTI, TRISTIA

ovine SHEEP(LIKE)

ovule EGG, EMBRYO, SEED, GERM, NIT

outer integument PRIMINE

ovum *See* "ovule"

owal(l)a tree BOBO

owing DUE, UNPAID, INDEBTED, OBLIGED, PAYABLE, ASCRIBABLE

owl LULU, UTUM, ULLET, BIRD, BARN, HAWK, SCREECH, SNOWY, BARRED, GNOME

and Pussycat author LEAR

Europe CUE

genus SYRNIUM, STRIX

hawk SURN

hoot of ULULU

parrot, N. Z. KAKAPO

pertaining to STRIGINE

plumed eye area DISK

short-eared MOMO

small HOWLET, UTUM

S. America UTUM

wailing of HOOT, ULULU

own HOLD, CONCEDE, AVOW, ADMIT, HAVE, POSSESS, CONFESS, RECOGNIZE, ACKNOWLEDGE, ALLOW, RETAIN, ASSENT, DIVULGE

combining form IDIO

ox(en) STEER, BEEVE, YAK, BULLOCK, BISON,

ZEBU, KINE, BULL, BOVINE, AUROCHS

cart ARABA, ARBA

combining form BOVI

extinct wild URUS

forest, Celebes ANOA

grunting YAK

India GUAR, GAYAL, ZEBU

kind of NEAT, NOWT

like BOVINE, SLOW

Malayan BANTENG, TSINE

pair of YOKE, SPAN

Rome URUS

stomach TRIPE

Tibet YAK, ZEBU

wild ancestor URUS

horned REEM

working AVER

oxaldehyde GLYOXAL

oxalic acid salt LEMON

oxalis OCA, SORREL, PLANT

oxen *See* "ox"

oxeye BOCE, BOGUE, DUNLIN, SANDPIPER, PLOVER, DAISY, CAMOMILE, FISH, BIRD, FLOWER

oxford SHOE, CLOTH, UNIVERSITY

alumnus (sister university) AUNT

exam GREATS

officer BEDEL

scholar DEMY

Oxford, *Earl of* HARLEY, ASQUITH

oxide CALX, RUST

oxidize CALCINE, RUST

oxter ARM, ARMPIT, HUG, EMBRACE, ENARM

oxybenzene PHENOL

oxygen, *allotropic* OZONE

binary compound OXIDE

metal compound OXID(E)

radical OXYL

oyer TRIAL, COURT, HEARING, PLEADING

oyes, oyez ATTEND, HEAR, ATTENTION

oyster BIVALVE, MOLLUSK

bed LAYER, STEW, CLAIRE, BANK

catcher TIRMA, BIRD

common family EDULIS

drill BORER

farm CLAIRE, PARK

fish TOAD, TAUTOG

genus OSTREA

grass KELP

ova SPAWN

plant SALSIFY

rake TONG

shell TEST, HUSK, SHUCK

spawn CLUTCH, OVA, SPAT

species MOLLUSCA

young SET, SPAT

oysterfish TAUTOG, TOAD

Oz books author BAUM

ozone AIR, ETHER, OXYGEN, GAS

P

P PEE, PI

pabulum FOOD, SUSTENANCE, FUEL, ALIMENT, MANNA, NUTRIMENT, NOURISHMENT, SUPPORT

paca LABBA, AGOUTI, CAVY, RODENT

pace TROT, GAIT, WALK, LOPE, STEP, TRACE, RUN, IMPETUS, ADVANCE, MEASURE, AMBLE, RACK, SPEED, RATE, TEMPO, CLIP, CANTER, GALLOP, PASSAGEWAY, NAVE

pachisi LUDO, GAME

pachyderm ELEPHANT, RHINO(CEROS), HIPPO(POTAMUS)

Pacific *island(s)* GUAM, WAKE, SAMOA, FIJI, SAIPAN, TAHITI, OKINAWA, UPOLU, KOMODO, TRUK, UVEA (UEA), YAP (UAP), LIFU, ELLICE, MUNGA, ARU, BALI, DUCIE, RAPA, ATOLL

capital NAHA, AGANA

pine HALA, MATSU

tree IPIL

pacifist BOLO

pacify QUIET, ASSUAGE, CONCILIATE, PROPITIATE, RECONCILE, CALM, MOLLIFY,

PLACATE, ABATE, ALLAY, TEMPER, APPEASE, SOFTEN, TRANQUILIZE, LULL, MODERATE, SOOTHE, ALLEVIATE, MITIGATE

pack STUFF, CRAM, FILL, (COM)PRESS, WAD, STOW, STEEVE, LOAD, TAMP, RAM, SQUEEZE, ARRANGE, CARRY, TOTE, GANG, FLOCK, DROVE, DECK, SET, SHOOK, TRUSS, BUNDLE, PACKAGE, BURDEN, BALE, MULTITUDE, CROWD, PREPARE
animal ASS, MULE, BURRO
horse SUMPTER

package BUNDLE, PACKET, BOX, CRATE, PARCEL, BALE, CARTON, BARREL, (EN)CASE, ENCLOSE
covered with hides SEROON, CEROON
for pepper, etc. ROBBIN

packing, *clay* LUTE

pact AGREEMENT, BARGAIN, TREATY, CARTEL, COVENANT, CONTRACT

pad MAT, QUILT, TABLET, CUSHION, LEAF, HORSE, FOOTFALL, THICKEN, TRAMP, CRAM, STUFF, COVER *See* "pack"
ring on harness pad TERRET

paddle SCULL, SPOON, SCOOP, OAR, BLADE, FLIPPER, WADE, DABBLE, SPANK, PUNISH

paddock FROG, PARK, FIELD, TOAD, LOT, YARD, PASTURE, ENCLOSURE

Paderewski opera MANRU

padre PRIEST, MONK, CHAPLAIN, CLERIC, FATHER

paean HYMN, SONG, ODE, PRAISE

pagan ETHNIC, HEATHEN, PAYNIM, GENTILE, IDOLATOR,

UNGODLY, IDOLATROUS, IRRELIGIOUS
god IDOL, BAAL

page CALL, SUMMON, BOY, CHILD, ATTENDANT, SERVANT, LEAF, RECORD, WRITING
left hand VERSO
number FOLIO
right hand RECTO
title RUBRIC

pageantry SHOW, PARADE, POMP, OSTENTATION, DISPLAY, SPLENDOR, MAGNIFICENCE, SPECTACLE

pagoda TA(A), TEMPLE, SUMMERHOUSE, TOWER, COIN
finial or ornament TEE

pagurian CRAB

Pahlavi's *country* IRAN

paillasse MATTRESS, PALLET, BED

paillette SPANGLE, PAILLON, SEQUIN

pain WOE, ANGUISH, DISTRESS, MISERY, PENALTY, AGONY, GRIEF, ANXIETY, THROE, STITCH, AIL, PANG, SORROW, ACHE, THROB, HURT, SMART, RANKLE, SUFFERING, DISCOMFORT, TORMENT, TORTURE, TWINGE, AFFLICTION
killer ANODYNE
reliever OPIATE

pains EFFORT, EXERTION, TROUBLE, LABOR, TOIL, WORK, CARE

paint LIMN, ROUGE, STAIN, COLOR, GLOSS, SMEAR, ENAMEL, PIGMENT, PICTURE, PORTRAY, DEPICT, SKETCH, DESCRIBE, BEAUTIFY, ADORN, TINGE, DELINEATE, REPRESENT, COVER, DECORATE, LIPSTICK
face ROUGE, FARD, PARGET
spreader SPATULA, ROLLER, BRUSH
with vermilion MINIATE

painting *method* GRISAILLE
on dry plaster SECCO
style GENRE, IMPASTO
technique TEMPERA
wall MURAL

pair COUPLE, MARRY, MATCH, MATES, DUO, TWINS, DYAD, BRACE, YOKE, SPAN, TEAM, TWOSOME
of units TWO, TWINS, TEAM, DUET, DYAD

paired GEMEL, MATED, WEDDED, MATCHED, TEAMED

Pakistan *city or town* LAHORE, MULTAN, DACCA, SIDI, DIR, KALAT, QUETTA
province SIND(H), PESHAWAR
state KALAT, SWAT

pal CHUM, CRONY, BUDDY, MATE, CONFEDERATE, COMPANION, FRIEND, PARTNER, ACCOMPLICE, ALLY, COMRADE

palace COURT, PRAETORIUM, MANSION
eastern SERAI

palaestra SCHOOL, GYM(NASIUM)

Palamon, *rival of* ARCITE

palanquin DOOLEE, DOOLIE, LITTER, STRETCHER, CONVEYANCE

palatable TASTY, SAPID, SAVORY, SPICY, AGREEABLE, ACCEPTABLE, GUSTABLE, RELISHABLE, TOOTHSOME, APPETIZING, DELICIOUS, LUSCIOUS, PLEASANT

palatal GUTTURAL, FRONT, VELAR

palate UVULA, VELUM, TASTE, RELISH

palatine PALATIAL, PALATAL, OFFICER, CAPE

palaver DISCUSS, DEBATE, PARLEY, TALK, CONFERENCE, CHAT, FLATTERY, TWADDLE, CHATTER, RIGMAROLE,

BALDERDASH,
CAJOLERY, FLUM-
MERY, COLLOQUY
pale HAGGARD, WORN,
ANEMIC, WHITISH,
PASTEL, ETIOLATED,
ASHEN, ASHY, PASTY,
STAKE, FENCE,
PICKET, LIVID, FAINT,
DIM, WAN, SALLOW,
MEALY, BLANCHED,
PALLID, COLORLESS,
WAXY, SICKLY, WEAK,
FEEBLE, REGION, EN-
CLOSURE, LIMIT,
LESSEN
palea WATTLE, DEW-
LAP, FOLD, BRACT,
SCALE, RAMENTUM
paleness ACHROMA
Palestine ISRAEL See
"Bible"
ancient country in
PHILISTIA, MOAB,
EDOM
city or town JAFFA,
HAIFA, HEBRON, AKIR
ancient DAN, CANA,
GATH
coin MIL
conquerer TURK
district GAZA, HAIFA
lake MEROM, HULE
mountain EBOL,
HERMON, TABOR,
NEBO, RAMON,
PISGAH, CARMEL,
ZION
part of CANAAN
port ACRE, JAFFA,
HAIFA, GAZA
weight ZUZA
Palestinian, *ancient*
AMORITE
paletot COAT, OVER-
COAT, GARMENT
palisade RIMER, CLIFF,
FENCE, DEFENSE,
PALING, STAKE,
STOCKADE, FORTIFY,
ENCLOSE, FORTIFICA-
TION
pall DULL, FAIL, GLUT,
GORGE, SATE, CLOY,
JADE, SMOKE,
MANTLE, FOG, COVER-
ING, CLOAK, CLOTH,
DISSPIRIT, DIS-
HEARTEN, SHROUD,
SATIETY
palladium *symbol* PD
Pallas ATHENA

pallet MATTRESS,
PAD, BED, BLANKET,
QUILT, PAILLASSE,
PAWL, PADDLE
palliate CLOAK, MASK,
MITIGATE, DIMINISH,
COVER, HIDE, VEIL,
GLOSS, SOFTEN,
CONCEAL, ABATE,
EXTENUATE, LESSEN,
DISGUISE, EXCUSE,
EASE, ALLEVIATE,
REDUCE, MODERATE
pallid THIN, WAN,
WAXEN See "pale"
pallion BIT, NODULE,
PELLET, PIECE
Pallu's *father* REUBEN
palm TREE, HAND,
CONCEAL, MANIPU-
LATE, STEAL, IMPOSE,
OBTRUDE, FOIST,
TOUCH, HANDLE,
LAUREL, PRIZE,
TROPHY, DOOM,
DOUM, TALA, ATAP,
NIPA, TARA, TALIERA,
SAGO, BRAB, FANLEAF,
ERYTHEA, ROYAL,
BETEL, COCO(NUT),
DATE, TALIPOT, TODDY
Africa DUM, DOOM,
DOUM, PALMYRA,
RAFFIA
  genus RAPHIA
areng GOMUTI
Arizona DATE
Asia BETEL, NIPA,
ARECA
betel PINANG, ARECA,
BONGA
book TALIERA, TARA
Brazil ASSAI, BACABA,
BABASSU, TUCUM(A),
JARA
cabbage PALMETTO,
SAW
Ceylon TALIPOT
Chile COQUITO
drink ASSAI, NIPA,
TODDY, SURA
dwarf fan genus
SABAL
E. India TALA,
TOKOPAT, NIPA
edible fruit of NIPA,
DATE, COCONUT
fan-leaf PALMETTO,
TALIPOT, ERYTHEA
  genus SABAL
feather GOMUTI
fiber DATIL, BURI,

TAL, RAFFIA,
TUCUM(A)
Florida ROYAL,
PALMETTO
fruit of See "edible
fruit" *above*
genus BACABA, AT-
TALEA, ARECA,
ARENGA, NIPA, COCOS,
SABAL, RAPHIA,
OENOCARPUS
gingerbread DOOM,
DOUM, DUM
leaf FROND, OL(L)A
lily TI, TOI
Malay GEBANG,
ARENG, ATAP, SAGO,
GOMUTI
mat PETATE, YAPA
New Zealand NIKAU
Nubian DOOM, DOUM
of hand VOLA,
THENAR
palmyra BRAB, TALA,
TALIPOT
  fiber TAL
pith SAGO
product of COPRA
Puerto Rico YAGUA,
YARAY
reedlike stem RATTAN
sago ARENG, GOMUTI,
IROK
sap TODDY
S. America DATIL,
ASSAI, COQUITO
spiny GRUGRU
starch SAGO, TALIPOT
stem CANE, RATTAN
sugar JAGGERY, GUR
toddy SURA
umbrella TALIPOT
W. Indies GRIGRI,
GRUGRU, YAGUA,
YARAY
wine TODDY, SURA
palmate WEBBED,
BROAD, FLAT, LOBED
palmetto SAW
  genus SERENOA
palmistry CHIROMANCY
palmyra tree TALA,
TALIPOT, BRAB
palp CAJOLE, PAT,
COAX, TOUCH,
ANTENNA, PALPUS,
FEEL, FLATTER
palpable TACTILE,
OBVIOUS, MANIFEST,
TANGIBLE, PATENT,
PLAIN, EVIDENT

palpitation QUIVER-(ING), PALMUS, BEAT, THROB(BING), PULSE, PULSATION, TREMBLE, FLUTTER

palter LIE, FIB, HAGGLE, TRIFLE, EQUIVOCATE, DODGE, SHIFT, CHAFFER, TRAFFIC, BARGAIN, PARLEY, ELUDE, QUIBBLE, FALSEHOOD

paltry PUNY, BASE, LOW, VILE, TRIFLING, CHILDISH, PITIFUL, PETTY, SORRY, SMALL, MEAN, LACKING, PICAYUNE, INSIGNIFICANT, TRASHY, WORTHLESS, DESPICABLE, UNIMPORTANT, CONTEMPTIBLE

paludal SWAMPY, FENNY, MARSHY, MALARIAL

pampas PLAINS
cat PAJERO

pamper BABY, INDULGE, CARESS, CODDLE, SPOIL, HUMOR, PET, DANDLE, COSSET, GRATIFY

pamphlet TRACT, ESSAY, TREATISE, BROCHURE, BOOKLET

pan POT, KETTLE, DISH, VESSEL, FACE, TAB, LAPPET, SUBSOIL, CRITICIZE, RIDICULE, RESULT, COOK, FRY, BOIL, TITLE

Pan FAUNUS, (THE)-ALL

panacea CURE-ALL, ELIXIR, CATHOLICON, NEPENTHE, SOLACE, REMEDY

panache PLUME, TUFT, FEATHERS, SWAGGER, ORNAMENT

Panama DARIEN, HAT
canal lake GATUN
city COLON
coin BALBOA
island REY
locks GATUN
port COLON
tree COPA, YAYA

Panay negrito ATI

pancake FROISE, FLAPJACK, CREPE, OVERTURN

panda WAH, BEARCAT

pandemonium DIN, CONFUSION, DISORDER

pander BAWD, PIMP, CATER, TOADY, FAWN, CRINGE, PROCURER

panegyric PRAISE, ELOGE, ENCOMIUM, LAUDATION, EULOGY

panel JURY, BOARD, TABLET, INSERT, PAD, CUSHION, SADDLE, HURDLE, SECTION, LIST, GROUP, PARTITION

pang ACHE, RACK, THROE, SORROW, AGONY, STITCH, SPASM, DISTRESS *See* "pain"

Pangim native GOAN

pangolin ANTEATER, MANIS

panhandle BEG, CADGE

panic FRIGHT, DREAD, CRISIS, TERROR, FRAY, FEAR, ALARM, FUNK, SCARE

pannier BASKET, DOSSER, FRAMEWORK, OVERSKIRT, CORBEIL

Panopolis *chief deity* MIN

panorama SCENE, VISTA, VIEW, SWEEP, PAINTING

pant ASPIRE, LONG, YEARN, DESIRE, PINE, PUFF, BLOW, GASP, HEAVE, THROB, HUFF, PALPITATE, PULSATE

panther COUGAR, LEOPARD, PARD, PUMA, CAT
like animal JAGUAR, OCELOT

pantry LARDER, AMBRY, CLOSET, SPENCE, BUTTERY, CUPBOARD

pants, *leather* CHAPS, CHAPARAJOS, CHAPARRERAS

papal APOSTOLIC, PONTIFICAL *See* "Pope"
book of edicts DECRETAL
cape or collar FANON
chancery DATARY
court SEE, CURIA

envoy ABLEGATE, NUNCIO
letter BULL
reformer GREGORY
scarf or veil ORALE
seal BULLA

papaya PAPAW, PAWPAW, FRUIT
genus CARICA

paper DOCUMENT, ESSAY, MONOGRAPH, WRITING, COMPOSITION, THEME, INSTRUMENT
cloth like TAPA, PAPYRUS
cutter SLITTER
damaged RETREE
folded once FOLIO
measure QUIRE, REAM
medicinal powders CHARTA
mulberry KOZO, TAPA
official TARGE, WHITE
size ATLAS, CAP, COPY, CROWN, IMPERIAL, FOOLSCAP
thin PELURE
twice pulled DOUBLE
untrimmed edge DECKLE

papilla PIMPLE, BUD

papyrus REED, PAPER, SCROLL

par MEDIAN, MEAN, LEVEL, NORMAL, EQUAL(ITY), VALUE, STANDARD
one under BIRDIE
two below EAGLE

parable APOLOGUE, FABLE, TALE, ALLEGORY, COMPARISON, SIMILITUDE
objective MORAL, PROVERB

parabole SIMILE

paraclete AIDER, PLEADER, ADVOCATE, COMFORTER, CONSOLER, INTERCESSOR

parade SHOW, REVIEW, DISPLAY, ARRAY, POMP, AIR, STRUT, WALK, FLAUNT, MARCH, VENT, FILE, OSTENTATION, EXHIBITION, PAGEANT, SPECTACLE, PROCESSION, FLOURISH, PRETENSION, SPLENDOR, MARSHAL

paradigm MODEL,
EXAMPLE, PATTERN
paradise BLISS, EDEN,
UTOPIA, ELYSIUM,
HEAVEN, GARDEN
Buddhist JODO,
GOKURAKU
paradisiac EDENIC
paradox ANOMALY,
CONTRADICTION,
ABSURDITY
paragon PATTERN,
RIVAL, EQUAL, NON-
PAREIL, PALADIN,
MODEL, TYPE, IDEAL,
NONESUCH, MASTER-
PIECE
paragram *See* "pun"
paragraph ARTICLE,
PLANK, CLAUSE,
PASSAGE, VERSE, ITEM,
SECTION, INDENT,
THEME, NOTICE
Paraguay *city or town*
ASUNCION, BELEN, ITA,
YUTY
Indian GUARANI
tea MATE, YERBA
parallel EQUAL,
SIMILAR, (A)LIKE,
SAME, MATCH, COR-
RESPOND, CONCUR-
RENT, ANALOGOUS,
COUNTERPART,
CORRELATIVE
render COLLIMATE
parallelogram
RHOMB(US)
paralysis STAGNATION,
INACTION, SHOCK,
PARESIS, PALSY,
STROKE
paralyze CRIPPLE,
NUMB, SCARE,
DEADEN, UNNERVE
paramount ABOVE,
UPWARD, SUPERIOR,
SUPREME
paramour LEMAN,
LOVER, MISTRESS,
CONCUBINE
parapet WALL, RAM-
PART, EARTHWORK,
BREASTWORK
dwarf wall BERM,
PODIUM
part of CRETE
V-shaped REDAN
parasite LEECH,
BUR(R), DRONE,
TOADY, BUG, VIRUS,
SYCOPHANT, SMUT,

RUST, FUNGUS, LOUSE,
FLEA, FLATTERER,
FAWNER, FLUNKY,
HANGER-ON,
SPONGE(R)
animal TICK, MITE,
FLEA, CUCKOO
blood FLUKE, TRYP
fungus LICHEN
internal ENTOZOA
marine REMORA,
SPONGE
plant THRIPS, APHID,
ENTOPHYTE
trout SUG
worm TRICHINA
paravane TORPEDO,
OTTER
Parcae *See* "Fates"
parcel BUNDLE, PIECE,
LAND, LOT, PART,
PORTION, SECTION,
PACK(AGE), PACKET,
ALLOT, DEAL, METE,
DOLE, RATION, GRANT,
AWARD, DIVIDE, COL-
LECTION, GROUP,
BATCH, DISTRIBUTE
parch TORREFY, DRY,
ROAST, SCORCH, BAKE,
SEAR, CHAR, SHRIVEL
parched ARID, DRY,
THIRSTY
parchment FOREL,
DEED, SKIN, VELLUM,
DIPLOMA, PAPER,
DOCUMENT, WRITING
manuscript
PALIMPSEST
roll PELL
pardi(e) INDEED,
VERILY, CERTAINLY,
SURELY
pardon FOREGO,
WAIVE, ABSOLVE,
SPARE, ACQUIT, FREE,
MERCY, REPRIEVE,
REMIT, AMNESTY,
EXCUSE, FORGIVE-
(NESS), TOLERATE,
RELEASE, REMISSION,
INDULGENCE, OVER-
LOOK, CONDONE
pardonable VENIAL,
EXCUSABLE
pare PEEL, RESECT,
SKIN, SHAVE, TRIM,
FLAY, CUT, CLIP,
SLICE, LESSEN, RE-
DUCE, DIMINISH,
DIVEST, SHORTEN,
DECREASE

parent DAD, SIRE, GENI-
TOR, PATER, MATER,
AUTHOR, CAUSE,
PRODUCER, SOURCE,
MOTHER, FATHER,
BEGETTER
female DAM, MATER,
MA(MA), MOTHER
undivided HOLETHNOS
parental affection
STORGE, PHILOPRO-
GENITIVENESS
parenthetical aside ER
parget PLASTER
pariah OUTCAST
Paris *airport* ORLY
designer, clothes
DIOR
district AUTEUIL
river SEINE
Roman name
LUTETIA
subway METRO
thug APACHE
Paris' *father* PRIAM
mother HECUBA
parity PAR, LEVEL,
EQUALITY, EQUIVA-
LENCE, ANALOGY,
EVENNESS, SAMENESS,
LIKENESS
park LEAVE, PLACE,
ZOO, GROVE, AREA,
VALLEY, BASIN,
CLAIRE, SETTLE,
ESTABLISH, PROME-
NADE
parley ARGUE, CON-
VERSE, TALK, CHAT,
TREAT, DISCOURSE,
DISCUSS, ADDRESS,
CONFER(ENCE)
parliament DIET,
LEGISLATURE, CON-
GRESS, DAIL, AS-
SEMBLY, CONFERENCE,
COUNCIL
parlor SALON, SALOON
Parnassian POET,
BUTTERFLY
parody SATIRE, SKIT,
IMITATION, TRAVESTY,
BURLESQUE,
CARICATURE, COPY
parol ORAL, UNWRIT-
TEN, NUNCUPATIVE,
PLEADING, VERBAL
paronomasia *See*
"pun"
paroxysm FIT, THROE,
ATTACK, AGONY,
SEIZURE, EMOTION,

SPASM, AGITATION,
CONVULSION,
EXACERBATION, OUT-
BURST
parrot LORY, ARA,
COCKATOO, TIRIBA,
POLL, KAKA, CORELLA,
ECHO, MIMIC, REPEAT,
BIRD
Africa JAKO
Brazil ARA, ARARA,
TIRIBA
fish LANIA, LORO,
SCAR(ID), SCARUS
gray JAKO
genus PSITTACUS
green CAGIT
hawk HIA
long-tailed MACAW
Malay LORY
monk LORO
N. Guinea LORIKEET,
LORY
N. Zealand KEA, KAKA
Philippine CAGIT
sheep-killing KEA
small LORILET,
PARAKEET
parry SHIFT,
REPARTEE, RETORT,
FEND, ELUDE, AVERT,
DEFLECT, FENCE,
EVADE, EVASION, PRE-
VENT, AVOID, DEFEND
Parsi priest MOBED
parsley *derivative*
APIOL(E)
genus SELINUM
parsnip, *water genus*
SIUM
parson bird POE, TUI,
ROOK
parsonage BENEFICE,
MANSE, RECTORY
part ROLE, ITEM,
SEGMENT, SLICE,
SHARE, TWIN, SEVER,
DIVORCE, SEPARATE,
DIE, REMNANT, PIECE,
SECTOR, SECTION,
PORTION, DETACH,
TEAR, REND, FRAG-
MENT, SCRAP, CRUMB,
MOIETY, FRACTION,
CONSTITUENT, ELE-
MENT, LOT, INTEREST,
CONCERN, QUARTER,
FACTION, REGION,
DISTRICT, DIVISION,
DISUNITE, SUNDER,
DISTRIBUTE, ALLOT,

DIVERGE, FUNCTION,
DUTY
that's kept RETENT
partake SHARE,
PARTICIPATE
partan CRAB
parted PARTITE,
CLOVEN, APART,
CLEFT, SEPARATED
partially HALF, SOME,
PARTLY
participate SHARE,
DIVIDE, PARTAKE,
COOPERATE
particle GRANULE,
SCINTILLA, ATOM,
SCRAP, SHRED, MITE,
IOTA, GEN, JOT,
TITTLE, PIECE, GRAIN,
MOTE, WHIT, BIT,
SPECK, FLECK,
MOLECULE, MORSEL,
DROP, SPARK, CRUMB
cosmic MESON
electrified ION
parti-colored PIED,
PIEBALD, VARIEGATED
particular ACCURATE,
EXACT, DETAIL(ED),
INDIVIDUAL, SEPARATE,
UNIQUE, LONE, STRICT,
CAREFUL, FUSSY,
SOLE, SINGULAR,
ITEM, (E)SPECIAL,
SPECIFIC, DISTINCT,
RESPECTIVE, ODD,
PECULIAR, CHARAC-
TERISTIC, PERSONAL,
PRIVATE, INTIMATE,
PRECISE, FASTIDIOUS,
FINICAL, INSTANCE,
REGARD, FEATURE
partisan SIDE, ZEALOT,
GUERILLA, ALLY, FOL-
LOWER, DISCIPLE, ITE,
FRIEND, ADHERENT,
CHAMPION, SUP-
PORTER, HALBERD
group CAMP, BLOC
partition WALL,
SCREEN, SCANTLE,
ALLOT, SEPT, DIVIDE,
BARRIER, SEVERANCE,
SEPARATION, APPOR-
TION
partlet HEN, BAND,
COLLAR, RUFF,
CHEMISETTE
partner ALLY, PAL,
MATE, PARD, CHUM,
ASSOCIATE, COL-
LEAGUE, PARTICIPANT,

SPOUSE, COMPANION,
CONSORT, COADJUTOR,
CONFEDERATE,
AUXILIARY, SHARER
partnership HUI,
CAHOOT, COMATES,
BUSINESS, FIRM, AL-
LIANCE, UNION, IN-
TEREST, CONNEC-
TION, ASSOCIATION,
COMPANY
partridge CHUKAR,
SEESEE, TITAR, YUTU,
FRANCOLIN, TINAMOU,
BIRD
call JUCK, JUKE
kind of GROUSE,
QUAIL, TINAMOU
sand SEESEE
party SQUAD, GALA,
SECT, TEA, SIDE,
CLIQUE, DANCE,
CIRCLE, BLOC,
FACTION, RING,
JUNTO, GROUP,
LEAGUE, CABAL,
COTERIE, TROOP, DE-
TACHMENT, COMPANY,
GATHERING, SOCIAL
giver HOST
house cleaning
WHANG
partylike GALA
parvenu ARRIVISTE,
SNOB, UPSTART
Pascal work PENSEES
pasha DEY, DOWLAH
pasquinade LAMPOON,
SATIRE, SQUIB,
PASQUIL
pass GAP, ROUTE,
GHAT, COL, WAY,
ROAD, AVENUE, DE-
FILE, TICKET,
LICENSE, PREDICA-
MENT, DIFFICULTY,
PINCH, STRAIT, CRISIS,
STATE, PLIGHT, LAPSE,
HAPPEN, DIE, GO,
SPEND, MOVE, WHILE,
PROMOTE, (E)LAPSE,
BYGO, RELAY, SKIP,
OMIT, ELIDE, PERMIT,
VANISH, TRANSFER,
CONVEY, ADVANCE,
GRADUATE, PROCEED,
DEVOLVE, FLIT, GLIDE,
SLIP, FADE, EXPIRE,
NEGLECT, OVERSTEP,
EXCEED, TRANSCEND
Alpine COL

by ELAPSE, IGNORE, OMIT
India, mountain GHAT
on RELAY, DIE
rope through REEVE
sudden LUNGE, THRUST
passable SOSO, ORDINARY, FAIR, TOLERABLE, MODERATE, MIDDLING, MEDIOCRE, SMALL, ADEQUATE, ACCEPTABLE, CURRENT, ADMISSIBLE, PRESENTABLE
passage ROUTE, HALL, AISLE, STRAIT, WAY, PORE, DUCT, ADIT, ATRIUM, GANGWAY, FARE, VOYAGE JOURNEY, TRANSIT, TRAVEL, DEFILE, GATE, DOOR, PATH, GAP, PASS, MIGRATION, CHANNEL, PART, THOROUGHFARE, CORRIDOR, CLAUSE, PARAGRAPH, TEXT, ENACTMENT, SANCTION, PROGRESS, OPENING
between two walls SLYPE, ARCADE
covered ARCADE
mine STOPE
one end closed IMPASSE, SAC
passageway ALLEY, AISLE, RAMP, HALL, SLIP *See* "passage"
passe ANTIQUATED, FADED, OUT, OBSOLETE, OUTMODED, WORN, AGED
passenger PILGRIM, TOURIST, FARE, TRAVELER, VOYAGER, WAYFARER, ITINERANT
passer of bad checks KITER
passeriform bird IRENA
passerine bird SPARROW, PITA, STARLING
passing DEATH, TRANSIENT, CURSORY, CASUAL, FLEETING, EPHEMERAL, EXCEEDINGLY, VERY, TEMPORARY, FORD
by or over PRETERITION, OMISSION
fashion FAD

passion LOVE, FERVOR, ARDOR, HEAT, PAIN, IRE, YEN, ANGER, TRIAL, AGONY, FEELING, LUST, SUFFERING, DESIRE, URGE, EMOTION, ZEAL, RAPTURE, TRANSPORT, EXCITEMENT, IMPULSE, AFFECTION, DEVOTION, VEHEMENCE, ENTHUSIASM
passive PATHIC, QUIET, INERT, STOIC, PATIENT, IDLE, SUPINE, LIFELESS, QUIESCENT, INACTIVE, RECEPTIVE, SUBMISSIVE, APATHETIC, OBEDIENT, YIELDING, PLIANT
Passover PASCH(A), FEAST
bread MATZOS, MATZOTH
commencement evening NISAN
first night of SEDER
pertaining to PASCHAL
songs of praise HALLEL
passport PASS, CONGE, PERMIT, LICENSE
endorsement VISA, VISE
passus CANTO
past ELD, (A)GONE, DEAD, SINCE, AGO, BEYOND, YORE, UP, AFTER, OVER, SPENT, ENDED, ACCOMPLISHED, ANCIENT, FORMER, BYGONE, OBSOLETE, BY, ELAPSED, HISTORY
tense PRETERIT(E)
paste GLUE, PAP, STICK, STRASS, GUM, CEMENT, ADHESIVE, IMITATION
rice AME
pastel TINT, CRAYON, WOAD, PALE, LIGHT
pastime SPORT, GAME, DIVERSION, AMUSEMENT, RECREATION
pastoral RURAL, COUNTRY, RUSTIC, POEM, SONG, BUCOLIC
cantata SERENATA

crook or staff PEDUM, CROSIER
god PAN
pertaining to AGRESTIC, RURAL, BUCOLIC, GEOPONIC
pipe REED, OAT
place ARCADIA
poem ECLOGUE, BUCOLIC, IDYL
pastry ECLAIR, PIE(S), TART(S), CAKE(S), FOOD, SWEETS, STRUDEL, FLAN, PUFF
pasture RANGE, AGIST, GRASS, GRAZE, LEA, HERBAGE, GRASSLAND
grass GRAMA, CLOVER, RYE
pasty DOUGHY, SOFT, MAGMA, PALE, WAN, STICKY, WHITE
pat CARESS, TIMELY, HAPPY, DAB, APT, TAP, FIT, LUMP, BUTTER, PERTINENT, SUITABLE, APPROPRIATE, OPPORTUNE, FIXED, IMMOVABLE, BLOW, STROKE
Patagonian *cattle* NIATA
cavy MARA
deity SETEBOS
rodent CAVY, MARA, CAPYBARA
patch MEND, DARN, FIELD, PLOT, PARCEL, TRACT, CLOUT, VAMP, REPAIR, PIECE, BLEMISH, SCRAP, BIT, REMNANT
trees or woods MOTT(E)
patchwork MEDLEY, JUMBLE, CENTO, HODGEPODGE, MIXTURE, VARIEGATION
patella KNEECAP, PAN, DISH, SESAMOID, ROTULA, KNEEPAN
paten DISC, DISK, PLATE, DISH
patent EVIDENT, OPEN, CLEAR, MANIFEST, SALIENT, PLAIN, BERAT, UNOBSTRUCTED, OBVIOUS, EXPANDED, APPARENT, CONSPICUOUS, UNCONCEALED, GLARING, NOTORIOUS, RIGHT,

PRIVILEGE, COPY-
RIGHT, GRANT,
LICENSE

path LANE, ROUTE,
TRAIL, BERM, ROAD-
(WAY), ORBIT, TRACK,
COURSE, FOOTWAY,
ACCESS, PASSAGE,
DIRECTION, BYWAY
math. LOCUS

pathetic TEARY, SAD,
TOUCHING, MOVING,
PLAINTIVE, EMO-
TIONAL, STIRRING,
PITIFUL

pathos, *false* BATHOS

patina DISH, PATEN,
FILM

patisserie BAKERY

patois ARGOT, JARGON,
SPEECH, CREOLE,
LINGO, CANT, PATTER,
SLANG, DIALECT

patriarch NASI,
FATHER, PATER, SIRE,
ELDER, VETERAN
Biblical ABRAHAM,
DAVID, JACOB
(ISRAEL), SHEM,
ISAAC

patriot REVERE, HALE,
OTIS, ALLEN

patron BACKER, ANGEL,
SPONSOR, BENEFAC-
TOR, ADVOCATE, CUS-
TOMER, CHAMPION,
SUPPORTER, GUARDIAN,
PROTECTOR *See*
"saint"

patronage EGIS, FAVOR,
HELP, PROTECTION,
GUARDIANSHIP,
SPONSORSHIP,
COUNTENANCE, SUP-
PORT, AID, ASSISTANCE,
INFLUENCE, EN-
COURAGEMENT, CON-
DESCENSION, AUTHOR-
ITY

patroon's *land* MANOR

pattern LAST, NORM,
SEME, FORM, DEVICE,
DEVISE, DESIGN,
SHAPE, MOTIF,
FIGURE, IDEA(L),
TEMPLATE, PARADIGM,
MODEL, MAP, FORMAT,
STENCIL, TYPE,
PARAGON, EXEMPLAR,
ARCHETYPE, SCALE,
PRECEDENT, DIE,
RULE, GUIDE, PLAN,

PROTOTYPE, ORIGINAL,
SPECIMEN, EXAMPLE,
SAMPLE, TENDENCY,
CHARACTERISTIC
flower beds PARTERRE

patulous GAPING,
OPEN, SPREADING,
EXPANDED, DISTENDED,
DIFFUSE

paucity DEARTH, FEW-
NESS, INSUFFICIENCY,
SCARCITY, EXIGUITY,
LACK, SCANTINESS

Paul SAUL
birthplace and city of
TARSUS
companion SILAS

pauldron SPLINT,
ARMOR

paulownia tree KIRI

pause INTERMIT, DE-
LAY, HESITATE, BREAK,
SWELL, LINGER,
DWELL, LULL, STAND,
CEASE, SELAH, REST,
REPOSE, STOP, RES-
PITE, RECESS,
STANCE, DESIST, WAIT,
TARRY, STAY, DEMUR,
WAVER, DELIBERATE,
CESSATION, INTERMIS-
SION, INTERVAL,
CAESURA, INTERRUP-
TION, HESITATION

pave TILE, COVER,
SURFACE, PREPARE,
SMOOTH

paver's *mallet* TUP

pavilion MARQUEE,
TABERNACLE, TENT,
SHELTER, ARBOR,
CANOPY, BANNER,
FLAG, COVERING, LIT-
TER, AURICLE, PAWL,
ARENA

paving stone FLAG,
PAVER, BRICK

paw FOOT, TOOL,
DUPE, HAND(LE),
CLAW, MAUL, TOUCH

pawl RATCHET, CLICK,
DETENT, TONGUE,
CATCH
gunlock SEAR

pawn LEND, PLEDGE,
GAGE, HOCK, WAGER,
HOSTAGE, DUPE,
PEACOCK, SECURITY,
EARNEST, CHESSMAN,
STAKE, RISK, HAZARD,
MAN
broker LENDER

Pawnee PANI, INDIAN
rite HAKO

pawpaw PAPAYA, TREE,
FRUIT

pax PEACE

pay ANTE, STIPEND,
TREAT, TIP, WAGE,
FEE, HIRE, SPEND,
SALARY, LIQUIDATE,
DEFRAY, RECOMPENSE,
COMPENSATE,
REQUITE, REWARD,
INDEMNIFY, EXPEND
attention HEED,
LISTEN
back REBATE, SETTLE,
REIMBURSE, REFUND
dirt ORE, GOLD
penalty of ABY

payable DUE, OWING,
OUTSTANDING,
PROFITABLE
unpaid balance
ARREARS

paymaster PURSER,
CASHIER, TREASURER

payment SCOT, CRO,
RENT, REQUITAL,
MAIL(L), TAC, FEE,
LIQUIDATION, DE-
FRAYAL, COMPENSA-
TION, RECOMPENSE,
HONORARIUM, RE-
WARD, REMUNERATION
demand DUN, BILL

paynim HEATHEN,
PAGAN, ETHNIC, IN-
FIDEL

Pb LEAD

pea LEGUME, SEED,
PULSE, PLANT
chick CICER, GRAM
heath CARMELE
India, split DAL
pigeon DAL
shaped PISIFORM
split DAL
tree AGATI

peace PAX, SERENITY,
NIRVANA, AMITY,
SILENCE, CALM,
QUIET, REPOSE, TRAN-
QUILLITY, CONCORD,
CONTENTMENT,
HARMONY, STILLNESS
goddess IRENE
symbol of TOGA,
OLIVE, DOVE

peaceable HENOTIC,
IRENIC, PLACID,
SERENE, CALM,

PACIFIC, TRANQUIL, UNDISTURBED

peaceful HALCYON, IRENIC(AL), PACIFIC, CALM, SERENE, GENTLE, MILD, COOL, STEADY, COMPOSED, FRIENDLY, AMICABLE, CONCORDANT, TRANQUIL, SMOOTH

peach CRAWFORD, ELBERTA, CROSBY, FREESTONE, CLINGSTONE, TREE, FRUIT
Australia QUANDONG
clingstone PAVY
origin ALMOND
stone PUTAMEN, PIT

peacock MAO, FOWL
blue PAON
butterfly IO
constellation PAVO
female HEN, PEAHEN
genus PAVO
Heraldic PAWN
like VAIN, PAVONINE

peag(e) TAX, TOLL, WAMPUM, PEDAGE

peak CLIMAX, POINT, SPIRE, CROWN, APEX, CUSP, CONE, ALP, TOR, TOP, PITON, CRAG, ZENITH, CREST, PINNACLE, SUMMIT, PROMONTORY, DWINDLE, HEIGHT, MAXIMUM
English SCAFELL
ornament EPI, FINIAL
rocky ALP, CRAG
Rocky Mountain PIKES, LOGAN

peaked WAN, WORN, TIRED, EMACIATED, THIN, POINTED *See* "pale"

peal ECHO, BOOM, CLAP, RING, RESOUND, TOLL, SALMON, GRILSE, THUNDER, ROAR

peanut GOOBER, GROUNDNUT, KATCHUNG, PLANT

pear SECKEL, SICKLE, TREE, FRUIT
cider PERRY
late autumn BOSC
prickly NOPAL, TUNA
genus OPUNTIA
shaped BULBOUS, PYRIFORM

pearl GEM, MARGARITE, ONION
eye CATARACT
imitation OLIVET, SEED
like NACRE, OLIVET
of great luster ORIENT

pearlwort *genus* SAGINA

pearly OPALINE, PELLUCID, NACREOUS, TRANSLUCENT, LIMPID, CLEAR

peart BRISK, CLEVER, (A)LIVE, ACTIVE, FRISKY, FLOURISHING, ALERT, QUICK, SMART

peasant CHURL, COOLIE, CARL, BOOR, COTTER, HIND, RUSTIC, SWAIN, PEON, COUNTRYMAN, TILLER, LABORER, FARMER
E. India RYOT
Egypt FELLAH
Eng. CARL, CHURL
Ireland KERN(E)
Scotland COTTER, COTTAR

pease *genus* PISUM, PLANT

peaseweep PEWIT, LAPWING, BIRD

peat TURF, GOR, FUEL
bog CESS, MOSS
cutter PINER
spade SLADE

peav(e)y HOOK, CANT HOOK, LEVER

pebble STONE, SCREE
fig-shaped SYCITE

pecan *tree* NOGAL, HICKORY

peccary JAVALI, TAJACU
genus TAYASSU

peck NIP, BITE, DAB, NAG, TWIT, NIBBLE, KISS, CARP, TEASE, MEASURE

pectinoid *bivalve* SCALLOP

peculiar ODD, UNIQUE, ERRATIC, QUEER, BIZARRE, PARTICULAR, SPECIAL, SPECIFIC, STRANGE, SINGULAR, UNCOMMON, ECCENTRIC, RARE, UNUSUAL, EXTRAOR-

DINARY, DISTINCTIVE, EXCEPTIONAL

peculiarity KINK, QUIRK, TRAIT, CHARACTERISTIC, INDIVIDUALITY, IDIOSYNCRACY, PARTICULARITY, DISTINCTIVENESS, SINGULARITY, PARTIALITY

pedal LEVER, TREADLE

pedant PRIG, TUTOR, PURIST, TEACHER, PEDAGOGUE, SCHOLAR, FORMALIST, PRECISIONIST

peddle SELL, VEND, HAWK, TRIFLE, RETAIL, PIDDLE, MEDDLE

pedestal GAINE, BASE, FOOT, SUPPORT, LEG, FOUNDATION
part of PLINTH, DADO, DIE, SURBASE, BASE
projecting SOCLE

pedicel STALK, STEM, FOOTSTALK

pedometer ODOGRAPH

peduncle PEDICEL, STALK, STEM, KNOT, PETIOLE, CRUS
plant SCAPE

peel FLAKE, EXCORIATE, RIND, SKIN, STRIP, HARL, PARE, SHOVEL, DECORTICATE, BARK, FLAY, HULL, DESQUAMATE, LAYER, UNCOVER

peep GLIMPSE, GLANCE, LOOK, VIEW, PRY, CHEEP, CHIRP, SPY, PULE, SKEG, CRY, EMERGE, CREVICE

peeper FROG, TOM

peepshow RAREE

peer GAZE, GAPE, STARE, LOOK, PEEK, PEEP, PRY, LORD, MATCH, EQUAL, EARL, NOBLE, CONTEMPORARY
lowest BARON
residence BARONY
wife of LADY
"Peer Gynt" *author* IBSEN
mother ASE
suite author GRIEG

peevish FRETFUL,
PETULANT, HUFFY,
SOUR, CROSS, PER-
VERSE, SULKY, TESTY,
NETTLED, QUERULOUS,
IRRITABLE, WASPISH,
SNAPPISH, PETTISH,
CAPTIOUS, CRUSTY,
CHURLISH, CRABBED,
CHOLERIC, IRASCIBLE,
SPLEENY, SPLENETIC

peewee LARK, LAP-
WING, PHOEBE, BIRD

peg DOWEL, LEG,
TOOTH, RESTRICT,
BIND, THROW, NOB,
BOLT, PIN, SPIKE,
HOB, TEE, KNAG,
PLUG, SUPPORT, PRE-
TEXT, REASON, STEP,
GRADE, DEGREE, CON-
FINE, STRIKE, HAM-
MER, PIERCE, NOTCH
mountain climber's
PITON
wood SKEG, SPILL,
DOWEL, NOG, SPILE

Pegu *See* "Burma"

peignoir WRAPPER,
NEGLIGEE, GOWN

pelagic MARINE,
OCEANIC, AQUATIC
phenomenon TIDE

pelf MONEY, LOOT,
LUCRE, WEALTH,
RICHES, GAIN, SPOILS,
BOOTY

Pelias' *son* ACASTUS

pelicanlike bird
SOLAN

pellet STONE, PILL,
BULLET, GRANULE,
SHOT, BALL, BOLUS

pellicle FILM, SKIN,
CUTICLE, SCUM,
MEMBRANE, COATING,
LAYER, CRUST

pellucid CLEAR, TRANS-
PARENT, CRYSTAL,
LIMPID, TRANSLUCENT

pelota *basket or
racquet* CESTA
court FRONTON

pelt SKIN, RIND, BARK,
PEEL, FELL, HIDE,
PEPPER, STONE, HURL,
HAIL

peltry FURS, HIDES,
SKINS, TRASH, REFUSE,
RUBBISH

pelvic bone ILIUM
pertaining to ILIAC

pen STYLUS, CONFINE,
JAIL, QUILL, COOP,
COTE, HUTCH, STY,
WRITE, STALL, CAGE,
CORRAL, FOLD, EN-
CLOSE, ENCLOSURE,
COMPOSE, INDITE, IN-
SCRIBE, IMPRISON,
INCARCERATE, CRIB,
PADDOCK, DAM, SWAN,
RESTRAIN
fish CRAWL
name See
"pseudonym"
point NIB, NEB

penalize FINE, MULCT,
RESTRICT, PUNISH,
AMERCE, HANDICAP

penalty FINE, AMAND,
CAIN, SENTENCE,
PUNISHMENT,
FORFEITURE, RET-
RIBUTION, DISAD-
VANTAGE, CHASTISE-
MENT

pend HANG, SWING,
DANGLE, FLAP, TRAIL

pendant EARRING, TAS-
SEL, TAG, AGLET, BOB,
LOP, CHANDELIER,
HANGING, FLAG

pending UNSETTLED,
UNDETERMINED,
UNDECIDED, OPEN,
HANGING, WAITING

pendulum weight BOB

Penelope's *father*
ICARIUS
husband ODYSSEUS
(ULYSSES)

penetrate DISCERN,
DETECT, REACH,
PROBE, INVADE, STEEP,
SOAK, DELVE, PIERCE,
PERMEATE, BORE,
ENTER, PERFORATE,
CUT, PERVADE, UNDER-
STAND, COMPREHEND,
DIFFUSE, IMBUE,
AFFECT

penetrating SHARP,
ACUTE, SHRILL, DEEP,
ASTUTE, KNOWING,
SHREWD, SUBTLE,
DISCERNING,
SAGACIOUS, PIERCING

penguin AUK, BIRD

penitence CONTRITION,
COMPUNCTION, RE-
MORSE, REGRET

penitent RUER, CON-
TRITE, SORRY, RE-

PENTANT, REMORSE-
FUL

penitential season
LENT

penman SCRIBE,
WRITER, AUTHOR,
COMPOSER, CAL-
LIGRAPHER, CHIROG-
RAPHER

penmanship HAND,
WRITING, CALLIG-
RAPHY, CHIROG-
RAPHY

pennant BANNER, EN-
SIGN, FLAG, GUIDON,
JACK, COLOR, PEN-
NON, STREAMER,
AWARD, PRIZE
pirates' ROGER
yacht BURGEE

Pennsylvania *borough*
MEDIA
city ERIE, CHESTER
county BUCKS, BERKS,
BLAIR, ELK, ERIE,
PIKE, TIOGA, YORK
sect AMISH

penny COPPER, SALTEE,
CENT, MONEY
Dutch STIVER
New Testament
DENARIUS

pension STIPEND,
ANNUITY, ALLOWANCE,
LODGINGHOUSE, IN-
COME, SUBSIDY

pentacle STAR,
SYMBOL, MEDAL,
PENTAGRAM,
PENTALPHA

Pentateuch TORA(H),
LAW

Pentheus' *mother*
AGAVE

penthouse LEAN-TO,
AERIE, SHED, ANNEX,
APARTMENT, DWELL-
ING, PENTIS

pentyl AMYL

penumbra SHADOW

penurious STINGY,
SCANTY, INDIGENT,
MEAN, CLOSE, TIGHT,
MISERLY, BARREN,
POOR, NIGGARDLY,
PARSIMONIOUS, IL-
LIBERAL, GRASPING,
NEAR

peon SERF, PEASANT,
SLAVE, THRALL, HAND,
LABORER
chess PAWN

peony MOUTAN,
PINY, PLANT, FLOWER
people(s) MULTITUDE,
RABBLE, MOB, STATE,
PERSONS, MANKIND,
NATION, VOTERS,
ANCESTRY, RELATIVES,
TRIBE, CLAN, FOLD,
DEMOS, KIN, LAITY,
RACE, FAMILY,
COUNTRY, POPULA-
TION, FOLKS,
POPULACE,
PROLETARIAT, CROWD,
MASSES, INDIVIDUALS,
BEINGS, COMMONAL-
ITY
ancient Asian SERES
German VOLK
group ETHOS
lowest order
CANAILLE, RABBLE,
MOB
Nigeria BENI(N)
Spain GENTE
pepper AVA, CAPSICUM,
PIMENTO, CONDIMENT,
CAYENNE, PAPRIKA,
KAVA, CAPSICIN,
SPICE, ATTACK, PELT
-and-salt GRAY
Australia KAVA
betel ITMO, IKMO
intoxicant KAVA
Java CUBEB
mild PAPRIKA
shrub KAVA
species BETEL,
CAYENNE
peppery CHOLERIC,
PUNGENT, HOT,
HASTY, ABRUPT,
FIERY, SPIRITED,
SNAPPISH, EXCITABLE,
PIQUANT, PASSIONATE,
ANGRY
perambulate WALK,
STROLL, AMBLE
perambulator PRAM,
CART, CARRIAGE,
STROLLER
perceive NOTE, VIEW,
ESPY, APPREHEND, UN-
DERSTAND, DISCERN,
KNOW, DESCRY, SEE,
SENSATE, NOTICE,
DISCOVER, RECOGNIZE,
DETECT, SPOT, OB-
SERVE, BEHOLD, FEEL,
SENSE, COMPREHEND,
APPRECIATE

perception TACT, EAR,
ACUMEN, SEEING,
KNOWLEDGE, INSIGHT,
IDEA, JUDGMENT, AP-
PREHENSION, AWARE-
NESS, DISCERNMENT,
COGNITION, UNDER-
STANDING, COMPRE-
HENSION, SENSATION,
CONSCIOUSNESS
perch AERIE, ROOST,
ROD, POLE, BAR,
HEIGHT, SIT, LAND,
(A)LIGHT, FISH
fish BARSE, OKOW,
POPE, MADO
genus PERCA
like DARTER
percolate SEEP,
STRAIN, RUN, GO,
TRANSUDE, OOZE,
MELT, FILTER, DRIP,
LEACH, EXUDE, DRAIN,
BREW, SIFT,
PERMEATE
percussion instrument
DRUM, TRAP, PIANO
perdition DESTRUC-
TION, WRECK, FALL,
HELL, LOSS, RUIN,
OVERTHROW, DOWN-
FALL, DEMOLITION,
DEATH, MISERY,
DAMNATION
peregrine FALCON,
HAWK, ALIEN,
FOREIGN(ER)
perfect MODEL, IDEAL,
INVIOLATE, SOLE,
SPOTLESS, UNDEFILED,
SOUND, HOLY, SHEER,
COMPLETE, FINISHED,
PURE, WHOLE,
SIMPLE, ENTIRE, IN-
TACT, ABSOLUTE,
BLAMELESS, FINISH,
ACCURATE, UTTER,
GREAT, CONSUMMATE,
EXQUISITE, FAULT-
LESS, EXPERT, FLAW-
LESS, RIGHTEOUS
perfection ACME,
IDEAL, VIRTUE, MERIT,
MATURITY, COM-
PLETION, CONSUM-
MATION, FAULTLESS-
NESS, CORRECTNESS,
EXCELLENCE
perfidy APOSTASY,
TREASON, TREACHERY,
FAITHLESSNESS, IN-

FIDELITY, DEFECTION,
DISLOYALTY
perforate ENTER, BORE,
ERODE, EAT, DRILL,
RIDDLE, PIERCE, GRID,
PRICK, PENETRATE,
PUNCTURE
perforated *block* NUT
marker STENCIL
sphere BEAD
perforation TRESIS,
HOLE, APERTURE
perform END, FINISH,
GAIN, REACH, FUL-
FILL, EFFECT, (EN)-
ACT, DO, PLAY, WORK,
EXECUTE, ACCOM-
PLISH, ACHIEVE,
TRANSACT, PRODUCE
performer ARTIST(E),
DOER, AGENT, ACTOR,
OPERATOR, EXECUTOR,
PLAYER, MUSICIAN,
STAR
perfume SCENT, ODOR,
SMELL, INCENSE,
AROMA, ATTAR, ES-
SENCE, REDOLENCE,
COLOGNE, FRAGRANCE,
BOUQUET
base MUSK
medicated
PASTIL(LE)
oriental MYRRH
pad SACHET
with burning spice
CENSE
perhaps PERCHANCE,
HAPLY, BELIKE, POS-
SIBLY, MAYBE, PROB-
ABLY, PERADVENTURE
pericline ALBITE
peril HAZARD,
JEOPARDY, RISK,
DANGER
perilous ICARIAN,
HAZARDOUS, DANGER-
OUS, RISKY, DREADFUL
perimeter BORDER,
AMBIT, CIRCUIT,
BOUNDARY, OUTLINE,
CIRCUMFERENCE,
PERIPHERY, RIM
period END, POINT,
DOT, TRACK, STAGE,
CYCLE, ERA, EPOCH,
EON, HOUR, DAY,
TIME, TERM, SPAN,
SPELL, SEASON, DATE,
DURATION, CON-
TINUANCE, LIMIT,
BOUND, CONCLUSION,

TERMINATION, DIVISION
of race's apex HEMERA
periodic ERAL, ANNUAL, ETESIAN, FITFUL, CYCLIC, RECURRENT, SEASONABLE, INTERMITTENT, REGULAR
periodical PAPER, JOURNAL, ORGAN, MAGAZINE, WEEKLY, MONTHLY, QUARTERLY, ANNUALLY, DAILY, HOURLY, CYCLIC, SERIAL, RECURRING, OFTEN
peripatetic WALKER, VAGRANT, RAMBLING, NOMAD(IC), ITINERANT, WANDERING, PEDESTRIAN, ARISTOTELIAN
peripheral EXTERNAL, DISTAL, DISTANT, CONFINED
periphery LIP, SPACE, AMBIT, PERIMETER, END, BOUND, EDGE, RIM, LIMIT, BOUNDARY, OUTSIDE, CIRCUMFERENCE, ENVIRONS
perish DECAY, DIE, ROT, WITHER, WASTE, SHRIVEL, EXPIRE, DECEASE
peritoneum, *fold of* OMENTUM
periwinkle MUSSEL, MYRTLE, SNAIL
permanent CHANGELESS, ABIDING, CONSTANT, LASTING, DURABLE, STABLE, STEADFAST, FIXED, ENDURING, CONTINUING, IMMUTABLE, PERPETUAL, INVARIABLE, PERSISTENT
condition HEXIS, STATUS
permeate PERVADE, SPREAD, IMBUE, FILL, STEEP, SOAK, SATURATE, DIFFUSE, PENETRATE
permission LIBERTY, GRACE, LEAVE, CONSENT, LICENSE,

PERMIT, ALLOWANCE, WARRANT, AUTHORIZATION, SUFFERANCE, TOLERATION
permit LEAVE, LICENSE, APPROVE, ALLOW, PASS, TOLERATE, SUFFER, LET, ENDURE, AUTHORIZE, WARRANT, GRANT, ADMIT, FRANCHISE, PATENT
pernicious EVIL, DEADLY, SINISTER, MALIGN, PAINFUL, NOISOME, BAD, HURTFUL, BALEFUL, DESTRUCTIVE, HARMFUL, DELETERIOUS, INJURIOUS, DETRIMENTAL, NOXIOUS, FATAL, RUINOUS
perpendicular ERECT, VERTICAL, SHEER, SINE, PLUMB, STEEP, ABRUPT, UPRIGHT, PRECIPITOUS
geometry APOTHEM
perpetuity ETERNITY, ENDLESSNESS, PERMANENCE
perplex UPSET, BALK, BAFFLE, BEWILDER, CONFOUND, EMBARRASS, CONFUSE, MYSTIFY, PUZZLE, FOOL, BESET, CRUX, TANGLE, COMPLICATE, INVOLVE, SNARL, DISTRACT, POSE, NONPLUS, CORNER, PLAGUE, VEX, HARASS, BOTHER
perplexed ASEA, KNOTTED, ANXIOUS, TROUBLED, INTRICATE, CONFUSED
perplexity STALEMATE, FOG, DOUBT, CONFUSION, INTRICACY, COMPLEXITY, COMPLICATION, ENTANGLEMENT, CONCERN, CARE, ANXIETY, DIFFICULTY, STRAIT, PICKLE, PLIGHT, DISORDER, PREDICAMENT
perquisite APPANAGE, FEE, PROFIT, BRIBE, SALARY, BONUS, TIP, RIGHT, INCOME, GAIN,

GRATUITY, PREROGATIVE
persecute PURSUE, BESET, HARASS, ABUSE, BAIT, RIDE, HOUND, HARRY, WRONG, HUNT, OPPRESS, TROUBLE, TORMENT, MOLEST, DISTRESS, WORRY, AFFLICT, ANNOY, PESTER, CHASE
Persephone's *parent* DEMETER, ZEUS *See under* "Proserpine"
Perseus' *mother* DANAE
Persia, Persian *See* "Iran"
persiflage BANTER, BADINAGE, FLIPPANCY, RAILLERY, RIDICULE, MOCKERY, PLEASANTRY
persist WEAR, INSIST, CONTINUE, REMAIN, ABIDE, STAY, PREVAIL, LAST, ENDURE, STICK
person BEING, ONE, BODY, MAN, WOMAN, CHILD, INDIVIDUAL, FELLOW, CHAP, SELF
of distinction NOTABLE, STAR, VIP
personage NIBS, CHARACTER, BIGWIG, INDIVIDUAL, PERSON, PEER, IMPERSONATION
personate APE, ACT, MIMIC, IMITATE, SIMULATE, REPRESENT, TYPIFY, FEIGN, PORTRAY
personified INCARNATE
light, Polynesian AO
personnel STAFF, FORCE, HANDS, FACULTY, ROSTER, MEN, CREW
perspective VIEW, VISTA, SLANT, SCOPE, PROSPECT, EXPECTATION, SCALE, PROPORTION, INTERRELATION, CONFIGURATION
perspicacious PENETRATING, ACUTE, KEEN, SHREWD, SHARP, ASTUTE, DISCERNING, CLEAR, LUCID, SAGACIOUS

perspicacity INSIGHT, ACUMEN, INTELLIGENCE, KEENNESS

perspiration SUDOR, SWEAT, EXUDATION

persuade URGE, WIN, INDUCE, ENTICE, PREVAIL, MOVE, DRIVE, IMPEL, LEAD, CONVINCE, COAX, INFLUENCE, INCITE, ACTUATE

pert IMPUDENT, BOLD, BRASH, DAPPER, LIVELY, BRISK, NIMBLE, SAUCY, SASSY, ARCH, SPRIGHTLY, FORWARD, IMPERTINENT, FLIPPANT, PRESUMING, PRESUMPTUOUS, DARING, OFFICIOUS, INSOLENT, DISCOURTEOUS

pertain REGARD, REFER, BELONG, RELATE, FIT, BEAR, APPLY

pertinent PAT, RELEVANT, RELATED, APT, ANENT, FIT(TING), HAPPY, TIMELY, APPROPRIATE, APPLICABLE, APROPOS, GERMANE, BELONGING, RELATIVE, CONGRUOUS

Peru(vian)
ancient INCA
bark CINCHONA
capital LIMA
city or town LIMA, ICA, PIURA, PUNO, CUZCO, PISCO
coin DINERO, LIBRA, PESETA, CENTAVO, SOL
dance CUECA
department See "province" below
early empire INCA
fog GARUA
goddess MAMA
hillock LOMA
Indian See under "Indian"
inn TAMBO
llama ALPACA, PACO
mark of nobility LLAUTU
partridge YUTU
plant OCA, ULLUCO, RHATANY
province or state ANCASH, TACNA, ICA,

LIMA, PIURA, CUZCO, LORETO
relic HUACO
river MARANON, SANTA, ICA, RIMAC, ACARA, OROTON, SAMA, PIURA
seaport PISCO
skin disease UTA
tribe INCA, CAMPA
volcano (EL)MISTI
wind SURES, PUNA

peruke HAIR, PERIWIG, WIG

peruse STUDY, SURVEY, CON, READ, SCAN, EXAMINE, SCRUTINIZE, OBSERVE, CONSIDER, INSPECT

pervade IMBUE, PERMEATE, EXTEND, FILL, DIFFUSE, SATURATE, INFUSE, PENETRATE, OVERSPREAD, INFILTRATE, INTERFUSE

perverse FORWARD, CROSS, AWRY, BALKY, UNRULY, MULISH, INTRACTABLE, UNREASONABLE, CONTRARY, STUBBORN, DISTORTED, HEADSTRONG, DOGGED, WICKED, WAYWARD, ERRING, PETULANT, CRANKY, WILLFUL, CHURLISH, SULKY

pesade REAR(ING)

Pescadores *island* HOKO
town MAKO

Peshkov, Aleksei Maksimovich GORKI (GORKY)

peso, *silver* DURO

pessimism GLOOM, DESPAIR, CYNICISM

pessimist CYNIC, GROUCH

pest BANE, PLAGUE, NUISANCE, PESTILENCE, SCOURGE, CURSE, INFLICTION, TROUBLE, ANNOYANCE, FLY, ANT, MOTH, FLEA, TICK, VERMIN, INSECT

pester VEX, BADGER, RIB, HARASS See "annoy"

pestilence PLAGUE, SCOURGE, EPIDEMIC, DISEASE, CALAMITY

pestle MASHER, MULLER, BRAYER, PILUM, GRIND, MIX, POUND, PULVERIZE
vessel MORTAR

pet CARESS, FONDLE, HUMOR, BABY, CADE, COSSET, LOVE, CODDLE, DANDLE, SULK, HUFF, MIFF, PEEVE, INDULGE, ANGER, FAVORITE

petals ALAE

petasus, petasos HAT, CAP

peter DWINDLE, FADE, WANE, FAIL, EXHAUST

Peter SIMON, ROCK, TSAR
father of JONAS

petiole STALK, PEDUNCLE, STEM, MESOPODIUM

petition PLEA, ASK, BEG, PRAY, SUE, PRAYER, SUIT, APPEAL, SOLICIT, REQUEST, ENTREATY, SUPPLICATE, SUPPLICATION

Petrarch's *beloved* LAURA

petrel TITI, BIRD

petrify FRIGHTEN, DAZE, STUPEFY, STUN, SHOCK, CALCIFY, LAPIDIFY, FOSSILIZE, ASTONISH, DUMFOUND, BENUMB, DEADEN, HARDEN, PARALYZE, SCARE, FREEZE, THRILL, AFFRIGHT

petrifying STONY, PETRESCENT

petrol GAS(OLINE)

petroleum *derivative* NAPHTHA, BUTANE

petticoat BALMORAL, JUPON, KIRTLE, UNDERSKIRT, WOMAN

pettish FRETFUL, PEEVISH, TESTY, IRASCIBLE, PETULANT

petty CHILDISH, FRIVOLOUS, TRIVIAL, PALTRY, LITTLE, MINUTE, PICAYUNE, SMALL, TRIFLING, SHALLOW, UNIMPORANT, INSIGNIFICANT, INCONSIDERABLE, NUGATORY petulant CROSS, PERT, SURLY, TESTY, PEEVISH, HUFFY, IRRITABLE, QUERULOUS, TOUCHY, WASPISH, CHOLERIC, SNAPPISH, CRABBED, CAPTIOUS, FRETFUL

pewit LAPWING, GULL, PEWEE, BIRD

peyote CACTUS, MESCAL, PEYOTL, PLANT

Phaedo's *school* ELIAN

phalanger TAPOA, MARSUPIAL

phantasm WRAITH, FETCH, GHOST, EIDOLON, VISION, SPECTER, APPARITION, PHANTOM, ILLUSION

phantom GHOST, SPIRIT, EIDOLON, SPECTER, VISION, APPARITION, IMAGE

Pharaoh RAMESES, RULER, KING

phase FORM, GUISE, ERA, SIDE, PART, POSTURE, LOOK, STATE, ASPECT, FACET, STAGE, STEP, SHAPE, ANGLE, CHAPTER, APPEARANCE, CONDITION, TRANSITION

pheasant CHEER, MONAL, MONAUL, FOWL, BIRD
  Africa, Asia TRAGOPAN
  Australia LEIPOA
  India MONAL
  nest NID(E)

phenol *derivative* SALOL, CRESOL

phenomenon MARVEL, EVENT, SIGHT, PRODIGY, MANIFESTATION, WONDER, MIRACLE

phenyl ARYL, TOLYL

philabeg KILT

philippic SCREED, TIRADE, INVECTIVE

Philippine, Filipino TAGAL, ATTA
  aborigine AETA, ATA, IFUGAO
  ancestral spirit ANITO
  ant, white ANAI, ANAY
  boat CASCO, VINTA, BANCA *See* "canoe" *below*

breadfruit CAMANSI, RIMA
buffalo CARABOU, TIMARAU
canoe VINTA, BANCA, BAROTO
cedar CALANTAS
century plant MAGUEY
chief, Moro DATO, DATTO, DATU
child BATA
Christianized tribe TAGALOG, VISAYAN
city or town ALBAY, CAVITE, MANILA, IRIGA, VIGAN, PALO, NAGA, BAGO, BOGO, CEBU, LANAO
coconut meat COPRA
coin PESO, CONANT
cyclone BAGUIO
dagger ITAC
dialect *See* "language" *below*
discoverer MAGELLAN
drink, alcoholic BENO, PANGASI
dwarf race NEGRITO, AETA
eight UALO
farmer TAO
fennel ANISE
fern NITO
fetish ANITO
fiber SABA, CASTULI, CAMANSI
food staple TARO, SABA
forest GUBAT
fort COT(T)A
gulf RAGAY, DAVAO
hardwood NARRA
headman DATO, DATTO, DATU
hemp ABACA
house BAHAY
idol ANITO
island SAMAR, CEBU, PANAY, NEGROS, LUZON, LEYTE, BOHOL, CUYO, JOLO
  group SULU
  largest LUZON, MINDANAO
knife BOLO, ITAC
lake TAAL, LANAO
language TAGAL(A), TAGALOG, IBANAG, BATAN, BIKOL, IGOROT, TINO, MORO

  (SULU), MANOBO, MONTES
lighter or barge CASCO
lighthouse FARO
liquor BENO, PANGASI
litter TALABON
lizard IBID
Luzon lake TAAL
  town VIGAN
measure APATAN, CHUPA
Moslem MORO
mountain peak APO
native ITA, MORO, AETA, ATA
negrito AETA, ATA, ITA, ATI, ATTA
nut PILI
oil CEBUR
  tree CEBUR
pagan ITALONE
palm NIPA, ANAHAU, ANAHAO
parrot CAGIT
peasant TAO
plant ALEM
plum DUHAT, LANSEH, LANSA
port ILOILO, CEBU, CAVITE
province ABRA, TARLAC, BATAAN, RIZAL, CAVITE, CEBU, LAGUNA, QUEZON, ALBAY, AKLAN, CAPIZ, ILOILO, BOHOL, LEYTE, SAMAR, SULU, AGUSAN, DAVAO, LANAO
rebel HUK
rice PAGA
river PASIG, ABRA
sapodilla CHICO
sash TAPIS
savage ATA, IGOROT
sea SULU
skirt SAYA
soap vine GOGO
soldier or brigand LADRONE
  barracks CUARTEL
stream ILOG
sweetsop ATES
thatch NIPA
town *See* "city" *above*
tree *See under* "tree"
tribe AETA, ATA, VISAYAN, MORO, ITA-

LONE, IGOROT(TE), IGOLOT, IFUGAO
vine IYO
volcano APO
water buffalo CARA-BAO
weapon BOLO
white man CACHIL
wine BENO
wood NARRA, EBONY, SANDAL, TEAK
Philippine-Malayan ITALONE
Philistine *deity* DAGON
Philomela's *sister* PROCNE
philosopher SOCRATES, PLATO, ZENO, BACON, SPINOZA, KANT, HEGEL, HUME
philosophical ERUDITE, SAPIENT, CALM, SE-RENE, RATIONAL, THOUGHTFUL, UN-RUFFLED, SEDATE, COOL, COLLECTED, TRANQUIL, IMPER-TURBABLE, TEMPER-ATE
element RECT
unit MONAD
philosophy, *ancient* STOIC, CYNIC
natural PHYSICS
school of ELEATIC
phlegmatic CALM, COOL, DULL, INERT, SLOW, INDIFFERENT, STOIC(AL), ALOOF, COMPOSED, STOLID, APATHETIC, SLUG-GISH, UNFEELING, IM-PASSIVE, IMPERTURBA-BLE
phloem TISSUE, BARK, BAST
phlogistic INFLAMMA-TORY
phoebad PROPHETESS, SEERESS
Phoebe ARTEMIS, DIANA, SELENE, MOON, PEWEE, FLYCATCHER, BIRD
Phoebus APOLLO, SUN, SOL
Phoenicia(n), *anc. city-state* TYRE, SIDON, ACRE, BYBLOS (GEBAL)
capital TYRE
dialect PUNIC

god BAAL
goddess BALTIS, ASTARTE
seaport SIDON
phonetic VOCAL, ORAL
notation ROMIC
sound PALATAL
photo STAT, FLASH, TINTYPE, MUG, FILM, PICTURE, SHOT, SNAP, LIKENESS
copy STAT
finish NOSE
solution HYPO
type of X-RAY
photography *inventor* TALBOT, DAGUERRE
photology OPTICS, PHOTICS
photometric unit PYR, RAD, LUX, LUMEN
phrase CLAUSE, MOTTO, EPIGRAM, TERM, STYLE, WRITE, EXPRESSION, MAXIM, IDIOM, SLOGAN, CATCHWORD, DICTION, WORD, DESCRIBE
style DICTION
phratry CLAN, CURIA, PHYLE, TRIBE
Phrygian *god* MEN, ATTIS, ATYS
king MIDAS
lunar god MEN
river MEANDER
town IPSUS
phylactery AMULET, CHARM, REMINDER, TALISMAN, SPELL
phyletic RACIAL, CLASSED, PHYLOGE-NETIC
physic DRUG, PILL, TREAT, PURGE, REM-EDY, MEDICINE, CA-THARTIC, RELIEVE, HEAL, CURE, PURGA-TIVE, LAXATIVE, APERIENT
physical EXAM(INA-TION), SOMAL, SO-MATIC, BODILY, NATU-RAL, MATERIAL, REAL, CORPOREAL, TRUE
physician(s) MEDIC, GALEN, DOCTOR, SUR-GEON, PRACTITIONER, CONSULTANT, HEALER, CURER
group AMA, PANEL, STAFF

pertaining to IATRIC
symbol CADUCEUS
physicist GALVANI, FARADAY, MARCONI, CURIE, BOYLE, NATU-RALIST, MATERIALIST, HYLOZOIST
atomic See "atomic"
physiognomy FACE, VISAGE, EXPRESSION, MIEN, FEATURES *See* "face"
physiological *person* BION
physostigmine ESERINE
pian FRAMBESIA, YAWS
pianissimo PP, SOFT(LY)
piano SOFT, LOW
early SPINET
pedal CELESTE
piaster, *1/120th of* ASPER
picaroon ROGUE, THIEF *See* "bandit"
pick GLEAN, CULL, CHOOSE, ELITE, CREAM, ELECT, OPT, TAKE, SEIZE, GRASP, SEEK, PLUCK, SELEC-T(ION), CHOICE, BEST, CUT, GATHER, DETACH, NIBBLE, PLECTRUM, PIERCE, INDENT, PENETRATE, COLLECT, PILFER, ROB, STEAL, TOOL
pickax(e) GURLET
picket SENTRY, GUARD, STAKE, PALING, PALE, POST, TETHER, FENCE, MARKER, BULLET, TERN, PATROL, SEN-TINEL, WATCHMAN
pickle SOUSE, PRE-SERVE, MARINATE, CORN, BRINE, VINE-GAR, PLIGHT, FIX, JAM, STRAIT, SCRAPE, MESS, PREDICAMENT, QUANDARY, DILEMMA
pickling *herb* DILL
pickpocket DIP, THIEF, WIRE
picnic JUNKET, OUT-ING, PARTY, GYPSY, EXCURSION, ENTER-TAINMENT
picture MOVIE, IMAGE, LIKENESS, SCENE, PASTEL, TABLEAU, PROFILE, VIEW, SCEN-

ERY, PAINTING, ETCH-
ING, ENGRAVING,
DRAWING, PRINT, POR-
TRAYAL, PORTRAI-
T(URE), DEPICT,
SHOT, PHOTO, SNAP
award OSCAR
border MAT
composite MONTAGE,
COLLAGE
moving CINEMA,
FILM, TV
wall MURAL
picturesque VIVID, AL-
LURING, STRIKING,
GRAPHIC, SCENIC,
QUAINT, STRANGE,
BEAUTIFUL, CHARM-
ING, COLORFUL
pie PATTY, TART, COB-
BLER, CHAOS, SNARL,
JUMBLE, PASTRY,
FOOD
meat PASTY, RISSOLE
piebald PINTADO, DAP-
PLED, PIED, PINTO,
MOTTLED, VARIE-
GATED, HETEROGENE-
OUS, MONGREL, SPOT-
TED, PATCHED
piece COIN, SCRAP,
PART, UNIT, ADJUNCT,
PORTION, DETAIL, SEC-
TOR, PARCEL, FRAG-
MENT, BIT, CHUNK,
HUNK, SHRED, ITEM,
ARTICLE, COMPOSI-
TION, TUNE, REPAIR,
PATCH, CUT, SLICE
armor CORSELET,
TANE, TACE
of eight PESO, REAL
out EKE, SUPPLE-
MENT
piecing out CANTLE,
EKING
pied PINTADO, DAP-
PLED, PINTO *See*
"piebald"
pieplant RHUBARB
pier STILT, ANTA,
SHAFT, BERTH, BUT-
TRESS, KEY, MOLE,
PILLAR, PILE, POST,
WHARF, SUPPORT,
DOCK, JETTY, WALL,
BREAKWATER, PILAS-
TER, GROIN
architectural ANTA
base SOCLE
pierce GORE, STICK,
LANCE, ENTER, CHILL,

STAB, BORE, SPEAR,
DISCERN *See* "pene-
trate"
piercing HIGH, KEEN,
SHRILL, TART, SHARP,
THORNY, PENETRAT-
ING, CUTTING
pig(s) HOG, SOW,
BACON, ELT, SHOAT,
BOAR, FARROW, BAR-
ROW, GILT, SWINE,
PORKER, PORK, MOLD,
BAR, INGOT, SLOB,
GLUTTON
female SOW, GILT
like animal PECCARY,
AARDVARK
litter FARROW
male BOAR, BARROW
of lead FOTHER
of metal INGOT, BAR
pickled feet of SOUSE
young GRICE, SHOAT,
ELT
pigeon DOVE, ISABEL,
PIPER, GOURA,
CUSHAT, POUTER,
CARRIER, HOMER, FAN-
TAIL, JACOBIN, NUN,
TRUMPETER, TURBIT,
TUMBLER
Australia WONGA
call COO
carrier HOMER, HOM-
ING
clay SKEET, TARGET
extinct DODO
fruit LUPE, KUKU
genus COLUMBA,
GOURA
hawk MERLIN
house COTE, ROOK-
(ERY)
pea DAL, TUR, GAN-
DUL
pertaining to PE-
RISTERONIC
short-beaked BARB
tooth-billed DODLET
variety NUN, RUFF,
TUMBLER, POUTER
wood KUKU
young PIPER
pigeonhole IGNORE,
FILE, LOSE, SHELF,
SHELVE, STORE,
CUBICLE, HOLE,
RECESS, COMPART-
MENT, ARRANGE,
ANALYZE, LABEL,
CLASSIFY, DEFER

pigment COLOR, STAIN,
DYE, TINT, PAINT, UM-
BER
black TAR, SOOT
blue IOLITE, BICE,
SMALT, AZURITE
board PALETTE
brown BISTER, UM-
BER
calico printing CAN-
ARIN(E)
coal tar ANILINE
cuttlefish SEPIA
earth OCHER, UMBER
lack of ACHROM(I)A
lake MADDER
orange-red REALGAR
pale yellow ETIOLIN
red LAKE, CHICA,
ROSET
white BARYTA, LEAD
without ALBINO,
ACHROMIC
yellow OCHER,
SIENNA
pigmy *See* "pygmy"
pignoration PIGNUS,
PAWNING, PLEDGING
pignus PAWN
pigpen REEVE, STY,
MESS, PIGGERY
pigtail CUE, QUEUE,
BRAID, PLAIT, ROPE
pike SHAFT, POLE,
STAFF, SPIKE, POINT,
SPEAR, ROD, ROAD
See "fish"
pilchard FUMADO,
SALMON
young SARDINE
pile PILLAR, TIMBER,
POLE, ACCUMULATE,
BANK, SHOCK, COCK,
FABRIC, GATHER,
HOARD, MASS, HEAP,
STACK, SHAG, NAP,
FORTUNE, HAIR, FUR,
PELAGE, FIBER, AMASS,
COLLECT(ION),
QUANTITY, LOT, BAT-
TERY, BUILDING,
BEAM, MONEY
driver RAM, GIN,
BEETLE, FISTUCA
of hay RICK, COCK,
STACK
of stones SCREE,
CAIRN
ram TUP
pilfer STEAL *See*
"filch"

pilgrim PALMER, TRAV-
ELER, WAYFARER,
CRUSADER
garb at Mecca
IHRAM
to Holy Land
PALMER
pilgrimage to Mecca
HADJ
pill BALL, BOLUS, PEL-
LET, PILULA, TABLET,
MEDICINE, REMEDY,
BOOR
pillage FORAY, RIFLE,
FLAY, HARRY, SACK,
ROB, LOOT, RAPINE,
(DE)SPOIL, SPOLIA-
TION, BOOTY, DEPRE-
DATION, PLUNDER-
(ING), PREY, STRIP
pillar SUPPORT, BEAM,
PIER, PEDESTAL, POST,
COLUMN, SHAFT
bearing notice STELE,
STELA
in Buddhist building
LAT
of ore JAM
stone STELA, STELE,
OBELISK, NEEDLE,
SHAFT
tapering OBELISK
with figures OSIRIDE
pillory STOCK,
CANGUE, YOKE,
FRAME
pilose HAIRY
pilot DIRECT(OR),
HANDLE, AVIATOR,
CONTROL, HELMSMAN,
GUIDE, LEAD, STEER,
HEAD, FLYER, LEADER,
CICERONE
pilous HAIRY
Piman *See under*
"Indian"
pimple PAPULE, QUAT,
BURL, STY, PUSTULE,
ERUPTION, BOIL,
SPOT, LESION
pin SECURE, HOLD,
TRANSFIX, FASTEN,
BROOCH, RIVET,
DOWEL, NOG, BOLT,
PEG, THOLE, SKEWER,
FEATHER, TRIFLE,
BADGE, NAIL, COTTER,
FID
machine COTTER
pivot PINTLE
rifle TIGE
Roman ACUS

small PEG, LILL
wooden FID, PEG,
COAG, COAK, DOWEL
pinafore SLIP, APRON,
TIER, GARMENT
pincer(s) TONG(s),
FORCEP(s), PLIERS,
ORGAN
claw CHELA
pinch STEAL, CRAMP,
NIP, STRAIN, STRESS,
TWEAK, RUB, STRAIT,
PASS, CRISIS, SAVE,
SCRIMP, ARREST, NAB,
SQUEEZE, COMPRESS,
OPPRESS, AFFLICT,
DISTRESS, EXTORT,
STINT, CONFINE,
LIMIT, PAIN, PANG,
HARDSHIP, EMER-
GENCY *See* "pilfer"
Pindaric form ODE
pine GRIEVE, LONG,
YEARN, THIRST, LAN-
GUISH, DROOP, FLAG,
WITHER, CHIR, CHEER
See under "tree"
tree genus ABIES
pineapple NANA, PINA,
ANANAS
genus PUYA
Pine Tree State MAINE
pinguefy FATTEN
pinguid ADIPOSE, FAT,
OILY, UNCTUOUS,
FERTILE, RICH
pinion WING,
FEATHER, QUILL, ARM
pink PUNCTURE,
STAB, PERFORATE,
SCALLOP, CORAL,
FLOWER, COLOR,
STYLISH, SMART
flower genus SILENE
pinkster AZALEA,
PLANT
pinna EAR, AURICLE,
FEATHER, WING, FIN,
LEAFLET, MOLLUSK
pinnacle TOP, CREST,
EPI, SPIRE, TURRET,
APEX, CROWN, ACME,
PEAK, ZENITH, SUM-
MIT
glacial ice SERAC
rocky TOR
pinniped SEAL, WAL-
RUS
pinocle *score* DIX
term MELD
pin point DOT, TRIFLE,
AIM, FIX

pintado SPOTTED,
PIED, PINTO, CHINTZ,
CERO, SIERRA, PETREL,
GUINEA, PIGEON,
FOWL, FISH
pintail DUCK, SMEE,
GROUSE, FOWL
pinto SPOTTED, PIE-
BALD, CALICO, PIED,
PINTADO, BEAN,
HORSE, INDIAN
pip ACE, HIT, SPEED,
SPECK, SPOT, SEED,
ROOT, PEEP, BREAK,
PEEVISHNESS, PIPPIN,
CHIRP, CRACK, BLOS-
SOM, SEGMENT
pipe BRIAR, BRIER,
DUDEEN, REED, TUBE,
FLUTE, CONDUIT, TRA-
CHEA, WHISTLE,
SOUND, CRY, NOTE,
CHIMNEY, FLUE, FLAG-
EOLET, OBOE,
HOOKA(H)
clay T.D.
fitting CROSS, TEE,
ELL, NIPPLE
flanged end TAFT
joint TEE, ELL
oriental NARG(H)ILE,
NARGILEH, HOOKA(H)
pastoral REED
peace CALUMET
player FIFER, PIPER,
FL(A)UTIST
shepherd's OAT, LARI-
GOT
short DUDEEN
stove CHIMNEY,
TEWEL, FLUE
Turkish CHIBOUK
water HOOKA(H),
NARGILE, NARGHILE
with socket ends HUB
pipefish SNACOT, EARL
pipit TITLARK, BIRD
genus ANTHUS
piquancy RACINESS,
KEENNESS, SAUCINESS,
PUNGENCY
piquant SPICY, SALTY,
ZESTY, TART, PUN-
GENT, PROVOCATIVE,
STIMULATING, BITING
pique PAIN, ROUSE,
CHAFE, GOAD, STING,
CUT, NETTLE, VEX,
OFFEND, IRRITATE,
FRET, HUFF, PROVOKE,
PRICK, RESENTMENT,
GRUDGE, UMBRAGE,

DISPLEASURE, EXCITE, ANGER
piquet *score* PIC
winning of all tricks CAPOT
pirate STEAL, ROB, PICAROON, CORSAIR, BUCCANEER, PRIVATEER, FREEBOOTER *See* "bandit"
flag of ROGER
gallows YARDARM
weapon SNEE
piraya, piranha CARIBE, FISH
piscine *propeller* FIN
Pisgah, *summit of* NEBO
pismire EMMET, ANT
pismo CLAM
pistil, *part of* CARPEL
pistol MAUSER, DAG, COLT, REVOLVER, GAT, IRON, DERRINGER, GUN, WAG, JOKER, WEAPON
case HOLSTER
old DAG
piston PLUNGER, VALVE, KNOB, PLUG
pit HOLE, CAVE, HELL, SEED, SUMP, FOVEA, MATCH, DENT, CAVITY, DEPRESSION, SHAFT, MINE, GRAVE, CORE, ABYSS, LACUNA, HOLLOW, DINT, INDENTATION, EXCAVATION, WELL, CRATER, GULF, CHASM, STONE
baking IMU, OVEN
bottomless ABADDON
peach PUTAMEN, SEED
theater PARQUET, PARTERRE, CIRCLE
pitch TAR, RESIN, SAP, GAME, TOSS, KEY, TONE, REGULATE, FALL, PLUNGE, DESCENT, SLOPE, DEPTH, GRADE, DIP, HURL, SLING, CAST, FIX, ERECT, THROW, FLING, SET, PAVE, TELL, RELATE, DECLIVITY, DEGREE, HEIGHT
cobbler's CODE
instrument for TONOMETER, PIPE
pitchblende *derivative* RADIUM, URANIUM

pitcher CROCK, EWER, OLLA, GORGE, JUG, PROCHOOS, TOSSER, BALLPLAYER, OLPE, JAR, CONTAINER
left-handed SOUTHPAW
plant NEPENTHE
shaped URCEOLATE
shaped like man BOGGLE, TOBY
shaped vessel AIGUIERE
pitfall TRAP, DECOY, GIN, SNARE, AMBUSH, SPRINGE, LURE, DANGER, TEMPTATION
pith NUB, JET, GIST, PULP, MARROW, MEDULLA, ESSENCE, CORE, KERNEL, FORCE, VIGOR, CENTER, NUCLEUS, QUINTESSENCE, SUBSTANCE
full of HEADY, MEATY, VIGOROUS, COGENT, TERSE, CONCISE
helmet TOPI, TOPEE
tree of Nile AMBASH, AMBATCH
pithy SHORT, CONCISE, VIGOROUS, TERSE, FORCIBLE, SENTENTIOUS, LACONIC, BRIEF, SUBSTANTIAL, HEADY, MEATY, COGENT
plant SOLA
pitiful PATHETIC, MOVING, TOUCHING, TENDER, PALTRY, DESPICABLE, LAMENTABLE, MEAN, BAD, CONTEMPTIBLE
pitiless STONY, HARD, MEAN, CRUEL, IMPLACABLE, MERCILESS, RELENTLESS, RUTHLESS, INEXORABLE, UNFEELING, REVENGEFUL
pittance BIT, MITE, ALMS, SONG, DOLE, ALLOWANCE, CHARITY, GIFT, TRIFLE, SCANTLING
pitted FOVEATE, PUNCTURED, FACED, MATCHED
Pittsburgh PGH

pity GRIEF, GRACE, RUTH, MERCY, YEARN, COMMISERATE, COMPASSION, CHARITY, SYMPATHY, HUMANITY, CONDOLENCE, REGRET, LAMENT
pivot TURN, FOCUS, AXLE, HINGE, AXIS, JOINT, SWIVEL, ROTATE, JUNCTION
pin PINTLE
pivotal POLAR, CENTRAL, CRUCIAL, DEPENDING
pivoted SWUNG, SWIVELED
pixy ELF, GOBLIN, SPRITE *See* "fairy"
placard TAG, BILL, NOTICE, POST(ER), AFFICHE, AD(VERTISEMENT), BROADSIDE, ANNOUNCE
placate CONCILIATE, CALM, PACIFY, SMOOTH, APPEASE, SOOTHE, FORGIVE
place(s) STEAD, PLOT, POSIT, SITUS, AREA, LOCUS, LOCI, SET, PUT, LAY, DEPOSIT, LIEU, SITE, POST, OFFICE, JOB, ASSIGN, SEAT, STATION, (AP)POINT, SECOND, STREET, PATIO, SQUARE, SITUATION, POSITION, LOCALITY, LOCATION, ORDER, RANK, LOCALE, DISTRICT, TRACT, SCENE, SPOT, PREMISES, VILLAGE, TOWN, CITY, FORTRESS, STATUS, RECOGNIZE, ARRANGE, DISPOSE
apart ENISLE, SEPARATE
beneath INFRAPOSE
camping ETAPE
combining form TOPO
frequented HAUNT, RESORT
hiding MEW, CAVE
in a row ALINE, ALIGN
intermediate LIMBO
market FORUM, MART, AGORA
meeting TRYST, RENDEZVOUS

of nether darkness
EREBUS

placid QUIET, COOL,
CALM, SERENE,
SUANT, MILD, EQUA-
BLE, UNRUFFLED,
PACIFIC, TRANQUIL,
UNDISTURBED, PEACE-
FUL, COMPOSED,
GENTLE

plagiarism CRIB, PI-
RACY, THEFT

plagiarist THIEF, BOR-
ROWER, PIRATE

plague TEASE, BOTHER,
BADGER, HARRY, HEC-
TOR, CURSE, DUN,
TWIT, PEST, WORRY,
ANNOY, GALL, PAIN,
FRET, DISEASE, CA-
LAMITY, EPIDEMIC,
PESTILENCE, AFFLIC-
TION, TORMENT,
TROUBLE, HARASS,
CHAFE

pertaining to LOIMIC

plaid MAUD, TARTAN,
CLOTH, FABRIC, GAR-
MENT

plain LLANO, PRAIRIE,
HEATH, WOLD, DOWN,
VELDT, STEPPE, LOW-
LAND, SIMPLE, BLUNT,
MERE, PATENT, OPEN,
CLEAR, FLAT, ARTLESS,
LEVEL, EVEN, FLUSH,
LUCID, FRANK, CANDID,
SMOOTH, HOMELY,
MANIFEST, UNMIS-
TAKABLE, APPARENT,
EVIDENT, DISTINCT,
OVERT, DOWNRIGHT,
ORDINARY, OBVIOUS,
INGENUOUS, OUT-
SPOKEN

Arctic TUNDRA

Argentina PAMPA

Asia CHOL

elevated MESA,
PLATEAU

Europe STEPPE

grassy CAMAS(S),
SAVANNA(H)

Italy CAMPAGNA

of Olympic games
ELIS

Russia STEPPE,
TUNDRA

salt-covered SALADA

small prairie PAMPA

S. Africa VELDT

Span. -Amer. LLANO,
VEGA

treeless SAVANNA(H),
VELDT, PAMPA,
LLANO, TUNDRA,
STEPPE, PRAIRIE

upland WOLD, WEALD,
MESA

plaintiff SUER, AC-
CUSER, PROSECUTOR,
COMPLAINANT

plaintive SAD, ELEGIAC,
WISTFUL, DOLEFUL,
MOURNFUL, SORROW-
FUL, PITEOUS,
MELANCHOLY, DISCON-
TENTED, PEEVISH,
QUERULOUS, FRETFUL,
CROSS

plait MILAN, PLEX,
WIMPLE, PLY, BRAID,
MAT, TWIST, CUE,
QUEUE, PLEAT

plaited KILTED,
BRAIDED, FOLDED, IN-
TERWOVEN, KNITTED

rope SENNIT

plan DESIGN, METHOD,
SCHEME, DRAFT,
DRAW(ING),
ITINERARY, PLAT,
OUTLINE, CHART,
PLOT, MAP, PURPOSE,
IDEA, SKETCH, DIA-
GRAM, LAYOUT, PROJ-
ECT, SYSTEM,
DEVICE, INTRIGUE,
CABAL, CONSPIRACY,
RACKET, CALCULATE,
DEVISE, PREMEDI-
TATE, CONSPIRE,
DRAW, CONCOCT,
ETTLE, HATCH

architecture EPURE

plane LEVEL, GRADE,
SHAVE, AERO, AIR-
CRAFT, SURFACE,
EVEN, FLAT, SMOOTH,
FLUSH, TREE, TOOL

chart MERCATOR

curve ELLIPSE

inclined RAMP, CHUTE

iron BIT

propulsion JET, ATOM

tree CHINAR,
PLATANUS

planet EARTH, WORLD,
STAR, MOON, URANUS,
NEPTUNE, MARS,
VENUS, PLUTO,
SATURN, MERCURY,
JUPITER

brightest VENUS

nearest sun MERCURY

recent PLUTO

red MARS

satellite MOON

planetarium ORREY

planisphere ASTROLABE

plank BOARD, TIMBER,
LUMBER

down PAY, ADVANCE,
DEPOSIT

planking, *breadth of*
STRAKE

plant(s) PLACE, IN-
SERT, SOW, SEED,
SETTLE, TREE, SHRUB,
HERB, FLORA,
VEGETABLE, FLOWER,
STOCK, FACTORY,
MILL *See* "shrub"

aconite BIKH

adapted to dryness
XEROPHYTE, CACTUS,
CACTI

Africa ARG(H)EL

agave PITA, DATIL
See "agave"

algae genus NOSTOC
See "alga"

alismaceous ALISMAD

Alpine EDELWEISS

ambrosia genus RAG-
WEED

ammoniac OSHAC

and animal life BIOTA

anise DILL, CUMIN,
ANET

apoplexy ESCA

appendage STIPULE

araceous CABBAGE,
LILY, TARO, ARUM

aralia FATSIA

aromatic ANISE,
MINT, NARD, LAVEN-
DER, TANSY, THYME,
TARRAGON

gum ARALIA

seed NARD, ANET

arrowroot ARARAO,
CANNA, TACCA, PIA,
MUSA *See* "arrow-
root"

arum family ARAD,
AROID, TARO

Asiatic fiber RAMIE

oil ODAL

Assam TEA, TCHE

aster family DAISY

astringent ALDER,
AVENS, SUMAC

auricula PRIMROSE

Australia CORREA, ALSTONIA
  genus HAKEA
bayonet DATIL
bean family LICORICE
benthonic ENALID
bitter RUE
  leaves TANSY
  vetch ERS
bodies without stems THALLI, ACAULES-CENTS
bog genus ABAMA, NARTHECIUM
bramble GORSE, THORN, BRIAR, FURZE
brassica COLE, RAPE, TURNIP, KALE, CABBAGE, RUTABAGA
broom HIRSE, CYTISUS, HEATHER, SPART
  Spain GENISTA, SPART
bud of CION
bulb CAMAS(S), CORM, CAMMAS, QUAMASH
burdock CLITE, LAPPA, HURR-BUR
burning bush WAHOO
cabbage family See "brassica" *above*
cactus CEREUS, DILDO, MESCAL, SAGUARO
  kind XEROPHYTE
  like CACTOID
  Mexico CHAUTE
  spineless CHAUTE
calyx leaf SEPAL
canna ACHIRA
capsule POD
castor KIKI
catchfly SILENE, CAMPION
catnip family NEP(ETA)
caustic MOXA
cell GAMETE
cellular flowerless LICHEN, MOSS
century AGAVE, ALOE, MAGUEY, PITA
chaffy scale PALEA
cherry, laurel CERASUS
Chinese RAMIE
chlorophyll lacking ALBINO
climbing BINE, VINE, LIANA, LIANE, IVY, PHILODENDRON

clover MEDIC, ALFALFA, LUCERN(E), MELILOT, ALSIKE, TREFOIL
clusters, flat top CYME
combining form PHYTO
corn lily IXIA
cruciferous ALYSSUM, CRESS
cryptogamous MOSS, FERN, ALGA(E)
cutter RARA, BIRD
cutting SLIP
cyperaceous SEDGE
desert AGAVE, CACTUS, ALHAGI
dill ANET
dipsacus TEASEL
disease BLISTER, ERINOSE, SMUT, FUNGUS, ROT, GALL, KERMES, SCALE
docklike SORREL
dogwood CORNUS, OSIER, CORNEL, SUMAC
dye-yielding MADDER, WOAD, HENNA, ANIL, ALKANET, SUMAC, CHAY
dwarf CUMIN, CUMMIN
E. India DEUTZIA, DA, MADAR, MUDAR, CREAT, REA, SESAME, SOLA, SUNN, AMBARY
Egypt CUM(M)IN
embryo PLANTULE
erica genus HEATH
euphorbia genus SPURGE
Europe AZAROLE, ALYSSUM, ORPINE
everlasting ORPINE
exudate RESIN, SAP, GUM
fabaceous ERS
fern TARA *See* "fern"
fiber ISTLE, PITA, RAMIE, SISAL, SIDA, FLAX, IXTLE, COTTON
flag, sweet CALAMUS
floating FROGBIT, LOTUS
flowerless FERN, LICHEN, MOSS, ACROGEN
fragrant root ORRIS
furze GORSE, ULEX, WHIN, WHUN

garlic, wild MOLY
genus AGAVE, ARUM, ERINGO, NOLANA, ULEX, MUSA
  isatis WOAD
  ulex FURZE
grain CORN, WHEAT, OAT, BARLEY, RYE
grass AVENA
growth, pertaining to VEGETAL
growing from inside ENDOGENIC
growth on GALL
habitat, adjustment to ECESIS
haw SLOE
Hawaii OLONA, TARO, KALO
hawthorne AZAROLE, MAYFLOWER
healing SANICLE
heather LING, ERICA, BESOM
honesty MOONWORT
hop vine stem BINE
hybridization XENIA
India See "E. India" *above*
indigo ANIL
interior chaff PALEA, PALET
ipecac genus EVEA, CEPHAELIS
Ireland symbol SHAMROCK
iris family IRID, ORRIS, FLAG, LIS
Japan AUCUBA, TEA
  quince genus CYDONIA
joining GRAFT
juice MILK, SAP, RESIN, GUM
leaf BLADE
  of betel palm BUYO
leguminous LENTIL, MEDIC, SENNA, PEA, BEAN, CLOVER, ALFALFA
lice or louse APHIS, APHID
life FLORA
liliaceous LEEK, ONION, SEGO, IRIS, TULIP, SOTOL, YUCCA
lilylike CAMA(S), ALOE, LOTUS, ASPHODEL, SQUILL, YUCCA
male MAS

malvaceous ALTHAEA, ESCOBA, MALLOW, OKRA
manioc CASSAVA, TAPIOCA
marine ENALID *See* "seaweed"
medicinal ARNICA, ALOE, ANISE, BONESET, SENNA, LOBELIA, GENTIAN, UIXI, TANSY, SQUILL, RUE, JALAP
menthaceous CATNIP, CATMINT, MINT
Mexico DATIL, CHIA, SALVIA, SABADILLA, AGAVE, SOTOL
mignonettelike WELA, WOALD, WOULD
millet, broomcorn HIRSE
mint, European LAVENDER
family BASIL, CATNIP, SAGE
mock orange SYRINGA
modified by environment ECAD
monkshood ATIS, ACONITE *See* "monkshood"
mosslike HEPATIC
mulberry, India ACH
multicellular METAPHYTE
muscus MOSS
mushroom MOREL *See* "mushroom"
mustard family CRESS, ALYSSUM
nepeta, nep CATNIP, CATMINT
noxious WEED, TARE
onionlike LEEK, CHIVE, SHALLOT
order ERICALES
organ(s) LEAF, STOMATA, PISTIL
Pacific thatch NETI
parsley annual ANISE, DILL
wild ELTROT
part AXIL, STIPEL
pepper AVA, KAVA
perennial CAREX, SEDUM
Peru RHATANY, OCA, ULLUCO
Philippine ALEM
pod BOLL
poisonous genus DATURA

to cattle LOCO
to fowls HENBANE
pore LENTICEL
prickly CACTUS, NETTLE, TEASEL, ROSE, BRIER, BRIAR
primrose PRIMULA, OXLIP *See* "primrose"
pungent MINT
rat poison OLEANDER
receptacle TORUS, VASE
rock LICHEN, MOSS
root RADIX
roselike AVENS
rose of Sharon ALTHEA
rye fungus ERGOT
sage, aromatic SALVIA
scalelike leaved SAVIN(E)
scales PALEAE, RAMENTA
sea, seaweed ALGA, ALGAE, ENALID *See* "seaweed"
secretion LERP, RESIN, SAP, MILK, LAAP, LAARP, LATEX
sedge genus CAREX, XYRIS, CYPERUS *See* "sedge"
seed GRAIN, NUT, BULB, PIP, BUTTON, PUTAMEN
organ PISTIL
seedless FERN
pertaining to AGAMIC
shoot SPRIG, STOLON, (S)CION, ROD, RUNNER
silene CAMPION
snake bite remedy GUACO
snakeroot SENECA, SENEGA, BUGBANE, BLOLLY
soap AMOLE
sour SOREL
S. Africa ALOE
spinachlike ORACH(E)
spring GORSE
starch-yielding PIA, TARO
stem BINE, CAULIS, SHAFT
joint NODE
tissue PITH
strawberry FRASIER

sun rose CISTUS, ROCKROSE
sweet bay genus LAURUS
sweet flag CALAMUS
tanning SUMAC(H)
tapioca CASSAVA
taro root EDDO(ES)
food from POI
thorny BUR(R), BRIAR, BRIER
tissue, relating to TAPETAL
trailing ARBUTUS
trifoliate SHAMROCK, CLOVER
tropical ALTEA, HAMELIA, TI, PALM, TARO, UDO, AGAVE
American CACOON, FUCHSIA
valerian NARD, HELIOTROPE
vine IVY, LIANA
vinegar flavoring TARRAGON
water ALGA, LOTUS
genus TRAPA
waterside SEDGE, REED
weed DOCK, TARE
wild growing AGRESTIAL
planter SEEDER, FARMER, SETTLER, SOWER
planters, *government by* PLANTOCRACY
plaque BROOCH, MEDAL, TABLET, PLATE, DISK, SLAB, ORNAMENT, BADGE
plash POOL, PUDDLE, LOP, PLOP
plasma QUARTZ, WHEY, SERUM, BLOOD, LYMPH, PROTOPLASM
plaster, *artist's* GESSO
coarse GROUT, PARGET, STUCCO
of paris GESSO
wax CERATE
plasterer's *glue* SIZE
plastic FORMATIVE, SUPPLE, ELASTIC, FLEXIBLE, FICTILE, SOFT, PLIABLE, DUCTILE, CREATIVE, PLIANT, LUCITE, VINYLITE, BAKELITE, ADAPTABLE, IMPRESSIONABLE, WAXY

clay PUG
repair paste SLURRY
plat BRAID, PLOT, MAP, PLAN, WEAVE
plate ILLUSTRATION, PRINT, LITHOGRAPH, LAYER, SHEATH(E), SLAB, FOOD, GRID, SHEET, DISC(US), LAMINA, SCUTE, PATEN, PLAQUE, TILE, DISH, PLATTER, UTENSIL, BASE, TEETH, GLASS, ARMOR
Eucharist PATEN
reptile's SCUTE, CARAPACE, SHELL
shaped like ship NEF
soap frame SESS
storage battery GRID
thin LAMELLA, LAMINA
plateau PLAIN, MESA, DOWNS, TABLELAND, STAGE, SUMMIT, HIGHLAND, PLATFORM, DISH, SALVER
platform ROSTRUM, ESTRADE, BASE, STAND, STAGE, PODIUM, POLICY, PLAN, SHELF, TERRACE, PORCH, DAIS, SCAFFOLD, FORUM, LYCEUM, DECK, PULPIT, ORATION, SCHEME
fort BARBETTE
mining SOLLAR, SOLLER
raised SOLEA, TRIBUNE, DAIS, STAND, PODIUM
platinum *symbol* PT
wire OESE
platitude TRUISM, BROMIDE, CLICHE
platoon UNIT, SQUAD, FORMATION, SUBDIVISION, SET, GROUP, TEAM, COTERIE, VOLLEY
Plato's *idea* EIDOS
knowledge, highest NOESIS
school ACADEME
work APOLOGY, CRITO, GORGIAS, MENO, PHAEDO, REPUBLIC, SOPHIST, TIMAEUS
platter LANX, RECORD, PLATE, DISH, DISK,

TRENCHER, RECORDING
shaped SCUTELLATE
play GAME, JEST, ROMP, FROLIC, FEIGN, (EN)ACT, (MELO)-DRAMA, SPORT, SWEEP, RANGE, RUN, FUN, TOY, SCENARIO, DISPORT, SKIP, FRISK, GAMBOL, REVEL, CAPER, TRIFLE, FLIRT, BET, DALLY, (IM)-PERSONATE, PERFORM, PRANK, PASTIME, COMEDY, TRAGEDY, FARCE, CONTEND, GAMBLE, DIVERSION, AMUSE(MENT), RECREATION, FREEDOM, ROOM, SCOPE, WAGER, EXERCISE, LOOSENESS, SLACK
badly STRUM, THRUM, MIFF, BOBBLE, ERR
complication of NODE
exhibiting STAGE
ground PARK, STADIUM, GRID, FIELD, YARD, COMMONS
mean trick SHAB
on words See "pun"
part in SCENE, SCENA, ROLE, BIT
part of EXODE, SCENE, ACT
silent PANTOMIME
playa BEACH, LAKE, BASIN
player(s) CAST, ACTOR, THESPIAN, STAR, PERFORMER, COMEDIENNE, TRAGEDIENNE, STARLET, IDLER, PIANIST, HARPIST
playing card *See under* "card"
plaything TRIFLE, DIE, BAUBLE, TOY
plea NOLO, SUIT, ENTREATY, REQUEST, EXCUSE, ALIBI, ANSWER, PRAYER, APPEAL, APOLOGY, ALLEGATION, ARGUMENT, PRETEXT, DEFENSE, JUSTIFICATION
to end ABATER
plead BEG, PRAY, SUE, APPEAL, ARGUE, REASON, ALLEGE, APOLOGIZE, REJOIN,

ENTREAT, PETITION, SUPPLICATE, IMPLORE, DEFEND
pleasant GENIAL, WINSOME, PLEASING, GENTLE, MILD, BALMY, KIND(LY), OBLIGING, AMIABLE, AGREEABLE, DELIGHTFUL, ENJOYABLE, SEEMLY, CHEERFUL, GAY, MERRY, AMUSING, GRATIFYING, JOCULAR, PLAYFUL
pleasantness CHEERFULNESS, AMENITY, GAIETY
please LIKE, PREFER, AMUSE, GRATIFY, ELATE, FANCY, WILE, DELIGHT, TICKLE, REGALE, EXALT, GLADDEN, SATISFY, CHOOSE
pleased SUITED, GLAD, HAPPY, GRATEFUL
pleasing ATTRACTIVE, NICE, ROSEATE, SOOTHING, AGREEABLE, ACCEPTABLE, WELCOME, CHARMING, DELIGHTFUL, PLEASANT
pleasure HAPPINESS, GLEE, GREE, GRACE, DELIGHT, JOY, BLISS, ENJOYMENT, SATISFACTION, JOLLITY, HILARITY, AMUSEMENT, SPORT, DIVERSION, DELECTATION, RECREATION, CHARM, GLADNESS
god of BES
pleated PLISSE, SHIRRED, FOLDED, PLAITED
plebiscite VOTE, MANDATE, REFERENDUM
pledge SWEAR, BET, GAGE, PLIGHT, PAWN, OATH, WAGE, TROTH, TOAST, VOW, TOKEN, BOND, BAIL, HOSTAGE, STAKE, HYPOTHECATE, DEPOSIT, COLLATERAL, EARNEST, SECURITY, GUARANTEE, SURETY, MORTGAGE, PROMISE, AFFIANCE, PAROLE

pledget SWAB, PLUG, COMPRESS, STOPPER, WAD

Pleiades ATLANTIDES
constellation TAURUS
daughters of Atlas and Pleione ALCYONE, CELAENO, ELECTRA, MAIA, MEROPE, STEROPE, ASTEROPE, TAYGETA

plenary FULL, COMPLETE, ABSOLUTE

plentiful COPIOUS, AMPLE, FULL, ABUNDANT, RIFE, PROLIFIC, LAVISH, LOTS, GOBS, ENOUGH, SUFFICIENT, FRUITFUL, OPULENT, PROFUSE, EXUBERANT

plenty GALORE, ABUNDANCE, PLENTITUDE, SUFFICIENCY, PROFUSION, AFFLUENCE, LUXURIANCE, AMPLITUDE

plenum PLETHORA, FULL(NESS), ASSEMBLY, SPACE

plethora FULLNESS, REPLETION, SUPERABUNDANCE, REDUNDANCY

plexiform COMPLICATED, INTRICATE, COMPLEX

plexus RETE, NETWORK, TANGLE

pliable WAXY, SOFT, PLIANT, PLASTIC, DUCTILE, MALLEABLE, LITHE, LIMBER, ELASTIC, FLEXIBLE, DOCILE, SUPPLE, YIELDING, ADAPTABLE, WORKABLE, COMPLIANT

pliant LITHE, PLASTIC, PLIABLE, FLEXIBLE, SUPPLE *See* "pliable"

plight SCRAPE, CASE, SITUATION, BETROTH(AL), PICKLE, FIX, JAM, PROMISE, PLEDGE, ENGAGE, PAWN, DILEMMA, PREDICAMENT, ENGAGEMENT, STATE

plinth SOCLE, ORLO, BASE, BLOCK, SUBBASE, SKIRTING, BASEBOARD
flat ORLO

plod TOIL, TRUDGE, SLOG, PEG, DRUDGE, THUD, WORK

plot CABAL, BREW, PACK, TRICK, MACHINATE, INTRIGUE, CONSPIRE, PLAN, CHART, LOT, MAP, PLAT, GRAPH, RUSE, SCENARIO, OUTLINE, DIAGRAM, DRAFT, SCHEME, CONSPIRACY, LOCATION, SITE, CONTRIVE, DEVISE
of a play NODE

plotinus work ENNEADS

plover DROME, SANDY, KILLDEER, PIPING, DOTTEREL, LAPWING, BIRD

plow DIG, TILL, ROVE, CULTIVATE, FURROW, FARM
blade or cutter SHARE, COLTER, COULTER
crosspiece BUCK
handle STILT
sole SLADE
subsoil MOLE
type SULKY, DISC, GANG
wooden part CHIP

plowed *land* ARADO, ARADA

plowland CARUCATE

plowman TILLER, FARMER

plowshare BLADE, COLTER, COULTER

pluck VALOR, GRIT, WILL, GUTS, SAND, FORTITUDE, SPIRIT, METTLE, COURAGE, BRAVERY, DARING, BACKBONE, DETERMINATION, NERVE, PICK, GARNER, STRIP, GATHER, CULL, FLEECE, TWITCH, TWANG

plucky BRAVE, DARING, GAME, NERVY, GRITTY

plug BUNG, TAP, SPILE, BOTT, WEDGE, STOP(PER), CORK, WAD, QUID, PEG, PLEDGET, ESTOP, CALK, CAULK, STOPPLE, OCCLUDE, CLOSE, TOIL, HORSE, JADE, SHOOT, RECOMMEND, BOOST
for cannon muzzle TAMPION
medicine CLOT, EMBOLUS, TAMPON, PLEDGET

plug-ugly ROWDY, THUG, RUFFIAN, GANGSTER

plum DAMSON, GAGE, PRUNE, DRUPE, FRUIT, PRIZE, LOMBOY
coco ICACO
date SAPOTE
dried PRUNE
Europe GAGE, BULLACE
green GAGE
Java JAMBOOL, JAMBUL
sapodilla LANZON, NISPERO, CHICO
seed PIT, PUTAMEN
W. Indies JOBO
wild SLOE

plumage ROBE, FEATHERS, DRESS, DOWN, ADORNMENT

plumbago GRAPHITE, LEAD

plumber PIPER

plume QUILL, FEATHER, EGRET, CREST, AIGRET, PRIDE, PREEN, PANACHE, TUFT

plump STOUT, FAT, BLUNT, CHUBBY, PURSY, TIDY, PLOP, PLUNGE, PORTLY, ROTUND, BURLY, BUXOM, DROP, FALL, SINK, SUDDENLY

plunder REAVE, RIFLE, BOOTY, PILLAGE, LOOT, SPOIL, STRIP, ROB, SACK, MARAUD, PREY, RAVAGE, DESPOIL, RAID, RANSACK

plunderer PIRATE,
RAIDER *See*
"bandit"
plunge FALL,
DIVE, DIP, SOUSE,
SINK, LUNGE,
PITCH, (IM)-
MERSE, SWOOP,
SUBMERGE, GAM-
BLE, HURRY, RUSH
plus AND, EXTRA,
OVER, POSITIVE,
MORE, SUPPLE-
MENTAL, ADDI-
TIONAL
Plutarch *work*
LIVES
Pluto ORCUS, DIS
kingdom of HADES
pluvial RAINY
ply LAYER, FOLD,
THICKNESS, WEB,
FOLLOW, EMPLOY,
SAIL, USE, WIELD,
HANDLE, URGE,
YIELD, COMPLY,
BEND, MOLD,
DOUBLE, WORK,
RUN, SHAPE, EX-
ERT, BENT, BIAS,
INCLINATION
pneuma SOUL,
SPIRIT, BREATH,
NEUME
poach MIX, COOK,
BOIL, STEAL, TRES-
PASS, INTRUDE,
ROB
pochard DUCK,
SMEE, FOWL
pocket BAG, POUCH,
BIN, PURSE, SAC,
CAVITY, VOID,
LODE, SOCKET,
HOLLOW, RECEP-
TACLE, STEAL,
CONCEAL, APPRO-
PRIATE, SUPPRESS,
KEEP, ENCLOSE
French POCHE
pocketbook BAG,
PURSE, MONEY
poco LITTLE,
SOMEWHAT,
SLIGHTLY
pod ARIL, BOLL,
SHUCK, RIND,
CAPSULE, FLOCK,
SCHOOL, SILIQUE,
POUCH, ENVELOPE,
SAC, HERD, COVER-
ING

tanning PIPI
podium DAIS,
PLATFORM
poem RIME,
RHYME, SONNET,
(EP)ODE, VERSE,
LAY, COMPOSITION,
BALLAD, ELEGY
bucolic ECLOGUE,
GEORGIC, IDYL
division CANTO
eight-line TRIOLET
epic EPODE,
EPOPEE, EPOS
fourteen-line SON-
NET
French DIT
heroic EPOS, EPIC
Icelandic EDDA
irregular DITHY-
RAMB
love SONNET
lyric ODE, ALBA
mournful ELEGY
narrative EPIC,
LAY
nonsensical LIM-
ERICK, DOGGEREL
Norse RUNE, SAGA
pastoral IDYL
patchwork CENTO
rural GEORGIC,
ECLOGUE
satirical IAMBIC
six stanzas SESTINA
small ODELET
Poe's *bird* RAVEN
heroine LENORE
poesy VERSE,
POETRY
poet IDYLIST, BARD,
SCOP, ODIST, METRIST,
RIMER, RHYMER,
MINSTREL, TROU-
BADOUR
German HEINE
Norse SCALD,
SKALD
poetaster RIMER,
RHYMER, SCALD,
VERSIFIER, DAB-
BLER *See* "poet"
poetic foot *See*
"metrical"
poetry POESY,
VERSE
division EPIC,
LYRIC, DRAMA,
SATIRE, ODE, ELEGY
early RUNE
god of BRAGI
line of STICH

muse of CALLIOPE,
ERATO, THALIA
poi, *source of* TARO
poignant SHARP,
KEEN, SEVERE,
ACUTE, PIERCING,
PENETRATING,
BITTER, INTENSE,
ACRID, PUNGENT,
STINGING, POINTED,
CUTTING, MOVING,
AFFECTING
point DOT, GIST,
JOT, PERIOD, AIM,
LEVEL, TRAIN,
LAY, STEER, PILOT,
GUIDE, ANGLE,
SLANT, OBJECT,
APEX, PRICKLE,
GOAL, SCORE,
PUNTO, TIP, BARB,
END, ACE, NEB,
FOCUS, SHARPEN,
DAGGER, BODKIN,
PIN, NEEDLE, NAIL,
TACK, PARTICULAR,
ITEM, DETAIL,
HINT, UNIT, SPOT,
LOCALITY, DIRECTION,
COURSE, PROJEC-
TION, FEATURE,
INDICATE
curve NODE
curve of two tangents
CRUNODE
highest APEX,
ZENITH, APOGEE
law RES
lowest NADIR,
PERIGEE
of land SPIT, HOOK
outside curve
ACNODE
pertaining to FOCAL
uniplanar UNODE
pointed AIMED,
TRAINED, LEVELED,
TERSE, BRIEF,
PIQUANT, PUNGENT,
POIGNANT, PIERC-
ING, STINGING,
PERTINENT, CON-
SPICUOUS, MARKED,
SIGNIFICANT, PUR-
POSEFUL, CONCISE,
CUSPATE, SHARP,
CONICAL, PIKED
arch OGEE, OGIVE
as a leaf APICULATE
end CUSP, BARB
missile DART, AR-
ROW

sharp ACUATE
spike PIKE, GOAD,
  SPEAR, ARROW
tip APICULUS
pointer DOG, ROD,
  STICK, HINT
  in synagogue YAD
  teacher's FESCUE,
  CUE
pointless INANE,
  SILLY, BLUNT,
  FLAT, DULL, OB-
  TUSE, VAPID, IN-
  SIPID, SENSELESS,
  MEANINGLESS
poise COMPOSURE,
  BALANCE, TACT,
  ADDRESS, APLOMB,
  DIGNITY, GRACE,
  WEIGH(T), EQUI-
  LIBRIUM, BEARING,
  CARRIAGE, STABIL-
  ITY
poison VIRUS,
  TOXIN, VENOM,
  BANE, GALL, TAINT,
  INFECT, POLLUTE,
  CORRUPT, TOXIC
  arrow INEE,
  WAGOGO See under
  "arrow"
  combining form
  TOXIC(O)
  deadly ARSENIC,
  BANE, INEE, UPAS
  hemlock CONIINE
  ivy genus RHUS
  rat SQUILL
  snake VENOM
poisoned arrow
  INEE, SUMPIT
poisonous TOXIC,
  FATAL, LETHAL,
  VIRULENT, VENOM-
  OUS, MALIGNANT,
  NOXIOUS, DEADLY,
  VIROSE
  alkaloid CONINE,
  CONIN(E), CURARE,
  CURARI
  fish of Japan FUGU
  fungus AMANITA
  gas ARSINE,
  PHOSGENE
  herb HENBANE
  lizard GILA
  plant MANDRAKE
  protein RICIN,
  ABRIN
    in castor bean
    RICIN

tree See under
  "tree"
poke BAG, JAB,
  CORE, HOOK,
  THRUST, PROD,
  PUNCH, PUSH,
  SHOVE, JOG, STIR,
  NUDGE, PRY,
  SEARCH, GROPE,
  POTTER, DAWDLE,
  BORE, INTRUDE,
  MEDDLE, LOITER,
  PUTTER
poker STAFF, ROD,
  STICK, DRAW,
  STUD, GAME
  call in SEE
  counter CHIP
  opener JACKS,
  PAIR
  stake ANTE, POT,
  KITTY
pokeweed SCOKE,
  POCAN, POKE
Poland, Polish
  SLAV, POLE,
  SARMATIA, POLSKA
  cake BABA
  capital WARSAW
  city or town LODZ,
  DANZIG, CRACOW,
  NYSA, PILA, LYCK,
  DUKLA, NAREV,
  OPOLE, TORUN
  coin DUCAT,
  GROSZ, ZLOT(Y),
  ABIA
  commune PLOCK,
  RADOM, RUDA,
  SOPOT, KUTNO
  composer CHOPIN
  dance POLKA
  island WOLIN
  king CONTI
  legislature SEJM
  (DIET), SENAT
  marshes PRIPET
  measure MORG,
  MILA, PRET, CAL
  monetary unit
  ZLOT(Y)
  nobleman STAROST
  river VISTULA,
  BUG, SAN, STYR,
  ODRA, PRIPET
  scientist CURIE
  weight LUT
Poland China HOG,
  PIG, SWINE
pole SPRIT, MAST,
  ROD, AXIS, SLAV,

CABER, PIVOT,
  EXTREMITY, HUB,
  SPAR, POST, SHAFT
  fish ROD, CANE
  memorial, Indian
  XAT
  negative CATHODE
  to pole AXAL,
  AXIAL
  positive ANODE
  rope dancing POY
  symbolic, or tribal
  TOTEM, XAT
polecat ZORIL, FER-
  RET, MUSANG,
  FITCHEW, SKUNK,
  CARNIVORE
polestar POLARIS,
  CYNOSURE, LODE-
  STAR
police(man) LAW,
  COP, BULL, BOBBY,
  PEELER, OFFICER,
  GUARD, WATCH-
  (MAN), CLEAN,
  SPRUCE, PATROL-
  (MAN)
  club BILLY,
  TRUNCHEON
  line CORDON
  organization PAL
  station TANA,
  BARRACKS
polish LUSTER,
  SHINE, BURNISH,
  LEVIGATE, SCOUR,
  BUFF, EMBELLISH,
  PERFECT, RENEW,
  ELEGANCE, GENTIL-
  ITY, CULTURE,
  REFINE(MENT),
  CIVILIZE, FURBISH,
  BRIGHTEN, GLAZE
polished FINE,
  GENTEEL, URBANE,
  GLOSSY, ELEGANT,
  REFINED, SMOOTH,
  SHINY, CIVIL, POLITE,
  LUSTROUS
polisher EMERY
polishing material
  EMERY, RABAT,
  SAND, PUMICE
polite CIVIL, GEN-
  TEEL, URBANE,
  GRACIOUS, GENTLE-
  (MANLY),
  CHIVALROUS,
  GALLANT, SUAVE,
  REFINED, COURTE-
  OUS, CORRECT, CUL-
  TURED, POLISHED

politic DISCREET, ARTFUL, WISE, SHREWD, ASTUTE, SUAVE, SAGACIOUS, EXPEDIENT, WARY, TACTFUL, PROVIDENT, DIPLOMATIC, CAUTIOUS, PRUDENT

political *division* WARD, HUNDRED, COUNTY, STATE, SHIRE, TOWN, CITY, PROVINCE, COMMUNITY NOME

faction BLOC, JUNTA, PARTY, CLAN

group CELL, BLOC

hack HEELER

list SLATE

party TORY, WHIG

poll HEAD, COUNT, LIST, CUT, TRIM

polled HORNLESS, SHORN, SHAVED, POLLARDED, SHAVEN

pollen *bearing* STAMINATE, ANTHERAL

part ANTHER

pollex THUMB, DIGIT, PHALANGE

polloi HOY

Pollux and Castor GEMINI, TWINS, DIOSCURI

Pollux's *brother* CASTOR

mother LEDA

Polo MARCO

polo *stick* MALLET

team FOUR

Polonius' *daughter* OPHELIA

poltroon CRAVEN, DASTARD, COWARD, IGNOBLE, ABJECT, SORRY, MEAN, MILKSOP, RECREANT, SNEAK, WRETCH

polygon, *certain* NGON

equal angles ISAGON

nine sides NONAGON

Polynesian MAORI, KANAKA, MALAYAN

banana FEI

beverage KAVA, KAWA

breech cloth MALO

burial place AHU

butterfly IO

chestnut RATA

clan or tribe ATI

common or profane NOA

creator of man TIKI

dance SIVA

demon ATUA

first man TIKI

fish AUA

food KAI, POI

garment PAREU, MALO

god ORO, MAUI, TANE, ATUA

goddess PELE

Hawaiian KANAKA

herb TARO, PIA

hero MAUI

island FIJI, HAWAII, EASTER, TAHITI, TONGA, U(V)EA, RAPA

loin cloth PAREU

magical power MANA

mound AHU

mulberry bark TAPA

native MAORI, MALAYAN

oven or pit UMU

pigeon LUPE

pine HALA

sky LANGI

stone heap AHU

supernatural force MANA

tree TI, IPIL

wages UTU

yam UBI, UVI

polyp ANEMONE, CORAL, HYDRA, TUMOR, HYDROID

pome PEAR, APPLE, QUINCE, FRUIT, BALL, GLOBE

Pomerania *island* RUGEN, USEDOM

river ODER

pomeranian DOG

pommel BEAT, FLAIL, FLOG, KNOB, CASCABEL, PROTUBERANCE, BRUISE

pomp PARADE, ARRAY, DISPLAY, RITUAL, FORM, SPLENDOR, GRANDEUR, OSTENTATION, SHOW, PRIDE, GLORY, GALA, PAGEANT, CORTEGE, PROCESSION, SPECTACLE, VANITY, VAINGLORY, STRUT, MAGNIFICENCE

pompano ALEWIFE, FISH, POPPYFISH

Pompeii *archeologist* MAU

pompous TURGID, AUGUST, VAIN, GRANDIOSE, FUSTIAN, OSTENTATIOUS

Ponchielli *opera* GIOCONDA

pond POOL, TARN, MERE, LOCHAN, LAKE, LAGOON,

ponder BROOD, MUSE, PORE, REFLECT, MEDITATE, EXAMINE, RUMINATE, WEIGH, THINK, STUDY, CONSIDER, CONTEMPLATE, DELIBERATE, COGITATE

ponderous DULL, ELEPHANTINE, HEAVY, VAST, HEFTY, BULKY, IMPORTANT, MOMENTOUS, WEIGHTY, MASSIVE, LABORED

poniard STYLET, DIRK, DAGGER

Pons LILY

pontiff BISHOP, PRIEST, POPE,

pony CRIB, GLASS, NAG, HORSE, BRONCO, CAYUSE, PINTO, SHETLAND, MUSTANG, SHELTY, TRANSLATION

pooh-pooh DERIDE, BAH, HOOT, DISDAIN

pool GAME, BILLIARDS, MERE, PLASHET, PUDDLE, TANK, TARN, POND, LAGOON, LOCH, RESERVOIR, KITTY,

ANTE, STAKE, CORNER,
CARTEL, COMBINE,
UNDERCUT, UNDER-
MINE, CONTRIBUTE
ball RINGER, EIGHT
  black EIGHT
game PIN, ROTATION,
  STRAIGHT
stick CUE
  support for BRIDGE
poon *tree* DILO
poor NEEDY, INDI-
  GENT, DEFICIENT,
  DESTITUTE, INADE-
  QUATE, WEAK,
  FLIMSY, BAD, SOSO,
  WRONG, UNHAPPY,
  SCANTY, FEEBLE,
  LEAN, THIN, MEA-
  GER, MEAN, IN-
  FERIOR, DEJECTED,
  EMACIATED, BAR-
  REN, STERILE, UN-
  FAVORABLE, UN-
  FORTUNATE, IMPOV-
  ERISHED, SICK(LY)
  John HAKE, COD,
    FISH
  player DUB, SCRUB
pop DAD, CRACK,
  SNAP, BURST, EX-
  PLODE, REPORT,
  CLAP, DETONATION,
  DRINK, SODA
pope RUFF, WEEVIL,
  SHRIKE, BIRD,
  BISHOP, PRIEST,
  PUFFIN
Pope('s) *cathedral*
  LATERAN
  collar ORALE, FANON
  court officer DATARY
  crown TIARA
  family name LEO,
    PIUS, URBAN,
    ADRIAN, PAUL
  letter from BRIEF
  name of 12 PIUS
  palace VATICAN
popinjay FOP, COX-
  COMB, DANDY, MAC-
  ARONI, PARROT,
  WOODPECKER, BIRD
poplar—ABELE, ALAMO,
  ASPEN, TULIP, LOM-
  BARDY, TREE
  Arab GARB, BAHAN
  balsam LIAR
  species BAHAN
  white ABELE
poppy PLANT,

FLOWER, OPIUM,
  CORN *See* "opium"
corn PONCEAU
genus PAPAVER
seed MAW, MOHN
poppycock BOSH, ROT,
  FOLLY, STUFF,
  NONSENSE, TRASH
populace CROWD,
  DEMOS, MOB,
  MASSES, RABBLE,
  COMMONALTY,
  PROLETARIAT,
  PEOPLE
popular ACCEPTED,
  LIKED, GENERAL,
  EPIDEMIC, DEMOTIC,
  COMMON, CURRENT,
  VULGAR, FASHION-
  ABLE, LAY, FAMIL-
  IAR, PLEASING,
  PRAISED, EASY,
  PLAIN, CHEAP,
  INFERIOR, PREV-
  ALENT, PLEBEIAN,
  PROLETARIAN,
  FAVORITE
popularity VOGUE,
  FAME, FAVOR,
  REPUTE, CELEBRITY
Poquelin, Jean Bap-
  tiste MOLIERE
porcelain ENAMEL-
  (WARE), CERAMICS,
  SEVRES, CHINA-
  (WARE), LIMOGES,
  EARTHENWARE
China JU, KO,
  CELADON
English SPODE
ingredient CLAY,
  KAOLIN
porch PORTICO,
  NARTHEX, STOOP,
  STOA, COLONNADE,
  VERANDA(H),
  PIAZZA, LOGGIA,
  GALLERY, ENTRANCE,
  VESTIBULE, PASSAGE,
  LANAI
swing GLIDER
toward west
  GALILEE
porcupine URSON,
  HEDGEHOG, RODENT
fish DIODON
grass genus STIPA
spine QUILL
pore STOMA, OSTIOLE,
  INTERSTICE, CON,
  STUDY, PONDER,
  GAZE, ORIFICE,

OPENING, FORAMEN,
  STARE, READ, RE-
  FLECT, MEDITATE
plant LENTICEL
porgy PARGO, SCUP,
  TAI, BREAM, FISH
pork *chop* GRISKIN
fish SISI
porpoise DOLPHIN,
  PELLOCK, CETACEAN,
  INIA
porridge BROSE,
  ATOLE, GROUT,
  POTTAGE, MUSH,
  POLENTA, BROTH,
  GRUEL, SOUP,
  HODGEPODGE
Porsena LARS
port LARBOARD,
  LEFT, HAVEN,
  HARBOR, REFUGE,
  BAY, COVE, INLET,
  WINE, CARRIAGE,
  MANNER, MIEN,
  BEARING, DEMEANOR,
  OPENING
Black Sea ODESSA
wine city DOURO
  shipping point
    OPORTO
portal GATE, ENTRY,
  POSTERN, OPENING,
  DOOR(WAY), EN-
  TRANCE, PASSAGE-
  WAY, ARCHWAY,
  MOUTH
portcullis GATE, BAR,
  HERSE, GRATING,
  DOOR
portend BODE, AUGUR,
  PRESAGE, OMEN,
  IMPORT, MEAN,
  DENOTE, FOREBODE,
  BETOKEN, FORETELL
portent OMEN, OS-
  TENT, MARVEL,
  SIGN, TOKEN, AUGURY,
  WARNING, PRODIGY
porter ALE, STOUT,
  HAMAL, CARRIER,
  SERVANT, JANITOR,
  GUARD, REDCAP,
  OSTIARY, DOOR-
  KEEPER, ATTENDANT,
  BEARER
portfolio CASE,
  OFFICE, LIST
Portia's *maid* NERISSA
portia *tree* BENDY
portico STOA, AR-
  CADE, PTERON
  See "porch"

inclosed space
PTEROMA, PERI-
DROME
long open VERANDA-
(H), XYST(US)
Roman ATRIUM
wing PTERON
portion DOOM, ALLOT-
(MENT), PARCEL,
RATION, HELPING,
SERVING, INHERIT-
ANCE, FATE, LOT,
DESTINY, DUE,
DOLE, SHARE, PIECE,
METE, PART, SOME,
FRAGMENT, BIT,
SCRAP, SECTION,
MORSEL, DIVISION,
DIVIDEND, QUOTA,
QUANTITY, DOWRY
portrait PAINTING
See "picture"
portray DELINEATE,
DRAW, DESCRIBE,
ACT, FORM, DEPICT,
LIMN *See* "picture"
Portugal, Portuguese
Atlantic islands
AZORES
boat MOLETA
cape ROCA
capital LISBON
old name
LUSITANIA
city or town OPORTO,
OVAR, LISBON, FARO,
EVORA, BRAGA
coin ESCUDO,
PATACA, CONTO,
COROA, CROWN,
TESTONE, DOBRA,
DOBRO
colony (*including
former*) DIU, GOA,
MACAO, TIMOR,
ANGOLA
commune BRAGA
explorer PO, CAO,
DIAZ, REAL *See*
"navigator" *below*
folk tune FADO
lady DONA
legislature CORTES
measure MEIO, BOTA,
SELAMIN, PE, VARA,
FANGA, GEIRA,
MILHA, MOIO, PALMO,
PIPA
monetary unit
ESCUDO
navigator MAGEL-
LAN, GAMA, DIAS

port FARO
province BEIRA,
ALGARVE, EVORA
river MINHO, TAGUS,
TAMEGA, DOURO
territory See
"colony" *above*
title DOM
weight GRAO,
LIBRA, ONCA,
MARCO
pose SIT, AIR, POS-
TURE, AFFECT-
(ATION), QUIZ,
MIEN, AFFIRM,
ASSERT, ATTITUDE,
POSITION, MANNER-
ISM, PUZZLE, BE-
WILDER, PERPLEX,
MYSTIFY, NONPLUS,
BAFFLE, MODEL
posed MODELED, SAT,
ATTITUDINIZED,
PROPOSED, PRO-
POUNDED
Poseidon NEPTUNE
parent CRONOS,
RHEA
poser FACER, STICK-
LER, QUESTION,
PUZZLE, PROBLEM
position POINT,
UBIETY, RANK,
COIGN(E), PLACE,
OFFICE, EMPLOY-
MENT, POST, BERTH,
BILLET, WORK, DUTY,
POSE, SITUS, STANCE,
SPOT, STAND, JOB,
STATION, SITUATION,
LOCALITY, SITE,
LOCUS, ATTITUDE,
POSTURE, BEARING,
STANDING, STATUS,
PROPOSITION, THESIS,
ASSERTION, STATE-
MENT
positive CERTAIN,
AFFIRMATIVE, FIRM,
THETIC, CONSTANT,
PLUS, SURE, REAL,
ACTUAL, DOGMATIC,
ABSOLUTE, EM-
PHATIC, CONFIDENT,
ASSURED, INDISPUTA-
BLE, EXPLICIT,
DEFINITE, PER-
EMPTORY, PHOTO,
ACTIVE, CONCRETE,
DECIDED, MATERIAL,
PRACTICAL, EFFEC-

TIVE, DECISIVE,
UNQUALIFIED
not MINUS
pole ANODE
saying DICTUM
positively CER-
TAINLY, ABSOLUTELY,
ACTUALLY, REALLY,
TRULY, INDUBI-
TABLY, EX-
TREMELY, OBVI-
OUSLY
positivism *founder*
COMTE
possess OCCUPY,
TAKE, OWN, HAVE,
ENJOY, HOLD, KEEP,
INFLUENCE, CON-
VINCE, MAINTAIN
possession, *assume
again* REVEST
legal TITLE, ESTATE
post MARKER, PILLAR,
STAKE, TIMBER,
NEWEL, XAT, OF-
FICE, PLACE, JOB,
BERTH, MAIL,
AFTER, COLUMN,
DISPATCH, HASTE,
STATION, SEND,
SUPPORT, PICKET,
PIER, POSITION,
BILLET, CHAPTER,
QUARTER, MES-
SENGER, PUBLISH,
COURIER, SPEED,
REGISTER, PROP,
ANNOUNCE, AD-
VERTISE, DENOUNCE,
FORT, CAMP, ENTER,
RECORD
for boat rope BOL-
LARD, CAPSTAN
Roman META
turning, airplane race
PYLON
poster SIGN, BILL,
BULLETIN, CARD,
PLACARD, STICKER,
DODGER, COURIER,
BROADSIDE, AF-
FICHE
postern GATE, DOOR,
PORTAL, BACK, SIDE,
PRIVATE, PASSAGE,
LESSER, INFERIOR
postpone SHELVE,
STAY, SUSPEND, DE-
LAY, PROROGUE
ADJOURN, DEFER,
TABLE, SLOW,
SLACKEN, RETARD,

PROCRASTINATE, SUBORDINATE
law REMAND, CONTINUE
postscript P.S., CODICIL
to a poem ENVOY, ENVOI
postulate POSIT, ASK, DEMAND, REQUIRE, ASSUME, SANCTION, SUPPOSITION, NOMINATE, CLAIM, STIPULATE, AXIOM
posture POSE, MOOD, FORM, STANCE, STAND, MIEN, ATTITUDE, POSITION, BEARING, CARRIAGE, SITUATION
figure in praying ORANT
posy NOSEGAY, CORSAGE, BOUQUET, FLOWER, MOTTO, LEGEND
pot CRUSE, JAR, OLLA, LOTA(H), BET, WAGER, STAKE, POOL, ANTE, KITTY, KETTLE, SAUCEPAN, SKILLET, JUG, CROCK, PLANT
chemical ALUDEL
potable ALE, WATER, BEER, BEVERAGE, DRINK(ABLE)
potash ALKALI, SALINE
potassium POTASH
compound ALUM, MURIATE
potato TUBER, OCA, IMO, SPUD, YAM, PLANT
disease CURL, POX
seed part EYE
sweet YAM, OCA
potency VIS, STRENGTH, POWER, MIGHT, EFFICACY, FORCE, INTENSITY, ENERGY, VIGOR, PUISSANCE
potent STRONG, COGENT, MIGHTY, ABLE, LUSTY, STURDY, POWERFUL, INFLUENTIAL, CONVINCING
potential energy ERGAL, LATENCY
pother ADO, ADD, STIR, WORRY, HARASS,

FUSS, BUSTLE, HASTE, PERPLEX, PUZZLE, TUMULT, TURMOIL, FLUTTER, CONFUSION, DISTURBANCE, COMMOTION, BESET, CONFUSE, BEWILDER, EXCITEMENT
potherb CHARD, WORT, KALE, SPINACH
pothook SCRAWL, ROD
potion DOSE, DRAM, DRAUGHT, DRAFT, DRINK, BEVERAGE, MEDICINE
potpourri MEDLEY, OLIO, MIX(TURE), JAR, ANTHOLOGY, PASTICCIO, HODGEPODGE, JUMBLE, SALMAGUNDI, MELANGE, MISHMASH, GALLIMAUFRY, FARRAGO
potsherd SHARD, FRAGMENT, BIT, PIECE, CHIP
potter MESS, TRIFLE, LOITER, PUTTER, DAWDLE, FIDDLE, SAUNTER, IDLE
English SPODE
pottery CERAMICS, DELFT, WARE, UDA, CELADON, PORCELAIN, EARTHENWARE
bit of broken SHARD
clay ARGIL, KAOLIN
in liquid state SLIP
dish RAMEKIN
fragment SHARD
glasslike VITREOUS
glazing term SLIP
Hindu UDA
mineral FELDSPAR
pertaining to CERAMIC
vessel for burning SAGGER
wheel DISK, LATHE, THROW
pouch BURSA, SAC(K), POD, BAG, PURSE, POCKET, SOCKET, MAILBAG
girdle GIPSER

Highlander's SPORRAN
poultry *breed* ANCONA, DORKING, LEGHORN
disease PIP, ROUP
farm HENNERY
pounce SPRING, LEAP, JUMP, GRASP, SEIZE, CLAW, TALON, SWOOP
Pound EZRA
pound RAM, BRAY, BEAT, THUMP, DRUM, STRIKE, COMMINUTE, PULVERIZE, BRUISE, TAMP, TRITURATE, PUMMEL, HAMMER, ASSAIL, WEIGHT
English QUID
pour DECANT, LIBATE, RAIN, FLOW, TEEM, STREAM, ISSUE, DISCHARGE, EMIT, SHED, RADIATE, GUSH
off DECANT
to the gods LIBATE
pourboire TIP, FEE, GIFT, GRATUITY, DOUCEUR
pourpoint GIPON, DOUBLET, JUPON
pout PIQUE, MOUE, MOPE, SULK
poverty DEARTH, LACK, INDIGENCE, PASS, PINCH, PAUCITY, NEED, RAGS, WANT, PENURY, STRAIT, DESTITUTION, PRIVATION, PAUPERISM, DEFICIENCY, SCARCITY, POORNESS, INSUFFICIENCY, TENUITY
powder TALC, DUST, GRIND, CORDITE, COSMETIC, POLLEN, PULVERIZE, TRITURATE
antiseptic BORON, ARISTOL
of aloes PICRA
smokeless FILITE, CORDITE
powdered, *heraldry* SEME
power CAPACITY, ABILITY, TALENT, GENIUS, FACULTY,

CAN, DINT, GIFT,
SWAY, FORCE, JET,
EMPIRE, NATION,
MIGHT, ENERGY,
REIGN, STEAM, ARM,
AUTHORITY, PO-
TENCY, PUISSANCE,
EFFICACY, EFFI-
CIENCY, STRENGTH,
VIGOR, CAPABILITY,
WARRANT, PREROGA-
TIVE, CONTROL
of attorney AGENT,
AUTHORITY
theoretical OD,
ODYL(E)
powerful STURDY,
STRONG, ROBUST,
LEONINE, DRASTIC,
POTENT, ABLE,
CAPABLE, MIGHTY,
CONVINCING, PUIS-
SANT, VIGOROUS,
MUSCULAR, SINEWY,
HERCULEAN, IN-
FLUENTIAL
practical VIRTUAL,
USEFUL, WORKABLE,
UTILE, PRAGMATIC-
(AL), EXPERI-
ENCED, VERSED,
PROFICIENT
example PRAXIS
joke HOAX, HUM-
BUG
practice HABIT,
DRILL, EXERCISE,
USE, WONT, CUS-
TOM, USAGE, MAN-
NER, METHOD,
PURSUIT, EXE-
CUTE, TRAIN, RE-
HEARSE, CONDUCT
for specific purpose
PRAXIS
praedial LANDED,
REAL
Prague PRAHA,
PRAG
prairie MESA,
PLAIN, CAMAS(S),
MEADOW, GRASS-
LAND
chicken GROUSE
clump of trees in
MOTTE
plant CAMAS(S)
State ILLINOIS
wolf COYOTE
praise EXALT, LAUD,
ACCLAIM, EULOGIZE,
EXTOL, KUDOS,

ADORE, APPLAUD,
APPROBATION, BLESS,
COMMEND, FLAT-
TER, GLORIFY,
HONOR, WORSHIP,
APPROVAL,
ENCOMIUM,
PANEGYRIC, TRIB-
UTE, MAGNIFY,
PLAUDIT, APPLAUSE,
COMMEND(ATION)
ascription of GLORIA
hunger for ESURI-
ENCE
prance CAPER,
SPRING, CAVORT,
GAMBOL, DANCE,
BOUND, SWAGGER,
PARADE, PESADE,
TITTUP
prandium REPAST,
DINNER, MEAL
prank JEST, ANTIC,
CAPER, JOG, SHINE,
DIDO, FROLIC, GAM-
BOL, TRICK, ESCA-
PADE, JOKE, ADORN,
BEDIZEN, SPANGLE
prase QUARTZ,
CHALCEDONY
prate GAB, YAP,
RANT *See* "chat-
ter"
prattle CLACK, GAB,
BLATHER *See*
"chatter"
pray BEG, ASK, SUE,
ENTREAT, PLEAD,
BESEECH, INVOKE,
PETITION, IMPLORE,
REQUEST, SOLICIT,
IMPORTUNE, SUP-
PLICATE
Yiddish DAVEN
prayer AVE, BENE,
CREDO, ORISON,
PLEA, SUIT, AP-
PEAL, VESPER,
INVOCATION,
LITANY, MATIN,
ENTREATY, PETI-
TION, REQUEST
beads ROSARY
book BREVIARY,
MISSAL, RITUAL,
PORTAS(S)
form LITANY
last of day COM-
PLIN(E)
Moham. call to
AZAN, ADAN
nine day NOVENA

rug or carpet
ASAN(A)
short GRACE,
BENEDICTION
praying figure
ORANT
preacher PRIEST,
PADRE, RABBI, MIN-
ISTER, PARSON,
See "clergyman"
preachment SERMON,
LECTURE, EXHORTA-
TION, DISCOURSE
prebendary CANON
precede FORERUN,
LEAD, OUTRANK,
EXCEL, ANTECEDE,
ANTEDATE, PREFACE,
INTRODUCE
precedence PRIORITY,
RIGHT, RULE, SUPERI-
ORITY, SUPREMACY,
RANK
preceding ABOVE,
PREVIOUS, PRIOR,
BEFORE, ANTECED-
ENT, PRECEDENT,
ANTERIOR,
PREFATORY, PRE-
LIMINARY, PRECUR-
SORY, EARLIER,
AFORESAID
precept ACT, CODE,
CANON, LAW,
MAXIM, RULE,
ORDER, AXIOM,
TENET, COMMAND,
INJUNCTION, PRIN-
CIPLE, INSTRUCTION,
MANDATE, BEHEST,
CHARGE, ORDI-
NANCE, WARRANT,
WRIT, DIRECTION
Hebrew SUTRA,
TORA(H)
precious DEAR, RARE,
COSTLY, CHOICE,
PRICELESS, VALUA-
BLE, BELOVED,
TREASURED, PAR-
TICULAR, FASTIDIOUS,
EXCELLENT
stone AGATE, OPAL,
JEWEL, RUBY, SARD,
TOPAZ, GEM, DIA-
MOND, SAPPHIRE,
AMETHYST, JADE,
EMERALD
precipice DROP,
BLUFF, CRAG,
LINN, CLIFF, PALI,

DECLIVITY, DESCENT, SLOPE

precipitate HASTE, SUDDEN, ABRUPT, DRIVE, FORCE, SPEED, RASH, HEADLONG, HASTY, HEADY, HURRY, ACCELER-ATE, EXPEDITE, QUICKEN, DISPATCH, IMPETUOUS, HEADSTRONG, IM-PULSIVE

precipitation RAIN, SNOW, SLEET, HAIL

precipitous SHEER, STEEP, HASTY, ABRUPT, HEAD-LONG, RASH, SUD-DEN

rock SCAR, STEEP, CRAG

precis EPITOME, AB-STRACT, SUMMARY

precise FORMAL, EVEN, PRIM, RIGHT, EXACT, ACCURATE, CORRECT, DEFINITE, DISTINCT, STRICT, PUNCTILIOUS, SCRUPULOUS, CERE-MONIOUS, PARTICU-LAR, OVERNICE

preclude (DE)BAR (E)STOP, PREVENT, AVERT, BLOCK, WARD, HINDER, CLOSE, IMPEDE, DETER, RESTRAIN, OBVIATE

preconceive IDEATE, THINK, PLAN, SCHEME, DREAM

precursor CRIER, HERALD, FORERUN-NER, HARBINGER, MESSENGER

predial *See* "praedial"

predicament SCRAPE, PASS, PLIGHT, FIX, JAM, STRAIT, PINCH, PICKLE, STATE, SITUATION, CONDITION, EX-TREMITY, DILEMMA, QUANDARY, CORNER, HOLE

predict FORETELL, AUGUR, BODE, OMEN, WARN, DIVINE, PROPHESY,

PRESAGE, PROGNOS-TICATE, SOOTHSAY, BETOKEN, FORECAST

predictor SEER, SAGE, SOOTHSAYER, FORECASTER

predispose SWAY, DISPOSE, TEND, IN-FLUENCE

predisposed PRONE, BIASED, PARTIAL, SOLD

preeminent CHIEF, PALMARY, SUPREME, PARAMOUNT, OUT-STANDING, SUPERIOR, PROMINENT, CELE-BRATED, EXCEL-LENT, PEERLESS, UNEQUALED, DISTINGUISHED, CONSUMMATE, TRANSCENDENT

preen PRIMP, PERK, PLUME, DRESS, SPRUCE, PRINK, TRIM, SMOOTH, PRIDE

preface OPEN, PREAMBLE, FRONT, PROEM, PRAYER, HERALD, BEGIN-(NING), ISAGOGUE, PROLUSION, INTRO-DUCTION, FOREWORD, PROLOGUE, PRELIMI-NARY, EXORDIUM, PRELUDE, BLESSING

prefecture, *Chinese* FU

Japanese KEN

prefer CHOOSE, (S)-ELECT, OPT, PICK, CULL, PROMOTE, FANCY, FAVOR, ADVANCE, RAISE, EXALT, OFFER, PRESENT, RECOM-MEND, LIKE

preference TASTE, LIKE, CHOICE, OPTION, FAVOR, PREDILECTION, FAVORITE, PRIOR-ITY, PICK

prefigure AUGUR, FORETELL, FORE-SHADOW, IMAGINE, SIGNIFY, INDICATE *See* "predict"

prefix *See word in-volved*

prejudice PARTIAL-ITY, LEANING,

FAVOR, BIAS, PREDI-LECTION, PREPOS-SESSION, DETRIMENT, PRESUMPTION

prelate PRIMATE, BISHOP, INGE, ARCH-BISHOP, CARDINAL, POPE, PONTIFF, ECCLESIASTIC, DIGNITARY, CLERIC

preliminary PREFA-TORY, FIRST, PROEMIAL, INTRO-DUCTORY, PRECUR-SORY *See* "preface"

prelude OVERTURE, PROEM, BEGINNING *See* "preface"

premature PRECO-CIOUS, UNSEASON-ABLE, UNTIMELY, PRECIPITATE, EARLY, UNRIPE

premise BASIS, CONDITION, PROP-OSITION, PRESUP-POSITION

premises GROUNDS, LAND, DATA, BUILD-INGS, DIGS

premium FEE, BONUS, AGIO, STAKE, PRIZE, AWARD, MEED, REWARD, RECOMPENSE, REMUNERATION, GUERDON, GIFT, BOUNTY, PAYMENT, LAGNIAPPE

preoccupied EN-GROSSED, LOST, ABSENT, ABSORBED, INATTENTIVE, ABSTRACTED, DREAMING, MUSING, UNOBSERVANT

prepare GIRD, FIT, FIX, PAVE, TRAIN, PRIME, ARRANGE, READY, EQUIP, ADAPT, ARM, AD-JUST, QUALIFY, INSTRUCT, PROVIDE, COMPOUND, PLAN

for the press EDIT, REVISE, REDACT

prepaschal era LENT

preposition EX-CEPT, BY, TO, IN, AT, UNTO, INTO, UPON, FOR, ON, OUT, OF, WITH, FROM, UNTIL presage BODE, OMEN, DIVINE, PORTEND, BETOKEN, PROPHESY, FOREBODE, FORETELL, PREDICT, SOOTHSAY, AUGUR, PROGNOSTICATE, FORECAST

prescribe ALLOT, ORDAIN, SET, URGE, DICTATE, DIRECT, RESTRAIN, CONFINE, OUTLAW, INVALIDATE, CONTROL, ADVOCATE, ORDER, ENJOIN, ADVISE, RECOMMEND

present CONFER, OFFER, TENDER, EXHIBIT, DISPLAY, GRANT, AWARD, CITE, DONATE, NOW, SHOW, FAVOR, BESTOW, BOON, GIFT, GIVE, LAGNIAPPE, DONATION, BENEFACTION, GRATUITY, LARGESS, DOUCEUR, BONUS, EXISTENT, ACTUAL, CONTEMPORARY, INTRODUCE, DELIVER, CONVEY, EXISTING
belonging to the CURRENT
time NONCE, NOW, TODAY

presently SOON, NOW, ANON, SHORTLY, IMMEDIATELY, DIRECTLY, FORTHWITH, CONSEQUENTLY

preservative VINEGAR, ALCOHOL, CREOSOTE

preserve PARK, JAM, CURE, TIN, CORN, SAVE, RESCUE, DELIVER, PROTECT, GUARD, JELLY, CONSERVE, MAINTAIN, KEEP, STORE, RESERVE, SANCTUARY, CAN, PICKLE, MARMALADE, MAINTAIN, RETAIN, UPHOLD, SHIELD, SPARE, DRY
in brine CORN, SALT, PICKLE
in oil MARINATE
President, U.S. *See under* "America"

nickname IKE, CAL, TEDDY, ABE
press CLOSET, WEDGE, CRAM, SQUEEZE, STAMP, CROWD, CLASP, IRON, FORCE, THRONG, URGE, SERRY, GOAD, CRUSH, COMPRESS, SMOOTH, FLATTEN, EMBRACE, CONSTRAIN, COMPEL, ENTREAT, STRAITS, DISTRESS, CUPBOARD, NEWSPAPERS, INSIST, HARASS
down TAMP, STOMP
famous ALDINE
together SERRY, BIND, BALE
pressing URGENT, EXIGENT, EXACTING, IMPORTUNATE, CRITICAL, RUSHING, IMPORTANT
pressure STRESS, STRAIN, INSTANCY, WEIGHT, RUSH, HURRY, FORCE, INFLUENCE, THRUST, COMPRESSION, SQUEEZING, OPPRESSION, DISTRESS, URGENCY, DISPATCH, CONSTRAINT, SQUEEZE, BURDEN
unit MESOBAR, ATMO, BARAD
prestige INFLUENCE, FAME, NOTE, BIAS, GLORY, POWER, CREDIT, ECLAT, RENOWN, REPUTATION, AUTHORITY
presumptive BRASH, ARROGANT, ICARIAN, DUE, PROBABLE, INFERRED, ASSUMED, SUPPOSED
presumptuous BRASH, BOLD, ARROGANT, INSOLENT, SASSY, SAUCY, BRASSY
pretend POSE, CLAIM, FEIGN, SIMULATE, ASSUME, SHAM, LIE, FAKE, AFFECT, CLOAK, MASK, DISSEMBLE, COUNTERFEIT

pretender COWAN, IDOL, SNOB, FRAUD, HYPOCRITE, QUACK, CLAIMANT, FAKER, DECEIVER
pretense CLAIM, PLEA, EXCUSE, CLOAK, FRAUD, AIR, COLOR, SHOW, ACT, POSE, RUSE, SHAM, CANT, FEINT, PRETEXT, SEMBLANCE, SIMULATION, SUBTERFUGE, FABRICATION, MAKESHIFT, ARTIFICE, AFFECTATION
pretentious GAUDY, ARTY, VAIN, SHOWY, ASSUMING, PRESUMING, AFFECTED, UNNATURAL, CONSPICUOUS, OSTENTATIOUS, TAWDRY, CONCEITED, POMPOUS, HAUGHTY
pretermit NEGLECT, OMIT, INTERRUPT, INTERMIT, SUSPEND, PASS
pretty BONNY, FAIR, COMELY, JOLI(E), WINSOME, DAINTY, PETITE, PLEASING, ATTRACTIVE, GOOD, FINE, EXCELLENT, MODERATELY
prevail DRIVE, SWAY, MOVE, ACTUATE, REIGN, BE, RULE, OBTAIN, WIN, EXIST, DOMINATE, INDUCE, OVERCOME, TRIUMPH, PREDOMINATE, SUCCEED, PERSUADE, INFLUENCE, MASTER
prevalent POPULAR, CUSTOMARY, CURRENT, USUAL, GENERAL, WIDESPREAD, RIFE, PREDOMINANT, SUCCESSFUL, EFFICACIOUS, EXTANT, INDIGENOUS
prevaricate EVADE, LIE, PALTER, CAVIL, QUIBBLE, FIB, DODGE, EQUIVOCATE, PETTIFOG, DEVIATE

prevent WARD, FOIL, BALK, THWART, DAM, WARN, FORESTALL, (E)STOP, (DE)BAR, AVERT, DETER, CHECK, OBSTRUCT, HINDER, PROHIBIT, IMPEDE, RESTRAIN, PRECLUDE, OBVIATE, INTERCEPT

legally ESTOP, DE-BAR, FORECLOSE

previous ERST, PRIOR, DONE, BE-FORE, PAST, OVER, FIRST, ANTECEDENT, FORMER, ANTERIOR, PRECEDING, FORE-GOING, PREMATURE, UNTIMELY, EARLIER

prey LOOT, ROB, SPOIL, VICTIM, KILL, QUARRY, PLUNDER, RAVIN, PRIZE, DEP-REDATION, RAVAGE, PILLAGE, RAPINE

bird of See under "bird"

upon FEED, RAVIN, RAVEN

Priam's *daughter* CASSANDRA

grandfather ILUS

son HECTOR, PARIS, TROILUS

wife HECUBA

price FARE, TOLL, RATE, COST, SUM, VALUE, WORTH, CHARGE, OUTLAY, EXPENSE, AMOUNT, CONSIDERATION, SACRIFICE

prick GAD, PIERCE, QUALM, SPUR, STICK, STING, WOUND, GOAD, BORE, DRILL, PERFORATE, PUNC-TURE, INCITE, URGE, REMORSE, STAB, PRICKLE

pricket BUCK, CANDLESTICK, DEER, SPIKE

prickle BRIAR, SPICULA, SETA, BARB, THORN, BUR(R), SPINE, ACANTHA, PRICK, POINT, PIERCE,

PROD, STING, TINGLE, SPICULE, BRISTLE

prickly SPINY, MURICATE, ECHI-NATE, THORNY, VEXATIOUS, SENSI-TIVE, HORRENT

animal HEDGEHOG, PORCUPINE

heat LICHEN, RASH, ACNE

pear NOPAL

plant NETTLE, NOPAL, CACTUS

seed coat BUR(R)

shrub BRIAR, ROSE

pride PLUME, PREEN, CONCEIT, VANITY, EGOTISM, AIRS, HAUGHTINESS, ARRO-GANCE, LORDLINESS, INSOLENCE, DISDAIN, OSTENTATION, DIS-PLAY, PIQUE, VAIN-GLORY

"Pride and Prejudice" *author* AUSTEN

character in DARCY, ELIZABETH

priest CURE, DRUID, ORATOR, ABBE, RABBI, LAMA, PADRE, CLERGYMAN, MIN-ISTER, DIVINE, PAS-TOR, PRESBYTER, EC-CLESIASTIC, HIERO-PHANT

army CHAPLAIN, PADRE

assistant ACOLYTE

cap BIRETTA

Celtic DRUID

Greek HIEROPHANT

Greek Catholic church PAPA

high AARON, ELI, PONTIFF

Jewish RABBI

mantle COPE, CAS-SOCK

Moham. IMA(U)M

Moro SARIP, PAN-DITA, PANDITO

neckpiece AMICE, STOLE

object URIM

office MATIN

of mysteries MYST

scarf MANIPLE, RABAT

surplice EPHOD

Tibetan LAMA

vestment ORALE, ALB, SCAPULAR

white collar AMICE

priestly SACERDOTAL, PONTIFICAL, HIERAT-IC(AL), CLERICAL

priestess, *Greek* AUGE

Roman VESTAL

priesthood, *Roman* SALII

prig PRIM, SMUG, PRUDE, FOP, THIEF, PILFERER, BUCK, DANDY, PRECISIAN

prim PRUDISH, SMUG, PROPER, PRECISE, NEAT, PRIG(GISH), DECOROUS, FORMAL, STIFF, STRAIT-LACED, SEDATE, FASTIDIOUS, PROUD

prima donna DIVA, LEAD, STAR, AC-TRESS

primary CHIEF, INI-TIAL, FIRST, ORIGI-NAL, FUNDAMENTAL, ELEMENTAL, PRIME-VAL, ELECTION, VOTE, PRIMITIVE, ABORIGINAL, PRIME, PRIMORDIAL, PRIS-TINE, FIRSTHAND, RADICAL, PRINCIPAL, LEADING

primate APE, MON-KEY, LEMUR, MAR-MOSET, MAN, ELDER, PRELATE, EXARCH, PATRIARCH, ARCH-BISHOP

prime FIRST, CHIEF, MAIN, BEST, FINEST, FRESH, VIGOROUS, CHARGE, PREPARE, TEACH, COACH, EX-CELLENT *See* "primary"

of life BLOOM, SPRING, HEYDAY

primer HORNBOOK, BOOK, CAP, TYPE, WAFER

primeval OLD, PRIS-TINE, NATIVE, AN-CIENT, FIRST *See* "primary"

primitive CRUDE, QUAINT, FIRST, PRIS-TINE, ORIGINAL, AN-CIENT, EARLIEST, PRIMARY, BASIC

PRIMEVAL, SIMPLE, PREHISTORIC, ANTIQUATED, UNSOPHISTICATED, WILD, PRIMORDIAL, ABORIGINAL, OLD

primordial ORIGINAL, FUNDAMENTAL, FIRST, PRIMITIVE, PRIMEVAL

primordium ANLAGE, EMBRYO, ORIGIN, BEGINNING, RUDIMENT, COMMENCEMENT

primrose OXLIP, COWSLIP, PRIMULA, POLYANTHUS, FLOWER

primp DRESS, PRINK *See* "preen"

prince RULER, CHIEF, LEADER, SATRAP, SOVEREIGN, MONARCH, DAUPHIN, PEER, NOBLE

Black EDWARD

Crown, Eng. WALES

of Darkness DEVIL, SATAN

of liars PINTO

opera IGOR

of the sonnet JOACHIM

Slavic KNEZ

principal CAPITAL, ARCH, CAPTAIN, TOP, HEAD, MAIN, CHIEF, TEACHER, FIRST, LEADING, HIGHEST, PRIME, FOREMOST, GREAT, ESSENTIAL, OUTSTANDING, IMPORTANT, PRIMARY, ORIGINAL

principality MONACO

principle TRUTH, LAW, RULE, TENET, BELIEF, ESSENCE, DOCTRINE, THEORUM, PRANA, SOURCE, ORIGIN, BASIS, CAUSE, FACULTY, ENDOWMENT, MAXIM, AXIOM, POSTULATE, CHARACTER

accepted AXIOM

prink PREEN, PRIMP, PRUNE

print MARK, PICTURE, PHOTO, DESIGN, ETCHING, FABRIC, STAMP, PUBLISH

printer's *direction* STET, DELE, CUT

error TYPO

helper AID, DEVIL

ink pad DABBER

mark See under "mark"

measure EM, EN, QUAD

mistake TYPO, PIE

plate STEREO

type mixed PIE, PI

printing EDITION

form DIE, CUT, FRAME

frame FRISKET, CHASE

hand instrument BRAYER, ROLLER

mark See under "mark"

metal block QUAD

mistake ERRATUM

press part PLATEN, ROUNCE

roller PLATEN, BRAYER

prior PAST, FORMER, ANTERIOR, ANTECEDENT, PRECEDING, EARLIER, PREVIOUS, FOREGOING, PRECURSORY, SUPERIOR, PRECEDENT, CLERIC, MONK, PRIEST

Priscilla's *husband* ALDEN, JOHN

prism PORRO

prison CLINK, BARS, JUG, CELL, COOP, QUOD, CAGE, PEN, STIR, BASTIL(L)E, GAOL *See* "jail"

Federal ATLANTA, ALCATRAZ, LEAVENWORTH, LEWISBURG

French BASTILLE

Latin for CARCER

London NEWGATE, GAOL

naval or ship's BRIG

sentence RAP

spy MOUTON

prisoner CON(VICT), JAILBIRD, LIFER, CAPTIVE

prissy NICE, PRECISE, PRIM, SISSIFIED, FINICKY

pristine EARLY, PRIMITIVE, PRIMEVAL, FRESH,

NEW, PURE, UNTOUCHED, UNSPOILED *See* "primary"

private PRIVY, COVERT, ESOTERIC, SECRET, SOLDIER, CONFIDENTIAL, SECLUDED, RETIRED, SEQUESTERED, PERSONAL, SEPARATE, SOLITARY, SPECIAL, HIDDEN

combining form IDIO

privateer PIRATE, KIDD, VESSEL, COMMANDER, CRUISE

privation LOSS, WANT, NEED, PINCH, STRAIT, POVERTY, DEPRIVATION, DESTITUTION, INDIGENCE, HARDSHIP

privet IBOTA, SHRUB, IBOLIUM

family OLIVE

fence HEDGE

privilege RIGHT, BOON, CLAIM, TITLE, PERMISSION, LIBERTY, FAVOR, CHARTER, FRANCHISE, PREROGATIVE, LICENSE, ADVANTAGE, EXEMPTION, PATENT, IMMUNITY, POWER, COPYRIGHT

English law SOC, SOKE

privy seal SIGNET

prize STAKE, REWARD, BONUS, AWARD, MEED, PALM, MEDAL, LOOT, SWAG, BOOTY, HONOR, TROPHY, CUP, LAURELS, PREMIUM, PLUM, LEVER, ESTEEM, CHERISH, CAPTURE

lottery TERN, PURSE

money PURSE, AWARD, STAKE, REWARD

pro FOR, CON, AYE, YES, AFFIRMATIVE, PROFESSIONAL, EXPERT

probability ODDS, FAVOR, VANTAGE, EXPECTATION, LIKE-

LIHOOD, CREDIBIL-
ITY, CHANCE, PRE-
SUMPTION, PROSPECT
probation TEST,
TRIAL, PAROLE, EX-
AMINATION
probe PROD, STAB,
SEARCH, TEST, SIFT,
INQUEST, PIERCE,
TRY, INVESTIGATE,
INVESTIGATION, IN-
QUIRY, EXAM(INA-
TION), DIG, SCRUTI-
NIZE, EXPLORE,
MEASURE
surgical STYLET,
TENT, ACUS
probity INTEGRITY,
HONESTY
problem PROPOSITION,
POSER, NUT, CRUX,
KNOT, RIDDLE,
ENIGMA, PUZZLE,
QUESTION, TOPIC,
MATTER, SITUATION
proboscis SNOUT,
TRUNK, NOSE, BEAK,
NIB, NEB, LORUM
monkey KAHA(U)
section LORE,
LORUM
Procavia HYRAX
one of CONY, DA-
MAN
proceed(s) (A)RISE,
GO, MOVE, RESULT,
ENSUE, FOLLOW,
ACT, FLOW, SPRING,
ISSUE, STEM,
WEND, PROCESS,
ADVANCE, CON-
TINUE, EMANATE,
CASH
proceeding STEP,
ACT, TRIAL, ACTION,
AFFAIR, DEED,
TRANSACTION, MEAS-
URE, EVENT
process WRIT, OR-
DER, COURSE,
METHOD, ADVANCE,
GROWTH, PROCE-
DURE, PROGRESS, IS-
SUANCE, EMANA-
TION, OUTGROWTH,
EXTENSION, MAN-
DATE, WARRANT,
PROJECTION
in organisms
MEIOSIS
procession TRAIN,
CORTEGE, FILE,

LITANY, PARADE,
MOTORCADE, RET-
INUE, CAVALCADE,
MARCH, GROUP,
FORMATION,
CEREMONY
prochein NEXT,
NEAREST, CLOSEST
proclaim CRY, AN-
NOUNCE, PUBLISH,
HERALD, VOICE,
VENT, UTTER,
PROMULGATE, DE-
CLARE, TELL,
ADVERTISE, TRUM-
PET, CIRCULATE,
BROADCAST,
MANIFEST, BLAZE,
REVEAL, NOTIFY
proclamation
AVOWAL, EDICT,
NOTICE, ANNOUNCE-
MENT, BLAZON,
PUBLICATION,
DECREE, MANI-
FESTO, ORDER,
LAW, NOTIFICATION
proclivity BENT,
BIAS, TENDENCY,
PRONENESS,
DISPOSITION
Procne's *husband*
TEREUS
procrastination
DELAY, INACTIVITY
procure BUY, HIRE,
GET, EFFECT,
GAIN, WIN, EARN,
ATTAIN, ACQUIRE,
OBTAIN, PURCHASE,
BORROW, CONTRIVE,
CAUSE
prod GOAD, URGE,
POKE, EGG, PRICK,
INCITE, THRUST,
DIG, REMINDER,
AWL, SKEWER
prodigal LAVISH,
SPENDER, LUSH,
AMPLE, LIBERAL,
EXTRAVAGANT,
UNRESTRAINED,
LUXURIANT,
SQUANDERING,
SPENDTHRIFT,
WASTER, PROFUSE,
WASTEFUL, RECK-
LESS
prodigy MARVEL,
MIRACLE, WONDER
produce BREED,
FORM, SHAPE,

CREATE, ENGENDER,
GENERATE, MAKE,
RAISE, GOODS,
YIELD, CROPS,
CAUSE, CARRY, EX-
HIBIT, SHOW, BEGET,
CONCEIVE, PRO-
CREATE, HATCH,
BEAR, FURNISH,
ORIGINATE, AC-
COMPLISH, MANU-
FACTURE, FABRI-
CATE, FASHION,
STOCK, MERCHAN-
DISE
product EFFECT,
HARVEST, RESULT,
WORKS, OPUS,
PROCEEDS, YIELD,
CROPS, FRUIT,
PRODUCE, GAIN,
RETURNS, PRODUC-
TION, OUTCOME,
ISSUE, CONSEQUENCE
proem PREAMBLE,
PREFACE, PRELUDE,
INTRODUCTION,
EXORDIUM, FORE-
WORD, PROLEGOME-
NON
profane VIOLATE,
DEFILE, POLLUTE,
DESECRATE, TEM-
PORAL, WORLDLY,
WICKED, UNGODLY
profess TEACH, AF-
FIRM, AVOW, OWN,
ADMIT, ACKNOWL-
EDGE, DECLARE,
PRETEND, PRACTICE,
FOLLOW, OBSERVE,
AVOUCH, (PRO)-
CLAIM, ALLEGE,
STATE
profession METIER,
CAREER, WORK,
ART, CRAFT, TRADE,
LAW, BAR, EMPLOY-
MENT, CALLING,
BUSINESS, DECLARA-
TION, PROTESTATION,
AVOWAL, FAITH,
RELIGION, OCCUPA-
TION, VOCATION
proficient SKILLED,
ADEPT, APT, EX-
PERT, VERSED,
DEXT(E)ROUS, CON-
VERSANT, COM-
PETENT, QUALIFIED,
ABLE, SKILLFUL

profile OUTLINE, SIZE, SHAPE, CONTOUR, FORM, DRAWING, GRAPH, CURVE, FIGURE, SILHOUETTE

profit BENEFIT, RETURN, GAIN, AVAIL, BOOT, MEND, NET, ADVANTAGE, VALUE, FRUIT, LUCRE, USE, SERVICE, INCREASE, WINNINGS

profitable FAT, GAINFUL, PAYING, BENEFICIAL, LUCRATIVE, ADVANTAGEOUS, PRODUCTIVE, REMUNERATIVE, USEFUL, HELPFUL, GOOD

profound DEEP, ABSTRUSE, RECONDITE, INTENSE, HEAVY, ABYSMAL, THOROUGH, EXHAUSTIVE, WISE, FATHOMLESS, LEARNED, ERUDITE, MYSTERIOUS, OCCULT, PENETRATING, SAGACIOUS

profuse LAVISH, LUSH, COPIOUS, LIBERAL, PRODIGAL, ABUNDANT, EXTRAVAGANT, EXUBERANT, BOUNTIFUL, WASTEFUL, OVERFLOWING, SPREADING

progeny SEED, ISSUE, CHILD(REN), OFFSPRING, SCION, DESCENDANTS, OFFSHOOT, RACE, FAMILY

prognosticate AUGUR, OMEN, PREDICT, DIVINE, FORETELL, PROPHESY, (FORE)BODE, FORECAST

program DRAFT, OUTLINE, CARD, MENU, EDICT, LIST, SYLLABUS, AGENDA, PLAN, ADVANCE, SCHEDULE, NOTICE, PROCLAMATION, PROSPECTUS, CATALOG(UE), PLAYBILL

progress ADVANCE, MOVE, DRIVE, RISE, GAIN, GROW(TH), MARCH, JOURNEY, TOUR, EXPEDITION, RATE, CIRCUIT, MOVEMENT, DEVELOPMENT, MOTION
planned TELESIS, TELESIA

prohibit (E)STOP, (DE)BAR, TABOO, TABU, VETO, FORBID, SHUT, ENJOIN, BAN, CURB, CHECK, HINDER, PREVENT, PRECLUDE, INTERDICT, EXCLUDE

prohibited ILLICIT, UNLAWFUL, TABU

prohibiting VETITIVE

prohibition TABOO, TABU, BAN, VETO

project PROTRUDE, BEETLE, JUT, JET, HURL, PITCH, PLAN, SCHEME, PLOT, PURPOSE, FLING, THROW, CONTRIVE, DEVISE, DESIGN, PATTERN, PROPOSAL, INTENTION, BULGE

projectile BOMB, MISSILE, ROCKET, BALL, BULLET, SHELL, SPEAR, ROCK, ARROW

projection PRONG, SNAG, CAM, SHELF, LEDGE, BARB, EAR, BULGE, FIN, LOBE, ARM, TOOTH, PROTUBERANCE, PROTRUSION, SPUR, JUTTY, DESIGN, SCHEME, PLAN

prolate, *opposed to* OBLATE

prolific TEEMING, FRUITFUL, FERTILE, FECUND, PROLIFEROUS, GENERATIVE, REPRODUCTIVE, PROPAGATIVE

prolix LONG, TEDIOUS, WEARISOME, PLEONASTIC, WORDY, VERBOSE, PROTRACTIVE, LENGTHY, TIRESOME, DIFFUSE,

LONGWINDED, EXTENDED

prolocutor ORATOR, ADVOCATE, CHAIRMAN, SPEAKER, SPOKESMAN

prolong LAST, ENDURE, PERSIST, PROTRACT, INCREASE, EXTEND, LENGTHEN, CONTINUE, SUSTAIN, POSTPONE, DETER

prom DANCE, PARTY, PROMENADE, BALL

promenade ALAMEDA, MALL, MARINA, PASEO, PRADO, GALLERY, WALK, PARADE, RIDE, DRIVE, PROM, BALL, DANCE, DISPLAY

prominence FAME, SALIENCE, PRESTIGE, EMINENCE, DISTINCTION, PROTUBERANCE, PROJECTION, CONSPICUOUSNESS, CELEBRITY *See* "promontory"

prominent SALIENT, SIGNAL, CHIEF, MAIN, OBVIOUS, HIGH, DISTINCT, PROTUBERANT, MARKED, OUTSTANDING, MANIFEST, NOTICEABLE, DISTINGUISHED, CELEBRATED, JUTTING, CONSPICUOUS

promise (A)VOW, HOPE, PLEDGE, PLIGHT, AGREE(MENT), CONSENT, ASSURE, DECLARATION, WORD, OATH, PAROLE, CONTRACT, EARNEST, FORETOKEN, ENGAGE(MENT), OFFER

promissory note PLEDGE, CHECK, IOU

promontory SPIT, CAPE, MOUNT, NESS, SKAW, LAND, POINT, CLIFF, NOUP, HEADLAND, PROMINENCE, JUTLAND, PROJECTION

promote SPEED, ASSIST, AID, BOOST,

FOSTER, ADVANCE,
INCREASE, AVAIL,
NURSE, HELP,
EXALT, IMPROVE,
ELEVATE, RAISE,
PREFER, FORWARD,
FURTHER, ENCOUR-
AGE, PATRONIZE,
DIGNIFY, GRADUATE
promotion ADVANCE-
MENT, RAISE,
BREVET, PREFER-
MENT, GRADUATION
prompt CUE, ANI-
MATE, EASY, SOON,
YARE, READY,
QUICK, APT, ADVISE,
EARLY, TELL,
ALERT, MOVE, URGE,
SPEEDY, SWIFT,
PUNCTUAL, EX-
PEDITIOUS, RE-
MIND(ER), IN-
STIGATE, INCITE,
PROVOKE, INSPIRE,
INDUCE, IMPEL
prompter AID, CUER,
READER
promulgate PRO-
CLAIM, PUBLISH,
ANNOUNCE, DE-
CLARE
prone DISPOSED,
ADDICTED, LIABLE,
OPEN, ABED, LEVEL,
APT, FLAT, LIKELY,
PROSTRATE, SUPINE,
INCLINED, PREDIS-
POSED, READY,
WILLING, RE-
CUMBENT, TENDING,
HORIZONTAL
face down PROS-
TRATE, FELL
face up SUPINE,
PASSIVE, DECUBITUS
prong FORK, NIB,
PEG, FANG, TINE,
HORN, ANTLER,
BRANCH, POINT
pronghorn CABREE,
CABRET, RUMINANT
pronoun ME, ITS,
YOU, HE, SHE, IT,
ANY, MINE, OUR(S),
MY, YOUR(S), HIM,
HER(S), WE, THOU,
THEE, THINE, YE,
THEY, THEIR, THEM
demonstrative THIS,
THAT, THESE,
THOSE

indefinite SOME,
ANY, ONE, EACH,
NONE, ALL,
BOTH
interrogative
WHO, WHAT, WHICH
personal YOU, HE,
SHE, WE, THEY, IT
pronounce DECLARE,
ARTICULATE, AF-
FIRM, ASSERT, UT-
TER, STRESS, SPEAK,
SAY, DELIVER,
DECLAIM, AN-
NOUNCE, SPECIFY,
RECITE, STATE
indistinctly SLUR
pronouncement(s)
DICTA, DICTUM,
OPINION, JUDGMENT,
ORDER, REMARK,
DECLARATION
pronunciation, *correct*
ORTHOEPY,
PHONOLOGY
proof ORDEAL, TRIAL,
TEST, EVIDENCE,
GROUND, REASON,
DEMONSTRATION,
CERTIFICATION,
ATTESTATION,
VERIFICATION,
TESTIMONY, CON-
FIRMATION, COR-
ROBORATION,
STRENGTH, DRAFT
proofreader's *mark*
DELE, CARET, STET,
TR
prop BRACE, GIB,
NOG, STAFF, HELP,
STAY, SHORE, RANCE,
STANCHION, STILT,
BOLSTER, TRUSS,
SUPPORT, ENCOUR-
AGE, UPHOLD, SUS-
TAIN, STRENGTHEN,
POLE, STAKE, COL-
UMN, UPRIGHT
propel MOVE, DRIVE,
FORCE, GUN, REV,
SHOVE, URGE, PUSH
propeller FIN, FAN,
OAR, DRIVER, BLADE,
SCREW, PROP, PAD-
DLE
propensity BENT,
INCLINATION,
TENDENCY
proper SEDATE,
WELL, MEET, RIGHT,
PRIM, FIT, DUE, APT,

DECENT, NICE, PE-
CULIAR, FITTING,
ACCURATE, SUITED,
ADAPTED, DISTINC-
TIVE, APPROPRIATE,
SUITABLE, PERTI-
NENT, EXACT, AP-
PLICABLE, CORRECT,
DECOROUS
property GOODS,
MONEY, RESOURCES,
WEALTH, QUALITY,
ASSET, TRAIT,
ESTATE, ATTRIBUTE,
POWER, CHATTEL,
LAND(S), CHARAC-
TERISTIC, POSSES-
SION(S), HOLD-
ING(S), BUILD-
ING(S), PECULIAR-
ITY, OWNERSHIP
act to regain RE-
PLEVIN
deceased wife's to
husband CURTESY
landed ESTATE,
REAL
law BONA
personal CHATTEL
real LAND(S),
ACREAGE
wanton destruction
of SABOTAGE,
ARSON
prophesy PROG-
NOSTICATE, AUGUR,
DIVINE, FORETELL,
PRESAGE, PREDICT,
DECLARE, FORECAST,
FOREBODE
prophet ORACLE,
AUGUR, SEER, SIBYL,
PREDICTOR, MO-
HAMMED, TEACHER,
LEADER
Bible AMOS, HOSEA,
SYRUS, ISAIAH,
JEREMIAH, EZEKIEL,
DANIEL, JOEL,
OBADIAH, JONAH,
MICAH, NAHUM,
MOSES, MALACHI,
HAGGAI
prophetess SEERESS,
PYTHONESS, SIBYL,
CASSANDRA,
SOOTHSAYER, IN-
TERPRETER,
PYTHIAN
prophetic VATIC-
(AL), PREDICTIVE,
INTERPRETATIVE,

PRESAGEFUL, DI-
VINATORY, PRESAG-
ING
prophetical PRE-
SCIENT, FATIDIC,
VATIC(AL),
ORACULAR
propinquity NEAR-
NESS, LIKENESS,
KINSHIP, APPROX-
IMATION, RELATION-
SHIP, NEIGHBOR-
HOOD, PROXIMITY,
AFFINITY, VICINITY
propitiate CONCILI-
ATE, PACIFY, CALM,
FORGIVE, ATONE,
ADJUST, SOOTHE,
APPEASE, RECON-
CILE, SATISFY
propitious KIND(LY),
MERCIFUL, TIMELY,
BENIGN, ROSY,
BENEVOLENT,
BENEFICIAL,
LUCKY, FAVORABLE,
AUSPICIOUS, HELP-
FUL, ADVANTA-
GEOUS, OPPORTUNE,
PROSPEROUS, PROM-
ISING
proportion SHARE,
PRO RATA, PART,
END, RATION, RATIO,
BALANCE, SIZE,
EXTENT, DIVIDEND,
DEGREE, QUOTA, LOT,
SYMMETRY, HAR-
MONY, QUANTITY,
AMOUNT, FORM,
SHAPE, ALLOTMENT
proposal OFFER,
MOVE, BID, FEELER,
OVERTURE, SUG-
GESTION, MOTION,
PROPOSITION, PLAN,
PROSPECTUS
proposition PLAN,
THESIS, PREMISE,
LEMMA, THEORUM,
PROJECT, UNDER-
TAKING, TOPIC,
PROBLEM, DEAL
See "proposal"
assumed to be true
LEMMA, AXIOM,
COROLLARY
secondary LEMMA
prosaic DULL, PROSY,
PLAIN, SOBER,
STOLID, UNEXCIT-
ING, HUMDRUM,

TIRESOME, TEDIOUS,
INSIPID, FLAT, PRO-
LIX, LONGWINDED,
COMMONPLACE,
DRY, JEJUNE,
LENGTHY
proscenium STAGE
area in front of
APRON
proscript INTERDICT,
EXILE, OUTLAW,
FORBID, BAN, TABU,
TABOO
prose form RO-
MANCE, ESSAY,
HISTORY, BIOGRAPHY
prosecute INDICT,
CHARGE, SUE,
PURSUE, PRACTICE,
FOLLOW, ACCUSE,
ARRAIGN
prosecution SUIT,
PROCESS, PROCEED-
ING, ARRAIGNMENT,
PURSUIT, UNDERTAK-
ING
prosecutor DA, SUER,
ATTORNEY, PLAIN-
TIFF
proselyte CONVERT
to Judaism GER
Proserpine KORE
husband PLUTO
mother CERES (DE-
METER)
prosody METER,
VERSE, SCANSION,
VERSIFICATION
prospect MINE,
SCENE, VIEW, VISTA,
HUNT, HOPE,
SEARCH, SURVEY,
LOOK, EXPLORE,
PROMISE, FUTURE,
FUTURITY,
PROBABILITY, EX-
PECTATION, LAND-
SCAPE, ASPECT,
FACE, OUTLOOK,
EXPOSURE, FORE-
SIGHT, ANTICIPA-
TION, EXAMINE
prospectus PLAN,
SCHEME, PROGRAM,
SKETCH, DESIGN,
BULLETIN, CATA-
LOG(UE), AN-
NOUNCEMENT,
LIST, COMPENDIUM,
OUTLINE
prosper SUCCEED,
FAVOR, SPEED,

THRIVE, WAX,
GROW, FLOURISH
prosperity LUCK,
HAP, WEAL, WEL-
FARE, THRIFT,
WEALTH, ADVANCE,
GAIN, PROGRESS,
SUCCESS, FORTUNE
god FREY
symbol TURQUOISE
Prospero's *sprite*
ARIEL
prosperous PALMY,
HAPPY, RICH,
SUCCESSFUL,
FLUSH, LUSH,
THRIVING, PLUSH,
FORTUNATE,
FLOURISHING,
AUSPICIOUS, LUCKY,
BLOOMING, HALCYON,
ROSY, BOOMING,
GOLDEN
prostrate BOW,
ABASE, FELL, FLAT,
PRONE, FALLEN,
SUPINE, LEVEL,
ABJECT, OVER-
THROW, DEMOLISH,
RECUMBENT,
PROCUMBENT,
HELPLESS, POWER-
LESS, LOW, DE-
PRESSED, EX-
HAUSTED
prosy DULL, DRY,
STUPID, JEJUNE,
TIRESOME, COM-
MONPLACE, UNIN-
TERESTING, TEDIOUS,
HEAVY, LIFELESS,
WEARY
protagonist HERO,
ACTOR, ADVOCATE,
CHAMPION, LEADER
protect CHERISH,
SHELTER, SHIELD,
SAVE, SCREEN,
SECURE, (SAFE)-
GUARD, KEEP,
PRESERVE, DEFEND,
COVER, HARBOR,
FOSTER, FORTIFY
protecting influence
(A)EGIS, SHIELD,
WING
protection WING,
APRON, BIB, DE-
FENSE, INFLUENCE,
LEE, SHELTER,
PASS(PORT),
SECURITY, PRESER-

VATION, SAFETY,
GUARD, SHIELD,
BULWARK, SAFE-
GUARD, GUARDIAN-
SHIP, UMBRELLA,
WRAP, COVER,
INSURANCE
right, Old Eng.
MUND
protein AMINE, AL-
BUMIN, GLOBULIN,
HISTON, CASEIN,
GLUTIN, FIBRIN,
LEGUMIN, MEAT,
EGG(S)
blood FIBRIN,
GLOBULIN
breakfast EGG
egg ALBUMIN
milk CASEIN
poison (castor bean)
RICIN(E)
source EGG, MEAT,
LENTILS, BEANS
protest DENY, AS-
SERT, AVER, AFFIRM,
OPPOSE, RESIST,
DEMUR, KICK, DE-
CLARE, ASSEVERATE,
DEPRECATE, OBJECT,
DISSENT, REMON-
STRATE, REPUDIATE,
PROFESS, REFUSAL
proteus OLM
protoactinium symbol
PA
protoplasm SPORE,
SARCODE, AMOEBA
protozoan LOBE,
AMOEBA, AMEBA,
MONER, PHYLUM,
RHIZOPOD
order of LOBOSA
protract DEFER, DE-
LAY, SPIN, STRETCH,
EXTEND, CONTINUE,
ELONGATE, POST-
PONE, PROLONG,
LENGTHEN
protrude JUT, PRO-
JECT, INTERFERE
protuberance HUNCH,
LOBE, SNAG, NODE,
PROMINENCE, HUMP,
BULGE, (K)NOB,
KNOT, KNURL,
GNARL, NUB, JAG,
PROTRUSION, LUMP,
BUNCH, SWELLING
occipital INION
rounded HUMP,
UMBO

proud LORDLY, VAIN,
ARROGANT,
HAUGHTY, HIGH,
GLAD, PLEASED,
HAPPY, PRESUMP-
TUOUS, LOFTY,
SUPERCILIOUS, CON-
CEITED, INDEPEND-
ENT, ELATED, EGO-
TISTICAL, DIGNIFIED
prove CONVINCE,
VERIFY, ESTABLISH,
SHOW, EVINCE, TRY,
TEST, DEMONSTRATE,
ASCERTAIN, JUSTIFY,
CONFIRM, MANI-
FEST, SUBSTANTIATE
provenance ORIGIN,
SOURCE
provender MEAT,
FOOD, GRUB, EATS,
CHOW, FODDER,
FORAGE, VIANDS,
HAY, STRAW, CORN,
OATS, GRAIN, FEED,
PROVISION(S)
proverb AXIOM,
ADAGE, APHORISM,
MAXIM, SAW, SAYING,
BYWORD, MOTTO,
PARABLE, TRUTH,
APOTHEGM
provide AGREE, SUP-
PLY, CATER, ENDOW,
FURNISH, GRANT,
ARRANGE, YIELD,
AFFORD, ENDURE,
PURVEY, PREPARE,
CONTRIBUTE, STOCK,
STIPULATE, GIVE,
BEQUEATH
provided BUT, IF,
BODEN, SOBEIT
provident CAREFUL,
PRUDENT, DISCREET,
CAUTIOUS, FARSEE-
ING, FRUGAL,
THRIFTY, WISE
province DISTRICT,
TRACT, REGION,
FIELD, BEAT, CIR-
CUIT, DUTY, OF-
FICE, SPHERE,
LIMIT, COUNTY,
DIVISION, CHARGE,
JURISDICTION, AREA,
TERRITORY, DOMAIN,
DEPENDENCY, COL-
ONY, DEPARTMENT
provincial NARROW,
LOCAL, RURAL,
RUSTIC, INSULAR,

BUCOLIC, COUNTRI-
FIED, UNSOPHISTI-
CATED, CRUDE, UN-
POLISHED, RE-
STRAINED, LIMITED,
VULGAR
provisions LARDER,
CATES, CHOW, EAT-
ABLES, SUPPLIES,
FOOD *See* "prov-
ender"
search for FORAGE
provoke UPSET,
PEEVE, EXCITE,
EVOKE, PIQUE, ROIL,
VEX, BAIT, SPUR, STIR,
NETTLE, NEEDLE,
AROUSE, IRE, MOVE,
INCITE, EXASPERATE,
ANGER, IRRITATE,
GOAD, INCENSE, OF-
FEND, AGGRAVATE,
TEMPT
prow PROA, STEM,
BOW, NOSE, BEAK
prowl STRAY, GAD,
ROVE, SNEAK, SLINK,
LURK, ROAM, RAM-
BLE, WANDER
proximal CLOSEST,
NEAREST, PROXI-
MATE, NEXT, IM-
MEDIATE
opposed to DISTAL
proxy AGENT, SUB,
DEPUTY, VOTE,
PROCTOR, VICAR,
FACTOR, SUBSTI-
TUTE, PROCURATOR,
ELECTION, BALLOT,
REPRESENTATIVE
prude PRIG, HYPO-
CRITE, PURIST
prudence CARE, WIS-
DOM, CAUTION,
DISCRETION, JUDG-
MENT, CIRCUM-
SPECTION, SKILL,
SAGACITY
prudent CAREFUL,
WISE, CAUTIOUS,
DISCREET, CIRCUM-
SPECT, SENSIBLE
prune PLUM, TRIM,
THIN, PRIME, PURGE,
LOP, REDUCE, PREEN,
PRIMP, DRESS,
PLUME, SHAPE,
SMOOTH
pruritus ITCH,
HIVES

Prussian *city* HALLE, ESSEN, AACHEN
lancer U(H)LAN
legislature LAND-TAG
seaport EMDEN
spa EMS
town BEECK
watering place EMS
prussic acid *discoverer* SCHEELE
pry OPEN, RAISE, SEEK, SNOOP, PEER, LEVER(AGE), MOVE, PRIZE, PRISE, SCRUTINIZE, PEEP, GAZE, EXAMINE, ENQUIRE, INSPECT, PROBE
psalm ODE, LAUD, CANON, ANTHEM, PRAISE, SONG, POEM, HYMN, CANTICLE, VERSE
dawn LAUDS
98th CANTATE
pseudo FAKE, MOCK, BOGUS, SHAM, FALSE, SPURIOUS, FEIGNED, COUNTERFEIT, SIMULATED
pseudologist LIAR
pseudonym ANONYM(E), ALIAS
Arouet VOLTAIRE
Charles Lamb ELIA
Clemens MARK TWAIN
Dickens BOZ
Dupin (Baroness Dudevant) GEORGE SAND
Humphreys, Mrs. RITA
psittaceous *bird* PARROT
psyche MIND, SOUL, BRAIN, WIT(S), SPIRIT
psychiatrist ALIENIST, ANALYST, FREUD, ADLER, BRILL, JUNG, MEYER
psychic emanation(s) AURA(E)
psychologist BINET, JAMES
child ILG
psychotic ODD, QUEER, MAD, MANIC, OFF, INSANE *See* "insane"

ptarmigan GROUSE, BIRD
pteric ALAR, WING-LIKE, ALATE
pteris FERN
rootstock ROI
pteropod MOLLUSK
genus CLIONE
pteroptochoid *bird* TURCO
ptisan TEA, TISANE
pub TAVERN
public PEOPLE, STATE, CIVIC, OVERT, FREE, COMMON, RABBLE, MASSES, MANKIND, AUDIENCE, OPEN, UNIVERSAL, INTERNATIONAL, GENERAL, KNOWN
accountant AUDITOR, CPA
land AGER, PARK, COMMONS
make PUBLISH, REVEAL, DISCLOSE, TELL, PRINT
performer ACTOR, ARTIST(E)
publication BOOK, PAPER, MAGAZINE, PAMPHLET
preliminary PRODROMUS
style FORMAT
publicist WRITER, SOLON, JOURNALIST, AGENT
publicity INK
publish DISCLOSE, DECLARE, CIRCULATE, ADVERTISE, REVEAL, TELL, DIVULGE, SPREAD, PROMULGATE, DELATE, BLAZON, PRINT, ISSUE, AIR, VENT, ANNOUNCE, DISSEMINATE, BLAZE, PROCLAIM
publisher's *announcement* BLURB
inscription COLOPHON
Puccini GIACOMO
heroine MIMI
opera BOHEME, TOSCA, MANON
puce UDA
pucker SHIRR, RUFFLE, CREASE, PURSE,

FOLD, BIND, GATHER, BULGE, WRINKLE, ANXIETY, PERPLEXITY, AGITATION, CORRUGATE, FURROW
puckered BULLATE, DRAWN, SOUR, GATHERED, WRINKLED
pudding SAGO, DUFF, MUSH, HOY, CUSTARD, DESSERT
puddle PLASHET, POOL, POND, QUAGMIRE, SINK, MESS
pueblo TOWN, VILLAGE
assembly room KIVA
Indian ZUNI, HOPI
See under "Indian"
in Luzon IMUS
puerile WEAK, BOYISH, FEEBLE, INFANTILE, SILLY, IMMATURE, RAW, CALLOW, GREEN, CHILDISH, JUVENILE, FOOLISH, TRIVIAL, UNTHINKING
Puerto Rico, *abracadabra* APIO
beverage MABI
breadfruit CASTANA
city or town ARECIBO, PONCE
conqueror MILES
island MONA
palm YAGUA, YARAY
plant APIO
porkfish SISI
puff BLOW, FLAM, PANT, WAFF, CLOUD, GASP, ELATE, WHIFF, POOH, EMIT, EXPEL, SMOKE, GUST, BREATH, INFLATE, SWELL, WAFT, CAKE, WIND, BOAST, PRAISE, FLATTER
bird BARBET
genus MONASA
hairdressing POUF
puffin AUK, BIRD
pug DOG, NOSE, TAMP, GRIND, TEMPER, PUGILIST, FIGHTER, BOXER
nose, having pug SIMOUS
pugil PINCH

pugilist PUG, BOXER, FIGHTER, CHAMPION

pugilistic FISTIC, BELLICOSE

puisne JUDGE, JUNIOR, SUBORDINATE, STUDENT, ASSOCIATE, YOUNGER

puissant STRONG, MIGHTY, POWERFUL

pulchritude BEAUTY, COMELINESS, GRACE, LOVELINESS, EXCELLENCE

pule WHIMPER, WHINE, PEEP, COMPLAIN, REPINE, CRY, SNIVEL

Pulex, *genus of* FLEAS

pull PLUCK, TOW, DRAW, YANK, TUG, JERK, DRAG, HAUL, GATHER, TEAR, REND, WRENCH, POWER, INFLUENCE, GRAFT

pulley SHEAVE, LEVER, WHEEL, ROPE, TACKLE
grooved FUSEE

pullman SLEEPER, CAR, DINER

pullulate BUD, SPROUT, GERMINATE, TEEM, SWARM

pulp POMACE, CHYME, PAP, MASS, MAGMA, PITH, TISSUE, MASH, MUSH

pulpit ROSTRUM, AMBO, DESK, LECTERN, PLATFORM, PREACHERS, PRIESTHOOD

pulpy *dregs* MAGMA
fruit FIG, POME, UVA, PEAR, APPLE
state, in a MASHED, FLESHY, SOFT

pulque MESCAL, STIMULANT, INTOXICANT, LIQUOR, DRINK

pulsate BEAT, THROB, VIBRATE, WAVER, PALPITATE, THUMP, OSCILLATE, THRILL

pulsatory RHYTHMIC, SYSTOLIC, THROBBING, PULSATING

pulse PULSATE, THROB, BEAT, QUIVER, RHYTHM, CADENCE, METER, ACCENT, PEA, BEAN, LENTIL
split DAL, PIGEON PEA

pulverize ATOMIZE, MULL, TRITURATE, MICRONIZE, BRAY, POWDER, GRIND, CRUSH, MILL, LEVIGATE, DISINTEGRATE, COMMINUTE, DEMOLISH
to smooth powder LEVIGATE

pulverulent DUSTY, POWDERED, POWDERY

puma COUGAR, PANTHER, CAT

pumice GLASS, STONE, LAVA, CLEAN, SMOOTH
powdered TALC

pump QUIZ, QUESTION, RAISE, SLIPPER, SHOE, INTERROGATE, INFLATE, SYRINGE
handle SWIPE
kind CHAIN, JET, FORCE, LIFT, AIR, BUCKET, SAND, SHELL, SUCTION
medical SYRINGE
plunger RAM

pumpkin PEPO, CUCURBITA, SQUASH, VEGETABLE, VINE
genus CUCURBITA
seed BUTTERFISH, FISH, SAILBOAT

pun MOT, EQUIVOQUE, NICK, PARAGRAM, PARONOMASIA, QUIP, ASSONANCE, QUIBBLE, WITTICISM, ADNOMINATION

punch STRIKE, HIT, POKE, GAD, PASTE, PRITCHEL, PIERCE, TOOL, BORE, DRINK, PROD, PERFORATE, PUNCTURE, STAMP, THRUST, BLOW, AWL, BUFFOON, CLOWN, JESTER, MOUNTEBANK

spiced NEGUS
Punch and Judy *dog* TOBY

puncheon AWL, CASK, POST, STAMP, DIE, PUNCH, TOOL

punctilious EXACT, NICE, STRICT, FUSSY, PRECISE, CEREMONIOUS, SCRUPULOUS, FORMAL, PARTICULAR, PUNCTUAL, CONSCIENTIOUS, OBSERVANT, ATTENTIVE

punctuation mark ACCENT, CARET, DASH, COLON, COMMA, PERIOD, SEMICOLON, PARENTHESES, APOSTROPHE, HYPHEN

puncture PIERCE, STAB, DRILL, PUNCH, BORE, PRICK, PERFORATE, HOLE, STING, FLAT

pundit SCHOLAR, NESTOR, LEARNER, TEACHER, SAGE, BRAHMIN

pung SLED, SLEIGH

pungent TANGY, PEPPERY, PIQUANT, ACRID, RACY, SPICY, BITING, STINGING, PAINFUL, SHARP, SARCASTIC, TART, KEEN, PIERCING, POIGNANT, IRRITATING, PENETRATING, STIMULATING, ACUTE

Punic *war, site of second* ZAMA
warrior SCIPIO

punish AMERCE, FINE, FRAP, CHASTEN, WREAK, MULCT, WHIP, REQUITE, CHASTISE, CASTIGATE, PENALIZE, CORRECT, DISCIPLINE, LASH, FLOG

punishment FINE, PENALTY, WRACK, PENANCE, JUDGMENT, NEMESIS,

RETRIBUTION,
INFLICTION
punitive PENAL,
VINDICTIVE, COR-
RECTIVE
Punjab *capital*
LAHORE
native JAT
river INDUS
state BAGUL
town SIMLA
warrior SIKH
punk AMADOU,
TINDER, TOUCH-
WOOD, FUEL, POOR,
WORTHLESS,
INFERIOR, MISERA-
BLE, CONCH
punkah FAN
punt BOAT, WAGON,
POLE, KICK, PROPEL,
HIT, DRIVE
pupil STUDENT,
TYRO, NEOPHYTE,
WARD, DISCIPLE,
SCHOLAR, LEARNER,
NOVICE, BEGINNER,
CATECHUMEN,
TRAINEE
French ELEVE,
ECOLIER
pupilage NONAGE
puppet VASSAL, TOOL,
DOLL, MARIONETTE,
JUDY, PUNCH,
PAWN, DUPE, EFFIGY
puppy WHELP, DOG,
FOP
purblind OBTUSE,
DULL, BLIND, SHORT-
SIGHTED, STUPID,
MYOPIC
purchasable VENAL,
CORRUPT, SALABLE,
MARKETABLE
purchase GET, OB-
TAIN, BUY, HIRE,
EMPLOY, BARGAIN,
ACQUIRE, PROCURE,
GAIN, BOOTY, AC-
QUISITION, PROPERTY
or sale of office
BARRATRY
pure STAINLESS,
UNMIXED, CANDID,
CLEAN, NEAT, TRUE,
SINCERE, GENUINE,
CLEAR, SHEER,
MERE, LUCID,
CHASTE, MORAL,
HOLY, INVIOLATE,
SIMPLE, IMMACU-

LATE, FAULTLESS,
REAL, PERFECT,
INNOCENT, GUILT-
LESS, ABSTRACT,
THEORETIC, UTTER,
UNDEFILED,
DOWNRIGHT,
ABSOLUTE, UN-
SULLIED, UN-
ALLOYED, UNADUL-
TERATED, VIRTUOUS,
DEVOUT
purfle PURL, BORDER,
ORNAMENT,
DECORATE, TRIM,
OUTLINE, HEM
purgative PURGE,
CATHARTIC, ABSTER-
GENT, LAXATIVE,
APERIENT, CLEANS-
ING, JALAP
purgatory LIMBO,
EREBUS, MISERY
purge PHYSIC, AB-
STERGE, FLUSH,
WASH, CLARIFY,
EVACUATE, DIS-
CHARGE, EMIT,
FIRE, ATONE,
CLEANSE, CLEAR,
PURIFY, DETERGE,
ABSOLVE, PARDON,
SHRIVE, CLEAN,
EXONERATE
purification PURGE,
CATHARSIS, LUS-
TRATION
purify CLEANSE, RE-
FINE, WASH, CLEAN,
EPURATE, LUSTRATE,
SPURGE, PURGE,
EXPURGATE
purl EDDY, FRILL,
MURMUR, STITCH,
BORDER, OUTLINE,
KNIT, RIB, SWIRL,
CURL
purlieu ENVIRON,
SUBURB, HAUNT,
NEIGHBORHOOD,
LOCALITY
purloin STEAL, FIN-
GER *See* "filch"
purple LILAC,
PUCE, TYRIAN,
AMARANTH,
MAGENTA, VIOLET,
MAUVE, RANK,
POWER, WEALTH,
DYE, CARDINALATE,
PIGMENT, LAV-
ENDER, UDA

black SLOE
dye CASSIUS
medic LUCERNE,
ALFALFA
ragwort JACOBY
seaweed SION,
LAVER
purple heart MEDAL,
AWARD, ORDER
purple-heart *genus*
COPAIVA, TREE,
WOOD
purport SENSE, FECK,
GIST, TENOR, VIEW,
SIGNIFY, MEAN-
(ING), IMPLY,
DRIFT, PURPOSE,
CONVEY, IMPORT,
PROFESS, IN-
TENT(ION),
TENDENCY, SUB-
STANCE
purpose AIM, PLAN,
PLOT, END, GOAL,
USE, DESIGN, PRO-
POSE, INTEND,
RESOLVE, INTENTION,
RESOLUTION,
DETERMINATION,
RELEVANCE, PUR-
PORT, MEANING, TALK
purposive TELIC,
TELEOLOGICAL
purpuraceous
TYRIAN, PURPLE
purse CRUMENAL,
PUCKER, WRINKLE,
BAG, MONEY, ANTE,
STAKE, BURSE,
BOURSE, POUCH,
POCKETBOOK, PORTE-
MONNAIE, TREAS-
URY, FINANCES,
MEANS, PRIZE,
REWARD, AWARD
purser BOUCHER,
BURSAR, CASHIER,
TREASURER, PAY-
MASTER
pursue TRAIL, TAG,
DOG, TAIL, HOUND,
RIDE, ENSUE, FOL-
LOW, PLOD, CHASE,
HUNT, SEEK, STALK,
PROCEED, PROSE-
CUTE, CONTINUE,
SHADOW, MAINTAIN,
CULTIVATE
pursuit WORK,
TRADE, METIER,
CHASE, QUEST,
OCCUPATION,

PROSECUTION,
BUSINESS, FAD,
PRACTICE, HOBBY,
CALLING,
(A)VOCATION

pursy OBESE, FAT,
STOUT, FLESHY,
PLUMP, PUDGY,
PUFFY, ASTHMATIC,
SWOLLEN, PURSED,
PUCKERED, BAGGY,
WEALTHY

purvey CATER,
PROVISION, SELL,
PANDER, FURNISH,
PROCURE, SUPPLY,
ASSIST, GET,
OBTAIN, PROVIDE

push GANG, IMPEL,
SHOVE, BOOST,
NUDGE, PROD, CRISIS,
THRUST, PROPEL,
MOVE, DRIVE, BACK,
PRESS, URGE,
PROSECUTE, EX-
TEND, PROMOTE,
STRESS, EXTREMITY,
EMERGENCY,
IMPULSE, ADVANCE,
INFLUENCE, OFFENSE

push-over SETUP,
EASY

put LAY, LAID, PLACE,
LOCATE, SET, PLANT,
FIX, DEPOSIT,
IMPOSE, CAST,
THROW, EXPRESS
away KEEP, STORE,
CACHE, HIDE,
BANK, RENOUNCE,
DISCARD, RESERVE
before or opposite
APPOSE, FACE
forth APPLY, EX-
ERT, SPROUT, DE-
VELOP, PROPOUND,
EXTRUDE
off DEFER, STALL,
DOFF
on ADORN, STAGE,
DON
out ANGER, EVICT,
FIRE, SACK, EJECT,
EXPEL, DISMISS,
DOUSE, EXTINGUISH

putamen PIT, SEED,
STONE, ENDOCARP,
MEMBRANE

putative REPUTED,
SUPPOSED, AT-
TRIBUTED

putrefaction ROT,
DECAY, DECOMPO-
SITION, DISINTEGRA-
TION

putrid RANK, BAD,
FOUL, SEPTIC,
FETID, FUSTY,
TAINTED, DECAYED,
DECOMPOSED, ROT-
TEN, PUTRIFIED,
CORRUPT, STINKING,
IMMORAL, VICIOUS,
OBSCENE, OFFENSIVE

puttee GAITER,
SPAT, LEGGING

puzzle CAP, CRUX,
GRIPE, NONPLUS,
EMBARRASS,
MYSTIFY,
POSE(R), REBUS,
PERPLEX, AMAZE,
RIDDLE, BEWILDER,
CONFUSE, EN-
TANGLE, COM-
PLICATE, BAFFLE,
DISCONCERT, DIS-
TRACT, ENIGMA,
QUANDARY, CON-
FUSION

pygarg ADDAX,
OSPREY

Pygmalion's *sister*
DIDO
statue GALATEA

pygmy DOKO, MINIM,
ATOMY, AKKA, SHORT,
DWARF, MIDGET,
RUNT, BATWA,
SMALL, NEGRITO
Congo people
ACHUAS

pylon MARKER,
POST, STAKE, TOWER,
GATEWAY, MONU-
MENT

Pylos *king* NESTOR

pyramid KHUFU,
INCREASE, ACCRUE,
TENT, HEAP, POINT
erector of largest
CHEOPS
province near
GIZEH
ruin, site of BE-
NARES

pyre BIER, PILE,
HEAP

Pyrenees, *highest
peak* ANETO
resort PAU

pyromaniac FIRE-
BUG, INCENDIARY

Pythagoras' *birth-
place* SAMOS

Pythias' *friend*
DAMON

python BOA, DRAGON,
SNAKE, MONSTER,
SERPENT, ANACONDA
slayer of APOLLO

pythonic ORACULAR,
INSPIRED, MON-
STROUS

pyx VESSEL, CASKET,
CIBORIUM, BINNA-
CLE, TABERNACLE,
BOX, CAPSA

Q

Q CUE, QUEUE

Q.E.D., *part of*
QUOD, ERAT,
DEMONSTRANDUM

qua AS, HERON,
BIRD

quack HUMBUG,
PRETENDER, FAKER,
CHARLATAN, IM-
POSTOR
grass COUCH

quad QUOD, TYPE,
PARK, COURT,
CAMPUS, HORSE,
IMPRISON

quadragesimal
FORTY, SERMON,
OFFERING

quadrangle COURT-
(YARD), TETRAGON,
ENCLOSURE, CAM-
PUS, SQUARE

quadrant SECTION,
FOURTH

quadrat EN, EM,
SPACER

quadrate AGREE,
SQUARE, ADAPT,
QUARTER, CONFORM,
BONE, SUIT, COR-
RESPOND, ADJUST

quadriga CHARIOT,
CAR

quadrilateral(s)
TESSARA, FIGURE

quadrille DANCE,
MUSIC, CARDS

quadroon MESTIZO,
METIS

quadrumane APELET,
APE, LEMUR,
MONKEY, PRIMATE

quadruped MAMMAL, HORSE, DOG, ASS, CAT, COW

quaere ASK, INQUIRE, SEEK, QUESTION, QUERY

quaff DRINK, SWILL, GUZZLE, DRAFT

quaggalike animal ZEBRA

quaggy QUEACHY, BOGGY, FENNY, SOFT, FLABBY, MARSHY, SWAMPY, SPONGY, YIELDING, MUDDY

quagmire BOG, FEN, MORASS, SWAMP, TRAP, MARSH, MUDHOLE, DIFFICULTY

quahog, quahaug CLAM

quail TURNIX, COLIN, LOWA, MASSENA, BIRD, RECOIL, COWER, FLINCH, QUAKE, CRINGE, SHRINK, BLENCH
flock of COVEY, BEVY
genus COTURNIX

quaint PRETTY, PROPER, ODD, PROUD, WISE, DROLL, QUEER, ELEGANT, FANCIFUL, REFINED, AFFECTED, STRANGE, PECULIAR, PLEASING, ATTRACTIVE

quake SHAKE, SHIVER, TREMBLE, QUIVER, SHUDDER, AGITATE, OSCILLATE
See "quail"

quaker FRIEND, SECT, HERON, ALBATROSS, BIRD, MOTH, LOCUST, GUN
founder of religion FOX

quaking TREPID, ASPEN, SHIVERING, TIMOROUS

qualified FIT, APT, ABLE, TRIED, TESTED, RESTRICTED, MODIFIED, COMPETENT, LIMITED, CAPABLE, CONDITIONAL, SUITABLE, ELIGIBLE, SKILLED, LICENSED

qualify LIMIT, VARY, TEMPER, MODIFY, ALTER, ADAPT, RESTRICT, DESCRIBE, PASS, FIT, NAME, EQUIP, CHARACTERIZE, SOFTEN, MITIGATE, DIMINISH, ASSUAGE, ABATE, PREPARE, RESTRAIN

quality CHARACTERISTIC, FEATURE, CALIBER, TRAIT, CLASS, STRAIN, ATTRIBUTE, BRAND, VIRTUE, GRADE, NATURE, PROFESSION, CAPACITY, OCCUPATION, RANK, POSITION, STANDARD, PROPERTY, DIFFERENCE
of tone TIMBRE, RESONANCE

qualm SCRUPLE, DOUBT, PANG, THROE, NAUSEA, PALL, REGRET, MISGIVING, COMPUNCTION, FEAR, DISBELIEF

quamash CAMAS(S), PLANT

quandary DILEMMA, STRAIT, PREDICAMENT, PASS, PICKLE, CRISIS, BEWILDERMENT, DIFFICULTY, PERPLEXITY, PLIGHT

quannet FILE

quant POLE, PUNT, PROPEL, CANE

quantity SIZE, MASS, SOME, DOSE, AMOUNT, ANY, LOT(S), KITTY, SCAD(S), SPATE, SUM, TOTAL, WHOLE, PORTION, BULK, EXTENT, AGGREGATE, NUMBER, VOLUME, WEIGHT
irrational SURD

Quapaw Indian OZARK, ARKANSAS

quarantine ISOLATE, RESTRAIN, INTERDICT, BAN, EXCLUDE

quarrel SPAT, BICKER, MELEE, FEUD, SCENE, CAVIL, TIFF, MIFF, ROW, BRAWL, FIGHT, (AF)FRAY, ALTERCATION, MISUNDERSTANDING, WRANGLE, SQUABBLE, CONTROVERSY, DISCORD, DISSENSION, DISPUTE, EMBROGLIO, STRIFE, DISAGREE, CLASH, ARGUE

quarrelsome BELLICOSE, CHOLERIC, LITIGIOUS, ADVERSE, HOSTILE, CONTENTIOUS

quarry DIG, CHASE, DELF, GAME, PREY, VICTIM, RAVIN, OBJECT

quarte CARTE

quarter DISTRICT, REGION, SECTION, AREA, LOCALITY, FOURTH, COIN, PERIOD, CLEMENCY, MERCY, TERRITORY, STATION, POSITION, LODGE, BILLET, MILDNESS
note CROCHET

quarters ABODE, BILLET, BIVOUAC, ROOMS, DIGS, HOUSE, DWELLING

quartet TETRAD, GROUP

quartodeciman PASCHITE, CONTROVERSY

quarts, *eight* PECK

quartz RUBASSE, JASPER, AGATE, FLINT, AMETHYST, CITRINE, TOPAZ, CRYSTAL, CHALCEDONY, CARNELIAN, SARD(ONYX), ONYX
flint SILEX
green PRASE, PLASMA
kind SARD, JASPER, SILICA
ruby red RUBASSE

quash CRUSH, ANNUL, ABATE, DROP, VOID, SUPPRESS, OVERTHROW,

SUBDUE, QUELL,
CANCEL, DESTROY
quat PIMPLE, PUS-
TULE, BLISTER,
BOIL
quatch BETRAY,
TATTLE
quaternion TETRAD,
QUATRAIN
turning factor VER-
SOR
quaver TREMOLO,
TRILL, SHAKE,
SWAY, QUAKE,
SHIVER, VIBRATE,
QUIVER, TREMBLE,
FEAR
quay LEVEE,
WHARF, PIER, KEY,
MOLE, LANDING,
DOCK
queachy FENNY,
BOGGY, SWAMPY,
WEAK, FEEBLE,
SMALL, MARSHY
quean JADE,
HUSSY, WENCH,
HARLOT
queasy DELICATE,
TICKLISH, NAU-
SEATED, SICK,
FASTIDIOUS,
SQUEAMISH,
HAZARDOUS, QUALM-
ISH, UNCOMFORTA-
BLE, RISKY
Quebec *peninsula*
GASPE
quebrith SULPHUR
Quechuan Indian
AYMARA, NASCAN,
YUNCA, INCA,
CHOLA
queen BELLE, CAT,
CARD, BEE, MON-
ARCH, RANK, GODDESS,
ANT, TERMITE,
RULER, SOVEREIGN,
RANI, RANEE, EM-
PRESS, REINE,
BEGUM, ANNE,
ELIZABETH,
VICTORIA
Queen *Anne's lace*
CARROT, PLANT
Elizabeth I ORIANA
Moslem BEGUM
of Greek gods HERA
of Hearts ELIZA-
BETH
of Isles ALBION

of Roman gods
JUNO
of Sheba BALKIS
of spades BASTA
of the Antilles
CUBA
of Thebes DIRCE
of the East
ZENOBIA
of the fairies
MAB, TITANIA
queenly REGAL,
REGINAL, NOBLE,
GRACIOUS, ROYAL
queen *pawn* FERS
queer UNIQUE,
STRANGE, EX-
TRAORDINARY, EC-
CENTRIC, SINGULAR,
QUAINT, DROLL,
FUNNY, SHADY,
ODD, PECULIAR,
CURIOUS, UNUSUAL,
SPURIOUS, SHAM,
SUSPICIOUS, QUES-
TIONABLE
quell QUIET, ALLAY,
END, SUBDUE,
SOOTHE, OVERPOWER,
SUPPRESS, DESTROY,
PACIFY, REPRESS,
QUASH, ASSUAGE,
CALM, CRUSH,
MODERATE, ABATE
quench COOL, SLAKE,
STIFLE, END, SUP-
PRESS, SATE, QUIET,
SUBDUE, EXTIN-
GUISH, CHECK,
DAMP(EN), SATI-
ATE, GRATIFY, AL-
LAY
quenelle FORCE-
MEAT, BALL, PASTE,
ENTREE, FOOD
quercus, *genus of*
OAK, EVERGREEN,
TREE
querl COIL, TWIST,
TWIRL
quern MILL, GRINDER
querulous PEEVISH,
HUFFY, TOUCHY,
FRETFUL, CRANKY,
WHINING, PETU-
LANT, IRRITABLE,
GROUCHY, PLAIN-
TIVE, CROSS, COM-
PLAINING, FASTIDI-
OUS
quest TEST, QUIZ,
SEARCH, SEEK,

PROBE, INQUIRE,
EXPLOIT, ADVEN-
TURE, ASK, GOAL,
EXAMINE, EX-
PEDITION, PROBLEM
question CHAL-
LENGE, DOUBT,
QUERY, CAVIL,
GRILL, NUT, PUZ-
ZLE, POSE(R),
QUIZ, WAVER,
ASK, INTERROGA-
TION, INQUIRY,
DEBATE, DISPUTE,
TOPIC, DISCUSSION,
PROBLEM, CHARGE,
ACCUSE
mark EROTEME
questionable MOOT,
EQUIVOCAL, DUBIOUS,
OBSCURE, VAGUE,
DEBATABLE, CON-
TROVERSIAL, PROB-
LEMATICAL, UN-
DECIDED, DISPUTABLE,
UNCERTAIN,
DOUBTFUL, FISHY,
DISREPUTABLE
questionnaire FORM,
LETTER, FEELER,
STRAW, INQUIRY,
BLANK
quetzal TROGON,
QUEZAL, BIRD
queue LINE, CUE, PIG-
TAIL, BRAID, STEM,
PLAIT
quib GUIDE, QUIP,
QUIBBLE, GIBE
quibble CARP,
CAVIL, EQUIVOCATE,
PUN, EVASION,
EQUIVOCATION,
SHUFFLE
quick VITAL, FLEET,
FAST, AGILE, READY,
RAPID, SHARP,
ACUTE, (A)LIVE,
SUDDEN, SNAPPY,
RUSHING, LIVELY,
ANIMATED, ACTIVE,
INTELLIGENT,
SPEEDY, APT, YARE,
DEFT, GAY,
ALERT, PROMPT,
FIERY, BURNING,
INTENSE, MOVING,
SHIFTING, YIELDING,
SWIFT, HASTY, IM-
PATIENT, PASSION-
ATE, EXPEDITIOUS,
SPRIGHTLY

quickly RAPIDLY, SOON, PROMPTLY, DEFTLY, ANON, APACE, ALIVE, PRESTO, IMMEDIATELY

quickness, *mental* NOUS, DISPATCH, ACUMEN, SAGACITY, PERSPICACITY, WIT

quicksand SYRTIS, TRAP, DANGER

quickset HEDGE, THICKET, HAWTHORN

quicksilver MERCURY

quid CUD, FID, SOMETHING, EXCHANGE, CHEW, POUND, BARTER

quiddity CAVIL, ESSENCE, NATURE, PECULIARITY, QUIBBLE, TRIFLE, DISTINCTION

quiddle DAWDLE, TRIFLE, QUIVER, SHIVER

quidnunc BUSYBODY, GOSSIP, FRUMP, TATTLER

quiescent LATENT, QUIET, STILL, INERT, PASSIVE, DORMANT, STATIC, SLEEPING, RESTING, MOTIONLESS, PLACID, UNRUFFLED, SERENE, INACTIVE, CALM, ASLEEP, ARRESTED

quiet STILL, SERENE, PLACID, MOUSY, SOOTHE, EASE, MUM, TUT, HALCYON, PEACE(FUL), ALLAY, NOISELESS, REPRESSED, PACIFY, SILENCE, SH, PSST, CALM, QUIESCENT, MOTIONLESS, HUSHED, GENTLE, MILD, CONTENTED, RETIRED, SECLUDED, UNRUFFLED, SMOOTH, REST, REPOSE, SETTLE, TRANQUIL(IZE), UNMOLESTED, LEISURE
place DELL, NOOK, DEN

quietus REPOSE, REST, DEATH, MORT, ACQUITTANCE, DISCHARGE, SETTLEMENT

quill(s) REMEX, REMIGES, FEATHER, PLUME, PEN, SPINE, TOOTHPICK, SPINDLE, BOBBIN
for playing spinnet SPINA
for winding silk COP
porcupine PEN, SPINE

quilt THROW, EIDER, DUVET, PATCHWORK, COMFORT(ER), COVER(LET), SEW, STITCH, BLANKET
down DUVET, EIDER

quince, *Bengal* BEL

quinoline *derivative* ANALGEN

quintessence ELIXIR, EXTRACT, ETHER, SUBSTANCE, PITH, HEART, CORE, ESSENCE, GIST, ATTAR

quip GIBE, MOT, TAUNT, RETORT
See "jest"

quirk CAPRICE, CONCEIT, ANGLE, TWIST, TURN, QUIP, GIBE, TAUNT, TRICK, EVASION, SHIFT, SUBTERFUGE, QUIBBLE, EQUIVOCATION, CHANNEL, GROOVE, JERK, TRAIT, PECULIARITY, SINGULARITY

quirt ROMAL, WHIP

quisling RAT, TRAITOR

quit ABANDON, FORSAKE, GO, RETIRE, SCRAM, DESIST, CLEAR, FREE, RID, STOP, CEASE, LEAVE, RESIGN, DEPART, DELIVER, RELEASE, RELIEVE, LIBERATE, DISCHARGE, REQUITE, REPAY, RENOUNCE, YIELD, SURRENDER, DISCONTINUE, RELINQUISH

quite VERY, WHOLLY, COMPLETELY, ENTIRELY

quiver ARROW, TREMOR, CASE, VIBRATE *See* "quail"

quivering ASPEN, SHAKING, TREMBLING, SHUDDERING, QUAKING, SHIVERING

quixotic UTOPIAN, ROMANTIC, VISIONARY, IDEALISTIC, UNPRACTICAL, QUEER, ECCENTRIC, MAD, RASH

quiz POSER, COACH, ASK, QUESTION, PROBE, EXAM, TEST, PUZZLE, ENIGMA, HOAX, BANTER, CHAFF, MOCK, RIDICULE
See "kid"

quod COURT, PRISON, JAIL, JUG

quodlibetic ACADEMIC

quoit DISC, DISCUS, CROMLECH
mark aimed at TEE
mark of MOT
pin HOB

quondam ONETIME, FORMER(LY), ONCE, OLD

quota SHARE, PROPORTION, CONTINGENT, DIVIDEND, RATING, PORTION

quotation PRICE, MOTTO, CITAL, EXCERPT, CITATION, EXTRACT, SELECTION, REFERENCE
developed into essay CHRIA
mark GUILLEMET

quote CITE, ADDUCE, REPEAT, EXTRACT, PARAPHRASE, REPORT, MENTION, NOTICE, OBSERVE, EXAMINE, NOTE, NAME, COPY

quotidian DAILY, ORDINARY, DIURNAL, TRIVIAL, COM-

R

R AR, RHO
Ra HORUS, ATEN, TEM, SHU
bull form of BACIS
consort MUT
father GEB (KEB, SEB)
mother NUT
rabbi TEACHER, MASTER, LORD, CLERGYMAN
rabbit CON(E)Y, HARE, LAPIN, TAPETI, BUNNY, LAGOMORPH, RODENT
eared LAGOTIC
fever TULAREMIA
fur LAPIN, CON(E)Y
genus LEPUS
home WARREN, HUTCH
tail FUD, SCUT
rabble HERD, CROWD, MOB, HORDE, POPULACE, COMMONALTY, DREGS, SCUM, TRASH, MASSES, CANAILLE, RIFFRAFF, VULGAR, COARSE, NOISY, DISORDERLY
Rabelaisian BAWDY
rabid MAD, RAMPANT, VIOLENT, FURIOUS, RAGING, FRANTIC, FANATICAL, INTOLERANT, FIERY, FRENZIED, VIRULENT, INSANE, EAGER, ZEALOUS
rabies LYSSA, LYTTA, MADNESS, HYDROPHOBIA
raccoon COON, MAPACH(E), MAMMAL
like animal COATI, PANDA
race PEOPLE, CASTE, SORT, STRAIN, ANCESTRY, PEDIGREE, LINE(AGE), NATION, FAMILY, MONPLACE, EVERYDAY

quotient RESULT
quotity GROUP, COLLECTION

TRIBE, CLAN, BREED, HOUSE, GROUP, HIE, SPRINT, COMPETE, RELAY, DASH, TROT, PACE, RUN, CONTEST, COMPETITION, CURRENT, (WATER)-COURSE, SPAN, CAREER, LANE, CHANNEL, GROOVE, PASSAGEWAY, CONDUIT, STREAM
boat REGATTA
channel FLUME
family ILK, STIRPS, BREED
gait TROT, PACE, GALLOP, RUN
mill FLUME, LADE, CHANNEL, CURRENT
pertaining to ETHNIC
science of ETHNOLOGY
single course HEAT, LAP
undivided parent HOLETHNOS
racecourse OVAL, TRACK, RACEWAY
marker META, PYLON, TAPE
race horse PACER, MUDDER, PLATER, TROTTER
raceme CLUSTER, SPIKE
race track OVAL, RING, TURF, DOWNS, ASCOT
England ASCOT, EPSOM
tipster TOUT
U.S. LAUREL, BOWIE, TROPICAL, PIMLICO, SARATOGA, JAMAICA, HIALEAH, AQUEDUCT, GOSHEN
Rachel's *father* LABAN
husband JACOB
sister LEAH
rachis SPINE, CHINE, BACKBONE
racial *group* CLAN, TRIBE, FAMILY, STRAIN
racing *colors* SILKS
forecaster TIPSTER, DOPESTER, TOUT
official TIMER, STARTER

rack GRILL, FRAME, FRAMEWORK, CLOUD, OPPRESS, TRY, PACE, AGONY, PAIN, STRAIN, TORTURE, TORMENT, ANGUISH, HARASS, EXCRUCIATE, WRENCH, SINGLE-FOOT, DESTRUCTION
for barrels JIB, GANTRY
for corn CRIB
for plates CREEL
racket SPAT, DIN, UPROAR, BABEL, REVEL, FUSS, NOISE, CLAMOR, HUBBUB, TUMULT, SCHEME, DODGE, TRICK, GAME, IMPOSTURE, AGITATION, DISCORD, GAMBLE
racquet BAT, RACKET
for pelota (jai alai) CESTA
racy FRESH, RICH, PIQUANT, PEPPY, PUNGENT, RISQUE, BRISK, STRONG, SPICY, FIERY, LIVELY, SPIRITED, ZESTFUL, NATURAL, UNSPOILED, STIMULATING, COLORFUL, VIGOROUS
Radames' *love* AIDA
raddle FENCE, HEDGE, REED, TWIG, STICK, ROD, BRANCH, HURDLE, DOOR, (INTER)-WEAVE, TWIST
radial QUADRANT, RAY, ROUND, BAR, ARTERY, SPREADING
velocity unit STROB
radian ARC
radiance LUSTER, BRIGHTNESS, REFULGENCE, BEAUTY, LIGHT, LAMBENCY, SHEEN, BRILLIANCE, LUMINOSITY, SPLENDOR, EFFULGENCE, GLARE, GLITTER

radiant BRIGHT,
LIVID, LAMBENT,
LUCENT, GLORIOUS,
AGLOW, BEAMY,
SHINING, BRILLIANT,
SPLENDID, RE-
SPLENDENT, LUS-
TROUS, LUMINOUS,
PLEASED, HAPPY,
ECSTATIC
radiate SPREAD,
GLOW, BEAM,
GLEAM, SHED,
SHINE, EMANATE,
GLITTER, ILLUMI-
NATE, DIFFUSE,
EMIT
radiating EMANANT
radical BASIC,
BASAL, VITAL, FULL,
WHOLE, ROOT, SIGN,
ULTRA, ORIGINAL,
FUNDAMENTAL,
CARDINAL, CAPITAL,
REVOLUTIONARY,
REBEL, RED, LEFT,
EXTREME
radicle ETYMON,
RADIX, ROOT(LET),
HYPOCOTYL, FIBER
radio *detector*
RADAR
frequency AUDIO
interference STATIC
rating HOOPER
tube GRID
wave MICRO, SHORT
radium *discoverer*
CURIE
emanation NITON
source CARNOTITE,
URANITE
radius SPOKE, EX-
TENT, RANGE,
SWEEP, KEN, ORBIT,
WIDTH, LENGTH
pertaining to
RADIAL
radix RADICAL,
ETYMON, ROOT,
BASE, CAUSE,
SOURCE, SUPPORT
radon NITON, RN
raffish LOW, IN-
FAMOUS, VULGAR,
WORTHLESS, FLASHY,
COMMON, FROWSY,
UNKEMPT, TAWDRY,
CHEAP, DISREPUTABLE
raffle CHANCE, LOT-
TERY, DRAWING,

GAMBLE, TANGLE,
JUMBLE
raft BARGE, CATA-
MARAN, FLOAT,
COLLECTION, TRANS-
PORT, BALSA,
QUANTITY, LOT(S),
GOBS
duck SCAUP, BLUE-
BILL, REDHEAD
log BRAIL
rafter BEAM, JOIST,
SUPPORT, FLY-
CATCHER
rag TATTER, TEASE,
CLOTH, TUNE
rage VOGUE, MODE,
WHIM, STYLE,
CRAZE, FAD, FASH-
ION, FURY, IRE,
ANGER, CRY, FRET,
FUROR, CHAFE,
FRENZY, STORM,
RANT, FUME, RAVE,
WRATH, VEHE-
MENCE, RAMPAGE,
EXCITEMENT, PAS-
SION, MADNESS,
EAGERNESS, MANIA,
BOIL, BLUSTER, EN-
THUSIASM, FERVOR,
RESE
ragged EROSE, TORN,
WORN, FRAYED,
SHABBY, TATTERED,
RENT, POOR, MEAN,
UNEVEN, JAGGED,
ROUGH, UNFINISHED,
IRREGULAR, DE-
FECTIVE, STRAG-
GLING, DISCORDANT,
DILAPIDATED,
HARSH
raging GRIM, RAMP-
ANT, INFURIATED,
INCENSED
ragout HARICOT,
STEW, HASH
of beef STEW,
GOULASH
of game SALMI
of mutton or lamb
HARICOT
ragweed *genus* IVA,
AMBROSIA, PLANT
ragwort JACOBY,
PLANT
raid ATTACK, ONSET,
FORAY, SIEGE, PIL-
LAGE, INVASION,
INROAD, INCURSION,
STEAL

rail BAR, JAW,
RANT, RATE,
REVILE, SCOFF,
CENSURE, RE-
PROACH, UPBRAID,
ABUSE, SCOLD,
FENCE
altar SEPTUM
bird *See under*
"bird"
Europe ORTOLAN
raillery BANTER,
PLAY, SATIRE,
RIDICULE, SPORT,
JEST, FUN, PERSI-
FLAGE, CHAFF,
PLEASANTRY
railroad HURRY,
RUSH, TRANSPORT,
SEND, EXPEDITE,
LINE, TRACK,
PENN(SY), MONON,
FRISCO
bridge TRESTLE
car DINER, SLEEPER,
CABOOSE, PULLMAN,
PARLOR
cross rail FROG
flare FUSEE
light FUSEE,
FLARE
tie SLEEPER, TIM-
BER
timber TIE,
SLEEPER
raiment DRESS,
ARRAY, TOGS,
VESTURE, GARB,
ATTIRE, CLOTHES,
CLOTHING, APPAREL,
HABILIMENTS,
COSTUME
rain SHOWER, POUR,
MIST, SEREIN,
DRIZZLE, SPRINKLE,
CLOUDBURST
after sunset SEREIN
bird PLOVER
fine MIST, SEREIN,
DRIZZLE, MIZZLE
forest SELVA
gauge UDOMETER,
PLUVIOGRAPH
pertaining to
PLUVIAL
tree SAMAN,
GENISARO, ZAMAN
rainbow ARC, IRIS,
ARCH
goddess IRIS
pertaining to
IRIDAL

raincoat SLICKER,
PONCHO, OILSKIN
Japan MINO
rainstorm PELTER,
SHOWER, CLOUD-
BURST, DOWNPOUR
rainy WET, MISTY,
SHOWERY
raise ROUSE, REAR,
(UP)LIFT, ELE-
VATE, BOOST, START,
GROW, BUILD,
PRODUCE, EXCITE,
RISE, AWAKEN,
HOIST, HEAVE,
ERECT, LEAVEN,
LIGHTEN, CON-
STRUCT, EXALT,
ADVANCE, PRO-
MOTE, ENHANCE,
STIR, BREED, CULTI-
VATE, HEIGHTEN,
MUSTER, GATHER,
COLLECT, PRESENT
to third power CUBE
raised HEFTED,
BRED, CULTIVATED,
GREW, CONVEX
with a bar LE-
VERED, PRIED
raising device JACK,
HOIST, CRANE, DER-
RICK, ELEVATOR
rajah's *wife* RANI,
RANEE
Rajmahal *creeper*
JITI
rake COMB, TOOL,
LECHER, SATYR,
ROUE, LIBERTINE,
DEBAUCHEE, IN-
CLINATION, SLOPE,
COLLECT, GATHER,
SCRAPE, SCRATCH,
SEARCH, SCOUR,
RANSACK
with gunfire
ENFILADE
rally RECOVER, STIR,
ASSEMBLY, COLLECT,
JOKE, BANTER,
(A)ROUSE, TWIT,
TAUNT, MOCK,
REVIVE, UNITE,
GATHER,
STRENGTHEN, RE-
CUPERATE, MEET-
ING, DERIDE, RID-
ICULE, ENCOURAGE
ram ARIES, CRAM,
STUFF, BUCK, PUN,
TUP, BUTT, TAMP,

WETHER, OVINE,
PISTON, STRIKE,
SHEEP, FORCE
headed god AMON,
AMEN
horn SHOPHAR,
SHOFAR
like ARIETINOUS
ramble STROLL,
PROWL, GAD, WAN-
DER, ROVE, SAUNTER,
STRAY, RANGE,
STRAGGLE, DIGRESS,
ROAM, HIKE
rame BRANCH, CRY,
SKELETON, SCREAM,
LIMB
ramekin PAN, DISH,
HASH
ramentum PALEA,
PALET, SCALE,
SHAVING, PARTICLE
Rameses' *goddess*
ANTA
ramification SPUR,
RAMUS, BRANCH-
(ING), FORK(ING),
OFFSHOOT, ARM,
DIVERGENCE, PART,
DIVISION, SEPARATION
rammed *earth* PISE
ramp SLOPE, IN-
CLINE, STAIR, WALL,
PASSAGE, PLAT-
FORM, GANGPLANK,
REARING, CRAWL,
ROMP, RAGE,
STORM, RAMPAGE,
SCUD
rampant RIFE, RANK,
TEEMING, LUXURI-
ANT, EXUBERANT,
FIERCE, UNCHECKED,
EXTRAVAGANT,
VIOLENT, PREV-
ALENT, WILD,
FERAL
rampart BULWARK,
MOLE, BARRICADE,
DEFENSE, FORT,
WALL, MOUND,
LINE, ESCARP, AG-
GER, PARAPET,
REDAN
detached RAVELIN
earthen BRAY
ground around
ESCARP
palisaded VALLUM
part of SPUR
raised work AGGER
V-shaped REDAN

ramus BRANCH,
DIVISION, FORK,
RAMIFICATION,
PROJECTION
rance MARBLE,
STONE
ranch FARM,
HACIENDA
rancid FETID, RANK,
FUSTY, STALE,
FROWSTY, MUSTY,
UNPLEASANT, OF-
FENSIVE, OBNOXIOUS,
UNCLEAN, SPOILED,
SOUR
rancor ENMITY,
HATE, GALL,
SPITE, SPLEEN,
MALICE, GRUDGE,
MALIGNITY, MA-
LEVOLENCE, VENOM,
ANIMOSITY
rand MARGIN,
BORDER, EDGE,
RIDGE, STRIP
random CASUAL,
CHANCE, PURPOSE-
LESS, HAPHAZARD
randy COARSE,
VULGAR, DISOR-
DERLY, SHREW
range STOVE, OVEN,
RADIUS, KEN,
SCOPE, ORBIT,
GAMUT, AREA, SPAN,
ARRAY, SORT, LINE,
ROW, TIER, GAD,
ROAM, STRAY, GRAZE,
EXCURSION, RAM-
BLE, CLASS, RANK,
COMPASS, REACH,
REGION, SERIES,
EXTENT, DISTANCE,
DIRECTION
finder SIGHT
rank COARSE, GROSS,
VULGAR, MUSTY,
RANCID, FETID,
DANK, CLASS, STA-
TION, GRADE, POSI-
TION, ESTATE, FILE,
ROW, TIER, WILD,
INDECENT, DEGREE,
RATE, RATING, OR-
DER, LUSH,
LUXURIANT,
EXUBERANT, DENSE,
VIGOROUS, UTTER,
FLAGRANT, ABSO-
LUTE, DOWNRIGHT,
GLARING, ABUN-
DANT

rankle GALL, FESTER,
PAIN, INJURE,
ULCERATE, IN-
FLAME, IRRITATE
ransack LOOT, RAKE,
RIFLE, PILLAGE,
SEARCH, EXPLORE,
PLUNDER, SACK,
RAVAGE, STRIP,
RUMMAGE
rant BOMBAST,
SCOLD, SPOUT, DE-
CLAIM, RAVE,
VOCIFERATE, RAIL,
DISCOURSE, BLUSTER
rap KNOCK, BOP,
CLOUT, BOX, STRIKE,
CRITICIZE, THUMP,
THWACK, WHACK,
CUFF, CENSURE,
COIN
rapacious GREEDY,
VORACIOUS, AVARI-
CIOUS, PREDACEOUS,
GRASPING, COVET-
OUS, RAVENOUS
raphe SEAM, LINE,
SUTURE, JOINT
rapid FAST, QUICK,
SWIFT, APACE,
AGILE, FLEET,
BRISK, SPEEDY, HASTY,
HURRIED
river RIP
rapids, *narrow*
DALLES
rapier VERDUN,
BILBO, SWORD
blade heel RICASSO
Raptores *bird* HAWK,
EAGLE, OWL, VUL-
TURE
rare INFREQUENT,
UNIQUE, PRECIOUS,
SCARCE, SLIGHT,
SLIM, THIN, EX-
CELLENT,
EXTRAORDINARY,
STRANGE, CURIOUS,
UNDERDONE, FINE,
CAPITAL, UNUSUAL,
EXCLUSIVE, UNCOM-
MON
element ERBIUM,
THORITE, YTTRIUM
object CURIO
violin AMATI
rascal DOG, ROGUE,
IMP, SCAMP,
KNAVE, VARLET,
SCAPIN, SCALAWAG,
MISCREANT

rascally MEAN,
FALSE, TRICKISH,
DISHONEST, BASE,
KNAVISH, UN-
PRINCIPLED
rase *See under* "raze"
rash HASTY, IMPET-
UOUS, FOOLHARDY,
IMPRUDENT, ICAR-
IAN, MAD, WILD,
GIDDY, RECKLESS,
ECZEMA, ERUPTION,
HEADLONG,
PRECIPITATE, IN-
JUDICIOUS, INDIS-
CREET, IMPULSIVE,
INCAUTIOUS, VEN-
TURESOME, HEED-
LESS, CARELESS,
UNWARY, (AD)VEN-
TUROUS
rashness ACRISY,
ACRASY
rasorial *bird See*
"gallinae"
rasp GRATE, FILE,
OFFEND, SCRAPE
raspberry *genus*
RUBUS
rat RODENT, DE-
SERTER, TRAITOR,
QUISLING, APOSTATE,
SNOB
genus SPALAX,
MUS
kind of MOLE,
HAMSTER
ratafia CURACAO,
NOYAU, CORDIAL,
LIQUEUR
ratchet CLICK,
DETENT, PAWL
rate LEVY, TAX,
CESS, TOLL, VALUE,
PRICE, RANK, RATIO,
ASSESS, ESTIMATE,
COST, CHARGE, AP-
PORTION, APPRAISE,
STANDING, WORTH,
VALUATION, EVALU-
ATE, PROPORTION,
DEGREE, IMPOST,
ACCOUNT, REPRI-
MAND, CHIDE,
SCOLD, JAW, RAIL,
REVILE
of exchange AGIO,
BATTA
rather THAN, ERE,
INSTEAD, SOME-
WHAT, SOONER,
PREFERABLY

ratify APPROVE,
SANCTION, SETTLE,
CONFIRM, AFFIRM,
PASS, SEAL, CONSENT,
SUBSTANTIATE,
ENDORSE, COR-
ROBORATE, ESTAB-
LISH, VALIDATE,
AUTHORIZE, SUBSCRIBE
ratio RATE, RELA-
TION, DEGREE,
PROPORTION, QUOTA,
PERCENTAGE *See*
"rate"
mathematical PI
ration DOLE, DEAL,
DIVIDE, ALLOT, LIMIT,
METE, SHARE, POR-
TION, ALLOWANCE,
FOOD *See* "rate"
rational JUDICIOUS,
REASONABLE, SANE,
SOUND, WISE, IN-
TELLECTUAL, JUST,
RIGHT, NORMAL,
EQUITABLE, FAIR, FIT,
PROPER, INTELLIGENT,
SENSIBLE, LOGICAL
principle LOGOS
rations DIET, FOOD,
FORAGE
ratite bird MOA,
EMU, EMEU,
OSTRICH, CASSO-
WARY
ratoon SPROUT,
SHOOT, SPRING,
CULTIVATE
rattan CANE, WHIP,
LASH, NOOSE, THONG,
WICKER, PALM
rattle RALE, CLACK,
RICK, NOISE, TOY,
PRATTLE, FAZE,
ADDLE, UPSET,
CHATTER, GAB,
CLATTER, ROUSE,
DISCONCERT,
CONFUSE, AGITATE,
RACKET, UPROAR,
MARACA,
SISTRUM
rattlepate ASS, DOLT,
CHATTERER
rattlesnake CROTA-
LUS, SISTRURUS,
SIDEWINDER,
BLACK, DIAMOND-
BACK, MASSASAUGA
ratwa MUNTJAC

raucous HARSH, HOARSE, ROUGH, DRY, STRIDENT, HUSKY

ravage RAVEN, SACK, WASTE, OVERRUN, RAZE, LOOT, ROB, RUIN, SPOIL, DEVASTATE, DESTROY, DESPOIL, RANSACK, DESOLATE, PILLAGE, HARRY, PLUNDER, DESTRUCTION, HAVOC

rave BLUSTER, RAGE, STORM, RANT, FUME, DECLAIM

ravel FRAY, SLEAVE, UNTWIST, UNWIND, UNWEAVE, DISENTANGLE, CRUMBLE, BREAK, SLOUGH, UNTANGLE

ravelin OUTWORK, FORT, DEMILUNE

ravelings LINT, THREADS

raven *genus* CORVUS, CORVIDAE
Hawaii ALALA
of Odin HUGIN
"Raven" *author* POE
heroine LENORE

ravine GULCH, GULLY, LIN, DITCH, ARROYO, GORGE, GAP, NULLAH
Africa WADI, WADY

raw BLEAK, RUDE, SORE, LEAN, NUDE, UNCOOKED, CALLOW, GREEN, UNRIPE, CHAFED, ABRADED, INEXPERIENCED, UNSKILLED, UNPREPARED, UNSEASONED, UNTRIED, CRUDE, COLD, CHILLY, DAMP, CUTTING, INCLEMENT

ray BEAM, SKATE, GLEAM, STREAK, SHAFT, EMANATION, LIGHT, GLIMMER
bishop OBISPO
fish SKATE, DORN
penetrating GAMMA
spectrum ACTINIC
thornback DORN, FISH

rayed *badge* STAR

rayon CELANESE,

ACETATE, VISCOSE, CLOTH

raze, rase DEMOLISH, DEVASTATE, LEVEL, ERASE, EFFECT, RUIN, WRECK, DESTROY, OBLITERATE, SUBVERT, OVERTHROW, PROSTRATE

razor SHAVER, CLAM
sharpen HONE, STROP

razorback HOG, FINBACK, WHALE, RIDGE, ROUSTABOUT, RORQUAL

razz DERIDE, RIDICULE, CHAFF, BANTER, TEASE

re ANENT, ABOUT, CONCERNING

rea TURMERIC

reach STRETCH, ADVENE, ACCOMPLISH, GAIN, SPAN, ATTAIN, GET, FULFILL, RANGE, SCOPE, KEN, RADIUS, ORBIT, AREA, EXTEND, STRIKE, HIT, TOUCH, GRASP, SEIZE, DELIVER, ARRIVE, COME, INFLUENCE, IMPRESS, ACHIEVE, POSSESS, EXPANSE, PROMONTORY, VISTA

reaction REFLEX, TROPISM, REPONSE, TENDENCY, IMPRESSION, INFLUENCE, REBOUND, RECOIL, CHANGE

read NOTE, STUDY, RECITE, CON, PERUSE, SKIM, RELATE, INTERPRET, DECIPHER, SOLVE, DISCOVER, REGISTER, INDICATE, MEASURE, LEARN
inability to ALEXIA
metrically SCAN
publicly PRELECT, LECTURE, RECITE, PRAELECT
superficially SKIM

reader PRIMER, BOOK, LECTOR, TEACHER, PRELECTOR, PRAELECTOR,

ELOCUTIONIST, LECTURER
Eastern Church ANAGNOST

readily EASILY, QUICKLY, WILLINGLY, PROMPTLY, CHEERFULLY

readiness ALACRITY, FACILITY, PROMPTNESS, PROMPTITUDE, APTITUDE, EASE

reading desk LECTERN, AMBO, PULPIT

ready SET, PROMPT, QUICKLY, YARE, WILLING, HANDY, CONVENIENT, RIPE, PRIME, APT, ALERT, PREPARED, EQUIPPED, SUPPLIED, LIABLE, LIKELY, INCLINED, DISPOSED, DEXT(E)ROUS, OPPORTUNE, AVAILABLE, EAGER, FACILE, CHEERFUL, UNHESITATING

real AUTHENTIC, PURE, TRUE, CERTAIN, ACTUAL, SURE, GENUINE, SINCERE, UNAFFECTED, VERITABLE, INTRINSIC, COIN

reality FACT, TRUTH, BEING, ACTUALITY

realize PERCEIVE, APPREHEND, FULFILL, THINK, EFFECT, ACCOMPLISH, GAIN, KNOW, SENSE, WIN, ACQUIRE, OBTAIN, CONCEIVE, UNDERSTAND

really INDEED, ACTUALLY, TRULY, ABSOLUTELY, POSITIVELY, VERILY, GENUINELY

realm DOMINION, EMPIRE, TERRITORY, SPHERE, AREA, DOMAIN, REGION, KINGDOM, JURISDICTION, PROVINCE, COUNTRY, DEPARTMENT, PEOPLE, PROPERTY
of Jamshid PERIS

ream WIDEN, BORE, STRETCH, LOTS, BEVEL, COUNTER-SINK

reanimate RALLY, LIVEN, RESUSCITATE, REVIVE, REINVIGOR-ATE, CHEER, PEP

reap ACQUIRE, MOW, GATHER, HARVEST, GLEAN

rear ERECT, BREED, AFTER, BACK, (BE)HIND, DERRI-ERE, ELEVATE, NURTURE, NURSE, TRAIN, STERN, EDUCATE, POSTERIOR, HINDMOST, LIFT, CONSTRUCT, FOSTER, INSTRUCT, BUILD, TEACH, ESTABLISH
by horse PESADE, STEND
toward the ABAFT, AFT, ASTERN, POSTERIORLY

rearhorse MANTIS, INSECT

reason LOGIC, SAN-ITY, MIND, BRAIN, NOUS, INTELLECT, SENSE, UNDER-STANDING, THINK, CONSIDER, WISDOM, GROUNDS, PROOF, AIM, MOTIVE, BASIS, ARGUE, CAUSE, OBJECT, PURPOSE, EXPLANATION, JUSTIFICATION, RATIONALITY, DIS-CUSS, DEBATE
higher NOUS
want of AMENTIA, MANIA

reasonable JUST, AGREEABLE, PROPER, ACCEPTABLE, MOD-ERATE, SENSIBLE, SANE

reata ROPE, LARIAT, LASSO, RIATA

reave BREAK, REND, TEAR, UNRAVEL, DEPRIVE

rebec SAROD, LYRE, VIOLIN, FIDDLE, REBAB

Rebecca's *brother* LABAN
son ESAU, JACOB

rebel ARISE, RISE, RESIST, REVOLT, DEFY, RED, INSUR-GENT, MUTINEER

rebellion REVOLU-TION, PUTSCH, TREASON, MUTINY, REVOLT, INSUR-RECTION, SEDITION, WAR, CONTUMACY

rebound RICOCHET, REACT, BOUNCE, CAROM, RECOIL, RESILE, SPRING, SKIP, REVERBERATE, ECHO, RESILIENCE, REACTION, KICK

rebuff CHIDE, SLAP, CHECK, SNUB, RE-PEL, REPULSE, REJECT, REFUSE, CENSURE

rebuke REPROACH, REPRIMAND, AD-MONISH, SLAP, CHIDE, SCOLD, (BE)RATE, REPROVE, BLAME, REPREHEND, CRITICIZE, CENSURE, UPBRAID

recall REMEMBER, REPEAL, ANNUL, ENCORE, RECOLLECT, REVOKE, RETRACT, WITHDRAW, AB-NEGATE, RESCIND, APPLAUSE, CANCEL

recant ABJURE, RE-TRACT, DISAVOW, RENOUNCE, WITH-DRAW, REPUDIATE, REVOKE

recapitulate RE-HEARSE, REPEAT, REVIEW, RESTATE, SUMMARIZE, REIT-ERATE, DESCRIBE

recede RETREAT, GO, DEPART, EBB, WITHDRAW, BACK, RETIRE, RETRO-GRADE, REGRESS

receive ADMIT, CON-TAIN, OBTAIN, AC-QUIRE, ACCEPT, HOLD, GET, TAKE, DERIVE, GAIN, POCKET, SHELVE, ENTERTAIN, WEL-COME, GREET, EX-PERIENCE, UNDERGO, BELIEVE, ADOPT

receiver, *property in trust* BAILEE, TRUSTEE, CON-SERVATOR
stolen goods FENCE

recent FRESH, NEW, LATE, MODERN, NEOTERIC, NOVEL, YOUNG, DECEASED
combining form NEO

receptacle HANAPER, CONTAINER, URN, BIN, BAG, SACK, VASE, BOX, CRATE, SAFE, VAULT, POT, CASE, BASKET, HAMPER, REPOSI-TORY, HOLDER, CHEST

reception PARTY, SOIREE, OVATION, COLLATION, TEA, FETE, FEAST, LEVEE, AT HOME, RECEIPT, WEL-COME, ENTERTAIN-MENT, ACCEPTANCE, ADMISSION, AP-PREHENSION, INTUITION

recess BAY, CRYPT, NICHE, NOOK, ALCOVE, BREAK, SINUS, CLEFT, CAVITY, RETREAT, CORNER, INTERMIS-SION, RESPITE, INTERVAL, SECLU-SION

Rechabite *lodge* TENT

recherché RARE, UNCOMMON, CHOICE, FRESH, NEW, NOVEL, FARFETCHED, FINE, GOOD

recidivate (RE)-LAPSE, BACKSLIDE

recipe FORMULA, PRESCRIPTION, RECEIPT, PATTERN

recipient HEIR, DONEE, RECEIVER

reciprocate BANDY, EXCHANGE, RETURN, SHARE, INTER-CHANGE, REQUITE, REPAY, RETALIATE

recital STORY, NARRATION, NARRA-

TIVE, CONCERT,
MUSICALE, RE-
HEARSAL, REPETI-
TION, ENUMERATION,
READING

recitative, *music*
SCENA

recite QUOTE, SAY,
REPEAT, SPEAK,
TELL, COUNT, RE-
HEARSE, NARRATE,
RELATE, READ,
ENUMERATE, RE-
COUNT, RECAPITU-
LATE

reckless MADCAP,
RASH, HOTSPUR,
PERDU, DARING,
HASTY, CARELESS,
NEGLECTFUL,
INDIFFERENT,
INCONSIDERATE,
HEEDLESS, REGARD-
LESS

reckon FIGURE,
DEEM, IMPUTE,
OPINE, COMPUTE,
THINK, COUNT,
CALCULATE, CON-
SIDER, REGARD, RE-
PUTE, CLASS, EVAL-
UATE, SUPPOSE,
GUESS, NUMBER,
BELIEVE, EXPECT

reckoning PENALTY,
TAB, TALE, DATE,
POST, SHOT, COUNT,
CALCULATION, AC-
COUNTING, REWARD,
PAYMENT
device ABACUS

reclaim REDEEM,
RECOVER, RENEW,
TAKE, RESTORE,
SAVE, RESCUE,
TRAIN, REFORM,
REGENERATE, RE-
PAIR, TAME

reclaimed *land*
POLDER

reclining ABED,
PRONE, SUPINE,
RECUMBENT, REST-
ING, REPOSING,
RELAXING

recluse ANCHORITE,
EREMITE, HERMIT,
ASCETIC, MONK,
NUN, SEQUESTERED,
SOLITARY,
CLOISTERED, IN-
CLUSUS, ANCHORET

recognize SPOT,
OWN, SALUTE,
GREET, ADMIT,
NOTE, NOTICE, SEE,
ACKNOWLEDGE

recoil SHY, KICK,
RESILE, WINCE,
QUAIL, BALK,
FALTER, DEFY, RE-
TREAT, SHRINK,
REBOUND, RE-
ACT(ION), RICO-
CHET, BOOMERANG,
REPERCUSSION

recollection
ANAMNESIS,
MEMORY, REMEM-
BRANCE, RALLY,
RECOVERY,
MEDITATION,
CONCENTRATION,
REMINISCENCE

recommend ADVISE,
INTRODUCE, AP-
PROVE

recommit REMAND

recompense (RE)-
PAY, WAGE, HIRE,
MEED, GUERDON,
REWARD, REQUITE,
COMPENSATE,
REIMBURSE
Irish ERIC

reconcile ATONE,
SETTLE, PACIFY,
AGREE, RESTORE,
CONCILIATE, AD-
JUST, ACCORD,
SQUARE, RECTIFY,
PLACATE, PROPITI-
ATE, REUNITE,
HARMONIZE, APPEASE

reconnoiter SPY,
SCOUT, INSPECT,
SURVEY, SCAN, EX-
AMINE, INQUIRE

record CALENDAR,
SCROLL, CATALOG,
CHRONICLE, HIS-
TORY, CHART,
REGISTER, LIST,
ACTA, DISK, PLAT-
TER, DIARY, NOTE,
ARCHIVE, ANNALS,
AGENDA, LEGEND,
FILE, MINUTE,
ENTER, LOG, TAPE,
ENTRY, DOCKET,
ESTREAT, ALMANAC,
ENROL(L), DOCU-
MENT, TRANSCRIP-
T(ION), INSTRUMENT

of events FASTI,
HISTORY
police BLOTTER
ship's LOG

recorded *proceeding*
ACTUS

recount TELL, RE-
LATE, NARRATE,
RECITE, STATE,
REPORT, ENUMERATE,
DESCRIBE, DETAIL,
PARTICULARIZE,
ITEMIZE

recover RALLY,
RETRIEVE, RESTORE,
RECOUP, REGAIN,
OFFSET, RETOP,
CURE, HEAL,
OVERCOME, RESCUE,
DELIVER, RECAP-
TURE, RETAKE,
RECRUIT, RESUME,
REPOSSESS, REDEEM,
GET

recovery, *law*
TROVER

recreant APOSTATE,
COWARD, TIMID,
TAME, ABJECT,
DASTARD, RENEGADE,
BACKSLIDER, KNAVE,
BASE, CRAVEN,
TREACHEROUS,
PUSILLANIMOUS,
FAITHLESS, UN-
TRUE

recrement SCORIA,
REFUSE, DROSS,
SPUME, SCUM,
DREGS

recruit BOOT, TYRO,
ROOKIE, LEARNER,
SOLDIER, ENLIST,
SUPPLY, REINFORCE,
GATHER, ASSEM-
BLE, REFRESH,
REVIVE, RENEW,
TRAINEE

rectifier DIODE

rectify EMEND,
AMEND, CORRECT,
ADJUST, REMEDY,
REDRESS, MEND,
BETTER, IMPROVE,
REFORM, REGU-
LATE, STRAIGHTEN,
REPAIR, FIX

recuperation LYSIS,
REST, RECOVERY,
RESTORATION,
CONVALESCENCE

recurring *pattern*
CYCLE
red COLOR, RADICAL,
COMMUNIST, BLUSH-
ING, RUDDY, RUBI-
CUND, FLUSHED,
CRIMSON, PINK,
CARMINE, MAGENTA,
CERISE, CORAL,
ERIC
redact REVISE, EDIT,
DRAFT, PEN
redbird CARDINAL,
TANAGER
redbud *tree* JUDAS
redcap PORTER
Red Cross, American,
founder BARTON
Redcross *knight*
GEORGE
wife UNA
reddish brown
AUBURN, RUSSET,
SORREL
rede EXPLAIN,
INTERPRET, ADVISE,
COUNSEL, RELATE,
PROVERB, SAW,
PLAN, STORY
redeem RANSOM,
DELIVER, SAVE,
FREE, RECOVER,
REPURCHASE,
REGAIN, RETRIEVE,
LIBERATE, RE-
CLAIM, REINSTATE,
OFFSET, COMPEN-
SATE, ATONE, FUL-
FILL, RESTORE
Redeemer, *Hebrew*
GOEL
redeye RUDD, FISH,
SUNFISH, VIREO, COP-
PERHEAD, WHISKEY
red-faced BLOWZED,
RUBESCENT,
FLUSHED
redmouth GRUNT,
FISH
redolence ODOR,
SCENT, AROMA,
SMELL, FRAGRANCE,
PERFUME
redolent AROMATIC,
SCENTED, BALMY,
SPICY, FRAGRANT,
ODORIFEROUS
redouble REPEAT,
INGEMINATE, RE-
TRACE, REDUPLICATE,
REECHO, REPRODUCE,
REITERATE

redoubtable FOR-
MIDABLE, DREAD,
FEARSOME
Red Sea *island*
PERIM
redshank CLEE,
BIRD
reduce DIMINISH,
ABATE, SHRINK,
DEFEAT, ABASE,
DEGRADE, SUBDUE,
DEPRIVE, IMPAIR,
THIN, CURTAIL,
SLIM, ALLAY,
DERATE, LOWER,
PARE, DIET, LESS-
EN, MINIMIZE,
SUBJUGATE, CON-
QUER, DISCOUNT,
SHORTEN, SUBJECT,
WEAKEN
sail REEF
to half DIMIDIATE
reduction CUT, SLASH
redundant EXU-
BERANT, EXTRA,
SPARE, WORDY,
PROLIX, EXCESSIVE,
PLEONASTIC,
PLETHORIC, SUPER-
ABUNDANT, SUPER-
FLUOUS, LAVISH,
VERBOSE
reduplicate REPEAT,
ITERATE, REDOUBLE,
COPY
ree ARIKARA, SHEEP-
FOLD, RUFF, SAND-
PIPER, BIRD
reed PIPE, SLEY,
STEM, CULM, GRASS,
THATCH, ARROW
buck BOHOR, NAGOR
loom SLEY
salt concretion on
ADARCE
reef SHOAL, CAY,
KEY, BANK, BAR,
SPIT, ATOLL, RIDGE
a sail SHORTEN,
FURL
mining LODE, RIDGE,
VEIN
reefer ETON, COAT,
JACKET, MIDSHIP-
MAN, MINER,
OYSTER, SMOKE
reek FUME, SMOKE,
STEAM, SMELL,
VAPOR, EXHALATION
reel TEETER, DANCE,
ROCK, SPIN, STAG-

GER, SWAY, SPOOL,
WHEEL, ROLL, WINCH,
WINDLASS, TOTTER,
FALTER, WHIRL,
WAVER
fishing PIRN
used in dyeing
WINCE
yarn SWIFT
reem URUS, UNICORN
refectory, *monastery*
FRATER
refer ASCRIBE, IM-
PUTE, ALLUDE,
ATTRIBUTE, CON-
SULT, ASSIGN,
SEND, PERTAIN,
ADVERT, RESORT,
TURN, QUOTE, CITE,
APPLY, APPEAL,
RELATE, POINT,
CHARGE, DIRECT,
CONSIGN, CONCERN
referee JUDGE,
UMPIRE, UMP,
MODERATOR, ARBI-
TER, ARBITRATOR
refine CLARIFY,
CULTIVATE,
CHASTEN, SMELT,
PURIFY, POLISH,
CLEANSE, CLEAN
reflect DELIBERATE,
THINK, PONDER,
CONSIDER, STUDY,
WEIGH, MUSE,
SHINE, COGITATE,
MEDITATE, RUMI-
NATE, MIRROR,
IMITATE, COPY,
CONTEMPLATE
reflection ECHO,
IMAGE, CONSIDERA-
TION, CONTEMPLA-
TION, LIKENESS,
ASPERSION,
CENSURE, SHADOW,
DISPARAGEMENT,
CRITICISM, RE-
PROACH
reform CORRECT,
RECTIFY, AMEND,
REMODEL, IM-
PROVE, CONVERT
reformer AMENDER,
REVISER, LUTHER
refracting *device*
LENS
refraction, *pertaining*
to ANACLASTIC
refractor PRISM,
LENS, TELESCOPE

refractory OBSTI-
NATE, DISOBEDIENT,
RESTIVE, WILLFUL,
CONTRARY, REBEL-
LIOUS, STUBBORN,
PERVERSE, MULISH,
HEADSTRONG,
CANTANKEROUS,
UNRULY, INTRAC-
TABLE, MUTINOUS

refrain STOP, CEASE,
DESIST, FORBEAR,
ABSTAIN, AVOID-
ANCE, SONG, ARIA,
FA LA
music DERRY,
EPODE, EPISTROPHE,
FA LA, ARIA, SONG

refuge SANCTUARY,
PROTECTION, DEN,
LAIR, PORT, ARK,
ASYLUM, HARBOR,
HAVEN, SHELTER,
COVE, COVER, RE-
TREAT, SAFETY,
SECURITY,
STRONGHOLD,
COVERT, RESOURCE,
RECOURSE

refund REBATE,
RESTORE, REPAY,
REIMBURSE, RE-
TURN

refurbish RENOVATE,
RENEW, REPAIR

refuse DECLINE,
REJECT, RENOUNCE,
RESIGN, SPURN,
REPUDIATE, DENY,
ABANDON, REVOKE,
WITHHOLD, TRASH,
SCUM, OFFAL,
COOM(B), WASTE,
GARBAGE, DREGS,
GROUNDS, SCORIA,
LEES, LEAVINGS,
JUNK, ORTS, RE-
MAINS, ASHES,
CLINKERS
from coffee beans
TRIAGE
metal SCORIA,
DROSS, SLAG

refute DISPROVE,
REBUT, DENY,
OVERTHROW,
CONFUTE

regal KINGLY,
ROYAL, STATELY,
AUGUST, IMPERIAL,
IMPOSING, NOBLE,
SPLENDID, GRAND

regale FETE, DIVERT,
FEAST, TREAT,
ENTERTAIN,
GRATIFY, DELIGHT,
BANQUET

regard EYE, SEE,
DEEM, ESTEEM,
HONOR, KEEP,
NOTE, RESPECT,
ADMIRE, RATE,
HEED, VALUE,
PRIZE, PERTAIN,
FAVOR, VIEW, GAZE,
OBSERVE, NOTICE,
(RE)MARK, MIND,
BEHOLD, OBEY,
CONCERN, CON-
SIDER(ATION),
REVERENCE, AF-
FECTION, JUDGE,
LOVE, APPROBATION

regatta RACE

regent GOVERNOR,
RULER, MASTER,
DIRECTOR, SUPERIN-
TENDENT, DEPUTY

regent *of the sun*
URIEL

regimen DIET, SYS-
TEM, COURSE,
REMEDY, CONTROL,
REGULATION,
HYGIENE

regiment, *framework*
CADRE

regina QUEEN

region CLIME, ZONE,
DISTRICT, AREA,
LAND, REALM,
BELT, SPACE, TRACT,
SECTOR, SECTION,
PURLIEU, DIVISION,
TERRITORY, COUN-
TRY, PROVINCE,
QUARTER, LOCALITY,
LOCALE, SPHERE

register ROSTER,
ROTA, LIST, TABLE,
INDEX, ROLL, AN-
NALS, ARCHIVES,
CHRONICLE, EN-
ROL(L), MATRICU-
LATE
historic ROTULET
legal DOCKET,
AGENDA
of deaths NECROL-
OGY

regret RUE, REPENT,
REMORSE, GRIEF,
WOE, DEPLORE,
SORROW, LAMENTA-

TION, PENITENCE,
COMPUNCTION,
REPINING

regular HABITUAL,
SYMMETRICAL,
NORMAL, USUAL,
NATURAL, FIXED,
SET, TYPICAL,
PERIODIC, CONVEN-
TIONAL, ORDINARY,
ORDERLY, ESTAB-
LISHED, METHOD-
ICAL, SYSTEMATIC,
UNIFORM, COM-
PLETE

regularly DULY,
ORDERLY, LAW-
FULLY, CORRECTLY,
PROPERLY, OF-
FICIAL

regulate FIX, ORDER,
DISPOSE, ADJUST,
DIRECT, ARRANGE,
CONDUCT, TIME,
GUIDE, MANAGE,
GOVERN, RULE,
METHODIZE, CON-
TROL, STANDARD-
IZE, SYSTEMATIZE

rehearse DRILL,
PRACTICE, SAY,
TRAIN, RECITE,
REPORT, REPEAT,
NARRATE, RELATE,
RECOUNT, DE-
SCRIBE, PORTRAY,
RECAPITULATE,
PREPARE, COACH

reign RULE, GOVERN,
PREVAIL, EXIST,
CONTROL, DOMIN-
ION, SOVEREIGNTY,
SWAY, INFLUENCE,
TERM, AUTHORITY
pertaining to
REGNAL

reigning REGNANT,
EXISTING

reimburse (RE)PAY,
OFFSET, REQUITE,
REFUND, RESTORE,
COMPENSATE, IN-
DEMNIFY

Reims, *former name*
REMI

reincarnating *princi-
ple* MANAS,
BUDDHI

reindeer CARIBOU

reins HAUNCHES,
LOINS, LEASHES,

CONTROLS, CURBS,
CHECKS, RESTRAINS
reinstate REHIRE,
RESTORE, REVEST,
REPLACE, REIN-
STALL
reiterate DRUM,
HARP, REPEAT,
RECAPITULATE,
REHEARSE, RESTATE
reject DECLINE,
DENY, JILT, RE-
FUSE, CAST, SHED,
OUST, SPURN, REPEL,
DISCARD, DISMISS,
EJECT, CASHIER,
REPUDIATE, RE-
BUFF, DISALLOW,
EXCLUDE
rejoice ELATE,
EXULT, PLEASE,
GLADDEN, EXHIL-
ARATE, CHEER,
GRATIFY, ENRAP-
TURE, DELIGHT,
JUBILATE
relate UNITE, LINK,
JOIN, APPLY, PER-
TAIN, TELL, RECITE,
STATE, REPORT,
RECOUNT, REHEARSE,
DESCRIBE, NARRATE,
CONNECT, DETAIL,
REFER
related GERMAN(E),
TOLD, (A)KIN, AL-
LIED, SEPTAL, CON-
NECTED, COGNATE,
CONSANGUINEOUS
by blood AKIN,
AGNATE, COGNATE,
SEPTAL
by marriage IN-LAW
on mother's side
ENATIC
to the country
PRAEDIAL
relation SIB, KIN,
CONNECTION, REL-
ATIVE, KINDRED,
KINSMAN, ACCOUNT,
RECITAL, NARRA-
TIVE, CHRONICLE,
STORY, PERTINENCE,
REFERENCE, RE-
SPECT
relational CAUSAL,
KIN
relative KIN(DRED),
EME, RELEVANT,
PERTINENT, COM-
PARATIVE, APPROXI-

MATE, RELATION,
SIB(LING), PARENT,
UNCLE, AUNT
amount RATIO,
RATION
favor to NEPOTISM
rank DEGREE
relax LOOSEN,
SLACKEN, BASK,
OPEN, DIVERT,
ABATE, RELIEVE,
STOP, MITIGATE,
UNBRACE, UN-
STRAIN, WEAKEN,
REMIT, MODERATE,
SOFTEN, RELENT
relay of horses
REMUDA
release PAROLE,
DISCHARGE, DROP,
FREE, EMANCIPATE,
DELIVER(ANCE),
EXTRICATE, UN-
BIND, UNDO, UNTIE,
REST, TRIP, LOOSE,
RELENT, ACQUIT,
EXEMPT, REMIT,
REMISE, LIBERATE,
RELIEVE, RELIN-
QUISH, DISENGAGE,
UNBURDEN, FORGIVE
relent SOFTEN,
MELT, SLACKEN,
EASE, THAW, ABATE,
WANE, EBB, YIELD,
DEFER, BOW, RE-
LAX, FORBEAR,
DISSOLVE, MODIFY,
MODERATE
relevant APPLICA-
BLE, GERMAN(E),
APROPOS, ALLIED,
FIT, PERTINENT,
PROPER, RELATIVE,
APT, SUITABLE, AP-
PROPRIATE, CON-
GRUOUS
reliable STEADY,
TRUSTWORTHY,
DEPENDABLE
reliance FAITH,
TRUST, HOPE,
CREDIT, BELIEF,
DEPENDENCE, CON-
FIDENCE, ASSURANCE,
CREDENCE, EXPECTA-
TION
relic(s) CURIO,
MEMORIAL, TOKEN,
REMAINS, REM-
NANT, SOUVENIR,
MEMENTO, MONU-

MENT, ANTIQUITY,
FRAGMENT, RESI-
DUE, KEEPSAKE
cabinet RELIQUARY
relict WIDOW,
WIDOWER, SURVI-
VOR
relief DOLE, EASE,
SPELL, SOLACE,
RELEASE, SUCCOR,
HELP, ASSISTANCE,
AID, SUPPORT, DE-
LIVERANCE, ALLE-
VIATION, COMFORT,
PALLIATION, REM-
EDY, REDRESS
ornamental FRET,
RELIEVO
relieve EASE, ALLAY,
ALLEVIATE,
LESSEN, RELAX,
TEMPER, LIGHTEN,
REDUCE, SUCCOR,
AID, HELP, ASSIST,
COMFORT, AS-
SUAGE, INDEMNIFY,
SUSTAIN, DIMINISH,
REMEDY, REDRESS,
CURE, IMPROVE
religieuse NUN,
SISTER
religieux MONK
religion PIETY,
FAITH, TRUST, SECT,
CULT, CREED,
GODLINESS, DE-
VOUTNESS, SANCTITY
religious belief
DEISM, CREED,
CREDO
brother FRA,
FRIAR, MONK
brotherhood
SODALITY
devotee FAKIR
devotion NOVENA
doctrine RITE,
CULT(US), CREED
fair MELA
flagellants ALBI
hermit MONK
jurist, Roman
GAIUS
law, Roman FAS
observance FAST,
LENT, PURIM
offering OBLATION,
TITHE, DEODAND
order TEMPLARS,
MARIST, OBLATE,
BABISM
ancient ESSENE

service, directory of
ORDO
relinquish CEDE,
YIELD, LET, WAIVE,
DEMIT, SHED, CAST,
LEAVE, RESIGN,
QUIT, RETIRE,
DESIST, FORSAKE,
RECANT, ABANDON,
SURRENDER, VA-
CATE, DESERT,
RENOUNCE, ABDI-
CATE, FOREGO,
WITHDRAW
reliquary ARCA,
CHEST, SHRINE,
BOX, CASKET
relish SAVOR,
GUSTO, ZEST,
SAUCE, TANG,
FANCY, TASTE,
PLEASURE, DELIGHT,
FLAVOR, ENJOY-
MENT, LIKING,
DASH, GRATIFICA-
TION, APPETITE,
INCLINATIOŃ, CON-
DIMENT, AP-
PETIZER
reluctant UNWILL-
ING, AVERSE,
LOATH, CHARY,
WARY, DISIN-
CLINED, INDIS-
POSED, HESITANT
rely LEAN, TRUST,
BANK, DEPEND,
COUNT, EXPECT,
RECKON, HOPE,
AWAIT, REST,
CONFIDE, REPOSE
remain (A)BIDE,
STAND, LAST,
LODGE, REST,
TARRY, LINGER,
THOLE, STAY, WAIT,
CONTINUE, EXIST,
ENDURE, SURVIVE,
DWELL, PERSIST
remainder BALANCE,
LEAVINGS, RESI-
DUE, REMNANT,
SURPLUS, RESI-
DUUM, ASH, AR-
REAR, REST,
SCRAPS, FRAG-
MENTS, LEFT-
OVER, OVERAGE,
ESTATE
*after dividing a
number* UNITATE

remains ASHES,
CORPSE, REST,
DUST, RUINS,
RELICS, LEES,
DREGS, REFUSE,
BONES, FOSSILS,
VESTIGE
remark OBSERVE,
COMMENT(ARY),
NOTE, HEED, SAY,
SEE, MOT, SALLY,
DISCERN, NOTICE,
STATE, ANNOTA-
TION, ASSERTION,
GLOSS
Remarque ERICH
remedy MEDICINE,
CURE, AID, HELP,
ACTION, PHYSIC,
HEAL, ANTIDOTE,
PATCH, FIX, ANTI-
TOXIN, CORRECT,
RELIEVE, REDRESS,
DOCTOR, RESTORA-
TIVE, REPAIR,
NOSTRUM, RELIEF,
REPARATION
imaginary ELIXIR,
PANACEA,
PLACEBO
mysterious
ARCANUM
quack NOSTRUM,
PLACEBO
soothing BALM,
SOP
susceptible of
SANABLE, DURABLE,
TRACTABLE
remember RETAIN,
RECALL, MIND,
RECOLLECT, REM-
INISCE, BETHINK,
REMIND, REWARD
remembrance
TOKEN, GIFT,
TROPHY, SOUVENIR,
MEDAL, CUP,
REMINISCENCE,
RECOLLECTION,
RETROSPECT,
MEMENTO, MEMORY,
CONSIDERATION, KEEP-
SAKE, REMINDER,
REWARD
remex FEATHER,
QUILL
reminder CUE, HINT,
MEMENTO, SOU-
VENIR, NOTE,
MEMO, STRING

remiss LAX, SLACK,
LAZY, LOOSE, IN-
ATTENTIVE, DILA-
TORY, DERELICT,
BACKWARD, IN-
DOLENT, NEGLIGENT,
CARELESS, THOUGHT-
LESS, SHIFTLESS,
LANGUID, NEGLECT-
FUL, IDLE
remit SEND, TRANS-
MIT, ANNUL, PAR-
DON, POSTPONE,
PAY
remnant(s) END,
RAG, RESIDUE, ORT,
PART, PIECE, RELIC,
REST, ODDMENT,
SCRAP, REMAINDER,
TRACE, DREGS, LEFT-
OVER, FRAGMENT,
BIT, SUGGESTION
remora PEGA,
PEGADOR, SUCKER,
FISH, CLOG, DRAG,
DELAY, HINDRANCE,
OBSTRUCTION
remorse REGRET,
PITY, SORROW,
GRIEF, QUALM,
COMPASSION,
PENITENCE,
COMPUNCTION, AN-
GUISH, CONTRITION,
REPENTANCE
remote ALIEN,
SLIGHT, FORANE,
FAR, DISTANT,
FOREIGN, SEPARATE,
ULTERIOR, AWAY,
APART, OFF,
SECLUDED, AB-
STRACTED, ALOOF,
INACCESSIBLE,
UNRELATED, IN-
DIRECT
goal or end THULE
remove MOVE, SHIFT,
TRANSFER, UPROOT,
PART, SEVER, DIS-
PLACE, ABOLISH,
CANCEL, DELE(TE),
CHANGE, ERASE,
RID, FIRE, SACK,
OUST, KILL, DOFF,
STRIP, DISLODGE,
TRANSPORT, TRANS-
PLANT, EXTRACT,
WITHDRAW, AB-
STRACT, DISMISS,
CASHIER, DEPOSE,

ASSASSINATE, DE-
PART, DISAPPEAR
legally ELOIN,
ELOIGN, OUST,
DISBAR
renumeration FEE,
EMOLUMENT,
PAY, REWARD,
BOUNTY, HONORAR-
IUM, COMPENSATION,
REQUITAL, REIM-
BURSEMENT,
SATISFACTION,
PAYMENT, RECOM-
PENSE
Remus' *brother*
ROMULUS
rend WREST, TEAR,
SPLIT, CHOP, RIP,
RIVE, BREAK, BURST,
CLEAVE, WREND,
UPROOT, SUNDER,
RUPTURE, FRAC-
TURE, LACERATE
render CONSTRUE,
TRY, YIELD, FUR-
NISH, BESTOW,
MELT, PROVIDE,
GIVE, PAY, PRESENT,
DELIVER, TRANS-
MIT, CLARIFY,
SURRENDER, STATE,
RETURN, RESTORE,
CONTRIBUTE,
INTERPRET, PLAY,
RECITE, PERFORM,
REQUITE, TRANSLATE,
EXPRESS
rendezvous DATE,
REFUGE, TRYST,
RESORT, PLACE,
MEETING, APPOINT-
MENT
renegade APOSTATE,
RAT, REBEL, DE-
SERTER, TURNCOAT,
TRAITOR
renew MEND, RE-
PAIR, RESTORE, RE-
FORM, REVISE,
REASSUME, RE-
JUVENATE, REGEN-
ERATE, REBUILD,
REVIVE, REFRESH,
RENOVATE, RESUME,
CONTINUE, ENLIVEN
wine STUM
rennet FERMENT,
APPLE, RENNIN,
CURDLER
renounce REJECT,
ABJURE, ABNEGATE,

REMIT, FOREGO,
SPURN, RENEGE,
RESIGN, REFUSE,
RENAY, ABANDON,
DISCLAIM, REPUDI-
ATE, WAIVE,
RELINQUISH, CEDE,
DISOWN, DENY,
FORSWEAR, FOR-
SAKE, RECANT
renovate RENEW,
REPAIR, FIX,
MEND, PATCH,
POLISH, REDO,
RESTORE, REFRESH,
REVIVE
renown GLORY,
FAME, NOTE,
HONOR, ECLAT,
REPUTATION,
CELEBRITY, AC-
CLAIM
rent INCOME, HIRE,
LEASE, LET, SPLIT,
HOLE, SLIT,
RIP(PED), REVENUE,
RUPTURE, TEAR,
TORN
renter LESSEE,
TENANT, OCCUPANT
repair MEND, DOC-
TOR, DARN, FIX,
PATCH, RENEW,
RESTORE *See*
"remedy"
repand BENT,
WAVY, UNEVEN,
UNDULATING
reparation REDRESS,
AMENDS, REQUITAL,
ATONEMENT,
RECOMPENSE,
RESTITUTION, RE-
WARD, BALM,
BOT(E), INDEMNITY
repartee WIT,
HUMOR, IRONY,
SATIRE, SALLY,
BANTER, RETORT,
RIPOSTE, REPLY, RE-
JOINDER
repast LUNCH,
TIFFIN, TREAT,
MEAL, FEED, FOOD,
VICTUALS, FEAST,
BANQUET, ENTER-
TAINMENT
between meals
COLLATION, SNACK
repay REFUND, PAY,
SATISFY, AVENGE,
REQUITE, RETALI-

ATE, MEED, RECOM-
PENSE, RETURN,
COMPENSATE,
REMUNERATE,
REIMBURSE
repeal ABOLISH, CAN-
CEL, RECALL, ANNUL,
ABROGATE, RESCIND,
REVOKE
repeat RECUR, REDO,
RETELL, (RE)ITER-
ATE, ECHO, ENCORE,
DIN, RAME, QUOTE,
CITE, IMITATE,
RECITE, MIMIC,
RECAPITULATE
mark NNE, DC, DS
repeatedly OFT,
OFTEN, FREQUENTLY
repeater PISTOL,
RIFLE, FIREARM,
RECIDIVIST, WATCH
repel CHECK, VAN-
QUISH, BEAT, RE-
PULSE, RESIST,
DISGUST, REVOLT,
OPPOSED, REJECT,
REBUFF
repent GRIEVE, RUE,
REGRET, ATONE
repetition ROTE, ECHO,
ANAPHORA, COPY,
(RE)ITERATION,
REDUNDANCY,
REPRODUCTION,
REPLICA, ENCORE,
RECAPITULATION
of homologous parts
MERISM
of idea TAUTOLOGY
repine FRET, MOPE,
GRIEVE, RUE, COM-
PLAIN, GRUMBLE,
LAMENT, LANGUISH
replace REFUND,
RESTORE, SUPER-
SEDE, CHANGE,
REINSTATE, RESET,
SUPPLANT, DIS-
PLACE
replete FULL, SATED,
ABOUNDING, COM-
PLETE, SURFEITED,
GORGED, GLUTTED,
BLOATED, FAT,
STOUT
repletion SATIETY,
FULLNESS,
PLETHORA, PRO-
FUSION
replica DUPLICATE,
COPY, IMAGE, BIS,

CARBON, ECTYPE, FACSIMILE

reply ECHO, RETORT, ANSWER, RESPONSE, RESPOND, REJOIN(DER), REPARTEE

report CANARD, BRUIT, STORY, RELATE, RECORD, RUMOR, POP, CARD, NOISE, CRY, TALE, TALK, ANNOUNCE, DECLARE, BROADCAST, ACCOUNT, HEARSAY, GOSSIP, EXPLOSION, FAME, STATEMENT, REPUTATION
legislative CAHIER
official HANSARD, MINUTES, RECORD

repose TRUST, CONFIDE, LEISURE, SIT, EASE, RELY, REST, PEACE, RECLINE, SLEEP, SLUMBER, TRANQUILLITY, RELAXATION, LIE, PLACE, QUIESCENCE

reposit REPLACE, DEPOSIT, STORE

represent ACT, EXHIBIT, IMITATE, PERSONATE, PORTRAY, TYPIFY, EXEMPLIFY, DEPICT, DESCRIBE, BETOKEN, SYMBOLIZE, ILLUSTRATE

representative AGENT, DELEGATE, DEPUTY, SUBSTITUTE, LEGATE, ENVOY, PROXY

repress CHECK, CURB, REIN, CRUSH, STIFLE, SILENCE, BRIDLE, SUBDUE, SUPPRESS, QUELL, OVERPOWER, RESTRAIN

reprimand CHIDE, REPROVE, SLATE, REBUKE, CENSURE, REPROACH, UPBRAID, PUNISH, ADMONISH, REPREHEND, SCOLD, LECTURE

reproach BLAME, CHIDE, CENSURE, REBUKE, CONDEMN, REVILE, REPREHEND, SCOLD, REPRIMAND, (BE)RATE, ACCUSE, REPROOF

reproduction COPY, CARBON, ECTYPE, PHOTO *See* "replica"

reproof REBUKE, CENSURE, SNUB *See* "reproach"

reptile LIZARD, TOAD, FROG, NEWT, WORM, SNAKE, ALLIGATOR, CROCODILE, CREEPING, CRAWLING, LOW, GROVELING, DESPICABLE, REPTANT, KNAVE *See* "snake"
edible TURTLE
Nile CROC(ODILE)
pertaining to SAURIAN, OPHIDIAN
scale SCUTE, SCUTUM

"Republic" *author* PLATO

repudiate RECANT, REJECT, DENY, ABJURE, ABANDON, SPURN, REFUSE, DISCARD, DISCLAIM, RENOUNCE, DISAVOW, DISOWN, ABROGATE

repugnance DISTASTE, DISGUST, HATE, HOSTILITY, HATRED, LOATHING, ABHORRENCE, ANTAGONISM, AVERSION, ANTIPATHY, RELUCTANCE, REPULSION, DISLIKE

repulse REPEL, BEAT, REJECT, REBUFF

repulsion AVERSION, DISGUST *See* "repugnance"

repulsive UGLY, HATEFUL, UNSAVORY, NASTY

reputation REPUTE, ODOR, NAME, FAME, CREDIT, WEIGHT, ECLAT, HONOR, RENOWN, GLORY, DISTINCTION, ESTEEM, CELEBRITY, CHARACTER

repute CHARACTER, ODOR, CREDIT, WORD, FAME, RENOWN, HONOR

request SOLICIT, INVITE, SUE, APPEAL, PLEA, ASK, BEG, SUIT, PRAY, PETITION, ENTREATY, BESEECH, INVITATION, SUPPLICATION, DEMAND, ORDER
formal ROGATION

requin SHARK

require DEMAND, NEED, DICTATE, EXACT, CLAIM, WANT, LACK, NECESSITATE, ASK, ENJOIN, COMPEL, FORCE

requite AVENGE, REWARD, ATONE, WAR, RETALIATE, (RE)PAY, REVENGE, PUNISH, RECOMPENSE, COMPENSATE, RECIPROCATE, SATISFY

res THING, OBJECT

rescind ANNUL, RECALL, RECANT, REPEAL, ABROGATE, VACATE, ABOLISH, REVOKE, CANCEL, VOID, COUNTERMAND

rescue RECLAIM, DELIVER, RANSOM, SAVE, AID, FREE, LIBERATE, REDEEM, EXTRICATE, RELEASE, RECOVER

research INQUIRY, STUDY, INQUEST, PROBE, INVESTIGATION, SCRUTINY, ANALYSIS, TEST, EXPLORATION, EXAMINATION

resemblance IMAGE, LIKENESS, ANALOGY, SIMILARITY, SIMILITUDE, FACSIMILE, AFFINITY, AGREEMENT
one bearing RINGER

resentment DUDG-
EON, HATRED,
ANGER, UMBRAGE,
PIQUE, HUFF,
ANIMUS, INDIGNA-
TION, IRRITATION,
ANIMOSITY, RANCOR,
GRUDGE, ANNOY-
ANCE, VEXATION,
CHOLER, GALL, IRE,
ACRIMONY, SPLEEN,
DISPLEASURE

reserve WITHHOLD,
STOCK, STORE, BACK-
LOG, KEEP, SAVE,
RETAIN, FUND,
SUPPLY, SAVINGS,
SILENCE, RETI-
CENCE, RESTRAINT,
DIFFIDENCE, SHY-
NESS, CONSTRAINT,
COLDNESS

reserved SILENT,
CLOSE, SHY, ALOOF,
DISTANT, KEPT,
MODEST, COY,
RESTRAINED, CAU-
TIOUS, COLD, UN-
SOCIABLE, RETI-
CENT, OFFISH,
DEMURE, UNCOM-
MUNICATIVE

reservoir BASIN,
STORE, SUMP,
POND, CAVITY,
CISTERN, TANK,
RESERVE, SUPPLY

reside LIVE,
(A)BIDE, DWELL,
LODGE, STAY, STOP,
INHABIT, ROOM,
SOJOURN, REMAIN

residence DOMICILE,
HOME, ABODE, SEAT,
DWELLING, HOUSE,
STAY, HABITATION,
MANSION, LODGING

resident BURGESS,
CIT, PRESENT,
INHERENT, DWELL-
ING, LESSEE,
FIXED, FIRM,
TENANT, OCCUPANT

residue ASH(ES),
ORTS, REMAINDER,
SORDES, REMNANT,
REST, SURPLUS,
GUM, TAR, EXU-
DATE, RELICS,
SLUDGE, RESIDUUM,
REMAINS, LEAVINGS,
EXCESS, DREGS,

SLAG, LEES, CIN-
DERS, SEDIMENT

resign QUIT, DEMIT,
ABDICATE, YIELD,
CEDE, WAIVE, RE-
TIRE, SURRENDER,
RELINQUISH, SUB-
MIT, ABANDON,
RENOUNCE, WITH-
DRAW

resiliency TONE,
ELASTICITY, BUOY-
ANCY

resin ELEMI, GUM,
LAC, TAR, AMBER,
PITCH, EXUDATE,
COPAL, DAMMAR,
MASTIC, ROSIN

allogach ALOE
calabar bean ES-
ERIN, PHYSOSTIG-
MINE
Chian turpentine
ALK
fossil AMBER,
GLESSITE
fragrant ELEMI
gum DAMMAR,
GUGAL, MASTIC
incense SANDARAC
pungent MYRRH
varnish ANIME

resinous *tree*
BALSAM, PINE, FIR

resist REBEL, STAY,
STEM, FEND, OP-
POSE, DEFEND, COM-
BAT, FOIL, WITH-
STAND, PREVENT,
MEET, DEFEAT,
FRUSTRATE, DIS-
OBEY, REFUSE,
FIGHT

resolute GRITTY,
FIRM, STANCH,
TRUE, BOLD, LEAL,
LOYAL, POSITIVE,
BRAVE, OBSTINATE,
UNSHAKEN, DETER-
MINED, DECIDED,
RESOLVED, STEAD-
FAST, FIXED,
CONSTANT, STOUT,
GAME, RIGID,
HARD

resolution WILL,
VIGOR, PLUCK,
GRIT, METTLE,
SPIRIT, PROPOSAL,
STAMINA, SCHEME,
PERSEVERANCE,
FORTITUDE, PUR-

POSE, STRENGTH,
ANALYSIS, DISEN-
TANGLEMENT,
TOPIC

resort PURLIEU,
ABODE, DIVE, GO,
SPA, INN, HAUNT,
SHORE, REFER,
APPLY, SHIFT,
RESOURCE, REFUGE,
RECOURSE, DEN,
JOINT, RETREAT

resound ECHO,
PEAL, CLANG, ROAR,
REVERBERATE,
RING, CELEBRATE,
EXTOL

resounding PLAN-
GENT

resource(s) DEVICE,
MEANS, SAVINGS,
ASSETS, FUNDS,
MONEY, EXPEDIENT,
CONTRIVANCE,
RESORT, SUPPLY,
WEALTH, ESTATE

resourceful FERTILE,
SHARP, APT

respect REGARD,
ESTEEM, REVERE,
AWE, FEAR, NOTICE,
HEED, CONCERN,
OBSERVE, VENERATE,
REVERENCE, FAVOR,
HONOR, CONSIDERA-
TION, DEFERENCE
act of DEVOIR

respire LIVE,
BREATHE, INHALE,
EXHALE

respite BREAK, LULL,
REST, STAY, PAUSE,
DELAY, RECESS, IN-
TERVAL, STOP, INTER-
MISSION, REPRIEVE,
POSTPONEMENT,
SUSPENSION,
FORBEARANCE

resplendent AUREATE,
GORGEOUS, GRAND,
SUPERB, BRIGHT,
BRILLIANT,
SPLENDID, SHINING,
RADIANT, LUSTROUS,
LUMINOUS, EFFUL-
GENT, GLORIOUS,
GLITTERING,
DAZZLING

respond (RE)ACT,
ECHO, REPLY,
REJOIN, ANSWER,
FEEL, WRITE

response REPLY, RETORT, ANSWER, ANTIPHON, ANTHEM, REACTION, LETTER

responsibility CHARGE, ONUS, ACCOUNTABILITY, OBLIGATION, TRUST, DUTY, (RE)LIABILITY

rest BASE, SUPPORT, REPOSE, HALT, RELAX, UNBEND, ABIDE, STOP, SURPLUS, CEASE, EASE, LIE, EXCESS, SIESTA, SEAT, SIT, RELY, LEAN, RECLINE, SLEEP, REMAINDER, SHELTER, LODGING, INN, SLUMBER, QUIET, TRANQUILLITY, INTERVAL, PAUSE, STILLNESS, INTERMISSION, PERCH, CESSATION, INACTION

in reading CAESURA
musket or gun GAFFLE, CROC

restaurant CAFE, BISTRO, EATERY, DINER, CHOPHOUSE, CAFETERIA

resthouse KHAN, CHAN, INN

resting ABED, SLEEPING, ASLEEP, DORMANT, QUIESCENT, LATENT

restive FRETFUL, MULISH, IMPATIENT, BALKY, STUBBORN, NERVOUS, PERSISTENT, REFRACTORY, RECALCITRANT, UNEASY, OBSTINATE, PERVERSE, DISOBEDIENT

restore STET, RENEW, SAVE, RESCUE, REVIVE, REPAIR, FIX, MEND, REPLACE, REFUND, REPAY, REINSTATE, RECOVER, HEAL, CURE, RETURN, REBUILD, RECONSTRUCT

restrain FETTER, BRIDLE, REIN,

BLOCK, CHECK, ARREST, DETER, BIND, STEM, TETHER, AWE, CURB, ENJOIN, DISSUADE, ABRIDGE, INHIBIT, CONTROL, RESTRICT, LIMIT, CONFINE, IMPRISON, LEASH, BATE

restraint CURB, BIT, TRAMMEL, FORCE, DURESS, REPRESSION, LIMITATION, CONFINEMENT, TABU, LAW, ORDER, WRIT, SHACKLE, ECONOMY, CONSTRAINT, RETICENCE

restrict BIND, RESTRAIN, CHECK, LIMIT, TIE, CRAMP, CURB, COERCE, REPRESS, CIRCUMSCRIBE, STRAITEN, STINT, CONFINE, HINDER, PROHIBIT, BAN, MODIFY, QUALIFY

result EVENT, UPSHOT, OUTCOME, CONCLUSION, DECISION, SCORE, ENSUE, PRODUCT, EFFECT, END, ISSUE, TOTAL, FRUIT, PROCEED, FOLLOW, ACCRUE, SPRING, ARISE, CONSEQUENCE, SUM

resume REPEAT, ABSTRACT, RENEW, REOPEN, RECOMMENCE, CONTINUE, SUMMARIZE, REOCCUPY

resumé ABRIDGMENT, SUMMARY, EPITOME, SYNOPSIS

ret ROT, SOAK, STEEP, SOP, SOG, DAMPEN

retable SHELF, LEDGE, GRADIN, PREDELLA, FRAMEWORK

retail VEND, SELL, TRADE, HAWK, PEDDLE, RELATE, REPEAT, BARTER, DISTRIBUTE

retain KEEP, SAVE, HOLD, OWN, ENJOY, REMEMBER, MAINTAIN, PRESERVE,

RESERVE, HUSBAND, RECOLLECT, ENGAGE, HIRE, EMPLOY

retainers RETINUE, TRAIN, CORTEGE, ATTENDANTS, ADHERENTS, SERVANTS, DEPENDENTS

retaliation TALION, REPRISAL, REQUITAL, REVENGE, RETRIBUTION, PUNISHMENT

retard LESSEN, ARREST, CHECK, STUNT, CLOG, FETTER, BALK, POSTPONE, SLOW, DELAY, IMPEDE, HINDER, OBSTRUCT, SLACKEN, DEFER, PROCRASTINATE, RESTRAIN, BRAKE

retardation LAG, DELAY, DECREASE, HINDRANCE

retch HAWK, VOMIT, GAG, HEAVE, STRAIN

rete NETWORK, PLEXUS

retiary NETLIKE, TELAR, MESHED

reticule BAG, ETUI, (WORK)BASKET, CABAS, SATCHEL

reticulum MITOME, NETWORK, TISSUE, STRAND

retinaculum FRENUM, GLAND, FUNICLE, BAND

retinue CREW, GANG, ESCORT, TRAIN, SUITE, CORTEGE, FOLLOWERS, ENTOURAGE, STAFF, ATTENDANTS, SERVANTS

retired ABED, LONE, WITHDRAWN, GONE, OTIOSE, REMOVED, SECLUDED, SOLITARY, SEQUESTERED, QUIET, HIDDEN

one who has EMERITUS

retort SALLY, REPARTEE, REPLY, QUIP, RIPOST(E), ALEMBIC, CRUCIBLE,

VIAL, ANSWER,
RETALIATION
retract DISAVOW,
RECANT, RECALL,
REVOKE, ABJURE,
RECEDE, ABANDON,
DISOWN, RENOUNCE,
ANNUL, REPUDI-
ATE
retreat WITHDRAW,
ARBOR, SHELTER,
ASYLUM, ROUT,
DEN, REFUGE, LAIR,
NOOK, SANCTUM,
PRIVACY, SOLITUDE,
PORT, HAVEN, ARK,
NEST, RETIRE,
RECEDE, ESCAPE
underground ABRI,
CAVE
retrench ABRIDGE,
CLIP, CUT, REDUCE,
CURTAIL, DECREASE,
LESSEN, SHORTEN,
DOCK, DIMINISH,
PARE, REMOVE,
ECONOMIZE
retribution RE-
QUITAL, NEMESIS,
REVENGE, REDRESS,
REPAYMENT,
RECOMPENSE, RE-
WARD, PUNISH-
MENT, COMPENSA-
TION, RETALIATION,
VENGEANCE,
PENALTY
of law KARMA
retrieve RECOVER,
RESTORE, REGAIN,
RECOUP, FIND,
RECRUIT, REPAIR,
REVIVE, REMEDY,
RECUPERATE
retrograde DETERI-
ORATE, RECEDE,
SLOW, DECLINE,
(RE)LAPSE, REAR-
WARD, BACKWARD,
DECADENT, INVERSE,
CATABOLIC, DEGEN-
ERATE, RETROGRES-
SION, INVERTED
return (RE)PAY,
YIELD, REQUITE,
RECUR, RE-ELECT,
REVERT, REAPPEAR,
ANSWER, REPLY,
RESPOND, RETORT,
REVISIT, RENDER,
RECOMPENSE
thrust RIPOSTE

returning REDIENT
reveal INFORM,
DIVULGE, PUBLISH,
DISCLOSE, AIR,
BETRAY, IMPART,
EXHIBIT, SHOW,
TELL, OPEN, BARE,
DISCOVER, UNVEIL,
UNMASK, UNCOVER,
EXPOSE, DISPLAY
revel RIOT, SPREE,
LARK, CAROUSAL,
ORGY, FEAST,
FESTIVITY, SATUR-
NALIA, MERRY-
MAKING, CONVIV-
IALITY, REVELRY,
CELEBRATION,
CARNIVAL
revelation ORACLE,
DISCLOSURE, DIS-
COVERY, GOSPEL
revelry *cry* EVOE
revenant EIDOLON,
GHOST, APPARITION,
SPECTER, RECUR-
RING, SPIRIT
revenue TAXES,
INCOME, YIELD,
RENTAL, FUNDS,
MONEY, RECEIPTS,
RETURN, PROFIT,
ASSETS, PRODUCE,
FRUITS, PROCEEDS
bishop's, first year
ANNAT(ES)
revere ADMIRE, DE-
FER, HONOR, ADORE,
WORSHIP, ESTEEM,
CHERISH, PRIZE,
VENERATE, HALLOW,
LOVE, RESPECT
reverence WORSHIP,
AWE, FEAR, HONOR,
PIETY, REGARD,
VENERATION,
ADORATION,
HOMAGE, RESPECT,
DEFERENCE
reverie FANCY,
DREAM, FANTASY,
NOTION, VISION
revers LAPEL
reverse ANNUL,
VACATE, UNDO,
OBVERSE, BACK,
REAR, INVERT, UP-
SET, TRANSPOSE,
OVERTHROW,
SUBVERT, REPEAL,
REVOKE, RESCIND,
RETRACT, OPPOSITE,

CONVERSE, CONTRARY,
MISFORTUNE, MIS-
HAP, TRIAL,
ADVERSITY, DEFEAT
reversion (RE)LAPSE,
ESCHEAT, ATAVISM,
REMAINDER,
THROWBACK
to type ATAVISM
revert RETURN,
RECUR, UNDO,
(RE)LAPSE,
ESCHEAT, REVOKE,
REVERSE, ANNUL,
ADVERT, REVEST
music ANTISTRO-
PHE
to state ESCHEAT
to type ATAVISM
revile ASPERSE,
VILIFY, ABUSE,
RAIL *See* "berate"
revise EDIT, COR-
RECT, ALTER, RE-
NEW, PATCH,
MODIFY, CHANGE,
IMPROVE, AMEND,
EMEND, REVIEW,
REDACT, REAR-
RANGE, REEXAMINE
revive REANIMATE,
RESUSCITATE, PERK,
RENEW, RALLY, RE-
VIVIFY, REINVIGOR-
ATE, REINSPIRIT,
ROUSE, QUICKEN,
REFRESH, RECALL,
REKINDLE, RECOVER,
ENLIVEN
revoke ABJURE, AN-
NUL, RENEGE, RE-
PEAL, ADEEM,
RECALL, RECANT,
RETRACT, CANCEL,
RESCIND, ABROGATE,
ABOLISH, COUNTER-
MAND
revolt NAUSEATE,
REBEL, PUTSCH,
MUTINY, RECOIL,
REPEL, SHOCK,
DISGUST, SICKEN,
DESERT
revolution REV,
CYCLE, GYRE,
REVOLT, PUTSCH,
MUTINY, UPRISING,
ROTATION, CIRCUIT,
WAR, CHANGE,
GYRATION, INSUR-
RECTION, REBEL-
LION

Revolution *essayist*
  PAYNE
spy ANDRE
revolutionist MARAT,
  REB
revolve GYRATE,
  WHEEL, PIRL, SPIN,
  SWING, TURN,
  CIRCLE, REFLECT,
  REASON, ROTATE,
  ROLL, CIRCULATE,
  CONSIDER, MEDITATE,
  PONDER, RUMINATE
revolver GUN, ROD,
  GAT, COLT, PISTOL,
  FIREARM, WEAPON
reward GUERDON,
  MEED, REQUITE, REC-
  OMPENSE, UTU, PAY,
  PRIZE, YIELD,
  BONUS, OSCAR,
  MEDAL, CUP,
  COMPENSATION,
  REMUNERATION,
  INDEMNITY,
  PREMIUM, BOUNTY,
  GRATUITY, TIP
rex KING
rhea EMU, EMEU,
  NANDU, OSTRICH
Rhea OPS
rhetorical ORATORI-
  CAL, ORNATE,
  FLORID, FLOWERY,
  FLUENT, BARONIAL,
  DECLAMATORY
figure LITOTES
rheum(a) CATARRH,
  COLD
rhinal NASAL,
  NARIAL
Rhine *tributary*
  AAR(E), ILL, LAHN,
  MAIN, RUHR, WAAL
rhinoceros ABADA,
  BORELE
black BORELE
cousin of TAPIR
rhizome ROOT,
  BULB, CORM,
  TUBER
Rhode Island *county*
  KENT, BRISTOL
insurrectionist
  DORR
Rhodesian *town*
  NDOLA
rhomb(us) CIRCLE,
  WHEEL, LOZENGE
rhoncus SNORING,
  RALE

Rhone *tributary*
  ARVE, ISERE,
  SAONE, GARD, ARLY,
  AIN, DROME
rhubarb, *acid of*
  RHEUM
genus RHEUM
rhus *genus* IVY,
  SUMAC
rhyming *scheme*
  TERCET
rhythm MEASURE,
  LILT, BEAT,
  CADENCE, ICTUS,
  SWING, MELODY
  See "meter"
ria INLET, CREEK
rialto BRIDGE, MART,
  EXCHANGE,
  ISLAND, THEATER
riant GAY, LAUGH-
  ING
rib TEASE, BONE,
  COSTA, WIFE, SUP-
  PORT *See*
  "kid"
having COSTATE
pertaining to
  COSTAL
ribald JOCULAR,
  GROSS, VULGAR,
  COARSE, LEWD,
  OBSCENE, VILE,
  FILTHY, LOOSE,
  INDECENT, RAW,
  IRREVERENT, OF-
  FENSIVE
ribbed RIDGED,
  FURROWED, SUP-
  PORTED
fabric REP(P),
  TWILL, FAILLE
ribbon BAND,
  STRIP(E), FILLET,
  COQUE, DECORA-
  TION
badge CORDON
for binding LISERE
like TAENIOID
rice PADDY, CEREAL,
  GRASS, GRAIN
boiled with meat
  PILAU, PILAF
drink SAKE,
  PANGASI
field PADDY
inferior CHIT
in husks PALAY
paste AME
polishings DARAC
refuse SHUDE,
  SHOOD

rich WEALTHY,
  LUSH, OPULENT,
  AFFLUENT, FLUSH,
  PROSPEROUS, SUMP-
  TUOUS, LUXURIOUS,
  COSTLY, VALUABLE,
  ABUNDANT, PLUSHY,
  FERTILE, SUPERB,
  AMPLE, SAVORY,
  COPIOUS, FECUND,
  FAT, EXPENSIVE,
  NOURISHING
man MIDAS,
  CROESUS, NABOB,
  PLUTOCRAT
Richelieu *successor*
  MAZARIN
riches PELF, LUCRE,
  OPULENCE, WEALTH,
  FORTUNE
demon of MAMMON
worship of
  PLUTOMANIA
rick HEAP, PILE,
  CORD, STACK
rickety SHAKY,
  TOTTERING, FRAIL,
  TUMBLEDOWN,
  FEEBLE, WEAK,
  UNSTABLE, UN-
  SOUND, IMPERFECT
ricochet CAROM,
  GLANCE, REBOUND,
  SKIP
rid PURGE, CLEAR,
  EJECT, FREE,
  EXPEL, KILL, VAN-
  ISH, DELIVER, DIS-
  ENCUMBER, DIS-
  BURDEN, DISPATCH,
  DESTROY, LIBERATE,
  LOOSE, RELINQUISH
riddle REBUS,
  ENIGMA, CRUX,
  SIEVE, PIERCE,
  SIFT, PROBLEM,
  PUZZLE, QUESTION,
  MYSTERY, CONUN-
  DRUM, PERFORATE
ride *See* "bait"
ridge(s) ARETE,
  CHINE, WELT,
  SPINE, ESKER,
  SPUR, WALE,
  ELEVATION, RIB,
  WEAL, RANGE,
  CREST, PROMINENCE
anatomical SPINE,
  STRIA
camp's RIDEAU
circular, on shells

PILAE
cloth WALE
drift KAME, OS, OSAR
furrow between two PORCATE
low RAND, PARMA, CUESTA
of glacial drift OSAR, OS, ESKER, KAME
relating to CARINAL
rounded GYRI, GYRUS
sand OS, OSAR
shell VARIX, VARICES, PILAE
skin WELT, WALE
ridicule RIDE, MOCK, RAZZ, DERIDE, DERISION, GUY, ROAST, BANTER, PAN, TWIT, LEER, TAUNT, CHAFF, RAILLERY, SARCASM, GIBE
personified MOMUS
ridiculous ABSURD, FUNNY, IRONIC, DROLL, TRIVIAL, COMIC, FOOLISH, SILLY, LUDICROUS, TRIFLING, LAUGHABLE, PREPOSTEROUS, FARCICAL, RISIBLE, WAGGISH, NONSENSICAL, GROTESQUE
riding *breeches* HABIT, JODHPURS, LEVIS
school MANEGE
whip QUIRT, CROP
rifle CARBINE, MAUSER, JAGER, MUSKET, GUN, FIREARM, WEAPON, STRIP, ROB, STEAL See "pilfer"
ball MINIE
converted breech loader SNIDER
magazine MAUSER
pin TIGE
rift CLEFT, GAP, LAG, RIMA, SPLIT, FISSURE, CRACK, RENT, BREACH, OPENING, CHINK, CREVICE, CRANNY, SEPARATION, BREAK

rig LATEEN, BEDIZEN, EQUIP, FIX, OUTFIT, DRESS, CLOTHE, PREPARE, TEAM, CHEAT, SWINDLE, FIT, ASSEMBLE, ADJUST
Riga *native* LETT, LATVIAN
rigging, *part of* SPAR, GEAR, ROPES
right DROIT, DEXTER, EQUITABLE, TRUE, JUST, LAWFUL, LEGAL, LEGITIMATE, CORRECT, FAULTLESS, DEXTRAL, STRAIGHT, FITTING, APPROPRIATE, SUITABLE, PROPER, PAT, NICE, PRECISE(LY), MEET, EXACT(LY), AMEND, AVENGE, REDRESS, EMEND, GEE, CLAIM, PREROGATIVE, CONSERVATIVE, GOOD
combining form DEXTRO
hand DEXTER
hand page RECTO
law DROIT
pertaining to DEXTER
precedence PAS
rightist TORY, CONSERVATIVE, REACTIONARY
rights JURA
rigid HARD, STRINGENT, AUSTERE, STIFF, SET, TENSE, STRICT, STARK, FIRM, SOLID, STRONG, FIXED, INFLEXIBLE, UNPLIANT, UNBENDING, SEVERE, RIGOROUS, STERN, PRECISE, EXACT, STUBBORN
Rigoletto's *daughter* GILDA
rigorous DRASTIC, STIFF, STERN See "rigid"
Rijeka FIUME
rile ANGER, OFFEND, ROIL, ANNOY, IRRITATE, VEX See "vex"

rim EDGE, LIP, BRIM, BRINK, FLANGE, VERGE, BORDER, MARGIN
shield ORLE
wheel FELLOE, FELLY, TIRE
rime HOAR, FROST, RUNG, FREEZE, CONGEAL, CHINK, CRACK, RHYME
rimes, *book of* EDDA
Rinaldo's *steed* BAJARDO, BAYARD
rind BARK, CRUST, EPICARP, CORTEX, HUSK, PEEL, SKIN, HULL, SHELL, INTEGUMENT
ring PEAL, TOLL, CLANK, CHIME, JINGLE, KNELL, (RE)SOUND, BLOC, FACTION, CABAL, JUNTO, CLIQUE, COTERIE, SET, ANNULET, ARENA, LOOP, RINK, CIRCLE(T), HOOP, GIRDLE, RACECOURSE, BAND, SURROUND, ENCIRCLE
dove CUSHAT
gem setting BEZEL, CHATON
harness pad TERRET
lamp flame CRIC
rope GROMMET
seal SIGNET
stone of CHATON, GEM
wedding BAND
ringlet CURL, LOCK, TRESS, CRISP
rings, *interlocking* GIMMAL
ring-shaped ANNULAR, CIRCULAR, CIRCINATE
ring-tailed *animal* LEMUR, (RAC)COON
ringworm TINEA, SERPIGO, FUNGUS
rinse SLUICE, ABSTERGE, LAVE, CLEANSE, WASH
riot BRAWL, ROW, FRACAS, FRAY, TUMULT, UPROAR, DISTURBANCE,

COMMOTION,
BROIL, MELEE,
PANDEMONIUM,
REVELRY, DISSIPA-
TION, CAROUSAL,
EXCESS, CON-
FUSION, MUTINY
riotous WANTON,
LUXURIANT,
BOISTEROUS, UN-
RESTRAINED,
PROFLIGATE, TUR-
BULENT, LOUD,
DISORDERLY,
SEDITIOUS
rip SPLIT, SEVER,
CUT, REND, CLEAVE,
RIVE, TEAR, PART,
SCAMP, CHEAT,
LIBERTINE, DE-
BAUCHEE, DIVIDE,
OPEN
ripa SHORE, COAST,
BEACH, STRAND,
BANK
ripe MATURE(D),
MELLOW, ADULT,
FIT, FULL, PRE-
PARED, READY,
DEVELOPED, EX-
PERIENCED
ripen AGE, MATURE,
DEVELOP, MELLOW,
FIT, PREPARE,
PERFECT, IM-
PROVE, GROW
ripened *stalk*
STRAW
ripening *agent* AGER
ripple PURL,
COMB, FRET, RIFF,
LAP, WAVE, SURGE,
BABBLE, GURGLE,
DIMPLE, UNDULA-
TION, BILLOW
rise TOWER, GROW,
SOAR, LOOM, HILL,
SPRING, ORIGINATE,
DERIVE, FLOW,
STEM, SURGE,
APPEAR, RESURGE,
ASCENT, EMERGE,
CLIMB, LIFT,
ASCEND, MOUNT,
LEVITATE, CLAM-
BER, THRIVE,
PROSPER,
GRADE, SLOPE,
BEGIN, START,
GROW, INCREASE,
PROGRESS, REVOLT

riser TREAD, STEP,
PIPE
risible FUNNY, AB-
SURD, DROLL,
LAUGHABLE,
RIDICULOUS, AMUS-
ING
rising GROWING,
ASCENDANT, SUR-
GENT, ORTIVE,
MONTANT, ASCENT,
BOIL, ABSCESS
risk DARE, (EN)-
DANGER, PERIL,
CHANCE, WAGER,
PLIGHT, HAZARD,
VENTURE, JEOP-
ARDY
rite(s) SACRA-
(MENT), CERE-
MONY, CUSTOM,
FORM, FUNERAL,
OBSERVANCE, PRO-
CEDURE, RITUAL,
SOLEMNITY,
SACRUM
ritual CEREMONY,
NOVENA, CULT,
RITE, LITURGY,
FORM, PRAYER,
OBSERVANCE, PRO-
CEDURE
rival EMULATE,
EVEN, FOE,
MATCH, EXCEL,
PEER, COMPETE,
VIE, COPE, FIGHT,
ENEMY, OUTSHINE,
COMPETITOR, AN-
TAGONIST, OP-
PONENT, OPPOSE
riven CLEFT, RENT,
SPLIT
river(s) RIO,
STREAM, CREEK
bank LEVEE,
RAND, RIPA
  pertaining to
  RIPARIAN
bottom land
HOLM
Caesar crossed
RUBICON
channels ALVEI
dragon CROC
duck TEAL
gauge NILOMETER
horse HIPPO
inlet SLOUGH,
BAYOU
island HOLM, AIT

lake formed by
OXBOW
Lochinvar's
ESK(E)
mouth BOCA,
ESTUARY, DELTA,
LADE
near sea EA
nymph NAIS,
NAIAD
of forgetfulness
LETHE
passage through
FORD
pertaining to
RIPARIAN, AMNIC
siren LORELEI
Thames at Oxford
ISIS
underworld STYX
widening of ESS
river(s), *geographical
distribution*
*Abyssinia See
"Ethiopia" below*
Africa NILE,
VAAL, CONGO,
NIGER, SOBAT,
PIBOR, BARO, OMO,
BENIN, SENEGAL,
GABUN, LINDI,
RUAHA, SABI(E),
UELE (WELLE),
TANA, MONO,
RIET, JUBA, JUR,
ATHI
Alabama COOSA
Alaska YUKON
Albania DRIN
Argentina TEUCO,
DULCE, PARANA
Arizona GILA,
SALT
Armenia ARAS
Asia ILI, YALU,
AMUR
Australia SWAN,
HUON, DALY,
NAMOI, ROPER
Austria DRAVE,
ISER, SAVE
(SAVA), ENNS,
RABA, LECH,
TRAUN, RAAB, MUR
Bavaria ISER
(ISAR), SAALE
Belgium SENNE,
YSER, MEUSE, LYS,
DYLE, OISE, RUPEL
Bohemia ELBE,
ISER (ISAR), EGER,
MOLDAU

Bolivia BENI,
ORTON
Borneo KAJAN
Brazil PARU, PARA,
PARDO, DOCE,
TIETE, TEFE, IVAI,
IRIRI, AMAZON,
XINGU, PARANA
Bulgaria MESTA
Burma NMAI,
MALI, IRAWADI
California KERN,
PITT
Cambodia
MEKONG
Canada BOW, HAY,
MILK, OGOKI, NASS,
PEEL, LIARD, SEAL
Chile ITATA, LOA,
BIOBIO, BUENO
China MIN, HAN,
PEI, AMUR, HWAI,
KWEI, LWAN, WEI,
LEI, CANTON, TUNG,
LIN, LI (WU),
SIND, YELLOW
(HWANG), TARIM,
TZU (TZE), SI, BO,
HWEI, PEH (PEI),
COI
Colombia TOMO,
META, PATTIA,
CAUCA, ATROTO, SINU,
ATRATO
Colorado LAR-
AMIE, ARKANSAS
Crimea ALMA
Czechoslovakia
MOLDAU, ODER,
IPOLY, EGER, GRAN,
NITRA, HRON, ISER,
VAH (VAG, WAAG),
ELBE (LABE)
Damascus ABANA
Dutch See
"Netherlands"
below
Egypt NILE
England EXE,
AVON, OUSE, TYNE,
WEAR, URE, NEN,
YARE, TAMAR,
STOUR, TAW, TEES,
TRENT, EDEN,
THAMES, NENE,
WYE, CAM
Est(h)onia PARNU,
NARVA
Ethiopia GIBE,
JUBA, RAHAD,
BARO, WEBBE,

GIUBO, OMO,
ABBAI
Finland KEMI,
OULU
France AIN, LYS,
AIRE, AUBE, AUDE,
CHER, INDRE, SAVE,
LOIR, OISE, SAAR,
YSER, ISERE, LOIRE,
SEINE, MOSELLE,
AISNE, RHONE,
VESLE, MARNE,
SOMME, VAR(O),
RANCE, GERS, LOT
Germany PEENE,
NAHE, NAB (NAAB),
MOSEL, SAAR, ELBE,
ODER, SPREE, REMS,
EMS, EGER (ISAR),
MAIN, RUR (RUHR),
WERRA, RHINE,
ELDE, NEISSE
(NYSA)
Ghent LYS
Greece MESTA,
LERNA
Hades STYX,
ACHERON, LETHE
Holland See
"Netherlands" *be-*
low
Hungary RAAB,
RABA, UNA, DRAVE,
THEISS (TISZA),
MURES
India SIND, GANGES,
KABUL, INDUS,
SWAT, FALAR, KEN,
LUNI, GUMTI,
KISTNA, SURMA,
TISTA, MAHI,
SON(E), TAPTI,
SARDA
Indo-China HUE
Iran TAB (ZUHREH),
ZAB, KARUN
Ireland LEE, ERNE,
MOY, SUIR, NORE,
BANN
Italy PAIVE, ADIGE,
DORA, ARNO, ORCA,
ADDA, OGLIO, LIRI,
NERA, TIBER,
PANARO, SALSO,
RENO
Java SOLO
Kenya TANA,
ATHI
Korea KUM
(KIM), YALU
(AMNOK)
Latvia AA

Manchuria LIAO,
FUYU, YALU (AMNOK)
Mesopotamia
TIGRIS, EUPHRA-
TES
Mexico TONTO,
FUERTE, SALADO,
CONCHOS, YAQUI
Michigan CASS
Minnesota SAUK
Mongolia PEI, ORON
Montana TETON
Moravia ODER,
ZLIN
Nebraska PLATTE,
LOUP, NEMAHA
Nepal KOSI
(KUSI), RAPTI
Netherlands EMS,
LEK, SCHELDT,
MAAS, WAAL, SENTA
New Guinea
SEPIK, FLY,
RAMU, POTARO
North Carolina
NEUSE, TAR, HAW
Norway TANA
(TENO), RANA,
KLAR
Pakistan SWAT,
KABUL, HAB
Persia See "Iran"
above
Peru MARANON,
ACARI, OROTON,
SAMA, PIURA,
SANTA, KA, RIMAC,
ENE
Philippines ABRA,
PASIG
Phrygian
MEANDER
Poland VISTULA,
BUG, SAN, PROSNA,
STOLPE, STYR, NYSA,
NOGAT, BOBR
(BOBER), PRIPET
Portugal SADO,
GEBA, TAGUS,
MINHO (MINO)
Rhodesia SAVE
(SABI)
Romania or Rumania
SERETH, SIRET, OLT
(ALT), JIU, PRUT(H)
Russia OB, RION
(PHASIS), NEVA,
OM, OKA, UFA,
URAL, DON, TEREK,
LENA, ROS, RHA,
KAMA, DUNA,
SEIM, ONEGA,

VOLGA, DVINA,
ONON, ZEYA, YANA,
VAKSH, VAKH, STRY,
STYR, SYAS, OSKOL,
TURA, TAZ, TOBOL,
TADVA, MSTA,
MEZEN, KURA,
KUMA, KUBAN,
KARA, KHETA,
KEMA, KET, KEM,
EMBA, PSEL, SURA,
CHU, ALMA, BUG,
MAYA, ONON, SULA,
SVIR, IOM, ISERET,
SOSVA, OREL,
See under
"Ukraine" *below*
Scotland NITH,
DEE, TAY, DOON,
SPEY, AFTON,
ESK(E), TEVOIT,
EDEN
Siam MENAM
See "Thailand"
below
Siberia AMUR, LENA,
OB, OBI, OKA, PIT
See "Russia" *above*
Sicily MAZZARO,
ACIS
S. America
ORINOCO, PLATA,
AMAZON *See*
country involved
S. Carolina
SALUDA, PEEDEE
Spain SEGRE,
EBRO, TAGUS,
TINTO, JALON,
DUERO, MINHO
Sudan JUR
Sumatra MUSI
(MOESI)
Sweden UME,
LULE, LAGAN,
KLAR, GOTA, DAL,
PITE
Switzerland
AAR(E), REUSS,
THUR, SAANE
Tagalog ILOO
Tanganyika
RUAHA
Texas PECOS,
NUECES, BRAZOS,
TRINITY
Thailand MUN,
MENAM, NAN, CHI,
YOM, PING
Tibet INDUS,
MEKONG

to Adriatic Sea
PO, PIAVE, BOSNA,
ADIGE, DRIN(I),
KERKA (KRKA),
RENO
to Aegean Sea
VARDAR, MARISTA,
STRUMA
to Arctic Ocean
DVINA, TANA
(TENO), MEZEN,
PECHORA, ONEGA,
OB, LENA
to Baltic Sea
ODER (ODRA),
PEENE, WISLA,
DVINA
to Black Sea
DANUBE, PRUT,
BUG, DON, DNIESTER,
KUBAN, INGUR,
RION (PHASIS),
DNIEPER (DNEPR)
to Caspian Sea
EMBA, URAL, KURA,
VOLGA, TEREK,
ARAS, KUMA
to Danube ARGES,
DRAVA (DRAVE,
DRAU), ILLER, INN,
IPEL (IPOLY),
PRUT(H), SAVA
(SAVE), TRAUN,
VAH (VAG, WAAG),
JUI (SCHYL), NAB
(NAAB), RABA
(RAAB), ENNS
to Dead Sea
JORDAN, ARNON
to Dnieper BUG,
DESNA, PSEL
(PSIOL), SULA
to Elbe ELDE,
HAVEL, ISER,
MULDE, OHRE
(EGER), SAALE
to English Channel
EXE, ORNE, RANCE,
SEINE, SOMME
to Lake Balkhash ILI
to Loire INDRE,
CHER
to Mediterranean
Sea AUDE,
RHONE, JUCAR,
EBRO, NILE, VAR(O)
to North Sea
ELBE, WESER, EMS,
RHINE, ALLER, DEE,
TEES, MEUSE (MAAS),
EIDER, TYNE

to Rhine AAR(E),
ILL, LAHN, MAIN,
RUHR, WAAL
to Rhone AIN,
DROME, ISERE,
ARVE, ARLY, GARD
to Seine AUBE,
EURE, MARNE,
OISE
to Somme ANCRE
to Vistula BUG,
DRWECA, SAN
to Volga KAMA,
OKA, SURA
to Yangtze HAN,
KAN, MIN
Turkey MESTA,
ZAAB, SARUS, IRIS
Tuscany ORCIA,
ARNO
Ukraine BUG,
PRUT, DNIESTER,
DNIEPER, PSEL,
INGUL, SULA, STYR
Umbria TEVERE
Venezuela
ORINOCO, CARONI
Virginia DAN
Wales NEATH, USK,
LUG(G), DIFI
(DOVEY)
Westphalia EMS
Yugoslavia UNA,
TIMOK, TIMIS,
IBAR, DRINA, SAVA
(SAVE, SAU),
KULPA (KULLPA),
MUR (MURA),
BOSNA, VARDAR
riviere NECKLACE
rivulet RILL,
BROOK, STREAM,
CREEK, RUN(NEL),
BURN
road ESTRADA,
AGGER, DRIVE,
ALLEY, LANE, ITER,
DRANG, WAY,
PASSAGE, PATH,
TRAIL, COURSE,
HIGHWAY, PIKE,
STREET, TRACK,
ROUTE, RTE,
THOROUGHFARE
country LANE
military AGGER
paving material
TARMAC, ASPHALT,
TAR
Roman ITER
roam STROLL, ERR,
GAD, RANGE, ROVE,

STRAY, MEANDER,
RAMBLE, WANDER,
PROWL, STRAGGLE
roan HORSE,
SHEEPSKIN
roar NOISE, BAWL,
BELLOW, SHOUT,
DIN, BRAY, BOOM,
OUTCRY, THUNDER,
LAUGH
roast COOK, PARCH,
GRILL, BROIL,
BANTER, BAKE,
RIDICULE, CRITI-
CIZE
meat on stick
CABOB, KABOB
stick for roasting
SPIT
rob STEAL, DESPOIL,
FLEECE, RIFLE
See "loot"
robbed, *music*
RUBATO
robber *See*
"bandit"
robbery PIRACY,
THEFT, LARCENY,
DEPREDATION,
SPOLIATION, PIL-
LAGE, PLUNDER
robe MANTLE,
CLOAK, GOWN,
PURPLE, CLOTHE,
ARRAY, DRESS, VEST,
ATTIRE, GARMENT,
COSTUME, APPAREL
bishop's See under
"bishop"
camel's hair ABA
light, loose CAMIS
woman's CYMAR,
SIMAR, KIMONO
robin *genus* TURDUS
Robin Goodfellow
PUCK, FAIRY,
SPRITE, HOBGOBLIN
Robin Hood's *love*
MARIAN
friar TUCK
"Robinson Crusoe"
author DEFOE
character FRIDAY
roble BEECH, OAK
robot GOLEM,
AUTOMATON
play about RUR
robust SOUND, HALE,
RUGGED, SINEWY,
MUSCULAR, VIGOR-
OUS, WELL, STRONG,

STOUT, HUSKY,
ATHLETIC, BRAWNY,
STALWART, HARDY,
STURDY, POWER-
FUL, LUSTY, HEARTY
roc SIMBURG(H),
BIRD
rock SWING, SWAY,
SHAKE, TEETER,
STONE, TRAP,
TRASS, MINERAL
See "marble"
and gravel (*glacial*)
MORAINE
beds, pertaining to
STRATAL
black igneous
BASALT
cavity DRUSE,
GEODE, VUG(G),
VUGH
clay GANISTER
combining form
PETRO
*concretions cemented
together* OOLITE
crystal ingredient
SILICA, QUARTZ
dark BASALT,
CHERT, WHIN
decayed GEEST,
LATERITE, CLAY
finely broken
SAND, CLAY
fish RASHER,
REINA, RENA
flintlike CHERT,
QUARTZ
fossil SHALE
geyser formation
SINTER
glacial MORAINE
granitelike GNEISS,
DIORITE, QUARTZ
hard WHIN, FLINT,
CHERT, QUARTZ
igneous BASALT,
FLINT, PERIDOT,
TRAP, DIORITE,
CHRYSOLITE, DA-
CITE, BOSS, GRANITE,
QUARTZ, URTITE
jutting CRAG, TOR
laminated SHALE,
SLATE, MICA
mica DIORITE,
BIOTITE, SILICATE
peak TOR, CRAG
pinnacle SCAR,
NEEDLE
plant MOSS,
LICHEN

projecting TOR,
CRAG
suffix ITE
that splits SCHIST,
MICA
volcanic DACITE,
LAVA, TRACHYTE,
DOMITE, TUFF, TUFA
weed FUNGUS,
MOSS, LICHEN
wren TURCO, BIRD
rocket PROJECTILE,
MISSILE, WEAPON,
FIREWORK, NIKE,
ATLAS, THOR,
JUPITER, MER-
CURY, ICBM,
(A)RISE, TOWER,
SOAR, LARKSPUR
rocky HARD, STONY,
DIZZY, SHAKY,
WEAK, UNFEELING,
FLINTY, CRAGGY,
RUGGED, ROUGH,
STUBBORN, OBDU-
RATE
eminence SCAR,
TOR, CRAG
pinnacle SCAR, TOR
Rocky Ford MELON,
CANTALOUPE
rocoa, rocou AN-
NATTO
rod POLE, STAFF,
PERCH, GAT, BAR,
WAND, SWITCH,
GUN, TWIG, STICK,
CANE, SHAFT,
FERULE, MEASURE,
SCEPTER, CROP,
PISTOL, REVOLVER,
SUPPORT
chastening FERULE
divination by
RHABDOMANCY,
DOWSING
fishing, reel on
TROLL
like RHABDO(I)
movable PISTON
rode goose BRANT
rodent HARE, RAB-
BIT, CON(E)Y,
SQUIRREL, PICA,
RAT, CAVY, MOUSE,
HUTIA, JUTIA, POR-
CUPINE, BEAVER,
GNAWING, CORRODING
aquatic BEAVER,
MUSKRAT
Belgian LEPORIDE

bushy-tailed
MARMOT
Europe CON(E)Y,
LEROT
genus LEPUS,
MUS, GLIRES
geomyoid GOPHER
gnawing MOLE,
RAT, MOUSE,
BEAVER
jumping JERBOA
genus DIPUS
mouselike VOLE
muroid or murine
RAT
rabbitlike PIKA
Russian ZOKOR
S. Amer. CAPYBARA,
COYPU, AGOUTI,
PACA
W. Indies HUTIA
rods, *160 square*
ACRE
roe OVA, EGGS,
SPAWN, CAVIAR
rogation LITANY,
SUPPLICATION,
REQUEST, WORSHIP,
PRAYER
rogue SCAMP,
SCOUNDREL,
TRICKSTER, IMP,
PICARO, WAG,
KNAVE, VAGRANT,
BEGGAR, VAGABOND,
TRAMP, CHEAT,
RASCAL, SWINDLER,
SHARPER
pertaining to
PICARESQUE
roguish ARCH,
PAWKY, SLY,
IMPISH, DISHONEST,
SPORTIVE, PUCK-
ISH, WAGGISH,
WANTON, KNAVISH,
MISCHIEVOUS,
PLAYFUL
roister REVEL,
SPREE, BLUSTER,
SWAGGER, BRAG,
BULLY
Roland's *destroyer*
GANELON, GANO
role CHARACTER,
PART, PERSON, IM-
PERSONATION,
FUNCTION, BUSI-
NESS
roll SCROLL, CADRE,
BOLT, TOSS, ROSTER,
RECORD, TRUNDLE,

FURL, LURCH, BUN,
LIST, ROTA, TROLL,
TRILL, MOVE, PRO-
GRESS, MONEY,
TURN, REVOLVE,
WHIRL, CURL,
WIND, WHEEL,
ROTATE, GYRATE,
WRAP, BREAD,
BISCUIT
of hair CHIGNON,
BUN
up FURL, AMASS,
ACCUMULATE
roller WAVE, BIL-
LOW, BREAKER,
CYLINDER, WHEEL,
CASTER
romaine COS, PLANT,
LETTUCE
Roman LATIN,
NOBLE, BRAVE,
STERN, SEVERE,
DISTINGUISHED,
PAPAL *See*
"Latin"
album ALBE
amphitheater seat
SELLA
ancient territory
DACIA, NUMIDIA
arch abutment
ALETTE
assembly COMITIA,
FORUM, CURIATA,
CENTURIATA,
TRIBUTA
author VARRO,
PLUTARCH, GAIUS,
LIVY, SALLUST,
SENECA, OVID,
VERGIL
barracks CANABA,
CANNABA
basilica LATERAN
baths THERMAE
bishop POPE
block of houses
INSULA
book cover
DIPTYCH
box, papyrus
CAPSA
boxing glove
CESTUS
bronze AES
building INSULA
calendar EPHEM-
ERIS
cap PILEUS
chariot ES-
SED(E), ESSEDA, BIGA

chest CIST
chief meal CENA
circus barrier
SPINA
post META
citadel ARX
clan GENS
cloak SAGUM,
ABOLLA, PLANETA
coat PAENULA
coin AUREUS,
SESTERCE, SEXTANS,
SOLIDUS, SEMIS, AS,
AES, DENIER
collar RABAT
comic afterpiece
EXODE
comic poet
TERENCE
concert hall
ODEUM
consul CINNA,
SCIPIO, MARIUS
court(s) FORUM,
TRIBUNAL
open ATRIA,
ATRIUM
Cupid EROS
dagger SICA
date IDES, NONE(S),
CALENDS
dead, abode of
ORCUS
deity LAR *See*
under "god" *or*
"goddess"
Diana ARTEMIS
dictator SULLA
dirk SICA
dish PATERA,
LANX
diviner AUSPEX
division CENTURY,
CURIA
domestic god
LAR(ES)
earthwork AGGER
emperor OTTO,
TITUS, OTHO
empress EUDOCIA
(ATHENAIS)
entrance ATRIUM
family CENCI,
ORSINI, SAVELLI
farce EXODE
fates PARCAE
See "fates"
festival(s) VOTA,
FERIA, FERIAE
Furies DIRAE
See "Furies"

gambling cube
TESSERA
games LUDI
garment PALLA,
STOLE, PLANETA,
TOGA, TUNIC,
SAGUM, SYNTHESIS,
PAENULA, TRABEA
general MARIUS,
SULLA
geographer MELA
ghosts LEMURES
goal post META
god or goddess
See under "god" *or*
"goddess"
governor PRO-
CONSUL, LEGATUS,
PROCURATOR,
PILATE
guard LICTOR
hairpin ACUS
hall, public
ODEUM
handle ANSA
hat PETASUS,
PETASOS, GALEA
hero HORATIUS
highway VIA, ITER
hill AVENTINE,
CAELIAN, PALATINE,
QUIRINAL, CAPITO-
LINE, ESQUILINE,
VIMINAL
historian SALLUST,
LIVY, PLUTARCH
holiday(s) IDES,
FERIA, FERIAE
javelin(s) PILUM,
PILA
judge EDILE,
AEDILE, JUDEX
jurist GAIUS
king NUMA
lands acquired in
war AGER
law LEX, JUS
divine FAS
leader DUX
legendary nymph
EGERIA
legion division
COHORT, CENTURY,
CURIA, MANIPLE
libation vessel
PATERA
libra AS, POUND
magistrate CENSOR,
EDILE, PRAETOR,
TRIBUNE
maid who opened

city to Sabines
TARPEIA
market FORUM,
EMPORIUM
meal CENA, CIBUS,
PRANDIUM, FARINA
measure URN(A),
STADIUM, GRADUS,
CLIMA, PES, LIBRA,
RASTA, SALTUS,
MODIUS, PALMIPES,
PALMUS, PASSUS,
PERTICA, POLLEX,
ACTUS, COTYLE,
CUBITUS, CULEUS,
JUGER, LEUGA,
LIGULA, UNCIA
foot PES
military cloak
SAGUM
insignia PHALERA
money See "coin"
above
month MARTIUS,
APRILIS, MAIUS,
JUNIUS, QUINTILIS,
SEXTILIS
first day of
CALENDS
mound AGGER
naturalist PLINY
needle ACUS
nymph, legendary
EGERIA
official EDILE,
LICTOR *See*
"magistrate" *above*
orator CICERO,
CATO
ornament PATERA
palace LATERAN,
CHIGI
patriot CATO
pax IRENE
peasant, female
COLONA
people, early SABINES,
ETRUSCANS
philosopher CATO,
SENECA
plate PATERA
platter LANX
pledge PIGNUS
poet VERGIL
(VIRGIL), JUVENAL,
TERENCE, LUCAN,
CINNA, OVID, HORACE
port OSTIA
pound AS, LIBRA
priest FLAMEN
priestly official
AUGUR

priests of Faunus
LUPERCI
province DACIA,
NUMIDIA, ARMENIA,
ASSYRIA, GAUL
provisions AN-
NONA
rampart AGGER
register ALBE
road ITER, VIA
famous APPIAN
military AGGER
sacrificial plate
PATERNA
seat SELLA
Senate and People
SPQR
senate house CURIA
senator CATO
shield(s) SCUTA,
SCUTUM, CLIPEUS,
PARMA, PELTA
sacred ANCILE
shop TABERNA
show place CIRCUS
social group
GENS
spirits of dead
LEMURES, MANES
sports official
ASIARCH
street(s) CORSO,
VIA, VICUS, PLATEA
sword GLADIUS,
ENSIS
tablet ALBUM
tenement house
INSULA
theater ODEUM
token or ticket
TESSERA
treasurer QUAESTOR
tribal division(s)
CURIA, CURIAE
tunic PALLA
vessel PATERA,
AMPHORA, LANX
vestment TOGA
See "garment"
above
virgin warrior, myth.
CAMILLA
war machine
TEREBRA
weight AS, LIBRA,
BES, SOLIDUS,
DODRANS, DUELLA,
DEUNX, OBOLUS,
SEMIS, SEPTUS,
SEXIS, SEXTANS,
TRIENS, UNCIA
well curb PUTEAL

world of dead
ORCUS
writer MACER
See "author" *above*
writing tablet
DIPTYCH
romance NOVEL,
GEST, FANTASY,
TALE, STORY,
FABLE, FALSEHOOD,
AFFAIRE (D'AMOUR),
COURT, WOO
language CATALAN,
SPANISH, FRENCH
tale of GEST(E)
verse form
SESTINA
Romanian *city*
ARAD, TORDA
See "Rumania"
Rome, *conqueror*
ALARIC *See*
"Roman"
lake near NEMI,
ALBANO
legendary founder
ROMULUS, REMUS
port of OSTIA
"Romeo and Juliet"
character PARIS,
CAPULET, MON-
TAGUE, TYBALT
romp PLAY, SPORT,
CAPER, FROLIC,
GAMBOL, HOYDEN
Romulus' *brother*
REMUS
rondure CIRCLE,
ROUNDNESS,
PLUMPNESS, SPHERE
rone THICKET,
BRAKE, BRUSHWOOD
ronin OUTCAST,
OUTLAW
rood CROSS, CRUCI-
FIX, MEASURE
roof TOP, DOME,
COVER(ING), GAM-
BREL, CUPOLA,
MANSARD, SUMMIT,
SHELTER, HOUSE,
DWELLING, HOME
angle HIP
covering for apex
EPI
edge EAVE
finial or ornament
EPI
of mouth PALATE
of World PAMIR
raised border
COAMING

rounded DOME,
CUPOLA
top COMB, RIDGE
rook CROW, RAVEN,
CASTLE, SWIN-
DLE(R), CHEAT,
CUB, SHARPER,
STEAL, GAME
room SALA, AULA,
ATRIUM, CHAMBER,
APARTMENT, COM-
PARTMENT, SPACE,
SCOPE, PLACE, OP-
PORTUNITY, LODGE,
QUARTER, EXTENT,
EXPANSE, CAPACITY,
ACCOMMODATION,
COMPASS, FIELD,
RANGE, LEEWAY,
LATITUDE
for household goods
EW(E)RY
India KIVA
rooming house
PENSION
rooms SUITE, LODGING,
FLAT, DIGS, APART-
MENT, QUARTERS
roomy AMPLE, WIDE,
SPACIOUS, LARGE, CA-
PACIOUS, EXTENSIVE,
BROAD, COMMODIOUS,
COMFORTABLE, VAST
roorback LIE, FICTION,
FALSEHOOD, CANARD
roost POLE, PERCH,
LODGING, SUPPORT,
GARRET, ABODE, NEST,
(A)LIGHT, LAND, SIT,
SLEEP
root ORIGIN, SOURCE,
BASIS, GROUND, CORE,
BASE, BOTTOM,
FOUNDATION, CAUSE,
REASON, MOTIVE,
RADICAL, RADIX,
ETYMON, RHYZOME,
ANCESTOR, CHEER,
PLANT, START, STEM,
IMPLANT, IMBED,
SETTLE, SET, FIX, DIG,
BURROW, GRUB,
APPLAUD, ENCOURAGE
combining form
RHIZ(O and A)
drug JALAP, SENEGA,
POKE, SQUAW
edible OCA, POTATO,
TARO, TAM, CARROT
fern ROI
footed RHIZOME
fragrant ORRIS
in cough mixture

SENEGA
of a word ETYMON
out ERADICATE, EX-
TERMINATE
plant RADIX
pungent TARO,
GINGER
used in tonic GEN-
TIAN, ATIS (ATEES),
POKE
rootlet RADICEL
rope TETHER, LASSO,
RIATA, HAWSER, CORD,
LARIAT, MARLINE,
BIGHT, LINE, CABLE,
REATA, TIE, BIND,
STAY, FASTEN, CURB,
RESTRAIN, ENSNARE
animal's TETHER,
HALTER
fasten ship's tackle
LANYARD
grass SOGA, MUNJ
guy STAY, CABLE,
VANG
lead or guiding
LONGE, REIN
loop BIGHT, FRAP
make turn with
BELAY
nautical VANG, HAW-
SER, RATLIN(E)
splicer's tool FID
stay GUY
tie with LASH,
TETHER, HOBBLE
unite SPLICE
roric DEWY, RORAL,
RORY
rorqual WHALE, FIN-
BACK
rosary BEADS, CHAP-
LET, GARLAND, DEVO-
TION
bead GAUD(Y), AVE
rose RHODA
apple POMA ROSA
fruit of HIP
of Sharon ALTHEA
ornament
ROSETTE
petal oil ATTAR,
OTTO
rosin *See* "resin"
Rosinante HORSE,
STEED, PLUG, NAG,
JADE
rosolic *acid*
AURIN(E)
roster LIST, ROLL,
ROTA, SLATE,
REGISTER, AGENDA

rostrum DAIS, TRIBUNE, STAGE, PULPIT, PLATFORM, BEAK, SNOUT, PROW

rosy BRIGHT, FAVORABLE, FLATTERING, AURORAL, PINK, FINE, DANDY, OPTIMISTIC, BLOOMING, RUDDY, BLUSHING, ROSEATE, RED, FLUSHED, FLORID, RUBICUND

rot NONSENSE, WASTE, DECAY, SPOIL, DECOMPOSE

rota LIST, COURT *See* "roster"

rotate BIRL, SLUE, GYRATE, ROLL, ROTE, WHIZ, CIRCLE, SPIN, WHIRL, TURN, ALTERNATE, REVOLVE, WHEEL, TWIRL, CIRCUMVOLVE, OSCILLATE, CIRCULATE

rotating piece ROTOR, CAM, WHEEL

rotation TORQUE, GYRATION, REVOLUTION, PIROUETTE, VORTEX, EDDY, CHANGE

rotten PUTRID, BAD, FOUL, CARIOUS, DECAYED, CORRUPT, FETID, OFFENSIVE, DECOMPOSED, RANK, PUTRESCENT, TAINTED, DIRTY, DISEASED

rove *See* "roam"

roue RAKE, DEBAUCHEE, LIBERTINE

rouge RED, REDDEN, POLISH, COSMETIC, PAINT

rough SCABROUS, HOARSE, RASPY, RUDE, GRUFF, CURT, BLUNT, HILLY, AGRESTIC, UNEVEN, RUGGED, BOORISH, SEAMY, HARSH, COARSE, SHAGGY, JAGGED, INEQUAL, BROKEN, CHOPPY, RUFFLED, CRUDE, JARRING,

BOISTEROUS, TURBULENT, HARD, STERN, SEVERE, APPROXIMATE, ROWDY, VIOLENT, RAUCOUS

cloth TERRY

copy DRAFT

hair SHAG

roughen NURL, CHAP, FRAY, GNAW

roulette *bet* BAS, CARRE, ROUGE, NOIR

Roumania *See* "Rumania"

round CYCLE, RONDA, ORBED, BOUT, GLOBATE, GLOBULAR, CIRCULAR, CURVED, DANCE, REVOLUTION, ROTUND, SONG, CIRCUIT, SPHERICAL, PLUMP, BULBOUS, RUNG, AROUND, ABOUT, TRAVERSE, COURSE, SERIES, CARTRIDGE, SHELL

music TROLL, ROTA

of ladder RUNG

protuberance LOBE, UMBO

room ROTUNDA

up RODEO

roundabout INDIRECT, WINDING, AMBIENT, DEVIOUS, CIRCUITOUS, CIRCUMLOCUTION, JACKET

rounded, *and notched* RETUSE

combining form GYRO

projection LOBE, UMBO

rouse STIR, KINDLE, WAKE, EXCITE, HIE, START, STIMULATE *See* "rally"

Rousseau *hero* EMILE

rout SCATTER, DEBACLE, CHASE, DEFEAT, BEAT, LICK, OVERPOWER, OVERTHROW, VANQUISH, DISORDER

route ROAD, PATH, LINE, WAY, COURSE,

PASSAGE, ITINERARY, CIRCUIT, JOURNEY, TRIP, SEND, DIRECT, ARTERY

routine HABIT, ROTE, RUT, REGULAR, PRACTICE, GROOVE, WONT, COURSE, METHOD, SYSTEM, PROCEDURE, UNIFORM, PERIODIC, CUSTOM(ARY)

rove RANGE, GAD, WANDER *See* "roam"

rover PILGRIM, NOMAD, PIRATE, WAIF, DOG, RAMBLER, WANDERER, STRAGGLER, FREEBOOTER, VAGRANT, TRAVELER, SAILOR

row LINE, FILE, TIER, RANK, OAR, SCULL, STREET, NAVIGATE, FIGHT, FRACAS *See* "brawl"

boat CANOE, GIG, RANDAN

form in a (A)LINE, ALIGN

rowan SORB, ASH, TREE

rowdy THUG, RUFFIAN, PLUG-UGLY, HOODLUM, ROUGH, BULLY, ROISTERER, BLUSTERER

rowel PRICK, URGE, SPUR, WHEEL, GOAD, MULLET

rowen CROP, FIELD, AFTERMATH, STUBBLE

rower OAR

rowing *match* REGATTA

rowlock *support* POPPET, THOLE, FULCRUM

royal AUGUST, KINGLY, QUEENLY, REGAL, MAJESTIC, IMPERIAL, STATELY, SUPERB, MAGNIFICENT, PRINCELY, SPLENDID, COURTLY

bay LAUREL, SHRUB

blue SMALT, HATHOR, COLOR

crown TIARA
house STEWART, TUDOR, WINDSOR
officer PALATINE
title SIRE, REGENT
rub SMEAR, GRATE, BUFF, SHINE, SCRAPE, CHAFE, ABRADE, MASSAGE, BURNISH, SMOOTH, POLISH, GRAZE, HINDRANCE, DILEMMA, DIFFICULTY, OBSTACLE
out ERASE, EXPUNGE, OBLITERATE, EFFACE, CANCEL
"Rubaiyat" *author* OMAR
rubber LATEX, CAOUTCHOUC, ARCTIC, GALOSH, SHOE
city AKRON
fruit jar ring LUTE
hard EBONITE, VULCANITE
lining GASKET
sap LATEX
synthetic BUNA
tree PARA, SERINGA, ULE, CAUCHO
  genus FICUS
rubbish TRASH, JUNK, RUBBLE, SCREE, ROT, DROSS, WASTE, REFUSE, DEBRIS, LITTER, SCORIA, TRIPE
mining STENT, SLAG
rubella MEASLES, RUBEOLA
rubicund RED(DISH), FLORID, RUDDY, ROSY, FLUSHED, RUBESCENT, ERUBESCENT
rubiginous RUSTY, REDDISH, BROWN, RUFOUS, TAWNY
rubric TITLE, RED, FLOURISH, HEAD, PARAPH, CATEGORY, HEADING, LETTER
book of ORDO
ruby SPINEL, RUBASSE, BALAS, GEM, STONE
rudder *control*

mechanism HELM, TILLER
rude CRUDE, HARSH, RAW, CALLOW, GREEN, ROUGH, UNCIVIL, IMPOLITE, ABUSIVE, IMPUDENT, GRUFF, VIOLENT, DISRESPECTFUL, RUGGED, UNPOLISHED, INELEGANT, UNCOUTH, VULGAR, BOORISH, CLUMSY, DISCORDANT, UNCIVILIZED, UNTRAINED, FLIPPANT, SAUCY, SASSY, SAVAGE
rudiment ANLAGE, GERM, EMBRYO, ABC, ELEMENTAL, FUNDAMENTAL, ROOT, SEED, BEGINNING
rudimentary BASIC, GERMINAL, EMBRYONIC, ELEMENTARY, INITIAL, PRIMARY, CAUSAL, VESTIGIAL
rue DEPLORE, REGRET, LAMENT, REPENT, GRIEVE, BITTERNESS, DISAPPOINTMENT
herb HARMEL
  genus RUTA
rueful SORRY, SAD, DOLEFUL, MOURNFUL, WOEFUL, PENITENT, DISMAL, LUGUBRIOUS, PITIABLE, LAMENTABLE, MELANCHOLY, REGRETFUL
ruff BIRD, FISH, COLLAR, TRUMP
female REE, REEVE
ruffle RUCHE, CRIMP, VEX, ROIL, DERANGE, BRISTLE, STRUT, FRET, IRRITATE, NETTLE, DISTURB, AGITATE, RUMPLE, SHUFFLE, SWAGGER, FRILL, RIPPLE, PUCKER, WRINKLE, ANNOY
neck JABOT, RUCHE, RUFF
rufous REDDISH,

TAWNY, RUBIGINOUS, RUSTY
rug RUNNER, MAT, COVERING, ROBE, WRAP
Rugby SCHOOL, FOOTBALL, FIVES
halfback SCRUM
tackling MAUL
Rugen Island *cape or promontory* ARKONA
town on BERGEN
rugged ASPER, CRAGGY, HARDY, ROUGH, HARSH, BURLY, SCRAGGY, COARSE, RUDE, IRREGULAR, UNEVEN, UNKEMPT, SURLY, SOUR, CRABBED, AUSTERE, UNCIVIL, VIGOROUS, ROBUST, STRONG, STURDY, SHAGGY
Ruhr *city* HAMM
ruin DEFEAT, WRECK, RAZE, FALL, COLLAPSE, DECAY, BANE, SPOIL, WRACK, UNDO, DOWNFALL, PERDITION, DESTROY, SUBVERT, DEMOLISH, FAILURE, DESTRUCTION, HAVOC, DILAPIDATION
ruined GONE, WRECKED, HOPELESS
ruins DEBRIS, ASHES, REMAINS
rule GUIDE, CONTROL, HABIT, ORDER, GOVERN, CANON, CODE, PRECEPT, LEAD, LAW, NORM, SWAY, MAXIM, COMMAND, STANDARD, FORMULA, METHOD, CRITERION, DECIDE, PREVAIL, PRINCIPLE, REGULATION
"Rule Britannia" *composer* ARNE
ruler EMIR, MIN, PRINCE, QUEEN, KING, MONARCH, POTENTATE, PRESIDENT, GOVERNOR, CHIEF, DESPOT, REGENT, AMEER, NAWAB

Moslem EMIR, CALIPH, SULTAN
of gods ZEUS
religious body HIERARCH
wife of EMPRESS, QUEEN, RANEE, RANI, TSARINA
"Rules of Order"
author ROBERTS
ruling, *act of* REGLE
rum *from molasses* TAFIA
Rumanian *city or town* ARAD, DEVA, CLW, AIUD, HUSI, SIGHET, IASI, TORDA, GALATI
coin BAN, LEY, LEU, AS, UNCIA, TRIENS
mountain NEGOI
pass ROSU
queen, former MARIE
river See under "river"
rumen CUD, STOMACH, PAUNCH
ruminant ALPACA, GOAT, LLAMA, CAMEL, YAK, BISON, BUFFALO, DEER, COW, SHEEP, EWE, BOS, GIRAFFE
division UNGULATA, BOS
genus CAPRA, BOS
second stomach RETICULUM
third stomach OMASUM
Tibet SEROW, TAKIN
ruminate CHEW, REFLECT, MUSE, MULL, PONDER, WEIGH, THINK, MEDITATE, CONSIDER, COGITATE
rummy ODD, QUEER, SOT, GAME, DRUNKARD
rumor TALK, BRUIT, STORY, NORATE, NOISE, REPORT, GOSSIP, HEARSAY, TIDINGS, NOTORIETY

personified FAMA
rumple TOUSLE, CREASE, MUSS, RUFFLE, WRINKLE, CRINKLE, CRUMPLE
rumpus FRACAS, ROW, DISTURBANCE
See "brawl"
run GO, OPERATE, PROPEL, TRIP, SPRING, RACE, PLY, HIE, SCUD, TROT, GAD, FLOW, LOPE, ROUTE, COURSE, SCAMPER, BROOK, STREAM, PANIC, RANGE
away ELOPE, DECAMP, FLEE, ESCAPE, FLY, SCUD
for office STAND
runes, *inventor (Norse myth.)* DVALIN
rung STEP, SPOKE, ROUND
runnel BROOK, CHANNEL, RIVULET, STREAM, CREEK
runner MAT, RUG, SCARF, RACER, MILER, COURIER, CANDIDATE, WHIPPET, HORSE, MESSENGER, SUPERVISOR, BRANCH, CONDUIT, STOLON, SMUGGLER
of plant STOLON
runt DWARF, PIGMY, CHIT, ELF
of a brood WRIG
runway RAMP, PATH, GROOVE, (AIR)STRIP, TRAIL, ROAD, TRACK, CHANNEL, TARMAC
rupee LAC, LAKH, COIN
1/16th of ANNA
rupture FRACTURE, BREAK, HERNIA, RIFT, RENT, RHEXIS, QUARREL, SPLIT, BREACH, DISRUPTION, BURST, FEUD
rural BUCOLIC, GEORGIC, PASTORAL, RUSTIC, COUNTRY, AGRARIAN, AGRICULTURAL, VILLATIC

deity PAN, FAUN(US)
pertaining to AGRESTIC, RUSTIC(AL)
poem GEORGIC, ECLOGUE, PASTORAL
rush SPATE, PRESS, SURGE, CHARGE, SPURT, HURRY, RUN, GRASS, STAMPEDE, HURTLE, ONSET, ATTACK, DEFEAT, HASTE(N)
basket FRAIL
Russell, *pen name* AE
Russell's *viper* DABOIA
Russia(n) RUSS, RED, MUSCOVY, MOSCOVITE, BYZANTINE, SOVIET, SIBERIAN, UKRAINIAN
alcoholic beverage KVASS, VODKA
aristocrat BOYAR, KNEEZE
assembly RADA, DUMA
autonomous region BASHKIR, YAKUT, MORDZIN, TUVA, UZBEK
barrow KURGAN
bay KOLA
beer KVASS
carriage TARANTAS(S), TROIKA
caviar IKRA
cereal grain EMMER, DURUM
city or town ORSK, GORI, MINSK, IOSH, SUMY, AKA, SEROV, SHUYA, OM, UKHTA, ORSHA, OREL, VOLSK, OMSK, KIEV, LIDA, KURSK, KOVEL, LYSVA, LVOV, LUTSK, PSKOV, PENZA, OSA, KOLA, RIGA, UMAN, ISKER, CHITA, BISK, BAKU, ROVNO, RZHEV
clover OREL
coal area DONETS (DONBAS)

coin DENESHKA, POLUSKA, POLTINA, KOPEC(K), RUBLE, IMPERIAL, ABASSI, ALTINIK, BISTI, GROSH, PIATAK, SHAUR
committee TSIK
community MIR
convict shelter ETAPE
cooperative society ARTEL
Cossack TATAR
council DUMA, SOVIET
  political RADA
dance KOLO, COSAQUE, GOPAK
decree UKASE
desert TUNDRA
devil CHORT
district STEPPE, KARELIA *See* "region" *below*
drink VODKA, KVASS
edict UKASE
emperor, former TSAR, CZAR, TZAR
empress TZARINA, TZARITZA
fiddle GUDOK
fish STERLET
fur KARAKUL
guild ARTEL
gulf AZOV, MEZEN
hemp RINE
holy picture IKON
imperial order UKASE
inland sea ARAL, AZOV
labor assn. ARTEL
lake See under "lake"
landed proprietor BOYAR
leather JUFTI, BULGAR, SHAGREEN, YUFT
legislature RADA, DUMA
liquor VODKA, KVASS
log hut ISBA
measure STOF(F), FOUTE, LOOF, SAGENE, FUT, OSMINA, LINIA, PAJAK, PALETZ, QUAR,

STEKAR, TSARKL, UEDRO, VERST
mile (approx.) VERST
monetary unit RUBLE
most northern town KOLA
mountains ALAI, URAL
musical instrument GUSLE, GUDOK, BALALAIKA
negative NYET
novelist TOLSTOI, TOLSTOY, GORKI
oil center BAKU
opera BORIS
parliament DUMA
peasant KULAK
peninsula CRIMEA, KOLA, YAMAL
people SLAVS
plane MIG
police OGPU, NKVD
port OKHA, ODESSA
prison or stockade ETAPE
province ABASIA, ARMENIA, BUGHDAN, DONBASS, GALICIA, GEORGIA, GURIA, INGUSH, KABARDIA (KABARDA), KARELIA, KARTHLI, (KARTILI(A)), KAVKAZ, KIRGIZ, LAPLAND, MOLDAU, OSETIYA, POLESIA, SIBERIA, UKRAINE, YAKUTIA, PODOLIA
river See under "river"
rodent ZOKOR
ruler, former IVAN, PETER
sea AZOV, AZOF, ARAL
secret service OGPU, CHEKA, MVD
soup BORSCH
stockade ETAPE
tavern CABACK, KABAK
tax OBROK
tea urn SAMOVAR

town See "city" *above*
trade union ARTEL
Ukraine council RADA
vehicle TROIKA, TARANTAS(S), TELEGA
wagon TELEGA
weight LOT, POOD, PUD, DULA, DOLA, FUNT, LANA, LAST, LOF, ONCE, SOL
wheat EMMER, DURUM
whip KNOUT, PLET(E)
wolfhound ALAN, BORZOI, (PSOVIE)
yes DA
russud FORAGE, GRAIN
rust CORRODE, EAT, WEAKEN, IM-PAIR, ERODE, VERDIGRIS, INACTION, IDLENESS, INERTIA, COLOR, DEGENERATE, DECAY, CANKER, OXIDATE, OXIDATION, PATINA
on bronze, etc. PATINA
plant BLIGHT, FUNGUS, FERRUGO
Rustam's *father* ZAL
son SOHRAB
rustic BOOR, GEO-PONIC, BUCOLIC, SYLVAN, RURAL, RUBE, PLAIN, CLOWN, YOKEL, UNPOLISHED, AWKWARD, BUMP-KIN, HAYSEED, PEASANT, RUDE, ARTLESS, COARSE, VILLATIC
lover SILVESTER, SWAIN
pipe REED, CORN
poet CARL
rustle SWISH, FROUFROU, STIR, STEAL, HURRY
rustling SOFT, GEN-TLE, MURMURING, SUSURROUS, WHIS-PERING
rut ROUTINE, GROOVE, PATH, FURROW,

TRACK, HABIT,
IMPASSE, CHANNEL
rutabaga TURNIP
ruthless *See*
"savage"
Ruth's *husband* BOAZ
mother-in-law
NAOMI
son OBED
rutilate GLOW,
GLITTER, SHINE
Ruy Diaz de Bivar
CID
rye *beard* AWN
fungus ERGOT
genus SECALE
ryot PEASANT,
TENANT, SERVANT

S

S ESS, SIGMA
curve OGEE
shaped like an
SIGMATE, SIGMOID
sable SOBOL, EBON,
MARTEN, BLACK,
DARK, FUR, FISH,
DUSKY, SOMBER
Alaskan SKUNK,
RACCOON
American MARTEN
genus MUSTELA
Sabrina *river*
SEVERN
sabulous FLOURY,
SANDY, DUSTY,
GRITTY, ARENACEOUS
sac POUCH, ASCUS,
BURSA, CYST,
CAVITY, VESICLE,
POCKET, BAG
sacaton GRASS
saccharine SWEET,
HONEYED, SWEET-
ENING
sacerdotal PRIESTLY,
CLERICAL
sachet PAD, SAC, BAG,
PERFUME, RETI-
CULE, SCENT
sack BAG, POUCH,
POKE, BED, WINE,
LOOT, FIRE, DIS-
CHARGE, PLUNDER,
ROB, DROP, CASHIER,
SPOLIATION,
DESTRUCTION,
HAVOC, DIS-
MISS(AL), JILT,
SHERRY

fiber JUTE,
GUNNY
sackbut TROMBONE
sacrament SERVICE,
RITE, HOST, CERE-
MONY, EUCHARIST,
SOLEMNITY,
COMMUNION,
MASS, TOKEN,
SYMBOL, BAPTISM,
PLEDGE, COVENANT,
MARRIAGE
sacrarium CHANCEL,
PISCINA, SANCTU-
ARY, VESTRY,
SHRINE, SACRISTY,
TABERNACLE
sacred HOLY,
DIVINE, CON-
SECRATED, REVERED,
CHERISHED, VALUED,
SACROSANCT, HAL-
LOWED, VENERABLE,
SAINTED, INVIOLATE,
DEDICATED,
VENERATED
bean LOTUS
bird IBIS
bull APIS, HAPI,
ZEBU
cantata MOTET
casket CIST, PYX
combining form
HIERO
Egyptian bird IBIS
fig tree PIPAL
grove, Greece
ALTIS
image PIETA, ICON,
IKON
instrument URIM
lily LOTUS
music MOTET
not PROFANE
place SHRINE,
TEMPLE
river, NILE
scripture KORAN,
BIBLE
things, traffic in
SIMONY
wine vessel AMA
word OM
sacrifice FOREGO,
YIELD, RESIGN,
IMMOLATE,
OBLATION, LOSS,
PRIVATION, SUR-
RENDER, VICTIM,
OFFERING
sacristy, *relating to*
VESTRAL

sacrosanct HOLY,
INVIOLABLE, SACRED
sad BLUE, BAD, DIRE,
SORRY, WAN, DULL,
GLOOMY, GRAVE,
DEJECTED, DISMAL,
SORROWFUL, SOM-
BER, MELANCHOLY,
MOURNFUL, DOWN-
CAST, DISCONSOLATE,
DEPRESSED, DE-
SPONDENT, MIRTH-
LESS, PAINFUL,
LUGUBRIOUS,
DOLENT, DOLEFUL,
UNHAPPY
combining form
TRAGI
cry ALAS, ALACK
music MESTO
saddle, *bag for*
ALFORJA, POUCH
blanket CORONA,
TILPAH
boot GAMBADO
bow POMMEL
cloth PANEL,
SHABRACK, BLANKET
girth CINCH
hind bow CANTLE
horn POMMEL
horses REMUDA,
PALFREYS
knob POMMEL
light PILCH, PIL-
LION
pack APAREJO
pad PANEL,
SHABRACK, BURR,
BLANKET
part CANTLE,
POMMEL, STIRRUP,
CINCH
place behind CROUP
pommel CRUTCH,
TORE, KNOB
rear part CANTLE
strap GIRTH, CINCH,
LATIGO
saddler LORIMER
sadness PATHOS,
GLOOM, DOLOR, SOR-
ROW, VAPORS, GRIEF,
WOE, BLUES,
DUMPS, DEJECTION,
UNHAPPINESS
safari HUNT,
JOURNEY, TREK,
EXPEDITION,
EXCURSION
safe VAULT, CUP-
BOARD, SECURE, RE-

LIABLE, TAME, TRIED, COFFER, CHEST, STRONGBOX, SURE, UNHARMED, TRUSTWORTHY, CERTAIN

blower YEGG

conduct CONVOY, COWLE, PASS(PORT)

keeping CUSTODY

safeguard PROTECT, DEFEND

safety *lamp* DAVEY

pin, forerunner of FIBULA

saffron YELLOW

plant CROCUS

sag LULL, SETTLE, SLOUCH, BEND, WILT, SINK, DROOP, DIP, CURVE, HANG

in timber SNY

saga EPIC, TALE, STORY, MYTH, LEGEND, TRADITION

Norse myth. EDDA

sagacious WISE, SAPIENT, WITTY, SAGE, ASTUTE, KEEN, SHARP, SHREWD, DISCERNING, INTELLIGENT, JUDICIOUS, PROPHETIC

sagacity ACUMEN, KEN, WISDOM, ACUTENESS, PERSPICACITY, INSIGHT, PENETRATION, JUDGMENT

sage SALVIA, HERB, SEASONING, WISE, SOLON, SAPIENT, SANE, PRUDENT, SAVANT, PUNDIT, PROFOUND, DISCERNING

genus SALVIA

hen GROUSE

of Pylos NESTOR

one of the seven SOLON

Sagebrush State NEVADA

sagitta ARROW, KEYSTONE, CONSTELLATION

saguaro CACTUS

saiga AHU, ANTELOPE

sail CANVAS, GLIDE, FLOAT, FLY, SKIM, DART, NAVIGATE, SCUD, CRUISE

center BUNT

cloth DUCK, CANVAS

corner CLEW

edge of square LEECH

four-sided LUGSAIL

furl REEF, MAINE

kind of JIB, SPANKER

line EARING

nearest wind LUFF

slack part of SLAB

square LUG

triangular JIB, LATEEN

with wind abeam LASK

sailboat SAPIT, SKIFF, YACHT, BARK, SCHOONER, KETCH *See* "boat"

race REGATTA

sailing vessel BUGEYE, SETEE, BUCKEYE *See* "boat"

Levant SAIC

sailor(s) MARINER, MIDDY, SALT, GOB, TAR, TOTY, JACK, SEAMAN, TARPOT

amusement SCRIMSHAW

call AHOY

E. India LASCAR

female WAVE

meeting GAM

mess tub KID

potion GROG

saint ELMO

saint(s) ELMO, OLAF, CANONIZE, HOLY, ANGEL, SANCTIFIED

Andrew's cross SALTIRE, SALTIER

beggars and cripples GILES

biographies of HAGIOGRAPHY, HAGIOLOGY

casket for relics of CHASSE

catalog of DIPTYCH

Catherine's home SIENNA

Elmo's fire CORPOSANT

England (patron) ANNE, GEORGE

George, rescued SABRA

John's bread CAROB, ALGAROBA

lawyers, patron IVES

memorial of RELIC

painted ICON

relic box CHASSE

Saens' opera DELILAH (SAMSON AND)

sailors, patron ELMO

Vitus dance CHOREA

worship of DULIA

Saipan *town* GARAPAN

sake BEHALF, BENEFIT, SCORE, ACCOUNT, INTEREST, OBJECTIVE, PURPOSE, ADVANTAGE, BEVERAGE

Sakhalin Gulf *river* AMUR

salaam CONGE, BOW, BEND, NOD, OBEISANCE, SALUTE, SALUTATION, CURTS(E)Y

salable VENAL, VENDIBLE, SUITABLE, MARKETABLE, PURCHASABLE, GOOD

salad ENDIVE, CRESS, CABBAGE, LETTUCE, SLAW, MIXTURE

salamander EFT, NEWT, TRITON, AMPHIBIAN, STOVE

Mexico AXOLOTL

order of CAUDATA, URODELA

salami SAUSAGE, SALAME

salary PAY, HIRE, STIPEND, WAGE(S), FEE, ALLOWANCE, HONORARIUM, COMPENSATION, RECOMPENSE

sale AUCTION, DEAL, VEND, HANDSEL, BARTER, TRADE, EXCHANGE, DEMAND, DISPOSAL

salesman CLERK

salicylic acid *deriv.* ASPIRIN

salient STRIKING, CONSPICUOUS, LEAPING, BOUNDING, JUMPING, JETTING, PROJECTING, PROMINENT, NOTICEABLE, RAMPANT, MANIFEST, IMPORTANT, SHARP

salientia ANURA

saliferous SALINE, SALTY

saline(e) POTASH

saline *solution* BRINE

salix ITEA, OSIER, WILLOW, CATKIN, SALLOW

sallow WAN, PASTY, GRAY, YELLOWISH, MUDDY, PALLID, WILLOW, COLORLESS

sally ISSUE, JEST, LEAP, SORTIE, START, DASH, ESCAPADE, EXCURSION, DIGRESSION, FROLIC, JOKE, QUIP, WITTICISM, RUSH, ATTACK, FRAY

salmagundi HASH, OLIO, MEDLEY, POTPOURRI, MIXTURE, FARRAGO, JUMBLE, HODGEPODGE, GALLIMAUFRY, MELANGE, MISHMASH

salmi RAGOUT

salmoid *fish* GWYNIAD, CHAR, TROUT, NELMA, WHITE, POLLAN, POWAN

salmon NERKA, GILLING, KETA, HADDO, QUINNAT
dog KETA
female BAGGIT, RAUN
first year SMELT
Japanese MASU
kind DOG, QUINNAT
male GIB, KIPPER, COCK
Norway LAX
pool STELL
second year SPROD, GILLING
silver COHO

third year MORT
troutlike SEWEN
two-year-old SMOLT, GILLING
young ALEVIN, JERKIN, PARR, ESSLING, GRILSE, PINK, SAMLET

salmonoid *See* "salmoid"

salon PARTY, HALL, LEVEE, PARLOR, RECEPTION, ASSEMBLY, EXHIBITION

saloon BAR, GROGGERY, PUB, CABIN

salt KERN, FLAVOR, HUMOR, SAVOR, SENSE, SALINE, BRINY, TASTE, WIT, BRINE, SAILOR, TAR, MARINER, GOB, SEAMAN, CONDIMENT, PRESERVE, CURE, CORN, SAL, SEASON, HALITE
alkaline BORAX
bed VAT
cellar SHAKER
factory SALTERN
lake CHOTT
marsh SALINA
mineral astringent ALUM
pertaining to HALOID, SALINE
rock HALITE
spring LICK, SALINE
tax GABELLE
tree ATLE(E)
water BRINE, SEA, OCEAN
works SALINA, SALTERY
  pond of SUMP

saltant LEAPING, DANCING, JUMPING, SALIENT

saltpeter NITER

saltwort KALI, GLASSWORT, PLANT, HERB

salty BRINY, RACY, PIQUANT, SHARP, BRACKISH
efflorescence REH

salutary GOOD, HEALTHFUL, HEALING, USEFUL, CORRECTIVE, BENEFICIAL, TONIC,

HEALTHY, SALUBRIOUS, WHOLESOME, CURATIVE, MEDICINAL, RESTORATIVE, REMEDIAL

salutation SALAAM, SALUTE, PROSIT, AVE, ALOHA, HI, HELLO, SIR, GREETING, ACHARA, WELCOME

salute AVE, CURTSY, HAIL, BOW, DIP, TOAST, KISS, SALVO, ADDRESS, ACCOST, WELCOME, CONGRATULATE, COMPLIMENT, GREET(ING), SALUTATION

salvage SAVE, RESCUE, RECLAIM

salve OINTMENT, BALM, CURE, PLASTER, TREAT, FLATTER, CERATE, ANOINT, HEAL, QUIET, ALLAY, ASSUAGE, SOOTHE, REMEDY, RELIEVE

salver TRAY, WAITER

salvia CHIA, PLANT

samara, *fruit of* ELM, ASH, MAPLE

samarium *symbol* SM, SA

Sambal *language* TINO

sambar *deer* ELK, RUSA, MAHA

sambucus ELDER, BUSH

same ONE, COGNATE, DITTO, ILK, IDENTICAL, SIMILAR, IDEM, (A)LIKE, EQUAL, PEER, VERY, EQUIVALENT, EQUALLY, JUST, LIKEWISE, EVEN, AKIN
combining form ISO, HOMO
place, in IBID

sameness PARITY, IDENTITY, MONOTONY, SIMILARITY, RESEMBLANCE, CORRESPONDENCE, LIKENESS, ONENESS

samisen BANJO

samlet PARR,
SALMON
Samoa(n) POLYNE-
SIAN See
"Polynesia"
barn owl LULU
bird IAO, MANUAO
capital APIA
cloth TAPA
council FONO
island MANUA,
TUTUILA
mollusk ASI
owl LULU
political structure
FONO
seaport APIA
warrior TOA
samovar URN,
TEAPOT
sample PATTERN,
SWATCH, SLIP,
TASTE, TEST,
EXAMINE, PART,
PARCEL, EXAMPLE,
CASE, TRY, SPECI-
MEN, PIECE,
PORTION
Samson's *city*
ZORAH
father MANOAH
Samuel's *father*
ELKANAH
home RAMAH
mother HANNAH
teacher ELI
Samurai, *ostracized*
RONIN
sanction AMEN,
FIAT, ABET, EN-
DORSE, RATIFY,
ALLOW, LICENSE,
APPROVE, CON-
FIRM(ATION), EN-
COURAGE, PERMIT,
COUNTENANCE,
SUPPORT, AUTHOR-
ITY, PENALTY,
PUNISHMENT, AP-
PROBATION
sanctuary HARBOR,
SHELTER, ASYLUM,
COVER, RETREAT,
CHURCH, SHRINE,
ADYTUM, ALTAR,
HAVEN, FANE,
TEMPLE, ARK,
HOME, REFUGE,
PROTECTION
Hebrew BAMAH
inner part
PENETRALIA

sanctum *of temple*
ADYTUM
sand SILICA, GRIT,
PLUCK, COURAGE,
GUTS, SPIRIT,
METTLE, GRAVEL,
POWDER
bank HURST,
SHOAL
bar REEF, SHOAL
drift ESKER
dune DENE,
MEDANO
expanses DUNES,
DESERTS, BEACHES
flea CHIGOE,
CHIGGER
hill DUNE, DENE
island BAR
mineral ISERINE
particles SILT,
GRAINS
quick BOG,
SYRTIS,
ridge(s) ASAR,
KAME, OS, OSAR
sea bottom PAAR
snake genus ERYX
sandal(s) BUSKIN,
SOCK, SHOE, SLIPPER,
MOCCASIN
winged TALARIA
sandalwood ALGUM,
ALMUG, MAIRE
genus SANTALUM
red color from
SANTALIN
sandarac ARAR,
ALERCE, REALGAR,
RESIN, TREE
wood ALERCE
sand bar REEF, SPIT,
SHOAL, BEACH
sandpiper STIB,
DUNIN, REE(VE),
TEREK, RUFF,
STINT, KNOT,
SANDERLING, BIRD
Arctic KNOT
Europe RUFF,
TEREK
female REE(VE)
march PECTORAL
Old World TEREK
small PUME,
STINT
sandstone GRIT,
MEDINA, ROCK
Sandwich *island*
HAWAII, OAHU,
MAUI See
"Hawaii"

sandy ARENACEOUS,
ARENOSE, SABULOUS,
GRITTY, UNSTABLE,
SHIFTING, PLUCKY
drift DENE,
ESKER, DUNE
region, France
(LES) LANDES
ridge ESKER
tract DENE, DUNE,
DESERT, BEACH
sane WISE, RIGHT,
GOOD, RATIONAL,
SOBER, HEALTHY,
LUCID, SAGE,
SOUND, REASON-
ABLE, SENSIBLE
sangalike *animal*
ZEBU, OX
sang-froid
PHLEGM, APLOMB,
COOLNESS, COM-
POSURE, INDIFFER-
ENCE, UNCONCERN
sangreal See "grail"
sanguine RED, GORY,
BLOODY, CHEERFUL,
PLETHORIC, CER-
TAIN, WARM, CON-
FIDENT, OPTIMISTIC,
HOPEFUL, ARDENT
sanity REASON,
LUCIDITY, NOR-
MALITY, SOUND-
NESS, RATIONALITY,
WHOLESOMENESS,
COMPETENCE
Sankhya *philos. term*
GUNA
Sanskrit VEDIC,
INDIC, LANGUAGE
college TOL
deity ADITI
dialect PALI,
VEDIC
god INDRA, VAYU
goddess DEVI,
UMA, ADATI
metrical unit
MATRA
verse SLOKA
Santa Maria *tree*
CALABA
sap JUICE, LYMPH,
ESSENCE, BLOOD,
FLUID, ENERVATE,
WEAKEN, WRECK,
DRAIN, UNDER-
MINE, UNSETTLE,
VITALITY, VIGOR,
ENERGY, TRENCH,
SIMPLETON, FOOL

spout SPILE
sapajou MONKEY,
  GRISON
sapid TASTY,
  SAVORY, ZESTFUL,
  PALATABLE, EN-
  GAGING
sapience SENSE,
  WISDOM, TASTE,
  JUDGMENT,
  KNOWLEDGE,
  SAGACITY, INTEL-
  LIGENCE
sapiens, *homo* MAN
sapient WISE, SAGE,
  SAGACIOUS, DIS-
  CERNING
sapiutan ANOA, OX,
  BUFFALO
sapodilla CHICO,
  NISPERO, TREE,
  FRUIT
  juice CHICLE
sapor SAVOR,
  FLAVOR, GUSTO,
  RELISH, TASTE
Sappho's *home*
  LESBOS
sappy JUICY, LUSH,
  SUCCULENT, VITAL,
  PITHY, SENTI-
  MENTAL, SILLY,
  FOOLISH
sapwood BLEA,
  ALBURNUM
Saracen MOOR,
  PAGAN, HEATHEN,
  ARAB, MOSLEM
  leader SALADIN
Sarah's *handmaid*
  HAGAR
sarcasm IRONY,
  SATIRE, WIT,
  BANTER, RIDICULE,
  TAUNT, GIBE, RE-
  BUKE, CENSURE,
  DETRACTION
sarcastic CAUSTIC,
  SARDONIC, IRONICAL,
  CUTTING *See*
  "sardonic"
sarcophagus *roof*
  TEGURIUM
sardine BANG,
  PILCHARD, AN-
  CHOVY, FISH
Sardinian *seaport*
  BOSA
  structure
  NURAGH(E),
  NORAGHE

sardonic CYNICAL,
  DRY, ACRID,
  BITTER, SARCASTIC,
  IRONIC, DERISIVE,
  BITING, SCORNFUL
Sardou *drama*
  FEDORA
  heroine TOSCA
Sargasso SEA,
  GULFWEED
Sargon's *capital or*
  country AKKAD
sartor TAILOR
sash CUMMERBUND,
  GIRDLE, OBI, BELT,
  FRAME, GATE,
  BAND, SCARF, STRIP,
  CORD
  weight MOUSE
Saskatchewan *capital*
  REGINA
sassafras *oil*
  SAFROL(E)
  tea SALOOP
  tree AGUE
Satan LUCIFER,
  TEMPTER, BELIAL,
  DEVIL, REPROBATE,
  APOLLYON,
  ARCHFIEND *See*
  "devil"
  Arab EBLIS
  before fall AZAZEL
  demon of anger
  ASMODEUS
  of bottomless pit
  ABADDON,
  APOLLYON
  Scot. DEIL
satanic VICIOUS,
  DIABOLIC, MA-
  LEVOLENT, EVIL,
  BAD, WICKED
satchel ETUI, CABAS,
  ETWEE, BAG,
  SACK, RETICULE,
  VALISE
sate SATISFY, CLOY,
  GLUT, SURFEIT,
  PALL, SATIATE,
  GORGE, STUFF,
  CRAM, GRATIFY
sated BLASE,
  STUFFED, GORGED
satellite LUNA,
  MOON, ORB,
  VOTARY, FAN,
  ATTENDANT, FOL-
  LOWER, RETAINER,
  ECHO, COMPANION,
  SPUTNIK, ATLAS

Uranus TITANIA,
  ARIEL, OBERON
satiate SATE, CLOY,
  GLUT, GORGE,
  SATISFY, SATURATE,
  SURFEIT, OVERFILL,
  PALL
satin(y) ETOILE,
  SILK, DAMASK,
  CLOTH, SMOOTH,
  SOFT, GLOSSY
satire IRONY, WIT,
  SKIT, HUMOR,
  RIDICULE, SARCASM,
  INVECTIVE,
  PHILIPPIC, DIATRIBE,
  LAMPOON, PAS-
  QUINADE, BUR-
  LESQUE, CARICATURE
satirical WRY, DRY,
  ABUSIVE, CAUSTIC,
  SARCASTIC, TAUNT-
  ING, CENSORIOUS,
  CUTTING, BITING,
  POIGNANT
satirist VOLTAIRE,
  SHAW, POPE,
  SWIFT
satirize GRIND,
  LAMPOON, LASH,
  CENSURE, ABUSE,
  RIDICULE, DETRACT
satisfaction AMENDS,
  COMFORT, PAYMENT,
  CONTENT, GRATIFI-
  CATION, SATIETY,
  PLEASURE, APOLOGY,
  REQUITAL, RE-
  DRESS, ATONEMENT,
  SETTLEMENT,
  INDEMNIFICATION,
  REMUNERATION,
  REPARATION
  combat for DUEL
  Maori UTU
  payment for killing
  CRO
satisfactory NICE,
  GOOD, NEAT, FINE
satisfy (RE)PAY,
  ATONE, MEET,
  CLOY, SATE, GLUT,
  SUIT, DO, PLEASE,
  PACIFY, PROVE,
  SUFFICE, REWARD,
  GRATIFY, APPEASE,
  SATIATE, CONVINCE,
  PERSUADE, ASSURE,
  COMPENSATE,
  SETTLE
satrap MIR, GOV-
  ERNOR, SULTAN,

DESPOT, RULER,
VICEROY
saturate DRENCH,
SEETHE, SOG, SOAK,
STEEP, WET, RET,
FILL, PENETRATE,
IMPREGNATE,
SATIATE
saturnalia FESTIVAL,
CARNIVAL,
ORGIES, REVELS,
FEASTS, GAMES
saturnine GLUM,
MOROSE, DULL,
DOUR, SURLY,
HEAVY, GLOOMY,
SOMBER, SULLEN,
SLUGGISH, GRAVE,
TACITURN
Saturn's *moon*
JAPETUS, DIONE,
MIMAS, RHEA,
TITAN
ring projection
ANSA
wife OPS
satyr SILENUS, FAUN,
BUTTERFLY, APE,
LIBERTINE, DEMON
sauce GRAVY,
CURRY, FLAVOR,
TOBASCO, SEA-
SONING, RELISH,
CONDIMENT,
DRESSING, ADJUNCT
Chinese SOY
fish ALEC, TARTAR,
ANCHOVY, SOY, GARUM
meat TOBASCO,
TOMATO
white vegetable
VELOUTE
saucepan SKILLET,
POSNET, SPIDER
saucy SASSY,
BRASH, COCKY,
CHIC, BOLD, PERT,
ARCH, INSOLENT,
AIRY, PIQUANT,
MALAPERT, IM-
PUDENT, IMPER-
TINENT, CAVALIER,
RUDE, FORWARD,
DISRESPECTFUL,
FLIPPANT, FRESH
Saudi Arabia *state*
ASIR *See* "Arabia"
sauger PERCH, FISH
Saul's *father* KISH
general ABNER
grandfather
ABIEL, NER

herdsman DOEG
successor DAVID
Sault Ste. Marie SOO
saunter AMBLE,
LOITER, LAG,
POTTER, STROLL,
WALK, DAWDLE,
RAMBLE, RANGE,
STRAY, LOUNGE
saurel XUREL,
SCAD, POMPANO,
FISH
saurian LIZARD,
REPTILE, DINOSAUR
sausage SALAMI,
BOLOGNA, FRANK-
(FURTER)
sauté FRY, COOK
sautoir CHAIN,
RIBBON
savage YAHOO, BAR-
BARIAN, WILD,
FIERCE, FERAL,
FELL, PITILESS,
CRUEL, ROUGH,
HARSH, GRIM,
RUGGED, UNTAMED,
VIOLENT, RUDE,
UNRESTRAINED,
FEROCIOUS, IN-
HUMAN, UN-
CIVILIZED, BRUTISH,
BARBAROUS,
BRUTAL
Island language
NIUE
savant *See* "wise
man"
save BUT, EXCEPT,
DELIVER, FREE,
PROTECT, KEEP,
HAVE, HOLD,
PRESERVE, RESCUE,
REDEEM, SPARE,
SALVAGE, RECOVER,
HOARD, STORE,
ECONOMIZE, RETAIN,
EXCLUDE, CAN,
FREEZE, TIN
savin(e) CEDAR,
JUNIPER, TREE
saving CHARY,
FRUGAL, THRIFTY,
CAREFUL, ECO-
NOMICAL, RESERV-
ING, REDEEMING,
EXCEPT
savoir-faire TACT,
POISE, ADDRESS,
GRACE, EASE,
SKILL

savor RELISH, FLA-
VOR, SMELL,
SMACK, ODOR, TASTE,
TINGE, TANG, FEEL-
ING, TONE, AURA,
SCENT, GOUT
savory GUSTABLE,
SAPID, TASTY, GOOD,
NICE, DAINTY,
RICH, LUSCIOUS,
PALATABLE, AGREE-
ABLE, PIQUANT,
DELICIOUS, FLA-
VORFUL, APPETIZ-
ING, MINT, SALTY
saw SAYING, AXIOM,
ADAGE, MOTTO,
MAXIM, PROVERB,
APHORISM, EPI-
GRAM, TOOL, CUT
buck TENSPOT
crosscut BRIAR
cut or groove KERF
dust COOM, SCOBS,
FILINGS
fish RAY
organ SERRA
horse BUCK, JACK,
TRESTLE
like part SERRA
mill gate SASH
palmetto SCRUB,
PALM
surgical TREPHINE,
TREPAN
saw-whet OWL,
BIRD
saxhorn TUBA,
ALTHORN
saxifrage SESELI,
PLANT, FLOWER
Saxon(y) SAS-
SENACH, SAXE
coin SCEAT
king INE, OTTO
swineherd GURTH
town AUE
say SPEAK, TELL,
AVER, UTTER, DE-
CLARE, PRONOUNCE,
EXPRESS, ALLEGE,
AFFIRM, REPEAT,
RECITE, ASSERT,
SUPPOSE, ASSUME
saying(s) DIT,
ANA, APHORISM,
ASSERTION *See*
"saw"
of religious teacher
LOGIA
scab CRUST, ES-
CHAR, MANGE, RAT,

APOSTATE, SCOUN-
DREL, STRIKE-
BREAKER
scabbard SHEATH,
PILCHER
scabies ITCH,
TINEA, MANGE
scad(s) OODLE(S),
LOT(S), GOB(S),
SAUREL, FISH
scale FLAKE, RUST,
EXFOLIATE, SLOUGH,
RATIO, CLIMB,
BALANCE, MOUNT,
ASCEND, GAUGE,
SERIES, GAMUT,
REDUCE, SCUTE,
SQUAMA, LAYER,
PLATE, LAMINA,
FILM, COATING,
COVERING, IN-
CRUSTATION, BRACT,
PEEL, PARE, HUSK,
LADDER, STANDARD,
PROPORTION,
RULE(R), SIZE,
EXTENT
bony SCUTUM
chafflike PALEA
combining form
LEPIS
fish GANOID
having SCUTATE,
LEPROSE
like LEPROSE
measuring BAL-
ANCE, VERNIER
minerals, hardness of
MOHS
musical GAMUT
third tone
MEDIANT
under blossom
PALEA
scale beetle TIGER
scales LIBRA,
RAMENTA, SCURF
on stems of ferns
CHAFF
scallop CRENA,
QUIN, MOLLUSK,
BIVALVE, INDENT,
NOTCH, COOK
cut PINK
scalloped CRENATE,
PINKED
scalp *disease* FAVUS,
DANDRUFF, SCURF
scalpel BISTOURY,
LANCET, KNIFE
scaly BASE, STINGY,
MEAN, LAMINAR,

LEPROSE, SCUTATE,
FLAKY
scamp SCALAWAG,
KNAVE, RASCAL,
RIP, ROGUE, SKIMP,
SLIGHT, CHEAT,
SWINDLER, SHARPER,
TRICKSTER, SCOUN-
DREL, BACALAO
scamper HIE, SCUD,
RUN, FLY, HASTEN,
SPEED
scandalize MALIGN,
REVILE, VILIFY,
SHOCK, TRADUCE,
OFFEND, SLANDER,
DISGRACE
Scandanavian
NORSE(MAN), DANE,
SWEDE, LAPP
See "Norse"
coin KRONA
goblin NIS
god or goddess
See under "god" *or*
"goddess"
heaven ASGARD
language NORSE
legend EDDA, SAGA
measure ALEN
musician and poet
SKALD, SCALD
name NILS, OLE
nation or tribe
GEATAS
navigator ERIC
sea monster, myth.
KRAKEN
territorial division
AMT
weight LOD
scansores, *order of*
TOUCAN, TROGON,
CUCKOO, WOOD-
PECKER, BIRD
scant CHARY, STINT,
FEW, RARE, SPARE,
SPARSE, MEAGER,
LITTLE, INSUFFI-
CIENT, INADEQUATE,
LACKING
scanty *See* "scant"
scapegoat DUPE,
VICTIM, SUBSTITUTE
scar BLEMISH, CICA-
TRIX, MARK, MAR,
DISFIGURE, CLIFF,
CRAG, INJURY,
FLAW, DEFECT,
WOUND
resembling ULOID,
CICATRICIAL

scarce RARE, SPAR-
ING, SCANTY,
BARELY, DEFI-
CIENT, WANTING,
UNCOMMON, IN-
FREQUENT, INSUF-
FICIENT
scarcity WANT,
PAUCITY, DEARTH,
RARITY, INSUFFI-
CIENCY
scare DAUNT,
FRIGHT(EN),
PANIC, COW,
ALARM, STARTLE,
APPALL, TERROR,
SHOO, AFFRIGHT,
INTIMIDATE, TER-
RIFY
scarecrow EFFIGY,
GUY, MALKIN, OGRE,
GHOST, BUGABOO,
SPECTER
scarf ASCOT, SASH,
TIPPET, BOA, STOLE,
MUFFLER, CRAVAT,
TIE, RUNNER, NECK-
ERCHIEF, TURBAN
bird CORMORANT,
SHAG
clerical MANIPLE,
RABAT, STOLE
military SASH
Pope FANON, ORALE
woman's NUBIA,
BOA, TIPPET, STOLE
scarfskin CUTICLE,
EPIDERMIS
Scarlett's *home* TARA
scary EERIE, ANX-
IOUS, FRIGHTFUL,
ALARMING, SPOOKY
scatter SOW, DEAL,
LITTER, SPRAY,
SPREAD, TED,
(BE)STREW,
DISPEL, DISPERSE, BE-
GONE, SCAT, STROW,
CAST, SPRINKLE,
BROADCAST, DISSIPATE,
DIFFUSE, SEPARATE,
DISTRIBUTE, DIS-
BAND, DERANGE,
ROUT, WASTE
scattered SPORADIC,
SPARSE, SPARSILE,
INFREQUENT,
DISRUPTED, DIS-
TRACTED, RAM-
BLING, IRREGULAR,
SEME
scattering DIASPORA

scenario SCRIPT,
PLAY, PLOT,
LIBRETTO, OUTLINE,
SYNOPSIS
scene VIEW,
TABLOID, VISTA,
EVENT, EXHIBITION,
SIGHT, LOCALITY,
PLACE, STAGE,
ACTION, (LAND)-
SCAPE, PAINT-
ING, PHOTO,
SPECTACLE, SHOW,
PAGEANT, REPRE-
SENTATION, DIS-
PLAY, SETTING,
QUARREL, EPISODE
scenery DIORAMA,
VIEW, SHOW,
PROPS, LANDSCAPE
scent AROMA,
SMELL, ODOR,
NOSE, TRAIL, AURA,
FLAIR, NIDOR,
ESSENCE, EFFLU-
VIUM, INCENSE,
TRACK, FRA-
GRANCE, REDO-
LENCE, PERFUME,
SIGN, INKLING,
INTIMATION,
BOUQUET
bag SACHET
scatter CENSE
scented OLENT,
ODOROUS, ARO-
MATIC, REDOLENT,
FRAGRANT, SPICY
scepter ROD, WAND,
BATON, MACE,
SOVEREIGNTY,
AUTHORITY, STAFF,
FASCES
schedule CARD, LIST,
PLAN, TARIFF,
SLATE, ROLL,
ROSTER, AGENDA,
PROGRAM, MENU,
CATALOG(UE),
INVENTORY,
REGISTER, (TIME)-
TABLE
scheme PLAN,
AIM, CABAL,
ANGLE, CONTRIVE,
WEB, PLOT, DESIGN,
PROJECT, DEVICE,
DEVISE, SHIFT,
ASPIRE, SKETCH,
DIAGRAM, INTRIGUE,
PROGRAM, SYSTEM,
ARRANGEMENT,

COMPLEXITY,
DIVERSION, LARK,
PURPOSE, THEORY,
STRATAGEM,
CONSPIRACY,
MACHINATION
schemer ARTIST,
PLOTTER, FIGARO
Schenectady *college*
UNION
schism DISSENT,
RENT, SPLIT, SECT,
SEPARATION,
DISUNION, DISCORD,
FACTION, DIVISION
schist SLATE, MICA,
HORNBLENDE
schizocarp REGMA,
COCCI, FRUIT
Schleswig-Holstein
capital KIEL
schmaltz CORN,
SENTIMENTALITY
scholar(s) PEDANT,
SAGE, STUDENT,
SABORA, SAVANT,
PUPIL, DISCIPLE,
LEARNER, PUNDIT
day EXTERN
Moslem, body of
ULEMA
scholarly ACADEMIC,
PHILOMATHIC,
ERUDITE, SCHOLAS-
TIC, LEARNED,
STUDIOUS
scholarship LEARN-
ING, KNOWLEDGE,
ERUDITION, LORE,
AID, BURSE, AC-
COMPLISHMENTS,
GRANT, FOUNDA-
TION
school PREP,
ACADEMY, COL-
LEGE, LYCEE,
LYCEUM, GYMNA-
SIUM, UNIVERSITY,
SEMINARY, INSTI-
TUTE, DROVE, BEVY,
FLOCK, HERD, SECT,
MULTITUDE, COM-
PANY, TEACH, TRAIN,
DRILL, GUIDE,
EDUCATE, DISCI-
PLINE
England ETON,
OXFORD
fishes SHOAL
France ECOLE,
LYCEE
grounds CAMPUS

group PTA
master PROF,
TEACHER, PEDANT
of fishes SHOAL
of whales GAM
*philosophers, pertain-
ing to* ELEATIC
religious
SEMINARY
riding MANEGE
secondary LYCEE,
COLLEGE, ACADEMY,
UNIVERSITY
schooner MUG *See*
"boat"
schottische POLKA,
DANCE
science ART, PRO-
FICIENCY,
KNOWLEDGE, SKILL,
LORE, ABILITY,
STUDY
of behavior ETHICS
of dining ARIS-
TOLOGY
of happiness
EUDAEMONICS
of healing
IATROLOGY
of man ETHNOLOGY
of self-defense
JUDO
of virtue ARETAICS
of words SEMAN-
TICS
sciential CAPABLE,
ABLE, COMPETENT,
KNOWING
scientific EXACT,
SOUND, ACCURATE,
EFFICIENT,
SKILLFUL
scientist SAVANT,
RESEARCHER
scilicet VIDELICET,
VIZ, IE, SC(T),
NAMELY, SCIL
scimitar SWORD,
SAX, TURK, SABER,
BILLHOOK
scintilla IOTA, TRACE,
WHIT, RAY, PAR-
TICLE, SPARK, BIT,
GLIMMER, JOT,
SHADOW, TITTLE,
SCRAP, ATOM
scion TWIG, GRAFT,
HEIR, SLIP, SON,
CUTTING, SHOOT,
SPROUT, DESCENDANT,
CHILD
Scipio AFRICANUS

scissors SHEARS, SNIPS

scoff SNEER, GIBE, FLOUT, FAIL, DERIDE, FLEER, RIDICULE, MOCK, SCORN, JEER, TAUNT

scold RAIL, RANT, (BE)RATE, CHIDE, NAG, JAW, REPROVE, CENSURE, REPRIMAND, BLAME, REBUKE, SHREW, VIXEN, VIRAGO, TERMAGANT

scombroid fish TUNA, BONITO, MACKEREL

sconce HELMET, HEAD, TOP, TRICK, CANDLESTICK, FINE, AMERCE, MULCT, COVER, SHELTER, REDOUBT, ENTRENCH, SCREEN, BRACKET

scoop BAIL, DIP, GOUGE, CHISEL, DIG, LADE, SPOON, LADLE, DIPPER, SHOVEL, EXCAVATE, STORY

scope FIELD, AMBIT, AREA, AIM, RANGE, LEEWAY, PLAY, REACH, SWEEP, ORBIT, ROOM, OPPORTUNITY, TRACT, LENGTH, EXTENT, SPACE, VENT, MARGIN, LIBERTY, LATITUDE, FREEDOM

scorch SEAR, CHAR, PARCH, SINGE, WITHER, BURN, BLISTER, ROAST

score GRUDGE, MARK, RUN, TALLY, NOTCH, GROOVE, TAB, CHALK, COUNT, POINT, MUSIC, CRITICIZE, ASSAIL, TWENTY, (BE)RATE, INCISION, ACCOUNT, CHARGE, DEBT, RECKONING, REASON, MOTIVE, GROUND, CONSIDERATION, SAKE, SCRATCH, FURROW, EXCO-

RIATE, GOAL, DOWN, RUN

scoria AA, LAVA, DROSS, SLAG

scorify SMELT, REDUCE

scorpion SCOURGE, LIZARD, WHIP, ARACHNID, CATAPULT, ONAGER
fish LAPON
stinger of TELSON
water genus NEPA

Scotch-Irish ERSE

scoter COOT, DUCK, FOWL
genus FULICA

Scotland, Scottish, Scot SCOTIA, ALBA, CALEDONIA(N), GAEL, PICT, CELT, MAC
accent BUR(R)
alluvial land CARSE
askew or awry AGEE
attendant GILLIE, GILLY
author BARRY, SCOTT
bailiff REEVE
bank BRAE
beg SORN
bound STEND, LOUP
brain HARN
brat GETT, GAITT
broadsword CLAYMORE
brow of hill SNAB
brownie NIS
cake SCONE, BAP, FARL(E)
cape WRATH
chalk CAUK
channel MINCH
chest KIST
chief THANE
child BAIRN, GETT, GAITT
church KIRK
city or town AYR, ALLOA
coin LION, BODLE, DEMY, ECU, PLACK, RIDER
congess MOD
contend KEMP
counsel REDE
county AYR
cup TASS
dagger SKEAN

dance FLING
decorum MENSE
dining room SPENCE
earnest money ARLES
endure DREE
explorer RAE
extra ORRA
eye EE
faithful LEAL
farmer CROFTER, COTTER
festival MOD
fireplace INGLE
firth KYLE
flinch BLUNK
game SHINTY, SHINNY
girl KIMMER, CUMMER, LASS
good-humored CROUSE
grandchild OY, OYE, OE
haul of fish DRAVE
have HAE
heavy THARF
highlander GAEL, CATERAN
hillside BRAE
historian HUME, SKENE
intend ETTLE
island ARRAN, BUTE *See* "Hebrides"
jump LOUP, STEND
keen SNELL
kilt FILIBEG
kindred SIB
king BRUCE
labor, day's DARG
lake LIN, LOCH, LOUGH, GARE, GAIR, AWE, FYNE, NEVIS, OICH, RYAN, SLOY, MAREE, NESS
landholder LAIRD, THANE
land tax CESS
land tenure FEU
language CELTIC
leap LOUP, STEND
liberator BRUCE
limestone CAUK
lord LAIRD
love LOE
lowlander SASSENACH
low river land CARSE

magistrate BAILIE
marauder CATERAN
market (*place*)
  TRONE
measure COP,
  FIRLOT, BOLL,
  NOGGIN, LIPPY,
  LIPPIE
mismanage
  BLUNK
mist DROW
money See "coin"
  above
mouth of river
  BEAL
muddled REE
mud rake CLAUT
murder fine CRO
negative DINNA,
  NAE
nimble GLEG
nobleman LAIRD,
  THANE
oak EIK
odd ORRA
one YIN, ANE
outlaw ROB ROY, DHU
pantry SPENCE
parish SCONE
peasant COTTER
philosopher HUME
physicist WATT
pillory JOUGS
plaid TARTAN
plant HEATHER
plunder REIF
poet BURNS, MOIR,
  HOGG
pole CABER
pool LIN
porridge BROSE
pouch SPORRAN
propriety MENSE
prove PREE
pudding HAGGIS
purpose ETTLE
race ILK
relieve LISS
river See under
  "river"
robbery REIF
scone FARL, FARLE
scythe handle
  SNEAD
seaport LARGS,
  OBAN, LEVEN
self SEL
servant GILLY,
  GILLIE
sharp SNELL
shawl MAUD
shelter SHEAL

small SMA
song STROUD
sore SAIR
sound JURA
stiff, unbending
  THARF
tenant CROFT, COT-
  TER
test PREE
tithe TEIND
to TAE
toil DARG
town BURGH
trial PREE
tribal payment
  CRO
trousers TREWS
uncle EME
undergo DREE
unit ANE, YIN
unroof or uncover
  TIRR
vigor VIR
warrior KEMP
water sprite
  KELPIE
weighing machine
  TRONE
weight TRONE,
  DROP
whine YIRN
world WARL
yell GOWL
Scott *character* DHU,
  AMY
work MARMION,
  IVANHOE, TALISMAN,
  ROB ROY
scoundrel HEEL, CAD,
  KNAVE, ROGUE,
  VARLET, VILLAIN,
  RASCAL, SCAMP,
  CHEAT, TRICKSTER,
  SWINDLER, MIS-
  CREANT, REPROBATE
scour SEEK, PURGE,
  CLEAN, CLEANSE,
  SCRUB, BURNISH,
  POLISH, SAND, RUB,
  BRIGHTEN, ROVE,
  RANGE, SEARCH
scourge WHIP,
  HARRY, FLAY,
  BANE, FLOG, SWINGE,
  LASH, PUNISH,
  CHASTISE, AFFLICT,
  DEVASTATE
Scourge of God
  ATTILA
scout LOOK, SEEK,
  GUIDE, AGENT,
  FLOUT, SCORN,

  SPURN, SPY, FEL-
  LOW, PAL, RECON-
  NOITER, RIDICULE,
  DERIDE, EMISSARY,
  MESSENGER
scow BOAT, BARGE
scowl MOUE, LOWER,
  FROWN, GLARE,
  GLOWER, STARE
scram DECAMP,
  VAMOOSE, SCAT, GO,
  LEAVE, QUIT,
  ELOPE, FLEE, ESCAPE
scramble STRUGGLE,
  SCRAPE, SWARM,
  MUSS, STRIVE,
  CLIMB, CLAMBER,
  SCRABBLE, SPREAD,
  SCALE, TRAVERSE,
  MIX, JOSTLE, PUSH,
  HASTE
scrap FRAGMENT,
  DRIBLET, MORSEL,
  END, ORT, JOT,
  SPECK, BIT, PIECE,
  RAG, JUNK, SCANT-
  LING, CRUMB, BITE,
  MOUTHFUL, LEFT-
  OVER, BRAWL,
  FIGHT
scrape GRAZE, RASP,
  ABRADE, EKE, RUB,
  ERASE, SCRATCH,
  FIX, PLIGHT, JAM,
  PICKLE, GRATE,
  DIFFICULTY, MESS
  bottom DREDGE
scrapings RAMENTA,
  DUST, LEAVINGS,
  CHAFF, SOUND,
  EARNINGS, SAVINGS,
  SHAVINGS, FILINGS
scratch GRATE,
  SCORE, MAR, PIT,
  SCARIFY, RUB, MARK,
  WRITE, GROOVE,
  SCRIBBLE, WOUND,
  RAKE, CANCEL,
  SCRAPE, LACERA-
  TION, INCISION,
  ERASE, EXPUNGE,
  OBLITERATE, TEAR,
  ROUGHEN, DIG,
  ABRADE, RIST
scratching ground *for*
  food RASORIAL
scrawl POTHOOK,
  SCRIBBLE, WRITE
scrawny BONY,
  LANK, SKINNY,
  SPARE, THIN,

SCRAGGY, RAW-
BONED, SCRANNY
screech SHRIEK,
YELL, CRY,
SCREAM
screed HARANGUE,
DIATRIBE, TIRADE
screen MASK, VEIL,
HIDE, SIFT, BLIND,
SHELTER, SHADE,
WINNOW, CLOAK,
GRILLE, PAVIS(E),
SHIELD, PRO-
TECT(ION), SIEVE,
NETTING, PARTI-
TION, MOVIES,
CINEMA, CONCEAL,
CLEAN, BOLT,
TROMMEL
canvas PAVISADE
chancel REREDOS,
JUBE
ecclesiastical
PARCLOSE, PERCLOSE
hall SPIER
mesh LAUN
wind PARAVENT
screw SPIRAL,
HELIX, TWIST,
FASTEN(ER),
JACK, TURN,
WAGE, HIRE, FEE,
CRUSTACEAN,
CONTORTION, NAG,
BARGAINER,
SKINFLINT,
PROP(ELLER)
scribble SCRAWL,
SCRATCH, MARK,
CARD, SCRABBLE
scribe EZRA, CLERK,
SCRIVENER, WRITER,
PENMAN, AUTHOR,
JOURNALIST
scrimmage FIGHT,
ROW, TUSSLE, BAT-
TLE, SKIRMISH,
SCUFFLE, BRAWL,
MELEE, STRUGGLE
scrip BAG, SCRAP,
CURRENCY, MONEY,
CERTIFICATE, LIST,
MEMORANDUM,
DOCUMENT,
SATCHEL
script WRITING,
TYPE, DOCUMENT
angular RONDE
scriptural *interpreter*
EXEGETE
scripture BIBLE,

TEXT, WRITING,
WORD
occult interpretation
CABALA
version of ITALIA,
VULGATE, DOUAY
scrivello TUSK
scrobiculate PITTED,
FURROWED, FOVEATE
scroll VOLUTE, LIST,
ROLL, FLOURISH,
DESIGN, SCHEDULE,
DRAFT, OUTLINE,
STREAMER, BUNDLE
scromboid *fish* CERO
scrouge CROWD,
SQUEEZE, PRESS
scrounge PILFER,
SEARCH, CADGE,
SPONGE, PRY
scrub SCOUR, SWAB,
MOP, CLEAN,
BRUSH, SMALL,
MEAN, INFERIOR,
MALLEE, BUSH,
MONGREL, UNDER-
SIZED, PALTRY,
DRUDGE, BRIGHTEN
scrubby STUNTED,
SMALL, INFERIOR
scruff NAPE, SCUFF,
CRUST, COATING,
FILM, SCUM, DROSS,
REFUSE, SLUR
scruple DOUBT,
WEIGHT, QUALM,
DEMUR, BALK,
WAVER, HESITA-
TION, UNCERTAINTY
scrupulous STAID,
SHY, PUNCTILIOUS,
CONSCIENTIOUS,
EXACT
scrutinize AUDIT,
PROBE, EYE, PRY,
SCAN, SIFT,
EXAMINE, STUDY,
WEIGH, INVESTIGATE,
EXPLORE, INSPECT
scryer SEER
scud DART, FLASH,
SKIM, FLY, CLOUD,
RUN, SAIL, SPEED
scuffle MELEE,
TUSSLE, FRAY,
STRUGGLE,
SHUFFLE, SCRIM-
MAGE, FIGHT
scull PADDLE,
SPOON, OAR, RACE,
ROW(BOAT)

scullion SERVANT,
MENIAL, WRETCH
sculp CHISEL,
CARVE, ENGRAVE
sculptor RODIN,
PHIDIAS, IMAGER,
ARTIST, MICHELAN-
GELO
chisel of EBAUCHOIR
sculpture, *blow cement*
on KIBOSH
in high relief
ALTO-RELIEVO
pertaining to
GLYPHIC
scum DROSS, FOAM,
FROTH, REFUSE,
RABBLE, FILM,
SCORIA, DIRT, SCURF
scup BREAM, FISH
scurrility *See*
"abuse"
scurry HIE,
HASTE(N), SKELTER,
SCUTTLE, DART,
DASH, HURRY,
SCOUR, FLURRY
scurvy SCORBUTUS,
LOW, MEAN, BASE,
VILE, SORRY, CHEAP,
SCURF(Y),
CONTEMPTIBLE,
DISCOURTEOUS
scutage FEE, TAX,
IMPOST, LEVY
scutate SCALY,
PELTATE
scutcheon, *voided*
ORLE
scuttle HOD, SINK,
BUSTLE, RUN,
WITHDRAW,
HATCHWAY, DESTROY
scuttlebutt RUMOR,
GOSSIP
scutum SHIELD,
PLATE, SCUTE
scythe SY, SYE,
SNATH, TOOL
handle SNATH,
SNEAD
sweep of SWATH
sea MAIN, LAKE,
OCEAN, DEEP, SURF,
WAVE, BILLOW, SURGE,
ADRIATIC, AEGEAN,
ARABIAN, AZANIAN,
AZOV, BALTIC,
BANDA, BARENTS,
BERING, BLACK,
CANDIA, CARIBBEAN,
CASPIAN, CHINA,

CELEBES, CORAL,
DEAD, IONIAN,
IRISH, JAPAN, KARA,
MARMARA, NORTH,
RED, OKHOTSK, ROSS,
SULU, TASMAN,
TIMOR, WHITE,
GALILEE (now Lake
Tiberius)
anemone ACTINIA,
POLYP, OPELET
animal CORAL
See under "mammal"
Antarctic ROSS
arm of FJORD,
FIORD, FIRTH, BAY,
SINUS *See* "inlet"
below
bird See under
"bird"
Black EUXINE
combining form HALI
cow DUGONG,
MANATEE
cucumber TREPANG
dog MARINE, SAILOR,
GOB, TAR
duck SCOTER, COOT,
EIDER
Dyak IBAN
eagle ERN(E)
ear ABALONE
fish See under
"fish"
god or goddess See
under "god" *or*
"goddess"
goods sunk at
LIGAN, LAGAN,
LAGEND
green CELADON
gull MEW
inland ARAL, AZOV,
AZOF, DEAD, SALTON,
GALILEE, CASPIAN
inlet FJORD, FIORD,
RIA, COVE, BAY,
FIRTH, SINUS
lemon DORIS
lettuce genus ULVA
mammal See under
"mammal"
mew GULL
mile KNOT, NAUT
monster CETE,
KRAKEN
nettle ACALEPH,
MEDUSA, JELLYFISH
nymph GALATEA,
NEREID
old man of PROTEUS
onion SQUILL

organisms NEKTON
pertaining to
OCEANIC, MARINE,
MARINAL, PELAGIC,
NAVAL, NAUTICAL,
THALASSIC
robber PIRATE,
CORSAIR
skeleton CORAL
slug TREPANG,
NUDIBRANCH
genus DOTO
snail WHELK, WILK
snake KERRIL
swallow TERN
swimming organisms
NEKTON
unicorn NARWHAL
urchin ECHINID,
ECHINITE
water BRINE, SALT
weed See "sea-
weed"
worm LURG, SAO,
ANNELID
seagirt land ISLE
seal SIGNET, DIE,
STAMP, WAFER,
OTARY, SETTLE,
SHUT, FASTEN,
SECURE, (EN)-
CLOSE, AUTHENTICA-
TION, CONFIRMATION,
PLEDGE, ASSUR-
ANCE, RATIFY,
CACHET
bearded MAKLUK,
URSUK
decorated with
SIGILLATE
eared OTARY
flock or herd POD
fur URSAL
genus OTARIA,
PHOCA
letter CACHET
official SIGNET
papal letter BULLA
pertaining to
PHOCINE
signet SIGIL
young PUP
sealing wax LAC
seam RAPHE, JOINT,
SUTURE, WRINKLE,
LAYER, CREASE,
LINE, RIDGE, FIS-
SURE, SCAR,
JUNCTURE, GROOVE,
CREVICE, STRATUM
pertaining to
SUTURAL

tapering DART
sea-maid SIREN,
MERMAID, NYMPH
seaman JACK, SALT,
TAR, GOB, MARINER,
SAILOR, SEAFARER
chapel for BETHEL
saint of ELMO
sear BRAISE, DEAD,
DRY, ARID, WITHER,
CAUTERIZE, BURN,
CHAR, SINGE, BRAND,
BLIGHT, PARCH,
CATCH
search HUNT, SEEK,
SCAN, PROBE, FER-
RET, LOOK, EXAMINE,
INQUIRE, EXPLORE,
RANSACK, SCRUTI-
NIZE, SIFT, INSPECT,
FORAGE, QUEST,
PURSUIT, SEEKING,
SCRUTINY, SURVEY,
INVESTIGATION
seashore STRAND,
COAST, BEACH
pertaining to LIT-
TORAL
season AGE, CURE,
SALT, MATURE,
RIPEN, SPICE, TIME,
TRAIN, DRILL,
TEMPER, INURE,
DEVIL, CORN, FALL,
SPRING, AUTUMN,
SUMMER, WINTER,
TERM, INTERVAL,
SPELL, PERIOD,
HABITUATE, AC-
CUSTOM, HARDEN
seasoning BASIL,
SAGE, RELISH, SALT,
THYME, CONDI-
MENT, SPICE,
FLAVORING, SAUCE
seat(s) SETTEE,
SELLA, ASANA,
PEW(AGE),
LOCATION, BENCH,
SITE, CHAIR, STOOL,
PLACE, STATION,
ABODE, DWELLING,
RESIDENCE, HOUSE,
BOTTOM, FUNDA-
MENTAL, THRONE,
CAPITAL, SUPPORT,
INSTALL
chancel SEDILE
justice BANC
of honor CURULE
tier of GRADIN

seawan, sewan
WAMPUM,
BEADS, MONEY
seaweed WRACK,
ORE, ALGA(E),
ULVA, VAREC,
LAVER, DULSE,
LIMU, KELP, CUVY
derivative BARILLA
edible DULSE,
LAVER, LIMU, KELP
genus ALARIA
Japan NORI
leaf FROND
pertaining to
ALGOUS
product AGAR,
GELOSE
purple LAVER, NORI
red DULSE,
DELISK
substance found on
ALGIN
Seb *See* "Geb"
sec DRY, WINE
seckel PEAR
secluded REMOTE,
ISOLATED, CLOIS-
TERED, COVERT,
SOLITARY, RETIRED,
WITHDRAWN,
REMOVED, SE-
QUESTERED, PRI-
VATE, EMBOWERED,
SCREENED, HIDDEN
second HANDLE,
BACK, SUPPORT,
ABET, AID(E),
JIFFY, FLASH,
TRICE, INSTANT,
NEXT, FORWARD,
PROMOTE, (AN)-
OTHER, SUBORDINATE,
INFERIOR, BACKER,
ASSISTANT,
ENCOURAGE,
FURTHER, SUSTAIN
combining form
DEUTER(O)
growth crop
ROWEN
helping OVERS
preparation HASH
secondary MINOR,
DERIVATIVE, FOL-
LOWING, ACCESSORY,
SUBJECT, SUBORDI-
NATE, INFERIOR,
SATELLITE
proposition LEMMA
secret RUNE, COV-
ERT, MYSTIC,

HIDDEN, LATENT,
FURTIVE, SECLUDED,
ARCANE, CRYPTIC,
PRIVY, OCCULT, UN-
SEEN, VEILED,
CLANDESTINE, CON-
CEALED, SHROUDED,
MYSTERIOUS, SUR-
REPTITIOUS, INTIMATE,
UNDERHAND,
ABSTRUSE,
RECONDITE,
ARCANUM, KEY,
RIDDLE
agent SPY
council of state
JUNTO, CABAL
place ADYTUM,
SANCTUM
secretary DESK,
AMANUENSIS,
RECORDER, OFFICER,
AIDE, ASSISTANT
secrete HIDE, CONCEAL,
MASK, CACHE, BURY,
DISGUISE, EXCRETE,
EXUDE
secretion, *plant*
LERP, RESIN, SAP,
MILK, LAAP, LAARP,
JUICE, GUM,
LATEX, CHICLE
secrets ARCANA
sect CULT, CHURCH,
SCHOOL, FACTION,
ORDER, PARTY, DE-
NOMINATION,
CLASS, GROUP
sectarian HERETIC,
BIGOT, ZEALOT, DIS-
SENTER, NONCON-
FORMIST
section PART, SEG-
MENT, PANEL, AREA,
FEN, UNIT, PIECE,
CHAPTER, TOWNSHIP,
SPECIMEN, SECTOR,
PORTION, MEMBER,
SLICE, DIVISION,
CUTTING
sector ARC, SECTION,
AREA *See*
"section"
secular LAIC(AL),
LAY, MUNDANE,
WORLDLY, PROFANE,
TEMPORAL,
EARTHLY, CIVIL
secure FIX, NAIL,
BIND, MOOR, FIRM,
TIE, RIVET, PIN,
FAST(EN), ROPE,

ATTAIN, GET, CATCH,
PROTECT, ANNEX,
SEIZE, SAFE, BELAY,
FIRM, SOLID, SURE,
ASSURED, CONFI-
DENT, UNDISTURBED,
RESTRAIN
security GAGE, BOND,
PLEDGE, SURETY,
SHELTER, SAFETY,
TOKEN, BAIL, PRO-
TECTION, DEFENSE,
GUARD, GUARANTEE
sedate QUIET,
STAID, STILL, CALM,
SOLEMN, SOBER,
DEMURE, GRAVE,
SERENE, COMPOSED,
SETTLED, UNRUFFLED,
SERIOUS, PLACID,
TRANQUIL, THOUGHT-
FUL, DISPASSION-
ATE, UNOBTRUSIVE,
DIGNIFIED
sedative BROMIDE,
ANODYNE, NERVINE,
SOOTHING, LENITIVE,
PALLIATIVE, OPIATE,
REMEDY
sedge MATI, CAREX,
FLAG, GRASS
like genus XYRIS,
CYPERUS, CAREX
sediment MAGMA,
LEES, SILT, LOESS,
DREGS, SETTLINGS,
GROUNDS, FECULA,
FAEX
see MEET, (E)SPY,
VIDE, VIEW, DIS-
CERN, CALL, RE-
GARD, LOOK, NOTICE,
NOTE, KNOW, RE-
MARK, WATCH,
GAZE, GAPE, STARE,
GLARE, BEHOLD,
DESCRY, PERCEIVE,
UNDERSTAND, EYE
holy DIOCESE,
BISHOPRIC, SEAT
seed OVULE, GRAIN,
GERM, SOURCE,
SOW, PIT, PUTAMEN,
NUT, BULB, CORM,
TUBER, ORIGIN,
EMBRYO, KERNEL,
ACORN, PROGENY,
DESCENDANTS,
OFFSPRING
apple PIT
bearing organ
PISTIL

coating (IN)-
TEGUMENT, TESTA
covering ARIL,
TESTA, SHELL, PEEL,
HULL, HUSK,
BUR(R), SHUCK
edible PEA, BEAN,
LENTIL, NUT,
WHEAT, RICE, OAT,
CORN
immature OVULE
one-celled CARPEL
poppy MAW
primitive SPORE
remove GIN
scars HILA
small PIP
two-valved
LEGUME
vessel SILICLE,
BUR(R), POD,
CAPSULE, SILIQUE
seedcake WIG(G)
seed coat, *broken*
BRAN
seedless *plant*
FERN
seedy WORN,
THREADBARE,
SHABBY, DINGY,
TACKY, OLD, FADED,
WRETCHED, DEBIL-
ITATED, NEEDY
seek HUNT, EXPLORE,
SEARCH, TRY, ESSAY,
ASPIRE, SOLICIT,
INQUIRE, FISH,
PURSUE, PRY,
PROBE, BEG, EN-
DEAVOR, REQUEST,
BESEECH, ENTREAT,
ATTEMPT, COURT,
WOO, PROSPECT
seel BLIND, CLOSE,
LIST, PITCH, ROLL
seem LOOK, APPEAR,
PRETEND, FEIGN
seeming GUISE,
LOOK, QUASI, SHOW,
LIKE, APPARENT,
APPEARANCE, OS-
TENSIBLE, PRETENDED,
SEMBLANCE,
OPINION
seemly PROPER,
MEET, NICE, DE-
CENT, FIT, COMELY,
DECOROUS, FITTING,
BEFITTING, BE-
COMING, SUITABLE,
APPROPRIATE, CON-
GRUOUS, FAIR,

HANDSOME, PLEAS-
ING, EXPEDIENT,
DUE
seep PERCOLATE,
OOZE, SOAK, DRAIN,
DRIP, LEAK
seer PROPHET,
GAZER, PREDICTOR,
FORETELLER, DI-
VINER, SOOTHSAYER,
ORACLE, SORCERER
seeress PHOEBAD,
SAGA, SIBYL,
PROPHETESS
seesaw TEETER,
TILT, VACILLATE,
WAVER, CROSSRUFF,
ALTERNATE, RE-
CIPROCATE
seethe FUME, BOIL,
STEW, COOK, SOAK,
SATURATE, FOAM,
BUBBLE, RAGE,
RAVE
segment SOMITE,
TELSON, CANTLE,
SECTOR, META-
MERE, PART, ARC,
PORTION, PIECE,
SECTION, WARD,
DIVISION, ITEM,
PARAGRAPH, CHAP-
TER, VERSE, FRAC-
TION, FRAGMENT,
PARCEL
body SOMATOME
seine NET, SAGENE,
TRAWL, RIVER
Seine *tributary*
EURE, OISE, MARNE,
AUBE
seize CATCH, BIND,
FASTEN, TAKE,
GRAB, COP, TRAP,
YOKE, ARREST,
USURP, CLUTCH,
REAVE, NAB, GRASP,
GRIP, APPREHEND,
CAPTURE, ROB,
SNATCH, CON-
FISCATE, IMPOUND,
ANNEX, HENT
for debt DISTRAIN,
EMBARGO, ATTACH
seizure FIT, STROKE,
ATTACK, SPELL,
CAPTURE, APPRO-
PRIATION, RETEN-
TION, CONFISCA-
TION, SEIZIN
Selassie HAILE

select PICK, OPT,
CULL, ELITE,
CHOOSE, CREAM,
GOOD, TAKE, VOTE,
ELECT, CHOICE,
RARE, BEST, PRE-
FER, EXCLUSIVE,
CHOSEN, SUPERIOR
selenium *symbol* SE
self EGO, ID, PER-
SON, VERY, SAME,
IDENTICAL
assertion EGOISM,
VANITY
combining form
AUT(O)
deification AUTO-
THEISM
denial ASCETICISM
derived existence
ASEITY
fear of AUTO-
PHOBIA
knowledge AUTOL-
OGY
murderer SUICIDE,
FELO-DE-SE
self-confidence
BALANCE, APLOMB
self-esteem PRIDE,
EGO(T)ISM,
VANITY, COM-
PLACENCY, VAIN-
GLORY, ASSURANCE
sell VEND, BARTER,
CANT, MARKET,
TRANSFER, AUC-
TION, TRADE, CON-
VEY, DEED, CHEAT,
TRICK, JOKE, EX-
CHANGE, HAWK,
PEDDLE, BETRAY,
DECEIVE, GULL,
CONVINCE, PERSUADE,
BARGAIN
over official rate
SCALP
seller COSTER,
VENDER, VENDOR,
MERCHANT,
DEALER, TRADES-
MAN, PEDDLER
selvage EDGE, LIST,
BORDER, FRINGE,
SELVEDGE
semblance GUISE,
SHOW, LOOK, AS-
PECT, IMAGE,
POSE, FORM, FIGURE,
SHAPE, PICTURE,
LIKENESS, COPY,
SIMILARITY, AP-

PEARANCE, EX-
TERIOR, COUNTE-
NANCE, FACE, AP-
PARITION, SEEM-
ING, PRETENSE
Semele's *sister* INO
semester TERM,
COURSE, HALF,
PERIOD
semidiameter RA-
DIUS
Seminole Indian *chief*
OSCEOLA
Semiramis' *husband*
NINUS
Semite HEBREW,
ARAB, JEW
Semitic *god* BAAL
language GEEZ,
HARARI, GHESE,
ARABIC *See under*
"language"
weight GERAH,
MINA, SHEKEL
semolina SUJEE,
FLOUR, SIZINGS,
MIDDLINGS, SUJI,
GROATS
sempiternal EVER,
ENDLESS, EVER-
LASTING, ETERNAL,
PERPETUAL
Senate and Roman
People SPQR
senate *house* CURIA
oratory DEBATE
senatorship TOGA,
CHAIR, SEAT
send MAIL, TRANS-
FER, EMIT, ISSUE,
TRANSMIT, FLING,
HURL, THROW,
PROPEL, MOVE,
AFFECT, CONVEY,
DISPATCH, CONSIGN,
COMMIT, DRIVE,
DISMISS, EJECT
back REMIT,
REMAND
senescent SENILE,
OLD, AGED, AGING
senility CADUCITY,
DOTAGE, AGE, IN-
FIRMITY, DE-
CREPITUDE
senior AINE, ELDER,
OLDER, SUPERIOR,
DEAN, MASTER,
STUDENT, PARENT
member DEAN
seniority RANK,
AGE, PRIORITY,

ELDERSHIP, SUPERI-
ORITY
senna CASSIA,
REMEDY
sennet SPET, FISH,
CALL
sensational LURID,
SCANDALOUS, EXCIT-
ING, THRILLING,
WONDERFUL,
MELODRAMATIC,
EMOTIONAL
sense FEEL(ING),
FLAIR, SAPIENCE,
FACULTY, VIEW,
WISDOM, BRAIN,
WIT(S), SIGHT,
SMELL, HEARING,
INTUITION, SUS-
PECT, TASTE,
PERCEPTION, AP-
PRECIATION, COM-
PREHEND, TOUCH,
MEANING
organ SENSILLA,
NOSE, EYE, EAR,
SKIN, RECEPTOR
senseless FATUOUS,
DULL, INEPT, STU-
PID, IDIOTIC,
ABSURD, INSENSATE,
UNFEELING, FOOL-
ISH, IRRATIONAL,
UNWISE
sensible AWARE,
WISE, JUDICIOUS,
DISCREET, SAGE,
SAGACIOUS, INTEL-
LIGENT, RATIONAL,
SENSITIVE, REA-
SONABLE
sentence JUDGE,
RAP, TERM, DOOM,
ADAGE, JUDGMENT,
CONDEMN, DECISION
analyze PARSE
balance PARISON
concluding
EPILOG(UE)
*consisting of one
word* MONEPIC
construction
SYNTAX
latter clause in
APODOSIS
part WORD, PHRASE,
CLAUSE, SUBJECT,
PREDICATE, NOUN,
VERB, ADJECTIVE,
ADVERB
type COMPOUND,

COMPLEX,
SIMPLE
sententious CURT,
PITHY, TERSE,
WISE, LACONIC,
SUCCINCT, CON-
CISE, APHORISTIC
sentiment MOTTO,
MAXIM, TOAST,
OPINION, EMOTION,
NOTION, IDEA, VIEW,
BELIEF, FEELING,
SENSIBILITY, SENTI-
MENTALITY
strong EMOTION,
IRE, FEELING
sentimental *song(s)*
STREPHONADE,
SERENADE, BLUES
sentinel SENTRY,
GUARD, PICKET,
SOLDIER, WATCH,
VEDETTE, VIDETTE,
PATROL, KEEPER,
WARDEN
sentry KITE, WATCH,
SOLDIER, GUARD
See "sentinel"
sepal LEAF, PETAL
separate DISCON-
NECT, DIVORCE,
WITHDRAW, DIS-
JOIN, CLEAVE,
SPLIT, RETIRE,
SINGLE, DISCRETE,
INDIVIDUAL, PAR-
TICULAR, DISCON-
NECT(ED), ISO-
LATE(D), REND,
SPLIT, SEVER(AL),
FORK, PART, SORT,
DIVIDE, SOLE, LONE,
DETACH, DISEN-
GAGE(D), DISAS-
SOCIATE, SUNDER,
ELIMINATE, ALONE,
SEGREGATE(D),
DISTINGUISH, IN-
TERVENE, DISTINCT,
SECLUDED, SOLI-
TARY, BISECT,
DIVERGE
separated FREE,
ALONE, LONE,
SHREDDED, PARTED
separation SCHISM,
DIVORCE, SECLUSION,
SEVERING, DIS-
JUNCTION, DIS-
UNION
separatist HERETIC,
PILGRIM, DISSENTER,

NONCONFORMIST,
SECTARY
sepia DUN, BROWN,
INK, PIGMENT,
CUTTLEBONE
sepiolite MEER-
SCHAUM
sept CLAN, TRIBE,
RACE, FAMILY,
GROUP, SEVEN,
CLASS, KIN
septic PUTRID,
ROTTEN
poisoning PYEMIA
septuple SEVEN-
FOLD
sepulchre URN,
TOMB, VAULT,
GRAVE, COFFIN
chest CIST, COFFIN
subterranean vault
CATACOMB
sequence CYCLE,
GAMUT, SERIES,
STRAIGHT, ORDER,
SUCCESSION, CHAIN,
SET, SUITE, TRAIN,
FOLLOWING, PRO-
GRESSION, GRADA-
TION, SEQUEL, RUN
3-card TIERCE
sequester ISOLATE,
INSULATE, ENISLE,
SEPARATE, CON-
FISCATE, RETIRE,
WITHDRAW, SE-
CLUDE, SEIZE, CON-
DEMN
sequin DISK, COIN,
SPANGLE
seraglio HAREM
serai CARAVANSARY,
INN, KHAN, REST-
HOUSE
seraph ANGEL,
CHERUB
Serb SLAV
coin DINAR, PARA
sere *See* "sear"
serenade NOCTURNE,
SONG *See* "house-
warming"
serene CALM,
PLACID, CLEAR,
HALCYON, STILL,
COOL, EASY, TRAN-
QUIL, QUIET, UN-
RUFFLED, CONTENT,
PEACEFUL, UN-
PERTURBED, UN-
DISTURBED, STEADY

serf HELOT, COLONA,
ESNE, PEON,
THRALL, VASSAL,
SLAVE, VILLEIN,
COLONUS, NEIF,
LITUS
female NEIFE,
COLONA
feudal law VILLEIN
Sparta HELOT
serfdom, *one born in*
NEIF, NEIFE
sergeant NONCOM,
OFFICER
fish COBIA, COAL
Serian SERIC
seric SILKEN
series *See* "sequence"
of discussions
SYMPOSIUM
of events EPOS
of steps SCALE,
LADDER
serious EARNEST,
DEMURE, GRAVE,
IMPORTANT, DAN-
GEROUS, GREAT,
SOLEMN, ASCETIC,
DEEP, STERN,
SEVERE, STAID,
SOBER, SEDATE,
WEIGHTY, MO-
MENTOUS, THOUGHT-
FUL
serment OATH,
SACRAMENT
sermon HOMILY,
DISCOURSE, SPEECH,
TALK, LECTURE,
REPROOF, EXHORTA-
TION, LESSON, DIS-
SERTATION
serotine BAT
serow JAGLA,
GORAL, ANTELOPE
serpent *See* "snake"
combining form
OPHI(O)
thousand-headed
SESHA, ANANTA
serpentine SINUOUS,
ZIGZAG, CIR-
CUITOUS, INDIRECT,
DEVIOUS, SUBTLE,
MEANDERING,
WINDING, TORTUOUS,
WILY, DIABOLIC,
SNAKY
serpentlike ANGUINE,
OPHIDIAN
serpigo TETTER,

RINGWORM, HERPES,
TINEA
serranoid *fish* LATES
Serv *See* "Serb"
servant PAGE, MAN,
BOY, AMAH, MAID,
VALET, FLUNKY,
HELP, MENIAL,
BUTLER, CHEF,
FACTOTUM, AT-
TENDANT, BONNE,
DOMESTIC, DRUDGE
See "serf"
inferior COISTRIL,
COISTREL
of nobleman
EQUERRY
serve AVAIL, LADLE,
DEAL, MINISTER,
SUCCOR, SUFFICE,
PLAY, DO, WAIT,
(AT)TEND, BENE-
FIT, HELP, PRO-
MOTE, AID, ASSIST,
WORK, OBLIGE, AD-
VANCE, FORWARD,
ANSWER, FURTHER,
OBEY
server LADLE, TRAY,
WAITER, SALVER,
UTENSIL, PLAYER
service(s) DUTY,
DEVOTION, AVAIL,
PROFIT, ADVANTAGE,
UTILITY, WORK, SET,
RITUAL, RITE(S),
USE, HELP, AID,
LABOR, MINISTRA-
TION, OFFICE, BUSI-
NESS, GAIN, ARMY,
NAVY, LIGHT, GAS,
TELEPHONE, MA-
RINES, ASSISTANCE,
MINISTRY
charge FEE, TIP
for dead DIRGE,
SONG, THRENODY
R. C. Church
TENEBRAE
servile SYCOPHANTIC,
ABJECT, MENIAL,
BASE, MEAN,
SLAVISH, OBSE-
QUIOUS, CRINGING,
FAWNING, SUB-
MISSIVE, SUBSER-
VIENT
Servite MENDICANT
sesame *grass* GAMA
oil BENI, BENEE
paste (pulp)
TAHIN, TAHEEN

plant TIL, TEEL
sesquipedal DWARF
session SEANCE, COUNCIL, ASSEMBLY, VESTRY, MEETING, SITTING, TERM, ASSIZE
set JELL, HARDEN, LAY, PLANT, POST, PIT, PLACE, SERIES, GANG, SUIT(E), CHAIN, STRING, ASSIGN, ADJUST, DEFINE, FIX, FIRM, SETTLE, CLIQUE, CIRCLE, GEL, STATION, LOCATE, ESTABLISH, PREPARE
apart TABOO, RESERVE
at naught OVERRIDE, VETO, DISREGARD, DESPISE
down RECORD, WRITE
firmly POSIT, PLANT
in groove DADO
in order FILE, POST, (A)LINE, ADJUST, ARRANGE
on fire TIND, KINDLE, LIGHT
out EMBARK, PLANT, PUBLISH, PROCLAIM
up RIG, ERECT, ESTABLISH, FOUND
seta BRISTLE, HAIR, SPINE, CHAETA
Seth's *father* ADAM
son ENOS
setting MILIEU, TRAP, HARDENING, INSERTION, MOUNTING, ENVIRONMENT
settle PAY, LOCATE, SAG, DECIDE, ADJUST, SEAT, NEST, FIX, SINK, SET, MOOR, RIVET, RULE, JUDGE, DETERMINE, CONFIRM, REGULATE, ESTABLISH, BENCH, END, CLOSE, COLONIZE, SUBSIDE, CHOOSE
settlement COLONY, PAYMENT, LIQUIDATION, VILLAGE, TOWN, COMMUNITY,

LOCATION, DREGS, COMPACT
settler BOOMER, COLONIST, SQUATTER
settlings *See* "sediment"
set-to BOUT, CONTEST, FIGHT, COMBAT, CONFLICT
seven VII, SEPT, HEBDOMAD, HEPTAD
against Thebes, one of TYDEUS, ADRASTUS
combining form HEPTA, SEPT(A)
day fever SEPTAN
days, every HEBDOMADAL, WEEKLY
group of HEPTAD, PLEIAD, SEPTET
languages, book in HEPTAGLOT
sevenfold SEPTULE
seventh son SEER
severe STERN, ACUTE, DRASTIC, TRYING, RIGID, HARSH, ASCETIC, GRIM, HARD, COLD, ARCTIC, EXTREME, AUSTERE, STIFF, EXACTING, STRICT, RIGOROUS, UNRELENTING, VIOLENT
Greek ARISTARCHUS
severity RIGOR, CRUELTY, STRINGENCY, BITTERNESS, DIFFICULTY, HARSHNESS
sew BASTE, SUTURE, STITCH, PATCH, MEND, TACK
with gathers FULL, SHIRR
sewer DRAIN, SINK, CLOACA
sewing machine *inventor* HOWE, ELIAS
sex GENDER, KIND
sexagesimal SIXTIETH
sexes, *common to both* EPICENE
sexton JANITOR, BEETLE, SACRISTAN
Seychelles *island* MAHE, ALDABRA

shab SCAB, ITCH, HERPES, SCRATCH
shabby RATTY, DOWDY, SEEDY, TACKY, SCURVY, WORN, CONTEMPTIBLE, DRAB, MEAN, SOILED, PALTRY, STINGY, RAGGED, THREADBARE, BEGGARLY, POOR, DESPICABLE
woman DOWD
shack SHED, CABIN, HUT, HOVEL, SHANTY
shackle GYVE, BIND, CHAIN, TRAMMEL, FETTER, HANDCUFF, MANACLE *See* "check"
shad ALOSE, ALEWIFE, ALLICE, CRAPPIE, FISH
England ALLICE, ALLIS
Europe ALOSE, ALLICE, ALOSA, CHAD
genus ALOSA
shaddock PUMELO, POMELO, TREE, FRUIT
shade VEIL, VISOR, BLIND, SHELTER, SWALE, SHIELD, UMBRAGE, SCREEN, UMBRELLA, CURTAIN, TINGE, NUANCE, DEGREE, TONE, COLOR, TINT, UMBRA, DASH, STREAK, HUE, GHOST, SPIRIT, SPECTER, SHADOW, PROTECT, ECLIPSE, DULL, OBSCURITY
shaded *walk* ARCADE, MALL
shadow SHADE, UMBRA, TRACE, DOG, SCUG, TAIL, TRAIL, FORM, FIGURE, SHAPE, OUTLINE, GHOST, SPIRIT, SPECTER, ADUMBRATION, OBSCURITY, SHELTER, VESTIGE, REMNANT
dark cone of UMBRA
eclipse UMBRA

man *without*
ASCIAN
thrown opposite
ways ANTISCIAN
shadows, *fight with*
SCIAMACHY
projecting
SKIAGRAPHY
Shadwell, Thos. OG
shady ADUMBRAL,
ELMY, HIDDEN,
COOL, DARK,
QUESTIONABLE,
SHADOWY, UM-
BRAGEOUS, UN-
RELIABLE,
DISREPUTABLE
shaft ARROW,
GROOVE, SPIRE,
SPEAR, DART,
MISSILE, COLUMN,
PILLAR, STEM,
TUNNEL, WEAPON,
OPENING, EX-
CAVATION, RAY,
HANDLE, STELE,
FLAGSTAFF, THILL,
POLE, PIT
column SCAPE
of cart THILL,
TONGUE
of feather SCAPE
plant AXIS
shafter HORSE
shag PILE, HAIR,
WOOL, NAP,
CORMORANT
shaggy HIRSUTE,
BUSHY, NAPPY,
UNKEMPT, UN-
POLISHED, CON-
FUSED, ROUGH
shake ROCK,
AGITATE, JAR,
JOLT, SHED, TRILL,
QUAKE, QUIVER, TOT-
TER, AROUSE, SWAY,
CONVULSE, STAGGER,
FRIGHTEN, DAUNT,
WAVE, OSCILLATE,
VIBRATE, SWING,
SHUDDER
Shakers *founder* LEE
Shakespearean *theater*
GLOBE
villain IAGO
Shakespeare's *wife*
ANNE
shale BAT, SHUCK,
ROCK, SLATE
shall CAN, MUST,

WILL, PROMISE,
COMMAND
shallot ESCHALOT,
ONION, SCALLION
shallow TRIVIAL,
SLIGHT, INANE,
CURSORY, HOLLOW,
EMPTY, TRIFLING,
PETTY, SHOAL,
SUPERFICIAL,
SILLY, SIMPLE,
IGNORANT,
FRIVOLOUS,
FOOLISH
channel LAGOON
sham APE, DUMMY,
FAKE, FEIGN,
FARCE, MOCK, PRE-
TENSE, FRAUD, TRICK,
COUNTERFEIT,
SUBSTITUTE,
IMITATION, DECEIT,
HOAX, DECEPTION
Shamash's *consort*
AI, AYA
shamble SHUFFLE,
WALK, STOOL,
HOBBLE, ABATTOIR
shame FIE, ODIUM,
DISGRACE, HUMILI-
ATE, GUILT, ABASE,
INDECENCY,
ABASHMENT,
MORTIFICATION,
CONFUSION,
DISHONOR, SCANDAL,
INFAMY, DISRE-
PUTE, IGNOMINY
shameful GROSS,
VILE, DISHONORABLE,
INDECENT, OUTRA-
GEOUS, BASE,
DEGRADING,
OFFENSIVE,
DISGRACEFUL
shampoo WASH,
LAVE, RINSE,
TRIPSIS, CLEANSE
Shan TAI *See*
"Thailand"
Shang *dynasty* YIN
shanghai DRUG, SHIP,
KIDNAP, SLINGSHOT
shank CRUS, GAM,
GAMB, LEG, TARSUS,
SHAFT, PEDICEL,
SHIN, METATARSUS,
TIBIA, SUPPORT
pertaining to
CRURAL
yellow TATTLER

shantung TUSSAH,
SILK, PONGEE
shanty HOVEL, HUT,
SHED, SHACK,
CABIN, LEAN-TO
shape REGULATE,
MODIFY, PATTERN,
OUTLINE, FIGURE,
PROFILE, MAKE,
FORGE, DESIGN,
FORM, GUISE,
FRAME, MO(U)LD,
CUT, MODEL, PLAN,
CREATE, ADJUST,
DIRECT, ASPECT, IN-
CLINE, STATE
shapeless AMOR-
PHOUS, CRUDE,
UGLY
shaping *core* AME
machine EDGER
shard FRAGMENT,
SHELL, SCALE,
PIECE, POTSHERD
share DOLE, LOT,
PART, QUOTA, RATION,
IMPART, DIVIDE,
PARTAKE, SLICE,
(AP)PORTION,
DISTRIBUTE,
DIVIDEND, PARTICI-
PATE
shark TOPE, GALEUS,
RHINA, MAKO,
SOUP-FIN,
PORBEAGLE, ANGEL,
ROGUE, EXPERT,
CHEAT, SWINDLER
adherent fish
REMORA
blue MAKO
nurse GATA
small LAMIA, TOPE
whale MHOR
sharp NOTE, SMART,
KEEN, EAGER,
EDGY, ACID, ALERT,
ACUTE, SLY, WILY,
BITING, ACERB,
CAUSTIC, CUTTING,
PIERCING, STABBING,
CUTE, PRETTY
combining form
ACET(O), OXY
sighted LYNCEAN
to taste ACERB,
ACID, ACRID
sharpen STROP,
WHET, GRIND,
HONE, EDGE, POINT,
INTENSIFY,
EXCITE

sharpened *lightly* ACUTATE

sharpening *of note* ECBOLE

sharper GYP, CHEAT, KNAVE, ROGUE, SWINDLER, TRICKSTER, SHARK

sharpshooter JAGER, SNIPER, SHOT, MARKSMAN

shatter DASH, SMASH, DESTROY, BREAK, CRUMBLE, DISSIPATE, BURST, CRACK, SPLIT, WRECK, IMPAIR, SPLINTER

shave CUT, PARE, SHEAR, SLICE, CHEAT, STRIP, TONSURE, REDUCE, SHORTEN, GRAZE

shaveling FRIAR, MONK, PRIEST, HYPOCRITE, TIME-SERVER

shavetail MULE, ENSIGN, LIEUTEN-ANT

shawl PAISLEY, MANTLE, WRAP
gray plaid MAUD
Mexican MANTA, SERAPE

sheaf KERN, BUNDLE, BALE, QUANTITY

shear CLIP, TRIM, REDUCE, SHORTEN, SHAVE, CUT, STRIP, FLEECE, PLUNDER, DEFRAUD, PARTING, FORK

sheatfish SOM

sheath OCREA, SLEEVE, CASE, THECA, TUBE, SCABBARD, SPATHE, LORICA, ENVELOPE, WRAP(PER)
botany OCREA

sheathe INCASE, COVER, CONCEAL, HIDE, CLOTHE

Sheba SABA

shebang SHOP, AFFAIR, THING, BUSINESS, ESTABLISH-MENT, CONTRIVANCE, OUTFIT, CONCERN

shed SLOUGH, SPILL, EFFUSE, JUNK, MO(U)LT, DOFF, SCRAP, CAST, POUR, EMIT, DIFFUSE, LEAN-TO, OUTBUILDING, HUT, EXUVIATE
dugout ABRI

sheen GLOSS, SPLENDOR, LUSTER, LUSTRE, POLISH, GLAZE, GLARE, LIGHT, BRIGHTNESS, SHINE, RADIANT, GLITTERING, FAIR

sheep MERINO, FLOCK
black ROUE
cry BLAT, BLEAT, MAA, BAA
disease BANE, SCAB, SHAB, BLAST, GID, ROT, COE, CORE
English CHEVOIT, DISHLEY
female EWE
fleece KET, WOOL
fly FAG, BOT
fold COTE
genus OVIS
hardy type KARAKUL
India SHA
keeper ABEL, SHEPHERD
leather ROAN, KID
leg hair GARE
Leicester DISHLEY
liniment EIK
male BUCK, RAM, TUP, HEDER, WETHER
mange SCAB
mountain IBEX, BIGHORN
nahoor SHA
pen COTE, FOLD, FANK *See* "sheepfold"
pertaining to ARIES, OVINE
pet COSSET
second year TEG
shorn HOG
skin ROAN, KID, PELT, BASAN (BASIL), DONGOLA, DIPLOMA
Tibet and India SHA, URIAL
tick KEB, KED
two-year-old HOB,

BIDENT
white MERINO
wild AOUDAD (ARUI), ARGAL, URIAL, RASSE, BHARAL, MOUFLON, SHA, NAHOOR
wool-producing MERINO
yearling HOGGET, TAG
young LAMB, (Y)EANLING

sheepfold COTE, KRAAL, FANK, REE(VE), PEN

sheeplike OVINE, TIMID, DOCILE, MEEK

sheepskin DIPLOMA, PARCHMENT, LEATHER
flexible ROAN

sheer UTTER, MERE, SIMPLE, THIN, STEEP, PURE, ABRUPT, TURN, DEFLECT, DIVERT, AVERT, SWERVE, UNMIXED, UN-DILUTED, UN-QUALIFIED, DOWN-RIGHT, ABSOLUTE, PERPENDICULAR, TRANSPARENT, DIAPHANOUS, FINE, QUITE, DEVIATE, COMPLETE

sheet LAYER, COVERING, PAPER, EXPANSE
12-folded DUODECIMO

sheeting PERCALE, LINEN, ROOFING, LINING

shekel, ½ BEKAH
1/20 GERAH

shelf LEDGE, REEF, SHOAL, BRACKET, SANDBANK, BED-ROCK, MANTELPIECE
embankment BERM(E)
on the RETIRED, PAWNED

shell CARAPACE, COWRY, SHARD, SHOT, BOMB, SAC(K), STRAFE, SHUCK, STRIP, POD, HULL, HUSK, HIDE, CASE,

COAT, SKIN, CASING,
ARMOR, COVER,
BURR,
BOMB(ARD)
beads PEAG,
WAMPUM
cast off SHED,
EXUVIATE,
EXFOLIATE
covered with
LORICATE
ear ORMER,
ABALONE
explosive BOMB,
GRENADE
fish BARNACLE,
PIPI, NACRE,
OYSTER, COCKLE,
MUSSEL, SHRIMP,
CRAB, LOBSTER,
ABALONE, LIMPET,
SCALLOP, CLAM
groove(s) of LIRA,
VARICES, VARIX
Indian coast
CHANK
large CONCH
marine TRITON,
CONCH, WHELK
money COWRY,
WAMPUM, COWRIE,
COLCOL, SE(A)WAN,
PEAG(E), UHLLO
shelldrake DUCK
Shelley *drama*
(THE) CENCI
shelter SHIELD,
PROTECT, LODGE,
HOUSE, BOARD,
ASYLUM, COVER,
LEE, COTE,
POUND, TENT,
HOSTEL, SCREEN,
COVERT, ABRI,
DUGOUT, HAVEN,
HARBOR, CAVE,
ARK, REFUGE,
RETREAT,
SANCTUARY, ROOF,
DEFENSE, SECURITY,
UMBRELLA, SHED,
SAFETY, PROTEC-
TION, DEFEND
cattle STELL,
STALL, BARN
nautical LEE
toward ALEE
Shem's *father* NOAH
son ELAM, ARAM,
LUD, ASSHUR,
ARPHAXAD

sheol HELL, HADES,
UNDERWORLD
shepherd PASTOR,
HERD(ER), GUIDE,
WATCH, TEND,
HERDSMAN,
LEAD(ER), DIRECT
god PAN
shepherd's *club*
MULLEIN, PLANT
pipe REED,
LARIGOT, OAT,
MUSETTE
rod TEASEL,
PLANT
staff KENT, CROOK
sherbet DRINK, ICE,
DESSERT
sheriff REEVE,
OFFICER, DEPUTY,
ELISOR
helper(s) POSSE,
DEPUTY
substitute ELISOR
"Sherlock Holmes"
author DOYLE
sherry WINE,
OLOROSO, XERES,
SOLERA
Shetland *bay* VOE
court president
FOUD
fishing grounds
HAAF
freehold right UDAL
*governor or magis-
trate* FOUD
island YELL, UNST
measure URE
pasture HOGA
tax SCAT
viol GUE
shibboleth SLOGAN,
PASSWORD,
CRITERION, TEST
shield (E)SCUTCH-
EON, SCUTUM, ECU,
PAVIS, SCUTE,
TARGE, EGIS, AEGIS,
ARMOR, BUCKLER,
APRON, BIB, HANDLE,
COVER, SHADE,
SHELTER, SAFE-
GUARD, PROTECT,
DEFEND, GUARD,
SAVE, AVERT,
FORBID, SCREEN
Athena's AEGIS
band across FESS
below dam APRON
border ORLE
boss UMBO

division ENTE,
PALY
fillet ORLE
on insect's head
CLYPEUS
Roman SCUTE,
SCUTUM, TESTUDO
sacred ANCILE
shaped SCUTATE,
THYROID, PELTATE,
CLYPEATE
small ECU
strap ENARME
shift FEND, STIR,
VEER, BAFFLE,
ALTER, VARY,
SWERVE, DEVICE,
TRICK, MOVE,
WILE, SUBSTITUTE,
DEVIATE, SHUNT,
CAMISE, SMOCK,
SLIP, CHEMISE,
CHANGE, SHUFFLE,
CONTRIVE, TRANS-
FER
position GYBE,
JIBE
shill ACCOMPLICE,
DUPE
shilling BOB
five DECUS
1/12 PENNY
twenty POUND
twenty-one GUINEA
twenty-two FLORIN
shilly-shally TRIFLE,
HESITATE, VACIL-
LATE, WAVER,
IRRESOLUTION
shin SHANK, CLIMB,
CRUS, TIBIA
pertaining to TIBIAL
plaster SCRIP,
MONEY
shindig, shindy
RIOT, ROW, PARTY,
RUMPUS, DANCE
shine TWINKLE,
GLOW, BEAM,
RADIATE, SPARKLE,
CORUSCATE, FUR-
BISH, POLISH, BUFF,
GLISTEN, GLITTER,
RUTILATE, BURNISH,
GLOSS, GLAZE,
LUSTER, EXCEL,
STAR, GLINT
shiner MINNOW,
CHUB, ROACH,
FISH, MENHADEN,
BOOTBLACK, COIN,
EYE

shingle CLAPBOARD, SIGN, FACIA, ROOF, BOB, WOOD, SIGNBOARD, HAIRCUT, WHIP, CHASTISE, CUT, CLIP
shingles ZONA, HERPES
shining GLARY, AGLOW, LUCID, GLOSSY, NITID, RESPLENDENT, EFFULGENT, FULGID See "shine"
Shinto gods KAMI
 spirits of dead heroes KAMI
 temple SHA
 gateway to TORII
ship(s) ARGOSY, FLEET, NAVY, SLOOP, SAIL, CRAFT, VESSEL, LINER, BARK, SCOW, OILER, JUNK, BRIG, SEND, MAIL, CORACLE, DONI, HOY, LUGGER, TARTAN, GALLEY, GALIOT, KOFF, YANKY See "boat"
 afterpart SKAG, SKEG, STERN, AFT
 ancient NEF, GALLEON
 Arab DHOW
 back end STERN, SKEG, SKAG
 bend plank of SNY
 berth SLIP, DOCK
 Biblical ARK
 boat for GIG, JOLLY, YAWL
 body HULL, HULK
 bottom, to clean BREAM
 bow STEM
 canvas SAIL
 channel GAT
 China JUNK, SAMPAN
 clock NEF
 crew leader BOSUN
 curved timber LOOF, APRON
 desert CAMEL
 drain SCUPPER
 Dutch YANKY
 employee STEWARD, HAND, SEAMAN, ABLE, MATE, PURSER

floor DECK
fraud BARRATRY
fuel OIL, COAL, OILER, TENDER
fur-hunting SEALER
galley CABOOSE
iron-clad MONITOR, MERRIMAC
jail BRIG
keel SKEG
left side PORT
lifting device DAVIT, CAMEL
lowest part BILGE
medieval DROMON, XEBEC, ASEC, BIREME, GALIOT, TRIREME, UNIREME
mid-part WAIST
mooring place DOCK, BERTH, SLIP, PORT, HARBOR
mortgage BOTTOMRY
oar-propelled GALLEY, TRIREME, UNIREME, BIREME
passage for GAT
platform DECK
pole MAST
prow STEM, BOW, NOSE
record book LOG
rope SHROUD
section HOLD, DECK
table frame FIDDLE
timber MAST, BIBB, SPAR, BITT
wheel HELM
worm BORER, TOREDO
shipshape NEAT, TAUT, TRIG, TIDY, SNUG
shipwreck, goods lost in FLOTSAM
shirk EVADE, SHUN, SLACK, DODGE, MALINGER, AVOID, GOLDBRICK
shirt KAMIS, CAMISA, SKIVVY, BLOUSE, CAMISE
 bosom PLASTRON
 false front DICKY
 long loose KAMIS
shiver QUIVER, TOTTER, VIBRATE, SHAKE, QUAKE, SPLINTER, SHUDDER,

TREMBLE, FRAGMENT, SHALE
shoal CROWD, HOST, HORDE, REEF, DROVE, BAR, SHALLOW, SPIT, BANK
shoat PIG, HOG, SHOTE
shock SURPRISE, DISGUST, HORRIFY, IMPACT, BLOW, COLLISION, TRAUMA, JAR, STARTLE, BRUNT, SCANDALIZE DISMAY, CONCUSSION, CROWD, HEAP, STACK, MOP, JOLT
shocking BAD, PAINFUL, UGLY, SCANDALOUS
shod CALCED
shoe BLUCHER, SLIPPER, MULE, BOOT, CLOG, BALMORAL, OXFORD, CASING, SANDAL
 aid HORN
 cleat CALK
 clog PATTEN, CHOPINE, SABOT
 coarse BROGAN, STOGY
 covering PRUNELLA, GAITER, SPAT
 edge WELT
 form LAST
 front VAMP
 gym SNEAKER
 heavy BROGAN
 high BUSKIN, BOOT
 house MULE, SLIPPER, MOYLE
 lace LATCHET, STRING
 low PUMP, SLIPPER, SANDAL
 margin RAND
 mule's PLANCH
 part SOLE, RAND, CALK, VAMP, WELT, HEEL
 stiffener COUNTER
 strip WELT, RAND
 thick-soled CHOPINE
 wiper MAT
 wooden GETA, SABOT, CLOG, SECQUE, PATTEN
shoebill STORK

shoeholder TREE
shoelace *tag* AGLET
shoemaker SOUTER,
CRISPIN, SUTOR,
SOUTAR, FISH, COB-
BLER
awl ELSEN
nail SPARABLE
oil stone SLIP
patron saint CRISPIN
Spain ZAPATERO
tool AWL, LAST
shoestring LACE,
LACET, THONG
shogun TYCOON,
CHIEF, GOVERNOR
shola JUNGLE,
THICKET
shooi SKUA, JAEGER,
BIRD
shoot SNIPE, FIRE,
KILL, DISCHARGE,
SPRIG, BUD, RATOON,
CHIT, TILLER,
TWIG, DART,
SPROUT, FLY,
SCUD, SPEED, HURRY,
LIMB, BRANCH,
BOUGH, SCION,
OFFSPRING,
GERMINATE
edible UDO
from cover SNIPE
long flexible
VIMEN, STOLON,
VINE
plant SCION, CION,
ROD, STOLON,
RUNNER
shooting *gallery* TIR
iron PISTOL,
REVOLVER, GAT,
GUN, FIREARM,
WEAPON
match SKEET, TIR,
SHOOT
star METEOR,
COWSLIP, PLANT
shop BUSINESS,
STORE, MART,
OFFICE, FACTORY,
BURSE, PLANT,
MILL, EMPORIUM,
BUY, TRADE
shopping, *mad for*
ONIOMANIA
shore BANK, COAST,
MARGE, PLAYA,
LAND, SUPPORT,
BRINK, STRAND,
BEACH, RIPA,

PROP, BUTTRESS,
STAY
bird AVOCET,
CURLEW, SAND-
PIPER, PLOVER,
SNIPE *See under*
"bird"
pertaining to LIT-
TORAL
short BRIEF,
FRIABLE, CONCISE,
TERSE, CRISP, ABRUPT,
CURT, CROSS,
LITTLE, LACKING,
QUICK, SCANTY,
CURTAILED,
SUCCINCT, CON-
DENSED, LACONIC,
SNAPPISH, UN-
CIVIL, BRITTLE
and fat PODGY,
PUDGY
legged BREVIPED
lived EPHEMERAL,
TRANSIENT,
FLEETING
napped RAS
of breath DYSPNEIC
sighted MYOPIC
shortage LACK,
DEFICIT, WANT,
ULLAGE, DEFICIENCY,
INSUFFICIENCY
shorten CUT, DOCK,
LOP, LESSEN,
CURTAIL, DEPRIVE,
ABBREVIATE, TELE-
SCOPE, ABRIDGE,
DIMINISH, REDUCE,
RETRENCH, APOCO-
PATE, ELIDE
shortening *of syllables*
SYSTOLE, APOCOPA-
TION
shorthand *system*
GREGG, PITMAN
short-leafed *internode*
ROSETTE
shortly SOON, ANON,
NEXT, BRIEFLY,
QUICKLY, CURTLY,
ABRUPTLY, RUDELY
Shoshonean INDIAN,
PAIUTE, UTE, HOPI,
PIMA, MOKI,
MOQUI, MONO,
BANNOCK
shot HYPO, DRINK,
CHARGE, SHELL,
LEAD, PELLET,
BALL, BULLET,
MISSILE, BB, DIS-

CHARGE, MARKS-
MAN, RANGE,
SCOPE, REACH,
GUESS
and shell AMMO
sizes BB, FF, TT
shou DEER
should OUGHT, MUST
shoulder *badge*
EPAULET
belt BALDRIC, SASH
blade SCAPULA,
OMOPLATE, BONE
combining form
OM(O)
inflammation
OMITIS, OMALGIA
muscle DELTOID
of a bastion EPAULE
of a road BERM
pertaining to
SCAPULAR
to shoulder SERRIED
yoke pail COWL,
SOE
shout CRY, SCREAM,
CALL, BAWL, YELL,
ROAR, EXCLAIM,
VOCIFERATE, OUT-
CRY, REJOICE, *See*
"cry"
shove JOSTLE,
ELBOW, PUSH,
THRUST, PROPEL,
AID, BOOST, ABET
shovel HAT, SCOOP,
SPADE, TOOL
show ARRAY,
EVINCE, TEACH,
PLAY, MOVIE, LEGIT,
POMP, REVEAL,
PROVE, GUIDE,
CONDUCT, DISPLAY,
OFFER, TENDER,
EXPOSE, PARADE,
FLAUNT, EXHIBIT,
FAIR, DIVULGE,
EXPLAIN, DEMON-
STRATE, PRETENSE,
OSTENTATION,
DISCLOSE
ring ARENA,
CIRCUS
stage LEGIT
street RAREE
showcase, *glass*
VITRINE
shower MISLE,
SPRINKLE, RAIN,
SPATE, PARTY,
BATH, FLOW, RUSH,
SPRAY, SCATTER,

MIZZLE, ABUN-
DANCE
of meteors
ANDROMEDE
showy GARISH, ARTY,
GAY, POMPOUS,
LOUD, OSTENTATIOUS,
BARONIAL, TINSEL,
GAUDY, SPORTY,
FLASHY, SWANK,
ORNATE, BEDIZ-
ENED, DASHY
shrapnel SHELL
shred RAG, RIP,
SNIP, STRIP, TAG,
WISP, TEAR, SCRAP,
FRAGMENT, BIT,
PIECE, TATTER,
PARTICLE, STRING,
FILAMENT
shrew ERD, SCOLD,
VIXEN, VIRAGO,
TARTAR, XANTIPPE,
TERMAGANT, SPIT-
FIRE, RANDY
Europe ERD
fictional KATE
(KATRINA)
long-tailed SOREX
shrewd FOXY,
CLEVER, KEEN,
WISE, CANNY,
SLY, CUTE, WILY,
ASTUTE, SAPIENT,
ARTFUL, CUNNING,
SUBTLE, CRAFTY,
ARCH, SAGACIOUS,
SAGE, KNOWING
shrill STRIDENT,
SHARP, PIPING,
PIERCING, KEEN,
PENETRATING,
ACUTE, BITING,
POIGNANT
shrimp PRAWN,
DWARF, PE(E)WEE,
CRUSTACEAN
brine ARTEMIA
Burma NAPEE,
BALACHAN
fisherman NETTER
shrine ALTAR,
ADYTUM, CHASSE,
TOMB, MEMORIAL,
SANCTUARY, IMAGE,
ARK, NAOS, RELI-
QUARY, TEMPLE,
CHAPEL
shrink SHRIVEL,
RECOIL, QUAIL,
WINCE, CONTRACT,
REDUCE, DIMINISH,

DECREASE, DWINDLE,
FLINCH, PARCH,
WRINKLE, ATROPHY,
WASTE, WITHDRAW
shrinking COY, SHY,
TIMID
shrivel PARCH,
WIZEN, WITHER, SEAR,
CRINE, WRINKLE
See "shrink"
shriveled SERE, THIN,
SMALL, WRINKLED
shroff BANKER,
MONEYCHANGER
shroud COWL, MASK,
CEREMENT, VEIL,
PALL, ENVELOPE,
HIDE, SCREEN,
SHELTER, COVERING
shrub(s) BUSH,
TOD, BOSCAGE,
FRUTEX, FOLIAGE,
ELDER, YEW, LILAC,
SALAL, ERICA *See*
"plant"
Adam's needle
YUCCA
Africa IBOGA,
BOCCA
America (U.S.)
ILEX, SALAL,
ITEA, RHUS, SAVIN(E)
apricot genus
PRUNUS
Arabian leaves
KAFTA, KAT
tea KAT
aromatic LAVEN-
DER, SASSAFRAS
Asia (T)CHE,
TEA, BAGO,
DEUTZIA,
WEIGEL(I)A,
KAFTA, KAT, SAVIN(E),
RUTA, AUCUBA
bean family ULEX
berry SALAL,
HOLLY
burning bush
WAHOO
bushy CADE, SAVIN,
TOD
California SALAL
cedar SAVIN(E)
cherry genus
CERASUS,
PRUNUS
China TEA,
(T)CHE, FATSIA,
KERRIA
Congo BOCCA
dogwood CORNUS

England HEATH
Europe CADE,
CISTUS, RUTA,
OLEA, ALDER,
CAPER, SAVIN(E)
evergreen CEDAR,
HOLLY, ILEX,
CAMELIA, CISTUS,
FATSIA, HEATH,
JASMINE, BOX,
LAUREL, MYRTLE,
YEW, SALAL,
PEPINO
fence HEDGE, BOX
flowering AZALEA,
LILAC, SPIRAEA,
PRIVET, SYRINGA,
OLEANDER,
FORSYTHIA
genus ITEA, ROSA,
RUTA, SUMAC,
SPIRAEA, OLEA,
RHUS, SIDA, RIBES,
ARALIA, DEUTZIA,
PYRUS, PRUNUS,
CISTUS, GENISTA
hardy ALTHAEA,
HEATHER
Hawaii AKALA
holly ILEX
Japan ACUBA,
KERRIA
Java UPAS
liliaceous TI
maple genus ACER
medical CUBEB,
BOCCA, SOMA
Mediterranean
CAPER
Mexico CEIBA
narcotic KAT,
KAFTA, COCA
N. Zealand TUTU,
RAMARAMA, TI,
GRAMA
olive OLEA
oriental HENNA
peach genus
PRUNUS
pepper KAVA
periwinkle VINCA
Peru MATICO
plum genus PRUNUS
poison SUMAC,
IVY, RHUS
prickly BRAMBLE,
HAW, ROSE, BRIAR
quince, Jap.
CYDONIA
relating to BOS-
CAGE
sambucus ELDER

silklike fiber
ANABO, CEIBA
S. America
PEPINO, MATE,
MATICO, CEIBA
spiny ULEX,
FURZE, GORSE,
ROSE, HAW,
BRAMBLE, BRIAR
stunted SCRUB,
SCRAG
tanning SUMAC
thick foilage TOD
thorny HAW,
BRAMBLE, BRIAR,
ROSE
W. Indies ANIL,
CASSAVA, EBOE,
ANNATTO
shudder QUIVER,
SHIVER, QUAKE,
TREMOR *See*
"shake"
shuffle SCUFF, RUSE,
MIX, DEAL, TRICK,
DRAG, CONFUSE,
SHIFT, PREVARICATE,
EQUIVOCATE, QUIB-
BLE, JUGGLE,
DERANGE, CHANGE
shun ESCHEW, ES-
CAPE, ELUDE,
AVOID, BALK, SHY,
IGNORE, CUT, SCORN,
REFRAIN, EVADE
Shunammite
ABISHAG
shunt BYPASS,
SWITCH, DODGE,
FLINCH, SIDETRACK,
SHIFT, TRANSFER,
DEVIATE
Shushan SUSA
shut CLOSE, FOLD,
CEASE, BLOCK, BAR,
SEAL, STOP, PRO-
HIBIT, EXCLUDE,
SECURE, FASTEN,
BLOCKADE, CONFINE
out OCCLUDE, EX-
CLUDE, PRECLUDE,
BAN, BAR
up DAM, CAGE,
PEN, IMMURE, EN-
CLOSE, CONFINE,
IMPRISON, SILENCE,
INCARCERATE
shuttle SLIDE,
LOOPER, FLUTE
shy COY, TIMID,
MODEST, WARY,
CHARY, BALK, BASH-

FUL, JIB, RE-
SERVED, DIFFIDENT,
SHEEPISH, SHRINK-
ING, SHAMEFACED,
UNOBTRUSIVE, UN-
ASSUMING, DEMURE,
AVOID, SHUN
Shylock's *daughter*
JESSICA
friend TUBAL
Siam, Siamese *See*
"Thailand"
twins CHANG, ENG
sib KINSMAN, RELA-
TIVE, (A)KIN,
BROTHER, SISTER
Siberian *blizzard*
BURAN *See*
"Russia"
city OMSK
fish NELMA
gulf OB
native TATAR,
YAKOOT, YAKUT, YUIT
squirrel MINIVER,
CALABER
swampy forest region
TAIGA
tent YURT
warehouse ETAPE
wild sheep ARGALI
sibilance mark
CEDILLA
sibilate HISH, HISS,
SISS
sibling SIS, TWIN,
BROTHER, SISTER,
RELATIVE, KINSMAN
sibyl SEERESS,
ORACLE, WITCH,
PROPHETESS,
SORCERESS, FOR-
TUNETELLER
sic EXACT, THUS, SO,
SUCH
sicca SEAL, DIE,
STAMP, RUPEE
siccity DRYNESS,
ARIDITY, DROUGHT
Sicily, Sicilian, *ancient*
town HYBLA
ash MANNA
bull PHALARIS
capital PALERMO
commune RAGUSA
province ENNA
river ACIS, MAZ-
ZARO
secret society
MAFIA
town ENNA
tyrant PHALARIS

sickle CROOK, HOOK,
SPUR, FEATHER,
SCYTHE, TOOL
shaped FALCATE,
FALCIFORM,
HOOKED
sickness *excuse*
AEGER
Sicyon *king* EPOPEUS
side LATUS, SECT,
FLANK, EDGE, JOIN,
AGREE, PHASE,
ASPECT, FACET,
ANGLE, LATERAL,
VERGE, MARGIN,
BORDER, SURFACE,
FACTION
pertaining to
COSTAL, LATERAL
towards LATERAD
side-kick PAL, CHUM,
FRIEND, BUDDY,
PARTNER, ASSISTANT,
CONFEDERATE,
COMPANION
sidero, *combining*
form for IRON
sides, *having unequal*
SCALENE
sideslip SKID, DIGRES-
SION
sidetrack SHUNT,
DISTRACT, DIVERT,
SWITCH
sidewalk *edge* CURB
sidewise ASLANT,
ASKANCE, SLYLY,
OBLIQUELY, IN-
DIRECTLY, LATER-
ALLY
sidle EDGE, CANT,
SKEW, DEVIATE
Sidon SAIDA
siecle CENTURY,
GENERATION, AGE,
HUNDRED
Siegfried, *slayer of*
HAGEN
sword BALMUNG
Siegmund's *sword*
GRAM
Siena *marble* BROC-
ATELLE
siesta NAP, REST,
LULL, BREAK, DOZE,
SLEEP
sieve RIDDLE, BOLT,
TAMIS, SCREEN,
SIFT(ER),
STRAIN(ER), COL-
ANDER, TATTLER,

GOSSIP, BASKET,
CLEAN, TROMMEL
for clay LAUN
like CRIBIFORM
sifac, sifaka LEMUR
siffleur WHISTLER
Sif's *husband* THOR
son ULL
sift BOLT, SORT,
SIEVE, WINNOW,
SCREEN, ANALYZE,
DISSECT, REE,
SEPARATE, PART,
INQUIRE, PROBE,
CLEAN
sifter *See* "sieve"
sigh SOB, MOAN,
LONG, GROAN,
THIRST, GRIEVE,
MOURN, SUSPIRA-
TION, COMPLAIN,
LAMENT
sight SENSE, PER-
CEPTION, VISION,
VISTA, VIEW, LOOK,
GLIMPSE, SEE,
SCENE, AIM, SPEC-
TACLE, SHOW, EX-
HIBITION
sigil SEAL, SIG-
NATURE, SIGNET,
IMAGE
sigmoid CURVE, ESS
sign CUE, TOKEN,
OMEN, SEAL, SYM-
BOL, MARK, BADGE,
NOTE, GESTURE,
DEVICE, MOTION,
HIRE, ENGAGE,
SHINGLE, EMBLEM,
INDICATION, SYMP-
TOM, MANIFESTA-
TION, SIGNAL,
BEACON, PORTENT,
AUGURY, PRESAGE,
SUBSCRIBE, IN-
DORSE, (UNDER)-
WRITE, TRACE,
VESTIGE
magic RUNE, SIGIL
math. PLUS,
MINUS, EQUAL
music SEGNO,
PRESA
pertaining to
SEMIC
signal FLAG, CUR-
FEW, HORN, TOOT,
CUE, PST, FLARE,
GLARE, MARK, GES-
TURE, ALERT, MO-
TION, ALARM,

SALIENT, SIGN,
EMINENT, FAMOUS,
TOKEN, INDICATION,
NOTABLE, IMPORTANT,
CONSPICUOUS, WARN-
ING
flag ENSIGN
light FLARE,
FUSEE
railroad FUSEE
spirit's TAP, RAP
warning CUE, SOS,
PHAROS, ALARM,
ALERT, STOP
signature HAND, SEAL,
SIGIL, NAME, MARK,
SUBSCRIPTION, IN-
SCRIPTION
signed ONOMATOUS,
INDORSED, SUB-
SCRIBED
not ANONYMOUS
significant COGENT,
TELLING, VALID,
SOUND, IMPORTANT,
INDICATIVE,
WEIGHTY, MO-
MENTOUS, POR-
TENTOUS, MEAN-
INGFUL, MEATY
signify DENOTE,
MEAN, SHOW, IM-
PORT, IMPLY, IN-
FORM, DECLARE,
ALLUDE, CONVEY,
MATTER, EXPRESS,
BETOKEN, INDICATE,
SUGGEST, COM-
MUNICATE, AN-
NOUNCE, FORE-
SHOW, INTIMATE
Sigurd's *foster
father* REGINN
silage FODDER, FEED
"Silas Marner"
author ELIOT
silence HUSH, OYER,
OYEZ, OBLIVION,
LULL, QUIET, STILL-
(NESS), GAG,
QUIESCENCE, CALM,
PEACE, APHONY
music TACET
silene CAMPION,
PINK, PLANT,
FLOWER
silent TACIT, MUM,
MUTE, WORDLESS,
TACITURN, RETI-
CENT, SECRETIVE,
STILL, QUIET,
CALM, UNSPOKEN,

NOISELESS, HUSHED,
SPEECHLESS, RE-
SERVED
Silesian *town* OELS,
OPOLE, OPAVA
silica OPAL, QUARTZ,
MICA, TALC, CERITE
silk, *brown* MUGA
cocoon BAVE
corded FAILLE
fabric TASH,
SAMITE, SATIN,
MOFF, PEKIN,
CAFFA, SENDAL,
SURAH, TAFFETA,
FOULARD, MOIRE,
GROS, PONGEE,
TIRAZ
fibers FLOSS
filling BRIN, TRAM,
BAVE
from silkworms
CRIN
gelatin SERICIN
half-mask of LOUP
hat CASTOR, TILE,
TOPPER
heavy GROS,
CAMACA
India ROMAL,
RUMAL, MUGA
material See
"fabric" *above*
moth TUSSAH,
ERIA, MUGA
package of MOCHE
plant RAMIE
raw GREGE
reeling FILATURE
substitute RAYON,
NYLON
thread FLOSS, TRAM
tied and dried
BATIK
tree CEIBA
voile NINON
unravel SLEAVE
waste NOIL
watered MOIRE,
TABBY
silken SERIC, SLEEK,
SLICK, SATINY,
SOFT, SMOOTH,
GLOSSY
silkweed MILKWEED,
PLANT
silkworm ERI(A),
MUGA, TUSSER,
TUSSUR
Assam ERI(A)

China AILANTHUS, SINA, TUSSUR, TUSSER
disease PEBRINE, UJI
genus BOMBYX
home ASSAM
organ of FILATOR
relating to BOMBIC
sill EDGE, LEDGE, THRESHOLD
silly ASININE, STUPID, DAFT, INANE, DULL, DENSE, DUMB, FOOLISH, FATUOUS, ABSURD, INSANE, SENSELESS, WITLESS, CHILDISH, BRAINLESS, SHALLOW, FRIVOLOUS, NONSENSICAL, INDISCREET, IMPRUDENT
silt MIRE, LEES, DREGS, WASH, DRIFT, SEDIMENT, DEPOSIT, ALLUVIUM, MUD, DIRT
silver ARGENT(UM), AG, PLATE, SERVICE, MONEY, COINS, CHANGE
alloy ALBATA
amalgam cone PINA
citrate ITROL
fish TARPON, INSECT
German ALBATA
gilded VERMEIL
in alchemy LUNA
ingots SYCEE
lace FILIGREE
lactate ACTOL
uncoined SYCEE, BULLION
weed TANSY, RUE
silverize PLATE
silverside SMELT, MINNOW, FISH
silversmith REVERE
silvery ARGENT, WHITE, GRAY, SHINING, CLEAR
simian APE, MONKEY, ANTHROPOID, SIMIOUS, APISH
similar AKIN, (A)LIKE, ANALOGOUS, SAME, EQUAL, SUCH,

RESEMBLING, PARALLEL
simile METAPHOR, PARABOLE, ANALOGY, COMPARISON
simitar *See* "scimitar"
simmer BOIL, SEETHE, BROOD, STEW, BUBBLE
Simon PETER, APOSTLE
simon-pure REAL, TRUE, GENUINE, AUTHENTIC, UNQUALIFIED
simoon, simoom STORM, WIND, TEBBAD
simple DULL, DENSE, STUPID, SHEER, SINGLE, SINGULAR, UNMIXED, SOLE, FACILE, LIGHT, CLEAR, PLAIN, LUCID, OPEN, NAIVE, NATURAL, FOOLISH, SILLY, OAFISH, MERE, EASY, PURE, UNCOMBINED, UNALLOYED, HOMESPUN, UNADORNED, UNAFFECTED, ARTLESS, INGENUOUS, UNSOPHISTICATED, INNOCENT
simpleton DAW, GUMP, ASS, FOOL, GAUP, GAWK, SIMP, MORON, OAF, BOOBY, GOOSE, NINNY, IDIOT
simulacrum UNREAL, IMAGE, ICON, MASK, SHAM, SEMBLANCE, PHANTOM, COUNTERFEIT
simulate SHAM, APE, FEIGN, MIMIC, ASSUME, MOCK, COPY, ACT, PRETEND, AFFECT, COUNTERFEIT, IMITATE
simulation FEINT, PRETENSE, CANT, SANCTIMONY, HYPOCRISY
simurg(h) ROC
sin PECCANCY, CRIME, ERR(OR), EVIL, FAULT, VICE,

LAPSE, SLIP, MISDEED, TRANSGRESS(ION), WICKEDNESS, WRONG, OFFENSE
confess SHRIVE
grief for ATTRITION
since AGO, AS, FOR, AFTER, LATER, HENCE, YET, BECAUSE, FROM, SYNE
sincere HONEST, REAL, PURE, SIMPLE, TRUE, EARNEST, OPEN, INTENSE, FRANK, PLAIN, CANDID, GENUINE, UNFEIGNED, UNAFFECTED, INGENUOUS, STRAIGHTFORWARD, ARTLESS, GUILELESS, UPRIGHT
sincerity CANDOR, INTEGRITY, HEARTINESS, PROBITY, VERACITY
Sind *prince* AMEER, AMIR
Sindbad's *transportation* ROC
sinecure CINCH, GRAVY, PIPE, SNAP
sinew MUSCLE, NERVE, TENDON, LIGAMENT
sinewy WIRY, HUSKY, BURLY, STRONG, STOUT, SOUND, MUSCULAR, BRAWNY, VIGOROUS, STURDY
sing CROON, YODLE, CAROL, CHORTLE, LILT, CHANT, LAUD, PRAISE, CHIRP, WARBLE, TROLL, HUM, EXULT, REJOICE
as a round TROLL
with trills ROULADE, WARBLE
singe SCORCH, BURN
singer CANTOR, BARD, CAROLER, DESCANTER, SONGSTER, CHANTEUSE,

VOCALIST, MINSTREL,
CANARY
female CHANTEUSE
singing, *suitable for*
MELIC, LYRIC
single SOLE, SOLO,
MONO, UNIT, APART,
ACE, (A)LONE,
ODD, ONE, SEPARATE,
SOLITARY, UNAL,
INDIVIDUAL, UNIQUE,
UNMARRIED, UN-
WEDDED, ISOLATED,
CELIBATE, HIT,
BUNT
not one of pair
AZYGOUS
out CHOOSE, SELECT,
OPT, PICK, CULL,
CITE
prefix MONO, UNI
singly APART, SOLO,
ALONE, UNAIDED
singular ISOLATED,
STRANGE, ODD,
UNIQUE, RARE,
QUEER, CURIOUS,
UNUSUAL, EXCEP-
TIONAL, EXTRAOR-
DINARY, REMARK-
ABLE, PECULIAR,
ECCENTRIC, BI-
ZARRE, FANTASTIC,
STRIKING
singult HIC, SIGH,
SOB
singultus HICCOUGHS,
HICCUPS
sinister BAD, EVIL,
OMINOUS, LEFT,
SECRET, FATEFUL,
PERVERSE, MALEVO-
LENT, UNLUCKY,
BALEFUL, DIS-
HONEST, ADVERSE,
CORRUPT, DISAS-
TROUS, VICIOUS,
MALIGN
sink DROOP, FLAG,
SAG, FALL, ENGULF,
BASIN, LESSEN,
DIMINISH, LOWER,
SUBSIDE, (SUB)-
MERGE, VANISH,
DESCEND, DROP,
DEBASE, DECEIVE,
FAIL
geology DOLINA
sinker BAGEL,
DOUGHNUT, LEAD,
DIPSY, WEIGHT,

PLUMMET, NAIL,
COOLER
sinning PECCANT
sinuous WAVY,
MAZY, CROOKED,
DEVIOUS, CIRCUI-
TOUS, WINDING,
CURVED, SERPEN-
TINE, TORTUOUS,
UNDULATING,
ERRING
sinus BAY, BEND,
CURVE, ANTRUM,
AMPULLA, ARM,
RECESS, SAC,
CAVITY, HOLLOW,
OPENING
Siouan INDIAN,
OTO(E), IOWA,
KAW, CROW, PONCA,
TETON *See under*
"Indian"
tribe TETON
sip LAP, SUCK, SUP,
GULP, DRINK, TASTE
sipper STRAW, TUBE
sippet CROUTON,
BIT, FRAGMENT
sire FATHER, PAR-
ENT, MAN, MALE,
LORD, KING, HORSE,
PROGENITOR, BE-
GET, BREED
siren CHARMER,
LORELEI, CIRCE,
ALARM, LURER,
ENTICER, MER-
MAID, TEMPTRESS,
SEDUCER, ALERT,
WARNING
Nile CLEO(PATRA)
Sirius CANICULA,
DOGSTAR
sirocco LESTE,
WIND, STORM
sisal HEMP, FIBER,
HENEQUEN
Sisera's *enemy*
BARAK
killer JAEL
siskin FINCH, BIRD
sissified PRISSY,
NICE, PRIM, EF-
FEMINATE
sister SOROR, NUN,
SIB, KIN, NURSE,
SIBLING
sistrum RATTLE
sit REST, HATCH,
FIT, SUIT, CONVENE,
MEET, POSE, PERCH,
STAY, REMAIN,

SETTLE, ABIDE,
BROOD, INCUBATE,
SQUAT
Sitatunga NAKONG,
ANTELOPE
site SEAT, SITUS,
POSITION, PLACE,
AREA, STANCE,
LOCATION, SITUATION,
LOCALITY, SPOT,
LOT
Sitsang TIBET
sitting SEDENT,
SESSION, INCUBA-
TION, POSE, SEATED,
CONVOCATION
situation CASE, POST,
STATE, STRAIT,
JOB, PLACE, SITE,
PLIGHT, STATUS,
PASS, CRISIS,
BERTH, POSITION,
WORK, METIER,
SEAT, PERCH, STA-
TION, LOCATION,
LOCALITY
situs SITE, POSITION,
LOCATION
Siva, *trident*
TRISUL(A)
wife KALI, SATI,
DEVI, UMA, DURGA,
SAKTI
six VI, SENARY
combining form
HEX(A)
dice SISE, BOXCAR
footed HEXAPOD
group of HEXAD,
SENARY
of a kind SEXTU-
PLET
on basis of
SENARY
players SESTET,
SEXTET
sixpence TANNER
sixty, sixties SAROS,
SEXAGENARY
person in SEX-
AGENARIAN
size CALIBER,
BULK, SPACE, MASS,
LIMIT, GAUGE,
MAGNITUDE, AREA,
EXTENT, VOLUME,
SPREAD, STRETCH,
WIDTH, BIGNESS,
AMPLITUDE, DIMEN-
SION(S), EXPANSE,
PROPORTIONS,
CONDITION

sizing SEALER,
  GLUE, PORTION,
  ALLOTMENT
skate RAY, SKIM,
  HORSE, PLUG, SKID,
  MISER
  place to RINK,
  ARENA, POND
skedaddle BOLT,
  FLEE, SNEAK, SCAT,
  SCURRY, SCAMPER
skegger PARR, FISH
skein HANK, MESH,
  WEB, RAP, COIL
skeleton BONES,
  CAGE, CADRE,
  FRAME(WORK),
  SKETCH, DRAUGHT,
  OUTLINE, REMAINS,
  PLAN
  organization CADRE
  sea SHELL, SPICULE,
  SPONGE
skelp SQUALL,
  STRIKE, THRASH,
  SLAP, SPANK, BLOW,
  STRIDE, RAINFALL
skeptic APORETIC,
  DOUBTER, AGNOSTIC,
  QUESTIONER, UNBE-
  LIEVER, FREE-
  THINKER, INFIDEL
sketch CHART, IDEA,
  MAP, SKIT, PLAN,
  PRECIS, APERCU,
  DESCRIPTION, DI-
  GEST, PLOT, TRACE,
  DELINEATION,
  DRAUGHT, POR-
  TRAYAL, DRAFT,
  OUTLINE, DRAW,
  LIMN, DESCRIBE
skewer PIN, SKIVER,
  ROD
ski, *marker for*
  SITZMARK
  run SCHUSS
  zig-zag SLALOM
skid SLIP, SLIDE,
  GLIDE, COAST, DRAG,
  RUNNER, SCUD
skill APTITUDE,
  KNACK, ART, CRAFT,
  FINESSE, DEXTER-
  ITY, INGENUITY,
  FACILITY, ABILITY,
  ADDRESS, PRO-
  FICIENCY, TECH-
  NIQUE, EXPERT-
  NESS
skillful DEFT,
  DAEDAL, APT, FIT,

  EXPERT, HANDY,
  TRAINED, TACTFUL,
  VERSED, ABLE,
  CLEVER, COM-
  PETENT, ADROIT,
  ADEPT
skim SKIP, SCUD,
  FLIT, SCOOP, FLY,
  DART, BRUSH,
  GLIDE, SUMMARIZE
skin(s) BARK,
  RIND, DERM(A),
  (IN)TEGUMENT,
  HIDE, CUTIS, EPI-
  DERMIS, HUSK,
  HULL, STRIP, FELL,
  FLAY, PELT, PEEL,
  DECORTICATE, PARE,
  CHEAT, SWINDLE
  animal PELLAGE,
  PELT, COAT, FUR,
  HIDE
  beaver PLEW
  combining form
  CUTI, DERM(A)
  decoration TATTOO
  destitute of
  APELLOUS
  disease FAVUS,
  TETTER, ACNE,
  TINEA, ECZEMA,
  SCALL, SCABIES,
  BOIL, IMPETIGO,
  DERMATITIS
  dryness XEROSIS
  eruption MACULA,
  RASH, HIVES, ACNE
  exudation SWEAT,
  SUDOR, PERSPIRA-
  TION
  finishing TAN,
  TAW
  fold PLICA
  layer CUTIS, TEGU-
  MENT, (EPI)-
  DERM, CORIUM
  of dark MELANIC
  oil SEBUM
  outer layer
  EPICARP
  pertaining to
  DERMIC, DERMAL,
  CUTICULAR
  redness RUBOR
  rug of KAROSS
  secretion SEBUM
  spot on TACHE,
  MACULA, PETECHIA
skinflint MISER,
  CHEAT, NIGGARD,
  CHURL, CURMUDG-
  EON

skink ADDA, LIZARD
skip OMIT, SPRING,
  FLIT, FLEE, ELIDE,
  CAPER, ELOPE,
  RICOCHET, LEAP,
  JUMP, PASS,
  BOUND, HOP,
  FRISK, GAMBOL,
  DISREGARD,
  NEGLECT, MISS,
  ESCAPE, BY-PASS,
  FOREGO
skipjack BONITO,
  ELATER, SAURY,
  SAUREL, ALEWIFE,
  FISH, (SAIL)BOAT,
  UPSTART, FOP,
  RUNNER
skipper RAIS,
  SERANG, CAPTAIN,
  MASTER, COM-
  MANDER, BUTTER-
  FLY
skirl PIPE, SCREAM,
  SHRIEK, TONE
skirmish CLASH, FRAY,
  TILT, BRUSH,
  MELEE, CONTEST,
  FIGHT, BOUT,
  BATTLE, EN-
  GAGEMENT, VELITA-
  TION, CONFLICT,
  COMBAT, ENCOUNTER,
  FLOURISH, BRAWL
skirt SARONG,
  DIRNDL, KILT,
  FUSTANELLA,
  PETTICOAT, EDGE,
  BORDER, MARGIN,
  FRINGE
  armor TASSE(T)
  attached to coat
  PEPLUM
  ballet TUTU
  Burmese ENGI
  section PANEL,
  GORE
  short KILT, TUTU
skit CAPER, JOKE,
  QUIP, LIBEL, PLAY,
  SQUIB, SKETCH,
  PARODY, SATIRE,
  BURLESQUE, DANCE,
  JIBE, FLOUNCE,
  ASPERSE
skivvy SHIRT
skittles (NINE)-
  PINS
skoal SLAINTE,
  HEALTH, HAIL,
  TOAST, SALUTATION

skulk LURK, HIDE, STEAL, COUCH, SLINK, SNEAK, SHIRK, MALINGER

skull HEAD, CRANIUM
bone SPHENOID, PARIETAL, NASAL, OCCIPITAL, ETHMOID
cavity FOSSA, FORAMEN
point of juncture SUTURE, BREGMA, PTERION
protuberance INION
vault of CALVARIUM

skunk ANNA, CHINCHE, POLECAT, BEAT, DEFEAT, CAD
like ZORIL
Mexico CONEPATE

sky WELKIN, VAULT, HEAVEN, AZURE, BLUE, FIRMAMENT, SUMMIT
blue AZURE, CELESTE, CERULEAN
combining form URAN(O)
highest point ZENITH

skylark PIPIT, LARK, BIRD, FROLIC, CAROUSE, SPORT
genus ALAUDA

slab, *flooring* DALLE
like STELAR
of marble TABLET, STELE, DALLE, PLAQUE

slack LAX, SLOW, LOOSE, REMISS, LAZY, EASY, FEEBLE, LISTLESS, CARELESS, NEGLIGENT, DULL, SLUGGISH, RELAXED, INADEQUATE, DILATORY, INACTIVE, WEAK, INERT

slacken SLOW, ABATE, CURB, EASE, RELAX, REMIT, LETUP, RETARD, MODERATE, WEAKEN, SLAG, LOOSEN

slacks PANTS, TROUSERS, DUFFS

slade PEAT, GLEN

slag DROSS, SCORIA, LAVA, CINDER(S), REFUSE, CLINKER, EMBERS, SLACKEN

slam RAP, SHUT, DEFEAT, BANG, BLOW, IMPACT, CRITICIZE, ABUSE
to make a VOLE

slander MALIGN, DEFAME, BELIE, HIT, ABUSE, OFFEND, REVILE, ASPERSE, LIBEL, SMEAR, CALUMNIATE, VILIFY, DECRY, TRADUCE, DEROGATE, BLACKEN, INSULT

slang LINGO, CANT, ARGOT, PATOIS, JARGON, CHEAT, SWINDLE, DUPE

slant OPINION, ATTITUDE, BIAS, TILT, SLOPE, VIEW, INCLINATION, LIST, LEAN, STAND, ANGLE, BEVEL, ASKEW, GRADE, GLANCE

slanted ATILT, BEVELED, SLOPED, BIASED
walk RAMP

slap SPANK, SMACK, SWAT, CUFF, BLOW, REPRIMAND, PUNISH *See* "hit"

slash JAG, REDUCE *See* "cut"

slat(s) SLOT, STAVE, LATH, TRANSOM, BLIND, SHUTTER, STRIP, FLAP, STRIKE, BAR, SLAB, RIB

slate ROLL, LIST, SLAB, AGENDA, FILE, ROCK, ROOF, BOARD, TILE, PLAN
hammer SAX
tool ZAX, SAX

slattern MOPSY, HAG, CRONE, SLUT, DRAB, SLOVEN, TROLLOP, IDLER, TRIFLER

Slav VEND, WEND, CROAT, SERB, SORB, BULGAR, POLE, BOHEMIAN, SLOVAK, RUSSIAN

slave *See* "serf"
block CATASTA
female ODALISK, ODALISQUE, NEIFE
Greek IAMBE, HELOT, BAUBO
slaves, dealer in MANGO

Slavic *race* LETT
See "Slav"

Slavic-German WEND

slaw SALAD, RELISH, CABBAGE

slay KILL, LYNCH, MURDER, DESTROY, EXTERMINATE, SLAUGHTER, ANNIHILATE, BUTCHER, ASSASSINATE, MASSACRE
by suffocation BURKE

sled PUNG, SKID, TOBOGGAN, SLEIGH, CUTTER, COASTER
See "sleigh"
log TODE, TRAVOIS
Swiss LUGE

sleeky SLY, SLICK, OILY, BLAND, OBSEQUIOUS, SMOOTH, GLOSSY, SILKY, UNCTUOUS, CRAFTY

sleep DOZE, SOPOR, REST, NOD, NAP, REPOSE, DORMANCY, QUIESCENCE, NARCOSE, FLOP, WINK, SLUMBER, SNOOZE, LETHARGY, DROWSE, SIESTA, SOMNOLENCE
causing NARCOTIC, SOPORIFIC
combining form HYPN(O)
deep SOPOR, STUPOR, COMA
deity SOMNUS, HYPNOS, MORPHEUS
inducing SOPORIFIC
insensibility CARUS, COMA
midday SIESTA
prolonged SOPOR
walker SOMNAMBULIST, NOCTAMBULIST

wander in DWALE
sleeper DRONE,
SUPPORT, BEAM,
TIE, TIMBER,
SLUMBERER,
SHARK, DORMOUSE
sleeping DORMANT,
LATENT,
QUIESCENT
pill SOPORIFIC
place BERTH, BED,
COUCH, PAD, BUNK
platform, Siberia
NARE
sickness source
TSETSE
sleepy OSCITANT,
DROWSY, NARCOTIC,
COMATOSE,
LETHARGIC, SLUG-
GISH, SOPORIFEROUS,
SOMNOLENT, PHLEG-
MATIC
sleeve DOLMAN,
ARM, PIPE,
CYLINDER, CHAN-
NEL, TUBE,
MANDREL, THIMBLE
badge CHEVRON
hole for SCYE
sleeveless *garment*
ABA, CAPE,
MANTLE, STOLE
sleigh SLED, PUNG
box PUNG
runner SHOE
sidepiece RAVE
slender FINE, LANK,
TRIM, SVELTE,
RARE, SPARE, LEAN,
THIN, SLIM, REEDY,
WISPY, FRAIL,
LITHE, SLIGHT,
SPINDLING, SKINNY,
NARROW, WEAK,
FEEBLE, MEAGER,
SMALL, INADEQUATE,
FRUGAL, ABSTEMI-
OUS, LISSOM(E),
LIMITED
finial EPI
sleuth DETECTIVE,
TEC, DICK, HAWK-
SHAW, COP, GUM-
SHOE
hound TALBOT,
BLOODHOUND
slice CUT, SLAB,
GASH, LAYER,
PIECE, SECTION,
PARE, SEVER,
DIVIDE, STROKE

bacon RASHER
meat COLP,
COLLOP
slide SKID, SLUE,
CHUTE, SKIP, SKATE,
COAST, GLISSADE,
SLIP, GLIDE
slight CUT, SNUB,
IGNORE, OMIT,
NEGLECT, SLENDER,
SLIM, FRAIL, SCANT,
FORGET, SUPERFI-
CIAL, TRIFLING,
PETTY, PALTRY,
UNIMPORTANT,
DISDAIN, OVERLOOK,
SLUR, FEEBLE
slim THIN, FRAIL,
WEAK, MEAGER,
SCANT, SLENDER,
DIET *See*
"slight"
slime OOZE, MIRE,
MUD, MUCK, FILTH,
ICHOR, SILT,
MUCOUS
slimsy FRAIL,
FLIMSY
slink CRAWL, CREEP,
STEAL, GLIDE,
LURK, SNEAK
slip SOLECISM,
GAFFE, ERR(OR),
LAPSE, BULL,
GLIDE, BONER,
BLUNDER, MISTAKE,
MISSTEP, TRIP,
OVERSIGHT,
CHEMISE, SLIDE,
SLUE, FAULT, VICE,
CUTTING, DOCK,
BERTH, TWIG,
SHOOT, SCION
leather REIN,
LEASH, STRAP
slipper SANDAL,
MOYLE, MULE,
SHOE
slippery SLICK, SLY,
ELUSIVE, GLIB,
FICKLE, SHIFTY,
GLASSY, SMOOTH,
SLITHERY, UNSTABLE,
ICY, UNSAFE, CRAFTY,
EELY, EVASIVE,
UNRELIABLE, SLEEK,
TRICKY, GREASY,
TREACHEROUS
slit SLASH, GASH,
VENT, CRACK,
CLEFT, SUNDER,
REND, SPLIT, CUT,

CLEAVE, SEVER,
FISSURE, INCISION,
APERTURE, OPEN-
ING, CHINK
slither SIDLE, SLIDE,
SLIP, GLIDE, SKID,
CRAWL, RUBBLE,
RUBBISH, SPLINTER
sloe HAW, PLUM,
BLACKTHORN, GIN
slogan CRY, MOTTO,
CATCHWORD,
WATCHWORD,
MAXIM
slope SCARP,
GRADIENT, GLACIS,
CANT, SLANT,
PEAK, ALP, RAMP,
SPLAY, TILT, TIP,
PITCH, GRADE, RISE,
LEAN, HILL, VEER,
INCLINE, DECLIVITY
fort GLACIS
of land VERSANT
sloping *bank* BRAE
sloth LORIS, INERTIA,
LAZINESS, TARDI-
NESS, INDOLENCE,
SLUGGISHNESS,
IDLENESS
three-toed AI
two-toed UNAU
slough SWAMP, BOG,
MARSH, SHED,
CAST *See* "shed"
sloughing ECDYSIS
sloven(ly)
SLOUCH(Y),
SLATTERN, FROWSY,
PHLEGMATIC, UN-
TIDY, SLOPPY,
SLIPSHOD, UNKEMPT
slow DILATORY,
INACTIVE, SLACK,
DELAY, RELAX,
LATE, RETARD,
POKY, INERT,
LESSEN, REDUCE,
HINDER, SLUGGISH,
BEHIND, TARDY,
DULL, TORPID,
STUPID, PHLEGMATIC,
LINGERING,
GRADUAL, DELIBER-
ATE, WEARISOME,
UNPROGRESSIVE
music LARGO, ADAGIO,
LENTO, TARDO
slowpoke SNAIL
sludge MIRE, PASTE,
MUD, ICE, SLOSH,

SLUSH, OOZE, SLOB,
SEDIMENT
slue TWIST, TURN,
VEER, PIVOT,
SWING, SLIP, SLIDE
slug BASH, DRONE,
SNAIL, BULLET,
SLAP, SWAT, CLOUT,
STRIKE, HIT, SMITE,
BEAT, BAT, DRINK,
NUGGET, SLUGGARD,
LARVA, MOLLUSK
genus LIMAX
sea TREPANG,
NUDIBRANCH, DOTO
sluggish *See* "slow"
sluice DRENCH, WET,
CHANNEL, OPEN-
ING, VENT,
FLOODGATE, CUR-
RENT, TROUGH,
FLUME, WASH,
SCOUR, EAT, SWILL,
CONDUIT, SEWER
slumber *See*
"sleep"
slur ELIDE, IN-
NUENDO, DIG, BLUR,
SKIM, SKIP, GLOSS,
SLIGHT, ASPERSE,
TRADUCE, DIS-
PARAGE, DEPRECIATE,
CALUMNIATE,
REPROACH, STIGMA,
MACULE, STAIN,
BLOT, INSULT,
SLANDER
sly CRAFTY, FOXY,
ASTUTE, WISE,
SHREWD, WARY,
WILY, ARCH,
CAGEY, COVERT,
SNEAKY, CLEVER,
CUTE, CUNNING,
ARTFUL, INSIDIOUS,
SUBTLE, STEALTHY,
UNDERHAND,
CLANDESTINE,
FURTIVE, SKILLFUL
look LEER, OGLE
smack KISS, TANG,
TASTE, BUSS, SLAP,
BOAT, SLOOP, BLOW,
SAVOR, RELISH,
DASH, FLAVOR,
TINCTURE, SNAP,
CRACK, CUTTER,
TINGE, TRACE,
SMATTERING,
STRIKE
small SCANTY,
LITTLE, LIL, TOT,

TINY, PINK, PETITE,
WEE, MINISCULE,
DINKY, DIMINUTIVE,
MINIATURE,
LILLIPUTIAN,
MINUTE, PETTY,
TRIFLING, TRIVIAL,
SELFISH, ILLIBERAL,
PALTRY, MICRO-
SCOPIC, MINOR,
SLIGHT, LIMITED,
COMMON
amount DROP,
DRAM, MINIM,
TRACE, MITE, IOTA
bunch WISP
case ETUI
coin MITE
combining form
MICRO, OLIG(O)
cube(s) DIE, DICE
smallage CELERY,
PARSLEY
smaller, *combining*
form MIO
smallpox VARIOLA
smaragd EMERALD,
BERYL
smart BRIGHT,
ALERT, ASTUTE,
NATTY, TRIG, ACUTE,
APT, CHIC,
TRIM, WITTY, PERT,
CLEVER, STYLISH,
NIFTY, POSH, STING,
HURT, ADROIT,
INTELLIGENT,
DEXT(E)ROUS,
SPRUCE, DAPPER,
BRILLIANT, SHARP,
SHREWD, PAIN
smash STAVE,
BASH, FALL, RUIN,
CRUSH, HIT, BREAK,
MASH, SHATTER,
CRASH, DESTROY,
WRECK, COLLAPSE,
BANKRUPTCY,
BEVERAGE, SUC-
CESS
smear DAUB,
GAUM, GLAIR,
ANOINT, MALIGN,
SPOT, STAIN,
SMUDGE, BEGRIME,
SOIL, BLOTCH,
SULLY, DEFAME,
SMIRCH, DEFILE,
POLLUTE, BLOT,
COVER
smell DETECT,
STENCH, ODOR,

SCENT, FLAIR,
SNIFF, AROMA,
SAVOR, PERFUME,
ESSENCE, FRA-
GRANCE, BOUQUET,
REDOLENCE, FUME,
FUST, NIDOR
bad, combining form
OZO
combining form
OSMO
having disagreeable
OLID, FETID, BAD,
FOUL
offensive REEK,
FETOR, NIDOR
smelt FISH, SCORIFY,
FUSE, MELT,
REFINE, FLUX
fish See under
"fish"
smelting *by-product*
SLAG
mixture MATTE
smile FAVOR,
SNEER, LAUGH,
GRIN, BEAM,
SMIRK, SIMPER
smirch SULLY,
STAIN, TARNISH,
BLACKEN, BLOT,
SMEAR, DEGRADE
See "smear"
smirk LEER, SIMPER,
GRIN, SMILE
smite AFFECT,
STRIKE, ENAMOR
See "hit"
smock CAMISE,
SHIFT, CHEMISE,
TUNIC, GARMENT,
ROBE
smog FOG, MIST,
HAZE, BRUME
smoke CURE,
SMUDGE, REEK,
FUME, VAPOR,
SMOTHER
colored FUMOUS
smoky REEKY,
FUMID, THICK,
TARNISHED,
BLACKENED,
SUSPICIOUS
City PITTSBURGH,
PGH
smolt SALMON
smooth SAND,
PLANE, LEVEL,
FLUSH, SLICK, EASY,
LIGHT, SIMPLE,
SUAVE, PLACID,

SERENE, EQUABLE, FLAT, EVEN, IRON, OILY, LENE, SUANT, BLAND, GLIB, URBANE, GLOSS, CALM, PALLIATE, PLACATE, GLOSSY, SATINY, UNINTER-RUPTED
combining form LEI(O)
consonant LENE
music LEGATO
smoothing tool PLANE, IRON
smother STIFLE, CHOKE, SUFFOCATE, OVERLIE, SMOLDER, SUPPRESS, REPRESS, KILL
smudge SMOKE, SPOT, SOOT, DIRT, GRIME, STAIN, SOIL, BLOT, SMUT, SMUTCH
smug SLEEK, TRIM, NEAT, PRIGGISH, AFFECTED
Smyrna IZMIR
Sn TIN
snack CANAPE, SHARE, BIT, BITE, REPAST, LUNCH, EAT
snail WHELK, CERION, HELICID, HELIX, SLUG, GASTROPOD, MOL-LUSK, THAIS
clam-killing WINKLE
genus NERITA, TRITON, MITRA
marine WHELK
pond CORET
snake ASP, BOA, ADDER, VIPER, REPTILE, OPHIDIAN, WORM, COLUBER, INGRATE *See* "serpent"
Asia DABOIA, JESSUR
bite antidote CEDRON
  plant GUACO
black RACER, LORA
boa ABOMA
charmer's flute PUNGI
Cuba JUBA

deadly COBRA, MAMBA, TAPA, CORAL, KRAIT
Egypt HAJE, ASP
eyes AMBSACE, ONES
Florida MOCCASIN, CORAL
genus BOA, ERYX
hooded COBRA
India KRAIT, DABOIA, COBRA
lizard SEPS
monster ELLOPS
python ANACONDA
relating to SERPEN-TINE, ANGUINEAL, OPHIDIAN
root SANICLE, ASARUM, PLANT, SENECA, SENEGA, BUGBANE, BLOLLY
sand genus ERYX
S. America ABOMA, BOM, LORA
thousand-headed S(H)ESHA, ANANTA
tree LORA
snake-haired *woman* GORGON, EURYALE, STHENO, MEDUSA
snakelike OPHIDIAN, APODAL, SERPEN-TINE, COLUBRINE
snap CRACKLE, POP, PEP, ELAN, BREAK, COOKIE, SPARK, PHOTO, SINECURE
with finger FILLIP
snapper PARGO, FISH
black fin SESI
snappish EDGY, IRED, HUFFY, FRETFUL, CROSS, CURT, SHORT, PEEVISH
snare DRUM, BAG, NAB, COP, DECOY, TRICK, RUSE, LURE, NOOSE, WILE, MESH, WEB, NET, TRAP, GIN, GUM, CATCH, PITFALL
snarl TANGLE, GNAR(L), GNARR, GROWL, KNOT, CHAOS, PIE, DISCORD
snatch SEIZE, STEAL, EREPT *See* "grab"

sneak SPY, LURK, SLINK, SNOOP, SKULK, STEAL
snee DIRK, DAGGER
sneer FLEER, SCORN, GIBE, JIBE *See* "scoff"
snell SNOOD, GUT
snib SNUB, REPROOF, CHECK
sniff SMELL, NOSE, SCENT, SNUFF, PERCEIVE
snip CLIP, CUT, LOB, BIT, SHORTEN, CINCH
snipe *See under* "bird"
cry SCAPE
hawk HARRIER
snivel MUCUS, WHINE, CRY, WEEP
snob TOADY, PARVENU, SWELL
snobbish UPPISH, PROUD, ARROGANT
snood FILLET, SNELL, HAIRNET
snoop LURK, PRY, PROWL, PROBE
snoot FACE, NOSE, SNOUT
snore RALE, RHONCHUS, SNIFF
snout FRONT, NOSE, NOZZLE, SNOOT
snow FIRN, SLEET, PASH, NEVE
field of FIRN, NEVE
fly genus BOREUS
granular NEVE
house IGLU, IGLO(O)
living in NIVAL
mouse VOLE
runner SKI, SKEE, SLED
vehicle PUNG, SLED, SLEIGH
snowflake CRYSTAL, FINCH, BIRD
snowman, *abominable* YETI
snowshoe PAC, PATTEN, SKI
snowy PURE, NIVAL, NIVEOUS, SPOTLESS, WHITE
snub SLAP, REPROOF, REBUFF, CUT, SLIGHT, SNOOT, HUMILIATE

snuff RAPPEE,
NOSE, SCENT, SNIFF,
SMELL, EXTINGUISH
bean CACOON
box MULL
snug COSY, COZY,
TAUT, TRIM, NEAT,
TRIG, TIDY, SPAN,
CLOSE, SECURE,
TIGHT, CLOSED, SAFE,
CONTENT, COMFORT-
ABLE
SO ERGO, THUS, SAE,
SIC, AS, HENCE,
THEREFORE
be it AMEN
much TANTO
soak WET, SOP,
STEEP, SATURATE,
RET, SOG, SOUSE,
DIP, IMBRUE, TOPER,
TIPPLER
flax RET
in brine MARINATE,
SALT, CORN
soap SAPO, SUDS,
CASTILE, FLATTERY,
RUB
convert into
SAPONIFY
fish JABON
frame bar SESS
plant AMOLE
vine GOGO
soapstone TALC
soapsuds FOAM,
FROTH, LATHER
soar (A)RISE, SAIL,
FLOAT, WING,
TOWER, FLIT, FLY,
GLIDE
sob SIMPER, SITHE,
MOAN, CRY, WEEP,
SIGH, WAIL,
WHIMPER
sobby DAMP, WET
sober CALM, COOL,
COLLECTED, STAID,
GRAVE, SEDATE,
STEADY, TEMPERATE,
SOLEMN, SOMBER,
MODERATE, SANE,
WISE, ABSTINENT
sobriquet ALIAS,
AGNAME, HANDLE,
APPELLATION,
HYPOCORISTIC
social TEA, CLAN,
TRIBAL, CASTE,
FRIENDLY, PARTY,
GENIAL, CORDIAL
entrance DEBUT

group TRIBE,
FAMILY, CLAN,
COTERIE
insect ANT
outcast PARIAH,
LEPER
standing RANK,
CASTE, ESTATE
swell SNOB
system REGIME
unit SEPT, FAMILY
society FOLK, LODGE,
ETHNOS, ORDER,
BUND, ELITE,
GENTRY, CLASS,
CLUB, FELLOWSHIP,
UNION, PARTY,
MANKIND
entrance DEBUT
German BUND
Italy MAFIA
Society island TAHITI
sock, *goat's hair*
UDO
symbol of tragedy
BUSKIN
sockdolager FACER,
ONER, ROUSER
socket MORTISE,
ORBIT, PAN, POD,
CAVITY, SPACE,
TUBE, OUTLET,
RECEPTACLE
Socrates' *disciple*
PLATO
wife XANTHIPPE
sod CLOD, DIVOT,
SWARD, PEAT,
TURF, GRASS, LAND
Old IRELAND,
EIRE, ERIN
soda SALERATUS,
ALKALI, BICARB, POP
plant BARILLA
seaweed VAREC
sodalite LENAD
sodden DULL, SOGGY,
DOUGHY, MOIST,
BLOATED
sodium *chloride*
SALT, SAL
compound SODA
nitrate NITER,
NITRE
oxide SODA
symbol NA
Sodom *king* BERA
sofa SETTEE,
CANAPE, DIVAN,
COUCH, SEAT,
DAVENPORT

soft LOW, EASY,
WAXY, LIMP,
DULCET, BLAND,
MILD, BALMY,
SMOOTH, DELICATE,
GENTLE, WEAK,
TENDER, LENIENT
drink ADE, POP,
COLA, SODA, TONIC
feathers DOWN
soap BLARNEY,
BLANDISH
soften MITIGATE,
THAW, RELENT,
MELT, TEMPER,
RELAX, MUTE,
PALLIATE
by kneading MA-
LAXATE
skins TAW, TAN
softening LENITIVE,
EMULSIVE
soggy DOUGHY,
DAMP, DULL, WET,
HEAVY, SODDEN
soigne TIDY, NEAT
soil GLEBE, LAND,
LOAM, MARL,
HUMUS, SOD, EARTH,
DIRT, GROUND,
BEFOUL, DEFILE,
DIRTY, POLLUTE,
(BE)GRIME, SPOIL
chalky MALM
sojourn LIVE, TARRY,
STAY, ABIDE, LODGE,
STOP, DWELL,
TENANT
solace CHEER,
SOOTHE, CONSOLE,
CALM, COMFORT,
ALLAY, CONSOLA-
TION, RELIEF, EASE
solan GANNET,
GOOSE, FOWL
solar *deity* RA,
HELIOS *See*
"god(s), sun"
disk ATEN, ATON
excess over lunar
year EPACT
solder FUSE, BRAZE,
UNITE, WELD,
JOIN, CEMENT
soldier VET, CADET,
CHASSEUR, GI,
WARRIOR, PRIVATE,
POILU, SEPOY,
ANZAC, ZOUAVE
Asian ROK
Australian ANZAC
bandit LADRONE

barrack BILLET
cavalry UHLAN
France POILU,
  ZOUAVE
Gaelic KERN
Indo-British SEPOY
irregular CROAT
Morocco ASKAR
overcoat for CAPOTE
Roman body COHORT
Thrace MYRMIDON
sole ONE, ONLY,
  MERE, FISH,
  (A)LONE, SINGLE,
  SLADE, SELECT
  of foot VOLA, PELMA
    pertaining to
      PLANTAR
  thin inner RAND
solecism ERROR,
  LAPSE, SLIP,
  GAFFE, BONER
solement ONLY,
  SOLELY
solemn AUGUST,
  GRAVE, SOBER,
  SERIOUS, FORMAL,
  SEDATE, DEVOUT,
  CEREMONIOUS,
  STATELY, IMPOR-
  TANT, REVERENTIAL
  declaration OATH
solenodon AGOUTI,
  ALMIQUE
solicit APPLY, ASK,
  BEG, SUE, BID, COURT,
  WOO, IMPLORE,
  REQUEST, PETITION,
  INVITE, BESEECH,
  PLEAD, ENTREAT,
  SUPPLICATE, URGE,
  LURE
solicitation CANVASS,
  PETITION, PLEA,
  ENTREATY
solicitude CARE,
  CONCERN, HEED,
  ANXIETY, DESIRE
solid HARD, FIRM,
  REAL, WHOLE,
  DENSE, VALID,
  CLOSE, COMPACT,
  UNBROKEN, ENTIRE,
  SUBSTANTIAL,
  UNANIMOUS, SET
  combining form
    STEREO
  geometric CONE,
    CUBE, PRISM,
    SPHERE
solidification
  GELATION, UNION

solidify SET, GEL,
  JELL, HARDEN
solitary (A)LONE,
  ONLY, SOLO, SOLE,
  SINGLE, UNIQUE,
  SEPARATED
  combining form
    EREMO
sollar BRATTICE,
  GALLERY, PLATFORM
solo SONG, ARIA,
  (A)LONE, SELF,
  FLIGHT
  music ARIOSO,
    SCENA
Solomon *gulf* KULA,
  HUON
  island SAVO, GIZO,
    BUKA
  volcano BALBI
Solomon's *ally*
  HIRAM
  father DAVID
  gold obtained from
    OPHIR
solon SAGE, SENATOR,
  LEGISLATOR
solution KEY, AN-
  SWER, SOLUTE,
  LIQUID, EXPLANA-
  TION
  strength of TITER,
    PROOF
solve DETECT, EX-
  PLAIN, DECIPHER,
  ANSWER, UNDO,
  WORK, RESOLVE,
  UNRAVEL, SETTLE,
  CLEAR, UNFOLD,
  INTERPRET, DIS-
  COVER
solvent WATER,
  ACETONE, ALCOHOL
Somaliland *capital*
  MOGADISHU
  coin BESA
  seaport BERBERA
Somalis ASHA
somber SERIOUS,
  GLOOMY, DARK,
  SAD, GRAVE,
  MELANCHOLY,
  GRAY
sombrerite OSITE
some ANY, ONE,
  SEVERAL, PART,
  PORTION, PIECE,
  APPROXIMATELY
somersault FLIP,
  LEAP, REVERSAL,
  SOMERSET

somite MEROSOME,
  METAMERE
Somme *tributary*
  ANCRE
son HEIR, MALE,
  FITZ, MAC, NATIVE,
  YOUTH, BOY, FILS
  of Judah ER
  youngest CADET
sonance SOUND,
  TUNE, NOISE
sonata, *closing* CODA,
  RONDO
  part of RONDO
song(s) AIR, DITTY,
  CHANT, ROUND,
  CAROL, ANTHEM,
  BALLAD, MELOS,
  RONDO, ARIA, LAY,
  LYRIC, STRAIN,
  ARIETTA
  after EPODE
  bird See under
    "bird"
  Christmas NOEL,
    CAROL, WASSAIL
  depressing BLUES
  evening SERENA
  for two GYMEL,
    DUET
  French CHANSON
  German LIED(ER)
  Italian CANZONE
  mystic RUNE
  of departure ALBA
  of lament
    THRENODY, THRENOS,
    DIRGE
  of praise PEAN,
    PAEAN, CAROL,
    HYMN
  of Solomon
    CANTICLE
  of triumph PAEAN
  operatic ARIA
  pertaining to
    MELIC
  sacred ANTHEM,
    MOTET, PSALM,
    HYMN
  sad DIRGE
  solo voices GLEE
songcraft POESY
songlike ARIOSE,
  LYRICAL
"Song of Bernadette"
  author WERFEL
sonnet *ending* CODA
  first 8 lines OCTET
  last 6 lines SESTET
sonorous VIBRANT,
  RICH, RESONANT

soon EARLY,
SHORTLY, ERELONG,
PRONTO, ANON,
PROMPT, QUICK(LY)
sooner RATHER,
FIRST, ERST, ERE
soot COOM, GRIME,
SMUT, DIRT
particle ISEL,
IZLE
sooth AUGURY,
SWEET, TRUTH
soothe CALM,
QUIET, CONSOLE,
ALLAY, REASSURE,
EASE, COMPOSE,
TRANQUILIZE,
RELIEVE, FLATTER
soothing LENITIVE,
BALMY, SEDATIVE
soothsayer DIVINE,
AUGUR, SEER,
CHALDEAN, AUSPEX,
ORACLE
sooty FULGINOUS,
STAINED, DUSTY,
BLACK
sophism ELENCHUS,
FALLACY, PARALO-
GISM
sopor CARUS, COMA,
LETHARGY, SLEEP,
STUPOR, SLUMBER
soporific ANODYNE,
OPIATE, NARCOTIC
soprano PONS,
CANTO, TREBLE,
VOICE
sora CRAKE, RAIL,
BIRD
sorcerer MAGE,
MAGI, WIZARD,
CONJURER
sorceress LAMIA,
CIRCE, USHA,
HELIOS
sordid MEAN, BASE,
DIRTY, FOUL, AB-
JECT, VENAL,
CHEAP, MERCE-
NARY, MUDDY, VILE
sore PAINFUL,
SENSITIVE, TENDER,
MAD, PEEVED, AN-
NOYED, VEXED,
ULCER, LESION
sorghum IMPHEE,
CANE, SYRUP,
MOLASSES
fodder FETERITA
grain SORGO, CUSH,
MILO, DURRA

sorite HEAP, MASS,
COLLECTION
sorrel OCA, OXALIS,
PLANT, ROSELLE,
BROWN, HORSE
sorrow CRY, WEEP,
WAIL, AGONY,
DOLE, SADNESS,
GRIEVE, DOLOR,
LAMENT, CARE,
GRIEF, RUE, WOE,
DISTRESS, MISERY
sorrowful DOLENT,
SAD, FORGIVING
sorry POOR, PALTRY,
PETTY, MEAN, SAD,
REGRETFUL, PITIFUL,
DISMAL, MELAN-
CHOLY, WRETCHED,
GRIEVED, CONTRITE
sort BLEND, CULL,
ILK, STRAIN,
SPECIES, SEPARATE,
CLASS(IFY), GRADE,
FILE, KIND, TYPE,
GROUP, CHARACTER,
ARRANGE
sortie RAID, FORAY,
SALLY
sortilege LOT,
SORCERY, DIVINA-
TION
so-so AVERAGE,
TOLERABLE, FAIR,
MEDIUM, PASSABLE,
INTERMEDIATE,
TRIFLING, SMALL
sot TOPER, TIPPLER,
BIBBER, SOAK,
DRUNK(ARD)
sough SOG, SIGH,
RUSTLE, WHIZ,
MURMUR, DRAIN,
SEWER, CHANNEL
soul EGO, ELAN, AME,
SPIRIT, ATMAN,
PNEUMA, BEING,
MIND, WIT(S),
ESSENCE, INTELLECT
personified ALMA,
PSYCHE
Sanskrit ATMAN
symbolized, Egypt
BA
sound HALE, TONE,
BONG, BAY, AUDIO,
KLOP, UTTER,
PLUMB, VALID,
SOLID, ROBUST,
LUSTY, COGENT,
STRAIT, SUBSTAN-
TIAL, HEALTHY,

SANE, WHOLE-
(SOME), FIRM,
SAFE, STRONG,
STABLE, FATHOM,
PERFECT, ORTHODOX
adventitious RALE,
MURMUR
derisive CATCALL,
BOO
detective SONAR,
RADAR
harsh GRATE,
GRIND
hoof beats CLOP
loud BLARE
metallic CLANG,
CLINK, TING
of drinking GLUB
pertaining to
SONANT
waves of AUDIO
soup PUREE, POT-
(T)AGE, BROTH,
BISQUE, CON-
SOMME, FOOD,
LIQUID
thick PUREE,
BISQUE
vessel TUREEN
sour HARSH, COLD,
UNKIND, MOROSE,
DOUR, SHARP,
GLUM, HARD, SUL-
LEN, ACID, ACERB,
WRY, ACRID, TART,
DRY, ACETOSE, EM-
BITTERED
as of stomach
ACOR
gum tree NYSSA
like ACETOSE
milk BLEEZE,
CLABBER
drink LEBAN,
TAYIR, TYRE
voice GRUM, GRUFF
source ORIGIN,
FONT, SPRING,
SEED, ROOT, CAUSE,
FOUNT(AIN), BE-
GINNING
soursop ANONA,
ANNONA, TREE,
FRUIT
soutache BRAID
soutane CASSOCK
South DIXIE, AUSTER
Africa BOER *See*
"Africa"
America LATIN
See "America"

Carolina county
AIKEN, DILLON,
HORRY, LEE, SALUDA,
SUMPTER, UNION,
YORK
Dakota county
BRULE, CLAY, DAY,
DEUEL, HAND,
HYDE, LAKE, TODD,
TRIPP
Sea island drink
AVA
southern AUSTRAL,
TORRID, MERIDIO-
NAL
southwester SQUAM,
HAT, STORM
souvenir RELIC,
CURIO, MEMENTO,
KEEPSAKE, BIBELOT,
TOKEN
sovereign SUPREME,
FREE, ROYAL,
PRINCELY, IM-
PERIAL, COIN,
HIGHEST, PARA-
MOUNT, SUPERIOR,
AUTHORITATIVE
See "king"
coin SKIV
sovereignty STATE,
DYNASTY, SWAY,
CONTROL, POWER,
DOMINION, AUTHOR-
ITY
Soviet *See* "Russia"
news agency TASS
paper PRAVDA,
IZVESTIA
Union founder
LENIN
SOW PLANT, SCATTER,
SEED, STREW, DIS-
SEMINATE, PIG,
HOG
young ELT, GILT,
PIG
soybean SOYA, SOJA
tablet TORFU
spa BATH, PAX,
SPRING, BADEN,
EMS
England BATH
space PERIOD,
TIME, EXPANSE,
INTERVAL, AREA,
LACUNA, ROOM,
CONCOURSE, OPEN,
EXTENT, HIATUS,
SEPARATE
between bird's eye

and bill LORE,
LORA
between triglyphs
METOPE
pertaining to SPA-
TIAL, AREAL,
LACUNAL
small AREOLA,
PORE
theory PLENISM
vehicle ROCKET,
SATELLITE, MER-
CURY, SPUTNIK
spaceman *See under*
"astronaut"
spade CARD, SHOVEL,
DIG, DELVE, GRUB
peat SLADE
spagyric ALCHEMIC,
CHEMICAL
Spain *See* "Spanish"
spalacid MOLE, RAT
spall GALLET, CHIP,
SPLINTER
span BRIDGE,
PERIOD, TEAM,
YOKE, SPACE,
SPREAD, MEASURE,
DISTANCE, ARCH,
GIRDER, ROOF,
STRETCH
in inches NINE
spangle STAR,
SEQUIN, GLISTEN,
GLITTER, ORNAMENT
Spanish, Spaniard,
Spain IBERIA, SENOR,
IBERIAN, DIEGO,
PICT, ESPANA
ancient kingdom
ARAGON
article LA, UN, UNO,
EL, LOS, LAS
as COMO
aunt TIA
bad MALO
bath tub BANO,
BANERA
bay BAHIA, BISCAY
bayonet YUCCA,
PLANT
beach PLAYA
bean HABA,
FRIJOL(E)
because PORQUE
belle MAJA
blanket SERAPE,
MANTA
blind CIEGO
bonnet GORRA
boy NINO,
MUCHACHO

brigand LADRONE
brush CEPILLO
bull TORO
bullring COSO
calico PERCAL,
ZARAZA
canyon CANON,
CAJON
card game OMBRE,
MONTE
castle ALCAZAR
cat GATO
cellist CASALS
cheap BARATO
chest CAJA
chief JEFE,
ADALID, CID
church IGLESIA
city AVILA, RONDA,
CIUDAD, MADRID,
LEON, TOLEDO,
CADIZ, ALCOY, LUGO
See "town" *below*
cloak CAPA, MANTA
cloth, wool PANO
coin DINERO,
CENTAVO, PISTOLE,
DOBLA, PESETA,
PESO, DURO, REAL,
DUBLOON, CENTEN,
CENTIMO, DECIMA,
DECIMO, PIASTER,
VELLON
old CUARTO,
DOBLA, PISTOLE
cold FRIO
collar CUELLO
commander CAID
commune ALCOY,
ELDA, GRADU, LENA,
JAEN, LORCA,
OLIVA, OSUNA, REUS,
RUTE, SUECA,
TELDE, TINEO,
UBEDA, YECLA,
VICH, UTRERA
council JUNTA,
CONSEJO
court PATIO
cowboy GAUCHO
cucumber PEPINO
dance DANZAR,
JALEO, BOLERO,
JOTA, CARIOCA
dining room
COMEDOR
dish OLLA
dollar PESO, DURO,
PIASTER
dramatist VEGA
drink PULQUE
duke ALBA

eight OCHO

explorer BALBOA, COLON

fabric CREA

farm HACIENDA

feast day FIESTA

fireplace (hearth) FOGON

flat lowland (marsh, or swamp) MARISMA

fleet ARMADA, FLOTA

friend AMIGO

gambling game MONTE

game PELOTA

gentleman SENOR, GRANDEE

goodbye ADIOS

governess DUENNA, AYA

gruel ATOLE

gypsy GITANO

harbor PUERTO

hat BOINA, SOM- BRERO

hearth FOGON

hero CID

hill CERRO, COLINA

holiday FIESTA

horse JENNET, CABALLO

hot CALIDO

house CASITA, CASA

Indian IND(I)O

inn POSADA, VENTA

interjection MANO, OLE

island(s) IBIZA, MALLORCA, MENORCA, BAL- EARIC, CANARY

jar BUCARO, OLLA, TINAJA

judge JUEZ

kettle TETERA

kettledrum ATABEL, TIMBAL

king REY

kingdom CASTILE, ARAGON, LEON

knife NAVAJA, CUCHILLO

lace ENCAJE

lady DAMA, SENORA, DONA

lake LAGO

landmark MOJON, MARCA, COTO, LINDE

legal affair ACTO

legislature CORTES

lighthouse FARO

linen HILO, LIENZO, CREA

little POCO

man DON, SENOR, HOMBRE

manager GERENTE

mantle CAPA

mattress COLCHON

mayor ALCALDE

meadow VEGA, PRADO

measure DEDO, ESTADEL, PIE, CODO, COPA, VARA, LINEA, FANEGA, LIBRA, MILLA, YUGADA

missile BOLA

monetary unit PESETA

month MES

Moorish capital (former) CORDOVA kingdom (former) GRANADA

mountain range SIERRA

mouth BOCA

Northern, old name ARAGON

novelist MIGUEL, IBANEZ, CERVANTES

now AHORA

nun AVILA, MONJA

officer ALCALDE

old VIEJO

open space COSO

pack saddle ALBARDA

painter GOYA, PICASSO, MIRO

people GENTE

plantation HACIENDA

poet VEGA

police RURALE

polite CORTES

post office CORREO

pot OLLA

pretty LINDO, BONITO, BELLO

province AVILA, GALICIA, ALAVA, SORIA

public garden ALAMEDA

purse BOLSA

queen REGINA, REINA

raisin PASA

rapier ESTOQUE, ESPADIN

red ROJO

relay horses REMUDA

ribbon CINTA

river RIO, EBRO, TAGUS, DUERO, MINHO, SEGRE

road CAMINO

sailing vessel ZABRA

saint TERESA, DOMINIC, EULALIA

seaport PALOS, ADRA, BILBAO, MALAGA, VIGO, MATARO

servant MOZO, CRIADO

shawl MANTA, SERAPE

sheep MERINO

sheet SABANA

sherry OLOROSO, XERES, JEREZ

ship GALLEON, BUQUE, BARCO, BARCA, NAVE

shirt CAMISA

shoe ZAPATO

shop TIENDA

sitting room SALA

six SEIS

soprano BORI, TIPLE

stock farm RANCHO

sword BILBO, ESPADA

table cloth MANTEL

the EL, LA, LOS, LAS

thimble DEDAL

thus ASI

title HIDALGO, DON, DONA, SENOR

town LORCA, IRUN, CABRA, BAZA, REUS, MULA, LUGO, LEON, LENA, LOJA, JAEN, ELCHE

trench TAJO, SURCAR

very MUY

vessel GALLEON See "ship" above

waistcoat CHALECO, CHUPA

walking stick BASTON

warm CALIENTE

watch RELOJ

watchtower ATA-
LAYA, TORRE,
MIRADOR
water AGUA
weight ONZA, AR-
ROBA, GRANO,
MARCO, TOMIN,
ADARME, BARRIL,
DINERO, LIBRA,
PUNTO, QUARTO
wine TINTA,
OLOROSO, XERES,
VINO, TINTO, BUAL,
JEREZ
woman gaily dressed
MAJA
work OBRA, LABRAR,
OPERAR
spank SLAP, CANE,
FLOG, CHASTISE,
PUNISH
spanker SAIL
spanking FRESH,
VIGOROUS, QUICK,
STOUT, BRISK,
LIVELY, GOOD,
LARGE
spanner WRENCH,
TOOL
spar BOX, MAST,
RUNG, BOOM, YARD,
SPRIT, POLE,
WRANGLE, GAFF,
BARITE, MINERAL,
BEAM, CONTEND,
QUARREL
extremity YARDARM
small SPRIT
upper GAFF, TOP-
MAST
spare SCANTY,
EXTRA, MEAGER,
SPARSE, SLENDER,
BONY, SCANT, LEAN,
THIN, LANK(Y),
GAUNT, STINGY,
FORBEAR, ADDI-
TIONAL, SAVE,
PARSIMONY, GIVE,
EXEMPT, TIRE
spark ARC, TRACE,
FLASH, IOTA, JOT,
GLEAM, GLINT,
GLISTEN, WOO,
SCINTILLATE,
EMBER
sparkle GLEAM,
FLASH, GLINT,
CORUSCATE, GLISTEN
sparoid fish PORGY,
SAR, TAI, SARGO(N),
SALEMA

Spartan HARDY,
STOIC, BRAVE,
SEVERE, GREEK
bondsman HELOT
king LEONIDAS,
AGIS, MENELAUS
lawgiver LYCURGUS
magistrate EPHOR
slave ILOT, HELOT
tyrant NABIS
spasm GRIP, THROE,
FIT, CONVULSION,
TIC, JERK, SEIZURE,
AGITATION
type TONIC,
CLONIC
spat GAITER, ROW,
TIFF, BICKER,
QUARREL
spate FLOOD,
FRESHET, OVER-
FLOW, ABUNDANCE,
GUSH
spatter SLOSH,
SPOIL, SPLASH,
SPRINKLE, SULLY,
DEFAME
spatula THIBLE,
SPADE, TOOL
spawn CLUTCH,
EGGS, OVA, ROE,
YIELD, OFFSPRING
up river to
ANADROMOUS
speak ORATE, AC-
COST, LISP, CARP,
MOOT, TALK, UTTER,
TELL, REVEAL,
BRUIT, SAY, BARK,
DECLAIM, ARTICU-
LATE
combining form
LALO
inability to
ALALIA
manner of TONE,
TENOR
noisily RANT,
FUME, RAVE
with interruption
HAW, HEM
speaker LOCUTOR,
AUDIO, CHAIRMAN,
LECTURER
spear GORE, PIERCE,
STAFF, PIKE, AS-
SAGAI, ASSEGAI,
HALBERD, BAYONET,
SPROUT, SHOOT,
STALK, WEAPON
fish GIG, TREN,
GAFF

long LANCE
Neptune's TRIDENT
shaped HASTATE
three-pronged
LEISTER, TRIDENT
specialty FORTE,
TALENT, PRO-
FESSION, WORK,
METIER
specie CASH, COIN,
MONEY
species SORT, CLASS,
VARIETY, CATE-
GORY, GENUS,
KIND, GENRE
groups of GENERA
kindred COGENERIC
modified by environ-
ment ECAD
specific PARTICULAR,
PRECISE, DEFINITE,
EXPLICIT, SPECIAL,
REMEDY
specimen CAST,
COPY, SLIDE, EX-
AMPLE, SAMPLE,
CASE, MODEL
specious OSTENSIBLE,
PLAUSIBLE, GOOD,
RIGHT, VAIN,
EMPTY, IDLE,
PROBABLE
speck JOT, DOT,
WHIT, BIT, MOTE,
SPOT, STAIN,
PARTICLE, BLEMISH
speckled PIED,
DOTTED, MOTTLED,
VARIEGATED
spectacle PAGEANT,
SCENE, SHOW,
SIGHT, DISPLAY,
VIEW, EXHIBI-
TION, LENS, GLASS,
DRAMA
specter PHANTOM,
APPARITION, FETCH,
SHADE, SPOOK,
SHADOW, MANES,
WRAITH, BOGEY,
GHOST, SPIRIT,
EIDOLON
spectral EERIE,
GHOSTLY, GHASTLY,
SPOOKY
spectrum VIOLET,
INDIGO, BLUE,
YELLOW, GREEN,
ORANGE, RED,
LIGHT, COLORS
speculate THINK,
PONDER, GAMBLE,

MUSE, REFLECT,
WEIGH, STUDY,
MEDITATE, GUESS,
SUPPOSE
speculum MIRROR,
DIOPTRON
speech VOICE, LIP,
SONANT, TALK,
SERMON, UTTER-
ANCE, ADDRESS,
ARTICULATION,
LECTURE
art of RHETORIC
blunder SOLECISM
boastful KOMPOL-
OGY, RODOMONTADE,
BLUSTER
combining form
LOGO
defect LISP,
ALOGIA, STUTTER,
STAMMER
figurative RHESIS,
TROPE
figure of ZEUGMA,
LITOTES, TROPE,
METAPHOR
forms IDIOMS
local PATOIS
long SPIEL
loss APHASIA,
ALALIA, MUTE
part of NOUN,
VERB
set RHESIS
violent TIRADE
voiceless element
SURD
with full breathing
ASPIRATE
speechless DUMB,
MUTE, SILENT
speed VELOCITY,
PROGRESS, PACE,
TEMPO, ACTIVITY,
EXPEDITE, HASTEN,
RUN, HASTE, RACE,
RATE, HIE, FLY,
RUSH
at full AMAIN
speedily APACE,
PROMPTLY
speedy SWIFT,
NIMBLE, ADEPT,
FAST, FLYING,
EXPEDITIOUS
speer SCREEN,
PARTITION, QUERY,
QUIZ, ASK, INQUIRE,
SEEK
spell CHARM, FIT,
SEIZURE, WRITE,

DECIPHER, BE-
WITCH, TEACH,
PERIOD, ATTACK,
SWAY, FASCINATION
spelt WHEAT,
CEREAL, GRAIN
spelter ZINC, INGOT
spelunker's *milieu*
CAVE
spend PASS, WHILE,
EXERT, LOSE, EMIT,
PAY, CONSUME,
EXHAUST, DISBURSE
spendthrift WASTREL,
PRODIGAL
Spenserian *character*
UNA
spent EFFETE,
CONSUMED,
EVANID, FATIGUED,
EXHAUSTED, WEAK,
TIRED
sphere FIELD,
RANGE, ORBIT,
BALL, ORB, GLOBE,
WORLD, BUSINESS,
REACH, SCOPE,
COMPASS, SPACE,
REGION, PROVINCE
of action ARENA,
THEATER, DOMAIN
steel, magnetic
TERRELLA
spherical GLOBATE,
GLOBOSE, ROTUND,
ORBICULAR, ROUND,
DISCOID
aberration, free from
APLANATIC
sphinx MONSTER,
ENIGMA, MOTH
spice TANG, MULL,
MACE, NUTMEG,
PEPPER, SEASON,
CLOVE, DASH, CON-
DIMENT, SEASON-
ING
Biblical CASSIA,
BALSAM
mill QUERN
package for
ROBBIN
spicknel MEUM,
HERB, PLANT
spicule ROD, ASTER,
NEEDLE, SPINE,
SCLERITE, PRICKLE,
BARB
sponge CYMBA
spicy RACY, SPIR-
ITED, FRAGRANT,
FLAVORED, WITTY,

SHARP, AROMATIC,
EXCITING
spider ARACHNID,
MITE, SCORPION,
SKILLET
appendages
CHELICERA
crab MAIAN
genus MAIA
genus AGALENA,
ARANEA
nest NIDUS
order ARACHNIDA
study of ARANEOL-
OGY
three-legged TRIVET
venomous TARAN-
TULA
web-spinning
RETIARY, TELERIAN
spigot PLUG, FAUCET,
TAP, DOSSIL, SPILE,
SPOUT, COCK, VALVE,
NOZZLE, VENT,
OUTLET
spike SPADIX, NAIL,
BARB, EAR, TINE,
SPINE, HORN,
ANTLER, STAB,
PIERCE
bill GODWIT, BIRD
lavender MINT
liquids LACE
spikenard ARALIA,
BALM, OINTMENT,
NARD, PLANT
spill SLOP, SHED,
SPLASH, ESCAPE,
TELL, BROOK, LEAK,
WASTE
spin BIRL, GYRATE,
ROTATE, REEL,
WHIRL, NARRATE,
TELL
spinach, *mountain*
ORACH(E)
spinal RACHIDIAN,
VERTEBRAL
areas CERVICAL,
DORSAL, LUMBAR,
SACRAL
cord MEDULLA,
MYELON
disease MYELITIS,
POLIO
layer DURA
spindle HASP, AXLE,
MANDREL, PIN,
SHAFT, SPOOL,
SLENDER, ROD,
AXIS, STEM, STALK

hollow TRIBLET,
SPOOL, CORE
lathe SANDRIL
spine QUILL, AXON,
ACICULA, NEEDLE,
RACHIS, CHINE, FIN,
VERTEBRA, SPIC-
ULE, RIDGE, COUR-
AGE, BACKBONE
animal CHINE,
RACHIS
spinel, *ruby* BALAS
spinetail DUCK
spinner SPIDER, TOP,
FISHHOOK, FLY
spinning *machine*
JENNY, MULE,
THROSTLE
rod SPINDLE
spinous THORNY,
PRICKLY, POINTED,
SHARP, BARBED
Spinoza *work* ETHICS
spiracle PORE,
ORIFICE
spiral COIL, HELIX,
HELICAL, SPRING,
WINDING
formation VOLUTE
spire STEEPLE, SUM-
MIT, PINNACLE,
CURL, WHORL,
PEAK
apex EPI
spiric *body* TORE
spirit(s) MIND,
SPECTER, SPOOK,
HAUNT, GENIE,
METTLE, GRIT,
SAND, GUTS, ZEAL,
ARDOR, SPUNK,
HEART, PEP, VERVE,
SOUL, ELIXIR, ELAN,
VIM, LIFE, MORALE,
METAL, COURAGE,
ENTHUSIASM,
GHOST, LIQUOR,
ESSENCE
air ARIEL
Arab myth.
AFREET, JINN
evil DEMON, DEVIL
female BANSHEE,
UNDINE
good NORM,
EUDAEMON
impish PO
lamp ETNA
like ETHEREAL
malignant KER
night-walking
LEMURES

of a people ETHOS
of censure MOMUS
of dead ancestors
MANES
of fire AGNI,
GENIE
of infatuation ATE
spirited RACY,
FERVENT, BOLD,
GAME, GAMY, EA-
GER, FIERY,
SPUNKY, ANIMATED,
ACTIVE
horse STEED
spiritless AMORT,
COLD, FLAT, LIFE-
LESS, DULL, TAME,
STUPID, CRASS,
WANING, DEJECTED,
SAD, COWARDLY
spiritual ANGELIC,
INCORPOREAL,
INNER, HOLY, PURE,
SACRED, DIVINE,
CELESTIAL, DEVOUT
beings ENS
spiritualist *meeting*
SEANCE
spiteful CATTY,
ENVIOUS, MEAN
spitfire NIPPER,
FIERY
spitter BROCK, DEER
spittoon CUSPIDOR
splash DAUB,
SPATTER, SPILL
splay FLAN, BEVEL,
CARVE, SPREAD
spleen MELANCHOLY,
GRUDGE, SPITE,
MALICE, HATRED,
ANGER, IRE, MILT
pertaining to LIENAL
splendid SHINING,
AUREATE,
SUPERB, NICE,
GORGEOUS, FINE,
BRIGHT, EMINENT,
LUSTROUS,
MAGNIFICENT,
GLORIOUS, IMPOSING
splendor ECLAT,
POMP, GLORY,
MAGNIFICENCE
splice JOIN,
UNITE, MARRY, WED,
UNION, REPAIR,
FIX
splinter SLIVER,
SHATTER,
SEPARATE, RIVE

split SEPARATE,
BREAK, TEAR, PART,
SEVER, DIVIDE,
CLEAVE, RIFT,
CHAP, RIVE,
SCHISM, REND,
BISECT
in two parts
BIFID, CLOVEN,
BIPARTITE, HALVED,
BISECTED
splotch *See* "stain"
spoil(s) DESTROY,
INJURE, BOTCH,
DEFILE, CORRUPT,
DECAY, INDULGE,
BABY, WRECK,
LOOT, PRIZE,
SWAG, PELF, MAR,
ROT, IMPAIR,
RUIN, SOUR, ROB,
PLUNDER
eggs ADDLE
spoke RAY, RUNG,
BAR, PIN, ROD,
STAKE, RADIUS,
SAID
spoken ORAL,
PAROLE, SAID
sponge(s) BADIAGA,
ASCON, LOOFA(H),
ZIMOCCA,
ASCONES, SYCONES,
PORIFERA, SYCON,
MOISTEN, CLEAN,
WASH, CLEANSE,
BATHE, CADGE,
MOOCH, SWAB,
OBLITERATE, ERASE
calcareous LEUCON
opening(s)
APOPYLE, PORES
orifice OSCULUM,
OSTIOLE
vegetable LOOFA,
LOOFAH
spongewood SOLA
spongy PITHY,
POROUS, BIBU-
LOUS, ABSORBENT,
LIGHT, SOFT,
ELASTIC
sponsor PATRON,
ANGEL, SURETY,
BACKER, GODPARENT,
ENDORSER
sponsorship EGIS
spooky WEIRD,
EERIE, GHOSTLY
spoon LADLE, TROLL,
OAR, PEN, DISH,

SCOOP, DIP, BAIL, CLUB, WOO

spoonbill AJAJA, SCAUP, JABIRU, DUCK

Spoon River *poet* MASTERS

spore(s) SORI, CARPEL, GERM, SEED, FUNGUS, FUNGI

case(s) ASCI, ASCUS, THECA

like structure CYST

sporont ZYGOTE, GAMONT

sport TRIFLE, JEST, PLAY, FROLIC, ROMP, FUN, GAME, GOLF, POLO, DIVERSION, PASTIME, AMUSEMENT

field ARENA, RINK, GYM, STADIUM

shirt TEE

sports *association* PGA, AAU, TEAM

event MEET, GAME, RACE

sporty FLASHY, GAY, LOUD, SHOWY

spot FISH, DOT, SPECK(LE), SITE, PLACE, LOCALITY, MACULE, MACULA, MOTTLE, FLECK, STAIN, DEFECT, FAULT, BLOTCH, BLOT, FLAW, DISCOVER, SEE, NOTE, ESPY, FIND, MARK, BLEMISH, SULLY

on playing card PIP

spotlight ARC, BEAM

spotted BLENNY, MACULOSE, DAPPLE(D), PIED, SULLIED, TARNISHED, NOTED, ESPIED, BLEMISHED, VARIEGATED, DAMAGED

beast PARD, LEOPARD, CHITAL

fever TYPHUS, TICK

spouse MATE, WIFE, HUSBAND, FERE

spout ORATE, STREAM, NOZZLE, GARGOYLE, EMIT, SPILE, GEAT, JET, PIPE, TUBA, CONDUIT, MOUTH

spray SPUME, ATOMIZE, SCATTER, BRANCH, TWIG, FOAM

sea LIPPER, SURF

spread SIZE, RANGE, REACH, SCOPE, STRETCH, AREA, DISPERSE, RADIATE, PROMULGATE, BRUIT, WIDEN, SPLAY(ED), COVER, FEAST, MEAL, FLARE, SET, DELATE, FAN, NORATE, BRAY, SMEAR, STREW, DEPLOY, PROLONG, UNFURL, EXPAND, EXPANSION, DIFFUSE, DIFFERENCE, CIRCULATE, DILATE, PUBLISH

as plaster TEER

for drying TED, THIN

loosely STREW, SCATTER

rumor BRUIT, GOSSIP

spreading out RADIAL

spree BENDER, BINGE, LARK, ORGY, WASSAIL, FROLIC, CAROUSAL, BAT

sprightly LIVELY, BRISK, AIRY, GAY, SMART, PERT, TID, AGILE, JAUNTY, SPRY, ANIMATED, VIVACIOUS

spring LAVANT, GEYSER, FONT, SPA, DART(LE), (A)RISE, BEGIN, GROW, SEEP, STEM, ISSUE, ROOT, CAUSE, LEAP, SALTATION, BOUND, SOURCE, (RE)COIL, STEND

back RESILE, RECOIL

board BATULE

deposit from TRONA, URAO

like VERNAL

springe GIN, NOOSE, SNARE, TRAP, SPRY

sprinkle SOW, FLOUR, DREDGE, SPLASH, DRENCH, WET, SAND, BEDEW, BEDROP, STREW, RAIN, SCATTER, BAPTIZE

with flour DREDGE

sprinkled SEME

sprinkling SEME, ASPERSION, SPRAY

sprite DEMON, BROWNIE, ELF, FAY, PIXY, PIXIE, GOBLIN, ARIEL, HOB, IMP, KELPY, NIX(IE), FAIRY

fairy ELF, FAY, PIXIE

mischievous PUCK, GOBLIN, GREMLIN

water NIX, UNDINE

sprocket TOOTH, CAM

architecture COIN, SPRIT

sprout SHOOT, BURGEON, BUD, GROW, GERMINATE, CHIT

sugar cane RATOON

spruce TIDY, DAPPER, SMUG, TRIG, SMART, TRIM, NEAT, TREE

genus PICEA

Norway ABIES

tree LARCH

white EPINETTE

sprue THRUSH, PSILOSIS

spry AGILE, BRISK, ALIVE, NIMBLE, QUICK, ACTIVE

spume SCUM, FOAM, FROTH, LAVA, LATHER, SUDS, YEAST

spunk COURAGE, GRIT, SAND, AMADOU, TINDER, SPIRIT, METTLE, PLUCK, GALL

spur URGE, INCITE, PRICK, GOAD, STIMULUS, ROWEL, BRANCH, MOTIVE, CALCAR

having SPICATE

mountain ARETE
on gamecock GAFF
railroad SIDING
wheel ROWEL
spurge FOAM,
  MILKWEED,
  EUPHORBIA,
  PLANT
spurious FALSE,
  IMITATION,
  FORGED, PHONY,
  FAKE, PSEUDO,
  SHAM, COUNTERFEIT,
  TIN, ARTIFICIAL,
  FRAUD, BOGUS,
  SNIDE, DECEPTIVE
spurn FLOUT, RE-
  JECT, REPEL,
  SCORN, REFUSE,
  DISDAIN
spurt GUSH, BURST,
  JET, SPOUT, HASTE
spy PEEK, PEER,
  PRY, EXAMINE,
  INSPECT, SEE,
  INFORMER, AGENT,
  SCOUT, EMISSARY,
  ANDRE, WORM
  Biblical CALEB
squab PIGEON,
  PIPER, FLEDGLING,
  CUSHION, CHAIR,
  STOOL, SOFA,
  CRUSH, SLOP, FAT
squad TEAM, POSSE,
  GROUP, TROOP
squall GALE, GUST,
  STORM, RAIN, CRY,
  MEWL
squander WASTE,
  SPEND, DISSIPATE,
  MISUSE
square CENTARE,
  PLAZA, COURT,
  QUADRATE,
  AREA, AGREE,
  TALLY, JIBE,
  MATCH, EQUAL,
  EVEN, JUST, FAIR,
  HONEST, DEPENDA-
  BLE, SETTLE
squared *circle*
  ARENA, RING
squash PEPO,
  CYMLING, CUSHAW,
  PLANT, MASH,
  CRUSH, SQUEEZE,
  SQUELCH, GAME
squaw MAHALA,
  MAHALY, WIFE,
  WOMAN, FEMALE

squeak CREAK,
  CROAK, INFORM
squeeze EXTORT,
  EXTRACT, GRIP,
  PINCH, PRESS,
  HUG, JAM, CON-
  TRACT, CONDENSE,
  EMBRACE
squid LOLIGO,
  CUTTLEFISH,
  MOLLUSK
squiggle ESS,
  SQUIRM, WRIGGLE
squill *genus* SCILLA,
  PLANT
squilla PRAWN,
  SHRIMP,
  CRUSTACEAN
squint PEER,
  GOGGLE,
  STRABISMUS,
  ESOTROPIA,
  EXOTROPIA
squire BEAU,
  ESCORT, GALLANT,
  ATTEND(ANT),
  TITLE
squirrel, *African*
  XERUS
  burrowing GOPHER
  fish SERRANO,
  MARIAN
  flying, Amer.
  ASSAPAN
    India TAGUAN
  fur, Siberia
  CALABAR, CALABER
  genus SCIURUS
  ground GOPHER,
  SUSLIK, SOUSLIK
  nest DRAY, DREY
  pelt or skin
  CALABAR,
  CALABER, VAIR
  Siberian MINIVER,
  MENIVER
stab PIERCE, SPIT,
  GORE, STICK, WOUND,
  HURT, PAUNCH,
  KNIFE, KNIVE, TRY,
  ATTEMPT, KILL,
  INJURE
  fencing PINK,
  STOCCADE
stabilize STEADY,
  POISE, FIRM,
  ADJUST, FIX,
  TRIM, BALANCE,
  REGULATE
stable STALL,
  BARN, BYRE, MEW,
  LASTING, FIRM,

  STEADY, FIXED,
  CONSTANT, SOUND
  make FIRM,
  STEADY, SUPPORT
stableman
  (H)OSTLER, GROOM
  royal AVENER
staccato SHARP,
  ABRUPT, DETACHED
  opposite to LEGATO,
  TENUTO
stack RICK, PILE,
  HEAP, CHIMNEY,
  SCINTLE, SHOCK
staddle CRUTCH,
  STAFF, FRAME, TREE
stadium COURSE,
  ARENA, OVAL, FIELD,
  TRACK, STAGE, COIN
staff MACE, CANE,
  WAND, STICK, CLUB,
  CUDGEL, SHAFT,
  POLE, ROD, BALLOW,
  CREW, RETINUE,
  SUPPORT
  bishop's BACULUS,
  ROD, CROSIER,
  CROZIER
  carried by bacchantes
  THYRSUS
  mountain climbing
  PITON
  officer's MACE,
  SCEPTER
  royal SCEPTER,
  SCEPTRE
  shepherd's CROOK,
  MULLEIN
  spiked ANKUS
Staffordshire *district*
  LEEK
stag HART, SPADE,
  HORSE, PARTY,
  DEER
  with cast antlers
  POLLARD
stage ARENA,
  SCENE, SPAN,
  LEGIT, THEATER,
  DRAMA, BOARDS,
  STEP, PHASE,
  APRON, DAIS,
  PULPIT, FORUM,
  PROSCENIUM,
  PLATFORM, SCAFFOLD,
  ENACT, DEGREE
  area in front of
  APRON, PIT
  call on trumpet
  SENNET
  direction EXEUNT,
  EXIT, ENTER,

MANET, SENNET,
SOLUS
extra SUPER,
SUPE
horn signal SENNET
pertaining to
SCENICAL
raised DAIS,
ESTRADE
remains MANET
scenery SET,
SETTINGS, PROPS
side scene COULISSE
speech to audience
ASIDE
washout HAM
whisper ASIDE
stagger LURCH,
STARTLE, STOT,
REEL, VACILLATE,
DOUBT, HESITATE,
GUESS, SURPRISE,
TOTTER
staghorn SUMAC,
BUSH
stagnation STASIS,
DULLNESS, STAND-
STILL, TORPOR
stagy ASSUMED,
THEATRICAL,
AFFECTED
staid DECOROUS,
SEDATE, GRAVE,
SOBER, COOL, STEADY,
SETTLED, SERIOUS,
COMPOSED, CALM,
SOLEMN
stain SOIL, SPOT,
IMBUE, BLOT, DYE,
SULLY, SMUDGE,
TINGE, MARK,
SIGN, STIGMA,
TINT, CORRUPT,
TARNISH, BLOTCH,
SMIRCH, BLEMISH,
DISCOLOR(ATION),
MACULATE,
DISGRACE, DEFILE
stair STEP, STY,
STILE, STAGE,
DEGREE, LADDER
part RISER, TREAD,
NEWEL
post NEWEL
staircase, *exterior*
PERRON
moving ESCALATOR
stake POT, WAGER,
ANTE, BET, RISK,
VENTURE, KITTY,
PALISADE, PEG,

POLE, STOB, PILE,
BOUND, MARK
resembling PALAR
swordsman's PEL
stale BANAL, FUSTY,
TRITE, STAGNANT,
VAPID, FLAT, DRY,
OLD, TASTELESS,
MUSTY, MO(U)LDY,
COMMON, THREAD-
BARE, HACKNEYED,
INSIPID, FLAVORLESS
stalemate CHECK,
IMPASSE, CRISIS
stalk(s) HAULM,
CANE, PEDICEL,
PEDUNCLE, CAULIS,
PETIOLE, REED,
PREY, DOG, HUNT,
STRIDE, STRUT,
MARCH
grass STRAW, CULM
leaf PETIOLE, STEM
plant AXIS, STEM
short STIPE
small PEDICEL
sugar cane RATOON
stall BOOTH, CRIB,
LOGE, MANGER,
SEAT, STOP, DELAY,
PRETENSE, MIRE,
CHECK
stamen, *summit*
ANTHER
stamina GRIT, VIGOR,
STRENGTH, POWER
stammer HAW, HEM,
STUTTER, HESITATE,
FAFFLE, PSELLISM
stamp MOLD, FORM,
PULVERIZE, MARK,
BRAND, STIGMATIZE,
IMPRESS, STRIKE,
PESTLE, SEAL,
PRINT, LABEL,
KIND, SORT,
POSTAGE, DIE,
INCUSE, TREAD
border TRESURE
out CANCEL,
SCOTCH, ERASE,
KILL, EXTERMINATE
with die IMPRINT,
EMBOSS
stampede DEBACLE,
ROUT, RIOT, RUN,
RUSH
stanch LOYAL, LEAL,
TRIED, STOUT,
STEM, STOP, TRUE,
QUELL, HONEST,
STEADY, STEADFAST,

FIRM, CONSTANT,
FAITHFUL
stand TABLE, BASE,
SUPPORT, EASEL,
TABO(U)RET,
TRIVET, TRIPOD,
STALL, TOLERATE,
ENDURE, TREAT,
ABIDE, BROOK,
SUFFER, BEAR,
HALT, (A)RISE,
POSITION
cuplike ZARF
inability to ABASIA,
ASTASIA
ornamental
ETAGERE,
EPERGNE
three-legged
TRIPOD, TRIVET,
TEAPOY
top of wooden CRISS
standard MEASURE,
MEAN, LAW,
AXIOM, MODEL,
COLOR, JACK,
GAUGE, STAND,
FRAME, EXAMPLE,
EMBLEM, CRITERION,
CANON, GONFALON,
ENSIGN, FLAG, PAR,
RULE(R), TYPE,
IDEAL, NORM, UNIT
bearer VEXILLARY
Turkish ALEM
standing RANK,
STATUS, PRESTIGE,
ERECT, DEGREE,
SITUATION, VERTICAL,
CONTINUING,
SETTLED, PERMA-
NENT, ESTABLISHED,
FIXED, IMMOVABLE,
LASTING, DURABLE,
POSITION, REPUTA-
TION, MOTIONLESS,
STAGNANT
out SALIENT,
AWAY, JUT, BEETLE
with feet on ground
STATANT
Standish's *wife* ROSE
stand-offish ALOOF,
RESERVED, COOL,
COY
stannum TIN
stanza STROPHE,
VERSE, STAVE
eight line TRIOLET,
OCTAVE
last ENVOY
ten line DECALET

two line DISTICH,
COUPLET
stapes STIRRUP,
OSSICLE, BONE
staple NAIL, FIBER,
LOOP, GOODS, MART,
ITEM
star(s) ASTERISK,
PLANET, ACTOR,
SUN, NOVA, ORB,
COMET, METEOR,
DECORATION,
BADGE, WORLD,
ORNAMENT, DESTINY,
LUMINARY
brightest SIRIUS
brilliant NOVA(E)
combining form
ASTR(O)
covered with SEME
dog SIRIUS, SOTHIS
evening VENUS,
HESPERUS, HESPER,
MERCURY, MOON
facet PANE
feathered
COMATULA
first magnitude
ALPHA
five or more points
MULLET
fixed ADIB,
ARCTURUS, VEGA
followers MAGI
heroic ESTOILE
in Aquarius SKAT,
ANCHA
in Aquilla(e)
ALTAIR, DENEB
in Argo NAOS,
MARKEB
in Big Dipper PHAD
in Bootis IZAR
in Centauri AGENA
in Cetus MIRA
in Cygnus SADR
in Draconis
ETAMIN, RASTABAN
in Leo(nis) REGULUS,
DUHR
in Medusa head
ALGOL
in Orion RIGEL
in Pegasus ENIF
(ENRI)
in Perseus ATIK
(ATTIK)
in Scorpio ANTARES,
LESUTH
in Swan SADR
in Taurus HYADES,
PLEIAD

in Ursa Minor
POLARIS, CYNOSURE
like PLANETOID,
ASTRAL, STELLAR,
STELLATE,
SIDEREAL, POINTED
morning PHOSPHOR,
VENUS, MARS,
JUPITER, SATURN,
MERCURY, LUCIFER
new NOVA(E)
path ORBIT
relating to See
"like" *above*
Serpens ALYA
shaped ASTERIOD,
STELLATE
figure ETOILE
shooting LEONID
six-pointed ESTOILE,
ETOILE, PENTACLE
sudden brilliant
NOVA
variable MIRA
starch ARUM,
FARINA, CASSAVA,
AMYL, SAGO,
AMULUM, BACKBONE,
FORMALITY,
STIFFEN
like ARUM,
INULIN, AMYLOSE,
AMYLOID
soluble AMIDIN
starchy STIFF,
PRIM, PRECISE,
FORMAL, PROUD,
AMYLOID
stare GAWK, GAZE,
GAPE, LOOK, GLARE,
PEER, WATCH, SEE,
OGLE
starfish ASTERID
stark BARE, STIFF,
RIGID, TENSE,
FIXED, SET,
STUBBORN,
SEVERE, UTTERLY,
VERY, COMPLETE
starling SALI,
MINA, MYNA,
STARNEL, BIRD
start ROUSE, ONSET,
JERK, JUMP,
LEAP, BEGIN,
ORIGINATE, FOUND,
STRIKE, ENTER,
BEGINNING, SPURT
starting point
DATA, MARKER,
SCRATCH, LINF

startle ALARM,
SHOCK, SCARE,
AROUSE, STIR,
DISTURB, EXCITE
starvation INEDIA,
WANT, PENURY,
FAMINE
starwort ASTER,
FLOWER, PLANT
state RELATE, TELL,
ANNOUNCE, SAY,
AVOW, AVER,
SPECIFY, SITUATION,
CONDITION,
STATUS, ASPECT,
PLIGHT, PASS,
CRISIS, LOT, CASE,
MOOD, ESTRE,
ETAT, GOVERNMENT,
ESTATE, MODE,
UTTER, DECLARE,
PREDICAMENT,
REALM, NATION,
AFFIRM
Beaver OREGON
Beehive UTAH
Buckeye OHIO
Cotton ALABAMA
Diamond DELA-
WARE
Equality WYOMING
Free MARYLAND
Gem IDAHO
Green Mountain
VERMONT
Hawkeye IOWA
Lake MICHIGAN
Lizard ALABAMA
Lobster MAINE
Lone Star TEXAS
Mountain
MONTANA
of mind MOOD,
HUMOR
Peninsula
FLORIDA
pertaining to CIVIL
Pine Tree MAINE
Sooner OKLAHOMA
Sunset ARIZONA
Swiss federal
CANTON
Treasure
MONTANA
stately LOFTY,
DIGNIFIED,
AUGUST, REGAL,
TOGATED, GRAND,
NOBLE, TALL,
STRAIGHT, PROUD,
MAJESTIC, POMPOUS
woman JUNO

statement BILL, ACCOUNT, ACCT, DICTUM, DESCRIPTION, EXPLANATION, RECITAL, REMARK, PRECIS

static, *opposed to* KINETIC

station STOP, TERMINAL, DEPOT, RANK, SET, RANGE, POST, WORK, POSITION, PLACE, LOCATION, SITUATION, SEAT, OFFICE, FUNCTION, STANDING, DEGREE

stationary STATIC, FIXED, STILL, STANDING, SET, STABLE, PERMANENT, MOTIONLESS, QUIESCENT, ARRESTED

point on curve SPINODE

statue ACROLITH, SCULPTURE, EFFIGY, IMAGE, ICON, MASK, FIGURINE, BUST, DOLL

pedestal projecting member SOCLE

praying ORANT

primitive XOANON

weeping NIOBE

status RATING, RANK, CASTE, POSITION, SITUATION, LEVEL, REPUTE

statute LAW, EDICT, DECREE, ORDINANCE, ACT, REGULATION, CANON, ORDER, BILL

staunch STEM, STEADY *See* "stanch"

stave STRIP, BASH, LAG, STAP, POLE, VERSE, SHATTER, SMASH

of cask LAG

stay PREVENT, HINDER, SLOW, TARRY, LINGER, LAG, LIVE, DWELL, RESIDE, REMAIN, CURB, WAIT, (A)BIDE, BRACE, PROP, GUY, ROPE, CHECK, STOP,

LAST, VISIT, SUPPORT, HALT, POSTPONE, TABLE, CONTINUE

staylace AGLET, AIGLET

stead LIEU, SERVICE, ADVANTAGE, AVAIL, PLACE, ROOM, VICE

steady EVEN, STABLE, RELIABLE, STANCH, SOBER, STAID, REGULAR, FIRM, GUY, FIXED, RESOLUTE, PERIODIC, UNDEVIATING, UNIFORM, CONSTANT, STEADFAST

not ASTATIC, UNSTABLE, SHAKY

steak TUCKET, SIRLOIN, FLANK

steal CRIB, PILFER, SNITCH, PURLOIN, EMBEZZLE, LOOT, RUSTLE, ROB, COP, LIFT *See* "filch"

from ship's galley MANAVEL

game POACH

stealthy FURTIVE, SLY, WILY, FOXY, UNDERHAND(ED), CLANDESTINE, SKULKING, CAUTIOUS, CUNNING, SURREPTITIOUS

steam VAPOR, MIST, FUME, REEK, FOG, GAS, STUFA, SMOKE, EXHALATION, EFFLUVIUM, EVAPORATE

combining form ATMO

jet of volcanic STUFA

organ CALLIOPE

steaming device AGER

steatite TALC

steed CHARGER, HORSE, PEGASUS, COB, NAG

steel TOLEDO, DAMASK, DAMASCUS, INVAR, SWORD, HARDEN, INURE

armor plate TACE, TASSE

German metallurgy STAHL, SIDERURGY

pour melted in water TEEM

process BESSEMER, CEMENTATION

protecting coating BARFF

steelyard *weight* PEA

steep SHEER, ABRUPT, EXPENSIVE, DEAR, COSTLY, HEIGHT, HIGH, IMBUE, RET, SOAK, BREW

hillside BRAE, CLEVE

in lime BOWK

slope SCARP

steeper TEAPOT

steeple SPIRE, TOWER, FLECHE, MINARET

steer PILOT, GUIDE, CONN, HELM, LEAD, DIRECT, GOVERN, RULE, CONTROL, OX, BOVINE, STOT, BULLOCK

into wind LUFF

wildly YAW

steeve CRAM, LADE, PACK, STOW, STUFF, DERRICK

stein FLAGON, SCHOONER, MUG, CUP

stele SLAB, PILLAR, MONUMENT

Steller's *sea cow* RYTINA

stem BASE, PROW, BINE, REED, SHAFT, CANE, STALK, TRUNK, STRAW, SPRING, (A)RISE, FLOW, STOP, ISSUE, ORIGIN(ATE), ARREST, STANCH

of joints, relating to NODAL

plant BINE, CAULIS, SHAFT

rudimentary CAULICLE

sheath OCREA

short fleshy
TIGELLA, TUBER,
CORM
without ACAULES-
CENT
stench SMELL,
FETOR, ODOR,
STINK
Stendhal, (de) BEYLE
character JULIEN-
(SOREL), FABRICE
steno, *combining form*
for NARROW,
LITTLE, CLOSE
stentorian LOUD,
CLARION
step(s) RANK,
PLATEAU, DANCE,
STAGE, GRADE,
STILE, STRIDE,
GAIT, PACE, PAS,
TRAMPLE, DEGREE,
LADDER, STAIR
arrangement of
troops ECHELON
dance PAS, CHASSE
ladder, kind of
TRAP
ladder's RUNG,
RIME
outdoor PERRON,
STILE
over fence STILE
pertaining to RISER,
TREAD
to mark TOE
stepmother, *pertain-*
ing to NOVERCAL
sterile ARID,
ASCEPTIC, DRY,
VAIN, EXIGUOUS,
BARREN, UN-
FRUITFUL, UN-
PRODUCTIVE
stern AFT, REAR,
(A)BAFT, GRIM,
SEVERE, HARD,
RIGID, STRICT,
FORBIDDING,
AUSTERE, DOUR,
UNKIND, UNFEEL-
ING, INFLEXIBLE,
STEADFAST,
UNCOMPROMISING,
RIGOROUS
toward (A)BAFT,
AFT, REAR,
CAUDAL
sterne character
TOBY, TRISTRAM-
(SHANDY), (DR)SLOP,
(CPL)TRIM

sternutation SNEEZE
stertor SNORE
stevedore STORER,
STOWER, LADER,
UN(LOADER)
Stevenson's *abode*
SAMOA
character HYDE,
JEKYLL
grave site APIA
stew OLLA, OLIO,
HARICOT, POT,
RAGOUT, BURGOO,
MATELOTE,
PREDICAMENT,
IMPASSE, BOIL,
STEEP, WORRY,
FRET, SEETHE,
SIMMER, CON-
FUSION, DIFFICULTY
steward SENESCHAL,
REEVE, TREASURER,
AGENT, FACTOR,
CHAMBERLAIN,
MANCIPLE,
PURVEYOR,
MANAGER,
CUSTODIAN,
DIRECTOR
of royalty DAPIFER
stewardly FRUGAL,
SPARING
stib DUNLIN, BIRD
stibium ANTIMONY
stich LINE, VERSE
stick BAT, WAND,
CANE, FAGOT,
BATON, BAR, TIE,
BIND, FIX, CLING,
CLEAVE, GLUE,
STAB, ADHERE,
ENDURE, STAY
bundle of sticks
FAGOT
fishing ROD, GAD,
CANE, POLE
hurling JAVELIN
jumping POGO
sticky GOOEY,
LIMY, TACKY,
TREACLY, GUMMY,
VISCID, GLUEY,
HUMID, MOIST,
ADHESIVE,
GLUTINOUS,
VISCOUS
stiff DRUNK, RIGID,
RIGESCENT, TENSE,
STARK, SOLID,
STOUT, FRIGID,
COLD, DIFFICULT,
COOL, BODY,

CORPSE, PRIM,
HARD, PROPER,
FIRM, STARCHY,
INFLEXIBLE,
STUBBORN, STRONG,
SEVERE, POMPOUS
stiffen BRACE,
STARCH, INSPISSATE,
HARDEN, OSSIFY,
GEL, SET
stigma BLEMISH,
STAIN, BLOT,
BRAND, ODIUM,
SHAME, DISGRACE,
DISHONOR, TAINT
stigmatize BRAND,
TAINT, MARK,
DEFAME, DISCREDIT
stiletto DIRK,
STYLET, WEAPON
still HUSH, QUIET,
SHH, CALM, PSST,
COSH, DRIP, DUMB,
PACIFIC, MUM,
SILENT, PLACID,
YET, EVEN, BUT,
NEVERTHELESS,
MUTE, INERT,
QUIESCENT, NOT-
WITHSTANDING
cap of ALEMBIC
stillicide DRIP,
DROP
stilt POGO, POLE,
POST, CRUTCH,
BIRD
stimulant COFFEE,
TEA, LIQUOR, SPUR,
GOAD, MOTIVE,
WHIP, QUIRT
coffee CAFFEIN
tea THEIN
stimulate ANIMATE,
AROUSE, ENCOURAGE,
STIR, URGE, GOAD,
SPUR, WHET, FAN,
PIQUE, EXCITE,
ENERGIZE, INSPIRIT,
INFLAME, KINDLE,
INCITE
stimulus FILLIP,
INCENTIVE
threshold LIMEN
sting SMART, GOAD,
PRICK, BURN, TANG,
GALL, CHEAT,
BARB, TINGLE,
NETTLE, HURT,
PAIN, EXCITE
of insect ICTUS
ray OBISPO, SEPHEN

stinger WASP, HORNET

stinging CAUSTIC, SHARP, ACID, HOT

stingy CLOSE, TIGHT, MEAGER, MEAN, NIGGARDLY, PENURIOUS, PARSIMONIOUS, GRUDGING, MISERLY

stint JOB, CHORE, DUTY, TASK, SCANT, SCRIMP, LIMIT, RESTRICT

stipe PETIOLE, STALK, STEM, SUPPORT

stipend PAY, SALARY, WAGE, PREBEND, PENSION, FEE, HIRE, SCREW, HONORARIUM, ALLOWANCE
Scot. ANNAT

stipulate ITEMIZE, AGREE, PARTICULARIZE, NAME, POSTULATE

stipulation IF, CLAUSE, CONTRACT

stir RILE, ROIL, (A)ROUSE, RALLY, ADO, MOVE, FUSS, ROUST, CAROUSE, PRISON, JAIL, AGITATE, BUZZ, INFLAME, INCITE, GOAD, PROD, MIX, BUSTLE, INSTIGATE
up, as colors TEER

stirps RACE, STOCK, FAMILY, ANCESTRY

stirrup, leather covering TAPADERA
straps CHAPELET

stitch PUNTO, ACHE, CRICK, PAIN, SEW, BASTE, PANG, THROE
bird IHI
knitting FESTON, PURL

stitched fold TUCK

stoa PORTICO, PROMENADE

stoat ERMINE, WEASEL

stock LINEAGE, FAMILY, PLANT, CERTIFICATE, BOND, SHARE, ANIMALS, CATTLE, STEM, TRUNK, HANDLE, STORE, RACE, BREED, CRAVAT, NECKCLOTH, CAPITAL, FUND, PRINCIPAL, SUPPLY, HOARD, RESERVE, MERCHANDISE, GOODS
family STIRPS
feed for hire AGIST

stockade FORT, ETAPE, PEN, BULWARK, REDOUBT

stocking SOCK, SHINNER, HOSE
clock of COIN

stockjobbing AGIOTAGE

stocky PLUMP, STOUT, FAT, STUB, SQUAT, SHORT, PURSY

stoker, glass works TEASER

stole ORARY, FUR, ORARION, SURPLICE, WRAP, SCARF

stolen property LOOT, PELF
receiver of FENCE

stolid DULL, ADAMANT, BRUTISH, HEAVY

stoma OSTIOLE, PORE, MOUTH, OS

stomach PAUNCH, ABDOMEN, CRAW, MAW, RUMEN, POUCH, ENDURE, ABIDE
bird's CROP, MAW, CRAW
combining form GASTRO
lower opening PYLORUS
ruminant's OMASUM, PAUNCH
second RETICULUM
third OMASUM, OMASA (PL.)

stomp See "stamp"

stone GEM, JEWEL, PIT, SEED, PEBBLE, MINERAL, ROCK, FLINT, LAPIS, COBBLE, ORE, BOULDER, TRAP, MARBLE, GRAVEL, CENOTAPH, ADAMANT
age PALEOLITHIC
new NEOLITHIC
and wood figure ACROLITH
orgillaceous SHALE
Biblical EZEL, PETER
carved in relief CAMEO
chip NIG, SPALL
chisel CELT
combining form LAPIO, LITH(O)
convert(ing) into LAPIDIFIC, PETRIFY
cutter MASON, LAPICIDE
receptacle or vessel for SEBILLA
dish COMAL
dress NIG, SCABBLE, DAB, NIDGE
Egyptian language, clew of ROSETTA
engraving INTAGLIO
face ASHLAR
for grinding corn MANO
fragments of BRASH, CHIPS, SAND
green BERYL, OLIVINE
hammer KEVEL
hard ADAMANT, FLINT, QUARTZ
heap SCREE, CAIRN
hewn ASHLAR
hollow GEODE
implement CELT, NEOLITH, ARROW
like LITHOID
monument MENHIR
nodule GEODE
of or pertaining to LAPIDARY
paving SETT, FLAG, PITCHER
pestle MULLER
philosopher's CARMOT, ELIXIR
pillar-shaped HERMA
porous LAVA
quarry LATOMY
red SARD, SPINEL
semi-precious SARD, TOPAZ, AGATE, ONYX
set PAVER

sharpening HONE, WHET
slab or tablet STELA, STELE, PLAQUE
squared ASHLAR
throwing engine ONAGER
trim NIG, DRESS, DAB, SCABBLE, NIDGE
woman turned into NIOBE
worker MASON
yellow TOPAZ, CITRINE
stonecrop SEDUM, ORPIN, ROSEWOOD, TREE
stone to death LAPIDATE
stoneware GRES, POTTERY
stony NIOBEAN, PETROUS, PITILESS, HARD, ROCKY, MALEVOLENT
concretion CALCULUS, TARTAR
ridge RAND
stool TABORET, BENCH, SEAT, STUMP, CROCK, DECOY, DUPE, STOOGE
foot CRICKET, TABORET, HASSOCK, OTTOMAN
pigeon NARK, DECOY, PEACHER
support TRIVET
stoop BEND, BOW, DEIGN, SUBMIT, CONDESCEND, PORCH, PIAZZA, GALLERY, LOGGIA
stop CHECK, CLOSE, PLUG, STEM, STALL, AVAST, (AR)REST, WOA, QUIT, BALK, DAM, HALT, STANCH, CEASE, FOIL, DESIST, FINISH, END, SHUT, HOLD, PAUSE, STATION
stopgap MAKESHIFT, SHIFT, RESORT, EXPEDIENT
stoppage JAM, HALT, CESSATION
stopper BUNG, CORK, SPILE, PLUG,

WAD, PAD, STOPPLE
stop-watch TIMER
storax EXUDATE, GUM
store SHOP, MART, BIN, FUND, RESERVE, CASH, HUSBAND, KEEP, STOCK, HOARD, HEAP, PACK, SUPPLY, COLLECTION, CACHE, POST
military CANTEEN
public ETAPE
storehouse BARN, SILO, ETAPE, GRANARY, MAGAZINE, WAREHOUSE, REPOSITORY, DEPOT, GODOWN
for wool LANARY
stork ADJUTANT, JABIRU, MARABOU, BIRD
like HERON, IBIS, PELARGIC
storksbill *genus* ERODIUM, PLANT
storm FUME, RAGE, OUTBREAK, ORAGE, RANT, FLOOD, BLOW, SNOW, RAIN, WIND, TEMPEST, ASSAULT, COMMOTION, OUTBURST, ATTACK, GALE, HURRICANE, TORNADO, TYPHOON, SQUALL, WHIRLWIND, BLIZZARD, DISTURBANCE
on Steppes BURAN
Turkey SAMIEL
story ANECDOTE, EPIC, PLOT, ARTICLE, LIE, FIB, REPORT, VERSION, NOVEL, NARRATIVE, HOAX, SAGA, FABLE, TALE, LORE, JEREMIAD, ANALOGY, PARABLE, LEGEND, TIER, FLOOR, YARN, PLOT, CANARD, CHRONICLE
short CONTE
teller RACONTEUR, RELATER, FIBBER
stoss, *opposite to* LEE
stot BULL, OX

stound STOP, PAIN, ACHE
stout ALE, PORTER, BOLD, FAT, OBESE, STRONG, RESOLUTE, TOUGH, STANCH, ROBUST, BRAVE, THICK, PROUD, FODGEL, BOCK, HUSKY, AUGUST, CORPULENT, PYKNIC
stove KILN, ETNA, OVEN, RANGE, FURNACE, LATROBE, HEATER
stow STEEVE, LADE, PACK, HIDE, LODGE
Stowe *character* EVA, TOM, SIMON (LEGREE)
heroine EVA
straggler NOMAD, STRAY, TRAMP, VAGABOND
straight LINEAL, RECT, DIRECT, ERECT, EVEN, SEQUENCE, RIGHT, TRUE, FAIR, HONEST, UPRIGHT, ACCURATE, NEAT, VERTICAL
line(s) over algebraic terms VINCULUM, VINCULA
passage ENFILADE
straighten ALIGN, CORRECT, COMPOSE, RECTIFY, ALINE
strain TENSION, SONG, LINE, STOCK, RACE, SIFT, CLEAN, OVERDO, WEAKEN, STRESS, FILTER, SIEVE, PERCOLATE, EXAGGERATE, TRY, HEAVE, BREED, TUNE, MELODY, COLATE, WRENCH, EFFORT
strainer SIEVE, TAMIS, COLANDER, FILTER
strait(s) NECK, NARROW(s), SOUND, CHANNEL, PHARE, ISTHMUS, AREA, PASS, PINCH, RIGOR, POVERTY, DIFFICULTY

strand COAST,
BEACH, BANK, RIPA,
SAND, THREAD,
STRING, FIBER,
ROPE, SHORE, PLY
strange FOREIGN,
NEW, QUEER,
QUAINT, ATYPIC,
BIZARRE, OUTRE,
ALIEN, TRAMON-
TANE, EXOTIC,
UNCO, NOVEL, ODD,
RARE, OUTLANDISH,
EXTRAORDINARY,
PECULIAR, SINGU-
LAR, PRETERNATU-
RAL, UNIQUE,
ERRATIC
stranger, *combining
form* XENO
strangle GARROTE,
CHOKE, STIFLE,
SUFFOCATE, RE-
PRESS, THROTTLE,
SUPPRESS
strap LEASH, STROP,
THONG, BAND,
LATIGO, LIGATURE,
FASTEN, BIND,
BEAT, FLOG,
PUNISH
arm shield ENARME
bridle REIN
shaped LORATE,
LIGULATE, LIGULAR
strass PASTE, GLASS
strata, *pertaining to*
STRATAL, TERRANE,
ERIAN
stratagem FINESSE,
TRAP, COUP, PLAY,
WILE, TRICK,
PLOT, SHIFT,
MANEUVER, ARTI-
FICE, PLAN, RUSE,
SCHEME, DODGE
strategus GENERAL,
COMMANDER
stratum BED, LAYER,
DEPOSIT, SEAM
relating to STRATAL,
ZONE
thin FOLIUM, SHEET
Strauss *composition*
SALOME, ELEKTRA,
WALTZ
straw CULM, STALK,
STEM, TRIFLE,
OMEN, SIGN, FIG,
FARTHING, SNAP
coat, Jap. MINO

color FLAXY,
FLAXEN
hat BAKU, BOATER,
PANAMA
to protect plants
MULCH
strawberry *genus*
FRAGARIA
like fruit ETAERIO
tree ARBUTUS
stray WAIF, STRAG-
GLER, GAD, SIN,
DEVIATE, WANDER,
DOGIE *See*
"roam"
animal CAVY,
DOGIE
streak LINE, STRIA,
STRIP, VEIN, BAND,
TRAIT, TOUCH,
TINGE, LAYER,
DASH, SHADE,
TRACE, SEAM,
STRIPE, MARK
narrow STRIA,
GROOVE
wood FLECK, ROE
stream RUN, EMIT,
POUR, FLOW,
SPRUIT, ARROYO,
RIVER, CREEK, RILL,
BROOK, CURRENT,
FLOOD, TIDE, FLUX,
DRIFT, CHANNEL,
TORRENT, BRANCH,
FORK
bed CHANNEL,
COULEE
of forgetfulness
LETHE
Scot. SIKE
streamlet RILL
streams, *meeting*
CONFLUX
street ROAD(WAY),
PARKWAY, BLOCK,
PLACE, VIA, CALLE,
LANE, DRIVE, ALLEY,
AVENUE, TERRACE
car TRAM
urchin ARAB,
GAMIN
strength POWER, WILL
BRAWN, SINEW,
VIS, MAIN, STHENIA,
THEW, VIGOR,
BEEF, FORCE,
MIGHT, ENERGY,
ARM, MEANS, AS-
SETS, FORTITUDE
of liquid PROOF
strengthen BRACE,

FORTIFY, INCREASE,
LACE
stress EMPHASIS,
PRESSURE, STRAIN,
URGENCY, WEIGHT
See "strain"
music ARSIS
of voice ICTUS
stressed syllable
ARSIS
stretch DISTEND,
EXTEND, TIGHTEN,
REACH, SIZE, EX-
TENT, EXPANSE,
SPREAD, STRAIN,
LENGTHEN, ELON-
GATE, WIDEN, EXPAND,
EXAGGERATE, PRO-
TRACT, EKE
stretched TAUT
out PROLATE, PRONE,
SUPINE, PORRECT
stretcher LITTER
strewing SEME,
LITTERING
strewn *with flowers,
or stars* SEME
stria FILLET, RIDGE,
STRIPE, STREAK
strict NICE, RIGOR-
OUS, RIGID, STERN,
STRAIGHT, PRECISE,
EXACT, HARD,
ASCETIC, SEVERE,
VIGOROUS, STRIN-
GENT, ACCURATE,
PURITANIC, ORTHODOX
stride STEP, PACE,
WALK, STRADDLE,
PROGRESS, STALK
strident HARSH,
UNEVEN, ROUGH,
GRATING, SHRILL
strife CLASH, WAR,
COMBAT, FEUD,
BATTLE, CONTEST,
SPAT, DISCORD,
QUARREL, STRUGGLE,
CONTENTION, CON-
FLICT, DISSENTION,
COMPETITION
evil RIOT, WAR
strigose ROUGH,
SHARP, HISPID
strike SMITE, BAT,
RAP, CONK, SLUG,
SOCK, SWAT, WHACK,
WHAM, CLOUT,
BASH, LAM, RAM,
BUFFET *See* "hit"
gently PUTT, PAT,
BUMP, DAB

out DELE(TE),
ERASE, EFFACE
out a vowel ELIDE
sharply SMITE,
SLAP, PELT(ER)
to and fro BANDY
strikebreaker RAT,
FINK, SCAB, GOON
striking NOTABLE,
IMPRESSIVE, DASH-
ING, ASTONISHING,
WONDERFUL,
EXTRAORDINARY,
REMARKABLE, SUR-
PRISING
string TWINE,
THREAD, CORD,
FILAMENT, SERIES,
SUCCESSION, ROW,
LINE, SET, CHAIN,
TRAIN, STRETCH,
DROVE
stringed instrument
See "musical in-
strument"
stringent TIGHT,
STRICT, RIGID,
STERN, CLOSE,
SEVERE, RIGOROUS,
COMPULSORY
stringy ROPY, LEAN,
LANK
strip LATHE, FLAY,
PEEL, STRAKE, FIL-
LET, BARE, DIVEST,
PARE, WELT, ROB,
DESPOIL, UNCOVER,
DENUDE, BAND,
RIBBON, HULL, EX-
POSE, DISROBE, LOOT,
RANSACK, DEVAS-
TATE, UNRIG,
DISARM, DEPRIVE,
UNDRESS, PLUCK
wood LATH, SLAT,
STAVE
stripe BAR, RIDGE,
WEAL, WELT, WALE,
FILLET, BAND,
RIBBON, SORT, TYPE,
KIND, KIDNEY, ILK,
STREAK, INSIGNE
of color, zool.
PLAGA
thread-like STRIA
stripes, *marked with*
LINEATE
stripling BOY, LAD,
YOUTH
strive EXERT,
STRAIN, TRY, ESSAY,
WORK, CONTEND,

FIGHT, TOIL, LABOR,
COMPETE, VIE,
COPE, ENDEAVOR,
AIM, STRUGGLE,
ATTEMPT, CON-
TEST, TUSSLE,
WRESTLE
strobile CONE
stroke ICTUS, SHOCK,
COUP, MASSE, BLOW,
BEAT, FEAT, MARK,
PALSY, CARESS,
SOOTHE, TOUCH,
SUCCESS
cutting CHOP,
SLICE
golf BAFF
short FLIP, PUTT,
WHISK
stroll AMBLE,
PROMENADE, SAUN-
TER, RAMBLE,
WANDER, ROVE,
ROAM, STRAGGLE,
RANGE
strong BRISK, HARD,
FIRM, FERE, HALE,
VIRILE, STOUT,
TOUGH, LUSTY,
SOUND, HARDY,
ARDENT, HUSKY,
POWERFUL, MUS-
CULAR, ROBUST,
VIGOROUS, WIRY,
SINEWY, BRAWNY,
HERCULEAN,
STALWART, POTENT,
ENERGETIC
arm man GOON,
BOUNCER
box SAFE
drink SPIRITS
flavored RACY, ACRID,
PUNGENT
man ATLAS, SAMPSON,
SAMSON
muscles THEWS,
BRAWN
point FORTE
stronghold CITADEL,
SAFE, FASTNESS,
MUNIMENT,
FORT(RESS), CASTLE,
FORTIFICATION,
BULWARK, DONJON
strontium *symbol* SR
strop HONE,
SHARPEN, STRAP
struck SMOTE, SMIT,
SHUT
struggle COPE, VIE,
CONTEST, LABOR,

FOUNDER, FIGHT,
WRESTLE, ENDEAVOR,
AIM, STRIVE,
WRITHE
struggle *à deux*
DUEL
Stuarts, *last of* ANNE
stubble EDDISH,
BEARD, STUMP, RE-
MAINS
field, unplowed
ROWEN
of wheat ARRISH
tuft MANE
stubborn ORNERY,
SOT, HARD, MULISH,
UNYIELDING, IN-
FLEXIBLE, OBSTI-
NATE, OBDURATE,
WILLFUL, HEAD-
STRONG, DOGGED,
PERSISTENT,
REFRACTORY,
RESISTANT
stuck FROZEN,
FIXED, MIRED
stud BOSS, POST,
KNOB, NAIL, HORSE,
PROP, SUPPORT
with nails CLOUT
student PLEBE,
CADET, PUPIL,
DISCIPLE,
SCHOLAR, COED,
LEARNER, TRAINEE
French ELEVE
group CLASS,
SEMINAR
in charge MONITOR
quarters DORM
studio ATELIER,
ROOM, WORKSHOP,
OFFICE
study PEN, ROOM,
CON, EYE, PORE,
EXAMINE, PLAN,
DEVISE, PONDER,
MUSE, THINK,
WEIGH, CONSIDER,
BONE, LEARN,
RESEARCH, IN-
VESTIGATE, EX-
ERCISE, MEDITATE,
REFLECT(ION),
CONTEMPLATE,
STUDIO, LIBRARY,
OFFICE, SKETCH
group SEMINAR,
CLASS
music ETUDE
of sacred edifices
NAOLOGY

stuff SATE, CRAM, FILL, RAM, WAD, SATIATE, STOW, STODGE, DISTEND, PACK, GORGE, FABRIC, GORMANDIZE, MATERIAL, RUBBISH, SUBSTANCE, TEXTURE, OVEREAT

stulm ADIT, PASSAGE(WAY), ENTRANCE

stump SNAG, STUB, BUTT, SCRAB, PUZZLE
of branch SKEG

stun *See "stupefy"*

stunning FINE, GRAND, WONDERFUL, DAZZLING, DEAFENING, STUPEFYING, STRIKING, ATTRACTIVE, ASTONISHING

stunt ATROPHY, DWARF, CROWD, CHECK, CRAMP, SAP, WEAKEN, STINT, TRICK, JOKE, FEAT

stunted SCRUB, DWARFED, SMALL

stupefy STUN, DRUG, DOPE, PALL, DULL, BEMUSE, DEADEN, BESOT, DAZE, MAZE, NUMB, MUDDLE, CONFUSE

stupid DUMB, SILLY, STOLID, HEBETATE, SLUGGISH, DULL, CRASS, VOID, BLANK, DENSE, EMPTY, SENSELESS, WITLESS, INEPT, ASININE, SLOW, INANE, OBTUSE, DOLTISH
as a goose ANSERINE
person ASS, OAF, LOON, COOT, FATHEAD, CLOD, GOOSE

stupor SOPOR, TORPOR, (NAR)-COMA, DAZE, LETHARGY, TRANCE, NARCOSIS, INSENSIBILITY
in a condition of NARCOSE

sturdy FIRM, HARDY, ENDURING, STRONG, LUSTY, ROBUST, STOUT, STALWART, BRAWNY, MUSCULAR, THICKSET, POWERFUL

sturgeon STERLET, BELUGA, ELOPS, FISH
genus ACIPENSER
large HAUSEN
roe CAVIAR
small STERLET
species OSSETER
white BELUGA, HUSO

sty SHED, PEN, HORDEOLUM, RISING, PUSTULE, QUAT, BOIL, PIMPLE, PIGGERY

style NAME, TITLE, TECHNIQUE, TON, FASHION, DICTION, VOGUE, ART, WAY, FORM, GENRE, MODE, FAD, RAGE, MANNER, CRY

styled YCLEPT, CALLED, NAMED, FORMED

stylet STILETTO, DAGGER, TROCAR, PONIARD, AWL
surgical TROCAR, PROBE

stylish SWANKY, DRESSY, DAPPER, CHIC, NATTY, NIFTY, POSH, ALAMODE, FASHIONABLE, MODISH, ELEGANT, SMART

stylized *flower* LIS

stymie BALK, CHECK, STOP, IMPEDE

styptic ALUM, ASTRINGENT

Styx RIVER, STREAM, NYMPH
ferryman CHARON
locale HADES
pertaining to STYGIAN

suave BLAND, OILY, GENIAL, SILKY, SLEEK, URBANE, SMOOTH, MANNERED, UNCTUOUS, POLITE

subbase PLINTH

subdue DOWN, AWE, QUASH, QUELL, CALM, CENSOR, SOBER, TAME, ROUT, BEAT, LICK, CONQUER, REDUCE

subject PRONE, THEME, TOPIC, ENTHRALL, TAKE, TEXT, SERVANT, LIEGE, OPEN, LIABLE, APT, LIKELY, SERVILE, VASSAL

subjoin ADD, APPEND, ANNEX, AFFIX, UNITE, ATTACH

subjugate MASTER, OVERAWE, COW, BEAT, LICK, DEFEAT, ENSLAVE

sublime LOFTY, HIGH, EMPYREAL, IDEAL, NOBLE, EXALTED, MAJESTIC

submarine NAUTILUS
tube SNORKEL

submerged AWASH, SUNK, IMMERSED

submission VAIL, OBEDIENCE, COMPLIANCE
act of CURTS(E)Y, KNEEL

submit RELENT, DEFER, ABIDE, BEAR, CEDE, BEND, OBEY, BOW, SURRENDER, YIELD, LOWER, SUBDUE, SOFTEN, RESIGN

subordinate UNDER, LOWER, AIDE, INFERIOR

subservient SERVILE, OILY, OBSEQUIOUS

subside ABATE, EBB, FALL, LANGUISH, WANE, SETTLE, RELAPSE, SINK, DECREASE

subsist LIVE, FARE, BE, EXIST, CONTINUE

substance MEAT, HEART, FIBER, GIST, SUM, BASIS, GROUND, MATERIAL, MATTER, TEXTURE, WEALTH

substantiate
  VERIFY, PROVE,
  CONFIRM, TEST
substantive NOUN,
  PRONOUN, FIRM,
  SOLID, LASTING
substitute VICE,
  ERSATZ, SUB,
  STAND-IN, PROXY,
  SUPPLANT,
  DEPUTY, MEANS,
  REPLACE
subterfuge EXCUSE,
  PRETENSE, FRAUD,
  TRICK, RUSE,
  BLIND, EVASION,
  SHIFT, REFUGE
subterranean
  PLUTONIC, HIDDEN,
  SECRET, ABYSMAL,
  SUNK
subt(i)le TENUOUS,
  AIRY, CRAFTY,
  DELICATE,
  ETHEREAL, WILY,
  RARIFIED, ELUSIVE
  emanation AURA,
  ATMOSPHERE
  influence AURA
  variation NUANCE
suburb PURLIEU,
  URBAN, TOWN,
  ENVIRON
subvention AID,
  BOUNTY, SUBSIDY,
  GRANT, ENDOW-
  MENT
subvert CORRUPT,
  RAZE, DESTROY,
  UPSET, RUIN,
  OVERTHROW,
  OVERTURN
subway TUBE,
  METRO, IRT, BMT
  entrance KIOSK
  Paris METRO
succeed GET,
  ENSUE, FOLLOW,
  PROVE, GAIN, WIN,
  ATTAIN, ACCOMPLISH,
  THRIVE, PROSPER
success HIT, LUCK,
  WOW, FORTUNE,
  FIND
  in love symbol
  EMERALD
  symbol of PALM,
  TROPHY, MEDAL,
  COMMENDATION,
  CITATION
successful LUCKY,

FORTUNATE,
  HAPPY, PROSPEROUS
successive AROW,
  SERIATE, SERIAL,
  CONSECUTIVE
successor HEIR,
  RELIEF, FOLLOWER
succinct CRISP,
  SHORT, BRIEF,
  TERSE, CURT,
  BLUNT, PITHY,
  CONCISE, LACONIC,
  COMPACT
succor HELP, AID,
  RELIEF, SERVE,
  ASSIST(ANCE)
succulent LUSH,
  JUICY, PAPPY,
  NUTRITIVE
  fruit UVA
succumb DIE,
  YIELD, FAIL,
  SUBMIT, BOW,
  DEFER, SURRENDER,
  CAPITULATE
suck ABSORB,
  IMBIBE, ENGULF,
  DRINK
sucking fish REMORA
suction INTAKE
Sudan(ese) MOSSI,
  FULA(H),
  HAMITES, TIBBU,
  TAUREG
  lake NO
  language MO(LE),
  EWE, TSHI, KRU, IBO,
  EFIK, VAK, VEI
  mountain(s)
  NUBA
  region SEGU
sudarium NAPKIN,
  VERONICA,
  HANDKERCHIEF
Sudra *caste member*
  PALLI
suds FOAM, FROTH,
  LATHER, SCUM,
  YEAST, BEER
sue ASK, CLAIM,
  SUIT, COURT, BEG,
  WOO, PRAY, PLEAD,
  PROSECUTE,
  SOLICIT, PETITION,
  APPEAL, IMPLORE
suffer BEAR,
  PERMIT, TOLERATE,
  STAND, BROOK,
  ALLOW, ACHE,
  PAIN, BIDE, LET,
  STARVE, UNDERGO,
  EXPERIENCE,

ENDURE, SUPPORT,
  STOMACH
suffering EXTREMITY,
  ILL, SICK
  combining form
  PATHO
sufficient BASTANT,
  ENOW, FIT, AMPLE,
  FULL, ENOUGH,
  MEET, ADEQUATE,
  COMMENSURATE
suffix AFFIX, AT-
  TACH, ATION, INE,
  OCK, NESS, ADD,
  SUBJOIN
  abounding in FUL,
  ULENT
  action ENCE
  adjective ENT, IAL,
  IAN, IC, IL, ILE,
  IVE, INE
  agent ATOR
  alcohol OL
  animal realm ALIA
  diminutive ULE, ETTE
  disciple ITE, IST
  equality ENT
  follower ITE, IST
  foot PED
  full of ITOUS, OSE
  geology period
  CENE
  jurisdiction RIC
  like INE, OID, AR, IC
  medical OMA, ITIS,
  ALGIA
  noun ING
  pertaining to ESE,
  IC
  too much ARD,
  ART
  verbal ISE, ESCE
suffocate BURKE,
  SMOTHER, STRANGLE,
  STIFLE, CHOKE,
  ASPHYXIATE
  partial APNOEA,
  FAINT, SWOON
suffrage BALLOT,
  VOTE, FRANCHISE,
  ASSENT, VOICE,
  APPROVAL
suffuse COVER,
  SPILL, IMBUE,
  INFUSE, BATHE,
  BLUSH, COLOR,
  SPREAD, POUR
Sufi *disciple* MURID
sugar OSE, BIOSE,
  SUCROSE, KETOSE,
  SWEETEN

and molasses
MELADA
artificial MANNOSE,
ALLOSE, GLUCOSE,
SACCHARIN
brown PANELA, RAW
burnt CARAMEL
cane SUCROSE
refuse BAGASSE
stalk RATOON
cleaning ELUTION
containing 12 atoms
BIOSE
crystalline MALTOSE
evaporating pan in
mfg. of TACHE
form of OSE
fruit KETOSE,
LEVULOSE,
FRUCTOSE
grape MALTOSE
DEXTROSE
lump LOAF, CUBE
milk LACTOSE
raw CASSONADE,
MUSCOVADO,
BROWN
refining box
ELUTOR
sack BAYON
solution SYRUP
source SAP, BEET,
CANE, MAPLE
works, W. Indies
USINE
suggest PROPOSE,
CONNOTE, ALLUDE,
IMPORT, PROMPT,
INSPIRE, IMPLY,
HINT, INTIMATE,
INSINUATE,
PROPOUND, RECOM-
MEND, ADVISE,
COUNSEL
suggestion CUE,
CLUE, HINT, TIP,
WRINKLE, NOTION,
IDEA, TOUCH,
SHADE, DASH,
TINGE, INTIMATION,
ALLUSION, INKLING,
REMINDER, ADVICE
suicidal DEADLY,
LETHAL, BRASH,
RASH, FATAL
suid HOG, BOAR,
SWINE
sui juris ADULT,
RESPONSIBLE
suit HIT, AGREE,
ADAPT, FIT,
BEFIT, CAUSE,

CASE, SET,
SERIES, BECOME,
ATTIRE, DRESS,
WOOING, REQUEST,
PETITION, ENTREATY,
SUPPLICATION,
COURTSHIP,
PROSECUTION,
TRIAL, CLOTHING,
COSTUME, HABIT
suitable IDEAL,
MEET, FIT, APT, PAT,
BECOMING,
EXPEDIENT,
ADEQUATE, PROPER,
APPROPRIATE,
(BE)FITTING,
CONGRUOUS,
SEEMLY
suitcase(s) BAG,
GRIP, VALISE,
RETICULE, LUGGAGE
suite ROOMS,
FURNITURE, SET,
RETINUE, STAFF,
TRAIN, SERIES,
CHAIN, ESCORT,
CONVOY, FOLLOWERS,
CORTEGE
suitor AMOROSO,
SWAIN, WOOER,
LOVER, BEAU,
SWEETHEART,
STEADY, ADMIRER,
FLAME
sulcate CLEFT,
FURROWED,
GROOVED, FLUTED
sulk HUFF, POUT,
MOPE, FROWN,
SCOWL
sulky PLOW, CAR-
RIAGE, GIG, GLUM,
SNUFFY, CROSS,
TESTY, MOROSE,
SURLY, MOODY,
CHURLISH,
GROUCHY, SULLEN
sullage MUD,
SEWAGE, SILT,
SCUM, SLAG, DROSS
sullen SOUR,
SULKY, POUTY,
GLUM, SURLY,
DOUR, MOODY,
GRIM, MOROSE,
SAD, SATURNINE,
CROSS
sulphate, *barium*
BARYTA
calcium GYPSUM
double ALUM

sulphide *calcium,*
HEPAR
iron TROILITE
lead GALENA
zinc BLENDE
sulphur QUEBRINTH
alloy NIELLO
sulphuric acid VITRIOL
Sultanate KOWAIT,
OMAN, MAHRA
sultry HOT, MOIST,
CLOSE, DAMP, STILL,
SENSUAL, COARSE,
LURID, STUFFY,
HUMID, STIFLING,
OPPRESSIVE, MUGGY,
SWELTERING
Sulu Archipelago
island JOLO
Moslem MORO
sum WHOLE,
QUANTITY, FIGURE,
CAST, FOOT, ADD,
AMOUNT, TOTAL,
GIST, RECAP,
MONEY
sumac *genus* RHUS
Sumatra island group
SUNDA *See*
"Sunda"
island NIAS
lake TOBA
Sumatran MALAYAN,
LAMPONG, REJANG,
BAT(T)AK, BATTA
deity ABU
kingdom ACHIN,
ATJEH
language NIAS(ESE)
measure ETTO,
JANKAL, PAKHA,
SUKAT, TUB, TUNG
weight CANDIL
wild cat BALU
Sumer, *ancient city*
ERIDU
summary DIGEST,
PRECIS, COMPEND,
BRIEF, SPEEDY,
SUCCINCT,
ABRIDG(E)MENT,
COMPENDIUM,
ABSTRACT,
EPITOME,
SYNOPSIS,
SYLLABUS, IMMEDI-
ATE
summer, *French*
ETE
house ARBOR,
PERGOLA, GAZEBO,

BELVEDERE, BOWER
pertaining to ESTIVAL
summit CROWN, CAP, PEAK, TOP, ACME, PINNACLE, APEX, VERTEX, SPIRE, APOGEE, ZENITH, POINT
summon INVITE, AROUSE, INVOKE, CONVOKE, CONVENE, CALL, SIGNAL, CITE, EVOKE, EVOCATE, PAGE, MUSTER, BID, ORDER, IMPLORE, ENTREAT
to court CITE, SIST
sump BOG, PIT, POOL, WELL, EXCAVATION
sumpter PACK HORSE, MULE
sun SOL, STAR, LUMINARY
bow IRIS
burn HELIOSIS, TAN
circle around HALO
combining form HELIO
crossing equator EQUINOX
disk ATEN
fish ROACH, OPAH, MOLA
god, goddess See under "god" or "goddess"
greatest distance from APSIS
luminous envelope of CORONA
path ECLIPTIC
personified TITAN, APOLLO
pertaining to SOLAR
room(s) SOLARIUM, SOLARIA
spots UMBRA, FACULA, LUCULE, MACULA
standing still SOLSTICE
worship HELIOLATRY, SABIANISM
Sunda island TIMOR, BALI, SUMATRA, LAMBOK, JAVA, CELEBES,

BORNEO, RAOUL, NIAS
Sunday SABBATH
low QUASIMODO
pertaining to DOMINICAL
sunder PART, SEVER, BREAK, DIVIDE, REND, RIVE, CLEAVE, SPLIT, SEPARATE
sundial *index* GNOMON
sundry's *companion* ALL
sunflower, *maid turned into* CLYTIE
State KANSAS
sunken fence AHA, HAHA, HAWHAW
sunn HEMP, SANA, PLANT, FIBER
sunrise *song* AUBADE
sunset TWILIGHT, DUSK, EVENING, CURFEW, NIGHTFALL
pertaining to CREPUSCULAR, ACRONICAL
toward WEST
sup DINE, DRINK, SIP, SNACK, FEED, EAT
supawn MUSH
super ULTRA, RICH, GRAND, SUPERIOR, EXTRA
superabundance PLETHORA, PLENTY, LOTS, GOBS, EXCESS, OVERFLOW, SUPERFLUITY, REDUNDANCE
superannuated ANILE, SENILE, AGED, OLD, RETIRED, DECREPIT, ANTIQUATED, PASSE
superfine LUXE, EXTRA, NICE, PLUSH, RICH, EXCELLENT, CHOICE, PRIME, SUPERIOR
superfluous OVER, EXTRA, REDUNDANT, SPARE, LAVISH, DE TROP, EXCESSIVE, PROFUSE

superintend BOSS, REGULATE, RUN, OVERSEE, CONDUCT, GUIDE, LEAD, CONTROL, DIRECT
superior DIRECTOR, BOSS, FINER, PREFERABLE, GRANDER, UPPER, EXCELLENT, PARAMOUNT, ABOVE, PREEMINENT, OVER, MERITORIOUS
Superior LAKE
superiority MASTERY, ODDS, EDGE, PRECEDENCE, ADVANTAGE, PREDOMINANCE, SUPREMACY, EXCELLENCE, WORTHINESS
superlative EMINENT, SUPREME, HIGHEST, UTMOST, ACME, PEAK, GREATEST, TRANSCENDENT, PEERLESS, CONSUMMATE, INCOMPARABLE
absolute ELATIVE
suffix EST
supernatural HYPERPHYSICAL, MAGIC, OCCULT, EERIE, ABNORMAL, MIRACULOUS, MARVELOUS, UNEARTHLY, METAPHYSICAL, PRETERNATURAL
being GOD, GODDESS, ATUA, TROLL, BANSHEE, ANGEL
superscribe ADDRESS, MARK, DIRECT
supersede OMIT, SUPPLANT, DISPLACE, OVERRIDE, REPLACE, VOID, ANNUL
superstitious, *relating to* GOETIC
supervisor PROCTOR, MONITOR, BOSS, TEACHER, DIRECTOR, MASTER, SUPERINTENDENT, GUIDE
supine INERT, LISTLESS, PRONE, ABED, PROSTRATE,

RECUMBENT,
HORIZONTAL,
INDOLENT, SLUGGISH,
LAZY, SLOTHFUL,
TORPID, LANGUID,
APATHETIC,
LETHARGIC,
OTIOSE, SERVILE
supple PLIANT,
LITHE, LISSOM(E),
LIMBER, SUBMISSIVE,
AGILE, NIMBLE,
PLIABLE, FLEXIBLE,
COMPLACENT,
YIELDING, SOFT
supplement ADD-
(ITION), EKE,
APPENDIX,
ADJUNCT, POSTSCRIPT,
SEQUEL
supplicate BEG,
BESEECH, CONJURE,
PRAY, PLEAD, SUE,
ASK, APPEAL,
PETITION, CRAVE
supplication AVE,
PETITION, PRAYER,
LITANY, ENTREATY,
SOLICITATION,
REQUEST
supplied FED, DOSED,
PRESCRIBED,
FURNISHED
supplies STORES,
GOODS, FEEDS,
ESTOVERS, ORD-
NANCE, STOCK,
PROVISIONS, AID,
FOOD
supply FEED, GRIST,
CATER, FURNISH,
HELP, FILL,
RELIEVE, RELIEF,
PROVIDE, EQUIP,
ACCOMMODATE,
FUND, GIVE
support KEEP,
BOARD, AID, TENON,
LEG, LIMB, PEG,
BASE, PROP, SHORE,
RIB, BEAR, STAY,
STRUT, BACK, ABET,
BUOY, SECOND,
SUSTAIN, UPHOLD,
BRACE, PATRONIZE,
CHAMPION,
FURTHER, PATRON-
AGE
for statue PEDES-
TAL, SOCLE
one-legged UNIPOD

slab PLANCH,
TRAY
suppose SURMISE,
DEEM, OPINE,
WEEN, TROW, WIS,
THINK, IMAGINE,
PRESUME, CONSIDER,
JUDGE, CONJECTURE,
ASSUME, PREDICATE,
SUSPECT, GUESS
supposition IF,
THEORY, SURMISE,
CONJECTURE,
GUESSWORK,
HYPOTHESIS
suppress SMOTHER,
BAN, CHECK,
QUASH, QUELL,
REPRESS, CRUSH,
OVERPOWER, SUBDUE,
OVERWHELM,
WITHHOLD,
RESTRAIN
suppurate FESTER,
MATURATE
suppuration PUS,
MATTER
suprarenal gland
ADRENAL
supreme PRIME,
PARAMOUNT,
ABSOLUTE, IMPERIAL,
FIRST, UTMOST,
CAPITAL,
HIGH(EST), CHIEF,
PEERLESS, PRE-
EMINENT
Supreme Court
NINE
suras, *114* KORAN
surcease REST, STOP,
END, ABATE,
RELIEF, RESPITE,
CESSATION
surcoat CYCLAS,
JUPON, GARMENT
surd VOICELESS,
MUTE
mutes, one of
TENUIS
sure SAFE, CERTAIN,
ASSURED, SECURE,
GENUINE, REAL,
TRUE, CONFIDENT,
POSITIVE, CONVINCED,
STABLE, UNERRING,
AUTHENTIC, ACTUAL,
UNFAILING
surety SPONSOR,
BOND, BAIL, PLEDGE,
FACT, GUARANTY,
VOUCHER, HOSTAGE,

ASSURANCE, CER-
TAINTY, SAFETY
suretyship, *Canada*
AVAL
surf FOAM, SPRAY,
WAVES
noise ROTE, SURGE
surface VENEER,
EXTERIOR, FACET,
NAPPE, PAVE, PLAT,
SIDE, OUTSIDE,
SUPERFICIAL
between two flutes of
shaft ORLO
flat PAGINA,
PLANE, TABULAR
growing above
EPIGEOUS
pertaining to
ACROTIC, OBVERSE
small AREOLA,
FACET
water's RYME
surfeit SATE, GLUT,
CLOY, JADE, PALL,
GORGE, SATIATE,
SATISFY
surfeited BLASE,
COMPLETE, REPLETE
surge GUSH, SWELL,
RUSH, WAVE, TIDE,
BILLOW, GURGITATE,
(A)RISE, SOAR
surgeon fish TANG,
BARBER
surgery, *father of*
modern PARE
surgical *appliance*
SPLINT, BRACE,
CRUTCH
file XYSTER
hammer PLESSOR
hook TENACULUM
knife FLEAM,
SCALPEL, LANCET,
CATLIN
operation
RESECTION
plug TAMPON
probe ACUS,
STYLET, TENT
puncture CENTESIS
saw TREPAN,
TREPHINE
scraper XYSTER
stitch SUTURE
stylet TROCAR
thread SETON
Surinam *capital*
PARAMARIBO
coin BIT
hut BENAB

toad PIPA(L)
tribe BONI, DJUKA
wood QUASSIA,
LANA
surly CROSS, DOUR,
RUDE, GRUFF, CRUSTY,
GRUM, GLUM,
MOROSE, UNKIND,
SULLEN, CRABBED,
TESTY, TOUCHY,
PEEVISH, SNAPPISH,
UNCIVIL, GRUMPY,
GROUCHY,
CHURLISH, SOUR
surmise DEEM,
THINK, FANCY,
OPINE, GUESS,
INFER, GATHER,
IMAGINE, SUSPECT,
CONJECTURE,
SUPPOSE, PRESUME,
PRESUMPTION,
ASSUME, ASSUMP-
TION, SCENT,
SUPPOSITION,
SUSPICION
surmount CONQUER,
CROWN, CAP,
SCALE, ROUT, BEAT,
LICK, CLIMB,
VAULT, OVERCOME,
VANQUISH, MASTER,
SURPASS, SUBDUE,
ASCEND
surname AGNOMEN,
EPONYM,
PATRONYM,
APPELLATION,
COGNOMEN
surpass BEAT,
EXCEL, LEAD, TOP,
CAP, OUTDO,
OUTSHINE, WIN,
EXCEED, SURMOUNT,
ECLIPSE, TRANSCEND
surplice COTTA,
PELISSE, VESTMENT
surplus EXTRA,
SPARE, OVER, REST,
EXCESS, REMAINDER,
RESERVE,
SUPERABUNDANCE,
GLUT
surprise FLOOR,
STUN, AMAZE, AWE,
START, DAZE, SHOCK,
BLOW
surrealist DALI
surrender RESIGN,
LEAVE, WAIVE,
REMISE, CESSION,
CEDE, REMIT, YIELD,

ABANDON, GIVE,
SUBMIT, CAPITULATE,
RELINQUISH
surreptitious
FURTIVE, SLY,
SECRET, COVERT,
UNDERHAND(ED),
STEALTHY,
DECEPTIVE
surround HEDGE,
HEM, BESET, RING,
ENCLOSE, COMPASS,
(EN)CIRCLE, EN-
CASE, CIRCUMSCRIBE
surrounding AMBI-
ENT, ZONE,
BESETTING
Surry *parish* KEW
surtax AGIO, EXTRA,
LEVY
surtout COAT
survey VISTA, POLL,
VIEW, PLOT, LOOK,
PLAN, ESPY, SEE,
REVIEW, SCRUTINIZE,
EXAMINE, SCAN,
MEASURE,
EXAMINATION,
PROBE, STUDY,
INSPECTION, PROSPECT
surveying GEODESY
instrument ALIDADE,
THEODOLITE,
TRANSIT, STADIA,
ROD
rod STADIA
surveyor(s)
ARPENTEUR
assistant RODMAN,
LINEMAN
measure LINK,
ROD, CHAIN, ACRE
survive LIVE,
PERSIST, ABIDE,
LAST, ENDURE,
OUTLIVE, OUTWEAR,
REMAIN, STAND,
STAY
survivor of race LIF
suspend HANG,
DEFER, HALT,
SLING, STAY, EJECT,
OUST, DEBAR,
WITHHOLD, POST-
PONE, DELAY, AD-
JOURN, INTERRUPT,
HINDER, CONTINUE
suspended PENSILE,
PENDENT, PENDANT,
TABLED, HALTED
suspender BRACE

suspension HALT,
DELAY, RESPITE,
CESSATION, STOP, IN-
TERRUPTION, RECESS,
TABLE, CLOTURE,
CONTINUANCE
of proceedings SIST,
ARREST, CONTINU-
ANCE, CLOTURE,
TABLE
suspicion HINT,
FEAR, MISTRUST,
DISTRUST, TOUCH,
TRACE, SOUPCON,
DOUBT, DASH, SHADE,
APPREHENSION,
INKLING, JEALOUSY
suspicious FISHY,
LEERY, SKEPTICAL,
DISTRUSTFUL,
DOUBTFUL, JEALOUS
Sussex borough
HOVE
sustained, *music*
TENUTO
susulike DOLPHIN
susurrant MURMUR-
ING, RUSTLING
sutler's *shop* CAN-
TEEN
sutor COBBLER,
SYRUP
suture RAPHE, SEAM,
SEW, JOINT,
JUNCTION, UNION
suzerain LIEGE,
LORD, NOBLEMAN
swab EPAULET, MOP,
MALKIN, WIPE,
CLEAN, WASH,
SPONGE, LOUT,
LUBBER
swaddle BAND, WRAP,
BANDAGE, CLOTHE
swag BOOTY,
PLUNDER, BOODLE,
SPOILS, LOOT,
STRUT, FLOURISH,
BRAG
swagger STRUT,
BOAST, BULLY,
BLUSTER, PRANCE,
SWELL, AIR, AR-
ROGANCE, BRAG-
GADOCIO
swaggering THRASON-
ICAL
swain BEAU, FLAME,
DAMON, GALLANT,
LAD, LOVER,
SQUIRE, YOUTH,

BOY, PEASANT,
SUITOR, RUSTIC
swallow BOLT,
GULP, ABSORB,
DRINK, BELIEVE,
IMBIBE, BIRD *See
under* "bird"
chimney SWIFT
swamp BOG, FEN,
MORASS, QUAGMIRE,
SLOUGH, DEFEAT
See "marsh"
belt, India TERAI
gas MIASMA,
METHANE
grass SEDGE, REED
land MAREMMA,
TUNDRA, SLASH,
MARSH, MUSKEG
muddy SLOUGH
plant SOLA
relating to MIASMA
Virginia DISMAL
swampy PALUDAL,
ULIGINOUS,
ULIGINOSE
swan *female* PEN
genus OLOR,
CYGNUS
male COB
whistling HOOPER,
OLOR
wild ELK, HOOPER
young CYGNET
Swan of Eternity
HANSA
swanky POSH, LUSH,
RICH, LUXURIOUS
"Swann's Way"
author PROUST
swap TRADE, EX-
CHANGE, BARTER,
BANDY
sward TURF, SOD,
GRASS, LAWN
swarm CLOUD,
CROWD, TEEM,
HERD, HIVE, SNEE,
SNY, PACK, FLOCK,
BEVY, THRONG,
HORDE, MIGRATE,
MOVE, CLIMB, SHIN,
MOUNT, COLLECTION
swarming ALIVE,
TEEMING, BUSTLING
swathe WRAP,
BANDAGE, BIND,
SWADDLE, CLOTHE,
PATH
sway ROCK, RULE,
VEER, WAVER,
BRANDISH, INFLU-

ENCE, WAVE,
AUTHORITY, POWER,
DOMINION,
SOVEREIGNTY *See*
"swing"
swear PROMISE,
INVOKE, CURSE,
DEPOSE, AFFIRM,
ATTEST, AVER, VOW,
DEPONE, TESTIFY,
BLASPHEME
falsely SLANDER,
PERJURE
sweat SUDOR,
EXUDE, PERSPIRE,
EXTORT, LABOR,
TOIL, DRUDGERY
Sweden, Swedish
SVERIGE
administrative
province LAN,
LAEN
body guard DRABANT
city or town
SOLNA, LUND,
MALMO, FALON
See "seaport" *below*
coin KRONA, ORE,
KRONE
explorer HEDIN
family VASA
farm TORP, THORP
king ERIC
lake MALAR,
ASNEN
legislature DIET
(RIKSDAG),
FORSTA, ANDRA
(KAMMAREN)
manual training
SLOYD
measure AMAR, AM,
REF, ALN, FOT, MIL,
TUM, KAPP, FAMN,
STANG
Nightingale LIND,
JENNY
philologist IHRE
royal guard
DRABANT
seaport MALMO,
VISBY, UMEA,
PITEA
territorial division
LAN, LAEN
town See "city"
above
weight ORT, STEN,
PUND
sweep OAR, DUST,
DRIVE, WIN, CLEAN,
CLEARANCE,

SPREAD, SCOPE,
SPACE, RANGE,
REACH, KEN, ORB,
BRUSH, GRAZE,
SCOUR
sweeping COMPRE-
HENSIVE, BROAD,
GENERAL, COMPLETE
sweepstakes LOTTERY,
RACE, ANTE, BET
sweet(s) HONEY,
DULCET, NICE,
SMOOTH, EASY,
PLEASING, AGREE-
ABLE, SUGARED,
PLEASANT,
DARLING, CANDY,
DESSERT,
MELODIOUS, LOVELY,
PASTRY
flag CALAMUS
potato YAM,
BATATA, PATAT,
OCARINA
smelling OLENT
sweetbread RIS, RIS
DE VEAU, RUSK,
THYMUS
sweetfish AYU
sweetheart LEMAN,
MISTRESS, VALEN-
TINE, (LADY)LOVE,
FLAME, DEAR,
DARLING, CHERI(E),
LOVER
female AMARYLLIS,
FLAME, SIS,
INAMORATA
male BEAU, SPARK,
SWAIN, ENAMORATO
See "beau"
Scot. JO
sweetmeat(s) CAKE,
CATES, CONFECTION,
CANDY, CARAMEL,
DESSERT, PASTRY
sweetsop ANNONA,
ATTA, ATES, TREE,
FRUIT
swell ENLARGE,
INCREASE, INFLATE,
DILATE, SURGE,
BULGE, EXPAND,
BILLOW, DISTEND,
FOP, NOB, STRUT,
PUFF, GRAND, GREAT,
PRETTY, STYLISH
of sea SURF, RISE,
WAVE
on plants GALL
swelling LUMP,
NODE, BLAIN,

EDEMA, STY,
BUBO, DROPSY,
TORUS, BULGE,
KNOT, PROTUBER-
ANCE
pertaining to
NODAL
swelter SWEAT,
ROAST, LANGUISH,
PERSPIRE, OP-
PRESSED
sweltering HOT,
HUMID
swerve YAW, SHIFT,
VEER, DEVIATE,
BEND, DIGRESS,
TURN, SHEER,
DEFLECT
swift FLEET, FAST,
QUICK, RAPID, BIRD
footed ALIPED,
ARIEL, MERCURY
swiftly APACE,
RAPID, FAST
Swift's *animal*
YAHOO
lady friend STELLA
pen name DRAPIER
swim DIP, CRAWL,
FLOAT, OVERFLOW,
ABOUND
swimmer LEANDER,
DUCK
swimming NATANT
bird See under
"bird"
swindle TRICK,
BAM, BUNCO,
GYP, CON, CHEAT,
COZEN, DECEIVE,
DUPE, GULL,
HOAX, VICTIMIZE,
CHOUSE, EMBEZZLE,
FORGE, (DE)FRAUD
swindler COZENER,
SHARK, SHARPER,
KNAVE, IMPOSTOR,
CHEAT, THIEF
swine HOG, PIG, SOW,
BOAR, SUID
breed ESSEX,
DUROC, CHESTER
female SOW, GILT
fever ROUGET,
CHOLERA
genus SUS
like PORCINE
male BOAR
young PIG, SHOAT
swineherd, *Odyssey*
EUMAEUS

swing SLUE, VEER,
SWAY, WAG, OSCIL-
LATE, HANG,
DANGLE, PIVOT,
TURN, LILT, SCOPE,
RANGE, WAVE,
WIELD, PLY, ROCK,
SHAKE
music JAZZ, JIVE
swink LABOR, TOIL,
WORK, GRIND,
DRUDGE
swipe STRIKE,
WIPE, RUB
swirl EDDY, CURL,
TWIST
Swiss, Switzerland
HELVETIA, SUISSE
archer TELL
author WYSS
canton BERN,
GLARUS, BASEL,
URI, VAUD, NYON,
TICINO, VALAIS,
ZUG
capital BERN(E)
card game JASS
city or town NYON,
SURAT, BIEL,
BERN(E), CHUR,
COIRE, LOCARNO,
BASLE, THUN
coin FRANC, BATZ,
HALLAR, RAPP
commune SION,
THUN, USTER,
VEVEY, CHUR,
AARAU
cottage CHALET
district CANTON
herdsman SENN
lake BIENNE,
LUCERNE, ZUG,
LEMAN (GENEVA),
MORAT, THUN
measure SAUM,
ELLE, IMMI, IMI,
POT
mountain(s) ALPS,
SENTIS, TODI, JURA,
DOM, RIG(H)I,
EIGER, ADULA
pass GEMMI,
SIMPLON
peak RIGI
poet AMIEL
political division
URI
river AAR(E),
REUSS, SAANE, THUR
scientist HALLER
theologian VINET

town See "city"
above
tunnel SIMPLON
switch TWIG, ROD,
CANE, BIRCH,
SPRIG, SHUNT,
SHIFT, BEAT, WHIP,
FLOG
switchback CHUTE,
TURN
switchman SHUNTER
Switzerland *See*
"Swiss"
swivel PILOT, TURN,
SWING, TRAVERSE,
HINGE
swollen TUMID,
TURGID, BLOATED,
BOLLEN, BULBOUS,
EXPANDED, PROUD
swoop DESCEND,
SEIZE, SOUSE,
POUNCE, DART
sword BILBO, DIRK,
FOIL, PATA,
BLADE, BRAND,
SABER, SABRE,
CUTLAS(S),
BAYONET, RAPIER,
ESTOC, SCIMITAR,
KUKRI, YATAGHAN
ancient ESTOC,
TUCK
Arthur's EXCALIBUR
blade, heel TALON
curved SABER,
SCIMITAR
cutting CUTLASS
dueling EPEE,
FOIL
dummy PEL
fencing EPEE, FOIL
finest steel TOLEDO
handle HAFT, HILT
heel TALON
heraldry BADELAIRE
Highland CLAY-
MORE
long thin RAPIER
loop for FROG
Malay CREESE
matador's
ESTOQUE, ESTOC
medieval ESTOC,
FALX, FALCHION
Norse myth. GRAM
of death MORGLAY
of God KHALED
of mercy CURTEIN
of St. George
ASKELON

of Siegfried GRAM,
BALMUNG
oriental SCIMITAR,
SIMITAR
pole GLAIVE
shaped ENSATE,
ENSIFORM,
XIPHOID, GLADIATE
short DIRK,
BAYONET, KUKRI
Turkish YATAGHAN
two-edged PATA
two-handled
SPADONE, SPADROON,
ESPADON
weakest part
FOIBLE
swordfish DORADO,
ESPADON
swordsman's *stake*
PEL
sworn to secrecy
TILED
sybarite EPICURE,
VOLUPTUARY,
SENSUALIST
sycamine MULBERRY
sycophant FLUNKY,
SPANIEL, PARASITE,
TOADY, LEECH,
SPONGE, ACCUSER,
SLANDERER, IN-
FORMER, TALE-
BEARER, FLATTERER
syllable, *accented*
THESIS (formerly),
ARSIS
added to word
PREFIX, SUFFIX
Buddhist OM
last ULTIMA
last but one
PENULT
last but two
ANTEPENULT
lengthening of
ECTASIS
music TRA
omission of last
APOCOPE, APOCOPA-
TION
omit, omission
ELIDE, ELISION,
SYNCOPE
pertaining to
DACTYLIC
short MORA
shortening of
SYSTOLE
unaccented
ATONIC, THESIS

syllabus APERCU,
PRECIS, ABSTRACT,
TABLE, DIGEST,
ABRIDGMENT,
OUTLINE, EPITOME,
LIST, SUMMARY,
COMPEND(IUM),
SYNOPSIS, BREVIARY
syllogism LEMMA,
EPICHIREMA,
EPICHEIREMA
series of SORITES
sylph PIXIE, ELF,
FAY *See* "fairy"
sylvan deity PAN,
FAUN, FAUNUS,
SATURN, SATYR
symbol OM, TOKEN,
PALM, EMBLEM,
SIGN, TOTEM,
MARK, BADGE,
BUTTON, TYPE,
MOTIF, FIGURE,
ENSIGNE
mathematical DIGIT,
NUMBER, FIGURE,
OPERAND, PLUS,
MINUS, EQUAL
of authority MACE,
FASCES, BADGE,
STAR, INSIGNE,
STRIPE
*of early Christian
church* ORANT
symmetrical SPHER-
ICAL, REGULAR,
EVEN, ROUND,
PROPORTIONAL,
BALANCED, EQUAL
anti ANTIMERE
sympathetic HU-
MAN, KIND, TEN-
DER, WARM, CON-
GENIAL, COMPAS-
SIONATE
sympathy CONSENT,
PITY, CONDOLENCE,
BENEVOLENCE,
COMPASSION, COM-
MISERATION, HEART
lack of DYSPATHY
symptom NOTE,
SIGN, TOKEN, MARK,
ALARM, WARNING,
BADGE, INDICA-
TION, FEVER
synagogue SHUL
ancient founder
EZRA
officer PARNAS
pointer YAD

synancioid fish
LAFF
syncope ELISION,
FAINT
syne AGO, SINCE
synodontoid fish
TIRU
synopsis ABSTRACT,
DIGEST, EPITOME,
CONSPECTUS, BRIEF,
PRECIS, APERCU,
SUMMARY, SYL-
LABUS, OUTLINE
Syracuse *master*
DION
Syria(n), *ancient
name* ARAM
bear DUB(B)
buried city DURA
capital, ancient
ANTIOCH
city or town
HOMS (EMESA)
god HADAD, GAD,
RIMMON
Hebrew name
ARAM
king HAZAEL
metal cloth ACCA
script PESHITO,
SERTA
sect DRUSE
weight COLA,
ZURLO
Syringa LILAC,
SHRUB
Syro-Phoenecian
goddess of love
ASTARTE
sun god BAAL
syrup HONEY, SOR-
GHUM, MAPLE,
TREACLE
system ISM, METHOD,
ORDER, RULE,
REGIMEN, PLAN,
SCHEME, DESIGN,
MODE, ARRANGEMENT
geological TRIAS
of rule REGIME
of rules CODE
of worship CULT
systematics TAXON-
OMY
syzygy DIPODY
szopelka OBOE

T

T TEE, TAU
taa PAGODA
tab FLAP, PAN,

STRIP, LABEL, TAG,
TONGUE, LATCHET,
AGLET, AIGLET,
CHECK, BILL
shoe LATCHET,
LACE, STRAP,
AIGLET, AGLET
tabard CAPE,
MANTLE, CLOAK,
JACKET, GOWN,
COAT
tabby cloth MOIRE,
MOREEN
tabby moth *genus*
AGLOSSA
taberna BOOTH,
TENT, TAVERN,
SHOP
tabernacle KIRK,
TEMPLE, CHURCH,
TENT
table BOARD, DESK,
FOOD, CHART,
LIST, ROLL,
ROSTER, ROTA,
CANON, POSTPONE,
STATEMENT,
SYNOPSIS
calculating
ABACUS
centerpiece
EPERGNE
cloth for wiping
FILE, NAPKIN
communion ALTAR
game POOL
linen NAPERY
philosopher
DEIPNOSOPHIST
three-legged
TRIVET, TRIPOD
workman's SIEGE,
BENCH
tableau PICTURE,
SCENE, PORTRAIT,
TABLE, LIST
tableland MESA,
PLATEAU, PLAIN,
PAMIR
Central Asia
PAMIRS
S. Africa KAROO
tablet PILL,
LOZENGE, TROCHE,
PAD, STILE, SHEET,
LEAF, MEMORIAL,
PLAQUE, SLAB
stone STELE, SLAB
symbolic PAX
taboo, tabu BAN,
BAR, INTERDICT,

FORBID, CENSURE,
PROHIBIT
tabor DRUM, ATABAL,
TAMBOURINE,
TIMBREL, CAMP,
FORT
tacit SILENT, IM-
PLIED, INFERRED,
UNDERSTOOD
taciturn RESERVED,
MUTE, DUMB,
CLOSE, CURT,
SILENT, RETICENT
tack SECURE, AN-
NEX, NAIL, LAVEER,
JIBE, BASTE, YAW,
PATH, JOIN
glazier's BRAD
tackle TRY, ATTACK,
GRAPPLE, GEAR,
TOOLS, OUTFIT,
YOKE, PULLEY, STOP,
GRASP, PLAYER
tacky DOWDY,
SEEDY, STICKY
tael, *1/10th* MACE
taffeta SAMITE,
FABRIC, CLOTH,
SILK
taffy BLARNEY,
FLATTERY, CANDY
tag RAG, FRAZZLE,
STUB, TAB, FLAP,
LABEL, TAIL, LOOP,
APPEND, JOIN,
GAME
metal AIGLET,
AGLET
Tagalog MALAYAN
child BATA, ANAC
good MABUTI
peasant TAO
mother INA
wine ALAC
Tahiti *apple* HEVI
canoe PAHI
capital PAPEETE
centipede VERI
god TAAROA
robe MARO
Tai *See* "Thailand"
tail CAUDA, SCUT,
END, TAG, FOLLOW,
TRAIL, DOG, AP-
PENDAGE, REAR,
SHADOW, PENDANT
boar's WREATH
furry SCUT
having a CAUDATE
pertaining to
CAUDAL
short SCUT, BUN

without ACAUDAL,
ACAUDATE, ANUROUS
amphibian family
RANIDAE, FROG,
TENREC
tailleurs AMPHIBIAN,
ANURA, FROGS
tailor SARTOR,
DRAPER, FASHION,
MAKE, FIT
iron GOOSE
lapboard PANEL
taint BLEMISH,
CONTAMINATE,
CORRUPT, STAIN
tainted BAD
Taiwan FORMOSA
Taj Mahal *site* AGRA
take NAB, OCCUPY,
ACCEPT, BAG,
ADOPT, GRAB, HOG,
USURP, CATCH,
STEAL, EMBEZZLE,
RECEIVE, SEIZE,
GRASP, CARRY, COP,
ARREST, TOTE,
SWALLOW, GAIN,
ENDURE, PHOTO-
GRAPH, CAPTURE,
CAPTIVATE
advantage of
ABUSE, MISUSE
away HEAVE,
WREST, ADEEM,
REMOVE
back RECANT,
RETRACT, RETURN
off DOFF, FLIGHT,
FLEE, BURLESQUE,
MIMIC, APE
possession SEIZE,
ESCHEAT
talapoin GUENON,
MONK, MONKEY
talc AGALITE,
STEATITE, SOAP-
STONE, POWDER
tale GESTE, YARN,
RECITAL, CONTE,
MYTH, LIE, FICTION,
FABLE, STORY,
SAGA, NOVEL,
LEGEND, ANECDOTE,
NARRATIVE
adventure
GEST(E)
bearer QUIDNUNC,
BLABBER, GOSSIP,
TATTLER
medieval LAI
Norse SAGA

of sorrow JERE-
MIAD
traditional SAGA
talent FLAIR,
GENIUS, TURN,
GIFT, CRAFT, BENT,
ART, SKILL, APTI-
TUDE, ABILITY,
ENDOWMENT,
FACULTY, KNACK
1/60 of MINA
taliera PALM, TARA
talipot PALM
talisman AMULET,
CHARM, FETISH,
GRIGRI, PHYLACTERY
talismanic MAGICAL
stone AGATE
talk SPEECH, AD-
DRESS, LECTURE,
SERMON, DISCUSS,
LANGUAGE, DIALECT,
LINGO, BLABBER,
GAB, CRACK, HARP,
CHAT, PALAVER,
SPEAK, PRATE,
SPIEL, RUMOR, RAVE,
RANT, CHIN,
BLATHER, DROOL,
DRIVEL, PRATTLE,
COLLOQUY, CON-
VERSE, DISCOURSE,
PARLANCE, CON-
VERSATION
freely DESCANT
talking *bird See*
under "bird"
horse See under
"horse"
tall HIGH, LOFTY
tallow SUET, LARD,
SEVUM, FAT,
GREASE
tree CERA
tally MATCH, AGREE,
SUIT, POINT, SCORE,
SQUARE, RUN,
NOTCH, GIBE, JIBE,
EQUAL, LIST
Talmud *commentary*
GEMARA
parts in GEMARA,
MISHNAH
title ABBA
talon CLAW, FANG,
NAIL, HAND, FOOT
Talos' *slayer*
DAEDALUS
tam BERET, CAP
tamarack LARCH,
TREE

tamarisk salt tree
ATLE(E)
tambourine DAIRA,
TABOR, TIMBREL,
WEIGHT
vibrant effect
TRAVALE
tame MILD, DOMES-
TICATE(D), CIVI-
LIZE(D), SUBDUE(D),
SUBJUGATE(D),
OVERCOME, TRAIN,
VAPID, DULL,
INERT, GENTLE,
DOCILE, HARMLESS
"Taming of the Shrew"
character
BAPTISTA, SLY,
GREMIO, TRANIO,
BIANCA, KATHERINA
(KATE)
tamper TINKER,
ALTER, MEDDLE,
MOLEST, INTERFERE,
MACHINATE, PLOT,
BRIBE
tan BUFF, BRONZE,
TAW, DUN, CHASTISE
tanager LINDO,
HABIA, BIRD
tang SAVOR, TASTE,
ZEST, BITE, ODOR,
FLAVOR
Tanganyika *moun-*
tain MERU
peak KIBO
Tangier *measure*
KULA, MUDD
tangle TRAP, SNARE,
SHAG, KNOT, SLEAVE,
MAT, WEAVE,
CONFUSE, PERPLEX,
EMBROIL, CON-
FUSION, DERANGE
tangy RACY, SPICY,
ZESTFUL
Tanis ZOAN
tank VAT, POND,
POOL, RESERVOIR,
VEHICLE
weapon BAZOOKA
tankard HANAP,
GOBLET, FACER,
VESSEL
tanker OILER, SHIP
tanner's *gum* KINO
shrub SUMAC,
SUMACH
solution AMALTAS,
BATE
substance SPLATE
Tanoan INDIAN,

ISLETA *See*
"Indian(s), Pueblo"
tantalize PLAGUE,
TEASE, VEX, TOR-
MENT, ANNOY,
HARASS, EXCITE
Tantalus' *daughter*
NIOBE
father ZEUS
son PELOPS
tantivy RAPID,
SWIFT, HASTE(N),
SPEEDY, GALLOP
tantrum FIT, SPELL,
ANGER, RAGE, HUFF,
MIFF, CAPRICE
Taoism, *right conduct*
TE
tap COCK, SPILE,
PLUG, FAUCET,
SPIGOT, SOUND,
RAP, DANCE, BAR,
STRIKE, PUNCTURE,
NUT, TOUCH
tape, *needle*
BODKIN
taper SHARPEN,
DIMINISH, LESSEN,
CANDLE, NARROW
tapered TERETE
tapering CONICAL,
FUSIFORM, SPIRED
piece SHIM
tapestry FABRIC,
DOSSER, ARRAS,
TAPIS, TEXTILE
comb REED
kind GOBELIN,
BRUGES
warp thread LISSE
tapeworm TAENIA,
CESTODE, ENTOZOAN
genus TAENIA
tapioca *like food*
SALEP
source CASSAVA
tapir ANTA, SELA-
DANG, SALADANG
tappet LEVER, CAM
Tapuyan INDIAN, GE
tar PITCH, SAILOR,
MARINER, GOB,
JACK, SALT, SEAMAN
See under "sailor"
mineral BREA,
MALTHA, PITCH
product of CREOSOL,
CREOSOTE
Taṛaf *subdivision*
DHER

Taranaki *volcano*
EGMONT
tarboosh TURBAN,
FEZ
tardy SLOW, LATE,
LAGGING, DILATORY
tare VETCH, WEED,
PLANT
target MARK, AIM,
BUTT, GOAL, BIRD,
OBJECTIVE
tarnish TAINT,
STAIN, DULL, DIM,
SPOT, DISCOLOR,
SOIL, DISGRACE
taro GABI, PLANT,
KOKO
dish (paste) POI
root(s) EDDO(ES)
W. Indies TANIA
tarpon SABALO,
ELOPS, FISH
genus ELOPS
related to CHIRO
tarradiddle LIE, FIB
tarry STAY, WAIT,
IDLE, LAG, DALLY,
DELAY, DETAIN,
LINGER, (A)BIDE,
REMAIN
tarsus ANKLE,
SHANK, HOCK,
TALUS
Tarsus *governor*
CLEON
tart PIE, ACID, SOUR,
ACERB, PERT,
SAUCY, CURT,
BLUNT, SEVERE,
CUTTING, PIERCING,
PAINFUL
tartan PLAID, SHEET,
FABRIC, BOAT
Tartar HU, TURK,
TATAR
dynasty WEI, KIN
horseman COSSACK
king KHAN
militiaman U(H)LAN
nobleman MURZA
tribe SHOR, TOBA,
SHORTZY
tartar ARGOL, CAL-
CULUS
Tartarus HADES
Tartini's *B-flat* ZA
Tartufe *maid*
DORINE
task STINT, CHORE,
JOB, METIER, FEAT,
DEED, DUTY,
WORK, CHARE,

LABOR, DRUDGERY,
TOIL, UNDERTAKING,
ENTERPRISE, AS-
SIGNMENT, BUSINESS
punishing PENSUM
taken to LECTURE,
SCOLD
Tasmania *cape*
GRIM
capital HOBART
tassel THRUM,
CORDELLE, TAG
taste SUP, SIP,
PALATE, SAMPLE,
SAVOR, SAPOR,
SMACK, TANG,
RELISH, GUSTO,
ZEST, LIKING,
APTITUDE
absence of AGEUSIA,
AGEUSTIA
delighting the
FRIAND
French SOUPCON
strong TANG
tasteful NEAT,
SAPID, SAVORY,
FINE, ARTISTIC,
DAINTY, DELICATE,
NICE, FIT, APT,
FLAVORFUL
tasteless WATERY,
FLAT, VAPID, IN-
SIPID, VULGAR,
INARTISTIC
tasty *See* "tasteful"
Tatar *See* "Tartar"
tatter RAG, PATCH,
SHRED
tattle DIVULGE, TELL,
BLAB, GOSSIP, TALK,
PRATE, CHATTER,
PRATTLE, JABBER,
INFORM
tattler BLAB,
QUIDNUNC, GOSSIP,
TELLTALE
tau *cross* ANKH,
CRUX, TACE,
CRUCIFIX
taunt SNEER, JEER,
GIBE, JIBE, TWIT,
QUIP, DERIDE, RAG
taurine BOVINE,
BULL, TAURUS
taurotragus ELAND,
OREAS
taut FIRM, TENSE,
TIDY, SNUG, TIGHT,
STRETCHED
tautog CHUB,
BLACKFISH

tavern CABARET,
INN, PUB, TAP,
HOTEL, SALOON,
ROADHOUSE
Spain TAMBO
taw MARBLE, TAN,
TOUGHEN, HARDEN,
SHOOTER
tawdry TINSEL,
LOUD, CHEAP,
VULGAR, GAUDY,
FLASHY, SHOWY
tawny TIGRINE,
RUBIATE, SWARTHY,
SWART, OLIVE,
DUSKY, TANNED,
FULVID
tax DUTY, LEVY,
ASSESS, CESS, SCAT,
SCOT, CUSTOM,
TRIBUTE, FINE,
TAILAGE, TOLE,
EXCISE, FEE, RATAL,
EXACTION, STENT,
IMPOST, STRAIN,
LOAD, BURDEN
assess on default
DOOMAGE
church TITHE
feudal TALLAGE,
TAILAGE
on hides HIDAGE,
salt GABELLE
Scot. STENT
anc. tribal CRO,
GALNES
taxite LAVA
taxus *genus* YEW
tazza BOWL, CUP,
VASE
tea TISANE, CAM-
BRIC, CHA, YERBA,
KAT, PEKOE, BOHEA
See "reception"
Asia CHA, OOLONG,
CONGO(U), HYSON
See "China" *below*
black PEKOE
bowl CHAWAN
box CADDY
Brazil holly MATE,
YERBA
caffein in THEIN(E)
China HYSON,
CONGO(U), BOHEA,
OOPAK, OOLONG
drug in THEIN(E)
extract ADENINE
Formosa OOLONG
genus THEA
Labrador LEDUM
plant KAT, THEA

rolled CHA, TCHA
table TEAPOY
urn SAMOVAR
weak BLASH
teacake SCONE
"Tea House" *location*
NAHA, OKINAWA
teach EDIFY, COACH,
SCHOOL, PRIME,
TUTOR, DRILL,
MONITOR, TRAIN,
NURTURE, LECTURE,
DIRECT, CONDUCT,
GUIDE, COUNSEL,
DISCIPLINE, IN-
STRUCT, ENLIGHTEN,
EDUCATE, INFORM,
INDOCTRINATE
teachable AMENABLE,
PLIANT, APT,
FITTING
teacher PEDAGOG(UE),
MASTER, PUNDIT,
DOCTOR, DOCENT,
SCRIBE, INSTRUCTOR,
LECTURER, PRE-
CEPTOR, EDUCATOR,
PREACHER
Jewish RAB(BI)
Moslem ALIM,
MULLA, MULLAH,
MOLLA(H)
teachers' *group* NEA
teal DUCK, FOWL
team JOIN, PAIR,
SPAN, BROOD, SIDE,
NINE, GROUP,
YOKE, SQUAD, CREW,
BRACE, SET
tear DROP, BEAD,
SNAG, RENT, REND,
RIP, RIVE, SPLIT,
SEPARATE, DIS-
RUPT, PART, RACE,
FLY, BINGE, TOOT,
SPREE, JAG, SLIT,
SLASH, LACERATE
French LARME
heraldry LARME
up by roots ASSART,
ARACE, PLUCK,
ARACHE
tear-droplike figure
LARME
tearful MOIST,
MAUDLIN, WEEP-
ING, SAD, SORROWFUL
pertaining to
LACRIMAL
tease PESTER, TWIT,
BAIT, VEX, BEG,
JOSH, ANNOY, IR-

RITATE, RAG,
RIB, BANTER,
HECTOR, NAG,
WORRY, FRET,
CHAFF, GALL,
TANTALIZE, TOR-
MENT
teasel BONSET,
HERB, PLANT
ted SPREAD, SCATTER
tedious PROSY,
DRY, DULL, DREARY,
SLOW, FLAT, TIRE-
SOME, IRKSOME,
BORING, PEEVISH,
LONG
tedium ENNUI,
BOREDOM
teem ABOUND,
OVERFLOW, POUR,
SWARM
teenager's *party*
HOP, PROM, BASH
teeter ROCK, SWAY,
SEESAW *See*
"shake"
teeth TUSKS,
IVORY, GRINDERS,
DENTURES
cavity tissue PULP
*concretion or deposit
on* TARTAR,
CALCULUS
decay or disease of
CARIES
double GRINDERS,
MOLARS
false DENTURE,
PLATE
grinding of
BRUXISM
hard tissue DENTINE
having all alike
ISODONT
long-pointed
TUSKS, FANGS
sockets ALVEOLI
without EDENTU-
LOUS, EDENTATED
teetotum TOY, TOP
tegula ALULA, AP-
PENDAGE, TILE
tegument ARIL,
CORTEX, SKIN,
MEMBRANE, COAT,
COVER
tela MEMBRANE,
TISSUE
telamon ATLAS,
COLUMN, PILASTER
Telamon's *brother*
PELEUS

companion HER-
CULES
son AJAX
telegram CABLE,
DISPATCH, WIRE,
MESSAGE
telegraph *code*
MORSE
instrument, part of
ANVIL, TAPPER, KEY
inventor MORSE
teleost fish APODA,
EEL
telephone CALL,
PHONE, DIAL, BUZZ,
RING
inventor BELL
telephotographic lens
ADON
telescope GLASS,
FOLD, COLLAPSE,
ABRIDGE, LENS
site PALOMAR
television VIDEO, TV
cable COAXIAL
interference SNOW
network ABC, CBS,
NBC
tell RECITE, SAY,
RELATE, OWN,
SPEAK, NARRATE,
DIVULGE, EXPLAIN,
UTTER
on someone PEACH,
SQUEAL, BLAB
telling POTENT,
SOUND, VALID,
CONGENT, IM-
PORTANT, EFFEC-
TIVE, TIMELY,
RELEVANT,
PERTINENT
Tell's *home* URI
telluride HESSITE,
ALTAITE
telson SOMITE,
SEGMENT
of king crab PLEON
temblor TREMOR,
QUAKE
temerarious RASH,
RECKLESS
temerity NERVE,
BRASS, GALL,
CHEEK, RASHNESS,
BOLDNESS
temper HUMOR,
VEIN, MOOD, DIS-
POSITION, RAGE,
DANDER, TANTRUM,
MIX, MODERATE,
ANNEAL, NATURE,

SOFTEN, MOISTEN,
(AT)TUNE, ADJUST,
MITIGATE
temperament CRASIS,
DISPOSITION, MOOD,
NATURE, CONSTITU-
TION
tempest GALE,
BLAST, ORAGE,
STORM, RAGE,
TUMULT, TURMOIL,
WIND, EXCITEMENT
Cuba BAYAMO
"Tempest, The,"
character in
ALONSO, ANTONIO,
PROSPERO, CALIBAN,
ARIEL, IRIS, JUNO,
CERES
temple HUACA,
CHURCH, NAOS,
TABERNACLE
See "church"
builder, early Jewish
MICAH
chief chamber
NAOS, CELLA
Chinese PAGODA,
TAA
gateway TORII
Hawaii HEIAU
inner CELLA
Mexico TEOCALLI
Mohammedan
MOSQUE, MOSK
pertaining to
HIERON
portico NARTHEX
Shinto SHA
Siam VAT, WAT
vestibule PRONAOS
tempo TIME, BEAT,
RATE, PACE, PULSE,
RHYTHM, SPEED
rapid PRESTO
very slow GRAVE
temporary TRAN-
SIENT, PASSING,
EVANESCENT,
FLEETING
tempt (AL)LURE,
DECOY, ENTICE,
SEDUCE, BAIT,
INDUCE, INCITE
temptation LURE,
ENTICEMENT
tempus TIME
ten DECAD
acres DECARE
century note
GRAND
decibels BEL

gallon hat SOM-
BRERO
prefix DEC(A),
DEKA
square chains ACRE
thousand MYRIAD,
GRAND
years DECENNIUM,
DECADE
tenacity PLUCK,
GRIT, SAND, METTLE,
NERVE, ADHESIVE-
NESS, COHESIVE-
NESS
tenant RENTER,
LESSEE, VILLEIN,
OCCUPANT
farm CROFT
feudal VASSAL,
SOCAGER, LEUD(E)
neglect to pay rent
CESSER
tribute, French
CENS
tend SHIELD,
GUARD, NURSE,
FOSTER, CARE, FEED,
NURTURE, MINISTER,
SERVE, AID, LEAN,
MIND, WATCH,
BEND
tendency TREND,
BENT, DRIFT,
BIAS, TENOR, TURN,
INCLINATION,
PROCLIVITY, PRO-
PENSITY
tender KIND, SOFT,
PRESENT, OFFER,
SORE, BID, PROFFER,
BOAT, WARM,
MILD, MONEY,
GENTLE, YOUTHFUL,
WEAK, DELICATE,
SENSITIVE, SYM-
PATHETIC
music AMOROSO
tending toward an
end TELIC
tendon SINEW,
THEW
broad, flat
APONEUROSIS
tendril STIPULE,
CURL, CLIMBER,
ROOT, SHOOT,
BRANCH, CIRRUS,
SPRIG
tenfold DECUPLE,
DENARY
Tennessee *county*
CLAY, DYER,

GILES, KNOX,
LAKE, POLK,
RHEA, SCOTT
first governor
SEVIER
old name FRANK-
LIN
tennis *champion*
RIGGS, TRABERT,
HOAD
cup DAVIS
like game FIVES
point ACE
score LOVE,
DEUCE
stroke LOB, CUT
Tennyson *heroine*
MAUD, ENID
tenon COG, TOOTH,
TUSK
tenor DRIFT,
INTENT, PURPORT,
MOOD, EFFECT,
COURSE, TREND,
IMPORT, SINGER,
CARUSO
violin ALTO
tense VERB, RAPT,
TAUT, RIGID, STIFF,
FIRM, HARD, TIGHT
grammar PRESENT,
FUTURE, PAST,
PERFECT
tenseness RIGOR
tensile DUCTILE
tent PROBE, LODGE,
SHELTER, COVERING,
CANOPY, MARQUEE
circular YURT
covering FLY,
TILT
dweller SCENITE,
KEDAR, NOMAD,
ARAB
India PAWL
Indian TEPEE,
TEEPEE, WIGWAM
large field
MARQUEE
Maker OMAR
Mogul YURT
tentacle FEELER,
HAIR, PALP,
TENDRIL
without ACEROUS
tenterhooks STRAIN,
ANXIETY
on AGOG, ANXIOUS
tenth, *combining*
form DECI
part TITHE

tenuity POVERTY,
INDIGENCE, RARITY,
THINNESS
tenuous THIN, SLIM,
SLENDER, FINE,
DELICATE, WEAK,
RARE
tenure of land
SOCAGE
tepid WARM, MILD
tequila MESCAL,
DRINK
teraph IMAGE, IDOL
terbium symbol TB
terebinth TEIL,
TREE, TURPENTINE
teredo BORER,
SHIPWORM, WORM
tergal BACK, DORSAL,
ABORAL
tergiversate
EQUIVOCATE, LIE,
SHUFFLE, DESERT,
SHIFT, RETREAT
term PERIOD,
BOUNDARY,
SESSION, NAME,
LIMIT, SEMESTER,
WORD, RHEMA,
END, BOUND,
DURATION, EX-
PRESS, STATE, CALL
in office TENURE
math. SINE, COSINE
of life SANDS, AGE
school SEMESTER
termagant SHREW,
VIRAGO, VIXEN,
SCOLD
terminal DEPOT,
STATION, END,
FINAL, LAST,
POLE
negative CATHODE
of a leaf APICULUS
positive ANODE
terminate CLOSE,
END, CEASE,
FINISH, STOP
termination END,
SUFFIX, AMEN,
BOUND, FINIAL, FINIS
termite ANAI,
ANAY, ANT
tern PIRR, KIP,
NODDY, STARN,
DARR, FOWL
genus ANOUS,
STERNA
Hawaii NOIO

ternary TRIAD,
THREEFOLD,
TRIPLE
terpene NEROL
terra EARTH, SOD,
LAND
terrace DAIS
PLATEAU, BERM(E),
BANK, BALCONY,
GALLERY, PORTICO,
PLAIN, STREET,
WAY
in series PARTERRE
terrapin EMYD,
TORTOISE, TURTLE
order CHELONIA
red-billed SLIDER
terrestrial EARTHY,
GEAL, MUNDANE,
WORLDLY, HUMAN
terrible DIRE, FEAR-
FUL, GRIM,
SHOCKING,
FRIGHTFUL,
HORRIBLE, AP-
PALLING, DREADFUL
The IVAN
terrier DANDIE,
SKYE, IRISH,
SCOTCH, FOX, DOG
terrify COW, PANIC,
APPAL(L), DAUNT,
FRIGHTEN
territory GROUND,
AREA, REGION,
DISTRICT
terror APPREHENSION,
ALARM, FRIGHT,
DREAD
terrorist GOON,
ALARMIST
terse CRISP, SHORT,
BRIEF, CURT,
PITHY, SUCCINCT,
LACONIC, COM-
PACT, CONCISE
tertiary period
PLIOCENE,
NEOCENE
tesselate TILE,
MOSAIC
test TRIAL, TRY-
(OUT), INQUIRY,
ASSAY, EXPERIMENT,
EXAM(INE),
QUIZ, ESSAY,
ORAL, ANALYSIS,
CRITERION,
STANDARD, NORM
orally QUIZ
pot CRUCIBLE
testament WILL,

COVENANT,
DISPENSATION
*New or Old See
under* "new" *or*
"old"
testator LEGATOR
tester CEIL,
CANOPY, PROVER
testifier DEPONENT,
WITNESS
testify DEPOSE,
DEPONE, AVOW,
AVER, STATE,
DECLARE, SWEAR,
AFFIRM
testimonial TOKEN,
SYMBOL, TRIBUTE,
EVIDENCE, WAR-
RANT, RECOMMEN-
DATION, COMMEN-
DATION
testy TOUCHY,
CRANKY, CROSS,
CHOLERIC, FRETFUL,
PEEVISH,
PETULANT,
IRASCIBLE, IRRITA-
BLE
tether BIND, LEASH,
TIE, CONFINE,
LIMIT, RESTRAIN,
ROPE, SCOPE,
RANGE
Tethys' *brother*
CRONUS
father URANUS
husband OCEANUS
tetrachord, *music*
MESON, NETE
tetrad FOUR,
QUADRIVALENT
tetter ECZEMA,
FRET, HERPES,
LICHEN, PSORIASIS
Teutonic *anc. tribe*
UBI(I)
barbarian GOTH
divinity, god See
"god" *or* "goddess"
legendary hero
OFFA
letter RUNE
people GEPIDAE
tewel BORE, FUNNEL,
TUYERE, LOUVRE,
HOLE, VENT
Texas *city* WACO,
ENNIS, AUSTIN,
DALLAS, ABILENE,
LAREDO
county SABINE,
FRIO, KNOX, BEE,

BELL, BEXAR, CLAY,
CASS, COKE, ERATH,
GAIZA, GRAY, HALE,
HALL, HAYS, HILL,
HOOD, HUNT, JACK,
KENT, KERR, KING,
LAMB, LEE, LEON,
LYNN, PECOS, POLK,
RAINS, REAL, RUSK,
WARD, WEBB, WISE,
WOOD
fever carrier TICK
flowering shrub
BARETTA
island PADRE
river PECOS,
NEUCES, BRAZOS,
TRINITY
shrine ALAMO
university RICE,
TCU, SMU
text TOPIC, THEME,
SUBJECT, VERSE,
VERSION, BOOK
textile CLOTH,
FABRIC, FIBER
dealer MERCER
worker REEDER,
REEDMAN
texture NAP, WALE,
WEB, WOOF, GRAIN,
WEAVE, QUALITY
Thackeray character
ESMOND, BECKY
(SHARP), AMELIA
Thailand SIAM,
TAI(S), THAI(S)
coin FUANG, ATT,
BHAT, TICAL,
BIA, CATTY
garment PANUNG
group KUI
isthmus KRA
language LAO, TAI
measure SESTI,
KEN, SAT, RAI, SEN,
SOK, YOT(E), COHI,
CAN, NIOU, KEUP,
LEENG, TANAN,
TANG, VOUAH
native LAO
river MENAM,
NAN, MUN, CHI,
YOM, PING
twins CHANG, ENG
weight CATTY,
COYAN, BAT,
FUANG, GRANI,
PAY
thalassic PELAGIC,
MARINE, NERITIC,
OCEANIC

Thalia's *sister* ERATO
Thames *at Oxford*
ISIS
estuary sandbank
NORE
Thanatos *personified*
DEATH
thanks GRACE,
GRAMERCY,
GRATITUDE
thankless UN-
GRATEFUL
person INGRATE
that WHICH, WHO, SO,
AS, WHAT, BECAUSE
is ID EST, IE
thatch *grass* NETI
palm NIPA
thaumaturgy MAGIC
theatre, theater
ODEON, ODEUM,
LEGIT, STAGE,
ARENA, DRAMA,
OPERA, CINEMA,
MOVIE
award TONY,
OSCAR
classic LYCEUM
curtain TEASER
district RIALTO
extra SUPE,
SUPER
floor PIT
Greek ODEON,
ODEUM
group ANTA
low class GAFF
part of SCENA,
STAGE
stall LOGE
theatrical VIVID,
ARTIFICIAL, STAGY,
DRAMATIC,
SHOWY
art HISTRIONICS
entertainment
REVUE, SHOW
role INGENUE,
PART
tour ROAD
Thebes, *blind sooth-
sayer of* TIRESIAS
deity MUT, AMEN,
AMENT, AMON
founder CADMUS
goddess MUT
king CREON,
OEDIPUS, LYCUS
LAIUS
one of 7 against
TYDEUS
theca CELL,

CAPSULE, CASE,
SHEATH, SAC
theme MOTIF, TEXT,
THESIS, TOPIC, SONG,
PAPER, ESSAY,
ARTICLE, MATTER
then SOON, NEXT,
SO, THEREFORE,
BESIDES
music POI
theodolite ALIDADE,
TRANSIT
theologian DIVINE,
CALVIN, LUTHER,
CLERIC *See*
"clergyman"
theorbo LUTE
theoretical
ACADEMIC,
SPECULATIVE,
IDEAL
power ODYL(E)
theory ISM, PLAN,
IDEA, DOCTRINE,
SPECULATION,
HYPOTHESIS,
SCHEME, PRINCIPLE
therapy CURE,
TREATMENT,
MEDICINE
there YON, THAT,
THENCE, YONDER,
THITHER, AT
therefore THEN,
ERGO, SO, HENCE,
SINCE, ACCORDINGLY,
CONSEQUENTLY
thersitical ABUSIVE,
SCURRILOUS
thesaurus LEXICON,
CYCLOPEDIA
Theseus' *father*
AEGEUS
thesis ESSAY,
THEME, ARTICLE,
PAPER, TREATISE,
MONOGRAPH,
DISSERTATION
opposite to ARSIS
thespian ACTOR,
ACTRESS, TRAGIC,
PLAYER, TROUPER,
MIME, DRAMATIC
Thessaly *mountain*
OSSA
Thetis' *husband*
PELEUS
theurgy MAGIC
thew MUSCLE,
SINEW
thick HEAVY,
CROWDED, SQUAT,

COMPACT, CLOSE,
CHUMMY, CON-
DENSED, DENSE,
DULL, TURBID,
ROILY, GRUMOUS,
CRASS, GROSS,
SOLID, NUMEROUS
thicken INSPISSATE,
CLOT, CURDLE,
CAKE, SOLIDIFY,
DRY, STIFFEN,
HARDEN
thicket COPSE, BOSK,
JUNGLE, COVERT,
HEDGE, BRUSH,
COPPICE, CHAPARRAL,
GROVE, SPINNEY
thickness LAYER,
PLY, STRATUM
thief FAGAN,
FILCHER, PIRATE,
CROOK *See*
"bandit"
thieve's *Latin* SLANG,
CANT
thigh HAM, FEMUR,
MEROS, COXA
combining form
MER(O)
thill SHAFT
thimble SPUT, CAP,
RING, BUSHING,
FERRULE
rigger CHEAT,
SWINDLER
thin DIM, RARE,
LATHY, LANK,
SCRAGGY, FINE,
WATER, SHEER,
BONY, MEAGER,
DILUTE, LEAN,
SPARSE, TENUOUS,
RAREFY, LESSEN,
GAUNT, SPARE,
SLIM, SLENDER,
SCANTY
disk WAFER
layer FILM
Man's dog ASTA
wife NORA
muslin MULL
plate SHIM, TILE,
TAGGER
scale LAMELLA,
LAMINA, FLAKE
toned REEDY, PIPING
thing(s) ENTITY,
BEING, DEED, ACT,
ITEM, GEAR, TRAPS,
AFFAIR, OBJECT,
ARTICLE, NOUN, MAT-
TER

done ACTA
found TROVE
law RES, CHOSE
of little value
STIVER, TRINKET
to be done AGENDUM,
AGENDA
thingamajig GADGET,
GISMO, GIZMO
think OPINE,
IDEATE, CONSIDER,
TROW, MUSE, REASON,
BROOD, MULL,
SUPPOSE, RECALL,
RECOLLECT, IN-
TEND, BELIEVE,
FANCY, WEIGH,
STUDY, GUESS,
JUDGE, INFER,
MEDITATE, PLAN,
SCHEME, ANALYZE,
IMAGINE, ESTIMATE,
COGITATE, CON-
TEMPLATE
thinness TENUITY
third *day* TERTIAN
in music TIERCE
power CUBE
row CEE
stage AUTUMN
thirsty ARID, DRY,
PARCHED, KEEN,
AVID, EAGER
this HOC, HERE
one HAEC
Thisbe, *loved by*
PYRAMUS
thistledown TUFTS,
PAPPUS
thistle *family*
ARNICA, COSMOS
like plant genus
CARLINA
thither THERE,
YON(D), TO,
TOWARD
thole FULCRUM,
OARLOCK, PIN,
FID, BEAR, ENDURE
Thomas opera
MIGNON
thong KNOUT,
STRAP, WHIP,
ROMAL, LASH,
LEASH, QUIRT
ox-hide RIEM
shaped LORATE
S. Africa RIEM
Thor *See* "Thor's"
thorax CHEST
thorn BRIAR, BRIER,
SPINE, STOB,

PRICKLE, VEXATION,
TROUBLE
apple METEL,
DATURA
back RAY, ROKER,
SKATE, FISH
combining form
SPINI
Jerusalem RETAMA
like SPINA,
SPINATE
thorofare WAY,
AVENUE, PIKE *See*
"street"
thoroughwort
BONESET, PLANT
thorp HAMLET,
VILLAGE, TOWN
Thor's *father* ODIN
stepson ULL
wife SIF
thought IDEA,
CONCEPT, NOTION,
VIEW, BELIEF,
COGITATION,
CONCEPTION,
OPINION, CEREBRA-
TION, REFLECTION
force PHRENISM
thousand MIL,
MILLE
combining form
MILLI, KILO
dollars GRAND
headed snake
SHESHA, SESHA
years CHILIAD,
MILLENNIUM
thousandth
MILLESIMAL
of an inch MIL
Thrace *musician*
ORPHEUS
town SESTOS
thrall ESNE, SERF,
VASSAL, PEON *See*
"slave"
thrash TROUNCE,
BELABOR, CANE,
DRUDGE, FLAIL, TAN,
FLOG, LAM,
FLOURISH, DRUB,
WAVE
thread LISLE, REEVE,
STAMEN, LINE,
CORD, TWINE,
FILAMENT, FIBER
ball CLEW, CLUE
combining form
NEMA, MIT(O)
cross WOOF,
RETICLE, WEFT

guiding CLEW
lengthwise WARP
like NEMALINE,
   FILOSE, LINEAR,
   FILAR
linen INKLE
process HAIR
shoe latchet LINGEL,
   LINGLE, LACE
silk TRAM
surgical SETON
testing device
   SERIMETER
worm FILARIA,
   NEMATODE
threadbare TRITE,
   SHABBY, COMMON-
   (PLACE), SERE,
   MEAN, THIN,
   SCANTY, WORN,
   HACKNEYED
threat MENACE, DARE
three TER, TRIA,
   TRIO, TRI, TRIN, III
dimensional SOLID,
   STEREO
fold TERNAL,
   TREBLE, TRINE,
   TERNATE
group of TERN,
   TRIAD, TRIO
in one TRIUNE, OIL
knotted TRINODAL
of a kind LEASH
penny THRIP
prefix TER, TRI(O)
spot TREY
toed bird STILT
threnody LAMENT,
   REQUIEM, DIRGE
thresh FLAIL, BEAT,
   BEST
threshold SILL,
   GATE, EVE, DOOR,
   ENTRANCE, BEGIN-
   NING
thrice, *prefix* TER,
   TRI
thrifty PRUDENT,
   SAVING, ECONOMICAL
thrill STIR, FLUSH,
   QUIVER, TREMOR,
   VIBRATE, KICK,
   BOOT
thrilling ELECTRIC,
   VIBRATING, MOVING
thrive WAX,
   PROSPER, GROW,
   SUCCEED, FLOURISH
throat GORGE,
   GULLET, NECK,
   MAW, GULA,

TRACHEA, FAUCES,
   PHARNYX, INLET,
   PASSAGE
affection ANGINA
Latin GULA
pertaining to GULAR,
   ESOPHAGEAL,
   JUGULAR
soreness or swelling
   FROG
to clear HAWK
throb PULSE, ACHE
   See "beat"
throe PANG, PAIN,
   RACK, STITCH,
   DISTRESS, SPASM *See*
   "ache"
throne ASANA,
   SEAT, CHAIR,
   SOVEREIGNTY,
   EXALT
throng HOST, CREW,
   ARMY, HORDE,
   SWARM, PRESS,
   CROWD, MULTITUDE
   See "mob"
throstle THRUSH,
   BIRD
through BY, VIA,
   PER, WITH, OVER,
   AMONG, FINAL,
   FINISHED, INTO,
   ACROSS, DURING
combining form
   DI(A)
throw WRAP
   SPREAD, QUILT,
   COP, CAST, HEAVE,
   TOSS, PEG, FLING,
   SLING, PITCH, HURL,
   KEST
obliquely DEAL,
   TOSS, SKEW
out BOUNCE, FIRE,
   SACK, EJECT,
   EVICT, DISBAR,
   UNFROCK
thrum TASSEL
thrush OUZEL,
   OUSEL, ROBIN,
   MAVIS, VEERY,
   MISSEL, THROSTLE,
   SHAMA, BIRD
Bengal ant NURANG
disease APHTHA,
   APTHA, SOOR
genus TURDUS
ground PITTA
Hawaii OMAO,
   OLOMAO
India SHAMA

song VEERY,
   MAVIS
Wilson's VEERY
thrust JAB, DIG, DART,
   ONSET, STAB,
   ENTER, PIERCE,
   PROPEL, PUSH,
   SHOVE, SHEAR,
   STRESS, STRAIN
aside SHOVE, SHUNT
thud BUMP, BEAT,
   BLOW
thug GUNMAN,
   RUFFIAN, YEGG,
   GOON *See* "bandit"
thulium *symbol* TM
thumb POLLEX,
   DIGIT, HANDLE,
   PHALANX
pertaining to
   THENAR
Thummin, *associated*
   with URIM
thump BANG, KNOCK,
   BEAT, PUNISH
thunder THOR, ROLL,
   RANT, NOISE, ROAR
thunderfish ROACH,
   RAAD
thurible CENSER
thurify CENSE,
   SCATTER
Thuringia *city* JENA,
   WEIMAR, GERA,
   GOTHA
thus HENCE, SIC, SO,
   YET, ERGO,
   CONSEQUENTLY
Latin ITA, SIC
thwack CLUB,
   POMMEL, MAUL,
   RAP, THRASH,
   WHACK
thwart BAFFLE, BALK,
   SPITE, FRUSTRATE,
   OBSTRUCT *See*
   "foil"
tiara CROWN,
   FRONTLET, CORNET,
   MITER
Tibet SITSANG
antelope GOA
beer CHANG
capital LASSA
   (LHASA)
chief POMBO
city LASSA
   (LHASA)
Lama DALAI
ox YAK
priest LAMA

ruminant TAKIN, SEROW
sheep See under "sheep"
wild ass KIANG
wild cat MANUL
tibia CNEMIS, SHIN, BONE
pertaining to CNEMIAL
Tibur, *anc., name for* TIVOLI
tic TWITCH(ING), JUMP, JERK
Malay LATA(H)
tick ACARID, MITE, KED, INSECT, CLICK, TAP, COVER, SOUND
fowl ARGAS
genus ARGAS, CIMEX, IXODIDAE, IXODES
sheep KED
S. Amer. CARAPATO
ticket LIST, SLATE, NOTE, SLIP, BALLOT, COUPON, CARD, TAG, LABEL, PASS, SCHEDULE, PLAN
sell illegally SCALP
tickle TITILLATE, EXCITE, PLEASE, AMUSE, DIVERT
tidal *flow* ESTUARY, SURGE, BORE, EBB, EAGRE, NEAP
wave EAGRE, AIGRE
tide FLOW, CUR-RENT, FLOOD, CHANCE, STREAM, TIME, EBB, NEAP
low NEAP
tiding(s) ADVICE, NEWS, SLOGAN, REPORT, WORD, GOSPEL, EVANGEL, RUMOR
tidy PRIM, SPRUCE, NEAT, TED, TRIM, SNUG, TRIG, ORDERLY
make REDD
tie LINK, BOND, ASCOT, BIND, DRAW, TRUSS, STALEMATE, TETHER, LIGATE, EQUAL, BEAM, RIVET, MOOR, JOIN, ATTACH, LINK, MARRY, CRAVAT, RELATION
as a sail TRICE

breaking game RUBBER
up ROPE, TRUSS, BIND
tied EVEN
tier RANK, ROW, SERIES, LAYER
Tierra del Fuegian ONA
tiff HUFF, PET, SPAT, QUARREL, BOUT *See* "brawl"
tiffin LUNCHEON, REPAST, TEA
tiger SHER, SHIR, FELINE, CAT
American JAGUAR
family FELIDAE
S. Amer. CHATI
tight SNUG, TAUT, DRUNK, STINGY, CLOSE, TENSE, FIRM, RIGID, CHEAP
person PIKER, NIGGARD
tighten LACE, STRAIGHTEN, TAUTEN, STRETCH, DRAW, CONTRACT
as a drum FRAP
nautical FRAP
tightwad PIKER, SKINFLINT, MISER
til SESAME, PLANT
tile, *curved* PANTILE
large SLAB
marble memorial DALLE
pattern MOSAIC
pertaining to TEGULAR
roofing PANTILE
tiler DOORKEEPER, KILN, OVEN
till (UN)TO, WHILE, BEFORE, FARM, PLOW, CULTIVATE, DRAWER, TRAY
tillage, *fit for* ARABLE
tilled land ARADA
tiller HELM, FARMER, SHOOT, SAPLING, PLOWMAN, HANDLE, LEVER
tilt HEEL, LIST, TIP, JOUST, CANT, SLOPE, CAREEN, SLANT, LEAN, DUEL
timber WOOD, LUM-BER, LOG(S), BEAM, FOREST,

TREES, MATERIAL(S)
convex CAMBER
decay ROT
ship's SPAR, BITT
support CORBEL, BEAM, T-BAR
tree See under "tree"
wolf LOBO
timbre TONE, RING, CLANG, PITCH, QUALITY
time PERIOD, SEASON, AGE, DATE, SPELL, EPOCH, ERA, TENSE, TEMPO, BEAT, DURATION, LEISURE
before EVE
being NONCE
division EON, YEAR, DAY, HOUR, EST, CST, WST, MST
error in order of ANACHRONISM
fast LENT, DST
in music TEMPO, BEAT, LILT, RHYTHM
measure of See under "measure"
out RECESS, BREAK, FIVE
past AGO, YORE
pertaining to ERAL
timely EARLY, PAT, PROMPT, TOPICAL, MEET, LUCKY, OPPORTUNE, SEA-SONAL
timepiece CLOCK, WATCH, HOROLOGUE, SUNDIAL, CHRONOM-ETER
water CLEPSYDRA
timid WEAK, PAVID, SCARY, FAINT, SHEEPISH, HENNY, TREPID, SHY, MOUSY, AFRAID, WARY, CHARY, FEARFUL, TIMOROUS, COWARDLY, SHRINKING, RETIRING
timon HELM, RUDDER
"Timon of Athens"
character LUCIUS, CAPHIS, TITUS, FLAVIUS
Timor *coin* AVO

timorous *See* "timid"

timpano DRUM, KETTLEDRUM

tin STANNUM, METAL, PRESERVE, CAN, COAT, INFERIOR, SPURIOUS
box TRUMMEL
fish TORPEDO
foil for mirrors TAIN
mine STANNERY
Pan Alley group ASCAP
pertaining to STANNIC
sheet LATTEN
symbol SN

tinamou YUTU, BIRD

tinct IMBUE, SHADE, HUE, TINT

tincture DASH, TOUCH, TINGE, TRACE, TINT, IMBUE, MIXTURE

tinder AMADOU, PUNK, KINDLING, FUEL

tine BIT, PRONG, TOOTH, POINT, FANG, SPIKE

tined, *three* TRIDENTATE

tinge TOUCH, HUE, STREAK, SHADE, TAINT, DASH, TRACE, STAIN, TINT, CAST, COLOR, DYE, IMBUE, SMACK

tint NUANCE, SHADE, COLOR, TONE, STAIN, HUE, CAST, DYE, BLUSH, TINGE

tintinnabulum BELL

tiny MINUTE, PETITE, TEENY, WEE, SMALL, LITTLE
creature ATOMY, MINIMUS

tip END, LIST, CANT HEEL, POINT, CUE, HINT, CAREEN, APEX, TILT, TOE, SLANT, SLOPE, LEAN, EXTREMITY, SUMMIT, GRATUITY, BONUS

tippet AMICE, SCARF, MUFFLER, FUR, CAPE

tipple NIP, GILL, SIP, TOPE, GUZZLE, DRINK

tippler TOPER, PIGEON, WINER, SOT, SOAK, STRICKER

tipster TOUT

tipsy REE, DRUNK, GROGGY, MERRY, TIGHT

tiptop APEX A-ONE, ACE, STAR, GOOD

tirade SCREED, SPEECH, HARANGUE

tire BORE, TUCKER, FAG, IRK, JADE, FATIGUE, WEARY, EXHAUST, SHOE, TREAD, PALL
casing SHOE
saver RECAP, RETREAD
support RIM

tissue BAST, FAT, TELA, NET, FABRIC, WEB, FIBER, MEAT, TEXTURE
connecting TENDON, STROMA
decay CARIES, ATROPHY
hardening SCLEROSIS
pertaining to TELAR
weblike TELA, PLEXUS

Titan OCEANUS, HYPERION, ATLAS, MISSILE, RHEA, IAPETUS, THEMIS, COEUS, TETHYS, THEIA, PHOEBE, CREUS, MNEMOSYNE, GIGANTIC, CRONUS (SATURN), PROMETHEUS *See* "giant"
female DIONE, RHEA
Hindu myth. BANA
parents of URANUS, GAEA, GE

Titania's *husband* OBERON

titanic HUGE, ENORMOUS, VAST, GIGANTIC, COLOSSAL *See* "huge"

titanium, *principal ore* ILMENITE

tithe TENTH, TAX, DECIMAL, LEVY, RATE, TOLL, CESS

titi MONKEY

titivate SPRUCE, CULTIVATE, TIDY

titlark PIPIT, BIRD

title DEED, NAME, TERM, MUNIMENT, MARK, CAPTION, RANK, CLAIM, RIGHT, HEADING, HEADLINE, INSCRIPTION, APPELLATION, EPITHET, COGNOMEN, DESIGNATION, TITULUS, LABEL, DUKE, DAME, LADY, LORD, BARON
church PRIMATE, BISHOP
eastern AGA, BABA, BWANA
of dignity SIR, ESQUIRE, SIRE, DAN, DON
of respect AGA
Spain DON, DONA, SENOR
Turkey AGHA, BABA

titled DEEDED, NAMED

titmouse TOMTIT, NUN, YAUP, BIRD

Tito BROZ, JOSEPH

titter TEEHEE, GIGGLE, LAUGH

tittle GOSSIP, IOTA, JOT, WHIT, BIT, MITE, ATOM, WHISPER

tittup CAPER, PRANCE

titular (COG) NOMINAL

titulus TITLE

Titus Andronicus *queen* TAMORA

Tivoli, *anc. Roman name* TIBUR

Tlingit TONGAS, TLINKIT, INDIAN

tmesis DIACOPE

T.N.T. TRINITROTOLUENE, TOLUENE, TROTOL, EXPLOSIVE

to AT, FORWARD, ON, THITHER, FOR, UNTO, TOWARD(S), NEAR, CLOSE

be, French ETRE
Latin ESSE
each his own SUUM
CIQUE
the point AD REM
wit NAMELY,
SCILICET,
VIDELICET, VIZ
toad AGUA, PIPA,
BUFONID, RANA,
FROG
fish SAPO, SARPO
largest AGUA
order of ANURA
tongueless genus
AGLOSSA
tree HYLA
toady PAWN,
LEECH, FAWN,
COWER
toast BROWN,
WARM, TAN,
SKOAL, PLEDGE,
ROAST, CELEBRATE,
BREAD
tobacco CAPORAL,
UPPOWOC, LATAKIA,
CAPA, KNASTER,
VUELTA, PLANT,
BURLEY
ash DOTTLE,
DOTTEL
chew QUID
coarse CAPORAL
kiln OAST
left in pipe DOTTLE,
DOTTEL
low grade SHAG
plant, heart of leaf
RATOON
pouch DOSS
shreds SHAG
toby CIGAR, MUG,
DOG
tode SLED
toe DACTYL,
PHALANX, DIGIT,
OBEY
great HALLUX
small MINIMUS
toga ROBE, TRABEA,
CANDIDA, GOWN,
GARB
Arab ABA
together UNION,
MASS, (CON)-
JOINTLY, MUTUALLY,
ACCOMPANYING
prefix CON, COM
toggery, togs GARB,
CLOTHES, DRESS

toggle COTTER, KEY,
BOLT, ROD, PIN,
SCREW
Togo *seaport* LOME
town HO
toil WORK, PLOD,
LABOR, DRUDGE(RY),
GRIND, TURMOIL,
TRAVAIL, EXERTION,
ACTIVITY
toilet case ETUI,
ETWEE
toils SNARE, NET,
TRAP, WEB, GRIP
token SCRIP, TICKET,
AMULET, BADGE,
INDEX, SIGN,
OMEN, MARK,
PLEDGE, PAWN,
INDICATION,
EVIDENCE,
MEMORIAL,
SOUVENIR, ME-
MENTO, KEEPSAKE,
REMINDER, TESSERA,
SYMBOL, EMBLEM
of respect ACCOLADE
taker IRT
Tokyo, *old name*
YED(D)O
tolerable SOSO, IN-
DIFFERENT, PASSA-
BLE, MIDDLING,
FAIR, SUPPORTABLE,
ENDURABLE, AC-
CEPTABLE, SATIS-
FACTORY
tolerate ENDURE,
SUBMIT, SUFFER,
STAND, ALLOW,
ABIDE, BEAR,
BROOK, PERMIT,
CONDONE, ACCEPT
toll LEVY, RATE,
CESS, DUTY, TITHE,
FEE, TAX, TAILAGE,
RING, KNELL, IM-
POST, EXCISE, SOUND
Toltec *anc. capital*
TULA
tolypeutine APAR,
ARMADILLO
Tom Tulliver's *river*
FLOSS
tomb MASTABA,
CRYPT, GRAVE,
LAIR, CENOTAPH,
CATACOMB
for bones of dead
OSSUARY
Moslem TABUT

tomboy HOYDEN,
ROMP, GIRL
tomcat GIB
Tom of Lincoln
BELL
tomorrow MANANA,
MORNING, MORROW
tone(s) KEY,
ENERGY, VIGOR,
SOUND, PITCH,
TINT, SHADE, HUE,
FEEL, SAVOR,
QUALITY, MOOD,
ATTITUDE, STYLE,
SPIRIT, COLOR,
HARMONY
artificial unit NIL
down MUTE
eight DIATONIC
eighth UNCA
lack of ATONY,
MUTE
rhythmical
CADENCE
series OCTAVE
variation NUANCE
toneless ATONIC,
MUTE, DEAF
Tonga island TOFUA
tongue DIALECT,
TAB, FLAP, GLOSSUS,
LORRIKER, IDIOM,
VOICE, LANGUAGE,
PRATE, PROJECTION,
GLOSSA
bone HYOID
combining form
GLOSSO
fish SOLE
pertaining to
GLOSSAL
projection on
PAPILLA
tip CORONA
wagon or vehicle
NEAP
tonguelike process
LIGULA
tonic PEP, VIGOR,
ELIXIR, ROBORANT,
BRACER, POP, SODA,
REMEDY, HEALTHY
Tonkin *capital*
HANOI
native THO
tonsil AMYGDALA,
GLAND
too ALSO, AND, ELSE,
OVER, BESIDES,
THEN, LIKEWISE,

EXCESSIVELY,
VERY, OVERLY
much NIMIETY
tool(s) PAWN, RAT,
PUPPET, DUPE,
REBEL, DEVICE,
GADGET, AGENT,
IMPLEMENT,
CATSPAW, APPARA-
TUS, GEAR, IN-
STRUMENT
ability to use
CHRESTIC
bookbinder's
GOUGE
boring AWL, BIT,
AUGER, DRILL,
GIMLET, REAMER
box CHEST, KIT
cleaving FROW,
FROE, AX(E),
WEDGE, HATCHET
cutting DIE, AX(E),
SAW, ADZ(E),
RAZOR, KNIFE,
SHEARS
edge BIT
engraver's BURIN
flat SPATULA
garden TROWEL,
HOE, RAKE, SPADE
grass SICKLE,
SCYTHE
kit ETUI, CHEST
marble worker's
FRAISE
metal DOLLY,
SWAGE, LATHE
mining GAD, PICK
shaping LATHE,
SWAGE
theft of RATTEN
trimming AX(E),
SAW
tooth CANINE, TUSK,
COG, INCISOR, MOLAR,
FANG, DENS, APPE-
TITE *See* "teeth"
canine CUSPID
cavity or decay
CARIES
combining form
ODONTO
gear wheel COG
grinding surface
MENSA
having but one
MONODONT
like DENTAL,
DENTATE
long TUSK, FANG
molar WANG

part of DENTINE,
ROOT, CUSP, TRIGON
point CUSP
projecting SNAG,
BUCK
pulp NERVE
sockets ALVEOLI
wheel GEAR, COG,
CAM
toothache ODON-
TALGIA
toothed SERRATED,
DENTATE
toothless EDENTATE,
EDENTULOUS
top APEX, VERTEX,
EXCEL, CAP, LID,
ACE, CREST,
SUMMIT, ACME,
HEAD, COVER, TUFT,
BEST, TOY, RIDGE,
TIP
of suit ACE
ornament EPI,
FINIAL
tops A-ONE, ACE,
BEST, EXCELLENT,
SUPREME
tope RIG, STUPA,
SHARK, WREN,
SHRINE, GROVE,
GARMENT, BOAT
(JUNK)
toper BOOZER, SOT,
DRUNK, SOAK,
TIPPLER
topi HELMET
topic ITEM, THEME,
TEXT, HEAD, SUB-
JECT, QUESTION,
ISSUE, POINT
topical THEMATIC,
LOCAL
topics THEMATA
topnotch A-ONE,
CREST, ACE
topsy-turvy ASKEW,
AWRY, INVERTED
tor CRAG, PINNACLE,
PEAK
tora TETEL, ANTELOPE
torbernite URANITE
torch CRESSET, LAN-
TERN, LAMP, FLARE,
FLASH (LIGHT)
toreador, torero
BULLFIGHTER
torment TEASE, BAIT,
DEVIL, AGONY,
PLAGUE, BADGER
See "rack"
tormina COLIC

torn RIVEN, RENT,
SPLIT
torpedo MINE, PE-
TARD, MISSILE, DETO-
NATOR, WEAPON
fish RAY
front end NOSE
torpor SLEEP, COMA,
STUPOR, DULLNESS,
APATHY, LETHARGY,
INDIFFERENCE,
STAGNATION
torque STRAIN,
TWIST, COLLAR,
NECKLACE
torrent FLOOD, FLOW,
STREAM, SPATE,
CASCADE, DOWNPOUR
torrid SULTRY, ARID,
TROPICAL, HOT,
PARCHING, SCORCH-
ING, BURNING
tortoise EMYD, TUR-
TLE, TERRAPIN
genus EMYS
gopher or land
MUNGOFA
marsh genus EMYS
order CHELONIA
shell CARAPACE
W. Indies HICATEE
torture MARTYR,
PAIN, FLAY, CRU-
ELTY, SUFFERING,
TORMENT *See*
"rack"
toss ROLL, BANDY,
TAVE, FLING, FLIP,
HURL *See* "throw"
tosspot DRUNKARD,
SOT, TOPER
total ADD, UTTER,
ENTIRE, WHOLE, ALL,
MASS, SUM, FIGURE,
COMPLETE, AGGRE-
GATE, CAST, FOOT
totem XAT, POLE, EM-
BLEM, FIGURE
totter REEL, ROCK,
SHAKE, WAVER,
WEAKEN
toucan ARACARI,
TOCO, BIRD
touch FEEL, ABUT,
SHAVE, PALP, IM-
PINGE, TINGE, SHADE,
DASH, VEIN, MEET,
TIG, CONTACT,
TRACE, BORDER,
IMPRESS
combining form
TAC

examine by PAL-
PATE
France SOUPCON
organ for PALP,
FEELER, ANTENNA
pertaining to HAP-
TIC, TACTILE
perceptible by PAL-
PABLE, TACTILE
touchan *See* "toucan"
touchdown GOAL,
SCORE
touchhole VENT
touching ATTINGENT,
TANGENT, SAD, PITI-
FUL, MOVING, TEN-
DER, PATHETIC
touchstone BASANITE,
TEST, CRITERION
touchwood AMADOU,
PUNK, TINDER
pertaining to AGARIC
tough WIRY, WITHY,
STIFF, STOUT,
STURDY, STRONG,
HARD, ROWDY, BULLY,
FIRM, RUFFIAN,
TENACIOUS, HARD-
BOILED, SEVERE
toughen TAW, SEASON,
INURE, TRAIN
toupee WIG
tournament CONTEST,
JOUST, MATCH,
MEET
tourniquet BANDAGE,
GARROT
tow DRAW, HAUL,
PULL, DRAG, TUG, FI-
BER, FLAXEN, YEL-
LOW, BARGE
rope TEW
towai KAMAHI, TREE
toward(s) LATERAD,
TO, NEAR, GAIN, FAC-
ING
center ENTAD
exterior ECTAD
mouth ORAD
prefix AD, OC, OB
stern AFT, ABAFT,
ASTERN
towel CLEAN, DRY,
WIPER, HUCK, RAG,
LINEN, CLOTH
fabric TERRY, LINEN
tower SPIRE, DOME,
CUPOLA, BABEL,
MINARET, TURRET,
TOR, TORRION,
MOUNT, SOAR, (A)-
RISE, SURGE

Buddhist TOPE
circular DOME
glacial ice SERAC
India MINARET
MINAR
kind of IVORY
medieval DONJON
pyramidal SIKHRA,
SIKHARA, SIKARA
small TURRET
small round RON-
DEL
Spain ATALAYA
spirical STEEPLE,
CUPOLA
towhee CHEWINK,
FINCH, BIRD
town, pertaining to
OPPIDAN, CIVIC,
URBAN
township DEME, DIS-
TRICT, AREA
townsman RESIDENT,
CIT, CITIZEN
at Eton College OP-
PIDAN
toxin VENOM, POI-
SON, VIRUS, BANE,
RICIN
alkaloid ABRIN,
BRUCIN, VENOM
protein ABRIN
toxophilite CUPID,
EROS
toy PLAY, FONDLE,
PET, TRIFLE, DALLY,
DOLL, BAUBLE, TOP,
IMITATION
trabea TOGA
trace HINT, SCENT,
TINGE, VESTIGE,
TRACK, TRAIL, SIGN,
MARK, TOKEN, DRAW,
SKETCH, CLEW, FOL-
LOW, COPY, SPOOR,
DELINEATE
trachyte DOMITE
track RUT, FOOT-
PRINT, TRAIL, SCENT,
WAKE, RAILS, TURF,
PATH, COURSE, OR-
BIT, TRACE, VESTIGE,
MARK, SPOOR, SLOT
animal's PUG, MARK,
SPOOR, SLOT
deer SLOT, SPOOR
railroad SIDING
ship's WAKE
tract LOT, AREA,
ZONE, STRETCH,
SECTOR, TREATISE,
REGION, BOOK

tractate TREATISE,
DISCUSSION, ESSAY
trade SWAP, JOB,
DEAL, CRAFT, METIER,
COMMERCE, OCCU-
PATION, PURSUIT,
BUSINESS, EXCHANGE,
SALE, SELL, ART,
WORK, BARTER,
TRAFFIC
France METIER
trademark BRAND,
SYMBOL
trader BROKER,
AGENT, MERCHANT,
MONGER
tradesman ARTISAN,
CIT, MERCHANT
trading post MART,
STATION, FORT, CAN-
TEEN
tradition CODE, CUS-
TOM, MORES, DOC-
TRINE, USAGE, MYTH,
(FOLK)LORE
traduce DEFAME,
SLANDER
traffic COMMERCE,
TRADE, DEALINGS,
BUY, SELL
tragacanth GUM,
TREE, SHRUB
tragopan PHEASANT,
FOWL
trail SPOOR, ABATURE,
DOG, DRAG, FOIL,
LAG, PUG, SLOT,
TRAPES, TRAIPSE,
TRUDGE, FOLLOW
train COACH, SERIES,
SET, TEACH, SCHOOL,
DRILL, AIM, LEVEL,
DIRECT, SUITE,
CHAIN, NURTURE,
REAR, CORTEGE,
RETINUE, BREED,
DRESS, SEQUEL,
PREPARE
fast LIMITED
overhead EL
slow LOCAL
track SIDING
underground TUBE,
METRO, SUBWAY
trained BRED, EDU-
CATED, AIMED
traitor RAT, KNAVE,
JUDAS
tramp STEAMER,
HOBO, NOMAD,
BEGGAR, TREAD,
VAGRANT, VAGABOND,

BUM, PAD, STROLL,
STEP, HIKE
trance RAPTUS,
SWOON, DAZE,
STUPOR, ECSTASY,
COMA, HYPNOSIS
tranquil SERENE,
EASY, LOWN, PEACE-
FUL, CALM, STILL,
SMOOTH, SOFT,
GENTLE, MILD,
UNDISTURBED, QUIET
transact DEAL, DO,
TREAT, CONDUCT,
NEGOTIATE, ACCOM-
PLISH, EXECUTE
transaction DEED,
DEAL, ACT(UM),
SALE, AFFAIR, PRO-
CEEDING, EVENT,
ACTION
transcend EXCEL,
OUTDO, CAP, EXCEED,
OVERSTEP, SURPASS
transcript RECORD,
COPY, APOGRAPH,
CARBON, REPLICA,
DUPLICATE, WRITING
transept PLAGE, ARMS,
WINGS
transfer CEDE,
CARRY, SHIFT,
DEED, ALIEN,
DEPUTE, GRANT,
GIVE, (RE)MOVE,
LET, CONVEY,
TICKET, PASS
design DECAL
legal DEED, LEASE,
ALIENATION
transfix HOLD,
PIERCE, NAIL,
IMPALE, PIN, STAB,
SPEAR
transform TURN,
ALTER, CONVERT,
CHANGE
transgress OFFEND,
DISOBEY, INFRINGE,
VIOLATE, INFRACT,
SIN, ERR
transition FLUX,
CHANGE, RISE, FALL,
PASSAGE
translate CHANGE,
INTERPRET, RENDER,
DECODE, TRANSFORM
translation PONY,
PHASE, VERSION,
PARAPHRASE
transmit CARRY,
BEAR, SEND, MAIL,

POST, WIRE, PHONE,
TRANSFER, CONDUCT,
REMIT, ENCLOSE
transmitting device
MIKE, RADIO, TV
transparent (PEL)
LUCID, CRYSTAL,
CLEAR, DIAPHANOUS,
LIMPID, LUMINOUS,
LUSTROUS, TRANS-
LUCENT, OBVIOUS
mineral MICA,
QUARTZ
transport SHIP,
VESSEL, RAPT(URE),
DELIGHT, CARRY,
BEAR, EXILE,
BANISH, MOVE,
TRANSFER
transportation
TICKET, RIDE, PASS,
CONVEYANCE
Transvaal *gold region*
RAND
legislature RAAD
Transylvanian *city*
CLUJ
trap NAIL, NET, PIT,
WEEL, GIN, SPRINGE,
TOIL, WEIR, WEB,
CREEL, CARRIAGE
See "snare"
fish WEIR, NET,
FYKE
trapshooting SKEET
trash RIFFRAFF,
JUNK, RUBBISH,
REFUSE, ASHES,
WASTE, DROSS,
NONSENSE,
BALDER-
DASH, DIRT
trashy WORTHLESS,
TRUMPERY, POOR,
USELESS, TRIFLING,
FLIMSY, PALTRY,
CHEAP
travel TOUR, MUSH,
TREK, WEND, TRIP,
MOVE, JOURNEY,
PEREGRINATE
pertaining to
VIATIC
traveler(s) NOMAD,
TOURIST, VIATOR,
PILGRIM
commercial AGENT,
DRUMMER, BAGMAN
company of CARAVAN,
SAFARI
traverse CROSS, FORD,
RANGE, PATROL,

DENY, REBUT, REFUTE,
PASS
rear PARADOS
travesty PARODY,
CARICATURE,
LAMPOON, MIMIC,
BURLESQUE, SATIRE
like PARODIC
trawl DRAGNET,
FISH, TROLL, NET
tray SALVER, HOD,
SERVER
treacherous *person*
JUDAS
treacle MOLASSES,
SYRUP
tread PAD, CRUSH,
DANCE, STEP, WALK,
TRAMPLE, PACE,
STAMP, TRAMP,
SOLE, TIRE
treadle PEDAL
treasure STORE,
HOARD, PRIZE,
CHERISH, VALUE,
ESTEEM, COIN,
GEMS, RICHES,
WEALTH, MONEY
treasurer BURSAR,
COMPTROLLER
treasury BANK,
BURSE, VAULT,
SAFE, CHEST, FISC,
EXCHEQUER, PURSE,
FUNDS, MONEY
treat DOSE, DEAL,
DOCTOR, MANIPULATE,
USE, PARLEY, CONFER,
NEGOTIATE, REGALE,
MANAGE, BARGAIN
badly FRAME,
MISUSE, MAN-
HANDLE, MALPRAC-
TICE
treatise BOOK, THESIS,
TRACT, ESSAY,
DISCOURSE, EXPO-
SITION
elementary DONET,
GRAMMAR, PRIMER
on fruit trees
POMONA
on trees SYLVA,
SILVA
preface to ISAGO-
GE
treatment USAGE,
REMEDY, THERAPY,
MANAGEMENT,
USE
treaty MISE,
PROTOCOL, (COM)-

PACT, CARTEL,
AGREEMENT
treble LATTEN,
SOPRANO, TRIPLE,
THREEFOLD
tree(s) TIMBER,
WOOD, TRAP, CORNER,
PEDIGREE, BOSCAGE,
FOREST
*Abyssinia, dried
flower* CUSSO
acacia BABUL,
SIRIS, COOBA(H)
Australia MYALL
Africa MOLI, AKEE,
BAOBAB, COLA,
OCHNA, SIRIS, BITO,
COPAIVA, SOKA,
ARTAR, ABURA, AFARA
alder ARN
genus ALNUS
algarroba CAROB,
CALDEN
allspice PIMENTO
apple SORB, SHEA
genus MALUS
ash ROWAN, SORB,
ARTAR, RONE *See*
"ash"
Asia OLAX, TI, ACLE,
DITA, SIRIS, BITO,
ASOK(A), MEDLAR,
ASAK, NARRA, BANYAN
aspen APS, POPLAR
Australia MYALL,
BOREE, MARARA,
GMELINA, WILGA
See under "Austra-
lia
babul GARAD
balsam TOLU *See*
"balsam"
poplar LIARD
bark TAN, CRUT
bay LAUREL
bee LINDEN
beech FAGUS, BUCK,
MYRTLE
Chile ROBLE
Bengal quince BEL,
BAEL
betel ARECA
birch BETULA
black gum NYSSA,
TUPELO
haw SLOE
branches RANAGE
Brazil ULE, UHLE,
ANDA, APA, HEVEA,
ARAROBA, WALLABA
buckwheat TITI

Buddhist sacred
PIPAL
bully BALATA
butter SHEA, FULWA,
PHULWARA
cabbage ANGELIN
(YABA)
candlenut KUKUI,
AMA, BANKUL
carica PAPAYA, PAW-
PAW
Cent. Amer. TUNO,
TUNU, AMATE,
CORTEZ, BANAK,
BALSA
oil EBO(E)
Ceylon TALA
Chile MUERMO
(ULMO), ROBLE
COLEU, PELU,
ALERCE, ALERSE
China GINKGO,
KINKAN, NIKKO,
KUMQUAT
cocoa CACAO
coffee CHICOT
coniferous FIR, PINE,
LARCH, TSUGA,
THUJA, CEDAR,
SPRUCE
coral DAPDAP
cordage SIDA
cotton, E. India
SIMAL
cottonwood ALAMO
custard SWEETSOP,
ANNOA, ATTA, ATES
dead RAMPIKE,
RAMPICK
devil DITA
devil's cotton ABROMA
dogbane species
APOCYNUM, DITA
dogwood genus
CORNUS
drupe bearing BITO
dwarf ARBUSCLE,
BUSH
dyewood TUA
E. Africa MOLI
E. India ACH, ASOKA,
BANYAN, DEODAR,
ALOE, POON, SAL,
TEAK, TOON, MEE,
NEEM, SIRIS, ACANA,
ABROMA, FIG
elm genus CELTIS,
ULMUS
eucalyptus GUM,
YATE
evergreen FIR, HOLM,
OLIVE, YEW, PINE,

MASTIC, CEDAR,
CAROB, SAVIN(E),
ABROMA, HOLLY
N. Zealand TARATA
exudation RESIN,
SAP, GUM, LATEX,
CHICLE
fabaceous AGATI
fig, sacred PIPAL
fir BALSAM
fir genus ABIES
Florida GOMART
flowering CATALPA,
TULIP, MIMOSA
forgetfulness LOTUS
fraxinus ASH
gamboge family
CALABA
genip wood LANA
genus MABA, CITRUS,
ULMUS, OWENIA,
ACER, TREMA,
STYRAX
gingerbread DOOM,
DUM
glasswort JUME,
KALI
grove TOPE
Guiana MORA, ICICA,
GENIP
Guinea AKEE
gum BABUL, BUMBO,
XYLAN, NYSSA,
BALATA, TUART,
TOOART
black NYSSA,
TUPELO,
haw SLOE
Hawaii KOA, OHIA,
MAJAGUA, HAU
hickory species
PECAN, CARYA
holly HOLM, ILEX
species YAPON,
YAUPON
honeyberry GENIP
India BANYAN, BEYR,
SAL, MAHWA, BEL,
DAR, TALA, ALUS,
AMPAC, TEAK,
SISSOO, PIPAL, DHAK,
TOON, SAIN, POON,
OADAL, NIM, NEEM,
KOKRA, ENG *See*
"E. India" *above*
Japan HINOKI, SUGI,
GINKGO, AKEKI, CYCAS
Javanese UPAS
Joshua YUCCA,
REDBUD
laurel BAY
light wood BALSA

lime TEIL, BASS,
LINDEN
linden LIN(N),
LIME, TEIL
live oak ENCINA
locust ACACIA, CAROB,
KOWHAI, COURBARIL
  pod CAROB
loquat BIWA
lotus SADR, JUJUBE
madder family
BANGCAL, CHINCONA
Malay OHIA, DUKU,
DURIAN, TERAP,
UPAS, LANSEH
Maori RATA
maple genus ACER
margosa NEEM, NIM
marmalade MAMEY,
CHICO, SAPOTE,
ACHRAS
Mediterranean
OLEA, CAROB
Mexico ABETO,
FUSTIC
  pine OCOTE, OKOTE,
  rubber ULE
mimosaceous SIRIS,
ACACIA, GAMA
moss USNEA, LICHEN
moth EGGER
mulberry, India
AAL, AL, ACH
  genus MORUS
N. Zealand AKE,
WHAU, HINAU,
KAURI, TOTARA,
TI, RATA, MAIRE,
PELU, PUKA, MIRO,
NGAIO, KIO
oak, Calif. live
ENCINA
  Calif. white ROBLE
  Europe HOLM
  holm HOLLY
  Jerusalem AMBROSE
oil EBO(E), MAHWA,
TUNG, POON
olive genus OLEA
palm See "palm"
palmyra TALA,
TALIPOT, BRAB
papaya CARICA,
PAWPAW, PAPAW
pea AGATI
pear PYRUS, SECKEL
  prickly NOPAL
pepperidge TUPELO
pertaining to
ARBOREAL
Philippine ANAGAP,
BETIS, TUA, YATE,

SUPA, ALLE, DAO,
DITA, IPIL, LIGAS,
IBA, LEBUR
pinaceous KAURI,
SEQUOIA
pine OCATE
  Asian MATSU
  beverage PINA
  China and Japan
  MATSU
  exudate RESIN
  family CEDAR,
  CONIFER
  grove PINETUM
  Mexico OCOTE,
  OKOTE
  Spain PINO
  strobile CONE
  tar extract RETENE
plane CHINAR,
PLATANUS
plum genus PRUNUS
  wild SLOE
poisonous SASSY,
BUNK, UPAS, HEM-
LOCK
Polynesia IPIL, TI
poon DILO
poplar ASPEN,
ABELE, ALAMO
quercus genus OAK
quinine CINCHONA
rain SAMAN, GENI-
SARO, ZAMAN
redbud JUDAS
resinous BALSAM,
PINE
rose family, Europe
MEDLAR
rowan ASH, SORB
rows of STICH
rubber PARA,
CAUCHO, ULE, SE-
RINGA
salt ATLE(E)
sandalwood ALGUM,
ALMUG
  N. Zealand MAIRE
sandarac ARAR
sapodilla SAPOTA
sassafras AGUE
science of SILVICS
service SORB
shade ASH, MAPLE,
OAK, ELM
shea KARITE
shoot LOT
soapbark QUILLAI
sour gourd BAOBAB
sour gum NYSSA,
TUPELO

S. Amer. EBO, CA-
CAO, APA, JUME, UM-
BRA, BALSA, CAOBA,
CHICHA, CLUSIA,
PEKEA, TALA, GAMA
spruce LARCH, EPI-
NETTE *See under*
"spruce"
stately PALM
strawberry ARBUTUS
swamp ALDER
tallow CERA
tamarack, Amer.
LARCH
tamarisk ATLE,
ATLEE
taxus genus YEW
thorn, Jerusalem
RETAMA
timber, China
KAYA
  forest ASH, RATA,
  OAK
  Hawaii KOA
  INDIA, DAR, SAL,
  BWA, KINO
  inferior ANAM
  N. Zealand RIMU,
  KAURI, RATA
  Pacific IPIL
  Philippine LA-
  NETE, AMAGA
  S. Amer. PEKEA,
  TALA
toad genus HYLA
Trinidad MORA
tropical COLA, CO-
LIMA, INGA, ANU-
BING, CYCAS, CLUSIA
  America BALSA,
  DALI, CEDRON,
  SAPOTA, PAWPAW,
  PAPAW
trunk BOLE, CABER
tupelo NYSSA
W. Africa AKEE,
BUMBO
W. Indies ACANA,
BALATA, SAPOTE,
GENIP, ANGELIN,
MORA, AUSU, BALSA,
CALABA, BONACE,
YACCA
willow OSIER
  genus ITEA
treeless *plain*
PAMPAS, LLANO,
TUNDRA, STEPPE,
PRAIRIE, SAVANNA(H)
treenail NOG, PIN,
SPIKE, PEG

trees, *to grub or clear of* ASSART
trefoil CLOVER, ARCH, MEDIC, PLANT
trellis ARBOR, ESPALIER, PERGOLA, LATTICE
tremble DODDER, JAR, QUAKE, THRILL *See* "shake"
tremendous GIGANTIC, TITANIC, HUGE, VAST, ALARMING, TERRIFIC *See* "huge"
tremulous ASPEN, QUAKY, WAVERING, TREMANDO, QUIVERING, AGITATED, NERVOUS
trench DITCH, FOSS(E), LEAT, MOAT, FURROW
trenchant KEEN, SHARP, BITING, CRISP, ACUTE, ACRID, CUTTING, CONCISE
trencher PLATTER, PLATE, VIANDS
trend DIRECTION, COURSE, SWING, TENDENCY, TENOR, DRIFT, TIDE, BENT, VEIN
trespass OFFENSE, INVADE, POACH, ENCROACH, SIN, TRENCH, TRANSGRESS
triad TRINARY, TRIO, THREE, TRINE, TRINITY
trial CROSS, DOOM, ESSAY, TEST, HEARING, EXAM(INATION), AFFLICTION, AGONY, EFFORT, ORDEAL, EXPERIMENT, LAWSUIT
pertaining to EMPIRIC
triangle TRINITY, TRIGON
draw circle in ESCRIBE
insert GORE
side of LEG
type SCALENE, OBTUSE
unequal SCALENE
triangular *insert* GUSSET, GORE
piece in sail GORE
sail LATEEN, SPINNAKER

shaped DELTOID, SCALENE
tribe CLAN, RACE, FAMILY, HORDE, SIB, SEPT, GROUP, CLASS, ASSEMBLAGE
Gaul REMI
symbol of TOTEM
tribunal FORUM, BAR, COURT, SEAT, BENCH
tribute GIFT, OVATION, HOMAGE, TAX *See* "tax"
trick ARTIFICE, PRANK, DO, GULL, FLAM, HOAX, WILE, GAG, RUSE, STRATAGEM, DODGE, JEST, DIDO, FRAUD, FEINT, STUNT, DECEIVE, KNACK
trickery ART, LEGERDEMAIN, DECEIT, FRAUD, GUILE, SHAM, FORGERY, FINERY
trickle DRIP, SEEP, DROP, FLOW, OOZE, PERCOLATE
tricks, *play mean on* SHAB
win all SLAM, CAPOT
tricky QUIRKY, CRAFTY, SNIDE, FOXY, WILY, SLY, UNRELIABLE, DISHONEST
trident LEISTER, SPEAR, FORK, GIG
tried KNOWN, RELIABLE, TRUSTWORTHY
Trieste *measure* ORNE, ORNA
trifle DALLY, MONKEY, PALTER, STRAW, BIT, PIN, TOY, POTTER, FLIRT, DAWDLE
insignificant FICO
trifling PALTRY, PIFFLE, PETTY, INANE, LITTLE, SHALLOW, FRIVOLOUS, CHILDISH, TRIVIAL
trifoliate *plant* CLOVER, SHAMROCK
trig NEAT, SMART, TRIM, TIDY, SNUG, SPRUCE, NATTY
trigger CATCH, LEVER, START

triglyphs, *space between* METOPE
trigo WHEAT
trigon TRINE, HARP, LYRE, TRIANGLE, GAME
trigonometric *figure* SINE, COSINE
trill SHAKE, TREMBLE, ROLL, TWIRL, WARBLE, QUAVER, TREMOLO
trillion, *combining form* TREGA
trim TIDY, NEAT, NIFTY, PERK, FIX, POISE, PRUNE, EDGE, PREEN, CLIP, LOP, CUT, ADORN, BEAUTIFY
coin NIG
dress GIMP, RUCHE, LACE, SEQUIN
lace GARD, JABOT
trine TRIPLE, TRIO
Trinidad *gulf* PARIA
tree MORA
trinity THREE, TRIAD
trinket BAUBLE, BIJOU, BIBELOT, ORNAMENT, TOY, GAUD, TAHLI
trio THREE
triode CATHODE, GRID, PLATE
trip TOUR, JAUNT, CRUISE, ERR, MISSTEP, MISTAKE, DANCE, STUMBLE, FALL, HALT, SKIP, HOP, CAPER, FRISK
triphthong TRIGRAPH
triple TRIN, TRINE, THREE(FOLD), THIRD, HIT
crown TIARA
grass CLOVER, SHAMROCK
triplet(s) TERCET, TRIN(E), SIBLINGS
one of TRINE
tripod EASEL, SPIDER, TRIVET
Tripoli *coin* PIASTRE
measure DRA(A)
ruler DEY
triptych TABLET, PICTURE, CARVING
trisaccharide TRIOSE
trismus LOCKJAW, TETANUS

tristful SAD, GLOOMY, SORROWFUL

Tristram's *beloved* ISOLT, ISEULT, ISOLDE

"Tristram Shandy" *author* STERNE

trite OLD, DULL, BANAL, STALE, FLAT, JEJUNE, FRAYED, RUSTY, HACKNEYED, THREADBARE, COMMON, STEREOTYPED, WORN-OUT
expression CLICHE, CORN

triton EFT, NEWT

triturate GRIND, BRAY, PULVERIZE, BRUISE, THRASH, RUB

triumph JOY, WIN, EXULT, BOAST, VICTORY, ACHIEVE

trivet KNIFE, TRIPOD, STOOL, STAND

trivial MEAN, PETTY, NOMINAL, SMALL, FUTILE, VAIN, CHILDISH, LITTLE, SHALLOW, BANAL, PALTRY, LEGER, UNIMPORTANT, INSIGNIFICANT

troche PASTILE, TABLET, LOZENGE

trochilus SCOTIA, WARBLER, HUMMINGBIRD

trochlea PULLY

trogon QUETZAL, BIRD

"Troilus and Cressida" *character* HECTOR, PARIS, AJAX, NESTOR, HELEN

Troilus' *father* PRIAM

Trojan DARDAN, ILIAN
epic ILIAD
hero AENEAS, HECTOR
horse builder EPEUS
slave SINON
warrior AGENOR

troll GNOME, WARBLE, SING, SPIN, FISH

trolley BARROW, LACE, TRAM, CAR, CART, WHEEL

trombone *mouthpiece* BOCAL

trommel SIEVE, SCREEN

trona URAO

troop BAND, PARTY, CROWD, HORDE, MARCH, PARADE

troops ARMY, BATTERY, SQUAD, REGIMENT, BRIGADE
German division TAXIS
group BAND, ARMS, ARMY, BRIGADE
quarters ETAPE, BARRACKS, CAMP
reserve ECHELON

trop MANY, TOO

trope EUOUAE

trophy SCALP, CUP, MEDAL, TOKEN, PRIZE, AWARD, OSCAR, MEMORIAL, SPOILS, REWARD, PALM

tropical *bird See under* "bird"
clay LATERITE
disease SPRUE, YAWS
fish See under "fish"
plant See under "plant"
tree See under "tree"

tropo, *combining form for* TURN

Tros' *son* ILUS

trot HASTEN, RUN, JOG, PACE, DANCE, CANTER

Trotsky LEON

troubadour POET, MINSTREL, JONGLEUR

trouble ADO, AIL, PAIN, WOE, WORRY, COIL, DISTRESS, GRIEF, DIFFICULTY *See* "annoy"

trough HOD, MANGER, STRAKE, CHANNEL, GROOVE, BASIN, GUTTER, CONDUIT
between waves VALLEY
inclined CHUTE
mining SLUICE

trousers SLACKS, PANTS

trout SEWEN, LONGE, TOGUE, RAINBOW, SPECKLED, BROOK, MALMA, FISH
Britain SEWEN, SEWIN
Lake Tahoe POGY
parasite SUG

Troy ILION, ILIUM, TROAS
defender ENEAS, AENEAS
founder ILUS
mythological TROS
Greek general AGAMEMNON
king PARIS, PRIAM
mountain IDA
pertaining to ILIAC
region TROAD

truant VAGRANT, STRAGGLER, TRIVANT, TRAMP, MICHE, HOBO, BUM

truce LULL, TREVE, BREAK, ARMISTICE, RESPITE, CESSATION, BREATHER

truck RUBBISH, VAN, LORRY, CART, MOVE, PRODUCE, DOLLY, WAGON, BARTER, TRADE, TRAFFIC, VEHICLE
trailer SEMI

truckle CRINGE, NUCKLE, YIELD, BEND, KNEEL

trudge SLOG, PLOD, PACE, WALK, TRAMP, HIKE

true LEAL, VERY, GERMANE, STANCH, RIGHT, ALINE, LOYAL, FAITHFUL, HONEST, JUST, CORRECT, REAL, ACTUAL, STRAIGHT, CONSTANT, STEADFAST, GENUINE, VERITABLE, HONORABLE, UPRIGHT, ACCURATE, LEGITIMATE, ORTHODOX, OFFICIAL, EXACT

truffle(s) FUNGUS, FUNGI, EARTHNUT, TUBER, MUSHROOM

truism AXIOM, POSTULATE, PLATITUDE

truly AMEN, YEA,
  VERILY, REALLY,
  LEGALLY, DULY,
  RIGHTLY
Truman's *birthplace*
  LAMAR
trumpery SHOWY,
  TRASHY, WORTH-
  LESS
trumpet HORN, BUGLE,
  CLARION, TUBA, TUBE,
  LURE
  bell of CODON
  blare TANTARA
  call SENNET
  mouth CODON
  shell TRITON
trumpet-creeper
  TECOMA, PLANT
trumpeter AGAMI,
  TROUT, BIRD,
  FISH
  perch MADO
trundle CART, WHEEL,
  ROLL, TRUCK
  as ore RULL
trunk STEM, BOLE,
  CABER, COFFER,
  STOCK, CHEST,
  TORSO, BODY, BOX
  animal's TORSO,
  SOMA, SNOUT
trust CARTEL, MO-
  NOPOLY, HOPE,
  CREDIT, CREDENCE,
  FAITH, ASSURANCE,
  BELIEF, CORNER
trusty TRIED, LOYAL,
  STANCH, CONVICT
truth DEED, FEALTY,
  TAO, FACT, VERITY,
  REALITY, VERACITY
  Chinese philosophy
  TAO
  drug PENTOTHAL
truthful RELIABLE,
  VERACIOUS, TRUST-
  WORTHY, SINCERE,
  HONEST
try ESSAY, ATTEMPT,
  ENDEAVOR, ASPIRE,
  STRIVE, TRIAL, ET-
  TLE, PUT, SAY, HEAR,
  TEST, TAX, BESET,
  JUDGE, AFFLICT,
  AIM, STAB *See*
  "rack"
  again RETEST, RE-
  TASTE, REPEAT
  for luck HANDSEL
tsetse fly KIVU, MAU,
  MUSCID

disease caused by
  ENCEPHALITIS,
  NAGANA
  genus GLOSSINA
T-shaped TAU
tsine BANTENG, OX
tub BATH(E), WASH,
  BOAT, CASK, POT,
  SHIP, HOD, TUN, VAT,
  VESSEL, CONTAINER
  small wooden KID,
  FIRKIN
tuba *mouthpiece*
  BOCAL
Tubal's *grandfather*
  NOAH
tube DUCT, BOUCH,
  PIPE, HOSE, CYLIN-
  DER, MAIN,
  BRONCHUS, STRAW
  flexible HOSE
  for winding silk
  COP
  glass PIPETTE, SIP-
  PER
  music SALPINX
  priming AUGET
tuber EDDO, JALAP,
  OCA, POTATO, TARO,
  YAM, NODE, TRUFFLE,
  BEET
  orchid SALEP
tubiform TUBATE
tuck FOLD, LAP, PLEAT
  WRAP, COVER, EN-
  CLOSE, CRAM, STUFF,
  HIDE, INSERT
  up KILT, COVER
tuckahoe PORIA,
  ARUM, PLANT
tufa ROCK, TOPH(E)
tuff DETRITUS, ROCK
tuft CREST, TUSSOCK,
  BUNCH, WISP,
  GOATEE, BEARD
  bird's head COP,
  CREST
  botany COMA
  feathers ALULA
  milkweed COMA
tufted COMOSE,
  CRESTED
tug EFFORT, PULL,
  TRACE, TOIL, TOW,
  DRAG, DRAW, BOAT,
  HAUL, ROPE, CHAIN,
  STRAP
tule BULRUSH
  genus SCIRPUS
  root WAPATOO
tulle LACE, NET,
  MESH

tumble FLOP, ROLL,
  FALL, DROP, LEAP,
  DISORDER, TOUSLE,
  FAIL
tumbler DOVE, GLASS,
  ACROBAT, LEVER,
  SLIDE
tumbleweed
  AMARANTH, BUGSEED,
  PIGWEED
tumbrel CART
tumeric *See* "tur-
  meric"
tumor YAW, WEN,
  CANCER, SWELLING,
  KELOID, MORO,
  PHYMA
  fleshy SARCOMA
  glandular ADENOMA
  small WEN, PAPILLA
  suffix OMA
tumult BABEL, DIN,
  FRAY, RIOT, FIGHT,
  FERMENT, UPROAR,
  STRIFE, TURMOIL,
  AGITATION, COM-
  MOTION, HUBBUB,
  DISTURBANCE, RE-
  VOLT
tumulus BARROW,
  MOUND, BANK, DUNE,
  HILLOCK
tun, *half* PIPE
  shell, fossil DOLITE
tune ARIA, SONANCE,
  LILT, AIR, STRAIN,
  SONG, KEY, MELODY,
  ADJUST, FIX,
  ADAPT, CORRESPOND
  to lower pitch
  ANESIS
tung *oil product*
  VARNISH
tungsten WOLFRAM
tunic ACTON, CHITON,
  SHIRT, COAT, STOLE,
  CAMISA, PALLA,
  SMOCK, TOGA,
  BLOUSE, GARMENT
  medieval GIPON,
  JUPON
tunicate SALP(A),
  BULB
Tunisia *measure* ZAH,
  SAA(H)
  port SFAX
  ruler BEY, DEY
  town BIZERTE,
  SFAX, SOUSSE
  (SUSA)

tunnel ADIT, TUBE,
  PASSAGE(WAY)
  train, Alps CENIS
tup RAM, BUTT
tupelo NYSSA, GUM,
  TREE
turban HAT, CAP, FEZ,
  PATA, MANDIL,
  SCARF
  flower TULIP
turbid ROILED,
  FECULENT, MUDDY,
  ROILY, DARK, MURKY,
  DIRTY, FOUL,
  CLOUDY, DISTURBED,
  UNSETTLED
turbot FLATFISH
turbulent VIOLENT,
  DISORDERLY, WILD,
  MAD, AGITATED,
  RIOTOUS, DISORDERED,
  UNSETTLED
turdidae, *family*
  THRUSH, BIRD
turf SOD, PEAT, CESS,
  DIVOT, SWARD, PLOT,
  GRASS, TRACK
turgid SWOLLEN,
  BLOATED, POMPOUS,
  BOMBASTIC, TUMID,
  DISTENDED
Turk *See* "Turkish"
Turkestan *native*
  SART
  river ILI (KULJA)
turkey, *male* TOM
  young POLT
Turkey, Turkish, Turk
  OSMANLI, OTTOMAN,
  TATAR, TARTAR,
  (THE) PORTE
  army district ORDU
    officer, former
    AG(H)A, ZAIM
  brandy RAKI, RAKEE
  cap FEZ, CALPAC
  cape BABA
  capital ANKARA
  caravansary IMARET
  cavalryman SPAHI
  chief ZAIM
  city or town ADANA,
    KARS, EDESSA, ZILE,
    ANKARA, TOKAT, TIRE,
    SIIRT (SERT),
    SESTOS, SIVAS
    (SEBASTE)
  coin ASPER, PARA,
    LIRA, ATILIK, PIASTER,
    ONLIK, YUZLUK,
    AKCHEH, BESHLIK,
    IKLIK, PURSE

college ULEMA
commander AG(H)A,
  SIRDAR, ZAIM
decree IRADE,
  FIRMAN
district ORDU
fermented drink
  BOZA, AIRAN
flag ALEM
founder OSMAN
free land MULK
garment DOLMAN
general KAMAL,
  AG(H)A, PASHA
government PORTE
  house KONAK,
  YALI
governor BEY, DEY,
  SULTAN, PASHA,
  BASHAW, WALI
gulf COS, IZMIR
harem SERAI
  ladies of KADEIN
headgear FEZ
high official
  PASHA, BASHAW
hill DAGH
hospice IMARET
house SELAMLIK
imperial standard
  ALEM
inn IMARET, SERAI
javelin JAREED,
  JARRID, JEREED
judge CADI, AG(H)A
lake VAN
leader AGA, KEMAL,
  OSMAN, AGHA
liquor RAKI, RAKEE
magistrate CADI,
  AGA, AGHA
measure ALMUD,
  DJERI, KILO, OKA,
  ARSHIN, FORTIN,
  HATT, NUL, PARMACK
military district
  ORDU
minister VIZIR
money of account
  ASPER
mountain ARARAT,
  DAGH
name ALI
non-moslem RAIA
officer ATABEG,
  ATABEK, AG(H)A,
  PASHA, ZAIM, SIRDAR
official EMIR,
  OSMANLI *See*
  "governor" *above*
palace SERAI

parade of troops
  ALAI
peasant RAYA
pipe CHIBOUK
prayer rug MELAS,
  MELES
prefect WALI
province or division
  VILAYET
regiment ALAI
reservist REDIF
royal grant FIRMAN
rug KONIA
sailing vessel SAIC
sea MARMARA
seaport ISMIR
  (SMYRNA), FOCA
soldier(s) NIZAM,
  REDIF, UHLAN
standard ALEM,
  TOUG
storm SAMIEL
sultan SELIM, CALIF,
  CALIPH, PASHA
summer residence,
  government YALI
sword YATAGHAN
tambourine DAIRA,
  DAIRE
tax AVANIA
title EMIR, EMEER,
  AG(H)A, PASHA,
  BASHAW, BEY, DEY
  of honor GHAZI,
  AG(H)A
  of respect BABA,
  BEY
town See "city"
  above
tribesman KURD,
  GHUZ
villayet ADANA,
  ANGORA
weight CHEQUI,
  KARAT, ROTL, OKA,
  KILEH, MAUND, OCK,
  TCHEKE, MISKAL,
  ROTOLO, MANE,
  CANTAR, CEQUI,
  DEUKE
turmeric REA, ANGO,
  OLENA, CURCUMA
  India HULDEE
turmoil AGITATION,
  WELTER, DISTURB-
  ANCE, FERMENT,
  CONFUSION, TUMULT
turn BEND, SLEW,
  SLUE, VEER, CHANGE,
  (RE)VERT, GYRATE,
  ROTATE, BENT, TAL-
  ENT, DEVIATE,

SOUR, CURVE,
HINGE, PIVOT
around GYRE, SLUE
aside DIVERT,
SWERVE, DETOUR,
SHUNT, VEER
frontward OBVERT
inside out EVERT,
INVERT
left HAW, PORT
out of course SLUE,
VEER, DEVIATE
outward EVERT
over KEEL, SPILL
rapidly WHIRL, TIRL,
SPIN
right GEE, STAR-
BOARD
to side SPLAY
turncoat RENEGADE,
DESERTER, RAT
turning point CRISIS
turnip NAPE, SWEDE,
RUTABAGA
shaped NAPIFORM
wild NAVEW, RAPE
turnkey JAILOR
turnover TART, CAKE
turnpike RTE, PIKE,
ROAD, HIGHWAY,
THOROFARE
turnstone PLOVER,
REDLEG, BIRD
turpentine, *chian*
TEREBINTH
distillate GALIPOT,
RESIN, ROSIN, CHIAN
resin ALK, GALIPOT,
PITCH
tree TARATA,
TEREBINTH, PINE
turret TOWER, LATHE,
MINARET, TOURELLE
revolving armored
CUPOLA
turtle COOTER, JURARA,
TERRAPIN
back CARAPACE
fresh-water EMYD
genus EMYS,
CHELONE
giant ARRAU
hawksbill CARET
marine CARETTA
shell CARAPACE
snapping TORUP
S. Amer. MATAMATA
Tuscan wine
CHIANTI
tusk RAZOR, FANG,
IVORY, TOOTH,
INCISOR, TENON

tussis COUGH
tussock THICKET,
BRUSH(WOOD), TUFT,
CLUMP
tutelary *deity, deities*
LARES, GENII,
DAEMON, PENATES
tutor DOCENT,
MENTOR, TEACH-
(ER), COACH,
GOVERNOR, PEDAGOG-
(UE), INSTRUCT(OR)
tutta ALL, WHOLE
tuyere NOZZLE,
TEWEL, PIPE, TEW
twaddle DRIVEL,
FUSTIAN, ROT,
BABBLE
twang PLUNK,
SOUND, NASALITY,
TWANK, TWANGLE,
PUNGENCY
tweak PINCH
tweezer PINCHERS,
PINCERS
"Twelfth Night"
character ORSINO,
VIOLA, OLIVIA
twelfth *part* UNCIA
twentieth *drachma*
OBOL
twenty SCORE,
CORGE, XX
combining form
ICOSA
fourth part CARAT,
KARAT
pertaining to
ICOSIAN
quires REAM
years VICENNIAL
twibil CHISEL,
MATTOCK
twice, *prefix* BI, DI,
BIS
music BIS
twig(s) SHOOT,
ROD, BRANCH, CHILD,
SWITCH, WITHE,
SLIP, OFFSHOOT
*excessive develop-
ment of* PLICA
flexible OSIER
made of VIRGAL,
WATTLED
twilight DUSK,
SHADED, DIM,
OBSCURE, EVENING
pertaining to
CREPUSCULAR
twin(s) COUPLE,
TWO, GEMEL,

DUPLICATE,
SIMILAR, CARBON,
DUAL, SIBLINGS
crystal MACLE
Siamese CHANG,
ENG
zodiac GEMINI
twine TWIST,
WREATHE, WIND,
COIL, CORD, THREAD,
STRING
hank of RAN, BALL
twinge PAIN, PANG,
QUALM, TIC, ACHE,
STITCH, THROE
twining *stem* BINE,
VINE
twink WINK,
NICTITATE
twinkle BLINK, WINK,
FLASH, GLEAM,
GLINT, SHINE, SCIN-
TILLATE, SPARKLE
twirl TURN, SPIN,
WHIRL, ROTATE *See*
"circle"
twist WARP, TURN,
SLUE, SLEW, DANCE,
SQUIRM, SKEW,
SPIN, WHIRL, TWEAK,
CURL, BEND, CURVE,
GNARL, CONTORT,
WIND, DISTORT,
DEVIATE, OLIVER
horsehair SETON
in rope GRIND
inward INTORT
to and fro WRENCH,
WRIGGLE
twisted TORC,
TORTILE, (A)WRY,
LOXIC
cord TORSADE,
ROPE
roll of cotton SLUB
spirally TORSE
twit TAUNT, BANTER,
TEASE, BLAME,
UPBRAID, DERIDE
See "josh"
twitch JERK, TUG,
TWEAK, VELLICATE,
TIC, PULL, YANK
twitter GIGGLE,
CHIRP, TITTER
two PAIR, BRACE,
TWINS, TEAM
and one-half inches
NAIL
celled BILOCULAR
colors DICHROMIC

consisting of DYAD,
BIVALENT
edged ANCIPITAL
fingered BIDIGITATE
fold BINAL, DUAL,
BINARY, DUPLE(X),
DOUBLE, DIDYMOUS
footed BIPED
forked BIFURCATED
handed AMBIDEX-
TROUS, BIMANUAL
animals BIMANA
headed ANCIPITAL
herrings, oysters,
etc. WARP
months, containing
two BIMESTRIAL
of a kind BRACE,
PAIR, TWINS, YOKE,
TEAM, COUPLE
pronged weapon
BIDENT
"Two Gentlemen of
Verona" *character*
PROTEUS, THURIO,
SPEED, JULIA,
SYLVIA
"Two Years Before
the Mast" *author*
DANA
Tyche FORTUNE
tycoon NABOB,
SHOGUN, BARON, VIP
tylopod CAMEL
Tyndareus' *step-child*
HELEN
wife LEDA
type GENRE, TOKEN,
KIND, SORT, BRAND,
NATURE, STRIPE,
PATTERN, KIDNEY,
ILK, MODEL, PRINT,
IDENTIFY, CLASS-
(IFY), SPECIES
assortment FONT
blank QUAD
box(es) for CASE
collection FONT
face KERN, RUNIC
frame CHASE
jumbled PI(E)
kind ELITE, IONIC,
PICA, RONDE, PEARL,
AGATE, MINION
measure EN, EM
metal piece QUAD
mold MATRIX
part of NICK, FACE,
FOOT
script RONDE
set FONT

size AGATE, PEARL,
PICA, NORM,
PRIMER, MINION,
BREVIER, NON-
PAREIL, DIAMOND,
RUBY
slanted ITALIC
square EM
style CASLON, IONIC,
ALDINE, SCRIPT,
RONDE, RUNIC,
ITALIC
tray GALLEY
written RONDE,
SCRIPT
typewriter *roller*
PLATEN
type ELITE, PICA
typical REGULAR,
USUAL, GENERAL,
CHARACTERISTIC,
EMBLEMATIC,
SYMBOLIC,
REPRESENTATIVE
example NORM
Tyr ZEUS, JUPITER,
TIW, DYAUS, TIU
tyrant DESPOT,
DICTATOR, OLIGARCH,
OPRESSOR
of Syracuse HIERO,
GELO(N)
tyre MILK, CURDS,
WINE
Tyre *king* HIRAM
princess DIDO
town SOUR, ZOR,
(ES) SUR
tyro NOVICE,
AMATEUR,
ABECEDARIAN, TIRO,
BEGINNER, LEARNER,
NEOPHYTE

U

U UPSILON
uberous FRUITFUL,
ABUNDANT, COPIOUS
ubiquitous OMNI-
PRESENT
Uchean YUCHI,
INDIAN
Uffizi GALLERY
Uganda *native* KOPI
ugliness *symbol*
TOAD
ugly SURLY, VICIOUS,
HOMELY, INELEGANT,
REPULSIVE,
DISPLEASING,

UNSIGHTLY,
HIDEOUS, DANGER-
OUS, BAD, EVIL
Uintah UTE
Ukraine *city or town*
SUMY, ROVNO, LVOV,
ODESSA
holy city KIEV
legislature RADA
money of account
GRIVNA
ulcer SORE, LESION
ule, *derivative of*
LATEX
ulema, *leader of*
IMAM
ulex FURZE, PLANT
ulexite TIZA, BORATE
ullage WANTAGE,
DEFICIENCY,
SHORTAGE
ulmacae *family* ELM
ulna CUBITUS, BONE
Ultima Thule
ICELAND
ultimate END, LAST,
FINAL, TERMINAL,
CONCLUSIVE,
MAXIMUM,
ELEMENTAL,
PRIMARY
atom MONAD
ultimatum DEMAND,
ORDER, OFFER
ultra TOP, A-ONE,
BEST, RADICAL,
EXTREME, BEYOND,
SUPERIOR
ululate BELLOW, CRY,
HOWL, ROAR, WAIL,
LAMENT
Ulysses ODYSSEUS
See "Odysseus"
antagonist IRUS
dog ARGUS
father LAERTES
swineherd EUMAEUS
voyage ODYSSEY
wife PENELOPE
umbelliferlike
CELERY
umber SHADE, DUSKY,
CHESTNUT, BROWN,
FISH
umbo BEAK, BOSS,
KNOB, SPIKE, STUD
umbrage HUFF,
OFFENSE, SHADE,
SHADOW, PIQUE,
DISPLEASURE,
RESENTMENT

umbrella *finial* TEE
grass MILLET
large PARASOL,
GAMP
tree MAGNOLIA,
CATALPA
umbrette BIRD
umpire REF(EREE),
ARBITER, JUDGE,
UMP
unaccented ATONIC
opposed to THESIS
part of bar, music
ARSIS
unadorned STARK,
BALD, BARE, PLAIN,
SIMPLE, NAKED
unadulterated CLEAR,
TRUE, FRANK, PURE,
GENUINE
Unalaska *native*
ALEUT
unanimous ONE,
SOLID, AGREED,
MUTUAL
unappropriated
OPEN, ORPHAN
unaspirated LENE
unassuming
MODEST, OPEN,
PLAIN, HUMBLE,
SHY, DIFFIDENT
unau SLOTH
unavowed ULTERIOR
unaware IGNORANT,
UNWARY
unbeliever HERETIC,
SKEPTIC, KAFIR,
KAFFIR, INFIDEL,
PAGAN, ATHEIST
unbend REST, RELAX,
THAW, STRAIGHTEN,
REPOSE
unbleached BEIGE,
ECRU
unblenched
UNDAUNTED
unbranched *antler*
DAG
unbroken CON-
TINUOUS, INTACT,
WHOLE, ENTIRE,
REGULAR, SMOOTH
unburden FREE,
DISCLOSE, UNLOAD,
EASE, REVEAL,
RELIEVE
unbury EXHUME
uncanny UNCO,
WEIRD, EERIE, ODD,
QUEER, MYSTERIOUS

unceremonious(ly)
ABRUPT, SLY(LY),
INFORMAL
uncertain VARIABLE,
VAGUE, ERRING,
CHANGING, DOUBT-
FUL, PRECARIOUS,
DUBIOUS, IRREGULAR
uncivil RUDE, BLUNT,
BOORISH, BLUFF,
GRUFF, HAUGHTY,
DISCOURTEOUS,
DISRESPECTFUL,
VULGAR
uncivilized one
SAVAGE, BRUTE
uncle NUNKS, OOM,
SAM, EME
pertaining to
AVUNCULAR
Scot. EAM, EME,
YEME
unclean VILE, DIRTY,
FILTHY, FOUL, SUL-
LIED
unclose OPE(N),
SPREAD
unclothe TIRL, DI-
VEST, STRIP
unco UNCANNY,
STRANGE
uncommon ODD,
PECULIAR, STRANGE,
SPECIAL, RARE,
SCARCE, CHOICE,
UNCO, EXTRAORDI-
NARY, SINGULAR
uncompromising IN-
FLEXIBLE, RIGID,
STRICT, UNYIELDING,
SEVERE
unconcerned INSOU-
CIANT, FREE, OPEN,
CALM, SERENE,
APATHETIC, IN-
DIFFERENT, CARE-
LESS, INSENSIBLE
unconscious IG-
NORANT, UNAWARE,
INSENSIBLE
unconventional
INFORMAL, FREE,
EASY, OUTRE, DEGAGE
uncouth RUDE,
GAUCHE, UNGAINLY,
AWKWARD, VULGAR
uncover UNFOLD,
DISCLOSE, OPEN,
BARE, DIVEST, EX-
POSE, REVEAL, STRIP
uncritical NAIVE,
PLEASED

unction UNGENT,
SOOTHING, ENELE
administer ANELE,
ENELE
unctuous GREASY,
OILY, PINGUID,
BLAND, SUAVE, SALVY,
SLEEK, SOAPY,
SOOTHING, HYPO-
CRITICAL
waxy mixture
CERATE, LANOLIN
uncultivated FAL-
LOW, WILD
uncultured WILD,
PHILISTINE, RUDE,
ROUGH, BRUTISH,
IGNORANT
undaunted BOLD,
SPARTAN, FEARLESS,
BRAVE, STANCH,
INTREPID
undecided IRRESO-
LUTE, WAVERING,
PENDING, DILEMMA,
UNCERTAIN
under SOTTO, INFE-
RIOR, NEATH, SUB,
NETHER, BELOW,
BENEATH, SUBORDI-
NATE, LOWER, LESS
prefix SUB, HYPO
side VENTRAL,
BELLY
undercover *agent(s)*
SPY, FBI, OGPU,
POLICE
underdone RARE,
PARTIAL, INCOM-
PLETE
undergo BARE, STAND,
PASS, SURVIVE, SUF-
FER, ENDURE
cell destruction LYSE
underground *bulb*
ROOT, POTATO, CORM,
TUBER
product MINERAL,
OIL, COAL, ORE
underhand COVERT,
SECRET, UNFAIR,
SLY, TRICKY, WILY
underline MARK,
SCORE, EMPHASIZE
undermine THWART,
SAP, CRIPPLE,
WEAKEN, IMPAIR,
EXCAVATE
undersong TIERCE
understand SENSE,
KNOW, KEN, FEEL,
SEE, REALIZE,

SOLVE, APPREHEND,
COMPREHEND,
SAVVY, GRASP
understanding EN-
TENTE, AGREEMENT,
CONTRACT, REASON,
INTELLECT, FAC-
ULTY, MIND, JUDG-
MENT, PERCEPTION,
ACCORD, SYMPA-
THETIC, INTELLI-
GENCE
understatement
LITOTES
understood ASSUMED,
IMPLIED, TACIT,
AGREED
undertake ESSAY,
ATTEMPT, POSTU-
LATE, TRY, ENGAGE,
CONTRACT, COVENANT,
PROMISE, BEGIN,
AGREE, EMBARK
undertaking ACT,
AVOWAL, AVAL,
MOOD, JOB, RISK,
OBLIGATION, TASK,
VENTURE, ENTER-
PRISE, BUSINESS
zealous CRUSADE
undertow EDDY,
VORTEX, RIPTIDE,
CURRENT
underworld EREBUS,
SHEOL *See* "Hades"
Egypt DUAT,
AMENTI
god DIS, PLUTO,
OSIRIS
goddess HEL
relating to spirits of
CHTHONIAN
underwrite FINANCE,
INSURE, BACK,
ABET, FOOT
undeserving INDIGN,
UNWORTHY
undeveloped LATENT,
RAW, WILD, EM-
BRYO, RUDIMENTARY
undiluted RAW, PURE,
NEAT, THICK
undine NYMPH,
GNOME, SYLPH
undo LOOSE, RUIN,
DESTROY, OPEN,
UNTIE, UNFASTEN,
ANNUL, SOLVE
undomesticated
FERAL, WILD
undone LOST, RARE,
RUINED, OPENED

undraped NUDE,
BARE
undressed *fur* PELT,
HIDE
undulating VIBRAT-
ING, WAVY, RIPPLING
undulation TREMOLO,
HEAVE, SURGE,
WAVE, SWELL
undyed CORAH,
PLAIN, TRUE
undying IMMORTAL,
AMARANTHINE, LAST-
ING, ETERNAL, PER-
PETUAL, IMMUTABLE
unearth EXHUME,
FIND, DETECT, ROOT,
DISCOVER, DELVE,
REVEAL, EXPOSE,
UNCOVER
unearthly EERIE,
WEIRD, SUPERNATU-
RAL
uneasiness MALAISE,
UNREST, WORRY,
ANXIETY
uneasy RESTIVE
uneducated
BENIGHTED, RUDE,
CRUDE, CALLOW,
GREEN, IGNORANT,
UNPREPARED
unemployed FREE,
IDLE, OTIOSE, LAZY,
INACTIVE
unending BOUNDLESS,
TIMELESS
unequal DISPARATE,
ODD, UNFAIR, IR-
REGULAR, INSUF-
FICIENT, UNEVEN,
INADEQUATE
condition ODDS
side and angle
SCALENE
triangle SCALENE
uneven EROSE, ODD,
ROUGH, HARSH,
VARIABLE, SPAS-
MODIC, RAGGED,
UNFAIR, DIVERSE
unexciting TAME,
BORING
unexpected SUDDEN,
UNFORESEEN, RARE
unfadable FAST
unfading *flower*
AMARANTH
unfair PARTIAL,
FOUL, UNJUST,
DISHONEST,
WRONG(FUL)

unfamed HUMBLE,
LOWLY
unfashionable ILL,
BAD, PASSE, SHAPE-
LESS, DEFORMED,
VULGAR
unfasten *See under*
"open" LOOSE,
UNCLASP
unfeathered
PLUCKED, BARE
unfeeling CALLOUS,
BRUTAL, STOIC,
HARD, FELL, COLD,
CRUEL, APATHETIC,
INSENSATE
unfettered LOOSE,
FREE
unfilled cavity VUGG
unfit DENATURED,
INEPT, UNSUIT-
ABLE, INAPT, IM-
PROPER, DIS-
QUALIFIED, CRIP-
PLED, UNTIMELY,
WRONG, IMPOTENT,
INCOMPETENT, DIS-
ABLED
unflattering FRANK,
BLUNT, OPEN,
CANDID
unfledged *bird*
EYAS, QUAB
unfold EVOLUTE,
DEPLOY, EVOLVE,
DEVELOP, UNFURL,
OPEN, UNROLL,
EXPAND, DISCLOSE,
REVEAL, SPREAD,
DISPLAY
unforeseen CHANCE,
LUCK, UNEXPECTED
unfounded FALSE,
UNTRUE
unfragrant OLID,
FETID
unfrequented
SOLITARY, LONELY
unfriendly INIMICAL,
HOSTILE, WILD, ICY,
ALIEN, SAVAGE, UN-
CIVIL, OPPOSED,
MALEVOLENT
unfruitful STERILE,
ACARPOUS, BARREN,
UNPRODUCTIVE
unfurl UNFOLD, DIS-
CLOSE, OPEN, UN-
ROLL, UNWIND
ungainly GAWKY,
WEEDY, CLUMSY,
LEGGY

ungirt LOOSE, UNTIE, UNKNOT, UNBIND, SLACKEN
ungrateful THANKLESS, INGRATEFUL
unguent NARD, CHRISM, SALVE, OINTMENT, POMADE
ungula CLAW, HOOF, NAIL, TALON
ungulate TAPIR, SWINE, HORSE, COW, RUMINANT
unhappiness DOLOR, WORRY, WOE, GRIEF, MISERY, UNREST
unhappy SAD, INEPT, WRETCHED, PAINFUL, DISTRESSED, DISMAL, DREAR, DEJECTED
unhealable RAW, INSANABLE, INTRACTABLE
unheard SURD, DEAF, UNKNOWN, UNPRECEDENTED
unhorse OVERTHROW, FREE, TOPPLE
unicellular *animals* OOZOA, PROTOZOA
  plant SPORE
unicorn REEM, MONOCEROS, MONSTER
  fish LIJA, UNIE, NARWHAL(E), NARWAL
uniform STABLE, EQUAL, EVEN, LEVEL, CONSTANT, (A)LIKE, SIMILAR, STEADY, UNVARIED, REGULAR, SYMMETRICAL, CONSISTENT, UNCHANGING, EQUABLE, LIVERY, GARB
  color FLAT
unimportant MINOR
uninflected APTOTIC
unintelligent BRUTISH, DULL, DUMB, IGNORANT
union FUSION, LEAGUE, MERGER, LIAISON, LINK(AGE), AMALGAM, CIO, AFL, ACCORD, HARMONY, JUNCTION, RAPHE, SEAM, ALLIANCE, MARRIAGE, ENSIGN,

FLAG, JACK, COMBINATION, UNITY, COALITION, CONFEDERACY, ASSOCIATION
  political BLOC
  Russia ARTEL
  trade GUILD, HANSE
uniplanar *point* UNODE
unique (A)LONE, SINGLE, SOLE, RARE, ONLY, ODD, QUEER, QUAINT, CHOICE, UNCOMMON, ORIGINAL, UNEQUAL, MATCHLESS, EXCEPTIONAL
  person ONER
unit ACE, ONE, SYLLABLE, INDIVIDUAL
  caloric THERM, THERME
  electric COULOMB, AMPERE, MHO, OHM, PROTON, VOLT, WATT, WEBER, HENRY, REL
  electrical capacity FARAD
    conductivity MHO
    pressure BARAD
    resistance OHM
  energy ERG, JOULE, QUANTUM
  force DYNE, OD, TONAL, VOLT
  heat CALORY, CALORIE, THERM(E)
  hypothetical ID, IDIC, OD
  illumination PHOT, LUZ
  inductance HENRY
  kinetic energy ERG
  light LUMEN, LUX, PYR, PHOT
  magnetic field, or flux GAUSS, MAXWELL
    potential GILBERT
  magnetism GAUSS, KAPP, WEBER, OERSTED
  mathematical RADIX
  meter MORA, STERE
  of angular velocity STROB
  of discourse WORD
  power WATT

  pressure BARAD, BARIE
  reluctance OERSTED, REL
  resistance OHM
  social SEPT, CLAN, FAMILY
  speed VELO
  ultimate MONAD
  velocity KIN, VELO
  weight MAUND, CARAT, CRITH, DRAM
  wire MIL
  work ERG(ON), KILERG, JOULE
unite LINK, (CON)JOIN, MIX, MARRY, BLEND, COMBINE, COHERE, FUSE, WED, ALLY, SOLDER, MERGE, YOKE, CONNECT, INCORPORATE, ASSOCIATE, AMALGAMATE, WELD, FEDERATE, COALESCE, CONSOLIDATE, ADD, EMBODY
united ONE, WEDDED
United States *See* "America"
unity UNION, ONE
univalent *element* MONAD
universal GENERIC, COSMIC, COMMON, CATHOLIC
  writing PASIGRAPHY
universe COSMOS, MACROCOSM, EARTH, WORLD, CREATION, SPAN
  combining form COSMO
  pertaining to COSMIC
university *group* SEMINAR, FRAT
  governor REGENT
  growing body of SENATUS
  officer PRES, DEAN, BEADLE, BURSAR
unjudiciousness ACRISY
unjust PARTIAL, UNFAIR, DISHONEST, FOUL, BIASED
unkeeled RATITE
unkempt ROUGH, SHAGGY, UNTIDY, LAX, SLACK,

TOUSLED, RUFFLED, UNCLEAN, DIRTY

unkeyed ATONAL, HARSH, SOUR

unkind BRUTAL, CRUEL, FELL, HARSH, HARD, SEVERE

unknown, *Latin* IGNOTUS

person ICONNU, IGNOTE

quantity in an equation COSS

unlawful ILLICIT, ILLEGAL, CONTRABAND, ILLEGITIMATE

unlearn FORGET

unleavened AZYMOUS

bread AZYM(E), MATZOS, MATZOTH

unless NISI, EXCEPT-(ING), SAVE, THAT, LEST

unlike DIVERSE, SUNDRY, ODD, ALIEN, DIFFERENT, DISSIMILAR

unlimited INDEFINITE, FREE, BOUNDLESS

unload REMOVE, RID, SELL, DISENCUMBER, EJECT

unlock OPE, OPEN, SOLVE, DISCLOSE, UNFASTEN, DISCOVER, INTERPRET

unlooked for CHANCE, HAP, HAPPEN, SERENDIPITOUS

unlucky FEY, ILL, DISASTROUS

unmarried CELIBATE, SOLE, SINGLE

unmatched ODD, AZYGOUS, SINGLE

unmetrical *composition* PROSE

unmixed SHEER, RAW

unmoved DEAD, INERT, SERENE, RESOLUTE, FIRM, CALM, APATHETIC, OBSTINATE

unorganized MESSY, ACOSMIC

unpaid DUE

unplowed FALLOW, LEA, UNTILLED

unpolished *See* "unrefined"

unqualified UNFIT, SHEER, PLENARY, INCOMPETENT, INEXPERT

unravel FEAZE, SOLVE, OPE(N), UNTIE, INTERPRET

unreal STRANGE, DELUSIVE, CHAOTIC, ARTIFICIAL, WHIMSICAL, IMAGINARY

unrefined RAW, RIBALD, RUDE, CRUDE, GROSS, CRASS, SAVAGE

unroll DEVELOP, EVOLUTE, UNFURL, SPREAD, EXHIBIT, DISCOVER, OPEN, DISPLAY

unruffled CALM, SERENE, STILL, SEDATE, COOL, PLACID, QUIET, UNAFFECTED

unruly LAWLESS, TURBULENT, WILD, WILLFUL, FERAL, REFRACTORY, DISOBEDIENT, VIOLENT

unsatisfactory MEASLY, BAD, POOR, FAILING

unseasoned UNTIMELY, GREEN, RAW

unsheathe DRAW, REMOVE

unshorn *sheep* TEG

unsightly UGLY

unskil(l)ful MALADROIT, AWKWARD, INEPT, GAUCHE, BUNGLING

unskilled INAPT, INEPT, PUISNE, RAW, IGNORANT, INEXPERT, CLUMSY

unsociable SHY, RESERVED

unsophisticated NAIVE, SHY, NATURAL, SIMPLE, CANDID, FRANK, OPEN, ARTLESS, INGENUOUS, GENUINE, PURE, GUILELESS, INNOCENT, UNWORLDLY, INEXPERIENCED

unspeakable VILE, BAD, UNUTTERABLE, INEFFABLE, INDESCRIBABLE

unspoken TACIT, UNUTTERED, SECRET

unstable ASTATIC, INFIRM, LABILE, INCONSTANT, CHANGEABLE, FICKLE, PRECARIOUS, SHAKY, UNSTEADY, INSECURE, UNSAFE, UNBALANCED, WEAK, VACILLATING, ERRATIC, FLUCTUATING

unsuitable INEPT, INAPT, UNFIT, GAUCHE, INAPPROPRIATE, UNSATISFACTORY, IMPROPER, UNBECOMING

unsullied PRISTINE, PURE, CLEAN

untamed FERINE, FERAL, WILD, RAW, CALLOUS, UNBROKEN, FIERCE, UNSUBDUED, FEROCIOUS

untanned *skin* KIP, HIDE, SHAGREEN, PELT

unthinking PUERILE, HEEDLESS, RASH, THOUGHTLESS, CARELESS, INCONSIDERATE, MECHANICAL, AUTOMATIC, CASUAL

untidy MESSY, LITTERED, SLOPPY, SLOVENLY, DISORDERLY, DOWDY, FRUMPY, UNKEMPT, CARELESS

untie FREE, LOOSE, UNKNOT, SOLVE, DISCLOSE, DIVORCE, UNFASTEN, LOOSEN, UNFOLD, RESOLVE, CLEAR, LIBERATE

until HENT, TILL, WHEN, FORMERLY

untold VAST, COUNTLESS, SECRET, UNNUMBERED, UNREVEALED, INNUMERABLE, BOUNDLESS, INCALCULABLE, UNINFORMED

untouched PURE, PRISTINE, INTACT,

UNAFFECTED, UN-
HARMED, UNIN-
JURED, INSENSIBLE
untrained RAW, UN-
DISCIPLINED, INEX-
PERIENCED, IGNO-
RANT, GREEN, UN-
BROKEN
untwist FAG, FEAZE,
LOOSE, DISENTANGLE,
(UN)RAVEL, FREE,
UNTANGLE,
STRAIGHTEN
Unungun ALEUT
unusual NOVEL,
EXOTIC, ODD, OUTRE,
RARE, ANOMALOUS,
UNCOMMON,
RECHERCHE, FUNNY,
SINGULAR, RE-
MARKABLE, STRANGE,
CURIOUS, EXTRAOR-
DINARY, ABNOR-
MAL, EXCEPTIONAL
unvitiated PURE,
PRISTINE
unvoiced SURD, SE-
CRET, TACIT, UN-
UTTERED
unwholesome ILL,
BAD, NOISOME, DE-
CAYED, CORRUPT,
UNHEALTHY, UN-
HEALTHFUL, NOXIOUS,
DELETERIOUS, BANE-
FUL, POISONOUS,
PERNICIOUS, TAINTED,
IMMORAL, IN-
SALUBRIOUS
unwilling LOATH,
ESCHEW, AVERSE,
RELUCTANT, DIS-
INCLINED, GRUDGING,
INDISPOSED
unwise AMISS, SILLY,
IMPOLITIC, IN-
SIPIENT, FOOLISH,
INJUDICIOUS, IN-
DISCREET, IM-
PRUDENT
unwonted RARE,
UNUSED, UNUSUAL,
UNCOMMON
unworthy INDIGN,
BAD, UNFIT,
WORTHLESS, UN-
DESERVING, UNBE-
COMING, UNSEEMLY,
VILE, DESPICABLE,
DISHONORABLE,
CONTEMPTIBLE

unwrinkled SMOOTH,
UNFURROWED
unwritten PAROL,
BLANK, TACIT,
ORAL, TRADITIONAL
unyielding ADAMANT,
FIRM, IRON, STIFF,
INFLEXIBLE,
STANCH, DETER-
MINED, INDOMITABLE,
UNCOMPROMISING,
TENACIOUS, STUB-
BORN, OBSTINATE,
HEADSTRONG, HARD
upas tree *poison gum*
ANTIAR
upbraid *See* "scold"
Uphanishad ISHA
upholstery *fabric*
TOURNAY, LAMPAS,
TABARET, SCRIM
hanging VALANCE
upland DOWN, MESA,
INTERIOR, RIDGE,
PLATEAU, INLAND
Upolu *capital* APIA
upon ON, ONTO,
ABOVE, ATOP, OVER,
prefix EPI, SUR,
SUPRA
upper BUNK, BERTH,
HIGHER, OVER, ABOVE,
SUPERIOR, IN-
NERMOST
uppermost TOP,
HIGHEST, FIRST,
LOFTIEST, TOP-
MOST, FOREMOST,
SUPREME
uppish PROUD,
ASSUMING, PRETEN-
TIOUS, SNOBBISH,
ARROGANT, HAUGHTY
upright HONEST,
JUST, MORAL, FAIR,
NOBLE, GRAND,
ERECT, PERPENDIC-
ULAR, VERTICAL,
HONORABLE, CON-
SCIENTIOUS, TRUST-
WORTHY, VIRTUOUS
support JAMB,
STUD
uprising REVOLT,
MUTINY, PUTSCH,
ACCLIVITY, ASCENT,
INSURRECTION,
REBELLION
uproar DIN, HUBBUB,
NOISE, RIOT, ADO,
BABEL, RACKET,
TUMULT, DISTURB-

ANCE, COMMOTION,
CONFUSION, TURMOIL,
PANDEMONIUM,
CLAMOR, DISORDER
upshot RESULT,
CONCLUSION, LIMIT
upsilon-shaped
HYOID
upstanding *See*
"upright"
upstart PARVENU,
SNOB, SAFFRON
up to TILL, UNTIL
upupoid bird
HOOPOE
upward *bend in lumber*
SNY
upward, *combining
form* ANO
uraeus ASP, EMBLEM
uranium CARNOTITE
Uranus' *daughter*
RHEA
wife GAEA, GE
urban *division* WARD
inhabitant CIT
urbane CIVIL, BLAND,
POLITE, SUAVE,
COURTEOUS,
MANNERLY, RE-
FINED, POLISHED
urchin GAMIN, ARAB,
IMP, CHILD, BRAT,
HEDGEHOG
Urd URTH
urde CLECHE,
POINTED, CROSSED
uredo HIVES,
URTICARIA
urge INCITE, EGG,
GOAD, HIE, ABET,
DESIRE, LUST,
PASSION, ANIMATE,
SPUR, DRIVE, PUSH,
PRESS, PLY, YEN,
PLOD, IMPEL,
INSTIGATE, STIMU-
LATE, ENCOURAGE,
INDUCE
urgent EXIGENT,
IMPORTANT, PRESS-
ING, RUSHING,
COGENT, CRITICAL,
IMPORTUNATE,
IMPERATIVE,
IMMEDIATE
urial OORIAL, SHA,
SHEEP
urn CAPANNA,
CAPANNE, VESSEL
See "vase"
copper SAMOVAR

shaped URCEOLATE
shaped organ
 URCEOLUS
urodele EFT, NEWT,
 SALAMANDER
uroxanthin INDICAN
Ursa DIPPER, BEAR,
 CONSTELLATION
Urth NORN
urticaria HIVES,
 UREDO
Uruguay *city or town*
 SALTO, ROCHA,
 RIVERA, MINAS,
 MELO
 department ARTIGAS,
 FLORES, RIVERA,
 ROCHA, SALTO
urus AUROCHS, TUR,
 OX
usage WONT, HABIT,
 MANNER, WAY,
 FORM, PRACTICE,
 CUSTOM, METHOD,
 TREATMENT,
 UTILITY, ADVANTAGE
usance USAGE,
 USURY, USE, TIME
use AVAIL, EMPLOY,
 EXHAUST, TREAT,
 WONT, CONSUME,
 APPLY, PLY, WIELD,
 FORM, MANIPULATE,
 OCCUPY, NECESSITY,
 SPEND, PRACTICE,
 HABIT, CUSTOM,
 EXERCISE, APPLICA-
 TION
useful UTILE, GOOD,
 HELPFUL, SERVICE-
 ABLE, PROFITABLE,
 ADVANTAGEOUS,
 REMUNERATIVE,
 PRACTICAL, BENE-
 FICIAL, EFFECTIVE
useless IDLE,
 UNUTILE, NULL,
 OTIOSE, VOID,
 FRUITLESS, BOOTLESS,
 INEFFECTUAL,
 WORTHLESS,
 UNSERVICEABLE
Ushas' *father* BANA
usher SEAT, SHOW,
 ESCORT, DOOR-
 KEEPER, TILER,
 ATTENDANT,
 HERALD, PRECURSOR,
 INTRODUCE
Usnech's *son* NOISE
Uspallata Pass ANDES

USSR *See* "Russia"
 news agent TASS
ustulate SCORCHED,
 SEARED, DISCOLORED
usual COMMON,
 CUSTOMARY, HABIT-
 UAL, ORDINARY
usurp GRAB, ASSUME,
 SEIZE, TAKE,
 ARROGATE,
 APPROPRIATE
Utah *canyon* ECHO
 county CACHE,
 IRON, JUAB, KANE,
 PIUTE, RICH, WEBER
 State flower SEGO
 town OREM, LEHI
utmost EXTREME,
 MAXIMUM, END,
 LAST, FINAL, BEST,
 LIMIT, EXTENT,
 FARTHEST, HIGHEST,
 GREATEST, FULLEST
"Utopia" *author*
 MORE
utopian IDEAL(ISTIC),
 VISIONARY, EDENIC,
 CHIMERICAL
utricle BAG, SAC,
 CELL, CAVITY,
 VESICLE
utter SHEER, MERE,
 BRAY, EMIT, MOOT,
 STARK, DRAWL,
 INTONATE, PERFECT,
 VENT, VOICE,
 PUBLISH, VOCIFERATE,
 SAY, BID, BLURT,
 REMOTE, COMPLETE,
 TOTAL, ENTIRE,
 ABSOLUTE, EXTREME,
 UNUSUAL, PREEMP-
 TORY, UNCONDI-
 TIONAL
utterly STARK,
 SHEER, FULLY,
 TOTALLY, ENTIRELY,
 QUITE, WHOLLY
uvula CION
uxor WIFE

V

V VEE, FIVE
 shaped piece
 WEDGE
vacancy VOID, BLANK,
 GAP, OPENING,
 SPACE, LEISURE,
 EMPTINESS, CHASM,
 VACUUM, INANITY,

 IDLENESS, BARREN-
 NESS, VACUITY
vacant INANE, VOID,
 EMPTY, OPEN,
 FREE, BLANK, IDLE,
 BARE, BARREN,
 UNFILLED, DESTI-
 TUTE, DEVOID, FREE,
 LEISURE, UN-
 EMPLOYED, DIS-
 ENGAGED, VACUOUS,
 FOOLISH, SILLY,
 UNTENANTED
vacate ANNUL,
 MOVE, CANCEL,
 DEPART
vacation RECESS,
 SPELL, HOLIDAY,
 REST, RESPITE,
 INTERMISSION
vacillate SEESAW,
 WAVER, FLUCTUATE,
 TEETER, OSCILLATE,
 HESITATE, WOBBLE,
 WAG, WAVE
vacuity INANITY,
 VACANCY, STUPID-
 ITY *See* "vacancy"
vacuous STUPID,
 EMPTY, INANE
vacuum VOID, SPACE,
 CAVITY, HOLE, HOL-
 LOW, POCKET, GAP,
 CLEANER, VACUITY
 opposite of
 PLENUM
 tube DIODE,
 TETRODE
vadium BAIL, PLEDGE,
 PAWN
vagabond BUM,
 WASTREL, LOREL,
 RODNEY, STRAGGLER,
 HOBO, VAGRANT,
 TRAMP, ROVER,
 TRUANT, ROGUE,
 NOMADIC, HOME-
 LESS, SCAMP,
 RASCAL, WANDERER
vagans QUINTUS
vagrant *See* "vaga-
 bond"
vague DIM, HAZY,
 OBSCURE, LOOSE,
 DARK, DREAMY,
 LAX, CRYPTIC,
 UNCERTAIN,
 UNSETTLED,
 UNFIXED, AMBIGU-
 OUS, CONFUSED,
 SHADOWY, INDIS-
 TINCT

vain EMPTY, IDLE, PROUD, FUTILE, TRIVIAL, UNREAL, UNAVAILING, UNREWARDED, CONCEITED, UNIMPORTANT, OVERWEANING, USELESS, FOOLISH, WORTHLESS, SILLY, VAPID
boasting FANFARONADE

vainglory GASCONADE, POMP, SHOW, PRIDE, VANITY, PARADE, RODOMONTADE, CONCEIT

vale DALE, DELL, DINGLE, GLEN, VALLEY, ADIEU, FAREWELL

valediction ADIEU, FAREWELL

valentine GIFT, LOVE, TOKEN, GREETING, CARD

valerian NARD, HELIOTROPE, PLANT

valet MAN, CRISPIN, SQUIRE, SERVANT, FLUNKY, LACKEY, ATTENDANT

Valetta *native* MALTESE

valid SOUND, COGENT, LEGAL, LICIT, JUST, LOGICAL, SOLID, GOOD, EFFICIENT, EFFECTIVE, EFFICACIOUS, WEIGHTY, LAWFUL, BINDING, OFFICIAL
mode of third figure FERISON
not NULL, VOID

validate ATTEST, RATIFY, SEAL, CONFIRM, SUBSTANTIATE

validity FORCE, COGENCY, SOUNDNESS, JUSTNESS, STRENGTH, AUTHORITY

valise, *small* ETUI, ETWEE, BAG, PORTMANTEAU

Vali's *father* ODIN

Valkyrie NORN, DIS

valley DALE, VALE, GLEN, DELL, SWALE, DINGLE, GORGE,

GULCH, RAVINE, CANYON
between volcanic cones ATRIO
Biblical BACA
deep COULEE, CANYON
England DEAN, DENE
Hinnom GEHENNA
in Argolis NEMEA
India DHOON
Levant WADI, WADY
moon RILL(E)
S. Africa VAAL
stream CREEK, COULEE

valorous HEROIC, GALLANT, BRAVE, BOLD, INTREPID, COURAGEOUS, STOUT, DAUNTLESS, DOUGHTY

value ADMIRE, ESTEEM, CARAT, STERLING, PAR, WORTH, PRICE, COST, WEIGHT, RATE, ASSESS, JUDGE, CHERISH, PRIZE, IMPORTANCE, UTILITY, ESTIMATE, APPRAISE, EVALUATE, RESPECT
assay LEY
excessively OVERRATE
least possible RAP, PLACK, TRIFLE, NOMINAL

valueless BAFF, WORTHLESS, MISERABLE, TRASHY

valve COCK, TAP, FAUCET, OUTLET
sliding PISTON

vamoose GO, SCRAM, DECAMP

vampire BAT, LAMIA, FLIRT, GHOUL, TEMPTRESS, EXTORTIONER

van FORE, FRONT, HEAD, TRUCK, DRAY, LORRY
opposite REAR

van Gogh *city* ARLES

vane FAN, FLAG, PENNON, WEATHERCOCK, BLADE, FEATHER

vang ROPE, GUY

vanish FLY, FADE, PASS, EVANESCE, MELT, SINK, FLEE, DISSOLVE, DEPART, RECEDE, DIE, DISAPPEAR, EVAPORATE

vanity SHAM, PRIDE, EGOISM, EGOTISM, ARROGANCE, EMPTINESS, FUTILITY, FALSITY, CONCEIT
box DORINE, ETUI, ETWEE

"Vanity Fair"
character SHARP, BECKY

vantage, *place of* COIGN(E)

vapid POINTLESS, STALE, FLAT, INSIPID, DULL, INANE, JEJUNE, BANAL, TAME, DEAD, SPIRITLESS, TASTELESS

vapor RACK, REEK, FOG, GAS, HAZE, STEAM, MIST, MOISTURE, SMOKE, EXHALATION, PHANTASM, BUBBLE, EVAPORATION, FUME
combining form ATM(O)
pressure indicator TONOMETER

vaporous STEAMY, CLOUDY, INDISTINCT, UNREAL, FOGGY, MISTY, MOIST, ETHEREAL, UNSUBSTANTIAL, VAIN

Varangians ROS

variable PROTEAN, MOBILE, MUTABLE, FICKLE, FITFUL, CHANGEABLE, IRRESOLUTE, UNSTEADY, INCONSTANT, ABERRANT, SHIFTY, CAPRICIOUS, UNSTABLE, RESTLESS, WAVERING, SHIFTING

variance *in text of author* LECTION

variegate FRET, DIVERSIFY, DAPPLE,

SPOT, VARY, MOTTLE,
FLECK, SPECKLE
variegated PIED,
PINTO, DIVERSE,
MOTLEY
variety KIND, CLASS,
BRAND, VERSATILITY,
DIVERSITY,
INTERMIXTURE,
VARIATION,
DIFFERENCE, MIX-
TURE, MEDLEY
various DIVERSE,
SEVERAL, MANY,
DIVERS, DIFFERENT,
MANIFOLD, MULTI-
FORM
combining form
VARI
varnish SHELLAC,
JAPAN, POLISH,
GLOSS, PALLIATE,
EMBELLISH,
FURBISH, ADORN,
EXCUSE
ingredient LAC,
COPAL, ELEMI
vas DUCT, VESSEL,
VEIN, SURETY,
PLEDGE
vascular, *pertaining*
to HEMAL, HEMIC
vase DIOTA, JAR,
URN
bronze ECHEA
Egypt and Etruscan
CANOPIC
Greek DEINOS,
DINOS, PELIKE
handle ANSA
ornamental
EPERGNE
used as cinerary urn
D(E)INOS,
CANOPIC
as oil vessel
ASKOS
with separate cover
POTICHE
vassal SLAVE,
LIEGEMAN, SERF,
THRALL, HELOT,
TENANT, SUBJECT,
RETAINER, SERVANT,
FEUDATORY, BONDS-
MAN
vassalage, *subject to*
ENFEOFF
vast HUGE, UNTOLD,
GREAT, BIG, LARGE,
IMMENSE, ENOR-
MOUS, MIGHTY,

SPACIOUS,
EXTENSIVE,
INFINITE, BOUND-
LESS *See* "huge"
vat TUB, CISTERN,
KEEL, TANK, TUN,
BAC, BARREL
beer GAAL, GYLE
bleaching KIER,
KEIR
for mash KEEVE
Vatican *chapel*
SISTINE
vaticinator ORACLE,
PREDICTOR,
PHOPHET
vault FORNIX, CELLAR,
ARCH, CRYPT,
CAVE, SPRING, LEAP,
CURVET, TOMB,
CRATER, CEILING,
niche CATACOMB
vaulted CONCAVE,
DOMED, ARCHED,
CUPOLAR, CURVED
recess APSE
roof CAMERA
vaunt BRAG, CROW,
VAPOR *See* "boast"
veal CALF, MEAT
forequarters RACK
like VITULINE
vector CARRIER, HOST
opposite of SCALAR
Vedic-Aryan *dialect*
PALI
cosmic order RITA
Vedic *god See under*
"god"
sky serpent AHI
veer SLUE, WEAR,
YAW, SWAY,
SWERVE *See*
"shift"
Vega *constellation*
LYRA
vegetable PLANT,
PEA, UDO, POTATO,
LOMENT, LEGUME,
OKRA, CHARD, FOOD,
CABBAGE, TURNIP,
BEAN, CELERY, LET-
TUCE
mold HUMUS
onionlike LEEK,
SHALLOT, GARLIC
pod PEASE, HULL
rubbish WRACK
tracing paper ECU
vegetate HIBERNATE,
GROW

vegetation HERBAGE,
FLORA
floating SUDD
vehemence HEAT,
FORCE, ZEAL, ARDOR,
FIRE, ENTHUSIASM,
VIOLENCE, IMPETU-
OSITY, FURY, FERVOR,
PASSION, INTENSITY
vehement HOT, AR-
DENT, EAGER, IN-
TENSE, FIERCE,
IMPETUOUS, FURIOUS,
VIOLENT, URGENT,
PASSIONATE,
ZEALOUS, FERVID
vehicle CAR, AUTO,
SLED, VAN, TANK,
JEEP, BUS, TRUCK,
TAXI, CYCLE, DEVICE,
MEANS, AGENT,
CARRIAGE, CON-
VEYANCE *See*
"carriage"
India TONGA
pole NEAP, SHAFT,
TONGUE
public BUS, TAXI,
TRAIN, PLANE, CAB
snow PUNG, SLED,
SLEIGH
veil NET, FILM,
CLOAK, MESH, PRE-
TENSE, CONCEAL,
HIDE, DISGUISE,
SCREEN, COVER-
(ING), CURTAIN,
CAUL
head CAUL
fungi VELUM
papal ORALE
veiled HIDDEN,
VELATE, INCOGNITO,
CURTAINED
vein BENT, TENOR,
STRIA, MOOD, HUMOR,
STRAIN, STREAK,
TINGE, TOUCH,
SHADE, LODE, CAVA,
FISSURE, CAVITY,
CREVICE, VARIEGATION,
CHANNEL
enlarged VARIX
Latin VENULA,
VENA
metal LODE
mining LODE
neck JUGULAR
ore LODE, BONANZA
veinless AVENOUS
veinstone GANGUE,
MATRIX

veld(t) *See* "grass-
land"
vellicate TIC, TWICH,
PLUCK
vellum PARCHMENT,
PAPER, SKIN, MEM-
BRANE
venal HIRELING,
CORRUPT, SORDID,
SALABLE, MERCENARY,
VENDIBLE
vend SELL, PEDDLE,
BARTER, TRADE,
AUCTION, HAWK
vender SELLER,
MERCHANT, TRADER
vendetta FEUD
veneer SHELL,
ENAMEL, LAC, COAT-
ING, POLISH, OVER-
LAY, COAT, PRE-
TENSE, LAYER,
COVERING
venerable OLD(EN),
AUGUST, WISE,
SAGE, HOAR(Y),
ANCIENT, AGED, RE-
SPECTED, PATRIARCHAL
venerate REVERE,
LOVE, RESPECT,
ADORE, PRIZE, VALUE,
ESTEEM *See*
"worship"
veneration ESTEEM,
AWE, DULIA, HONOR,
RESPECT, DEVOTION,
REVERENCE
of angels and saints
DULIA
of God only LATRIA
Venetian *barge*
BUCENTAUR
boat GONDOLA
bridge RIALTO
coin DUCAT, GAZ-
ZETTA, OSELLA,
BEZZO, GROSSO,
CROISAT
district RIALTO
judge DOGE
medal OSELLA,
OSELA
nobleman DOGE
ruler PODESTA, DOGE
song BARCAROLE
traveler POLO,
MARCO
water street RIO
watering place LIDO
Venezuela *city or*
town CARACAS,
AROA, CORO

coin PESO, BOLIVAR,
CENTIMO
god TSUMA
grassy plain LLANO
hero BOLIVAR
Indian TIMOTE,
CARIB
language PUME
mountain (EL) PAO
river ORINOCO,
CARONI
state LARA, BOLIVAR,
ZULIA, FALCON,
APURE, SUCRE,
MONGAS, BARINAS
town See "city"
above
tree BALATA
venom GALL,
MALICE, VIRUS,
POISON, BANE,
TOXIN, SPITE,
RANCOR, VIRULENCE,
MALIGNITY
vent EMIT, BUNG,
SAY, SPIRACLE, UTTER,
AIR, REVEAL, HOLE,
OPENING, APERTURE,
OUTLET, EGRESS,
EMIT, EJECT,
PUBLISH, FLUE
ventilated AIRED,
OXYGENATED, AER-
ATED, FRESHENED
ventral HEMAL,
STERNAL, ABDOMI-
NAL
ventricles, *roof of*
TELA
venture CHANCE,
RISK, PERIL, DARE,
WAGE, BOLD, BRAVE,
HAZARD, STAKE,
UNDERTAKING,
ENTERPRISE,
SPECULATION,
DANGER, JEOPARDY,
GAMBLE,
PROJECT
Venus VESPER,
ASTARTE, APHRODITE
boy beloved by
ADONIS
epithet of
CYTHEREA
fly trap DIONAEA,
PLANT
girdle CESTUS
mother DIONE
planet LUCIFER,
PHOSPHOR
son CUPID

veracious TRUE,
VERILY, TRUTHFUL,
ACCURATE, RELIABLE
veranda LANAI,
PYAL, STOA, STOOP,
PORCH, PIAZZA,
PATIO, LOGGIA,
PORTICO, GALLERY
verb RHEMA, WORD,
VOCABLE
form TENSE
verbal ORAL, TACIT,
LITERAL, SPOKEN,
PAROL
noun GERUND
quibble PUN, SHIFT,
SOPHISM, WORDI-
NESS, VERBOSITY
rhythm METER
suffix ESCE, ISE
verbenaceae LANTANA,
TECTONA, PLANTS
verbiage PROLIXITY,
VERBOSITY, WORDI-
NESS, REDUNDANCY
verbose PROLIX,
WORDY, VOLUBLE,
TALKATIVE, LOQUA-
CIOUS, TEDIOUS
verd(ant) GREEN,
FRESH, RAW
Verdi *opera* AIDA,
OTHELLO, ERNANI,
RIGOLETTO, FALSTAFF,
(LA) TRAVIATA
character in AM-
NERIS, RAMADES,
AIDA
first opera OBERTO
verdigris RUST, FILM,
PATINA, PIGMENT,
DRUG, DEPOSIT
verecund MODEST,
SHY, BASHFUL
verge BRINK, EDGE,
MARGIN, TOP,
LIMIT, (B)RIM,
BORDER, SKIRT, ROD,
STAFF, BOUNDARY,
RANGE, SCOPE, CIR-
CUMFERENCE
of authority WAND
Vergil POET
birthplace GAUL
family name MARO
hero AENEAS
patron MAECENAS
queen DIDO
verify (AT)TEST,
PROVE, AUDIT, CON-
FIRM, SUBSTANTIATE,

AUTHENTICATE,
CORRECT
verily YEA, AMEN,
INDEED, CERTAINLY,
ASSUREDLY, TRULY,
REALLY, POSITIVELY
verisimilitude POS-
SIBILITY, TRUTH,
VERITY, PROBABILITY,
LIKELIHOOD
veritable REAL,
ACTUAL, GENUINE
verity FACT, HON-
ESTY, TRUTH,
REALITY
vermiform LONG,
SLENDER, THIN,
FLEXIBLE, WORM-
LIKE, VERMICULAR,
SINUOUS, WIND-
ING
vermilion RED, PIG-
MENT, PAINT
Vermont *city* BARRE,
LYNDON
county ESSEX,
ORANGE, ORLEANS
vernacular DIALECT,
CANT, ARGOT,
SLANG, PATTER,
PATOIS, NATIVE,
INDIGENOUS, LOCAL,
VULGAR, IDIOM
vernal GREEN,
YOUTHFUL, SPRING-
LIKE
versation WINDING,
TURNING
verse POEM, METER,
POETRY, JINGLE,
RIME, RHYME, STICH,
RONDEL, STROPHE,
STAVE, LINE, STANZA,
POESY, TEXT, DIVISION
break in CAESURA
form TROCHEE,
ANAPAEST, DACTYL,
SPONDEE, IAMB,
IONIC
pertaining to ODIC
group STROPHE
having 8 feet
OCTAMETER
3 feet TRIPODY
2 feet DIPODY
Horace EPODE
nonsensical DOG-
GEREL, LIMERICK
of 4 meters TETRAM-
ETER
3 feet TRIMETER

2 measures
DIMETER
pause in CAESURA
pertaining to PALI-
NODIC
romance form
SESTINA
six-line SESTINA
stress, pertaining to
ICTIC
three-line TERCET
unit FOOT
with hidden motto
ACROSTIC
versed ADEPT,
SKILLED, ERUDITE,
PROFICIENT, SKILL-
FUL, ACCOMPLISHED,
TRAINED, CLEVER
versification
ORTHOMETRY,
POETRY
versifier BARD, POET,
POETASTER, RIME-
STER, RHYMER,
RHYMESTER
version FORM, EDI-
TION, TRANSLATION,
DESCRIPTION, AC-
COUNT, REPORT,
STORY, INTERPRETA-
TION, TURNING
Bible VULGATE
See "Bible"
Latin ITALA
verso BACK, REVERSE
versus AGAINST, VS
vertebra SPONDYL,
SPINE, CHINE, SEG-
MENT *See*
"spine"
vertebrate *axis* AXON
vertex APEX, TOP,
SUMMIT, ZENITH,
CULMINATION
vertical PLUMB,
UPRIGHT, STRAIGHT,
STANDING, PER-
PENDICULAR, ERECT
timber BITT, JAMB
verticillate WHORLED
vertigo DIZZINESS,
GIDDINESS, DINUS,
INSTABILITY, STAG-
GERS, CONFUSION
verve ZIP, ELAN,
PEP, SPIRIT, ZEST,
APTITUDE, TALENT,
ANIMATION, EN-
THUSIASM, VIVACITY,
VIGOR, ENERGY,
FEELING

act with EMOTE
very REAL, TRUE,
ACTUAL, EXTREMELY,
SAME, GENUINE,
TRES, EXCEEDINGLY,
ABSOLUTELY, QUITE,
UTTERLY, IDENTICAL,
TRULY, SO
much, combining
form ERI
vesicle CYST, SAC,
CAVITY, HOLLOW,
BLADDER, BLISTER,
BLEB
vespa WASP
vesper STAR, EVENING,
PRAYER, HESPER,
VENUS, HYMN
Vespucci AMERIGO
vessel(s) URN, DIOTA,
CASK, VAS, PAN, POT,
VAT, MUG, BOWL,
CONTAINER *See*
"ship"
amount needed to fill
ULLAGE
anatomical VAS(A),
ARTERY, VEIN
assaying CUPEL
baptismal FONT
beer STEIN, POURIE,
MUG, KEG, SEIDEL,
TOBY, FLAGON,
SCHOONER
Biblical ARK
broad shallow PAN
combining form
VASO
cuplike ZARF
cylindrical glass
BOCAL
deep table TUREEN
drinking GOURD,
JORUM, STEIN, TANK-
ARD, STOUP (STOOP),
AMPULLA, CUP,
GLASS, MUG, FLAGON,
TOBY, SEIDEL,
FLASK, SCHOONER
earthen CROCK,
PANKIN
ecclesiastical AMA,
PYX
edge LIP
filter glass ALUDEL
for ale or wine
JUBBE, STEIN
for holding illumi-
nant CRESSET
for napkins, etc.
NEF, RING

for oil CUP, CRUSE, FONT
for refining CUPEL
for sugar or molasses refining ELUTOR
glass BOCAL, GOBLET, TUMBLER, BEAKER
heating ETNA
large TANK, VAT, TUB
liquor FLAGON *See* "drinking" *above*
sacred PIX, PYX
saucerlike PATERA
small NOG, NOGGIN, SHOT, PONY
stone or clay STEAN, STEEN, URN
vinegar CRUET
wine service AMA
wooden COGUE, PIGGIN, SKEEL, KITTY, MAZER, SOE
vessels *fitted into each other* ALUDEL, NEST(ED)
vest ROBE, DRESS, ATTIRE, JACKET, CASSOCK, ARRAY, GARB, GARMENT, WAISTCOAT, ENDOW, FURNISH, GIVE, GRANT, ENCOMPASS, SURROUND
stuffed ACTON, BORE
woolen GILET, LINDER, WAISTCOAT
Vesta HESTIA, MATCH, TAPER
vestal VIRGINAL, PURE, CHASTE, NUN
vestibule HALL, LOBBY, FOYER, ENTRY, NARTHEX, ANTEROOM, PORCH, PASSAGE, ENTRANCE
vestige RELIC, SIGN, TRACE, TRACK, SHRED, FRAGMENT, TINCTURE, PRINT, STAMP, MARK, TOKEN, EVIDENCE
vestment DRESS, CHASUBLE, HABIT, EPHOD, SCAPULAR, GREMIAL, UNIFORM, GARMENT, ROBE, FROCK
alblike SACCOS
Arab ABA
clerical ALB, AMICE, COPE, CASSOCK

eucharistic MANIPLE
liturgical COPE
outer CHASUBLE
priest SURPLICE, ALB, STOLE, FROCK
white ALB
vestry SACRISTY, CHAPEL
vesuvianite IDOCRASE
vetch AKRA, TARE, FITCH, PLANT
bitter ERS
common genus SATIVA
vetiver CUSCUS, BENA, KHUSKHUS, GRASS
veto KILL, QUASH, DENY, PROHIBIT, INTERDICT(ION), FORBID, NEGATIVE
vex HARASS, CARK, FRET, RILE, GALL, ROIL, IRK, NETTLE, IRE, PUZZLE, PROVOKE, DISQUIET *See* "annoy"
vexation CHAFE, CHAGRIN, IRRITATION, ANNOYANCE, TROUBLE, DISPLEASURE, PIQUE, AGITATION, AFFLICTION, DISTRESS, DISCOMFIT, NUISANCE, MORTIFICATION
vexatious PESKY, PESTIFEROUS, PROVOKING, AGGRAVATING
vial CRUET, AMPULE, PHIAL, BOTTLE, AMPOULE
viand(s) CATE, FARE, FOOD, EATS, CHOW, GRUB, VICTUALS *See* "food"
viatic JOURNEYING, TRAVELING
viator TRAVELER, WAYFARER, TOURIST
Viaud LOTI
vibrant RESONANT, SONOROUS, PULSING, THRILLING, RESOUNDING, ANIMATED, LIVELY, THROBBING, VIGOROUS
vibrate OSCILLATE, THRILL, JAR, RESONATE, TIRL, QUAVER, THROB, BEAT, FLUC-

TUATE, BRANDISH, QUIVER, UNDULATE, WAVER
music TREMOLO
vicar PASTOR, CURATE, DEPUTY, VICEREGENT, PROXY, SUBSTITUTE, CLERGYMAN
vice PLACE, STEAD, SIN, FLAW, EVIL, ILL, FAILING, DEPRAVITY, WICKEDNESS, CORRUPTION, DEFORMITY, TAINT, IMPERFECTION, INIQUITY, CRIME, SUCCEEDING, IMMORALITY, DEFECT
king VICEROY
president VEEP
viceroy VALI, BUTTERFLY
victim GULL, DUPE, PREY, CULLY, SACRIFICE, MARTYR
victor CONQUEROR, MASTER, WINNER, CHAMPION, VANQUISHER
garland BAY, LAUREL
victorine PEACH, TIPPET
victory AWARD, NIKE, PALM, CONQUEST, SUCCESS, TRIUMPH, MASTERY, ACHIEVEMENT
celebrating EPINICION
crown LAUREL, BAY
English CRECY, CRESSY
hymn of EPINICION
memorial ARCH, TROPHY, SCALP
sign of VEE, BIDIGITATION
victual(s) EAT(S), FEED, FOOD, KAI, CHOW, GRUB, VIANDS
videlicet VIZ, NAMELY
vie LIFE, RIVAL, COMPETE, EMULATE, CONTEND, MATCH, STRIVE
Vienna WIEN
park PRATER
Vietnam *city or town* NGAI, HANOI, HUE, RON, SAIGON *See* "Indo-China"
region TONKIN

river SEN, MEKONG
tribe THO, THAI,
  MOI
view VISTA, SEE, EYE,
  KEN, LOOK, SIGHT,
  PEEK, OPINION,
  BELIEF, IDEA, SCAN,
  SURVEY, GLIMPSE,
  SCENE, OGLE,
  WITNESS, BEHOLD,
  EXAMINATION,
  PROSPECT, REPRE-
  SENTATION, SKETCH,
  JUDGMENT,
  EXPECTATION,
  PANORAMA
vigil PATROL, WATCH,
  WAKEFULNESS,
  SLEEPLESSNESS,
  CARE
vigilant AWAKE,
  ALERT, WARY, AGOG,
  SHARP, KEEN, AVID,
  WATCHFUL,
  ATTENTIVE,
  OBSERVANT,
  CIRCUMSPECT,
  WAKEFUL, CAUTIOUS
person ARGUS
vigilantes POSSE
vigor FORCE,
  STAMINA, STHENIA,
  SPIRIT, ESPRIT, VIR,
  ENERGY, LIFE, VIM,
  PEP, ZIP, STRENGTH,
  POWER, VALIDITY,
  MIGHT, POTENCY,
  HEALTH, SOUNDNESS,
  VITALITY
vigorous HALE,
  COGENT, STRONG,
  LUSTY, STOUT,
  ATHLETIC, ROBUST,
  ACTIVE, POWERFUL,
  VIRILE, FORCIBLE,
  STRENUOUS,
  VEHEMENT,
  HEALTHY, STURDY,
  LIVELY, POTENT,
  HARDY, ZEALOUS
Viking PIRATE,
  ROVER
poet SKALD, SCALD
vile BAD, BRUTISH,
  COMMON, IMMORAL,
  POOR, DEGRADED,
  DEPRAVED, LOW,
  ABJECT, MEAN,
  WILE, BASE,
  REPULSIVE, WICKED,
  IMPURE, EVIL,
  DESPICABLE,

PALTRY, CONTEMPTI-
  BLE, BEGGARLY,
  ODIOUS,
  GROVELLING, FOUL,
  OBSCENE
vilify ABUSE,
  MALIGN, REVILE,
  TRADUCE, LIBEL,
  DEFAME, SLANDER,
  ASPERSE, CALUMNI-
  ATE, VITUPERATE,
  DISPARAGE, CENSURE,
  DENIGRATE
village TOWN,
  HAMLET, DORP, VILL,
  THORP, BURG, DUMP,
  ALDEA, SETTLEMENT
Africa KRAAL, STAD
fortified BURG
Russian MIR
Spanish ALDEA
villain KNAVE, ROGUE,
  RASCAL, BOOR,
  SCOUNDREL, SCAMP,
  REPROBATE, RUF-
  FIAN, MISCREANT
of "Othello" IAGO
villatic RURAL,
  RUSTIC
villein CHURL, CARL,
  ESNE, SERF, HELOT,
  THRALL, SLAVE, PEON,
  PEASANT
vim *See* "vigor"
vinculum FRENUM,
  BAND, BRACE, BOND,
  UNION
vindicate JUSTIFY,
  AVENGE, REVENGE,
  ACQUIT, DEFEND,
  UPHOLD, SUPPORT,
  SUSTAIN, MAINTAIN,
  ABSOLVE, CLEAR
vine(s) LIANA,
  LIANE, IVY, TWINE,
  GRAPE, HOP
combining form
  VITI
covered with
  IVIED
E. India SOMA, ODAL
fruit bearing GRAPE,
  CUPSEED
parasite APHIS,
  APHID
part of CIRRUS,
  TENDRIL
support RISEL,
  TRELLIS,
tropical LIANA
twining BINE

woody CUPSEED
  genus HEDERA
vinegar ACETUM,
  EISEL
bottle CRUET
combining form
  ACET(O)
dregs MOTHER
of ale ALEGAR
preserve in MARI-
  NATE, PICKLE
vineyards, *protector of*
  PRIAPUS
vinous WINY
  grosbeak MORO,
  BIRD
viol RUANA, SARINDA,
  REBEC
progenitor of REBEC
viola ALTA, GAMBA,
  ALTO
violate ABUSE,
  POLLUTE, DESECRATE,
  DEFILE, PROFANE,
  RAVISH, DEBAUCH,
  INFRINGE, TRANS-
  GRESS, DISHONOR
violation BREACH,
  SIN, VICE, CRIME,
  DESECRATION,
  INFRINGEMENT,
  TRANSGRESSION,
  PROFANATION,
  IRREVERENCE,
  DISTURBANCE
sentence structure
  ANACOLUTHON
violent WILD, HOT,
  RAGING, MAD,
  MANIC, IRATE,
  FORCIBLE, ACUTE,
  FRANTIC, FURIOUS,
  SEVERE, VEHEMENT,
  GREAT, EXTREME,
  INTENSE, VIVID,
  LOUD, UNNATURAL,
  ABNORMAL, FIERCE,
  SAVAGE, TURBULENT,
  TEMPESTUOUS,
  STORMY
Norseman
  BERSERKER
violently AMAIN
violet MAUVE,
  PLANT, FLOWER,
  PIGMENT
dye ARCHIL
oil from leaves
  IRONE
violin, *baritone*
  CELLO

bow, combining form
ARC(O)
famous AMATI,
STRAD, CREMONA
first REBEC, REBAB
like ROCTA
part of NECK
player See
"violinist"
pressure on bow
SACCADE
progenitor of REBAB,
REBEC
sound post AME
string GUT
tenor ALTO
violinist NERO, BULL,
OLE, AUER,
KREISLER
viper ADDER, ASP,
CERASTES, SNAKE,
SERPENT, BOA,
RACER *See* "snake"
E. India KUPPER
genus ECHIS
Russell's KATUKA
virago FURY,
RULLION, VIXEN,
TERMAGANT, SCOLD,
SHREW, BARGE,
XANTIPPE
Virgil *See* "Vergil"
virgin NEW, FRESH,
PURE, VESTAL,
CHASTE, MAID(EN),
LASS, DAMSEL,
MADONNA, MODEST,
UNADULTERATED
mourning PIETA
warrior, Aeneid
CAMILLA
Virgin island
TORTOLA, (ST.)
CROIX
Virginia DARE
county BATH,
BLAND, CRAIG,
ESSEX, FLOYD,
GILES, HENRY,
HENRICO, LEE,
LOUISA, PAGE, SCOTT,
SMYTH, SURRY,
SUSSEX, WISE,
WYTHE, YORK
creeper AMPELOPSIS,
IVY, WOODBINE,
PLANT
juniper CEDAR
pine LOBLOLLY
swamp DISMAL
wake-robin ARUM,
PLANT

willow ITEA
woodcock PEEWEE,
PEWEE
virile STRONG,
MANLY, MASCULINE,
MASTERFUL, FORCE-
FUL
virtu CURIO, RELIC,
ANTIQUE
virulence HATRED,
TOXICITY,
MALIGNANCY
virulent POISONOUS,
VENOMOUS,
NOXIOUS, DEADLY,
TOXIC, RABID,
BITTER, HOSTILE,
ACRIMONIOUS
virus POISON, VENOM,
GERM, TOXIN,
DISEASE
ailment FLU,
HERPES
visage FACE, MAP,
ASPECT, FRONT,
GUISE, MUG, PUSS,
COUNTENANCE,
APPEARANCE,
SEMBLANCE
viscid THICK,
STICKY,
GLUTINOUS
viscous SLIMY,
ROPY, STICKY,
GLUEY, SIZY, VISCID,
GLUTINOUS
vise CLAMP, WINCH,
TOOL
cap CHUCK
Vishnu, *incarnation*
KRISHNA, RAMA
serpent NAGA
Soul of Universe
VASU
visible PATENT,
OBVIOUS, OPEN,
APPARENT,
MANIFEST,
PERCEPTIBLE,
DISCOVERABLE
to naked eye
MACROSCOPIC
Visigoth TEUTON,
GOTH
king ALARIC
vision DREAM,
SIGHT, VIEW,
FANCY, MIRAGE,
PHANTOM, APPARI-
TION, SPECTER,
GHOST, CHIMERA,
ILLUSION,

HALLUCINATION,
EYESIGHT,
DISCERNMENT,
FORESIGHT,
PERCEPTION
combining form
OPTO
double DIPLOPIA
pertaining to OPTIC
poor ANOPIA,
AMBLYOPIA
visionary FEY, IDEAL,
DREAMY, DREAMER,
FANCIFUL, UTOPIAN,
FANTASTIC, UNREAL,
DELUSIVE,
ROMANTIC,
IMAGINARY, IMPRAC-
TICAL, CHIMERICAL,
DELUSIONAL,
HETERODOX
visit CALL, STAY,
SEE, AFFLICT,
SOJOURN, INSPECT,
BENEFIT, BLESS,
TRAVEL
between whale ships
GAM
visor, *helmet* UMBREL
vista SCAPE, SCENE,
VIEW, SIGHT,
PROSPECT, OUTLOOK,
PERSPECTIVE
Vistula *tributary*
SAN, BUG, DRWECA
vita LIFE
"Vita Nuova" *author*
DANTE
vital MORTAL,
IMPORTANT,
NECESSARY,
ESSENTIAL, LIVING,
ANIMATE(D),
ENERGETIC, FATAL,
FLOURISHING,
INVIGORATING,
FUNDAMENTAL,
REQUISITE, INDIS-
PENSABLE, EXIGENT,
IMPERATIVE
air OXYGEN
energy HORME
fluid SAP, BLOOD,
LYMPH
force NEURISM,
VIS
growth force
BATHMISM
juice BLOOD, SAP,
LYMPH
strength STAMINA

vitality LIFE, SAP,
STRENGTH, PEP,
ZIP, ENDURANCE
See "vigor"
pertaining to
VIABLE
vitamin NIACIN,
FLAVIN, BIOTIN
vitellus YOLK
vitiate SPOIL,
POLLUTE, VOID,
TAINT, CORRUPT,
IMPAIR, DEFILE,
CONTAMINATE,
DEBASE, DEPRAVE,
PERVERT, INVALI-
DATE
vitreous GLASSY,
HARD
sodium carbonate
TRONA
stone APATITE
vitriform *mineral*
SPAR
vitrine SHOWCASE
vitriol CAUSTIC,
ACID
vituperation REBUKE,
BLAME, ABUSE,
CENSURE, RAILING,
INVECTIVE
vivacity DASH, ELAN,
VERVE, PEP, ZIP,
SPRIGHTLINESS,
LIVELINESS *See*
"vigor"
vivandiere SUTLER
vivary, vivarium
PARK, WARREN, ZOO,
ENCLOSURE, BOX,
POND
vivid LIVE, GRAPHIC,
SHARP, KEEN,
ACUTE, CLEAR,
LUCID, SPIRITED,
FRESH, LIVELY,
INTENSE, BRIGHT,
STRIKING, COLORFUL,
RICH, GLOWING,
DISTINCT, STRONG
vixen SHREW,
VIRAGO, SCOLD,
BARGE *See* "virago"
Vladimir Ilich
Ulyanov LENIN
vocabulary LEXICON,
DICTION(ARY),
STYLE, WORDBOOK,
LANGUAGE
vocal SONANT, ORAL,
FLUENT, VERBAL,
PHONETIC,

VOICED, CLAMOROUS,
ELOQUENT
composition MOTET,
SONG
flourish ROULADE
vocally, utter
PHONATE, ARTICULATE
voe BAY, CREEK,
INLET
vogue CUSTOM,
FASHION, FAVOR,
POPULARITY
voice VOX, KEY,
SAY, TENOR, ALTO,
BASS, EMIT,
SOPRANO, TELL,
SPEAK, TALK, SOUND,
SPEECH, UTTERANCE,
WISH, CHOICE,
OPINION, VOTE,
SUFFRAGE, ARTICULA-
TION, EXPRESSION,
TONGUE, OPTION,
PREFERENCE, TONE,
INTONATION,
ANNOUNCE, DIVULGE,
RUMOR
inflection TONE,
INTONATION
loss of APHONIA,
ANAUDIA
natural DIPETTO
person with loud or
powerful STENTOR
voiceless ANAUDIA,
SPIRATE, SURD,
APHONETIC, SILENT,
MUTE, DUMB
consonant SURD
sound TENUIS
void ABOLISH, NULL,
VAIN, ANNUL, VETO,
QUASH, ABYSS,
EMPTY, VACANT,
BLANK, BARE,
BARREN, VACUUM,
UNOCCUPIED,
UNEMPLOYED, IDLE,
DESTITUTE, DEVOID,
INEFFECTUAL,
USELESS, VACATE,
LEAVE, NULLIFY
voided *escutcheon*
ORLE
volatile AIRY,
CHANGEABLE,
VAPOROUS, FITFUL,
FLIGHTY, MERCURIAL,
FICKLE, FLYING,
VOLANT, LIGHT-
HEARTED, BUOYANT,

FRIVOLOUS, GIDDY,
CAPRICIOUS
volatilize EXHALE,
ATOMIZE, EVAPORATE
volcanic *ejection*
BELCH, LAVA
fragments of lava
LAPILLI
glass PERLITE,
OBSIDIAN
lava ingredients
LAPILLI, PUMICE,
SCORIA, MUD, ROCK
mud MOYA, SALSE
rock PERLITE,
RHYOLITE, LATITE
saucer CRATER
scoria SLAG
vent CRATER
volcano, *Alaska*
PAVLOF, KATMAI,
OKMOK
Cape Verde FOGO
Colombia HUILA,
PURACE, PASTO
Costa Rica POAS,
BARBA
Ecuador SANGAY
El Salvador IZALCO
fluid rock LAVA
goddess, Hawaii
PELE
Guatemala
ATITLAN, FUEGO
Hawaii MAUNA
(LOA), MAUNA(KEA)
Iceland ASKJA,
HEKLA
Indonesia AWU
(AWOE), RAUNG
Italy ETNA,
VESUVIUS, STROM-
BOLI
Japan ASAMA, FUJI,
ASO(SAN), MIHARA
Java GEDE,
RAUNG, KELUT,
BROMO, MERAPI,
SEMERU
Kuril Islands FUYO
Martinique PELEE
Mexico COLIMA,
TUXTLA
Mindanao APO
mouth of
FUMAROLE, CRATER
New Hebrides
LOPEVI
Nicaragua TELICA,
NEGRO
Peru MISTI

Philippines APO,
HIBOK, TAAL, MAYON,
ASKJA
Sicily ETNA
slag SCORIA
Solomon Islands
BALBI
steam from STUFA
Volga, *anc. city on*
SARAI
tributary KAMA,
SURA, OKA
volition WILL,
CONATION, CHOICE,
ELECTION,
DETERMINATION,
PREFERENCE
volley SALVO, BURST
volplane GLIDE
Volsunga *king* ATLI
volt AMPERE, WATT,
OHM, TURN, CIRCLE
Voltaire *novel*
CANDIDE, ZADIG
name AROUET
volti TURN
voluble FLUENT,
GLIB, ROTATING,
REVOLVING, TALKA-
TIVE, LOQUACIOUS
volume BULK,
CUBAGE, MO, TOME,
MASS, EXTENT,
BOOK, SIZE, ROLL,
SCROLL, AGGREGATE,
QUANTITY,
DIMENSIONS,
AMPLITUDE, VAST-
NESS
in ten parts
DECAMERON
measure See under
"measure"
volumetric *analysis*
TITRATE
Volund's *brother*
EGIL
volunteer OFFER,
ENLIST, ENROLL
volute CILERY,
MOLLUSK, SCROLL,
SPIRAL, WHORL,
UNIVALVE
voodooism OBEAH,
FETISHISM
fetish MOJO, OBI,
JUJU
voracious EDACIOUS,
EAGER, GREEDY,
RAVENOUS,
RAPACIOUS,
GLUTTONOUS,

HUNGRY, INSATIABLE,
IMMODERATE
vortex EDDY, GYRE,
WHIRLPOOL,
MAELSTROM,
TORNADO, WHIRL-
WIND
votary FAN,
DEVOTEE, ITE,
ADDICT, FIEND,
ZEALOT, BUFF,
ADHERENT,
ENTHUSIAST
vote BALLOT, STRAW,
NAME, NAY,
SUFFRAGE, VOICE,
TICKET
of assent NOD,
YEA, AYE
receptacle for votes
SITULA, BOX
register of POLL
vouch BACK, ATTEST,
SPONSOR, ABET,
UPHOLD, VERIFY,
SUPPORT, MAINTAIN,
GUARANTEE
voucher STATEMENT,
CHIT, NOTE, BILL,
RECEIPT, RELEASE
vouchsafe BESTOW,
CONCEDE, DEIGN,
GRANT, GIVE,
STOOP, FAVOR,
CONDESCEND,
YIELD, ALLOW
vow OATH, SWEAR,
PROMISE, PLEDGE,
ASSERTION,
ASSEVERATION,
DEDICATE,
CONSECRATE, DEVOTE
*dedicated or promised
by* VOTIVE
vowel(s), *change in,
German* UMLAUT
contraction of two
CRASIS
drop final ELIDE
gradation ABLAUT
group of two
DIGRAPH
line over MACRON,
TILDE
omission APHESIS
point, Hebrew
(T)SERE
short BREVE
sign DIAERESIS
sound, pertaining to
VOCAL
Vulcan HEPHAESTUS,

BLACKSMITH, METAL-
WORKER
son CACUS
wife VENUS, MAIA
vulcanite EBONITE
vulgar GROSS, LEWD,
RIBALD, MEAN,
COMMON, COARSE,
LOW, BASE, VILE,
GENERAL, ORDINARY,
PUBLIC, POPULAR,
CUSTOMARY,
COMMONPLACE,
VERNACULAR,
UNREFINED, BOORISH,
OFFENSIVE, OBSCENE,
RANDY
looking DOWDY,
FRUMPY
Vulgate ITALA
vulpine FOXY, WILY,
ALOPECOID, CUNNING,
CRAFTY, ARTFUL,
SLY
vulture CONDOR,
PAPA, URUBU,
BUZZARD, HARPY,
BIRD
king PAPA
Old World GRIFFON

W

W WEN (old Eng.)
waag GRIVET,
MONKEY
wabble TITTER,
VACILLATE, OSCIL-
LATE, SWAY, WOBBLE
wachna COD
wacky ERRATIC,
FOOLISH, CRAZY,
DISORDERED
wad MONEY, MASS,
PACK, LUMP, PAD,
STUFF, PLUG, TUFT,
BUNDLE, STOPPER,
WEALTH, LINE
Wadai Moslem
MABA
wade FORD, PLODGE
wadi, wady
CHANNEL, VALLEY,
GORGE, RIVER,
OASIS
wading *bird See
under* "bird"
wafer DISK, HOST,
SEAL, CANDY, CAKE,
BISCUIT, CRACKER,
LAMINA, SCALE
box PYX

waffle (BATTER)CAKE, GOPHER

waft CARRY, BREATH, ODOR, CONVEY, TRANSPORT, TRANSMIT, SIGNAL, BECKONING, WHIFF, BLOW

wag WAVE, NOD, ROGUE, WIT, JOKER, CARD, SHAKE, VIBRATE, OSCILLATE, SWAY, SIGNAL

wage(s) HIRE, PAY, STIPEND, FEE, SCREW, SALARY, EMOLUMENT
N. Zealand UTU

wager RISK, BET, PLEDGE, STAKE, HAZARD, POT, ANTE, PRIZE, VENTURE

waggish ARCH, JOCULAR, ROUGISH, JOLLY, WITTY, COMIC, SPORTIVE, MISCHIEVOUS, FROLICSOME, HUMOROUS

Wagner *hero* TRISTRAM
heroine ISOLDE, ELSA
opera RIENZI, PARSIFAL

wagon TRAM, TONGA, VAN, DRAY, CART, CAR, CAISSON, CHARIOT, COACH, LORRY, TRUCK, WAIN
India TONGA
oriental covered ARABA
pin CLEVIS
pole NEAP
shaft THILL, BLADE
springless, Russia TELEGA
thill BLADE, SHAFT
tongue NEAP, POLE

wahoo PETO, FISH, BUSH, ELM, BUCKTHORN, BASSWOOD

waif GAMIN, STRAFE, STRAY, WANDERER, CASTAWAY, FOUNDLING

wail HOWL, SOB, ULULATE, MOAN, BAWL See "lament"

wain CART, WAGON

wainscot CEIL, PANEL, MOTH

waist BODICE, BASQUE, GARIBALDI, GIRTH, CAMISE, BLOUSE, SHIRT

waistband BELT, SASH, OBI, CUMMERBUND

waistcoat DOUBLET, VEST, GILET, JERKIN
unlined SINGLET

wait (A)BIDE, LINGER, STAY, TARRY, REMAIN, EXPECT, HOPE, DELAY, LOITER, PAUSE, BREAK

waiter TRAY, SALVER, GARCON, ATTENDANT, SERVANT, LACKEY, STEWARD

waive FOREGO, RELINQUISH, CEDE, YIELD, RESIGN, ABANDON, SURRENDER, FORSAKE, DISREGARD, RENOUNCE, REPUDIATE, POSTPONE, DEFER

Wakashan AHT, INDIAN

wake-robin ARUM, CUCKOOPINT, TRILLIUM, ORCHIS, PLANT

waken (A)ROUSE, WAKE, STIR, EXCITE, FIRE

Waldensian LEONIST

wale RIB, WELT, STREAK, MARK, RIDGE, STRIPE, WHEAL, GRAIN

Wales, Welsh CAMBRIA, CYMRI(C), TAFFY, CELT, CAMBRIAN, CYMRY
boat CORACLE
dialect CYMRIC
district MOLD, RHYL
floral emblem LEEK
hamlet TREF
island CALDY
lake BALA
language CELTIC
legendary prince MADOC
musical assembly EISTEDDFOD
onion CIBOL

people of South SILURES
prince IDRIS
zone of OLENUS

walk AMBLE, PACE, HIKE, GAD, TRAMP, TREAD, MUSH, PLOD, GAIT, STROLL, SAUNTER, STRUT, PARADE, PERAMBULATE, PEREGRINATE, TRAVEL, CONDUCT, BEHAVIOR, AVENUE, PROMENADE, STATUS, BEAT, ROUND
affectedly MINCE
incapacity to ABASIA
lamely LIMP
public PROMENADE, ALAMEDA, ESPLANADE, PRADO, MALL
reeling LURCH
shaded MALL, ALAMEDA

walking PASSANT, PERIPATETIC
like a bear PLANTIGRADE
stick STILT, CANE, CRUTCH

wall(s) SIDE, BARRIER, CLIFF, FENCE, RAMPART, ENCLOSE, ENCLOSURE, LEVEE, DEFENSE, PARAPET
arena (Rome) SPINA
dividing SEPTUM, SEPTA, PARTITION
enclose in MURE
inner ESCARP, PARTITION
ornament PLAQUE, PICTURE, TABLET, MURAL
outer face of PARAMENT
panel WAINSCOT
pertaining to MURAL
piece TEMPLET, TEMPLATE
section DADO, PANEL
squeeze against MURE
trim DADO

wallaba APA, TREE

wallaby KANGAROO

wallaroo KANGAROO

Wallis island UVEA (UEA)

wallow WELTER,
TOSS, ROLL, GROVEL,
FLOUNDER, SURGE,
BILLOW

walnut *skin* ZEST,
HULL, SHELL

walrus MORSE,
MAMMAL
herd POD
order BRUTA

wampum BEADS,
SE(A)WAN, PEAG(E),
ROANOKE, MONEY

wan PALE, FADED,
PALLID, ASHY, LIVID,
ASHEN, SICKLY,
LANGUID, LUSTER-
LESS, DIM

wand BATON,
CADUCEUS, ROD,
MACE, SCEPTER,
BAGUET, CANE,
POINTER, POLE,
STAFF, VERGE
royal MACE,
SCEPTER
short CUDGEL,
TRUNCHEON

wander STRAY, RAM-
BLE, ROAM, GAD,
MOON, RANGE,
ROVE, TRAIPSE,
ERR, DIGRESS,
TRAVEL, STROLL,
SAUNTER, DEPART,
DEVIATE, RAVE,
CIRCULATE, TRAVERSE
aimlessly DIVAGATE,
GAD, TRAIPSE
widely ROAM,
PEREGRINATE,
RANGE
winding course
SCAMANDER, MEAN-
DER

wanderer ARAB,
NOMAD, TRUANT,
VAG(RANT),
RAMBLER, STRAGGLER,
ROVER, COVENANTER,
TRAVELER, BUTTER-
FLY, ITINERANT, GAD-
ABOUT, VAGABOND

wandering ODYSSEY,
ERRANT, VAGRANT,
NOMADIC, DELIRIOUS,
ROVING, TRAVELING,
STRAYING, DEVIOUS
religious votary
PALMER

"Wandering Jew"
author SUE

plant ZEBRINA, IVY

wane DECLINE,
PETER, ABATE, EBB,
FADE, LESSEN, DE-
CREASE, DECAY,
WILT
opposed to WAX

want DESIRE, NEED,
PENURY, ABSENCE,
POVERTY, PINCH,
LACK, MISS, CRAVE,
COVET, LONG,
YEARN, WISH, PINE,
THIRST, REQUIRE,
DESTITUTION, DE-
FICIENCY, INDIGENCE,
SCARCITY

wanting SHY,
DEFICIENT, INCOM-
PLETE, ABSENT

wanton FREE, RAMP-
ANT, WILD, RANK,
IMPISH, UNRULY,
LOOSE, HEEDLESS,
RECKLESS, UNDIS-
CIPLINED, REFRAC-
TORY, SPORTIVE,
FROLICSOME, PLAY-
FUL, UNCHASTE,
LEWD, LUSTFUL,
UNRESTRAINED,
LASCIVIOUS, LECHER-
OUS, LICENTIOUS,
SENSUAL, INSOLENT,
MALICIOUS, EXTRAVA-
GANT, LAVISH,
PRODIGAL, IMMORAL,
CAPRICIOUS, WAY-
WARD

wapiti STAG, DEER,
ELK

war STRIFE, CON-
FLICT *See*
"battle"
agency OSS, NSA
agreement in CARTEL
club MACE
engine See under
"engine"
garb, Roman
SAGUM
god MARS, ARES
See under "god"
machine TANK, ONA-
GER *See under*
"military"
religious CRUSADE
trophy SCALP,
MEDAL, RIBBON
vessel CORVETTE,
FRIGATE, SUB

"War and Peace"
author TOLSTOI

warble SING, CAROL,
TRILL, YODEL, CHIRP

warbler PIPIT, BIRD

ward STAVE (OFF),
FEND, FENCE,
PARRY, PARISH,
AREA, DIVISION, COR-
RIDOR, ROOM, BLOCK,
AVERT, MINOR, HEIR,
DEFEND, PROTECT,
WATCH, CARE, GUARD,
PROTECTION, CUS-
TODY, SAFEGUARD,
REPEL, DISTRICT,
PRECINCT
politician HEELER

warden RANGER,
GUARD(IAN), KEEPER,
CUSTODIAN, CURATOR,
SUPERINTENDENT

warder MACE, STAFF,
WATCHMAN, BUL-
WARK, STRONGHOLD,
WARDEN, GUARD,
KEEPER

wardrobe ALMIRAH,
AMBRY, CABINET,
APPAREL, CLOSET,
CLOTHESPRESS,
BEDROOM

warehouse STORE,
GODOWN, DEPOT,
ETAPE, MART
France ENTREPOT
Russia ETAPE

warfare CRUSADE,
STRIFE, STRUGGLE,
CONTEST, HOSTILI-
TIES, CONFLICT

warlike MARTIAL,
MILITANT, BELLI-
COSE, COMBATIVE,
SOLDIERLY, BELLIG-
ERENT

warm ALIVE, MILD,
CALID, HUMID,
MUGGY, TEPID,
TOASTY, TENDER,
SINCERE, GLOWING,
FLUSHED, GENIAL,
GRATEFUL, HOT,
IRASCIBLE, ANGRY,
HEATED, FERVENT,
SYMPATHETIC,
AMOROUS, PAS-
SIONATE, CLEMENT,
ENTHUSIASTIC
growing CALESCENT
moderately TEPID
Spanish CALIENTE

warmed over RE-
CHAUFFE
warmth ARDOR, ELAN,
ZEAL, HEAT, LIFE,
PASSION, GLOW,
ENERGY, EMOTION,
FERVOR, ENTHU-
SIASM, IRRITATION,
ANGER, FERVENCY,
VEHEMENCE, ANIMA-
TION, EXCITEMENT
pertaining to
THERMAL
warn ADMONISH,
APPRISE, PREVISE,
ADVISE, FLAG, SIG-
NAL, CAUTION,
COUNSEL, REPRE-
HEND, NOTIFY,
INFORM
warning CAVEAT,
ALARM, TOCSIN,
ALERT, COUNSEL,
OMEN, BEACON,
SIREN, BLINKER,
EXAMPLE, FLAG,
CAUTION, ADMONI-
TION, NOTICE, SUM-
MONS, AUGURY
warp DEFLECT,
BEND, TWIST, CAST,
BIAS, DISTORT,
SWAY, TURN, MAR,
DAMAGE, CONTORT,
SHRIVEL, CONTRACT,
WRINKLE, PERVERT,
MISINTERPRET,
INFLUENCE
in weaving CRAM
thread (loom)
STAMEN
*threads, tapestry
weaving* LEASE
yarn ABB
warragal DINGO,
MYALL, DOG
warrant(s) BERAT,
WRIT, ENSURE,
PLEVIN, JUSTIFY,
JUSTIFICATION,
COMMISSION,
GUARANTEE, AU-
THORIZATION, SANC-
TION, GUARANTY,
SECURITY, CERTIFI-
CATE, VOUCHER,
DOCUMENT, ATTEST
warren HUTCH,
RABBITRY, TENE-
MENT
warrior SPAHI, GI,
VET, SOLDIER,

SAILOR, FIGHTER,
VETERAN
fabled female
ASLAUGA, AMAZON
professional
GLADIATOR, HESSIAN
warship FRIGATE,
GALLEON
deck of ORLOP
low-decked RAZEE
three bank TRIREME
two bank BIREME
wart TUMOR, VER-
RUCA, SYCOMA
Warwickshire
borough RUGBY
wary CANNY, WISE,
ALERT, CAGY,
CHARY, PRUDENT,
SCRUPULOUS, CAU-
TIOUS, CAREFUL,
CIRCUMSPECT,
WATCHFUL, DIS-
CREET
wash RINSE, LEACH,
LAVE, TINT, DRIFT,
SILT, OVERLAY,
PURIFY, BATHE,
CLEAN(SE),
LAUNDER, PURGE,
LOTION
washings BATHS,
LAVAGE, SLUICE,
ABLUTIONS, TUB-
BINGS, SHOWERS
Washington *county*
ADAMS, FERRY,
GRANT, KING,
LEWIS, PIERCE,
YAKIMA
town PASCO
Washington, George,
portraitist for
STUART
wasp HORNET, JIGA,
VESPA, WHAMP,
INSECT
waste LOSS, IDLE,
FRITTER, SPILL,
ATROPHY, CHAFF,
RAVAGE, SPOIL, SACK,
LOOT, SCUM, DROSS,
DEBRIS, DREGS,
REFUSE, DEVASTATE,
DWINDLE, ROT, NEG-
LECT, SQUANDER,
WILD, UNCULTIVATED,
BARREN, TREELESS,
DESOLATE, DIMINISH,
CONSUME, SPEND,
EMACIATE, DISSIPATE,
DEMOLISH, EXHAUST,

EXPEND, DESERT,
WILDERNESS, RUIN,
PRODIGALITY, HAVOC,
DESTRUCTION, DECAY,
GARBAGE
allowance for TRET
fiber NOIL
matter DROSS,
DEBRIS, REFUSE,
DREGS, ASHES, GAR-
BAGE
silk FRISON
to lay HAVOC, SACK,
SPOIL, RAVAGE
wasted GUANT, POOR,
SPARE, LANK, WORN,
EMACIATED, SQUAN-
DERED, WEAK, DE-
TERIORATED, ATRO-
PHIED
wasteful PRODIGAL,
LAVISH, EXTRAVA-
GANT, IMPROVIDENT,
THRIFTLESS
wasteland MOOR,
SWAMP, DESERT,
WILDERNESS
wastrel VAGABOND,
VAGRANT, OUTCAST,
WAIF, PRODIGAL,
PROFLIGATE, WASTER,
SPENDTHRIFT
watch LOOK, VIGIL,
EYE, TEND, SPY,
GAZE, STARE, SEE,
GUARD, SENTRY,
SHIELD, CLOCK,
HOROLOGE, HEED,
OBSERVE, MIND,
MARK, TIMEPIECE
chain ALBERT
charm FOB
mounted VEDETTE
pocket FOB
pin STUD
tower BEACON,
MIRADOR
watchdog, *Hel's*
GARM(R)
watchful ALERT,
WARY, VIGILANT,
READY, CAUTIOUS,
ATTENTIVE
guardian ARGUS
watchman GUARD,
SENTINEL, KEEPER,
WARDEN, SUPER
Greek myth.
CERBERUS
night SERENO, SEN-
TRY
Norse HEIMDALL(R)

watchtower MIRADOR, BEACON, LIGHT-HOUSE, LOOKOUT

watchword SHIB-BOLETH, SIGNAL

water RAIN, SEA, HOH, LAKE, RIVER, POND, POOL, IRRIGA-TION, DILUTE, AQUA, EAU

bag CHAGUL

body of OCEAN, SEA, POND, POOL, LAKE, RIVER

brash PYROSIS

combining form HYDRO

course FLUX, RACE, CANAL, WADI, RILL, RIA, NULLAH

covered by AWASH, FLOODED

fall CASCADE, LIN(N), CATARACT

gauge UDOMETER

hen COOT, GALLI-NULE, FOWL

jar BANGA, LOTA(H)

lifting engine NORIA, RAM, SHADOOF, SAKIEH

lily LOTUS *See under "lily"*

mineral VICHY, SELTZER, SELTERS, PULLNA

mix with SLAKE, DILUTE

nymph NAIAD, UNDINE, ARIEL, KELPIE, NIX(IE)

opening GAT

ouzel THRUSH, BIRD, DIPPER

passage STRAIT, SLUICE, CANAL, CHANNEL

plant ALGA, LOTUS, SUDD

genus TRAPA

raising device SAKIEH *See "lift-ing engine" above*

rat VOLE, MUSKRAT

receptacle FONT, BASIN, BUCKET, PAIL

search for DOWSE

sound of PLASH

spirit See "nymph" above

spout SPATE, GAR-GOYLE

sprite See "nymph" above

vessel LOTA(H), AFTABA

wheel NORIA, TUR-BINE

Egypt SAKIEH

Water Bearer AQUARIUS, CON-STELLATION

water cress *genus* RORIPA

watering place SPA, SPRING, BADEN, OASIS, WELL, PUMP, BAR

waterless ANHYDROUS, DRY, ARID

watershed DIVIDE

waterway CHANNEL, CANAL, RIVER, STRAIT, STREAM

waterwort *family* ELATINE

watery HYDROGE-NOUS, SEROUS, WEAK, SOGGY, VAPID, THIN, MOIST, WET

wattle DEWLAP, LAP-PET, HURDLE

fish BARBEL

fowl GILL, LAPPET

wave BRANDISH, FLOURISH, SIGNAL, GREET, SWELL, RIPPLE, BILLOW, SWING, SWAY, FAL-TER, FLOAT, FLUTTER, UNDULATE, WAVER, VACILLATE, BREAKER, SURGE

combining form ONDO

crest COMB

tidal EAGRE

top CREST, COMB

violent BORE

wavelike molding CYMA

waver TEETER, VEER, SWAY, FLAG, FALTER, FLICKER, HESITATE, VACILLATE, FLUCTUATE, TOTTER, REEL, UNDULATE, OSCILLATE

wavy UNDE, ONDY, UNDATE, ONDOYANT

as of leaves REPAND

wax CERE, GROW,

PELA, OIL, FAT, GUM, GREASE, INCREASE

bees, acid of CEROTIC

candle CIERGE

China PELA

cobbler's CODE

cover with CERE

figure CEROPLAST

match VESTA

ointment CERATE

opposed to WANE

pertaining to CERAL

unguent CEROMA

yellow CERESIN

waxwing CEDAR, BIRD

waxy CERAL, PLIABLE, VISCID, ADHESIVE, SOFT, YIELDING, IM-PRESSIBLE,

appearance PALLID, PALE, SODDEN

way LANE, STREET, CHANNEL, ROAD, PATH, VIA, WONT, MODE, ROUTE, COURSE, PASS, ARTERY, METHOD, PASSAGE, TRACK, TRAIL, PRO-GRESSION, PLAN, JOURNEY, FASHION, STYLE, SCHEME, DEVICE, HIGHWAY, AVENUE, ALLEY, HABIT, CHARACTER-ISTIC

out EGRESS, EXIT

wayfarer VIATOR, TRAVELER, TOURIST, NOMAD, TRAMP, TRANSIENT, PASSEN-GER, PILGRIM, ITINERANT, VOYAGER

waylay AMBUSH, TOB, SEIZE, ATTACK, ASSAIL, BESET, SUR-PRISE

wayward PERVERSE, UNRULY, FICKLE, UNSTEADY, CAPRI-CIOUS, STUBBORN, HEADSTRONG, RE-FRACTORY, IN-TRACTABLE, WILLFUL, FROWARD, DIS-OBEDIENT

we EDITOR, OUR-SELVES

Latin NOS

weak DEBILE, FADE, PECCABLE, PUNY,

WAN, FLAT, FRAIL,
ANEMIC, WATERY,
IRRESOLUTE, SOFT,
ANILE, FEEBLE,
INFIRM, DEBILITATED,
EXHAUSTED, LOW,
FAINT, PLIABLE,
SIMPLE, FOOLISH,
UNSOUND, DECRIPIT

weaken ENERVATE,
ENFEEBLE, SAP, UN-
MAN, DILUTE, WATER,
THIN, UNDERMINE,
DEBILITATE, DIMIN-
ISH

weakling PULER,
SISSY

weakness ASTHENIA,
FAULT, ATONY,
FOIBLE, FRAILTY,
IMPOTENCE, DE-
BILITY, INFIRMITY,
DECREPITUDE
of organ or muscle
ATONY

weal SUCCESS, WEL-
FARE, STATE, STRIPE,
WALE, WELT, PROS-
PERITY

wealth ESTATE,
CAPITAL, RICHES,
FORTUNE, MONEY,
AFFLUENCE, TREAS-
URE, FUNDS, GOODS,
PROPERTY, OPULENCE,
ABUNDANCE, POS-
SESSIONS
combining form
PLUTO
mad pursuit of
PLUTOMANIA
opposed to ILLTH
person of MAG-
NATE
worship of
PLUTOLATRY

wealthy SOLID, RICH,
HEELED, (F)LUSH

wean CHILD, INFANT,
DETACH, ALIENATE,
WITHDRAW

weapon ARM, CLUB,
SWORD, SPEAR, PIS-
TOL, GAT, IM-
PLEMENT, TALON,
CLAW, BEAK, SPUR,
GUN
daggerlike BALARAO
gaucho BOLA(S)
long-handled
HALBERD

medieval ONCIN,
CROSSBOW
prehistoric CELT,
ROCK, CLUB
single-edged BOLO,
MACHETE
war, early POLEAX(E)
wooden BOW,
MACANA, CLUB

wear USE, RUB,
CHAFE, FRET, LAST,
FRAY, ABRADE, COR-
RODE, ERODE, EAT,
RUST, BEAR, SHOW,
IMPAIR, WASTE,
CLOTHES, GARMENTS,
CONSUME

wearied IRKED,
FAGGED, JADED,
FATIGUED, BORED,
TIRED, EXHAUSTED,
WORN, SPENT,
SURFEITED

weariness ENNUI,
FATIGUE, LASSITUDE,
TEDIUM

wearisome TEDIOUS,
DREE, STUPID,
DULL, BORED,
MONOTONOUS, TIRE-
SOME, ARDUOUS,
LABORIOUS, HUM-
DRUM, IRKSOME

weary TIRE, BORE,
JADE, PALL, FAG,
EXHAUST, IRK,
FATIGUE

weasel VARE, ERMINE,
FERRET, RASSE
like MINK, FERRET,
TAYRA, TAIRA,
OTTER, STOAT

weather *map line*
ISOBAR

weathercock FANE,
VANE

weave ENTWINE,
MAT, PLAIT, REEL,
SPIN, KNIT, BRAID,
INTERLACE, FASHION,
DEVISE, PRODUCE
together PLAIT
twigs WATTLE

weaverbird MAYA,
BAYA, TAHA, MUNIA

weaver's *reed* SLEY

weaving, *batten or lay*
LATHE
cylinder BEAM
frame LOOM
term LISSE, LEASE

tool EVENER, SHUT-
TLE
together PLEXURE

web NET, TELA, TIS-
SUE, SCHEME, SNARE,
TEXTURE, STRUC-
TURE, GOSSAMER
pertaining to
RETIARY, TELAR

webbing, *bird's foot*
PALAMA

weblike TELARY,
RETIARY

wed JOIN, ESPOUSE,
MARRY, WIVE, TIE,
HITCH, COUPLE,
UNITE

wedding *gift, prenup-
tial* MAHR
ring BAND
snow RICE

wedge QUOIN, COIGN,
COTTER, GIB, KEY,
STOW, CHOCK, JAM,
SLIVER, SHIM
like contrivance
CLEAT
shaped CUNEATE,
SPHENOID, CUNEI-
FORM

wee LITTLE, SMALL,
TINY, PETITE, MI-
NUTE, DIMINUTIVE,
MICROSCOPIC,
LILLIPUTIAN

weed TARE, HOE,
CULL, DOCK, DARNEL,
EXTIRPATE, PLAN-
TAIN, ERADICATE,
CIGAR
asthma LOBELIA
Biblical TARE
May MARUTA
prickly BUR(R),
NETTLE
wiry grass DARNEL

week SENNET, SEN-
NIGHT, HEBDOMAD
day, pertaining to
FERIAL
having intervals of
SEPTAN, HEBDOMADAL

weekly HEBDOMADAL

ween EXPECT,
FANCY, THINK

weep WAIL, SOB, CRY,
BLUBBER, BOOHOO
See "lament"

weevil BOUD, CUR-
CULIO *See* "beetle"
cotton boll PICUDO
plum TURK

weft WOOF, FILLING, WEB, FILM, CLOUD, SHOOT, YARN

weigh CONSIDER, STUDY, PONDER, MUSE, POISE, STRESS, EXAMINE, MEASURE
down OPPRESS, DEPRESS, OVERBALANCE

weight TROY, HEFT, LOAD, WORTH, VALUE, SIZE, PRESTIGE, CREDIT, INCUBUS, PEISE, GRAVITY, AVOIRDUPOIS, INFLUENCE *See country involved*
allowance TARE, TRET
ancient MINA
apothecary OBOL(E), GRAM
balance RIDER
combining form BARO
deduction for TARE, TRET
after tare SUTTLE
determined by PONDERAL
down BALLAST
equal ISOBARIC
gems CARAT
gold or silver, India TOLA
measure of GRAM, MINIM, TON, BALE, METAGE, OUNCE, POUND, CARAT, KILO
metric unit KILO
of lead CHAR, PIG
of 100 pounds CENTRAL
relating to BARIC
sash cord MOUSE
system of TROY
wool, cheese, etc. CLOVE, NAIL, TOD

weighty ONEROUS, SOLID, HEAVY, HEFTY, PONDEROUS, MASSIVE, UNWIELDY, IMPORTANT, GRAVE, INFLUENTIAL, SIGNIFICANT, MOMENTOUS

weir BARRIER, DAM, NET, SEINE, TRAP, FISHPOND

weird EERIE, EERY, AWFUL, ODD, QUEER, UNCANNY, ELDRITCH, SPOOKY, UNEARTHLY

weka RAIL, BIRD

weld ARC, FUSE, SOLDER, BIND, UNITE, ROCKET, DYESTUFF, CONSOLIDATE

welfare SUCCESS, SELE, WEAL, HEALTH, HAPPINESS, PROSPERITY

welkin HEAVEN, SKY, VAULT, AIR, ATMOSPHERE

well HOLE, SHAFT, SPRING, GAY, HALE, FONT, SOUND, BIEN, FOUNT(AIN), RESERVOIR, ISSUE, FLOW, POUR, SATISFACTORY, SUITABLE, PROPER, HEALTHY, ACCEPTABLE, ADEQUATE
boring drill JAR
born NOBLE, EUGENIC
done BRAVO, GOOD
feeling EUPHORIA
pit SUMP
up WALL

Welland CANAL, CITY, RIVER

wellaway ALAS, WOE, REGRET, ALACKADAY

Welsh *See* "Wales"
rabbit, rarebit CHEESE (DISH)

Welshman CAMBRIAN, CELT *See* "Wales"

welt FRINGE, HEM, LASH, WALE, STRIP, SWELLING, EDGE, BORDER, RIDGE, TURMOIL, CONFUSION

welter ROLL, TUMBLE, WALLOW, SLOUGH, GROVEL, TOSS

wen MOLE, TALPA, CLYER, TUMOR, CYST, EXCRESCENCE, RUNE

wend GO, PASS, SHIFT, TURN, ALTER, CHANGE, PROCEED, DEPART, TRAVEL

Wend of Saxony SORB, SLAV

wergild FINE, CRO

Wessex *king* INE

West Africa
ASHANTEE *See* "Africa"

western HESPERIAN, OCCIDENTAL

W. Indies ANTILLES
bayberry AUSU
bird TODY, ANI
fish CERO, SESI, PEGA, PETO, RONCO, PINTADO, MARIAN, PEGADOR
idol ZEMI
Indian CARIB
island NEVIS, ARUBA, TOBAGO, CUBA, SABA, HISPANOLA, JAMAICA
liquor MOBBY, RUM
native (Indian) CARIB
rodent HUTIA
shark GATA
sorcery OBEAH
sugar works USINE
tree CALABA, BONACE *See* "tree"

West Pointer CADET, PLEBE
first year PLEBE
mascot MULE
second year YEARLING

W. Virginia *county* CLAY, GRANT, HARDY, LEWIS, LOGAN, MASON, MINGO, OHIO, ROANE, TYLER, WIRT, WOOD

wet SOPPING, DANK, SOAK, MOIST, HUMID, SATURATE, IMMERSE, DRENCH, RAINY, DAMP, WRONG, MISGUIDED, CRAZY
as flax RET

wether SHEEP, RAM, EUNUCH

whack STRIKE, SLAP
up SHARE, DIVIDE

whale(s) BLUE, SPERM, CETE, CETACEAN, GRASO, CACHALOT, MAMMAL
Arctic ORC
carcass KRANG, KRENG
combining form CET(O)

constellation
  CETUS
fat CETIN
female COW
finback GRASO
food BRIT, HERRING,
  SPRAT
genus INIA
herd of GAM, POD
killer GRAMPUS,
  ORCA
oil cask RIER
pertaining to
  CETIC
school of POD,
  GAM
secretion
  AMBERGRIS
skin SCULP
sperm CACHALOT
strip blubber from
  FLENSE
tail part of FLUKE
whalebone BALEEN
whale shark MHOR
whang CHUNK,
  BANG, STRIKE,
  THONG, STRIP,
  SLICE, PARTY,
  IMPACT, BLOW
whangee, wanghee
  BAMBOO, CANE
wharf DOCK, JETTY,
  KEY, QUAY, PIER,
  LANDING
elevated staging
  STAITH
space QUAYAGE
what EH, HOW,
  WHICH, WHATEVER
whatnot CABINET,
  STAND, ETAGERE,
  SHELF, THING,
  OBJECT, ARTICLE,
  MISCELLANY
whaup CURLEW,
  BIRD
wheal WALE, RIDGE,
  STRIPE, WELT,
  WHELK, MARK,
  SWELLING, URTICA
wheat DURUM,
  SPELT, EMMER,
  GRAIN
beard AWN
cracked GROATS
disease BUNT,
  SMUT, ERGOT, RUST,
  FUNGUS, AECIUM
German SPELT,
  EMMER

gritty part
  SEMOLINA
head EAR, SPIKE
India SUJEE, SUJI
kind of SPELT,
  DURUM, EMMER,
  EINKORN, POULARD,
  KANRED, FULTZ
outer coat BRAN
primary product of
  FLOUR
repository ELEVATOR,
  BIN
Russian EMMER,
  DURUM
secondary product
  BRAN, MIDDLINGS,
  GROATS, OIL
substance in GLUTEN,
  STARCH, PROTEIN
trade, abbr. AT
wheatear CHACK,
  BILL, BIRD
wheedle BAM,
  BLANDISH,
  INVEIGLE, COAX,
  FLATTER, CAJOLE,
  ENTICE, HUMOR,
  COURT, LURE
wheel(s) HELM,
  PULLY, REVOLVE,
  SPROCKET, DISK,
  CIRCLE, BIKE,
  CYCLE, SPIN, TURN,
  TWIRL, ROTATE,
  GYRATE, AXIS,
  PIVOT, CASTER,
  WHIRL, ROLL,
  BICYCLE
band TIRE
center HUB, NAVE
check SPRAG,
  BRAKE
combining form
  TROCH(O)
fifth SPARE
furniture CASTER
grooved SHEAVE,
  PULLY
iron tire STRAKE
part HUB, HUBCAP,
  SPOKE, AXLE
projection CAM,
  GEAR
resembling TROCHAL
shaft AXLE
shaped ROTIFORM
ship's HELM
spiked COG, ROWEL
spoke RADIUS
spur ROWEL
swivel CASTER

teeth of sprocket
  wheel WHELP
toothed COG,
  ROWEL
tread TIRE
turbine ROTOR
water NORIA
wheeze GASP, PUFF,
  GAG, DEVICE, DODGE,
  TRICK, JOKE
whelk PIMPLE,
  PUSTULE, SNAIL,
  WHEAL, PROTUBER-
  ANCE
whelp CHIT, PUP(PY,)
  CUB, YOUTH, CHILD,
  RIB, RIDGE, DOG,
  ROGUE
when AS, WHEREAS,
  WHILE, THO, WHERE-
  UPON, ALTHOUGH
whenever ONCE
wherefore WHY,
  BECAUSE, SO,
  THEREFORE
whereness UBIETY
wherewithall MEANS,
  MONEY
wherry BOAT, BARGE,
  LIGHTER
whet STIR, EGG,
  INCITE, STIMULATE,
  SHARPEN, HONE,
  GRIND, ROUSE,
  QUICKEN, AROUSE,
  PROVOKE, ANIMATE,
  KINDLE, INSPIRE,
  EXCITE
whether EITHER, IF,
  ALTERNATIVE
whey SERUM
whiff PUFF, ODOR,
  SMELL, WAFT, GUST,
  SAVOR, SMACK,
  INSTANT, JIFFY,
  FAN, WIND
whiffle SHIFT,
  VACILLATE, WAVER,
  TURN, VEER,
  FLICKER, FLUTTER
Whig poet OG,
  SHADWELL
while WHENAS, AS,
  UNTIL, DURING,
  INTERVAL, MEAN-
  TIME, SPEND, PASS,
  BEGUILE, WHILST
whilom FORMER,
  SOMETIME, ONCE,
  ERST
whim CAPRICE,
  FREAK, FANCY,

VAGARY, IDEA, HUMOR,
WHIMSEY, NOTION,
DESIRE, QUIRK,
WINCH, CHIMERA
whimper CRY, MEWL,
PULE, SNIFF, WAIL,
WHINE, COMPLAIN
whimsey CROCHET,
HUMOR, FANCY,
FREAK, NOTION
See "whim"
whimsical FREAKISH,
NOTIONAL, ODD,
DROLL, QUEER,
CAPRICIOUS,
SINGULAR, STRANGE,
FANCIFUL,
FANTASTIC, ERRATIC,
QUAINT
whin FURZE, GORSE,
ROCK, BIRD
whine CRY, PULE,
SNIVEL, WHIMPER,
WAIL, GRUMBLE,
COMPLAIN
whinny HINNY,
NEIGH
whip BEAT, LASH,
STRIKE, PUNISH,
FLAGELLATE, CROP,
KNOUT, QUIRT,
CAT, GOAD, STICK,
FLOG, DEFEAT,
HASTEN, FLAGELLUM
cowboy CHICOTE
handle CROP
rawhide SJAMBOK,
KNOUT, QUIRT,
THONG
Russia KNOUT
whir BIRR, REVOLVE,
TURN, BUZZ, WHIZZ,
HURRY, COMMOTION
whirl SPIN, TURN,
GYRE, GYRATE,
REEL, ROTATE,
ROTATION
whirlpool GORCE,
EDDY, VORTEX,
MAELSTROM,
GURGE, SWIRL
whirlwind, *Faroe
islands* OE
whisk *broom*
RINGE
whisker, *fish* BARBEL
whist *declaration*
MISERE
dummy MORT
holding TENACE
whit ATOM, BIT,
IOTA, JOT, MITE,

SPECK, TITTLE,
PARTICLE, GRAIN,
SCRAP, SCINTILLA
white FAIR,
HONORABLE, HOAR(Y),
ALABASTER, PALE,
PALLID, ASHEN, WAN,
COLORLESS, SNOWY,
IVORY, SILVERY,
CHALKY, CHASTE,
INNOCENT,
CAUCASIAN, NIVEOUS
and Indian GRIFFE
combining form
ALB(O), LEUC(O)
egg GLAIR
fish ATINGA,
CISCO, POLLAN
flecked ROAN
matter ALBA
vestment ALB
with age HOAR(Y)
White House *designer*
HOBAN
whiten ETIOLATE,
BLEACH, BLANCH,
ALBIFY
whiting-pout BIB,
FISH
whitish HOARY,
ALBESCENT, PALE
mineral TRONA-
(URAO). *See under*
"mineral"
Whitman WALT
Whitsunday
PENTECOST,
WHITSUNTIDE
whittle PARE, CUT,
TRIM, CARVE,
SHAPE, REDUCE,
REMOVE
whiz(z) PURR,
HUM, BUZZ, HISS,
BARGAIN, CORKER,
WHIR
who THAT, WHICH
whole AGGREGATE,
MASS, INTEGER,
ENTIRE, PURE,
UNCUT, ALL, SUM,
INTACT, SOUND,
WELL, TOTAL(ITY),
ENTIRE(TY),
COMPLETE, PERFECT,
UNIMPAIRED,
UNDAMAGED,
UNITY, HEALTHY
combining form
TOTO, TOTI
wholesale BULK,

ABUNDANT, SWEEP-
ING, LOTS, GOBS
wholesome SALU-
BRIOUS, SALUTARY,
HEALTHFUL, SOUND
wholly ALL, QUITE,
FULLY, THOROUGHLY,
SOLELY, COMPLETELY,
ENTIRELY
whoop CALL,
PURSUE, URGE,
SHOUT, HOOT,
HALLOO, YELL,
CHEER, PRAISE,
HOOPOE
whooping cough
PERTUSSIS
whop STRIKE, BEAT,
THRASH, FLOP,
SHAKE, DASH, CAST,
SURPASS
whorl TURN,
VOLUTION, SPIRAL,
COIL, VERTICIL
wicked VILE, CRUEL,
IMPIOUS, SINFUL,
EVIL, BAD, ILL,
IMMORAL, CRIMINAL,
GUILTY, UNJUST,
INIQUITOUS, UNHOLY,
PROFANE, VICIOUS,
ATROCIOUS,
NEFARIOUS,
HEINOUS, FLAGRANT,
IRRELIGIOUS
wickedness BELIAL
wicker TWIG, OSIER,
WITHE
basket PANNIER,
KISH
cradle BASSINET
hut JACAL
wicket ARCH, GATE,
HOOP, WINDOW,
DOOR, LOOPHOLE
widen SPREAD,
BROADEN, EXPAND,
REAM, EXTEND,
DILATE, ENLARGE,
SPLAY
widgeon DUCK,
SMEE, BALDPATE
widow RELICT
widowhood VIDUAGE
widow's *dower right*
TERCE
mite LEPTON
wield PLY, USE,
SWING, HANDLE,
MANAGE, CONTROL,
RULE, COMMAND,
BRANDISH, FLOURISH,

MANIPULATE, SWAY,
EXERCISE
wife FRAU, RIB,
BRIDE, SPOUSE,
CONSORT, MATE,
UXOR, FERE
bequest to DOT,
DOWRY,
killer UXORICIDE
Latin for UXOR
pertaining to
UXORIAL
rajah's RANI,
RANEE
sacrifice, India
SUTTEE
wig PERUKE,
TOUPEE, JAW,
BERATE, SCOLD,
PERIWIG, GIZZ
worsted JASEY
wigwam TEPEE,
HUT, LODGE, TENT,
CABIN, HOGAN,
PUEBLO, WICKIUP
wild UNEXPLORED,
FERAL, FIERCE,
DISSOLUTE,
PRODIGAL, EAGER,
EXCITED, MAD,
SAVAGE, UN-
CONTROLLED,
FANTASTIC, VISIONARY,
UNDOMESTICATED,
UNTAMED, ROUGH,
UNCULTIVATED,
UNCIVILIZED,
FEROCIOUS,
BARBAROUS, GIDDY,
RECKLESS, BOISTER-
OUS, NATIVE,
WASTE, DESOLATE,
VIOLENT, STORMY,
AMUCK, RABID
growing in fields
AGRARIAN
wildcat LYNX, CHAUS,
EYRA, BALU, BOBCAT,
UNRELIABLE,
IRRESPONSIBLE,
UNSOUND
wildebeest GNU
wile ART, RUSE,
TOY, TRICK, FEINT,
FRAUD, STRATAGEM,
ARTIFICE, DECEIT,
GUILE, SNARE
will BEHEST,
VOLITION, DESIGN,
TESTAMENT, WISH,
DESIRE, INCLINA-
TION, PURPOSE,

CHOICE, DETERMINA-
TION, POWER,
COMMAND,
RESOLUTION
addition to CODICIL
convey by DEVISE
having made
TESTATE
loss of ABULIA
maker of TESTATOR
wil(l)ful STUBBORN,
HEADSTRONG,
UNRULY, OBSTINATE
willing FAVORABLE,
PRONE, FAIN,
INCLINED, DISPOSED,
COMPLIANT,
AMENABLE, READY,
EAGER, AGREEABLE,
UNFORCED,
VOLUNTARY
willingly READILY,
GLADLY, LIEF,
CHEERFULLY,
FREELY
willow SALIX, ITEA,
OSIER, TREE
catkin RAG, AMENT
Europe SALLOW
genus ITEA, SALIX
plaited WICKER
spike CATKIN
twig WITHE,
SALLOW
Virginia ITEA
willowy SVELTE,
SLENDER, SUPPLE,
PLIANT, FLEXIBLE,
GRACEFUL, LISSOME
willy-nilly VACIL-
LATING, UNCERTAIN,
TORNADO, CYCLONE
Wilson's *thrush*
VEERY, BIRD
wily ASTUTE,
CRAFTY, FOXY,
ARTFUL, SLY,
POLITIC, INSIDIOUS,
SUBTLE, ARCH,
DESIGNING, TRICKY,
CUNNING
wimple GORGET,
WRAP, FOLD,
CURVE, WRINKLE
win GAIN, ACQUIRE,
GET, OBTAIN, SECURE,
DRUB, EARN, ATTAIN,
TRIUMPH, PREVAIL,
SUCCEED, ACHIEVE
wince RECOIL, REEL,
FLINCH, QUAIL,

CRINGE, SHRINK,
SHY
wind GALE, GUST,
BLAST, SAMIEL,
NOTUS, ZEPHYR,
TYPHOON, BREATH,
STRENGTH, SCENT,
ODOR, STORM,
SQUALL, SARSAR,
SIMOON, BISE,
TEBBAD, SIROCCO,
LESTE, PONENTE,
TEMPEST, TORNADO,
BREEZE, BORA,
TWINE, VINE, COIL,
LOOP, TWIST, CURL,
CROOK, BEND,
CHINOOK
Adriatic BORA
Alpine BORA, FOEHN
Asia MONSOON,
BURAN
away from ALEE
Chile and Peru
SURES
cloud SCUD
coastal, Chile and
Peru SURES
cold BISE, MISTRAL,
PUNA, SARSAR,
LEVANTER, GREGALE
desert SIMOON,
SIROCCO
dry BORA
east EURUS, LESTE
Egypt K(H)AMSIN
equatorial TRADE
Europe BISE
flower ANEMONE,
GENTIAN
gentle AURA,
ZEPHYR
god of EURUS *See*
under "god"
hot SIMOON, SIROCCO,
KAMSIN, SOLANO
instrument PIPE,
HORN, BUGLE, OR-
GAN
Madeira LESTE
Malta GREGALE,
LEVANTER
Medit. MISTRAL,
LEVANTER, ETESIAN,
SOLANO, GREGALE
north BOREAS,
ETESIAN
northeast, personi-
fied CAECIAS
northwest ETESIAN
pertaining to
ANEMONAL, VENTAL

Peru PUNA, SURES
Rocky Mtn. CHINOOK
science of
  ANEMOLOGY
sheltered from
  ALEE
south NOTUS, AUSTER
  Europe BISE
southeast EURUS,
  SOLANO
southwest AFER,
  NOTUS, PAMPERO,
  AUSTER
summer ZEPHYR
Switzerland BISE
tower BADGIR
warm, dry CHINOOK
west FAVONIUS,
  ZEPHYR, PONENTE
windfall BOON, VAIL,
  FORTUNE, LUCK,
  CHANCE, GODSEND,
  GIFT
windflower ANEMONE,
  GENTIAN
winding AMBAGE,
  SPIRAL, SNAKY, TURN-
  ING, MEANDERING,
  CONVOLUTION,
  CONTORTION,
  SINUOUS, SERPENTINE,
  CIRCUITOUS
windlass CRAB,
  CAPSTAN, REEL,
  WINCH
window OPENING,
  APERTURE, FENESTRA,
  ORIEL, CASEMENT,
  DORMER
bay ORIEL
ledge SILL
oval dormer OXEYE
roof SKYLIGHT,
  DORMER
weight MOUSE
worker GLAZIER
windrow SWATH,
  TRENCH
windward AWEATHER
opposed to LEEWARD
Windward Islands
  GRENADA, (ST.)
  LUCIA
wine(s) ASTI,
  NEGUS, VINO,
  MEDOC, MOSELLE,
  VIN(UM), SEVE,
  SEC, SACK
Bordeaux class or
  type COSNE, BAR-
  SAC, BERGERAC,
  BOURG, CABERNET,

CARIGNAN, CHARBONO,
CHIANTI, GLENPARA,
GRAVES, MALBEC,
MATARO, MEDOC,
MERLOT, CLARET,
FLOIRAC, PONTAC,
SAUTERNE
bottle MAGNUM
Burgundy class or
  type CHABLIS,
  BEAUNE, BEZIERS,
  MACON, MEUNIER,
  MUSIGNY, PINOTS,
  POMARD, SAVIGNY,
  TONNERRE, VOLNAY
cask LEAGUER, BOSS,
  BUTT
combining form
  OEN(O)
cup AMA
dealer COOPER,
  VINTNER
delicacy, France
  SEVE
deposit ARGOL, LEES
  from new GRIFFE
dipper OLPE
disease CASSE
dregs MARC, SALIN,
  VINASSE
dry SACK, SEC, BRUT
Eucharist KRAMA
Europe MUSCA-
  T(EL) *See country*
  involved
evaporation ULLAGE
flat VAP
flavoring of
  DOSAGE
French MADEIRA,
  MEDOC, BOIS *See*
  "Bordeau" *and*
  "Burgundy" *above*
glass RUMMER
heavy TOKAY
honey and MULSE
hot NEGUS
Hungary TOKAY
India SHRAB
jug OLPE
leather bag for
  ASKOS
list CARD
Madeira type or class
  BUAL, CANARY,
  GOMERA, MALMSEY,
  MARSALA
making, pertaining to
  OENOPOETIC, VINTAGE
measure AAM, PIPE,
  ORNA
  in cask BUTT

merchant VINTNER,
  COOPER
new MUST
pertaining to VINIC,
  VINOUS, VINTAGE
pitcher OLPE, OLLA
receptacle AMA
red PORT, TINTA,
  CLARET, CHIANTI
renew STUM
Rhine class or type
  RHENISH, HOCK,
  BURGER, RIESLING,
  RULANDER, STEIN
sampler TASTER
sherry OLOROSO,
  XERES, TENT,
  SHIRAZ, MONTILLA,
  MALAGA, JEREZ,
  FALERNO, ALISO
Spain MASDEU, TENT,
  XERES *See under*
  "Spain"
spiced SANGAREE,
  NECTAR
strength SEVE
sweet ALICANT(E),
  MUSCAT, PORT,
  MULSE, CANARY,
  ANGELICA, BARI, COT-
  NAR, FALERNO,
  IONA, LUNEL,
  MALMSEY, MOSELLE,
  PONTAC, TENT,
  TOKAY
Tagalog ALAC
unfermented MUST
vessel AMA, CRATER,
  AMPHORE
white HOCK, MALAGA,
  ALISO, BARSAC,
  BERGERAC, BOUZY,
  CHABLIS, FARNESE,
  FORST, LUNEL,
  MALAGA, MARSALA,
  MONTILLA, MOSELLE,
  ORVIETO, RIESLING,
  SANTERROT,
  SAUTERNE, SHERRY,
  VERDAL
with honey MULSE
wines, *study of*
  ENOLOGY,
  OENOLOGY
wing(s) ALULA, ALA,
  ALAE, PINION, ELL,
  ARM, FLANK, ANNEX,
  DIVISION, ADJUNCT,
  SAIL, ALETTE, EX-
  TENSION, PENNON,
  FLIGHT, VANE, FAC-
  TION

closed PLIE
divested of DEALATE
false ALULA
feather PENNA
like ALAR
part FLANK, AILERON
tip, pertaining to
ALULAR
winged ALATE,
PENNATE
boots TALARIA
cap of Mercury
PETASOS
fruit SAMARA
horse PEGASUS
manikin or figure
KER
monster HARPY
two DIPTERAL
heraldry VOL
victory NIKE
wing-footed ALIPED
wingless DEALATE,
APTERAL, EXALATE
bird KIWI
invertebrates
APTERA
wink TWINKLE,
FLICKER, OVERLOOK,
BAT, NICTATE,
NICTITATE, NAP,
BLINK, GLEAM, FLASH,
TWITCH
winner FIRST, ACE,
EARNER, VICTOR,
HIGH, FACEMAN
"Winnie the Pooh"
author MILNE
winning three numbers
TERN
winnow CULL, SIFT,
WIM, FAN, STIR,
SIEVE, SCREEN, BOLT,
SEPARATE, ANALYZE,
ASSORT, ELIMINATE,
SELECT, DISPERSE,
SCATTER, FLY, GLEAN
winsome BONNY,
ATTRACTIVE, GRA-
CIOUS, CAPTIVATING,
CHARMING, PLEASANT,
BLITHE, LOVABLE,
PRETTY, PLEASING
winter, pertaining to
HIEMAL, HIBERNAL
"Winter's Tale" char-
acter LEONTES,
CAMILLO, DION,
PERDITA, EMILIA,
MOPSA, DORCAS
wipe ERASE, RUB,
EFFACE, DRY, SWAB,

MOP, CLEAN,
OBLITERATE,
EXPUNGE
wire, bacteriologist's
OESE
measure MIL
platinum looped
OESE
worm MYRIAPOD,
MILLEPEDE
wireless RADIO, TV
Wisconsin county
DANE, DOOR, DUNN,
IOWA, IRON, POLK,
ROCK, RUSK, VILAS,
WOOD
Indian SAC
town or city BELOIT,
RIPON, RACINE
wisdom GNOSIS, LORE,
SAPIENCE, SENSE,
SAGACITY, PRUDENCE,
JUDGMENT See
"learning"
god See under
"god"
tooth MOLAR
wise SAPIENT, SANE,
ERUDITE, HEP, DEEP,
SENSIBLE, SAGE,
SAGACIOUS, ALERT,
BRIGHT, SMART, DIS-
CREET, JUDICIOUS,
PROFOUND, DISCERN-
ING, RATIONAL,
COGNIZANT, IN-
FORMED, LEARNED,
CIRCUMSPECT
man NESTOR, ORACLE,
SAVANT, SAGE, SOLON,
SOLOMON, MAGUS
men MAGI, WITAN
saying ADAGE, SAW,
MAXIM
wish DESIRE, ASPIRE,
VOTE, WANT, CRAVE
See "covet"
tense expressing
OPTATIVE
wishbone FURCULUM
wishy-washy FORCE-
LESS, INANE, VAPID,
FLAT, BANAL,
JEJUNE, THIN, PALE,
WEAK, FEEBLE,
SICKLY, WATERY,
DILUTED, INSIPID
wit(s) FUN, SALT,
HUMOR, IRONY,
WAG, SENSE, GRAIN,
MIND, SOUL, SHARP-

NESS, ALERTNESS,
SATIRE, INTELLECT,
INTELLIGENCE, FACE-
TIOUSNESS, DROLLERY,
SAGACITY
feeblest form PUN
witch HECATE, HAG,
LAMIA, SIREN, HEX,
SORCERESS, EN-
CHANTRESS,
CHARMER, SIBYL,
CRONE
city SALEM
famous LILITH,
CIRCE
male WARLOCK
witchcraft SORCERY,
MAGIC, NECROMANCY,
CHARM, SPELL
witch hazel HORN-
BEAM, SHRUB, TREE,
ASTRINGENT
genus HAMAMELIS
with AMONG, BY,
PLUS, THROUGH,
ALONG, AMIDST,
ACCOMPANYING, BE-
SIDE
prefix COM, COL,
SYN
withdraw DECAMP,
DEPART, LEAVE,
RECEDE, RETIRE,
AVOID, DISAVOW,
QUIT, RETRACT,
DEPORT, SECEDE,
GO, DEDUCT,
RECANT, REVOKE,
RELINQUISH, RESIGN,
ABJURE, RETREAT,
REMOVE
wither SHRIVEL,
WASTE, FADE, SERE,
DECAY, DROOP,
SHRINK, WILT, LAN-
GUISH, ATROPHY
within IN, INNER,
INTO, ON, INSIDE,
DURING, INWARDLY,
INTERNALLY, IN-
DOORS
combining form
END(O), ESO
without OUTSIDE,
EXTERNAL, BEYOND,
EXEMPT, LACKING,
MINUS, UNLESS
combining form
ECT(O)
fluid ANEROID
French SANS
inclination ACLINIC

Latin SINE
limitation of time
AORIST, ETERNAL
polarity ASTATIC
prefix ECT(O)
purpose IDLY
ribs DECOSTATE
withstand LAST,
OPPOSE, ENDURE,
BIDE, RESIST, BEAR,
FACE, DEFY, CON-
FRONT
witness OBSERVE,
SEE, TESTIFY, ATTEST,
TESTE, VOUCH, SUB-
SCRIBE, TESTIMONY,
EVIDENCE, PROOF,
CONFIRMATION,
DEPONENT, BE-
HOLDER, ONLOOKER,
SPECTATOR,
VOUCHER
witticism PUN, JOKE,
QUIP, MOT, GAG,
SALLY, JEST, CON-
CEIT
Witt's *planetoid*
EROS
witty DROLL, JOCOSE,
HUMOROUS, FACE-
TIOUS, JOCULAR,
WAGGISH, FUNNY
remark QUIP, MOT,
PUN
reply REPARTEE,
RIPOSTE
saying MOT, QUIP,
PUN
wivern DRAGON
wizard SHAMAN,
FIEND, SORCERER,
PELLAR, SEER, SAGE,
EXPERT, ADEPT,
MAGE, MAGUS,
MAGICIAN, CON-
JURER, ENCHANTER,
NECROMANCER,
DIVINER
wizen DRY, WITHER,
SHRIVEL, SHRINK
woad GLASTUM, DYE,
HERB
woe BANE, GRIEF,
AFFLICTION, DOLE,
AGONY, SORROW,
DISTRESS, TRIBULA-
TION, ANGUISH,
TORTURE, MISERY,
UNHAPPINESS,
TROUBLE, HEARTACHE
woebegone SORRY,
DEJECTED,

WRETCHED, MISER-
ABLE, DISCONSOLATE,
SAD, FORLORN,
MELANCHOLY,
DOWNCAST, CREST-
FALLEN
woeful SAD, SORROW-
FUL, MOURNFUL,
UNHAPPY, PALTRY,
MISERABLE, DE-
PLORABLE, PITIFUL,
WRETCHED
wold DOWNS, UP-
LAND
wolf COYOTE, LOBO,
ROUE
genus CANIS
head of HURE
myth. WEREWOLF
Odin's GERE
timber LOBO
wolfbane ACONITE
See "monkshood"
wolfhound BORZOI,
ALAN
wolfish LUPINE,
FEROCIOUS, RAVEN-
OUS
wolflike THOOID,
LUPINE
wolframite CAL
wolfsbane ACONITE,
MONKSHOOD, PLANT
Wolsey's *birthplace*
IPSWICH
wolverine CARCAJOU,
GLUTTON
genus GULO
woman, women
LADY, FEMALE,
FEM(M)E, WIFE,
MISTRESS, PARA-
MOUR
adviser EGERIA
apartment SERAGL-
IO, ZENANA,
HAREM, THALAMUS
beautiful HOURI,
PERI, BELLE, VENUS,
APHRODITE
beloved INAMORATA
club for SORORITY
combining form
GYN(O)
explorer OSA
fond of PHILOGY-
NIST
furious MENAD,
MAENAD
hater MISOGYNIST
ill-tempered SHREW,

VIRAGO, VIXEN,
TERMAGANT
killing FEMICIDE
lawyer PORTIA
malicious CAT
noble DUCHESS,
LADY, DAME
old CRONE, GAMMER,
HAG, VECKE
ruler MATRIARCH,
QUEEN
sailor WAVE, SPAR
soldier WAC, WAAC
England WREN
suffrage leader
ANTHONY, MOTT,
STONE, STANTON
wonder AWE, RARITY,
MUSE, ASTONISHMENT,
AMAZEMENT, SUR-
PRISE, PRODIGY,
MARVEL, MIRACLE,
PHENOMENON,
PONDER, MEDITATE,
SPECULATE
world PHAROS
wonderful SWELL,
GREAT, DANDY,
MIRIFIC, UNIQUE,
EXTRAORDINARY,
GRAND, STUPEN-
DOUS, MIRACULOUS,
ADMIRABLE, EXCEL-
LENT, AMAZING,
MARVELOUS
wont HABIT, USE,
CUSTOM, USAGE,
PRACTICE
woo SEEK, COURT,
SUE, LURE, SOLICIT,
BEG, ADDRESS, IM-
PORTUNE, ENTREAT,
INVITE
wood(s) TREES, FOR-
EST, TIMBER, LUM-
BER, FUEL, GROVE,
SILVAN, SYLVAN
See "wooden"
agalloch(um)
GAROO, ALOES
ball of KNUR
billet of SPRAG
black EBONY
block, small DOOK,
NOG
combining form
LIGN(I), XYLO
core AME
demon NAT
engraving XYLOGRA-
PHY

flexible WILLOW, OSIER, EDDER
fragrant CEDAR
grove NEMORA
gum XYLAN, RESIN
hard NARRA, EBONY, MAHOGANY, OAK
hen WEKAS
horse TRESTLE
India KOKRA, ENG, SAL
knot NODE, GNUR, BURL
light BALSA
overlaying VENEER
peg in boat THOLE
pertaining to woods or grove NEMORAL
pin BOG, FID, SPILE, BUNG, STOPPER
sandarac ALERCE, ARAR, REALGAR
shoe GETA, SABOT, CLOG, SECQUE, PATTEN
sorrel OCA, OXALIS, PLANT
streak in ROE, FLECK
strip BATTEN, SLAT, LATH, SPLINE
stripe in ROE, FLECK
wheel GLAZER
woodbine CREEPER, JASMINE, HONEYSUCKLE
woodchuck MARMOT
wooden STIFF, RIGID, SEDATE, UNMOVABLE, DULL, STUPID, STOLID, SOLID, TENSE, FIRM, HARD, AWKWARD, CLUMSY, UNGAINLY, EXPRESSIONLESS, SPIRITLESS, LIFELESS *See* "wood"
brick DOOK, NOG
bowl KITTY, MAZER
bucket or pail SOE
peg or pin SKEG, FID, SPILE, THOLE
vessel PIGGIN, SOE, COGUE, SKEEL
woodland *deity See under* "god"
landscape BOSCAGE
woodpecker YAFFLE, JYNX, AWL, CHAB, PICULET, TAPPER, FLICKER, WRYNECK, SAPSUCKER, BIRD
genus PICUS

group PICI
types DOWNY, PILEATED, HAIRY, IMPERIAL, RED-HEADED
wood-robin MIRO, THRUSH, BIRD
wood wind instrument OBOE, BASSOON
woody LIGNEOUS, XYLOID, SYLVAN, PITHY
tissue XYLEM
woof WEFT, FABRIC, TEXTURE, FILLING
wool YARN, HAIR, ANGORA, DOWN, FUR, FLEECE
blemish MOTE
coarse GARE
comb CARD
deposit in SUINT
detached lock FRIB
fabric See under "woolen"
fat LANOLIN, SUET
grower SHEEP, RANCHER
inferior CLEAMER, HEAD
knot BURL, NEP, NOIL
measure HEER
new VIRGIN
old weight TOD
on sheep's leg GARE
package FADGE
reclaimed MUNGO, SHODDY
separated by combing NOIL
skirtings BROKE
to tease out TUM, CARD
twisted roll SLUB
undyed BEIGE
unravel TEASE
woolen *fabric* ETAMINE, FRISCA, CASHMERE, TARTAN, CASHA, SERGE, TRICOT, BEIGE, KERSEY, MOREEN, YERGA, SATARA, RATINE, MERINO, COTTA, YERGA
strainer TAMIS
thread YARN
vest LINDER
waste FUD
watered MOREEN

woolly LANOSE, LANATE, FLOCCULENT, FLOCCOSE, WARM, SOFT, TOSY
covering FLEECE
pyrol URD
word(s) NEWS, TERM, IDIOM, RHEMA, REPORT, REPUTE, TALK, EXPRESSION, NAME, UTTERANCE, PHRASE, INFORMATION, MESSAGE, PROMISE, PLEDGE, SIGNAL, COUNTERSIGN, COMMAND
blindness ALEXIA
book LEXICON, THESAURUS, DICTIONARY
combining form LOG(O), VERBO
compound, separation of TMESIS
deletion of last letter of APOCOPE
derived from another PARONYM
figurative use of TROPE
formed for an occasion NONCE
for word LITERAL
having same sound, different meaning HOMONYM
imitative ONOMATOPE, ECHOIC
invent new COIN
last syllable of ULTIMA
magical PRESTO, SESAME, ABRACADABRA
meaning, pertaining to SEMANTIC
mishearing or misapprehension of OTOSIS
misuse of MALAPROPISM, CATACHRESIS
new NEOLOGISM
of action VERB
of God LOGOS
of honor PLEDGE, OATH, PAROLE
of mouth ORAL, PAROLE, PAROL
of sanction AMEN, YEA, VERILY

of unknown meaning
SELAH
*omission middle
letter* SYNCOPE
opposite meaning
ANTONYM
oral PAROL(E)
order of MORPHEME
puzzle ANAGRAM,
REBUS, ACROSTIC,
CHARADE
repetition of PLOCE
root form ETYM,
ETYMON
sign LOGOGRAM
smallest division
MORPHEME
*spelled alike, pro-
nounced differently*
HETERONYM
square PALIN-
DROME
that unites COPULA
used for another
METONYM
use of long
SESQUIPEDALIA
with no TACIT
wordiness PLEONASM,
PROLIXITY, VER-
BIAGE, VERBOSITY,
LOQUACIOUSNESS
wordless TACIT
words, *new, doctrine
of* NEOLOGY
wordy PROLIX,
VERBOSE, DIFFUSE,
WINDY, GAR-
RULOUS, TALKATIVE,
LOQUACIOUS
work OPUS, CHORE,
TOIL, EFFORT,
TRADE, JOB, LABOR,
GRIND, KARMA,
ERGON, ACT, RUN,
OPERATE, PAINS,
TASK, DUTY,
METIER, CALLING,
CRAFT, ART, MOIL,
SLAVE, FAG, GRUB,
STRIVE, ENDEAVOR,
EXERTION, OCCUPA-
TION, EMPLOYMENT,
BUSINESS, FUNCTION,
DRUDGE(RY)
aimlessly POTTER
by day CHARE
disposition toward
ERGASIA
hard MINE, MOIL,
LABOR, SLAVE, TOIL

musical OPUS,
OPERA, SONATA
perseveringly
TOIL, PEG, PLY
steadily PLY
unit ERG(ON)
workbag RETICULE,
ETUI, ETWEE
work horse CAPO
workman HAND,
ARTIFICER, ARTISAN,
NAVVY, MECHANIC,
LABORER,
OPERATOR, WRIGHT,
PEON, CRAFTSMAN
workmen GANG,
FORCE, MEN,
HANDS, CREW
works PLANT, SHOP,
MILL, MECHANISM,
FACTORY, DEEDS,
BOOKS
workshop ATELIER,
PLANT, LAB(ORA-
TORY), STUDIO
world REALM,
COSMOS, EARTH,
GLOBE, MACROCOSM,
UNIVERSE, CREA-
TION, NATURE,
SPHERE, HUMANITY,
MANKIND, PUBLIC,
CAREER
worldly MUNDANE,
TERRENE, PROFANE,
EARTHLY, SOPHIS-
TICATED, TER-
RESTRIAL, HUMAN,
SECULAR, CARNAL
world's *biggest land
mass* EURASIA
World War II *battle*
BULGE, NORMANDY,
WARSAW, OREL,
ANZIO, CASSINO,
SICILY, BATAAN,
TARAWA, OKINAWA
world-wide ECU-
MENIC, PANDEMIC,
PLANETARY
worm ANNELID,
NAID, LURG,
FLUKE, ESS, LEECH,
NEMA(TODE),
CRAWL, CREEP,
EXTRACT, INCH,
INSINUATE,
WRITHE, WRIGGLE,
LARVA, GRUB,
MAGGOT, WRETCH
Africa LOA
bait LURG, MAD

blind ORVET
combining form
VERMI
earth MAD
edible PALOLO, IPO
eye infecting LOA
fluke PLAICE
fresh water NAID
mud IPO, LOA
round ASCARID,
NEMA(TODE)
sea SAO, LURG
ship BORER,
TEREDO
silk ERI(A)
snaillike SLUG
threadlike FILARIA
track NEREITE
worm-eating *mammal*
MOLE
wormwood *prepara-
tion* MOXA
worn USED, TIRED,
JADED, FATIGUED,
TATTERED, AT-
TRITE, ABRADED,
EATEN, EROSE,
SPENT, EFFETE,
PASSE, SEEDY,
IMPAIRED, WASTED,
EXHAUSTED, CON-
SUMED, THREAD-
BARE, SHABBY,
DILAPIDATED, FRAYED
worried FAZED,
ANNOYED, ANXIOUS,
AFRAID, FEARFUL
worry CARK, BAIT,
FRET, HARRY,
BOTHER, CARE,
VEX, FEAR, MAUL
See "annoy"
worship SERVE,
HONOR, TITLE,
REVERE, ADORE,
LATRIA, EXALT,
IDOLIZE, ADORA-
TION, DEVOTION,
HOMAGE, DIS-
CIPLINE
angels and saints
DULIA
house of BETHEL,
CHURCH, SYNA-
GOGUE, TEMPLE,
MOSQUE
object IDOL
place of ALTAR
system of FETISH,
CULT, RITUAL,
RELIGION
to God only LATRIA

worst BEAT, ROUT, DEFEAT, CONQUER, FOIL, OVERCOME, OVERTHROW, SUBJUGATE, VANQUISH, QUELL, MASTER, BEST

worth USE, MERIT, VALUE, COST, VIRTUE, INTEGRITY, PRICE, CREDIT, ESTIMATION, DESERT, IMPORTANCE, EXCELLENCE, USEFULNESS, WEALTH, RICHES

thing of little STIVER, RAP, TRIFLE

worthless RACA, PUTRID, JUNK, IDLE, FUTILE, PALTRY, SCURVY, BASE, VALUELESS, USELESS, VILE, MEAN, UNDESERVING, NUGATORY, IGNOBLE, ABJECT, TRASHY, FLIMSY, PIDDLING, AMBSACE

fellow BUM, JAVEL, LOSEL, TRAMP, SCAMP, KNAVE

leaving CHAFF, ORT, TRASH, RUBBISH

object LEMON

rock GANGUE, SLAG

worthy GOOD, FITTING, NOBLE, HONORABLE, ESTEEMED, MERITORIOUS, DESERVING, ESTIMABLE, EXCELLENT, VIRTUOUS, EXEMPLARY, VALUABLE

wou-wou APE, GIBBON

wound VULNUS, LESION, SCATHE, OFFEND, GALL, SORE, TRAUMA, HURT, HARM, INJURE, INJURY, CUT, STAB, DAMAGE, DETRIMENT, DISTRESS

discharge from ICHOR, PUS, SERUM

heraldry VULN

lint to dilate TENT

mark SCAR, CICATRIX

wrack SEAWEED, KELP, EELGRASS, DESTRUCTION, RUIN, WRECK, RAZE

wraith SPECTER, APPARITION, GHOST, SPIRIT, VISION

wrangle BRAWL, SPAR, BICKER, DISPUTE *See* "quarrel"

wrap CAPE, CLOAK, SHAWL, OVERCOAT, CLOTHE, COVER, CONCEAL, HIDE, ROLL, FOLD, FURL, SWATHE, BOA, ENVELOP, LAP

fishing line with wire GANGE

long loose PELISSE

wrapper KIMONO, PEIGNOIR, CARTON, PAPER, BARK, SKIN, ENVELOPE, COVERING

for fabrics TILLOT

wrath ANGER, RAGE, INDIGNATION, IRE, FURY, CHOLER, EXASPERATION, IRRITATION, RESENTMENT

wreath CHAPLET, ANADEM, CROWN, GARLAND, FESTOON, BAY, LAUREL, LEI, TROPHY

bay LAUREL

Hawaii LEI

heraldry TORSE

wreck RUIN, SMASH, UNDO, HULK, RAZE, RASE, SHATTER, BREAK, DESTROY, DESOLATION, STRAND, FOUNDER, BLIGHT, BLAST, DISABLE, DEMOLISH, DAMAGE

wren *Australian* EMU

genus NANNUS

wrench STRAIN, SPRAIN, TWIST, YANK, TOOL, SPANNER, DISTORTION, TWINGE, WREST,

SNATCH, JERK, PULL, TEAR, DISTORT

wrest ELICIT, REND, WRING, WRENCH, TEAR, DISTORT

wrestling *arena* RING, PALAESTRA

hold NELSON

pad MAT

wretch CAITIFF, SKUNK, SCOUNDREL, OUTCAST, PARIAH, VICTIM, SUFFERER

Hindu PARIAH

scabby RONYON

wretched PALTRY, SAD, FORLORN, ABJECT, MEAN, DESPICABLE, UNHAPPY, UNFORTUNATE, MISERABLE, AFFLICTED, DISTRESSED, DEJECTED, WOEFUL, GRIEVOUS, CALAMITOUS, BASE, CONTEMPTIBLE, WORTHLESS

wrinkle ANGLE, SEAM, CREASE, RUCK, RUGA, CORRUGATION, RIDGE, FURROW, PUCKER, FOLD

facial LINE

wrinkled RUGATE, RUGOSE, RUGOUS, CORRUGATED, PUCKERED, LINED

free from being ERUGATE, SMOOTH

wrist CARPUS, JOINT

bone CARPAL

writ PROCESS, ORDER, PRECEPT, CAPIAS, SUBPOENA, SCRIPTURE, DOCUMENT, DEED, SUMMONS

concluding clause TESTE

of execution ELEGIT

order for CAPIAS, BREVE, PRECIPE

server SHERIFF, ELISOR

to arrest CAPIAS, WARRANT

write SCRIVE, INDITE, PEN, SCRAWL,

COMPOSE, IN-
SCRIBE, SCRIBBLE,
DRAFT, RECORD,
SCRIBE, TYPE
writer SCRIBE,
AUTHOR, RHETO-
RICIAN, COMPOSER,
PENMAN, SCRIVENER,
CORRESPONDENT,
POET, NOVELIST
American POE,
JAMES, DANA,
HARTE, STOWE,
CABELL *See under*
"America"
English LAMB,
HARDY, GRAY
See under "English"
French RENAN,
ZOLA, VERNE *See*
under "French"
Irish-born SHAW
Norway IBSEN
of poems ELEGIST,
ODIST, POET
Scotch SCOTT,
BARRIE
writing TEXT, HAND,
OPUS, WORK, BOOK,
LEGEND, POEM,
STORY, CHIROG-
RAPHY, PENMAN-
SHIP, CALLIGRAPHY,
DOCUMENT,
MANUSCRIPT, PUB-
LICATION, COM-
POSITION, INSCRIP-
TION
cipher CRYPTOG-
RAPHY
combining form
GRAPH(O)
desk ESCRITOIRE,
SECRETARY
instrument PEN,
STYLUS, PENCIL
on the wall MENE,
TEKEL, UPHARSIN
used in ancient
manuscript
UNCIAL
written above
SUPRASCRIPT,
SUPRA, SUPER-
SCRIPT
not ORAL, PAROL(E),
LEGENDARY
under SUBSCRIPT,
SIGN
wrong EVIL, SIN,
CHEAT, VICE, HARM,
HURT, INJURE,

TORT, AMISS, OUT,
FALSE, BAD, POOR,
UNFIT, INAPT, UN-
JUST, UNFAIR,
INEQUITABLE,
WICKED, INAP-
PROPRIATE, UN-
SUITABLE, IM-
PROPER, INCOR-
RECT, INACCURATE,
ERRONEOUS, MIS-
TAKEN, FAULTY,
UNTRUE, CRIME,
VILLAINY, TRANSGRES-
SION, MISDEED, OP-
PRESS, ABUSE, IM-
MORAL
civil TORT,
MALUM
prefix MIS, MAL
wroth ANGERED,
IREFUL, IRED,
INDIGNANT, EXAS-
PERATED
wry OBLIQUE,
DISTORTED
wryneck TORTICOL-
LIS, LOXIA, WOOD-
PECKER, BIRD
genus JYNX
Wurttemburg *measure*
IMI
Wycliffe *disciple*
LOLLARD, HUSSITE
Wyoming *city*
LARAMIE, CASPER
county PARK,
PLATTE, TETON,
UINTA, CROOK
mountains TETON,
LARAMIE

X

X EX, CHI, TEN
Xanadu *sacred river*
ALPH
Xant(h)ippe's *hus-*
band SOCRATES
xanthous YELLOW,
MONGOLIAN
Xavier (ST.)
FRANCIS, FRANCISCO
xenium PRESENT,
GIFT
xenodochy HOSPI-
TALITY
xenon *symbol* XE
Xeres SHERRY,
WINE
site of bridge of
ABYDOS

xerophyte CACTUS
xerotic DRY, SEC
Xingu *river tribe*
ANETO
xiphoid ENSIFORM,
STERNUM, BONE,
SWORDLIKE,
BREASTBONE
xylo, *combining form*
WOOD
xyloidlike LIGNEOUS,
WOODY
xylonite CELLULOID
xylophone MARIMBA,
GIGELIRA
xyster SCRAPER
xystus PORTICO,
HALL, TERRACE,
WALK, PORCH, STOA

Y

Y WY(E)
yabbi DASYURE,
WOLF, THYLACINE,
MARSUPIAL
yacht *basin*
MARINA
flag or pennant
BURGEE
yaffle WOODPECKER,
BIRD
yahoo SAVAGE,
BRUTE, RUSTIC,
CLOWN, LOUT,
BUMPKIN
Yahveh YHVH,
YHWH, JEHOVAH,
YAHWE, GOD
yak OX, SARLAK,
SARLYK
Yaksha DRYAD,
GNOME, FAIRY
Yale ELI
yam BONIATA,
POTATO, TUBER
Hawaii HOI
Malay UVI
Philippine UBI, UBE
Yangtze River
KIANG
tributary HAN,
KAN, MIN
yap BARK, YELP,
CHATTER, GAB,
SCOLD, HOODLUM
stone money FEI
yard SPAR, PATIO,
GARTH, GARDEN,
ENCLOSURE, COM-
POUND, COURT,

CLOSE, MEASURE,
LAWN
enclosed GARTH,
PATIO
1¼th ELL
1/16th NAIL
5½ PERCH, ROD,
POLE
measure STICK,
RULER, VERGE,
GAUGE
sail tackle TYE
yarn FIB, STORY,
TALE, THREAD,
WOOL, WORSTED,
NARRATIVE, FAB-
RICATION, SAGA,
EXAGGERATION
ball of CLEW
bleached SPINEL
conical roll COP
measure LEA,
HEER
projection KNOP
quantity of SKEIN
reel PIRN
skein HANK, RAP
spindle HASP
twist SLUB
twisted CREWEL
warp ABB
waste THRUM
wind, to WARP
winder PIRNER
yarrow MILFOIL,
HERB
like SNEEZEWORT
yashmak VEIL
yatag(h)an BALAS,
SWORD, SCIMITAR,
SABER
yaup SHOUT, YELL,
BAWL, YAP, YELP,
CRY
yaupon CASSINE,
HOLLY, CASSINA,
TREE
yaw DEVIATE,
STEER, ZIGZAG,
TUMOR, BLISTER
yawn GAPE, OSCI-
TATE, CHASM,
SPLIT, PART
yaws FRAMBESIA,
PIAN, DISEASE
y-clept STYLED,
CALLED, NAMED
ye THEE, THOU,
YOU
yea PRO, FOR, YES,
TRULY

year, *excess solar*
over lunar EPACT
in this HOC ANNO
Mayan HAAB
¼ of RAITH,
TRIMESTER,
QUARTER
½ of SEMESTER
yearly *festival, High-*
lander MOD
payment SENS
yearn HANKER,
WISH, CRAVE,
ACHE, PAIN, LONG,
PANT, PANG *See*
"want"
years, *1000* CHILIAD,
MILLENNIUM
yeast BARM,
LEAVEN, FERMENT,
RISING
brewer's LOB, BARM
cake, Japan KOJI
yell SHOUT, CRY,
SCREAM, CALL,
YELP, ROAR,
SHRIEK, SCREECH,
BAWL, HOWL,
BELLOW, CHEER
yellow CHROME,
GULL, AMBER,
FLAXEN, ICTERINE,
OCHER, CITRINE,
JAUNE, COW-
ARDLY, MEAN,
GOLDEN, SAFFRON,
AUREATE, JAUN-
DICED, JEALOUS,
CRAVEN, FULVOUS,
FAVEL
alloy BRASS,
SIMILOR
as butter BLAKE
brown TOPAZ
combining form
LUTEO, XANTH(O)
egg YOLK
India PURREE
jacket HORNET,
INSECT
king's ORPIMENT
ochre SIL
pale, pigment
ETIOLIN
pertaining to
XANTHIC
race MONGOL
River HWANG HO
yellowhammer
SKITE, FLICKER,
FINCH, BUNTING,
BIRD

State ALABAMA
yellowish SALLOW,
LUTESCENT, JAUN-
DICED, OLIVE, TAN,
BEIGE, SANDY
yelp BARK, YIP, YAP,
YAUP, KI-YI, YAWP,
CRY
Yemen *capital*
SANA(A)
resident ARAB,
YEMENI(TE)
ruler IMAM
seaport MOCHA,
MUKHA
yen LUST, URGE,
DESIRE, HANKER,
YEARN, COIN
See "want"
1/100 SEN
yerba MATE, TEA
yercum, *bark* MUDAR
yes YEA, AYE, INDEED,
TRUE, TRULY,
SURE, JA
yesterday, *pertaining to*
HESTERNAL
yet E'EN, THO, AGAIN,
BUT, STILL, THOUGH,
NEVERTHELESS,
HOWEVER, NOT-
WITHSTANDING,
BESIDES, HITHERTO
yew CONIFER, TREE,
EVERGREEN
genus TAXUS
yield DEFER, BEAR,
FOREGO, OUTPUT,
BOW, CROP, CEDE,
RELENT, SOFTEN,
GIVE, ACCEDE,
PRODUCE, FURNISH,
RENDER, CON-
CEDE, ACKNOWL-
EDGE, RELINQUISH,
SURRENDER, SUB-
MIT, SUCCUMB,
CAPITULATE,
RESIGN, QUIT
yielding SOFT,
PLIANT, SUPPLE,
COMPLYING,
OBEDIENT, AC-
COMMODATING,
COMPLAISANT
yogi SWAMI
yoke CANGUE,
PILLORY, UNION,
BOND, LINK, TIE,
JOIN, PAIR, TEAM,
WED, COUPLE,

BRACE, HARNESS,
CONNECT
bar, S. Africa SKEY
combining form
ZYGO
yokel BOOR, BUMP-
KIN, HICK, RUSTIC,
PLOWBOY
yore ELD, ERST,
AGO, BEFORE,
FORMERLY
Yorkshire *district*
OTLEY, SELBY,
SCALBY
young GREEN,
FRESH, NEW,
YOUTHFUL, JUVE-
NILE, IMMATURE,
INEXPERIENCED,
OFFSPRING
animal WHELP,
CALF, KID, BABE,
CHICK, COLT, CUB
bring forth YEAN,
EAN
fox CUB
hare LEVERET
herring BRIT
man ADONIS, BOY,
CHAP, LAD
salmon PARR
squab PIPER
younger JUNIOR,
PUISNE
son CADET
youngster BABY,
LAD, TAD, SHAVER,
KID, TOT, YOUTH,
BOY, ADOLESCENT,
YOUNKER, COLT,
FILLY
youth GOSSOON,
ALADDIN, LAD, BOY,
GIRL, TEENAGER,
STRIPLING,
YOUNGSTER,
YOUNKER
goddess of HEBE
shelter HOSTEL
youthful YOUNG,
BOYISH, MAIDEN,
EARLY, JUVENILE,
CHILDISH,
CALLOW, PUERILE,
ADOLESCENT,
GREEN
yow OUCH
Yuan TAEL
Yucatan *capital*
MERIDA
city or town
UXMAL

Indian MAYA
yucca *fiber* ISOTE,
IZOTE
like plant SOTOL
Yugoslav(ia, ian)
CROAT, TITO, SERB,
SLOVENE
city or town SENTA,
BOR, SAVA, BOSNA,
VARSAC, TROGIR,
NIS(H)
coin DINAR
island PAGO, VIS,
HVAR, CRES,
SOLTA, SUSAK
(SUSAC), RAB
(ARBE), KRK
measure OKA, RIF
native CROAT
province BANAT
river DRINA, SAVA,
VARDAR, BOSNA
seaport POLA,
SPLIT, ZADAR
(ZARA), SUSAK
weight DRAMM
Yutang LIN

Z

Z ZED, IZZARD
zac IBEX,
ZEBUDER, GOAT
zacate GRASS, HAY,
HERBAGE, FORAGE
zachun BITO, OIL
Zagreus DIONYSUS
Zambal MALAYAN,
SAMBAL
language TINO
Zambales *capital* IBA
zanje CANAL, DITCH
zany COMIC, FOOL,
BUFFOON, CLOWN,
ANTIC, JESTER,
SIMPLETON,
CRAZY
Zanzibar *sultan*
SAYID
zarf CUP, HOLDER,
STAND
zeal SOUL, ARDOR,
FERVOR, GUSTO,
ZEST, FORCE,
EAGERNESS,
WARMTH, ENERGY,
ENTHUSIASM,
PASSION, FEELING
Zealand Island *fiord*
ISSE
zealot FAN,
DEVOTEE, PARTISAN,

DISCIPLE, BUFF,
VOTARY, BIGOT
religious FANATIC
zebra, *Burchell's*
DAUW
extinct QUAGGA
wood ARAROBA
zebu YAK, ZO,
ZOH, ZOBO
zebuder ZAC,
IBEX, GOAT
zenana HAREM,
SERAGLIO
zenith TOP, PRIME,
ACME, APEX,
CLIMAX, APOGEE,
SUMMIT, PINNACLE,
CULMINATION
opposite to NADIR,
PERIGEE
Zeno, *follower of*
STOIC
zephyr AURA, WIND,
BREEZE
zero CIPHER, NONE,
NAUGHT, NIL,
BLANK, NOTHING,
OUGHT, HOUR,
NULLITY, NADIR
zest ZIP, FLAVOR,
RELISH, TASTE,
TANG, ZEAL, ARDOR,
SPIRIT, KICK,
GUSTO, GLEE,
RAPTURE, SAVOR
Zeus ZAN, JUPITER,
ALASTOR
attendant NIKE
attribute AEGIS
beloved by IO,
LEDA, EUROPA
brother HADES
consort HERA
daughter PER-
SEPHONE, ARTEMIS,
APHRODITE
epithet ALASTOR
festival in honor
NEMEAN
maid loved by IO,
LEDA, EUROPA
messenger IRIS
mother RHEA
oracle seat DODONA
princess beloved by
EUROPA
sister HERA
son AEACUS,
APOLLO, ARES,
PERSEUS, HERMES,
ARGUS, HERCULES

wife DIONE, HERA, LETO, MAIA, METIS, THEMIS, SELEME, DEMETER, ALCMENE, EURYNOME

zigzag TACK, SWERVE, YAW, AWRY

zinc SPELTER, ZN
alloy BIDRI, PAKTONG, TUTENAG
and copper OROIDE
arsenite ADAMINE, ADAMITE
silicate CALAMINE

zingel PERCH, FISH

zip PEP, HISS, ELAN, ENERGY, SNAP, VIM

zirconium *symbol* ZR

zizany COCKLE, TARES, DARNEL, WEED

Zobeide's *half sister* AMINA

zodiac *sign* CRAB, LEO, LIBRA, PISCES, GEMINI, RAM, VIRGO, TAURUS, SCORPIO, CANCER

Zola EMILE
novel NANA

zone ISLE, BELT, CLIME, BERTH, WARD, AREA, BAND, TRACT, REGION, SECTOR, DISTRICT, DIVIDE, GIRDLE

ZOO VIVARIUM

zoogeographic *division*, EOGAEA

zooid of coral growth POLYPITE

zoological vessel ARK

zoril POLECAT, MARIPUT, ZORILLA

Zoroastrian PARSEE, PARSI

bible AVESTA
scripture AVESTA
translation ZEND

zoster BELT, GIRDLE

zuche STUMP

Zuider ZEE

zuisin WIDGEON, DUCK

zules ROOK

Zulu *army* IMPI
headman INDUNA
marauder VITI
meeting INDABA
spear ASSAGAI

zygoma BONE

zymogen, *substance actuating* KINASE

zymome GLUTENIN

zythepsary BREWERY

zythum BEER

exciting